# THE LANDMARK
# XENOPHON'S ANABASIS

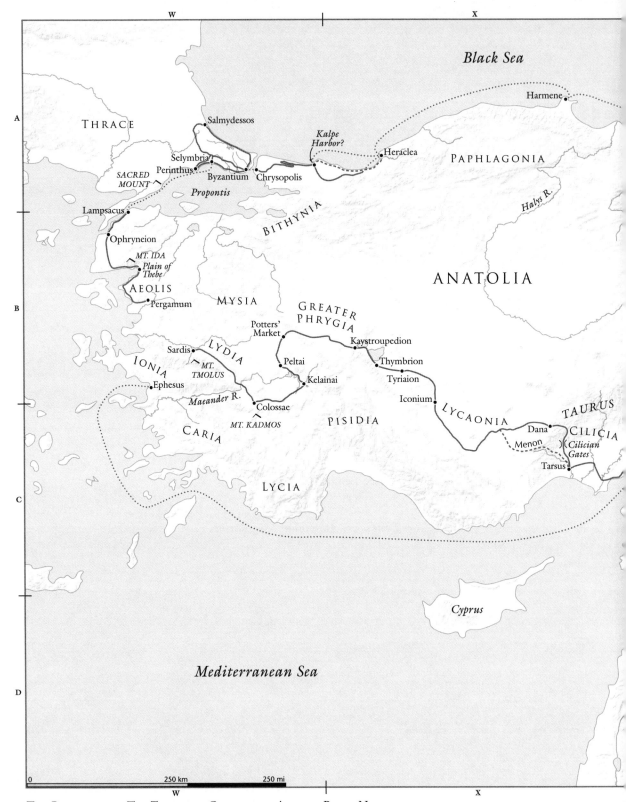

THE ROUTE OF THE TEN THOUSAND GREEKS WITH ANCIENT PLACE-NAMES

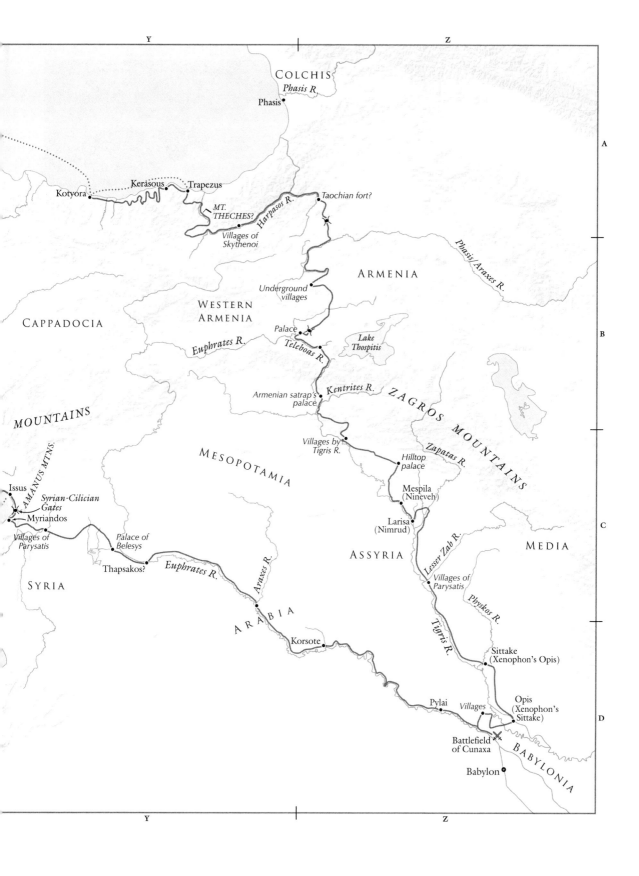

COLCHIS

*Phasis R.*

Phasis

Trapezus

Kerásous

Kotyora

*MT.
THECHES?*

*Harpasos R.*

Taochian fort?

*Villages of
Skythenoi*

ARMENIA

*Phasis/Araxes R.*

*Underground
villages*

WESTERN
ARMENIA

CAPPADOCIA

*Euphrates R.*

Palace

*Teleboas R.*

*Lake
Thospitis*

*Kentrites R.*

*Armenian satrap's
palace*

ZAGROS MOUNTAINS

*Villages by
Tigris R.*

*Zapatas R.*

*Hilltop
palace*

MOUNTAINS

Mespila
(Nineveh)

Issus

*AMANUS MTNS.*

*Syrian-Cilician
Gates*

Myriandos

Larisa
(Nimrud)

MEDIA

*Villages of
Parysatis*

ASSYRIA

MESOPOTAMIA

Palace of
Belesys

*Lesser Zab R.*

*Villages of
Parysatis*

SYRIA

Thapsakos?

*Euphrates R.*

*Araxes R.*

*Physkos R.*

ARABIA

*Tigris R.*

Korsote

Sittake
(Xenophon's Opis)

Pylai

*Villages*

Opis
(Xenophon's
Sittake)

Battlefield
of Cunaxa

BABYLONIA

Babylon

# THE LANDMARK
# XENOPHON'S
# *Anabasis*

A New Translation by David Thomas

with Maps, Annotations, Appendices, and Encyclopedic Index

Edited by Shane Brennan and David Thomas

Series Editor Robert B. Strassler

PANTHEON BOOKS · NEW YORK

Frontispiece: bust of Xenophon from the Bibliotheca Alexandrina Antiquities Museum.

A cataloging-in-publication record has been created for this book by the Library of Congress.

ISBN: 978-0-307-90685-4

*Designed by Kim Llewellyn*
*Maps by Beehive Mapping*
*Photo research by Ingrid MacGillis*
*Index by David Thomas*

www.pantheonbooks.com

Printed in the United States of America

First Edition

1st Printing

# CONTENTS

# INTRODUCTION

### Shane Brennan

§1.1. In the late spring of 401, mercenaries from Greece began landing on the shores of western Anatolia.[a] Together with Greeks from the cities along the coast, they were headed inland to the city of Sardis, where a young Persian prince named Cyrus[b] was organizing a military expedition. The men believed they were being recruited to help subdue a troublesome tribe, the Pisidians,[c] but Cyrus in fact had a more ambitious and daring plan in mind.

§1.2. Three years earlier Cyrus' father, King Darius II,[a] had died. Though the eldest son Artaxerxes[b] was the appointed successor, some in the court believed that Cyrus had a better claim to the throne. It was said he was more able in military matters and more suited to rule an empire; his very name recalled the glories of the founder of the Persian Empire 150 years before, Cyrus the Great.[c] Nevertheless, Artaxerxes did become King,[d] and shortly thereafter he arrested Cyrus on suspicion of plotting against him. He would have put his brother to death except for the intervention of their mother, Queen Parysatis, who even persuaded Artaxerxes to allow Cyrus to assume his former position as satrap of Lydia, Greater Phrygia, and Cappadocia.[e] On his return the dishonored prince determined never again to be in his brother's power. He proceeded secretly to hire contingents of Greek soldiers

NOTE: Unless otherwise specified, all dates in this volume are B.C.E. (Before the Common Era) and all text references are to Xenophon's *Anabasis*.

Intro.1.1a The term Anatolia ("the land where the sun rises" in Greek) is often used to refer to the territory approximately covered by the Asian part of modern Turkey, though some historians prefer to call this Asia Minor. Neither term was yet in use in Classical antiquity. Greece: Ref. Map 2. Western Anatolia: Intro. Map 3.1.

Intro.1.1b On Cyrus the Younger, see Appendix W: Brief Biographies of Selected Characters in *Anabasis*, §10. Sardis: Intro. Map 3.1.

Intro.1.1c Pisidia: Map 1.2.13, AX.

Intro.1.2a On Darius II, see Appendix W, §11.

Intro.1.2b On Artaxerxes, see Appendix W, §6.

Intro.1.2c On Cyrus the Great, also known as Cyrus the Elder, see Appendix W, §9. Persian Empire: Intro. Map 4.6 and Ref. Map 9.

Intro.1.2d The Greeks called the Persian monarch "the King," or sometimes "the Great King," so distinguishing him from the rulers of lesser kingdoms.

Intro.1.2e Satrap: provincial governor; see further §4.2. On Greater Phrygia, see n. 1.2.6a. The events surrounding the succession at the court are reflected only dimly in the sources we have: see *Anabasis* 1.1.3; Plutarch, *Life of Artaxerxes* 3.3–4 (in Appendix T: Selections from Plutarch's *Life of Artaxerxes*). On Parysatis, see Appendix W, §26. Lydia, Greater Phrygia: Intro. Map 4.6. Cappadocia: Book 1 map.

with the intention of joining them with his own troops, and set in motion a plan to seize the Persian throne.

§1.3. The success of Cyrus' plan depended on three elements: surprise, speed, and superior troops. The King's full army was large but had to be brought together from different parts of the empire, a task that could take several months, by which time Cyrus believed he could already be in Babylonia.ᵃ He could also have some confidence in the quality of his strike force: the Greek hoplites,ᵇ heavily armed infantrymen who would make up the bulk of his attack troops, were formidable when fighting in close formation. While they were skilled in the use of their arms—a large circular shield, a six- to eight-foot-long spear, and a single-sided slashing sword—it was when fighting as a phalanxᶜ that hoplites were the most potent. The power of the phalanx lay in coordination, formation, and discipline, each man literally covering his neighbor with his shield and preventing any break in the line. Rightly or wrongly, Cyrus seems to have believed that with this select force he could break through the enemy center where Artaxerxes would be positioned, an event that might in turn cause the entire enemy line to collapse.

§1.4. However, significant obstacles stood in his way, and the odds could not be said to have been in his favor. Once Cyrus had assembled his army, he would have to lead it across the Taurus Mountains, through the deserts of northern Syria, and down along the empty left bank of the Euphrates River into Babylonia.ᵃ In addition, speed became even more vital because Tissaphernes, a rival governor in the region, realizing that Cyrus' army was too large for merely subduing a local people, had ridden off to warn the King.ᵇ At some stage as well, Cyrus would have to inform the soldiers of his true purpose and persuade them to go along with his plan. His own troops would be obliged to obey, but his Greek mercenaries, who were free men, would not be easily persuaded: to most, the idea of traveling deep into the King's lands and engaging his army there would have seemed foolhardy. Among these Greek soldiers—known both as the Cyreans, after their employer, and later as the Ten Thousand, their (approximate) number—was a young Athenian named Xenophon, who many years later would recount his own story of the expedition, the *Kyrou Anabasis* (which could be translated as *Cyrus' March Up-Country*).ᶜ

§1.5. Xenophon's book has come down to us in seven sections, themselves usually referred to as books. As with other texts from antiquity, this division is generally

Intro.1.3a This historic region was close to the Persian heartland; its capital, Babylon, was an important center of the empire, and Cyrus evidently believed his brother would be there; see 1.4.11. Babylonia, Babylon: Intro. Map 4.6.

Intro.1.3b Hoplites: the term "hoplite" (*hoplitēs*) is a reference to the equipment used by this soldier, from the Greek *hopla*, "a set of tools." For more on hoplites and other combatants, see Appendix H: Infantry and Cavalry in *Anabasis* (on hoplites, §§2–3). See Figure 1.2.16 for an image of a hoplite.

Intro.1.3c For more on the phalanx, see Appendix H, §§13–15.

Intro.1.4a Euphrates River: Intro. Map 4.6. Taurus Mountains, Syria: Map 1.4.1, AX, BX.

Intro.1.4b Tissaphernes hastens to warn the King: 1.2.4.

The first-century Greek author Diodorus (*Library of History* 14.22; in Appendix S: Selections from Diodorus), writes that Artaxerxes had learned of Cyrus' plan from another western satrap, Pharnabazos. For more on Tissaphernes and Pharnabazos, see Appendix W: Brief Biographies, §§37, 27.

Intro.1.4c The word *anabasis* literally means "going up," that is, traveling away from the sea. *Kyrou Anabasis* may or may not be Xenophon's title, though giving a prose work a title does seem to have been an innovation of around this time. The title *Anabasis* first appears in Diogenes Laertius' third-century c.e. biography of the author (2.57; in Appendix V: Diogenes Laertius' *Life of Xenophon*).

considered to be the work not of the author but of later editors.[a] An oddity with the title, *Cyrus' March Up-Country*, is that the march up-country—from Sardis to Babylonia[b]—takes up just the first book of the narrative. The remaining six books recount the homeward journey of the Greeks after the battle in Babylonia: Books 2–4 cover the retreat to the Black Sea (*katabasis*), Books 5–6 the march and sea voyage along the Black Sea coast (*parabasis*), and Book 7 the army's time in Thrace.[c]

### *Anabasis* Past and Present

§1.6. Xenophon's account, having engaged readers down the centuries, has furthermore proved to be a mine of information for scholars and travelers. Taking in much of what was the western Persian Empire—today Turkey, Syria, and Iraq[a]—the story provides a firsthand report of places and peoples encountered and is one of the earliest records of the natural and human environments of the region. For instance, the author names and provides the width of many major rivers, describes in detail the date harvest in Mesopotamia,[b] and names animals that are no longer present in the area. On the Black Sea coast, he describes such phenomena as hallucinogenic honey and whistled speech, both of which can be found in the same localities today.[c] His account of a desperate week fighting the Kardouchoi in eastern Anatolia may be the first written description of the ancestors of the modern Kurds.[d] Later encounters with various tribes[e] are poignant in that little is heard of these peoples again in the historical record; in some cases virtually the only trace of them now is found in the pages of Xenophon's book. Taking his *Anabasis* in hand, I set off myself twenty years ago to explore on foot what survives of his descriptions and to see whether the route he outlines could still be followed. I was pleasantly surprised. Striking features, such as a booming fountain by the roadside in western Turkey, plains as flat as the sea in Syria, and deserted ancient ruins on the banks of the Tigris in Iraq, remained almost exactly as Xenophon saw them 2,500 years ago.[f] The entire journey, starting in Sardis and ending in Istanbul (ancient Byzantium),[g] took me fourteen months and covered about 3,200 miles on foot, plus a sea voyage of about 230 miles along part of the southern Black Sea coast. These figures for time and distance match quite closely those that one can derive from Xenophon's record.

Intro.1.5a A full treatment of the text's history and transmission is given in the Translator's Notes, §§10–17.

Intro.1.5b For the route of the march up-country, see Book 1 map.

Intro.1.5c Just as *anabasis* means "going up," *katabasis* means "going down," that is, traveling from the interior to the sea. *Parabasis* is here used in the sense of "going alongside," traveling parallel to the seacoast. Black Sea (Pontus Euxinus in the *Barrington Atlas*), Thrace: Intro. Map 4.6. The whole route is shown with ancient place-names on Ref. Map 7 and with modern ones on Ref. Map 8.

Intro.1.6a The following locations appear on Ref. Map 8: Turkey, BX; Syria, DY; Iraq, DZ.

Intro.1.6b Major rivers: for example, the Euphrates, Maeander (Map 1.2.10, AX), and the Halys (Book 6 map). Mesopotamia: Intro. Map 4.6.

Intro.1.6c Hallucinogenic honey: 4.8.20–21 (in Kolchoi territory, Map 4.7.25); for more, see Appendix Q: The Chronology of the March, §§8–10. Whistled speech: 5.4.31 (in Mossynoeci territory, Map 5.4.1). Whistled speech is practiced in the Turkish village of Kuşköy, "bird village" (Ref. Map 8, AY). See Brennan 2016.

Intro.1.6d Kardouchoi territory: Map 4.4.3. Eastern Anatolia: Intro Map 4.6.

Intro.1.6e For example, the Taochoi and Eastern Chalybes and the Mossynoeci. Territories of the Taochoi, Eastern Chalybes (not listed in the *Barrington Atlas*): Map 4.7.1.

Intro.1.6f Roadside fountain: 1.2.13 (at the Fountain of Midas, Map 1.2.13, AX). Deserted ruins: 3.4.7 (at Larisa/Nimrud, Book 3 map).

Intro.1.6g Byzantium changed names over the course of history, becoming Constantinople under the reign of the Emperor Constantine in the fourth century C.E., and then, officially in the twentieth century, Istanbul. Byzantium: Intro. Map 4.6.

§1.7. Aside from the effects of massive dam building in eastern Turkey, perhaps all that had really changed was that the world I passed through held considerably less danger than it did for the Ten Thousand, about a third of whom did not make it back to the Aegean Sea.[a] Even if that is no longer true due to the situations in Syria and Iraq, Western travelers in much of the region today are probably safer than they are on their own streets, and they will certainly benefit from a level of hospitality they would rarely find at home. As it did for Xenophon, the memory of the experience remains vivid for me years afterward and, I hope, has helped to enhance some of the details in this volume.

### Xenophon the Athenian

§2.1. Had Xenophon written his account of the expedition shortly after its conclusion, his book would probably have been quite straightforward, grounded in the raw experience of the march and its trials. But it was thirty years or more before the work was published,[a] a period in which he witnessed great changes and momentous events in the world around him. The result of the gap in time between event and authorship is a rich work that weaves many of the writer's personal concerns and interests into the narrative of the march. A review of Xenophon's life and times allows us to appreciate the impact that they came to have on his writings.[b]

§2.2. The closing years of the fifth century were a time of great uncertainty for the city-states[a] of Greece. Athens, which had been the outstanding economic, cultural, and naval power in the Aegean region, was in turmoil, ground down by the military might of Sparta and the purse of the Persian King.[b] Sparta, together with its allies in the Peloponnese, had been at war with Athens and its imperial subjects on and off for more than a quarter of a century[c] and had now realized its avowed aim in the war: to defeat the Athenians and liberate those Greeks under its subjection. Yet no one was sure what would follow. Sparta did not have the experience or the institutions that were ideally needed for the hegemonic role it now seemed poised to assume throughout mainland Greece and the Aegean.[d] And how would such a role square with the aim of liberty for the Greeks? Moreover, how would Sparta deal with Persia? Many Greeks must have thought that Artaxerxes would expect some form of payback for his state's decisive support in the ultimate phase of the war. If some were optimistic for the future, many more would have been anxious about what the end of the war would mean for themselves and their city. One of these Greeks was Xenophon, an ambitious young man who was an associate of the philosopher Socrates.[e] It was against this background that he came to join Cyrus.

Intro.1.7a  Aegean Sea: Intro. Map 3.1.
Intro.2.1a  For the dating of *Anabasis*, see §6.2.
Intro.2.1b  For more than this brief review, see Anderson 1974; also Higgins 1977, a more unorthodox treatment.
Intro.2.2a  For more on the city-state (*polis*), see *"polis"* in the Glossary.
Intro.2.2b  The Persians had loomed large in Greek affairs since the invasions of Darius I (490) and Xerxes (480) at the beginning of the

century. Darius I reigned from 522 to 486. On Xerxes, see Appendix W: Brief Biographies, §38. Athens, Sparta: Intro. Map 3.1.
Intro.2.2c  The Peloponnesian War lasted from 431 to 404. Peloponnese: Intro. Map 3.1.
Intro.2.2d  For more on Sparta and its rule, see Appendix B: Xenophon and Sparta.
Intro.2.2e  On Socrates, see §2.9–12 and Appendix A: Xenophon and Socrates.

### Sources for Xenophon's Life

§2.3. Most of what we know about Xenophon derives from his own writings. Several of the fourteen books or handbooks he wrote, including *Anabasis*, furnish evidence about his life.[a] In some instances the detail seems plainly autobiographical, while in others arguments can be made that he is referring to personal experience. However, the detail provided cannot always be taken at face value. Xenophon's representation of himself in *Anabasis* has a distinct exemplary quality: a good case can be made that the Xenophon portrayed in the text is primarily being put forward as a model pupil of Socrates who applies the lessons of his teacher to the extreme situations he confronts.

§2.4. One complete biography of Xenophon survives from antiquity. This was written by Diogenes Laertius, a third-century C.E. Greek author from Cilicia, who compiled a work called *Lives of Eminent Philosophers*.[a] As we tend to think of Xenophon primarily as a soldier and a historian, his inclusion in this work may seem odd, but in antiquity he was known first and foremost as a philosopher.

§2.5. Diogenes derived the material for his subjects from a variety of sources. He specifically names ten of them in the biography of Xenophon and alludes to several others. While some of these will have drawn their detail from Xenophon's writings, other sources seem to have been completely independent. Not all of the sources are today regarded as reliable, and obvious mistakes by Diogenes himself have further diluted the value of his work.[a] However, he did have access to high-grade material now lost to us.[b]

### Early Years

§2.6. Xenophon was born probably in the early 420s, which means he would have been in his late twenties when he joined Cyrus' expedition. Diogenes gives his father's name as Gryllos and writes that he belonged to the deme of Erchia, an agricultural district some twelve miles from the city.[a] The family must have been prosperous, given that Xenophon took several horses with him on Cyrus' expedition.[b] His guest-friendship with Proxenos of Boeotia may be further evidence of his elite status, since the relationship quite likely marks his family as being well connected in high-status networks across the region.[c]

Intro.2.3a  For Xenophon's works, see the List of Xenophon's Writings.

Intro.2.4a  See Appendix V: Diogenes. On Diogenes, see Ancient Sources Cited in this Edition. Cilicia: Intro. Map 4.6.

Intro.2.5a  For example, had Diogenes checked sources available to him, he would have seen that the date he gave for Xenophon's death (360/59: 2.56, in Appendix V) could not have been correct, as certain events that Xenophon describes in his writings occurred after 359.

Intro.2.5b  One example is a speech concerning Xenophon's family by the fourth-century Athens-based speechwriter Dinarchus: Diogenes Laertius 2.52 (in Appendix V).

Intro.2.6a  Twelve miles/19 kilometers. Paternity, deme: Diogenes Laertius 2.48 (in Appendix V). Erchia: Map 1.2.1, AY.

Intro.2.6b  Xenophon's horses: 3.3.19. Horse ownership in the ancient world was a traditional indica-

tor of wealth. In the fourth century, a horse would have cost a minimum of 100 Athenian drachmas, the equivalent of ten months' wages for a skilled craftsman. A good horse sold for 500 drachmas and the best could fetch twice that. On drachmas, see Appendix O: Ancient Greek and Persian Units of Measurement, §11.

Intro.2.6c  Xenophon as guest-friend of Proxenos: 3.1.4. Guest-friendship was an ancient support system whereby the parties undertook to provide assistance and hospitality to one another as the need arose. By and large it was based on status and cut across ethnic boundaries. Thus Cyrus, a Persian, had guest-friend relations with a Thessalian (1.1.10) and a Boeotian (1.1.11), among others. For more on guest-friends, see the Glossary. On Proxenos, see Appendix W: Brief Biographies, §29. Thessaly, Boeotia: Intro. Map 3.1.

§2.7. With the outbreak of the Peloponnesian War in 431, the Athenian countryside was subjected to annual raids by Sparta and its allies. While before 413 these meant that Xenophon's deme was unsafe for only part of the year, as landowners his family would have suffered directly as a result of their harvests' being damaged. The situation deteriorated further from 413, when the Spartans permanently established themselves in Attica and Athenians were forced to live year-round inside the city's walls. On account of the war some believe that Xenophon grew up in the city; even if he did, he evidently retained a strong connection with the countryside, as is shown by the intimate knowledge of it that he displays in two of his works, namely, *Oikonomikos* (*On the Management of the Household*) and *Kynegetikos* (*On Hunting*).

§2.8. The sons of wealthy fifth-century Athenians were typically educated in literacy, arithmetic, music, and physical activities. Music, including dance, was an integral part of Athenian life and featured in the city's many festivals and theatrical performances. In later life Xenophon showed an appreciation for dance in particular, and even a flair for choreography, as is evident in his advice to cavalry commanders about public displays.[a] Physical education, likewise, brought benefits to both the individual and his country in a world where war was more common than peace and an army needed a regular supply of trained and fit soldiers. The performance of Xenophon's character in *Anabasis* testifies to this grounding: at various stages he represents himself as fit, as when toiling up a hillside in full armor, and as hardy, rising at dawn without his cloak to chop wood in freezing winter conditions.[b]

### Xenophon's Relationship with Socrates

§2.9. Many of Xenophon's writings bear a philosophical stamp. His interests were predominantly in ethics and in the problem of how to rule, with a noticeable coolness toward inquiry that did not have a practical end. That his teacher Socrates' influence endured throughout Xenophon's life is most obvious in the writings he produced toward the end of it; specifically, in four of his works he explicitly defends the memory of the great philosopher and promotes the value of his teachings: *Apologia Sokratous* (*Defense of Socrates*), *Memorabilia* (*Recollections of Socrates*), *Oikonomikos*, and *Symposion* (*The Drinking Party*). Some have argued that other works by Xenophon are Socratic too, notably *Kyroupaideia* (*The Education of Cyrus*), whose chief character, a fictionalized version of Cyrus the Great, may be an embodiment of the philosopher's teachings. As we see later, a similar case may be made for *Anabasis*.[a]

§2.10. The degree to which Xenophon was a participant in Socrates' circle is a much-debated subject among modern scholars. Although in *Memorabilia*, his book of recollections of Socrates, Xenophon only once takes part in a conversation, the impression given by this work is that he was often in attendance while others talked.[a]

Intro.2.8a Dance: *Anabasis* 6.1.5–13. Public displays: *Hipparchikos* (*Cavalry Commander*) 3.10–12.
Intro.2.8b Toiling up a hillside: 3.4.47–49. Chopping wood: 4.4.12.
Intro.2.9a For this argument, see §8.12–14, and in more detail, Brennan forthcoming.
Intro.2.10a Xenophon in conversation with Socrates: *Memorabilia* 1.3.8–13. Xenophon's atten-

dance at talks in *Memorabilia* (Marchant/ Loeb translation): "For I myself never heard Socrates indulge in the practice" (1.2.31); "I will first state what I once heard him say" (1.4.2); "The following conversation between him [Socrates] and Euthydemus I heard myself" (4.3.2).

FIGURE INTRO.2.9.
BUST OF THE PHILOSOPHER
SOCRATES. ALTHOUGH THIS IS A
ROMAN COPY, THE ORIGINAL IS
BELIEVED TO BE FROM THE EARLY
FOURTH CENTURY AND TO DEPICT
SOCRATES FAIRLY REALISTICALLY.
LATER IN THE FOURTH CENTURY,
A DIFFERENT, IDEALISTIC TYPE OF
BUST OF SOCRATES BECAME POPULAR.

To be set against this, however, is his seemingly impossible claim in *Oikonomikos* that he was present when Socrates referred to the death of Cyrus.[b] Xenophon was on the battlefield with Cyrus when the latter was killed and had not yet returned to Greece two years later when Socrates was executed by the Athenian democracy (in 399). Equally, if we assume that Xenophon was in his late twenties at the time of Cyrus' expedition (401), he would have been far too young to have been present—as he implies he was—at the conversation between Socrates and his friends recounted in *Symposion*, which is set in 422.[c]

§2.11. The most significant piece of evidence concerning the relationship between Xenophon and Socrates comes from *Anabasis* 3.1.4–7. After receiving a letter from his guest-friend Proxenos that promised to make him a friend of Cyrus if he came to Sardis, Xenophon consulted Socrates on the matter. Socrates—worried that associating with Cyrus could cause trouble for Xenophon at Athens, since the prince had supported the Spartans in the recent war—advised him to ask the oracle at Delphi[a] whether

Intro.2.10b  Xenophon present: *Oikonomikos* (*On the Management of the Household*) 1.1. Death of Cyrus the Younger: *Oikonomikos* 4.18.

Intro.2.10c  Xenophon present: *Symposion* 1.1. Plato, another principal source for the life and teachings of Socrates, does not mention Xenophon in any of his works (which also include a *Symposion*). But this may not be proof of Xenophon's remoteness from the Socratic circle so much as a result of personal friction between Xenophon and Plato, as mentioned in Diogenes Laertius 2.57 (in Appendix V: Diogenes), 3.34; see also the second-century C.E. Roman writer Aulus Gellius' *Attic Nights* 14.3.

Intro.2.11a  On oracles, see Appendix G: Divinity and Divining. Delphi: Intro. Map 3.1.

he should undertake the journey. In *Memorabilia* Xenophon writes that Socrates dealt with close friends in this manner, which implies that he himself was one of them.[b] When he visited the oracle, however, he did not ask whether he should or should not join Cyrus but, rather, asked to which of the gods he should sacrifice for a successful journey. When Socrates learned about this, he was annoyed, but he then accepted the situation, an outcome that indicates an avuncular relationship between them.

§2.12. It is on the later retreat of the Greeks from Mesopotamia that Xenophon matures as a character; and by introducing his mentor into the narrative at the point when he himself steps up to lead the army, he means to signal that his success in leading it to safety is owed in some important part to his training with Socrates.

### The Athenian Democracy

§2.13. An element of Xenophon's background that is sometimes underappreciated is the influence of the Athenian political system. Up to the end of the Peloponnesian War (except for a short interval in 411), Athens remained a direct democracy, in which adult male citizens gathered in assembly and voted on motions after listening to arguments from all sides. The ability to present cases for or against motions to a popular audience was thus a critical ingredient of political effectiveness, and the most accomplished speakers were often the most powerful politicians.

§2.14. Xenophon, as a leader of the Ten Thousand, skillfully employs democratic methods in his political arena: the army as an assembly.[a] As he tells it, early in the retreat it is he who takes the initiative in rallying and leading the army after its key commanders have been seized by the Persians. His initial address to fellow officers leads to a speech to a full assembly of the army, where he speaks persuasively on how they are to extricate themselves from the Persians and reach their homes safely. When he concludes with a request for a show of hands, the whole assembly approves his proposals. Throughout the ensuing retreat, we witness how Xenophon handles the soldiers effectively by using democratic methods. At Trapezus, on the Black Sea,[b] for example, he puts forward a series of measures that are to be taken while the army waits for ships to take it home. Each proposal is in turn approved. However, the men strongly object to his final recommendation, that they repair roads along the coast as a contingency against insufficient sea transport, as they do not want even to consider more marching: "As Xenophon perceived that they were gripped by folly, he did not put anything to a vote on this topic but instead persuaded the cities [along the coast] to mend the roads voluntarily, saying that they would more quickly be rid of the army if the roads were made passable."[c] So either his proposals are approved by the assembly or he works around it to achieve his objective. Xenophon's successful leadership invites comparison to his descriptions of other leaders on the march, notably Cyrus and the Spartans Klearchos and Cheirisophos.[d]

Intro.2.11b  Socrates advises close friends to go to Delphi: *Memorabilia* (*Recollections of Socrates*) 1.1.6.
Intro.2.14a  In his account Xenophon delivers more speeches than anyone else, some of them very long.

Intro.2.14b  Trapezus: Ref. Map 7, AY.
Intro.2.14c  Proposal not put to the vote: 5.1.14.
Intro.2.14d  On Xenophon's leadership, see §8.2–5. On Cyrus the Younger, Klearchos, and Cheirisophos, see Appendix W: Brief Biographies, §§10, 20, 7.

## Xenophon and the Thirty

§2.15. After its victory in the Peloponnesian War (431–404), Sparta suppressed the Athenian democracy. The Spartan general Lysander demanded that a ruling body of thirty Athenian citizens be installed, ostensibly for the purpose of establishing a new constitution. Sparta favored oligarchies, and those appointed to power in Athens were of like mind.[a] The brief reign of the Thirty, as this body was called, proved harsh and arbitrary. The regime executed some 1,500 citizens and exiled many others, confiscating their property. In 403 its leader, Kritias, was killed in a decisive battle with the democratic opposition;[b] by the end of that year, the Athenian democracy had been restored, albeit restricted in its foreign policy by a treaty with Sparta[c] and by the ever-present threat of Spartan military sanction.

§2.16. From Xenophon's account in his *Hellenika* of the postwar period in Athens, it seems probable that, as a cavalryman, he played a role in the enforcement of the Thirty's rule. The cavalry functioned as an armed wing of the Thirty, and several passages in *Hellenika* suggest that he himself was involved in violent episodes; for example, he describes one occasion when the democrats ambushed the cavalry, and another when the cavalry killed a group of citizens who were going to their farms for provisions.[a] The stories as they are told give the impression of being reports of personal experience, and though in the case of a talented writer, vividness need not depend on autopsy, it is not just that quality here that points to personal experience but the particularity of the detail in an otherwise not especially full narrative. The lengthy section on the Thirty in *Hellenika* has a distinctly apologetic character, quite likely intended by Xenophon to portray himself as a reluctant affiliate of the regime.[b] The extent to which he was involved with the Thirty would have been an important factor in determining his future in the city following the restoration of the democracy. Another would have been his continuing links to figures perceived as anti-democratic. His teacher Socrates, who worried about the dangers of popular power, argued that the state should be led by those who had appropriate expertise to rule, not necessarily those elected by the people.

§2.17. Under these circumstances it is not surprising that in spring 401 Xenophon was well motivated to act on Proxenos' letter and leave Athens to meet Cyrus. While there had been a formal reconciliation between the democrats and all but the most extreme oligarchs, the prospects for an active future in the city's life did not look good for members of the Thirty's cavalry force. Bearing out that assessment is the Athenians' dispatch in 399 of a force of three hundred horsemen to fight with Sparta against the Persians in western Anatolia.[a] Xenophon later wrote of this force:

Intro.2.15a Athens, when it had been an imperial power, had likewise favored constitutions similar to its own and tended to impose democracies on its allies. On Sparta's political system, see Appendix B: Xenophon and Sparta, §§12–17.

Intro.2.15b Kritias was a prominent associate of Socrates. This may help to explain why the democracy later indicted Socrates for having corrupted the youth.

Intro.2.15c The treaty that concluded the Peloponnesian War imposed several obligations on the Athenians, including provisions that they were to "have the same friends and enemies as the Spartans; and . . . be willing to follow the Spartans as their leaders on land or sea, on whatever campaign the Spartans should order them" (*Hellenika* 2.2.20; Marincola/Landmark translation).

Intro.2.16a Ambush: *Hellenika* 2.4.6. Killing of citizens: *Hellenika* 2.4.26.

Intro.2.16b The Thirty in *Hellenika*: 2.3.11–2.4.43.

Intro.2.17a Western Anatolia: Intro. Map 3.1.

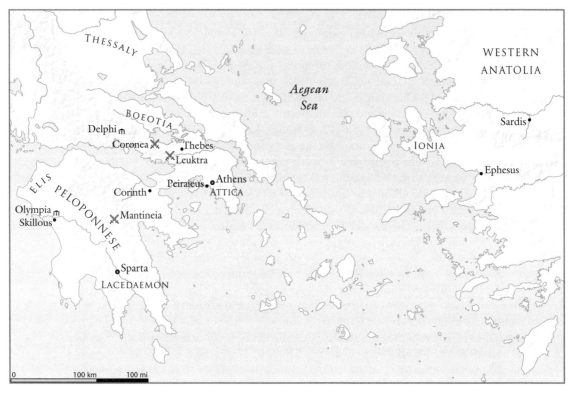

caption
INTRO. MAP 3.1. SITES LINKED WITH XENOPHON.

"The Athenians sent those who had served in the cavalry under the Thirty, for they thought that it would be advantageous to the people if these men went abroad and died there."[b] For years afterward service in the cavalry during the reign of the Thirty was invoked as grounds for denying admission to public office.[c]

### Xenophon the Exile

§3.1. At some time in 399 or later, Xenophon was exiled from Athens. We know from a passage in *Anabasis* (7.7.57), dateable to the spring of 399, that the relevant decree cannot have been passed earlier: Xenophon, in Thrace[a] with the remnants of the Ten Thousand but preparing to return home, remarks that "no motion regarding his exile had yet been put to the vote at Athens." This wording may indicate that it was then imminent but some think that the decree of exile had still not been passed when he first returned to Greece with the Spartan army in 394, on the ground that it was then that he made a dedication in the Athenian treasury at Del-

Intro.2.17b  Cavalry sent abroad: *Hellenika* 3.1.4 (Marincola/Landmark translation).
Intro.2.17c  In a speech (*On the Scrutiny of Evandros*), dated to 382, the Athenian orator Lysias writes: "Suppose that he were now under scrutiny for admission to the Council, and

he had his name registered on the tablets as having served in the cavalry under the Thirty: even without an accuser you would reject him" (Lysias 26.10; Lamb/Loeb translation).
Intro.3.1a  Thrace: Intro. Map 4.6.

phi.[b] If indeed it had not, then it must have been passed shortly after this point. As the Spartan army passed through Boeotia, it fought a battle at Coronea[c] with a coalition of Greek cities that included Athens. Although Xenophon may not have actually fought in the battle, his presence on the victorious Spartan side was likely to have been construed as treasonous by the Athenians.

§3.2. In two brief mentions of the exile in *Anabasis* (5.3.7, 7.7.57), Xenophon gives no reason for it, nor does he refer to his exile in any of his other writings. Diogenes Laertius says that it was on account of favoritism toward Sparta, but subsequently, in an epigram at the end of the same work, he writes that it was because of Xenophon's friendship with Cyrus.[a] If treason of some kind was the formal basis of the decree against him, then both of the named causes are plausible. The reason for the decree would be clearer if its date could be established. A later banishment, in 394 or 393, would argue for Xenophon's close ties with Sparta at a time when the states were in conflict again, while an earlier one, in 399 or 398, would point to association with Cyrus the Younger. Cyrus had been instrumental in bringing about Athens' defeat in the Peloponnesian War, and Xenophon's involvement with him only three years after the defeat would have rankled many in the city.[b] Some scholars have tried to square the evidence by suggesting intermediate dates, 396 or 395, during which both of these factors might have played a part.[c]

§3.3. That the Athenians took the trouble to exile Xenophon indicates that he may have been a more significant figure before he left home than has been assumed. Or perhaps events on the march or after it elevated him to a level of prominence that warranted a public decree. In the mid-390s he was openly linked with the Spartan king Agesilaos,[a] which would certainly have rendered his name recognizable in Athens. While that association may suggest a later date for the decree, the dispatch of the three hundred horsemen and the execution of Socrates in 399 strongly point to an early date, when the decree would form part of a decisive push against those seen as a threat to the democracy. This could be so even if the official rationale was different.

§3.4. Sometime after the battle of Coronea in 394, Xenophon went with Agesilaos to Sparta and for his service was awarded an estate at Skillous in Elis, near Olympia.[a] There is some debate about when he went to live on the estate, but he was probably settled there by the early 380s. By his own account, his time at Skillous

Intro.3.1b  Dedication at Delphi: 5.3.5. Those who argue that the exile decree came after this say that cities that paid for treasuries at Delphi bearing their names subsequently controlled them and would refuse dedications from exiles. But it is more likely that once built, the treasuries were handed over to the god—that is, to the control of his priests. Even if the Athenians had in theory claimed veto rights over dedications, it would have been difficult to stop Xenophon from making one if he turned up at Delphi in 394 alongside the Spartan army. Delphi: Intro. Map 3.1.

Intro.3.1c  This battle was one of the major set pieces of the Corinthian War (395–386), so named because much of the land fighting took place in the region of Corinth. Boeotia, Coronea, Corinth: Intro. Map 3.1.

Intro.3.2a  Diogenes Laertius on cause of exile: favoritism toward Sparta, 2.51; friendship with Cyrus, 2.58 (both in Appendix V: Diogenes). Pausanias, a second-century C.E. author of a famous travel guide to Greece, also cites Xenophon's links with Cyrus as the cause (5.6.5), as does Dio Chrysostom (*Orations* 8.1), a Greek orator and philosopher from Prusa (Ref. Map 4.2, AY), who lived in the first to second century C.E.

Intro.3.2b  Socrates' concern when Xenophon sought his advice about joining the expedition was that association with the prince could get him into trouble: 3.1.5.

Intro.3.2c  See Thomas 2009, §4.3.

Intro.3.3a  On Agesilaos, see Appendix W: Brief Biographies, §2.

Intro.3.4a  Estate at Skillous: *Anabasis* 5.3.7, Diogenes Laertius 2.52 (in Appendix V: Diogenes). Skillous, Elis, Olympia: Intro. Map 3.1.

was idyllic.[b] He writes that he used his share of money from a sale of slaves on the Black Sea to build a small-scale copy of the famous temple to Artemis at Ephesus, and that he organized an annual festival in her honor.[c] Together with his two sons, he hunted wild animals—boars, gazelles, deer—and cultivated fruit trees and vines.[d] He does not mention his wife, but in his biography Diogenes Laertius, who gives her name as Philesia, writes that she went with him to Skillous.[e] We might suppose that *Oikonomikos* (*On the Management of the Household*), Xenophon's essay on estate management, is based in part on their experiences there and that it was in the relative quiet of Skillous that he began his writing career in earnest.

§3.5. When the Spartan army was decisively defeated by Thebes at the battle of Leuktra in 371,[a] it seems probable that Xenophon and his family were forced to leave their estate. Diogenes says that the Eleians marched against Skillous and that Xenophon made his way to Corinth, where he stayed until he died.[b] However, the second-century C.E. travel writer Pausanias writes that after trying him for having received land from the Spartans, the Eleians pardoned Xenophon, and he remained on the estate for the rest of his life, though this claim is widely disbelieved.[c] Diogenes also writes that the decree of exile against him was repealed; and on this basis, and in light of the Athenocentric character of Xenophon's *Poroi* (*Ways and Means*) and *Hipparchikos* (*Cavalry Commander*), both written not earlier than the 360s, it has been argued that he returned to his home city.[d]

§3.6. Even if we don't really know where he went next, we do know that Xenophon continued writing until at least 356 or 355, since there are passages in his *Poroi* that refer to events in those years.[a] This suggests he did find somewhere to settle, but it is also possible that he moved from place to place with only a simple set of possessions. Poverty, after all, was a part of the fate that had been foretold for him prior to the beginning of his journey up-country with Cyrus: "He recalled that when he was setting out from Ephesus to join Cyrus, an eagle called out to him from the right while, however, it was sitting; at this, the seer who was escorting him had said that it was a great omen, signifying something not merely private, and of high repute; but also full of toil and suffering, as the other birds are prone to attack

Intro.3.4b  Xenophon and his estate: 5.3.7–13.
Intro.3.4c  Sale of slaves: 5.3.4. A portion from the sale went to Apollo at Delphi, discussed in §3.1. Xenophon informs us at 5.3.5 that the votive offering at Delphi was inscribed with his name and that of Proxenos, his guest-friend. Annual festival: 5.3.9. Ephesus: Intro. Map 3.1.
Intro.3.4d  One of Xenophon's sons, Gryllos, was killed while serving in the Athenian cavalry at the battle of Mantineia (362) in which Thebes (Intro. Map 3.1) and its allies fought against Sparta and Athens and their supporters. Following his death numerous authors wrote epitaphs and eulogies, and a painting for the Athens agora (marketplace) was commissioned. Diogenes (2.55, in Appendix V: Diogenes) remarks that Aristotle said these public displays were partly out of respect for the father.
Intro.3.4e  Xenophon's wife, Philesia: Diogenes 2.52 (in Appendix V). Mantineia: Intro. Map 3.1.
Intro.3.5a  This battle, the first major defeat of the Spartan army in two hundred years, ended Spartan hegemony in Greece. Leuktra: Intro. Map 3.1.
Intro.3.5b  Xenophon at Corinth: Diogenes Laertius 2.53, 2.56 (in Appendix V).
Intro.3.5c  Eleians pardon Xenophon: Pausanias 5.6.6. Pausanias adds that Xenophon's grave is to be seen a short distance from the sanctuary to Artemis that he built. However, many scholars suspect that this passage merely shows the Eleians taking advantage of Xenophon's subsequent fame and placing themselves in a favorable light.
Intro.3.5d  Decree of exile repealed: Diogenes Laertius 2.59 (in Appendix V: Diogenes). The repeal is thought to have happened either as a result of some clause in the King's Peace of 387/6, a Spartan-led peace negotiated with Persia, or at some time in the early 360s—not later than 362, when Xenophon's sons were fighting for Athens in the Mantineian War.
Intro.3.6a  Dateable passages in *Poroi* (*Ways and Means*): 5.9, 5.12.

the sitting eagle. However, he had added that the omen did not portend wealth, for the eagle gets its food supplies only when in flight."[b] It may be that the sign at Ephesus applied not only to the journey at hand but to the rest of Xenophon's life. At least from his time with the Ten Thousand, hardship, danger, and poverty would never be far away from him. However, as the eagle also portended, Xenophon would earn enduring fame.

## The Persian Empire

### Sources of Information

§4.1. Our knowledge of the empire founded by Cyrus the Great in the sixth century, and ended by Alexander the Great in the fourth, derives from a range of sources: archaeological, documentary (royal administrative documents), iconographic, and literary.[a] It bears mention that while they left a rich architectural and artistic legacy, the Persians neither wrote down their stories nor, apparently, maintained annals, as for instance the Assyrian kings before them had done.[b] Hence our image of Persia has been substantially shaped by what others—predominantly Greeks, such as Xenophon, Herodotus, and Ctesias—have written about it.[c] While advances in Persian studies continue to roll back this influence, it is important to note the foreign cultural and historical contexts in which these works were produced, and indeed the individual motivations of the writers, where these can be discerned. To touch on the case of Ctesias, Artaxerxes' physician, in his *Persika* he portrays Parysatis,[d] the mother of King Artaxerxes and Cyrus the Younger, as a scheming monster. Perhaps she was, but this portrait is as likely to be the result of Ctesias' penchant for colorful characters and events.

### Imperial Organization

§4.2. Control of the empire, which stretched from the Hellespont to the Indus River and from the Aral Sea to the first cataract of the Nile, was effected through a system of provincial governors, known as satraps.[a] These were appointed by the King and were predominantly drawn from the Persian elite. We meet several of them in *Anabasis*, the most prominent of whom are Pharnabazos and Tissaphernes.[b]

Intro.3.6b  Great omen: 6.1.23.

Intro.4.1a  For more on the empire, see Appendix C: The Persian Empire. On Cyrus the Great, see Appendix W: Brief Biographies, §9. Persian Empire: Intro. Map 4.6 and Ref. Map 9.

Intro.4.1b  Diodorus Siculus writes that Ctesias, Artaxerxes' Greek physician, claimed he had access to "the royal records, in which the Persians in accordance with a certain law of theirs kept an account of their ancient affairs" (Diodorus 2.32.4; Oldfather/Loeb translation; compare 2.22.5). There was also a tradition in late antiquity that an archive of annals was destroyed when Alexander burned down Persepolis in 330. Nevertheless, many scholars are skeptical about the existence of such records, even if the existence of extensive archival material,

such as the administrative records at Persepolis, is proven. Persepolis, Assyria: Intro. Map 4.6.

Intro.4.1c  Other sources are the Biblical books of Ezra, Nehemiah, and Esther. On Ctesias and his history, *Persika*, see Appendix W, §8, and Ancient Sources Cited in this Edition. For extracts from the surviving fragments, see Appendix U: Selections from Photius' Synopsis of Ctesias' *Persika*.

Intro.4.1d  On Parysatis, see Appendix W, §26.

Intro.4.2a  For more on satraps, see the Glossary. Hellespont: Intro. Map 4.6. Indus River, Aral Sea: Ref. Map 9, BZ, AY. Nile River: Intro. Map 4.6.

Intro.4.2b  On Tissaphernes and Pharnabazos, see Appendix W, §37, 27.

Pharnabazos had control of Hellespontine Phrygia and Bithynia continuously from 413, while at various times Tissaphernes governed Lydia and the Ionian coast. Herodotus (3.89–94) tells us that Darius I organized the empire into twenty satrapies, though this arrangement shifted over time as territories were merged, divided up, or lost.[c]

§4.3. The satraps were directly accountable to the King, who received regular reports about them from officials whom the Greeks referred to as the King's Eyes and the King's Ears.[a] The satraps had a range of responsibilities, chief among them security and taxation. Security included the maintenance of order and the protection of imperial property; those on the margins of the empire were the first line of defense against outside incursion, so their effectiveness and loyalty were particularly critical.[b] The most important duty of the satrap was collection and remittance of the tribute, a centrally determined tax levied on his province. This was in addition to the obligation to provide levies for the royal army when required, and could take the form of money or goods.[c] The tribute enabled the construction of temples and roads, paid for armies and fleets, and allowed the state to project influence beyond its boundaries.[d] The Kings accumulated wealth from it on a massive scale.[e]

§4.4. The imposition of the imperial system on subject peoples seems not to have been repressive: local rulers continued to exercise real authority and could prefer loyalty to rebellion when crises arose. In some cases the King permitted existing dynasties to be autonomous, as in Cyprus and in Cilicia, whose ruler (and his wife) Cyrus the Younger encountered in the march up-country.[a] These monarchs were de facto satraps, and as such their positions were dependent on remittance of the tribute and fulfillment of other obligations.

## Communications

§4.5. The nature of the empire brought significant challenges in communication. Not only did the great distances between the center and the outlying provinces constitute an obstacle, but in many cases so too did the terrain itself: mountains, rivers,

Intro.4.2c  On Hellespontine Phrygia, see n. 1.2.6a. Lydia, Ionia, Hellespontine Phrygia, Bithynia: Intro. Map 4.6.

Intro.4.3a  See Xenophon, *Kyroupaideia* (*The Education of Cyrus*) 8.2.10–12.

Intro.4.3b  The King himself maintained a standing army, which spearheaded offensive campaigns. The elite force known as the Immortals formed part of this. See Figure Intro.4.2. For more about the Persian military, see Appendix D: The Persian Army.

Intro.4.3c  In Appendix C: The Persian Empire, §20, Christopher Tuplin remarks that the tribute might have been not an obligation from city to King but a debt from satrap to King relating to the extent of authority granted personally to the satrap by the King.

Intro.4.3d  Plutarch, a Greek writer and polymath of around 100 C.E., describes in his *Life of Agesilaos* (15.6) how the Persians dealt with an invasion in the 390s led by the Spartan king Agesilaos (for the Cyreans and this campaign, see the Epilogue, §3): "Persian coins were

stamped with the figure of an archer, and Agesilaos said, as he was breaking camp, that the King was driving him out of Asia with ten thousand 'archers'; for so much money had been sent to Athens and Thebes and distributed among the popular leaders there, and as a consequence those peoples made war upon the Spartans" (Perrin/Loeb translation, slightly modified).

Intro.4.3e  Diodorus (17.71.2) gives a possible indication of the scale of this wealth when he writes that Alexander carted off from Persepolis 120,000 talents' worth of silver, assembling a vast number of mules and three thousand pack camels to do so. (The weight of the talent varied, depending on the standard being used. On the Euboic-Attic standard, 120,000 talents would have amounted to about 3,000 tons/2,720 metric tons. For the talent and this standard, see Appendix O: Measurements, §§10–11.)

Intro.4.4a  Cyrus and the Cilician royals: 1.2.12–27. Cyprus, Cilicia: Intro. Map 4.6.

FIGURE INTRO 4.2. PERSEPOLIS. THE PERSIAN ELITE FORCE KNOWN AS THE IMMORTALS (TOP). BOTTOM: TRIBUTE BEARERS IN PROCESSION.

and deserts remained natural boundaries even if they no longer formed political ones. From his travels in the interior, Xenophon observed that "the Great King's empire was strong in the magnitude of its territory and the number of its people, but weak from its extended lines of communication and the dispersal of its forces."[a] But although the King needed time to muster his forces and move them into place, the travel infrastructure was second to none. Building on preexisting networks, such as those developed in eastern Anatolia and Mesopotamia by the Assyrians,[b] the Persians expanded road links so that even remote areas of the empire were connected to the center. These "royal roads" were usually made of compacted dirt and were suitable for use year-round. An integral feature of the network was a system of way stations that facilitated the progress of royal armies and enabled rapid transit for messengers. These were typically situated a day's travel from one another, and as well as providing food and shelter for those on official business, their presence enhanced security along the routes for all travelers.

§4.6. The royal road about which we know the most is the one described by Herodotus that ran some 1,500 miles from Susa, in the Persian heartland in western Iran, to Sardis, at the western end of the empire.[a] The Ten Thousand started off on this road, but since Cyrus wished to conceal his intentions, he did not remain on it for long.[b] The journey from Sardis to Susa ordinarily took about ninety days by foot, but it could be done faster, as it was by the royal messengers on horseback.[c] Still faster (although limited) communication was achieved through the use of fire beacons.[d]

§4.7. Sea communications were not critical for Persia, a land empire with its heart in the interior, though some if not all of the satraps with territory bordering the sea maintained naval forces. Twenty-five of Cyrus the Younger's ships joined his expedition in the Gulf of Issus, having sailed from Ephesus with the aim of helping to take the Syrian-Cilician Gates.[a] More significant in terms of communications was travel

Intro.4.5a Dispersal of forces: 1.5.9. Xenophon was correct in his observation, though it may have been intended to increase the reader's interest in what has come to be termed panhellenism, an ideology that agitated for a unified Greek campaign against Persia. This was in vogue around the time he was writing *Anabasis* in the 370s/360s, although Xenophon seems not to have been a straightforward advocate of it. For more, see Appendix E: Panhellenism. For discussion of Xenophon's writing motivations, see §6.4–7.

Intro.4.5b These ancient networks remained the basis of the regional road system up until the advent of the modern highway, when engineers began to bulldoze and blast to make way for straight lines through the landscape. Eastern Anatolia, Mesopotamia, Assyria: Intro. Map 4.6.

Intro.4.6a The Royal Road: Herodotus 5.52–53. The author reports it as being 13,500 stades long, which equates to some 1,500 miles/2,400 kilometers; see Appendix O: Measurements, §5. The road linked a number of important sites in Anatolia. Royal Road, Susa, Sardis: Intro. Map 4.6.

Intro.4.6b On their way back, the army rejoined the Royal Road between Kainai and Mespila (Ref. Map 9, CX) and after a detour came back to it

briefly again near the Tigris River crossroads (3.5.15). Xenophon's Kainai (Ashur in the *Barrington Atlas*): Book 2 map. Xenophon's Mespila (Nineveh): Map 3.5.15.

Intro.4.6c Herodotus writes of the royal courier system: "There is nothing that travels faster, and yet is mortal, than these couriers; the Persians invented this system, which works as follows. It is said that there are as many horses and men posted at intervals as there are days required for the entire journey, so that one horse and one man are assigned to each day. And neither snow nor rain nor heat nor dark of night keeps them from completing their appointed course as swiftly as possible" (Herodotus 8.98.1; Purvis/Landmark translation).

Intro.4.6d According to a Greek text falsely attributed to Aristotle (*De Mundo* 398a30–34), these formed a chain "from the boundaries of the empire to Susa and Ecbatana, so that the King, on the very same day, knew all that was news in Asia" (author's translation).

Intro.4.7a Ships join Cyrus: 1.4.2–5. Gulf of Issus (Issicus Sinus in the *Barrington Atlas*), Syrian-Cilician Gates (a pass on the Mediterranean coast between Cilicia and Syria; Kilikiai Pylai in the *Barrington Atlas*, Map 67 C3), Ephesus: Intro. Map 4.6.

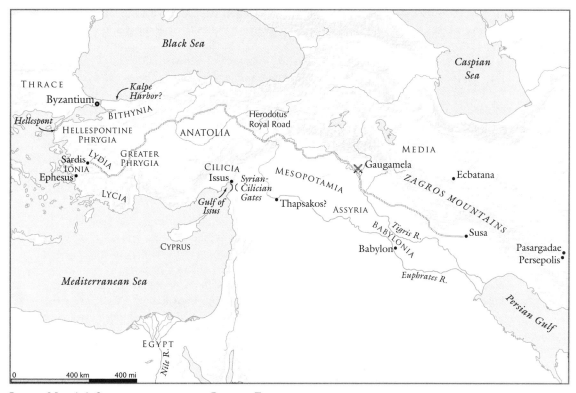

INTRO. MAP 4.6. SELECTED SITES IN THE PERSIAN EMPIRE.

by river. The Euphrates in particular was an important artery, and a ferry service from points along the middle part of the river operated downstream to Babylonia.[b] Cyrus, who crossed the river at Thapsakos,[c] did not avail himself of this channel in his haste to get to Babylonia, but clearly logistical requirements—the need to transport thousands of troops, equipment, and pack animals—would have made any such attempt extremely difficult.

## How Greeks and Persians Saw Each Other

§5.1. A common Greek word for a foreigner was *barbaros*, "barbarian." The onomatopoeic term described those who spoke languages unintelligible to the Greeks ("bar-bar-bar"). It was not originally pejorative, but it acquired something of this sense in the fifth century following the Persian invasions, first by Darius I in 490 and then by his son Xerxes I in 480. The pejorative overtones were especially marked

Intro.4.7b  Euphrates River, Babylonia: Intro. Map 4.6.
Intro.4.7c  Ferry service: in 395–394 the Athenian admiral Konon used this to sail down the Euphrates to meet with the King (Diodorus 14.81.4–6).

Thapsakos, possible location: Intro. Map 4.6 (not listed in the *Barrington Atlas*). For discussion about this site, see Appendix P: The Route of the Ten Thousand, §§4–5.

among the Athenians, whose sacred sanctuaries had been destroyed in the campaign of King Xerxes.[a] The impact of the Persian penetration of their acropolis, the religious and historical heart of the city, is hard to overstate. Before the invasions Athenians' self-identity could be said to have been an aggregate of many small features on which they agreed and disagreed with their generally similar Greek neighbors and rivals; after the invasions it came to be fashioned more by contrast with the barbarian as their polar opposite. Athenians came to be publicly imagined as democratic, athletic, warlike, frugal, and free; the barbarian, as powerless, weak, cowardly, decadent, and slavish.

§5.2. In visual terms the Persians depicted outsiders by differentiating them into types. Monumental reliefs showing subject peoples give each group a distinctive costume, although it is not always clear which people is being represented.[a] In Persian records the Greeks appear as the Yauna, an undifferentiated ethnic group on the western Anatolian seaboard.[b] It is striking that not a single extant Persian document refers to any of the Greek mainland states. Aeschylus, one of the great fifth-century Athenian tragedians, may have intended to portray the Persian King's mother as ignorant when he has her ask the whereabouts of Athens, but he may also have been hinting at the geopolitical reality.[c] In what may be another instance of subversive political commentary, Herodotus writes that Cyrus the Great had to ask who the Spartans were when he received a threat delivered by one of their messengers; the historian later reports that another Persian King, Darius I, had never before heard of Athens when he learned that it was the Athenians who, with the Ionians, had burned the temple of Kybele at Sardis.[d] This last act surely brought the Athenians to the attention of the Persians, but it is doubtful that they ever assumed the same prominence in the Persian mind as the Persians did in the Greek.

§5.3. A remarkable, and perhaps related, feature of Xenophon's account of Cyrus' expedition is how little he says about the Asian troops in the army; in contrast to the wealth of information he supplies on the Greeks, we learn virtually nothing about this force from him.[a] His silence on the subject is nevertheless consistent with contemporary historiography, where we regularly encounter the numberless horde. A striking example in Herodotus is where he cites an inscription set up at Thermopylae after the famous battle there with King Xerxes in 480: "Three million foes were once fought right here by four thousand men from the Peloponnese."[b]

---

Intro.5.1a  See Figure Intro.5.1 for a depiction of Greek superiority over Persians.

Intro.5.2a  For an image of a procession of tribute bearers at Persepolis, see Figure Intro.4.2 (bottom).

Intro.5.2b  Darius I's Bisutun Inscription—a trilingual text carved into a cliffside recording the King's achievements—lists the territories of the empire, with those surrounding the imperial center named first; in Kuhrt 2007, 141–58. The arrangement may reflect a perceived hierarchy of civilizations, with those on the periphery on the lowest rung; see also Herodotus 1.134. Bisutun: Ref. Map 9, CX. Western Anatolia: Intro. Map 3.1.

Intro.5.2c  "Where in the world do men say this Athens is?" (Aeschylus, *Persians* 231; author's translation)

Intro.5.2d  Cyrus the Great asks who the Spartans were:

Herodotus 1.152–53. Darius ignorant of Athens: Herodotus 5.105. Kybele was an ancient Anatolian mother goddess. Ionia, Sardis: Intro. Map 3.1.

Intro.5.3a  Diodorus, in his first-century summary of the march, is more informative, and by virtue of his account, we can make a decent guess as to who made up the Asian part of Cyrus' army: Phrygians (Greater Phrygia), Lydians (Intro. Map 4.6), Paphlagonians (Ref. Map 5, AX), and Persians; see Appendix S: Diodorus, 14.22.5–6.

Intro.5.3b  Three million foes: Herodotus 7.228.1 (Purvis/Landmark translation). The modern historian of Persia, Pierre Briant, refers to this convention as "a deeply rooted *topos*" (Briant 2002, 686). Thermopylae: Map 5.3.7, BX. Peloponnese: Intro. Map 3.1.

FIGURE INTRO.5.1. TWO SIDES OF AN ATHENIAN RED-FIGURE WINE VESSEL C. 460 DEPICTING GREEK SUPERIORITY OVER BARBARIANS IN THE WAKE OF THE ATHENIAN VICTORY AT THE BATTLE OF THE EURYMEDON RIVER.

Xenophon writes that Artaxerxes' army numbered 1.2 million in 401, although as one of the army's four divisions was late arriving, only nine hundred thousand were present for the eventual battle at Cunaxa.[c] As to Cyrus' native force, all Xenophon tells us is that "the number of barbarians with Cyrus was one hundred thousand, plus around twenty scythed chariots."[d] Its actual number is likely to have been no more than twenty thousand. A considerably larger force would have introduced logistical and command-and-control issues that are not in Xenophon's narrative, and he would almost certainly have noted such difficulties had there been any, because it is clear from *Anabasis* that he was keenly interested in problems of army leadership. Just on the logistics, the King's army must have been much smaller than the reported million or so; about sixty thousand may be the correct order of magnitude.

Intro. 5.3c  Size of the King's army: *Anabasis* 1.7.11–12. Two other Greek sources—Plutarch (drawing on Ctesias) and Diodorus (citing Ephorus, a fourth-century historian whose works are lost)—provide a less fanciful figure for the King's army: four hundred thousand (Plutarch, *Life of Artaxerxes* 13.3, in Appendix T: Plutarch; Diodorus 14.22.2, in Appendix S: Diodorus). Battlefield of Cunaxa: Map 1.5.1, inset.

Intro.5.3d  Size of Cyrus' native army: 1.7.10. Scythed chariots are described at 1.8.10.

§5.4. The average Athenian's hostile view of the Persians and their subject peoples was not uniformly held among Greeks. Some cities—Thebes,[a] for example—had not opposed the invading Persian army in 480 (though some Thebans had done so unofficially) and had subsequently retained friendly links with the King. Nor did all Athenian writers, or even all those writing for an Athenian audience, unthinkingly adopt the prevailing view. Xenophon's own reports from his travels in the Persian Empire are a case in point. While for various literary reasons he skimps on descriptions of Cyrus' native force, his depictions of foreign peoples encountered on the retreat are frequently nuanced and nearly always founded on experience. He clearly respects the Kardouchoi as proud and fierce warriors never subjected by the King, while he reports the opinion of the soldiers that the Mossynoeci, hill dwellers with a liking for outdoor sex and dancing with the severed heads of captured enemies, were "the most barbarous" of all the peoples whom the Greeks encountered.[b] As to Xenophon's portrayal of Persians, there is little negative stereotyping, and the individuals he describes almost always display values admired by Greeks. More generally, if, as some suggest, there was a scheme in the Greek mind whereby the sea and its periphery represented civilization (Hellenism) and the remote interior its antithesis (barbarism), it did not find a faithful reflection in *Anabasis*.

### Xenophon the Writer

§6.1. Xenophon was the author of fourteen works that we know of, all of which have come down to us.[a] Modern scholars have found it difficult to establish their chronology, as evidence from the works themselves and limited biographical information rarely give conclusive proof of their dates of composition. Nonetheless, even if scholars disagree on the relative chronology, few dispute the idea that Xenophon wrote fairly late in his life. The desire to date individual books stems from the benefit of being able to situate them in a personal and historical context. If we could establish the dates of authorship, or even approximate periods of composition, it would help us to know more about how and why Xenophon wrote a particular work.

§6.2. Although *Anabasis* is vividly written, there is little doubt that it was composed long after the events of 401–399 that it describes. The author's nostalgic tone in his description of his later life at Skillous (5.3.7–13), and in particular the use of the imperfect tense in all the verbs in the original Greek of 5.3.9–10, suggest that it was written after he had left his estate, although it might well have been a work in progress when he left. On balance, a time period from the late 370s to the early 360s seems to be a reasonable estimate. That would fit well with a remark by Xenophon on the journey (6.6.9) referring to Sparta's then being the leading power in Aegean Greece, the implication being that it was not at the time of writing (see further §3.5).

§6.3. Why did Xenophon choose to write his account some thirty years after the expedition ended? Clearly the story of the Ten Thousand was important to him in itself, but as we'll see, the events of 401–399 also allowed him to express other concerns.

Intro.5.4a Thebes: Intro. Map 3.1.
Intro.5.4b Encounter with the Kardouchoi: 4.1.5–4.3.34.
    Kardouchoi never subjected by the King: 3.5.16. "The most barbarous" Mossynoeci:
    5.4.34. Kardouchoi territory: Map 4.4.3.
    Mossynoeci territory: Map 5.4.1.
Intro.6.1a See the List of Xenophon's Writings following the Introduction.

### Writing Agenda

§6.4. Xenophon's writings span a wide range of genres—biography, history, historical fiction, philosophical dialogue, technical treatise, travelogue—but a number of themes and concerns persistently recur. Moral philosophy and leadership are particularly pervasive, as, at a more mundane level, is the advantage to be derived from horsemanship and the appropriate deployment of cavalry. Sparta is another topic that turns up again and again. Xenophon regularly provides character descriptions or anecdotes that go beyond the immediate needs of the main narrative, often with a didactic purpose but sometimes to stand as memorials of the individuals concerned. This interest in remembrance points to a further key theme, apologia. This manifests itself primarily as Xenophon's self-defense and, in the Socratic works, defense of his teacher. The recognition of these recurring themes and concerns has led to a view that much of Xenophon's work is the product of a single literary project, although to be sure individual works may place more emphasis on one or another of them.

§6.5. One distinctive characteristic of Xenophon's writing just touched on is its didactic orientation. *Hipparchikos* (*Cavalry Commander*) and *Kynegetikos* (*On Hunting*), for instance, are concerned with practical instruction; *Kyroupaideia* (*The Education of Cyrus*) highlights the conduct of an ideal leader; while the Socratic works *Apologia Sokratous* (*Defense of Socrates*), *Symposion* (*The Drinking Party*), *Memorabilia* (*Recollections of Socrates*), *Oikonomikos* (*On the Management of the Household*) provide guidance on moral and practical questions together with defending the philosopher. As is shown in §8.2–6, one of his preoccupations in *Anabasis* is to provide models for military leadership. Given his Socratic background and Socrates' concern with improving those around him, it is no surprise that Xenophon sought to pass on to his readers what he had learned.

§6.6. Many of Xenophon's works are inspired and shaped by personal experience, notably by his early association with Socrates and by his experiences of war. His abiding interest in political philosophy may be a product of both. Time and again the problem of how to rule—whether households, animals, armies, kingdoms, or, ultimately, oneself—surfaces in his works. Thus, for example, *Kyroupaideia* sets up (and then arguably knocks down or undermines) a pattern of ideal leadership in the person of a largely fictionalized Cyrus the Great. It opens with a reference to the overthrow of democracies by those who prefer to live under any regime but a democratic one, and shortly afterward it refers to the typical brevity of rule by those who aspire to act as tyrants. The installation and deposition of the Thirty (§2.15) were quite likely in Xenophon's mind. Turning to the everyday, *Oikonomikos* deals with the problem of how to rule a household, making clear in its concluding passage that the author sees similarities between the role of the householder and that of the general or political leader.

§6.7. Exile surely shaped the writings of Xenophon, banished from his homeland in the 390s and driven from Skillous,[a] his adopted home of about twenty years, in 371. His expulsion from his native city must have weighed heavily on him. He may

Intro.6.7a  Skillous: Intro. Map 3.1.

have felt that the exile decree was unjust and been motivated to set the record straight. There is certainly a case for interpreting *Anabasis*, the only work of his that refers to the exile, as Xenophon's defense against the accusations, whatever they might have been. In the narrative he deals carefully with his associations with Cyrus the Younger and with Sparta, for one or both of which his fellow citizens found fault with him. That he does not defend himself overtly may be due to the repeal of the decree,[b] or perhaps it is a measure of his contempt for the charge against him. Alternatively, his silence could mark his obedience to the laws of the city, a virtue championed by his teacher Socrates in both word and deed.

### Literary Method

§6.8. Hallmarks of Xenophon's writing include experimentation with form and narrative, a subtle yet lively style,[a] and the use of such devices as exemplars and "literary apologia." Without question, Xenophon was a talented writer, but he doubtless benefited as well from the competitive literary environment of the day, in which authors strove to distinguish themselves with their innovations.[b]

§6.9. In the emerging field of historiography, Xenophon differed in important ways from his predecessors. In contrast to Hecataeus,[a] Herodotus, and Thucydides, who open their histories with succinct programmatic statements, he begins his in the middle of events, with no indication of his objectives as an author. That almost all of his other works indicate at the outset what is to follow emphasizes the exceptional nature of his authorial decisions in *Anabasis* and *Hellenika*. Perhaps Xenophon meant to imply that his concept of the genre was different from theirs. His apparently idiosyncratic, unsystematic treatment of events in *Hellenika* does put him at odds with the methodical history of Thucydides.[b] Indeed, many fourth-century writers tended to change the way historical truth was presented. Accuracy was increasingly marginalized as writers sought to manipulate the past for the purpose of moral instruction. In *Hellenika* Xenophon, to an even greater extent than any of his predecessors, shaped his narrative more by moralizing factors than by the analysis of important events. For example, he is more likely to feature historical episodes where the unjust come to grief or an individual's lack of discipline brings grief to others[c] than are those whose works place less emphasis on such ethical content. The likely cause of this his-

Intro.6.7b  Repeal of exile decree: Diogenes Laertius 2.59 (in Appendix V: Diogenes). See further n. Intro.3.5d.

Intro.6.8a  For more on Xenophon's style, see the Translator's Notes, §§1–9.

Intro.6.8b  On rivalry between Xenophon and Plato, see Diogenes Laertius 3.34.

Intro.6.9a  Hecataeus of Miletus was a mythographer, genealogist, and geographical writer who lived in the late sixth to the early fifth century. Miletus: Map 1.2.10, BX.

Intro.6.9b  Most notably Xenophon leaves out important events, ones that Thucydides, one expects, would have included. Prominent in this regard are the liberation of Messenia (Map 1.2.1, BX) by Thebes, the foundation of the Second Athenian League, and the capture of Samos (Map 1.2.10, AX). Still, in

characterizing *Hellenika*, we shouldn't think of it as ahistorical: for example, as with Thucydides, Xenophon frequently refers to documentary sources—letters, decrees, inscriptions—in his narrative. In Appendix N: Xenophon and the Development of Classical Historiography, §2, John Dillery notes that Xenophon's omission of a preface in *Hellenika* suggests that the work was intended as a continuation of Thucydides' history, which ends around the time that *Hellenika* starts.

Intro.6.9c  For instance, the story of the Spartan commander Alketas, whose infatuation with a boy led to a prisoner escape and the revolt of Oreos (*Hellenika* 5.4.56–57). Oreos: Ref. Map 2, BY.

toriographical change (if we assume a change and not just individual turns) was the profound social, economic, and political upheaval of the later fifth century; as a writer in the first half of the fourth century, Xenophon was part of an intellectual milieu that sought to reinvigorate moral fiber and that embraced morally driven exemplary writing as a way of promoting personal excellence.

§6.10. While he was not unique in this, Xenophon believed strongly in the power of example to affect human behavior. Commenting in *Kyroupaideia* (*The Education of Cyrus*) on the moral downfall of the people of Asia, he writes that they turned to wickedness because they witnessed it in their rulers: "For, whatever the character of the rulers is, such also that of the people under them for the most part becomes."[a] A close reading of *Anabasis* reveals the extent to which it is shaped by paradigm; as I argue in §8.12–14, Xenophon represents himself as a model student of Socrates. But it is not just characters in *Anabasis* that have a distinctly exemplary quality; so too do many of the episodes and events described and even some of the places, such as Kalpe Harbor on the Black Sea and the estate at Skillous, both of which are depicted in ideal terms.[b] Xenophon frequently uses exempla to help realize his didactic aims on the subject of leadership, as we can discern with Cyrus, Klearchos, Tissaphernes,[c] and the character of Xenophon. In virtually all cases, I believe we have elaboration rather than invention, with characters, episodes, and places regularly configured to serve his agenda.

§6.11. Several literary innovations first appear in *Anabasis*. In Michael Flower's analysis of Xenophon's approach to history, he suggests that the author created a category of "microhistory (which treats of an isolated event in great detail)," as opposed to "macrohistory (which provides a grand narrative)."[a] Arguably another first is the author's apparent use of a pseudonym. Xenophon, it seems, was among the earliest writers in the Western tradition to use a pen name. In *Anabasis* he provides no detail about the narrator of the story (Xenophon is a character in it and is formally introduced in the third person at 3.1.4), but in *Hellenika* he writes that one Themistogenes of Syracuse authored an account of Cyrus' march up-country and the retreat of his Greeks to the sea.[b] The notion that Xenophon is here using Themistogenes as a pseudonym for himself has been current since at least the first century C.E.[c] and is the most widely accepted explanation for the statement in *Hellenika*.[d] Finally, as I argue in §8.12–14, in the burgeoning field of Socratic literature, Xenophon provided a novel means of defending his teacher, linking Xenophon

Intro.6.10a   Character of the rulers: *Kyroupaideia* (*The Education of Cyrus*) 8.8.5 (Miller/Loeb translation).

Intro.6.10b   Neither the location of the harbor nor the actual estate in Skillous have been certainly identified. Kalpe Harbor, possible location: Intro. Map 4.6. Skillous: Intro. Map 3.1.

Intro.6.10c   On Cyrus, Klearchos, and Tissaphernes, see Appendix W: Brief Biographies, §§10, 20, 37.

Intro.6.11a   Flower 2012, 47–51; for the quotation, see p. 48.

Intro.6.11b   Themistogenes: *Hellenika* 3.1.2. Syracuse: Ref. Map 1, BW.

Intro.6.11c   See Plutarch, *Moralia* 345e.

Intro.6.11d   Other explanations have been suggested for

the *Hellenika* passage: both Themistogenes and Xenophon wrote accounts but the former's is lost; the passage is an interpolation; the name Themistogenes is the result of a copyist's error and the relevant clause at 3.1.2 should read: "this has been written, rightfully and dutifully, by one of Cyrus' men"; by naming Themistogenes as the narrator of *Anabasis*, Xenophon means to distinguish between the narrator of the text and himself as its author, thus warning readers that he himself does not necessarily agree with everything *Anabasis* says. For this last explanation, see McCloskey 2017.

the character's leadership success on the retreat to the guidance and instruction given by the philosopher in Xenophon the author's other Socratic works.

### *Anabasis:* The March Record

§7.1. One of the best-known features of Xenophon's text is his march record. From Sardis, where the expedition began, until its effective completion at Byzantium, the author supplies more or less a point-to-point log of the journey; that is, he names landmarks or cities to which the army marched and tells us the number of days taken and, more often than not, the distance covered.[a] Frequently he provides additional information, such as the width of rivers, descriptions of landscapes, and environmental conditions. In the first four books, covering the march up-country and the retreat to the Black Sea, he recorded his distances mostly by a combination of two units of measure: the *stathmos* and the parasang.

§7.2. The Greek term *stathmos* denotes both a stopping station on the road and the distance traveled between two such points. A day's travel usually, but not always, equated to a *stathmos*. The second-century C.E. author Arrian, in his book describing the campaigns of Alexander the Great, provides an example in which, by moving quickly, one detachment covered two or three *stathmoi* a day for several days together.[a]

§7.3. The parasang was a Persian measure that is not perfectly understood. A number of modern writers think that it was time based, one formula being "the distance covered by an army in one hour's marching." By this definition the parasang as a unit of length would vary with terrain, weather, and season (as the ancient hour's length varied with the season). Some Classical Greek writers, on the other hand, took the parasang to be a fixed unit of distance. Herodotus and Strabo equated it with thirty stades, about 3.4 miles/5.5 kilometers, although Strabo added that it could also be forty or sixty stades.[a] Using the more common figure of thirty stades, these two readings of the parasang—temporal and spatial—are reasonably concordant: a soldier in full kit walking on a track would typically cover a little over 3 miles/4.8 kilometers, roughly the same as thirty stades, in one hour.

§7.4. It would not be surprising if Xenophon, like Herodotus and Strabo, understood the parasang as a unit of distance. When the thirty-stades formula is applied to his march record in *Anabasis*, it does indeed result in close fits for many sections of the route. However, that is not the case for the whole route, and it may be that we are looking at a time-based version of the measure, the parasang distance in places

---

Intro.7.1a  Sardis, Byzantium: Ref. Map 7, BW, AW.

Intro.7.2a  Arrian, *Anabasis Alexandrou* (Alexander's march up-country): 3.29.7. The title references Xenophon's and is intended to make a parallel between the two works and their authors; see Appendix R: The Legacy of Xenophon's *Anabasis*, §2, and for more detailed discussion, the Introduction by Paul Cartledge, §1.1–3, in Romm 2010. In this edition, *stathmoi* is translated as "days' march." For more on the *stathmos*, see Appendix O: Measurements, §6.

Intro.7.3a  Strabo (c. 64? B.C.E.–c. 24 C.E.) was a Greek

historian and geographer. His best-known work, the *Geography*, provides detailed information on peoples and countries of the ancient world. Parasang equals 30 stades: Herodotus 2.6.3, 5.53, 6.42.2. Parasang equals 30, 40, or 60 stades: Strabo 11.11.5. One stade is about 200 yards/180 meters; 1 parasang on this basis would equal 6,000 yards/5,485 meters—that is, around 3.4 miles/5.5 kilometers. For more on the stade and the parasang, see Appendix O, §§5, 7–8, respectively.

being less than thirty stades because of difficult terrain.[a] Alternatively, the difficult circumstances might have resulted in an impression of longer toil in the writer's mind, so leading to an inflated number of parasangs for the march segment.[b] In this volume we have taken the definition of the parasang to include terrain as a factor: the distance covered by a traveler in an hour over a particular terrain in normal conditions. For example, a four-mile/six-kilometer hike on level ground might take one parasang, while a mountain march of the same distance might take two. In practice, there is no difference in the mileage figures to be derived from Xenophon's parasangs whether one assumes that in difficult terrain people had a tendency to overstate the number of parasangs or whether the definition of the parasang itself took the terrain into account.

§7.5. Some scholars think that Xenophon's parasang also had literary functions. For example, its fluctuation and absence in the remoter stages of the retreat are intended to reflect the army's disorientation as it struggles to escape from the interior.[a] Then, once the army reaches the sea at Trapezus[b] and marches along the Black Sea coast (in Books 5 and 6), Xenophon does not use the parasang at all, instead describing progress in terms of days and, occasionally, in stades. One explanation for this could be that the army was now in the vicinity of Greek colonies and only on the periphery of the King's control. Thus it suggests a link in Xenophon's mind between the empire and the Persian measure and that, by abandoning it, he meant to underline the changed political environment.

### The Diary Question

§7.6. The gap in time between the end of the expedition and the publication of Xenophon's account raises questions about the source(s) for his march record and its accuracy. Even if he had written some form of aide-mémoire immediately after the expedition, it would be extraordinary for him to recall the course of more than three thousand miles/4,825 kilometers from memory. For this reason it has been argued that he must have kept a diary. Edward Bunbury wrote in his classic *History of Ancient Geography*, "...the whole series of marches and distances traversed could hardly have been preserved otherwise than by being committed to writing at the time."[a]

§7.7. Doubts about whether Xenophon kept a diary arise principally from the practical difficulties that would have been involved in maintaining one. For an individual to maintain one consistently over the long period of the march would have

Intro.7.4a  For example, at 1.5.5, Xenophon says the army crossed a remote desert stretch, 90 parasangs in thirteen days. This segment, Korsote to Pylai, is about 210 miles/340 kilometers long, a rate of 2.3 miles/3.7 kilometers to the 30-stade parasang compared to a standard rate of 3.4 miles/5.5 kilometers (Korsote to Pylai: Map 1.5.1 and inset, *Halting places 23–24*).

Intro.7.4b  The phenomenon is illustrated by the case of a British military expedition to Abyssinia (modern Ethiopia) in the nineteenth century. Bunbury (1879, 362) reports that experienced officers estimated the distances they marched per day through difficult terrain to be 16 or 18 miles/26 or 29 kilometers, but when these journeys were measured, the actual daily progress amounted only to 8 or 9 miles/13 or 14 kilometers.

Intro.7.5a  An instance would be the desperate crossing of Kardouchoi territory in Book 4 where the parasang is not used at all. Kardouchoi territory: Map 4.4.3, *Halting place 42*. For the measure having a literary function in *Anabasis*, see Rood 2010b and Purves 2010.

Intro.7.5b  Trapezus: Ref. Map 7, AY.

Intro.7.6a  "the whole series of marches": Bunbury 1879, 359.

required great discipline; in the face of the elements and the enemy, a stock of good fortune—not to mention papyri to write on—would also have been needed. It is worth noting that there is only one reference to anyone writing on the march, this, ironically, relating to a barbarian noble who wrote secretly to the King.[a]

§7.8. What are the alternatives? Perhaps someone else on the march kept a journal that Xenophon copied. This person is unlikely to have been a "diarist," but he could have been an official whose records related to the logistics of the march. Cyrus would have had to keep a payroll for his mercenaries, and it is apparent that the Greeks, at least in the later stages of their journey, kept their own records. At Kerasous, a Greek city to the west of Trapezus, a count was taken of the army, and the money raised from the sale of prisoners was distributed among the soldiers; earlier, on their arrival in Trapezus, it was agreed to maintain the crews of confiscated ships from the "common fund."[a] These reports indicate the maintenance of a treasury function, which may have included a payroll and other information on progress.

§7.9. Another explanation could be that Xenophon accessed information from oral and written sources. He could, for example, have cross-checked his own recollections with those of comrades, a method liable to yield good if limited results; he might have obtained further detail by interviewing foreigners—exiles, traders, slaves—some of whom would have had intimate knowledge of the topography of their native lands. Xenophon himself alludes to such a possibility in a poignant passage in Book 4. The army is confronted by yet another hostile tribe, and a clash seems imminent, when a Makronian peltast, who had been a slave in Athens, approaches him and says "that he recognized the language the people were speaking. 'I think,' he said, 'that this is my native country, and unless there is something to prevent it, I would like to talk to them.'"[a]

§7.10. As to written sources, Ctesias gave details of imperial routes in his *Persika*,[a] and Xenophon does refer to this work (though not in connection with distances or routes) in *Anabasis* at 1.8.27. Other potential sources were Hecataeus, on the geography of the continent, and Herodotus, on the Persian Royal Road.[b] It is worth noting that by the late 370s, when Xenophon probably began writing his account, he would have had access to a growing number of written sources. While most of the early fourth-century writers' works have not come down to us, one we do know of is that of the so-called Oxyrhynchus historian, whose history probably covered the period from 411 to 386.[c] From the recovered papyri of this history, it is evident that the author was well informed about Persia and that he had knowledge of the topography of Anatolia. Beyond Greece, although Persian sources would have

Intro.7.7a  The letter of Orontas: 1.6.3.
Intro.7.8a  Count taken: 5.3.3–4. The "common fund": 5.1.12. Kerasous: Map 5.4.1.
Intro.7.9a  Makronian peltast: 4.8.4–5. Peltasts: light-armed infantrymen; for more, see Appendix H: Infantry and Cavalry in *Anabasis*, §§4–5. Makrones territory: Map 4.7.1, inset.
Intro.7.10a  Ctesias' statistics for imperial routes are referred to in Photius §76 (not in Appendix U: Photius' Synopsis of Ctesias' *Persika*).
Intro.7.10b  For Hecataeus, see n. Intro.6.9a. Herodotus

on the Persian Royal Road: 5.52–53. Royal Road: Intro. Map 4.6.
Intro.7.10c  The Oxyrhynchus historian, whose name is not known, wrote a history of Greece that has survived only in fragments. This was published quite possibly by the end of the 370s, though conceivably as late as 346. For more on this important work and on the possible identity of the author, see Appendix M: Other Ancient Sources on the Ten Thousand, §11.

been more difficult to access and use, we know from the archives at Persepolis that the royal administration maintained extensive records, including travel-related material; an example that has been part of a recent archival study is a document in which Arshama, the satrap of Egypt, authorizes his steward to draw daily travel rations from a series of officials along his route from Babylonia.[d]

§7.11. It is quite likely that Xenophon drew on travelogues and gazetteers that were in circulation. There are indications of their usage in the text—for instance, in the formulaic descriptions he often applies to cities, expressed by one or a combination of three adjectives: *oikoumenos* (populous), *megas* (big), and *eudaimōn* (prosperous). Then there are his detailed descriptions of Larisa and Mespila, the large deserted or partly deserted cities on the Tigris River.[a] Of Larisa he writes, "The width of its wall was twenty-five feet/eight meters, its height one hundred/ thirty meters; the circuit around it was two parasangs"; and of Mespila, "The foundation was of dressed stone containing many crushed shells, fifty feet/fifteen meters in width and fifty in height, and on top of this was a brick wall, fifty feet in width and a hundred in height. The circuit around the perimeter was six parasangs."[b] Xenophon was doubtless struck by the exceptional size of the sites, but as George Cawkwell remarked, the Ten Thousand were not tourists and it is hard to imagine Xenophon pacing around the perimeter of these cities to gather data for a diary while Tissaphernes' army harried the rear guard.[c]

§7.12. In light of the available sources on the one hand, and the challenges of maintaining a diary on the other, my view is that Xenophon did not keep one, not systematically anyway. Nevertheless it is possible that the answer to the diary question lies somewhere in the middle ground: Xenophon could have made, or copied, some rudimentary notes en route and later, with the aid of memory and written and oral sources, fleshed these out.

### Reliability of the March Record

§7.13. However Xenophon produced his march record, some doubt its reliability. Given his moralizing tendency in *Hellenika*, it could be that he is not primarily concerned with completeness and accuracy but that the record instead acts as a backdrop for the major themes in the narrative, indicated in §6.4 and discussed in §8. As has been said, some consider that Xenophon uses units of measurement possibly even more for literary reasons than for the hard information they convey.

§7.14. One way to test the record, and test whether he intended it to accurately reflect the course of the journey, is to check the detail provided in the account against the territories through which the army passed. A high degree of harmony between his descriptions and distances and what we can observe now would point to an intention to leave a verifiable record of the army's progress. If there were little agreement, then little weight could be placed on the record, and indeed we could

Intro.7.10d  Arshama document: Kuhrt 2007, 739–741, recently studied in Tuplin and Ma, 2020. Persepolis, Babylonia, Egypt: Intro. Map 4.6.

Intro.7.11a  Larisa (Xenophon's name for the ancient city referred to as Nimrud today), Mespila (Xenophon's name for ancient Nineveh), Tigris River: Book 3 map.

Intro.7.11b  City descriptions: Larisa, 3.4.7; Mespila, 3.4.10–11.

Intro.7.11c  Ten Thousand not tourists: George Cawkwell, "When, How and Why Did Xenophon Write the *Anabasis*?" in Lane Fox, 2004, 52. On Tissaphernes, see Appendix W: Brief Biographies, §37.

set aside the whole question of a route diary.[a] A cursory look at the map shows that the geographical detail is not mere fantasy, but the important question of how accurate it is still remains. Three different sections of the route from Sardis to the Black Sea (Books 1–4) are examined in §7.15–18.[b]

§7.15. The first half of Book 1 describes the journey across southern Anatolia, a region with a long and continuous settlement history, and therefore a promising testing ground. Xenophon's record of the stages there includes several points on the Royal Road and a number of cities and physical features whose locations are known. Although he does not define the parasang, if we work on the basis that it represents an hour's walk over the terrain in question under normal conditions, then his travel figures in the main closely approximate the modern road distances.[a] One of the first to satisfy himself as to the faithfulness of the record here was the nineteenth-century English traveler William Hamilton, who, with the aid of the map that he used on his own journeys, reconstructed the segments from Kelainai to Iconium by measuring out the figures given by Xenophon between these fixed points.[b]

§7.16. Book 2 describes the march out of Babylonia and north along the Tigris River. This is another section that offers favorable opportunities for testing, since it is likely that the army was mostly following well-defined routes, including Herodotus' Royal Road for some of the time. At first sight the result is rather negative: Xenophon's account as it stands does not map well onto the historical geography. However, this simple conclusion can be mitigated if one or two adjustments are made. The first is that Xenophon seems to have reversed the names of two of the towns that the army came across, making them pass by Sittake first and Opis second, when it should be the other way around.[a] A second adjustment should be made because when we add up the figures Xenophon gives for the journey from crossing the Tigris in Babylonia to reaching the crossing of the Zapatas River, the total appears to be too small by about 16 miles/25 kilometers, or one or two days' travel depending on the circumstances.[b] Possibly this is connected with the fact that Xenophon does not mention the army's crossing of the Lesser Zab River,[c] which lay directly in its path; but it is not clear that these two phenomena are connected, since at the time of year the army crossed it, the river would have been fairly

Intro.7.14a If another contemporary account of the march were available, it would also provide a check on Xenophon's record. Some consider that such an alternative account lies behind Diodorus in his universal history (Diodorus 14.19–31, 14.37; in Appendix S: Diodorus); if it does, then that account for the most part was consistent with Xenophon's. For other possible sources on the march, see Appendix M: Other Ancient Sources on the Ten Thousand.
Intro.7.14b The route from Sardis to the Black Sea: see Ref. Map 7.
Intro.7.15a Twenty-first-century infrastructure development in Turkey has seen traditional routes replaced by new highways, though the old roads mostly remain in use; see also n. Intro.4.5b.

Intro.7.15b See Hamilton 1842, vol. 2, 198–205. For this segment of the march, Kelainai (Map 1.2.10, AY, *Halting place 4*) to Iconium (Map 1.2.13, AX, *Halting place 10*), see *Anabasis* 1.2.10–19.
Intro.7.16a Sittake (Xenophon's Opis): 2.4.13; Opis (Xenophon's Sittake): 2.4.25. Sittake, Opis: Map 2.3.14, *Halting places 32, 31*. Sittake is not listed in the *Barrington Atlas*.
Intro.7.16b Crossing the Tigris: 2.4.24 (Map 2.4.27, *Halting place 31*). Reaching the crossing of the Zapatas: 2.5.1 (Map 2.4.27, *Halting place 34*). For further discussion, see Appendix Q: The Chronology of the March, §11.
Intro.7.16c Lesser Zab River (Zabas Mikros in the *Barrington Atlas*): Map 2.4.27, *Halting place 33*.

insignificant. All the same, the proven discrepancy concerns only one, or possibly two days among many.[d]

§7.17. The trek across eastern Anatolia to the Black Sea,[a] recounted in Book 4, is the most difficult to check because the information given is very limited. From the crossing of the Kentrites River in southeastern Anatolia to the army's arrival at Trapezus, only one settlement (Gymnias), one mountain (Theches), and five rivers (Tigris, Teleboas, Euphrates, Phasis, and Harpasos) are named.[b] The lack of detail may point to the comparative unfamiliarity of the region to the Greeks, or to Xenophon's being distracted by events on the ground, or to both. If, however, Xenophon's information comes in part from external sources rather than solely from a diary, the problem of the record's sparseness grows more acute. Eastern Anatolia may have been distant from Greece, but that did not make it a barbarian wilderness; indeed, Xenophon's own account demonstrates that it was not. We know from Book 4 that the region contained several satrapies and, at the lower end of the administrative hierarchy, villages that provided tribute to the king.[c] Accordingly, we should expect that information concerning routes in the region was discoverable. On the hypothesis that external sources were important in assembling the record generally, it would follow that Xenophon here ignored information that he could have utilized. That in turn would fit with the view that the narrative in Book 4 is sketchy for a literary reason—namely, that the very absence of travel detail brings out a sense of the army's being adrift.

§7.18. Even so, over this long stretch, Xenophon does maintain his count of days and, for the majority of the stages, the number of parasangs traveled, so ensuring a certain continuity in the march record. Although we lack the means to verify these numbers, the chronology of the march provides an external check. Using seasonal indicators, we are able to assign windows of time to certain episodes described by Xenophon. Examples are the relative depth of the Tigris River when the army considers fording it near the crossroads; the presence of snow in Western Armenia and its evident absence in any notable quantity in the area of Mount Theches; and the strength of the "mad honey" the troops ate near Trapezus.[a] If we line up the chronological markers across the route and overlay his count of days, we can check the integrity of the record. By way of illustration, taking the first example, the army's sounding of the Tigris River depth indicates high water, which occurs in spring, so if Xenophon's count of days had us near the crossroads in autumn or early winter, then we would suspect there was time missing from the record; similarly, if

Intro.7.16d The flaws discussed in this paragraph are cited by those who believe there was no diary to support their argument, for had one been kept on a regular basis, it is unlikely these errors would have occurred.

Intro.7.17a Eastern Anatolia: Intro. Map 4.6.

Intro.7.17b All locations mentioned here can be found on Book 4 map.

Intro.7.17c Provinces of the Persian Empire were known as satrapies, their governors as satraps. Before the Achaemenids, the Persian kings of this period, the region had been administered first by Assyrians, then Medes,

each of whom maintained a substantial road network. For more on the Achaemenids, see the Glossary.

Intro.7.18a Depth of Tigris near crossroads: 3.5.7–11 (Map 3.4.24, *Halting place 41*). Snow in Western Armenia: 4.4.8, 4.4.11, 4.5.1, 4.5.3–6, 4.5.12–19 (Maps 4.4.3, 4.7.1, *Halting places 47–51*). No mention of snow near Mt. Theches: 4.7.19–27, esp. 4.7.25 (Map 4.7.1, inset, *Halting places 58–59*). "Mad honey"/hallucinogenic honey: 4.8.20–21 (in Kolchoi territory: Map 4.7.1, inset). For discussion, see Appendix Q: The Chronology of the March, §§8–9.

we were there in summer, we might think he had added a chunk of time. But the event will fit well enough if the army reached the place in February, as is compatible with the rest of Xenophon's chronological indications. Evaluation of the markers indicates generally that the record provides a fair reflection of the progress of the journey.[b]

§7.19. Since Xenophon went to some lengths to produce a faithful march record, we are bound to ask what his aim was in doing so. One is tempted to take the view that this sort of documenting is what we would expect of a historiographical work, but this may be anachronistic and, as we saw in §6.9, Xenophon's approach to writing about the past differed somewhat from others'. One possible answer as to his purpose is that the record serves to commemorate the journey for posterity: that the route is in many parts retraceable offers the prospect of an intimate connection between past and present. Just as a visitor to the ruins of ancient cities is bound to call to mind their past inhabitants, something Xenophon did himself when he saw Larisa and Mespila,[a] so those crossing the path of the Ten Thousand would remember the deeds of the army.[b] Xenophon certainly envisaged commemoration as being one of history's functions, as may be seen from a passage in *Hellenika* about Phleious, in the Peloponnese, which remained steadfastly loyal to its ally Sparta when under attack.[c] Xenophon remarks: "Now if a great city does some fine deed, all the historians record it; but I think that if a small city has accomplished many fine deeds, it is even more fitting to make them known."[d]

§7.20. Another possible explanation for the record could be that Xenophon intended it to be a practical road map into, and out of, the Persian interior. During the first half of the fourth century, exponents of an ideology often referred to by modern scholars as panhellenism argued for the unification of Greece to enable it to fight a war of conquest against the Persians. Aspects of this ideology arguably surface in *Anabasis*, though Xenophon does not seem to have been a straightforward advocate for it.[a]

§7.21. A further possibility is suggested by the evidence of the author's body of work as a whole, in which, as has been remarked in §6.5, practical and moral instruction were important ends. An outstanding feature of Xenophon's literary method in *Anabasis* is his setting of exemplars in *real* contexts: by marrying one form of truth with another, he aims to lend greater force to the embedded lessons of the narrative.

Intro.7.18b Some have argued strongly that there is in fact information missing from the record: see Robin Lane Fox, "Introduction" in Lane Fox 2004, esp. 35–46. For the chronology as an external check on the record, see further Appendix Q: The Chronology of the March.
Intro.7.19a Recalling ancient inhabitants of Larisa (Nimrud) and Mespila (Nineveh): 3.4.7–8, 3.4.11–12.
Intro.7.19b Arrian may have been one of the earliest to seek out a location on the march. In his *Periplus ponti Euxini* (*Voyage Around the Black Sea*), written in the second century C.E., he described how he looked down on the sea from the same place as Xenophon (1.1); see Appendix P: The Route of the Ten Thousand, n. P.1b. Note also Arrian, *Anabasis*

*Alexandrou* 2.7.8–9, and Plutarch, *Life of Antony* 45.6, and see Appendix R: The Legacy of Xenophon's *Anabasis*. In the modern era, many have tried to follow in the army's footsteps. See, for instance, the accounts in Kinneir 1818, Ainsworth 1854, Layard 1853, and, in more recent times, Manfredi 1986, Brennan 2005, Waterfield 2006.
Intro.7.19c Phleious, Peloponnese: Map 1.2.1, AY, BX.
Intro.7.19d Small city accomplished fine deeds: Xenophon, *Hellenika* 7.2.1 (Marincola/Landmark translation). Incidentally, the Ten Thousand on the retreat are often described by later commentators as a moving city, although Xenophon himself does not use this description.
Intro.7.20a See further Appendix E: Panhellenism.

## *Anabasis:* Themes

§8.1. We saw in §6.4 how certain themes and concerns underlie Xenophon's diverse output. A number of these are evident in *Anabasis,* namely horsemanship, relations between gods and men, Sparta, memorialization, military leadership, and apologia. Of these, the last two are the most prominent. Leadership is a central theme in many of Xenophon's writings; the range of contexts in which it is treated—military, household, kingship—shows his wide-ranging interest in the problem of how to rule. Apologia most obviously appears in the Socratic works, where Xenophon defends his teacher;[a] but elsewhere in his writings he defends himself and other historical figures. With regard to himself, he does this in a characteristically subtle manner, which usually depends on context rather than open appeal. However, on occasion he can be relatively direct—for example, in the story of the slaughter of some innocent countrymen in his extensive account of the rule of the Thirty in *Hellenika.*[b] Here he implies strongly that some ordinary horsemen, of whom we are to understand that he was one, were not complicit in the excesses of the regime. In *Anabasis* we encounter both personal and Socratic defense.[c]

### *Leaders and Leadership*

§8.2. Xenophon's interest in leadership is exemplified in *Anabasis* by his treatment of commanders and the problem of how to lead armies. A considerable amount of the narrative is devoted to describing both the characters and the actions of leaders in the story, whereas relatively little space is given to ordinary soldiers. Up to the events on the banks of the Zapatas River, when Xenophon becomes, by his own account, one of the army's leaders, his name appears in the narrative in only three places;[a] but after that episode, he has cause to mention himself by name more than 240 times. An examination of the travelogue confirms the importance of the leadership theme, as evidently route description and geographical detail are frequently abbreviated, or omitted altogether, in favor of accounts of incidents involving the expedition leaders. One example from the army's march up-country (§8.3) and one from its retreat with Xenophon (§8.4) illustrate this.

§8.3. During the long march through the western desert bordering Babylonia,[a] Xenophon describes how Cyrus deals with Orontas, a noble in his entourage who planned to go over to the King with a thousand cavalry. On learning of the plot, Cyrus arrests Orontas, and following a trial held in his tent, he is found guilty and executed.[b] Xenophon might have accounted for the episode in as few words as those used here; and, since the event was precipitated by the discovery of horse tracks belonging to the King's men,[c] we would expect narrative attention to refocus on the

---

Intro.8.1a  Defense in the explicitly Socratic works mentioned in §6.5—*Apologia Sokratous* (*Defense of Socrates*), *Memorabilia* (*Recollections of Socrates*), *Symposion* (*The Drinking Party*), and *Oikonomikos* (*On the Management of the Household*)—is a mix of engagement with the charges made against the philosopher at his trial in 399 and promotion of the value of his teaching to his countrymen.

Intro.8.1b  Account of the Thirty: *Hellenika* 2.3.11–2.4.43. The particular incident occurs at 2.4.26. See further §2.16.

Intro.8.1c  The discussions about leadership and apologia in *Anabasis* that follow are detailed in Brennan forthcoming.

Intro.8.2a  Three previous mentions: 1.8.15–16, 2.4.15, 2.5.37–41. Zapatas (modern Greater Zab) River: Book 2 map.

Intro.8.3a  Babylonia: Intro. Map 4.6.

Intro.8.3b  Trial of Orontas: 1.6.

Intro.8.3c  Sightings of horse tracks: 1.6.1.

impending battle, the climax of the march. Instead, he writes in detail about the trial, because it speaks to his leadership theme. On one hand he highlights Cyrus' commitment to justice; on the other, he raises a question about his judgment as a leader, for we learn that Orontas had already betrayed him on two previous occasions. Cyrus' misplaced trust is spelled out by Klearchos, the only Greek in attendance at the trial, who counsels Cyrus "to do away with this man as quickly as possible, so that it is no longer necessary to be on our guard against him."[d]

§8.4. The second example occurs on the banks of the Zapatas River. Tissaphernes has seized their generals and the Greeks must reorganize themselves and escape across the river before the Persians attack.[a] Xenophon devotes considerable space to this critical juncture, most of it taken up with speeches that he himself makes to the army.[b] These addresses serve to establish his importance as an actor in the story and to emphasize his own style of leadership, where speech is the preferred method of persuasion. In his treatment of the episode at the Zapatas, however, he neglects to tell us how the army actually crossed the river, a significant tributary of the Tigris; we may contrast his silence here with the detail he later provides on the crossing of the Kentrites River, where the army found itself trapped between two enemies.[c] Presumably pontoon bridges spanned the Zapatas,[d] and it seems likely that to avoid a showdown with desperate men, the Persians did not block access to them. Xenophon may therefore have considered the episode unnoteworthy, as it afforded little opportunity for instruction on leadership. He would, in short, rather dwell on difficulties they overcame than difficulties they fortunately didn't have to face. The omission is thus an example of how the dominance of the leadership theme has displaced—in this case historically important—journey detail.

§8.5. Throughout *Anabasis*, one of Xenophon's concerns is to highlight the respective strengths and weaknesses of individual leaders and thereby create a record to serve as thoughtful and instructive material for aspiring commanders. Another didactic aim is to critique the different styles of leadership of the successive leaders of the expedition.[a] Cyrus is royalty and rules on an oriental model: for example, he orders his entourage to go down into the mud to free some wagons but does not go himself.[b] Klearchos (and later Cheirisophos) is a product of the Spartan militaristic tradition; they lead from the front and often beat those who are not pulling their weight.[c] Xenophon, by contrast, is an Athenian citizen and a pupil of Socrates who prefers to use words instead of a baton to achieve his ends.[d] The treatment of leadership in *Anabasis*, then, is as much a study of the effectiveness of leadership styles as it is a

---

Intro.8.3d    Klearchos' counsel: 1.6.9.

Intro.8.4a    Tissaphernes seizes generals at Zapatas River: 2.5.31–32.

Intro.8.4b    Xenophon's speeches: 3.1.15–25, 3.1.35–45, 3.2.7–32, 3.2.34–39.

Intro.8.4c    Zapatas River crossing: 3.3.6 (Map 3.4.24, *Halting place 34*); Tigris River: Map 3.4.24. Army trapped at the Kentrites River: 4.3.3–7 (Map 4.4.3, *Halting place 43*).

Intro.8.4d    Pontoon bridges across rivers: Tigris at Opis, 2.4.17; Physkos at Sittake: 2.4.25; all on Book 2 map.

Intro.8.5a    On the death of Cyrus, at the battle of Cunaxa (Book 1 map), Klearchos the Spartan assumed the de facto leadership of the Greek mercenaries (2.2.5). After his seizure on the Zapatas River (2.5.31–32), a collective command was formed, although in Xenophon's narrative Cheirisophos the Spartan, leading the vanguard, and Xenophon himself, taking the rear, have singularly prominent roles in this.

Intro.8.5b    Example of Cyrus' leadership style: 1.5.7–8.

Intro.8.5c    Spartan leadership: 2.3.11, 4.6.2. On Cheirisophos, see Appendix W: Brief Biographies, §7.

Intro.8.5d    Xenophon's leadership style: for example, 3.4.46–48.

practical exercise in learning from the successes and failures of outstanding men. The subtle, though unambiguous, conclusion of Xenophon's exposition is that the optimal style is the one he himself represents. It is Xenophon, the democratic exponent and the embodiment of virtuous behavior, who successfully leads the army back to western Anatolia[e] from the heart of the barbarian world. This implicit conclusion in turn leads us on to the second key theme of *Anabasis*: apologia.

## Apologia

### Personal Apologia

§8.6. Through his self-representation and choice of events for the narrative of *Anabasis*, Xenophon mounts both a personal defense and, as we'll see in §8.12–14, a defense of Socrates. Already in antiquity it was thought that he had written his account of Cyrus' expedition with his own reputation in mind. Explaining the use of a pseudonym, Plutarch says Xenophon's purpose was "to win greater credence for his narrative by referring to himself in the third person,"[a] so that his outstanding performance on the retreat would not be undermined by his being the narrator of his own deeds. A modern take is that Xenophon wrote *Anabasis* with the aim of setting the record straight: his account of a nearly flawless achievement on his own part in helping to lead the Greeks homeward is a response to a portrayal of his role in another published account of the march that in his eyes did not do him justice. There are several potential candidates for such a work.[b] Stephanus, the sixth-century C.E. Byzantine lexicographer, mentions four fragments of a *Kyrou Anabasis* by Sophainetos, probably the Stymphalian general in Xenophon's account, though some scholars think this was a much later literary exercise and others that the evidence is too thin to infer a substantial work.[c] Ctesias' *Persika* contained an account of the battle of Cunaxa[d] and other information related to the march, and as remarked earlier, there were many historians in the field in the fourth century. One mentioned at §7.10, whose book may have included detail on the expedition, is the Oxyrhynchus historian.[e] Yet, set against this, there is no proof that any of these accounts were expressly unfavorable to Xenophon. Moreover, the histories by the Oxyrhynchus writer and others covering Greek affairs would have merely summarized the march as an episode in a wider narrative, mitigating any grievance Xenophon could reasonably have felt if they did not mention him much, or at all.

§8.7. Whatever the strengths of the respective arguments for and against an alternative published version that moved Xenophon to write his own, his text certainly does contain substantial evidence of self-defense. At several points Xenophon defends himself in lengthy speeches against charges that have been brought against him in the course of the retreat. The most serious of these are *hybris* (translated in this volume as "arrogant willfulness") and corruption, both damaging accusations to a man

---

Intro.8.5e  Western Anatolia: Intro. Map 3.1.
Intro.8.6a  "To win greater credence": Plutarch, *Moralia* 345e (Babbit/Loeb translation). On Xenophon's use of a pseudonym (Themistogenes), in connection with *Anabasis*, see §6.11.
Intro.8.6b  For a full discussion about this subject, see Appendix M: Other Ancient Sources on the

Ten Thousand.
Intro.8.6c  On Sophainetos, see Appendix W: Brief Biographies, §32. Byzantium: Book 1 map. Stymphalos: Map 1.2.1, AY.
Intro.8.6d  Battlefield of Cunaxa: Book 1 map.
Intro.8.6e  The Oxyrhynchus Historian may have published his work by 370; see n. Intro.7.10c.

whose writings promote virtuous conduct.[a] That he should go to great lengths to rebut these charges and justify his actions reveals the depth of his concern about what was being said, whether in another account or perhaps even an oral version that had gained currency at home.

§8.8. There is also likely to be an element of "literary apologia," whereby an author introduces a (quite possibly genuine) charge and uses it as the basis for a defense that he has adapted to facilitate his self-justification. The intention could be to bring out one specific personal or professional quality or to highlight several. A possible example in *Anabasis* is the aforementioned corruption charge, where the unnamed Arcadian[a] who accuses Xenophon of profiting at the expense of the men incidentally provides evidence of one of his key leadership qualities: "You know, Lacedaemonians,[b] as far as we are concerned, we would have been in your service long ago if Xenophon had not used his persuasive powers to bring us away here." Given what we know of the circumstances, it is likely that the Arcadian really did accuse Xenophon of corruption, and Xenophon may have taken the chance here to mark one of his leadership skills or he may be faithfully reporting his accuser. But what's notable is the comprehensive treatment that follows, this enabling the author to highlight his virtue and demonstrate that private gain is not a motivating factor in his actions. He is thus emphasizing features of his character that were in harmony with Socrates' teaching, something entirely natural if at the time of writing he was looking at ways to underscore his Socratic identity.

§8.9. Literary apologia may help to explain the lateness of Xenophon's response to charges about the author's personal conduct, which ordinarily one might think would be much less relevant years after the event. However, if Xenophon adapted the attacks and his defense to support more general aims of his writing, such as reinforcing his representation as a Socratic, that oddity is resolved.

§8.10. There were other subjects too on which Xenophon took the opportunity to defend himself when writing this account. One was the rumor of his having been in paid service with Cyrus in 401, together with his having actually been in paid service with the Spartan expeditionary force from 399. For wealthy and high-status individuals in the ancient world, paid employment was not well looked upon, one reason being that it implied dependency.[a] Another issue with Cyrus was the lack of a legitimate basis for his attempt on the throne, it being apparently driven by his own ambition; association with him was therefore particularly awkward for Xenophon as a follower of Socrates, who in word and deed observed meticulous obedience to the laws.

§8.11. There is also Xenophon's exile from Athens to consider. Even though the decree of exile had probably been repealed by the time he began to write in earnest in the 370s,[a] given the gravity of the original event, it would not be surprising if it

Intro.8.7a  Accusations of *hybris:* 5.8.1; of corruption, 7.6.9–10. For more on *hybris,* see the Glossary.
Intro.8.8a  Arcadia: Ref. Map 2, CX.
Intro.8.8b  The terms Lacedaemon and Sparta are nearly synonymous for most purposes, but strictly speaking, Lacedaemon is a state and territorial designation. Sparta was the most important city within that state. For more

detail on the distinction, see Appendix B: Xenophon and Sparta, §§18–19. Lacedaemon: Intro. Map 3.1.
Intro.8.10a  Xenophon's defense: not a mercenary, 3.1.4, 6.4.8; not in need of Spartan employment owing to a successful raid, 7.8.23.
Intro.8.11a  Diogenes Laertius says the decree was repealed (2.59; in Appendix V: Diogenes); see §3.5.

impacted his writing. There is considerable evidence in fact that he used the narrative in *Anabasis* both to justify his association with Cyrus the Younger and to distance himself from Sparta, his links with one or the other being the most likely basis for the formal charge against him (see §3.2). In the latter case, Xenophon is at pains to portray his relationship with the Spartan commanders on the retreat as problematic, each regarding the other with a clear degree of distrust.[b] As for Cyrus, in the prince's obituary at 1.9, Xenophon describes him as a noble and virtuous leader, so someone with whom it would be quite natural for any young man keen to develop himself to want to associate; on the question of the expedition's legitimacy, the characterization in the obituary also serves to obfuscate the reason for Cyrus' attempt on the throne. This artful passing over is evident again in his silence on the question of Cyrus' role in Athens' defeat to Sparta. Xenophon would without doubt have regarded his banishment from Athens as a stain on his character, but it would be typical of him to engage with it indirectly, undermining the charge with substantial contrary evidence. The exile, the cause of which may or may not be rooted in the march, alerts us to the fact that the telling of the story of the Ten Thousand provided him with a means to address personal issues that did not all arise solely from his participation in the march.

### Defense of Socrates

§8.12. Xenophon in *Anabasis* portrays himself as more than an average leader. Indeed, his energy and foresight at times verge on the superhuman. Italo Calvino writes that "on occasions Xenophon appears to be one of those heroes from children's comics, who in every episode appear to survive against impossible odds."[a] George Cawkwell remarks that "he never seems to make a mistake. Both in counsel and in action, Xenophon was always right."[b] It is hard not to conclude, as many have done, that in his narrative, Xenophon's aim is to represent his own role in the successful retreat as highly significant—whether this is part of his personal apologetic agenda or is simply to be attributed to vanity. A further element in the explanation, which could conceivably be an alternative explanation, is that Xenophon's character as portrayed in the story is an exemplar, a model pupil of Socrates behaving as such a pupil should in these types of situations. His performance is a faithful enactment of the advice Xenophon has Socrates give on generalship in *Memorabilia*[c] and is true to ethical precepts promoted by the philosopher. The overall success of his leadership therefore constitutes a testament to the value of the Socratic training, demonstrating that it produces young men capable of doing good for their friends and their communities. Whether or not Xenophon was, in fact, an outstanding pupil of Socrates, his character in *Anabasis* acts like one, and in this way the work functions as a defense of his teacher. Specifically, by his own conduct as a young Athenian, Xenophon furnishes evidence against the charges that Socrates had corrupted the youth of the city and was impious; more generally, in the contest for Socrates' legacy, he is providing

---

Intro.8.11b  Distrust between Xenophon and Spartans: 3.4.38–39, 4.1.15–21, 6.1.16–32.
Intro.8.12a  Impossible odds: Calvino 1999, 20.

Intro.8.12b  Xenophon always right: Cawkwell in Lane Fox 2004, 60.
Intro.8.12c  Socrates on generalship: *Memorabilia* 3.1–5.

a reflected image of him to stand and be evaluated against other versions in circulation at the time of writing in the 370s/360s.

§8.13. Socrates' introduction into the story comes alongside Xenophon's own formal introduction in Book 3, following the seizure of the Greek commanders on the banks of the Zapatas River. After supplying his name, ethnicity, and military status, Xenophon diverts us from the desperate circumstances of the army by providing a vivid flashback about his consultation with Socrates on whether or not to join Cyrus.[a] This consultation has been interpreted by some scholars as support for the view that he was a prominent pupil of Socrates, and for the claim that his association with Cyrus constituted the cause of his banishment from Athens.[b] Xenophon may well have wished to provide grounds for these inferences, but the prime function of the episode in the narrative is to situate Socrates at the heart of his decision to join Cyrus. Among several of the important effects that flow from this, one is to highlight the enterprise's philosophical aspect, reinforced in the same passage by the reference to Proxenos, who was a pupil of the sophist Gorgias, and by the statement that Xenophon did not join Cyrus for a military purpose: "He did not accompany the army as a general, nor as a captain, nor as an ordinary soldier."[c] Another is that by the concern he shows for Xenophon in this passage, Socrates becomes a presence that will be linked to the trials his pupil is fated to undergo in the months ahead. Conscious of the close relationship between the men, more in the public eye with Xenophon's contributions to the growing body of Socratic literature,[d] the contemporary reader was primed to link the young man's performance to the instruction of his teacher.

§8.14. This key passage, then, establishes the backstory against which Xenophon intends the account to be read: having consulted Socrates and visited the oracle, the young Athenian sets off for Asia to learn what he can from a Persian prince educated at the court.[a] However, his personal journey sees him caught up in a mercenary enterprise against the King, leading to the critical juncture at the opening of Book 3. With Cyrus dead and the Greek high command decapitated, Xenophon finds himself in mortal peril in a land far from Greece. Awakening from a dream that night by the river, he articulates his new reality, his linear analysis and self-questioning already displaying his Socratic training:

Intro.8.13a  Conversation with Socrates: 3.1.4–5.
Intro.8.13b  On Xenophon's relationship with Socrates, see §2.9–12, noting the reference to *Memorabilia* 1.1.6 on how Socrates dealt with close friends; in their meeting Socrates expressed concern that association with Cyrus could land Xenophon in trouble with the Athenians.
Intro.8.13c  Not for military purpose: 3.1.4. On Proxenos, see Appendix W: Brief Biographies, §29. Gorgias was a famous sophist (from *sophos*, "wise") and orator from Leontini in Sicily (Ref. Map 1, BW). He came to Athens in 427 and taught his craft to paying customers. The sophists acquired something of a bad reputation, with detractors claiming that they taught their students how to make the worse argument appear the better and

the better the worse.
Intro.8.13d  Although not certain, there is a good case for *Apologia Sokratous* (*Defense of Socrates*) having been published in the late 370s, before *Anabasis*. It's possible that Xenophon's recollections of Socrates, *Memorabilia*, as a whole or in part, also predated *Anabasis*. See the List of Xenophon's Writings for estimates of dates of composition.
Intro.8.14a  Educated at the royal court: 1.9.3. Cyrus' qualities are described in Xenophon's obituary of the prince at *Anabasis* 1.9 and alluded to by Socrates himself in *Oikonomikos* (*On the Management of the Household*) 4.18: "if Cyrus had only lived, it seems that he would surely have proved an excellent ruler" (Marchant, Henderson/Loeb translation).

Why am I lying down? The night is far advanced, and it is likely that along with the day will come the enemy. If we fall into the hands of the King, what is to stop us from having to behold all the most grievous sights imaginable, from suffering all the most terrible torments, and from dying in the course of humiliating maltreatment? Nobody is making preparations or paying attention to how we may defend ourselves, but instead we are lying around as if it were possible to live in peace and quiet. Take me, for example: From what city am I expecting the general to come to take action here? What age am I waiting to reach? For I shall not grow any older if I hand myself over to the enemy today![b]

So the student is impelled into action. Rising, he calls together the captains of his slain companion, Proxenos, and urges them to take their fate in hand. "Let us not wait for other people to approach us and summon us to perform noble deeds—let us ourselves take the lead in rousing the others to reveal their worth."[c] Xenophon is appointed the leader of Proxenos' contingent, and following a conclave of generals and captains, an assembly of the entire army is called. The young Athenian puts on his finest armor and prepares to address the soldiers. His character and learning are now to be tested in the crucible of war. The outcome will bear on how history judges him and, ultimately, Socrates.[d]

Intro.8.14b    "Why am I lying down?": 3.1.13–14.
Intro.8.14c    Summon to noble deeds: 3.1.24.
Intro.8.14d    The question of Xenophon's readiness for leadership and his maturity is debated. My view is that Xenophon sets off as knowledgeable and keen but lacking in experience and still somewhat immature; he himself seems to be pointing to the latter in relating the fact of his disobedience to Socrates regarding the oracle. In the course of the journey, he learns and develops as a character. However, Robin Waterfield believes that Xenophon embarked on the journey fully formed, as it were, as a leader; see Appendix A: Xenophon and Socrates, §26.

# LIST OF XENOPHON'S
# WRITINGS

*Agesilaos,* published after 360: An encomium of the Spartan King Agesilaos.

*Apologia Sokratous* (*Defense of Socrates*), late 370s?: An account of Socrates' defense speech at his trial at Athens in 399. Socrates explains why he prefers death to continued life.

*Hellenika* (*History of Greece*), Books 1–2.3.10 written in the 380s, Books 2.3.11–7, in the early 350s: Xenophon's contemporary history, with particular reference to relations between Sparta and Athens covering the period 411–362. This work is more concerned with highlighting moral virtue and failings than with full coverage of historically important events.

*Hieron,* published 360 or later?: The lyric poet Simonides of Keos gives advice on ruling to Hieron, a fifth-century Syracusan tyrant. A quasi-Socratic work concerned with political philosophy and statesmanship.

*Hipparchikos* (*Cavalry Commander*), 365–364: An instructional handbook on cavalry command.

*Kynegetikos* (*On Hunting*), late 390s: An instructional handbook on hunting and the breeding and training of hunting dogs.

*Kyrou Anabasis* (*The March Up-Country of Cyrus*), published early 360s: *Kyrou Anabasis* is the title given in the manuscripts but it is almost always abbreviated to just *Anabasis.* Other common titles given to English translations of the book are *The Persian Expedition* and *The Expedition of Cyrus.* Beyond the march itself, subjects include military leadership, defense of Xenophon's reputation, defense of Socrates, commentary on Spartan hegemony of Greece in the aftermath of the Peloponnesian War, memorialization.

*Kyroupaideia* (*The Education of Cyrus*), completed shortly after 362: A fictionalized account of the life of Cyrus the Great/the Elder, founder of the Persian (Achaemenid) Empire. A historical novel, military manual, and moral treatise incorporating leadership and political philosophy.

*Lakedaimonion Politeia* (*Constitution of the Lacedaemonians*), 378–377: Showing how Sparta's civil and military institutions are the basis of its success as a state. The penultimate chapter denounces contemporary Spartans for disregarding the ideals of their forefathers.

NOTE: UNLESS OTHERWISE SPECIFIED, ALL DATES IN THIS VOLUME ARE B.C.E. (BEFORE THE COMMON ERA). An *Athenaion Politeia,* "*Constitution of the* Athenians," was included among Xenophon's writings in antiquity but is thought by modern scholars not to be his.

**Memorabilia** (Latin), *Apomnemoneumata* (Greek), *"Recollections"* [*of Socrates*], early 360s?: The author's recollections of Socrates' teachings and personal virtue.

**Oikonomikos** (*On the Management of the Household*), mid 360s?: Advice on farming and household management involving Socrates.

**Peri Hippikes** (*On Horsemanship*), late 360s?: Instruction on horsemanship and on buying and looking after horses; companion piece to *Hipparchikos* (*Cavalry Commander*), which it postdates.

**Poroi** (*Ways and Means*), 355: Advice on ways to increase the revenues and boost the economy of Athens. The author shows that peace is more profitable than war.

**Symposion** (*The Drinking Party* or *Symposium*), mid-360s?: Portrait of Socrates at leisure.

# EDITORS' PREFACE

## Shane Brennan and David Thomas

### Features of this Edition

§1. *The Landmark Xenophon's* Anabasis is the sixth volume in the Landmark series, preceded by works by Thucydides, Herodotus, Arrian, and Julius Caesar, and another work by Xenophon, the *Hellenika*. All these volumes have shared the common goal of making the ancient text accessible and comprehensible to the general reader and all have employed similar means to achieve that end.

§2. **Maps** have been the key feature of every Landmark volume to date, and this fact made *Anabasis*, the story of a long journey through unfamiliar lands, a natural subject for the series. So here too there are good, clear maps, specially drawn according to the editors' specifications, on which all the known place-names mentioned by Xenophon may be found together with plenty of signposts to guide the reader to the right map. These map features are more fully explained in §§15–22.

§3. The **Introduction** describes what is known about Xenophon, sets his work in its time and place, gives further background information about it, and examines the themes that it explores, including ones that may not be obvious at first sight.

§4. Copious **footnotes** on issues that may be found difficult or obscure in the text, or which answer questions that may naturally occur to readers, are to be found on the same page on which the issue was raised and refer the reader to both internal and external resources as appropriate. In accordance with the policy of the series, it has not been assumed that the reader will start at the beginning of the volume and read straight through. Footnotes have been provided on the basis that different readers might start at different places. The key points of the narrative, as it unfolds, together with the date and location of the relevant events, are brought out in **running heads** on each page and in **side notes** to each paragraph of the translation. In accordance with ancient tradition and modern practice, Xenophon's text is divided into seven units known as "books" and these have then been subdivided by later editors into chapters and sections, the standard system for which was devised in the early nineteenth century. We have made further use of these divisions by gathering together the main elements of the narrative in the **Summary by Book and Chapter**. This feature permits the reader to scan the flow of the narrative and quickly locate events in the text by book and chapter.

**Sample Running Head and Side Note**

| BOOK ONE | ARABIAN DESERT | *Severe food shortages* |
|---|---|---|

| | |
|---|---|
| 1.5.4–8 | Book/Chapter/Section(s) |
| November 401 | Date |
| ARABIAN DESERT | Location(s) |
| *Korsote (23)–Pylai (24)* | Location(s) with beginning halting place number(s) |
| On a long march through desert terrain, many animals die from starvation and grain runs short for the soldiers. | Summary of action |

§5. This volume is illustrated with a number of images of **objects and artwork** specific to the time period and subject of the narrative, which help the reader understand concepts and practices that are foreign to us but were familiar features of the ancient world. The volume also includes **photographs** of some of the places that Xenophon visited. All these illustrations are included for their relevance to the story that Xenophon tells.

§6. **Appendices.** In a suite of **appendices**, leading scholars in their respective fields explain various political, cultural, and conceptual features of Xenophon's world which are likely to be unfamiliar to the modern lay reader, and they describe how his narrative relates to these features and how subsequent authors have appropriated Xenophon's *Anabasis* for their own purposes. Also included in the appendices are discussions by the editors of problems which the narrative presents for anyone trying to sort out its relationship to other accounts of the same events, as well as its chronology, geography, and estimates of troop strengths. Where there is a passage in the translation which is specifically illuminated by something in an appendix, the footnotes to the translation make that clear.

§7. **Translations of parallel passages by other ancient authors.** Some of the events covered in *Anabasis* are narrated by other ancient authors. Appendices S–U present translations by Peter Green and Pamela Mensch of relevant parts of the works of Diodorus Siculus, Plutarch, and Photius. Appendix V consists of the Loeb translation of almost the whole of Diogenes Laertius' *Life of Xenophon*. Footnotes throughout the main text point out parallel passages in these other works.

§8. **Appendix W** consists of **brief biographies of selected characters**, supplementing what Xenophon has to say about them with information from other sources, where that is available. Footnotes alert the reader to where this appendix incorporates supplementary material or editorial assessment.

§9. Xenophon's narrative is supplemented by an **Epilogue**, which describes briefly what subsequently happened to the principal surviving actors in the story. A catalog of all **Ancient Sources** cited in this edition gives short accounts of their lives and works. The **Glossary** gives further explanations of technical terms found in the text in those cases where something is said at greater length than is suitable for a footnote.

§10. **Translator's Notes.** While all Landmark translators have varied to some degree from the published version of the Greek text that they have chosen as their basis, the number of variances in this translation is unusually high. Our Translator's Notes therefore explain how it comes about that other published texts are open to such a degree of amendment, as well as saying more about the principles on which this translation is based. Although a knowledge of Greek is required to follow the table of variances itself, the rest of the Translator's Notes have been written so as to be accessible to the general reader.

§11. The **Bibliography** makes no attempt at fullness. It is organized in two sections. The first contains items that the general reader of *Anabasis* may find especially helpful. The second lists works of specialized interest, together with all books and articles cited in the editorial material. Full references to books and articles cited in the editorial material are provided only in the Bibliography, while the footnotes to the text specify only the author in question and the date of the relevant work.

§12. The **Index** to the translated text is a very full one, not only citing the relevant references to key words by book, chapter, and section but also setting out briefly what will be found in each place if the reader looks up the citation. In addition to historical and mythological persons, places, and objects, the Index in this case includes entries for a high number of abstract ideas, as befits the work of a writer with a strong interest in philosophy.

§13. The **spelling of proper names** of individual people and the titles of literary works has been conformed to follow the *Oxford Classical Dictionary* where the name or title is included in that work, with the exception of the works of Xenophon himself, for which the reader is referred to the **List of Xenophon's Writings**. Where the *Oxford Classical Dictionary* does not provide the answer, Greek transliteration is used. For the spelling of place-names and ethnic names, see §14.

### The Map Scheme and Route of the Army

§14. In accordance with the usual Landmark practice, the default position for the attribution of **place-names** and **ethnic names** on our maps, and for the way they are spelled, is the *Barrington Atlas of the Greek and Roman World*. However, we have departed from the *Atlas*'s locations in a number of instances, which are all clearly noted. As with previous Landmark editions, we have avoided referring to seas with the Latin word *mare* or to mountains with the Latin words *mons* or *montes*. More familiar forms have also been used for a small number of place-names, such as Athens and the Zagros Mountains. Other departures from the *Barrington Atlas* have been needed because of fairly recent discoveries or because the location it assigns relates to a period earlier or later than the fourth century B.C.E.; on at least one occasion we have simply disagreed with the choice that it makes. Such discrepancies have been indicated in the footnotes; the footnotes also indicate places to which the *Barrington Atlas* does not assign a location.

§15. For map iconography, see the **Key to Maps**, placed at the end of the front matter.

§16. The narrative is tracked by **maps** spread at intervals through the volume, bringing the journey into clearer focus. Those placed within the text include almost all the names of the peoples and places mentioned in Xenophon's narrative, including some places which are far away from the route Xenophon took but which he mentions for other reasons, typically because he is naming the place from which a particular character came. Landmark maps follow a telescoping scheme of **locator**, **main**, and **inset maps**. On the first occurrence of any place-name or ethnic name, a **footnote** points the reader to the most convenient map on which to locate it. The footnotes below correspond to the Sample Route Map 1.5.1:

> 1.2.13a   Babylonia: Map 1.5.1 and inset.
> 1.4.11c   Babylon: Map 1.5.1 and locator.
> 1.5.10a   Charmande, possible location: Map 1.5.1.
> 1.6.6a    Sardis: Map 1.5.1, locator.

Maps with many labels or large in scope are marked in quadrants and location coordinates are given in the footnotes. For names that are repeated at some distance from the original occurrence, the information is given again for the convenience of the reader.

§17. **The Route.** Determining where the army's route went and when the army traveled along each section of it is by no means straightforward, and the route line shown on our maps and the monthly dates given in our side notes are often subject to doubt.ª Probably no two scholars have ever agreed on every aspect of the route, so our maps can represent only our best estimate and should not be taken as claiming authority, let alone certainty.

§18. In recounting the army's march, Xenophon breaks up the route into segments; he tells us how many days it took the army to march through each of them, and for many of them he also gives us a measure of the distance covered in doing this. For example, at 1.2.5 he writes, "Meanwhile, Cyrus started out from Sardis with those whom I have mentioned. He pushed on through Lydia for three days' march, covering twenty-two parasangs, to the river Maeander."ª We have assigned numbers on our maps to the places where the army halted at the beginning and

EP.17a   This is explained more fully in Appendix P: The Route of the Ten Thousand and Appendix Q: The Chronology of the March.

EP.18a   For an explanation of *stathmos*, the Greek term Xenophon uses (translated in this edition as "day's march"), see the Introduction, §7.2, and Appendix O: Ancient Greek and Persian Units of Measurement, §6. On the parasang, see the Introduction, §7.3–5, Appendix O, §§7–8. Distances in the *Anabasis* text have been converted to their US equivalents.

## Sample Route Map

**Locator Map**
The inner rectangle shows the location and boundaries of the main map.

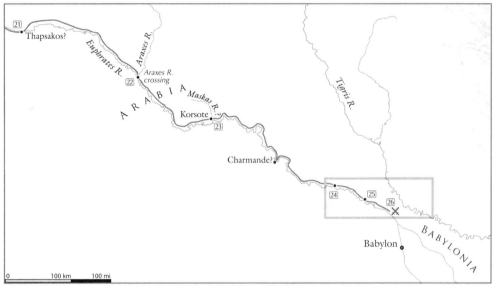

**Main Map**
Numbered locations indicate halting places.

**Inset Map**
Detail of area in rectangle on main map.

SAMPLE ROUTE MAP 1.5.1. *ANABASIS:* FROM THAPSAKOS TO THE BATTLEFIELD OF CUNAXA, *HALTING PLACES 21–26.*

end of each of these segments, referred to as **halting place numbers**. Thus in this example Sardis is given the number 1 and the crossing of the Maeander River is given the number 2. These numbers usually correspond to a named city, town, or village, but where no ancient name can be assigned to a place, an identifying feature or event in the narrative such as "River crossing," "Army divides," or "Guide runs off" is used to label the relevant halting place. The halting place numbers appear in boxes on the maps and in italics in side notes and footnotes. A map showing all of them, accompanied by a list of these locations, appears as Reference Map 10.

§19. For our purposes, we have called the span between each halting place a segment, which is identified in italics in the side notes by its beginning halting place number. Xenophon clearly marks out separate segments of the march almost continuously until Book 7, where there are gaps except for its last chapter. Where this information is missing, some editorial judgment has had to be applied to identify the most appropriate locations to mark as halting places.

§20. **Route Maps.** On the opening left-hand page of each of the seven books into which the narrative is divided, the reader will find a **book map**[a] showing the portion of the Greek army's route that is described in that book, with the route line marked on it and the beginning and ending halting place number. A locator map in the top left-hand corner of each of these opening maps shows how the route distance covered by that map relates to the entire route described in the *Anabasis*. Within each book more detailed maps contain between them all the place-names referred to in the book in connection with the army's route. On these **detailed route maps**[b] we indicate the start and finish of each of these march segments by assigning a halting place number to its starting point.

§21. **Other maps.** Maps without halting place numbers provide context for sites mentioned by Xenophon or relate to topics discussed in the Introduction or the appendices. Altogether, the maps of Greek sites show all the places from which named members of the Greek army originated. Another map depicts the four main routes that intersect at the Tigris River. Diagrams depict troop movements at the battle of Cunaxa and at the conflict at Byzantium.

§22. **Reference Maps and Directory.** At the back of the volume will be found a set of Reference Maps stretching from Sicily and Italy in the west to the Indus River in the east, encompassing not only Persia but almost the entire known world of the ancient Greeks. The names of all the places and peoples[a] mentioned anywhere in the volume, not only in Xenophon's text but also in the supporting material, are included in one of these reference maps and in the Directory. The Directory lists alphabetically all the toponyms occurring anywhere in the volume and the map number and quadrant of each on one of the reference maps. Two maps show the full extent of the route of the army proposed in this edition; one displays the **route with ancient place-names** for selected places on or near it, the other the whole **route with modern place-names**.

---

EP.20a  See Sample Book 1 map.
EP.20b  See Sample Route Map 1.5.1.

EP.22a  There are four exceptions—three of them tribes whose identity is in doubt.

## Sample Book Map

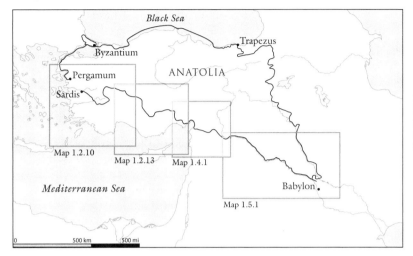

**Locator Map**
The rectangles in the locator map indicate the location and boundaries of the detailed route maps.

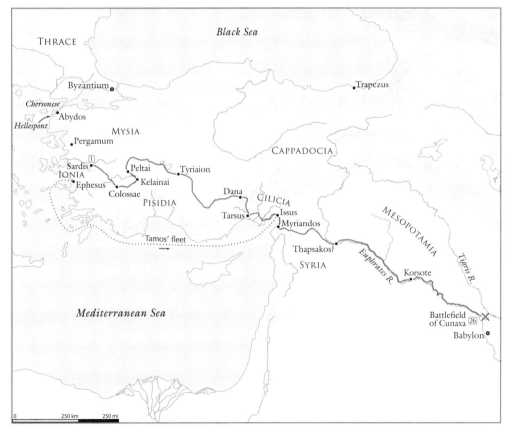

**Main Map**
Shows the portion of route covered in the book with beginning and ending halting place numbers.

SAMPLE BOOK 1 MAP. *ANABASIS:* FROM SARDIS TO THE BATTLEFIED OF CUNAXA, *HALTING PLACES 1–26.*

**Editors' Responsibilities**

With the exception of the Index, the two co-editors of this volume have worked closely together on every page and every map, indeed every line and every word, of the volume. Beyond the named individual contributions as listed in the Contents, Shane Brennan is responsible for the determination of the route in Books 1–6 and David Thomas for the determination of the route in Book 7. He is also responsible for the Index.

Both co-editors take joint responsibility for all other text in the volume. Notwithstanding this, Shane Brennan led on the topographic element of the footnotes and the List of Xenophon's Writings. He also provided almost all of the photographs of places on the route. David Thomas led on the historical element of the footnotes and the Summary by Book and Chapter.

Editorial disagreements with contributors are not stated, except that footnotes point out where two opposing positions are expressed within the volume itself.

Finally, the co-editors should say that Bob Strassler, the Series Editor and originator of the Landmark concept, has played a part in the production of the book which goes far beyond the normal line of duty of series editors. He too has worked over every line of the book with the co-editors, in the case of some important aspects of the book several times. He has managed the mapping process and the final choice of illustrations. Throughout, he has been keen to remind us of the all-important aim of producing an accessible text and the clearest possible maps.

# ACKNOWLEDGMENTS

*From David Thomas*

I am grateful to all our Appendix writers, not only for the quality of the final products, but also for the speed with which they produced their first drafts and responded to editorial queries and the patience with which they endured subsequent delays. Paul Cartledge, John Dillery, Michael Flower, Peter Krentz, John Lee, Thomas Martin, Tim Rood, and Christopher Tuplin also responded to queries beyond their own Appendices. In addition, Nick Cahill, Stephanie Dalley, Roland Enmarch, Deborah Gera, Luuk Huitink, David Gilman Romano, Roel Konijnendijk, William Mack, Robert Parker, Ellen Perry, Julian Reade, Tracey Rihll, and Nigel Wilson kindly answered queries in their areas of expertise. In addition, I am deeply grateful to Christopher Carey, Leofranc Holford-Strevens, Tim Rood, and Christopher Tuplin for reviewing some of my proposals for changes to the standard Greek text and for persuading me out of the most foolish of them. The last two also kindly read the Translator's Notes. Of course, none of these people can be held responsible for what we have then done. On top of that, Luuk Huitink and Tim Rood generously made their commentary on *Anabasis* Book 3 for the Cambridge Greek and Latin Classics series (the so-called "Green and Yellow" series) available prior to its publication. Michael Flower, Neill Fox, Peter Krentz, John Webster, and especially and repeatedly David Gray assisted this quite definitely British translator on matters of US idiom. David Gray also read the entire translation at a late stage, as did Ann Widdecombe despite her many other commitments. Her copious and typically trenchant comments have improved the product in the many cases where they were heeded; she will have to forgive me where they were not.

Much of the work in preparing the translation, the underlying Greek text, and the supporting editorial material was carried out in the Sackler Library in Oxford and the Combined Library of the Institute of Classical Studies and the Societies for the Promotion of Hellenic and of Roman Studies in Bloomsbury, London. I would like to register my especial gratitude to the successive Librarians of the latter, and to their staff, in particular Christopher Ashill, Paul Jackson, and above all the endlessly helpful Sue Willetts. The former Hon. Librarian, Michael Crawford, added encouragement and hospitality. I would also like to thank the late Mark Donovan and the other partners of Altima LLP for their generous parting gift of a copy of the first English translation of *Anabasis*, that of John Bingham in 1623. Frances Thomas baked emmer bread for me (see *Anabasis* 5.4.27), provided hands-on experience with sheep (particularly helpful in making sense of *Anabasis* 6.4.20), and abstained from resorting to divorce lawyers on finding herself to be a "Landmark widow."

Ingrid MacGillis, Pat Larash, and Kim Llewellyn have hunted out illustrations and their copyright holders, sometimes following up our suggestions and sometimes bringing new material to the table to enhance the book's informativeness and aesthetic quality. In her role as book designer Kim Llewellyn has been a constant source of creative ideas for resolving matters ranging from material placement to captioning; she also succeeded in tying together in a seamless way the many different strands that constitute the volume, and has latterly been so heavily involved in the process of bringing the work to completion that she might almost be regarded as the volume's fourth editor. My thanks are also due to Candice Gianetti and Chris Jerome, for their diligence as copy editors, imposing consistency and uncovering the inaccurate or unclear, and to Kelly Sandefer and Jonathan Wyss of Beehive Mapping for the production of the maps. Further, I should acknowledge the part played by Chris Carruth in producing a first draft of the Index, without which the final Index would have been much more difficult for me to prepare.

My co-editor Shane Brennan has been a congenial colleague over the years, putting up with my irritability and tantrums with scarcely a protest and himself never jibbing at repetitive and sometimes obtuse cross-examination about the route as revealed by his travels, even though exclusively offered from the comfort of my study. I am very grateful for the opportunity to share in his virtually unique personal familiarity with the whole of the route which Xenophon took. Bob Strassler's vision was the indispensable foundation of the Landmark series, just as his experience, drive, and passion to keep the needs of the general reader to the fore were key in bringing the work to fruition.

But above all my thanks are due to George Cawkwell for the inspiration and insight into the late fifth and early fourth century B.C.E., and in particular into its Xenophontic aspects, that he provided in lectures and tutorials almost fifty years ago; for his peremptory command, when I retired from the City of London, that I should take up serious academic study again; for introducing me to Bob Strassler and the Landmark series; and for his constant support and frequent hospitality. It is the simple truth to say that my part in this book was written for him. Sadly, he did not live to see the completed work.

## From Shane Brennan

I would like firstly to echo David Thomas' thanks to all of the contributors to the volume for the very high quality of their work and for their patience in staying the course with us. Likewise, the production team at Landmark have been solidly behind us through the project, being notably creative and responsive in dealing with the material from initial map drafts to final book design.

I am very grateful to everyone who helped me to explore sections of Xenophon's route that I had been unable to investigate properly on my original journey following the army in 2000/01. In 2018 Cengiz Çakmak and İffet Özgönul joined me on the first stage of Xenophon's journey in Anatolia, from the port of Ephesus to Sardis. Thanks also to Cengiz for the image of the Thynian plain in Thrace, included in Book 7. In spring 2017, Christopher Tuplin agreed to join a trip to the highlands south of Trabzon from where the Ten Thousand saw the sea. Even if we didn't do so from the same spot, it was a memorable week, one in which I learned a great deal about the indispensable qualities for historical research, among them precision, perseverance, and context. The fruits of that trip are partly reflected in Appendix P: The Route of the Ten Thousand, and more fully in a forthcoming co-authored book chapter and a journal article. On the excursion numerous people went out of their way to help us and I would especially like to thank Hayrettin Karagöz of Maçka Kaymakamlığı, Yiğit Yavuz of Turkish radio TRT Trabzon, and the Jandarma at Araklı.

In January 2016, Murdoch MacLeod accompanied me with his camera on a visit to the Kars region in eastern Anatolia, a bitterly cold experience but recalled as a warm one for his companionship. Map 4.7.1 shows an alternative route for a part of the retreat that might have passed through this area. Further afield in Iran, I am very grateful to Alireza Askari Chaverdi for sharing his learning and for numerous excursions to sites in the Achaemenid heartland. In Shiraz, thanks to Batul and Zari, and in Esfahan, Reza and Maede.

Much of the work for the book was completed while I worked at Mardin Artuklu University in Turkey (2011–16). I would like to record my gratitude to all of my colleagues in the History Department for their encouragement, together with Abdurrahman Adak, Rysbek and Elvira Alimov, Ramazan Aras, Ercan Aslanacier, Ali Asker Bal, Recep Bindak, Ibrahim Bor, Can and Emel Bulgu, Hıdır Çakmak, Kürşat and Elaine Çevik, Bülent and Ebru Diken, Halil Ibrahim Duzenli, Lokman Ece, Bezhat Ekinci, Çaybahçe Fehmi, Tayfun Gürkaş, Kahveci Murat, Elif Keser Kayaalp, Ersin Kılınç, Ayşe Küçükkirca, Murat Küçük, Mel abi, Şahin and Metin Migros, Haji Murat, Dukkan Navaf, Ömer Oruç, Hatip Özer, Sedat Özer, Edip Özkan, Zeynep Sayın, Mark Soileau, Tacettin the Greek, Hasan Tekgüç, Selim Temo, and Habip Türker. Still in Turkey, I have benefited greatly over the years from knowledge about the country's past shared with me by Mehmet Ali Kaya (Izmir), Turhan Kaçar, Nezih Başgelen, Ayşegül Yılmaz, Ülker Sayın (Istanbul), Meral Gürbüz (Eskişehir), Nabi Evren (Şile), Müslüm Yücel (Urfa), Mehmet Akbaş, Marc Herzog (Antep),

Gülşen Laleoğlu (Diyarbakır), Nursun Emren (Kadıköy), İsmail Hakkı Özçelik (Kaçkar Dağları), and Meriç Kükrer (Isparta).

Throughout the course of the project, a longer one than either of us had envisaged, David Thomas, my co-editor, was a meticulous collaborator and extremely generous with the time and thought he gave to supporting my work on the book. I am very grateful also to Bob Strassler, the series editor, for giving me the opportunity to work on the book back in 2010 when I had not yet finished my doctorate. Many thanks to David Schmidt, Sabrina Joseph, and Elham Seyedsayamdost at the American University in Dubai for their support and understanding. I am also grateful to the university library staff—Elizabeth, Chrisa, Jana, and Sunil—and to Nazanin, Stavros, Ioannis, Pedro, Biju, and Kausalya.

Finally, my dad and sister in Ireland have, as always, been unfailingly supportive, and my part in the book is dedicated to them.


*From Robert B. Strassler*

My first and strongest thanks must go to the Editors of this Landmark Edition. Shane Brennan's first-hand experience of the terrain and his knowledge of the text provided extraordinary insights into the problems and possibilities that must have guided the Greeks on their long journey home. David Thomas is a superb scholar, an expert editor, and a talented translator. His erudition, knowledge of the Classical period, and command of both ancient Greek and modern English were essential to the book's success. This edition is, of course, the product of their labor in every way. I must also express my thanks and admiration for the editorial and management skills displayed by Kim Llewellyn, whose role in this effort far exceeded her title of Page Designer. I can state with certainty that without her expertise and energy, this volume would never have reached completion. I am also very grateful to Kelly Sandefer and Jonathan Wyss of Beehive Mapping who transformed rough topographical indications into accurate and elegant maps, despite being inundated over several years with changes of mind about the precise route and the best arrangement of maps to display it.

I would like finally to express my thanks to Edward Kastenmeier, my own editor at Pantheon, for his kind advice, support, and flexibility as we struggled to predict for him when the book would be completed, and I am aware of and very grateful for the efforts of Lisa Montebello and Altie Karper of Penguin Random House to produce the finished volume.

# SUMMARY BY BOOK AND CHAPTER

*ANABASIS*

**Book 1: Sardis to Cunaxa**

| Book/ Chap./Sect. | Location | Date | Event |
|---|---|---|---|
| 1.1–5 | PERSIA | 405–404 | Death of King Darius and accession of his elder son Artaxerxes. Cyrus, the younger son, plots to supplant him. |
| 1.1.6–11 | WESTERN ANATOLIA | 403–402 | On the pretext of a quarrel with the satrap Tissaphernes, Cyrus arranges for troops to be mobilized. |
| 1.2.1–4 | SARDIS | Spring 401 | Cyrus summons his troops. Tissaphernes warns Artaxerxes. |
| 1.2.5–20 | SARDIS–DANA | May–August | Cyrus' army sets out. He marches through Anatolia and reviews his troops at Tyriaion. |
| 1.2.21–27 | CILICIA | August | Cyrus forces his way through mountains to Tarsus and meets the ruler of Cilicia, Syennesis. |
| 1.3 | TARSUS | August–September | The Greek troops refuse to go farther until, manipulated by Klearchos, they accept the promise of more pay from Cyrus. |
| 1.4.1–11 | TARSUS–THAPSAKOS | September–October | Cyrus' army advances from Cilicia to Syria and onward to the crossing of the Euphrates River, never meeting any opposition. |
| 1.4.12–19 | THAPSAKOS | October | The Greek troops again refuse to go farther but are again persuaded to do so by promises of more pay. They cross the Euphrates River. |
| 1.5 | THAPSAKOS–CHARMANDE | October–November | Cyrus' army marches through desert along the north bank of the Euphrates. Challenges include mud and lack of food. Cyrus has to intervene to prevent armed conflict between his Greek commanders. |
| 1.6 | APPROACH TO BABYLONIA | November | Plot of Orontas against Cyrus is uncovered. The trial and execution of Orontas. |
| 1.7 | BABYLONIA | November | The two armies close on each other amidst uncertainty as to whether there will be a battle. |

| Book/<br>Chap./Sect. | Location | Date | Event |
|---|---|---|---|
| 1.8 | BATTLEFIELD OF CUNAXA | November 401 | Battle between Cyrus and Artaxerxes. Cyrus orders his Greek troops to attack Artaxerxes in the center of the enemy line, but instead they keep by the Euphrates and chase Tissaphernes' men off the battlefield. Cyrus himself is killed in the center charging at his brother. |
| 1.9 | | | The obituary of Cyrus. |
| 1.10 | BATTLEFIELD OF CUNAXA | November | Standoff between the Greeks and Artaxerxes after the main battle. |

## KATABASIS: BABYLONIA TO THE BLACK SEA
## Book 2: Cunaxa to the Zapatos River Crossing

| | | | |
|---|---|---|---|
| 2.1 | BATTLEFIELD OF CUNAXA | November | The Greeks learn that Cyrus is dead. Diplomatic fencing between Klearchos and Artaxerxes' Greek envoy, Phalinos. |
| 2.2 | BABYLONIA | November | The Greeks join up with Cyrus' Persian supporter Ariaios and start to retreat as best they can. |
| 2.3.1–16 | BABYLONIA | November–December | Klearchos accepts Artaxerxes' offer of a temporary truce in return for being led to food supplies. |
| 2.3.17–28 | BABYLONIA | November–December | Tissaphernes negotiates a more comprehensive truce whereby he will guide the Greeks back to the Aegean. |
| 2.4 | MESOPOTAMIA | December–January | After an initial delay, the Greeks march north out of Babylonia and through Media, guided by Tissaphernes. An air of mutual suspicion grows. |
| 2.5 | ZAPATAS RIVER | January 400 | Tissaphernes deceives Klearchos and lures him to his death together with four of the other Greek generals and many captains. |
| 2.6 | | | Obituaries of Klearchos and generals Proxenos and Menon. |

## Book 3: The Zapatos River Crossing to Western Armenia

| | | | |
|---|---|---|---|
| 3.1.1–3 | ZAPATAS RIVER | January | Distress and confusion of the Greek army. |
| 3.1.4–10 | ATHENS-DELPHI-SARDIS | *flashback* Spring 401 | Xenophon, after consulting Socrates but not following his advice faithfully, joins his friend Proxenos in Cyrus' entourage in Sardis. |
| 3.1.11–47 | ZAPATAS RIVER | January 400 | Inspired by a dream, Xenophon restores the morale of Proxenos' officers, goes on to exhort an assembly of all the officers presided over by Cheirisophos, and is elected one of the new generals. |
| 3.2 | ZAPATAS RIVER | January | Xenophon delivers a morale-boosting but also practical speech to an assembly of the whole army presided over by Cheirisophos. |
| 3.3 | ZAPATAS RIVER | January | The army crosses river and advances northward, beset by the Persians. |
| 3.4 | NEAR TIGRIS RIVER | January–February | The army advances past Larisa (Nimrud) and Mespila (Nineveh) and through high hills to the north, pursued and obstructed by Tissaphernes. |
| 3.5 | TIGRIS RIVER | February | Without a clear passage westward across the river, the generals decide to go north through the mountains. |

| Book/Chap./Sect. | Location | Date | Event |
|---|---|---|---|
| **Book 4: Western Armenia to Trapezus** | | | |
| 4.1 | KARDOUCHOI TERRITORY | February 400 | The Greeks ascend into Kardouchoi territory and begin to make their way through it despite the hostility of the tribesmen. |
| 4.2.1–22 | KARDOUCHOI TERRITORY | February | Sent on a diversion, Xenophon and the rearguard fight their way through. |
| 4.2.23–28 | KARDOUCHOI TERRITORY | February | Xenophon and Cheirisophos cooperate in their ongoing progress through the tribal lands. |
| 4.3 | KENTRITES RIVER | February | The army forces its way across the Kentrites River. Outstanding tactics of Xenophon. |
| 4.4 | ARMENIA | February | The army's progress is hampered by heavy snow. The Greeks capture the camp of the Persian deputy satrap Tiribazos. |
| 4.5 | ARMENIA | March | Snow causes increasing problems, but army reaches well-supplied underground villages where the soldiers feast and rest. |
| 4.6 | VICINITY OF PHASIS RIVER | March–April | Despite losing its guide, the army reaches and proceeds along the Phasis River, eventually fighting its way over a pass to its north. Further tactical success of Xenophon. |
| 4.7.1–14 | TAOCHOI TERRITORY | April | Led by officers from Xenophon's rearguard, the Greeks capture the Taochian stronghold. |
| 4.7.15–18 | [E.] CHALYBES TERRITORY | April | The Greeks force their way onward despite opposition from the fierce Chalybes. |
| 4.7.19–27 | MT. THECHES | May | The Greeks at last see the Black Sea. |
| 4.8.1–8 | MAKRONES TERRITORY | May | The Greeks make friends with the Makrones and are assisted through their territory. |
| 4.8.9–19 | MAKRONES-KOLCHOI BOUNDARY | May | The Kolchoi block the army's progress over a ridge. The army, deployed in column in accordance with Xenophon's advice, sweeps them away. |
| 4.8.20–21 | KOLCHOI TERRITORY | May | Many soldiers become ill after eating "mad honey." |
| 4.8.22–28 | TRAPEZUS | May–June | The army reaches the Black Sea coast and celebrates with games of thanksgiving. |

*PARABASIS:* THE BLACK SEA COAST, EAST TO WEST
**Book 5: Trapezus to Kotyora**

| Book/Chap./Sect. | Location | Date | Event |
|---|---|---|---|
| 5.1 | TRAPEZUS | June | Cheirisophos goes off to find ships for transport. The army debates its course of action in the meantime. |
| 5.2 | DRILAI TERRITORY | June | Xenophon leads an only partly successful expedition against nearby tribespeople. |

| Book/<br>Chap./Sect. | Location | Date | Event |
|---|---|---|---|
| 5.3.1–4 | KERASOUS | June 400 | A count is taken of the army, numbering 8,600, and its plunder divided. |
| 5.3.5–13 | SKILLOUS | *flash-forward*<br>388?–370 | Xenophon's idyllic subsequent life (for a time) and faithful service to the goddess Artemis. |
| 5.4 | MOSSYNOECI TERRITORY | July 400 | After a false start, the army defeats the dominant group among the Mossynoeci with the aid of rival tribesmen. Strange customs of the Mossynoeci. |
| 5.5 | KOTYORA | July–August | The army proceeds to Kotyora, where ambassadors from Sinope, led by Hekatonymos, make threats against them but are seen off by Xenophon. |
| 5.6.1–14 | KOTYORA | July–August | Hekatonymos' advice that the army should continue by sea is accepted. |
| 5.6.15–37 | KOTYORA | July–August | Xenophon's dream of founding a city on the Black Sea coast is undermined by the seer Silanos. |
| 5.7.1–12 | KOTYORA | July–August | Xenophon defends himself against charges that he wants to take the army "back to Phasis." |
| 5.7.13–35 | KOTYORA | July–August | Xenophon complains about the lawless behavior of Klearetos and his comrades at Kerasous and the army as a whole in Kotyora against Zelarchos. |
| 5.8 | KOTYORA | July–August | By skillful cross-examination, Xenophon defeats accusations against him of willful violence during the winter march through the Armenian snow. |

## Book 6: Kotyora to Chrysopolis

| Book/<br>Chap./Sect. | Location | Date | Event |
|---|---|---|---|
| 6.1–14 | KOTYORA | August | The army leaders throw a banquet for Paphlagonian envoys at which spectacular dances are put on. |
| 6.1.15–16 | HARMENE (PORT OF SINOPE) | September | Cheirisophos returns with just one ship. |
| 6.1.17–33 | HARMENE (PORT OF SINOPE) | September | Xenophon deflects an attempt to make him commander in chief. Instead Cheirisophos is elected. |
| 6.2 | HERACLEA | September | The army splits into three amidst recriminations. |
| 6.3.1–9 | BITHYNIAN THRACE | September | The Arcadian contingent comes to disaster. |
| 6.3.10 | BITHYNIAN THRACE | September | Cheirisophos marches to Kalpe Harbor without incident. |
| 6.3.10–26 | BITHYNIAN THRACE | September | Xenophon marches to the aid of the Arcadians and relieves the pressure on them. |
| 6.4 | KALPE HARBOR | September | Death of Cheirisophos. The army, now reunited, is restricted to Kalpe Harbor by hostile omens, despite the lack of supplies there. |
| 6.5 | KALPE HARBOR | September | Once the omens improve, Xenophon leads out an expedition to bury the dead and obtain supplies. Through his leadership, the Greeks defeat the Bithynians and Pharnabazos' cavalry. |

| Book/ Chap./Sect. | Location | Date | Event |
|---|---|---|---|
| 6.6.1–10 | KALPE HARBOR | September– October 400 | The Spartan harmost Kleandros arrives and is met by a riot. |
| 6.6.11–34 | KALPE HARBOR | October | Xenophon's diplomatic skills persuade Kleandros not to punish the alleged leaders of the riot. |
| 6.6.35–38 | KALPE HARBOR | October | Xenophon and Kleandros formally pledge friendship. The army travels overland to the crossing point to Europe. |

### THRACE, THE TROAD, AND MYSIA
### Book 7: Chrysopolis to Pergamum

| | | | |
|---|---|---|---|
| 7.1 | CHRYSOPOLIS– BYZANTIUM | Late October | Very serious riot at Byzantium against the Spartan admiral Anaxibios. Xenophon resolves to leave the army and sail away with Anaxibios. |
| 7.2.1–16 | COASTAL THRACE | Early November | When Pharnabazos fails to pay Anaxibios the bribes he has promised him, Anaxibios sends Xenophon back to the army. |
| 7.2.17–38 | COASTAL THRACE | November– December? | Xenophon and selected officers visit Seuthes, a Thracian warlord, who wishes to enlist them to recover his lost domains. |
| 7.3.1–34 | COASTAL THRACE | December? | The army agrees to join Seuthes, who throws a banquet for leading Greeks and others at which gifts are given and speeches made. Strange customs of the Thracians. |
| 7.3.35–48 | THYNIAN PLAIN | December? | Seuthes and the Greeks march by night to the Thynian Plain and occupy the villages there, taking much plunder. |
| 7.4.1–11 | THYNIAN PLAIN | December? | Extreme cold of Thrace in winter. Further assault by Seuthes and the Greeks on Thynian villages. |
| 7.4.12–24 | THYNIAN PLAIN | December? | Failed night attack by Thynoi on Xenophon. Thynoi submit to Seuthes. |
| 7.5 | THE DELTA– SALMYDESSOS– SELYMBRIA | December?– February 399 | Further successful campaign by Seuthes and the Greeks amid increasing recriminations about insufficient pay for the army being provided from the profits. |
| 7.6 | SELYMBRIA | March | The Spartans Charminos and Polynikos arrive to take the army into Spartan service against Persia. In a long speech, Xenophon answers the soldiers' bitter complaints against him. |
| 7.7.1–19 | COASTAL THRACE | March | The Thracian Medosades complains about the army's occupation of his villages. Xenophon convinces a senior Odrysian nobleman that this is unjust. |
| 7.7.20–57 | COASTAL THRACE | March | Backed by the power of Sparta, Xenophon lectures Seuthes and persuades him to supply an installment of the army's overdue pay. |
| 7.8.1–8 | THE TROAD– AEOLIS–MYSIA | March | The army crosses back to Asia and marches from Lampsakos to Pergamum. Xenophon's poverty is made clear to his old seer Eukleides. |
| 7.8.9–23 | PERGAMUM | March | Xenophon and his men capture the Persian grandee Asidates, making Xenophon a rich man. |
| 7.8.24–26 | PERGAMUM | March | The Spartan commander Thibron takes over the army. |

# KEY TO MAPS AND DIAGRAMS

## Map Configurations

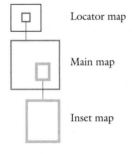

Locator map

Main map

Inset map

## Typography

| | |
|---|---|
| ANATOLIA | Major region |
| CAPPADOCIA | Region |
| Sardis | City |
| Tarsus | Town |
| Skythenoi | Tribe |
| *Euphrates R.* | River, body of water |
| *Cyprus* | Island, promontory |
| *MT. IDA* | Mountain |

## Cultural Features

● •   City, town

✗   Battle site

═══   Road

▭▭▭▭   Wall or fortification

## Natural Features

⌢   Mountain

≍   Pass

⌒   River

⬭   Coastline or lake
(approx. extent in Classical period)

## Route Features

⑩   Halting place

———   Land route

- - - - -   Alternate or additional
land route

·······   Sea route

## Military Units

▭   Infantry

▱   Cavalry

▮ ▮ ▮   Chariots

# BOOK ONE

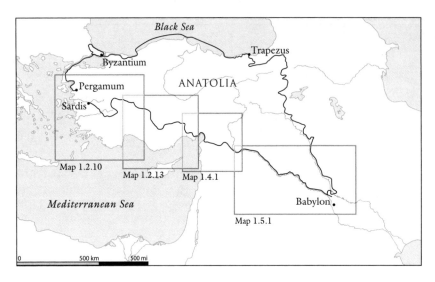

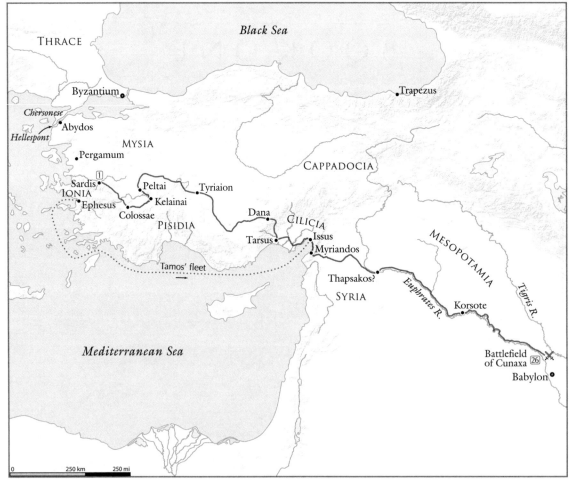

BOOK 1. *ANABASIS:* FROM SARDIS TO THE BATTLE OF CUNAXA, *HALTING PLACES 1–26.*

<sub>D</sub>arius and Parysatis had two sons, the elder called Artaxerxes, the younger Cyrus.[a] When Darius fell ill and suspected that it was the end of his life, he wanted his two sons, both of them, to be with him. [2] His elder son happened to be with him already, so he sent for Cyrus from the province over which he had made him satrap (he had also appointed him general of all those whose muster point was the plain of Kastolos).[a] Accordingly Cyrus went up into the interior,[b] taking Tissaphernes with him in the belief that he was a friend, as well as three hundred Greek hoplites, whose commander was Xenias of Parrasia.[c] [3] After Darius died and Artaxerxes succeeded to the kingship, Tissaphernes maligned Cyrus to his brother on the ground that he was plotting against the King. Artaxerxes was persuaded of this and arrested Cyrus, intending to put him to death; but their mother successfully pleaded on his behalf, and so he sent him back again to his province. [4] Departing as he did, dishonored and having been put in great danger, Cyrus set about planning how to avoid ever again being at his brother's mercy, and how instead to become King in his place if he could.

1.1.1–5
405–404
PERSIA
Following King Darius' death, his younger son Cyrus plans to supplant the new Great King, his elder brother, Artaxerxes.

NOTE: Unless otherwise indicated, all dates are B.C.E., and all citations are to Xenophon's *Anabasis*. The determination of the army's route and stopping places are based on the editors' calculations and estimates from data taken from *Anabasis*. Nonetheless, the route line shown on our maps and the monthly dates given in our side notes are often subject to doubt. Our best estimates should not be taken as authoritative or certain. See the Editors' Preface, §§17–20.

1.1.1a Darius II, King of the Persians (r. 424/3 to 405/4). Parysatis was his half sister and wife. For a brief account of Darius' family and reign, Parysatis' conduct after *Anabasis*, and Artaxerxes' very long reign (405/4–359/8), see Appendix W: Brief Biographies of Selected Characters in *Anabasis:* Darius II, §11; Parysatis, §26; Artaxerxes, §6; Cyrus the Younger, §10. For background on the Persian Empire (Ref. Map 9), see the Introduction, §4.1–7, and Appendix C: The Persian Empire.

1.1.2a Satraps were provincial governors of the Persian Empire. For more on them, see the Glossary and Appendix C, §9. Cyrus was satrap of Lydia, Greater Phrygia, and Cappadocia, and general of "all those assigned to muster in the plain of Kastolos" (1.9.7). On this role, see Appendix D: The Persian Army, §9. This unusually powerful role is mentioned in Xenophon's *Hellenika* (1.4.3), using the term *karanos*, on which, see the Glossary. Cappadocia: Book 1 map. Lydia, plain of Kastolos: Map 1.2.10, AX (Kastolou Pedion in the *Barrington Atlas*). Greater Phrygia (see n. 1.2.6a): Map 1.2.10, AY.

1.1.2b The work takes its title from the Greek term for "going up into the interior," *anabasis*, on which see further the Introduction, §1.4–5.

1.1.2c Tissaphernes, powerful Persian official in Western Anatolia from 413 to 395; see Appendix W, §37. "Anatolia" is roughly synonymous with "Asia Minor"; both were used in very late antiquity. Hoplites were heavily armed infantry who fought in close formation; see Appendix H: Infantry and Cavalry in *Anabasis*, §§2–3. Anatolia: Book 1 map, locator. Parrasia (in Arcadia): Map 1.2.1, BX.

3

Indeed, their mother, Parysatis, was on Cyrus' side, for she loved him rather than Artaxerxes, even though it was Artaxerxes who was the King. [5] When people came to Cyrus from the King, he used to send them back to the interior having treated them all so well that from then on they were his friends rather than the King's. In addition, he used to take care that the barbarians[a] at his own court should be fit and ready to wage war and favorably disposed toward him.

[6] He went to work putting together a force of Greeks, but as much as he possibly could, he disguised his purpose so as to surprise a completely unprepared King. So this was how he proceeded to collect them: Turning to all the garrisons he had in the cities, he gave instructions to each of the garrison commanders to secure the greatest number and highest quality of men from the Peloponnese[a] that he could, on the ground that Tissaphernes had designs on the cities. The Ionian cities had indeed of old been granted by the King to Tissaphernes, but they had then revolted to Cyrus, all except Miletus;[b] [7] in the case of Miletus, Tissaphernes had realized in advance that the Milesians were resolved on the same step, and he had put some of them to death and exiled others. Cyrus took in the exiles, assembled an army, and set about besieging Miletus both by land and by sea in an effort to restore those who had been expelled—and this served him as another excuse to gather an army. [8] He sent to the King to say he thought that, as he was the King's brother, these cities should be given to him rather than be ruled by Tissaphernes, and his mother was in league with him on this. Consequently the King did not perceive the plot against himself but thought that if Cyrus was making war on Tissaphernes, he was running through his money on the expenses of the campaign; and so Artaxerxes was not at all displeased at their fighting one another. This was especially the case as Cyrus continued to send the King the tribute that fell due from the cities that belonged to Tissaphernes but were in fact in Cyrus' own hands.[a]

[9] Another army was being assembled for Cyrus in the Chersonese on the other side of the strait from Abydos[a] in the following way: Klearchos was

**1.1.6–8**
**403–402**
SARDIS–IONIA
Cyrus gathers troops on the pretext of a quarrel with Tissaphernes.

**1.1.9–11**
**403–402**
SARDIS–THRACIAN
CHERSONESE–THESSALY
Cyrus funds Klearchos and Aristippos and asks other friends to assemble troops for him.

1.1.5a   Although, following the Persian Wars of the early fifth century, many Greeks (perhaps especially Athenians) became contemptuous of non-Greeks, the word "barbarians" (*barbaroi*) did not in itself carry the full overtones of savagery in Greek that it does in English; for more, see the Introduction, §5.1.

1.1.6a   The Peloponnese region was a traditional recruiting ground for mercenaries, notably so in the fourth century. Soldiers looking for work would often gather at ports on the southern coast. Peloponnese: Map 1.2.1, BX.

1.1.6b   In 413 King Darius ordered Tissaphernes to revive Persian claims over the Greek cities of the coast, which is probably what Xenophon refers to when he says Tissaphernes was granted the cities "of old" at 1.1.6. However, most scholars prefer

to date this grant to 405 or later because from 407 to 405 Cyrus was the ultimate overlord of the cities. But even though Tissaphernes was then subordinate to him, Cyrus did not reverse previous grants to him across the board, else he could not at that time have believed Tissaphernes to be a friend at 1.1.2. Ionia, Miletus: Map 1.2.10, AX, BX. For a coin of Tissaphernes, see Figure 1.1.6.

1.1.8a   Although the Persian Kings' central control over the provinces was often quite lax, they were insistent on the flow of tribute: for more on tribute, see the Introduction, §4.3, and Appendix C: The Persian Empire, §§20–21.

1.1.9a   Chersonese, Abydos: Book 1 map. The Hellespont runs between them.

a Lacedaemonian exile[b] whom Cyrus had met and admired, and to whom he gave ten thousand darics.[c] Klearchos took the gold and used the money to assemble an army. Making the Chersonese his base, he proceeded to wage war on the Thracians who live farther inland from the Hellespont, and thus helped the Greeks in that area.[d] Consequently the cities around the Hellespont also willingly provided him with money to feed the soldiers; but again, the army that was being maintained in this way was surreptitiously for Cyrus' benefit. [10] Aristippos the Thessalian also happened to be a guest-friend of Cyrus', and as he was under pressure from those of the opposite faction at home, he went to Cyrus and asked him for two thousand mercenaries and three months' pay for them, saying that in this way he would be able to overcome the other faction.[a] Cyrus gave him four thousand mercenaries and six months' pay, and he asked him not to come to terms with his opponents without consulting him first. In this way, once again, the army in Thessaly was being maintained for Cyrus' benefit unnoticed. [11] Cyrus also told Proxenos the Boeotian,[a] another guest-friend of his, to come and support him with as many men as he could obtain, on the pretext that he wanted to make an expedition against the Pisidians, who were, he said, making trouble for the territory under his control; and he told Sophainetos the Stymphalian and Socrates the Achaean,[b] who were also his guest-friends, to come with as many men as they too could obtain, on the pretext that he was going to make war on Tissaphernes in company with the Milesian exiles. So they set about doing just that.

[1] When Cyrus decided it was time to make his way to the interior, he used the pretext of wanting to expel the Pisidians altogether from his land, and he gathered together his troops, both barbarians and Greeks, as if it were the Pisidians he was going to attack. At this point he also sent instructions to Klearchos and Aristippos: to Klearchos, to come with the entire army that was with him; to Aristippos, to come to terms with his rivals at home and send Cyrus the army that he had. Cyrus also sent instructions to

FIGURE 1.1.6. COIN OF THE SATRAPAL GOVERNMENT OF TISSAPHERNES FROM THE BEGINNING OF THE FOURTH CENTURY. THIS HAS BEEN CLAIMED TO BE A PORTRAIT OF HIM.

1.2.1–3
Spring 401
SARDIS
Cyrus summons the troops he has been recruiting.

1.1.9b The terms Lacedaemon and Sparta are nearly synonymous. Lacedaemon is a state and territorial designation. Sparta was the most important city within it; see Appendix B: Xenophon and Sparta, §§18–19. For Klearchos' career as a Spartan officer and harmost (governor) of Byzantium, see Appendix W: Brief Biographies, §20; also note particularly Diodorus Siculus 14.12.2–9 (in Appendix S: Selections from Diodorus). Byzantium: Book 1 map. Lacedaemon, Sparta: Map 1.2.1, BX, BY.

1.1.9c The gold daric, equivalent to 25 Attic drachmas, was the standard large coin of the Persian empire; for more, see Appendix O: Ancient Greek and Persian Units of Measurement, §§13–14, and Figure O.13.

1.1.9d Thrace, Hellespont: Book 1 map.

1.1.10a Guest-friend: someone with whom there is a bond of ritualized friendship of a type that was common between prominent men

of different cities; see the Glossary. For more on Aristippos' role within Thessaly and the identity of the opponents who were putting him under pressure, see Appendix W, §5. Thessaly: Map 5.3.7, AX.

1.1.11a For a discussion of Proxenos' conduct on the expedition, including the little about him found in other sources, see Appendix W, §29. Boeotia: Map 1.2.1, AY.

1.1.11b For discussion of Sophainetos' age and Xenophon's attitude toward him, see Appendix W, §32. For Sophainetos' possible authorship of a rival account of the expedition, see Appendix M: Other Ancient Sources on the Ten Thousand. Very little is known about "Socrates the Achaean"—he is a different man from the famous philosopher, Socrates of Athens. Pisidia: Map 1.2.13, AX. The following locations appear on Map 1.2.1: Achaea, AX; Stymphalos, Athens, AY.

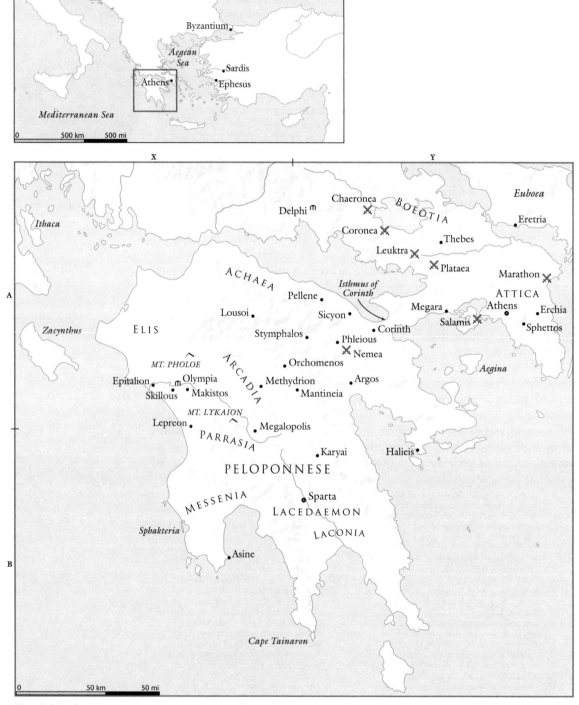

MAP 1.2.1. SITES IN CENTRAL AND SOUTHERN GREECE.

FIGURE 1.2.4. OVERVIEW OF SARDIS WITH THE TEMPLE OF ARTEMIS IN THE FOREGROUND.

Xenias the Arcadian[a]—who had earlier been appointed the commander of the mercenary forces stationed in the cities on Cyrus' behalf—to come with his troops, except for the minimum needed to guard each city's acropolis.[b] [2] He also sent for the troops besieging Miletus and told the exiles to come on the campaign with him, promising them that if he successfully achieved his campaign aims, he would not rest until he had restored them to their homes. They were glad to obey him, as they trusted him, and presented themselves at Sardis[a] with their weapons. [3] Xenias came to Sardis to support him with the hoplites from the cities to the number of four thousand; Proxenos was there too, with fifteen hundred hoplites and five hundred light-armed infantry;[a] Socrates the Achaean arrived with about five hundred hoplites, as did Pasion the Megarian with three hundred hoplites and three hundred

1.2.1a　Xenias the Arcadian was previously mentioned at 1.1.2 under the designation Xenias of Parrasia, the specific district in Arcadia from which he came.
1.2.1b　Acropolis: the citadel or high point of a city; for more, see the Glossary. Arcadia: Map 1.2.1, AX.
1.2.2a　Sardis was the historic capital of Lydia, captured by the Persians under Cyrus the Elder in 546 and now the place of the younger Cyrus' administration and the main Persian center for western Anatolia. On Cyrus the Elder, see Appendix W: Brief

Biographies, §9. Sardis: Map 1.2.10, AX, *Halting place 1.*
1.2.3a　Light-armed infantry: there were various types, depending on the protective weaponry and clothing they had. The Greek word here, *gymnētes*, indicates that Proxenos' light-armed troops had little or no protection; the peltasts, mentioned shortly afterward as coming with Pasion, had more. For a list of the Greek contingents in Cyrus' army and their sequence of assembly, see Appendix I: Infantry and Cavalry in *Anabasis*, Table I.4.

peltasts[b]—both he and Socrates had been among those who were campaigning around Miletus.[c]

So these troops arrived at Sardis to assist Cyrus; [4] but when Tissaphernes realized what was happening, he concluded that the preparations were greater than were required for an attack on the Pisidians, and he made his way to the King as fast as he possibly could, together with about five hundred cavalry.[a] [5] The King on his side, when he heard from Tissaphernes about Cyrus' armament, set about making counterpreparations.

Meanwhile, Cyrus started out from Sardis with those whom I have mentioned. He pushed on[a] through Lydia[b] for three days' march, covering twenty-two parasangs,[c] to the river Maeander.[d] The width of this is two hundred feet,[e] and there was a pontoon bridge over it made up of seven boats. [6] Having crossed this, he pushed on through Phrygia for one day's march, covering eight parasangs, to Colossae,[a] a populous city, prosperous and large. There he remained for seven days. Here Menon the Thessalian arrived with a thousand hoplites and five hundred peltasts, Dolopians and Ainians and Olynthians.[b] [7] From there Cyrus pushed on for three days' march, covering twenty parasangs, to Kelainai,[a] a populous city in Phrygia,

**1.2.4–5**
**May 401**
SARDIS–PERSIA
Tissaphernes warns the King about Cyrus. Cyrus sets out from Sardis.

**1.2.6–9**
**May–July 401**
SARDIS–PHRYGIA
*Sardis (1)–Kelainai (4)*
Other forces join Cyrus, and he conducts a review of his troops when staying in Kelainai. They total about thirteen thousand.

1.2.3b   Peltasts: light-armed infantry typically carrying a light crescent-shaped shield called a *peltē*, though Xenophon sometimes uses the term more generally to cover yet lighter infantry; for more, see Appendix H: Infantry and Cavalry in *Anabasis*, §§4–5. Megara: Map 1.2.1, AY.

1.2.3c   The manuscripts have an extra clause here saying that Sophainetos arrived at this point with his troops. For why this should be rejected, see Appendix I: The Size and Makeup of the Ten Thousand, §4.

1.2.4a   Tissaphernes likely followed the Royal Road described by the fifth-century historian Herodotus (5.52). Herodotus' Royal Road: Intro. Map 4.6. On travel in the empire, see the Introduction, §4.5–7.

1.2.5a   In Book 1 Cyrus is repeatedly said to "push on" (*exelaunei*), stressing his vigorous leadership. In subsequent books, when he is no longer there to provide that leadership, the verb "make their way" (*eporeuthēsan*) is instead used in connection with the army's movements, having not been employed much in Book 1. The contrast is no doubt intended to be significant and has therefore been systematically reflected in the translation. (Translator's note) See further the Translator's Notes, §5.

1.2.5b   Lydia was once the kingdom of King Croesus (ruled c. 560–546), whose legendary wealth became proverbial. Lydia: Map 1.2.10, AX.

1.2.5c   The parasang is a Persian unit for measuring travel, typically of about 3 miles/5 kilometers, but it is controversial whether it measures hours spent traveling, distance traveled, or a combination of the two: see the Introduction, §7.3–5, and Appendix O: Measurements, §§7–8. For the nuances of

the Greek word *stathmos*, here translated "days' march," see the Introduction, §7.2, and Appendix O, §6.

1.2.5d   For much of its course, the river flows through low-lying plains and valleys, a factor that explains its proverbial winding course to the sea. Maeander River: Map 1.2.10, AX, *Halting place 2*.

1.2.5e   Two hundred feet/61 meters: the Greek text says 2 *plethra*; see Appendix O, §§2–3.

1.2.6a   The site of Colossae, overlooked by the imposing Mount Kadmos, is today surrounded by some of the finest cherry orchards in Anatolia. By the time of the events of *Anabasis*, the extensive area known as Phrygia was divided in two for Persian administrative purposes. In this edition, "Hellespontine Phrygia" is used for the more northerly satrapy and "Greater Phrygia" for the more southerly one. The following locations appear on Map 1.2.10: Greater Phrygia, Colossae (*Halting place 3*), AY; Mt. Kadmos, BY. Hellespontine Phrygia: Ref. Map 4.1, BX, Ref. Map 4.2, AX.

1.2.6b   Presumably Menon led these troops rather than Aristippos himself because the political situation in Thessaly was too fragile for Aristippos to risk leaving home. Note also that Menon brings little more than a third of the four thousand mercenaries for whom Cyrus had provided six months' pay (1.1.10). For the explanation, see Appendix W: Brief Biographies, §5 (Aristippos). For more on Menon, see Appendix W, §23. The following locations appear on Map 5.3.7: Dolopia, Ainis, BX; Olynthos, AX.

1.2.7a   Kelainai: Map 1.2.10, AY, *Halting place 4*.

large and prosperous. Cyrus had a palace here and an extensive park full of wild animals,[b] which he used to hunt on horseback whenever he wanted to exercise himself and his horses. The river Maeander flows through the middle of the park, and its springs come up in the palace grounds; it flows through the city of Kelainai as well. [8] There is also a fortified palace belonging to the Great King in Kelainai, by the springs of the river Marsyas[a] under the citadel. This river too flows through the city, and it empties into the Maeander: its width is twenty-five feet.[b] Here, it is said, Marsyas entered into his famous contest of skill with Apollo,[c] and Apollo, after defeating him, flayed him and hung up his skin in the cavern from which the river springs: it is because of this that the river is called Marsyas. [9] Xerxes is said to have built this fortified palace there, and also the citadel of Kelainai, when he was retreating from Greece after being worsted in the battle.[a] There Cyrus remained for thirty days, during which time Klearchos, the Lacedaemonian exile, arrived with a thousand hoplites, eight hundred Thracian peltasts, and two hundred Cretan archers.[b] At the same time, Sosis the Syracusan[c] arrived with three hundred hoplites, and Sophainetos with a thousand Arcadian hoplites. Also here, Cyrus held a review and took a head count of the Greeks in his park, and there were altogether eleven thousand hoplites and about two thousand peltasts.[d]

[10] From there Cyrus pushed on for two days' march, covering ten parasangs, to Peltai, a populous city.[a] There he remained for three days, in the course of which Xenias the Arcadian performed the Lykaian sacrifices[b] and organized a contest. The prizes were golden coronets,[c] and Cyrus himself

1.2.10
July 401
PHRYGIA
*Peltai (5)–
Potters' Market (6)*
Sacrifices and games
at Peltai.

1.2.7b Parks (*paradeisoi*) like this were a feature of Persian administrative centers; possibly they were intended as re-creations of Iranian highland pastures where the court traditionally spent summers; for more, see Appendix C: The Persian Empire, §6.

1.2.8a The Greeks called the Persian monarch "the King," or sometimes "the Great King," so distinguishing him from the heads of lesser kingdoms. Marsyas River: Map 1.2.10, AY.

1.2.8b Twenty-five feet/8 meters: the Greek text says twenty-five *podes;* see Appendix O: Measurements, §§2–3.

1.2.8c In this mythical musical contest, the god Apollo played the lyre, while the pipes were played by Marsyas son of Silenus. Silenus was a drunken companion to the god Dionysus and the leader or father of the satyrs, half men and half animals. The contest is also referred to at Herodotus 7.26.3, where Kelainai is mentioned, and in Diodorus 3.58.3–3.59.5.

1.2.9a The naval battle of Salamis in 480 was seen by the Athenians, who were the biggest contributors to the Greek fleet, as the turning point in King Xerxes' expedition against Greece. On Xerxes, see Appendix W: Brief Biographies, §38. Salamis: Map 1.2.1, AY.

1.2.9b Crete: Map 5.3.7, locator.

1.2.9c Syracuse: Map 5.3.7, locator.

1.2.9d For discussion of the accuracy of this figure of 13,000, see Appendix I: The Size and Makeup of the Ten Thousand, §4.

1.2.10a Up to this point, Cyrus had been marching east–southeast more or less directly toward Pisidia, but he turned back here in a north-westerly direction, making a detour even as regards the route he eventually took, since there should have been a serviceable road northeast from Kelainai to Kaystroupedion (see n. 1.2.11a), which he reaches at 1.2.11. Peltai, approximate location, *Halting place 5* (not listed in the *Barrington Atlas*), Pisidia: Map 1.2.10, AY, BY.

1.2.10b The Lykaian sacrifices were performed in honor of Zeus Lykaios, whose cult center was on Mount Lykaion in Arcadia. The open-air festival there was an important focus of identity for the Arcadians, who were divided into many small city-states (*poleis*) at the time. Some argue that the timing of the festival provides evidence for the chronology of the march: see Appendix Q: The Chronology of the March, §§4–5. Mt. Lykaion: Map 1.2.1, AX.

1.2.10c At the major games in mainland Greece the prizes were wreaths made of aromatic foliage from wild olive, bay, or pine trees, or from wild celery; coronets at other Greek athletic games were usually made of bronze. Cyrus was therefore showing his generosity by having some of them made of gold.

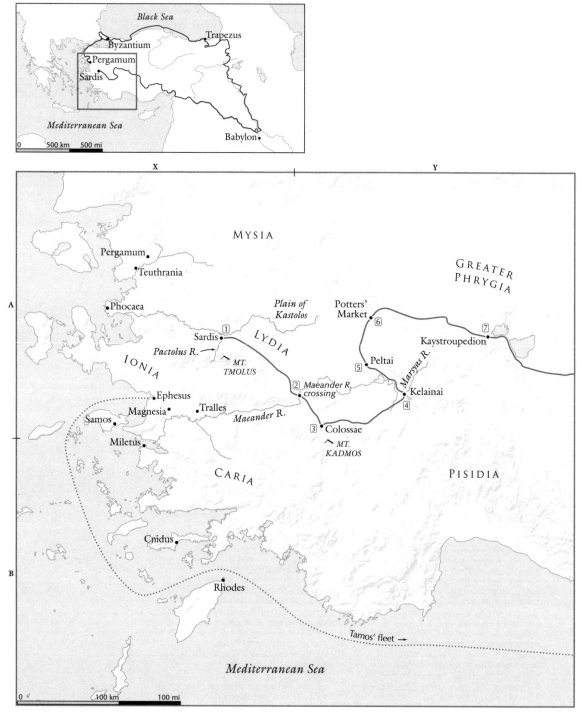

MAP 1.2.10. *ANABASIS:* FROM SARDIS TO KAYSTROUPEDION, *HALTING PLACES 1–7.*

was one of the spectators. From there he pushed on for two days' march, covering twelve parasangs, to Potters' Market, a populous city, the last in this direction before Mysian country,[d] [11] and from there he pushed on for three days' march, covering thirty parasangs, to Kaystroupedion,[a] a populous city. There he remained for five days.

At this point more than three months' pay was owing to the soldiers, and they went many times to Cyrus' quarters and demanded it. He put them off by telling them of his hopes; and it was clear he was distressed, for it was not Cyrus' way to fail to hand out what he had. [12] Here Epyaxa, the wife of Syennesis, king of Cilicia,[a] arrived, having come to see Cyrus, and it was said she gave him a great deal of money. At any rate Cyrus then gave four months' pay to the army. The Cilician queen had her own guard, made up of Cilicians and Aspendians;[b] it was said that Cyrus even slept with her.

[13] From there he pushed on for two days' march, covering ten parasangs, to Thymbrion, a populous city.[a] There by the side of the road was a fountain, called the Fountain of Midas, the Phrygian king, at which Midas is said to have caught the satyr by mixing the water of the fountain with wine.[b] [14] From there he pushed on for two days' march, covering ten parasangs, to Tyriaion,[a] a populous city. There he remained for three days.

The Cilician queen is said to have asked Cyrus to put his army on show for her; so, wishing to make a suitable display, he held a review of his Greek and barbarian soldiers on the plain. [15] He ordered the Greeks to be drawn up according to their rule for battle and to stand at halt, and for each general to marshal his own troops. Accordingly, they were drawn up four-deep:[a] Menon and those with him held the right wing, Klearchos and his

1.2.11–12
July 401
PHRYGIA
*Kaystroupedion (7)*
Cyrus experiences a cash crisis.

1.2.13–14
July 401
PHRYGIA
*Thymbrion (8)–*
*Tyriaion (9)*
Cyrus pushes on past the Fountain of Midas at Thymbrion.

1.2.15–18
Late July 401
TYRIAION
Cyrus puts on a review of the army for the Cilician queen's benefit.

1.2.10d  The location of Potters' Market is disputed. In this region of Turkey in particular there are many archaeological sites, some unmarked, so in the absence of a persuasive identifier such as an inscription or an abundance of ceramic or numismatic evidence, matching text to site is difficult. Potters' Market: Map 1.2.10, AY, *Halting place 6* (Keramon Agora in the *Barrington Atlas*, Greek for "Potters' Market"). Mysia: Map 1.2.10, AX.

1.2.11a  Kaystroupedion: Map 1.2.10, AY, *Halting place 7* (not listed in the *Barrington Atlas*). Kaystroupedion means "plain of Kaystros," referring to the Kaystros River.

1.2.12a  Cilicia enjoyed considerable autonomy within the Persian Empire. For more on Epyaxa's ancestry and on the policy that Syennesis was pursuing, see Appendix W: Brief Biographies, §14. Cilicia: Map 1.2.13, AY.

1.2.12b  Aspendos: Map 1.2.13, BX.

1.2.13a  Cyrus was now moving along a more direct though more difficult route toward Babylonia (Map 1.5.1 and inset) via the Taurus Mountains (Map 1.2.13, AY). The more regular way was the Royal Road

identified by Herodotus (Ref. Map 9, CW–CY). Thymbrion: Map 1.2.13, AX, *Halting place 8* (not listed in the *Barrington Atlas*).

1.2.13b  Up until 2001 there was a booming fountain in the vicinity, outside the village of Ulupınar ("great spring"), but this has now dried up. The story of Midas tells how the god Dionysus rewarded King Midas for releasing the captured satyr Silenus by giving him the "golden touch," whereby everything Midas touched turned to gold. The story explained the origin of the gold in the Pactolus River, which flows through Sardis. Pactolus River: Map 1.2.10, AX. Fountain of Midas: Map 1.2.13, AX.

1.2.14a  Tyriaion: Map 1.2.13, AX, *Halting place 9.*

1.2.15a  The main body of heavy-armed troops was usually drawn up eight-deep, so four-deep was far shallower than usual. It has been suggested that Cyrus' Greeks were deliberately drilled to be drawn up in this way, in the belief that depth was not required because they would not be facing heavy infantry of similar quality, and the greater width of the line would allow them to outflank even much more numerous troops when the critical battle came.

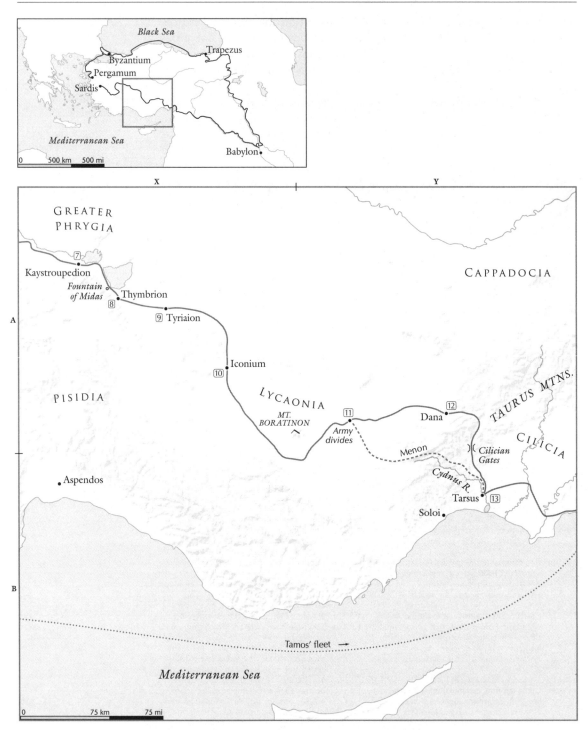

MAP 1.2.13. *ANABASIS:* FROM KAYSTROUPEDION TO TARSUS, *HALTING PLACES 7–13.*

FIGURE 1.2.16. THIS FIFTH-CENTURY CUP, UNFORTUNATELY NOW LOST, DEPICTS A HOPLITE WITH ALL HIS EQUIPMENT —SHIELD, SPEAR, BODY ARMOR, HELMET, AND GREAVES.

troops the left, and the other generals the center.[b] [16] So Cyrus then conducted his review, taking the barbarians first, who paraded past him drawn up in squadrons of cavalry and regular units of infantry. Next he reviewed the Greeks by driving past them, he himself in a chariot and the queen in a covered carriage. All the soldiers wore bronze helmets, red tunics,[a] and greaves[b] and paraded with their shields out of their storage covers.[c] [17] When he had driven past all of them, he halted his chariot in front of the phalanx, in the middle, and sent his interpreter Pigres to the Greek generals to order them to level arms and set the whole phalanx in

1.2.15b The right wing was the place of honor. It seems at this stage Menon was thought of as senior to Klearchos, although the latter had brought more troops with him than Menon and eventually it was Klearchos who became the Greek general on whom Cyrus most relied. On Menon and Klearchos, see Appendix W: Brief Biographies, §§23, 20.

1.2.16a Red tunics were characteristic of Spartans in particular. Cyrus' troops must have been instructed to wear them on this occasion because the variety of body armor worn by different soldiers would have destroyed the impression of unity

that Cyrus no doubt intended to create. Sparta: Map 1.2.1, BY.

1.2.16b Greaves (bronze shinguards) were one element of the hoplite panoply that soldiers often did not bother to buy or wear. Perhaps Cyrus had provided them to those who did not have them already. A soldier wearing the complete panoply is depicted in Figure 1.2.16.

1.2.16c Evidently hoplite shields were normally kept inside covers when not actually being used in combat. They were presumably stored in them at night and during a march when combat was not imminent.

FIGURE 1.2.19. TOWARD ICONIUM: THE ARMY COVERS TWENTY PARASANGS IN THREE DAYS.

motion.[a] The generals gave instructions to the soldiers to this effect, and when the trumpet sounded, they advanced with weapons leveled. From this start they went forward faster and faster, shouting as they went, and so, with its own momentum, their charge brought the soldiers right up to the camp tents. [18] There was a great panic among the barbarians, and the Cilician queen fled in her carriage, while the traders fled from the market, leaving behind the goods they had brought for sale.[a] The Greeks went to their tents laughing. When the Cilician queen saw the splendor and discipline of the army, she was amazed, and Cyrus was pleased when he saw the fear that the Greeks inspired in the barbarians.

[19] From there he pushed on for three days' march, covering twenty parasangs, to Iconium,[a] the last city in Phrygia, where he remained for three days. From there he pushed on through Lycaonia[b] for five days' march, covering thirty parasangs. He turned this land over to the Greeks to plunder, on the ground that it was enemy territory.[c] [20] Cyrus sent the Cilician queen away from there to Cilicia by the quickest route, and with her he sent soldiers who were in Menon's section, together with Menon himself.[a] Cyrus then pushed on with the rest of the army through Cappadocia for four days'

1.2.19–20
August 401
PHRYGIA–LYCAONIA–
CAPPADOCIA
*Iconium (10)–Dana (12)*
Cyrus approaches the
passes over to Cilicia.
*Army divides (11)*
Menon departs on a
separate route.

1.2.17a  Phalanx: a body of troops drawn up across a broad front in close formation; for more, see Appendix H: Infantry and Cavalry in *Anabasis*, §§13–15. Xenophon does not record Pigres' ethnic origin, but scholars think he was from Caria (Map 1.2.10, BX).
1.2.18a  The traders were present because it was normal in Greek armies for the soldiers to buy their own provisions and other supplies: see Appendix O: Measurements, §19.
1.2.19a  Iconium: Map 1.2.13, AX, *Halting place 10.*
1.2.19b  Lycaonia: Map 1.2.13, AX.

1.2.19c  See 3.2.23. Though the Lycaonians lived within Cyrus' satrapy of Cappadocia, they, like the Pisidians, had not been subdued by the Persians.
1.2.20a  To get to Cilicia, the army had to cross the Taurus Mountains (1.2.21). The principal route for armies and caravans was the so-called Cilician Gates (see Figure 1.2.22). Menon's party went by a more southerly route, starting from *Halting place 11*, Map 1.2.13, AY, which was unsuitable for the larger force because of the terrain.

march, covering twenty-five parasangs, to Dana,[b] a populous city, large and prosperous. There they remained for three days, during which time Cyrus put to death a Persian man, Megaphernes, who was a royal scribe,[c] and also another leading figure among his subordinate officials,[d] both of whom he accused of plotting against him.

[21] From there they set about trying to force their way into Cilicia.[a] The approach route was a wagon road that was exceedingly steep and, if anyone was blocking it, impossible for an army to get through. Syennesis[b] was also said to be on the heights guarding the approach; as a consequence Cyrus remained in the plain for a day. On the next day a messenger came, saying that Syennesis had left the heights, since he had learned that Menon's army was already in Cilicia on the inner side of the mountains and he was hearing that triremes belonging to the Lacedaemonians and to Cyrus himself were sailing around from Ionia to Cilicia.[c] [22] However that might be,[a] Cyrus went up into the mountains with no one stopping him, and he saw the tents where the Cilicians had been keeping guard. From there he proceeded to descend into an extensive, beautiful, and well-watered plain, which is full of all sorts of trees and vines and grows a great deal of sesame, foxtail millet, proso millet, wheat, and barley.[b] A mountain range encloses it securely, towering up on every side from sea to sea.[c] [23] Having made his descent through this plain, he pushed on for a total of four days' march, covering twenty-five parasangs, to Tarsus,[a] a great and prosperous city in Cilicia. That was where the palace of Syennesis, the king of the Cilicians, was located, and through the middle of the city flows a river called Cydnus, two hundred feet

1.2.21–24
August 401
CILICIA
*Tarsus (13)*
Cyrus' army, let into
Cilicia by Syennesis,
reaches Tarsus.

1.2.20b   Cappadocia, Dana (probable location, *Halting place 12;* a major source of controversy): Map 1.2.13, AY.

1.2.20c   On the scribe (*phoinikistēs*), see Appendix C: The Persian Empire, §8.

1.2.20d   This man, identified as a *hyparchos* (see the Glossary), was probably a high-ranking local official, according to Christopher Tuplin in Appendix C, §10.

1.2.21a   Epyaxa, the queen of Cilicia, had cooperated with the army. Evidently Cyrus expected Synnesis' Cilicians to oppose his transit of the pass; see further n. 1.2.22a.

1.2.21b   Syennesis: the king of Cilicia, as mentioned at 1.2.12.

1.2.21c   Triremes: long warships with three banks of oars, the standard military vessels at this period; for more, see the Glossary. Ionia: Map 1.2.10, AX.

1.2.22a   The alternative explanation was that Syennesis was playing a double game with both of them and wanted to do just enough to excuse himself to Artaxerxes but not so much that he alienated Cyrus; that is what is suggested by Ctesias (in Appendix U: Photius' Synopsis of Ctesias' *Persika*, §63) and by Diodorus 14.20.3 (in Appendix S: Diodorus). It is not clear whether Syennesis was successful in thus hedging his bets: native dynasts continued to rule

Cilicia, but as far as we know they were not subsequently called Syennesis, perhaps indicating a change of status or of dynasty or both.

1.2.22b   The Cilician plain (Map 1.4.1, AX) remains one of Anatolia's richest and most heavily cultivated regions. Foxtail millet and proso millet are types of cereal grass sown in early summer and harvested in late summer. For the difference between them, see "millet" in the Glossary.

1.2.22c   A mountain range: this refers to part of the Taurus Mountains. Diodorus 14.20.1 (in Appendix S: Diodorus) says that at this point the army went through the Cilician Gates, a natural pass and a striking pinch point on the main road to Cilicia. Xenophon does not mention the Cilician Gates: this is strange if he himself passed through them rather than going around by a slightly different route, but he often omits things that one would have thought it was inevitable to include. Cilician Gates: Map 1.2.13, BY. See Figure 1.2.22.

1.2.23a   Despite appearances, these four days must represent the whole journey from Dana to Tarsus. Tarsus: Map 1.2.13, BY, *Halting place 13.*

FIGURE 1.2.22. THE
CILICIAN GATES, THE
MAIN PASS THROUGH THE
TAURUS MOUNTAINS
FROM CENTRAL ANATOLIA
TO CILICIA, AS SEEN IN A
1909 PHOTOGRAPH.

1.2.25–26
August 401
TARSUS
Menon's army, having
suffered losses in the
mountains, takes its
revenge.

in width.[b] [24] The inhabitants of Tarsus, along with Syennesis himself, abandoned their city for a secure stronghold in the mountains, with the exception of the small tradesmen; the people who lived by the sea in Soloi and Issus[a] also remained where they were.

[25] Epyaxa, the wife of Syennesis, reached Tarsus five days earlier than Cyrus, but in crossing the mountains into the plain, two companies from Menon's army were destroyed. Some said that while engaged in a little plundering, they had been cut to pieces by the Cilicians; others, that they had lagged behind and had been destroyed after wandering around, unable to find the rest of the army or the right tracks. Whatever the precise story, those concerned amounted to a hundred hoplites. [26] When the others arrived, they sacked the city of Tarsus, angry because of the destruction of their fellow soldiers, and they also sacked the palace inside the city.

Once Cyrus had pushed right into the city, he repeatedly sent for Syennesis to come to him. But Syennesis said he had never before put himself

1.2.23b  Two hundred feet/61 meters: the Greek text says 2 *plethra;* see Appendix O: Measurements, §§2–3. Cydnus River: Map 1.2.13, BY.
1.2.24a  These "people who lived by the sea" were

a fair distance from Tarsus (about 25 and 75 miles/40 and 121 kilometers, respectively). Soloi: Map 1.2.13, BY. Issus: Map 1.4.1, AX, *Halting place 16.*

into the hands of anyone who was more powerful than he was; and he was unwilling to go to Cyrus on this occasion until his wife persuaded him and he received pledges of good faith. [27] When after all this they met each other, Syennesis gave Cyrus a great deal of money for the army, and Cyrus granted him gifts such as are thought honorable at the court of the King: a horse with a golden bit, a golden necklace, armlets, a golden dagger, and a Persian robe.[a] He also granted him the right not to have his country plundered anymore[b] and to recover the slaves that had been seized as booty if the Cilicians came across them anywhere.

[1] Cyrus and the army remained there for twenty days, for the soldiers said they were not going any farther. They already suspected that they were being led against the King, and they said they had not been hired for that. Klearchos was the first to try to force his own soldiers to go on, but they started to throw things at him and at the draft animals carrying his baggage whenever they began to move forward. [2] On this occasion Klearchos only just escaped from being stoned to death, but later on, when he realized that he was not going to be able to succeed by force, he called together an assembly of his soldiers. To begin with, he stood there in tears for a long time. When they saw it, they were amazed and fell silent, and then he spoke as follows:

[3] "Brave soldiers, do not be amazed that I take badly what is going on now. Cyrus became my guest-friend, and among other ways in which he honored me, though I was an exile from my native land, he gave me ten thousand darics.[a] Once I had taken the money, I did not stockpile it for my private use, nor did I squander any of it on luxury, but, over time, I spent it on pay for you. [4] Initially I waged war on the Thracians and, along with you, proceeded to exact revenge on them on behalf of Greece, driving them out of the Chersonese when they wanted to deprive the Greeks who live there of their land.[a] When Cyrus sent for me, I took you with me and set off on the way, in order to repay him for his kind treatment of me by helping him if he needed anything. [5] Since you do not want to accompany him on his way any farther, of necessity I shall have either to betray you and continue to enjoy Cyrus' friendship, or to break my word to him and stay with you. I do not know if I shall in truth be doing what is right, but whether I am or no, I will choose you and I will suffer along with you whatever it may be necessary to suffer. Nobody shall ever say that, having led Greeks to the lands of the barbarians, I betrayed the Greeks and chose the friendship of the barbarians instead. [6] Rather than that, since you do not wish to obey me or follow me, I will follow along with you and take the necessary conse-

1.2.27
Late August 401
TARSUS
Cyrus meets Syennesis, king of Cilicia. They exchange gifts.

1.3.1–2
August–September 401
TARSUS
The Greek soldiers mutiny.

1.3.3–6
September 401
TARSUS
Klearchos plays on his men's emotions, pretending to break with Cyrus.

---

1.2.27a  On royal gifts, see Appendix C: The Persian Empire, §4.
1.2.27b  Over and above ordinary taxation, the Great King was entitled to take supplies for his court and his army from the vicinities through which he passed without paying for them. In granting Syennesis a right not to be plundered, Cyrus is

perhaps indicating that he releases the Cilicians from this obligation.
1.3.3a  The gold daric, equivalent to 25 Attic drachmas, was the standard large coin of the Persian empire; for more, see Appendix O: Measurements, §13–14.
1.3.4a  Thrace, Chersonese: Book 1 map.

quences. I regard you as being my fatherland, my friends, and my allies, and with your assistance I think I would be held in honor wherever I might be; but if I were left without you, I think I would not be powerful enough either to help a friend or to ward off an enemy. So think of me as someone who will go wherever you may go."

1.3.7–9
September 401
TARSUS
Klearchos reassures Cyrus
that he has the situation
under control.

[7] That was his speech. The soldiers—both his own troops and the others who heard of it—praised him for refusing to make his way to where the King was; and more than two thousand took their weapons and baggage from the sections of Xenias and Pasion and encamped near Klearchos. [8] Cyrus was at a loss at these events and, in his distress, sent repeatedly for Klearchos. He refused to go, but at the same time he sent a messenger to Cyrus behind the soldiers' backs to tell him to keep his spirits up, as things would turn out all right. He told him to continue to send for him but said he would not go. [9] After this he brought together his own soldiers and those who had come over to him and any of the others who wanted to come to the meeting, and spoke as follows:

1.3.10–12
September 401
TARSUS
Klearchos exposes the
difficulties of deserting
Cyrus at this point.

"Brave soldiers, it is clear that Cyrus' stance toward us is the same as ours toward him: we are no longer his soldiers—obviously, since we are not following along with him—and he is no longer our paymaster. [10] However, I know that he thinks he is being wronged by us, and for that reason even when he sends for me, I do not want to go. Most of all this is because I am ashamed, knowing in my own heart that I lied to him in every respect, but on top of that, it is because I am also afraid that he might seize me and punish me for the wrongs he thinks I have done him. [11] So it seems to me that this is no time for us to sleep or be careless of our own affairs; we need instead to discuss what we have to do under the circumstances. And at any rate as long as we remain here, it seems to me we must look out for how we are to do so as safely as possible, and if we decide to leave now, for how we shall leave as safely as possible. And also for how we are going to obtain food supplies, since without those it's no use having either generals or rank-and-file soldiers. [12] Cyrus is a man who is a highly worthwhile friend to anyone who is a friend of his, but he is also the most awkward of enemies to anyone to whom he is hostile, and he has infantry, cavalry, and naval forces at his disposal that all of us alike see and know well; indeed, to my mind we don't seem to be camped very far away from him. And so now is the time for any of you to suggest what he reckons to be best."

1.3.13–14
September 401
TARSUS
An absurd proposal
points up the weakness
of the Greeks' position.

[13] Having said this, he broke off. After this some people stood up spontaneously in order to say what their judgment was, while others did so prompted by him, making clear what a problem it would be, without Cyrus' goodwill, either to stay or to go. [14] One of them, pretending to be keen on making his way as quickly as possible back to Greece, actually proposed

that they should first choose new generals with the utmost speed if Klearchos did not want to lead them back home; and that they should then buy their food supplies in the market (which was in the barbarian army's encampment) and pack up and, after that, go and ask Cyrus for transport ships in order to set sail. And if he didn't give them ships, they should ask Cyrus for a guide who would lead them away through friendly territory. If he didn't give them a guide either, they should draw up in line of battle as soon as they could manage to do so—and also send troops ahead to occupy the heights so that they could not be taken beforehand by either Cyrus or the Cilicians, "many of whom, and much of their property," he added, "are in our possession, since we plundered them." That was the sort of thing this individual said.

[15] After him Klearchos spoke to this effect: "Let none of you say that I will undertake this command, for I see many reasons why it should not be me who does this. But I will obey whichever man you choose to the very best of my ability, to let you see that I know how to be ruled just as much as any other person."

[16] After Klearchos, another soldier stood up and pointed out the silliness of telling them to ask for transport ships, "as if Cyrus were making a voyage back again," and on the other hand, he pointed out how silly it would be to ask for a guide "from the very person whose enterprise we are ruining. And if we actually trust the guide Cyrus gives us (if he does give us one), we might just as well tell Cyrus to occupy the heights in advance for our benefit! [17] I would hesitate to embark on any transport ships that he might give us, in case he sank us with his triremes, and I would be afraid to follow any guide he might give us, in case he led us into a place from which it would not be possible to escape. On the contrary, if I was going away against Cyrus' wishes, I would want to conceal my departure from him, but that is not possible. [18] The whole idea is a load of nonsense, I say.

"I think men should go to Cyrus—whoever are suitable for the purpose—along with Klearchos and ask him how he wants to make use of us, and if the enterprise he has in mind is close enough to what he used mercenaries for in the past,[a] we too should follow him and not be greater cowards than those who accompanied him to the interior previously. [19] If, on the other hand, his enterprise seems greater than the previous one and involves more hard work and danger, we should expect that either he persuades us and leads us forward or he is persuaded by us and lets us depart in friendship. In this way, if we were to follow him, we would follow eagerly, as his friends, and if we departed, we would depart safely. But whatever he says in response should be reported back here, and when we have heard it, we can make up our minds in the light of it."

1.3.15
September 401
TARSUS
Klearchos refuses to lead the troops back.

1.3.16–19
September 401
TARSUS
A soldier argues for consultation with Cyrus about his intentions.

1.3.18a   Cyrus used mercenaries to accompany
            him when he went to see his dying father
            at 1.1.2.

1.3.20–21
September 401
TARSUS
Despite its suspicions,
the army accepts Cyrus'
assurances that he is
attacking Abrokomas
rather than the King
himself, and agrees to
go on.

1.4.1–3
September 401
TARSUS–ISSUS
*Psaros River (14)–Issus (16)*
A small Lacedaemonian
fleet meets the army at
Issus.

[20] That was what they decided, and they chose men and sent them along with Klearchos to ask Cyrus the questions the army had settled on. He answered that his current information was that Abrokomas, a man who was an enemy of his, was presently by the river Euphrates, twelve days' march away.[a] So, he said, he wanted to go after him, and if he was there, he said, he longed to give him his due punishment. If he fled, "we will have a discussion there in the light of that." [21] When they heard this, the delegates made their report to the soldiers, and they were suspicious that he was leading them against the King, but they still decided to follow him. However, they asked for more pay, and Cyrus promised to give them all half again as much as they had had before: a daric and a half per month for each soldier, rather than a daric.[a] At this stage nobody heard anyone say, at any rate openly, that he was leading them to attack the King.

[1] From there he pushed on for two days' march, covering ten parasangs, to the river Psaros, which was one hundred yards wide.[a] From there he pushed on for one day's march, covering five parasangs, to the river Pyramos, which was two hundred yards wide.[b] From there he pushed on for two days' march, covering fifteen parasangs, to Issus, the last city of Cilicia[c] along the coast, populous, large, and prosperous. [2] There they remained for three days, and the ships from the Peloponnese, thirty-five of them, arrived for Cyrus with Pythagoras of Lacedaemon in command of them as admiral.[a] Tamos of Egypt had been conducting them from Ephesus with twenty-five other ships belonging to Cyrus, with which Tamos had been besieging Miletus at the time when it was friendly to Tissaphernes and Tamos had been waging war against it in company with Cyrus.[b] [3] Cheirisophos[a] of Lacedaemon was also there on board ship, having been sent for by Cyrus with seven hundred hoplites under his command; he continued to be general over these

1.3.20a　Indeed the army was then about twelve days' march from northern crossings of the Euphrates, but the more southerly route that Cyrus followed was a nineteen days' march to the fording point. On the view taken in this edition, their crossing point was much farther downstream than the one closest to Anatolia and so was closer to Cyrus' real goal—Babylon. See Appendix P: The Route of the Army, §§4–5, and Map P.1 for a spread of possible crossing points on the Euphrates. On the office held by Abrokomas in 401, see Appendix W: Brief Biographies, §1. Anatolia, Babylon: Map 1.4.1, locator. Euphrates River: Map 1.4.1.

1.3.21a　One daric was about 25 drachmas, so the mercenaries' pay had been a little less than a drachma a day and was now quite a lot more. Soldiers could also hope to obtain money from booty. On the daric and drachma, as well as for discussion of how the rates compare with the evidence for other soldiers at the time and for civilian wages, see Appendix O: Measurements, §§11, 13–19.

1.4.1a　One hundred yards/91 meters: the Greek text says 3 *plethra;* see Appendix O, §§2–3. Psaros River: Map 1.4.1, AX, *Halting place 14.*

1.4.1b　Two hundred yards/183 meters: the Greek text says 1 stade; see Appendix O, §5. Pyramos River: Map 1.4.1, AX, *Halting place 15.*

1.4.1c　Issus (*Halting place 16*), Cilicia: Map 1.4.1, AX.

1.4.2a　Pythagoras was *nauarchos* (admiral) of Sparta, the commander in chief of the Spartan fleet for the year. (On the term *nauarchos,* see Appendix B: Xenophon and Sparta, §14.) He is referred to as Samios in Xenophon's *Hellenika* (3.1.1) and, presumably by a slip, as Samos in Diodorus (14.19.4–5; in Appendix S: Diodorus). Probably Pythagoras is a nickname given to Samios because of the Samian origin of the philosopher Pythagoras (after whom the Pythagorean theorem is named). Sparta, Peloponnese, Lacedaemon: Map 1.2.1, BY, BX.

1.4.2b　For Tamos' earlier career and his eventual miserable end, and on Tissaphernes, see Appendix W, §§34, 37. Egypt: Ref. Map 1, DX. Ephesus, Miletus: Map 1.2.10, AX, BX.

1.4.3a　On Cheirisophos, see Appendix W, §7.

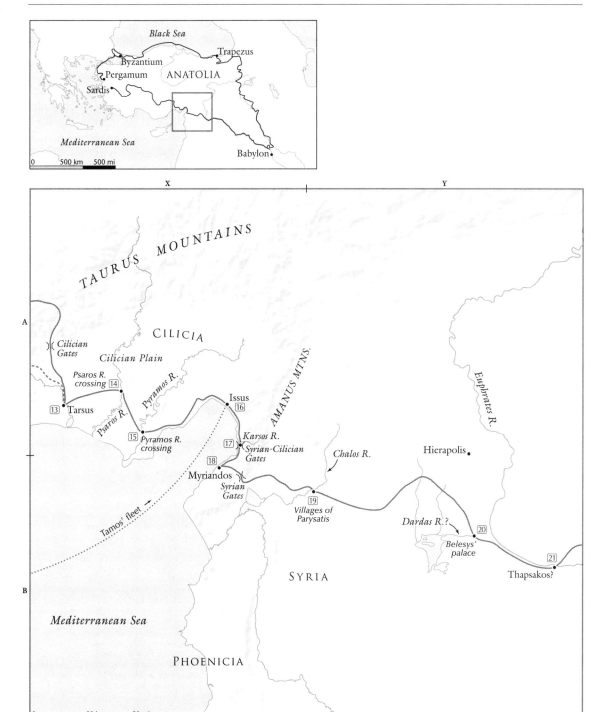

Map 1.4.1. *Anabasis:* from Tarsus to Thapsakos, *Halting places 13–21.*

within Cyrus' army. The ships lay at anchor near Cyrus' tent. There too came the Greek mercenaries who had been with Abrokomas, four hundred hoplites who, having deserted him for Cyrus, were now joining the expedition against the King.

[4] From there he pushed on for one day's march, covering five parasangs, to the Gates between Cilicia and Syria.[a] These consisted of two walls, and Syennesis and a garrison of Cilicians held the wall on the Cilician side, from which they were coming, while it was said that a garrison of the King's was guarding the wall on the other, Syrian, side. Through the space between these walls flows a river named Karsos, thirty yards or so[b] in width. The entire distance between the walls is just six hundred yards,[c] and it was not possible to force the position directly, as the passage through it was narrow and the walls came down to the sea, while above there were precipitous cliffs; in both walls gates were set. [5] Because of the nature of the passageway, Cyrus had sent for the ships, in order that he might disembark hoplites both between the Gates and on the far side of them. By that means they could pass through, having forcibly dislodged any enemy troops that were keeping guard on the Gates on the Syrian side, which is what Cyrus thought Abrokomas would be doing, since he had a large army. But Abrokomas did not do this; instead, when he heard that Cyrus was in Cilicia, he turned away from Phoenicia[a] and set about marching off to the King with what was said to be an army three hundred thousand strong.[b]

[6] From there Cyrus pushed on through Syria for one day's march, covering five parasangs, to Myriandos,[a] a city by the sea inhabited by Phoenicians. The place was a center for trade, and many cargo ships were at anchor there. There the troops remained for seven days, [7] during which time Xenias the Arcadian and Pasion the Megarian[a] embarked on a boat, loaded it with their most valuable belongings, and sailed off. At least to most people, it seemed that they did so out of a concern for their prestige, because when their soldiers had left them for Klearchos[b] with the idea of going back again to Greece and not attacking the King, Cyrus had subsequently let Klearchos keep them. However that might be, when they disappeared, a tale went around that Cyrus was pursuing them with triremes. Some people were pray-

1.4.4a The "Gates": the Syrian-Cilician Gates, two structures on either side of the Karsos River that marked Cilicia's southern border. The army was following a narrow coastal road between the Amanus Mountains and the Mediterranean Sea. The following locations appear on Map 1.4.1: Cilicia, Amanus Mtns., Syrian-Cilician Gates (*Halting place 17;* Kilikiai Pylai in the *Barrington Atlas,* Map 67 C3), Karsos River, AX; Syria, BY; Mediterranean Sea, BX.
1.4.4b Thirty yards or so: the Greek text says 1 *plethron;* see Appendix O: Measurements, §§2–3.
1.4.4c Six hundred yards/550 meters: the Greek

text says 3 stades; see Appendix O, §5.
1.4.5a Abrokomas was reported at 1.3.20 to be at a northern crossing of the Euphrates. His original plan presumably involved marching from there to Phoenicia, but it appears he altered it and instead went to a more southerly crossing of the river, where he burned the pontoon bridge (see 1.4.18). Phoenicia: Map 1.4.1, BX.
1.4.5b It would have been logistically impossible in ancient conditions for Abrokomas to have had such a large army; see n. 1.7.13a.
1.4.6a Myriandos: Map 1.4.1, BX, *Halting place 18.*
1.4.7a Arcadia, Megara: Map 1.2.1, AX, AY.
1.4.7b On Klearchos, see Appendix W: Brief Biographies, §20.

ing that they would be overtaken, on the ground that they were cowards, but others pitied them if they were captured.

[8] Cyrus called the generals together and said, "Xenias and Pasion have deserted us. But nevertheless they should be very well aware that they have not run away unnoticed—I know in what direction they are going. Nor have they eluded me in their flight—I have triremes that could catch their boat. All the same, for my part I will certainly not pursue them. Nobody shall say of me that I make use of people as long as they stay, but when they want to leave, I arrest them, mistreat them, and rob them of their property. No, let them go, knowing as they do that they have shown themselves worse people in their dealings with us than we have shown ourselves in our dealings with them. And even though I have their wives and children under guard in Tralles,[a] they shall not be deprived of them. On the contrary, they will receive them back, on account of their earlier meritorious conduct toward me." [9] Such was his speech: as for the Greeks, if anyone had been rather dispirited at the imminent march into the interior, on hearing of Cyrus' reaction, itself worthy of merit, they all now made their way forward with more zest and greater enthusiasm.

After these events Cyrus pushed on for four days' march, covering twenty parasangs, to the river Chalos, which was one hundred feet[a] in width and full of great tame fish. The Syrians regarded these as gods and would not allow them to be harmed; the same was true of the doves there.[b] The villages in which the troops took up their quarters belonged to Parysatis, having been given to her to pay for her girdles.[c] [10] From there he pushed on for five days' march, covering thirty parasangs, to the sources of the river Dardas, the width of which is one hundred feet.[a] There were the palace buildings belonging to Belesys, who had previously been ruler of Syria,[b] and a very large and beautiful park with everything in it that the different seasons

1.4.8
Late September 401
MYRIANDOS
Cyrus reacts magnanimously to the desertions.

1.4.9
October 401
CHALOS RIVER
*Villages of Parysatis (19)*
The army takes up quarters in Parysatis' villages by the Chalos River.

1.4.10
October 401
DARDAS RIVER
*Belesys' palace (20)*
Cyrus burns the palace of Syria's former ruler, Belesys, and fells the park's trees.

---

1.4.8a   Tralles: Map 1.2.10, AX.

1.4.9a   One hundred feet/30 meters: the Greek text says 1 *plethron;* see Appendix O: Measurements, §§2–3. Chalos River, probable location: Map 1.4.1, AY, *Halting place 19* (Oinoparas River in the *Barrington Atlas,* which locates the Chalos farther east).

1.4.9b   The second-century C.E. author Lucian writes at length on the Syrian taboos regarding fish in his *On the Syrian Goddess,* claiming that the sacred fish of Hierapolis (Map 1.4.1, AY) in Syria were so tame, they were said to answer to their names; he also confirms that Syrians regarded doves as untouchable and sacred, and apparently they thronged Syrian temples.

1.4.9c   Persian bureaucratic records show that the court had an elaborate system of allocations of food and clothing to the royal family and courtiers. In this instance, rather than hand out clothing when required, the King gave his mother the revocable use of various estates to achieve

the same purpose. (According to Plato, *Alcibiades* 123 b–c, other estates were assigned to pay for her veils and other wardrobe items.) Her servants administered these estates. Probably recipients of such grants were not limited to the ostensible rationale of the grant when deciding how to spend the revenues. On Parysatis, see Appendix W: Brief Biographies, §26.

1.4.10a   One hundred feet/30 meters: the Greek text says 1 *plethron;* see Appendix O, §§2–3. Dardas River, possible location: Map 1.4.1, BY, *Halting place 20.* (The *Barrington Atlas* identifies a different, though nearby, river as the Dardas.)

1.4.10b   A considerable cache of clay tablets concerning Belesys has been found under one of the citadels of Babylon, his place of origin and of which he was city governor between 421 and 414. He was satrap (provincial governor) of Syria between 407 and 401. For more on Belesys' past career as a Persian official, see Appendix C: The Persian Empire, §9.

1.4.11–13
October 401
EUPHRATES RIVER
*Thapsakos (21)*
The army marches on to
Thapsakos, where Cyrus
at last announces that he
is marching against the
King and promises the
Greeks more rewards.

produce. But Cyrus felled the park trees and burned down the palace buildings. [11] From there he pushed on for three days' march, covering fifteen
parasangs, to the river Euphrates, which is eight hundred yards[a] in width.
A great and prosperous city was situated there, called Thapsakos,[b] where they
remained for five days.

Cyrus sent for the Greek generals and explained that their road would
lead to Babylon[c] and to a confrontation against the Great King, and he told
them to say this to the soldiers and persuade them to follow along. [12] So
the generals called an assembly and made a report to this effect, but the
soldiers were annoyed with the generals and said that they had known this
long before but had been concealing it. They refused to go on unless someone gave them money, such as had been given to those who had accompanied Cyrus to the interior on the earlier occasion when he went to see his
father—and that had been given to them although they had not been going
to a battle but, on the contrary, Cyrus' father was calling him to come.[a] [13]
The generals proceeded to report all this to Cyrus, and he promised to give
each man five minas[a] of silver when they arrived in Babylon, and wages in full
until he brought the Greeks back to Ionia.[b] Most of the Greek army were
persuaded by this means, but before it was clear what the other soldiers were
going to do and whether they would follow Cyrus or not, Menon[c] called
together his own army, separately from the others, and made this speech:

1.4.14–15
October 401
THAPSAKOS
With crafty arguments,
Menon persuades his
men to cross the river
before the other Greeks.

[14] "Men, if you do what I say, then without any danger to yourselves
or any hard work, you will be honored by Cyrus more than the other
soldiers. So what is it that I am telling you to do? Right now Cyrus wants
the Greeks to follow him against the King, so I say that you ought to cross
the river Euphrates before it is clear what answer the other Greeks will give
him. [15] If they vote to follow him, it will seem that you are responsible,
through having been the first to cross over; and Cyrus will feel grateful to
you as the most enthusiastic of all and will reward you accordingly—and he
knows how to do that if anyone does! But if the others vote against, we
shall all of us go back together, but as he will regard you as his most trust-

1.4.11a  Eight hundred yards/730 meters: the
Greek text says 4 stades (this may well be
an exaggeration); see Appendix O:
Measurements, §5.
1.4.11b  Thapsakos (the name derives from a
Semitic word meaning "ford") was a transport hub for the Middle Euphrates. A ferry
service went downstream to Babylon from
here, and a pontoon bridge was usually in
place, though on this occasion the enemy
had burned it (1.4.18). The location of the
site is controversial; see Appendix P: The
Route of the Ten Thousand, §5. A notable
feature of the historical geography of
Mesopotamia is its comparative unfamiliarity to ancient Greek and Roman writers
whose works have survived, which sometimes makes it difficult to reconstruct the
history of names of important settlements.
Mesopotamia: Book 1 map. Thapsakos,
possible location: Map 1.4.1, BY, *Halting*

*place 21* (not listed in the *Barrington
Atlas*).
1.4.11c  Babylon: Map 1.5.1 and locator.
1.4.12a  Calling him to come: this refers to King
Darius' summons mentioned at 1.1.2.
1.4.13a  Five minas equals 500 drachmas; see
Appendix O, §§10–11.
1.4.13b  It does not seem likely that where their
final military activity was some distance
away from their original mustering point,
mercenaries could expect to be discharged
without payment for the return journey.
Rather than suggesting an unusual bonus,
more probably Cyrus is just being reassuring in view of the very long distance, in this
case from the battlefield to Ephesus, some
16,050 stades, or about 1,825 miles/2,935
kilometers. Ephesus: Book 1 map, DZ.
1.4.13c  On Menon: see Appendix W: Brief Biographies, §23.

worthy troops, the only ones who are obedient, he will make use of you both for garrisons and as officers, and if there is anything else you want, I am sure that you will obtain it from Cyrus, as he will be your friend."

[16] After hearing this speech, they were persuaded and crossed over the river before the others had given their answer. When Cyrus saw that they had crossed over, he was pleased and sent Glousa to Menon's army with this message: "Men, here and now it is I who praise you, but I will take care that you too shall praise me in future—or no longer believe me to be Cyrus!" [17] The soldiers for their part were in great hopes at this and prayed for his success, while it was said that he also sent magnificent gifts to Menon. After doing so, he crossed over, and the whole of the rest of the army all followed him as well, and as they crossed the river, the water reached no more than chest-high for any of them. [18] The inhabitants of Thapsakos maintained that never before had it been possible to cross the river on foot, but only by making use of boats, which on this occasion Abrokomas had burned when he went on from there previously, in order to stop Cyrus from crossing. It seemed indeed that it was a divine sign, and that the river had clearly drawn back for Cyrus as the future King.a

[19] From Thapsakos Cyrus pushed on through Syria for nine days' march, covering fifty parasangs, and they arrived at the river Araxes.a There were many villages there full of grain and wine, and they remained there for three days and stocked up on food. [1.5.1] From there he pushed on through Arabia, with the river Euphratesa on the right, for five days' march through empty country, covering thirty-five parasangs. In this area the land was an entirely level plain, as level as the sea, and full of wormwood; and whatever else grew there in the way of shrubs or reeds, every one of them was sweet-smelling, like an aromatic herb. [2] There were no trees whatsoever but all kinds of wild animals—great numbers of wild asses, and also many ostriches, and there were bustards and gazelles too.a The cavalrymen sometimes set off in pursuit of these wild animals, and when anyone pursued the asses, they

1.4.16–18
October 401
THAPSAKOS
The army crosses the
Euphrates River on foot.

1.4.19–1.5.3
October–November 401
SYRIA–ARABIA
*Araxes River crossing (22)*
The flora and fauna of
the Syrian desert.

1.4.16a   On Glous, a senior member of Cyrus' entourage, and his later career (ending around 380), see Appendix W: Brief Biographies, §34.

1.4.18a   The people of Thapsakos were probably engaging in flattery. The river is not fordable in spring and early summer, but would be in September/October, when it is likely that the army crossed (see Appendix Q: The Chronology of the March). Today dams in upper Mesopotamia, notably on the Euphrates and Tigris, greatly restrict the flow of rivers. Centuries after Xenophon, the variations in the level of the Euphrates enabled the inhabitants of its banks to flatter the Roman generals Lucullus (amazement that the river had fallen so he could cross) and Vitellius (amazement that the river had risen, allegedly portending a flood of success).

1.4.19a   On crossing the Araxes, Cyrus took the most direct, if more challenging, route to

Babylonia (Map 1.5.1 and inset), along the riverbank. Armies especially preferred the longer route northwest to the Tigris crossing, owing to easier terrain and greater ease in securing provisions. Abrokomas, after he had destroyed the pontoon bridge, took the longer way. Araxes River, probable location: Map 1.5.1, *Halting place 22* (Aborras/Chaboras River in the *Barrington Atlas*). Euphrates River: Map 1.5.1 and inset.

1.5.1a   Some scholars think Xenophon's use of Arabia for the area in question is inaccurate. However, Arabia could be used for any area over which Arab nomads roamed, so it extended much farther than the modern Saudi Arabia. Arabia: Map 1.5.1.

1.5.2a   Xenophon's report affords us a unique glimpse of the contemporary regional ecology. Other wild animals in northern Mesopotamia included lions and aurochs, the now extinct ancestor of domestic cattle, and possibly wolves (see 2.2.9 and n. 2.2.9a).

would run off and then stand still, for they ran much faster than the horses.[b] When the horses came close, they would do the same thing again, and it was not possible to catch them unless the horsemen posted themselves at intervals and hunted them in relays. The meat of those that were caught was very like venison but more tender. [3] But nobody caught an ostrich. Any of the horsemen who pursued one quickly broke off, for it would put a great distance between itself and its pursuers as it fled, which it did by running at speed and raising its wings, using them like a sail. However, if anyone is quick about getting the bustards to rise up into the air, it is possible to catch them, as they fly off only a short distance like partridges and also quickly flag. Their meat was very pleasant to eat.[a]

[4] Making their way through this land, they reached the river Maskas, about a hundred feet[a] or so in width. Here there was a large deserted city called Korsote;[b] the Maskas flowed around it in a circle. [5] They remained there for three days and stocked up on food.[a] From there Cyrus pushed on for thirteen days' march through empty country, covering ninety parasangs,[b] with the river Euphrates on the right, and arrived at Pylai.[c] In these marches many of the draft animals died of starvation, for there was no grazing and there were no trees at all, the entire land being barren.[d] (The inhabitants used to quarry millstones along the riverbank and shape them; they would take them to Babylon, sell them there, and by buying grain in return, sustain themselves.) [6] The army's supply of grain ran out, and it was not possible to buy it except in the market made by the Lydians, which was located in Cyrus' barbarian army and where a *kapithē* of wheat or barley cost as much as four *sigloi* (the *siglos* is worth seven and a half Attic obols, and the *kapithē* contained two Attic *choinikes*).[a] So the soldiers survived by eating meat.[b]

**1.5.4–6**
**November 401**
ARABIAN DESERT
*Korsote (23)–Pylai (24)*
On a long march through desert terrain, many animals die from starvation and grain runs short for the soldiers.

---

1.5.2b   These are wild asses, or onagers, which unlike domesticated asses (donkeys) run faster than the normal gallop of even the modern horse.

1.5.3a   The bustard does not live in Syria and Arabia all year round, but winters there. So Xenophon's mention of it here lends support to the late chronology adopted in this volume, on which see Appendix Q: The Chronology of the March.

1.5.4a   About a hundred feet/30 meters: the Greek text says about a *plethron;* see Appendix O: Measurements, §§2–3. Maskas River, possible location: Map 1.5.1 (not listed in the *Barrington Atlas*).

1.5.4b   Korsote, probable location: Map 1.5.1, *Halting place 23* (Haradu in the *Barrington Atlas*).

1.5.5a   While the city may have been, as Xenophon says, largely deserted at this period, the area around it cannot have been completely depopulated or the army could not have provisioned itself.

1.5.5b   According to the interpretation of the parasang in this volume (see the Introduction, §7.3–5), the relatively high number of parasangs recorded for this stage is explained by the difficulty of the terrain;

note the wadi (dried-up desert watercourse) described at 1.5.7–8. Thus the distance covered in the thirteen days is relatively shorter than an equivalent journey undertaken across "standard" terrain.

1.5.5c   Pylai ("the gates"), probable location: Map 1.5.1, inset, *Halting place 24* (not listed in the *Barrington Atlas*). In our suggested location, the name is explained because heights on either side press in on the river, forming a natural control point for river and land traffic, while beyond it the land flattens out into the fertile plains characteristic of Babylonia.

1.5.5d   For draft animals on the march, see Appendix J: A Soldier's View of the March, §§12–13.

1.5.6a   These prices were twenty to twenty-five times the normal price for grain meal in Athens, Thomas Martin estimates in Appendix O, §§19–20. On the *kapithē, siglos,* obol, and *choinix,* see Appendix O, §§20, 13–14, 11, and 20, respectively. Lydia: Map 1.2.10, AX.

1.5.6b   The Greeks were happy to eat meat; it was the *exclusive* reliance on it that was a hardship, as John Lee explains in Appendix J, §17.

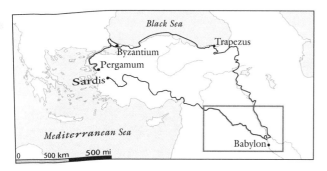

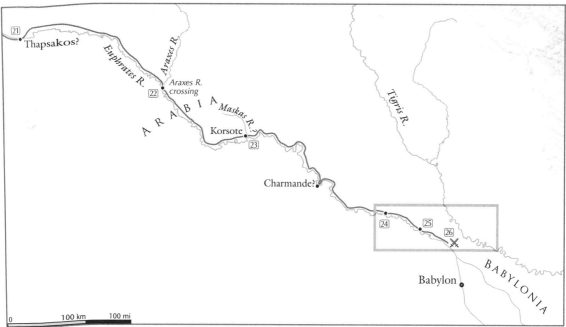

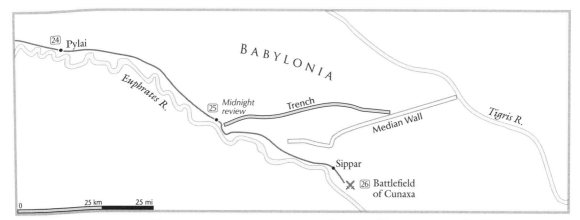

MAP 1.5.1. *ANABASIS:* FROM THAPSAKOS TO THE BATTLEFIELD OF CUNAXA, *HALTING PLACES 21–26.*

FIGURE 1.5.5. MIDDLE EUPHRATES: THE RIVER IN THIS PART OF ITS COURSE FORMS GIANT BENDS AND CAN EXTEND FOR SEVERAL HUNDRED FEET/ABOUT NINETY METERS FROM ONE BANK TO THE OTHER. CYRUS, TRAVELING ON THE FAR (LEFT) BANK, WOULD HAVE CUT THROUGH THE DESERT TO BRIDGE THESE MEANDERS.

1.5.7–9
November 401
ARABIAN DESERT
Cyrus overcomes the problem of getting his wagons through heavy mud by exerting discipline over the noblemen in his entourage.

[7] Sometimes during this stretch, he greatly extended the day's march whenever he wanted to carry on to reach water or fodder. On one occasion, because they were in a narrow place and the mud made it difficult for the wagons to get through, Cyrus halted, along with the highest-ranking and wealthiest members of his entourage, and gave Glous and Pigres the job of taking some of the barbarian soldiers and helping to extricate the wagons.[a] [8] When they seemed to him to be taking their time about it, he gave orders, as if in a temper, to the Persian nobles in his entourage to help get the wagons going. Then indeed one could see a bit of good discipline. Each nobleman threw off his purple robe wherever he happened to be standing, and they all rushed down an extremely steep hill, like people running for victory in the Games, with their expensive tunics and their embroidered trousers, some of them wearing necklaces and bracelets. They immediately leapt into the mud with these on and, more quickly than one might suppose, brought the wagons out onto higher ground. [9] In short, it was clear that Cyrus was in haste throughout the whole journey, and he did not linger anywhere unless pausing to stock up on food or for some other necessity, thinking that the faster he went, the more unprepared the King would be to do battle, while the more leisurely his pace, the larger would be the army that the King would gather. So anyone who considered the matter carefully could see that the Great King's empire was strong in the magnitude of its territory and the number of its people, but weak from its extended

1.5.7a   This incident serves as a chronological pointer, as the mud is likely to indicate recent rainfall and therefore suggests the autumn; for more, see Appendix Q: The    Chronology of the March. Pigres was previously referred to as an interpreter at 1.2.17.

FIGURE 1.5.10. JUBBAH ISLAND, MIDDLE EUPHRATES: NEAR THE SITE OF XENOPHON'S CHARMANDE, A LARGE AND PROSPEROUS CITY ON THE OTHER SIDE OF THE EUPHRATES. THE GREEKS CROSSED THE RIVER HERE ON RAFTS TO BUY WINE AND BREAD.

lines of communication and the dispersal of its forces if someone mounted a swift attack.[a]

[10] On the other side of the river Euphrates, during these desert marches, was a large and prosperous city called Charmande.[a] The soldiers obtained their food supplies from the market there, crossing the river on rafts in the following way: They filled hides, which they had for use as shelters, with light fodder and then gathered them together and stitched them up so that the water would not touch the dry hay.[b] It was on these that they used to cross the river and so acquire their supplies, both wine made from the kernel of the date palm and bread made from foxtail millet, as this type of grain was very plentiful in the land around.

[11] In this area a dispute of some sort arose between one of Menon's troops and a soldier from Klearchos' contingent, and Klearchos, judging that Menon's soldier was in the wrong, struck him several times.[a] That man then went to his own army and spoke about it, and when they heard his tale, the soldiers became angry and worked themselves up into a rage with Klearchos. [12] On the same day, Klearchos went to the river crossing and had a close look at the market there, and was then riding back to his own tent through Menon's army together with a few of his own staff; Cyrus had

1.5.10
November 401
CHARMANDE
The soldiers cross the river on rafts made of hay-stuffed hides to obtain supplies.

1.5.11–17
November 401
CHARMANDE
Cyrus intervenes to stop serious trouble between the Greek generals.

1.5.9a   For discussion of the empire's lines of communication, see the Introduction, §4.5. Scholars debate whether the Persian Empire was as vulnerable to Greek invasion in the early fourth century as Xenophon suggests; later in the century, it was conquered by Alexander the Great.
1.5.10a  Charmande, possible location: Map 1.5.1 (not listed in the *Barrington Atlas*). There

is no solid evidence for the site. It may have been opposite or slightly downstream from the island of Jubbah or farther downstream at modern Hit (for both, Ref. Map 8, DZ).
1.5.10b  Rafts of this kind (*kelleks*) were regularly used to cross the river up until the nineteenth century.
1.5.11a  On Menon and Klearchos, see Appendix W: Brief Biographies, §§23, 20.

not yet arrived but was still pressing forward to get there. One of Menon's soldiers, who was chopping wood, saw Klearchos as he rode through, and let fly at him with his axe. This soldier missed him, but first one and then another started to throw stones; a clamor arose, and then many more threw stones at him. [13] Klearchos made his escape to his own army and immediately called them to arms. He ordered the hoplites to remain there with their shields leaning against their knees while—taking the Thracians and the forty horsemen who were with him in his army, most of whom were also Thracians[a]—he himself rode toward Menon's troops, throwing them into a panic and Menon himself as well, and sending them running for their weapons; others just stood there, at a loss at the turn of affairs. [14] But Proxenos,[a] who happened to be later in arriving, along with a unit of hoplites that was following him, then immediately led his troops into the middle between the two sides, grounded arms,[b] and pleaded with Klearchos not to do this. Klearchos became angry, because Proxenos spoke mildly of what had happened to him when in fact he had only just escaped being stoned to death, and he told him to get out of the way. [15] At this point Cyrus himself came into camp and learned what was going on. He immediately took a light spear in each hand and rode forward into the middle with those of his trusted advisers who were there, and said: [16] "Klearchos and Proxenos, and you other Greeks who are here, you don't know what you are doing. If you take to fighting with each other, you should realize that on that day I shall be cut down and you too, not long after me, since if our affairs go badly, all these barbarians whom you see will be more hostile to us than the King's troops." [17] When Klearchos heard this, he came to his senses, and both parties broke off and put their weapons away in their proper places.

1.6.1–4
November 401
APPROACH TO BABYLONIA
A plot of Orontas against Cyrus is revealed.

[1] As they went on from there, they kept seeing the hoofprints and the dung of horses; the tracks seemed to indicate that there were about two thousand horses. As these enemy cavalrymen proceeded, they were burning the fodder and anything else that was useful. Orontas,[a] a Persian man closely related to the King by birth and said to be among the best of the Persians in warfare, devised a plot against Cyrus, even though he had been forgiven for previously making war on him. [2] He said to Cyrus that if Cyrus gave him a thousand horsemen, he would lay an ambush for the cavalrymen who were preemptively burning everything and would either kill them or take many of them alive, thus preventing them from setting fires as they approached; doing this, furthermore, would mean that they would no longer be able to

1.5.13a Klearchos doubtless called on Thracians rather than Greeks because Greeks might be inhibited about going to extremes against fellow Greeks in the same army, whereas he reckoned that Thracians could be relied on for whatever bloodthirsty deeds their master called on them to perform. Thrace: Book 1 map.
1.5.14a On Proxenos, see Appendix W: Brief Biographies, §29.
1.5.14b Grounded arms: Proxenos brought his soldiers to a halt and ordered them to hold

their weapons so that the butts of their spears and the bases of their shields touched the ground. In this way they did not present a directly threatening appearance but were still ready for immediate action on command.
1.6.1a *Anabasis* mentions two very senior Persians called Orontas. All we know about this one is contained in this chapter. It is the other one, a son-in-law of Artaxerxes, whose career is set out in Appendix W, §26. See further the Introduction, §8.3, for why Xenophon has included the story.

keep an eye on Cyrus' army and send full reports to the King. When Cyrus heard this, it seemed a useful plan, and he told him to take a detachment with him from each of the commanding officers. [3] Orontas, thinking that the horsemen were at his disposal, wrote a letter to the King to the effect that he would come to him with as many horsemen as he possibly could, but he urged the King to tell his own cavalry to welcome him as a friend. The letter also included reminders of his previous friendship and loyalty. He gave this letter to a man he could trust, or so he thought; but the man took the letter and gave it to Cyrus. [4] Having read the letter, Cyrus arrested Orontas, and in his tent he assembled the best Persians of those in his entourage, seven of them, and gave orders to the Greek generals to bring up hoplites and for them to stand in arms around his tent. The generals brought up about three thousand hoplites and set them in place as requested.

[5] Cyrus called Klearchos inside the tent to take part in his council, since he seemed, both to Cyrus and to the others, to be by far the foremost in prestige among the Greeks. When Klearchos emerged, he recounted to his friends what had happened during the trial of Orontas, for it was not a secret. He said that Cyrus had begun the conference like this: [6] "I have summoned you, my dear friends, in order to consider, with your assistance, what is just in the eyes both of human beings and of gods and to carry it through in the case of Orontas here. Originally my father gave him to me to be my subject. But then he waged war against me from his vantage point on the acropolis of Sardis,[a] having been assigned this task, as he himself has admitted, by my brother, and I was so successful in my operations against him that he thought it best to put an end to his war with me, and we shook hands with each other. [7] After this, Orontas," he said, "did I treat you unfairly in any respect?" Orontas answered that he had not.

Cyrus again asked, "Isn't it the case that later on—though, as you yourself agree, you had not suffered any unfairness at my hands—you deserted to the Mysians[a] and set about harming my lands in whatever way you could?"

"Yes," said Orontas.

"Isn't it the case," Cyrus said, "that when you again understood how little was your own power, you came to the altar of Artemis[b] and said that you were sorry, and after persuading me, you again gave me tokens of good faith and received them from me?" Orontas agreed that this was so.

[8] "Then," said Cyrus, "in what respect have you been treated unfairly by me, so that now for the third time you stand revealed as plotting against me?" And when Orontas said that he had not been treated unfairly in any way, Cyrus asked him: "So do you agree that you have been unfair in your treatment of me?"

"Necessarily so," said Orontas.

1.6.5–8
November 401
APPROACH TO BABYLONIA
The trial of Orontas:
Cyrus cross-examines
him.

1.6.6a  Acropolis: the citadel or high point of a city; see the Glossary. Sardis: Map 1.5.1, locator.
1.6.7a  Mysia: Map 1.2.10, AX.
1.6.7b  Though the most famous temple of Artemis as far as Greeks were concerned

was at Ephesus (Map 1.2.10, AX), Cyrus more likely means an altar at Sardis, his satrapal capital. Remains from a fifth- or late sixth-century altar were uncovered there, alongside a later temple to Artemis. For this later temple, see Figure 1.2.4.

As a result, Cyrus asked him again, "So might you now become an enemy to my brother and a friend and trusted adviser to me?"

Orontas answered, "Even if I would, Cyrus, to you I should not seem so."

[9] At this, Cyrus said to those who were present, "Such were the deeds of this man, and such are his words. Of all you assembled here, Klearchos, you give your judgment first, as you think fit." Klearchos said, "My advice is to do away with this man as quickly as possible, so that it is no longer necessary to be on our guard against him, but instead we can relax as far as he is concerned and feel free to do good to those who are our friends because they want to be."

[10] The others too joined in this judgment, Klearchos said, and at Cyrus' command they stood up and took Orontas by the belt,[a] thus passing the death sentence on him, every one of them, including his relatives. Then those to whom the task had been assigned led him out. When those who had previously been accustomed to bow low to him saw him, they bowed low to him[b] even then, although they knew that he was being led to his death. [11] Once he had been led into the tent of Artapatas, the most faithful of Cyrus' mace-bearers,[a] nobody ever saw Orontas again, alive or dead, nor did anyone speak with knowledge of how he died, different people making different guesses; and no grave for him was ever pointed out.

[1] From there Cyrus pushed on through Babylonia[a] for three days' march, covering twelve parasangs. In the course of the third day's march, he held a review of the Greeks and the barbarians on the plain around midnight, as he thought that the King would come with his army near dawn the next day and fight. He gave orders to Klearchos to lead out the right wing and to Menon of Thessaly[b] to lead out the left while he himself drew up his own troops.

[2] After the review some deserters from the Great King came in at daybreak the following day and gave Cyrus reports about the King's army. Cyrus called together the Greek generals and captains and got them to give their views about how he should conduct the battle, and he himself then went on to exhort them so as to boost their spirits, saying something like this:

[3] "Men of Greece, it is not because I lack people to enroll in my army that I am bringing you along here to be my allies in battle, but because I think that you are better and more effective than even a large number of barbarians. That was the reason that I took you on. So make sure that you are men worthy of the freedom that you possess, and because of which I count you as happy. You may be certain that I would choose freedom rather than all I have and much more besides.[a] [4] I know the sort of battle you

---

1.6.10a This was the regular Persian method of pronouncing the death sentence.

1.6.10b This is a reference to the Persian custom of *proskynēsis*, "a gesture of obeisance, sometimes involving prostration, made when approaching a social superior," as noted in Appendix C: The Persian Empire, n. C.3e, citing Herodotus 1.134. For the Greek attitude toward it, see 3.2.13 and n. 3.2.13c. See Figure 3.2.13

for a depiction of *proskynēsis*.

1.6.11a For the mace-bearers, see Appendix C, §7.
1.7.1a Babylonia: Map 1.5.1 and inset.
1.7.1b Thessaly: Map 5.3.7, AX.
1.7.3a Greeks perceived all Persians, even those of the highest rank, as slaves of the Great King; see 1.9.29 and n. 1.9.29a. Here, at 1.7.3, Xenophon makes Cyrus share this perception.

are going into, and I will teach you so that you may know too. Their numbers are large, and they will advance with a lot of shouting, but if you bear with this, in other respects I do believe I am ashamed at what sort of people you will find those who live in our country to be. If you are men and my affairs turn out well, I will make those of you who wish to go back home the objects of envy to the folks there; but I think I shall induce many to choose life with me rather than at home."

[5] At this point, one of those present, Gaulites, a Samian[a] exile who was a trusted adviser to Cyrus, said, "And yet, Cyrus, some people say that you promise a lot now because the situation is one of imminent danger, but that if things were to turn out well to any extent, they say, you would not remember your promises. And some say that even if you did remember and it was what you wanted to do, you would not be able to provide what you are promising."

[6] When he heard this, Cyrus said, "On the contrary, men, what is available for us is the land over which my father ruled, and that extends to the south to where human beings cannot live because of the burning heat, and to the north to where they cannot live because of the wintry cold, and my brother's friends are satraps[a] over absolutely everything that there is between the two. [7] If we are victorious, we shall necessarily put our own friends in control of these satrapies. So I am not afraid of not having something to give to each of my friends if things turn out well but, rather, of not having enough friends to whom to make gifts. And to each of you Greeks I will also give a golden crown."[a]

[8] When they heard this, they were much more enthusiastic and passed the news on to the others. Some of the other Greeks began coming up to him too, thinking they should know what would be in it for them if they prevailed, and he fulfilled the expectations of every one of them before he sent them away.

[9] Everyone who talked to Cyrus encouraged him not to take part in the battle but to post himself behind his troops. At this juncture Klearchos asked Cyrus a question along these lines: "Cyrus, do you really think your brother will fight you?" "Definitely," said Cyrus; "if indeed he is the son of Darius and Parysatis,[a] and my brother, I shall not obtain all this without a fight."

[10] Here in the review, the number of Greeks came to a total hoplite force of 10,400, together with 2,500 peltasts,[a] while the number of barbarians with Cyrus was 100,000, plus around 20 scythed chariots.[b] [11] People said that the enemy numbered 1,200,000, plus 200 scythed chariots. There

1.7.5–8
November 401
BABYLONIA
Prompted by Gaulites, Cyrus makes further promises.

1.7.9
November 401
BABYLONIA
Cyrus is sure they will have to fight.

1.7.10–13
November 401
BABYLONIA
The numbers of troops on both sides, the Greeks being some 12,900 strong.

1.7.5a  Samos: Map 1.2.10, AX.
1.7.6a  Satraps: governors of Persian provinces; see the Glossary.
1.7.7a  Although crowns of honor could be worth as much as 500 or 1,000 silver drachmas, they varied in weight, and crowns worth 100 silver drachmas are also attested. One hundred silver drachmas would still be a sizable bonus amounting to four months' pay for a soldier. On drachmas, see Appendix O: Measurements, §11.

1.7.9a  On Darius II and Parysatis, see Appendix W: Brief Biographies, §§11, 26.
1.7.10a  For discussion of the accuracy of this total of 12,900, see Appendix I: The Size and Makeup of the Ten Thousand, §§3–4. On hoplites (heavy-armed infantry) and peltasts (light-armed infantry), see Appendix H: Infantry and Cavalry in *Anabasis*, §§2–5.
1.7.10b  Scythed chariots: for a description, see 1.8.10.

were 6,000 cavalry as well, which Artagerses[a] commanded: these were stationed in front of the King himself. [12] There were four commanders of the King's army, each with 300,000 troops: Abrokomas, Tissaphernes, Gobryas,[a] and Arbakes.[b] Of these troops 900,000, together with 150 scythed chariots, were present for the battle, since Abrokomas arrived five days late, bringing his army from Phoenicia.[c] [13] This was the tenor of the reports made to Cyrus by those who had deserted from the Great King before the battle, and after the battle those of the enemy who had subsequently been captured reported the same.[a]

**1.7.14–16**
**November 401**
BABYLONIA
The army passes a bottle-neck created by a defensive trench.

[14] From there Cyrus pushed on for one day's march, covering three parasangs, with his entire army, both Greek and barbarian, drawn up in line of battle; for he thought that the King would fight that day, as at the mid-point of the day's march was a deep trench that had been dug out, in width thirty feet and in depth eighteen.[a] [15] The trench extended up through the plain for twelve parasangs, as far as the Median Wall.[a] [There indeed are the canals that flow from the river Tigris.[b] There are four of them, around a hundred feet[c] in width and very deep, and boats sail on them carrying grain. They empty into the Euphrates, and there are intervals of a parasang between each of them and bridges over them.][d] [16] The Great King had made this trench to serve as a defense when he learned that Cyrus was marching against

1.7.11a  According to Plutarch (*Life of Artaxerxes* 9; in Appendix T: Plutarch), Artagerses was one of the Kadousioi, a warlike people who lived in the mountains north of Media, probably to the southeast of the Caspian Sea (for all, see Map C.1). The Great Kings repeatedly campaigned against them, so it is striking that a Kadousian was the chief royal bodyguard.

1.7.12a  On Abrokomas and Tissaphernes, see Appendix W: Brief Biographies, §§1, 37. Gobryas here may well be the Gobryas who was governor of Babylonia in the early years of Darius II's reign.

1.7.12b  According to Plutarch, *Life of Artaxerxes* 14.2, the Median Arbakes, probably meaning this man, ran away to Cyrus in the course of the battle of Cunaxa (Map 1.5.1, inset) and, though allowed to live, was subjected to a humiliating punishment for cowardice. That he was not punished for treason might suggest that he deserted in the belief that Cyrus had actually killed Artaxerxes rather than just wounded him. For discussion of the nature of the units the four commanders led, see Appendix D: The Persian Army, §2.

1.7.12c  Phoenicia: Map 1.4.1, BX.

1.7.13a  Xenophon gives numbers for Cyrus' barbarian troops and the King's army that are too large to be logistically possible. It is common for Greek authors to inflate Persian numbers far beyond the bounds of possibility. In several ancient sources (see Appendix L: The Battle of

Cunaxa, §9, and Appendix M: Other Ancient Sources on the Ten Thousand) it is said that the King's army numbered 400,000; which is also far more than could have been supplied. Diodorus 14.19.7 (in Appendix S: Diodorus) says Cyrus had 70,000 barbarian troops, but numbers more like 20,000 are often preferred. See also the Introduction, §5.3.

1.7.14a  Thirty feet/9 meters, eighteen feet/ 5 meters: the Greek text says 5 and 3 *orguiai*, respectively; see Appendix O: Measurements, §§2–3.

1.7.15a  The wall is mentioned again at 2.4.12, and see n. 2.4.12a. It was probably built by the Babylonian king Nebuchadnezzar in the early sixth century. For the trench and the Median Wall, see Map 1.5.1, inset.

1.7.15b  Tigris River: Map 1.5.1 and inset.

1.7.15c  A hundred feet: the Greek text says a *plethron;* see Appendix O, §§2–3.

1.7.15d  This geographical note is rightly regarded as a later insertion by a scribe. It fits awkwardly into the context and appears to contradict the rest of the text about the width and purpose of channels in this part of Mesopotamia. Nevertheless, it may still represent the truth about some period in antiquity, perhaps indeed the fourth century B.C.E.—the ancient canal system of Babylonia is not yet clear to us and changed over time. (Translator's note) Mesopotamia: Book 1 map. Euphrates River: Map 1.5.1 and inset.

him.[a] There was a narrow passage by the Euphrates between the river and the trench, about twenty feet[b] in width. Naturally Cyrus and the army went through this passage and brought themselves to the inner side of the trench.

[17] In fact, the King did not fight that day; instead, many different tracks of retreating forces were evident, both of horses and of people. [18] Then Cyrus called for Silanos, the Ambracian seer, and gave him three thousand darics.[a] This was because on the eleventh day before that, Silanos had said to him while offering a sacrifice that the King would not fight in the next ten days, and Cyrus had said, "Then he will not fight at all if he does not fight in that time; if you prove to be telling me the truth, I promise you ten talents."[b] It was this amount of gold he then handed over, since the ten days had elapsed.

[19] Since the King did not try to stop Cyrus' army from crossing over at the trench, Cyrus and the others thought that he had given up the idea of fighting, and so on the following day Cyrus made his way forward rather slackly. [20] On the day after that, he continued on his journey seated in a chariot and with only a few troops in formation in front of him; most of his army made their way in great disorder, and many of the weapons were being carried for the soldiers on wagons and draft animals.

[1] It was already the time when the markets fill up,[a] and the halting place where Cyrus planned to break off was near, when Pategyas, a Persian man who was among Cyrus' trusted entourage, came into view galloping with all his might and his horse in a sweat. Immediately he began shouting in both Persian and Greek to everyone he fell in with that the King was advancing with a large army as if prepared to do battle.[b] [2] At this much confusion broke out; the Greeks, and everyone else, thought the enemy would fall on them at once, out of formation as they were. [3] Cyrus jumped down from his chariot, put on his breastplate, and mounted his horse; he took his light spears in both hands and started giving orders to all the others to put on their full armor and take up their respective places. [4] At this they then took up their positions in great haste,[a] Klearchos occupying the right wing

1.7.17–18
November 401
BABYLONIA
Cyrus rewards the seer Silanos for a true prophecy.

1.7.19–20
November 401
BABYLONIA
The army now advances carelessly.

1.8.1–7
November 401
BABYLONIA
*Battlefield of Cunaxa (26)*
Warned that the King's army is close, Cyrus makes his own dispositions.

1.7.16a A trench 12 parasangs long was a very large undertaking for the brief period Artaxerxes had to put his defenses in place. More probably, the trench was part of an existing but decayed defense system or canal (for both of which there is other evidence in this broad vicinity), which would explain why Cyrus seems to know about it well before he gets there. Xenophon may be wrong to mention Artaxerxes here, which is the view taken in Appendix D: The Persian Army, §15.

1.7.16b Twenty feet/6 meters: the Greek text says 20 *podes*.

1.7.18a The gold daric, equivalent to 25 Attic drachmas, was the standard large coin of the Persian empire; for more, see Appendix O: Measurements, §§13–14, and on this passage in particular, see n. O.14c. Ambracia: Map 5.3.7, AX.

1.7.18b On Silanos' prediction, see Appendix G:

Divinity and Divining, §8. On talents, see Appendix O, §§10–11.

1.8.1a Shortly before midday.

1.8.1b The battle that ensued, conventionally known as the battle of Cunaxa, is outlined in Diagram 1.8. For a detailed discussion, see Appendix L: The Battle of Cunaxa. The precise location of the battlefield is disputed; see Map 1.5.1 and inset, *Halting place 26*, for the view taken in this edition, which places it south of the Median Wall, some way from the village of Cunaxa.

1.8.4a To clarify what follows: the Paphlagonian horsemen and the peltasts were on the extreme right; next came the Greek hoplites, forming Cyrus' right, with subdivisions (from right to left) led by Klearchos, Proxenos, and Menon; then came Cyrus in the center of his line; finally, Ariaios led Cyrus' left wing.

of the line by the river Euphrates, Proxenos coming next and the others after him, while Menon and his army held the left wing of the Greek line.[b] [5] From Cyrus' barbarian troops, Paphlagonian[a] cavalry to the number of a thousand took up a position near Klearchos on the right, as did the Greek peltast contingent. On the left were Ariaios,[b] Cyrus' lieutenant, and the rest of the barbarian forces; [6] and Cyrus and his cavalry escort, as many as six hundred, were in the center, all in armor, with breastplates and thigh guards and all of them except Cyrus with helmets (he took up his position for battle with his head bare).[a] [7] All the horses with Cyrus had protective armor over their foreheads and chests, and the horsemen also had Greek sabers.

[8] It was already the middle of the day, and the enemy were not yet in sight. But as soon as it wore on into the afternoon, dust could be seen like a white cloud, and sometime later it was as if there was a sort of blackness in the plain extending over a long distance. As they came closer and closer, very soon a gleam of bronze would flash out, and the lances and the various units started to become distinct. [9] There were cavalrymen with white breastplates on the enemy's left; Tissaphernes was said to be their commander. Next to these were troops carrying wicker shields, and next to them hoplites[a] with wooden shields reaching to their feet; these were said to be Egyptians.[b] Others were cavalry, and others archers. All these, arranged by ethnicity, made their way forward, each ethnic group in a solid square of people.[c] [10] In front of them were chariots, separated some distance from each other, the so-called scythed chariots. They had knives projecting sideways from their axles and from under the charioteer's platform to the ground, so as to cut to pieces whatever they came across. The idea was for them to drive into the ranks of the Greeks and cut them to pieces. [11] But as for what Cyrus said when he called the Greeks together and encouraged them to bear with the shouting of the barbarians, this turned out to be false, for they did not advance with shouts but in silence, as far as feasible, and calmly, at a slow and steady pace.

1.8.12–13
November 401
BATTLEFIELD OF CUNAXA
Cyrus gives Klearchos his
orders for the battle, but
Klearchos does not follow
them.

[12] At this point Cyrus himself rode along the lines with Pigres, his interpreter, and three or four others and shouted to Klearchos to lead his army toward the enemy's center, because that was where the King was. "If we are victorious there," he said, "we have achieved everything." [13] Klearchos saw the dense mass in the center and heard from Cyrus that the King was

1.8.4b  On Klearchos, Proxenos, and Menon, see Appendix W: Brief Biographies, §§20, 29, 23.

1.8.5a  Paphlagonia: Book 6 map.

1.8.5b  For Ariaios' subsequent relations with Artaxerxes, see Appendix W, §4.

1.8.6a  At this point the manuscripts contain a note: "It is said that the other Persians too go into danger in war with their heads unprotected." Scholars agree that Xenophon did not write this; it is a comment that some scribe wrote in the margin of his copy, which subsequently got copied into the main body of

the text. Although there is evidence for Persian helmets, vase-paintings generally show Persians wearing hoods when fighting, so the scribal comment is correct.

1.8.9a  As this shows, Xenophon (like other Greek authors) does not reserve the term "hoplites" for Greek heavy infantry with shields of the standard Greek type but also uses it of foreign heavy infantry with larger shields.

1.8.9b  Egypt: Ref. Map 1, DX.

1.8.9c  On this passage, see Appendix D: The Persian Army, §2.

FIGURE 1.8.9. PERSIAN
WICKER SHIELD–BEARER.

beyond the Greek left wing (for the King was superior in numbers to such an extent that, though he held the center of his own troops, he was beyond Cyrus' left),[a] but all the same he did not want to draw his right wing away from the river, fearing that he might be encircled from both sides, and he answered Cyrus that he would take care that things went well.[b]

[14] At this critical juncture, the barbarian army was advancing steadily, but the Greek army was still in the same place, forming its line from those who were still coming up. Cyrus rode along, not very close to his own army, observing the scene and looking in both directions, both at the enemy troops and at his own. [15] Xenophon of Athens,[a] seeing him from the Greek army, came forward a little to meet him and asked if he had any message to pass on. Cyrus halted and told him to say to everyone that the sacred signs from the main sacrifice were favorable and the omens from the blood sacrifice were favorable too.[b] [16] As he said this, he heard a loud noise running through the ranks, and he asked what the noise was. Xenophon said that the

1.8.14–17
November 401
BATTLEFIELD OF CUNAXA
Conversation between
Cyrus and Xenophon.

1.8.13a  The interpretation of this passage is disputed among scholars. In Appendix L: The Battle of Cunaxa, §6, the view is taken that Xenophon means that Artaxerxes was beyond the left of Cyrus' own section of the battle line, rather than that he was beyond the left of the whole of Cyrus' battle line.

1.8.13b  Plutarch, in his *Life of Artaxerxes* 8.3–7 (in Appendix T: Selections from Plutarch's *Life of Artaxerxes*), blames Klearchos severely for not obeying Cyrus as his words implied he would do and thus, in effect, losing the battle for Cyrus; on this, see Appendix L, §§17–18.

1.8.15a  Xenophon of Athens: the author of this work; for more on his life, see the Introduction, §§2.6–12.

1.8.15b  Cyrus gives the results of two different sacrifices. In the main sacrifice, the omens (*hiera*) were derived from the state of the victim's entrails, whereas in blood sacrifices (*sphagia*) they were derived from the way the blood flowed from the knife wound that killed the victim. For the ancient practice of inferring the gods' will or predictions from features of animal sacrifice, see Appendix G: Divinity and Divining, §2, and Figures 2.1.9 (*hiera*) and 6.5.2 (both *hiera* and *sphagia*).

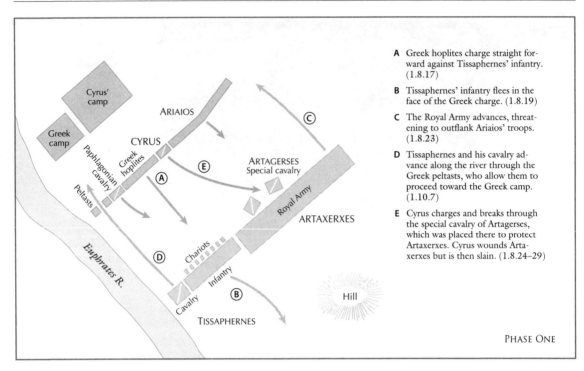

A  Greek hoplites charge straight forward against Tissaphernes' infantry. (1.8.17)

B  Tissaphernes' infantry flees in the face of the Greek charge. (1.8.19)

C  The Royal Army advances, threatening to outflank Ariaios' troops. (1.8.23)

D  Tissaphernes and his cavalry advance along the river through the Greek peltasts, who allow them to proceed toward the Greek camp. (1.10.7)

E  Cyrus charges and breaks through the special cavalry of Artagerses, which was placed there to protect Artaxerxes. Cyrus wounds Artaxerxes but is then slain. (1.8.24–29)

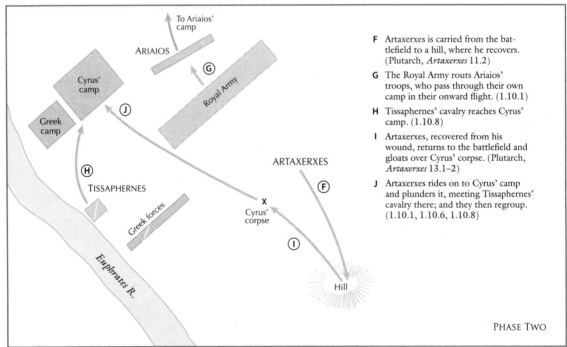

F  Artaxerxes is carried from the battlefield to a hill, where he recovers. (Plutarch, *Artaxerxes* 11.2)

G  The Royal Army routs Ariaios' troops, who pass through their own camp in their onward flight. (1.10.1)

H  Tissaphernes' cavalry reaches Cyrus' camp. (1.10.8)

I  Artaxerxes, recovered from his wound, returns to the battlefield and gloats over Cyrus' corpse. (Plutarch, *Artaxerxes* 13.1–2)

J  Artaxerxes rides on to Cyrus' camp and plunders it, meeting Tissaphernes' cavalry there; and they then regroup. (1.10.1, 1.10.6, 1.10.8)

DIAGRAM 1.8. THE BATTLE OF CUNAXA.

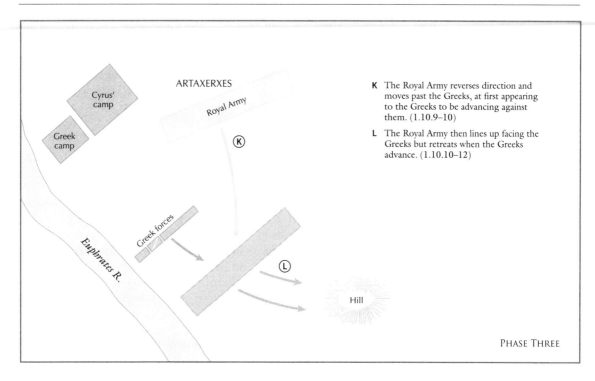

ARTAXERXES

Royal Army

Cyrus' camp

Greek camp

Euphrates R.

Greek forces

Hill

**K**   The Royal Army reverses direction and moves past the Greeks, at first appearing to the Greeks to be advancing against them. (1.10.9–10)

**L**   The Royal Army then lines up facing the Greeks but retreats when the Greeks advance. (1.10.10–12)

PHASE THREE

watchword was now being passed along for the second time.[a] Cyrus wondered on whose instruction this was being done, and he asked what the watchword was. Xenophon replied, "Zeus the Savior and Victory." [17] On hearing this, Cyrus said, "Well, I accept it, and let it be so." Having said this, he rode away to his own position. The two battle lines were now separated from each other by less than six or eight hundred yards[a] when the Greeks started singing a war hymn and began to move against the enemy. [18] As they proceeded on their way, a bulge appeared in the battle line, and those who were being left behind began to dash forward at a run. At the same time, they all cried out as if raising the battle cry to Enyalios[a] and all broke into a run. Some say they clashed their shields against their spears and startled the horses.[b] [19] When they were almost a bowshot away, the enemy

1.8.18–20
November 401
BATTLEFIELD OF CUNAXA
The Greeks are victorious in their sector.

1.8.16a   The watchword, having been passed from the first man to the last, was now being passed back from the last man to the first to confirm that it had been correctly received and understood. The primary purpose of the watchword was (in the absence of uniforms) to enable friends to be distinguished from foes. The watchword was not used only in battle (see 7.3.34). The particular watchword would often also be chosen, as here, for its encouraging effect.

1.8.17a   Six or eight hundred yards/550 or 730 meters: the Greek text says 3 or 4 stades; see Appendix O: Measurements, §5.

1.8.18a   Enyalios: a war god. In Homer and other literature, sometimes he is identified with or seen as an aspect of Ares. But despite not being treated separately in mythology, Enyalios had a cult separate from that of Ares, even within cities that also had Ares cults.

1.8.18b   This sentence is the only certain instance in *Anabasis* where the narrator speaks as though he was not himself present with the Greek army (though see also 5.4.34). As a consequence, it has been suggested that it was not written by Xenophon but is an insertion by a later scribe from another account of the battle. That could be right.

broke and fled. Then, naturally enough, the Greeks set about the pursuit with all their might, although shouting to one another not to run headlong but to follow in formation. [20] The chariots hurtled around, some among the enemy themselves; others, with no charioteers in them, among the Greeks too. Whenever they saw the chariots coming, they stood aside, but there was one soldier who was run down by a chariot, like someone on a racetrack in a daze. But they said that he was not injured in any way, nor were any of the other Greeks at all injured in this battle,[a] except that on the left wing someone was said to have been shot by an arrow.

1.8.21–23
November 401
BATTLEFIELD OF CUNAXA
Cyrus is pleased by the success of the Greeks, but fears the King's longer line will encircle them and attack from the rear.

[21] Cyrus was pleased when he saw that the Greeks were victorious over those opposite them and were mounting a pursuit, and he was already having homage paid him as King by those around him,[a] but he was not tempted to join the pursuit. Instead, accompanied by the unit of six hundred cavalry that he had with him in close order, he was watching carefully for what the King was going to do, as he knew that he would be occupying the center of the Persian army. [22] All the barbarian rulers lead their troops with themselves in the center, thinking that this puts them in the safest position, with the strength of their forces on either side, and also that should they need to send some message, the army would learn what it is in half the time.[a] [23] The King, then, naturally occupied the center of his army on this occasion and was nevertheless beyond Cyrus' left. Since nobody was making a direct frontal attack on him, nor on those of his troops that were drawn up in front of him, he began to bend his line around to achieve an encir-

1.8.24–29
November 401
BATTLEFIELD OF CUNAXA
Cyrus charges the King directly and wounds him but is himself killed in the melee.

clement. [24] At this Cyrus, struck by the fear that Artaxerxes[a] might get behind the Greek force and cut it to pieces, charged in the King's direction. Breaking into the enemy line with his six hundred cavalry, he defeated the troops drawn up in front of the King and turned the six thousand of them to flee, and it is said that he himself killed their commander, Artagerses, with his own hand. [25] When the rout occurred, Cyrus' six hundred started out in pursuit and spread out, except for a very small number left with him, more or less his so-called Table Companions.[a] [26] Left on his own with them, he caught sight of the King and the mass of troops around him, and imme-

1.8.20a  While it was remarkable for one side in a pitched battle to have virtually no casualties at all, there are similar instances; in 368, for example, the Spartans beat a larger Arcadian force without suffering a single casualty (Xenophon, *Hellenika* 7.1.31–32; Sparta, Arcadia: Map 1.2.1, BY, AY). In general, casualties chiefly occurred to a side that fled the battle, especially if it broke ranks in doing so.

1.8.21a  A further instance of *proskynēsis* (see 1.6.10), showing that what was involved varied depending on the degree to which the superior Persian outranked the inferior *mente ed.*

1.8.22a  At this period, by contrast, a Greek commander would typically take the position on or close to the extreme right.

1.8.24a  On Artaxerxes, see Appendix W: Brief Biographies, §6.

1.8.25a  As Xenophon implies by saying "so-called," being the Table Companion of the Great King, or as here of a comparable figure, was a recognized status, to or from which one could be promoted or demoted. However, it really did involve eating dinner with the relevant superior—though according to Heraclides of Cyme, writing probably in the mid- to late fourth century, the Table Companions of the King actually ate most of the time in the room next door to the King: *Die Fragmente der griechischen Historiker*, edited by F. Jacoby, 689 F2, translated in Kuhrt 2009, 610. Cyme: Ref. Map 4.1, CX, Ref. Map 4.2, BX.

FIGURE 1.8.29. THE *AKINAKĒS* OR CEREMONIAL DAGGER, TWO DETAILS FROM THE FRIEZES OF THE APADANA STAIRCASE IN PERSEPOLIS.

diately his self-control vanished. Calling out, "I see the man!" he rushed at the King and struck him in the chest, wounding him through his breastplate, as Ctesias the physician says (and he also says that he himself treated the wound).[a] [27] Someone threw a light spear with great force at Cyrus just as he struck the King, hitting Cyrus under the eye, and from that point the King and Cyrus and their respective entourages were all fighting together. How many of the King's entourage were killed is stated by Ctesias, who was with the King; on the other side, Cyrus himself was killed, and the best eight of his supporters lay dead upon his corpse.[a] [28] It is said that when Artapatas,[a] his most trusted companion-in-arms among the mace-bearers, saw that Cyrus had fallen, he leapt from his horse and threw himself on him. [29] Some say that the King ordered someone to slay him on top of

1.8.26a   Ctesias, a Greek who was Artaxerxes' physician, wrote a history of Persia that included an alleged eyewitness account of the battle of Cunaxa (on Ctesias, see Appendix W: Brief Biographies, §8). For excerpts of this work, see Appendices T: Plutarch, and U: Photius' Synopsis of Ctesias. See also Appendix M: Other Ancient Sources on the Ten Thousand, §1, and Appendix L: The Battle of Cunaxa, §§8–15.

1.8.27a   Unsurprisingly, in the circumstances of a heated battle, there is considerable variation in the sources as to exactly what happened leading up to Cyrus' death. In addition to the sources themselves in Appendices S: Diodorus, T: Plutarch (especially §§10–11), and U: Photius, see Appendix L: The Battle of Cunaxa, §10.

1.8.28a   Artapatas was previously mentioned as the executioner of Orontas at 1.6.11.

Cyrus, like a blood sacrifice; others, that he drew his ceremonial dagger[a] and slew himself. His dagger was made of gold, and he used to wear a necklace and bracelets and other jewelry like the noblest of the Persians, for he was honored by Cyrus because of his goodwill toward him and his trustworthiness.

**1.9.1–6**
CYRUS' OBITUARY
The events of Cyrus' boyhood.

[1] So this, then, was how Cyrus met his end, the most kingly man there had been among the Persians since Cyrus the Elder,[a] and the one who most deserved to rule, as is agreed among all those who had personal experience of him, so it would seem. [2] In the first place, while he was still a boy, at the time when he was being brought up with his brother and the other boys, he used to be thought the best of them all in everything. [3] All the boys among the Persian nobility are brought up in the King's palace,[a] where one may take on board many examples of prudent self-control and it is not possible to hear or see anything shameful. [4] The boys see, and also hear about, people being honored by the King and other people being dishonored, so that right away, though they are only boys, they are learning how to rule and to be ruled. [5] Here Cyrus seemed to be, first, the most modest of those of his own age, being more obedient to his elders even than those who were inferior in rank to him, and next, the fondest of horses and the one able to manage them in the best way. They used to judge him to be the keenest to learn the techniques of war, such as archery and throwing the javelin, and the one who practiced most. [6] When he reached the right age,[a] he was also the most avid of huntsmen and, in addition, the most eager to risk danger when stalking wild animals. There was one occasion when a bear was charging down on him, and he did not run away like a coward. On the contrary, he came to grips with it and was pulled down from his horse and injured; and the scars he bore from the incident remained visible on him. But he slew it in the end and indeed made the first person who came to his aid extremely fortunate in the eyes of many.

**1.9.7–13**
CYRUS' OBITUARY
Cyrus' trustworthiness and enmity toward malefactors.

[7] When he was sent down by his father to be satrap of Lydia, Phrygia, and Cappadocia and was also appointed general of all those assigned to muster in the plain of Kastolos,[a] from the first he showed that he attached great weight to keeping his word if he made peace with anyone or reached

1.8.29a Only the King could grant permission to wear this dagger, the *akinakēs*, so clearly Artapatas' dagger was granted to him by Cyrus, purporting to exercise royal prerogatives. It was therefore especially appropriate for Artapatas to use it in his final act of devotion to his dead master. See Figure 1.8.29 for images of *akinakēs*.

1.9.1a Cyrus the Elder: founder of the Persian Empire, otherwise known as Cyrus the Great. On his rise to power and his reign, see Appendix W: Brief Biographies, §9.

1.9.3a In the King's palace: literally, "at the gates of the King." On this phrase, see Appendix C: The Persian Empire, §§5–7.

1.9.6a The order of the narrative here suggests

that Cyrus hunted quite a lot in Persia before he was sent to the western provinces, which was probably in spring 407. But as he was born after his father became King in winter 424/3, that is a tight, though not impossible, fit with *Kyroupaideia* (*The Education of Cyrus*) 1.2.8, 1.2.9, where Xenophon describes his idealized Persians as beginning to hunt at sixteen or seventeen.

1.9.7a Lydia, Phrygia (meaning Greater Phrygia): Map 1.2.10, AX, AY. Cappadocia: Book 1 map. Plain of Kastolos: Map 1.2.10, AX (Kastolou Pedion in the *Barrington Atlas*).

an agreement with anyone or promised anyone anything. [8] And accordingly the cities trusted him, as is shown by their putting themselves under his authority, and men trusted him too. If anyone had become his enemy, once Cyrus had made peace with him he would be confident that he would not suffer any injury contrary to the peace terms. [9] As a consequence, when Cyrus declared war on Tissaphernes, all the cities willingly supported him rather than Tissaphernes, except for the Milesians:[a] they were afraid of Cyrus because he did not want to abandon the exiles, [10] for he showed by his actions, and he also stated, that he would never abandon anyone when once he had become their friend, not even if they became still fewer in number and fared still worse. [11] If anyone did him a good turn or a bad one, he was open about trying to outdo that person, and some people reported a prayer of his that he might live long enough to repay with interest both his benefactors and those who had harmed him. [12] And accordingly of all those in our time, he was the one man for whose sake so very many eagerly spent their money, gave up their cities, or risked their lives. [13] Yet there was no case at all for anyone to say that he let the evildoers and the unjust laugh at him; no, his punishments were utterly merciless. Often one could see along the high roads people who had had their feet or hands cut off or their eyes gouged out; and so it came about that in Cyrus' territory all those who were doing no wrong, whether Greek or barbarian, could make their way fearlessly wherever they wanted to go, together with whatever it was convenient for them to take with them.

[14] However, people agreed that he especially honored the warlike. He was at war with the Pisidians and Mysians[a] from the outset. So when he personally campaigned against those lands, if he saw people volunteering for dangerous tasks, he would make them the rulers of the country that he subdued; and he then honored them with other gifts, [15] so that it was evident that the good were the most prosperous and that the bad were thought fit to be their slaves. For this reason he had no shortage of volunteers for dangerous tasks whenever anyone thought that he would notice. [16] All the same, the quality he most valued in people was justice, and if he became aware of anyone who wanted to set an example of just behavior, he reckoned that it was more important than anything else to make him richer than those who loved to profit from injustice. [17] And accordingly many other matters were conducted for him with justice, and he managed an honest army. The generals and captains who had sailed to join him on account of money came to know that running their commands for Cyrus' benefit in an honorable way was more profitable than their monthly salary. [18] But then if anyone at all gave him honorable service when he had been assigned a duty, he never allowed that person's enthusiasm to go unrewarded; for that reason the very best staff officers were said to be available to Cyrus for every task. [19] If he

1.9.14–19
CYRUS' OBITUARY
Cyrus honored the warlike, the just, and the efficient.

1.9.9a  On Tissaphernes, see Appendix W: Brief Biographies, §37. Miletus: Map 1.2.10, BX.

1.9.14a  Pisidia: Map 1.2.13, AX. Mysia: Map 1.2.10, AX.

saw anyone who was a skillful and just administrator, providing the land of which he was in charge with resources and making it pay, he would never take any land away from him but would always hand more over, so that people used to be pleased to work hard and would confidently take on more. Again, no one in the least concealed from Cyrus what he had acquired, for he showed no envy of those who were clearly rich but tried, on the contrary, to make use of the wealth of those who were secreting it away.

[20] All that said, people agree that what he was definitely best at, more than anything else, was looking after all the friends he had made, knew to be well-disposed toward him, and judged to be in a position to assist him in whatever he wanted to accomplish. [21] Indeed, just as he thought he needed friends so as to obtain their assistance in his enterprises, he for his part would try not to be outdone in assisting his friends in whatever goals he saw each of them had set his heart on. [22] It was, I think, for many reasons that he was the man who received the most presents of any individual. More than anyone else, he was given to distributing presents to his friends; in doing so, he had an eye to each person's way of life and to what he saw that each one most needed. [23] This included whatever anyone sent him as suitable adornment for his person, either for war or just for finery; people said he remarked that his own body could not be adorned with all of these but that he thought that if his friends were finely arrayed, that was the greatest adornment for a man. [24] It is not remarkable that he used to outdo his friends in benefiting them in great matters, since after all he was more powerful, but by contrast it does seem admirable—to me, at least—that he also excelled in his solicitude for his friends and his eagerness to make himself congenial. [25] For Cyrus would often send them half-full casks of wine whenever he obtained a wine that was especially pleasant, saying that he had not come across a better wine than this for a long time. "So Cyrus has sent this to you and asks you to drink it today with your closest friends." [26] Often he would send his friends the other half of a goose he had eaten and half a loaf of bread or some other such dish, ordering the person who brought it to say, as he did so, "Cyrus was pleased with these, so he wants you too to taste them." [27] And whenever fodder was especially sparse, as he was able to procure it for himself because of the many staff officers he had and because of the attention he himself paid to the matter, he would send it out to his friends and tell them to throw this fodder to the horses they themselves rode, so that the horses that carried his friends should not go hungry. [28] If he was ever proceeding on his way and a very large number of people were likely to see him, he would call his friends to his side and engage them in earnest conversation, in order to make clear those whom he held in honor.

And so I for one judge that of all those of whom I have heard, no one was regarded as a friend by more people, whether Greeks or barbarians. [29] A proof of it is this: though Cyrus was the King's slave,[a] no one left him for the King, and only Orontas tried to (and Orontas quickly found that the very person he thought he could trust was friendlier to Cyrus than to himself).[b] But many left the King for Cyrus once the two of them had become enemies to each other, and furthermore these were the people with particularly high self-regard and who thought that because of their good qualities, they would obtain more honor at Cyrus' hands than at the King's. [30] A great proof that also became evident at the end of his life was that, as a good person himself, he could rightly judge who were trustworthy, well-disposed, and constant. [31] For when Cyrus died, all the friends and Table Companions around him also died fighting on his behalf, though Ariaios was an exception: he happened to be posted on the left as commander of the cavalry, and when he realized that Cyrus had fallen, he took to flight, together with the entire force he was leading.[a]

[1] Then Cyrus' head was cut off, and his right hand. The King, in his pursuit, broke into the Cyrean camp, and the troops with Ariaios no longer stood firm but fled through their own camp to the overnight halt from which they had started out;[a] people said that it was as much as four parasangs away. [2] The King and those with him seized a large amount of plunder, notably Cyrus' Phocaean concubine, who was said to be wise and beautiful.[a] [3] His Milesian concubine, the younger of the two,[a] was captured by the King's entourage but succeeded in escaping, though undressed, to join some of the Greeks in the baggage train who happened to have weapons and who, formed up in line against the plunderers, killed many of them, though some of them were also killed. In spite of this, they did not run off, but they saved her and also saved whatever other property and people were within their lines.

1.9.29–30
CYRUS' OBITUARY
Cyrus' friends' response
to his generosity.

1.10.1–3
November 401
BATTLEFIELD OF CUNAXA
The King rampages
through Cyrus' baggage
train.

---

1.9.29a   Cyrus was not Artaxerxes' chattel slave (see Appendix C: The Persian Empire, §3), but it is plausible enough that he was his *bandaka*, the Persian word used by King Darius I to refer to his generals and satraps. Although the King's generals and satraps were of high status relative to his other subjects, the word *bandaka*, to judge from equivalents offered in other languages, signifies an inferior person who is bound to obey without question.
1.9.29b   For the Orontas episode, see 1.6.
1.9.31a   On Ariaios, see Appendix W: Brief Biographies, §4. For various other ancient accounts of his performance, see Appendix L: The Battle of Cunaxa, §§11–12.
1.10.1a   The battle actions shown in Diagram 1.8 resume at this point. The Greeks subsequently joined Ariaios at the overnight halt from which they had started out (2.1.3, 2.2.8), so its location is marked on Map 2.3.14 as Camp, *Halting Place 27*.

1.10.2a   Other sources tell us that the Phocaean concubine's birth name was Milto but that once she became a kept woman, she was nicknamed Aspasia, after the beautiful and very clever mistress of the fifth-century Athenian political figure Pericles. Subsequently she became a favored concubine of Artaxerxes, and later still we are told that his eldest son, when proclaimed crown prince, asked for her to be given to him. Phocaea: Map 1.2.10, AX.
1.10.3a   The Persians, and particularly the Persian Kings, were famous for the large number of their concubines. Formal concubinage was not unknown to the law of Athens, though it was not widespread and operated on a smaller scale than among Persian royalty. So Xenophon would not have expected his readers to think it untoward for Cyrus to have (at least) two concubines living openly with him, though the greater the number, the more exotic it would have seemed.

**1.10.4–6**
November 401
BATTLEFIELD OF CUNAXA
Both sides maneuver to
improve their positions.

[4] At this point the King and the Greeks were about three and a half miles[a] apart from one another, the Greeks pursuing those in their sector as if they were victorious over all the enemy, the Persians engaged in plunder as if all of them were now victorious. [5] When the Greeks realized that the King was in their baggage train with his army, and the King on his side heard from Tissaphernes that the Greeks had won the victory over their particular opponents "and they are going forward in pursuit," the King then gathered his own troops and arranged them in line of battle, while Klearchos called to Proxenos[a]—who was closest to him—and started to confer about whether they should send some soldiers to the camp or whether they should all go there to give aid. [6] Meanwhile the King was clearly visible advancing again, directly behind them, or so it seemed. The Greeks wheeled around and set about preparing to engage him too, in the belief that this was his line of advance. But that was not in fact the route by which he was leading his army; instead he was leading it back along the same line by which he had originally advanced, outside the Greek left wing, once he had rounded up those who had deserted to the Greeks in the course of the battle, together with Tissaphernes and the troops with him.

**1.10.7–8**
November 401
BATTLEFIELD OF CUNAXA
Tissaphernes' part in
the battle.

[7] For Tissaphernes had not fled when the armies first engaged with each other but rode along the river, through where the Greek peltasts were stationed. As he rode through he killed nobody, but the Greeks parted on either side and proceeded to strike and spear his troops as they went past. Episthenes of Amphipolis[a] was the commander of the peltasts, and he was said to have revealed himself to be a person of sense. [8] So Tissaphernes escaped, though he had the worst of it, and he did not turn back again but arrived at the Greek camp and there came across the King, and they once more lined up their forces together and set about making their way back.[a]

**1.10.9–12**
November 401
BATTLEFIELD OF CUNAXA
The Greeks charge the
Persians successfully
once more.

[9] Since the Persians were in the vicinity of the Greek left wing,[a] the Greeks were afraid they might move toward the wing, fold around them from both sides, and cut them to pieces; so it seemed a good idea to roll up the wing and place the river behind them.[b] [10] While they were considering this, the King passed them by and set up his battle line opposite theirs in the same fashion as when he first assembled to fight the battle. When the Greeks saw that the King's troops were close by and drawn up in battle order, they again chanted a war hymn and attacked with yet more enthusiasm than before. [11] But again the barbarians did not withstand them, instead turning in flight from a greater distance than previously. The

1.10.4a   About 3.5 miles/5.5 kilometers: the Greek text says 30 stades; see Appendix O: Measurements, §5.
1.10.5a   On Klearchos and Proxenos, see Appendix W: Brief Biographies, §§18, 29.
1.10.7a   Amphipolis: Map 5.3.7, AX.
1.10.8a   Diodorus 14.23.6 (in Appendix S: Selections from Diodorus) arguably implies that, contrary to what Xenophon says here, Tissaphernes did not remain at the head of his cavalry; for more detail and speculation about what actually happened,

see Appendix L: The Battle of Cunaxa, §§11, 14–16.
1.10.9a   That is, what had originally been the left wing. But as the Greeks were now facing in the opposite direction, it was actually their right wing now.
1.10.9b   The net effect of the planned maneuver would have been to turn the line through 90 degrees, so that it now faced away from the river instead of being at right angles to it.

Greeks carried on the pursuit as far as a certain village, and there they halted, [12] as above the village was a hill[a] and on top of this the King's entourage rallied. No infantry remained among them, but the hilltop was covered with cavalry, so that the Greeks could not make out what was happening. They said they saw the royal standard, a golden eagle upon a shield with its wings outstretched.[b]

[13] When the Greeks began even so to advance again, the cavalry then left the hill too, no longer keeping together but different sections going in different directions. The hill was gradually denuded of cavalry, and in the end all of them had gone away. [14] So Klearchos did not continue to go up the hill but halted the army at its foot and sent Lykios the Syracusan[a] and one other to the top of the hill and ordered them to look down at what was beyond it and report back accordingly. [15] Lykios rode up, had a look, and reported back that they were fleeing with all their might. More or less at this point, the sun set. [16] The Greeks halted there, grounded their arms, and rested for a time. While they did this, they marveled that Cyrus was not to be seen anywhere and that nobody came from him. They did not realize that he was dead but imagined that he had gone in pursuit or had ridden on ahead to seize some position. [17] They deliberated whether to remain where they were and bring up the baggage train or to go back to the camp, and they decided to go back, arriving at their tents around suppertime. [18] Such was the end of that day.

They found that most of their possessions had been thoroughly plundered, especially anything to eat or drink. Cyrus had also provided wagons full of flour and wine, so that if ever shortage took severe hold of the army, these could be distributed to the Greeks (it was said that there were four hundred of these wagons), and these too the King's troops had plundered on this occasion. [19] And so most of the Greeks went without their evening meal, and they had also had no morning meal, for the King had made his appearance before the army broke off for the morning meal. So that was the condition in which they spent that night.

1.10.13–17
November 401
BATTLEFIELD OF CUNAXA
The Greeks are left in possession of the battle-field.

1.10.18–19
November 401
BATTLEFIELD OF CUNAXA
The Greeks find themselves short of food supplies.

1.10.12a  This hill is probably a tell: a mound of earth covering and built up by remnants of an ancient settlement. Many tells are visible in the plain of this part of Mesopotamia. For a tell located farther north, see Figure 3.4.7 (top), the tell of ancient Larisa/Nimrud.
1.10.12b  The precise text and translation of this passage are disputed. On the view taken here, Xenophon's point is not about how the emblem was made visible but solely about what it looked like. Inci-

dentally, the Persian royal standard did not always depict an eagle but sometimes a falcon or a griffin. The Greeks did not use military standards themselves. (Translator's note)
1.10.14a  Syracuse: Map 5.3.7, locator.

BOOK TWO

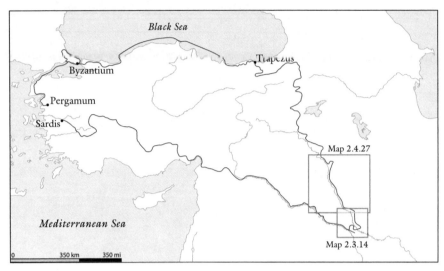

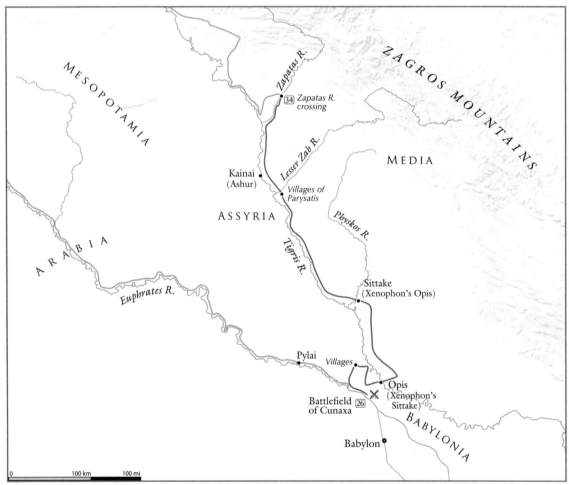

BOOK 2. *KATABASIS:* FROM THE BATTLEFIELD OF CUNAXA TO THE ZAPATAS RIVER, *HALTING PLACES 26–34.*

[So, then, in the preceding narrative, the author explained how the Greek contingent was gathered together for Cyrus' benefit when he launched his campaign against his brother Artaxerxes, what was done en route to the interior, how the battle went, how Cyrus met his end, and how the Greeks went to their camp and retired to rest, thinking that they had won a complete victory and that Cyrus was still alive.][a]

[2] When day broke, the generals had a meeting and were surprised to find that Cyrus had not sent anyone to indicate what they should do, nor had he made an appearance himself. So they decided that when they had packed up the baggage they had with them and armed themselves, they would go on until they met him. [3] They were already making a start as the sun rose when up came Prokles, the ruler of Teuthrania, who was a descendant of Damaratos the Laconian; with him came Glous son of Tamos.[a] These two gave them the news that Cyrus was dead. They also said that Ariaios[b] had fled and was now, together with the other barbarians, at the overnight halt from which they had set out on the previous day, and they reported that he had said he would wait for them that day in case it was their intention to come to him, but on the following day he would leave for Ionia,[c] where he had come from.

[4] When they heard this, the generals were distressed, as were the other Greeks when they learned the news. But Klearchos[a] said, "Well, we could

2.1.1
An ancient scribe's summary of the story so far.

2.1.2–3
November 401
BABYLONIA
*Battlefield of Cunaxa (26)*
The Greeks learn that Cyrus is dead.

2.1.4–6
November 401
BATTLEFIELD OF CUNAXA
Klearchos claims the victory and offers to make Ariaios King of the Persians.

NOTE: Unless otherwise indicated, all dates are B.C.E., and all citations are to Xenophon's *Anabasis*. The determination of the army's route and stopping places are based on the editors' calculations and estimates from data taken from *Anabasis*. Nonetheless, the route line shown on our maps and the monthly dates given in our side notes are often subject to doubt. Our best estimates should not be taken as authoritative or certain. See the Editors' Preface, §§17–20.

2.1.1a This is the first of the paragraphs occurring throughout the work that summarize the story so far. It appears in brackets because scholars generally agree these are later scribal insertions; for more, see the Translator's Notes, §13. On Cyrus and Artaxerxes,

see Appendix W: Brief Biographies of Selected Characters in *Anabasis*, §§10, 6.

2.1.3a On Prokles—the origin of his name, his ultimate allegiance to Greece, and his ancestor Damaratos (king of Sparta at the turn of the sixth to the fifth century, who was deposed and subsequently fled to Persia)—see Appendix W, §28. On the later career of Glous, his miserable end, and his father, Tamos, see Appendix W, §34. Teuthrania: Map 1.2.10, AX. Laconia: Map 1.2.1, BY.

2.1.3b For Ariaios' subsequent relations with Artaxerxes, see Appendix W, §4.

2.1.3c Ionia: Map 1.2.10, AX.

2.1.4a On Klearchos, see Appendix W, §20.

51

wish that Cyrus was alive; but since he is dead, report to Ariaios that we at least are victorious over the King, and, as you see, nobody is still in the field against us. If you had not come, we would now be making our way to attack the King. Our message to Ariaios is that if he comes here, we will set him on the royal throne, for to those who conquer in battle belongs the power to rule." [5] Having said this, he sent the messengers back, and with them Cheirisophos the Laconian and Menon the Thessalian[a]—and indeed Menon himself positively wanted to go, as he was personally friendly with Ariaios and a formal guest-friend[b] of his. [6] They went off, while Klearchos waited. The army provided itself with food as best it could by slaughtering oxen and donkeys from among the draft animals. For firewood, they advanced a short distance out of the lines to where the fighting had taken place and gathered the arrows, and there were many of them, which the Greeks had forced those who were deserting from the King to throw away.[a] They also gathered up the wickerwork shields and the wooden shields of the Egyptians;[b] and in addition there were many light, leather-covered shields and abandoned wagons to be carried off. Using all these as fuel to boil the meat, they got down to eating their meal for the day.

[7] It was already the late morning when heralds came from the King and Tissaphernes.[a] The rest of the heralds were barbarians, but one of them was a Greek, Phalinos, who was in Tissaphernes' entourage and held in honor by him, especially as he professed to be an expert on the subject of military formations and hoplite warfare.[b] [8] The heralds approached and summoned the Greek commanders. They said that the King ordered the Greeks—since he was the victor and had killed Cyrus—to give up their weapons, go and wait at the King's gates, and obtain what benefit they could. [9] So spoke the King's heralds, and the Greeks generally were depressed to hear it, but Klearchos still maintained the line that it was not for the victors to hand over their weapons. "But," he said to the others with him, "you, my fellow generals, should give whatever answers to these people you think best and most honorable. I shall be back very soon." He said this because he happened to have been offering a sacrifice, and one of his servants had now summoned

2.1.5a  On Menon's preexisting Persian relationships and on the justice or otherwise of Xenophon's portrait of him, see Appendix W: Brief Biographies, §23. For Diodorus Siculus' account of Cheirisophos' status within the army, see Appendix M: Other Ancient Sources on the Ten Thousand, §§3, 6. Thessaly: Map 5.3.7, AX.
2.1.5b  Guest-friend: someone with whom there is a bond of ritualized friendship, going beyond simple personal friendship, of a type that was common between prominent men of different cities; for more, see the Glossary.
2.1.6a  For these deserters, see 1.10.6, where Artaxerxes rounds them up again.
2.1.6b  See Figure 1.8.9 for an image of a Persian wicker shield-bearer. Egypt: Ref. Map 9, DW.

2.1.7a  On Tissaphernes, see Appendix W, §37.
2.1.7b  Hoplite: heavy-armed infantryman; for more, see Appendix H: Infantry and Cavalry in *Anabasis*, §§2–3. As Plutarch pointed out in the second century C.E. (*Life of Artaxerxes* 13.3–4; in Appendix T: Selections from Plutarch), Xenophon's implication that Phalinos was the only Greek in this deputation contradicts the account of the King's Greek doctor, Ctesias, who claimed to have been there himself. Plutarch took Xenophon to be deliberately contradicting Ctesias, thereby implying that Ctesias was prepared to lie. For further brief remarks about Phalinos, see Appendix D: The Persian Army, §14. On Ctesias, see Appendix W, §8.

FIGURE 2.1.9.
VASE, C. 525, BY THE
ANTIMENES PAINTER,
DEPICTING THE PRESENTA-
TION AND EXAMINATION
OF A LIVER FOR DIVINA-
TION (*HIERA*).

him to see the sacred entrails that had been removed from the victim.[a] [10] At this point, then, Kleanor the Arcadian, the oldest person present, answered that they would die before they handed over their weapons, and Proxenos the Theban said,[a] "Well, Phalinos, for my part I wonder whether the King is asking for our weapons on the basis that he is the conqueror or as gifts to be given to him out of friendship. For if he is the conqueror, why does he have to ask, rather than just come and take them? But if he wants to obtain them through persuasion, let him say what will be in it for the soldiers if they do him this favor." [11] To this Phalinos said, "The King regards himself as the victor, since he killed Cyrus. And indeed, is there anyone to contest his rule with him? He also thinks that you belong to him, since he has caught you in the middle of his territory, between uncrossable rivers, and he can lead against you a multitude of people so large that you would not be able to kill them even if he gave you the opportunity."

2.1.9a　In the usual form of divinatory sacrifice, the omens (*hiera*) were derived from the state of the victim's entrails. For more on divinatory sacrifice, see Appendix G: Divinity and Divining, §§2, 11–15. See Figure 2.1.9 for a divination scene.

2.1.10a　Kleanor was not a general at this point, since his election is recorded only later (3.1.47). The statement that he was the oldest person present also gives rise to a problem, as at 6.5.13 Sophainetos is said to be the oldest of the generals, and at 5.3.1 the same is said of both Sophainetos and Philesios. Perhaps these two happened to be absent from the group that received Phalinos. On Kleanor and Proxenos, see Appendix W: Brief Biographies, §§19, 29; on Sophainetos and his age, §32. Arcadia, Thebes: Map 1.2.1, AX, AY.

**2.1.12–13**
November 401
BATTLEFIELD OF CUNAXA
Theopompos gives reasons for refusing to hand over their weapons. Phalinos makes fun of him for speaking pretentiously.

**2.1.14**
November 401
BATTLEFIELD OF CUNAXA
Other Greek soldiers are more conciliatory.

**2.1.15–23**
November 401
BATTLEFIELD OF CUNAXA
Diplomatic fencing between Klearchos and Phalinos.

[12] After this speech, Theopompos of Athens[a] said, "Phalinos, as you see, nothing else is now any good to us except weapons and our own personal merits. We think that while we have our weapons, we could also put our personal merits to use; but that if we were to give up our weapons, we would also be deprived of our lives. So don't think that we are going to hand over to you the only things that are any good to us; instead, we will use them to extend the fight to the good things you possess." [13] When he heard this, Phalinos laughed and said, "Well, young man, you seem like a philosopher, and you speak quite charmingly, but be aware that you are a fool if you think that your personal merits and those of the others here could withstand the power of the King."[a]

[14] It has been reported that certain others spoke in a somewhat softer vein, to the effect that, as faithful as they had been to Cyrus, they could certainly be worth a lot to the King too if he wanted to become friends with them; and whether he wanted them to campaign in Egypt[a] or to use them in some other way, they could help him subdue his opponents.

[15] At just that point, Klearchos came back and asked if they had already given their answer. Phalinos took up his question and said, "As for these people, Klearchos, each one says something different; you tell us what you say." [16] In reply he said, "I was glad to see you, Phalinos, and I believe all these others were too, as you are a Greek and so are we—all those you see here. In the situation in which we find ourselves, we seek your advice about what we should do on the points you raise. [17] So, in the name of the gods, give us the advice that seems to you to be best and most honorable and that will bring you a great reputation for the future, when the story is told and retold. 'Phalinos,' people will say, 'was once sent from the King to order the Greeks to surrender their weapons, and he advised them, when they sought his advice, in such-and-such a way.' You know that whatever advice you give us will necessarily be reported in Greece."

[18] Klearchos led him on like this in the hope that, though he was on an embassy from the King, he would advise them not to surrender their weapons, thus making the Greeks more optimistic about their position. But against his expectation, Phalinos dodged out of it and said, [19] "My personal advice is not to surrender the weapons if there is one chance in a million for you to come off safely from a war with the King; but if in truth

2.1.12a Many scholars, including this edition's co-editor, Shane Brennan, have thought that Theopompos here is a pseudonym for Xenophon himself, and what the man says would be quite fitting in the mouth of Xenophon, who was, as Theopompos is described at 2.1.13, a "young man" who might well "seem like a philosopher" (for more, see Appendix A: Xenophon and Socrates, §§21–28). Xenophon uses a pseudonym for himself elsewhere, in connection with his authorship of *Anabasis* (see the Introduction, §6.11), and his willingness to do so may be relevant here; but the cases are different, as here the sugges-

tion is that he is using a pseudonym for himself within the narrative.
2.1.13a At this point Diodorus (14.25.6; in Appendix S: Selections from Diodorus) gives another general, Socrates of Achaea, an overly elaborate speech with no parallel in Xenophon.
2.1.14a Egypt had been part of the Persian Empire in the late sixth and through most of the fifth century, but at this point a native dynasty under Amyrtaios (ruled c. 404–c. 399) was in rebellion with increasing success, and Egyptian independence was in fact maintained throughout the first half of the fourth century.

there is no hope of safety with the King hostile, my advice is to save yourselves in whatever way is possible." [20] To this, Klearchos said, "Well, that's what you say. What you are to report back from us is that we think that, should it be necessary to be friends with the King, we would be more valuable friends if we had our weapons than if we had surrendered them to someone else; and we think that, should it be necessary to fight a war, we would likewise fight it better if we had our weapons than if we had surrendered them to someone else."

[21] Phalinos said, "We shall indeed report that back. But the King ordered us also to say this to you: that there would be a truce for you if you remain here but open war if you advance or go elsewhere. So speak about this issue too and whether you will be staying and there is a truce, or whether I am to report back that there is open war as far as you are concerned." [22] Klearchos answered, "Then report back on this that we think exactly the same as the King." "So what is that?" said Phalinos. To which the response of Klearchos was "If we remain here, a truce; if we retreat or advance—open war." [23] He again asked, "Am I to report back a truce, or open war?" and Klearchos again answered the same: "Staying put—truce; retreat or advance—open war." But he gave no clear clue as to what he would do.

[1] Phalinos then went away, together with his companions. On the other side, Prokles and Cheirisophos arrived from Ariaios, though Menon remained with him. They reported that Ariaios had said there were many Persians[a] who were better than he was and they would not stand for his being the King. "But if you want to go back with him, he tells you to come now, tonight. If not, he says he will be leaving early tomorrow." [2] Klearchos said, "Well, this is what he must do. If we come to him, just as you say; if we don't, do whatever you think is most advantageous for you." But he said nothing to them about what he would actually do.

[3] After this, and with the sun already setting, Klearchos assembled the generals and captains and said this to them: "Men, when I was offering a sacrifice to inquire about attacking the King, appropriate sacred signs were not forthcoming. And it was indeed reasonable that they should not be forthcoming, for as I now learn, between us and the King is the river Tigris,[a] so deep it is navigable by ships, which we could not cross except by boats, and we don't have boats. Of course, we can't remain here, as it's impossible to find food supplies; but the sacred signs were very favorable for us to go to Cyrus' friends. [4] So this is what it's necessary to do: Go away and make our evening meal with whatever anyone may have; and when the signal is given by trumpet to turn in, instead pack your things together. When the second signal is given, load them up onto the draft animals, and on the third signal, follow the vanguard, with the draft animals next to the river and the armed troops on the outside."

2.2.1–2
November 401
BATTLEFIELD OF CUNAXA
Ariaios rejects the Greeks' offer to make him King. He offers to lead them back to the coast.

2.2.3–4
November 401
BATTLEFIELD OF CUNAXA
Klearchos gives instructions for a speedy retreat.

2.2.1a  Persian Empire: Ref. Map 9.
2.2.3a  Tigris River: Book 2 map. The path of the river in its middle course has changed since

antiquity. Large sections of its former bed are still visible today between Samarra and Baghdad (Ref. Map 8, DZ).

2.2.5
November 401
BATTLEFIELD OF CUNAXA
Klearchos is now the
undisputed leader.

2.2.6
Scribal note on the
distances covered so far.

2.2.7–9
November 401
BABYLONIA
*Camp (27)*
The Greeks and Ariaios
swear an oath of loyalty
to each other.

2.2.10–12
November 401
BABYLONIA
Ariaios advises retreating
by a different route, and
as fast as possible.

[5] When they heard this, the generals and captains went away and did as instructed. And from then on Klearchos acted as the commander and they obeyed, not because they had elected him their commander but because they saw that he alone understood what the commander must understand, while the others did not have enough experience.

[6] [Reckoning the route by which they went from Ephesus[a] in Ionia as far as the battlefield, it turns out to be ninety-three days' march, 535 parasangs, about 1,825 miles.[b] From the battlefield they said it was about 40 miles[c] to Babylon.][d]

[7] At this point, when it became dark, Miltokythes the Thracian[a] deserted to the King with the roughly forty cavalry that he had with him, and about three hundred of the Thracian infantry. [8] Klearchos took the lead for the others in accordance with the directions he had given, and they followed. They reached as far as the first halting place and met Ariaios and his army about midnight.[a] The Greek troops grounded their arms in formation, and the generals and captains had a meeting with Ariaios, in the course of which the Greeks and Ariaios, together with the most important of those with him, swore not to betray each other and to be allies, and the barbarians swore in addition to guide them without trickery. [9] They swore these oaths after slitting the throats of a bull, a wolf,[a] a boar, and a ram over a shield, with the Greeks dipping a sword in the blood and the barbarians a lance.

[10] When these pledges had been given, Klearchos said, "Come, then, Ariaios, since you and we are to travel together, tell us what thoughts you have about the journey. Should we return by the same route we came by,[a] or do you have some other road in mind that seems to be better?" [11] Ariaios said, "If we go back the way we came, starvation would totally destroy us.

2.2.6a   Note that Xenophon elsewhere reckons the army's journey from Sardis, but here it is reckoned from Ephesus, which is where Xenophon places the beginning of his personal journey (6.1.23), rather than at Sardis, as the army as a whole did. Ephesus, Sardis: Book 1 map, AX.

2.2.6b   About 1,825 miles/2,935 kilometers: the Greek text says 16,050 stades; see Appendix O: Ancient Greek and Persian Units of Measurement, §5. On one common modern estimate of the parasang (a Persian unit for measuring travel) as typically about 3 miles/5 kilometers, 535 parasangs comes out at rather less than this, but there may be no discrepancy, since it is controversial whether the parasang measures hours spent traveling, distance traveled, or a combination of the two; see the Introduction, §7.3–5; Appendix O, §§7–8.

2.2.6c   Forty miles/64 kilometers: the Greek text says 360 stades. Plutarch, *Life of Artaxerxes* 8.2 (in Appendix T: Plutarch), in a passage in which he has just referred to Xenophon's account of the battle, says it was 500 stades. According to the view of the Babylonian section of the route taken in this edition, the text here is right, and Plutarch has

made some kind of mistake.

2.2.6d   This paragraph is generally regarded by editors as an insertion by a later scribe, along with the similar 5.5.4 and 7.8.26. It is certainly oddly located within the text, and the Plutarch passage referred to in n. 2.2.6c suggests that his copy of Xenophon did not have the sentence about the distance between the battlefield of Cunaxa and Babylon. The days'-march count looks to be a few days too high, even allowing for the journey from Ephesus to Sardis; some scholars claim that the parasang count is a little too low, but this is more disputable. Babylon: Book 2 map.

2.2.7a   Thrace: Map 5.3.7, AY.

2.2.8a   This is the beginning of the march down-country (*katabasis*).

2.2.9a   Wolf: the Greek word here (*lykos*) has been deleted by some scholars because wolves are not found in Mesopotamia today. But perhaps things were different in ancient times. Also, the Greek word has a somewhat wider meaning than "wolf" and could cover jackals, which are still found there.

2.2.10a   For the route they had taken on the march up-country, see the Book 1 map.

We have no food supplies left now, and for the last seventeen days' march here, there was nothing at all for us to take from the land. Where there was anything, we used it all up as we made our way through the country. We are now thinking of making our way back[a] by a longer route, but one on which we shall not be short of food supplies. [12] But in making our way, we must do so at the outset using the longest marches each day that we can, in order to be separated as far as possible from the royal army. Once we have a head start of two or three days on the road, the King will no longer be able to catch us, that's for sure. He will not dare to follow us with a small army, and with a large company he will not be able to make his own way quickly, and perhaps he too will fall short of food supplies. That's my personal opinion."

[13] This strategy amounted to nothing more than stealing off or turning in open flight, but fortune dictated a more honorable course of action. When day came, they set about making their way with the sun on their right, reckoning that they would come at sundown to villages in the Babylonian countryside,[a] and in this they were not mistaken. [14] But while it was still afternoon, they thought they saw enemy cavalry. Those of the Greeks who happened not to be in formation ran to take up their positions, and Ariaios, who was making his way in a wagon because he had been wounded, got down from it and put on his breastplate, and so did those with him. [15] But while they were arming, the scouts who had been sent on in advance returned and said that what the army had seen was not cavalry but draft animals grazing. Everyone realized at once that the King was encamped somewhere nearby, and indeed smoke could be seen in the villages not far off.

[16] Klearchos did not lead them against the enemy, for he knew that the soldiers were exhausted and without food, and it was already late. But he also did not change direction at all, taking care that he should not seem to be running away. Instead, he led them straight ahead to the closest villages as the sun set and settled down into quarters there with the first ranks, though the villages had been thoroughly ransacked by the King's army, who had even removed from the houses the wood that was there. [17] All the same, the vanguard did make camp there after a fashion, while the rearguard, as they came up in the darkness, set about bivouacking in different groups at random; they made a great amount of noise, calling to one another, so that the enemy too could hear it, and those of the enemy who were closest actually fled from their encampment. [18] This became clear on the next day, for no draft animals at all were any longer visible, nor a camp nor smoke anywhere near. Even the King, it appeared, had been struck by panic at the approach of the army; he showed this clearly by what he did on the following day.

*2.2.13–15*
*November 401*
BABYLONIA
Signs of the enemy army are spotted.

*2.2.16–18*
*November 401*
BABYLONIA
*Villages (28)*
The enemy panics at being near the Greeks and makes off in the night.

2.2.11a Here Xenophon several times uses one of his favorite words in *Anabasis*, *poreuesthai*, which we translate as "to make [one's] way"; see the Translator's Notes, §5. This passage is the first instance of this degree of repetition, and perhaps marks the change from when Cyrus imposed his plan of action, whereas now his previous subordinates have to work out the way forward for themselves.

2.2.13a Sun on their right: that is, northward. Babylonia: Map 2.3.14.

2.2.19–21
November 401
BABYLONIA
A similar panic in the
Greek army is skillfully
dealt with by Klearchos.

2.3.1–9
November 401
BABYLONIA
The King sends messen-
gers with an offer of a
truce, and Klearchos
accepts it.

[19] Nevertheless, as the night went on, fear also fell on the Greeks, and there was a hubbub and a din such as readily happens when a panic descends. [20] Klearchos ordered Tolmides of Elis, the best herald of his day, who was, as it happened, in his quarters, to call for silence and proclaim that the generals had an announcement to make: that whoever gave information as to who had let the donkey loose among the weapon stacks would receive a talent of silver as a reward.[a] [21] When the herald made this proclamation, the soldiers realized that their fears were empty and the officers were safe.

At sunrise Klearchos issued instructions for the Greeks to ground arms in the formation they had used in the battle. [1] I wrote earlier that the King was panic-stricken at the army's approach, and this was clear from the following: the day before, he had been sending orders to the Greeks to hand over their weapons, but now, as soon as the sun came up, he sent heralds about a truce. [2] When they came up to the advance sentries, they asked for the commanders, and when the sentries reported this, Klearchos, who happened at that point to be inspecting the ranks, told the sentries to order the heralds to wait until he was at leisure to receive them. [3] When he had organized the army so that in all respects it presented a fine appearance as a compact phalanx[a] and none of those without weapons were visible, he summoned the messengers, and he himself advanced toward them with the best-armed, most presentable soldiers. He also indicated to the other generals that they should do the same. [4] When he was near the messengers, he asked what they wanted. They explained that they had come to discuss a truce and were men who would be in a position to report the King's stance to the Greeks and vice versa. [5] Klearchos answered, "Then report to him that first there must be a battle, for there is no meal for us here, and there is no one who will dare to talk about truces to the Greeks without first providing a meal." [6] When they heard this, the messengers rode away and then came back quickly, from which it was clear that somewhere nearby was the King or someone else whom he had instructed to act in the matter. They said that the Greek stance seemed reasonable to the King and that they had come with guides who, if a truce were made, would lead them to where they might obtain food supplies. [7] Klearchos asked whether he would be making the truce just with the men who were coming and going or whether it would apply to all the others as well.[a] They said, "To everyone without exception, until your proposals are reported to the King." [8] When they said this, Klearchos had them removed and held a discussion, and it was thought best to make the truce quickly and then to go and take the food supplies in peace and quiet. [9] Klearchos said, "That's what I think too,

---

2.2.20a   Talent of silver: on this unit of currency, see Appendix O: Measurements, §§10–11. Elis: Map 1.2.1, AX.

2.3.3a   Phalanx: a body of troops drawn up across a broad front in close formation; for more, see Appendix H: Infantry and Cavalry,

§§13–15.

2.3.7a   Klearchos may suspect that the Persians will claim that the truce is restricted to the people in the immediate area and does not apply to their many soldiers in the wider region.

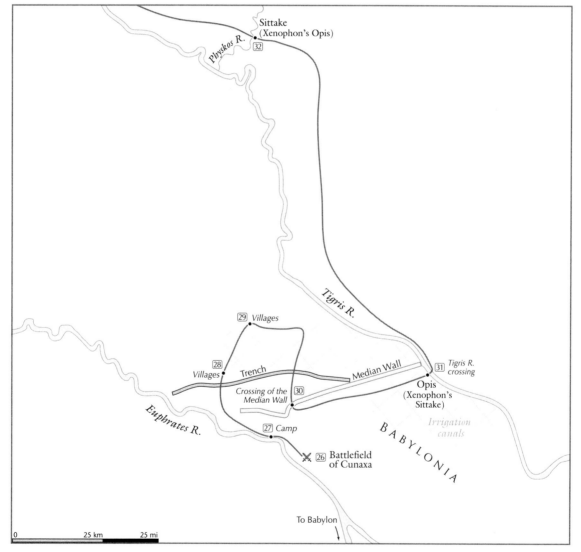

MAP 2.3.14. *KATABASIS:* FROM THE BATTLEFIELD OF CUNAXA TO SITTAKE, *HALTING PLACES 26–32.*

but I will not be particularly quick about saying so to them. Instead I will draw things out until the messengers become hesitant out of fear that we might reject making a truce—though I certainly imagine that the same fear will affect our own soldiers too."

When he thought the right time had come, he reported to the envoys that he would make a truce, and he pressed them to lead them to the food supplies immediately. [10] They led on; however, although Klearchos had entered into the truce, he kept the army in formation as he made his way forward, bringing up the rear himself. They kept coming upon ditches and canals full of water, which they could not cross except via bridges, though temporary crossings were made out of date palms that had fallen on the ground; others they themselves cut down. [11] Here one could readily see how Klearchos led his troops, with his spear in his left hand and his officer's baton in his right. If ever any of those posted to this task seemed to him to be slacking, he would pick out the right person and hit him, while at the same time he himself went into the mud and lent a hand, so that they were all ashamed not to be working hard along with him. [12] The troops who had been assigned to the task were those up to thirty years old, but when they saw Klearchos too working hard at it, the older troops also lent a hand.[a] [13] Klearchos worked all the harder because he was suspicious that the ditches were not always so full of water, for it was not the season for irrigating the plain;[a] his suspicion was that the King had let the water out into the plain to make it appear to the Greeks that there were many obstacles in the way of their journey.

[14] As they went on their way, they arrived at villages from which the guides indicated they should take their food supplies. There was a lot of grain there, wine from date palms, and vinegar boiled up from the same source. [15] As for the dates themselves, the sort that one can see in Greece were left for the servants, but those reserved for the masters were specially selected and were amazing in their size and quality, gleaming just like amber.[a] Some of them they would dry and store away as nibbles; they were pleasant with a drink but gave people headaches. [16] Here the soldiers also ate the cabbage of the palm[a] for the first time, and most people were amazed at its shape and its very particular taste, though it too was exceedingly liable to cause headaches. Where the cabbage had been removed from a palm tree, the whole tree would wither.

**2.3.10–13**
November–December 401
BABYLONIA
The army moves on. Xenophon gives an example of Klearchos' style of leadership.

**2.3.14–16**
November–December 401
BABYLONIA
*Villages with grain and dates* (29)
The soldiers sample the date palms of Babylonia.

2.3.12a Klearchos was about fifty (2.6.15), so one of the oldest soldiers in the army.

2.3.13a Irrigation would have been necessary only in the dry season, which would end with the rains coming in November. Klearchos' suspicion, therefore, suggests that it is this month or later that the army is in Babylonia. On chronological pointers in *Anabasis*, see Appendix Q: The Chronology of the March.

2.3.15a If dates were plentiful, that would indicate that the annual harvest in autumn was

under way if not completed. The mention of ripe, "gleaming" dates could push the date to later in the year as typically the fruit is dried for about two months to allow it to sweeten. Dates are edible straight from the tree but are bitter and liable to cause diarrhea.

2.3.16a Cabbage of the palm: the large terminal bud at the top of the palm tree's stem from which grows the tree's characteristic fan of leaves.

FIGURE 2.3.15. TWO IMAGES OF DATE
PALMS. RIGHT: ASSYRIAN SCRIBES TAKING
RECORDS, RELIEF FROM THE PALACE AT
NIMRUD, 730 B.C.E. BOTTOM: AERIAL
VIEW OF GROVES GROWING IN THE
TIGRIS RIVER FLOODPLAIN NEAR BAIJI,
NORTH OF BAGHDAD, IRAQ.

**2.3.17–20**
November–December 401
BABYLONIA
Tissaphernes claims to
have asked the King for
permission to help the
Greeks.

[17] There they remained for three days, during which time Tissaphernes arrived from the Great King, and also the brother of the King's wife and three other Persians, with many slaves in their train.[a] When the Greek generals met them, Tissaphernes spoke first, through an interpreter, along these lines: [18] "Men of Greece, my own home makes me a neighbor to Greece,[a] and when I saw that you had fallen into many unmanageable difficulties, I reckoned it would be a piece of luck if I could somehow claim from the King the boon of bringing you back safely to Greece. I think that this, if achieved, will be something not unworthy of thanks both in your own eyes and in those of the rest of Greece. [19] Realizing this, I set about registering my claim with the King, saying to him that it would be only fair for him to grant me a favor, because I was the first to bring the news that Cyrus was mounting a campaign against him, and when I arrived with the news, I also brought him concrete help. Furthermore, I alone of those posted opposite the Greeks did not flee, but I rode through the enemy lines and met the King in your camp,[a] where he came when he had killed Cyrus and pursued the barbarians who had been in Cyrus' army. He did so along with these people here with me now, who are extremely loyal to him. [20] He promised me that he would carefully consider my request but, meanwhile, told me to come and ask you why you had campaigned against him. And I advise you to answer him with moderation, in order to make it more doable for me to achieve a good result for you from him."

**2.3.21–24**
November–December 401
BABYLONIA
Klearchos answers diplo-
matically but firmly.

[21] At this the Greeks withdrew and held a discussion. Then they gave their answer, which Klearchos delivered: "We did not gather together in order to make war on the King, nor did we make our way to the interior to attack him. On the contrary, Cyrus found many pretexts, as you too know well, in order to take you unprepared and to bring us here. [22] However, when we eventually saw that he was in a terrible position, shame in the sight of the gods and of mankind kept us from betraying him, because we had in former times been willing recipients of his largesse. [23] But since Cyrus is dead, we are not contesting the King's right to rule, nor do we have any reason to wish to harm the King's territory; and we would not want to kill him but would just make our way home, unless someone harasses us. However, if anyone wrongs us, we will try to defend ourselves against him, with the aid of the gods; but if anyone takes the initiative in benefiting us, we will not be outdone by him in confer-

---

2.3.17a It is possible that the Great King's wife, Stateira, and her brother were related to Tissaphernes. Xenophon's mention of Stateira's brother may be one of Xenophon's quiet corrections of Ctesias (alongside 2.1.7), since the latter seems to have implied that all of Stateira's siblings had been killed by Parysatis (mother of Artaxerxes and Cyrus) in the preceding reign (Photius §56; not in Appendix U: Selections from Photius' Synopsis of Ctesias' *Persika*). On Tissaphernes, Parysatis, Artaxerxes, and Cyrus the Younger, see Appendix W: Brief Biographies, §§37, 26, 6, 10.

2.3.18a Tissaphernes' estates were in Caria (Xenophon, *Hellenika* 3.2.12), though he had been satrap (governor) of Sardis before Cyrus arrived in western Anatolia and was so again subsequently. Whichever location he has in mind, he calls himself a neighbor to Greece because he regards the Greeks of the Ionian seaboard as being part of Greece. The following locations appear on Map 1.2.10: Caria, BX; Sardis, Ionia, AX. Western Anatolia: Ref. Map 4.1, BY.

2.3.19a For doubts as to whether Xenophon is right about this, see Appendix L: The Battle of Cunaxa, §§14–15, 18–19.

ring benefits, up to the very limit of our ability." [24] So Klearchos said on his side, and when Tissaphernes heard it, he said, "I will report what you say to the King and bring his response back again to you. Until I come back, let the truce remain in force. We shall provide a market to sell you supplies."

[25] He did not come back that day or even on the next, so that the Greeks were anxious; but on the third day he appeared and said that he had come back having achieved his aim: the King had granted him the preservation of the Greeks, although very many people opposed it, saying that it would not be fitting for the King to allow those who had campaigned against him to go free. [26] Finally he said, "And now you can receive pledges from us that we really will ensure that the land is friendly to you and will lead you back to Greece without any trickery while providing you with a market. Wherever we do not provide a market, we shall allow you to take food supplies from the land. [27] But you too must swear to us that you really will make your way onward without doing any damage, as if going through friendly territory; that you will simply take food and drink only when we do not provide a market, and that if we do provide a market, you will obtain your food supplies by buying them." [28] They agreed on that and swore the oath; and Tissaphernes and the brother of the King's wife formally exchanged handshakes with the generals and captains of the Greeks.[a] After this Tissaphernes said, "Just for now I am going back to the King, but when I have carried through what I need to, I shall come back, having made everything ready to lead you back to Greece and to go myself to my own province."

[1] After all this the Greeks and Ariaios[a] waited around for Tissaphernes for more than twenty days, encamped close to each other. During this period Ariaios' brothers and other blood relations arrived to see him, and some other Persians arrived to see members of his entourage, encouraging them and in some cases bringing hand tokens[b] from the King assuring them that he would not bear ill will toward them for campaigning with Cyrus against him or for anything else in times gone by. [2] While this was happening, Ariaios' people became visibly less attentive to the Greeks; consequently, on this ground too they were upsetting the majority of the Greeks, who started to approach Klearchos and the other generals and say: [3] "Why are we staying here? Or do we not know that Artaxerxes would reckon that to destroy us would be worth all that he has in order to make the rest of the Greeks afraid to campaign against him, the Great King? As things stand, because his forces are dispersed, he is inducing us little by little to remain here, but once his army has been gathered together again, it's quite certain that he will attack us. [4] Perhaps he is digging trenches somewhere or building walls to make the route impassable, for he will never—voluntarily, at least—permit us to go to Greece and spread the report that, few as we are, we were

2.3.25–28
November–December 401
BABYLONIA
The Greeks and
Tissaphernes swear a
more detailed truce.

2.4.1–4
December 401
BABYLONIA
A long delay causes
suspicions among
the Greeks.

2.3.28a  See Figure 2.3.28 for an image of a pledg-
        ing ceremony.
2.4.1a   On Ariaios, see Appendix W: Brief Biogra-
        phies, §4.
2.4.1b   Hand tokens: when two parties could not

shake hands, because they were not in the
same place, they might instead, and with
similar symbolic force, exchange tokens in
the shape of a hand.

FIGURE 2.3.28. DETAIL OF
A MARBLE RELIEF, 403/2,
DEPICTING ATHENA
(RIGHT) SHAKING HANDS
WITH HERA AS A PLEDGE
OF THE SPECIAL RELATION-
SHIP BETWEEN THE ATHE-
NIANS AND SAMIANS.

2.4.5–7
December 401
BABYLONIA
Klearchos explains why
they have to cooperate
with Tissaphernes.

victorious over the power of the King at his own doors and then departed, having had a laugh at his expense."

[5] Klearchos replied to those who said this sort of thing, "I too am concerned about all this and more, but on the other hand, I bear in mind that if we go away now, it will seem that we are departing to carry on the war and that we are acting in breach of the truce. Other points are, first, that nobody will provide us with a market, nor is there anywhere from which we can obtain any food; next, that there will be no one to act as guide; on top of that, as soon as we do this, Ariaios will immediately cease to support us. So then we shall have no friend left, but even those who were friends previously will become our enemies. [6] Whether there is also some other river that we must cross, I don't know, but we do know that the Euphrates[a] is impossible to cross when there are enemies there to prevent it. And of course, if we did have to fight at all, there would be no cavalry to support us, while the enemy's cavalry is very numerous and should be rated very highly. So if we were victorious, whom would we manage to kill? Yet if we were defeated, none of us would survive. [7] Therefore, if the King, with so many circumstances working for him, does intend to destroy us, I for my part don't know why he would need to swear an oath, proffer his right

2.4.6a   Euphrates River: Map 2.3.14.

hand, perjure himself by the gods, and make his assurances of good faith untrustworthy in the eyes of Greeks and barbarians alike." Klearchos used many arguments of this sort.

[8] At this point Tissaphernes came back with his private force as if he were leaving for home, and Orontas[a] likewise came with his troops. Orontas also brought his new wife, the King's daughter,[b] with him. [9] So the Greeks now set out on their way from there without further delay, Tissaphernes taking the lead as well as providing a market for them. Ariaios, at the head of Cyrus' barbarian army, was also making his way back in the company of Tissaphernes and Orontas and used to make his camp along with them. [10] The Greeks were suspicious of them and journeyed with their own guides, keeping to themselves. The two parties would make camp separately, a parasang[a] and more apart. Both were on their guard against the other as if they were enemies, and this immediately created more suspicion. [11] Sometimes when they were gathering wood from the same place or collecting fodder and other such things, they came to blows, and this too provoked enmity.

[12] When they had traveled three days' march, they reached the so-called Median Wall and passed inside it.[a] It was built of baked bricks on a bitumen[b] base, twenty feet in width and one hundred in height.[c] Its length was said to be twenty parasangs, and it is no great distance from Babylon. [13] From there they made their way onward for two days' march, covering eight parasangs, and they crossed two canals, one by a bridge and the other spanned by seven boats.[a] These canals drew water from the river Tigris, and ditches were cut from them to run over the land, with large ditches to start with, then smaller ones, and finally small conduits like those used in Greece to water millet. They reached the river Tigris, by which was a large and populous city called Sittake,[b] a mile and three quarters[c] distant from the river.

---

**2.4.8–11**
December 401
BABYLONIA
Tissaphernes and
Orontas return.
The march resumes.

**2.4.12–14**
December 401
BABYLONIA
*Median Wall (30)–Opis*
*(Xenophon's Sittake) (31)*
The march to the
Tigris River.

---

2.4.8a   This Orontas (not the man put to death by Cyrus at 1.6) is brought in without introduction because he was a well-known figure to the original readers of the book, being *hyparchos* (lieutenant governor) of Mysia in the 370s and 360s. For more on this Orontas, see Appendix W: Brief Biographies, §25. Mysia: Map 1.2.10, AX.
2.4.8b   The wife's name was Rhodogyne.
2.4.10a   On the parasang (a Persian unit for measuring travel), see the Introduction, §7.3–5, and Appendix O: Measurements, §§7–8.
2.4.12a   Median Wall: previously mentioned at 1.7.15, the fortification is usually identified as a wall just north of Sippar, still visible in part, that was built by Babylonian king Nebuchadnezzar II (r. 605–562)—the Babylonian king who conquered Jerusalem in 587—probably, as the name suggests, to stop the Medes from raiding Babylonia. (For more on the Medes, see n. 2.4.27a.) As the army is said to be going "inside" the wall, it must have been traveling south at this point, presumably to reach what the Greeks were told was the best or only crossing of the Tigris. Median Wall: Map

2.3.14, *Halting place 30.* Sippar: Map 1.5.1, inset. Media, Babylonia: Map 2.4.27.
2.4.12b   Bitumen (asphalt) oozes naturally to the surface close to or possibly at Xenophon's Charmande (possible location: Map 1.5.1; not listed in the *Barrington Atlas*). Probably it was transported by boat down the Euphrates to sites in Babylonia.
2.4.12c   Twenty feet/6 meters, 100 feet/30 meters. Modern scholars agree that 100 feet is much too high for the wall as a whole, though the height of a special section, such as a tower or fortified gateway, might approach it.
2.4.13a   See Figure 2.4.13 for a modern bridge over the Tigris, part of it made from boats.
2.4.13b   Xenophon has probably confused Sittake, named by him here, with Opis, mentioned at 2.4.25. The location of Opis is definitely known, but that of Sittake is in dispute. We follow most scholars in locating Sittake north of Opis. Opis (Xenophon's Sittake): Map 2.3.14, *Halting Place 31.*
2.4.13c   A mile and three quarters/2.8 kilometers: the Greek text says 15 stades; see Appendix O: Measurements, §5.

FIGURE 2.4.13. A BRIDGE OF BOATS ON THE TIGRIS RIVER (MASONRY SECTION IN THE DISTANCE), MOSUL, IRAQ, 1920.

2.4.15–18
December 401
OPIS
(XENOPHON'S SITTAKE)
The strange incident of a
message from Ariaios.

[14] So the Greeks took up quarters by this city, near an extensive and beautiful park, thickly planted with all sorts of trees; the barbarians took up quarters once they had crossed the Tigris but were not, in fact, visible.

[15] After the evening meal, Proxenos and Xenophon happened to be taking a walk in front of the weapon stacks when an insignificant fellow came up and asked the sentries where he might find Proxenos or Klearchos; he was not looking for Menon, even though his message was from Ariaios, Menon's guest-friend.[a] [16] When Proxenos said, "I am the very person you are looking for," the fellow said, "Ariaios and Artaozos,[a] faithful supporters of Cyrus and well-disposed toward you, sent me, and they bid you take care in case the barbarians attack you in the night. There is a large army in the nearby park. [17] They also bid you send a guard to the pontoon bridge across the river Tigris, as Tissaphernes has in mind to cut it in the night, if he has the opportunity, so that you wouldn't be able to cross over but would be caught between the river and the canal." [18] When they heard this, they took him to Klearchos and recounted what he had said, and when Klearchos heard it, he became highly agitated and was full of fear.

2.4.15a   On Proxenos, Klearchos, Menon, and
Ariaios, see Appendix W: Brief Biographies,
§§29, 20, 23, 4.

2.4.16a   Nothing more is known of Artaozos
beyond this reference and the similar one
at 2.5.35.

[19] Among those present was a young man[a] who, after reflection, said that the attack and the cutting of the bridge were inconsistent with each other. "For it's clear that if they attack, they must either win or lose. Now, if they win, why is it necessary for them to cut the bridge? For even if there were many bridges, we would still have nowhere to flee to where we would be safe. [20] But if, on the contrary, we win, once the bridge has been cut, they will not have anywhere to which they can flee, nor will any of their numerous troops on the other side be able to come to help them once the bridge has been cut." [21] When Klearchos heard this, he asked the messenger how extensive the area between the Tigris and the canal was. He said that it was considerable: there were villages in it and many large cities.[a] [22] At that point the natural further conclusion was that the barbarians had sent the fellow as a subterfuge, because they were anxious in case the Greeks broke down the bridge and stayed on the island. There the Tigris would serve as a natural defense on one side and the canal on the other, and they would have food supplies from the wide acres of good land between the two, complete with peasants to till it; so it might then become a place of refuge for anyone who wanted to do the King harm.

[23] After this they took their rest, but they still sent troops to guard the bridge. Nobody mounted an attack from anywhere, and none of the enemy came up to the bridge, according to the reports of those guarding it. [24] When dawn came, they proceeded to cross the bridge, which was made up of thirty-seven boats roped together. They took the greatest possible care, for some of the Greeks in Tissaphernes' entourage were sending them messages that he intended to attack them as they crossed. But that was false, though while they were crossing, Glous put in an appearance with some others, watching to see if they were crossing the river; and when he saw that they were, he galloped off.[a]

[25] From the Tigris they made their way onward for four days' march, covering twenty parasangs, to the river Physkos, which is one hundred feet[a] wide. There was a bridge over it. There too was a great city named Opis.[b] Near here the Greeks encountered the bastard brother of Cyrus and Artaxerxes, bringing a large army from Susa and Ecbatana[c] in order to come to the King's

2.4.19–22
December 401
OPIS
(XENOPHON'S SITTAKE)
One man argues that
Ariaios' message is a
subterfuge.

2.4.23–24
December 401
OPIS
(XENOPHON'S SITTAKE)
The Greeks cross
the Tigris.

2.4.25–26
January 400
BABYLONIA–PHYSKOS RIVER
*Sittake (Xenophon's Opis) (32)*
By a ruse, the Greeks
give a Persian general an
exaggerated impression
of their numbers.

2.4.19a  A young man: many commentators think this was, in fact, Xenophon. They explain the author's choice not to give his name as a reluctance (for literary reasons) to take away from the impact of his character's dramatic step forward at the beginning of Book 3.

2.4.21a  Many large cities: most of these "cannot have been at all large," says Christopher Tuplin in Appendix C: The Persian Empire, §12.

2.4.24a  Subsequently the Greeks concluded they had been lured across the Tigris by deception. That implies that the subterfuge here was actually successful—that Klearchos was showing reluctance to cross the Tigris, but Tissaphernes made him worry that he

would be cut off in the "island," and thus he ignored what Xenophon describes above as "the natural further conclusion." On Glous, last mentioned at 2.1.3, see Appendix W: Brief Biographies, §34.

2.4.25a  One hundred feet/30 meters: the Greek text says a *plethron;* see Appendix O: Measurements, §§2–3. Physkos River: Map 2.4.27 (Radani in the *Barrington Atlas*).

2.4.25b  As remarked in n. 2.4.13b, Xenophon has probably confused Opis, named by him here, with Sittake. Sittake (Xenophon's Opis), probable (but disputed) location: Map 2.3.14, *Halting place 32* (not listed in the *Barrington Atlas*).

2.4.25c  Susa, Ecbatana: Ref. Map 9, CY, CX.

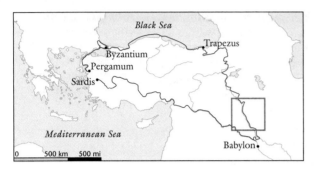

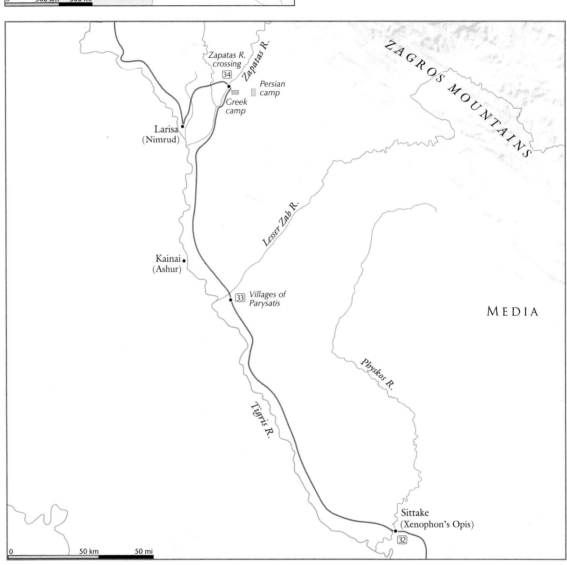

MAP 2.4.27. *KATABASIS:* FROM SITTAKE TO THE ZAPATAS RIVER, *HALTING PLACES 32–34.*

FIGURE 2.4.28. DETAIL OF A FRIEZE FROM THE NORTHWEST PALACE OF ASHURNASIRPAL II (883–859) IN NIMRUD (XENOPHON'S LARISA), DEPICTING SWIMMERS UNDER ATTACK AS THEY CROSS A RIVER TO SAFETY. THE TWO SWIMMERS USING INFLATED ANIMAL SKINS ARE BLOWING INTO THEM TO KEEP THEM BUOYANT. SUCH INFLATABLE SKINS WERE ALSO USED IN RAFTS (*KELLEKS*) TO CARRY TROOPS AND SUPPLIES AS MENTIONED HERE AND AT 1.5.10.

aid. He halted his force and sat watching the Greeks as they passed by. [26] Klearchos led them two abreast, halting from time to time as he made his way onward. As long as the vanguard of an army is at halt, of necessity there is a halt throughout the whole army for the same length of time; the natural effect of this was to make the army seem very large indeed even to the Greeks themselves, and to astonish the Persian as he watched.

[27] From there they made their way through an uninhabited part of Media[a] for six days' march, covering thirty parasangs, to the villages belonging to Parysatis, the mother of Cyrus and of the King.[b] In mockery of Cyrus,[c] Tissaphernes turned this over to the Greeks to take any plunder they wished, except for slaves.[d] There was a great deal of grain there, and sheep and other rich property. [28] From there they made their way through uninhabited

2.4.27–28
January 400
MEDIA
*Villages of Parysatis (33)*
The Greeks continue their march up the Tigris. Tissaphernes allows Greeks to plunder Queen Parysatis' villages.

2.4.27a   Media was the country of the Medes, an Iranian people who were in the ascendancy for the first half of the sixth century, prior to the Persians of the Achaemenid dynasty (see the Glossary). Their homeland was in the Zagros Mountains, centering on Ecbatana, well to the northwest of here. It seems from the mentions of Media and the Medes between here and 3.5.15 that by this time the term Media had come to include the area southwest of the mountains extending toward Babylonia, which before 612 had been the heartland of the empire of a different people, the Assyrians. Zagros Mountains, Media: Map 2.4.27.

2.4.27b   For more on Parysatis' conduct after these events, see the Epilogue, §2, and Appendix W: Brief Biographies, §26. Villages of

Parysatis, probable (but disputed) location: Map 2.4.27, *Halting place 33.*

2.4.27c   In mockery of Cyrus: because Cyrus was Parysatis' favorite (1.1.4). But perhaps in reality Tissaphernes intended to anger her against the Greeks, rather than to insult the Queen Mother.

2.4.27d   Some scholars have inferred that the villagers here were therefore already slaves, but in Appendix C: The Persian Empire, §22, Christopher Tuplin argues that all Xenophon means is that if the Greeks had carried them off, it would have been as slaves. By forbidding the Greeks to take the workforce captive, Tissaphernes had at least limited the damage to the longer-term productive potential of the estate.

country for four days' march, covering twenty parasangs, with the river Tigris on their left.[a] In the course of the first day's march, there was a large and prosperous city on the other side of the river, Kainai by name, from which the barbarians brought over bread, cheeses, and wine on rafts made of prepared hide.[b]

[1] After this they arrived at the river Zapatas, which has a width of four hundred feet.[a] Here they stayed for three days, during which time suspicions were rife but no open plot against the Greeks was evident. [2] So Klearchos decided to have a meeting with Tissaphernes and, if he could somehow, put a stop to the suspicions before war arose from them. He sent someone to say that he wanted to have a meeting with him, and Tissaphernes readily told him to come. [3] When the two of them met, Klearchos said this: "Tissaphernes, I know on my side that oaths have been made between us and pledges of good faith given that we shall not wrong each other, but I see that you are on guard against us like enemies, and since we see this, we in turn are on guard against you. [4] But since, when I look into it, I cannot detect that you are trying to do us harm, and I know clearly that we, at any rate, do not have anything of this kind in mind ourselves, I decided to come to you to discuss the situation, in order to eradicate the distrust between us if we could. [5] For I have also known people in the past who became afraid of one another, whether through slander or merely through becoming suspicious, and in their wish to strike first before they became the victim, they inflicted irreparable harm on those who neither intended nor indeed wanted to do anything of the kind. [6] So thinking that such misunderstandings would best be ended if we met personally, I have come here, and I want to show you that you are not right to distrust us.

[7] "First and most important, the oaths we swore to the gods prevent us from being enemies to each other: to my mind, no one conscious of having disregarded these could be at all happy. For I am well aware that in a war with the gods, no speed would be sufficient to permit a fugitive to escape, no place would be dark enough for him to steal off and hide, and he would have no possibility of removing himself to a secure stronghold. All things are subject to the gods in every way, and the gods rule everything and everywhere alike. [8] That's what I know about the gods and about oaths, in whose care we deposited the friendship we made with each other. And as for human considerations, I for my part think that in our present situation

**2.5.1–6**
January 400
MEDIA
*Zapatas river crossing (34)*
Klearchos goes from the Greek camp to the Persian one to meet with Tissaphernes.

**2.5.7–12**
January 400
ZAPATAS RIVER
Klearchos tries to reassure Tissaphernes about the Greeks' intentions.

2.4.28a  Here they must have crossed the Lesser Zab River. Most scholars agree that Xenophon's failure to record it is surprising, some taking the omission as evidence that he did not keep a diary—though if the river's winter volume today reflects that of ancient times, a crossing might have been undertaken on foot; see the Introduction, §7.16. It may be that Xenophon left out a section of the journey; see Appendix Q: The Chronology of the March, §12. The possibility of a recording error is underscored by the Opis/Sittake mixup (see nn. 2.4.13b, 2.4.25b). Lesser Zab River: Map 2.4.27

(Zabas Mikros in the *Barrington Atlas*).
2.4.28b  Kainai, Xenophon's name for ancient Ashur, which was the original capital of the Assyrians, was sacked in 614 but reoccupied later, if on a less grand basis (see Andrae 1938, 237–49). Kainai: Map 2.4.27 (Ashur in the *Barrington Atlas*). See Figure 2.4.28 for an Assyrian frieze depicting crossing a river using inflatable animal skins.
2.5.1a  Four hundred feet/122 meters: the Greek text says 4 *plethra;* see Appendix O: Measurements, §23. Zapatas (modern Greater Zab) River: Map 2.4.27. The armies camped near *Halting place 34.*

you are an extremely good thing for us. [9] With you the whole route is easy to travel, every river is passable, there is no shortage of food supplies. Without you we travel the route in the dark, as we don't know it at all; every river is difficult to cross; every crowd of people is fearsome; but most fearsome of all is solitude, for it is replete with all sorts of shortages. [10] Indeed, supposing that in some fit of madness we did slay you, that would be nothing other than slaying our benefactor and then entering a contest against the King himself, the most effective reserve[a] of all. There are many causes for hope, and of many different kinds, of which I would obviously be depriving myself if I were to try to do you any harm. I will set them out: [11] I set my heart upon Cyrus' becoming a friend to me because I thought that he was in the best position of anyone at that time to do good to someone if he wanted to, but I now see that you have the power and lands of Cyrus and have also preserved your own, while the power of the King, which Cyrus found hostile, is to you an ally. [12] Since this is the situation, who would be so mad as not to want to be your friend?

"But, in fact, I will say something else, which gives me hope that you too will want to be friends with us. [13] I know that the Mysians[a] are troublesome to you, and I think with my present forces I could humble them for you. I also know that the Pisidians[b] are troublesome, and I hear that there are many other tribes of that sort, and I think I could stop them from being a constant obstacle to your prosperity. And then there are the Egyptians,[c] with whom I understand that you have become especially infuriated recently: I do not see what forces you might prefer to use as your ally in punishing them rather than those I currently have with me. [14] But indeed, just considering your immediate neighbors, if you were to wish to be a friend to any of them, what a very great friend you would be if we were in your service; and if anyone else were to annoy you, how you could play the master over them! We would not serve you only for the sake of the pay but also because of the gratitude we would rightly have toward you because we would have been saved by you. [15] When I reflect on all these points, your distrust for us seems so remarkable that it would be with great pleasure that I would hear his name—the name of the person who is so clever a talker that he has persuaded you with his tales of our plots against you."

So that was what Klearchos said on his side. This was Tissaphernes' reply: [16] "How pleased I am, Klearchos, to hear such prudent words from you, for if you were to plan some evil against me when you recognize all this, by that very fact you would seem to me to be demonstrating evil intent against yourself. Take your turn in listening, and you will learn that any distrust of the King or of me on the part of you Greeks would not be fair. [17] If we wanted to destroy you, do we seem to you to be short of sufficient cavalry

2.5.13–15
January 400
ZAPATAS RIVER
Klearchos gives reasons why Tissaphernes should want to be friends with the Greeks.

2.5.16–23
January 400
ZAPATAS RIVER
Tissaphernes reassures Klearchos about Persian intentions and hints at his own ambitions.

---

2.5.10a  "Reserve": the Greek word here, *ephedros*, is a reference to wrestling contests in which two people fight and the winner then has to face a third person, the *ephedros*.

2.5.13a  Mysia: Map 1.2.10, AX.

2.5.13b  The Pisidians were the tribe that Cyrus ostensibly set out with the Greeks to subdue. Pisidia: Map 1.2.13, AX.

2.5.13c  Egypt: Ref. Map 9, DW.

or infantry or military equipment to have the capacity to harm you without there being any danger of our suffering any reprisal? [18] Or perhaps we seem to you to be lacking in places suitable to launch attacks on you? Don't you see how extensive are the plains across which you are making your way with such great toil even when they are friendly; how high are the mountains over which your way necessarily lies, which we could occupy in advance and render impassable to you; and how many are the rivers on whose banks we could regulate how many of you at a time we might want to fight? There are some of them that you would not manage to cross at all if we did not convey you over. [19] If we came off worse in all these places, still, at any rate, fire assuredly masters harvest, and by burning down all the crops, we could put starvation in the battle line against you. Even though you may be very good at fighting, you could not fight against that. [20] So with so many ways to wage war against you, none of which involve danger for us, how, then, could we possibly choose to destroy you by the one method of all of these that is impious in the eyes of the gods and disgraceful in the eyes of mankind? [21] It is among those who are altogether without resources, with no other devices available to them, and in the grip of necessity—and they would have to be worthless as well—that there are people who want to achieve something through perjury to the gods and deceit to mankind. No, Klearchos, we are not so irrational or so foolish.

[22] "But why, then, since it is possible to destroy you, did we not go ahead and do so? You should be aware that the reason we did not is my intense desire to become trustworthy in the eyes of the Greeks. Where Cyrus went up to the interior trusting in his foreign troops because of the pay he was giving them, I long to go back down to the coast strengthened by your support because of the good deeds I am doing for your sake. [23] You yourself have mentioned some of the respects in which you and your troops are useful to me, but I myself know the greatest: for only the King can wear the tiara upright on his head, but perhaps another, with your assistance, might readily wear it upright in his heart."[a]

2.5.24–26
January 400
ZAPATAS RIVER
Klearchos agrees to bring
all his officers to meet
with Tissaphernes.

[24] When he said this, he seemed to Klearchos to be speaking the truth. Klearchos then said, "So aren't those who are trying to make us enemies by their malignant reports, when there are such strong reasons for us to be friends, worthy of suffering the uttermost pains?"

[25] "And for my part," said Tissaphernes, "if you generals and captains want to come to me, I will openly name those who are telling me that you are plotting against me and against the army I have here with me."

[26] "For my part," said Klearchos, "I will bring them all, and I will show you in turn from what source I am hearing stories about you."

2.5.23a  For the tiara, or *kurbasia* (Figure 2.5.23), to be worn upright only by the Great King, see Appendix C: The Persian Empire, n. C.4a. What Tissaphernes means by referring to the upright tiara is disputed. Some think he is hinting that he secretly harbors ambitions to become the Great King himself, others that he has in mind only practical independence from the King's power. Perhaps he is being deliberately unclear.

[27] After these remarks, Tissaphernes, in an apparently affable mood, told him to stay for the time being, and he made him his companion at dinner. On the next day, Klearchos went back to the camp, and it was clear he thought that his relationship with Tissaphernes was an extremely friendly one. He reported at length all of Tissaphernes' remarks and said that those whom Tissaphernes was demanding should come to him must do so and that any of the Greeks who were clearly proved to be maligning their colleagues would have to be punished as traitors with evil intentions toward their fellow Greeks. [28] He suspected that Menon was the one doing the maligning, since he knew that, together with Ariaios, Menon had been having meetings with Tissaphernes, and also that Menon had been stirring up opposition to him and plotting against him so that he might draw the entire army over to himself and be friends with Tissaphernes.[a] [29] Klearchos too wanted the entire army to look just to himself and to be rid of the troublemakers. Some of the soldiers began to speak in opposition, saying that the captains and generals should not all go to Tissaphernes and that they did not trust him. [30] But Klearchos insisted vehemently[a] until he obtained agreement for five generals to go and twenty captains. In addition, about

2.5.27–30
January 400
ZAPATAS RIVER
Klearchos persuades the army to send most of the officers with him to Tissaphernes.

2.5.28a On Menon, Ariaios, and Tissaphernes, see Appendix W: Brief Biographies, §§23, 4, 37.
2.5.30a A different story was given by Artaxerxes' physician Ctesias. Photius represents Ctesias as saying that Menon, party to Tissaphernes' plot, was eager for the Greeks to go, and that Proxenos, deceived by a

trick, argued the same way, while Klearchos himself had forebodings and was reluctant to go. See Appendix U: Photius, §68. This is discussed further in Appendix W, Menon, §23. On Klearchos, Ctesias, and Proxenos, see Appendix W, §§20, 8, 29.

2.5.31–34
January 400
ZAPATAS RIVER
Tissaphernes arrests the
generals and kills their
entourage.

[31] When they reached Tissaphernes' threshold, the generals were called inside: Proxenos of Boeotia, Menon of Thessaly, Agias of Arcadia, Klearchos of Laconia, Socrates of Achaea.[a] Meanwhile the captains waited at the entrance. [32] Not long afterward, at a single signal, the Greeks inside were all arrested and the Greeks outside cut down. After this some of the barbarian cavalry rode across the plain killing every Greek, whether slave or free, whom they came across. [33] As the Greeks looked out from their camp, they wondered at the cavalry's movements and were puzzled about what was happening until Nikarchos of Arcadia arrived in flight. He had been wounded in the belly and held his guts in his hands, and he told them all that had happened. [34] At this the Greeks naturally ran for their weapons; all of them were astonished and thought that the enemy would immediately come to attack the camp.

2.5.35–39
January 400
ZAPATAS RIVER
Kleanor harangues a
Persian deputation for
their breach of trust.

[35] But they did not all come, only Ariaios and Artaozos and Mithradates, who had been Cyrus' most trusted companions. The person acting as interpreter for the Greeks said he also saw and recognized Tissaphernes' brother with them. Other Persians in armor followed along, as many as three hundred. [36] When they were close, they gave orders that if any of the Greeks was a general or a captain, he should approach, in order that he might be given the King's message. [37] After this Kleanor of Orchomenos and Sophainetos of Stymphalos came out cautiously in the capacity of generals; and with them came Xenophon of Athens, in order to find out what had happened to Proxenos.[a] Cheirisophos[b] happened to be away at the time in some village with other troops, foraging. [38] They took up a stand within hearing distance, and Ariaios spoke as follows: "Men of Greece, since Klearchos has been revealed as a perjurer and truce breaker, justice has been done to him and he is dead.[a] But Proxenos and Menon, by contrast, because they denounced his plot, are held in great honor.[b] As for you, the King demands your weapons, since he says they belong to him, especially as they previ-

2.5.30b  As if going to a market: presumably, then, they went lightly armed or even unarmed, and not in formation. Even so, the Persians may have regarded their presence as designed to intimidate.

2.5.31a  Agias is not mentioned prior to his arrest in the manuscript text. A likely explanation is that he took over the remaining soldiers of the generals Xenias and Pasion, who deserted the army at Myriandos in Syria (1.4.7; Map 1.4.1, BX, BY), and Xenophon has omitted mentioning it. But some editors instead substitute him for the manuscripts' mistaken reference to Sophainetos at 1.2.9. The following locations appear on Map 1.2.1: Arcadia, Achaea, AX; Boeotia, AY; Laconia, BY. Thessaly: Map 5.3.7, AX.

2.5.37a  Kleanor was not actually a general at this point; see n. 2.1.10a. On Sophainetos' generally poor relationship with Xenophon, see Appendix W: Brief Biographies, §33, 29; on Kleanor, §19. Orchomenos, Stym-

phalos: Map 1.2.1, AX, AY.

2.5.37b  On Cheirisophos, see Appendix W, §7.

2.5.38a  "He is dead": that wasn't true at this stage. Klearchos was not put to death until at least some weeks later, for Ctesias says he saw him in prison and was too frightened to assist him to commit suicide. (See Plutarch, *Life of Artaxerxes* 18 in Appendix T: Plutarch.) As this story is discreditable to Ctesias, it is likely to be true; and a delay before the execution of the generals would better fit the language of 2.6.1 and 3.1.29. Perhaps Xenophon is representing Ariaios as lying in this as in other matters.

2.5.38b  "Held in great honor": probably this is simply untrue, at any rate as regards Proxenos—a lie to soften up the remaining Greeks. But, as reported in n. 2.5.30a, Ctesias says that Proxenos, deceived by a trick, had argued alongside Menon that Klearchos should go to Tissaphernes on the fateful visit.

ously belonged to Cyrus, his slave."ᶜ [39] To this the Greeks answered, with Kleanor the Orchomenian as spokesman, "Ariaios, you worst of people, and those of you others who were friends of Cyrus', you who swore to us that you would acknowledge the same friends and enemies as we do—are you not ashamed before the gods and before mankind to have betrayed us and sided with Tissaphernes, that most godless and wicked person? You have destroyed the very men to whom you swore your oaths, and you have betrayed the rest of us as well by advancing against us in company with the enemy."

[40] Ariaios said, "It has become clear that Klearchos has for a long time been plotting against Tissaphernes and Orontasᵃ and against all of us who are associated with them." [41] Thereupon Xenophon said, "If indeed it is true that Klearchos was breaking the truce, contrary to his oaths, he has received justice, for it is just for perjurers to be wiped off the face of the earth. But Proxenos and Menon are both your benefactors and our generals, so send them here. It's clear that since they are on friendly terms, as you say, with both sides, they will try to give the best advice both to you and to us." [42] In response to this, the barbarians spoke among themselves for a long time and then went away without giving any answer.

[1] The generals, then, having been arrested by these means, were carried off to the King and met their end by being beheaded.ᵃ

One of these generals, Klearchos, seemed by common consent among all who knew him personally to be a man who was both a warlike person and a lover of war to an extreme extent. [2] This is clear from the fact that, while he remained with the Lacedaemonians as long as they were at war with the Athenians,ᵃ when peace came he persuaded his city that the Thracians were wronging the Greeks; and, having arranged the matter with the ephors as best he could, he set out on a voyage with a view to making war on the Thracians in defense of the Chersonese and Perinthus.ᵇ [3] But for some reason the ephors changed their minds after he had already left and tried to make him turn back from the Isthmus, and thereafter he no longer obeyed them but continued his voyage to the Hellespont.ᵃ [4] As a result, the Spartan government went so far as to condemn him to death for disobeying orders. Now an exile, he went to Cyrus. What words he used to persuade Cyrus have been recounted elsewhere, the outcome being that Cyrus gave him ten thou-

2.5.40–42
January 400
ZAPATAS RIVER
Xenophon's challenge silences the Persians.

2.6.1–6
OBITUARY OF KLEARCHOS
Klearchos' love of war.

2.5.38c   For Cyrus' status as "slave" to his brother the King, see n. 1.9.29a.

2.5.40a   On Orontas, see Appendix W: Brief Biographies, §25.

2.6.1a   But, as mentioned in n. 2.5.38a, the generals were executed only after some delay.

2.6.2a   The terms Lacedaemon and Sparta are nearly synonymous. Lacedaemon is a state and territorial designation. Sparta was the most important city within it; see Appendix B: Xenophon and Sparta, §§18–19. The Lacedaemonians and the Athenians were at war (known as the Peloponnesian War) from 431 to 421 and from 413 to the final Spartan victory in 404. The following locations appear on Map 1.2.1:

Lacedaemon, Peloponnese, BX; Sparta, BY.

2.6.2b   Ephors: the chief elected magistrates of Sparta and heads of the government, exercising military discipline over individual Spartan citizens; for more, see Appendix B: Xenophon and Sparta, §16. Thrace, Chersonese, Perinthus: Book 7 map.

2.6.3a   Klearchos made himself autocrat of Byzantium, which he ruled tyrannically until the Spartans expelled him from it; see Diodorus 14.12.2–7 (in Appendix S: Diodorus). Xenophon passes this over in silence. Most commentators agree that "the Isthmus" here refers to the Isthmus of Corinth: Map 1.2.1, AY. Byzantium, Hellespont: Book 1 map, AX.

sand darics.ᵃ [5] He took the darics, but he did not use them to live at his ease; on the contrary, with this money he collected an army and set about waging war against the Thracians. He defeated them in battle, and afterward he carried on harrying and pillaging them, continuing the war against them until Cyrus had need of his army. Then he left Thrace in order to wage war once more, this time alongside Cyrus. [6] So these seem to me to be the actions of a man who is a lover of war. When it is possible to live in peace without suffering shame or damage, nevertheless such a man chooses to be at war. When it is possible to live at ease, he wants to work hard, so long as it involves waging war. When it is possible to retain his money without danger, he chooses to diminish his wealth by going to war. Other people want to spend their money on boys or some other kind of pleasure; Klearchos wanted to spend his money on war.

[7] Thus he was a lover of war, but he also seemed to be someone who was warlike, in that he loved danger, he led his troops against the enemy both by day and by night, and he kept his wits about him in the worst of circumstances, as all those who were in his company on any of his campaigns used to agree. [8] He was also said to be suited to command, as far as anyone with the harsh temperament he had could be. On the one hand, he was as capable as anyone else of thinking through how the army could obtain its food supplies and of actually procuring them; on the other hand, he was also capable of impressing on those around him the lesson that Klearchos must be obeyed. [9] He achieved this by being harsh, for he was gloomy in appearance and rough in his speech, and he always used to punish troops severely and sometimes in anger, which on occasion even he regretted. [10] But he also punished on principle, for he thought that there was nothing to be gained from an undisciplined army; on the contrary, the story was that he even said that if a soldier was going to be on sentry duty, or avoid squabbles with his mates, or advance unhesitatingly against the enemy, it was necessary for him to fear his commander more than he feared his enemy. [11] So when things got really tough, the soldiers very much wanted to hear from him, and they would not accept anyone else. They said that his habitual gloom appeared at such times cheerfulness itself amid the expressions of the others, and his harshness seemed to be a strength when directed at the enemy, so that it appeared no longer harsh but a source of salvation. [12] But whenever they were out of the worst danger and it was possible to turn to others for leadership, many would desert him, for he had no charm but was always harsh and savage, so that the soldiers' attitude toward him was like that of boys toward their teacher. [13] And as a matter of fact, he never held his followers by friendship and goodwill. Those who associated with him did so because they had been put under his command by a city or out of poverty, or because they were constrained by some other necessity, and in

2.6.7–15

OBITUARY OF KLEARCHOS
His suitability for warfare.

2.6.4a   Recounted elsewhere: if Xenophon means in *Anabasis*, perhaps the reference is to an earlier draft, as there is no such account in the draft that we have, though the incident itself is narrated at 1.1.9. On darics, see Appendix O: Measurements, §§13–14.

his hands they were extremely obedient. [14] By the time they began to win victories over the enemy under his leadership, his presence had already had powerful effects in turning the soldiers he led into useful troops, for they had confidence in the face of the enemy, and their fear of punishment from him kept them in good order. [15] That, then, was the sort of commander he was, but they said that he did not at all like it when others gave him commands. He was around fifty years old when he met his end.

[16] From his earliest youth, Proxenos the Boeotian wanted to become a man capable of achieving great things, and because of this desire, he paid fees to Gorgias the Leontine.ª [17] Since he had kept company with Gorgias, he thought that he was already capable of acting as a commander and that friendly with leading people as he was, the benefit he could provide to them would be at least as much as any good they did for him; and so he embarked on this affair of Cyrus'. He thought he would thereby obtain a great name, great power, and much wealth. [18] But though he very much desired these things, he also made it quite clear that he would not wish to obtain any of them with the aid of wrongdoing; he thought that it was necessary to achieve them in company with justice and honor, and not otherwise. [19] He was capable of commanding good and honorable people,ª but by contrast he was not capable of instilling respect or fear toward himself in the ordinary soldiers; on the contrary, he stood in awe of his soldiers rather more than those under his command did of him, and it was clear he was more afraid of being disliked by his soldiers than his soldiers were of disobeying him. [20] He thought that in order to be and to appear to be fit for command, it was sufficient to praise those who acted well and to abstain from praising those who did wrong. As a result, the good and honorable people among his associates were well-disposed toward him, but the wrongdoers used to plot against him, thinking him easy to manipulate. When he died, he was about thirty.

[21] It was clear that Menon the Thessalian strongly desired money; he also desired command, in order to obtain further riches, and he desired prestige, in order to make yet more gains. He wished to be on friendly terms with the most powerful people, in order that when he did wrong, he would not have to pay the penalty for it. [22] He thought that the shortest road to achieve his desires was by way of perjury, lies, and deceit, and he regarded being straightforward and truthful as identical with being stupid. [23] It was manifest that he felt affection for no one, and if he said he was someone's friend, it became plain that he was plotting against him. He did not jeer at any of the enemy, but in conversation he was constantly jeering at all his companions. [24] He was not given to devising schemes for how to obtain the possessions of the enemy, for he thought that it was difficult to take what belonged to those who were on their guard; on the other hand,

2.6.16–20
OBITUARY OF PROXENOS
The strengths and weaknesses of his character.

2.6.21–27
OBITUARY OF MENON
His evil nature.

---

2.6.16a  Gorgias of Leontini (c. 485–c. 380) was a famous sophist. For Xenophon's and Plato's attitudes toward him, see Appendix W: Brief Biographies, §17. Leontini, Sicily: Ref. Map 1, BW.

2.6.19a  Good and honorable people: this phrase translates the Greek *kaloi kagathoi*. For more on this phrase, with special reference to this obituary of Proxenos, see the Glossary.

he thought he was the only one to realize that it was very easy to take what belonged to friends, as it lay unguarded. [25] He was afraid of all those whom he perceived to be perjurers and wrongdoers, regarding them as proof against attack, but if people respected the claims of religion and practiced truthfulness, he tried to exploit them, thinking them unmanly. [26] Just as other people glory in their reverence for the gods, truthfulness, and justice, so Menon used to glory in being able to deceive people, in fabricating lies, in mocking his friends—he always used to think that unless someone stopped at nothing to achieve his own ends, he was one of the uneducated. When he was trying to gain first place in friendship with people, he thought that maligning their existing friends was necessary in order to achieve this. [27] He worked to keep his soldiers obedient by participating in their crimes. He thought he should be honored and courted because he showed clearly that he would be both able and willing to commit more acts of injustice than anyone else. He used to reckon it a kindness on his part, whenever anyone detached himself from him, that though he had made use of them, he had not actually ruined them.

2.6.28–29
OBITUARY OF MENON
His sexual tastes and
hideous death.

[28] As regards the hidden aspects of his life, it is possible to be mistaken about him, but what everyone knows is this: while still in the flush of youth, he obtained the generalship of his foreign troops from Aristippos;[a] and likewise while still in the flush of youth, he became very close to Ariaios, despite his being a barbarian, because he knew that Ariaios liked pretty boys; and he himself, though he still lacked a beard, had a favorite called Tharypas, who was already bearded.[b] [29] When his fellow generals died because they had campaigned with Cyrus against the King, he was not put to death, though he had done the same as they had. But after the death of the others, he received his own punishment from the King and was put to death then. Unlike Klearchos and the other generals, he was not beheaded, which seems to be the quickest death there is; but he is said to have met the end befitting a villain, after being tortured alive for a year.[a]

2.6.30
OBITUARIES OF TWO
OTHER GENERALS

[30] Agias the Arcadian and Socrates the Achaean were also both put to death. Nobody used to make fun of either of them as a coward in war, nor did people speak ill of them for disloyalty to their friends. They were both around thirty-five years old.

2.6.28a Generalship of foreign troops: this appointment is not reported directly but can be inferred from the combination of 1.1.10, 1.2.1, and 1.2.6. For more on Aristippos and the Thessalian political context in which he operated, see Appendix W: Brief Biographies, §5.

2.6.28b Homosexual relationships between older and younger men are not in themselves unacceptable in Xenophon's eyes, but he regards Menon's three relationships as unacceptable. It is unacceptable for the younger man to permit the older man to penetrate him (which Xenophon hints must be the case between Menon and

Aristippos in order for Menon to have been shown such favor). It is also unacceptable for Menon, as a Greek, to encourage Ariaios, an older barbarian, to have a homosexual relationship with him. Finally, it is unacceptable for Menon, as a younger man than Tharypas, to be the dominant partner in their relationship, implying that he had chosen a passive partner who actually liked being penetrated.

2.6.29a It is not clear when or why Menon was put to death, as no other source mentions it. Maybe Xenophon is simply engaging in wishful thinking.

# BOOK THREE

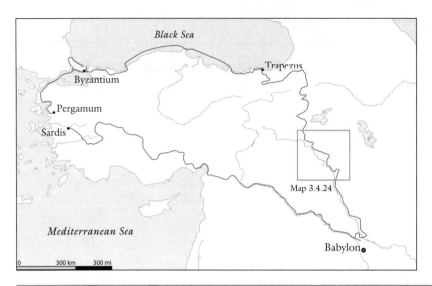

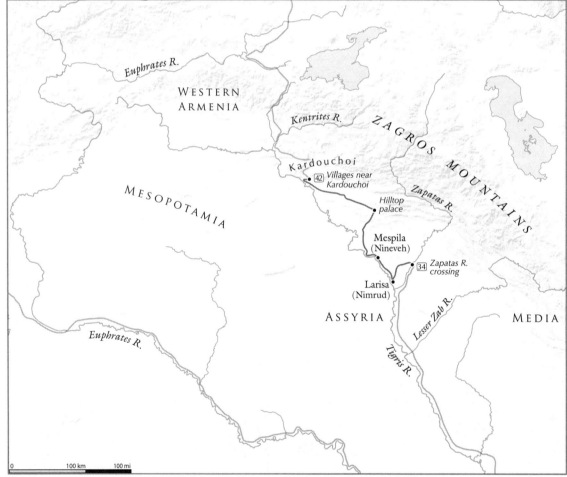

BOOK 3. *KATABASIS*: FROM THE ZAPATAS RIVER CROSSING TO KARDOUCHOI TERRITORY, *HALTING PLACES 34–42*.

[In the preceding narrative, the author has explained what the Greeks did in the course of their march into the interior with Cyrus up until the battle, and what happened when Cyrus was dead and the Greeks were returning in company with Tissaphernes in time of truce.]ᵃ

[2] Since the generals had been arrested and those of the captains and ordinary soldiers who had followed along with them had perished, the Greeks were in very great perplexity. They were at the very doors of the Great King, they reflected, and all around them were many different peoples and cities hostile to them; nobody was going to provide them with a market any longer, and they were separated from Greece by no less than a thousand miles;ᵃ they had no guide to show them the route, and there were rivers, impossible to cross, that barred the way home. Furthermore, the barbarians who had come up from the coastᵇ with Cyrus had also betrayed them, and they were alone by themselves, abandoned without a single horseman to act in support—because of which it was quite clear that if they won a victory, they would still not manage to kill a single enemy, but if they had the worst of it, none of them would escape with their lives.ᶜ [3] With these thoughts in their minds and with heavy hearts, few of them touched their meal for the evening and few kindled fires. Many did not come into the camp that

3.1.1
An ancient scribe's summary of the story so far.

3.1.2–3
January 400
MEDIA
*Zapatas River crossing (34)*
The Greeks are despondent following the arrest of the generals.

NOTE:   Unless otherwise indicated, all dates are B.C.E., and all citations are to Xenophon's *Anabasis*. The determination of the army's route and stopping places are based on the editors' calculations and estimates from data taken from *Anabasis*. Nonetheless, the route line shown on our maps and the monthly dates given in our side notes are often subject to doubt. Our best estimates should not be taken as authoritative or certain. See the Editors' Preface, §§17–20.

3.1.1a   This is the second of the paragraphs occurring throughout the work that summarize the story so far. It appears in brackets because scholars generally agree these are later scribal insertions; for more, see the Translator's Notes, §13. On Cyrus the Younger and Tissaphernes, see Appendix W: Brief Biographies of Selected Characters in *Anabasis*, §§10, 37.

3.1.2a   A thousand miles/1,600 kilometers: the Greek text says 10,000 stades; see Appendix O: Ancient Greek and Persian Units of Measurement, §5. For the soldiers' reliance on purchasing food for themselves in markets, see Appendix J: A Soldier's View of the March, §§14, 17; Appendix O, §19.

3.1.2b   The coast: the Aegean hinterland (Aegean Sea: Map 5.3.7, AY).

3.1.2c   One of the principal uses of cavalry at this period was to pursue defeated infantry. Once an infantry phalanx had been broken by the opposing phalanx, cavalry had the advantage of speed in pursuing the fleeing foot soldiers. On hoplites, see Appendix H: Infantry and Cavalry in *Anabasis*, §§2–3. On the phalanx, a body of troops drawn up across a broad front in close formation, see Appendix H, §§13–15.

night, each individual instead trying to take his rest where he happened to be. But they were unable to sleep because of their distress and longing for their native lands and their parents, wives, and children, whom they thought they would never see again. It was in this state of mind that they all tried to take their rest.

[4] In the army there was a certain Xenophon, an Athenian.[a] He did not accompany the army as a general, nor as a captain, nor as an ordinary soldier:[b] Proxenos, who was a long-standing guest-friend of his,[c] had sent for him to come from home, promising him that if he were to come, he would make him a friend of Cyrus'. Proxenos indeed said that he regarded Cyrus as more important to him than was his own native land. [5] However, when Xenophon read Proxenos' letter, he first discussed with Socrates the Athenian[a] what he would advise about the journey. Socrates was apprehensive that becoming a friend of Cyrus' would be something blameworthy in the eyes of the city of Athens because Cyrus was reputed to have assisted the Lacedaemonians wholeheartedly in their war against Athens,[b] and he counseled Xenophon to go to Delphi and take the god's advice about the journey.[c] [6] Xenophon went there and asked Apollo to which of the gods he should perform sacrifices and offer prayers in order to make the journey that he had in mind in accordance with the best and most honorable course of action, and then, his mission honorably accomplished, to reach safety again. Apollo in response told him the names of the gods to whom he should perform sacrifice. [7] After he had come back again, he recounted the oracle to Socrates, and when Socrates heard it, he strongly criticized Xenophon because he had not first asked whether it would be more fitting for him to make his way abroad or to remain at home, instead making his own judgment that he ought to go and inquiring only how he might make his way with the greatest honor. But since that was the question he had asked, he had to act, Socrates said, as the god had ordered him to. [8] Xenophon, for his part, accordingly offered sacrifices to the gods whom Apollo had ordained, and set sail; he caught up with Proxenos and Cyrus in Sardis[a] when they were about to depart along the road to the interior, and was introduced to

---

3.1.4a  In this famous passage, Xenophon introduces himself as if we have not heard of him before, although he has been mentioned several times already (at 1.8.15, 2.4.15, 2.5.37, 2.5.41). Perhaps this is just a way of underlining that he here becomes the most important figure in the narrative, but it is not clear that this explanation is right. Athens: Map 1.2.1, AY.

3.1.4b  In his Introduction (§8.13), Shane Brennan argues that this means Xenophon did not join Cyrus for a military purpose but out of interest in the prince's virtue. David Thomas on the other hand interprets this passage as a declaration that Xenophon was not part of the normal military structure and was not paid a salary, instead hoping to participate in the distribution of booty and other fruits of victory.

3.1.4c  Guest-friend: someone with whom there is a bond of ritualized friendship of a type that was common between prominent men of different cities; for more, see the Glossary. On Proxenos, see Appendix W: Brief Biographies, §29.

3.1.5a  For Socrates and Xenophon's relationship with him, see Appendix A: Xenophon and Socrates, and the Introduction, §2.9–12.

3.1.5b  Xenophon was subsequently exiled by the Athenians (5.3.7), so he may mean us to infer that Socrates was right. But for possible complications, see the Introduction, §3.2. Lacedaemon, Sparta, Peloponnese: Map 1.2.1, BY.

3.1.5c  For Apollo's oracle at Delphi, see briefly Appendix G: Divinity and Divining, §6. Delphi: Map 1.2.1, AY.

3.1.8a  Sardis: Book 1 map and locator.

Cyrus. [9] Proxenos was eager for him to stay with them, and Cyrus joined fully in his efforts. Cyrus said that as soon as the campaign was over, he would immediately let him go home. The expedition was said to be against Pisidia.[a] [10] Thus Xenophon, in truth, served in the army as the consequence of deceit, but not on the part of Proxenos (for he did not know the attack was being made against the King, nor did any other of the Greeks except Klearchos); though by the time that they reached Cilicia, it seemed clear to everyone that the expedition was against the King.[a] Unwilling though they were, and fearful of the journey, the majority still followed along from a sense of shame toward Cyrus and toward each other; and among these was Xenophon.

[11] At this time of perplexity, Xenophon was distressed just like the others and was unable to sleep; but when by luck he managed a little bit of sleep, he had a dream. It seemed to him that there was a clap of thunder and a lightning stroke fell on his ancestral home, and as a result, the whole house was ablaze with light. [12] Greatly afraid, he woke up immediately. He judged the dream a good one in one way, because in the midst of troubles and dangers, he had seemed to see a great light from Zeus. But looking at it from another point of view, he was also fearful, because the dream seemed to him to come from Zeus the King and the fire seemed to be blazing all around. This made him afraid that he might not get out of the land of the King but be penned in on all sides by various difficulties. [13] Now, what such a dream really means can be seen from what happened after it, which was as follows: First of all, the moment he woke up, the thought struck him, "Why am I lying down? The night is far advanced, and it is likely that along with the day will come the enemy. If we fall into the hands of the King, what is to stop us from having to behold all the most grievous sights imaginable, from suffering all the most terrible torments, and from dying in the course of humiliating maltreatment? [14] Nobody is making preparations or paying attention to how we may defend ourselves, but instead we are lying around as if it were possible to live in peace and quiet. Take me, for example: From what city am I expecting the general to come to take action here? What age am I waiting to reach?[a] For I shall not grow any older if I hand myself over to the enemy today!" [15] With this he stood up and called together, first of all, those who had acted as captains for Proxenos.

When they assembled, Xenophon spoke: "Brave captains: Speaking for myself, I am unable to sleep, and the same is true of you, I imagine; nor can

3.1.11–14
January 400
ZAPATAS RIVER
Xenophon sees his ancestral home in a dream.

3.1.15–18
ZAPATAS RIVER
Xenophon urges Proxenos' captains to remain optimistic.

3.1.9a   Pisidia: Map 1.2.13, AX.
3.1.10a   Contrary to Xenophon's account, Diodorus Siculus 14.19.9 (in Appendix S: Selections from Diodorus) says Cyrus disclosed the truth to the commanders generally, not just to Klearchos. Some have thought Xenophon rather naïve here; it would seem that he was relying on the assurances of Proxenos. On Klearchos, see Appendix W: Brief Biographies, §18. Cilicia: Map 1.4.1, AX.
3.1.14a   From this passage most scholars infer that Xenophon was just under thirty at the time;

being thirty or older was an important qualification for many civic responsibilities in Athens, probably including the generalship (although the direct evidence for that office is not very good). However, a few scholars take Xenophon's *Symposion* 1.1 to be historically accurate when it asserts that he was present at the events narrated in the dialogue, which purports to describe a drinking party in 422; they then infer that he was around forty when he joined Cyrus.

I continue lying down when I see the situation we are in. [16] It is clear that the enemy did not reveal their hostile intent until they thought their own position was fully prepared, but in response to this, none of us is taking any thought at all as to how we shall carry on the struggle as honorably as possible. [17] And yet if we give in and come into the hands of the King, what treatment do we think we shall receive? This is someone who, even when it was his own brother, born of the same mother, and already dead, cut off his head and his hand and impaled them;[a] while as for us, in whose case there is no protector at hand and who campaigned against Artaxerxes[b] with the aim of making him a slave instead of a king and of killing him if we could, what would you think we shall suffer? [18] Under the circumstances, wouldn't he go to any length, such as torturing us in the most extreme way, to instill in all mankind a fear of ever campaigning against him? Rather than that, we have to do everything we can to avoid coming into his hands.

[19] "In fact, as long as there was a truce, I myself never stopped lamenting our position and looking upon the King and those with him as supremely fortunate. I fully saw how extensive and how prosperous is the land they control, how abundant are their food supplies, how many retainers they have, how many livestock, how much gold, how much clothing. [20] And on the other hand, whenever I brought to mind the circumstances of our soldiers, I was all too well aware that we have no share in any of these good things unless we purchase it—and I knew that few of us still have what it would cost us—and furthermore, that our oaths now prevented us from acquiring food supplies in any other way than buying them; so, analyzing the situation like this, I was sometimes more afraid of the truce than I am now of open war. [21] However, since these people have broken the truce, it seems to me that their arrogant willfulness and our perplexity have both come to an end. These good things now lie between us like prizes in a competition about who prove to be the better men, we or they, a competition in which the gods are the umpires; and the gods, it seems likely, will be on our side. [22] For these people have sworn false oaths by them, whereas, though we could see all this plentiful bounty, we kept rigidly clear of it because of our own oaths to the gods. And so it seems to me that we can go into the contest with far greater confidence than these people can. [23] What's more, our bodies are better able than theirs to bear cold and heat and hard work, and, with the gods on our side, our spirits are better; and their men are more exposed to wounds and death

3.1.17a  Xenophon told us at 1.10.1 that Artaxerxes had Cyrus' head and hand cut off. Plutarch (*Life of Artaxerxes* 13.2; in Appendix T: Selections from Plutarch's *Life of Artaxerxes*) in part exculpates this (as he says it was a Persian custom) but in part heightens it, claiming that Artaxerxes personally seized the head by the hair and displayed it to his troops. (Plutarch presumably derived these details from Ctesias.) Neither passage refers to impaling.

3.1.17b  No protector at hand: Xenophon is thinking in particular of Queen Parysatis, mother of both Artaxerxes and Cyrus and chief advocate of Cyrus, her younger son. For the subsequent conduct of Parysatis, and on Artaxerxes, see Appendix W: Brief Biographies, §§26, 6.

than we are, if the gods continue to give us victory as they did before.[a]

[24] "But as perhaps others are also having the same thoughts, in heaven's name let us not wait for other people to approach us and summon us to perform noble deeds—let us ourselves take the lead in rousing the others to reveal their worth. Show yourselves to be the best of the captains, and deserve more to be generals than the generals themselves. [25] As for me, if you want to make the first move toward these goals, I am willing to follow you; but if you assign me the post of leader, I do not make the age I am an excuse for refusing it but think I am actually at the best time of life for warding off the evils that press on me."

[26] That was his speech, and after the captains heard it, they all urged him to take the lead, except for a certain Apollonides, who spoke in the Boeotian dialect.[a] This fellow said it was nonsense for anyone to say he could achieve safety other than by persuading the King, if that were possible, and at once he started to recount the difficulties. [27] However, Xenophon cut him short and said, "You most extraordinary person, you do not understand what you see or remember what you hear. Yet you too, just like these others, were right there when the King, after Cyrus' death, puffing himself up on that account, sent an order to us to hand over our weapons. [28] And when we did not hand them over but, fully prepared for battle, went and took up our quarters next to him, what did he not do—sending ambassadors and asking for truces and providing food supplies—until he obtained a truce? [29] But when the generals and captains trusted in the truce and went unarmed to talks with them, just as you are now telling us to do, isn't their situation now that—beaten, tormented, and subjected to outrages—they are not even allowed to die, though I should think they very much long for death in their misery? Knowing all this, how can you say that those who tell you to defend yourself are talking nonsense while you tell us to go back again and try persuasion? [30] Men, I think we should not admit this fellow into our ranks but should deprive him of his captaincy, pile baggage on his back, and use him in that capacity. He disgraces his native country and all Greece because of the sort of person he is, despite being a Greek."

[31] Agasias of Stymphalos took it up from there and said, "But the fellow has nothing to do with Boeotia, nor with Greece at all, for I have noticed that he has both ears pierced like a Lydian."[a] And indeed he had. [32] So they drove him away.

The rest of them did the rounds of the various units: wherever a general had survived, they would invite him to join them, and from units where the general was missing, they invited the deputy general; again, wherever a captain had survived, they invited the captain. [33] When they had all assem-

**3.1.26–31**
January 400
ZAPATAS RIVER
Apollonides, who advocates appeasement of the King, is stripped of his captaincy and driven away.

**3.1.32–33**
January 400
ZAPATAS RIVER
All the remaining senior officers assemble.

3.1.23a Xenophon implies here that Persian infantry generally had less protective body armor than Greek hoplites. Insofar as the Persian infantry was made up in large part of archers and slingers, this is no doubt true. But there were also Persian heavy infantrymen (1.8.9). For the mix of types

of infantry in the Persian forces, see Appendix D: The Persian Army, §12.
3.1.26a Boeotia: Map 1.2.1, AY.
3.1.31a The Greek stereotype of Lydians was that they were soft (see esp. Herodotus 1.155.4). Stymphalos: Map 1.2.1, AY. Lydia: Map 1.2.10, AX.

bled, they took their places in front of the weapon stacks, and the generals and captains who had assembled amounted to about a hundred in all. It was now almost the middle of the night.

[34] At this juncture Hieronymos of Elis, the oldest of Proxenos' captains, was the first to speak, as follows: "Generals and captains, when we saw the present circumstances, we thought we should have a meeting and summon you to it as well, in order to discuss whether there was any good we could do. Now, Xenophon," he said, "over to you. Speak here just as you did to us."

[35] After this introduction Xenophon said, "Now, we all, of course, know that the King and Tissaphernes seized those of us whom they could, and it is clear that they are plotting against the rest of us in order to destroy us if they can. We on our side, in my opinion, must do everything conceivable to avoid falling into the hands of the barbarians; on the contrary, we must work to have them in our power, if we can ever achieve it. [36] In the light of this, you should be well aware that you who have now gathered together in such numbers have a very great opportunity. The soldiers here all have their gaze fixed on you, and if they see you being fainthearted, they will all be cowardly; but if you show yourselves to be making preparations against the enemy and you summon the others to join you, there's no doubt about it: they will follow you and try to imitate you. [37] Perhaps indeed it is also only fair for you to excel them to some extent. You are generals, you are group commanders and captains; and when there was peace, you claimed a larger share of riches and honors than they did. Consequently, now, when there is war, it is necessary to expect you to be better than the crowd, to devise plans before they do, and to be foremost in hard work if any is needed anywhere.

[38] "Right now, first and foremost, I think that you would be doing a great service to the army if you were to take steps as quickly as possible to replace the generals and captains who have perished. For without leaders nothing either honorable or beneficial could be accomplished anywhere at all, to put it bluntly, and in warfare this is particularly true. Good order, it seems, saves people, while lack of order has already destroyed many. [39] When you have appointed as many officers as necessary, I think you would be acting very opportunely if you then assembled the rest of the soldiers and put some spirit into them. [40] For perhaps you too notice, as things stand, how listlessly they came into camp, how listlessly they went on guard; while they are in this frame of mind, I do not know what use anyone could make of them, whether the need to do so arose by night or by day. [41] But if anyone turns the soldiers' minds from merely brooding on what they are going to suffer, and instead gets them to concentrate on what they are going to do, they will be much more stouthearted. [42] You know, of course, that it is neither numbers nor brute force that brings victories in war; instead, whichever army, backed by the gods, advances against the enemy in the more vigorous spirit finds that their opponents do not generally wait to receive

3.1.34a For Hieronymos' precise place of origin and Xenophon's subtle presentation of    him, see n. 7.4.18a. Elis: Map 1.2.1, AX.

3.1.34
January 400
ZAPATAS RIVER
Hieronymos calls on Xenophon to speak.

3.1.35–44
January 400
ZAPATAS RIVER
Xenophon addresses the officers.

their charge. [43] I myself, men, have taken to heart that in war those who cast about by every means they can to remain alive are precisely those who generally meet a bad and shameful end. By contrast, I see that those who have learned that death is common to all and unavoidable for human beings, and who compete for the prize of an honorable death, are the ones who somehow or other reach old age and enjoy a happier existence as long as they live. [44] Having now learned these lessons, and since we are at such a critical juncture, we too must both be good men ourselves and also summon the others to join us." And with this he broke off his speech.

[45] After him Cheirisophos[a] spoke: "Well, Xenophon, previously I knew you only to this extent, that I used to hear of you as being an Athenian. But now I also praise you for your speech and actions, and I would wish that the majority were like you; that would be good for the army as a whole. [46] And now, men," he said, "let us not delay but, immediately on leaving the meeting, choose new officers, those who need to; and when you have made your choice, come to the center of the camp and bring those you have chosen; then we will assemble the other soldiers there. Tolmides the herald should be in attendance on us." [47] No sooner had he said this than he stood up, so that there should be no delay and they would carry out what was necessary. As a consequence leaders were chosen as follows: instead of Klearchos, Timasion of Dardanos; instead of Socrates, Xanthikles of Achaea; instead of Agias, Kleanor of Arcadia; instead of Menon, Philesios of Achaea; instead of Proxenos, Xenophon of Athens.[a]

[1] When they had been chosen, day was almost beginning to break; the leaders went to the center of the camp and decided to post advance guards and call the soldiers together. When the other soldiers had also assembled, first of all Cheirisophos the Lacedaemonian stood up and spoke as follows:

[2] "Brave soldiers, the current situation is difficult, now that we have lost such fine men as generals and captains and soldiers; and in addition to that, Ariaios' people, who were previously allies, have now betrayed us.[a] [3] All the same, it's necessary to prove ourselves good men in the present circumstances: not to give way but instead to try to save ourselves by a noble victory if we can; and if we cannot, at least to die nobly, never letting ourselves fall alive into the hands of the enemy. For I think that we would then suffer what I pray that the gods may inflict on those we hate."

[4] Directly after him, Kleanor the Orchomenian[a] stood up and spoke as follows: "Men, just look at the perjury and impiety of the King, and at the bad faith of Tissaphernes, who said that he was a neighbor of Greece[b] and would put a high value on saving us. He personally swore an oath to this effect, he personally gave us the pledge of his right hand—and he personally

---

3.1.45–47
January 400
ZAPATAS RIVER
Cheirisophos sums up. Five new generals are chosen.

3.2.1–3
January 400
ZAPATAS RIVER
The whole army assembles. Cheirisophos speaks first.

3.2.4–6
January 400
ZAPATAS RIVER
Kleanor speaks indignantly of Persian bad faith.

---

3.1.45a  On Cheirisophos, see Appendix W: Brief
        Biographies, §7.
3.1.47a  This Socrates is Socrates of Achaea, not
        the philosopher. On Kleanor and Menon,
        see Appendix W, §§19, 23. Dardanos:
        Map 5.3.7, AY. Achaea, Arcadia: Map

1.2.1, AX.
3.2.2a  On Ariaios and his subsequent relations
        with Artaxerxes, see Appendix W, §4.
3.2.4a  Orchomenos: Map 1.2.1, AX
3.2.4b  Tissaphernes said he was a neighbor of
        Greece at 2.3.18.

arrested the generals, having completely deceived them. He had no shame before Zeus the protector of guest-friendship, but even though he had eaten from the same table as Klearchos in particular, through these very actions he deceived the men and brought them to ruin. [5] And Ariaios, whom we wanted to set up as King and with whom we exchanged pledges not to betray each other, he too neither fears the gods nor feels shame for the memory of Cyrus; but though he was especially honored by him when Cyrus was alive, he now deserts to Cyrus' greatest enemies and tries to do harm to us, Cyrus' friends. [6] Well, may the gods take vengeance on these people! We, seeing all this, must never let ourselves be deceived again by them but, fighting as best we can, must suffer whatever fate the gods ordain."

[7] After him Xenophon stood up. He had arrayed himself for war as splendidly as he could, as he thought that if the gods granted success, the most splendid adornment was suitable for victory, but if he had to die, then, as he had thought himself worthy to wear the finest armor in life, he should meet his end wearing it. This was how he began his speech:[a] [8] "Kleanor speaks of the perjury and faithlessness of the barbarians, and these are well-known to you too, I think. If, then, we want to revert to being on friendly terms with them, we shall necessarily be in great despondency, since we see what has happened to the generals who, out of trust, put themselves into their hands. But if we concentrate on using our weapons to exact justice from them for what they did and on carrying on total war against them thereafter, with the aid of the gods we have many excellent grounds to hope for a safe return."

[9] As he was saying this, someone sneezed, and when the soldiers heard it, with a single impulse they all knelt and worshipped the god. Xenophon then went on: "It seems to me, men, that since an omen from Zeus the Savior manifested itself while we were speaking about our safe return,[a] we should vow to this god to perform a sacrifice for our safe delivery whenever we first arrive in friendly territory; and we should make a further vow to perform sacrifices to the other gods as well, to the best of our ability. Whoever thinks this a good idea, raise your hand." Every one of them raised their hands. As a result, they made the vows and sang a war hymn. When they had properly attended to the business of the gods, Xenophon began to speak again, as follows: [10] "What I was saying was that we had many excellent grounds to hope for a safe return. First, we are upholding our oaths to the gods, while the enemy have perjured themselves and broken the truce contrary to their oaths. In this situation, it is likely that the gods are opponents of the enemy and allies of ours, and they have the ability quickly to make the strong weak and to save the weak even in terrible cir-

3.2.7–13
January 400
ZAPATAS RIVER
Xenophon gives arguments for success, referring to the likely aid of the gods and the history of their ancestors.

3.2.7a  This speech is discussed in Appendix E: Panhellenism, §7, where Vivienne Gray counsels against taking its propaganda for Greek settlement in Mesopotamia (3.2.22–26) too seriously. Mesopotamia: Book 3 map.
3.2.9a  Although there are not many instances in Greek literature where sneezing is taken to be an omen (another, also in relation to returning to Greece from far away, is a sneeze by Odysseus' son, Telemachos, in Homer, *Odyssey* 17.541, when his mother, Penelope, refers to the possible return of Odysseus), it is evident from this passage that Greeks generally regarded it as being, under suitable circumstances, divinely sent. Presumably this was because sneezing is involuntary and can thus appear to come from an external force.

cumstances, whenever they want and without any effort. [11] Next, I shall remind you of the dangers our ancestors faced, so that you may know that it is appropriate for you to act as good men do and also that, with the aid of the gods, the good are saved even from very terrible troubles. For when the Persians and their followers came in overwhelming force on their expedition to annihilate Athens, the Athenians dared to withstand them and were victorious over them.ᵃ [12] They had made a vow to Artemis that however many of the enemy they slaughtered, they would sacrifice as many goats to the goddess; since they were unable to find sufficient goats, they decided to perform the sacrifice with five hundred goats each year, and they still carry out this sacrifice even now.ᵃ [13] Next, when Xerxes subsequently gathered together that innumerable army and attacked Greece, our ancestors were victorious over the ancestors of these people both on land and at sea.ᵃ Seeing the trophiesᵇ they put up provides evidence of this, but the greatest proof is the freedom of the cities in which you were born and brought up, for you kneel in worship to no human being as master but to the gods alone.ᶜ [14] Such are your ancestors.

"I do not say this in the least to imply that you are disgracing those ancestors; on the contrary, not many days since, you were arrayed in ranks against these people here, the descendants of those Persians of old, and with the aid of the gods, you were victorious over them, though they were many times your number. [15] On that occasion, when the issue was the kingship of Cyrus, you acted as good men do; and now, when the contest is about your own preservation, it is surely appropriate for you to be both better still and more eager. [16] And furthermore you should now also be more confident in relation to the enemy. For then, with no prior experience of them and despite seeing their uncountable numbers, you still dared to advance on them with the high spirit of your fathers; so now, when you have already made trial of them and found that they are unwilling to stand firm against you although they are many times your number, why should you be afraid of them any longer?

[17] "Nor indeed should you imagine that you are in a worse position because the Persians who were previously drawn up alongside us have now

3.2.14–21
January 400
ZAPATAS RIVER
Xenophon gives further arguments for why they should succeed.

3.2.11a  Xenophon is referring to the battle of Marathon, in 490, when the Athenians, together with the Plataeans, inflicted a severe defeat on an invading Persian army on the beach of Marathon (Marathon, Plataea: Map 1.2.1, AY). Persian Empire: Ref. Map 9.

3.2.12a  It is impossible that so many Persians were slain that the Athenians still owed Artemis any goats ninety years later. But the Athenians preferred to continue with the sacrifices even after they had discharged their vow, in order to advertise their heroism and piety. Herodotus (6.117.1) gives a figure of 6,400 for the Persian dead; on this basis, the vow would have been discharged as early as 478.

3.2.13a  On land, in 479 at the battle of Plataea; at sea, in 480 at the battle of Salamis (Map 1.2.1, AY). On Xerxes, see Appendix W: Brief Biographies, §38.

3.2.13b  Trophies: victorious Greeks put up a trophy—a captured helmet, shield, and other pieces of armor nailed to a tree or post—on the battlefield or, in the case of naval victories, on a nearby coast to establish the fact of their control of the area and to commemorate it thereafter. Where the battle was against other Greeks, the defeated enemy would not remove the trophy even if they regained control of the area.

3.2.13c  The Greek word *proskyneō*, translated here (and similarly at 3.2.9) as "kneel in worship," covers a range of obeisances the Persians made to their superiors at various social distances (see Appendix C: The Persian Empire, §3, esp. n. C.3e). The associated noun is *proskynēsis*. Greeks found this offensive, as they offered *proskynēsis* only to the statues of the gods. See Figure 3.2.13 for an example of *proskynēsis*.

FIGURE 3.2.13. A PERSIAN NOBLE BLOWS A KISS TO THE GREAT KING IN THE HONORIFIC GESTURE THE GREEKS CALLED *PROSKYNĒSIS*, AS DEPICTED IN A BAS RELIEF FROM PERSEPOLIS.

deserted. They are still worse than those who were overcome by you—at any rate, when they abandoned us, the troops they were avoiding were the troops we overcame. Where people are willing to take the lead in flight, it is far better to see them drawn up alongside the enemy than in our own ranks. [18] And if any of you are dispirited because we have no cavalry and among the enemy there are many, take this to heart: ten thousand cavalry are just the same thing as ten thousand human beings, as nobody ever dies in battle from being bitten or kicked by a horse; it is men who do whatever is done in battles. [19] Well, then, certainly compared to horsemen, we are on a much safer platform, for they are perched up on the horses, afraid not only of us but also of falling off; whereas we, firmly placed on the ground, will strike much more powerfully if anyone comes against us and will be much more likely to land our blow on target. In one point alone cavalry have the advantage: to flee is safer for them than for us.

[20] "But despite being in good heart as regards the fighting, you may be weighed down by the thought that Tissaphernes[a] will no longer be acting as

3.2.20a  On Tissaphernes, see Appendix W: Brief
         Biographies, §37.

your guide and the King will not be providing us with a market. If you are—and I say if—consider whether it is such a good thing to have Tissaphernes as a guide, someone who is clearly plotting against us. Isn't it better to use men we have captured, who guide us under our orders and who will know that if they make some mistake in what concerns us, they will find that to be a mistake for their own lives and limbs? [21] Consider further whether it is such a good thing to buy food supplies from the market, where these people give us small measures of food for large amounts of money, which we no longer have. Isn't it better for us just to take our food supplies, if we gain the upper hand, using however large a measure each one of us wants?

[22] "And if you understand that you are better off in these respects, but you think that the rivers are an insuperable obstacle and strongly suppose that you were deceived when you crossed over,[a] consider whether in reality this is not the stupidest thing the barbarians have done. On the one hand, even if rivers may be impossible to cross far from their sources, when one approaches closer to the sources, they all become fordable without even getting one's knees wet. [23] Then, on the other hand, even if the rivers bar our way through and no guide appears to help us, there is still no need for us to lose heart. For we know that the Mysians,[a] who we would not say are better than we are, inhabit many great and prosperous cities in the land of the King against the King's will. We know the same of the Pisidians, and we ourselves have seen how the Lycaonians have taken over the strong points in the plains and harvest the King's land.[b] [24] And speaking for myself, I would say that we should not make it clear that we have set out for home but instead should make preparations as if we were going to live somewhere around here. For I am sure that the King would provide the Mysians with many guides and many pledges of a genuine safe conduct abroad, and would go so far as to make a road for them if they wanted to depart riding in four-horse chariots! And I am sure he would be three times as glad to do this for us if he saw that we were preparing to stay. [25] But my real fear is that once we learn to live in idleness and spend our time in the midst of abundance, consorting with the big and beautiful Median and Persian women and girls, then, like the lotus-eaters, we shall forget the homeward road.[a] [26] So it seems to me fair and reasonable to try first to reach Greece and our people at home and show the Greeks that it is by their own choice that they are poor. For they could see citizens now living in hardship in Greece instead become rich once they have brought themselves here. But however that may be, what's clear, men, is that all these good things belong to those who are the stronger.

3.2.22–26
January 400
ZAPATAS RIVER
Xenophon argues that they can make the King glad to conduct them safely back to Greece.

FIGURE 3.2.25. ENGRAVED GEMSTONE FROM XENOPHON'S TIME DEPICTING A "BIG AND BEAUTIFUL" PERSIAN WOMAN.

3.2.22a  "Deceived when you crossed over": this prompts us to reconsider the mysterious incidents leading up to the crossing of the Tigris River at 2.4.24; see Map 2.3.14, Tigris River crossing at Opis (Xenophon's Sittake), *Halting place 31*.
3.2.23a  Mysia: Map 1.2.10, AX.
3.2.23b  For these peoples' independence from Persian control, see Appendix C: The Persian Empire, §17. Pisidia, Lycaonia: Map

1.2.13, AX.
3.2.25a  For a gemstone depicting a "big and beautiful" Persian woman, see Figure 3.2.25. The lotus-eaters appear in Homer's *Odyssey* 9.82–104. Those of Odysseus' men who join them in eating the lotus forget their homes and have to be dragged back aboard ship to continue their return voyage.

[27] "And now it's necessary to say how we might make our way on from here most securely and how we might fight most effectively, if we have to fight. In the first place, then," he said, "I think that we should burn the wagons we have so that it is not the draft animals that determine our strat- egy but instead we can make our way by whatever route best suits the army. Then I think we should burn the tents at the same time, for again with them comes the bother of carrying them, and they contribute nothing either to the fighting or to obtaining food supplies. [28] Going still further, let's also leave behind the superfluous equipment in the rest of the baggage, exclud- ing what we have for warfare or for food or drink, in order that as many as possible of us may be under arms, and as few as possible baggage carriers. For as you know, when people are conquered, everything they had becomes the property of others, but if we gain the upper hand, we should think of the enemy as having acted as our baggage carriers.

[29] "It remains for me to make what I think is actually the most impor- tant point of all. You are aware that our enemies did not dare to start making war on us until they had seized hold of the generals, thinking that while we had officers and were obedient to them, we were sufficiently strong to prevail in the war, but that when they had captured our officers, we would perish in anarchy and indiscipline. [30] It is therefore necessary for the officers now to become much more careful than their predecessors, and for the rank and file now to be much more orderly and obedient to their officers than they were before. [31] But in case someone is disobedient in future, you must vote here and now that whoever among you happens to be there at the time is to join the officer in punishing him; thus the enemy will find themselves very much mistaken. For then they will this very day see the one Klearchos[a] replaced by ten thousand who will not put up with any misbehavior.

[32] "But it is now time to bring my speech to a close and put it into practice, for perhaps the enemy will be near us very soon. So whoever thinks that my proposals are right should ratify them as soon as possible in order for them to be carried into effect. And if there is something better than this, even the rank-and-file soldier should not be afraid to teach us what it is, since we all want the whole army's safety."

[33] After this Cheirisophos said, "Well, if there is a need for anything beyond what Xenophon says, it will be possible to act on it presently. It seems best to me to vote to approve what has now been said as soon as pos- sible. So whoever thinks the same, raise your hand." Every one of them raised his hand.

[34] Xenophon stood up again and said, "Men, listen to what else I think is needed. It is clear that we have to make our way to where we shall have food supplies, and I hear that there are fine villages not much more than two miles[a] from here. [35] But I would not be surprised if the enemy—just

3.2.31a   On Klearchos, see Appendix W: Brief
          Biographies, §20.
3.2.34a   Not much more than 2 miles/3 kilome-

ters: the Greek text says not more than
20 stades; see Appendix O: Measurements, §5.

like cowardly dogs that pursue and, if they can, bite passersby but that take to flight when pursued—follow closely after us. [36] Perhaps, then, it will be safer for us to make our way once we have formed the armed troops into a hollow rectangle, so that the baggage carriers and the throng of noncombatants may be in a safer position.ᵃ So if we settle now who should lead the rectangle and keep the vanguard in order, who should be in charge of the flanks on either side, and who should guard the rear, we won't have to enter into discussions whenever the enemy approach but can immediately make use of the people who have been assigned these positions. [37] Now, if anyone sees any better plan, let's do it differently; but if not, Cheirisophos could take the lead, especially since he is a Lacedaemonian, and each of the flanks could be looked after by two of the oldest generals; while Timasion and I, as the youngest, could guard the rear, at any rate for now.ᵃ [38] Looking to the future, though we are trying out this formation, we shall keep what seems best under permanent review. If anyone sees another, better plan, let him speak up." Nobody spoke in opposition, so he then said, "Whoever agrees with this, raise your hand." It was so agreed.

[39] "So now, then," he said, "we have to go and do what has been agreed. Whoever among you wants to see his folks at home, remember to be a good man, for in no other way is it possible to achieve this; whoever wants to stay alive, let him strive to be victorious, for slaying others is the lot of the victors and being killed is the lot of the defeated; and if anyone wants riches, let him strive to prevail, for it belongs to the victors both to preserve their own possessions and to obtain those of the defeated."

[1] After these speeches they got up, went away, and began to set the wagons and tents on fire. The surplus equipment anyone needed was shared out among them, and the rest they threw onto the fire. When they had done this, they went on to prepare their main meal; and while they were in the middle of their preparations, Mithradatesᵃ came with about thirty cavalry, called the generals within earshot, and said, [2] "Men of Greece, I too was faithful to Cyrus, as you know, and am now well-disposed toward you. And here I am, though in great fear as long as I stay. So if I were to see you resolving on some safe course of action, I would join you, together with all my retainers. Tell me what you have in mind, as someone who is a friend and well-disposed and who would like to make the journey with you."

3.3.1–5
January 400
ZAPATAS RIVER
Mithradates pretends to be the Greeks' friend and is rebuffed.

3.2.36a "Hollow rectangle": the armed troops formed up to make four sides, leaving a space in the middle for the camp followers and baggage animals (hence the formation was "hollow"). In English "hollow square" is the more familiar military term, but an army moving forward, as the Greeks are doing here, is more likely to use an oblong formation. This passage is discussed in Appendix K: The Noncombatant Contingent of the Army, §3.

3.2.37a Cheirisophos is to take the lead because at this time Lacedaemon was the most powerful state in Greece and had the best-trained and most successful army. The youngest generals go to the rear because the rearguard is likely to require the most physical activity in chasing the enemy off and then retreating to rejoin the main body of troops. Diodorus 14.27.1 (see Appendix S: Selections from Diodorus) claims that Cheirisophos was chosen as supreme commander at this point (see Appendix M: Other Ancient Sources on the Ten Thousand, §§3, 6), but according to Xenophon, it was only at 6.1.32.

3.3.1a Mithradates was previously mentioned at 2.5.35 as one of Cyrus' most faithful friends.

[3] The generals discussed this and decided to give this answer, which was delivered by Cheirisophos: "What we think right, if a certain person allows us to go home, is to make our way through the country doing the least damage possible; but if anyone should block us from our route, we will fight it out with that person, using the utmost strength we can." [4] Mithradates' reaction was to try to read them a lesson on how there would be no way of reaching safety without the King's cooperation. Then, of course, it was clear to the generals that he had been sent with a secret purpose, in addition to which one of Tissaphernes' kinsmen had accompanied him to ensure his loyalty. [5] As a result, the generals decided that it was better to make a decree that the war was to be carried on without contact between the two sides as long as they were in the enemy's country, for the other side kept coming up and trying to corrupt the troops, and they did corrupt one captain, Nikarchos of Arcadia,[a] who went off in the night with about twenty people.

[6] After this they had their meal, and after crossing the river Zapatas,[a] they made their way onward in formation, with the draft animals and the crowd of noncombatants in the middle of the rectangle. They had not gone far when Mithradates put in another appearance, with about two hundred cavalry and as many as four hundred archers and stone slingers, very nimble troops and highly mobile. [7] He advanced under guise of being a friend to the Greeks, but when his troops had come close, suddenly some of them, both cavalry and infantry, began to fire arrows and others set about slinging stones, and they managed to wound some of the Greeks. The rearguard suffered badly, but they could not retaliate at all. For the javelin throwers had too short a range with their darts to reach the stone slingers, while the Cretan archers also had a shorter range than the Persians, and besides, as they were lightly armed, they had been shut in inside the hoplite rectangle.[a] [8] As a result, Xenophon decided that pursuit was necessary, and so the hoplites and peltasts[a] who were with him in the rearguard did mount pursuits; but though they did so, they did not succeed in catching any of the enemy. [9] This was because the Greeks had no cavalry and the rearguard could not catch the enemy infantry within a short distance, since the enemy turned in flight while still a long way off; to carry on the pursuit very far from the rest of the army was impossible. [10] Even as they fled, the bar-

3.3.6–11
January 400
ZAPATAS RIVER
*Zapatas River crossing (34) –Villages (35)*
The Persians harass the Greeks as they start their march north. Xenophon makes a tactical mistake.

---

3.3.5a  Though some scholars disagree, the Nikarchos here was probably the same one who alone had escaped the original massacre, though badly wounded, and brought news of it to the army at 2.5.33. While Persian propaganda may have played a role in the defection, Nikarchos' comrades may not have intended actually to go over to the Persians but simply meant to try to get their wounded captain and themselves away from what seemed an inevitable massacre; see Hyland 2010.

3.3.6a  Some commentators express surprise that more is not made of this crossing, and frustration that we are not told how it was

made, since the river is now too deep to ford even at its lowest season near or indeed a good way upstream from its confluence with the Tigris. Zapatas (modern Greater Zab) River: Map 3.4.24, *Halting place 34.*

3.3.7a  The two halves of this sentence have been reversed in translation to clarify the relative extent of defensive armor between the archers and the javelin throwers. Crete: Map 5.3.7, locator.

3.3.8a  Peltasts: light-armed infantry; for more, see Appendix H: Infantry and Cavalry in *Anabasis*, §§4–5.

barian cavalry were at the same time inflicting casualties on the Greeks by firing arrows behind them from their horses,[a] and as far forward as the Greeks went in their pursuit, they had to come back again the same distance under fire. [11] And so in the whole day they progressed only just under three miles, and though they did reach the villages[a] in the course of the afternoon, further dejection was the natural consequence. Cheirisophos and the oldest of the generals proceeded to blame Xenophon because he had gone away from the phalanx in pursuit and put himself in danger without being able to harm the enemy to any greater extent at all.

[12] When Xenophon heard this, he freely said that the criticisms were correct and the outcome itself bore witness to them. "But," he said, "I was forced to mount pursuits, since I could see that we were suffering badly in the position we were caught in, unable to retaliate at all. [13] About the occasions when we went in pursuit," he said, "it's true what you say: we were unable to do any harm to the enemy, and each time we came back again only with the utmost difficulty. [14] So thank the gods that the enemy did not come in great strength but with only a few troops, so that not much harm was done, and also because it has become clear what we need. [15] As things stand, the enemy on their side shoot arrows and sling stones farther than the Cretans can shoot back again, or than can be reached by people throwing missiles by hand; while from our point of view, whenever we pursue them, it's not possible to carry on the pursuit over ground far from the army, and when infantrymen pursue infantrymen who have a bowshot's start, they won't catch them within a short distance, even if they are quick. [16] So in our case, if we intend to prevent these people from being able to harm us as we make our way forward, we need to find both slingers and cavalry in the shortest time possible. I hear that there are Rhodians[a] in our army, and people say that most of them know how to use a sling and that their missiles carry twice as far as the Persian sling stones. [17] The Persians reach only a short distance, because in their slings they use hand-sized stones, but the Rhodians know how to use lead pellets as well.[a] [18] If, therefore, we have a review of which of them possess slings and we give them money for their slings and provide further money to anyone who volunteers to make more slings, and if we then work out some sort of further exemption for anyone who volunteers to be assigned the role of a slinger, perhaps people will come forward who have the capability to help us. [19] I observe that there are also horses with the army, some few of them my

3.3.12–20
January 400
NEAR ZAPATAS RIVER
Xenophon suggests putting together bodies of slingers and cavalry.

---

3.3.10a  This shows that the so-called Parthian shot predates the Parthians (the dominant power in Iran and much of Mesopotamia from around 148 B.C.E. to 224 C.E.), as Christopher Tuplin notes in Appendix D: The Persian Army, §17. Parthia: Ref. Map 9, BY. Iran, Mesopotamia: Ref. Map 8, BZ, CY.

3.3.11a  Just under 3 miles/5 kilometers: the Greek text says 25 stades; see Appendix O:

Measurements, §5. Villages: Map 3.4.24, *Halting place 35*.

3.3.16a  Rhodes: Map 1.2.10, BX.

3.3.17a  Lead pellets bearing Tissaphernes' name have survived from antiquity, so evidently at some stage the Persians did learn how to use them—perhaps picking up the technique from the Greeks on this occasion.

own, others left behind from those Klearchos had,[a] and many others that have been captured and are being used to carry baggage. So if we were to pick all these out, replace them with proper pack animals, and equip the horses to carry cavalrymen, perhaps they will give those running away some grief."

[20] This too seemed a good idea, and that same night two hundred slingers were identified, while fifty horses and horsemen passed inspection the following day. Leather jerkins[a] and breastplates were provided for these, and a cavalry commander was appointed, Lykios son of Polystratos, an Athenian.[b]

[1] They remained where they were for that day but made their way onward on the next, having risen earlier than usual, as it was necessary to cross a gully, where they feared that the enemy might fall on them as they went across. [2] When they had crossed it, Mithradates again put in an appearance, with a thousand horsemen and as many as four thousand archers and slingers. He had asked Tissaphernes for this many troops and had received them on the basis of promises that if he was assigned them, he would deliver the Greeks up to Tissaphernes. Though in the previous attack he had had only a few soldiers, he had suffered no casualties and was under the impression that he had inflicted a lot, so he despised the Greeks. [3] When the Greeks had crossed over the gully and were as much as a mile[a] farther on, Mithradates also proceeded to cross it with his force. Instructions for pursuit had been given to those of the peltasts and hoplites whose task it was, and the cavalry were told to set about the pursuit boldly, because a sufficient force was going to be following up. [4] When Mithradates had caught up and his sling stones and arrows were already reaching the Greek troops, the signal was given to the Greeks by trumpet, and immediately those to whom the orders had been given began their run all together, and the cavalry started on their gallop. The enemy did not wait to receive them but turned in flight back toward the gully. [5] Many of the infantry on the barbarian side were killed in this pursuit, and eighteen of the cavalry were taken alive in the gully. Without orders from their officers, the Greeks mutilated the dead, so that the sight should instill the greatest fear in the enemy.

[6] After this experience the enemy left, while the Greeks made their way in security for the rest of the day and came to the river Tigris.[a] [7] Here was a great deserted city: its name was Larisa, and in olden times Medes

---

3.3.19a  That Xenophon had several horses of his own with him shows his wealth and aristocratic status. By contrast, the horses Klearchos had are likely to have belonged to a cavalry detachment rather than to have been his own, as horse riding was not part of Spartan aristocratic culture (though chariot racing was for those who were very rich).

3.3.20a  For examples of non-metal armor, see Figure 4.7.15.

3.3.20b  Polystratos: quite possibly the Polystratos who was prosecuted, probably in the last decade of the fifth century, on some charge (not clear to us) arising from his having been a member of the brief oligarchic regime at Athens in 411 known as the Four Hundred.

3.4.3a  As much as a mile/1.5 kilometers: the Greek text says 8 stades; see Appendix O: Measurements, §5.

3.4.6a  Tigris River: Map 3.4.24.

FIGURE 3.4.7. TWO VIEWS OF NIMRUD (XENOPHON'S LARISA) IN THE EARLY TWENTIETH CENTURY. IN THEM, THE TELL (MOUND) OF THE ANCIENT CITY STILL RISES DRAMATICALLY FROM THE LANDSCAPE AS IT DID WHEN XENOPHON PASSED CLOSE BY. BOTTOM: OVERVIEW OF THE CITADEL WITH REMAINS OF THE ZIGGURAT IN THE FOREGROUND. THE TELL IS REPORTED TO HAVE BEEN DAMAGED IN THE RECENT REGIONAL HOSTILITIES.

inhabited it.[a] The width of its wall was twenty-five feet, its height one hundred; the circuit around it was two parasangs.[b] It was built with clay bricks on top of a stone foundation twenty feet[c] high. [8] This city was besieged by the King of the Persians at the time when the Persians were taking over the empire from the Medes, but he could not devise a method of capturing it; however, Helios covered it with a cloud and obliterated its features from sight until the people left it, and that is how it was captured.[a] [9] By the side of the city was a stone pyramid, one hundred feet in width and two hundred in height, upon which many of the barbarians had gathered, having fled from the neighboring villages.

3.4.10–12
January 400
TIGRIS PLAIN
*Mespila (Nineveh) (37)*
Xenophon describes a second city of the Medes and the fortification nearby.

[10] From there in one day's march, covering six parasangs, they made their way to a great deserted fortification, situated next to a city; the name of the city was Mespila, and Medes once inhabited it.[a] The foundation was of dressed stone containing many crushed shells, fifty feet in width and fifty in height,[b] [11] and on top of this was a brick wall fifty feet in width and a hundred in height. The circuit around the perimeter was six parasangs.[a] It is said that Medea, one of the king's wives, fled there for refuge at the time when the Medes were losing their empire at the hands of the Persians. [12] The King of the Persians set about besieging this city but could not capture it, either by direct assault or by a long siege; but the inhabitants were thunderstruck[a] at Zeus' hands, and in this way it was captured.

3.4.7a Most modern scholars identify Larisa with Kalhu (Biblical Calah), also known as Nimrud, capital of the Assyrians from c. 880 to c. 715 and still one of their great cities for the following century. Assyrian power collapsed suddenly in 612, when they were overcome by the Medes (see n. 2.4.27a), who sacked Larisa at that point. There is archaeological evidence that it was occupied on a humbler scale after this, though how continuously is not fully clear. It may not have been as deserted in 401/0 as Xenophon suggests—after all, he did not actually enter the city. In other respects, his description is largely consistent with the archaeology. Larisa (Nimrud): Map 3.4.24, *Halting place 36*. See Figure 3.4.7.
3.4.7b Width and height of wall: 25 feet/8 meters; 100 feet/30 meters. Perimeter of wall 2 parasangs: the parasang is a Persian unit for measuring travel, and a reasonable equivalent for the 2 parasangs here would be 6 miles/10 kilometers, but for the complications, see the Introduction, §7.3–5, and Appendix O: Measurements, §§7–8.
3.4.7c Stone foundation: 20 feet/6 meters.
3.4.8a Helios, the Greek sun god, may be named as the god who assists the Persians in this way because of the strong solar associations of the Persian god Mithra, important to the royal dynasty, who can also bring moisture (hence the cloud). But almost all scholars have preferred to emend the text so that the sun is being covered from the city by a cloud, rather than itself actively covering the city with a cloud.

3.4.10a Mespila is identified with the old Assyrian capital Nineveh. Like Larisa, Nineveh was sacked in 612. I take Xenophon to be differentiating the citadel (the "great deserted fortification," that is, the remains of the palace complex) from the lower city. Although the palace complex has been thoroughly excavated, much less has been done in the lower city, so archaeological verification is tenuous (Translator's note). Mespila (Nineveh): Map 3.4.24, *Halting place 37*.
3.4.10b Fifty feet/15 meters.
3.4.11a Xenophon's description of the city is accurate on the whole, though the perimeter measurement is greatly exaggerated (about 7.5 miles/12 kilometers is a common modern estimate). It is remarkable that he speaks of the Medes as its inhabitants, which they can have been only for a limited period starting in 612, rather than the Assyrians, who had previously lived there for so long.
3.4.12a Thunderstruck: Zeus was the Greek thunder god as well as the king of the gods, and the story probably envisaged a literal thunderbolt. In the version Xenophon was told, presumably it was wielded by a Mesopotamian or Persian thunder god. However, it is possible that the expression is metaphorical and the god is thought of as driving the inhabitants out of their wits. Whatever the details, Cyrus the Elder took Nineveh in 539; on him, see Appendix W: Brief Biographies, §9.

[13] From there they made their way in a single day's march, covering four parasangs. During this march Tissaphernes himself appeared, along with the cavalry he had brought from his satrapy, the force belonging to Orontas (that Orontas who was married to the King's daughter),[a] the barbarians with whom Cyrus had journeyed from the coast, the troops the King's brother had with him when he came to the King's aid,[b] and however many others the King had given him on top of all these, so that his army appeared enormous. [14] When he drew close, though he posted some of his units to the rear of the Greeks and brought up others on the flanks, he did not dare to make a direct assault and he did not want to run any great risks, so he passed the word for them to use their slings and bows. [15] The Rhodians and the archers had been posted throughout the Greek army, and the Rhodians hurled their slingshot pellets and the archers shot their arrows and none of them failed to hit a man, which was difficult to do, even if someone was trying hard to miss. Tissaphernes very quickly set about retreating beyond missile range, and the other units also retreated. [16] Then for the rest of the day the Greeks made their way onward while the Persians followed. The barbarians continued to bombard the Greeks with missiles from a distance but no longer inflicted any damage as a result, as the Rhodians with their slingshot pellets had a longer range than the Persians had, and most of the archers.[a] [17] The Persians had long bows too, and so the Cretans could make use of as many of their arrows as came into their hands; they carried on their fire by using the enemy arrows and took care to shoot them high and long.[a]

[18] That day, once the Greeks had reached some villages and were proceeding to encamp there, the barbarians withdrew, having had the worst of the exchanges of long-distance missiles. On the following day, the Greeks remained where they were and stocked up on food, as there was a lot of grain in the villages. In addition, they found there a large quantity of sinews for cord making, and also lead, which could be used in their slings.[a] The day after that, they set about making their way over the plain, and Tissaphernes followed, keeping up a long-distance barrage.

3.4.13–17
Late January 400
TIGRIS PLAIN
Tissaphernes and Orontas reappear, but the Greeks hold them off.

3.4.18
Late January 400
TIGRIS PLAIN
*Villages with grain (38)*
The Greeks stock up in some villages.

3.4.13a Satrapy: a province of the Persian Empire, governed by a satrap; for more, see the Glossary. This Orontas is not the man Cyrus executed (1.6) but the one mentioned at 2.4.8. On Orontas and Tissaphernes, see Appendix W, §§25, 37.
3.4.13b The Greeks met this brother and his army on their march out of Babylonia (Book 2 map; see 2.4.25).
3.4.16a If the text is sound, the Rhodian slingers had a longer range than the Persian slingers and than most of the archers, both the Persian ones and the Greek ones. That does not seem implausible. But many scholars have found the passage to be awkwardly expressed and have suspected corruption here, or that some words have dropped out.
3.4.17a Some scholars have given fanciful explanations of why the Greek archers shot high.

But arrows will carry farther if aimed slightly higher rather than directly at the target, owing to the force of gravity.
3.4.18a Sinews were needed primarily to make bowstrings. Some scholars say the lead in the villages also had a military purpose but at 3.3.17 Xenophon says that the Persians use sling stones rather than lead pellets. As mentioned in n. 3.3.17a, the troops certainly used lead pellets only a few years after this, but it has been argued that they borrowed the idea from the Ten Thousand. So it seems more likely that the lead in these villages was for beads or weights. In the manuscripts this sentence is found at the end of 3.4.17, but as suggested by Huitink and Rood 2019, it seems likely that it has been displaced.

**3.4.19–23**
**Late January 400**
TIGRIS PLAIN
The Greeks revise their
tactics.

[19] Here the Greeks discovered that a hollow formation that is a regular rectangle is a poor arrangement to use when the enemy are following. On the one hand, if ever the two wings draw together, either because the route becomes narrower or because the mountains or a bridge compel it, it is inevitable that the hoplites are jostled out of place, so that they make their way onward only with difficulty; they are simultaneously squeezed together and thrown into disorder, and so it is, again, inevitable that they come to be of no use, because they are out of formation. [20] But by contrast, when the wings separate, it's equally inevitable that those previously jostled out of place are now pulled apart, and the line between the flanks becomes sparse; those to whom this happens lose heart when the enemy is following them. And so whenever it was necessary to pass over a bridge or some other crossing, each soldier pressed on, wishing to be the first across, which gave the enemy a good opportunity to attack there. [21] When the generals realized this, they created six companies of a hundred men each, and they appointed captains for them and others to be lieutenants and platoon leaders.[a] Continuing on their way with this organization, these captains would keep back whenever the wings drew together, so as not to be a nuisance to them, and on these occasions they would lead their troops past the bottleneck independently of the wings.[b] [22] Conversely, whenever the sides of the hollow rectangle moved apart, they would once again fill up the ranks between them—if they were only somewhat spread out, in a single file per company; if they were more spread out, in a single file per half company; and if they were very spread out, in a single file per platoon—so that the space between the ranks was always filled in. [23] Even if it was necessary to pass over some crossing or bridge, they were not thrown into disorder, but the companies crossed over in turn; and if there was a weakness anywhere in some part of the line, these troops would come up to assist. They kept on their way in this manner for four days' march.

**3.4.24–30**
**Late January 400**
HILLS NORTH OF THE TIGRIS
*Villages by hilltop*
*palace (39)*
Fighting on the way
over high hills.

[24] While they were making their way[a] forward on the fifth day, they saw a sort of palace and many villages around it. The route to this stronghold lay through high hills, which ran down from the high ground on top of which

3.4.21a  A lieutenant (*pentēkontēr*) commanded fifty men, a platoon leader (*enōmotarchēs*) twenty-five.

3.4.21b  My interpretation of this text, which differs from that of other scholars, is this: three mobile units were normally stationed at the front of the army (3.4.43) and three at the rear. The formation was no longer strictly rectangular, as at 3.2.36, since these units stuck out from what had been the rectangle. When the army approached a pinch point, the mobile units disengaged from contact with the wings (temporarily moving sideways) and, Xenophon says, they held back until the rest of the

army marched past them. Then the six mobile units linked together and provided extra protection against a pursuing enemy while the army funneled down toward the pinch point. (Translator's note)

3.4.24a  In this passage Xenophon repeats his standard word for the progress of the army (*eporeuonto*), translated here as "making their way," even more than previously. The increase in repetition perhaps implies that now at last they are making good progress along the route they themselves have chosen. See further the Translator's Notes, §5.

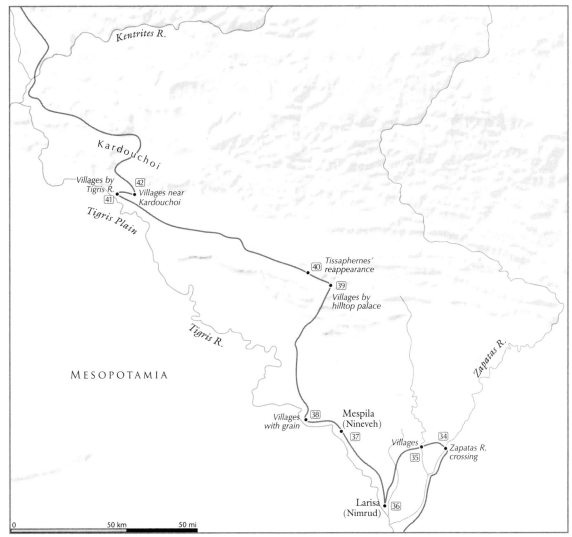

MAP 3.4.24. *KATABASIS:* FROM THE ZAPATAS RIVER CROSSING TO THE VILLAGES NEAR THE BORDER OF KARDOUCHOI TERRITORY, *HALTING PLACES 34–42.*

the stronghold was situated.[b] The Greeks were glad to see the hills, as was reasonable, since the enemy were horsemen. [25] But when, making their way from the plain, they had ascended the first hill and were coming down again in order to ascend the next one, there the barbarians went on the attack, throwing missiles from the top of the pass down the slope, slinging stones and firing arrows under the lash of whips.[a] [26] They succeeded in wounding many, and overpowered the Greek light-armed infantry, shutting them inside the rectangle of hoplites, with the result that, for that day, both the slingers and the archers were of no use at all, because they were in with the general throng. [27] And when, pressed as they were, the Greeks set to work mounting a pursuit, they reached the top of the pass only slowly, since they were hoplites, and the enemy quickly darted off. [28] Each time the hoplites came back and rejoined the main army, they had the same experience, and again on the second hill the same things occurred; and so in the case of the third hill, they decided not to move the soldiers from it until they had led the peltasts from the right side of the rectangle up to the high ground. [29] Once these troops were in position above the enemy troops following the Greeks, the enemy ceased to attack the Greek army in its descent, since they were afraid of being cut off and of having enemies on both sides of them. [30] So by making their way onward like this for the rest of the day—some on the route along the hills, the others proceeding in parallel above them along the mountainside—the Greeks reached the villages. There they appointed eight doctors,[a] as there were many who had been wounded.

3.4.31–36
February 400
HILLS NORTH OF THE TIGRIS
*Tissaphernes'
reappearance (40)*
After three days' recuperation, the Greeks make good progress on the fourth day.

[31] They remained there for three days, both on account of the wounded and because during this time they had plentiful food supplies, wheat meal, wine, and a lot of barley, which was in store for horses. These supplies had been brought together for the official acting as satrap of the territory.[a] On the fourth day, they descended to the plain. [32] But when Tissaphernes caught them with his forces,[a] necessity taught them to take up quarters in the first village they saw and not to make their way farther forward while fighting, as there were many noncombatants, some as a result of their wounds, some bearing the wounded, and some who had been handed the bearers' weapons. [33] When they had taken up their quarters and the bar-

3.4.24b　Hilltop palace: scholars usually locate this palace about 30 miles/48 kilometers northwest of our selected location (Map 3.4.24, *Halting place 39*), but in that location there do not seem to be enough ridges between the hilltop palace and the plain from which the Greeks viewed it. An in-person check of the lines of sight would confirm our choice, but currently, political instability prevents it. Our location implies very slow progress through the plain in the days before the army saw the palace, which fits better with Xenophon's narrative.

3.4.25a　Herodotus often represents Persian troops as being forced forward under the lash, as

at Thermopylae (Herodotus 7.233), though many modern scholars maintain that this is a fictional stereotype—a position this passage makes more difficult. For the Greek view of others, see the Introduction, §5.1. Thermopylae: Ref. Map 2, BY.

3.4.30a　Appointed eight doctors: as they were seemingly untrained, their function must have been more like that of medical orderlies than what we would understand as the role of a doctor.

3.4.31a　On such depots, see Appendix C: The Persian Empire, §22.

3.4.32a　Our view of where Tissaphernes reappeared is marked on Map 3.4.24 as *Halting place 40*.

barians approached the village and set to work attacking them from a distance with missiles, the Greeks had very much the upper hand, for it made a great difference to be defending themselves by means of sorties from a fixed position rather than fighting against the enemy's attacks while making their way onward. [34] When it was already afternoon, the time came for the enemy to go away, for the barbarians never set up their camp less than seven miles[a] from the Greek encampment, afraid that the Greeks would attack them in the night. [35] Persian armies are a disgrace at night. Their horses are tied up and generally have their legs shackled together to avoid their making off if they get loose; and if any disturbance occurs, the horse has to be saddled and bridled for its Persian rider, and then he has to mount it once he has put on his breastplate. It is difficult to do all this at night, especially when there is a disturbance. For this reason they would take up quarters far from the Greeks. [36] When the Greeks realized that the Persians wanted to go away and were passing the instruction through their ranks, within the enemy's hearing the herald made an announcement for the Greeks to pack up their baggage. For some time the barbarians put off their departure, but when it was already late, they went away, for they thought it not at all a good idea to make their way back to their camp in the dark. [37] As soon as the Greeks saw they were clearly going, they themselves harnessed up again and made their way onward, covering as much as seven miles.[a]

The armies were thus so far apart that on the next day the enemy did not appear, nor on the day after; but on the fourth day, the barbarians started out first by night and occupied a strong point high up above the route along which the Greeks were intending to go, a fingertip of high ground under which ran the descent to the plain. [38] When Cheirisophos[a] saw that this peak had been occupied in advance, he called Xenophon up from the rear and told him to bring the peltasts and attend him at the front. [39] Xenophon did not bring the peltasts, as he saw Tissaphernes and the whole enemy army making their appearance, but he himself rode up and asked, "Why are you calling me?" Cheirisophos said to him, "You can see: the hill above our descent has been occupied in advance, and it is impossible to go past it unless we knock them off it. [40] But why didn't you bring the peltasts?" Xenophon said he didn't think it a good idea to leave the rearguard without cover when the enemy were in view. "But it is indeed timely," he added, "to discuss how one might drive the men off the hill." [41] At this point Xenophon observed the summit of the mountain above their own army, and from it a byway to the hill where the enemy were, and he said, "The best thing, Cheirisophos, is for us to make haste to the top as quickly as we can, for if we occupy the summit, they will not be able to remain

3.4.37–45
February 400
HILLS NORTH OF THE TIGRIS
Xenophon advises on how to dislodge the enemy from some high ground and volunteers for the task.

---

3.4.34a   Seven miles/11 kilometers: the Greek text says 60 stades; see Appendix O: Measurements, §5.
3.4.37a   Seven miles/11 kilometers: the Greek text says 60 stades.
3.4.38a   On Cheirisophos, see Appendix W: Brief Biographies, §7.

above our route. Now, if you want, stay here with the main army, as I am willing to go that way, or, if you have a strong wish to do so, you go that way and I shall remain here." [42] "Well, then," said Cheirisophos, "I give you the choice." Xenophon said that, as he was the younger, he chose to go and told him to send with him men from the vanguard, for it would be a long business to obtain them from the rear. [43] So Cheirisophos sent the peltasts from the vanguard along with Xenophon and used the peltasts in the middle of the rectangle as replacements. He also gave orders that the three hundred picked troops he kept at the front of the rectangle should accompany Xenophon.

[44] They made their way from there as quickly as they possibly could, but when the enemy troops on the hill noticed the Greeks were heading to the top, they immediately set out on a race for the top themselves. [45] Here there was much shouting from the Greek army as they cheered on their party, and much shouting from those around Tissaphernes as they cheered on theirs.

[46] Xenophon was riding on horseback alongside his troops and calling out encouragement: "Men, think of this now as a race for Greece, toward your wives and children. Now is the time to go for it—after a brief effort now, there'll be no more fighting as we make our way for the rest of the journey." [47] But Soteridas the Sicyonian[a] said, "We are not on equal terms, Xenophon. You are riding on horseback, and I am laboring uphill with difficulty, carrying my shield." [48] When Xenophon heard this, he jumped down from his horse and pushed Soteridas away out of his place; he took his shield from him and set about making his way forward as fast as he could go with it. But he happened to be wearing his cavalry breastplate, and so he was weighed down.[a] He was encouraging those in front of him to lead on and those behind to overtake him, since he was having difficulty following in file, [49] but the other soldiers hit Soteridas and threw things at him and abused him until they forced him to take his shield back and make his way onward. Xenophon remounted and rode his horse up as long as the terrain allowed it, but when horses could go no farther, he left it behind and pressed onward on foot. And so they did reach the top before the enemy. [3.5.1] At this the barbarians unsurprisingly reversed course, and each began to flee as best he could, while the Greeks occupied the top of the mountain. Tissaphernes and Ariaios[a] and their entourages turned aside and went off by another route.

Xenophon leads by example, and his detachment successfully dislodges the enemy.

3.4.47a  By using "the Sicyonian" for an otherwise unmentioned figure, perhaps Xenophon is signaling the Sicyonians' generally poor reputation as soldiers (evident from *Hellenika* 4.4.10). Sicyon: Map 1.2.1, AY.

3.4.48a  Xenophon, it appears, is wearing armor that was either metal or had metallic elements. Metal armor was not a necessary choice for a cavalryman, but he could wear it without worrying as much as an infantry-

man would about its weight. The passage shows that any body armor the infantry wore was not so heavy. For more, see Appendix H: Infantry and Cavalry in *Anabasis*, §9, which takes a slightly different view and gives a different translation ("corslet" rather than "breastplate").

3.5.1a  On Ariaios, see Appendix W: Brief Biographies, §4.

The troops under Cheirisophos' command descended to the plain and set up camp in a village full of good things, and there were also many other villages well-stocked with good things in this plain by the river Tigris.[b] [2] During the afternoon the enemy suddenly appeared in the plain and cut to pieces some of the Greeks who were scattered over the plain in pursuit of plunder; and indeed many herds of cattle had been intercepted by Cheiri-sophos[a] as they were being taken across to the other side of the river. [3] Here Tissaphernes and those with him set to work firing the villages, and some of the Greeks became very dispirited, apprehensive that they would not have food supplies to take from there if the supplies were burned. [4] Meanwhile, Cheirisophos' troops were returning from their cattle rustling, and as they came back they met Xenophon; having made his descent into the plain, at that moment he was riding along his lines, saying, [5] "Men of Greece, do you see that they are already conceding that the land belongs to you? When the truce was made, they stipulated that there should be no setting fire to the King's lands, but now they themselves are setting his land on fire as if it belonged to someone else. But if they leave any food supplies anywhere for themselves, they will see us making our way there too. [6] However, Cheirisophos, it seems to me," he said, "that we should go to help fend off those who are starting the fires, as if we were defending our own property." Cheirisophos said, "No, that doesn't seem right to me at all. On the contrary," he said, "let us also set fires, and then the enemy will stop sooner."[a]

[7] When they went to their quarters, the generals and captains held a meeting while the rest concerned themselves with the food supplies. At the meeting there was much perplexity. On the one side, the mountains were extremely high;[a] and on the other, the river was so deep that when they tested the depth, their spears did not stick out at all above the water.[b] [8] As they were in a state of indecision, a certain man from Rhodes came up and said, "Men, I am willing to take you across, four thousand hoplites at a time,

3.5.2–6
February 400
TIGRIS PLAIN
*Villages by Tigris River (41)*
Skirmishes and Persian scorched-earth tactics.

3.5.7–12
February 400
TIGRIS PLAIN
A Rhodian makes an ingenious but impractical proposal for crossing the Tigris.

3.5.1b  Villages by the Tigris River: Map 3.4.24, *Halting place 41*.
3.5.2a  Xenophon's narrative here is not very clear in the transmitted text. "By Cheirisophos" has been added in the translation. In 3.5.4 the emendation "cattle rustling" (*boēlasias;* replacing "going to help," *boētheias*) has been accepted from the early twentieth-century scholar Wilhelm Gemoll. Another suggestion is that a sentence has dropped out somewhere in the passage; both ideas could be right. (Translator's note)
3.5.6a  Possibly Cheirisophos means that the sooner the Persians do the job that they have set about doing—burning the villages—the sooner they will be gone, but it is not at all clear how to take his remark.
3.5.7a  The mountains here rise steeply from the

Tigris River valley, about 3,000 feet/ 915 meters, and would have been a strik-ing sight for those who had just crossed the plain. But the highest mountains in the area are about 6,500 feet/1,980 meters, so Xenophon's characterization as "extremely high" is an exaggeration. Far-ther north in Armenia, around Lake Thospitis, the mountains range from 10,000 to more than 13,000 feet/3,050 to 3,962 meters. Armenia, Lake Thospi-tis: Ref. Map 6, AY, BY.
3.5.7b  Here the Tigris River is deepest in the winter months, which is evidence support-ing the "late" chronology explained in Appendix Q: The Chronology of the March. For more detailed argument on the relevance of this passage, see the Introduc-tion, §7.18.

if you supply me with what I need and provide me with a talent[a] as pay."
[9] Asked what he needed, he said, "I shall need two thousand bags made
of skin. I see many sheep here, and goats and oxen and asses, and if they are
skinned and the skins are inflated, it would easily provide a method of crossing. [10] I shall also need some of the ropes you use for the draft animals.
With these I will tie the bags to each other, and then, having moored each
bag in the river by fastening stones to it and casting them off into the water
like anchors, I will draw the bags across and, after securing each end to the
two riverbanks, I shall throw brushwood on top and cover it with earth.
[11] So you will see absolutely right away that you will not sink, for each
bag will buoy up two men, and the brushwood and earth will be there to
keep people from slipping." [12] When the generals heard this, they decided
that it was a charming idea but impossible in practice, since to prevent it
there was a large body of cavalry on the far side, which would immediately
stop the advance party from doing any of this.

[13] Hence, having burned down the village they were leaving, they
spent the following day retreating in the direction of Babylon to the villages
that had not been burned.[a] Consequently the enemy did not ride after them
but kept watch and seemed to be wondering where the Greeks would turn
next and what they had in mind. [14] Then, while the rest of the soldiers
were occupied with the food supplies, the generals held another meeting;
they brought in the captives they had taken and started to question them
about the varying nature of all the surrounding lands. [15] The prisoners
said that to the south was the road to Babylon and to Media, through which
the Greeks had come; the road to the east went to Susa and Ecbatana, where
it is said the King spends the summer and the spring; the road for anyone
crossing the river would lead to the west, to Lydia and Ionia.[a] Of the road
that turned through the mountains and to the north, they said that it led to
the Kardouchoi.[b] [16] They said that these people lived all over the mountains and were warlike, taking no notice of the King; on the contrary, a royal
army of 120,000 had once attacked them, but because of the harsh terrain,
not one of them had returned home. However, sometimes they made truces
with the satrap of the plain, and then the two sides would even mingle with
each other.

3.5.13–16
February 400
TIGRIS PLAIN
*Villages near
Kardouchoi (42)*
Captives advise the
Greeks on possible routes
onward.

3.5.8a   Talent: for this currency unit, see Appendix O: Measurements, §§10–11. Rhodes:
Map 1.2.10, BX.
3.5.13a  Babylon: Map 3.5.15, locator. Unburned
villages: Map 3.4.24, Villages near Kardouchoi, *Halting place 42.*
3.5.15a  In the *Kyroupaideia* (*The Education of
Cyrus*) 8.6.22, Xenophon writes that the
King spent three months of the spring in
Susa, two months of the summer in
Ecbatana, and seven months of the
winter in Babylon. The length of stay in
Babylon in particular seems dubious, as
does the failure to mention any time
spent in the heartland of Persia, at Perse-

polis or Pasargadae. However, we know
from many sources that the King did
move around quite a bit over his central
territories, though they are less categorical
about precise places and durations. Babylon, Media, Susa, Ecbatana, Lydia, Ionia,
Persepolis, Pasargadae: Map 3.5.15,
locator.
3.5.15b  For the roads the army had to choose
among, see Figure 3.5.15 and Map 3.5.15.
Kardouchoi territory: Map 3.5.15. Some
scholars make a connection between the
Kardouchoi and the modern Kurds, who
have lived in this area for many
centuries.

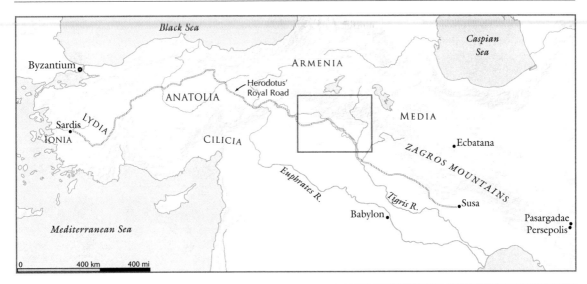

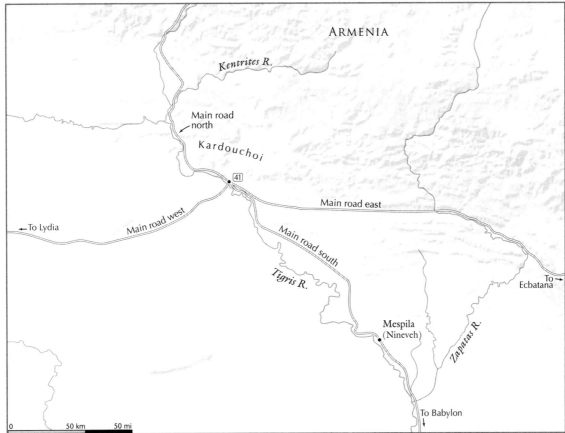

MAP 3.5.15. THE FOUR MAIN ROADS LEADING FROM THE TIGRIS RIVER CROSSROADS.

FIGURE 3.5.15. THE TIGRIS VALLEY LOOKING NORTH FROM THE CROSSROADS DESCRIBED AT 3.5.15, WHERE THE GENERALS DEBATED IN WHICH DIRECTION TO GO. THE GREEKS BACKTRACKED SLIGHTLY FROM HERE AND TRAVELED THROUGH THE MOUNTAINS OF THE KARDOUCHOI (AT RIGHT). THESE MOUNTAINS EXTEND FOR MANY MILES AND, AS XENOPHON SAYS AT 3.5.7, THEY WOULD HEM THE GREEKS IN IF THEY TRIED TO ADVANCE ALONG THE RIVERBANK.

3.5.17–18
February 400
TIGRIS PLAIN
The generals decide to travel to Armenia through Kardouchoi territory.

[17] When they heard these reports, the generals made those who said they knew the various different routes sit in separate groups, without making clear in which direction they meant to make their way. What the generals then decided was that they had to invade the Kardouchoi over the mountains, since the captives said that if they passed through them, they would come to Armenia, an extensive and prosperous land, of which Orontas was the ruler.[a] From there they said that it was easy to travel to wherever anyone wanted to make his way. [18] The generals offered a sacrifice to inquire about these points, in order to start the journey the moment that it seemed the right time,[a] as they were afraid that the pass over the mountains might be occupied before they reached it. They gave instructions that when people had had dinner, everyone was to pack up and take a rest and then follow whenever the instruction was given.

3.5.17a  The Orontas mentioned at 3.4.13, the King's son-in-law, not to be confused with the Orontas put to death by Cyrus at 1.6. Armenia: Map 3.5.15 and locator.
3.5.18a  It would be customary to offer a sacrifice before setting out on a further stage of the journey, in order to check the omens. This would usually be done just before they left, to get the freshest possible information from the gods, but on this occasion they did it early to avoid a last-minute holdup.

BOOK FOUR

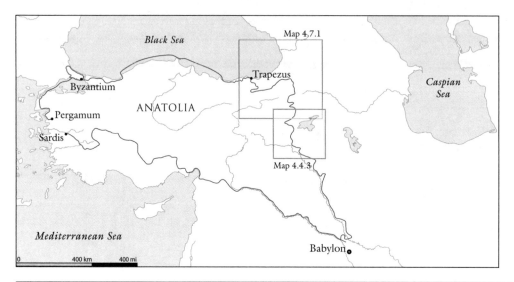

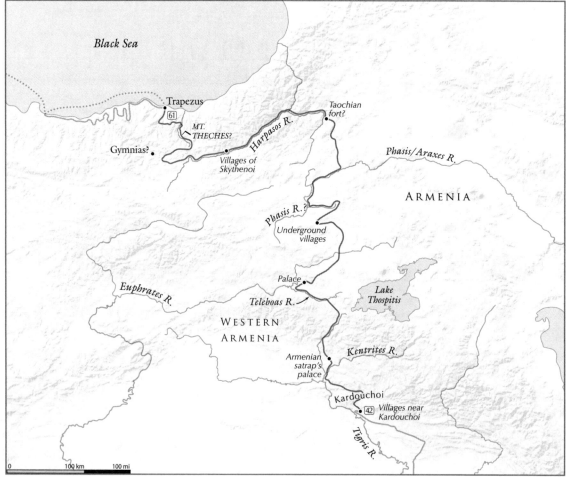

BOOK 4. *KATABASIS:* FROM THE VILLAGES NEAR THE KARDOUCHOI TO TRAPEZUS, *HALTING PLACES 42–61.*

[In the preceding narrative, the author has explained what happened on the march up into the interior leading to the battle, then what happened after the battle during the truce between the King and the Greeks who had journeyed up with Cyrus, and then how, after the King and Tissaphernes had broken the truce, war was waged against the Greeks as the Persian army followed them.[a] [2] And when the Greeks reached a point where the river Tigris was altogether impassable because of its depth and great size, and there was no way alongside it as the Kardouchian heights rose precipitously over the river, the generals naturally decided they had to make their way through the mountains.[a] [3] For what they were hearing from those they took prisoner was that if they managed to get through the Kardouchian mountains, then in Armenia[a] they could get across the headwaters of the Tigris if they wanted, and if they didn't want to, they could go around them. They were also told that the headwaters of the Euphrates were not far from those of the Tigris, and this is indeed the case.[b] [4] So now they are launching their assault on the Kardouchoi, trying simultaneously to escape notice and to get through before the enemy occupies the heights.][a]

[5] When it was around the last watch[a] and what remained of the night was just long enough for them to get across the plain under cover of darkness, the command was passed to the troops to get up and make their way onward, and they arrived at the mountain range just as day broke. [6] Once there Cheirisophos took the lead of the army with his own contingent and

4.1.1–4
An ancient scribe's summary of the story so far.

4.1.5–11
February 400
TIGRIS PLAIN–
KARDOUCHOI TERRITORY
*Villages near Kardouchoi (42)*
The Greeks leave the Tigris plain and enter the mountains.

NOTE:  Unless otherwise indicated, all dates are B.C.E., and all citations are to Xenophon's *Anabasis*. The determination of the army's route and stopping places are based on the editors' calculations and estimates from data taken from *Anabasis*. Nonetheless, the route line shown on our maps and the monthly dates given in our side notes are often subject to doubt. Our best estimates should not be taken as authoritative or certain. See the Editors' Preface, §§17–20.

4.1.1a  On King Artaxerxes, Cyrus the Younger, and Tissaphernes, see Appendix W: Brief Biographies of Selected Characters in *Anabasis*, §§6, 10, 37. Persian Empire: Ref. Map 9.

4.1.2a  Tigris River, Kardouchoi territory: Book 4 map.
4.1.3a  Armenia: Book 4 map.
4.1.3b  This sentence is new information not contained in Book 3, odd in a summary (but see n. 4.1.4a). Euphrates River: Book 4 map.
4.1.4a  This is the third of the passages occurring throughout the work that summarize the story so far. It appears in brackets because scholars generally agree that they are later scribal insertions; for more, see the Translator's Notes, §13.
4.1.5a  The last watch: the hours of darkness were divided into probably five watches. In February the last night watch would begin approximately three hours before dawn.

111

all the light-armed troops, while Xenophon followed with the rearguard hoplites[a] and without any of the light-armed contingent, as there seemed no danger that anyone behind would be pursuing them as they made their way up the hill. [7] In fact, Cheirisophos reached the top before any of the enemy noticed. Then he led on, a short distance in front, and as each contingent came over the brow of the hill, it descended after him and advanced to the villages lying in the nooks and recesses of the hills. [8] The Kardouchoi deserted their homes there and fled to the hilltops with their women and children. There were plenty of food supplies in the villages to take, and the houses were furnished with large numbers of bronze vessels; but the Greeks did not carry them off, nor did they pursue the people. They spared them in the hope that the Kardouchoi might be prepared to let them pass through their country as friends, since they were hostile to the King. [9] However, as regards the food supplies, they took whatever anyone came across, for necessity drove them. The Kardouchoi neither answered when they called nor gave any other sign of friendliness. [10] When the last of the Greeks came down from the top of the pass to the villages, they were already in darkness—for the path was narrow, and so their ascent and then descent to the villages had taken the whole day—and at that point some of the Kardouchoi gathered together and attacked these rear ranks. They killed some and severely wounded others with stones and arrows, though the attackers were few indeed, as the Greek army had come upon them unexpectedly. [11] But if they had brought together more fighters, there would have been a danger that a large part of the army would have been destroyed. That night the Greeks bivouacked in the villages just as they were, while the Kardouchoi lit a great circle of fires on the hilltops and kept each other in view.

4.1.12–14
February 400
KARDOUCHOI TERRITORY
The generals take steps
to reduce the army's
baggage train.

[12] At daybreak the Greek generals and captains met and decided to make their way[a] onward with only the strongest and most needed draft animals, leaving the others behind, and to send away all the recently taken captives in the army. [13] For the large numbers of draft animals and captives were slowing down the march, and those who were looking after them, also many in number, were noncombatants;[a] furthermore, the large number of people made it necessary to provide and carry double the food supplies. Once the decision had been taken, they had a herald announce their course of action. [14] When the troops had had their morning meal and were making their way onward, the generals surreptitiously took up a position where the path was narrow, and if they came across anything or anyone that had been proscribed but had not been let go, they deprived them of it. The troops obeyed, except where someone had concealed something, like a boy he especially fancied or a good-looking woman. During this day, as they

---

4.1.6a   Hoplites: heavy-armed infantry; for more,
           see Appendix H: Infantry and Cavalry in
           *Anabasis*, §§2–3. On Cheirisophos, see
           Appendix W: Brief Biographies, §7.
4.1.12a  In Book 4 Xenophon's use of the verb
           *poreuesthai*, in this translation rendered

"to make one's way," becomes insistent.
           See the Translator's Notes, §5, for this
           phenomenon and possible reasons.
4.1.13a  See Appendix K: The Noncombatant
           Contingent of the Army.

made their way onward, sometimes they had to fight a bit, but at other times they were left alone.

[15] The next day a heavy winter storm came on,[a] but they still had to make their way onward, as they had insufficient food supplies. Cheirisophos led, and Xenophon guarded the rear. [16] The enemy now began to attack them vigorously, and as the passes were narrow, they came up close, shooting arrows and slinging stones, so that, what with chasing off the enemy and then drawing back again, the Greeks were forced to make their way slowly. Many a time[a] when the enemy pressed them hard, Xenophon gave the order to wait where they stood. [17] Though on other occasions Cheirisophos waited when this happened and the word was passed to him, in one instance he did not wait but led his troops on quickly and passed the word back to Xenophon to follow, so that it was clear that something was the matter. There was no time to go to the front and see the cause of the haste, so the rearguard had to make their way in something very like flight. [18] And a good man died there, Kleonymos of Laconia, when an arrow pierced through his shield and jerkin into his rib cage; and so also Basias of Arcadia,[a] shot right through his head.

[19] When they reached the end of the day's march, Xenophon, just as he was, went straight up to Cheirisophos and began to blame him because he had not waited and they had been forced to fight while fleeing. "And now," he said, "two good and honorable men[a] are dead, and we were unable either to recover their bodies or to bury them." [20] In reply Cheirisophos said, "Look at the mountains and see how elsewhere they are altogether impassable; the only route is this one you see going straight up, and you can see on it the great crowd of people who have occupied it and stand guard over the road out. [21] That is why I was pressing on and why I didn't wait for you, so that I could get there first before the pass was occupied against us—the guides we have say there is no other road." [22] Xenophon said, "But I myself have two men who could act as guides. When the enemy were making life difficult for us, we set up an ambush, which also allowed us to draw breath, and we killed some of them and deliberately took others alive for this very reason, so that we could use guides who know the country."

[23] And immediately they brought forward the fellows and, taking them separately, set about questioning them as to whether they knew any route other than the obvious one. One of them denied it, even though many methods of inducing fear were brought to bear on him; and since he was saying nothing of any use, he was butchered in the sight of the other one. [24] The remaining prisoner now said that the reason the first prisoner had denied all knowledge was that the alternative route lay close to where his

4.1.15–18
February 400
KARDOUCHOI TERRITORY
Difficulties of coordination between vanguard and rearguard.

4.1.19–22
February 400
KARDOUCHOI TERRITORY
Xenophon is angry with Cheirisophos about unnecessary casualties.

4.1.23–28
February 400
KARDOUCHOI TERRITORY
Volunteers come forward for a special assignment, among them Aristeas of Chios, who has proved valuable to the army in this way before.

4.1.15a   "Heavy winter storm" is a chronological marker useful in determining the timing of the entire march; for more, see Appendix Q: The Chronology of the March, §§3, 6, 13–14.
4.1.16a   "Many a time" translates the Greek *tham-*

*ina*, a word with Homeric overtones.
4.1.18a   Laconia, Arcadia: Map 1.2.1, BY, AX.
4.1.19a   "Good and honorable men": for discussion of this phrase, see *kaloi kagathoi* in the Glossary.

daughter, who was married, happened to live with her husband; but he himself, he said, would lead them on a path along which even the draft animals could make their way. [25] Asked if there might be any place on it that was difficult to get past, he said there was a height that would be impossible to get by unless first some of them seized it. [26] So then they decided to call a meeting of captains, both peltasts and selected hoplites.[a] They explained the current situation and asked if anyone among them wanted to prove himself a good man by voluntarily undertaking to try going this way. [27] From among the hoplites, Aristonymos of Methydrion, an Arcadian, undertook to do this, as did Agasias of Stymphalos, another Arcadian, and also, but in rivalry with them, Kallimachos of Parrasia,[a] a third Arcadian, who said he wanted to try going this way once he had found further volunteers from the whole army. "I know," he said, "that many of the young men will follow my lead." [28] Thereupon they asked if any of the light-armed group commanders also wanted to go ahead with them, and Aristeas of Chios[a] undertook to do so. On many occasions he showed his great value to the army in deeds of this kind.

[1] It was already late afternoon, and they[a] told them to eat their meal quickly and be on their way. Having bound the guide and handed him over to the volunteers, they arranged with them that if they took the height, they would guard the place for the night and at break of day give a signal by trumpet.[b] Those on the height would fall upon the enemy who held the principal road out, while the generals[c] would advance to their assistance with the bulk of the army as quickly as they possibly could. [2] When they had made these arrangements, the volunteers, about two thousand in number, made their way forward while heavy rain fell; in the meantime Xenophon led off with the rearguard toward the principal road out, so that the enemy would keep their attention on that route and the volunteers going by the circuitous route would as far as possible escape notice. [3] The rearguard found themselves in a gully, and once they had crossed this, they needed to climb out up the steep slope; but at this point the barbarians started rolling boulders down on them, both larger and smaller ones. There were cartloads of these, which in their fall smashed against the rocks and were scattered like stones from slings. It was altogether impossible to draw nigh to the approach.[a] [4]

4.1.26a　On the difference between the peltasts (light-armed infantry) and the hoplites (heavy-armed infantry), see Appendix H: Infantry and Cavalry in *Anabasis*, esp. §§2–5. Presumably the exploit was thought to be more suitable for the light-armed troops, though it turned out that the hoplite officers were more eager to demonstrate their zeal.

4.1.27a　The following locations appear on Map 1.2.1: Methydrion, AX; Stymphalos, AY; Parrasia, BX.

4.1.28a　Chios: Map 5.3.7, BY.

4.2.1a　Xenophon does not make clear who the "they" giving the orders are; it could be just Xenophon and Cheirisophos, but it

could as well be all the generals. Indeed, for much of the retreat we are unclear whether it is just Xenophon and Cheirisophos or the generals as a whole who direct the army. Perhaps the obfuscation is deliberate. (Translator's note)

4.2.1b　For an image of a trumpet (*salpinx*), see Figure 4.2.1.

4.2.1c　The original says literally "they themselves" here; the explicit references to the generals and to the bulk of the army have been added in the translation.

4.2.3a　"Draw nigh": for discussion of Xenophon's occasional use of archaic or unusual vocabulary, see the Translator's Notes, §§4, 8.

FIGURE 4.2.1.
A SOLDIER BLOWING A
TRUMPET (*SALPINX*) AS
SHOWN ON AN ATHENIAN
DISH OF C. 520.

Thinking they could not succeed like this, some of the captains set about trying elsewhere, and they carried on until darkness fell. When they thought they would not be seen if they withdrew, they went back for their evening meal—the troops who formed the rearguard happened not to have had their morning meal either. But the enemy still carried on rolling down stones at intervals throughout the night, as was evident from the noise.

[5] The detachment with the guide circled around and surprised the enemy guards as they sat around a fire. Some they killed, the others they chased off, and then they stayed there, in the belief that they were occupying the highest point. [6] But they were not occupying it: there was a round hilltop above them past which ran the narrow path where the guards had been sitting. However, there was an approach route from there to the enemy who were settled on the main path. [7] They spent the night where they were, but when the day was just beginning to break, they made their way silently in formation toward the enemy; and there was also a thick mist, so they got close to them unobserved. When the two sides were in sight of each other, the trumpet was sounded and the Greeks raised the battle cry and set upon the fellows. They did not stay to receive the attack but aban-

4.2.5–9
February 400
KARDOUCHOI TERRITORY
Greek tactics are successful, and the enemy is dislodged.

115

doned the path, and in their flight a few were killed—only a few, as they were highly mobile. [8] When Cheirisophos' soldiers heard the trumpet, they immediately charged up along the obvious road, while other generals made their way by previously unused routes from wherever their own unit happened to be; and, climbing up as best they could, they hauled each other up using their spears—[9] and these were the first to join up with the detachment that had initially captured the position.

Xenophon, with half the rearguard, went the way the group with the guide had gone, as that was the best route for the draft animals, and he posted the other half of the rearguard behind the draft animals. [10] As they made their way onward, they came upon a ridge above the path, which had been occupied by the enemy. They would now either have to drive them off or end up separated from the other Greeks, and while they themselves might have made their way by the route the other troops had taken, the draft animals could get out only by this path. [11] So, after encouraging one another, they charged up the ridge in columns, not surrounding it but leaving an escape route for the enemy, should they wish to flee. [12] As long as they were climbing up, each soldier as best he could, the barbarians kept firing arrows and throwing stones at them, but rather than let them get near, they abandoned the place and fled. When the Greeks had passed by this ridge, they saw in front of them another occupied ridge, and again it was decided to make their way forward against it. [13] But Xenophon was anxious about leaving the ridge they had just taken bare of troops, in case the enemy recaptured it and attacked the draft animals as they went by, since, because of the narrowness of the path, they were spread out over a long distance as they made their way onward. So he left the captains Kephisodoros son of Kephisophon, an Athenian, Amphikrates son of Amphidemos, another Athenian, and Archagoras, an Argive[a] exile, there on the ridge while he himself made his way to the second ridge with the rest of the party, and they captured this by the same method.

[14] But there still remained a third hilltop for them to get past, by far the steepest of the three: this was the one rising above the guard that the volunteers had surprised in the night by their fire. [15] When the Greeks got close, the barbarians left the hilltop without a fight, which they all thought was extraordinary and supposed that they had left it in fear of being surrounded and besieged. But, in fact, they had seen from the height what was happening in the rear and were all going off to attack the rearguard.[a] [16] Xenophon then set about climbing up to the height with the youngest soldiers; the others he ordered to move on slowly so the detachments that were farthest behind could join up, and he said that once they had gone along the path and reached level ground, they were to halt under arms.

4.2.10–13
February 400
KARDOUCHOI TERRITORY
Initial good progress of the rearguard, which is protecting the baggage train.

4.2.14–16
February 400
KARDOUCHOI TERRITORY
After scaling the highest ridge, Xenophon gives orders to help the rearguard.

4.2.13a  Athens, Argos: Map 1.2.1, AY.
4.2.15a  "The rearguard" here refers to the troops with and behind the draft animals, at the very rear. (See 4.2.17 where "the rearguard" is mentioned again with this sense.)

The narrative shows that the Kardouchoi didn't proceed directly against these troops but first set about dislodging the Greek contingent stationed above them to guard their passage. (Translator's note)

[17] At this point Archagoras the Argive came up in flight and said that they had been dislodged from the first ridge and that Kephisodoros and Amphikrates were dead, along with the others, except for those who had leapt down the rocks and reached the rearguard. [18] The barbarians, having achieved this, came up onto a ridge separated from the round hilltop by a narrow divide, and Xenophon talked to them through an interpreter about a truce and asked for the bodies of the dead. [19] They said they would hand them over on condition that he did not set their homes on fire. To this Xenophon agreed. In the time it took for them to say this to each other and for the rest of the Greek army to pass by, everyone from the nearby districts had streamed in together. [20] Here the enemy made a stand. When the Greeks began to descend from the hilltop toward where their comrades had halted under arms, the enemy charged forward en masse in a great tumult, and when they were on the very highest point of the hilltop from which Xenophon was descending, they took to rolling rocks down the mountainside. They broke one soldier's leg, and at this point the shield-bearer who was carrying Xenophon's shield deserted him.[a] [21] But Eurylochos, a hoplite from Lousoi, in Arcadia,[a] ran up to him and provided cover for both of them as they withdrew, and the others also withdrew successfully to the troops who were drawn up in formation.

[22] As a result of this, the whole Greek army were now together again, and they billeted themselves in many fine houses that had abundant food supplies—and indeed lots of wine, stored in plaster-lined cisterns. [23] Xenophon and Cheirisophos arranged to hand over the guide once they had received the corpses, and, as far as they could, they did everything for the dead that it is customary to do for good men.

[24] On the next day, they made their way onward without a guide. The enemy kept up a constant fight and, by occupying every narrow place in advance, were always blocking the path ahead. [25] So whenever they blocked the vanguard, Xenophon, in the rear, would leave the track for the higher ground and dislodge what was obstructing the vanguard's onward route by trying to get above the force blocking them; [26] while whenever they attacked the rearguard, Cheirisophos would leave the track and try to get higher than the blocking force, in turn dislodging what was obstructing the rearguard's forward progress. Thus they constantly came to each other's assistance and put a lot of effort into supporting each other. [27] There were times when the barbarians gave them a great deal of trouble both as they went up and as they came down again, for they were light on their feet, with nothing other than bows and arrows and slingstones, and so even if they turned back in flight from close at hand, they could escape successfully. [28] They were very effective, especially as archers. They had bows nearly four and

4.2.17–21
February 400
KARDOUCHOI TERRITORY
The enemy counterattacks the rear, but Xenophon brings his men through.

4.2.22–23
February 400
KARDOUCHOI TERRITORY
The Greeks secure a respite.

4.2.24–28
February 400
KARDOUCHOI TERRITORY
The Greeks maneuver skillfully against the formidable Kardouchoi.

4.2.20a  This shield-bearer was probably a slave, likely brought by Xenophon from home to act as one of his personal servants. Although slave shield-bearers were fairly widespread in citizen armies, probably

only the officers among the Ten Thousand had them.
4.2.21a  Lousoi, Arcadia: Map 1.2.1, AX.

a half feet long, and three-foot arrows;[a] and whenever they shot, they would draw back their bowstrings by stepping forward with their left foot pressed against the bottom of the bow, and the arrows would go through shields and body armor. The Greeks used the arrows as javelins when they got hold of them, fitting them with throwing loops.[b] In these places the Cretans were the most useful troops; their leader was a Cretan called Stratokles.[c]

**4.3.1–2**
**February 400**
KARDOUCHOI TERRITORY–
HEIGHTS ABOVE
KENTRITES PLAIN
The Greeks reach apparent safety after continuous fighting with the Kardouchoi.

[1] By contrast,[a] that day they bivouacked in the villages above the plain extending along the river Kentrites.[b] Here the Greeks rested, happy to see the plain. (The river was two hundred feet wide and marks the boundary between Armenia and the land of the Kardouchoi, running at a distance of twelve hundred to fourteen hundred yards from the Kardouchian mountains.)[c] [2] So they then bivouacked very pleasantly, with ample food supplies and reminiscing a great deal about the hardships that were past. For the entire seven days[a] during which they had been making their way through the lands of the Kardouchoi, they had been fighting continuously and had sustained more damage than everything that they had suffered from the King and Tissaphernes. So now, thinking they were free from these problems, they slept soundly.

**4.3.3–7**
**February 400**
KENTRITES RIVER
The Greeks find themselves between two sets of enemies.

[3] But at daybreak they saw, some distance beyond the river, horsemen in full armor intent on stopping them from crossing; and they also saw infantry drawn up on the rising ground above the horsemen so as to prevent a breakout into Armenia.[a] [4] These were the troops of Orontas and Artouchas,[a] Armenians and Mardoi and Chaldaian mercenaries.[b] The Chaldaioi

4.2.28a Four and a half feet/1.5 meters, 3 feet/ 1 meter: the Greek text says *tripēchē* (3 *pēcheis*) and *dipēchē* (2 *pēcheis*). The *pēchus* was a measure of length notionally equivalent to a forearm; see Appendix O: Ancient Greek and Persian Units of Measurement, §§2–3.
4.2.28b Fixed throwing loops were fitted as an integral part of javelins in warfare to increase range. In the absence of integral loops, the Greeks here seem to have tied less permanent loops around the Persian arrows when reutilizing them as javelins, a technique employed by Greek athletes, who used loops on javelins that came off in flight in order to get the javelin to land point first, though such loops weren't nearly as good as fixed ones for increasing range. See Figure 4.3.28.
4.2.28c Crete: Map 5.3.7, locator.
4.3.1a "By contrast": the Greek phrase here, *d'au*, has given rise to debate among scholars. The likeliest explanation is that there is a contrast with something in a paragraph that has been lost in transmission; also see n. 4.3.2a. (Translator's note)
4.3.1b Kentrites River: Map 4.4.3.
4.3.1c Two hundred feet/61 meters: the Greek text says 2 *plethra*. Twelve hundred to 1,400 yards/0.7–0.8 mile: the Greek text says 6 or 7 stades. On *plethra* and stades, see Appendix O, §§2–3, 5. Kardouchoi territory: Map 4.4.3.
4.3.2a The entire seven days: the preceding narrative covers events of only five days. Probably a couple of paragraphs have fallen out of the text, but perhaps Xenophon made an understandable mistake, given the turbulence of the days the army spent among the Kardouchoi. Xenophon does not measure the army's journey here in parasangs (see n. 4.4.1a), perhaps because the Kardouchoi were independent of Persian control and parasang measurements were not readily available or possibly because Xenophon wanted to connect parasangs and Persia for literary reasons (a theme developed in Rood 2010b).
4.3.3a Armenia: Map 4.4.3.
4.3.4a For more on the later career of this Orontas, see Appendix W: Brief Biographies, §25; for the makeup of his troops, see Appendix D: The Persian Army, §6. Artouchas is not otherwise known.
4.3.4b The Chaldaioi mentioned here are not the Babylonian Chaldees familiar from the Bible, or the modern Chaldean Christians living in Iraq. Xenophon, in his *Kyroupaideia* (*The Education of Cyrus*), says the Chaldaioi came from mountainous country beyond Armenia (3.2) and emphasizes their warlike nature and liking for mercenary service (3.2.7, 3.2.25). They may be the same as the [Eastern] Chalybes, who in *Anabasis* at 4.5.34 are said to live beyond Armenia and at 4.7.15 are described as the most valiant natives the Greeks encountered. In the parallel passage to 4.7.15, Diodorus Siculus 14.29.2 uses the name Chaldaioi (Appendix S: Selections from Diodorus). [E.] Chalybes territory: Map 4.7.1, BX (not listed in the *Barrington Atlas*). Armenia, Mardoi territory: Map 4.4.3. Babylonia: Book 2 map. Iraq: Ref. Map 8, DZ.

FIGURE 4.3.1. THE KENTRITES RIVER FLOWING
WEST TO THE TIGRIS VALLEY (ABOVE). AFTER SEVEN
DAYS IN THE MOUNTAINS OF THE KARDOUCHOI
THE GREEKS CAMPED OVERLOOKING THE RIVER
PLAIN. LATER THEY CROSSED THE RIVER AND WENT
UP THE STEEP BANKS ON THE OTHER SIDE (4.3.23).
A FOURTH-CENTURY BOEOTIAN HELMET (RIGHT)
WAS FOUND IN 1854 IN THE KENTRITES RIVER,
NOT FAR FROM WHERE THE TEN THOUSAND MAY
HAVE CROSSED THE RIVER.

were said to be a free and valiant people; they were armed with lances and long wickerwork shields. [5] The rising ground on which they were drawn up was three hundred or four hundred feet[a] distant from the river. Just one route could be seen leading up that way, apparently man-made, and the Greeks attempted to get across by it. [6] But when they tried, they found that the water came above their chests and the riverbed was rough with great, slippery stones. Furthermore, they could not hold their shields in the water as they crossed, otherwise the river swept them away, and if anyone tried to carry his shield on his head, he became exposed to enemy arrows and other missiles. So they retreated and set up camp by the river. [7] In the place on the hillside where they had passed the previous night, they could see the Kardouchoi in large numbers, assembled in arms. At this, naturally enough, a great despondency came over the Greeks as they looked at the difficult ford in the river, then at the enemy intent on stopping them from getting across, and then back at the Kardouchoi to their rear, equally intent on attacking them as they were crossing over.

[8] So for that day and night, they stayed where they were, greatly at a loss. But Xenophon had a dream: he seemed to be bound in chains, but his chains burst into pieces of their own accord, so that he was released and could stride off[a] wherever he wanted. Just before dawn, he went to Cheirisophos[b] and said that he had hopes that all would be well, and recounted the dream to him. [9] Cheirisophos was delighted, and exactly at the crack of dawn, all the generals who were present set about offering sacrifice. The sacred signs were favorable right away with the first victim.[a] Then, as they left the sacred rites, the generals and captains passed the word to the army to prepare their morning meal.

[10] As Xenophon was having his morning meal, a couple of young men ran up to him, for everyone knew that they could approach him while he was at the morning or evening meal or indeed, if he were asleep, could wake him up and speak to him if anyone had something to say relevant to the campaign. [11] So on this occasion they said that they happened to be collecting dry sticks to make a fire, and after a time they noticed on the other bank, among crags of rock that came right down to the river, an old man and a woman and some young girls depositing what looked like bags of clothes in a cavern in the rock face. [12] As they watched, it occurred to them that this was a safe place to cross, being inaccessible to the enemy horsemen at this point. So, they said, they stripped and, carrying their daggers, forded the river naked so that they would be able to swim. But, in fact, they made their way over by foot, crossing right to the other side without getting their crotches wet; and once across, they took the clothes and came back again.

4.3.8–9
February 400
KENTRITES RIVER
Despite the dire outlook, there are good omens.

4.3.10–12
February 400
KENTRITES RIVER
Two young soldiers bring Xenophon news of a way across the river.

4.3.5a  Three hundred or 400 feet/91 or 122 meters: the Greek text says 3 or 4 *plethra*; see Appendix O: Measurements, §§2–3.

4.3.8a  "Stride off": the Greek, *diabainein*, involves a play on words, the same word meaning both "stride" and "get across," as in "get across the river," underlining the

good omen of the dream.

4.3.8b  On Cheirisophos, see Appendix W: Brief Biographies, §7.

4.3.9a  For more on sacrificial divination, see Appendix G: Divinity and Divining, §2. For an illustration of this type of sacrifice (*hiera*), see Figure 2.1.9.

[13] At this Xenophon immediately prepared a libation[a] for himself and bade the young men fill a cup and pray to the gods who had revealed the dream and the ford that they would also bring what else remained to a good conclusion. When he had poured the libation, he immediately led the young men to Cheirisophos, and they repeated their story. [14] On hearing it, Cheirisophos too made a libation. After the libations, they passed the word to the others to pack up their baggage, while they themselves called the generals together and discussed how they might best get across, defeat those in front of them, and avoid damage from those in their rear. [15] They decided that Cheirisophos would take the lead and go across with half the army, the other half would wait awhile with Xenophon, and the draft animals and the crowd of noncombatants would cross between the two of them.

[16] When this division had been put into effect properly, they got on their way. The two young men led them, keeping the river on the left. The route to the river crossing was about eight hundred yards[a] long. [17] As they made their way there, the squadrons of horsemen across the river moved in parallel with them. When the Greeks were down by the crossing, right on the banks of the river, they grounded arms, and Cheirisophos was the first to take up his weapons, once he had put on a garland[a] and stripped for action. He gave the word to all the others and ordered the captains to lead off in columns, some on his left and some on his right. The seers set about making a blood sacrifice[b] so that the blood ran into the river [18] while the enemy fired arrows and slingstones, though they were as yet out of range. [19] Since the omens from the blood sacrifice were favorable, all the soldiers chanted the war hymn and raised the battle cry, while the women called out together exultantly— every one of them—and there were a lot of kept women[a] with the army.

[20] Then Cheirisophos went into the water, followed by those with him. At the same time, Xenophon took the most mobile of the troops in the rearguard and began to run with all his might back again to the other ford, the one at the low point of the road that led out into the mountains of Armenia, trying to give the impression that he was going to cross over at that point and cut off the enemy horsemen who extended along the river. [21] When the enemy horsemen saw that Cheirisophos' troops were easily getting through the water and that Xenophon's troops were running back to where they had been earlier, they were afraid of being intercepted and fled with all

4.3.13–15
February 400
KENTRITES RIVER
Libations are poured for the gods. The generals plan tactics for the crossing.

4.3.16–23
February 400
KENTRITES RIVER
*Kentrites River crossing (43)*
The main body of the army crosses the river successfully.

4.3.13a  Libations consisted of ritually pouring a liquid—most often wine but sometimes water, oil, milk, or honey—onto the ground in honor of the gods (or sometimes heroes or the dead). Here a double libation is made, partly in thanksgiving for unexpected good news and partly to request success in the crossing that will follow.

4.3.16a  Eight hundred yards/730 meters: the Greek text says 4 stades; see Appendix O: Measurements, §5.

4.3.17a  Put on a garland: in Lacedaemon, where Cheirisophos is from, it was the custom for soldiers generally to wear a wreath during the prebattle sacrifice; see Xenophon,

*Constitution of the Lacedaemonians* 13.8. Plutarch (*Life of Lycurgus* 2.2) implies that they continued to wear these wreaths during the battle, but some scholars doubt this. Lacedaemon: Map 1.2.1, BX.

4.3.17b  For the blood sacrifice (*sphagia*) that was made before battle, see Appendix G: Divinity and Divining, §2, and Figure 6.5.8.

4.3.19a  "Kept women": the Greek word used here, *hetairai*, literally "female companions," indicates that the women were not prostitutes available to all and sundry. Emily Baraganwath emphasizes the role of these women as companions in Appendix K: The Noncombatant Contingent of the Army, §12.

their might for the road up from the river. When they got to the road, they hastened up it toward the highlands. [22] Lykios, in charge of the cavalry, and Aischines, in charge of the unit of peltasts with Cheirisophos, seeing them in full flight, went in pursuit, while the mass of the soldiers shouted out not to be left behind but to break out with their comrades toward the highlands. [23] Cheirisophos, however, once he had crossed the river, did not pursue the horsemen. Instead, from a standing start where the banks came down to the river, he immediately broke out toward the enemy infantry posted directly above them. They, seeing their own horsemen in flight and hoplites advancing on them, abandoned the heights above the river.

[24] Xenophon, when he had seen that all was going well on the other side of the river,[a] went back by the fastest route he could to the army as it was crossing over, for the Kardouchoi could already be seen descending to the plain in order to attack the rear ranks. [25] At this juncture Cheirisophos was occupying the heights, while Lykios, who had set about the pursuit with a small number of horsemen, had captured the stragglers among the enemy's baggage animals and with them some fine clothing and drinking cups. [26] And now, just as the Greek baggage animals and the throng of camp followers were crossing over, Xenophon instead wheeled around toward the Kardouchoi and set his troops in position opposite them. He gave the word to the captains that each of them should maneuver his company by platoon,[a] leading each platoon in turn to the left to form the line of battle. The captains and the platoon leaders were to advance toward the Kardouchoi, while the officers of the rear rank were to remain stationed by the river.[b] [27] When the Kardouchoi saw the rearguard stripped of the throng of camp followers and evidently now few in number, they came on more quickly still, chanting various battle songs. Cheirisophos, since he had secure control over the situation in his quarter, sent the peltasts, stone slingers, and archers over to Xenophon and ordered them to do whatever Xenophon might tell them. [28] When Xenophon saw the reinforcements coming across the river, he sent a messenger and ordered them not to come across but to stay where they were by the river; his further orders were that when

4.3.24a It is conceivable that the crossing was a good deal less orderly than in Xenophon's account. Perhaps he is more concerned with presenting exemplary military maneuvers than with historical accuracy. A Boeotian helmet discovered in the vicinity in the nineteenth century may be a relic of the event. Xenophon says the Boeotian type affords the best protection to all the parts above the breastplate without obstructing the sight: see *Peri Hippikes* (*On the Art of Horsemanship*) 12.3. See Figure 4.3.24. Boeotia: Ref. Map 2, BY.

4.3.26a Although Xenophon's rearguard units were organized in platoons, they had been specially assembled (3.4.21–22), so, as John Lee points out in Appendix J: A Soldier's View of the March, §4, it might not be safe to infer the same for the wider army.

4.3.26b Starting from where the main army was crossing, the men of the rearguard ran in column, company by company, back along the riverbank in the same formation that they would have marched down to the crossing, in a long line with a narrow front. Now Xenophon wants them to form up as a phalanx in line of battle (in Greek *epi phalaggos*) in order to present a broad front to the Kardouchoi. In line of battle, each platoon formed a file with its best man, an officer, in the front rank of the file. The platoon's second (or possibly the third) best man would be in the rear rank of the file; normally to ensure that men near the back of the formation did not try to run off, but here it enables Xenophon to use the reliable rear rank to fake an advance on the pursuing enemy.

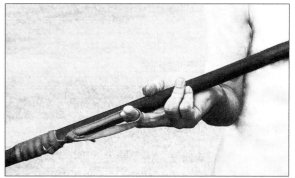

FIGURE 4.3.28. A WARRIOR PREPARING TO THROW
A SPEAR WITH THE *ANKYLĒ* LOOPED AROUND HIS
FINGERS AS DEPICTED ON A MID-SIXTH CENTURY
SIANA CUP (ABOVE). THE LEATHER THROWING LOOP
(RIGHT) HELPED CREATE A ROTATING MOTION
ABOUT THE SPEAR'S AXIS TO INCREASE THE DISTANCE
THE SPEAR WAS ABLE TO TRAVEL. IN COMBAT, THE
*ANKYLE* WAS PERMANENTLY ATTACHED TO THE SPEAR
FOR MILITARY READINESS.

his own troops began to cross, the reinforcements were to enter the river on the opposite side, advancing to the left and to the right of them. The reinforcements were to start as if about to come right across the river, the javelin-men with fingers through the throwing loop ready to throw,[a] the archers with their arrows on the string ready to shoot; but, in fact, they were not to advance far into the river. [29] To the troops with him, Xenophon gave instructions that as soon as the enemy's slingstones carried to them and they first heard the pellets rattle down on their shields, they should chant the war hymn and run toward the enemy; but when the enemy turned back and they heard the trumpeter sound the charge from the river, they should about-face by the right and, with the rear-rank officers in the lead, all run and cross the river as fast as possible, each soldier keeping to his own file so as not to get in each other's way; and he said that best among them would be the one who was first on the other side of the river.

[30] The Kardouchoi could see that the remaining troops were already few in number—for many even among those detailed to stay had gone, variously looking after the draft animals or the baggage or the kept women— and at this, naturally enough, they set about attacking boldly and began to use their slings and their bows. [31] But the Greeks chanted their war hymn and set off eagerly against them at a run. The enemy did not withstand their charge, since they were equipped suitably for the flying charges and retreats of mountain warfare but quite unsuitably for hand-to-hand fighting. [32] At this point the trumpeter blew the signal. And at that the enemy fled much faster still, while the Greeks turned around in the opposite direction and set about escaping across the river as fast as possible. [33] Some of the enemy, realizing this, ran back again toward the river and wounded a few Greeks with their arrows, but most of them were still visibly in flight even when the Greeks had already crossed to the other side. [34] But the reinforcements who had come to meet Xenophon's division, playing up their manliness and advancing farther than was sensible, consequently had to recross the river behind his troops, and some of these were wounded too.

4.4.1–6
February 400
ARMENIA
*Armenian satrap's palace (44)–
Tigris crossing (45)–
Teleboas crossing (46)*
The Greeks press on through Armenia. They come to an agreement with Tiribazos.

[1] When they had crossed the river, they formed up together at about midday and made their way through Armenia over a completely flat plain and gently rising hills for at least five parasangs,[a] there being no villages close to the river because of the wars against the Kardouchoi. [2] The first village they reached was a large one, with a palace for the satrap[a] and turrets on most of the houses; and food supplies were plentiful. [3] From here they made their way onward for two days' march, over ten parasangs, until they had crossed the headwaters of the river Tigris, and from there they made

4.3.28a On the throwing loop (*ankylē*), see n. 4.2.28b; also see Figure 4.3.28.

4.4.1a The parasang is a Persian unit for measuring travel, typically of around 3 miles/ 5 kilometers, but it is controversial whether it measures hours spent traveling, distance traveled, or a combination of the two; see the Introduction, §7.3–5, and Appendix O: Measurements, §§7–8. It is

an exaggeration to describe the plain to the north of the Kentrites as "completely flat"; in fact, from this point there is a steady rise into the highlands of Armenia.

4.4.2a Satrap: governor of a province of the Persian empire; for more, see the Glossary. Armenian satrap's palace, probable location: Map 4.4.3, *Halting place 44.*

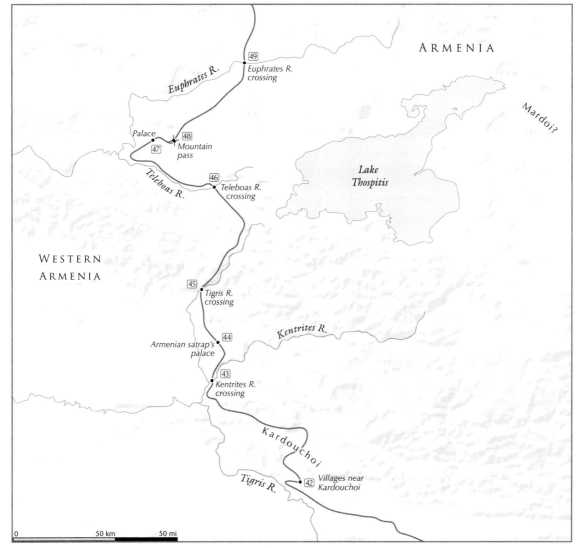

MAP 4.4.3. *KATABASIS:* FROM KARDOUCHOI TERRITORY TO THE EUPHRATES RIVER CROSSING, *HALTING PLACES 42–49.*

their way for three days, covering fifteen parasangs, to the river Teleboas, a beautiful river but not a big one, with many villages around it.[a] [4] This area was called Western Armenia.[a] Its lieutenant governor was Tiribazos,[b] who was a friend of the King himself: whenever he was present, it was he and no one else who helped the King mount his horse. [5] Tiribazos himself rode up with some horsemen and sent forward an interpreter to say that he would like to have a discussion with the army's leaders. The generals decided to hear what he had to say, and going up to within earshot, they asked what he wanted. [6] He said he would like both sides to agree to a sworn truce whereby he would not harm the Greeks and they would not burn the houses and would receive whatever food supplies they might need. These proposals seemed good ones to the generals, and they swore a truce on these terms.

[7] From there they made their way through the plain for three days' march, covering fifteen parasangs.[a] In the meantime, Tiribazos dogged their footsteps with his forces, keeping a distance of around a mile or so.[b] They eventually reached a palace[c] with many villages around it, full of food supplies in abundance. [8] While they camped there, there was a heavy snowfall in the night,[a] and just after dawn they decided that the various units, along with their respective generals, should be split up and billeted in the villages, as they saw no one hostile and they appeared to be safe from attack because of the great quantity of snow. [9] There they had access to good food supplies of every sort—animals for sacrifice, corn, old wines with a fine bouquet, dried grapes, all kinds of pulses. But several of those who had strayed from the camp reported that during the night they had seen many fires blazing. [10] Then it seemed to the generals that it was not safe to split up the troops in separate quarters, and they decided to bring the army together again. Accordingly, they reassembled, especially as the sky seemed to be clearing. [11] However, while they were spending the night there, a terrifying amount of snow fell and buried the weapon stacks, and the people too where they lay. The snow also meant that the draft animals could not move their legs.

4.4.7–13
Late February 400
ARMENIA
*Palace (47)*
The Greeks find plentiful supplies but encounter a heavy snowfall.

4.4.3a  Tigris headwaters crossing to the Teleboas River, Map 4.4.3, *Halting places 45–46*. This stretch of river is not identified in the *Barrington Atlas*. The name Tigris was usually applied in antiquity to a more westerly branch. Two days after crossing the river, the army would have come close to but not in sight of Lake Thospitis. As it turned west, its route descended onto a great expansive plain through which flowed the Teleboas River. Lake Thospitis: Map 4.4.3.

4.4.4a  Western Armenia was a subdivision within the satrapy of Armenia; see Map 4.4.3.

4.4.4b  For Tiribazos' eventful subsequent career and relations with Orontas, see Appendix W: Brief Biographies, §36.

4.4.7a  Initially in this section of the march the army was heading northwest toward the Euphrates River. It would have been natural, on reaching it, to cross and continue north-

west, yet instead it seems they turned northeast. The problem this presents is discussed in Appendix P: The Route of the Ten Thousand, §7, where it is suggested that their turn was part of the agreement with Tiribazos mentioned at 4.4.6 but Xenophon has suppressed it. Euphrates River: Map 4.4.3.

4.4.7b  Around a mile/1.5 kilometers: the Greek text says 10 stades; see Appendix O: Measurements, §5. The nature of Tiribazos' forces is discussed in Appendix D: The Persian Army, §5.

4.4.7c  Palace: Map 4.4.3, *Halting place 47*.

4.4.8a  Snowfall in this region starts in November, with the heaviest amounts typically seen in late winter. Xenophon's remarking on a huge fall at 4.4.11 would best fit with the profile for February and helps refine the chronology of the march; see Appendix Q: The Chronology of the March, §§3, 5.

There was great reluctance about getting up, as where the snow had fallen on people, it warmed them as they lay there, except where it slipped off. [12] But when Xenophon brought himself to stand up, though not fully dressed, and to begin to split wood, someone else also quickly got up and, taking over from him, went on with the wood splitting. Thereupon the others too stood up and set about lighting fires and greasing themselves: [13] for they found a large quantity of ointment there, used in those parts instead of olive oil and made of pork fat, sesame, extract of bitter almonds, and pistachio nuts; and they also found a more heavily perfumed oil made from the same ingredients.[a]

[14] After this they decided they had once again to disperse the soldiers' billets throughout the villages so as to get under cover. The soldiers then naturally made for the shelter of the houses and the food supplies in them with gusto and a lot of shouting. Out of crazy recklessness, some soldiers had set fire to their houses when they left them on the earlier occasion, and now they paid the price in having poor quarters. [15] At this point they sent Demokrates of Temnos[a] by night with some men to the mountains where those who had strayed from the camp had said they saw the fires, since even before this he had gained a reputation for accurate reconnaissance on many occasions. If something was so, he would report that it was so. If something was not so, he would report that it was not so. [16] When he had made his way there and back, though he said he did not see the fires, he had captured a man and come back with him in tow, carrying a Persian bow and quiver and a battle-axe, such as the Amazons have too.[a] [17] Asked where he was from, the prisoner said he was a Persian and was making his way from Tiribazos' camp in order to get food supplies. They interrogated him as to how large the army was and for what reason it had been brought together. [18] He replied that it was Tiribazos with his own forces as well as Chalybian and Taochian mercenaries; the pass over the mountain had a narrow stretch that travelers could not avoid, and he had made preparations to set upon the Greeks there.[a]

4.4.14–18
Late February 400
ARMENIA
Demokrates' reconnaissance discovers that Tiribazos is preparing an ambush.

4.4.13a  Ancient peoples habitually spread oil or grease over their skin to increase suppleness (especially before and after exercise), to combat dryness, and, in winter, to increase the retention of body heat.

4.4.15a  Temnos: Map 5.3.7, BY.

4.4.16a  Legends about Amazon warrior women from far away were, incidentally, widespread among the Greeks from at least Homer's time, and they were frequently depicted in combat with men in statuary and vase paintings. In referring matter-of-factly about their existence in the fifth century, Xenophon is not being credulous; only one ancient source expresses any doubts, the second-century C.E. historian of Alexander the Great, Arrian (*Anabasis Alexandrou* 7.13.4), and even he does not dispute that they once existed. The oldest stories were probably just myths, but it seems that there really were

warrior women among the Sauromatai who lived north of the Black Sea (Herodotus 4.110–117; Wheeler 2007, Appendix F: Rivers and Peoples of Scythia, §5). Sauromatai: Ref. Map 1, AY. Black Sea: Map 4.4.3, locator (Pontus in the *Barrington Atlas*).

4.4.18a  Perhaps Tiribazos hoped to destroy the Greeks when he directed them this way. It would have been harder to destroy them had he allowed them to cross the river at the foot of the plain, which was the logical way for the Greeks to proceed homeward. Xenophon does not explain why the Greeks accepted the route northeast over this mountain pass as the only way they could go. See Appendix P: The Route of the Ten Thousand, §6. [E.] Chalybes, Taochoi territories: Map 4.7.1, BY (the [Eastern] Chalybes are not listed in the *Barrington Atlas*).

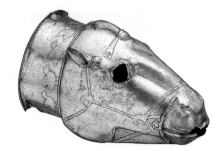

FIGURE 4.4.21. TWO ACHAEMENID DRINKING VESSELS (*RHYTONS*) FROM IRAN. AT LEFT, GOLD CUP IN THE SHAPE OF A LION'S FOREBODY, FIFTH OR FOURTH CENTURY; ABOVE, SILVER CUP IN THE SHAPE OF A HORSE'S HEAD WITH BRIDLE, C. FIFTH CENTURY.

**4.4.19–22**
**Late February 400**
ARMENIA
The Greek peltasts capture Tiribazos' camp, complete with luxury items.

[19] On hearing this, the generals decided to concentrate the army again; and as soon as they had done so, they left guards behind, with Sophainetos of Stymphalos[a] as general over those who were staying, and made their way onward with the fellow who had been captured as their guide. [20] When they were passing over the mountains, the peltasts, who were going on ahead, caught sight of the enemy camp; they did not wait for the hoplites but, shouting loudly, ran toward it. [21] When they heard the uproar, the barbarians did not stand their ground but broke into flight; nevertheless, some of the barbarians were killed, and some twenty horses were captured. They also captured the tent of Tiribazos, and in it couches with silver feet, drinking cups, and people calling themselves his bread makers and wine pourers.[a] [22] When the generals of the hoplites learned this, they decided to go back as fast as possible to their own camp, so as to avoid any surprise attack on the troops who had been left there. Immediately they sounded the recall by trumpet and returned, arriving in the camp on the same day.

**4.5.1–2**
**March 400**
ARMENIA
*Mountain pass (48)–*
*Euphrates crossing (49)*
The Greeks cross the Euphrates River.

[1] The following day it was decided that they should make their way onward as fast as they possibly could, before the enemy army reassembled and occupied the narrow places on the route. So they immediately packed up and set about making their way through the deep snow with a considerable number of guides, and that same day they crossed over the high point[a] where Tiribazos had been intending to attack them and pitched camp. [2] From there they made their way onward[a] for three desolate days' march, covering

4.4.19a For Xenophon's attitude toward Sophainetos, see Appendix W: Brief Biographies,
§32. Stymphalos: Map 1.2.1, AY.
4.4.21a The Greeks made much of what they saw
as excessive luxury among the Persian elite.
Although not showing the strong distaste
of some other authors, Xenophon is happy
to take the opportunity to report the
lifestyles of senior Persian officials even
while on campaign. See Figure 4.4.21 for
Persian gold and silver drinking vessels.
4.5.1a High point: Mountain pass, Map 4.4.3,

*Halting place 48.*
4.5.2a This passage (4.5.1–3) has the highest
concentration in *Anabasis* of Xenophon's
favorite verb, *poreuesthai*, in this edition
translated "to make one's way." For general
remarks as to why he does this, see the Translator's Notes, §5. Here it seems to emphasize
both that this part of the march was a hard,
boring slog and, conversely, that they were
nevertheless still progressing toward their
ultimate goal. (Translator's note)

fifteen parasangs, to the river Euphrates[b] and crossed it with the water at waist height.[c] The river's sources were said to be not much farther on.

[3] From there they continued to make their way through deep snow over level ground for three days' march, covering thirteen parasangs.[a] The third day's march was a difficult one, and a gale from the north blew straight at them, parching every living thing with windburn and numbing the people stiff. [4] At that, then, one of the seers prescribed a blood sacrifice to the wind and proceeded to carry it out; and it seemed clear to all of them that the severity of the wind slackened. The snow was six feet[a] deep, so that many of both the draft animals and the slaves perished, and about thirty of the soldiers. [5] They got through the night by keeping fires burning. There was a lot of wood at the place where they halted[a]—but those who came along late were left without any, and so those who had arrived earlier and whose fires were ablaze did not allow latecomers up to the fire unless they shared wheat with them or anything else edible that they might have. [6] Consequently they gave each other a share of what each group had. Where the fires were burning, the melting of the snow caused great hollows to appear, right down to the bare earth; from this it was possible to measure the depth of the snow.

[7] The following day they continued to make their way from there through the snow, and many people fainted from extreme hunger. Xenophon, in the rearguard, came upon people falling down and did not recognize the condition they were suffering from. [8] But when someone who was familiar with it told him that they were clearly fainting from starvation and if they ate something, they would get up, he went around among the draft animals looking for anything edible and set about distributing it. Back and forth he sent those who were capable of running so far, giving the food as they went to those who had fainted from starvation; [9] and once these people had eaten something, they would get up and make their way onward.

And as they made their way, Cheirisophos reached a village[a] about dusk, and outside its stockade captured some women and girls from the village at the well, about to carry back some water. [10] The women asked who they were, and the interpreter replied in Persian that they were making their way

---

**4.5.3–6**
March 400
ARMENIA NORTH OF
THE EUPHRATES
*Halt in snow? (50)*
The army faces difficult conditions because of strong winds and deep snow.

**4.5.7–8**
March 400
ARMENIA NORTH OF
THE EUPHRATES
Hunger adds to the army's difficulties. Xenophon organizes a simple food distribution.

**4.5.9–11**
March 400
ARMENIA NORTH OF
THE EUPHRATES
*Underground villages (51)*
The vanguard reaches shelter, but much of the army is unable to do so.

---

4.5.2b  Crossing of the Euphrates: Map 4.7.1, BY, *Halting place 49* (the *Barrington Atlas* labels the river Arsanias at this point, a name given to this stretch of it in later antiquity).

4.5.2c  At 3.2.22 Xenophon said, in a morale-raising speech to the troops, that they would be able to cross the river with the water reaching only to their knees, whereas when they actually come to the river, it turns out to be deeper. For other respects in which the speech did not represent the author's real views, see Appendix E: Panhellenism, §7.

4.5.3a  The text here is uncertain, and most modern editors mark the passage as corrupt. Most manuscripts say "fifteen

parasangs," but many scholars cannot believe that the army traveled as far as this in blizzard conditions. For more on the text and its transmission, see the Translator's Notes, §§10–18.

4.5.4a  Six feet/2 meters: the Greek text says 1 *orguia* (sometimes translated "fathom"); see Appendix O: Measurements, §§2–3.

4.5.5a  Halt in snow (north of the Euphrates), possible location: Map 4.7.1, BY, *Halting place 50.*

4.5.9a  On Cheirisophos, see Appendix W: Brief Biographies, §7. Underground villages: Map 4.7.1, BY, *Halting place 51;* Xenophon does not mention that the villages' houses are underground until 4.5.25.

from the King to the satrap. They answered that he was not there but about a parasang away.[a] Since it was late, the soldiers went with the water carriers into the stockade to see the village headman. [11] And so Cheirisophos and as many of the army as could do so encamped there, but among the other soldiers, those who could not manage to complete the journey spent the night without food or fire, and because of this some of the soldiers died of exposure.

[12] Following them came a band of the enemy, making off with those draft animals that were unable to go farther and fighting with each other over them. Soldiers fell behind if they had become snow blind or had their toes rot off their feet through frostbite, [13] but a soldier could protect his eyes from the snow glare if he kept something dark in front of him as he made his way, and he could protect his feet if he kept moving, never had a rest, and took his shoes off at night. [14] Those who slept with them still strapped up found that the leather straps bit into their feet and the shoes froze onto their flesh all around; this happened because these were primitive shoes made of freshly flayed oxhide, since their old footwear had worn out.[a]

[15] Under such pressure from the harsh conditions, some of the soldiers had been left behind. They noticed a dark patch of ground and inferred, because of the absence of snow, that it had melted. And they were right: this was because, close by in a wooded hollow, there was a hot spring throwing off steam.[a] So they turned aside and sat there, saying they would not go on. [16] But when Xenophon, coming up with the rearguard, saw them, he begged them, using all the arguments and wiles he could muster, not to stay behind, telling them that some of the enemy had banded together and were on their tail. In the end he got angry, but they told him to slit their throats, for they could not make their way onward any farther. [17] The best thing, then, seemed to be, if they could, to frighten the enemy tailing them and so prevent their attacking the sick and weary troops. It was already dark, and the enemy were approaching in a great hubbub as they wrangled over the booty they had taken. [18] So then the rearguard, who were in good health, got up and ran toward the enemy while the sick troops shouted as loud as they could and banged their shields against their spears. The enemy, in fear, hurled themselves down the snow into the wooded hollow, and none of them uttered a sound at all after that.

[19] So Xenophon and the troops with him said to the invalids that some people would come back for them the following day, and they them-

4.5.12–21
March 400
UNDERGROUND VILLAGES
Many soldiers suffer from frostbite, and some refuse to go on despite Xenophon's best efforts.

FIGURE 4.5.14. THE *KRĒPIS*, A TYPE OF SANDAL USED FOR LONG-DISTANCE TRAVEL, AS SHOWN ON A COLUMN FRAGMENT FROM THE TEMPLE OF ARTEMIS AT EPHESUS, C. 340–320.

4.5.10a  In Appendix D: The Persian Army, §13, Christopher Tuplin notes the women's seeming lack of surprise at the appearance of a force of Greek soldiers in search of the satrap.

4.5.14a  The usual shoe for long-distance travelers on foot was the *krēpis*, a type of sandal (Figure 4.5.14) with a network over much of the foot of fairly elaborate narrow straps and loops tightened with laces. The primitive shoes which the soldiers now wore

may have been no more than a sole and a pair of knotted broad straps. The extreme cold and wet would have made it difficult to undo the knot.

4.5.15a  Owing to its situation on major fault lines, Anatolia is rich in thermal springs. Over a thousand are known today, many in this region; however, seismic activity closes old and opens new ones over time. Anatolia: Ref. Map 7, BX.

selves continued to make their way onward. Before they had traveled half a mile,[a] they came upon soldiers at rest on the track in the snow all wrapped up, with no guard whatsoever set, and they tried to make them get up. But the soldiers said that those in front would not let them through. [20] Xenophon bypassed them and sent ahead the most vigorous of the peltasts, telling them to find out what the obstacle was. They reported back that the whole army was likewise at rest. [21] Consequently Xenophon's troops too bivouacked there, without fire or food, having posted such guards as they could. Around daybreak Xenophon sent the youngest of his troops to the invalids with orders to force them to stand up and go on.

[22] Meanwhile Cheirisophos sent some troops from the village to find out how things were with the troops at the rear. The latter were pleased to see them and handed over the invalids to them to take to the main camp while they made their own way there; and before they had traveled two and a half miles,[a] they were in the village where Cheirisophos was bivouacking. [23] When they all got together, they decided it was safe for the units to take up quarters dispersed through the different villages. Cheirisophos continued to stay where he was, while the other generals drew lots for the villages they could see and then made their way to them, each with his own troops. [24] At this point Polykrates, an Athenian captain, urged them to send him off separately; taking the mobile troops with him, he ran to the village that Xenophon had been allotted and captured all the villagers inside it, together with the village headman, seventeen colts that were being reared as tribute for the King,[a] and the headman's daughter, only nine days after her marriage. Her husband was off hunting hares and was not taken in the village.

[25] The houses were underground, with a mouth like that of a well but broadening out below. The entrances for the draft animals were dug out, while people went down a staircase.[a] In the houses were goats, sheep, cattle, poultry, and their young; all the livestock were reared inside on fodder. [26] Here there were also wheat and barley and beans, and barley wine in large bowls;[a] in the bowls the grains of barley floated level with the brim, and unjointed straws were left in them, some larger, some smaller. [27] Whenever anyone went to drink, he had to take these straws and suck the

4.5.22–24
March 400
UNDERGROUND VILLAGES
In the morning the generals divide up the available villages among their units.

4.5.25–27
March 400
UNDERGROUND VILLAGES
The Greeks drink barley wine in the underground houses of the Armenians.

---

4.5.19a  Half a mile/0.8 kilometer: the Greek text says 4 stades; see Appendix O: Measurements, §5.

4.5.22a  Two and a half miles/4 kilometers: the Greek text says 20 stades.

4.5.24a  According to the first-century geographer Strabo (11.14.9), every year the satrap of Armenia had to provide twenty thousand colts to be sacrificed during the festival of Mithra, a Persian warrior god and protector of the fields. Mithra had strong associations with the sun, so he is probably the Persian god who is referred to as Helios at 4.5.35, where a particular horse is said to be sacred to him. Figure 4.5.34 shows how the Persians naturally associated Armenians with horse rearing. For more on horses as tribute, see Appendix C: The

Persian Empire, §21.

4.5.25a  Traveling in this region in the nineteenth century, the British explorer and diplomat Robert Curzon described similar dwellings in use in the hills near Erzurum, with animals and people spending the winter in underground sites apparently as large as an acre (Curzon 1854, 45–51). Similar structures, known as "underground cities," can still be seen in areas of Cappadocia on the southern side of Anatolia; see Figure 4.5.25 for an example. Erzurum: Ref. Map 8, BY. Cappadocia: Book 1 map.

4.5.26a  Barley wine: actually a type of strong beer from eastern Anatolia, although this region was better known in antiquity for its production of wine (and see 4.2.22).

FIGURE 4.5.25.
UNDERGROUND
DWELLINGS LIKE THIS
HELD WINE PRESSES
AND ANIMAL STABLES.
ALTHOUGH APPARENTLY
ORIGINALLY HOLLOWED
OUT IN 800–700 B.C.E.,
THE UNDERGROUND
STRUCTURE IN THIS
FORM DATES FROM
1000 C.E.

4.5.28–33
March 400
UNDERGROUND VILLAGES
Xenophon and headman
visit Cheirisophos and are
feted in villages on the
way.

liquor up into his mouth. It was very strong if you didn't add water;[a] and very sweet was the draft to one who had learned the secret of drinking it.

[28] Xenophon made the headman of this village his companion for dinner and told him to take heart, saying that he would not be deprived of his children and that the Greeks would move on after replenishing his house with food supplies if it became clear, before they found themselves amid another tribe, that he had put the army onto something good. [29] He promised to do so and, to show his friendliness, told Xenophon where some wine was stored underground. So for that night in their various quarters, the soldiers slept amid plenty, with the headman kept under guard and his children with him under their eyes.

[30] On the following day, Xenophon took the headman and set out on his way to Cheirisophos. Whenever he went by a village, he would turn aside to see the troops quartered in it and found them everywhere feasting and in good spirits. In every village the troops would not let them go until they had laid out breakfast for them, [31] and in every village they laid out on the one table all sorts of meats—lamb, kid, pork, veal, poultry—together with many loaves of bread, some made of wheat and some of barley. [32] Whenever anyone wanted to toast someone to show his friendliness, he would pull him over to the wine bowl, where he had to bend his head over and drink in gulps like an ox. They offered the headman whatever he might want to take, but the only use he made of this offer was that whenever he saw any

4.5.27a  It was customary for Greeks to dilute their
        wine with water.

FIGURE 4.5.34. THREE ARMENIANS IN CHARACTERISTIC COSTUME LEAD A HORSE AS TRIBUTE FOR THE GREAT KING, AS DEPICTED IN THE FRIEZE ON THE APADANA EAST STAIRCASE IN PERSEPOLIS.

of his relatives, he always took them off with him. [33] When they came to Cheirisophos, Xenophon found him with his troops in their quarters, all crowned with garlands made of hay and with teenage Armenian boys serving them, dressed in their barbarian garments, to whom they made clear by gestures whatever they had to do, as if they were deaf.

[34] After Cheirisophos and Xenophon had greeted each other effusively, they jointly interrogated the village headman through their Persian-speaking interpreter as to what country they were in. He replied, "Armenia." They asked him for whom the horses were being reared, and he replied that they were tribute for the King. He said that the neighboring land belonged to the Chalybes[a] and explained where the road went. [35] At that point Xenophon went back with the headman to his household. He gave the headman a horse he had captured, a rather old one, to fatten up for sacrifice, because he had heard that it was sacred to Helios[a] and was fearful that it might die, as it had been badly affected by the journey. He took some of the colts himself and gave a colt to each of the other generals and captains. [36] The horses here were smaller than the Persian ones but much more high-spirited. The head-

4.5.34–36
March 400
UNDERGROUND VILLAGES
The village headman gives useful information and advice.

4.5.34a   When the army finally meets the [Eastern] Chalybes in their homeland (4.7.15), it seems not to be contiguous with that of the Armenians but on the farther side of the Taochoi. But the Greeks had gone a long way around from here, so we should not doubt the juxtaposition. [E.] Chalybes,

Taochoi territory: Map 4.7.1, BY (the [Eastern] Chalybes are not listed in the *Barrington Atlas*).
4.5.35a   Helios, the Greek sun god, here presumably stands for the Persian god Mithra; for more on Mithra and on horses sacred to the sun god, see n. 4.5.24a.

man then explained to him that they should tie bags around the feet of the horses and draft animals when they were leading them through the snow, as without these bags they would sink down in it up to the belly.

**4.6.1–3**
**March 400**
PHASIS RIVER
*Guide runs off*
*(52 or 52 Alt.)*
The village headman acts as guide but runs away after Cheirisophos strikes him.

[1] After they had been there seven days, Xenophon handed the headman over to Cheirisophos to act as guide, but he left the rest of his household behind except for the son, who was just coming into the bloom of youth. Him he handed over to Pleisthenes of Amphipolis[a] to guard, so that if the headman guided them properly, he could depart, taking his son with him as well. They brought as many contributions to his house as they possibly could, as if it were the treasury and they were tax collectors, and then harnessed up and set off on their way. [2] The headman, who was left unbound, led them through the snow, and they were on their third day's march when Cheirisophos got angry with him because he was not taking them to villages; but he said that there weren't any in this region. [3] Cheirisophos hit him, but he still did not tie him up. After this, the headman ran off in the night,[a] leaving his son behind. This incident—the combination of mistreating the guide and then being careless about him—was the only thing about which Cheirisophos and Xenophon had a serious disagreement during the whole journey. Pleisthenes fell in love with the boy and, when he got back home with him, found him very faithful.

**4.6.4–9**
**March 400**
PASS NORTH OF THE
PHASIS RIVER
*Army leaves river*
*(53 or 53 Alt.)*
Tribesmen block a strategic pass, and the generals take counsel on tactics.

[4] After this they made their way onward for seven days' march, at the rate of five parasangs a day, along the river Phasis,[a] which is about a hundred feet in width.[b] [5] From there they made their way onward for two days' march, covering ten parasangs.[a] On the pass to the plain beyond, the Chalybes,

4.6.1a Pleisthenes of Amphipolis: some manuscripts and editors give this man's name as Episthenes, presumably by identifying him with both the peltast commander Episthenes of Amphipolis (1.10.7) and the boy-lover Episthenes of Olynthos (7.4.7–11). Amphipolis: Map 5.3.7, AX.

4.6.3a Guide runs off: Map 4.7.1, BY, *Halting place 52* or *52 Alt*. The difference between these two locations is a side effect of a more basic difference, explained in n. 4.6.5a, about how far the army diverted from the direct route to the Black Sea.

4.6.4a The army, now without its guide, may have become confused here. This Phasis River in Armenia led to the Caspian Sea and for most of its course was known as the Araxes River (this edition differs from the *Barrington Atlas* about the precise point of changeover in 400). There was another Phasis River much farther north in Colchis that flowed into the Black Sea, and from a remark by the senior officer Neon reported at 5.7.1, it appears that the soldiers identified the two rivers and wrongly thought that if they followed the Phasis River in Armenia it would eventually bring them to the Black Sea; see Appendix P: The Route of the Ten Thousand, §9. The two Phasis Rivers, Map 4.7.1: in Armenia, BY; in Colchis, AY. Phasis/Araxes River: Book 4 map. Caspian Sea: Ref. Map 1, AZ.

4.6.4b A hundred feet/30 meters: the Greek text says 1 *plethron;* see Appendix O: Measurements, §§2–3. Diodorus 14.29.1 (in Appendix S: Diodorus) says the army stayed at the river for four days, although he does not say whether these were in addition to Xenophon's seven-day march along the river. For a discussion of this discrepancy in context, see Appendix M: Other Ancient Sources on the Ten Thousand, §5.

4.6.5a It seems that after seven days of marching along the river, and now traveling in a more or less easterly direction, the army realized it was off course and turned north, leaving the Phasis. Where it did so is controversial. On the main route in this edition, it went eastward only briefly, to *Halting place 53* on Map 4.7.1, AY, and then turned northward to a pass over the watershed, *Halting place 54* (see n. 4.6.27a). David Thomas, in common with some other scholars, thinks that the soldiers went about 80 miles farther east: the alternate route shown takes them down to *Halting place 53 Alt*., before they turn north to *Halting place 54 Alt*. Very likely the army's northward turn, wherever it was, was prompted by intelligence or local knowledge; in these remote areas it was probably normal practice to interrogate captives as to the surrounding territory (note Xenophon's reply to Cheirisophos at 4.6.17).

FIGURE 4.6.5. THE MODERN ÇAKIRBABA PASS, IN THE AREA WHERE XENOPHON SAYS THREE NATIVE TRIBES MADE A STAND AGAINST THE GREEKS BUT WERE OUTFLANKED. BEYOND THIS DIVIDE, ALL RIVERS FLOW INTO THE BLACK SEA.

Taochoi, and Phasianoi stood ready to meet them.[b] [6] When Cheirisophos saw the enemy on the pass, he stopped making his way forward and kept a distance of about three and a half miles,[a] in order not to get close to them while marching in column. He passed the word to the other generals to bring up their companies so as to form the army into line of battle. [7] When the rearguard had arrived, he called together the generals and the captains and said, "The enemy, as you see, are occupying the passes over the mountain. It's time to consider together how to carry on the contest as honorably as possible. [8] My thought is to pass the word to the soldiers to have their morning meal while we discuss whether to cross the mountain today or tomorrow." [9] "In my opinion," said Kleanor,[a] "as soon as we have eaten our breakfast, we should fully arm ourselves and attack the men as quickly as possible. If we fritter today away, the enemy, who can already see us, will grow bolder and most likely others will join them in larger numbers in view of their confidence."

[10] After him Xenophon spoke: "This is how I see it. If we really have to fight, our preparations must be directed to fighting as effectively as possible. But if our objective is to get over the pass as easily as we can, it seems to me that what we have to consider is how to sustain the minimum number of wounds and how to squander the minimum number of our men's lives. [11]

4.6.10–15
March 400
PASS NORTH OF THE
PHASIS RIVER
Xenophon offers sound
tactical advice and ribs
Cheirisophos.

4.6.5b  Phasianoi territories: Map 4.7.1, BY
(Phasioi in the *Barrington Atlas*).
4.6.6a  About three and a half miles/5.5 kilometers: the Greek text says 30 stades; see

Appendix O: Measurements, §5.
4.6.9a  On Kleanor, see Appendix W: Brief
Biographies, §19.

Now, the mountain we can see extends for more than seven miles,[a] but no men can be seen guarding it against us except on the road itself. So rather than fighting against easily defensible places and men who are ready for us, it is much better to try to take control of a bit of the deserted mountain by stealth, without being noticed, snatching it from the enemy by getting there first if we can. [12] It is much easier to go uphill without fighting than it is to go on the level where there are enemies on both sides; and even at night, if you aren't fighting, you can see what lies immediately ahead better than you can by day if you are in a battle. Similarly, as long as there's no fighting, rough country is not as uncomfortable for those going over it on foot as level ground is for those whose heads are being hit by missiles. [13] And to steal a position does not seem impossible to me, since our troops can go by night so as not to be seen, and they can go at a sufficient distance so as not to give a whisper or whiff of what they are doing. I would also think that if we pretended we were going to make an attack along the road, we might then usefully find the rest of the mountain more deserted, since the enemy would be even more likely to stay where they are in close order. [14] But why am I the one putting forward ideas about stealing? What I at any rate hear, Cheirisophos, is that you Lacedaemonians—you at least who are numbered among the *homoioi*[a]—practice stealing from your earliest boyhood, and that to steal things other than those that custom forbids is not disgraceful for you but something noble. [15] And so that you may steal as effectively as possible and make efforts to avoid detection, it is customary, I gather, for you to be whipped if you are caught stealing.[a] So now has come the time for you to show off your education and really take care that we are not caught as we steal part of the mountain, so that we shall not get a beating."

Cheirisophos ribs Xenophon in turn, and they agree on the arrangements.

[16] "But on the contrary," said Cheirisophos, "what I hear is that you Athenians are terribly clever at stealing public money, even though it's an especially terrible danger that the thief is running—and indeed I hear that this is especially true of the best among you, assuming that with you it is the best who are thought fit to rule. So it's time for you too to show off your education." [17] "Then," said Xenophon, "I am ready to go with the rearguard troops and seize the mountain once we have had our meal. I

---

4.6.11a Seven miles/11 kilometers: the Greek text says 60 stades.
4.6.14a *Homoioi*: this Greek word, translated sometimes as "the Equals" but more literally as "the Similars," refers to the relatively small (and at this period shrinking) group of full Spartan citizens who alone, among the highly stratified inhabitants of Laconia, had voting rights in the Spartan assembly. The truth is that the Spartans did not maintain anything close to political or social equality among their citizens and were growing more unequal at this period, but the fiction of near-equality was ideologically important to them; see Appendix

B: Xenophon and Sparta, §§19–20. Lacedaemon, Laconia: Map 1.2.1, BX, BY.
4.6.15a Teenage Spartans were apparently expected to practice their foraging skills by stealing food and supplies from country dwellings or from the official messes for Spartan adults. They were admired for successes but punished if caught. The actual extent of the custom is disputed by modern scholars. Xenophon's phrase "other than those that custom forbids" indicates that there was a limit on the sort of things that, and/or the circumstances in which, it was socially sanctioned for youngsters to steal; see Appendix B, §20.

even have guides, for the light-armed soldiers ambushed and captured some of the thieves who follow us, and from them I gather that the mountain is not impassable but provides grazing for goats and cattle. So if we just occupy a bit of the mountain, there will be accessible routes even for the draft animals. [18] I expect that the enemy will not hold their ground any longer, once they see us on the same level as them on the heights, since at the moment they don't want to come down and be on equal terms with us." [19] Cheirisophos replied, "Why is it necessary for you to go and abandon your post in the rearguard? Send others instead— unless perhaps there are some volunteers?" [20] At this Aristonymos of Methydrion came forward with his hoplites, Aristeas the Chian with his light-armed troops, and Nikomachos of Oeta,[a] also with light-armed troops. The arrangement they made for a signal was to set many fires blazing if and when they occupied the heights. [21] Once this had been settled, they all set about having their morning meal, and after the morning meal, Cheirisophos led out the whole army for a mile or so[a] toward the enemy, to make it seem as far as possible that they were going to attack by this route.

[22] When they had had their evening meal and night had fallen, the task force set off and occupied the mountain, while the others rested where they were. When the enemy realized that the mountain was held against them, they stayed wide awake and kept many fires burning during the night. [23] When day came, Cheirisophos offered sacrifice and led the main army along the road while the troops who had occupied the mountain advanced over the heights. [24] Most of the enemy waited on the mountain pass, but a party of them went to meet those coming over the heights. Before the main bodies of the two armies closed on each other, the detachments on the heights were fighting hand to hand, and the Greeks were victorious and started the pursuit. [25] Meanwhile the Greek force coming from the plain also quickened its pace as the peltasts broke into a run toward the enemy battle line and Cheirisophos followed with the hoplites at a quick march. [26] When the enemy on the road saw that their party on the higher ground was getting the worst of it, they fled. A few of them were killed, and a great number of wicker shields were captured, which the Greeks rendered useless by hacking them with their sabers. [27] When they had ascended the pass,[a] they performed a sacrifice and set up a trophy;[b] then

4.6.22–27
March–April 400
PASS NORTH OF THE
PHASIS RIVER–
TAOCHOI TERRITORY
*Pass to plain (54 or 54 Alt.)*
Xenophon's plan succeeds
and the Greeks take the
pass.

---

4.6.20a Methydrion: Map 1.2.1, AX. Chios, Mt. Oeta: Map 5.3.7, BY, BX.
4.6.21a A mile or so/1.5 kilometers: the Greek text says 10 stades; see Appendix O: Measurements, §5.
4.6.27a On this edition's proposed route, the ridge that the army crossed here (*Halting place 54*) was the modern Çakırbaba Pass, the watershed for basins feeding the Black and Caspian Seas. Once the Greeks had crossed it, their problems in finding a route to the Black Sea were

much reduced, as any watercourse they followed would ultimately lead them there. Pass to plain: Map 4.7.1, AY, *Halting place 54 or 54 Alt.* Çakırbaba Pass: Ref. Map 8, AZ; see Figure 4.6.5. Black and Caspian Seas: Map 4.7.1, locator.
4.6.27b Trophy: memorial set up by the victors of a battle, usually consisting of a post on which armor from the vanquished was hung; for more, see the Glossary.

they made their descent into the plain, where they came to villages full of many good things.[c]

4.7.1–7
April 400
TAOCHOI TERRITORY
*Taochian fort (55)*
Xenophon and
Cheirisophos plan how
to attack a stronghold
of the Taochoi.

[1] After this they made their way into the land of the Taochoi[a] for five days' march, covering thirty parasangs. Here food supplies were lacking, since the Taochoi lived in formidable strongholds in which they were also keeping their entire food supplies, having previously brought them up there. [2] So when the Greeks reached a stronghold that had no citadel and no houses but where men and women and many herds of animals were gathered, Cheirisophos[a] launched an attack against it immediately on his arrival, and when the first unit flagged, another one took up the attack and then yet another. (It was not possible to use the whole army and encircle the stronghold, because the land around it was precipitous.)[b]

[3] When Xenophon came up with the rearguard, both peltasts and hoplites, Cheirisophos said to him then and there, "You have come just at the right time. The place has to be taken—there are no food supplies for the army unless we capture it." [4] They began to plan the operation together on the spot, and when Xenophon asked what the obstacle was to getting inside, Cheirisophos replied, "There is just the one route up to it that you see, and when anyone attempts to advance along it, they roll rocks over the edge of that overhanging cliff there. And whoever gets caught by a rock ends up like this—" And with that, he pointed out people whose legs and ribs had been crushed. [5] "But if they used up their rocks," said Xenophon, "there is nothing else to hinder the advance, is there? The fact is, we don't see anyone opposing us beyond these few fellows, and only two or three of them are properly equipped. [6] And as you can see for yourself, the ground that has to be crossed under attack from their missiles is hardly a hundred and fifty feet across, and as much as a hundred feet[a] of that has plenty of cover, with great pine trees at intervals. If men stand behind the trees, how could they be hurt by rocks, whether they came flying through the air or were being rolled down upon them? So the rest amounts to fifty feet,[b] and we have to run across it whenever the rocks cease to come." [7] "But," said Cheirisophos, "whenever we start to advance toward cover, that instant the rocks start flying down in great numbers." "That would be the very thing we need," Xenophon replied, "as they will run out of rocks more quickly. But let's make our way to where it will be only a short distance for us to run across if we can do so and easier to retreat if we want to."

---

4.6.27c  Xenophon could have left out a few days here: Diodorus 14.29.1 (in Appendix S: Diodorus) says they occupied the inhabitants' properties for fifteen days. But since Diodorus is providing only a summary account, his total could include the days spent on the march up to the pass or subsequently through Taochoi territory. To place this in context, see Appendix M: Other Ancient Sources on the Ten Thousand, §5.

4.7.1a  Taochoi territory: Map 4.7.1, BY.

4.7.2a  On Cheirisophos, see Appendix W: Brief Biographies, §7.

4.7.2b  The rock outcrop at the junction of the rivers today called Oltu and Penek is a possible location for this Taochian fort: Map 4.7.1, BY, *Halting place 55*. Oltu and Penek Rivers: Ref. Map 8, AZ.

4.7.6a  A hundred and fifty feet/46 meters, 100 feet/30 meters: the Greek text says 1.5 *plethra*, 150 feet; see Appendix O: Measurements, §§2–3, 5.

4.7.6b  Fifty feet/15 meters.

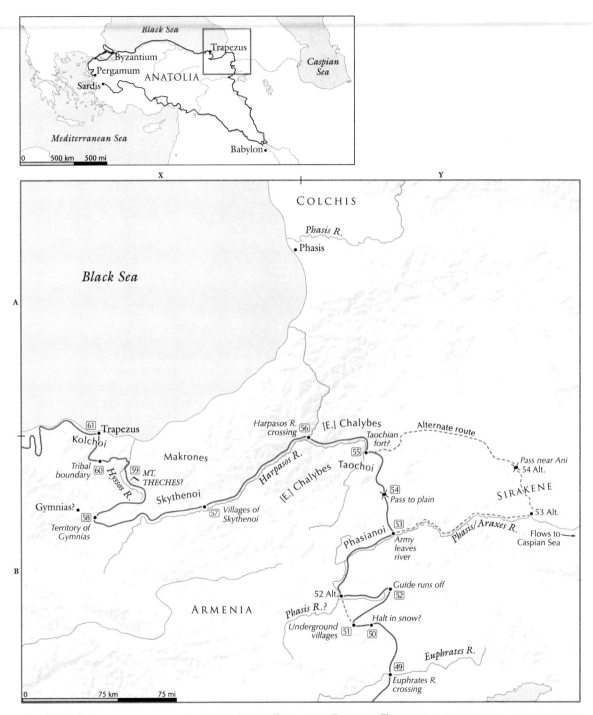

MAP 4.7.1. *KATABASIS:* FROM THE CROSSING OF THE EUPHRATES RIVER TO TRAPEZUS, INCLUDING ALTERNATE ROUTE ALONG THE PHASIS RIVER, *HALTING PLACES 49–61.*

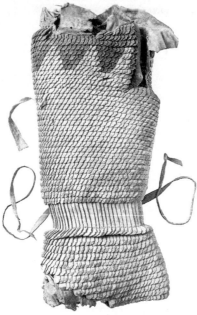

FIGURE 4.7.15. NONMETAL ARMOR WAS ADVANTAGEOUS TO THE INFANTRY BECAUSE OF ITS LIGHT WEIGHT, ASSISTING WITH MOBILITY AND ENDURANCE. LINEN ARMOR, AS SHOWN IN THIS EARLY FIFTH-CENTURY VASE PAINTING (LEFT), WOULD STAY RELATIVELY COOL IN HOT CLIMATES. LEATHER OR A COMBINATION OF MATERIALS WAS ALSO USED. THE SCYTHIAN OR SUBEIXI LEATHER SCALE ARMOR (RIGHT), EIGHTH TO THIRD CENTURY, IS THE BEST-PRESERVED SCALE ARMOR FROM ANTIQUITY.

4.7.8–12
April 400
TAOCHIAN FORT
Troops from the rearguard capture the stronghold. Xenophon emphasizes the competitive spirit of their officers.

[8] Consequently Cheirisophos and Xenophon made their way forward with Kallimachos of Parrasia,[a] a captain, whose turn it was that day to act as the senior officer among the captains of the rearguard while the other captains stayed in safety. After this, in fact, about seventy people set out under cover of the trees, not all together but one by one, each of them protecting himself as best he could. [9] Agasias of Stymphalos and Aristonymos of Methydrion,[a] who were also captains of the rearguard, and others too took their stand outside the trees, for no more than one company could stand among them in safety. [10] From his position there, Kallimachos engaged in a little ruse. He ran ahead from the tree under which he had been standing for two or three paces, and whenever the rocks began to fly, he quickly drew back. Each time he dashed forward, more than ten cartloads of boulders were wasted by the enemy. [11] When Agasias saw what Kallimachos was doing, and with the whole army looking on, he became afraid that he would not be the first to run across to the stronghold, and without calling for help from Aristonymos, even though he was next to him, or from Eurylochos the Lousian,[a] though they were comrades in arms, or from anyone else, he ran out by himself and set about overtaking them all. [12] When Kallimachos saw him going by, he grabbed hold of the rim of Agasias' shield; meanwhile Aristonymos of Methydrion ran past them, and so did Eurylochos of Lousoi, for all of these advanced their own claims to merit and used to compete keenly against one another. And vying in this manner, they captured

4.7.8a  Parrasia: Map 1.2.1, BX.
4.7.9a  Stymphalos, Methydrion: Map 1.2.1, AY, AX.
4.7.11a  Lousoi: Map 1.2.1, AX.

FIGURE 4.7.16. DETAIL OF
AN ATHENIAN BLACK-FIGURE
FUNERAL VASE 500–460,
SHOWING A WARRIOR WITH A
SEVERED HEAD AS XENOPHON
DESCRIBES AT 4.7.16 AND
5.4.17.

the place, for once they ran in, no further boulders came down from above.

[13] Here, as a result, there was a terrible spectacle. The women threw their children off the edge and flung themselves down after, and the men did likewise. Here too Aineias of Stymphalos, a captain, seeing a Taochian wearing a fine robe make a run to throw himself down, grabbed him in order to stop him. [14] But the Taochian dragged Aineias after him, and both went flying down the rocky cliff and were killed. From this place only a very few people were captured; but they acquired cattle and asses in great numbers, and also sheep.

[15] From there they made their way through the land of the Chalybes for seven days' march, covering fifteen parasangs.[a] These were the most valiant of all the peoples they passed through, and would fight hand to hand. They had linen body armor extending down to the waist, with thickly twisted cords instead of flaps.[b] [16] They also had greaves and helmets and

4.7.13–14
April 400
TAOCHIAN FORT
The shocking reaction
of the Taochoi.

4.7.15–18
April 400
[E.] CHALYBES TERRITORY–
SKYTHENOI TERRITORY
*Harpasos River*
*crossing (56)–*
*Skythenoi villages (57)*
The valor, armaments,
and savagery of the
Chalybes.

---

4.7.15a   Fifteen parasangs: all the manuscripts say 50
parasangs, but the Greeks surely could not
have traveled at over 7 parasangs a day
through the territory of the [Eastern]
Chalybes, a particularly ferocious tribe who
fought the Greeks hand to hand with some
success. This must have slowed the Greeks
down. Furthermore, on almost all scholars'
routes, there isn't room for 50 parasangs
between Taochoi territory and the Harpasos River (Map 4.7.1, BY, AX, *Halting*
*places 55–56*). Hence, this edition assumes
Xenophon wrote "fifteen" rather than
"fifty," a fairly easy corruption. (Translator's

note) [E.] Chalybes territory: Map 4.7.1, BY
(not listed in the *Barrington Atlas*).
4.7.15b   Metallic body armor had leather flaps at its
lower edge to protect the groin without
obstructing mobility. The Greeks retained
these flaps when linen body armor began
to be substituted, as was common by
Xenophon's time. Evidently the [Eastern]
Chalybes had a similar idea but carried out
in a different material (one would think it
would give less protection but more
mobility). See Figure 4.7.15 for examples
of nonmetal armor.

at their belts a small saber, the size of a Laconian curved knife,[a] with which they would slit the throats of those they could overpower; then they would cut off their heads and carry them with them as they went on their way, and they used to sing and dance whenever their enemies were likely to see them. They also had a spear, well over twenty feet long, with a point at only one end.[b] [17] They would stay inside their settlements, but when the Greeks marched past, they would follow, continually fighting with them. They lived in forts, and their food supplies had been carried up and stored in them, so that the Greeks could not get hold of anything from that region; instead, they lived on the herds they had captured from the Taochoi. [18] Leaving these people, the Greeks reached the river Harpasos, four hundred feet in width.[a] From there they made their way through the land of the Skythenoi for four days' march, covering twenty parasangs, going over a plain to some villages, where they stayed for three days and replenished their food stocks.[b]

[19] From there they completed four days' march, covering twenty parasangs, to a large, prosperous, and populous city called Gymnias.[a] The ruler of the region sent a guide to the Greeks from this place to lead them through another region, at war with his own tribe. [20] On his arrival the guide said that he would lead them in five days to a place from which they would see the sea, and if not, he undertook to forfeit his life.[a] At the head of the army, he thrust into enemy territory; and once he had done so, he kept encouraging them to set ablaze and lay waste the countryside, from which it became clear that he had come for this purpose, rather than through any goodwill toward the Greeks. [21] And they did reach the mountain on the fifth day: its name was Theches.[a]

4.7.16a  Greaves: bronze shin guards; see Figure 1.2.22. The length of the Laconian curved knife (*xuēlē*) is not known independently of this passage; for more on the *xuēlē*, see n. 4.8.25c. Laconia: Ref. Map 2, DY.

4.7.16b  Early modern pikes of this great length are attested. Xenophon notes the single point of the Chalybes spear in contrast to the Greek spear (*saurōtēr*), which also had a point on the butt (see Figure 5.4.12). He similarly notes the single point of the Mossynoecian spear at 5.4.12. Twenty feet/6 meters: these figures have been rounded down. The Greek text says 15 *pēcheis* (22.5 feet); see Appendix O: Measurements, §§2–3.

4.7.18a  Four hundred feet/122 meters. Harpasos River crossing: Map 4.7.1, AY, *Halting place 56*.

4.7.18b  It would have been a shorter route to the Black Sea if the army had followed the Harpasos River downstream, but instead it turned upstream. Skythenoi territory: Map 4.7.1, AX (located differently in the *Barrington Atlas*); Villages of the Skythenoi: *Halting place 57*.

4.7.19a  Gymnias: Map 4.7.1, BX, *Halting place 58*, shows the editors' hypothesis that the army

did not reach the city itself but camped near the eastern edge of its territory. The *Barrington Atlas* (Map 87 G4) places Gymnias about 80 miles/129 kilometers farther southeast than the location usually given by other scholars. Our route line places it yet farther to the northwest; it is impossible to make the atlas's location for Gymnias compatible with Xenophon's narrative.

4.7.20a  In Diodorus 14.29.3 (Appendix S: Diodorus) says this part of the journey took fifteen days. That might be because the guide took the army by long detours to ravage more of the lands of rival tribesmen, as David Thomas argues in Appendix M: Other Ancient Sources for the Ten Thousand, §5, giving reasons why Xenophon might be wrong here. Others say Diodorus was following Xenophon but made a slip.

4.7.21a  Mt. Theches, possible location: Map 4.7.1, BX, *Halting place 59*, Map 4.7.25 (located differently in the *Barrington Atlas*). The location of the mountain is a matter of dispute; for discussion, see Appendix P: The Route of the Ten Thousand, §§11–14. Diodorus 14.29.3 called it Mt. Chenion. See Figure 4.7.25. The editors identify the location as the northwesterly spur of modern Polut Daği.

MAP 4.7.25. THE JOURNEY TO THE BLACK SEA VIA MOUNT THECHES, SHOWING THE BOUNDARY RIVER THAT SEPARATED THE TRIBES.

When the vanguard got high up on the mountain,[b] a great clamor arose. [22] On hearing it, Xenophon and the rearguard thought that there were further enemies in front of them, in addition to those who were following behind them from the region in flames. By setting an ambush, the rearguard had killed several of the latter and taken others alive, and they had captured about twenty wicker shields covered with raw, shaggy oxhides. [23] Now the noise grew louder and nearer, and constantly, as the advancing ranks got closer to it, they would break into a run, speeding toward their comrades on the heights; it was their constant shouts that were the cause of the noise, which became much greater the more of them there were. [24] So it seemed to Xenophon that it was something really important, and mounting his horse and taking Lykios and the cavalry with him, he went to help. Very quickly they heard the soldiers shouting, "The sea, the sea!" and repeating it from one to the other like a watchword.[a] Then naturally all the rearguard started to run too, and the draft animals were urged on, as well as the horses. [25] When they all reached the summit, then and there they embraced each other, and generals and captains too, with tears in their eyes. Someone passed the word, and all of a sudden the soldiers began bringing stones and making a great cairn.[a] [26] On this they

4.7.21b  For the textual issue here, see the Translator's Notes, §16, and table.

4.7.24a  The watchword, when first given out, was audibly passed down the line (see 1.8.16) and was often chosen to lift the troops' spirits. For the famous cry "Thalassa! Thalassa!" ("The sea! The sea!"), see Appendix R: The Legacy of Xenophon's *Anabasis*, §§9, 13–14.

4.7.25a  That the soldiers could gather these stones shows there cannot have been much snow on the ground, indicating that we must be either in early winter or late spring, a point against the traditional chronology which brings them there in mid-winter. See further Appendix Q: The Chronology of the March, n. Q.3b, §§4, 7.

FIGURE 4.7.25. A SPUR OF MODERN POLUT DAĞI, THE MOUNTAIN THAT IS OUR PREFERRED CANDIDATE FOR MOUNT THECHES. THIS SPUR COULD BE THE PRECISE SITE FROM WHICH THE GREEKS FIRST SAW THE SEA.

proceeded to lay a large number of raw oxhides as thank offerings, together with walking staffs and the captured wicker shields, and the guide himself set about hacking the shields to pieces and encouraging the others to do so. [27] After this the Greeks sent the guide back with gifts from their common stock—a horse and a silver drinking cup and some Persian apparel and ten darics;[a] but he asked especially for their finger rings, and got many from the soldiers. He showed them a village where they could take up quarters and the road by which they would make their way to the land of the Makrones,[b] and then, when evening had fallen, he left, going off in the night.

[1] From there the Greeks made their way through the land of the Makrones for three days' march, covering ten parasangs. On the first day they reached the river that marks the boundary between the land of the Skythenoi and that of the Makrones.[a] [2] Above them on their right they had extremely difficult ground, and on their left they had another river.[a]

4.8.1–3
May 400
MT. THECHES–
HYSSOS RIVER
The Makrones are hostile at first.

4.7.27a  On darics, see Appendix O: Measurements, §§13–14, and Figure O.13.
4.7.27b  Makrones territory: Map 4.7.25; Map 4.7.1, BX.
4.8.1a  Skythenoi territory: Map 4.7.25; Map 4.7.1, BX. Boundary river between the Skythenoi and the Makrones (a tributary of the Hyssos), proposed location: Map 4.7.25; for more detail, see Appendix P: The Route of the Ten Thousand, §14.
4.8.2a  We identify this with the Hyssos River (Map 4.7.25; Map 4.7.1, BX). On our proposed route, the army descended from

Mt. Theches into the valley of the boundary river and had now reached the confluence with the Hyssos. We take it that Makrones territory lay partly to the east of the Hyssos, north of the boundary river, and partly to the west of the Hyssos, both to the north and to the south. The Makrones presumably chose to defend the boundary river, though it was only a tributary, rather than the Hyssos, the area's principal river, because the latter was a more formidable obstacle in itself.

144

Into this the boundary river poured its waters, which they had to get across. The river was overgrown with trees, individually slender but densely massed. When the Greeks got close, they set about cutting these down, keen to get out of the place as fast as possible. [3] The Makrones—with wicker shields and lances and tunics made of hair—were drawn up on the farther side of the crossing, and they were shouting encouragement to each other and throwing stones, which fell into the river; but they did not reach the Greeks, nor do any damage.

[4] At this point Xenophon was approached by one of the peltasts, a man claiming to have been a slave in Athens, who said that he recognized the language the people were speaking. "I think," he said, "that this is my native country, and unless there is something to prevent it, I would like to talk to them." [5] "Indeed, nothing prevents it," Xenophon replied. "Talk to them and first find out who they are." When the man asked them, they said, "Makrones." "Ask them, then," said Xenophon, "why they are drawn up against us and why they feel the need to be hostile to us." [6] They answered, "Because you are invading our territory." The generals told the man to say that they did not intend doing any harm, but having fought against the King, they were making their way out to Greece and wanted to reach the sea. [7] The tribesmen asked whether they would give pledges to that effect, and they said they were willing both to give and to receive them. Consequently the Makrones gave the Greeks a lance of the barbarian type and the Greeks gave them one of the Greek type, as they said these were their pledges of good faith, and both sides called on the gods to bear witness.

[8] After they had exchanged pledges, the Makrones immediately set about helping them cut down the trees and clearing the path to take them across the river, working side by side with the Greeks, and they provided them with a market[a] to the extent that they could, and in three days led them onward until they brought them to the boundary with the Kolchoi.[b] [9] Here there was a mountain that was huge[a] but accessible, and on it the Kolchoi had been drawn up for battle. At first the Greeks drew themselves up in line of battle opposite them, intending to advance in this formation toward the mountain, but then the generals decided to meet and discuss the most suitable method of contesting the position.

[10] So Xenophon said, "We should dissolve the line of battle and form the companies into columns. The line would be immediately broken up, for we will find that the mountain has no paths in one place and good paths up in another, and it will immediately lower morale for troops drawn up in line to see the line broken. [11] Next, if we advance drawn up many ranks deep,

| | |
|---|---|
| 4.8.4–7 | |
| May 400 | |
| MAKRONES TERRITORY | |
| A peltast brokers an agreement with the Makrones. | |

4.8.8–9
May 400
MAKRONES TERRITORY
*Makrones–Kolchoi boundary (60)*
The Greeks are now blocked by the Kolchoi.

4.8.10–13
May 400
MAKRONES–KOLCHOI BOUNDARY
Xenophon suggests novel tactics to deal with the steep ground.

---

4.8.8a  For the soldiers' reliance on purchasing food for themselves in markets, see Appendix J: A Soldier's View of the March, §§14, 17, and Appendix O: Measurements, §19.

4.8.8b  It is not clear whether the three days mentioned here are additional to the journey from Mt. Theches to the tribal boundary river (4.8.1) or include it. Kolchoi territory, Makrones–Kolchoi boundary: Map 4.7.25, *Halting place 60*.

4.8.9a  Huge mountain: although there is steep and mountainous ground in this area, Xenophon must be exaggerating somewhat, especially by comparison with some of the country through which they have passed.

the enemy will outnumber us at the point of contact and they will use their extra troops however they want. But if we were to proceed only a few ranks deep, it would not be at all remarkable if our line were cut through by a concentrated attack somewhere from both people and missiles; but if this happens anywhere, it will be bad for the whole line. [12] Instead, my advice is to form the companies into columns and, by leaving intervals between the columns, to cover such an extent of ground that the outermost companies are beyond the enemy wings. With this formation we will outflank the enemy's battle line, our best soldiers will go up first, leading their columns, and each captain will lead his troops wherever there may be good going. [13] It will not be easy for the enemy to get into the gaps between the columns with our companies on both sides of them, nor will it be easy to cut through a company as it goes forward in column. If any of the companies is hard-pressed, its neighbor will come over to support it. And if one of the companies is able to get to the top anywhere, not a single one of the enemy will stand his ground any longer, that's for sure."

[14] This plan was approved, and they started to form the companies into columns. As Xenophon was going back from the right wing to his position on the left,[a] he said to the soldiers, "Men, those you see over there are the only thing still keeping us from already being where we have long been striving to be. If we possibly can, we must eat them raw."[b]

[15] When each of the officers was in his right place and had formed his company into columns, there were around eighty companies of hoplites, each company having about a hundred troops in it. By contrast, they divided the peltasts and the archers in three, some beyond the left of the hoplites, some beyond the right, and some in the center, roughly six hundred of each.[a] [16] After this the generals passed on the word to offer a prayer, and when they had prayed and had chanted the war hymn, they moved off on their way. Both Cheirisophos and Xenophon and the peltasts with each of them made their way forward in positions that outflanked the enemy line, [17] and when the enemy saw them, they ran to right and left to meet them and thus broke up their formation, creating a big gap in the middle of their own line. [18] On seeing the enemy divided in two, the peltasts associated with the Arcadian contingent, whose leader was Aischines the Acarnanian,[a] thought they were in flight and began to run, cheering as they did so. These

4.8.14a The generals had evidently had their meeting on the extreme right wing. This was the normal place for the most senior commander, so where Cheirisophos had taken up his position with the vanguard became the location of the right wing of the line when the army deployed from its usual marching column into battle order, as it had done shortly before this, at 4.8.9. Each section of the army would then have fallen in on the vanguard's left in turn as it came up, so Xenophon's rearguard contingent would end up on the extreme left wing, to which he now returns.

4.8.14b "Eat them raw": a vigorous expression from popular speech (see, for example, Xenophon, *Hellenika* 3.3.6 and Homer's *Iliad* 4.35, 22.346–47, 24.212–13).

4.8.15a So there were about 8,000 hoplites now, as compared with 10,400 at the battle of Cunaxa (1.7.10), and about 1,800 peltasts. For the Greek contingents in Cyrus' army as originally assembled, see Appendix I: Infantry and Cavalry in *Anabasis*, §§3, 5, 8, Table I.4.

4.8.18a On the Arcadian contingent, see Appendix I, §§3, 9–11. Arcadia: Map 1.2.1, AX. Acarnania: Map 5.3.7, BX.

were the first to get to the top of the mountain, followed by the Arcadian hoplite contingent, whose leader was Kleanor the Orchomenian.[b] [19] As for the enemy, once the peltasts had begun to run, they didn't make a stand anywhere but turned in flight, each in a different direction.

Once the Greeks had ascended the ridge, they went on to encamp in many villages that had plentiful food supplies. [20] And though there was nothing else that at all surprised them, there were many swarms of bees[a] thereabouts, and all of the soldiers who ate the honeycombs began to behave crazily, started to vomit, and were subject to diarrhea, and none of them could stand up straight.[b] Those who had eaten only a little seemed like people who were extremely drunk, but those who had eaten a lot appeared to be mad—or even to be dying. [21] Many lay on the ground in this state as if they had been routed by an enemy, and there was much despondency. But on the following day, nobody had died, and round about the same time of day, they recovered their senses; and on the third day, or in some cases on the fourth, they got up just as if it had been an enchanted potion[a] that they had been drinking.

[22] From there they made their way onward for two days' march, covering seven parasangs, and came to the sea at Trapezus, a well-populated Greek city on the Black Sea that is a colony of Sinope in the land of the Kolchoi.[a] They stayed there for about thirty days in the Kolchoi's villages, [23] which they used as bases from which to plunder Kolchian territory. The Trapezountians provided an ongoing market for the encamped army, and they received the Greeks hospitably, giving them as tokens of their friendship[a] cattle and barley meal and wine. [24] They also undertook negotiations on behalf of those Kolchoi who lived nearby, for the most part in the plain; these too gave the Greeks cattle as tokens of friendship.

4.8.19–21
May 400
KOLCHOI TERRITORY
The Greeks encounter "mad honey."

4.8.22–24
May–June 400
BLACK SEA COAST
*Trapezus (61)*
The Greeks arrive at the Black Sea.

4.8.18b The hoplites in the middle of the Greek formation were Arcadians. The peltasts associated with them were, however, probably not Arcadians, as they were led by someone from Acarnania, which is not part of Arcadia. On Kleanor, see Appendix W: Brief Biographies, §19. Orchomenos: Map 1.2.1, AX.

4.8.20a "Swarms of bees": the Greek word used here, *smēnē*, can mean either "swarms" or "hives." "Swarms" was chosen for the translation because the soldiers, in the area for only a short time, were more likely to notice highly active bees than stable colonies, and thus be led to their honey.

4.8.20b The toxic effect of "mad honey" (*deli bal* in modern Turkish) is a recognized medical phenomenon, the result of bees feeding on the pollen of a species of rhododendron prevalent in, but not exclusive to, this part of the south coast of the Black Sea. This rhododendron flowers in May/early June, and many scholars argue that that is when the soldiers must have been in the area, on the ground that the honey is toxic only when fresh. This has been denied, but

whether or not the honey can produce the effect after time has elapsed, its toxicity is at any rate likely to be greater when it is fresh, and there is evidence in a pharmacology text from the first century C.E. that it varied over time (Dioscorides, *Materia medica* 2.82.4–5). For more, see Appendix Q: The Chronology of the March, §§8–9.

4.8.21a Enchanted potion: Xenophon probably expects readers to recall the potion that the enchantress Circe gave to Odysseus' men in Book 10 of Homer's *Odyssey*, which turned them into swine. However, the Greek word here, *pharmacopia*, can also mean "medicine" or "poison," somewhat like the English "drug." (Translator's note)

4.8.22a Here Xenophon uses the name "Euxine" for the Black Sea. This is the only time he does so in *Anabasis;* he normally refers to it more informally. Trapezus (*Halting place 61*), Black Sea: Map 4.7.1, AX, and locator. Sinope: Map 6.1.15, *Halting place 67.*

4.8.23a "Tokens of their friendship": the Greek word used is *xenia*, on which see "guest-friend" in the Glossary.

4.8.25–28
May–June 400
TRAPEZUS
Athletic contests are held
in celebration of their safe
arrival.

[25] After this they began to prepare the sacrifice that they had vowed to make.[a] Enough cattle had come to them to offer due safe-conduct thank offerings to Zeus the Savior and to Herakles and to discharge their vows to the other gods. They also held an athletic contest on the range of hills where they had taken up their quarters. They chose Drakontios, a Spartiate,[b] who had gone into exile from his home when still a boy, having struck another boy with a curved knife[c] and unintentionally killed him, to make the arrangements for the racetrack and preside over the contest. [26] When they had held the sacrifice, they handed the skins of the victims[a] over to Drakontios and told him to lead them to where the racetrack had been prepared. Drakontios pointed to where they happened to be standing: "This ridge," he said, "is excellent for running, wherever one may want." "But how, then," they said, "will they be able to wrestle in such a rough, hard place?" He replied, "The greater the grief for the one who is thrown." [27] The contests were a sprint race for the boys, most of them from the captives; a long-distance race run by more than sixty Cretans;[a] wrestling, boxing, and all-in fighting; and it was a fine spectacle. There were many entrants for the competitions and much eager rivalry among them, especially with their companions[b] looking on. [28] They also held horse races, in which they had to ride the horses down the slope, turn around in the sea, and bring them back up again to the altar. Going down, most of them were tossed about as they rode; and coming back up, it was hard for the horses to make their way over the steeply rising slope, even at a walking pace. At this there was much shouting and laughter and cheers of encouragement.

4.8.25a Sacrifice they'd vowed to make: these
vows were made at 3.2.9.
4.8.25b Spartiates were full citizens of Sparta, a
minority among the Lacedaemonians; see
Appendix B: Xenophon and Sparta, §§18–
19. The word covers the same group of
people as "the *homoioi*" at 4.6.14.
4.8.25c A curved knife: Drakontios used a Laconian *xuēlē*, previously mentioned at
4.7.16. This was a tool used for cutting or
slicing: the word *xuēlē* is said to mean
something similar to the Athenian word
for a cheese grater. It was not designed to
be a weapon, and perhaps only boys would
use it as such.
4.8.26a Gave Drakontios the skins: he is to distrib-

ute them to the victors as prizes, a common
practice in Greek athletic contests.
4.8.27a The sprint race (*stadion*) was 1 stade (200
yards/183 meters) long, the length of the
track at the stadium at Olympia; on stades,
see Appendix O: Measurements, §5. The
long-distance race (*dolichos*) was variable
in length, but 12 stades (1 mile 640
yards/2 kilometers) was typical. Olympia,
Crete: Map 5.3.7, BX, locator.
4.8.27b "Companions": some scholars think the
word (*hetairōn* in Greek) is chosen here
to refer (or at least allude) to the kept
women; for this view, see Appendix K:
The Noncombatant Contingent of the
Army, §12, n. K.12c.

BOOK FIVE

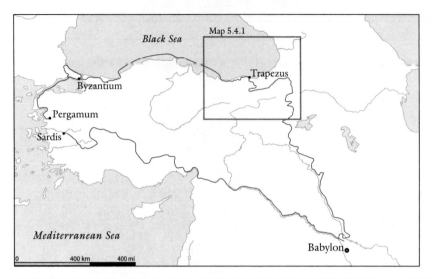

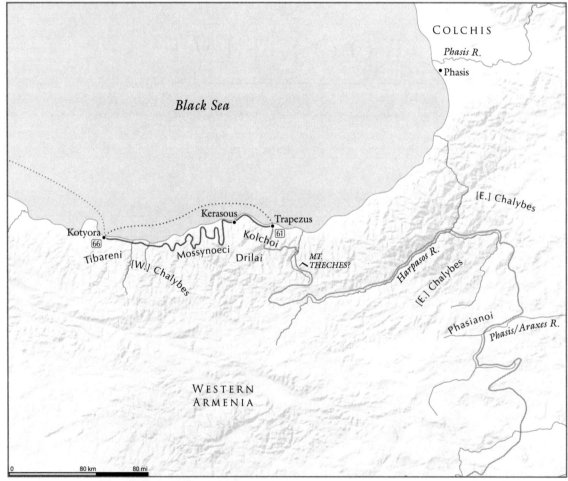

BOOK 5. *PARABASIS:* FROM TRAPEZUS TO KOTYORA, *HALTING PLACES 61–66.*

I[n the preceding narrative, the author has explained what the Greeks did in the course of their march with Cyrus up into the interior and what they did during their return journey all the way to the sea (the Black Sea, to be precise).[a] He has also explained how they came to the Greek city of Trapezus and how they carried out the sacrifices that they had vowed they would perform to give thanks for their deliverance in the place where they first reached friendly territory.][b]

[2] Following this, the Greeks held an assembly and started discussing the remainder of the journey. First to stand up was Antileon of Thurii,[a] and what he had to say for himself was this: "Now, men, I for one am already tired of packing up my kit and traveling on foot and running and bearing arms and keeping in formation and doing guard duty and fighting, and what I long for now is to have no more of these troubles, since we have reached the sea, and instead to sail the rest of the way and arrive in Greece stretched out at my ease, like Odysseus."[b] [3] When they heard this, the soldiers shouted out in an uproar that he spoke rightly, and someone else started to make a speech on the same lines, as indeed did everyone who came forward. Next Cheirisophos stood up and said, [4] "Men, I have a friend called Anaxibios who happens to be the current *nauarchos*.[a] So if you send me to him, I think I would come back both with triremes[b] and with

1+1

5.1.1
An ancient scribe's summary of the story so far.

5.1.2–4
June 400
BLACK SEA COAST
*Trapezus (61)*
The army wants to go on by sea. Cheirisophos says he can arrange this.

NOTE: Unless otherwise indicated, all dates are B.C.E., and all citations are to Xenophon's *Anabasis*. The determination of the army's route and stopping places are based on the editors' calculations and estimates from data taken from *Anabasis*. Nonetheless, the route line shown on our maps and the monthly dates given in our side notes are often subject to doubt. Our best estimates should not be taken as authoritative or certain. See the Editors' Preface, §§17–20.

5.1.1a  On Cyrus the Younger, see Appendix W: Brief Biographies of Selected Characters in *Anabasis*, §10. Black Sea: Book 5 map and locator.

5.1.1b  The army's vow: see 3.2.9. Trapezus: Book 5 map, *Halting place 61*. This is the fourth of the passages occurring throughout the work that summarize the story so far. It

appears in brackets because scholars generally agree that they are later scribal insertions; see the Translator's Notes, §13.

5.1.2a  Thurii: Map 5.3.7, locator.

5.1.2b  Odysseus, the hero of Homer's *Odyssey*, was transported by ship asleep by the (mythical) Phaeacians for the last leg of his otherwise eventful and arduous ten-year voyage home from Troy (*Odyssey* 13.70–124). Troy: Map 5.3.7, BY.

5.1.4a  On Anaxibios and his later career, see Appendix W, §3. He was based in Byzantium. For the *nauarchos*, or chief admiral of the Spartan fleet for the year, see Appendix B: Xenophon and Sparta, §14. Byzantium: Book 5 map, locator. Sparta: Map 5.3.7, BX.

5.1.4b  Triremes: long warships with three banks of oars; for more, see the Glossary. For an image of a warship, see Figure 5.8.20.

5.1.4. ATHENIAN BLACK-FIGURE DINOS DATED 525–500. A DINOS IS A ROUND-BOTTOMED BOWL DESIGNED TO SIT ON A STAND AND USED BOTH TO MIX WINE AND WATER AND AS A GOBLET TO DRINK FROM. THE IMAGE ON THE INSIDE OF THE RIM (LEFT) SHOWS A WARSHIP WITH ITS OARS AND BEAKED BOW. WHEN THE DINOS WAS FULL, THE SHIPS PAINTED ON ITS INNER SIDE WOULD APPEAR TO BE SAILING ON A WINE-DARK SEA.

merchant ships to ferry us. If you do indeed want to go by sea, wait until I come back. I will be quick." When they heard this, the soldiers were pleased and voted for him to set sail as soon as possible.

5.1.5–13
June 400
TRAPEZUS
Xenophon proposes ways to procure supplies and contingency plans during Cheirosophos' absence.

[5] After him Xenophon stood up and said, "Cheirisophos for his part is setting out to get merchant ships, while we stay put. So I will tell you what seems to me appropriate to do while we're waiting. [6] First, we must obtain our food supplies from enemy territory, as there is no adequate market hereabouts, and except for a few of us, we do not have the means to buy anything anyway. However, as the countryside is in enemy hands, there is a danger that many of you will be killed if you make your own way in search of food supplies in a careless fashion, without taking any precautions. [7] Rather than that, I suggest that, in order to ensure your safety, you should obtain food supplies through organized foraging parties instead of wandering around any which way; and I propose that we generals see to all this." This was resolved.

[8] "Then listen to what else I have to say. Some of you will be going out on plundering expeditions. So I think it is best that anyone who intends to set out from the camp tell us generals first, and also say where he is going, so that we can keep track of the numbers of those going out and those staying behind and can help with the preparations if anything is needed. Moreover, if there came a time when we had to go to the aid of some of these people, we would know where we had to go to assist them. Also, if any of the less experienced troops are trying their hand somewhere, we could give

them advice, while at the same time attempting to establish the strength of the enemy they would be attacking." This too was resolved.

[9] "Then consider this as well," he said. "There is plenty of opportunity for the enemy to plunder us, and they are plotting what harm they can do to us. Fair enough, since we have their property! What's more, they are perched above us. Under the circumstances, for us to have guards around the camp seems a necessity to me. If, then, we were to take turns acting as guards and as watchmen, the enemy would be less able to prey on us.

"And here is another proposal for you to look at. [10] If we knew for sure that Cheirisophos was going to come back with enough merchant ships, there would be no need for what I am about to say. But in fact, since this is uncertain, I think we should also try to get a fleet of merchant ships ready from our base here. For if he does come, as a result of already having ships, we shall sail without any arguments about the distribution of berths; and if he doesn't bring any ships with him, we shall use the ones we gather here. [11] I see merchant ships sailing by frequently, so if we asked the Trapezountians for some warships and were then to bring passing ships in to land and keep them under guard, removing their rudders, until there were enough to carry us, perhaps we would have no shortage of the means of transport we need." This too was resolved.

[12] "And consider," he went on, "whether it is not right for us to maintain from our common fund those whom we may force to land, during the time they have to wait on our account, and whether we shouldn't also establish a price that we'll pay for being transported. That way, by helping us, they too will gain a benefit." This too was resolved.

[13] "It further seems to me," he said, "that in case our efforts do not after all succeed in providing enough merchant ships, it would be a good idea for us to instruct the cities along the coast to mend the roads, which we hear are in poor condition for travelers.[a] The cities will obey, partly out of fear and partly because they want to be rid of us."

[14] At this the soldiers cried out that there was no need to go by road. As Xenophon perceived that they were being gripped by folly, he did not put anything to a vote on this topic but instead persuaded the cities to mend the roads voluntarily, saying that they would more quickly be rid of the army if the roads were made passable.

[15] They even obtained a fifty-oared ship from the Trapezountians and put Dexippos, a Laconian *perioikos*,[a] in charge of it. This individual neglected

5.1.14–17
June 400
TRAPEZUS
The army is determined to go by sea. Dexippos deserts with a fifty-oared ship; the men make further attempts to secure a fleet and obtain booty.

5.1.13a   The normal way of traveling along the coast here was by sea. Until modern times the land route was a trial because of the mountainous nature of the coastal hinterland. The heights in this region regularly press close against the sea and are punctuated by steep valleys through which fast rivers flow. As a result, land journeys were time consuming and arduous. Notwithstanding Xenophon's statement, it is doubtful that any meaningful road network existed.

5.1.15a   Fifty-oared ships (pentekonters) were the precursors of triremes and were old-fashioned by this time. *Perioikoi*: free Lacedaemonians inferior to the citizens of Sparta, Lacedaemon's principal city; see Appendix B: Xenophon and Sparta, §18. Laconia refers to the territories the Spartans held in the southeast quarter of the Peloponnese: Map 1.2.1, BY. For Dexippos' career prior to joining Cyrus' expedition, see Appendix W: Brief Biographies, §13.

his task of assembling merchant ships and, slipping off with the vessel, sailed right out of the Black Sea. So he got what he deserved afterward, when he was in Thrace carrying on some intrigue at the court of Seuthes and was killed by Nikandros the Laconian.[b] [16] They also obtained a thirty-oared ship, which they put under the command of Polykrates of Athens,[a] who brought ashore to the camp whatever merchant ships he could take. They removed the ships' cargoes, if they were carrying any, and set guards over them to keep them safe, while the merchant ships themselves they used for carrying supplies along the coast. [17] In the meantime the Greeks went out on plundering expeditions; some of them got hold of booty, some did not. Kleainetos led both his own company and another one against a difficult stronghold, where he himself was killed and many of those with him as well.[a]

5.2.1–2
June 400
TRAPEZUS–
DRILAI TERRITORY
Xenophon leads a plundering expedition against the Drilai.

[1] When it was no longer possible for them to seize food supplies and return to the camp the same day, Xenophon obtained Trapezountian guides and led half the army against the Drilai.[a] He left the other half to guard the camp, since the Kolchoi,[b] driven from their homes, had gathered in large numbers and were occupying the heights above them. [2] The Trapezountians did not lead them against tribes from whom it was easy to get provisions, as they were friendly toward those tribes; but they led them eagerly against the Drilai—at whose hands they had often suffered badly—to places that were mountainous and hard to access and against people who were the most warlike of those who live on the coast of the Black Sea.

5.2.3–6
June 400
DRILAI TERRITORY
The peltasts reach the main stronghold of the Drilai and get into difficulties.

[3] When the Greeks were in the high country, they found that the Drilai had gone away, having first set fire to all their strongholds that had seemed to them easy to capture, and there was nothing for the Greeks to take except the odd pig, ox, or other animal that had escaped from the fire. But there was one stronghold that was their main settlement, into which they had all streamed together. Around this lay an extremely deep ravine, and the routes across it to the stronghold were difficult to traverse. [4] The peltasts had run on, about two-thirds of a mile ahead of the hoplites,[a] and crossed the ravine; and seeing a great deal of livestock and other signs of wealth, they proceeded to attack the stronghold. Along with them there also followed a throng of spearmen, who had set out hastily, intent on obtaining the expected food supplies, and so the number of those who had crossed the ravine amounted to more than about one thousand people.[b] [5] But despite all their fighting, they could not capture the stronghold, for there was also a broad trench and, piled up behind it, an earth rampart with stakes set on the top and wooden

5.1.15b  Seuthes is a major character in Book 7; on him, see Appendix W: Brief Biographies, §30. Laconia was Spartan territory, so Nikandros was either a Spartan or a *perioikos* (see n. 5.1.15a). Thrace: Map 5.3.7, AY.
5.1.16a  Athens: Map 5.3.7, BX.
5.1.17a  The number of troops killed in this failed raid is discussed in Appendix I: The Size and Makeup of the Ten Thousand, §6.
5.2.1a  Drilai territory, probable location: Map 5.4.1 (located slightly differently in the *Barrington Atlas*).

5.2.1b  Kolchoi territory: Map 5.4.1.
5.2.4a  On peltasts (light-armed infantry) and hoplites (heavy-armed infantry), see Appendix H: Infantry and Cavalry in *Anabasis*, §§4–5, 2–3, respectively. About two-thirds of a mile/1 kilometer: the Greek text says 5 or 6 stades; see Appendix O: Ancient Greek and Persian Units of Measurement, §5.
5.2.4b  For discussion of the textual and other issues here, see Appendix I: The Size and Makeup of the Ten Thousand, §§5–8.

towers constructed at frequent intervals. So they began to try to retreat instead, but the enemy kept pressing them. [6] Since they could not run off, because they could make the descent from the stronghold to the ravine only in single file, they sent for Xenophon, who was leading the hoplites.

[7] On reaching Xenophon, the messenger said, "The place is full of a great deal of wealth, but we can't capture it—it's too strong. And it's not easy to get away, either, for they have come out against us and are putting up a fight, and the escape route is difficult." [8] When he heard this, Xenophon went forward to the ravine and ordered the hoplites to halt under arms, while he himself crossed over with the captains and spent some time working out whether it would be better to lead back the troops who had already crossed the ravine or to take the hoplites across it too, with the idea that in that way the stronghold might be captured. [9] Retreat seemed impossible without incurring many fatal casualties; the captains for their part thought they could take the place, and Xenophon himself agreed with their opinion. This was because he put his confidence in the sacred signs from the sacrifices, for the seers had made clear that while there would be a battle, the outcome of the expedition would be an honorable one. [10] He sent the captains back to bring over the hoplites, while he himself stayed where he was, having made every one of the peltasts draw back, and he did not allow any of them even to throw a javelin from a distance. [11] When the hoplites arrived, he ordered each of the captains to deploy his company in the way he thought would make it fight most effectively, since the captains positioned close to one another on this occasion were ones who used to vie with each other the whole time in the behavior befitting a man. [12] They set about deploying their companies while Xenophon gave instructions to all the peltasts to advance with fingers through the throwing loop, as it would be necessary to throw their javelins at the exact moment he gave the signal. Likewise, the archers were to have their arrows on the bowstrings, as it would also be necessary for them to shoot at the exact moment he gave the signal, and the light-armed[a] were to have their slings primed with stones; and he sent suitable officers to see to these arrangements.

[13] When everything was ready, the captains and their lieutenants and those who thought themselves to be as good as their officers were all drawn up together, and indeed could see each other clearly, since they were in a crescent formation because of the nature of the ground. [14] After they had sung the war hymn and the trumpet sounded, the hoplites simultaneously raised the battle cry to Enyalios[a] and set off at a run while the missiles began to fly: lances, arrows, slingshot pellets, and a very large number of stones thrown by hand; some people even used firebrands. [15] Under the impact of the huge

5.2.7–12
June 400
DRILAI TERRITORY
Xenophon comes to the rescue with the hoplites.

5.2.13–15
June 400
DRILAI TERRITORY
The hoplites storm the outer stockade of the Drilai.

5.2.12a  Xenophon sometimes uses "peltasts" as a broad term covering all light-armed troops and sometimes, as here, distinguishes peltasts with shields from those with no protective kit at all (called *gymnētes* in Greek).

5.2.14a  Enyalios: a war god. In literature this

appears to be just another name for Ares, but the evidence is that originally there were two separate gods, and even in Classical times there still seem to have been two separate cults. The cry to Enyalios is also mentioned at 1.8.18.

quantity of missiles, the enemy left the stockade and its towers, and so Agasias of Stymphalos and Philoxenos of Pellene[a] put aside their body armor and shields and, clad in only their tunics, climbed up the stockade; and then the soldiers set about drawing each other up, and soon yet others had climbed up without aid—and the place had been captured, or so it seemed.

**5.2.16–20**
**June 400**
DRILAI TERRITORY
Despite the peltasts' indiscipline, the outer area of the settlement is taken.

[16] Both the peltasts and the lighter-armed troops ran in, and each individual began to seize whatever he could, but Xenophon stood by the gates and kept outside as many of the hoplites as he could, because more of the enemy were starting to appear on various easily defensible heights. [17] Not much time had passed when loud shouting was heard from inside and soldiers came fleeing out, some managing to carry what they had taken but soon one or two who were wounded, and there was much jostling about the gateways. When they were questioned, the troops stumbling out all said that inside was a citadel where there were large numbers of the enemy, who ran out and rained blows on the crowd of people inside the stockade. [18] Thereupon, Xenophon ordered Tolmides the herald to announce that anyone who wanted any plunder should quickly make his way inside. Many did indeed rush inside, overcoming those stumbling out of the gates by pushing their way in and once more bottling up the enemy in the citadel. [19] Everything outside the citadel was systematically plundered and carried off by the Greeks, and the hoplites took up position, some by the stockade, others on the road leading to the citadel. [20] Xenophon and the captains kept on the lookout to see if it might be possible to capture the citadel, for in that way they would be secure, and unless they did so, to withdraw seemed to be extremely difficult. However, on considering the matter, they came to the conclusion that the place was completely impregnable.[a]

**5.2.21–27**
**June 400**
DRILAI TERRITORY
Xenophon extracts the troops from a difficult situation, thanks to guidance from the gods, and the city is burned down.

[21] Thereupon they began to prepare their retreat, and each unit proceeded to pull down the palisading in its vicinity; the captains set about sending away the troops who were ineffective and heavily laden, indeed the majority of the hoplites; they held back only those in whom each officer had confidence. [22] When they started to retreat, many tribesmen began running out from inside to attack them, armed with lances and wickerwork shields and wearing greaves and Paphlagonian helmets,[a] while others began to climb up onto the tops of the houses on each side of the track leading up to the citadel, [23] and hence it was not safe to mount a pursuit as far as the gates leading into the citadel. Furthermore, the enemy was throwing great logs down from above, so that there were difficulties for the Greeks whether they retreated or stood their ground; in addition, the approach of night alarmed them. [24] But as they fought on, at a loss as to what to do, some god gave them a means of salvation. All of a sudden, one of the houses on their right

5.2.15a  Stymphalos, Pellene: Map 1.2.1, AY.
5.2.20a  The valleys in this region are often bounded by steep rock faces, some enabling superior defensive structures to be built.
5.2.22a  Greaves were bronze shin guards. It seems from 5.4.13 that Paphlagonian helmets

had a crest (or topknot) in the middle and a shape very like a tiara (the Persian headdress, a type of soft headgear with flaps, on which see n. C.4a and Figure 2.5.23). Paphlagonia: Map 5.4.1, locator. Mossynoeci territory: Map 5.4.1.

blazed up, someone or other having set it on fire. As it was falling in, the enemy began to flee from the houses on the right. [25] Good fortune made Xenophon aware of this, and he ordered the troops to set the houses on the left on fire as well. The houses were made of wood, so they burned especially quickly, and the enemy therefore began to flee from these houses too. [26] The enemy facing them were now the only ones still causing trouble, and they were clearly going to attack the Greeks as they withdrew and in their subsequent descent. Hence Xenophon gave instructions that whoever happened to be beyond the range of the missiles was to get to work carrying logs into the middle ground between themselves and the enemy. When there were enough logs, they set them on fire, and they also proceeded to set fire to the houses by the palisade itself, in order that the enemy might be preoccupied with them. [27] By thus creating a belt of fire between themselves and the enemy, they made their way out of the place, though not without difficulty. The whole city was burned down, houses, towers, stockade, and everything else except the citadel.

[28] On the next day, the Greeks went away with the food supplies they had captured. But since they were worried about the descent to Trapezus,[a] which was steep and narrow, they set a fake ambush. [29] To do this, one man, a Mysian by race and Mysos by name, took fourteen or fifteen of the Cretans[a] and stayed behind in a dense thicket, where he pretended to try to escape the enemy's notice while the detachment's light shields, being bronze, gleamed through now and then. [30] The enemy, seeing this through the undergrowth, were afraid that it was an ambush, and meanwhile the army proceeded to make its descent. When it seemed that they had already gone far enough, Xenophon signaled to the Mysian to flee with all his might—whereupon he stood up and fled, together with his comrades. [31] The others (the Cretans)—because, as they said, they would certainly be captured if they just ran—turned out of the track into the woods and saved themselves by tumbling down through the wooded hollows there; but the Mysian fled down the track, shouting for help. [32] And they did come and help him, and picked him up wounded. Those who had come to help him then proceeded to retreat in their turn, step by step without turning their backs and under a hail of missiles, while some of the Cretans returned the enemy's arrow fire. In this way they all arrived safe back in the camp.[a]

[1] Since Cheirisophos had not come back, there were not enough merchant ships for them, and it was no longer possible to obtain food supplies, they now realized they had to leave. They put the sick on board the merchant ships they had, together with the troops over forty, the women and children, and whatever baggage that it was not essential to have with them. They also sent aboard Philesios and Sophainetos, the oldest of the generals, and ordered

**5.2.28–32**
**June 400**
DRILAI TERRITORY
Under cover of a pretend ambush, the Greeks manage to get back to camp safely.

**5.3.1–3**
**June 400**
TRAPEZUS–KERASOUS
*Kerasous (62)*
The Greeks resume their journey. A head count at Kerasous totals 8,600 men.

---

5.2.28a Trapezus: Map 5.4.1, *Halting place 61.*
5.2.29a The Cretans were famous as bowmen and supplied the army's archery force (1.2.9). Mysia: Map 7.8.7, BY. Crete: Map 5.3.7, locator.
5.2.32a All arrived safe: this is misleading. This

little party may have returned safely, but overall the Drilai must have inflicted major losses; see Appendix I: The Size and Makeup of the Ten Thousand, §§5–6.

them to look after all this while the rest of the army made its way onward by land (the route having now been made passable).[a] [2] Making their way like this, on the third day they reached Kerasous, a Greek city by the sea, a colony of the Sinopeans in the land of Kolchis.[a] [3] There they remained for ten days. A review under arms was held there, and a head count was taken, in which there turned out to be 8,600 troops. These were the survivors. The others had perished at the hands of the enemy or because of the snow or, in a few cases, through disease.

[4] In this place they also divided up the money derived from the sale of the captives. In addition, the generals divided up the tithe they had reserved for Apollo and for Ephesian Artemis,[a] each of them taking a share to keep safe for the gods, with Neon the Asinean taking Cheirisophos' share.[b] [5] Xenophon therefore had a votive offering made from Apollo's part of his share and dedicated it in the treasury of the Athenians in Delphi;[a] he inscribed on it his own name and that of Proxenos, who had died with Klearchos, for Proxenos had been his guest-friend.[b] [6] As for the part due to Ephesian Artemis, when Xenophon was coming away from Asia with Agesilaos on the journey to Boeotia,[a] he left it with Megabyzos,[b] warden of the temple of Artemis, because he thought he was going into danger, and he instructed him to give the money back to him if and when he was safe and sound; but if, on the other hand, anything were to happen to him, Megabyzos was to have something made that he thought would find favor with Artemis and dedicate it to the goddess. [7] When Xenophon was living as an exile[a]—he was resident by then in Skillous, where he had been settled by the Lacedae-

5.3.1a   On Sophainetos and the relative ages of the generals, see Appendix W: Brief Biographies, §32. Made passable: Xenophon claimed at 5.1.14 that he instigated these repairs. For the difficulties of the land journey, see n. 5.1.13a.

5.3.2a   Kerasous: Map 5.4.1, *Halting place 62.* Sinope: Map 6.1.15. Kolchis/Kolchoi territory: Map 5.4.1 (to be distinguished from Colchis on the east coast of the Black Sea).

5.3.4a   Tithe: it was standard in the ancient world to set aside one-tenth of the spoils of war for the gods as a thank offering. Ephesus housed probably the most famous temple of the goddess Artemis, sister of Apollo; see further at 5.3.12 and n. 5.3.12a. See Figure 5.3.4. Ephesus: Map 5.3.7, BY.

5.3.4b   The citizens of Asine were Lacedaemonians, but only *perioikoi* (free Lacedaemonians inferior to the citizens of Sparta, Lacedaemon's principal city). The terms Lacedaemon and Sparta are nearly synonymous for most purposes; see Appendix B: Xenophon and Sparta, §§18–19. On Cheirisophos, a Lacedaemonian, see Appendix W, §7. Asine: Map 1.2.1, BX.

5.3.5a   The treasury of the Athenians (Figure 5.3.5) was built as a repository of offerings by Athens and Athenians to Apollo of Delphi. For discussion of dating inferences for Xenophon's exile that have been drawn

from his offering there, see n. Intro.3.1b. Delphi: Map 5.3.7, BX.

5.3.5b   The execution of Klearchos and Proxenos by the Persians was reported at 2.6.1. Guest-friend: someone with whom there is a bond of ritualized friendship of a type that was common between prominent men of different cities; for more, see the Glossary. On Proxenos and Klearchos, see Appendix W, §§29, 20. Persian Empire: Ref. Map 9.

5.3.6a   Xenophon journeyed to Boeotia with Agesilaos of Sparta in 394, when the king led his army back to Greece because of a revolt against Spartan domination; for more, see the Introduction, §3.2–3; Appendix B: Xenophon and Sparta, §§9–10. On Agesilaos' reign, see Appendix W, §2. Boeotia: Map 1.2.1, AY.

5.3.6b   Megabyzos: the Greek transcription of a Persian name, though here it is probably the title of the temple warden rather than the name of the individual who held the office. Xenophon does not shy away from bringing out the strong Persian influence on the cult of his favorite goddess.

5.3.7a   Both the text here and its interpretation are disputed; some believe the passage shows that Xenophon was exiled as late as 394 or 393. This edition advocates earlier dates; see the Introduction, §3.2–3.

FIGURE 5.3.4A. MARBLE FRAGMENT FROM THE TEMPLE OF ARTEMIS
AT EPHESUS (TOP), 560–540 B.C.E., MEASURING 3.5 FEET/ABOUT
1 METER LONG. THE COLUMNS WITH THEIR LINTELS WERE CALCU-
LATED TO BE ALMOST 56 FEET/17 METERS TALL. ABOVE: TWO COINS
MINTED IN EPHESUS WITH THE IMAGE OF THE TEMPLE AND STATUE
(LEFT), 198–211 C.E., AND STATUE (RIGHT), 81–96 C.E.

FIGURE 5.3.4B. SECOND-CENTURY C.E. STATUE OF ARTEMIS FOUND AT
EPHESUS, PARTLY MODELED ON THE GREAT FOURTH-CENTURY B.C.E.
STATUE OF ARTEMIS IN HER TEMPLE THERE (THE TEMPLE BURNED
DOWN IN 356 B.C.E., BUT THE MAIN FEATURES OF THE STATUE AS IT
WAS AROUND 400 B.C.E. WERE PROBABLY KEPT THE SAME IN SUBSE-
QUENT REPRODUCTIONS). AS THE ROMAN-ERA STATUE SHOWS,
IN LINE WITH COINS FROM THE HELLENISTIC PERIOD, THE
CULT STATUE OF EPHESIAN ARTEMIS HAD A VERY
DISTINCTIVE FORM WITH WHAT LOOKS LIKE MULTIPLE
BREASTS, ALTHOUGH THEY LACK NIPPLES; ALL THE
STATUES ALSO DEPICT BEES ON THE SIDES OF THE
GODDESS' SKIRT. BELOW RIGHT: A COIN MINTED AT
EPHESUS WITH THE IMAGE OF A BEE, 390–380 B.C.E.

FIGURE 5.3.5. THE TREASURY OF THE ATHENIANS AT DELPHI.

monians near Olympia[b]—Megabyzos came to Olympia as a spectator of the Games[c] and gave Xenophon back the money he had deposited with him. Xenophon took the money and bought the goddess a plot of land where the god[d] ordained it.

5.3.8–13
June 400
SKILLOUS
*Flash-forward*
Xenophon compares Skillous with Ephesus and uses part of his share of the tithe to create a precinct for Artemis in Skillous.

[8] It happened that through the plot of land flowed the river Selinous; and in Ephesus also, close to the temple of Artemis, there flows a river Selinous.[a] There are fish in both rivers, and mussels; and in the plot of land in Skillous, there are also opportunities to hunt every kind of beast that is hunted. [9] From the sacred money Xenophon built both an altar and a shrine; and for the rest of his time there, he always took a tithe of the crops in their season from the surrounding fields and held a sacrifice to the goddess; and all the townspeople and the neighbors, both men and women, would share in the festival. The goddess would provide the banqueters with barley meal, loaves of bread, wine, dried fruits, and an allotted portion of the sacrificial victims taken from the sacred pasture and of the animals killed in the hunt. [10] For this purpose Xenophon's sons and the sons of the other

5.3.7b  On Xenophon's residence at Skillous, see the Introduction, §§6.2, 6.7. Skillous, Olympia: Map 5.3.7, BX. Lacedaemon: Map 1.2.1, BX.

5.3.7c  The year of these Olympic Games was probably 388, though some scholars also

consider 392 or 384 as possibilities.

5.3.7d  The god: Apollo, acting through the Delphic oracle.

5.3.8a  The Selinous River near Skillous is not shown on the maps owing to scale. The Selinous River near Ephesus: Ref. Map 4.2, DY.

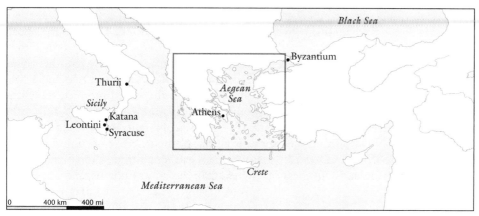

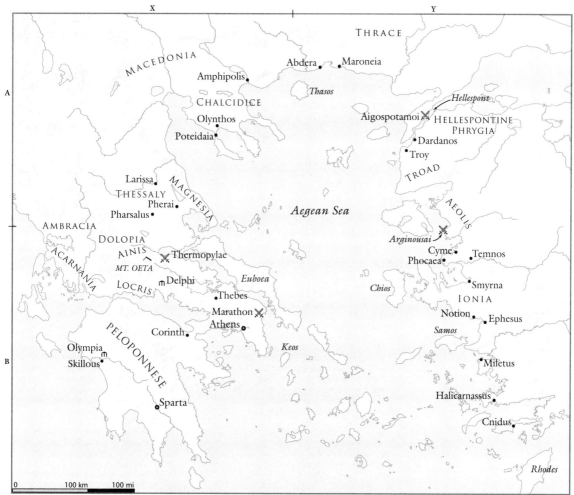

MAP 5.3.7. SITES IN GREECE AND THE AEGEAN.

townspeople used to organize a hunt for the festival, and there also hunted along with them those grown men who wanted to do so. Their quarry—boar and roe deer and fallow deer—was taken partly from the sacred precinct itself and partly also from Mount Pholoe.ᵃ [11] The place is on the road by which people make their way from Lacedaemon to Olympia, about two and a half milesᵃ from the temple of Zeus at Olympia. In the sacred precinct, there is a meadow and tree-covered hills, sufficient to support pigs and goats and cattle and horses, so that the draft animals of those coming to the festival have their feast too. [12] Around the shrine itself was planted a grove of cultivated trees, bearing in due season all sorts of fruit to eat. The shrine, though small, has been made in the likeness of its great counterpart at Ephesus, and the effigy, though made of cypress wood, is like the golden effigy at Ephesus.ᵃ [13] A stone tablet has been set up next to the shrine with this inscription: "The sacred place of Artemis. He who occupies it and reaps its fruits is to use the tenth part each year to perform sacrifices. From the balance he is to keep the shrine in repair. And if anyone does not do these things, the goddess will be mindful of it."

**5.4.1–10**
**July 400**
**BLACK SEA COAST**
*Kolchoi-Mossynoeci boundary (63)*
The Mossynoeci refuse to let the Greeks pass, but Xenophon negotiates successfully with a rival Mossynoecian group to the west.

[1] From Kerasous the same people were carried by sea as had been previously, while the rest made their way by land. [2] When they were on the frontier with the Mossynoeci,ᵃ they sent to them Timesitheos, a Trapezountian and a *proxenos* of the Mossynoeci at Trapezus,ᵇ asking whether they would be making their way through friendly or hostile territory. The Mossynoeci replied that they would not let them pass through, for they trusted in their strongholds. [3] At this point Timesitheos said that the tribesmen on the far side of these people, also Mossynoeci,ᵃ were enemies of theirs, and the Greeks decided to invite them over to see whether they might want to enter into an alliance. Timesitheos was sent to them and came back, bringing their leaders with him. [4] When they arrived, the leaders of these more westerly Mossynoeci and the generals of the Greeks held a meeting and Xenophon made a speech, with Timesitheos acting as his interpreter: [5]

5.3.10a Mt. Pholoe: Map 1.2.1, AX.
5.3.11a About 2.5 miles/4 kilometers: the Greek text says 20 stades; see Appendix O: Measurements, §5.
5.3.12a The cult statue of Artemis of Ephesus reputedly fell from the sky, so perhaps it was a meteorite or other unworked object. Xenophon's description shows that if so, it was housed within a distinctive golden effigy. But the effigy in Xenophon's time may not have been quite the same, since a great fire destroyed the temple in 356. See Figure 5.3.4.
5.4.2a Mossynoeci territory: Map 5.4.1. The boundaries of their territory are marked as *Halting places 63, 64.*
5.4.2b A *proxenos*—while residing in and owing primary loyalty to the city-state of which he was a citizen—was appointed to act in support of the people of a specific foreign

state in their dealings with the *proxenos'* city. In particular, he looked after them when they visited the city, whether as official envoys or in a private capacity. Through literary references and especially inscriptions, we know of several thousand cases in which city-states appointed citizens of other city-states to perform these functions for them. But here Timesitheos is the *proxenos* of a non-Greek people, the Mossynoeci, a less usual situation. For more on this office, see the Glossary. Trapezus: Map 5.4.1, *Halting place 61.*
5.4.3a "also Mossynoeci": they must have been Mossynoeci since Xenophon shortly afterward addresses them as such, but the Greek does not actually say so—these two words, and two similar expressions below, have been added to clarify the situation. (Translator's note)

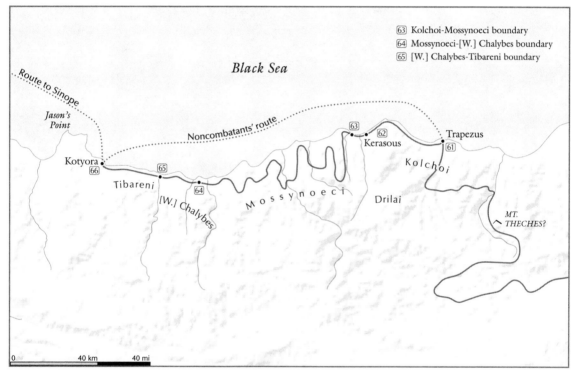

MAP 5.4.1. *PARABASIS:* TRAPEZUS TO KOTYORA, *HALTING PLACES 61–66.*

"Men of the Mossynoeci, as we don't have ships, we want a safe passage through, toward Greece, on foot. These people are stopping us, and we hear they are enemies of yours. [6] So if you want, you can ally yourselves with us, have your revenge if these people have ever done you any wrong, and in future treat them as your subjects. [7] If you refuse us, consider where else you could obtain so large a force as an ally." [8] To this speech the leader of the more westerly Mossynoeci answered that this was what they wanted and

163

FIGURE 5.4.12. GREEK THRUSTING SPEARS (LEFT) DEPICTED IN THE NORMAL POSITION USED BY HOPLITES ON A LATE FOURTH-CENTURY VASE FROM ITALY. THE BUTT-SPIKE OR *SAUROTĒR* APPEARS CLEARLY.

5.4.11–15
July 400
MOSSYNOECI TERRITORY
The rebel Mossynoeci
return with canoes and in
battle attire. They launch
an attack on their rivals,
who are in possession
of the Mossynoecian
mother-city.

they would accept the alliance. [9] "Come, then," said Xenophon; "tell us how you will want to make use of us if we become your allies, and how you will be able to work with us so we can get through." [10] They said, "Your enemies are also ours. There are enough of us to invade their territory from its other side and also to send to you here not only vessels but men as well who will fight alongside you and point out the route."

[11] They gave and received pledges confirming these terms and then departed. On the next day, they duly came with three hundred canoes, each hollowed out of a single log and with three men in it, of whom two disembarked and lined up, standing ready with their weapons, while the third stayed on board. [12] This last group took the boats and paddled off, while those who remained marshaled themselves into two lines, each of about a hundred people, facing each other like dancers in a chorus.[a] Each Mossynoecian had a wickerwork shield in the shape of an ivy leaf and covered with the hide of shaggy white oxen, and in his right hand a light spear nine feet[b]

5.4.12a While today a chorus suggests a group of singers for whom any dancing may be only incidental, ancient Greek choruses both sang and danced. They had prominent roles in tragedy and comedy, but in addition organized collective dancing outside the theater was very important in the life of many cities, especially Sparta. A modern parallel for the Mossynoeci here would be the lines of dancers who face one another in barn dances.

5.4.12b Nine feet/3 meters: the Greek text says 6 *pēcheis*. The *pēchus* was a measure of length notionally equivalent to a forearm; see Appendix O: Measurements, §§2–3.

long, with a lance head on top and the wooden shaft shaped into a ball at the butt.[c] [13] They had dressed in short, thigh-length tunics with the thickness of a linen bag for bedclothes, and on their heads they wore leather helmets, like Paphlagonian helmets, with a crest in the middle and a shape very like that of a tiara;[a] they also had battle-axes made of iron. [14] Then one of them started to lead off, and all the others moved forward too, singing in time as they went on their way. When they had passed through the ranks of the Greeks and their weapon stacks, they made their way straight on toward the enemy in the direction of a stronghold that seemed to be easily assailable. [15] This was situated in front of the city that they called their mother-city and that contained the highest ground in Mossynoeci territory.[a] In fact, it was about this place[b] that the Mossynoeci were fighting their war, for those who were in possession of it at any time were thought to have authority over all the Mossynoeci, and the tribesmen on the Greek side said that their enemies did not have the right to occupy it but, through seizing it when it was common property, now had more than their due.

[16] Some of the Greeks followed them, not assigned to that duty by the generals but in hope of plunder. All the time they were approaching, the enemy held their peace; but when they had come close to the stronghold, the enemy ran out and routed them. The enemy killed several of their fellow barbarians and some of the Greeks who had come up with them, and they carried on the pursuit until they saw the Greeks coming out to help their allies. [17] At that, they turned away and went back, and they cut off the heads of the corpses and displayed them to the Greeks and to their own Mossynoecian enemies, all the time dancing and singing to a kind of tune.[a] [18] The Greeks took it very hard that their allies' rout had made the enemy bolder and that the Greeks who had gone out with them had been put to flight even though there were quite a lot of them, something that had not previously happened in the course of the expedition.

[19] Xenophon called the Greeks together and said: "Brave soldiers, do not be downhearted because of what has happened. You should realize that there is good in what has occurred as well as bad. [20] First, you now know that those proposing to be our guides really are hostile to the people of whom we are forced to be enemies. Next, as for those Greeks who paid no heed to

5.4.16–18
July 400
MOSSYNOECI TERRITORY
The attack by the rebel Mossynoeci fails, even though some Greeks leave their posts in the army to accompany them.

5.4.19–21
July 400
MOSSYNOECI TERRITORY
Xenophon rallies the Greeks.

---

5.4.12c  The base of a Greek spear (the *sauròtèr*) was pointed, so that it could be stuck in the ground upright. In not having this pointed base, the Mossynoecian spear was like the Chalybian spear of 4.7.16, though much shorter. See Figure 5.4.12.

5.4.13a  On the Persian tiara, a type of soft headgear with flaps, see n. C.4a and Figure 2.5.3. Paphlagonia: Map 5.4.1, locator.

5.4.15a  If we take the Mossynoecian boundary to which the Greeks came at 5.4.2 to be marked by a river, it seems likely that the Mossynoeci with whom the Greeks allied had paddled up this river some way to negotiate with the Greek leaders. The

mother city was not very far from where they disembarked.

5.4.15b  This place was the stronghold (5.4.14), rather than the mother-city (as some commentators suggest). It seems that possession of it symbolically represented sovereignty over the totality of Mossynoecian tribes, but that while it had previously been under joint control it was now occupied by a representative of the tribe of the metropolis.

5.4.17a  See Figure 4.7.16 for a warrior wearing a crested helmet and carrying a severed head.

their posts alongside the rest of us but thought themselves capable of achieving the same success alongside the barbarians as they had with us—they have had their just deserts and so will be less likely to leave our ranks again. [21] But you must make ready to show our friends among the barbarians that you are mightier than they are, and also to make clear to the enemy that they are not fighting the same men now as when they fought against those who lacked discipline."

**5.4.22–26**
**July 400**
METROPOLIS OF THE
MOSSYNOECI
A properly organized
attack is successful.

[22] For that day, therefore, they remained as they were. But on the next day, once they had performed sacrifices and obtained favorable omens and had had their morning meal, they organized the companies as columns, posted the barbarians on the left in the same formation, and got on their way. They put archers between the companies, set back a little from the front rank of the hoplites, [23] since the enemy had some highly mobile warriors who would run down and pelt them with stones. So the archers and peltasts held these people in check while the rest of the Greek troops made their way forward at a steady pace. To begin with, their target was the stronghold from which on the previous day the barbarians on the Greek side had been turned in flight, along with the Greeks accompanying them, because that was where the enemy were drawn up against them now. [24] The enemy barbarians actually stood firm against the peltasts and carried on battling with them, but when the hoplites got near, they turned in flight. The peltasts immediately followed, pursuing the enemy up toward the city while the hoplites followed in formation. [25] When the Greeks were on the high ground near the houses of the mother-city, the enemy then managed to pull themselves together and began to fight back, hurling their light spears; they also had different spears, long thick pikes, which a man could carry only with difficulty, and with these they tried to defend themselves hand to hand. [26] But when the Greeks did not waver but continued to advance to close quarters, the barbarians, every one of whom had earlier abandoned the stronghold in front of the mother-city, now fled from the mother-city itself. Their king lives in a wooden tower built on the highest point, and all his subjects maintain him in common while he stays there, keeping guard over him. He did not want to leave, nor did the chief in the stronghold the Greeks had taken previously, so instead they were burned alive there together with their towers.[a]

**5.4.27–29**
**July 400**
METROPOLIS OF
THE MOSSYNOECI
The supplies captured
in the Mossynoecian
strongholds.

[27] In the course of plundering the strongholds, the Greeks found storeroom after storeroom in the houses full of piles of bread made from the previous year's flour, as the Mossynoeci told them, and they also found the new grain stored away with the stalks still attached; most of it was emmer.[a] [28] Pickled slices of dolphin meat were also found in two-handled jars, and

5.4.26a It sounds as though the Mossynoecian king was under a taboo, of a kind seen in a wide variety of cultures, against leaving his tower and setting foot on the ground. It further looks as if this applied not only to the king of the metropolis but also to the chief of what had once been (on our interpretation) the symbolic common possession of the whole tribe.

5.4.27a For emmer, see the Glossary. It seems that some of the current emmer crop has been harvested but not processed. The relevant harvest would have taken place in mid-July or August (but August dates would give rise to difficult chronological problems further down the line). On chronological markers in the text of *Anabasis*, see Appendix Q: The Chronology of the March, §3.

in other containers they found dolphin fat, which the Mossynoeci use just as Greeks use olive oil. [29] On the upper floors, there were lots of nuts, the flat kind without any division in them.[a] This they used for what was actually their main food, boiling and baking the nuts into loaves. Wine was also found that, taken neat, seemed to be sharp because of its roughness but when mixed with water had a good bouquet and a pleasant taste.

[30] After the Greeks had had their morning meal, they handed over the place to their allies among the Mossynoeci and began gradually to make their way onward. They approached various other strongholds belonging to those on the side of their Mossynoeci enemies, and in the case of the most readily accessible of them, the inhabitants either abandoned them or came over to the Greek side voluntarily. [31] Most of the strongholds fell into this category. The cities[a] were separated from each other by seven and a half miles, more or less, but by calling out to each other from high up, people could communicate from one city to the next, as the terrain consisted of lofty crags and hollow valleys.[b] [32] When, as they made their way onward, they were among friendly Mossynoeci, the latter showed off to them the plump children of their wealthy elite, who had been fed on boiled nuts. They were white and soft to an extraordinary degree, and almost as round as they were tall. Their backs were painted in many colors, while all over the front of them they sported flower tattoos. [33] The Mossynoeci also kept trying to have sex in public with the kept women whom the Greeks brought with them, for such was the custom among them. All the men and women were white-skinned. [34] The soldiers who came back from the expedition used to say that these were the most barbarous people they had passed through and the furthest removed from Greek customs, for when they were in a crowd, they did whatever others might do in solitude, and when they were by themselves, they behaved just as if they were in the company of others: they would talk to themselves and laugh at themselves and stand and dance wherever they happened to be, as if showing off to other people.

[1] It took an eight days' march for the Greeks to make their way through the land of the Mossynoeci, both the hostile and the friendly parts of this country, and then they reached the Chalybes.[a] These were few in number

5.4.30–34
July 400
MOSSYNOECI TERRITORY
Xenophon describes the extraordinary communication methods of the Mossynoeci and what the Greeks regard as their barbarous customs.

5.5.1–3
July 400
[W.] CHALYBES–
TIBARENI TERRITORIES
*Mossynoeci-[W.] Chalybes boundary (64)–Kotyora (66)*
The generals' plan to attack the Tibareni is blocked by bad omens.

5.4.29a These were probably a flatter type of hazelnuts stored by the Mossynoecians, although it is possible they are chestnuts native to the area, made into bread when there are shortages of cereals.

5.4.31a These settlements seem to have been smaller than cities; however, the Greek word used, *poleis* (city-states), indicates not size, but that the settlements had self-governing institutions. See *polis* in the Glossary.

5.4.31b Seven and a half miles/12 kilometers: the Greek text says 80 stades; see Appendix O: Measurements, §5. This distance is too far for human speech to carry, and has to be interpreted as the distance a traveler between the villages would traverse going up and down, while the calling distance

between successive ridges might be only half of that. Even so, 40 stades is still too great for normal human speech to be intelligible. But this can be achieved by special techniques such as whistled speech, and it is conceivable that Xenophon is referring to that practice, which may still be observed in this region. See Brennan 2016.

5.5.1a These [Western] Chalybes are to be distinguished from the [Eastern] Chalybes of 4.7.15. Other authors tell us of Chalybes who lived yet farther to the west, around the Thermodon River; it is these whose homeland is marked in the *Barrington Atlas*. [W.] Chalybes territory: Map 5.4.1. [E.] Chalybes territory: Book 5 map. Thermodon River: Map 6.1.15.

and subjects of the Mossynoeci, and most of them derived their livelihood from ironworking.[b] [2] From there they came to the Tibareni.[a]

The land of the Tibareni was much more level, and their strongholds, which were by the sea, were less readily defensible. The generals longed to attack the strongholds so that the army could obtain a little profit, and they would not accept the tokens of friendship that came from the Tibareni. Instead, ordering them to wait until they had deliberated, they proceeded to offer sacrifice.[b] [3] Yet though they performed many sacrifices, in the end the seers unanimously delivered their opinion that the gods would simply not countenance the campaign. Then of course they accepted the tokens of friendship, and making their way for two days as if through friendly territory, they came to Kotyora, a Greek city made up of colonists from Sinope,[a] who dwell in the land of the Tibareni.

[4] [Up to this point the army had traveled by land. There had been 122 days' worth of marching in the journey down from the battle in Babylon[a] as far as Kotyora, amounting to 620 parasangs, or rather more than two thousand miles.[b] They had spent eight months on the journey.][c]

[5] There they stayed for forty-five days. During this time the first thing they did was to perform a sacrifice to the gods; parades were held by groups of Greeks according to their ethnic origin,[a] and also athletic contests. [6] They took their food supplies partly from the territory of Paphlagonia[a] and partly from places belonging to the Kotyorites, since the Kotyorites did not provide them with a market, nor would they take the sick within the walls.

[7] At this point ambassadors came from Sinope, anxious about the city of the Kotyorites, which was a colony of the Sinopeans and paid a regular levy to them, and also about the countryside, because they had heard that it was being laid waste. They came into the camp and made a speech,

---

**5.5.4**
Scribal note on the distance traveled so far.

**5.5.5–6**
July–August 400
KOTYORA
The Greeks are delayed for a long time.

**5.5.7–12**
July–August 400
KOTYORA
Hekatonymos of Sinope criticizes the army and threatens to seek help against them from the Paphlagonians.

---

5.5.1b There is extensive archaeological evidence for ironworking in the southeast of the Black Sea area. Perhaps the Greeks applied the name "Chalybes" to tribesmen who were ironworkers rather than to members of a single ethnic group. That would help explain the dispersion of the name.

5.5.2a Tibareni territory: Map 5.4.1, a possible location for the boundary with the [Western] Chalybes is marked as *Halting place 65.*

5.5.2b Offer sacrifice: in order to get the good omens appropriate before launching any military enterprise.

5.5.3a Kotyora: Map 5.4.1, *Halting place 66.* Sinope: Map 6.1.15.

5.5.4a The battle, described at 1.8, 1.10, took place in the vicinity of Babylon, not actually at Babylon. The journey is said to be "down" from the battle because it was a journey to the sea. Babylon: Map 5.4.1, locator.

5.5.4b More than 2,000 miles/3,220 kilometers: the Greek text says 18,600 stades. The parasang is a Persian unit for measuring travel, typically of around 3 miles/5 kilometers, but it is controversial whether it measures hours spent traveling, distance

traveled, or a combination of the two. For more, see the Introduction, §7.3–5; Appendix O: Measurements, §§7–8.

5.5.4c This passage is generally believed to be a scribal insertion, along with 2.2.6 and 7.8.26, perhaps from a different fourth-century source. In particular, the parasangs look overstated and appear to be derived by multiplying the march days by five (with a small slip) rather than being in line with the narrative. Objection has also been made to the number of march days and the total duration as being overstated compared to the narrative, but Xenophon's own climatic pointers, on which, see Appendix Q: The Chronology of the March, show that the true duration can't be reached simply by adding up the figures he gives explicitly.

5.5.5a According to ethnic origin: that is, the Arcadians would hold one parade, the Achaeans another, perhaps the Thessalians all together a third, and so forth. That would be regardless of how they had been mixed together on the march or in line of battle. Arcadia, Achaea: Map 1.2.1, AX.

5.5.6a Paphlagonia: Map 5.4.1, locator.

their spokesman being Hekatonymos, who was thought to be a clever speaker:
[8] "Brave soldiers, the city of Sinope has sent us, first to praise you because
you are Greeks who have defeated barbarians, and secondly to rejoice with
you because you have reached here in safety after going through what we
hear were many appalling troubles. [9] We think that as we ourselves are
Greeks and you are Greeks, we should receive some benefit from you and not
suffer any harm, since never in any way did we initiate injury to you. [10]
These Kotyorites are colonists of ours, and we gave them this land once we
had cleared it of barbarians. For this reason they pay us a specified tribute,
as do the Kerasountians and the Trapezountians,ª and so whatever harm you
may do to these people, the state of Sinope considers itself to suffer. [11]
Now we hear that, having forced your way into the city, some of you occupy
quarters in the houses there, and that you take whatever you want by force
from places belonging to the Kotyorites without obtaining their consent.
[12] We do not appreciate this behavior, and if you carry on like this, it will
be necessary for us to make friends with Korylasª and his Paphlagonians and
with anyone else we can."

[13] In response to this, Xenophon stood up and spoke on behalf of the
soldiers: "We for our part, men of Sinope, have come back happy enough
that we have preserved ourselves and our weapons—it was not possible for
us at one and the same time both to fight the enemy and to acquire many
belongings and carry them along with us. [14] And as for the present situation, once we had reached the Greek cities, in Trapezus we got our food
supplies by purchasing them, as they provided us with a market, and in
return for the respect they showed us and the tokens of friendship they gave
the army, we in turn showed them respect; and indeed if any of the barbarians were friends of theirs, we kept away from them, but we did as much
harm as we could to the enemies of theirs against whom they led us. [15]
Ask them what sort of people they found us to be—there are some of them
here, whom their city sent with us out of friendship, to be our guides. [16]
But wherever we come where we do not have access to a market, whether in
barbarian territory or in Greek, we seize our food supplies, not out of arrogant willfulness but out of necessity. [17] Take the Kardouchoi, the Taochoi,
or the Chaldaioi:ª although they are not subjects of the King, nevertheless—
and despite their very real fearsomeness—we treated them as enemies because
of the necessity of obtaining food supplies, since they did not provide us with
a market. [18] By contrast, in the case of the Makrones,ª although they are
barbarians, we thought we should be friends with them, since they provided
a market as far as they could, and we seized none of their possessions.

5.5.13–23
July–August 400
KOTYORA
Xenophon defends the
army's behavior and calls
Hekatonymos' bluff.

5.5.10a  Kerasous (*Halting place 62*), Trapezus
        (*Halting place 61*): Map 5.4.1.
5.5.12a  Korylas was the ruler of Paphlagonia
        (6.1.2, 7.8.25).
5.5.17a  Food supplies taken: from the Kardouchoi,
        4.1.8–9; from the Taochoi, 4.7.14, 4.7.17.
        Chaldaioi: this is probably another name
        for the [Eastern] Chalybes, a hostile tribe
        whose lands they crossed at 4.7.15–17.

Kardouchoi territory: Map 4.4.3. [E.]
Chalybes, Taochoi territory: Map 4.7.1,
BX, BY (the *Barrington Atlas* does not
locate the [Eastern] Chalybes on its maps
and locates the Chaldaioi in a different
location, at Map 87 E4 [Chaldia]).
5.5.18a  Encounter with the Makrones: see 4.8.1–8.
        Makrones territory: Map 4.7.1, BX.

[19] "As for the Kotyorites, who you say belong to you, if we have taken anything of theirs, they are the ones responsible for it, since they did not conduct themselves toward us as friends but shut the gates and would not receive us inside or send a market outside. They claimed that the governor who came from you was the origin of these decisions. [20] As for your reference to people getting in by force and occupying quarters, we made the reasonable request that the sick be taken indoors, and when the townspeople would not open the gates, we got in where the state of the walls positively invited us in, but we did nothing else violent. The sick have quarters indoors at their own expense, and we garrison the gates in order that our sick should not be at the mercy of your governor, but instead it should be in our power to take them back whenever we choose. [21] The rest of us, as you see, have our quarters in the open air in military formation, ready, supposing anyone treats us well, to treat him well in return, and supposing anyone treats us badly, to defend ourselves. [22] And as for your threats that, if you see fit, you will make Korylas and his Paphlagonians your allies against us: if there was the need for it, we would certainly make war on both of you, for in the past we fought wars against others much more numerous than you. But supposing we were to decide to make the Paphlagonian our friend rather than yours [23] (and we hear that he covets your city and your strongholds on the coast), we would try to become his friends by working with him to achieve his desires."

5.5.24–25
July–August 400
KOTYORA
Good relations are established with Sinope and Kotyora.

[24] After this, Hekatonymos' fellow ambassadors made very clear their irritation at the way these speeches had gone, but another of the ambassadors came forward and said that they had not come to start a war but to show that they were our friends: "And if you come to Sinope,[a] we will receive you there with gifts of friendship, while right now we will order those on the spot here to give you what they can, for we see that all that you are saying is true." [25] After this, the Kotyorites[a] set about sending gifts of friendship and the Greek generals proceeded to entertain the Sinopean ambassadors as their guests; they talked to each other for a long time and in a friendly spirit and asked each other such detailed questions as they wished, both about the remaining journey and as regards other matters.

5.6.1–2
July–August 400
KOTYORA
The army asks the Sinopeans' advice on how best to go forward.

[1] That was how things turned out in the end on that day. On the next day, the generals assembled the soldiers, and the decision was made to call in the Sinopeans to discuss the remaining journey. If it were necessary to make their way by foot, it seemed that the Sinopeans would be useful because of their undoubted knowledge of Paphlagonia; while if by sea, it seemed they still needed them, as it appeared that they alone had the resources to provide sufficient merchant ships for the army. [2] So they

5.5.24a   Sinope: Book 6 map.
5.5.25a   Kotyora: Map 5.4.1, *Halting place 66.*

called the ambassadors and opened the discussion with them, saying they expected that, as Greeks dealing with Greeks, the Sinopeans would treat them handsomely at the outset of their relationship by being well-disposed toward them and giving them the best advice.

[3] Hekatonymos stood up and he began by defending his earlier statement that the Sinopeans would make friends with the Paphlagonian ruler, on the ground that he did not mean to imply that they would make war on the Greeks but, rather, meant to say that though it was possible for them to be friends with the barbarians, they would choose the Greeks instead. Then, when the Greeks started to tell him to give his advice, he called on heaven and spoke as follows: [4] "If I were to give you the advice that seems to me to be the best, may I obtain many benefits, but if not, may I suffer the reverse instead! For it seems to me that, in the words of the proverb, 'Sacred Counsel' itself is present here.[a] That is because if in the present circumstances I were found to have given good counsel, many are those who will praise me, but if the opposite, many are you who will curse me. [5] So, then, I realize that we for our part will have much more trouble if you are carried by sea, as we shall have to provide the vessels, whereas if you set out by land, you will have to do the fighting. Nevertheless, I must speak the facts as I know them, [6] being, as I am, familiar both with the land of the Paphlagonians and with their forces. For their land has both extremes: very fine plains and very high mountains.

[7] "In the first place, I know exactly where it is necessary to make your entry, for the only possible way in is where the horns of the mountain stand high above both sides of the road, and just a few troops, if they held those peaks, could prevail—all the people in the world could not get through if those positions were held against them. I could even show you the peaks, if you want to send someone with me. [8] And after that I know that there are plains, and also cavalry forces that the barbarians themselves think are stronger than all of the King's cavalry put together. Indeed, on a very recent occasion, these horsemen did not attend upon the King when he called for them, as their ruler thought it beneath him. [9] And even if you steal through the mountains, or occupy them before the enemy, and you prevail in the plain, despite fighting against their cavalry and more than twelve myriads[a] of foot soldiers, you will come to the rivers: first to the Thermodon, three hundred feet wide,[b] which I think is difficult to cross, especially with many enemies in front of you and many following behind; second, to the Iris, likewise three hundred feet wide; and third, to the Halys, whose width is no less than four hundred yards.[c] You could not cross this without boats, but who is going to provide them? And in the same way

5.6.3–10
July–August 400
KOTYORA
Hekatonymos makes a florid speech, urging them to go by sea.

---

5.6.4a The proverb was "Counsel is a sacred thing."
5.6.9a Twelve myriads: this would be 120,000 men, but the number should not be taken too seriously.
5.6.9b Three hundred feet/91 meters: the Greek text says 3 *plethra;* see Appendix O:

Measurements, §§2–3. Thermodon River: Map 6.1.15.
5.6.9c Four hundred yards/365 meters: the Greek text says 2 stades; see Appendix O, §5. Iris, Halys Rivers: Map 6.1.15.

the Parthenios[d] is also impassable, which you would come to, if you managed to cross the Halys. [10] So it is my opinion that the land route is not so much difficult for you as altogether impossible. But if you were to go by sea, it is possible to sail from here along the coast to Sinope, and from Sinope to Heraclea;[a] and from Heraclea there is no difficulty about the route either on foot or by sea, as there are many merchant ships in Heraclea too."

[11] When Hekatonymos had finished speaking, some people were suspicious that he spoke out of friendliness toward Korylas, as he was a *proxenos*[a] of Korylas at Sinope, and others even thought that he gave the advice he did in order to obtain bribes. Yet others were suspicious that he spoke as he did in case they did some harm to the territory of the Sinopeans if they went on foot. But however that might be, the Greeks voted to make the journey by sea.

[12] After the vote Xenophon said: "Sinopeans, the men have chosen the route for the journey that you advise. However, this is how things stand: Should it turn out that there are enough merchant ships for not one single person to be left behind here, we would go by sea. But if the plan should be for some of us to sail and some of us to be left behind, we would not embark on the ships. [13] For we know that wherever we are in a dominant position, we would be able both to preserve ourselves and to obtain food supplies, but if we are caught anywhere in smaller numbers than our enemies, it is quite clear that we shall be in the position of slaves." On hearing this, the ambassadors told the army to send its own ambassadors to Sinope, [14] and they sent Kallimachos of Arcadia, Ariston of Athens, and Samolas of Achaea. And off they went.

[15] Meanwhile, as Xenophon contemplated the many hoplites that the Greeks had, and also their many peltasts, archers, and slingers, and horsemen too, by now all really quite competent from the practice they had had, and as he noted that they were on the Black Sea,[a] where so large a force could not have been put together without considerable expense, it seemed to him that it would be a fine thing to add both territory and strength to Greece by their founding a city. [16] And he thought it would become a great city, when he took into account both their numbers and the people who lived in the neighborhood of the Black Sea. So before he spoke to any of the soldiers about it, he summoned Silanos, the Ambraciot who had been Cyrus' seer, and set about offering sacrifice to inquire about these matters.[a] [17] Silanos, fearing that the idea might be put into effect and that the

**5.6.11–14**
July–August 400
KOTYORA
Though suspicious, the army accepts Hekatonymos' advice, and an embassy is sent to Sinope to make arrangements.

**5.6.15–18**
July–August 400
KOTYORA
Xenophon thinks of founding a city and makes a preliminary sacrifice with Silanos as his seer.

5.6.9d   Parthenios River: Map 6.1.15. Halys River: Map 6.1.15. Four hundred yards: the Greek text says two stades.
5.6.10a   Heraclea: Map 6.1.15.
5.6.11a   It is not surprising that the army was suspicious of Hekatonymos' advice in view of his position as *proxenos* (see n. 5.4.2b) of Korylas.
5.6.15a   Black Sea: Map 5.4.1 and locator.
5.6.16a   Offering a divinatory sacrifice to see if the gods were happy with a proposed new city was a normal part of what its founder (the *oecist*) would do, but this

was supposed to be the final stage after human consensus had been reached, not a preemptive move by the person offering the sacrifice. Although Xenophon protests that he was only asking a preliminary question, it is not surprising the men were suspicious that he was jumping the gun. On divinatory sacrifices, see Appendix G: Divinity and Divining, esp. §10. On Cyrus the Younger, see Appendix W: Brief Biographies, §10. Ambracia: Map 5.3.7, AX.

army would settle down somewhere, told the troops a tale of how Xenophon wanted the army to settle down so he could found a city and obtain
power and a great name for himself. [18] Personally, Silanos wanted to reach
Greece as soon as possible: as recounted earlier, Cyrus had given him three
thousand darics, because when he was offering sacrifice on Cyrus' behalf, he
had spoken truly of the ten days;[a] and so far Silanos had succeeded in keeping them safe.

[19] When the soldiers heard what Silanos was saying, some of them
thought that it was best to remain there, but the majority did not. Timasion
the Dardanian and Thorax the Boeotian[a] told some merchants from Heraclea and Sinope who were present that unless they provided pay for the
army, so that they had food supplies when they sailed away, there would be
a considerable danger that such a great force would stay in the region of the
Black Sea. "For in the discussions that Xenophon is holding with us officers,
he is encouraging us to choose the moment when the merchant ships arrive
to say to the army, all of a sudden, [20] 'Men, at present we see that you are
without the means to obtain food supplies on the voyage or, once you have
departed homeward, to be of any advantage to your people at home. But if
you want to take your pick of the inhabited lands around the Black Sea and
capture wherever you fancy, and then go back home or stay here, just as
each of you wishes, here are ships at your disposal with which you can make
a sudden attack wherever you may want.' "

[21] When they heard this, the merchants reported back to their cities,
and Timasion, being a Dardanian, sent Eurymachos the Dardanian and also
Thorax the Boeotian with them to say the very same thing. On hearing
their account, the Sinopeans and Heracleans sent to Timasion and told him
to take their money and use his influence to get the army to sail away. [22]
He was well pleased to hear it, and spoke in the soldiers' assembly as follows:
"We must not turn our attention to staying here, men, and we should not
value anything more highly than Greece. I hear that some people are offering sacrifices as regards this issue without saying anything to you. [23] I
promise you, if you sail away, to provide each of you with pay of a Cyzicene
stater per month,[a] starting from the next new moon, and I will take you to
the Troad, from which I myself am an exile, and my city will be at your
disposal, as they will willingly have me back.[b] [24] I will personally lead you

5.6.19–20
July–August 400
KOTYORA
Timasion and Thorax
intrigue against
Xenophon's plan.

5.6.21–24
July–August 400
KOTYORA
Timasion makes the
soldiers a counterproposal.

---

5.6.18a   Cyrus' gift to Silanos: this story is narrated
at 1.7.18. Silanos prophesied that there
would be no battle between Cyrus and his
brother for the following ten days, and
Cyrus promised him 3,000 darics if this
turned out to be true, as it did (the battle
took place on the thirteenth day). The gold
daric, equivalent to 25 Attic drachmas, was
the standard large coin of the Persian
Empire; see Appendix O: Measurements,
§§11, 13–14, and Figure O.13.

5.6.19a   Dardanos: Map 5.3.7, AY. Boeotia: Map
1.2.1, AY.

5.6.23a   A Cyzicene stater per month: this rate is
broadly in line with what the soldiers were

originally promised by Cyrus before he
was compelled to increase his offer in
order to retain their services. On the
Cyzicene stater, see Appendix O: Measurements, §§12, 15, and see Figure 5.6.23.
Cyzicus: Book 7 map.

5.6.23b   Since Timasion is an exile, his fellow citizens might not be so willing to have him
back if he did not have several thousand
mercenaries behind him. On the other
hand, maybe he had enough past and
potential supporters within his city for him
and his men to obtain entry without a
fight. The Troad (the district around
Troy): Map 7.8.7, BX.

173

FIGURE 5.6.23. A CYZICENE STATER, SHOWING TWO DOLPHINS ALONGSIDE AND A TUNA BELOW THE BOW-RAM OF A WARSHIP (RIGHT). THE TUNA WAS KEY TO CYZICUS' WEALTH AND IS CHARACTERISTIC OF ITS COINS. THE BEARDED FIGURE HAS BEEN CLAIMED TO BE A PORTRAIT OF THE PERSIAN SATRAP PHARNABAZOS.

to where you can obtain a great deal of wealth. I know my way around Aeolis and Phrygia[a] and the Troad, and the whole of the province ruled by Pharnabazos, partly because I come from there and partly because I campaigned in that area with Klearchos and Derkylidas."[b]

5.6.25–26
July–August 400
KOTYORA
Thorax makes a further proposal.

[25] Thorax the Boeotian, who was always clashing with Xenophon over the management of the army, then stood up in his turn. He said that if they left the Black Sea, the Chersonese[a] would be open to them, a fine and prosperous country. Thus those who so wanted could settle there, and those who did not could go home. It was ridiculous, when there was plenty of land in Greece, more than enough for all, to be casting around in barbarian territory.[b] [26] "And until you find yourselves there," he said, "I promise the same pay to you as Timasion has done." He said this because he knew what the Heracleans and Sinopeans were offering to Timasion to sail away.

5.6.27–33
July–August 400
KOTYORA
Xenophon defends his actions but, as a better option seems to be available, withdraws his idea of founding a city.

[27] Meanwhile, Xenophon remained silent. Philesios stood up, as did Lykon, both Achaeans, and they went on about how dreadful it was that in private Xenophon was trying to persuade people to stay and was offering sacrifices with a view to remaining, but in public he said nothing about it. So Xenophon was forced to stand up and speak as follows: [28] "Men, I offer sacrifices, as you see, regarding as many subjects as I can, both on your behalf and on my own, in order that in speech and thought and deed I may succeed in working out whatever is going to be best and most honorable for you and for me. And recently I have been offering sacrifice about this very issue, whether it would be better to start to speak to you on this subject and set it in motion, or not to touch the matter at all. [29] Silanos the seer gave me the answer to the most important question by saying that the sacred signs were favorable, for he knew that I am not ignorant on these matters,

5.6.24a   Aeolis: Map 5.3.7, AY. The Phrygia referred to here is Hellespontine (or Lesser) Phrygia: Map 5.3.7, AY. This is to be distinguished from the Phrygia of 1.2.6 (sometimes known as Greater Phrygia, Map 1.2.10, AY). The relative positions of the two can be seen on Ref. Map 4, BX, BZ, respectively.

5.6.24b   On these campaigns and the careers of Pharnabazos, Klearchos, and Derkylidas,

see Appendix W: Brief Biographies, §§27, 20, 12.

5.6.25a   Chersonese: Book 7 map.

5.6.25b   The Thracian inhabitants of the Chersonese would not have agreed with Thorax that it was part of Greece, though he was not alone in seeking to colonize it: the Spartans already maintained a military presence there (7.1.13), which would no doubt have blocked Thorax' plans.

because I'm always present at the sacred rites. He said that some trick or plot against me was evident in the sacred signs, as well he might, knowing that he himself was plotting to malign me to you. For he was the one who produced the story that I intended to put my ideas into action without having first persuaded you. [30] For my part, if I saw that you were without resources, I would have looked into how we might manage things so that once you had captured a city, those who wanted to could sail off right away, while those not of that mind could leave once they had gained enough to be of some assistance to their people at home. [31] But since I see that the Heracleans and Sinopeans are sending you the merchant ships so that you can sail away, and that men are promising pay to you from the next new moon, it seems to me a fine thing for us not only to get safely to where we want to be but also to be paid for achieving our own salvation. So I am giving up my former plan myself, and as for anybody who approached me saying that it was necessary to put it into action, I say they too should give it up now.

[32] "For I know this: if you continue all together in great numbers, as you are now, I think you would both be held in respect and have food supplies, for it is given to those who are already strong and powerful also to take the possessions of the weaker. But if you were dispersed and your forces divided into small groups, you would not be able to obtain sustenance, nor would you enjoy an easy escape. [33] So I think, as you do, that we should travel away from here to Greece, and that if anyone stays here or is discovered deserting before the whole army has reached safety, he should be condemned as a wrongdoer. Whoever agrees with this," he said, "let him raise his hand." Every one of them put up their hands.

[34] Silanos, however, began shouting, and he tried to say that it would be right for whoever wanted to leave to do so. But the soldiers would not stand for it, instead threatening to punish him if they caught him running off. [35] Thereupon, when the Heracleans realized that the decision to sail away had been taken and Xenophon himself had put it to the vote, they did send the merchant ships, but they broke their word about the money they had promised to Timasion and Thorax. [36] At this, Timasion and Thorax were panic-stricken: they were afraid of the army's reaction, since they had promised them their pay. So they added to their number the other generals whom they had consulted about their previous actions, and that was all of them except Neon the Asinean (Cheirisophos was absent, and Neon was his deputy general);[a] and they came to Xenophon and said to him that they were very sorry. They now thought it best, they said, to sail to Phasis, since they had ships, and to take control of the land of the Phasians[b] [37] (at that time ruled by a grandson of Aietes).[a] Xenophon answered that he would

5.6.34–37
July–August 400
KOTYORA
Those who had led the opposition to Xenophon panic. They now secretly propose to conquer the territory of the Phasians.

---

5.6.36a  On Cheirisophos, see Appendix W: Brief
            Biographies, §7. Asine: Map 1.2.1, BX.
5.6.36b  Phasis/Phasian territory in Colchis:
            Book 5 map. The Phasis River here flows
            into the Black Sea.

5.6.37a  Grandson of Aietes: in mythology, Aietes
            was the father of the witch Medea, whom
            the hero Jason brought home from Colchis
            after she helped him overcome the dragon
            that was guarding the Golden Fleece.

not say anything to the army on this subject. "But you call them together," he said, "if you want to, and speak to them." At this, Timasion the Dardanian gave it as his opinion that they should not call a full assembly but that each should first try to persuade his own captains, and so they went away and set about doing this.

[1] So the soldiers found out what was afoot. Neon said that the other generals had been led astray by Xenophon, who planned to carry the soldiers back to Phasis[a] by deception. [2] When the soldiers heard this, they became angry, and meetings were held and clusters of troops gathered, and they gave the terrifying impression that they might repeat what they had done to the Kolchian heralds and the superintendents of the market.[a] [3] When Xenophon realized this, he decided to bring them together in formal assembly as quickly as possible, rather than allow them to meet of their own accord; and so he ordered the herald to call an assembly. [4] When they heard the herald, they congregated quickly and very readily. At this Xenophon did not denounce the generals for coming to him but spoke as follows:

[5] "I hear that someone is maligning me, men, asserting that I, of all people, intend to lead you to Phasis by deception. Hear me out, then, in the name of the gods, and if I stand revealed as a wrongdoer, there will be no need for me to go away from here before being duly punished. But if it is those who are maligning me who appear to you to be doing wrong, then deal with them as they deserve!

[6] "You know, of course," he said, "where the sun rises and where it sets, and that if anyone intends to go to Greece, he must make his way toward the evening sun, but if anyone wants to go to the barbarians, he must make his way in the opposite direction, toward the dawn. So is there anyone who could possibly deceive you into believing that where the sun rises, it is there that it sets, and that where it sets, it is from there that it rises? [7] Then again, you know this for sure, that the north wind carries one out of the Black Sea to Greece, and the south wind carries one farther into the Black Sea, to Phasis, and, as the proverb says, 'Fair sailing to Greece whene'er the north wind blows.' So how is it possible for anyone to deceive you into embarking when the south wind is blowing? [8] But, you may say, I will get you to embark when there is a calm. Well, then, I shall be sailing on one vessel and you on at least a hundred. How, then, could I force you to sail with me if you didn't want to, or bring you along

5.7.1a The officers proposed to sail to Colchian Phasis on the east coast of the Black Sea. But Neon says here that Xenophon wants to take them "back to Phasis," the Phasis River in Armenia where they were at 4.6.4. Neon was probably exploiting confusion on the part of the soldiers about the two rivers; they seem to have thought the Armenian Phasis ultimately flowed into the Black Sea. The two Phasis Rivers, Map 4.7.1: in Colchis, AY; in Armenia, BY.

5.7.2a Superintendents of the market: see n. 5.7.23a. The manuscripts add an explanation of what

Xenophon is cryptically referring to (he tells the story later, at 5.7.13–33): "Those who had not made their escape to the sea were stoned to death." These words have been deleted as a gloss, especially as this is not quite the same story as the one Xenophon subsequently tells us about either the Kolchian elders or the superintendents of the market. (Translator's note) Kolchoi territory/Kolchis: Map 5.4.1 (to be distinguished from Colchis on the east coast of the Black Sea).

by deception? [9] However, let's imagine that, deceived and bewitched by me, you have reached Phasis, and suppose also that we are disembarking on shore. You will, of course, perceive that you are not in Greece. And I, the deceiver, will be one single individual, and you, the deceived, will be nearly ten thousand in number, and with weapons. How could a man more readily devise his own punishment than by designing such plans for himself and for you?

[10] "But these are the tales of foolish men, jealous of me because I am held in honor by you. And yet they would not justly be jealous of me: do I prevent any of them from speaking, if any of them can say anything worthwhile in your meetings? Or from fighting, if any of them want to fight on your behalf and his own? Or from staying awake, preoccupied about your safety? Or again, do I stand in anyone's way when you are choosing leaders? I stand back—let him lead: only let it be apparent that he is doing you some good. [11] But as far as I am concerned, enough has been said on these topics. If any of you thinks that he could himself have been deceived in these ways or could deceive anyone else like this, let him speak and teach us how.

[12] "But when you have had enough of all this, do not leave before you have heard what sort of problem I see starting to develop in the army. If this goes any further and turns out as it seems to suggest, it will be time for us to make ourselves the topic of our debates, and how we can avoid displaying ourselves as the worst and most dishonorable of men in the eyes of both gods and humans, both friends and foes."

[13] When they heard this, the soldiers wondered what he was referring to and urged him to speak out.

At that, he began again: "You are aware, I suppose, that there were strongholds in the mountains occupied by barbarians who were friendly to the Kerasountians,[a] and people would come down from them and sell us animals for sacrifice and other things they had, and some of you too, I think, used to go to the closest of these places, buy something in the market there, and come back again. [14] When Klearetos the captain learned about this place, that it was small and also that no guard was set there as the inhabitants thought they were on friendly terms with us, he went there in the night to pillage it, without saying anything to us. [15] He intended, if he took this stronghold, not to return to the army again but to embark on a merchant ship in which his messmates[a] would just then be sailing off the coast, and having loaded it with whatever he had seized, to sail away, out of the Black Sea. This plan had been agreed between him and the messmates on the merchant ship, as I am now aware. [16] So he called together all those he had persuaded and led them to the place. But while he was on his

5.7.12
July–August 400
KOTYORA
Xenophon sees a problem developing in the army.

5.7.13–19
July–August 400
KOTYORA
Xenophon recounts an outrage that occurred at Kerasous.

5.7.13a  About forty days before this, they had stayed in Kerasous for ten days (5.3.2–3). Kerasous: Map 5.4.1, *Halting place 62*.
5.7.15a  Messmates (*suskēnoi*): within their companies, soldiers organized themselves into

small groups of men who ate together and helped each other with their daily needs. See Appendix J: A Soldier's View on the March, §§8–15, where John Lee emphasizes the importance of these groups.

way, day broke; the people gathered together and threw missiles from secure positions, and Klearetos was struck and killed, together with many of the others, though some few of the Greeks managed to return to Kerasous. [17] All this occurred on the day on which we were setting out for here on foot, and some of those who were going to sail along the coast were still in Kerasous, not yet having put to sea.

"After this, the Kerasountians tell me, men from the stronghold arrived, three of the elders, seeking admittance to our assembly. [18] Since they failed to catch us, they went on to say to the Kerasountians that they were at a loss to understand why we had decided to attack them. However, or so the Kerasountians later reported, when they themselves explained that the affair had not been undertaken as a result of a decision by the army as a whole, the three elders were pleased, and they intended to sail here with the aim of informing us of what had happened and, as regards the dead bodies, to tell those so minded to take them and bury them. [19] But some of the Greeks who had escaped from the failed attack happened to be still in Kerasous, and when they learned where the barbarians were going, they brazenly pelted them with stones and started to encourage the others to do the same. The men—the three ambassadors—actually died as a result of being stoned.

[20] "Since this had happened, the Kerasountians came to us and recounted the affair, and when we generals heard it, we were horrified at what had happened, and we entered into discussions with the Kerasountians as to how the Greek corpses might be buried. [21] We were holding our meeting outside the armed camp when suddenly we heard a great hubbub of 'Get them, get them! Stone them, stone them!' and shortly afterward, as one might expect, we saw many people running up with stones in their hands and others picking stones up. [22] The Kerasountians were afraid, as well they might be, since they would also have witnessed the affair in their own city, so they retreated to the ships. And, by Zeus, there were even some of us generals who were afraid. [23] Nevertheless, I went toward the mob and asked what was the matter. There were some of them who knew nothing about it, even though they were holding stones in their hands. When I did fall in with someone who knew, he told me that the market superintendents were treating the army appallingly.[a] [24] At this point someone saw the market superintendent, Zelarchos, slipping off toward the sea and raised a cry. When they heard this, they charged after him as if they had a wild boar or deer in their sights. [25] But the Kerasountians, when they saw the troops rushing toward them, evidently thought it was they who were the target of the charge, and they ran away in flight and ended up in the sea. Even some

5.7.20–26
July–August 400
KOTYORA
Xenophon recounts a further, more recent outrage arising from indiscipline.

5.7.23a   Market superintendents (*agoranomoi*) kept order in the marketplace, levied market dues, checked the quality of goods for sale, and in some cities ensured the fairness of weights and measures in use in the market (the same function is performed in Turkey today by municipal officials known as *zabita*). It's usually thought that the city provided the market superintendents, but it has been argued (O'Connor 2016) that in this instance they were officials of the army, elected by the soldiers but repudiated by them on this occasion.

of us ended up in the sea alongside them, and those who did not know how to swim drowned. [26] Now, what do you think about these people? They had done no wrong, but they feared some madness might have fallen on us, like rabid dogs.

"So if things like these are going to happen, stand back and see what will be the state of our army. [27] All of you collectively will not have the authority either to start a war against whomever you may wish or to put an end to it; but any individual who wishes to do so will lead an army against whatever target he wants. If any ambassadors were to come to you in search of peace or of anything else, those who so wish will kill them and so make sure that you do not hear what they were coming to say to you. [28] Furthermore, whatever leaders all of you as a body may elect will have no standing at all, but whoever elects himself general and takes it into his head to shout 'Stone him, stone him!' will thereby obtain the power to kill an officer—or for that matter any ordinary person from among you whom he may want to put to death without trial—if there are those who will obey him, as happened in the recent instances.

[29] "Consider what these self-elected generals have achieved for you. In the case of Zelarchos the market superintendent, if he has been doing you wrong, he has left by sea without giving you recompense; if he has done no wrong, he has fled from the army, fearing that he would be put to death unjustly and without trial. [30] In the case of those who stoned the ambassadors to death, their first achievement is that you are the only Greeks in the world for whom it is safe to go to Kerasous only when strong in numbers and weaponry, and their second achievement is that it is not safe for you, even if you bear a herald's staff,[a] to take up the corpses of your comrades, which earlier the very people who slew them were telling you to bury. For who will want to act as a herald when he himself has killed heralds? Instead, we asked the Kerasountians to bury them.

[31] "If these are honorable outcomes, then pass a decree to that effect. By voting in favor of such occurrences, you will be deliberately encouraging individuals to create their own private guards and to try to take up quarters only where they have control of the higher ground commanding the site. [32] However, if you think that such deeds are characteristic of wild beasts rather than of human beings, look into some way of putting a stop to them. Otherwise, in the name of Zeus, how shall we perform sacrifices to the gods with glad hearts when we are carrying out impious deeds? Or fight our enemies, seeing that we are slaughtering each other? [33] What friendly city will take us in if they see us display such utter lawlessness? Who will dare to provide a market for us if we show ourselves to be guilty of such offenses as regards the

5.7.27–33
July–August 400
KOTYORA
Xenophon draws the moral from these incidents.

5.7.30a   Heralds (*kērykes*) carried a staff (*kērykeion*) with a distinctive curled top (see Figure 5.7.30) and were regarded as inviolable. Their basic function was to make announcements; their inviolability stemmed from being used to carry messages between armies at war. Xenophon is exaggerating here when he says the Greek thugs had killed heralds. From earlier in the speech, it is evident that they had killed ambassadors, but that was bad enough; killing heralds was considered even worse.

FIGURE 5.7.30. HERALDS, ASSOCI-
ATED WITH THE MYTHOLOGICAL
HERMES, MESSENGER TO ZEUS,
CARRIED A DISTINCTIVE STAFF
(*KĒRYKEION*) AS A SYMBOL OF
THEIR AUTHORITY. TWO EARLY
FIFTH-CENTURY EXAMPLES OF
BRONZE STAFFS FROM SYRACUSE
(LEFT) AND SEGESTA, SICILY
(BELOW), CHARACTERISTICALLY
TERMINATE IN ENTWINED SNAKES.
RIGHT: HERMES WEARING WINGED
SANDALS ON A GREEK TERRA-COTTA
*LĒKYTHOS* (OIL FLASK), C. 480–470.

most serious matters? And where we thought we would obtain praise from everyone, who would praise us if this is the sort of people we are? Indeed, I know we ourselves would say that those who commit such acts are scum."

[34] At this they all got up and said that those who took the lead in these incidents should be punished, that from here on it should no longer be possible to initiate lawlessness, and that if anyone did so, he should be brought to trial for his life. Further, that the generals should make arrangements for all the trials, and that trials should also be held if anyone had been wronged in any other respect since the death of Cyrus;[a] and they appointed the captains to act as jurymen. [35] And at Xenophon's recommendation, and on the advice of the seers, it was also resolved to purify the army, and a formal purification took place.[a]

[1] It was further resolved that the generals too should stand trial for their conduct during the time that had passed. The verdict on them was that Philesios and Xanthikles were declared to owe twenty minas for their negligent guarding of the cargo from the merchant ships, that being the value of the cargo that had been lost, while Sophainetos was fined ten minas for neglect of the office to which he had been elected.[a] Some laid accusations against Xenophon, asserting that he had hit them, and they set about prosecuting the case on the basis that he had acted through arrogant willfulness.[b] [2] So Xenophon told the first spokesman to say where the assault had taken place. [3] He answered, "Where we were perishing with cold and the snow was very deep."[a] Xenophon said, "Really? Well, indeed, as it was the depth of winter at the time you are speaking about, and food had run out and it was not possible to get even a sniff of wine, and many people were exhausted by their labors and the enemy were following us, if in a time such as that I acted with arrogant willfulness, I agree that I am more willful than a donkey, and they say weariness finds no place in donkeys because of their willfulness. Nevertheless," he said, "go on and say for what reason you were struck. [4] Was it that I was asking you for something and took to hitting you when you wouldn't give it to me? Or was I asking for something back? Or were we fighting about a boy? Or was I drunk and disorderly?"

5.7.34–35
July–August 400
KOTYORA
Trials of the guilty are instituted and the army is purified by ritual.

5.8.1–4
July–August 400
KOTYORA
Xenophon addresses accusations of willful violence made against him. The generals also stand trial.

5.7.34a   On Cyrus the Younger, see Appendix W: Brief Biographies, §10.

5.7.35a   The army needed to be purified of the bloodguilt of murder, and perhaps more generally of illicit violence. There are a variety of Greek purification ceremonies, but most likely here, the army was made to pass between the split halves of a sacrificial victim, probably a dog (definitely a dog in the case of the Macedonian army).

5.8.1a   Cargo from commandeered merchant ships was put into storage at 5.1.16. As regards the charge against Sophainetos (see Appendix W, §32), most editors suggest that a word or words have been lost hereabouts, which might have made it clearer what his office had been; but it is generally assumed that it was his superintendence of the voyage at 5.3.1. For the mina, a medium-

sized unit of currency, see Appendix O: Measurements, §§10–11.

5.8.1b   "Arrogant willfulness" is used throughout this passage to translate the Greek *hybris*. This word is often used today (as "hubris") to mean great arrogance, usually suggesting the pride that comes before a fall—a usage deriving from studies of Greek tragedy. But the ancient usage was not as restricted, as can be seen from its application to donkeys at 5.8.3. In Athens *hybris* was also a prosecutable offense, something like "aggravated assault," assault that was carried out to demean the victim. (Translator's note) For more, see *hybris* in the Glossary.

5.8.3a   For the march in the snow referred to here, see 4.5.

5.8.5–12
July–August 400
KOTYORA
Xenophon exposes the
truth of the incident
through cross-examination.

[5] When he said it was none of these things, Xenophon asked him if he was a hoplite. "No," he said. "Then are you a peltast?" "Not quite," he said. "I was assigned the role of mule driver by my messmates—though I'm a free man."

[6] From that Xenophon recognized him and asked: "Are you the one who carried off the sick fellow?"

"Yes indeed, by Zeus," he said, "since you were forcing me to do so; and you threw my messmates' baggage around."

[7] "Threw it around?" said Xenophon. "This is the sort of throwing around that happened: I distributed the baggage to other people to carry and ordered them to bring it back to me, and when I got it back, I handed every single item over to you safe and sound, after you on your side produced the man for me to see. But, all of you," he continued, "listen to what sort of affair this turned out to be—it's worth hearing. [8] A man was on the point of being left behind because he was no longer able to make his way onward. All that I knew about the man was that he was one of us, and I forced you to carry him to avoid his meeting a bitter end, for enemies were pursuing us, as I recall."

The fellow agreed this was so.

[9] "And then," said Xenophon, "after I had sent you on ahead, I came along with the rearguard and caught up with you again, digging a hole in which to bury your fellow human being, and I stopped and praised you. [10] But as we stood around, the man flexed his leg, and the bystanders shouted out that the man was alive, and you said, 'He can be as alive as he likes, I'm not carrying him.' It was then that I hit you—what you say is true—for you seemed to me to look as though you knew that he was alive."

[11] "So what?" he said. "He died all the same, after I produced him to you."

"Why, yes," said Xenophon, "we shall all of us die: but is that a reason why we should be buried alive?"

[12] They all shouted out that Xenophon had hit the fellow less than he deserved, and Xenophon then told the others to say for what reason each of them had been struck.

5.8.13–22
July–August 400
KOTYORA
Xenophon defends himself
for taking stern measures
against indiscipline and
slackness.

When none of them stood up to speak, Xenophon said, [13] "Men, I agree that I hit men for indiscipline, those who were quite content to be kept safe by you—who stayed in formation as you made your way onward and who fought whenever necessary—while they left the ranks and ran ahead in hopes of getting their hands on plunder and obtaining an advantage over you. If we had all behaved like that, every one of us would have been killed. [14] And again, when someone was being a weakling and didn't want to stand up, leaving himself to be the prey of the enemy, then I struck him and forced him to make his way onward. For in the severe cold, I too once remained sitting down for a long time, waiting for people to pack themselves up for the march, and I noticed how difficult it was to get up and stretch my legs. [15] So I took my own experience to heart, and as a result I would harass anyone else whom I saw sitting down idly and behaving sluggishly, since moving about and acting as a man should do would have a healthy warming effect, while I could see that sitting down and resting were conducive to making the blood congeal and the toes rot, problems from which many suffered, as you too know well. [16] Perhaps indeed there was some other person whom I struck, someone lagging behind through laziness and preventing you in the vanguard and us in the rearguard from making our way forward: I struck him with my fist so that he should not be struck by the enemy with a lance. [17] And so as a consequence, now that they are safe, anyone who has had any unfair treatment from me can get recompense for it. But if they had fallen into the hands of the enemy, however much they had suffered, what recompense do they think they would have received?

[18] "My case is a straightforward one," he said. "It is this: if I punished anyone for a good reason, I for my part think I should pay the same compensation for it as parents pay their sons and teachers their pupils, and one might add that doctors burn and cut their patients for a good reason. [19] But if you think I acted in this way from arrogant willfulness, bear in mind that now, thanks to the gods, I am full of confidence, much more than I was then, and I am bolder now than then, and I drink more wine, but nevertheless I don't hit anyone, [20] for I see that you are in fair weather. But when there is a storm and a great sea is getting up, don't you know that for a mere nod the boatswain gets angry with those in the bows and the helmsman gets angry with those in the stern? For in such circumstances even small mistakes are enough to bring the whole ship to ruin. [21] And that I was right to hit these people was also the verdict you gave against them at the time: you were there, and you had swords rather than voting pebbles:[a] you could have come to their defense if you wanted to—though it's certainly true that while you didn't come to their defense, you didn't join me in hitting the undisciplined. [22] In that way you gave the rogues among them the opportunity to behave with arrogant willfulness themselves as a result of your laxity.

"For I think you will find, if you want to look into the matter, that it's the same people who were the worst behaved then and are the most arrogant and willful now. [23] At any rate, Boiskos the Thessalian[a] boxer contended then that he was too ill to carry a shield, and now, as I hear, he has stripped bare many of the Kotyorites. [24] So if you are prudent, you will treat him the opposite of how people treat dogs: they chain dangerous dogs during

5.8.23–24
July–August 400
KOTYORA
Xenophon attacks the behavior of Boiskos.

---

5.8.21a  Voting pebbles: in Athenian courts each juryman had two *psēphoi*, literally "pebbles" but in fact discs, hollow discs being votes for the prosecution and solid discs votes for the defense. A pair of urns was set up, and the juryman dropped the disc he intended to count into one of them, designated for effective votes; he put the other disc into the second urn, designated for wasted votes.

5.8.23a  Thessaly: Map 5.3.7, AX.

FIGURE 5.8.20. THE MODERN TRIREME *OLYMPIAS* UNDER SAIL. IT WAS FIRST LAUNCHED IN 1987 AND SAILED AS A SHIP OF THE GREEK NAVY.

5.8.25–26
July–August 400
KOTYORA
Xenophon completes his defense and is acquitted.

the day but let them loose at night, but this fellow, if you are prudent, you will tie up at night but let loose by day.[a]

[25] "Still," he said, "I am surprised that, though you remember if I made myself hateful to any of you and you don't keep quiet about it, if on the other hand I helped people through the winter weather or warded off the enemy from them or if I had a share in assisting the weak or those in need, none of them remembers it; and if I praised someone for some fine action or if I gave someone all the honor I could for being a good man, you remember none of these things. [26] But surely it is fine and just and righteous and more agreeable to remember good deeds rather than bad ones."

After his speech people in fact started to stand up and recall such occasions, and the upshot was that things went well.

5.8.24a  Tying up Boiskos at night: Xenophon proposes this because mugging people for their clothes (especially their cloaks) was particularly common at night. It was a

widespread form of robbery in ancient Greece because cloaks were costly and fairly easy to remove, and was often punishable by death.

184

# BOOK SIX

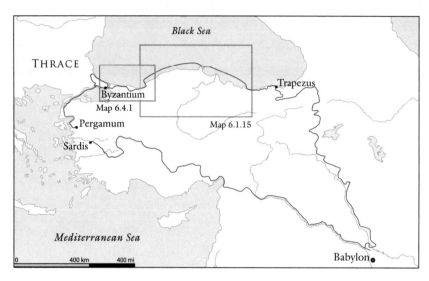

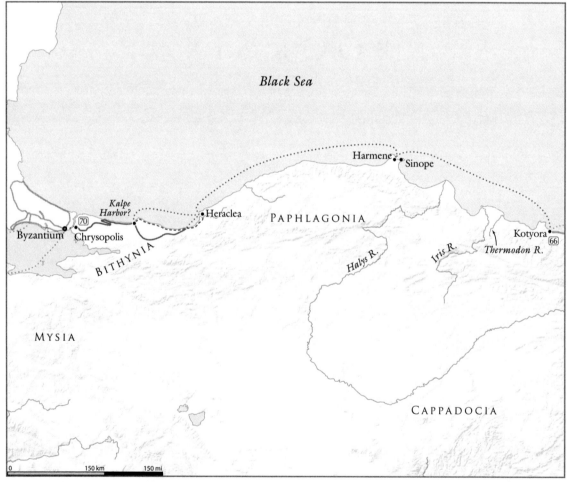

Book 6. *Parabasis:* from Kotyora to Chrysopolis, *Halting places 66–70.*

After this, as they whiled away their time, some of them kept alive by buying their supplies from the market, others by plundering Paphlagonian territory.[a] Gangs of Paphlagonians in their turn would steal the spoils back from the stragglers, and were very good at it; and during the night they would try to do harm to those quartered at a distance from the main body. For these reasons both sides maintained great hostility toward each other. [2] Korylas, the ruler of Paphlagonia at that time, sent ambassadors to the Greeks with horses and fine robes, who said that he was ready to agree not to do the Greeks wrong on the basis that he himself would not be wronged by them. [3] The generals answered that they would discuss the matter with the army, and they set about welcoming the ambassadors with a banquet, to which they also invited some of the men, those they thought most appropriate. [4] By sacrificing some of the cattle they had taken as booty, together with other sacrificial victims, they provided an adequate feast: they dined lying on beds of straw[a] and drank out of wine cups made of horn, which they came across in country areas.

[5] When libations had been offered and they had sung a war hymn, first to stand up were two Thracians,[a] who danced with their weapons to the sound of a pipe, lightly leaping high into the air and brandishing their sabers. Finally one of them struck the other so as to make it seem to everybody that a heavy blow had been landed on the man, [6] and the Paphlagonians actually cried out at it. But in fact the first had struck him in an artful way.[a] The first dancer stripped the second of his weapons and went out singing the Sitalkas song,[b] while some of the other Thracians carried out the second dancer as if he were dead, though he had not been hurt at all. [7] Next some Ainians and

NOTE:  Unless otherwise indicated, all dates are B.C.E., and all citations are to Xenophon's *Anabasis*. The determination of the army's route and stopping places are based on the editors' calculations and estimates from data taken from *Anabasis*. Nonetheless, the route line shown on our maps and the monthly dates given in our side notes are often subject to doubt. Our best estimates should not be taken as authoritative or certain. See the Editors' Preface, §§17–20.
6.1.1a  Paphlagonia: Book 6 map.

6.1.4a  Lying on beds of straw: Greeks ate formal meals reclining on couches; this is the best the men can do in the circumstances.
6.1.5a  Thrace: Book 6 map, locator.
6.1.6a  In the Greek text, this sentence appears at the end of 6.1.5; it has been moved in this translation. (Translator's note)
6.1.6b  Sitalkas song: Sitalkes was a very successful king of the Odrysian Thracians in the fifth century; this was presumably a victory song praising his exploits.

6.1.1–4
July–August 400
BLACK SEA COAST
*Kotyora (66)*
After initial hostilities, the Paphlagonians send ambassadors to the Greeks to make peace, and they are welcomed to a banquet.

6.1.5–8
August 400
KOTYORA
Thracians, Ainians, and Magnetes in the Greek army perform dances.

Magnetes stood up and began a dance in arms called the *karpaia*.[a] [8] The dance was performed like this: One dancer lays down his weapons and sets about sowing, driving a team of oxen, but as he does so he often turns around as if afraid while another dancer approaches in the guise of a brigand. When the first dancer catches sight of the second one, he snatches up his weapons and goes to confront him, doing battle with him for the team of oxen. And the dancers perform these moves keeping time to the pipe. The end of it is that the brigand ties up the other man and then leads away the team of oxen; or sometimes the plowman defeats the brigand and then yokes him with the oxen with his hands tied behind him and drives the team off.

[9] Next after this a Mysian[a] came in with a light shield in each hand, at one point dancing so as to mime two soldiers formed up against each other, at another using the shields as if against a single opponent, and at yet another whirling around and turning somersaults while still holding the shields, which made a fine spectacle. [10] Finally he danced the Persian dance, crouching down and jumping up while clashing the shields together.[a] And all this he did keeping time to the sound of the pipe. [11] Following on from this, the Mantineians and some of the other Arcadians[a] stood up in their full armor, as splendid as could be, and moved in time to a martial rhythm played on the pipe; they sang a war hymn and danced just as is done in religious processions.

When they saw all this, the Paphlagonians thought it an amazing thing that all the dances were performed in arms. [12] Then, seeing that they were astounded, the Mysian persuaded one of the Arcadians, who owned a dancing-girl, to let him bring her in. He had decked her out as splendidly as he could and given her a light shield, and she danced a Pyrrhic dance[a] nimbly. [13] At this there was much applause, and the Paphlagonians asked if the women also fought alongside them. The Greeks said that these were the women who had chased the Great King out of the camp.[a] This was the conclusion of the night's proceedings.

[14] On the next day, they brought the ambassadors before the army, and the soldiers adopted the proposal neither to do wrong to the Paphlagonians nor to be wronged by them. After that the ambassadors went on their way, while the Greeks, now that there seemed to be sufficient merchant ships available, went on board and sailed for a day and a night with a fair wind,

6.1.7a  *Karpaia:* this is the sole reference in ancient literature to this dance (except for later citations of this very passage). It is not clear what the name means or why it was assigned to this particular dance. Ainis, Magnesia: Map 5.3.7, BX, AX.
6.1.9a  Mysia: Book 6 map.
6.1.10a  Persian dance: during the festival of the Persian god Mithra, the Great King himself, and he alone, danced this strenuous dance; at other times its performance was widespread, partly (we are told) as an exercise in bodybuilding.
6.1.11a  Mantineia, Arcadia: Map 1.2.1, AY, AX.
6.1.12a  Pyrrhic dance (*Pyrrhiche*): another type of

war dance, illustrated in Figure 6.1.12. It involved crouching, leaping, and fast arm movements.
6.1.13a  We can take this as a joke. Xenophon's account of the King's movement to and away from the Greek camp at 1.10.1–11 does not give the women any role; nor indeed did the people in the camp chase the King away, though they did prevent him from plundering it freely. It was (allegedly) in fear of the main Greek army that he left the camp. For discussion of this passage, see Appendix K: The Noncombatant Contingent of the Army, §14.

FIGURE 6.1.12. THE PYRRHIC
DANCE (*PYRRHICHĒ*) AS
DEPICTED ON A DETAIL FROM
A DEDICATION BY THE SPON-
SOR ATARBOS, FOLLOWING
THE VICTORY OF HIS TEAM IN
VARIOUS DANCING CONTESTS,
323/2.

keeping Paphlagonia on their left.[a] [15] The following day they arrived at
Sinope and anchored at Harmene, Sinope's port.[a] The Sinopeans live in Paphlagonian territory and are Milesian colonists.[b] As tokens of their friendship
they sent the Greeks three thousand *medimnoi*[c] of barley and fifteen hundred jars of wine.

At this point Cheirisophos came with a single trireme.[d] [16] The soldiers
were full of expectation that he had come with something for them. But he
had brought nothing, though he reported that both Anaxibios the *nauarchos* and the others had praised them, and that Anaxibios had promised that
if they turned up outside the Black Sea, there would be pay for them.[a]

[17] The soldiers remained in this place, Harmene, for five days. As they
seemed to be getting near to Greece, the question of how they might arrive
home with something in hand now began to press on them even more than
it had previously.[a] [18] They therefore took the view that if they chose one

6.1.17–19
September 400
HARMENE
(PORT OF SINOPE)
The army decides it
wants a single leader, and
Xenophon is pressed to
take the post.

6.1.14a  Paphlagonia on their left: that is, they
sailed west.
6.1.15a  Sinope, Harmene: Map 6.1.15, *Halting
place 67*. Harmene (Armene in the *Barrington Atlas*) was about 6 miles/10 kilometers west of Sinope. The city's exposed
location, on the narrow neck of a peninsula jutting into the Black Sea, may
explain why the port was sited so far away.
6.1.15b  Miletus: Map 5.3.7, BY.
6.1.15c  *Medimnoi*: the *medimnos* was a unit of
volume or capacity, equal to about 1.5 US
bushels/51.5 liters; see Appendix O:
Ancient Greek and Persian Units of Measurement, §20.
6.1.15d  Trireme: long warship with three banks of
oars; for more, see the Glossary; see also

Figure 5.8.20. On Cheirisophos, see
Appendix W: Brief Biographies of Selected
Characters in *Anabasis*, §7.
6.1.16a  *Nauarchos*: chief admiral of the Spartan
fleet for the year; for more, see Appendix
B: Xenophon and Sparta, §14. For Anaxibios' later career, see Appendix W, §3.
6.1.17a  Although the army had passed through
the territories of several Greek colonies on
the coast of the Black Sea, Greece proper
was evidently not reckoned to begin until
Byzantium (Map 6.1.15, locator); see
6.6.12, 7.1.29. In Appendix C: The Persian Empire, §16, Christopher Tuplin
counsels against drawing the conclusion
that the Black Sea colonies were thought
to be subject to Persia.

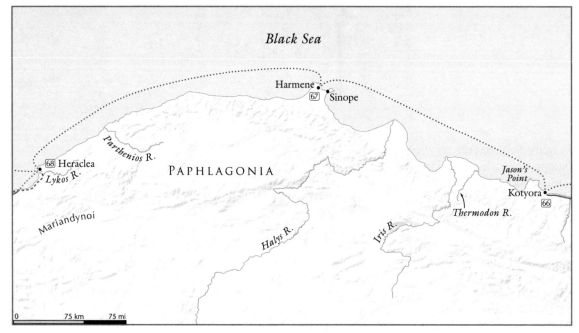

MAP 6.1.15. *PARABASIS:* FROM KOTYORA TO HERACLEA, *HALTING PLACES 66–68.*

commander, that individual would be better able than their existing joint command to put the army to use during both night and day: if it was necessary to conceal some aspect of its operations, he would be more likely to keep the matter secret, and if it was necessary to be preemptive, he would be less likely to act too late. For there would be no need to have discussions with each other, as what the one person decided would be put into effect—up until this, the generals used to do everything according to the opinion that prevailed after debate. [19] As they considered all this, they turned to Xenophon, and the captains started to go to him and say that this was the considered opinion of the army, each one showing his goodwill and seeking to persuade him to undertake the command.

FIGURE 6.1.23. ZEUS WITH AN EAGLE DEPICTED ON A LACONIAN CUP, C. 550. THE EAGLE WAS CONSIDERED THE BIRD OF ZEUS THE KING, WHOSE MESSAGE WAS TO BE DIVINED FROM ITS DIRECTION OF FLIGHT OR POSE.

[20] As for Xenophon, he was in a quandary. On the one hand, he wanted the post, thinking that he would thus gain greater honor in the eyes of his friends and that his name would reach his own city enhanced; and perhaps he might also become the cause of some benefit to the army. [21] Thoughts of this type strengthened him in his desire to become commander in chief. But on the other hand, whenever he reflected that for every human being it is unclear what the future will bring, and that for this reason there would be a danger of throwing away even the reputation he had already achieved, he was unclear which way to go. [22] And being at a loss, it seemed to him that it was best to consult the gods. He produced two sacrificial victims and set about sacrificing to Zeus the King, exactly as had been prescribed to him by the Delphic oracle.[a] (And indeed he considered that the dream he had seen when he began to establish himself in the joint management of the army was from this god.)[b] [23] Furthermore, he recalled that when he was setting out from Ephesus to join Cyrus, an eagle called out to him from the right while, however, it was sitting;[a] at this, the seer who was escorting him had said that it was a great omen, signifying some-

6.1.20–24
September 400
HARMENE
(PORT OF SINOPE)
Following adverse omens, Xenophon decides not to put himself forward.

6.1.22a  At 3.1.6 we were told that the oracle at Delphi had advised Xenophon to sacrifice to the gods, but we were not told which ones or in what circumstances he was to choose one rather than another. Evidently one of these gods was Zeus the King. In Appendix G: Divinity and Divining, §12, Michael Flower explains that Xenophon here sacrifices two victims because he had two questions to ask, as becomes clear at 6.1.24. Delphi:

Map 5.3.7, BX.
6.1.22b  For this dream, see 3.1.11.
6.1.23a  The Greeks took the appearance of birds as a sign from the gods (the right was the good side for bird omens), and seers could make elaborate inferences about them, as here. See Figure 6.1.23. On Cyrus the Younger, see Appendix W: Brief Biographies, §10. Ephesus: Map 5.3.7, BY.

thing not merely private, and of high repute; but also full of toil and suffering, as the other birds are prone to attack the sitting eagle. However, he had added that the omen did not portend wealth, for the eagle gets its food supplies only when in flight. [24] Accordingly, Xenophon set about offering sacrifices of this type, but the god gave him clear signs neither to seek the command nor to accept it if he was chosen. This, then, was the upshot.

[25] The army assembled, and everyone said one leader should be chosen; and when this had been decided, they proceeded to put Xenophon's name forward. Since it seemed clear that they were going to choose him if anyone put it to the vote, he stood up and spoke as follows:

[26] "Men, I for my part am pleased, as any human being in my position would be, to be honored by you, and I give thanks for it and I pray the gods grant to me to become a source of some good to you. However, it seems that for you to select me as commander when there is a man available who is a Lacedaemonian[a] is not going to be to your advantage, nor to mine. On the contrary, the result would be a lower chance of success if you needed something from them—while I believe that, in addition, it would not be at all safe for me. [27] For I observe that the Lacedaemonians did not cease waging war against my native land until they had made the whole city agree that they were to be their leaders too.[a] [28] When they did agree to this, the Lacedaemonians immediately stopped waging war and besieged the city no longer. So if, though aware of these facts, I were to seem by my conduct here to be reducing their reputation to impotence wherever I could do so, I think I would very quickly be brought to my senses. [29] As for your own view that there would be less dissension with one leader than with many, be assured that if you choose someone else, you will not find me leading a rival party, for I think that anyone who in wartime sets up in opposition to his commander is by the same token setting up in opposition to his own safety; but if you were to choose me, I would not be surprised if you were to find someone seriously upset with both you and me."

[30] After he had said this, even more people than before stood up and said that he should be the commander. Agasias of Stymphalos[a] said that it would be ridiculous if things were as Xenophon had indicated. Or would the Lacedaemonians also be angry if when people got together to have a party, they didn't choose a Lacedaemonian to be the master of ceremonies? "If things are really like this," he said, "it seems it is not possible for us to be

**6.1.25–29**
**September 400**
HARMENE
(PORT OF SINOPE)
Xenophon rejects the offer of the chief command.

**6.1.30–31**
**September 400**
HARMENE
(PORT OF SINOPE)
Pressed further to accept, Xenophon reveals the adverse omens.

6.1.26a　Lacedaemon is a state and territorial designation. Sparta was the most important city within it; for more on the distinction, see Appendix B: Xenophon and Sparta, §§18–19. Lacedaemon: Map 1.2.1, BX.
6.1.27a　"Made the whole city agree": a term of the peace treaty between Sparta and Xenophon's "native land," Athens, at the conclusion of the Peloponnesian

War in 404 (Xenophon, *Hellenika* 2.2.20). It is partly because Sparta had so recently been the decisive victor in this war that Xenophon says a Lacedaemonian was a more suitable commander than an Athenian for an army from all over Greece. Athens: Map 1.2.1, BY, AY.
6.1.30a　Stymphalos: Map 1.2.1, AY.

captains, because we are Arcadians."[b] At that, naturally enough, there was uproar, and loud shouts that Agasias spoke well.

[31] Since Xenophon saw that more was needed from him, he came forward and said, "But, so that you should know the exact situation, I swear to you, men, by all the gods and goddesses, that the real truth is that when I became aware of your inclination, I proceeded to offer some sacrifices to find out whether it would be better for you to entrust the command to me, and better for me to undertake it. And the gods indicated so clearly in the sacred signs that even a layman could tell that I have to keep away from this offer of one-man rule."[a]

[32] So as a result, they chose Cheirisophos. After he had been chosen, Cheirisophos came forward and said, "In fact, men, I assure you that I would not have stirred up dissension if you had chosen someone else. But on the other hand, you have done Xenophon a service," he said, "by not choosing him, since Dexippos[a] has already for some time been maligning him to Anaxibios as much as he can, even though I strenuously tried to silence him. Dexippos said that he was of the view that Xenophon wished to share the command of Klearchos' army with Timasion, though he is a Dardanian, rather than with himself, a Laconian.[b] [33] But since you have chosen me," he said, "I too will try to do you what good I can. So get yourselves ready to put to sea tomorrow, provided there is a fair wind. Our voyage will be to Heraclea, so everyone without exception should try to land there;[a] and once we have arrived there, we will discuss further plans."

[1] On the next day, they sailed from there for two days along the coast, carried on a following wind. [As they sailed along, they viewed Jason's Point, where the *Argo* is said to have anchored,[a] and the mouths of various rivers, first the Thermodon, then the Iris, then the Halys, and after the Halys, the Parthenios.][b] After their coastal voyage, they reached Heraclea, a

6.1.32–33
September 400
HARMENE
(PORT OF SINOPE)
The army chooses Cheirisophos, who accepts graciously.

6.2.1–3
September 400
BLACK SEA COAST
*Heraclea (68)*
The army sails to Heraclea.

6.1.30b  Arcadia: Map 1.2.1, AX.
6.1.31a  The sacrifice, rather than reasoned argument about politics, is the decisive consideration for the troops. See Appendix G: Divinity and Divining, §12.
6.1.32a  Dexippos previously appeared at 5.1.15; for his career prior to joining Cyrus' expedition and for suggestions that Xenophon's portrait of him may not be fair, see Appendix W: Brief Biographies, §13.
6.1.32b  On Klearchos, see Appendix W, §20. Timasion had been joint leader of the rearguard with Xenophon. He subsequently intrigued against Xenophon (5.6.19), but perhaps Dexippos did not know this, as he had left the army by then. Laconia is a strictly geographic term referring to the territories the Spartans held in the southeast quarter of the Peloponnese, as distinct from Messenia, the territory in the southwest that they subsequently conquered (for all locations, see Map 1.2.1, BX–BY). Dardanos: Map 5.3.7, AY.

6.1.33a  "Everyone without exception": this oddly emphatic phrase perhaps suggests that Cheirisophos suspected that some members of the army would want to sail farther toward the Bosphorus, stealing the Heracleans' ships. Heraclea: Map 6.1.15, *Halting place 68*. Bosphorus: Map 6.4.1, inset.
6.2.1a  Jason was a mythological hero who sailed to the east coast of the Black Sea and back in the ship *Argo*, leading the Argonauts in the quest for the Golden Fleece (see also n. 5.6.37a).
6.2.1b  This is a topographically impossible passage. The places mentioned, other than the Parthenios, lie between Kotyora and Sinope, not between Sinope and Heraclea. Scholars disagree as to whether memory has played a trick on Xenophon or the passage has been inserted by a later scribe— the view hesitantly taken in this edition. Jason's Point (Iasonion Pr. in the *Barrington Atlas*), Thermodon River, Iris River, Halys River, Parthenios River: Map 6.1.15.

FIGURE 6.2.2. HERAKLES LEADS THE DOG OF THE UNDERWORLD, CERBERUS, OUT OF HADES AS THE LATTER RESISTS. DETAIL OF A RED-FIGURE KRATER, C. 330–310.

Greek city, a colony of the Megarians, situated in the land of the Mariandynoi.[c] [2] They anchored by the Acherousian Chersonese,[a] where it is said Herakles descended to the Underworld to fetch the dog Cerberus,[b] and where they now show people the marks of the descent, to a depth of more than four hundred yards.[c] [3] Here the people of Heraclea sent the Greeks tokens of their friendship, consisting of three thousand *medimnoi*[a] of barley, two thousand jars of wine, twenty oxen, and a hundred sheep. A river called the Lykos flows through the plain here and is around two hundred feet in width.[b]

6.2.1c　Megara: Map 1.2.1, AY. Mariandynoi territory: Map 6.1.15.

6.2.2a　Acherousian Chersonese: Map 6.4.1. The Acheron River takes its name from one of the mythological rivers in the Underworld.

6.2.2b　The last of the mythological hero Herakles' famous "twelve labors" was to descend to the underworld to bring up the hellhound Cerberus. The inhabitants of Heraclea evidently claimed that Herakles' portal to the Underworld was in their territory, but it was more usual to place the portal in the southern Peloponnese, at Cape Tainaron (Map 1.2.1, BX). See Figure 6.2.2.

6.2.2c　More than four hundred yards/366 meters: the Greek text says more than 2 stades; see Appendix O: Measurements, §5. There is a ravine cut by the Acheron River about three hundred yards deep, which is reported to be pierced by three holes to the depth of about a further hundred yards.

6.2.3a　*Medimnoi*: the *medimnos* was a unit of volume or capacity, equal to about 1.5 US bushels/51.5 liters: see Appendix O, §20.

6.2.3b　Two hundred feet/61 meters: the Greek text says 2 *plethra*; see Appendix O, §§2–3. Lykos River: Map 6.1.15.

[4] The soldiers assembled and started to debate about the rest of the journey and whether they should make their way out of the Black Sea by land or by sea. Lykon of Achaea[a] stood up and said, "I am amazed, men, at the generals and their lack of effort to procure ration money for us. The friendship tokens do not amount to three days' worth of food for the army, and there is no place from which we can supply ourselves before we go on our way. So I think," he said, "we should ask the Heracleans for no less than three thousand Cyzicene staters."[b] [5] Another speaker said it should be no less than ten thousand staters, and they should choose ambassadors that very instant while the assembly was still meeting, send them to the city, learn whatever they had to report back, and deliberate accordingly. [6] At that they proceeded to put forward different people as ambassadors, in first place Cheirisophos, because he had been chosen as commander; and some put forward Xenophon. But both of them strongly resisted, for they were of the same opinion: that they should not compel a friendly Greek city to give what they did not wish to give. [7] Since these candidates seemed unenthusiastic, the soldiers sent Lykon of Achaea, Kallimachos of Parrasia, and Agasias of Stymphalos.[a] These three went and explained what had been resolved; and people said that Lykon also added threats if they did not do as asked. [8] Having heard them out, the Heracleans said they would discuss the matter; and they immediately gathered together their property from the fields and packed up the market and moved it inside the city; and the gates were shut, and people in arms began to appear on the walls.

[9] As a result, those who had stirred up all this blamed the generals for the ruin of their plans, and the Arcadians and Achaeans began to form a breakaway group, their ringleaders being Kallimachos the Parrasian and Lykon the Achaean. [10] Their arguments were that it was disgraceful that Peloponnesians and Lacedaemonians should be under the command of an Athenian[a] who was making no contribution to the army's forces, and that they had the hard work while others had the profits, even though it was they who had achieved the army's deliverance. For, they said, it was Arcadians and Achaeans who got things done, while the rest of the army amounted to nothing (and indeed, as a matter of fact, the Arcadians and Achaeans totaled more than half of the army). [11] So if they were prudent, they would band together and choose generals of their own and then make the journey by themselves and try to get hold of something good on the way. [12] That was the decision, and having deserted Cheirisophos—to the extent that there were any Arcadians and Achaeans with him—and also Xenophon, they did band together, and they chose ten generals of their own, who they voted

6.2.4–8
September 400
HERACLEA
The army demands money from the Heracleans, despite opposition from Cheirisophos and Xenophon.

6.2.9–12
September 400
HERACLEA
The Arcadians and Achaeans break away from the rest of the army.

6.2.4a   Achaea: Map 1.2.1, AX.
6.2.4b   At 5.6.23 the troops were offered 1 Cyzicene stater each a month on the basis of promises by the Heracleans, so 3,000 Cyzicenes would amount to about a fortnight's pay for the army; on the Cyzicene stater, see Appendix O: Measurements,

§§12, 15, and Figure 5.6.23.
6.2.7a   Parrasia, Stymphalos: Map 1.2.1, BX, AY.
6.2.10a  Xenophon is accused of having made no contribution to the army's forces because he brought no troops of his own with him when he came to Sardis. Peloponnese: Map 1.2.1, BX.

should act upon whatever the majority of them decided. So Cheirisophos' overall command was dissolved then and there on the sixth or seventh day from when he was elected.

6.2.13–19
September 400
BLACK SEA COAST
*Heraclea–*
*Kalpe Harbor (69)*
The army, totaling 8,540 men, splits into three groups and journeys on separately.

[13] Xenophon, however, wanted to make the journey in company with Cheirisophos, thinking that this would be safer than for each to set out on his own. But Neon[a] was arguing the case for making their way in separate contingents. He had heard from Cheirisophos that Kleandros, the harmost in Byzantium, was saying that he would come to Kalpe Harbor with triremes.[b] [14] So this was the reason for his advice, in order that only he and Cheirisophos and their soldiers should sail away on the triremes and no one else should participate.[a] Cheirisophos, partly through depression at what had happened and partly because of his consequent hatred for the army, allowed Neon to do whatever he wanted. [15] For a time Xenophon made an attempt to sail away and leave the army behind, but when he offered a sacrifice to Herakles the Leader, consulting him on whether it would be better and more fitting to soldier on with the troops who had remained or to leave them, the god indicated through the sacred signs that he should soldier on with them. [16] And thus the army came to be in three parts: one of Arcadians and Achaeans, more than 4,500 of them, all hoplites; another with Cheirisophos, 1,400 hoplites and 600 peltasts (Klearchos' Thracians); and a third with Xenophon, 1,700 hoplites and 300 peltasts.[a] But only Xenophon had cavalry, about 40 horsemen.

[17] The Arcadians, who managed to extract merchant ships from the Heracleans, were first to sail, with the idea of making a sudden attack on the Bithynians[a] and seizing as much as possible. They disembarked at Kalpe Harbor more or less in the middle of Bithynian Thrace. [18] Cheirisophos, on the other hand, started out from the city of Heraclea and from the outset made his way by land through the countryside; but once he had advanced into Thrace,[a] he went along the coast, as on top of everything else, he was ill. [19] Third, Xenophon obtained merchant ships, disembarked on the boundary between Thrace and the land of the Heracleans, and made his way through the interior.

6.2.13a  Neon was Cheirisophos' deputy.
6.2.13b  For the probable role of Kleandros in 406 and its implications, see Appendix W: Brief Biographies, §18. Harmost: a technical term (literally, "fixer") for a Spartan official resident abroad; see Appendix B: Xenophon and Sparta, §15. Byzantium: Map 6.4.1 and locator. Kalpe Harbor, possible location: Map 6.4.1, *Halting place 69*.
6.2.14a  Triremes were not designed to carry passengers, so the number of soldiers they could take was limited.
6.2.16a  Scholars dispute the figure of 4,500 Arcadian and Achaean hoplites. Cheirisophos' 600 peltasts were not in origin all Klearchos' Thracians, though those presumably constituted the core of them. For

explanation of the figures chosen in this edition, see Appendix I: The Size and Makeup of the Ten Thousand, §§9–11. On hoplites (heavy-armed infantry) and peltasts (light-armed infantry), see Appendix H: Infantry and Cavalry in *Anabasis*, §§2–5. Arcadia, Achaea: Map 1.2.1, AX. Thrace: Book 6 map, locator.
6.2.17a  The Bithynians were Thracian peoples who spread from Europe in northwestern Anatolia; hence this area is referred to as "Bithynian Thrace" in the next sentence and "Asian Thrace" at 6.4.1. They were relations of the Thynoi, who feature in Book 7. Bithynia/Bithynians: Map 6.4.1. Western Anatolia: Ref. Map 4, BY. Thynoi: Book 7 map.
6.2.18a  Thrace: meaning Bithynian Thrace.

[1] [So, then, in the preceding narrative, the author has explained in what way Cheirisophos' overall command came to an end and the Greek army split up.]ᵃ [2] Each of these groups did as follows: The Arcadians, after disembarking by night at Kalpe Harbor, made their way into the territory of the closest villages, about three milesᵃ from the sea. When it turned light, each general led his own company against a different village, though where the village seemed to be rather large, the generals led two companies put together. [3] They also agreed on a hill where they should all gather afterward. As their attack was a sudden one, they seized many slaves and were managing to corral many cattle and sheep. But those Thracians who had made their escape began to gather again; [4] and Thracians continued to escape out of the hands of the Greeks in large numbers, as they were peltasts outrunning hoplites. When they had assembled, they attacked first the company commanded by Smikres, one of the Arcadian generals, which was already going away to the agreed rendezvous, carrying off a lot of stuff. [5] And although the Greeks fought back for a time while making their way onward, the Thracians put them to flight as they crossed a gully, and killed Smikres himself and all the others in the company to the last man; and from another company belonging to one of the ten Arcadian generals, Hegesandros, they left alive only eight soldiers, including Hegesandros himself.

[6] The other companies got together, some with difficulty and some without, while the Thracians, once their good fortune had led them to this success, kept on shouting out to each other and continued to gather energetically through the night. Daybreak found them drawn up in a circle around the hill where the Greeks were encamped, with horsemen in large numbers and also peltasts, and all the time more were streaming in. They could safely mount attacks on the hoplites, [7] as the Greeks had not a single archer or javelin thrower or horseman. The Thracians, then, kept running or riding up and throwing their javelins, and whenever the Greeks counterattacked, they easily slipped away while others kept up the attack in another place. [8] Many of the Greeks were wounded but none of the enemy, so the Greeks could not move from the place; on the contrary, in the end the Thracians were barring them even from reaching their water supply. [9] Since they were in great straits, they opened negotiations about a truce, and while they came to agreement in other respects, the Thracians refused to give hostages as demanded by the Greeks, and on this point there was an impasse. That, then, was how matters stood with the Arcadians.

6.3.1–5
September 400
BITHYNIAN THRACE
Disaster overtakes the Arcadians at the hands of the Bithynian Thracians near Kalpe Harbor.

6.3.6–9
September 400
BITHYNIAN THRACE
The Arcadians are trapped on a hill without water by the Bithynian Thracians.

6.3.1a   Almost all scholars agree that the bracketed sentence, missing in about a third of the manuscripts, is an insertion by a later scribe. Although this is not the beginning of a new book, as are other such passages noted elsewhere, it is quite possible that

the divisions were different in antiquity (as is the case with Xenophon's *Hellenika*).

6.3.2a   About 3 miles/5 kilometers: the Greek text says 30 stades; see Appendix O: Measurements, §5.

6.3.10–11
September 400
BITHYNIAN THRACE
*Kalpe Harbor (69)*
Cheirisophos reaches
Kalpe Harbor. Xenophon
proceeds inland and learns
of the Arcadians' plight.

6.3.12–14
September 400
BITHYNIAN THRACE
Xenophon rallies his men
to go to the Arcadians'
rescue.

6.3.16–18
September 400
BITHYNIAN THRACE
Xenophon emphasizes
the dangers of leaving
the Arcadians to perish.

[10] Cheirisophos, making his way safely along the coast, arrived at Kalpe Harbor.

As for Xenophon, making his way through the interior, his cavalry, galloping on ahead, came upon some old men on their way somewhere or other. When they were brought to Xenophon, he asked them if they were aware of another army of Greeks. [11] They recounted all that had happened and said the other Greeks were now being besieged on a hill, with all the Thracians encircling them. Hearing this, he put the fellows under a strict guard so that they could act as guides to wherever there might be a need to go. Then he posted lookouts, assembled the soldiers, and said: [12] "Soldiers, some of the Arcadians have died, and the rest are under siege on a hilltop. It is my personal opinion that if they are wiped out, there is no safety for us either, since the enemy are so many and are now in such good heart. [13] So the best thing for us is to go as quickly as possible to help the men, so that if they are still alive, we can have them alongside us in the fight and not be left by ourselves, alone in our danger. [14] Yes, let us by all means make camp presently—provided we continue to advance right up to the time that seems best for our evening meal. And while we are making our way onward, Timasion is to ride ahead with the cavalry, though still keeping us in his sight, and is to scout out what lies in front of us so that nothing escapes our notice.ᵃ [16] <There is no real alternative to advancing against the enemy,>ᵃ for there is nowhere we could manage to run away to from here. It is a long way to go back again to Heraclea," he said, "and a long way to get through to Chrysopolis,ᵇ and the enemy are close by. The shortest route is to Kalpe Harbor, where we suppose that Cheirisophos is, if he has survived. But of course in that place there are no merchant ships in which we can sail away, and if we stay there, our supplies are insufficient even for one day. [17] It will be a bad business if the Arcadians under siege are wiped out and we go through the danger alongside just Cheirisophos' troops; better, then, if the Arcadians are saved and we all go to the same place together and achieve safety by our collective efforts. Come on, then, we must be on our way, having made up our minds either to die gloriously or to accomplish a most noble deed by saving so many Greeks. [18] Perhaps it is the god who is bringing this about, in his wish to humble those who boasted of their superior wisdom, and to give us the position of greater honor, since we make the gods our starting point.ᵃ However that may be, you must keep up and pay attention to carrying out your instructions."

6.3.14a  Section 15 has been transposed to follow section 15 and is renumbered as 18A for this edition. Since the nineteenth century, editors generally have agreed that the text in the manuscripts is in the wrong order here, though the preferred sequence varies by editor.

6.3.16a  Many editors move section 16 as well as section 15, but this produces an anticlimactic effect. My diagnosis is that a sentence has dropped out at the beginning of section 16. The words in angle brackets are my suggestion

about how the passage might have gone originally. (Translator's note)

6.3.16b  Heraclea (*Halting place 68*): Map 6.4.1; Chrysopolis (*Halting place 70*): Map 6.4.1 and inset.

6.3.18a  This could be a reference to disputes about whether it was right to extort money from friendly cities and tribes. Examples of this occur at 5.5.2–3, where the negative results of the sacrifices settled the matter, and at 6.2.6, where perhaps a revival of that argument met with scorn from the Arcadians.

[18A][a] Having delivered this speech, he began to lead them forward. He also sent people from the light-armed troops who were especially mobile out to the flanks of the army and onto the heights around in order to signal if they observed anything anywhere from anyplace, and he issued orders to burn absolutely everything combustible that they came across. [19] The cavalry, dispersing to the extent needed to do the job properly, set about the work of burning; the peltasts in their parallel progress along the heights were also burning everything combustible they saw; and the main force did so too, if they came across anything left over. The result was that it seemed the whole countryside was ablaze and that the army was particularly numerous. [20] When the time came, they broke off and encamped on a hill; they could see the enemy's fires about four and a half miles[a] away from them, and they themselves lit as many fires as they could. [21] Once they had very hastily taken their evening meal, the instruction was given to put out all the fires. They slept through the night, having posted sentries, and at daybreak they offered prayers to the gods; once they had arranged themselves in battle formation, they made their way onward as fast as they could go. [22] Timasion and the cavalry,[a] together with the guides, rode on ahead and, before they realized it, found themselves on the hilltop where the Greeks had been under siege. And neither the friendly army nor the hostile one were to be seen, only some old women and old men, a few sheep, and some cattle that had been left behind. They reported this to Xenophon and the main force.

[23] At first there was astonishment at whatever it was that had happened, but then they learned from those who had been left behind that the Thracians had gone away immediately after nightfall, and at dawn the Greeks too had gone, they said, but where to they did not know. [24] When Xenophon's troops heard this, and had eaten their meal, they packed up and made their way onward, wanting to join up with the others as quickly as possible at Kalpe Harbor. As they made their way there, they kept seeing the tracks left by the Arcadians and Achaeans on the way to Kalpe. When they caught up with them, the two groups were pleased to see each other and fell to greeting each other like brothers. [25] The Arcadians asked Xenophon's troops why they had extinguished their fires. "For," they said, "when we could no longer see the fires, we at first thought that you would attack the enemy during the night; and it was also for fear of this that the enemy went away, or so it seemed to us, for they left at roughly the same time. [26] But when you did not arrive and the time had run on, we began to think that you had learned of what had happened to us, had become afraid, and were making a run for it to the sea; and we decided not to be left behind by you. So for this reason we too made our way here."

**6.3.18A–21**
September 400
BITHYNIAN THRACE
Xenophon's men burn everything as they advance.

**6.3.22–23**
September 400
BITHYNIAN THRACE
Timasion's cavalry rides on ahead of the army only to find no trace of the Arcadians at the hill where the siege took place.

**6.3.24–26**
September 400
BITHYNIAN THRACE–
KALPE HARBOR
*Kalpe Harbor (69)*
Xenophon's men are reunited with the Arcadians.

---

6.3.18Aa  For the numeration of this section (6.3.15 in most editions), see nn. 6.3.14a, 6.3.16a.

6.3.20a  About four and a half miles/7 kilometers: the Greek text says 40 stades; see Appendix O: Measurements, §5.

6.3.22a  Previously Lykios son of Polystratos was the commander of the cavalry (appointed at 3.3.20). It is not clear whether he has died or whether Timasion displaced him for some reason.

[1] For that day they bivouacked there on the beach by the harbor. This place, which is called Kalpe Harbor, is in Asian Thrace, an area extending from the mouth of the Black Sea as far as Heraclea, on the right as one sails into the Black Sea.[a] [2] The voyage from Byzantium to Heraclea takes a trireme a very long day if only oars are used, and between the two there is no other city, either Greek or friendly to Greeks, only Bithynian Thracians,[a] who are said to maltreat Greeks terribly if they get hold of any of them, through shipwreck or otherwise. [3] Kalpe Harbor lies in the middle of the voyage between Heraclea and Byzantium, from whichever way one comes, and is a promontory in the sea, forming a stronghold. It consists partly of a sheer cliff extending out to sea, at its lowest no less than 120 feet in height, partly of a neck that reaches up from the stronghold to the mainland, about 400 feet[a] across; inside the neck there is a natural stronghold large enough to house ten thousand people. [4] There is a harbor under the cliff, with a beach facing west, and there is also a spring of fresh water that flows abundantly, right by the sea and commanded by the stronghold. There is a large amount of timber of various kinds, and especially a great deal of fine ship-building timber right by the sea. [5] The hilly country extends into the interior for about two and a quarter miles and is rich in soil and not stony, and the area along the coast for two and a half miles or so[a] is thickly wooded, with many huge trees of different kinds. [6] The rest of the countryside is beautiful and extensive, and there are many well-inhabited villages in it, for the earth here yields barley and wheat and all kinds of pulses, foxtail millet,[a] sesame, a sufficiency of figs, many vines producing agreeable wine, and everything else except olive trees. [7] That was what the country there was like.

The Greeks settled into their quarters on the beach by the sea, not wishing to camp in a place that might be turned into a settlement; indeed, they thought that even their coming there was part of a plot, the result of certain people's wish to found a city. [8] Most of the soldiers were not the kind of people who, in need of a livelihood, have sailed overseas for the pay, but they had done so on hearing of the personal merits of Cyrus;[a] some actually brought other men with them, and others had even spent their own money. Beyond these, there were yet others who had run away from their fathers and mothers; and some, hearing that people in Cyrus' following were doing very well, had left children behind, intending to come back when they had

6.4.1a   The description of Kalpe Harbor, although detailed, does not correspond to any current location along this stretch of the coast. This may be because of changes in the coastline, or it could be that the author adapted the natural features to give the impression of an ideal site for settlement though in fact no one in antiquity took up this idea; see Appendix P: The Route of the Ten Thousand, §17. Xenophon uses the terms Bithynian Thrace and Asian Thrace interchangeably.

6.4.2a   Normally, except in battles, both oars and sails would be used for sailing any distance,

but naturally there had to be sufficient wind to use the sails. Byzantium: Map 6.4.1 and inset. Bithynia/Bithynians: Map 6.4.1.

6.4.3a   One hundred twenty feet/37 meters, 400 feet/122 meters: the Greek text says 20 *orguiai* and 4 *plethra*, respectively; see Appendix O: Measurements, §§2–3.

6.4.5a   Two and a quarter miles/3.5 kilometers, 2.5 miles/4 kilometers: the Greek text says 20 stades and more than 20 stades, respectively; see Appendix O, §§2–3.

6.4.6a   On the varieties of millet, see the Glossary.

6.4.8a   On Cyrus the Younger, see Appendix W: Brief Biographies, §10.

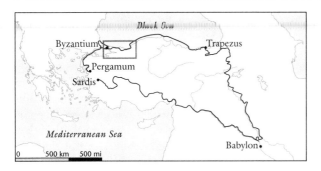

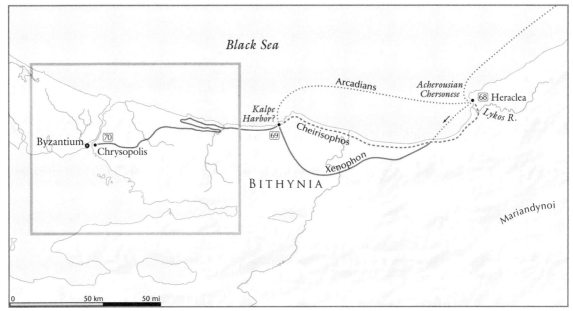

MAP 6.4.1. *PARABASIS:* FROM HERACLEA
TO CHRYSOPOLIS, *HALTING PLACES 68–70.*

acquired money to spend on them. These being the kinds of people they were, they longed to get safely back to Greece.

[9] The day after their reunion at Kalpe, Xenophon set about offering a sacrifice to inquire about the prospects of making an expedition, for it was a necessity to go out looking for food supplies, and he also had it in mind to bury the dead. Since appropriate sacred signs were forthcoming, the Arcadians too followed, and they buried most of the dead bodies one by one where they had fallen, for it was now the fifth day after the battle that they had lain there, and it was no longer possible to take them up. But they did gather together some of them from along the roadways and bury them as honorably as they could under the circumstances, and for those they could not find, they made a great cenotaph and placed wreaths on it.[a] [10] When they had done all this, they went back to the camp, and after they had eaten their evening meal, they went to sleep.

On the next day, all the soldiers assembled. It was especially Agasias, the Stymphalian captain, who took the lead, together with another of the captains, Hieronymos of Elis, and others who were the oldest of the Arcadians.[a] [11] They passed a decree that if in the future anyone made mention of dividing the army in two, he should be punished with death; that they should return to the way the army had been organized previously; and that the previous generals should be in charge. By this time Cheirisophos had died as a result of medicine that he drank while in a fever, and Neon of Asine[a] took over his contingent.

[12] After this Xenophon stood up and said, "Brave soldiers, the way things look, we shall have to make our onward journey on foot. There are no ships, and there is a pressing need to be on our way, as there are no food supplies for us if we remain. So we will offer sacrifice," he said, "and you must prepare yourselves for the fight of your lives, as the enemy's confidence is now high."

[13] The generals thereupon set about offering sacrifice, with Arexion of Arcadia present as seer (Silanos the Ambraciot[a] had some time before hired a merchant ship from Heraclea and deserted). But when they offered the sacrifice to inquire about their departure, appropriate sacred signs were not forthcoming, so they broke off for that day.[b] [14] There were some who dared to say that Xenophon, wishing to found a settlement in the stronghold, had persuaded the seer to say that the sacred signs had not been forthcoming in favor of departure. [15] Hence he had a public announcement made that whoever wanted could be present for the sacrifice on the following day, and passed the word that if anyone were a seer, he should attend in order to join in witnessing the sacred signs. He set about performing the sacrifice, and there were many people present there, [16] but the sacred signs were not forthcoming in favor of departure, even though he offered sacrifice for a second and third time. The soldiers took this badly, especially

6.4.9
September 400
KALPE HARBOR
The army buries the dead Arcadians to the extent possible.

6.4.10–11
September 400
KALPE HARBOR
The army formally reunites. Since Cheirisophos has died, Neon takes over his contingent.

6.4.12–16
September 400
KALPE HARBOR
Adverse sacrificial omens block their onward journey.

6.4.9a   For more about Greek funerary practices, see Appendix G: Divinity and Divining, §18.
6.4.10a  Stymphalos, Elis: Map 1.2.1, AY, AX.
6.4.11a  Asine: Map 1.2.1, BX.
6.4.13a  Ambracia: Map 5.3.7, AX.
6.4.13b  On divinatory practice, see Appendix G, esp. §§13–14.

as the food supplies which they had when they came had been exhausted, and there was as yet no market to be seen.

[17] After this they held a meeting, and Xenophon spoke again: "Men, you can see that the sacred signs are not yet forthcoming in favor of our journey, and I can see that you are in need of food supplies. So I think it necessary to offer a sacrifice to inquire about that in particular." [18] Someone got up and said, "In fact it's with good reason that the sacred signs are not forthcoming for us, for as I gathered from some merchant ship that by coincidence came here yesterday, Kleandros, the harmost at Byzantium,[a] intends to come here with merchant ships and triremes." [19] As a result, everyone decided to stay where they were, but it was still a necessity to venture out for food supplies. With this objective, Xenophon again offered a sacrifice and did so three times, but appropriate sacred signs were still not forthcoming. By this stage people were even coming to Xenophon's tent to say that they had no food supplies, but he refused to lead them out unless appropriate sacred signs were forthcoming.

[20] And again on the following day, he set about offering sacrifice, and because it mattered so much to them all, nearly the whole army stood in a circle around the place for the sacred rites.[a] But the victims had been found wanting.[b] The generals maintained their refusal to lead the army out, but they did call a meeting. [21] So Xenophon said, "Perhaps our enemies have gathered and there will be a need to fight. Therefore, if we were to deposit the baggage in the natural stronghold and go prepared for battle, perhaps the sacred signs would be more likely to turn out to our advantage." [22] On hearing this, the soldiers shouted out that there was no need to take anything into the stronghold; what was needed was to offer sacrifice as soon as possible. There were no more sheep or goats, but they bought some oxen that were being used to pull carts and set about offering the sacrifice. Xenophon asked Kleanor the Arcadian[a] to offer it, and to use special zeal, in case this made a difference. But even so, appropriate signs were not forthcoming at all.

[23] Neon, who had replaced Cheirisophos[a] as a general, saw the dire condition to which need had reduced all the people, and wishing to please them, he found some person or other from Heraclea who said that he knew of villages nearby from which it would be possible to obtain food supplies. Neon then had the herald announce that whoever so wished could go in search of food supplies, as there would be a guide. Accordingly, about two thousand people did go out, with short spears and wineskins and sacks and other con-

6.4.17–19
September 400
KALPE HARBOR
Further adverse omens dissuade the army from foraging for food supplies, and Xenophon is adamant the signs should be respected.

6.4.20–22
September 400
KALPE HARBOR
Continuing problems with omens, despite Xenophon's best efforts.

6.4.23–27
September 400
KALPE HARBOR
Neon's disastrous expedition in defiance of the omens, and its aftermath.

---

6.4.18a   Byzantium: Map 6.4.1 and locator.
6.4.20a   "Sacred rites": on this expression, here and at 6.5.2, see the Translator's Notes, §6, and n. TransNotes.6.b.
6.4.20b   "Victims had been found wanting": an obscure expression for the climax of these sacrificial problems. It sounds as if there were no suitable victims left at all; that this was found out only after the rituals had started suggests that there had been a number of prospective victims left after

the previous day's sacrifices but they collapsed or died overnight. Sudden widespread collapse across a flock of sheep is quite possible, for several diseases that run through sheep flocks, such as liver fluke, wreak major damage on the internal organs before the sheep show any external signs.
6.4.22a   On Kleanor, see Appendix W: Brief Biographies, §19.
6.4.23a   On Cheirisophos, see Appendix W, §7.

tainers. [24] When they were in the villages and were scattered about, the better to seize things, the enemy attacked them suddenly, Pharnabazos' cavalry[a] in the lead; they had come to the aid of the Bithynians, since, like the Bithynians, they wanted, if they could, to stop the Greeks from entering Phrygia.[b] These horsemen killed no fewer than five hundred of the men from the Greek army, but the rest escaped to the hills. [25] Afterward someone brought to the camp the news from those who had escaped. Since appropriate sacred signs had not been forthcoming that day, Xenophon took an ox from the cart it was yoked to, there being no other sacrificial animals, and made a blood sacrifice;[a] he then set out to the rescue, as did all the troops under thirty, every one of them. [26] They recovered the rest of the men and came back to the camp.

It was already about sunset, and the Greeks proceeded to eat their evening meal in great despondency. Suddenly, while they were doing so, some of the Bithynians made their way through the bushes and attacked the outlying guards, killing some and pursuing the others as far as the camp. [27] At the shouting that arose, all the Greeks ran for their weapons. It did not seem safe either to mount a pursuit or to move the camp by night, as the land around was thickly wooded, so they spent the night under arms with sufficient sentries keeping watch.

[1] In this way they passed the night. At daybreak the generals proceeded to lead them into the stronghold, and the troops picked up their weapons and baggage and set about following. Before it was the time for the morning meal, they had dug a defensive ditch across the approach to the stronghold and completely fenced off the whole place, leaving three gateways. Then a merchant ship came from Heraclea[a] with barley, animals for sacrifice, and wine. [2] Xenophon, who had risen early in the morning,[a] set about offering a sacrifice to inquire about the prospects for an expedition, and favorable sacred signs were forthcoming with the first victim.[b] Furthermore, just at the end of the sacred rites, the seer, Arexion of Parrasia, saw an

A fresh batch of sacrificial victims produce good omens at last, and the Greeks go out to bury the men who were killed the day before.

6.4.24a  On Pharnabazos' career as satrap (governor) of Hellespontine Phrygia (413– c. 390) and his even higher subsequent positions (c. 390–c. 373), see Appendix W: Brief Biographies, §27. On the composition of his forces, see Appendix D: The Persian Army, §7. For a coin of Pharnabazos, see Figure 5.6.23.

6.4.24b  (Hellespontine, or Lesser) Phrygia: Map 5.3.7, AY. This is to be distinguished from Greater Phrygia (Map 1.2.10, AY); see n. 1.2.6a.

6.4.25a  The blood sacrifice (*sphagia*) was used immediately before battles and was almost guaranteed not to produce bad omens, which is why Xenophon used it here in preference to inspection of the victim's entrails (*hiera*). He had not resorted to *sphagia* earlier because it was considered bad form except in narrowly defined, or altogether exceptional, circumstances. On these forms of sacrifice, see Appendix G:

Divinity and Divining, §2, and see Figure 6.5.2.

6.5.1a  Heraclea: Map 6.4.1, *Halting place 68*.

6.5.2a  Risen early in the morning: Xenophon presumably makes a point of this because this time, when it was still dark, was especially appropriate for making sacrifices before setting out: Xenophon, *Constitution of the Lacedaemonians* 13.3.

6.5.2b  The emphasis here perhaps implies that previously the gods had, in effect, been telling them to go into the stronghold. A more secular explanation might be that the old animals had been afflicted with a disease of the entrails, but the new ones, not having been pastured with them, had not had a chance to catch it. Since the divinatory signs were read from the entrails (see Figure 2.1.9), diseased entrails were liable to give bad signs (though disease was not the only source of negative signs).

FIGURE 6.5.2. TWO FORMS OF SACRIFICE. TOP: THE FINAL STAGE IN A DIVINATORY SAC-RIFICE (*HIERA*), AS SHOWN ON A LATE FIFTH-CENTURY VASE. AS THE GODDESS NIKE (VICTORY) FLIES ABOVE THE SCENE, THE OSPHUS (SACRUM) BONE OF THE SACRIFICED ANIMAL BENDS UPWARD WHEN HEATED ON THE ALTAR, WHICH WAS TAKEN TO BE THE CLINCHING SIGN OF GOOD OMENS. LEFT: THE *SPHAGIA*, OR PRE-BATTLE BLOOD SACRIFICE, AS SHOWN ON A FRAGMENT OF A TERRA-COTTA ATTIC KYLIX C. 490–480. HOW THE BLOOD SPURTED FROM THE RAM'S NECK WAS SEEN AS SIGNIFICANT.

eagle in an auspicious position[c] and told Xenophon to go ahead. [3] They crossed the ditch and grounded arms, and the generals then made a proclamation that once they had had their morning meal, the soldiers should go out on an expedition carrying their weapons, while the camp followers and the slaves should stay there. [4] All the other generals went on the expedition, but not Neon, as it seemed most suitable to leave him as guard over those in the camp.[a] And when Neon's captains and soldiers proceeded to abandon him because they were ashamed not to follow the others on their expedition, they left behind there only troops over the age of forty-five: these stayed behind, while the others made their way onward. [5] Before they had traveled a mile and a half,[a] the head of the column had already started to come across dead bodies. They went on until the rear of the column came up to the first corpses that had been spotted, from which point corpses lay on the ground for the whole extent of the column. They then brought the column to a halt and set about burying all the corpses where they lay.[a] [6] When they had buried the first ones, they moved forward, again proceeding until they could bring the rear to a halt by the first of the next batch of unburied corpses, when they set about burying them in the same way, as far as the army extended. But when they reached the road from the villages, where the dead bodies were lying close together, they gathered the corpses there into one place before burying them.

[7] It was already past the middle of the day; they had moved the army forward beyond the villages and were seizing any food supplies to be seen within the area the troops controlled when suddenly they saw the enemy coming down over the brow of some hills opposite, drawn up in line of battle. There were cavalry in large numbers and also infantry, as Spithridates and Rhathines[a] had come from Pharnabazos in full force. [8] When the enemy had the Greeks clearly in view, they halted, standing off from them as far as a mile and a half.[a] At this, Arexion, who was acting as seer for the Greeks, immediately made a blood sacrifice, and favorable omens were forthcoming from the blood sacrifice at the first attempt.[b] [9] Thereupon Xenophon said to the generals, "My fellow generals, it seems to me that we should post companies behind the phalanx[a] as reserves, so that they may come up to help the phalanx wherever may be necessary, and the enemy, their order

6.5.2c  See 6.1.23 on inferences from the appearance of birds. Parrasia: Map 1.2.1, BX.
6.5.4a  Left Neon in camp: presumably since what happened the day before had been his fault.
6.5.5a  A mile and a half/2.4 kilometers: the Greek text says 15 stades; see Appendix O: Measurements, §5.
6.5.5a  The last two sentences of 6.5.5 have been expanded in translation to make the narrative clearer. (Translator's note)
6.5.7a  For events in the 390s concerning Spithridates and Rhathines, see Appendix W: Brief Biographies, §33.
6.5.8a  A mile and a half/2.4 kilometers: the

Greek text says 15 stades.
6.5.8b  Favorable omens from blood sacrifice: as mentioned in n. 6.4.25a, that is what almost always occurred with the blood sacrifice (*sphagia*), though this passage implies that it did not do so every time. But given the trouble the Greeks had been having with obtaining propitious omens, it is not surprising they noted the fact.
6.5.9a  Phalanx: a body of troops drawn up across a broad front in close formation; for more, see Appendix H: Infantry and Cavalry in *Anabasis*, §§13–15.

already broken, will meet fresh troops still in formation." All agreed with these tactics. [10] "Then go first and lead the way against the enemy, the rest of you," he said, "and avoid standing at a halt, since we have seen the enemy and they have seen us; I will come on when I have separated out the rearmost companies in the way you agree."

[11] After this speech they went on ahead in a slow and orderly way while Xenophon detached the three last units, amounting to two hundred men each. He turned the first unit, led by Samolas of Achaea, to the right, to follow behind with a hundred-foot gap; the second unit, of which Pyrrhias of Arcadia was the leader, he separated so as to follow in the center; and the remaining unit, which was headed by Phrasias of Athens, he put on the left.[a] [12] In the course of the advance, those in front came upon a great wooded hollow that was difficult to cross, and they halted, unsure whether they ought to cross it. They passed the word back to the generals and captains to come up to the front. [13] Xenophon had wondered what was obstructing their progress, and quickly taking the summons on board, he rode on as fast as possible. When they met, Sophainetos, as the eldest of the generals,[a] said that it was not worth deliberating whether such a hollow place should be crossed.

[14] Xenophon replied vigorously, "On the contrary. Men, you know that in the past I have not advocated any avoidable danger to you, for I see you are in no need of a reputation for manliness; what you need is safety. [15] But the situation now is this: it is not possible to leave from here without a fight, for if we do not attack the enemy, they will follow us whenever we retreat and fall upon us. [16] Just visualize which would be better: advancing against these men with shields to the front, or shifting them to cover our backs when we see the enemy attacking. [17] For sure, you know, if anyone does, that retreating from the enemy is in no way honorable, whereas being in pursuit puts fighting spirit even into poorer troops. I at any rate would be more comfortable attacking with half the number of soldiers than I would be retreating with twice as many. And as regards the enemy troops here, I know that if we attack, you would not expect them to stand and receive us, while if we retreat, we all know that they will have the courage to pursue us.

[19A][a] "I for my part am amazed if anyone thinks that this wooded hollow is more terrifying than the other places through which we have made our way previously. [18] As for the fact that if we cross over, having a wooded hollow behind us would create difficulties in a retreat, well, for those about to enter battle, isn't that an opportunity to be seized? I would wish the enemy

6.5.11–13
September 400
KALPE HARBOR
The army is unsure whether to cross a wooded hollow, and Sophainetos objects to doing so.

6.5.14–21
September 400
KALPE HARBOR
Xenophon exhorts the army to cross the hollow.

6.5.11a   Hundred-foot/30-meter: the Greek text says 1 *plethron;* see Appendix O: Measurements, §§2–3. Achaea, Arcadia: Map 1.2.1, AX.

6.5.13a   For Xenophon's engagement with Sophainetos, see Appendix W: Brief Biographies, §32. Sophainetos' possible authorship of a rival account of the expedition is discussed in Appendix M: Other

Ancient Sources on the Ten Thousand, §§12–15.

6.5.19Aa   Several scholars think the first sentence of section 19 has been misplaced slightly; this edition moves it to a different location from the alternative printed by some previous editors. That is why verse 19A appears before verse 18. (Translator's note)

to have everything easy for retreating, while we should be taught from the very nature of the place that victory is our only safety. [19B] For how indeed is the plain to be crossed unless we defeat their cavalry? How are we to get back through the hills if all these peltasts are pursuing us? [20] Even if we do reach the sea in safety, how deep a hollow is the Black Sea! There we have no merchant ships to carry us, nor grain to live on if we stay, and the more quickly we find ourselves there, the more quickly we shall have to set out again for food supplies. [21] Surely it is better to fight now, when you have eaten, than tomorrow, when you will not have had a meal.

"Men, the sacred signs were favorable for us, the birds auspiciously placed, and the omens in the blood sacrifice very favorable—let's go for those men! Especially since they have seen us, we must not now let them have a pleasant meal this evening or settle into quarters wherever they want."

6.5.22–25
September 400
KALPE HARBOR
The Greeks cross the hollow and prepare for battle.

[22] As a result, the captains told him to lead the way, and nobody dissented. And he did lead the way, first giving instructions for each soldier to cross the hollow at whatever point he happened to be, for he thought the army would end up all together on the other side more quickly in this way than if they peeled off in single file by the bridge[a] over the hollow. [23] When they had crossed over, he made this speech as he passed along the battle line: "Men, remember how very many battles you have won, with the aid of the gods, by coming to close quarters, and remember too what happens to those who flee the enemy. Bear in mind also that we are at the very doors of Greece. [24] Now follow Herakles the Leader, and encourage each other by name. It will surely be pleasant to provide those whom you wish with a memory of yourself as someone who on this occasion said and did what was manly and noble." [25] While he rode along, he continued making this speech at the same time as leading them forward in line of battle, and having posted the peltasts on either flank, they set about making their way toward the enemy. The word was passed to keep their spears on the right shoulder until a signal should be given by trumpet, and then, lowering their spears for the attack, to follow at walking pace, and for no one to pursue at a run. After this the watchword[a] was passed along, "Zeus the Savior, Herakles the Leader." But the enemy stayed put, thinking that the position they occupied was a fine one.

6.5.26–32
September 400
KALPE HARBOR
The Greeks rout the enemy.

[26] When they drew near, the Greek peltasts raised the battle cry and began running toward the enemy before anyone ordered them to do so; but the enemy, both the cavalry and the mass of the Bithynians,[a] rushed forward to meet them and turned the peltasts to flight. [27] However, the hoplite phalanx came on for the encounter, making its way forward quickly; as the trumpet sounded, they sang a war hymn, and then they began to raise the battle cry, simultaneously lowering their spears into position—and

6.5.22a   The bridge: rather oddly, this bridge has not been mentioned previously, despite the use of the definite article.

6.5.25a   The primary purpose of the watchword was, in the absence of uniforms, to enable

friends to be distinguished from foes, but it was often chosen so as also to encourage the troops (see 1.8.16).

6.5.26a   Bithynia/Bithynians: Map 6.4.1.

at this point the enemy no longer stayed to receive them but broke into flight. [28] Timasion and the cavalry then set off in pursuit, and, few as they were, they killed as many as they could. The left wing of the enemy, which was the target of the Greek cavalry, was immediately scattered, but the right wing, not pursued so strongly, came to a halt together on a hill. [29] When the Greeks saw that they were standing their ground there, it seemed easiest and least dangerous to carry on the advance against them, so they sang a war hymn and immediately pressed on; and now the enemy did not stand their ground. At this the peltasts carried on the pursuit until the enemy right wing was likewise scattered; but few of the enemy were killed, as the large number of their cavalry made the peltasts fearful. [30] The Greeks saw that Pharnabazos' cavalry force remained intact as a unit and that the Bithynian horsemen were rallying to it and reviewing the unfolding situation from a nearby hill. At the sight of the enemy cavalry, the Greeks flagged, but nevertheless they decided that they had to advance against them as best they could, so that even if the enemy troops had recovered from their immediate panic, they should have no respite. [31] So they formed up and made their way forward. Seeing this, the enemy cavalry fled downhill as if they themselves were being pursued by cavalry, for there was a hollow there to give them cover, which the Greeks did not know about; but as it was late, the Greeks broke off their pursuit before they reached it. [32] They went back up to where the first engagement had occurred, raised a trophy,[a] and left for the coast about sunset. It was around six and a half miles[b] back to the camp.

[1] As a result, the enemy occupied themselves with their own affairs and set about taking their households and their moveable wealth as far away as they could. The Greeks for their part were waiting for Kleandros and the triremes and merchant ships to come; but they would go out each day with the draft animals and the slaves and carry off with impunity wheat and barley, wine, pulses, foxtail millet, and figs, as the countryside provided all good things except olive oil.[a] [2] Whenever the army stayed put for a rest, it was still permissible to mount raids for plunder, and those who went out on them used to keep the proceeds. But whenever the whole army went out, if someone then obtained something by going off by himself, it was taken to be common property. [3] By now there was an abundance of everything, for in addition to the raids, traders were arriving from the Greek cities from every side, and those who sailed by were happy to put in, hearing that a city was being founded and that there was a harbor. [4] And now those of the

6.6.1–4
September–October 400
KALPE HARBOR
The Greeks, now well supplied, continue to wait for Kleandros.

6.5.32a  Trophy: memorial set up by the victors of a battle, usually consisting of a post on which armor from the vanquished was hung; for more, see the Glossary.

6.5.32b  Six and a half miles/10.5 kilometers: the Greek text says 60 stades; see Appendix O: Measurements, §5.

6.6.1a  Xenophon does not include sesame among the crops they carried off, although it was listed as one of the benefits of the area at

6.4.6 and one could normally harvest millet and sesame at the same time. Grain crops can be processed with the portable hand mills the army would probably carry, but processing sesame requires an oil press, a much heavier item that the soldiers would be less likely to have with them. On Kleandros, the Lacedaemonian harmost in Byzantium, see Appendix W: Brief Biographies, §18; on Dexippos, §13.

enemy who lived nearby, hearing that Xenophon was turning the stronghold into a city, started to make approaches to him, asking what they had to do to be friends. He would make a point of bringing them before the soldiers.

6.6.5–11
October 400
KALPE HARBOR
Kleandros finally arrives.
He is greeted by a riot,
the result of arbitrary
action by Dexippos that
Xenophon's friend
Agasias resists.

[5] In the midst of this, Kleandros arrived with two triremes but no merchant ships, and it so happened that the main army was not there when he arrived. Certain others who had gone plundering in the hills had captured a large number of sheep, and, reluctant to have their plunder confiscated, they spoke to Dexippos, the individual who had run away with the fifty-oared ship[a] from Trapezus, and told him to keep the sheep safe for them and subsequently give them back after taking some for himself. [6] He immediately drove away the soldiers who were standing around and saying that the sheep were common property, and then he went straight to Kleandros and said that they were attempting a robbery. [7] Kleandros ordered him to bring the robber to him.[a] He seized hold of someone or other and was dragging him along when Agasias chanced by and took the soldier away from him, partly because he was one of the troops in his company. The other soldiers who were there tried to drive Dexippos off by throwing stones at him, calling him a traitor. Many of the crew from the triremes took fright and started to flee to the sea, and Kleandros also took to flight. [8] Xenophon and the other generals[a] set about putting a stop to all this while saying to Kleandros that there was nothing the matter, the army's decree was the cause of what had happened. [9] But Kleandros—who, stirred up by Dexippos, was in an excited state and ashamed of himself for having been frightened—said he would sail away and make a proclamation that no city was to receive them, as being enemies to all. At that time the Lacedaemonians ruled all the Greeks,[a] [10] and under the circumstances the affair looked like a dreadful mess for the Greek army; they begged him not to do this. He said that's what would happen unless someone handed over the person who had started throwing stones and the one who had taken the man from Dexippos. [11] The person whom he was demanding, Agasias, had been a friend to Xenophon throughout, and this was the reason why Dexippos was maligning him.

Since there was bemusement as a result of this, the commanders called

6.6.5a  Fifty-oared ships (penteconters) were the precursors of triremes and were old-fashioned by this time.

6.6.7a  Dexippos refers to robbers in the plural, Kleandros to just one robber. Perhaps this is simple carelessness on Xenophon's part; but possibly Kleandros was used to somewhat overdramatic behavior by Dexippos and wanted to avoid encouraging him to make mass arrests.

6.6.8a  The mention of the generals shows that the army as a whole must be back in camp, and perhaps that was already the case when Agasias made his appearance, though

Xenophon has not told us so. Perhaps he is just narrating carelessly, but perhaps he is obscuring the situation, which may not have been quite as black and white in terms of the rule laid down at 6.6.2 as he would like us to believe.

6.6.9a  "At that time the Lacedaemonians ruled": this implies that it was no longer true when Xenophon was writing; see Appendix B: Xenophon and Sparta, §11, where Paul Cartledge suggests that it points to a date for *Anabasis* after the battle of Leuktra in 371. Lacedaemon: Map 1.2.1, BX.

the army together. Some of them belittled Kleandros, but the incident did not seem trivial to Xenophon, who stood up and said, [12] "Brave soldiers, to me it does not seem a trivial matter if Kleandros goes away, as he says he will, with this sort of an opinion about us. For the Greek cities are now near at hand, and Lacedaemonians have the leading role in Greece; and they have enough power, each individual Lacedaemonian, to bring about what they want in all the cities. [13] So if he starts by excluding us from Byzantium[a] and next passes the word to the other harmosts not to receive us into their cities because we are lawless and disobedient to the Lacedaemonians, and if this tale about us then comes to the ears of Anaxibios the *nauarchos*,[b] there will be difficulties whether we stay here or sail away; for as you know, the Lacedaemonians rule both by land and now too by sea. [14] For sure, we must not end up excluding the rest of us from Greece on account of one or two men; rather, we have to obey Lacedaemonian commands, whatever they may be, for the cities from which we ourselves come obey them. [15] So then I myself—for I hear that Dexippos is saying to Kleandros that Agasias would not have acted as he did if I had not ordered him to do so—I myself clear both you and Agasias of the blame if Agasias himself says that I am in any sense the cause of what has happened. Moreover, I pronounce myself, if I set in motion stone throwing or any other violent action, to be worthy of the ultimate punishment, which I will freely undergo. [16] I say further that even if he blames someone else, Agasias should turn himself over to Kleandros to be his judge, for only in this way would you soldiers be cleared of the blame. As things now stand, it will be cruel if we, who thought we were going to gain both praise and honor in Greece, shall instead find that, unlike any other Greeks, we are excluded from Greek cities."

[17] After this speech Agasias rose and said, "Men, I swear by all that is holy that this is the real truth: Xenophon did not tell me to take the man from Dexippos, nor did anybody else from among you. When I saw a good man from my company being carried away by Dexippos, who you know betrayed you, it seemed a terrible thing to me, and I took the man from him, I admit it. [18] But don't you surrender me—I will give myself up, as Xenophon says, to Kleandros, for him to judge whatever he wants to do. Don't, for the sake of this incident, start a fight with the Lacedaemonians, but come safe and sound to wherever each one of you wishes. Nevertheless, choose from among yourselves those who will both speak and act on my behalf, and send them to Kleandros along with me in case I leave anything out." [19] When he said this, the army granted him the choice of those he wanted with him when he went, and he chose the generals.

After this, Agasias, the generals, and the man who had been rescued by Agasias made their way to Kleandros, and the generals made this speech:

6.6.12–16
October 400
KALPE HARBOR
Xenophon recommends that Agasias hand himself over to Kleandros.

6.6.17–19
October 400
KALPE HARBOR
Agasias agrees to surrender himself.

---

6.6.13a   Byzantium: Map 6.4.1 and locator.
6.6.13b   *Nauarchos:* chief admiral of the Spartan fleet for the year; see Appendix B:

Xenophon and Sparta, §14. On Anaxibios, see Appendix W: Brief Biographies, §3.

6.6.20–28
October 400
KALPE HARBOR
Agasias and the generals
plead their cause before
Kleandros.

[20] "The army has sent us to you, Kleandros, and they bid you, if you blame everyone, to act as the judge yourself and impose whatever punishment you wish. Or if you blame a particular individual or two or even more, they think it right that any such people should give themselves up to you for judgment. So, if you blame one of us, here we are in your presence; if you blame someone else, say so, for nobody who is willing to obey us will stay away."

[21] After this Agasias came forward and said, "I am the one, Kleandros, who took this man away from Dexippos as he was leading him off and who told the troops to use violence against Dexippos. [22] For I know this man to be a good man, and I know Dexippos too. He was chosen by the army to be in command of the fifty-oared ship that we had requested from the Trapezountians in order to gather merchant ships for our safe return, and he ran away instead and betrayed the soldiers with whose aid he had reached safety. [23] Because of him, we have in effect robbed the Trapezountians of their fifty-oared ship and appear to be bad people, while we ourselves, all of us, could have been wiped out as far as he was concerned. He was as aware as we were of the reports that if we left on foot, there was no way to cross the rivers and reach Greece safely. [24] So as that's the sort of person he is, I took the soldier out of his custody. If it had been you who had been carrying the soldier off, or anyone else from your staff, rather than one of those who deserted us, please be clear that I would have done none of these things. Just consider this: if you put me to death now, you will be killing a good man on account of a worthless coward."

[25] When he heard this speech, Kleandros said that Dexippos was not to be praised if he had acted in this way. Nevertheless (he said) he did not think that even if Dexippos were a thorough villain, he should have been made to suffer as a result of violence; rather, he should have been brought to trial first, "as you yourselves now think it right that you should be assigned a day in court. [26] So leave this man here now and go away; and when I tell you, attend here for my judgment. I no longer blame either the army as a whole or any other individual, since this fellow himself admits that it was he who took the man out of custody."

[27] The soldier who had been released then spoke: "As for me, Kleandros, in case you think that I was under arrest because I had done something wrong, I was neither hitting anyone nor throwing stones. I just said that the sheep were public property, as the soldiers had passed a decree that if anyone went plundering for his personal profit when the army had gone on an expedition, whatever he got should be public property. [28] That's what I said, and as a result Dexippos here grabbed hold of me and was leading me off in order that no one else should speak out; instead, since he himself had taken a cut of the booty, his aim was to keep it safe for those

who had plundered it, contrary to the ordinance."[a] To this Kleandros replied, "Well, then, since you are such a sharp fellow, stay here too, so that we may discuss your case as well."

[29] After this Kleandros and his staff had their meal, while Xenophon brought together the army and gave them the advice to send men to Kleandros to intercede for the men. [30] As a result they decided to send generals, captains, Drakontios the Spartiate,[a] and any of the other Greeks who seemed suitable to ask Kleandros, in every way they could, to release the two men. [31] When they came to him, Xenophon accordingly said, "Kleandros, you now have the men, and the army submits to you in whatever you want to do about them and also about the entire body of troops. But now they beg and beseech you to give them the two men and not to put them to death, for many times in the past they have worn themselves out for the army. [32] If they obtain this from you, they promise you in return that if you want to lead them and the gods are gracious to us, they will show you how well-behaved they are, every one of them, and will show also how, obedient to their leader, they are capable, with the assistance of the gods, of fearless resistance to the enemy. [33] This too they ask of you, that when you have joined them and become their commander, you make trial of the qualities of Dexippos and of the rest of us, and give each his due accordingly." [34] When Kleandros heard this, he said, "Now by the Twin Gods,[a] I can surely give you a swift answer. I give you the two men and I will also stay with you myself, and if the gods grant it, I will lead you out of here to Greece. Your words are very different from those that I have been hearing about you from some people, who said that you were alienating the army from the Lacedaemonians."

[35] After this they praised him and went away with the two men, while Kleandros set about offering a sacrifice to inquire about the journey; he associated with Xenophon on friendly terms, and they proceeded to enter into guest-friendship.[a] When he also saw the army carrying out their instructions in a disciplined way, his desire to become their leader grew even stronger. [36] But when on three successive days appropriate sacred signs

6.6.29–34
October 400
KALPE HARBOR
Xenophon leads the army's representatives in humbly submitting to Kleandros, who responds positively.

6.6.35–36
October 400
KALPE HARBOR
The omens prevent Kleandros from taking personal charge of the army.

---

6.6.28a    "The ordinance" refers to the decision (at 6.6.2) that when the army as a whole ventured out, any gains from private plundering parties would be shared with the rest of the army. The soldier here uses a word (*rhētra*) that was specifically used by Spartans for their laws. Possibly this is deliberate, to convey extra weight and solemnity to the Spartan Kleandros; it may be partly why Kleandros in the next sentence calls him by another typically Spartan word, *toros* ("sharp fellow"); on both words, see the Translator's Notes, §4. (Translator's note)

6.6.30a    Spartiates were full citizens of Sparta, a minority among the Lacedaemonians; see Appendix B: Xenophon and Sparta, §§18–19. Drakontios, who as a Spartiate

outranked Dexippos, was added to the deputation not because of his role within the army but because, even though he was an exile (see 4.8.25), his status would add weight to the generals' representations in Kleandros' eyes.

6.6.34a    The Twin Gods: Kastor and Polydeukes, twin sons of Zeus and the mythological Spartan queen Leda. They were also known as the Dioskouroi and were particularly important in Spartan culture. Leda was the mother of Helen, whose beauty caused the Trojan War.

6.6.35a    Guest-friendship: a guest-friend is someone with whom there is a bond of ritualized friendship of a type that was common between prominent men of different cities; for more, see the Glossary.

were not forthcoming for him when he offered his sacrifice, he called the generals together and said, "In my case the sacred offerings are not operating as they should for it to be me who leads the army away, but don't you lose heart on account of that: for it is to you, it seems, that it has been given to bring the men to safety. On your way, then! We for our part will receive you whenever you get there[a] in as handsome a fashion as we can."

6.6.37–38
Late October 400
BLACK SEA COAST
*Kalpe Harbor–
Chrysopolis (70)*
After a detour for plunder, the army finally reaches Chrysopolis.

[37] After this the soldiers passed a resolution to give him the sheep that were public property. He accepted the gift and then gave it back again to them. Then he sailed away. The soldiers distributed the grain they had gathered in and the other things they had obtained, and they then left, making their way through the territory of the Bithynians.[a] [38] Since, proceeding by the direct route, they came across no opportunity to have something in hand when they entered friendly territory, they decided to turn back again for a day and a night. Having done this, they captured many slaves and sheep, and they arrived on the sixth day at Chrysopolis, in Chalcedonia,[a] where they stayed for seven days, selling the plunder.

6.6.36a    "Whenever you get there": Kleandros means to Byzantium, his base as a harmost. Byzantium: Map 6.4.1 and locator.

6.6.37a    Bithynia/Bithynians: Map 6.4.1.

6.6.38a    Chrysopolis: Map 6.4.1 and inset, *Halting place 70.* Chalcedonia was the region centered on the city of Chalcedon (Map 6.4.1, inset), quite close to Chrysopolis.

# BOOK SEVEN

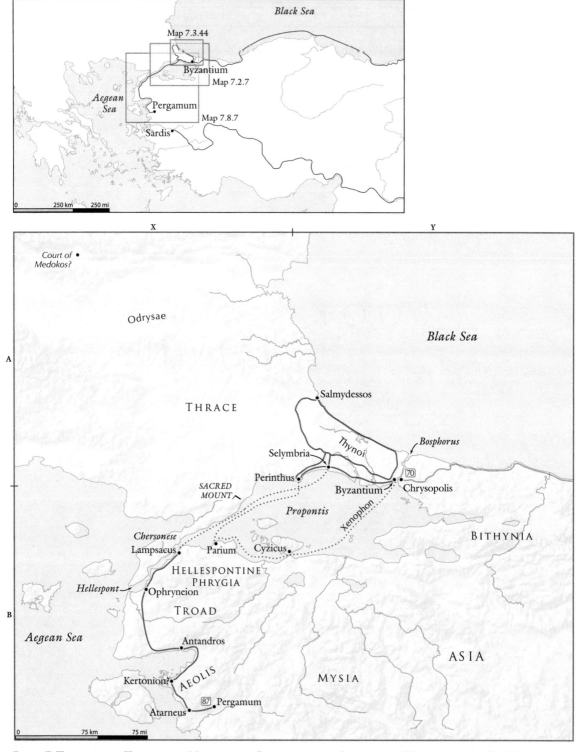

Black Sea

Map 7.3.44

Byzantium

Map 7.2.7

Aegean
Sea

Pergamum

Map 7.8.7

Sardis

0       250 km    250 mi

X                                                    Y

Court of
Medokos?

Odrysae

Black Sea

A

Salmydessos

THRACE

Thynoi

Bosphorus

Selymbria

SACRED
MOUNT

Perinthus

Byzantium

Chrysopolis

70

Propontis

Xenophon

BITHYNIA

Chersonese

Lampsacus

Parium

Cyzicus

HELLESPONTINE
PHRYGIA

Hellespont

Ophryneion

B

TROAD

Aegean Sea

Antandros

Kertonion

AEOLIS

MYSIA

ASIA

Atarneus

87

Pergamum

0       75 km    75 mi

BOOK 7. THRACE, THE TROAD, AND MYSIA: FROM CHRYSOPOLIS TO PERGAMUM, *HALTING PLACES 70–87.*

[In the preceding narrative, the author has explained what the Greeks did in the course of their march up into the interior with Cyrus leading to the battle, what they did during the return journey they made after Cyrus' death until they came to the Black Sea, and what they were doing as they were leaving the Black Sea region on foot and by ship, up to the point when they found themselves beyond the mouth of the sea in the Asian city of Chrysopolis.][a]

[2] Following on from this, Pharnabazos,[a] afraid that the army might campaign against his territory, sent to Anaxibios the *nauarchos*, who happened to be in Byzantium.[b] He asked that the army cross the straits out of Asia and promised to do everything for Anaxibios that he wanted.[c] [3] At this Anaxibios summoned the generals and captains to Byzantium and made promises to them that if they came across, there would be pay for the soldiers. [4] The others then said that they would give him a reply once they had discussed the request, but Xenophon told him that he would be leaving the army right then and wanted to sail away. However, Anaxibios ordered him to cross the straits with the army and only then to leave it. So Xenophon said that he would do that.

7.1.1
An ancient scribe's summary of the story so far.

7.1.2–4
Late October 400
CHRYSOPOLIS–BYZANTIUM
*Chrysopolis (70)*
Anaxibios the Spartan *nauarchos*, prompted by Pharnabazos, calls on the army to cross over to Byzantium.

NOTE: Unless otherwise indicated, all dates are B.C.E., and all citations are to Xenophon's *Anabasis*. The determination of the army's route and stopping places are based on the editors' calculations and estimates from data taken from *Anabasis*. Nonetheless, the route line shown on our maps and the monthly dates given in our side notes are often subject to doubt, and this is especially so in the case of Book 7. Our best estimates should not be taken as authoritative or certain. See the Editors' Preface, §§17–20.

7.1.1a The battle is described at 1.8, 1.10. This is the sixth and last of the paragraphs occurring through the work that summarize the story so far. It appears in brackets because scholars generally agree these paragraphs are later scribal insertions; see the Translator's Notes, §13. On Cyrus the Younger, see Appendix W: Brief Biographies of Selected Characters in *Anabasis*, §10. Black Sea (Pontus in the *Barrington Atlas*), Chrysopolis (*Halting place 70*): Book 7 map, AY.

7.1.2a Pharnabazos was the Persian satrap (governor) of Hellespontine Phrygia; on satraps, see the Glossary. For more on his career in this role from 413 to c. 390, and for his subsequent even higher position from c. 390 to c. 373, see Appendix W, §27. Hellespontine Phrygia: Book 7 map, BX.

7.1.2b *Nauarchos:* chief admiral of the Spartan fleet for the year; for more, see Appendix B: Xenophon and Sparta, §14. For Anaxibios' career after returning to Sparta, see Appendix W, §3. Byzantium was just across the Bosphorus straits from the army in Chrysopolis; see the Book 7 map, AY. Sparta: Map 5.3.7, BX.

7.1.2c Despite Sparta's support for Cyrus in 401 and its subsequent hostility to Persia from winter 400/399 to the King's Peace of 386, in autumn 400 the Spartans were still on good terms with Pharnabazos (especially, Xenophon implies here, when he offered them bribes). On the twists and turns of the relationship between Sparta and Persia, see Appendix B, §§5–10.

**7.1.5–6**
Late October 400
CHRYSOPOLIS
Xenophon declines
Seuthes' proposals for
cooperation.

**7.1.7**
Late October 400
CHRYSOPOLIS–BYZANTIUM
*Byzantium (71)*
Anaxibios' promises of
pay do not materialize.

**7.1.8–10**
Late October 400
BYZANTIUM
Xenophon discusses his
own departure with
Kleandros.

**7.1.11–13**
Late October 400
BYZANTIUM
Anaxibios, having cajoled
the army out of Byzan-
tium, again postpones
paying them.

[5] Seuthes the Thracian[a] sent Medosades to Xenophon and urged him to cooperate in encouraging the army to cross to Europe, saying that if he did so, he would not regret it. [6] Xenophon replied, "But the army will be crossing over in any event, so Seuthes should not reward either me or anyone else on that account. And when it has crossed over, I will be leaving, and he should approach the remaining officers in whatever way he thinks fit."

[7] After this all the soldiers crossed over to Byzantium. But Anaxibios did not give them pay. On top of that, he had the heralds announce that the soldiers were to take their weapons and their baggage and march out of the place, as he intended to send them away and at the same time would be taking a headcount. At this the soldiers were very upset, because they did not have money for purchasing supplies for the journey, and they began to pack up reluctantly.

[8] As he had become a guest-friend of Kleandros, the harmost[a] in Byzantium, Xenophon, with his own imminent departure by sea in mind, went to wish him goodbye. "Don't go," Kleandros told him. "If you do," he said, "you will be blamed for it, since even now some people are already blaming you because the army is not making its exit quickly."

[9] Xenophon replied, "But I am not at all the cause of this; the soldiers are in need of food for the journey, and because of this they have no heart for the march out."

[10] "All the same," said Kleandros, "my advice to you is to go out of the city as if you intended to make your way by land, and when the army is outside, to leave it at that point."

"Then we will go to Anaxibios," said Xenophon, "and arrange it like that." So they went and laid the matter before him.

[11] Anaxibios told Xenophon at some length to behave as Kleandros had suggested and to march them out, all packed up, double quick; and he added emphatically that anyone who was not present for the review and headcount would have himself to blame for the consequences. [12] At this they left the city, the generals first and then the others. And now all of them, except for a few, were outside, and Eteonikos[a] had taken his stand by the city gates so that when absolutely all of them were outside, he could close the gates and put the bar in place. [13] At this point Anaxibios called the generals and captains together and made a speech. "Take your food supplies," he said, "from the Thracian villages. There is a great deal of barley and wheat there, and other supplies as well. When you have taken them,

7.1.5a   On Seuthes, see Appendix F: Thrace and
         Appendix W: Brief Biographies, §30, which
         discusses his post-399 relations with his
         Odrysian overlord and with Athens (on the
         Odrysae, see n. 7.2.32b). Thrace, Odrysae/
         Odrysian territory: Book 7 map, AX.
7.1.8a   Harmost: a technical term (literally, "fixer")
         for a Spartan official resident abroad; see
         Appendix B: Xenophon and Sparta, §15.
         Guest-friend: someone with whom there
         was a bond of ritualized friendship of a type

that was common between prominent men
of different cities; see the Glossary. The
pledges of guest-friendship between Kleandros and Xenophon were exchanged at
6.6.35. On Kleandros, see Appendix W,
§18, which suggests from evidence about
his earlier career that he was predisposed to
sympathize with Xenophon.
7.1.12a  For Eteonikos' long military career before
         and after the events of *Anabasis*, see Appen-
         dix W, §15.

make your way to the Chersonese, where Kyniskos[a] is to give you pay."

[14] Some of the soldiers, on overhearing this, or perhaps it was one of the captains, spread the news through the army. Meantime the generals started to inquire about Seuthes and whether he was hostile or friendly; also whether it would be necessary to make their way via the Sacred Mount[a] or by going around through the middle of Thrace. [15] But while these people were still holding their discussion, the soldiers snatched up their weapons and ran headlong for the gates, intending to get inside the city wall again. When Eteonikos and those with him saw the hoplites[a] running toward them, they shut the gates and put the bar in place. [16] The soldiers began to hammer on the gates, saying that they were being treated very unfairly in being cast out to the enemy; and they declared that they would break down the gates if those inside would not open them willingly. [17] Others started to run down to the sea,[a] and they climbed over into the city along the break-water running out from the wall. Some of the soldiers happened to be still inside, and on seeing what was going on by the gates, they cut through the crossbar with axes[b] and threw the gates open—and in burst the troops.

[18] When Xenophon saw what was going on, he was afraid that the army would turn to looting and irreparable harm would be done to the city, to himself, and to the soldiers, so he started to run, charging in through the gates together with the mob. [19] As for the Byzantines, when they saw the army bursting in by force, they fled from the marketplace, some to the merchant ships, some to their homes; those who happened to be indoors ran outside; yet others set about launching the triremes,[a] supposing that in the ships they might be safe; and all of them thought that they had been ruined, believing that the city had been captured. [20] Eteonikos fled straight to the high ground, while Anaxibios ran down to the sea and sailed around to the acropolis in a fishing boat; he then immediately sent for guards from Chalcedon,[a] as the troops he had on the acropolis did not seem sufficient to contain the rioting men.

7.1.14–20
Late October 400
BYZANTIUM
Furious, the army breaks back into Byzantium, causing the Byzantines and the Spartan commanders to flee.

7.1.13a  Kyniskos may have been a relation of the Spartan king Agesilaos, since the latter had a sister called Kyniska. Chersonese: Book 7 map, BX.
7.1.14a  Sacred Mount: Book 7 map, BY (Hieron Mons in the *Barrington Atlas*).
7.1.15a  See Diagram 7.1.15. Hoplites: heavy-armed infantry; for more, see Appendix H: Infantry and Cavalry in *Anabasis*, §§2–3.
7.1.17a  Evidently unable to scale the city wall, the soldiers ran north to the Phosphorion Harbor. Although, as Diagram 7.1.15 shows, the main wall continued along the land side of the harbor, it seems that the breakwaters on either side of the harbor mouth were easier to climb. Presumably they were not as square and sheer to the ground as the main wall, or were lower at their seaward ends, or both. Once the soldiers had mounted the western break-water, they could run along the top until they reached its junction with the main wall and then drop down into the city.

7.1.17b  The soldiers inside the city could not simply lift the crossbar, because it would have been bolted to a keep on the gate frame with a bolt pin. The bolt pin was sunk through a hole in the crossbar into a socket in the keep; when it was in place, its top stood a little below the surface of the crossbar, and a special tube was required to lift it out. Doubtless Eteonikos still had the tube in his possession.
7.1.19a  Triremes: long warships with three banks of oars; for more, see the Glossary; see also Figure 5.8.20.
7.1.20a  Anaxibios probably ran north to the harbor, where some of the army were trying to break in, and was then rowed around the point, most likely to a cove just beyond it. This is no longer visible but a description from the 1540s C.E. mentions it. He then must have climbed a path up to the acropolis. Today the acropolis is occupied by the Ottoman Topkapı Palace. Chalcedon: Diagram 7.1.15, locator.

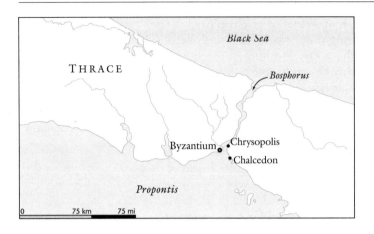

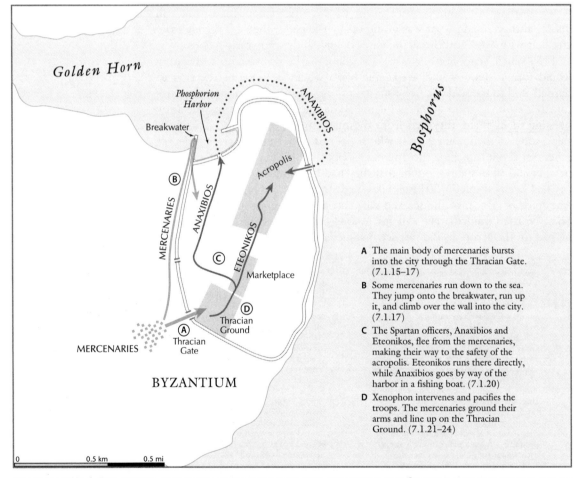

A  The main body of mercenaries bursts into the city through the Thracian Gate. (7.1.15–17)

B  Some mercenaries run down to the sea. They jump onto the breakwater, run up it, and climb over the wall into the city. (7.1.17)

C  The Spartan officers, Anaxibios and Eteonikos, flee from the mercenaries, making their way to the safety of the acropolis. Eteonikos runs there directly, while Anaxibios goes by way of the harbor in a fishing boat. (7.1.20)

D  Xenophon intervenes and pacifies the troops. The mercenaries ground their arms and line up on the Thracian Ground. (7.1.21–24)

DIAGRAM 7.1.15. BYZANTIUM: THE ARMY BREAKS BACK INTO THE CITY WHILE THE SPARTAN OFFICERS INSIDE FLEE TO THE SAFETY OF THE ACROPOLIS.

[21] When the soldiers saw Xenophon, they crowded around him in large numbers and said, "Now you can become a big man, Xenophon. You have a city, you have triremes, you have money, and you have all these men. Now, if you wanted, you would help us and we would make you great." [22] He replied, in an effort to calm them down, "Sure—what you say is a good idea, and I will do it; but if this is what you really want, then fall in and ground your arms as quickly as possible." Not only did he give these instructions personally; he also kept telling the others to pass on the word to ground arms. [23] The soldiers fell in by themselves, and in a short time the hoplites were drawn up eight-deep and the peltasts[a] had run across to either wing. [24] The place where they were, called the Thracian Ground,[a] is the finest possible location for holding a review, level and clear of houses. When they had laid down their weapons and been calmed down, Xenophon called the army together and spoke as follows:

[25] "Brave soldiers, I am not surprised that you are angry and that you think you are being treated dreadfully in being subjected to this deceit. But if we were to gratify our wrath and punish the Lacedaemonians[a] here present for their deception, and if we sacked the city—which is not at all to blame— bear in mind what will be the result. [26] We shall be proclaimed enemies of the Lacedaemonians and their allies, and from our memories of what we saw happen very recently, we can well imagine what sort of war might arise in consequence. [27] We Athenians went to war against the Lacedaemonians and their allies with no fewer than three hundred triremes, if one includes both those at sea and those in the docks; a great deal of money was kept on the acropolis, and state revenue used to come in from home and abroad to the tune of no less than a thousand talents a year.[a] We ruled over every one of the islands, and we held many cities in Asia and many others in Europe, and indeed this city of Byzantium itself, where we now are. And with all these advantages, we were ground down to exhaustion by the war,[b] as you are all aware. [28] So then what do we think would happen to us now, when the Lacedaemonians not only have their old allies on their side, but the Athenians and those who were formerly Athenian allies are all with them too? When, furthermore, Tissaphernes[a] and the other barbarians on the coast are all enemies of ours, and inland is the most hostile to us of all:

7.1.21–24
Late October 400
BYZANTIUM
The soldiers press Xenophon to take control of Byzantium. He assembles them on the Thracian Ground.

7.1.25–31
Late October 400
BYZANTIUM
Xenophon delivers a powerful speech, persuading the soldiers not to sack the city or attack the Spartans there.

7.1.23a  Peltasts: light-armed infantry; for more, see Appendix H: Infantry and Cavalry in *Anabasis*, §§4–5.
7.1.24a  Presumably this square was called "Thracian" because it was close to the Thracian Gate, which is mentioned by the third-century C.E. historian Cassius Dio (74.14.5 in Boissevain; 75.14.15 in Loeb). The gate led to the road from Byzantium to the interior of Thrace.
7.1.25a  The terms Lacedaemon and Sparta are nearly synonymous. Lacedaemon is a state and territorial designation. Sparta was the most important city within it; see Appendix B: Xenophon and Sparta, §§18–19. Lacedaemon, Sparta: Map 1.2.1, BX.

7.1.27a  On talents, see Appendix O: Ancient Greek and Persian Units of Measurement, §§10–11. Athens: Map 1.2.1, AY.
7.1.27b  The Peloponnesian War, between Athens and Sparta, which lasted, with two short breaks, from 431 to 404 and ended with the capture of almost all of the Athenian fleet, the collapse of Athens' empire over the Aegean Sea, and the destruction of the walls of Athens under the terms of the peace treaty. Aegean Sea: Map 5.3.7, AX.
7.1.28a  Tissaphernes had by now returned from the interior to his seaboard satrapy. On Tissaphernes, see Appendix W: Brief Biographies, §37.

the Great King himself, whom we set out to deprive of power and even to put to death if we could? With all these acting together, is anyone so senseless as to think that we would prevail? [29] Let us not, please God, go raving mad and perish shamefully as enemies of our native lands and even of our own friends and kinsmen, who all live in cities that will campaign against us. And they will be right to do so if—despite the fact that there was no barbarian city we wanted to occupy, though we had it in our power several times to do so—we nevertheless sack the first Greek city that we reach.[a] [30] So I for my part pray that I am ten thousand fathoms under the earth before I live to see such events brought about by you, and my advice to you is that since you are Greeks, you try to obtain justice by remaining obedient to the established leaders of the Greeks. Should you be unable to achieve that, we must still ensure that, wronged though we may be, we are at least not deprived of access to Greece. [31] And now it seems to me that we should send word to Anaxibios and say, 'We have not entered the city to do anything violent but to see if we can obtain any favor from you people; and if we cannot, then to make clear that we leave not because we have been tricked but out of obedience.' "

7.1.32–37
Late October 400
BYZANTIUM
The soldiers accept the traveling general Koiratadas as leader and exit Byzantium.

[32] This was agreed, and they sent Hieronymos of Elis to say so, together with Eurylochos of Lousoi and Philesios of Achaea.[a] They set off to say their piece, [33] and while the soldiers were still in session, Koiratadas of Thebes appeared.[a] Though he was not an exile, he was going around Greece seized with a desire for military office and proffering his services if either a city or a tribe was in need of a general.[b] On this occasion he came forward and said he would be ready to lead them to the Delta,[c] as it was called, of Thrace, where they might obtain many good things. He added that until they attained their destination,[d] he would provide as much food and drink as they could possibly want. [34] Simultaneously a reply arrived from Anaxibios, who answered that they would not regret their obedience but, on the contrary, he was sending a report of it to the authorities at Sparta[a] and he himself would consider how he could be of benefit to them. On hearing Koiratadas' speech and the message from Anaxibios, [35] the soldiers consequently accepted Koiratadas as general and went out beyond

7.1.29a  They had in fact visited or passed by several Greek cities on the Black Sea coast, but there are similar remarks at 6.1.17 and 6.6.12. It seems that Greece was thought of as beginning with Byzantium and the Bosphorus, though even around the Propontis (for these locations, see Map 7.2.7) and in the north Aegean, the coastal areas settled by Greeks were interspersed with territory controlled by Thracians and others.

7.1.32a  Elis, Lousoi, Achaea: Map 1.2.1, AX.

7.1.33a  On Koiratadas' pro-Spartan activities in 408 and 395, see Appendix W: Brief Biographies, §21. Thebes: Map 1.2.1, AY.

7.1.33b  If one wanted to be a general, the normal thing to do was to stand for election in

one's native city. Hawking oneself around was, Xenophon suggests, appropriate only if one was an exile, and so could not serve one's countrymen.

7.1.33c  The Delta was presumably so called because its boundaries formed a triangle, like the Greek letter delta (Δ). Delta, probable (though disputed) location: Map 7.2.7 (not listed in the *Barrington Atlas*).

7.1.33d  "attained their destination": the inflated word (Greek, *molōsin*) suggests the inflated pretensions of Koiratadas; see the Translator's Notes, §8.

7.1.34a  Sparta is not actually named in the Greek text here, the literal translation being "at home."

the city wall. Koiratadas made an agreement with them that he would present himself to the assembled force on the following day with sacrificial victims and a seer, together with food and drink for the army. [36] When they had left the city, Anaxibios closed the gates and had it proclaimed that if any of the soldiers were caught inside, they would be sold into slavery.

[37] On the following day, Koiratadas arrived with the sacrificial victims and the seer; twenty men were following him carrying barley meal, another twenty carrying wine, and three carrying consignments of olives, while one man carried the biggest load of garlic he could and another the equivalent in onions. Having set these down as if they were for distribution, he proceeded to offer sacrifice.

[38] Xenophon sent for Kleandros and told him to arrange for him to be allowed inside the city wall to reach the docks[a] and sail away from Byzantium. [39] Kleandros came and said, "Here I am, and I have made the arrangements, but only with very considerable difficulty. For Anaxibios[a] said that it was not expedient to have the soldiers close to the wall and Xenophon inside it, especially as the Byzantines are split into factions and behaving toward one another like criminals. However," Kleandros continued, "Anaxibios' ultimate orders were for you to come in if you intended to sail away in his company." [40] Xenophon accordingly said goodbye to the soldiers and left with Kleandros to go inside the wall.

Koiratadas for his part did not obtain favorable omens on the first day, and he did not distribute anything to the soldiers. On the next day, the animals for sacrifice were standing by the altar and Koiratadas was there as well, wearing a garland and about to perform a sacrifice, when Timasion the Dardanian, Neon the Asinean, and Kleanor the Orchomenian[a] came up and proceeded to tell him not to perform the sacrifice, as he would not be leading the army unless he gave them the food supplies. He ordered the supplies to be measured out. [41] But when his supply fell far short of being a day's rations for each of the soldiers, he took the sacrificial animals back again and went away, renouncing his appointment as general.

[1] Neon the Asinean, Phryniskos the Achaean, Kleanor the Orchomenian,[a] Philesios the Achaean, Xanthikles the Achaean, and Timasion the Dardanian remained in charge of the army, and they had advanced toward various Thracian villages in the vicinity of Byzantium and were camped out

7.1.38–39
Late October 400
BYZANTIUM
Xenophon arranges with Anaxibios to leave the army and go home.

7.1.40–41
Late October 400
BYZANTIUM
Unable to provide sufficient supplies, Koiratadas resigns his generalship.

7.2.1–4
Early November 400
COASTAL THRACE
*Camp near Byzantium (72)*
The army starts to break up.

7.1.38a  The words "to reach the docks" have been added to clarify why Xenophon first had to enter Byzantium in order to sail away from it. The docks were in the Phosphorion Harbor, which could be reached from the landward side only from inside the city. (Translator's note) On Kleandros, see Appendix W: Brief Biographies, §18.

7.1.39a  On Anaxibios, see Appendix W, §3.

7.1.40a  On Kleanor, see Appendix W, §19. Dardanos: Map 7.8.7, AX. Asine, Orchomenos: Map 1.2.1, BX, AX.

7.2.1a  The manuscripts here omit the names of two generals, Sophainetos and Kleanor, although we have not been told that they

have died, left, or been deposed. Kleanor is shown in the next sentence to have been a general at this time, so this edition follows a few earlier scholars in adding his name to the text as having fallen out in transmission. It has been suggested that Sophainetos must have left the army sometime after he was last mentioned, at 6.5.13, but given the loss of Kleanor's name, it is not clear that Sophainetos has left or been downgraded, though Phryniskos (who is new) might be replacing him. (Translator's note) On Sophainetos, see Appendix W, §32.

there.[b] [2] At this point the generals were divided into factions. Kleanor and Phryniskos wished to lead the army to Seuthes[a] as, in an effort to persuade them, he had given one a horse and the other a woman, while Neon wanted to take them to the Chersonese, thinking that if the army came under the control of Lacedaemonians, he would be put in overall charge of it; Timasion for his part was eager to cross back over to Asia, thinking that he might thus return home, [3] and this was what the soldiers wanted too. But as time wore on, many of them gave up, some selling their weapons around the countryside and then sailing away as best they could, others handing them over and merging into the cities. [4] Anaxibios was pleased when he heard that the army was disintegrating, for he thought that he would best please Pharnabazos[a] if this continued.

[5] As Anaxibios was sailing away from Byzantium, he was met at Cyzicus by Aristarchos, Kleandros' successor as harmost of Byzantium, and was told that his own successor as *nauarchos*, Polos, was already on the point of entering the Hellespont.[a] [6] Anaxibios gave orders to Aristarchos to sell into slavery as many of Cyrus' soldiers as he found lagging behind in Byzantium—Kleandros, by contrast, had not sold anyone but, out of pity, had been looking after the sick and forcing the inhabitants to receive them in their houses. As soon as Aristarchos arrived, he sold no fewer than four hundred. [7] Anaxibios sailed on to Parium and sent for Pharnabazos[a] in accordance with their agreement, but when Pharnabazos learned that Aristarchos had come to Byzantium as harmost and Anaxibios was no longer acting as *nauarchos*, he took no further notice of Anaxibios and set about making the same arrangements with Aristarchos about the Cyrean army as he had previously with Anaxibios.[b]

[8] In response to this, Anaxibios now called Xenophon over to him and ordered him to use every available ploy to sail to the army as quick as could be, to keep it together and to gather in as many of its dispersed elements as he possibly could, and then to lead it to Perinthus[a] and cross over to Asia as fast as possible. He provided him with a thirty-oared ship and sent a man with a letter to order the Perinthians to send Xenophon on to the army double-quick, using relays of horses. [9] So Xenophon sailed across and

7.2.1b  Camp (possible location, *Halting place 72*), Thrace: Map 7.2.7.
7.2.2a  On Seuthes, see Appendix W: Brief Biographies, §30.
7.2.4a  On Pharnabazos, see Appendix W, §27.
7.2.5a  Polos, otherwise unknown, arrives around the end of October or the beginning of November, as we can infer from the soldiers' claim shortly afterward that further sailing in the Aegean is now impossible (7.3.13). That would fit with an appointment early in October, roughly when the official Spartan year began (although some scholars deny that this was relevant for the *nauarchos*). This gives extra support to the chronology for Book 7, discussed in Appendix Q: The Chronology of the March, §14.

Xenophon's voyage with Anaxibios, Byzantium to Cyzicus to Parium: Map 7.2.7.
Hellespont: Book 7 map, BX.
7.2.7a  Pharnabazos was the Persian satrap of Hellespontine Phrygia: Map 7.2.7.
7.2.7b  At 7.1.2 Xenophon implies that Pharnabazos offered Anaxibios a bribe, on which he now reneged, which would account for Anaxibios' chagrin in what follows. When Anaxibios returned to Sparta, the Spartans were debating what to do about complaints by the Asian Greeks about aggressive behavior by Tissaphernes: it is not difficult to imagine that he added his voice to those urging Spartan intervention against Persia, which was agreed (7.6.1).
7.2.8a  Perinthus: Map 7.2.7, *Halting place 73*.

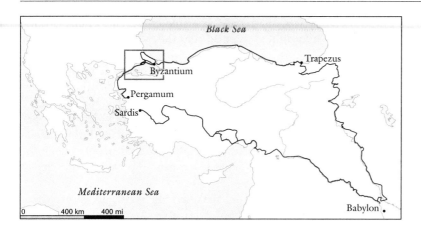

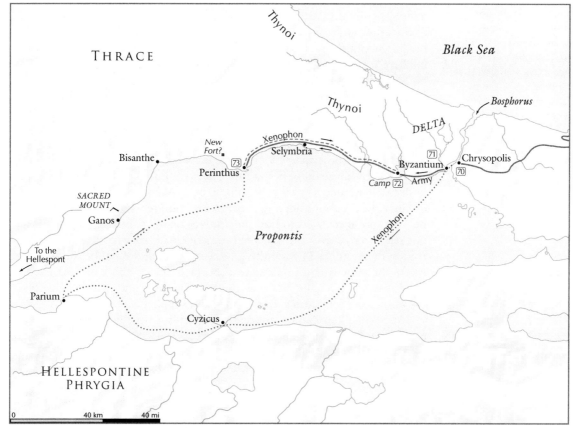

MAP 7.2.7. THRACE AND THE PROPONTIS: THE ARMY'S ROUTE FROM CHRYSOPOLIS TO PERINTHUS, *HALTING PLACES 70–73*, AND XENOPHON'S ROUTE AROUND THE PROPONTIS. After crossing over to Byzantium, the army camps among Thracian villages near the coast. Meanwhile Xenophon sails homeward, from Byzantium toward the Hellespont. Reaching Parium, he is ordered to return to duty by Anaxibios and instead must sail to Perinthus. From there he travels overland to reach the army camp *(73–72)*. Xenophon then leads the army to Perinthus *(73)*.

arrived where the army was quartered.ª The soldiers received him with joy and began following him right away, glad that they would be crossing over from Thrace to Asia.

**7.2.10–11**
**November 400**
CAMP NEAR BYZANTIUM–
SELYMBRIA–PERINTHUS
*Perinthus (73)*
Seuthes again tries and fails to persuade Xenophon to bring the army to him.

[10] When Seuthes heard that Xenophon had come back again, he sent Medosades to him by seaª to ask him to bring the army to Seuthes, making him whatever promises he thought would persuade him. Xenophon answered that nothing of that kind could be done, and when Medosades heard this, he went off. [11] As for the Greeks, when they arrived at Perinthus, Neon broke away and encamped separately with eight hundred people, while the rest of the army all stayed in the same place near the wall of the city of Perinthus.ª

**7.2.12–15**
**November–December 400**
PERINTHUS
The new harmost, Aristarchos, counter-mands Anaxibios' order to Xenophon. In the belief that Aristarchos is plotting against him, Xenophon considers whether to try to lead the army to Seuthes after all.

[12] After this Xenophon began to make arrangements about merchant ships so they could cross over as soon as possible. Meanwhile Aristarchos arrived from Byzantium with two triremes, and in obedience to Pharnabazos' wishes, he forbade the shipowners to carry the troops across; he then came to the army and said to the soldiers that they were not to cross over to Asia. [13] Xenophon was explaining that this was Anaxibios' order—"He sent me here for this reason"—but Aristarchos responded, "That's all very well, but Anaxibios is no longer *nauarchos*, and I am the harmost in these parts. If I catch any of you at sea, I will sink you." So saying, he withdrew within the city wall. [14] On the following day, he sent for the generals and captains of the army. They were already near the wall when someone sent a message out to Xenophon that if he came in, he would be arrested, and either something would happen to him there or he would be handed over to Pharnabazos himself. On hearing this, he sent the others ahead and said that he himself wanted to perform some sort of sacrifice. [15] Retiring some distance, he set about offering a sacrifice to inquire whether the gods would be with him if he tried to lead the army to Seuthes. For he saw that it was not safe to cross over the sea when someone with triremes was going to try to stop them, nor did he want to go to the Chersoneseª and be shut in there, where the army would suffer a great shortage of everything in a place where there was no choice but to obey the local harmost and it was highly likely the army would have no access to any food supplies.

**7.2.16–22**
**November–December 400**
COASTAL THRACE
Xenophon goes to visit Seuthes.

[16] While Xenophon was occupied in this way, the generals and captains came back from Aristarchos and detailed how he had ordered them to go away for the present and come back in the course of the afternoon. This made his plot against Xenophonª seem even clearer. [17] Since the sacred signs

7.2.9a   It is about fifty miles/30 kilometers from Perinthus to the army's camp. One can only guess why Anaxibios specified Perinthus rather than Selymbria, which would have cut the land travel by half. Camp (*Halting place 72*), Selymbria: Map 7.2.7.
7.2.10a   Perhaps Medosades came along the coast from one of Seuthes' three coastal forts mentioned at 7.5.8. We learn at 7.2.28 that Medosades came to Xenophon near Selymbria, so by then Xenophon and the army

had marched some way from their camp at *Halting place 72*.
7.2.11a   The army's length of stay at Perinthus is uncertain. See Appendix Q: The Chronology of the March, §14. The uncertainty here is the reason for the question marks in our side notes against the dates from 7.2.23 to 7.5.14.
7.2.15a   Chersonese: Book 7 map.
7.2.16a   "Against Xenophon" has been added in the translation to clarify the meaning.

were favorable for the safe passage of Xenophon and the army to Seuthes, Xenophon took with him Polykrates the Athenian captain and from each of the generals except Neon a man whom that general trusted, and set off in the night to travel the seven miles[a] to Seuthes' army. [18] When they were near it, Xenophon came across fires that had been left unattended, and at first he thought that Seuthes had moved elsewhere. But when he heard a commotion and became aware of Seuthes' people signaling to each other, he understood that the reason Seuthes had had the fires lit in front of the night sentries was so that the sentries, being in darkness, should not be seen and so it would not become clear how many of them there were and where exactly they were located; while on the other hand those approaching would not escape notice but would be easy to see in the light of the fires. [19] When he realized this, he sent forward an interpreter he happened to have with him and ordered him to say to Seuthes that Xenophon was there and wished to meet him. They asked if he was the Athenian from the army, [20] and when Xenophon said that he was, they leapt up and hurried off. A little while later about two hundred peltasts[a] appeared, and taking Xenophon and those with him in tow, they brought them to Seuthes. [21] He was in a tower, very well guarded, and there were horses all around the tower, ready bridled; for out of fearfulness he gave the horses fodder during the day[a] and at night he remained on his guard, with the horses ready to ride. [22] It was said that on an earlier occasion, Teres, his ancestor,[a] while in this part of the country with a large army, had many of his soldiers wiped out by the men thereabouts and was robbed of his baggage train; it was the Thynoi who did this, said to be the most warlike of all peoples, especially in night attacks.[b]

[23] When they were close, Seuthes told Xenophon to come in with two others, whomever he chose. Once the party was inside, first they all exchanged greetings, taking turns to drink hornfuls of wine to each other's health in accordance with Thracian custom; Medosades was also there with Seuthes, since he acted as his general-purpose ambassador.

[24] Next Xenophon began his opening remarks: "Seuthes, the first time you sent this fellow Medosades here to see me was when I was in Chalcedon;[a]

FIGURE 7.2.22. FIFTH-CENTURY LIFE-SIZED GOLD MASK, WHICH SOME HAVE ATTRIBUTED TO KING TERES I, UNEARTHED AT KAZANLAK.

7.2.23–30
December 400?
COASTAL THRACE
Seuthes welcomes Xenophon. Initial dialogue between Xenophon and Medosades.

7.2.17a  Seven miles/11 kilometers: the Greek text says 60 stades; see Appendix O: Measurements, §5.

7.2.20a  See Figure 7.4.4 (left) for a Thracian peltast.

7.2.21a  Normally horses graze by day and are given fodder at night. Seuthes keeps them close and has them fed during the day so they can be instantly ridden away at night without their riders' having to take time to put bits in their mouths.

7.2.22a  Teres ruled the Odrysae (see n. 7.2.32b) for many years in the early to mid-fifth century and was the father of Sitalkes (ruled c. 430). Thucydides 2.29.1–3 tells us that Teres was the first king to extend Odrysian power over other Thracian tribes. The precise genealogy between him and Xenophon's Seuthes is uncertain. Odrysae/Odrysian territory: Book 7 map, AX (the *Barrington Atlas* locates them in the eastern part of their realm). See Figure 7.2.22 for a mask of Teres.

7.2.22b  Night attacks by the Thynoi: see 7.4.14–18. Thynoi territory: Map 7.2.7. In later antiquity it seems they were restricted to the most northerly part of their original domain, to which area the *Barrington Atlas* assigns them.

7.2.24a  Xenophon was in Chrysopolis at the time (7.1.5–6); but the reference to Chalcedon is not a mistake, as Chrysopolis was in the territory of Chalcedon (6.6.38). Chalcedon, Chrysopolis: Map 7.3.44.

you were asking me to cooperate in encouraging the army to cross over from Asia and promising that if I did so, you would treat me well, or so Medosades here maintained."

[25] Having said this, he asked Medosades whether this was the truth. Medosades said it was. "Medosades here approached me again when I crossed back from Parium to rejoin the army, and promised that if I brought the army to you, you would treat me as a friend and brother and, in particular, you would hand over to me the strongholds on the coast that you control."[a] [26] At this point he again asked Medosades if that had been his message. He agreed that it had been. "Well, then," said Xenophon, "explain to Seuthes what answer I gave you the first time, in Chalcedon."

[27] "You answered that the army would be crossing over to Byzantium[a] and it would not be necessary to pay either you or anyone else on account of this; and you said that after you yourself had crossed over, you were going away. And it turned out just as you had been saying."

[28] "And what message did I give you," he said, "when you came to me not far from Selymbria?"[a]

"You said that the plan was impossible, and that when you reached Perinthus[b] with the army, you would all be crossing over to Asia."

[29] "So now," said Xenophon, "here I am and here too is Phryniskos, who is one of the generals, and Polykrates, one of the captains, and outside there are delegates from the generals, for each general the person he regards as the most trustworthy—each general, that is, except Neon the Laconian.[a] [30] So if you want our dealings to be yet more reliable, have them called in too. Polykrates, you go and say to them that I order them to put down their weapons, and come in again when you yourself have put down your saber."

**7.2.31–34**
December 400?
COASTAL THRACE
Seuthes explains that he wants to recover his father's lost domain.

[31] When Seuthes heard this, he said that he would not distrust any Athenian, since, he said, he knew that they were his kinsmen[a] and he believed that they were well-disposed friends. After this exchange, and when the necessary people had come in, Xenophon first asked Seuthes for what purpose he wanted to use the army.

[32] He replied: "Maisades was my father, and his domain consisted of

7.2.25a The strongholds on the coast are named at 7.5.8.
7.2.27a Byzantium: Map 7.2.7.
7.2.28a Selymbria: Map 7.2.7.
7.2.28b Perinthus: Map 7.2.7.
7.2.29a Neon was in fact from Asine in Messenia, as stated at 5.3.4 and elsewhere. Messenia and Laconia were two different areas within the state of Lacedaemon. Xenophon may be using "Laconian" somewhat loosely, as a synonym for "Lacedaemonian," or he may be indicating that though Neon's native city was in Messenia, his family were Laconian in origin. Asine, Messenia, Lacedaemon: Map 1.2.1, BX; Laconia, BY.

7.2.31a Kinship was claimed between Athens and the Odrysian Thracian royal house founded by Teres (see n. 7.2.22a on Teres and n. 7.2.32b on the Odrysae) on the ground that the mythical Athenian king Pandion had married his daughter Prokne to Tereus, a claim Thucydides (2.29) rebuts with detailed arguments; however, as the Athenians admitted Sadokos, son of Teres' son King Sitalkes, as an honorary citizen—ostensibly in part through accepting this mythical genealogy—it was in a sense true that Seuthes had an Athenian kinsman.

the Melanditai, the Thynoi, and the Tranipsai.ᵃ So it was from the country hereabouts that my father was expelled when the affairs of the Odrysae were ailing,ᵇ and he himself died of a disease, while I was brought up as an orphan at the court of Medokos, who is now the king.ᶜ [33] Once I became a youth, I could not bear to live with my eyes fixed on someone else's table. I took to sitting on the same bench as Medokos and entreating him as a suppliant to give me however many men he could in order for me to revenge myself, to the extent I was able to, on those who had thrown us out. That way I would not have to live with my eyes fixed on his table like a dog. [34] As a result, he gave me the men and the horses that you will see when day has dawned. And now, with them at my disposal, I live by plundering my own ancestral lands. But if you were to join me, I think that with the aid of the gods I should easily recover my domain. That is what I ask of you."

[35] "So," said Xenophon, "what would you be able to give the army and the captains and the generals if we did come? State it so that these people can report back."

[36] He promised to give each soldier a Cyzicene stater,ᵃ each captain double, and each general double again, and as much land as they wanted and teams of oxen and a fortified stronghold on the coast.

[37] "If we try for this but do not succeed," said Xenophon, "owing to some degree of panic about the Lacedaemonian reaction, will you receive into the area under your control whoever wanted to escape to you?"

[38] Seuthes said, "More than that, I will take you as brothers and table companions, and you shall share in everything without exception that we can acquire. To you personally, Xenophon, I will also give my daughter,ᵃ

7.2.35–38
December 400?
COASTAL THRACE
Seuthes explains how he will reward the soldiers. He offers Xenophon his daughter and a stronghold.

7.2.32a  Xenophon's near-contemporary Theopompus wrote that the Tranipsai were a tribe of the Thynoi (F. Jacoby, *Die Fragmente der griechischen Historiker*, Theopompus, historian number 128, fragment 16). Probably he said this as part of a detailed account of the Ten Thousand, now lost except for this and other tiny fragments; see Appendix M: Other Ancient Sources on the Ten Thousand, §10. Melanditai, Tranipsai territories, possible locations: Ref. Map 3, CZ, BZ (neither is listed in the *Barrington Atlas*).
7.2.32b  The Odrysae's affairs were ailing: this was during the reign of an earlier Seuthes (Seuthes I, r. 424–c. 410). The Odrysae were the dominant Thracian tribe in the mid-fifth century and again in the early to mid-fourth century. For a discussion of the extent to which central control slipped, see Appendix F: Thrace, §3. Odrysae/Odrysian territory: Book 7 map (the *Barrington Atlas* label for them is in the eastern part of their realm).
7.2.32c  For more on the subsequent relations

between Medokos and Seuthes, see Appendix W: Brief Biographies, §§22, 30.
7.2.36a  Seuthes means a Cyzicene stater per month, as is explicit at 5.6.23. The promised pay seems to have been similar to the basic pay of a daric a month that they originally had from Cyrus at 1.3.21, perhaps slightly more. The gold daric, the standard large coin of the Persian Empire, was equivalent to 25 Attic drachmas. On the Cyzicene stater, see Appendix O: Measurements, §§12, 15, and Figure 5.6.23; on the daric, §§11, 13–14, and Figure O.13.
7.2.38a  Give Xenophon his daughter: it seems that this was a regular Thracian practice. Herodotus 6.39.2 tells of the Athenian Miltiades' marriage to a Thracian princess around 516. Demosthenes 23.129 mentions the Thracian marriages of the fourth-century mercenary commanders Charidemos and Iphikrates; the latter's marriage, in about 387, was, we learn from other sources, to a daughter of Seuthes.

and if you have a daughter of your own, I will buy her from you in accordance with Thracian custom;[b] and as a dwelling place I will give you Bisanthe,[c] which is the finest of my strongholds on the coast."

**7.3.1–6**
**December 400?**
COASTAL THRACE
Xenophon explains to the army the choice it has to make between Aristarchos and Seuthes.

[1] When they had heard all this and exchanged handshakes,[a] they rode off. Even before daybreak they had made it back to camp, and each delegate reported to whoever had sent him. [2] When day came, Aristarchos again sent for the generals and captains, but they decided to be done with going back and forth to him, and called the army together. Everyone assembled except for Neon's troops, who kept their distance, a mile or so[a] away. [3] When they had assembled, Xenophon stood up and spoke as follows:

"Men, Aristarchos here, with his triremes, is blocking us from sailing across where we want to, so that it is not safe to embark on merchant ships. This same person orders us to force our way to the Chersonese via the Sacred Mount.[a] If we get control of the mountain and reach the Chersonese, he says that he will no longer sell us into slavery, as he did in Byzantium, and no longer act deceptively, but that instead you shall receive pay and he will no longer overlook the shortage of food supplies, as he does now. [4] That's what Aristarchos is saying. On the other side, Seuthes says that if you go over to him, he will treat you well. So now consider whether you prefer to remain here and reach a resolution on this now or do so only after going back for food supplies. [5] To my mind, since we have no money to buy supplies in the market, and those around here will not let us take food supplies without money, the best course of action is to go back to the villages where the inhabitants are weaker and will let you take supplies from them; there, with food supplies in your possession, when you hear what anyone wants from you, you can choose whatever you think best. [6] Whoever of you thinks this is a good idea," he said, "raise your hands." Every one of them raised his hand. "Well, then," he said, "go away and pack up, and when the instruction is given, follow the leader."

**7.3.7–9**
**December 400?**
COASTAL THRACE
Seuthes meets the army and says he will lead them to food supplies.

[7] Afterward Xenophon began to lead them out, and they followed. Neon, and others from Aristarchos, tried to persuade them to turn back, but they would not take any notice. When they had gone on as far as three and a half miles,[a] Seuthes met them. On seeing him, Xenophon told him to

---

7.2.38b Buy Xenophon's daughter: Herodotus 5.6.1 states that the Thracians "sell their children for export abroad" and that "they purchase their wives…from the women's parents for very high prices" (Purvis/Landmark translation). Seuthes seems to envisage that both he and Xenophon will enter into polygamous child marriages, but Xenophon would not have done so: the Athenians, who were prepared to betroth their children formally at very young ages, would not actually have married them off before puberty, and they did not practice polygamy. Possibly Seuthes is simply making a diplomatic proposal that he knows will not be taken up.

7.2.38c Originally the city of Bisanthe had been a subcolony from Perinthus. It, or at least a fort in its territory, had been occupied by

the Athenian politician and general Alcibiades during part of the previous decade; see n. 7.3.19a. Perinthus, Bisanthe: Map 7.2.7.

7.3.1a For the Greeks, a handshake was not commonplace. Even when not accompanied by the further rituals that would constitute guest-friendship, it was always a significant act, sealing a done deal or marking a firm relationship. See Figure 2.3.28.

7.3.2a A mile or so/1.6 kilometers: the Greek text says 10 stades; see Appendix O: Measurements, §5.

7.3.3a The route by the Sacred Mount would have been the more difficult one. Chersonese, Sacred Mount (Hieron Mons in the *Barrington Atlas*): Map 7.2.7.

7.3.7a Three and a half miles/5.6 kilometers: the Greek text says 30 stades; see Appendix O, §5.

ride up so that he might say to him what seemed advantageous with the maximum number of people listening.[b]

[8] When Seuthes came up, Xenophon said, "We are making our way to where it is likely that the army will have provisions; once there, on hearing from you and from the Laconian's[a] people, we will choose whatever seems to be best. So if you lead us to where food supplies are most plentiful, we shall think that you are treating us like guest-friends."

[9] To this Seuthes said, "Well, I know many villages close together that are full of food supplies and just far enough away from us that you could cover the distance and still be in time for a tasty morning meal."

"Then lead on," said Xenophon.

[10] When they reached the villages[a] in the course of the afternoon, the soldiers assembled and Seuthes spoke to them as follows: "Men, I need you to campaign alongside me, and I promise to give you soldiers a Cyzicene stater[b] each, and to captains and generals the usual supplements, and I will reward the deserving over and above that. You shall have food and drink if you take it from the country, just as on this occasion. Whatever may be captured, I shall expect to keep in my own hands so that, by disposing of it, I can provide your agreed pay. [11] We Thracians will be capable of pursuing and flushing out fugitives and runaways, but if anyone makes a stand, we will try to get the better of them with your assistance."

[12] Xenophon asked in reply, "How far from the sea would you expect the army to follow along with you?"

Seuthes answered, "No more than seven days' journey, mostly less."

[13] After these speeches, the floor was thrown open to whoever wanted to speak, and many people spoke to the same effect: that the terms Seuthes was offering matched anything they could possibly do for him. For it was now winter, and it was impossible for anyone who wished to sail away to do so. Furthermore, they could not continue to remain in friendly territory if that meant they could stay alive only by purchasing their food; and in hostile territory it was safer to spend their time and feed themselves in Seuthes' company than by themselves. With so many good points in favor of working with Seuthes, if they were to obtain pay in addition, it would seem like a lucky bonus. [14] In the light of these arguments, Xenophon said, "If anyone wants to speak against the proposal, speak now. But if not, let's have a vote on it." Since nobody did speak against it, he put it to the vote, and it was so resolved; and he at once said to Seuthes that they would campaign along with him.

7.3.10–14
December 400?
COASTAL THRACE
*Villages with supplies (74)*
The army enthusiastically votes to accept Seuthes' proposals.

7.3.7b  It is not clear from the Greek whether it is Xenophon or Seuthes who is to say what seems advantageous. Scholars disagree both about this and about the envisaged content of the message. Whatever the precise meaning, it feels as if this conversation is for public consumption and does not necessarily correspond to the private understanding between Xenophon and Seuthes. (Translator's note)

7.3.8a  By "the Laconian," Xenophon presumably means Aristarchos rather than Neon

and, if so, to refer to such a high-status Spartan as if he were some ordinary inhabitant of Laconia seems like an insult, prompted by Aristarchos' recent behavior. For more on the relevant status distinctions, see Appendix B: Xenophon and Sparta, §§18–19.

7.3.10a  Villages with supplies, probable location: Map 7.3.44, *Halting place 74.*

7.3.10b  As at 7.2.36, one Cyzicene stater is meant to be a monthly wage and not just a one-off payment.

7.3.15–20
December 400?
COASTAL THRACE
The officers go to
Seuthes' quarters for the
evening meal, and Hera-
kleides, his right-hand
man, encourages the
guests to give Seuthes
presents.

[15] After this the others took up quarters according to their respective units, while Seuthes invited the generals and captains for the evening meal, as he was occupying a village nearby. [16] As they were at the entrance waiting to go in for the meal, there stood a certain Herakleides from Maroneia.[a] This fellow came up to each of the guests who he thought had something to give to Seuthes. First he approached some Parians, who were there to negotiate friendly relations with Medokos, the king of the Odrysae,[b] and were bringing gifts for him and his wife; to them he went on about how Medokos was inland, twelve days' journey from the sea,[c] whereas Seuthes, having obtained the services of the army, would be ruler of the coastland. [17] "And as he is your neighbor, he will be the one most capable of doing you good or harm. So if you are prudent, it is to him that you will give what you are bringing. That is a better way of sorting out your affairs than if you make gifts to Medokos, who lives so far away." This, then, was the line he took to persuade the Parians. [18] Next it was the turn of Timasion the Dardanian to be approached, since Herakleides had heard he had goblets and barbarian carpets, and his story to him was that it was customary, whenever Seuthes invited people to dine with him, for the guests to give him presents.[a] "And if he becomes a great figure in these parts, he will have the resources both to restore you to your home and to make you rich here." Such were the ways in which he courted the guests on Seuthes' behalf, going up to one after another.

[19] When he came to Xenophon, the line was this: "You come from the greatest city and your name is greatest in Seuthes' eyes, and perhaps you will be expecting to receive forts in this country, such as others of your people also received,[a] and land too. Then it is appropriate for you to show your esteem for Seuthes in the most magnificent way. [20] I am giving you this advice because I am well-disposed toward you, for I know well that the

7.3.16a For a discussion of what reaction we are intended to have to Herakleides' conduct, see Appendix F: Thrace, §9. Maroneia: Map 5.3.7, AY (the *Barrington Atlas* gives the location to which it later moved).
7.3.16b Parium: Map 7.2.7, Book 7 map. Odrysae/Odrysian territory: Book 7 map.
7.3.16c Court of Medokos, possible location: Book 7 map. This tentative proposal would place Medokos' court in the vicinity of the late fourth-century Odrysian capital Seuthopolis. Seuthopolis was built later on a new site by a later king, Seuthes III, but it may give a clue to what the Odrysae regarded as their heartland. To judge from the journey times given by Thucydides at 2.97.1–2, where he discusses the extent of the Odrysian empire in 429/8, the district in which Seuthopolis later stood was around nine days' travel on foot from where Seuthes is based at this point. But if twelve days were literally correct, that would place Medokos' court in the extreme north-

western corner of Odrysae territory, near Mt. Skombros (Ref. Map 3, BX); so it is almost certain that Herakleides was exaggerating.
7.3.18a Customary to give presents: quite likely this is true, as Thucydides, who had property and influence in Thrace, notes at 2.97.4 that the Thracian custom regarding royal gifts was diametrically opposed to the Persian. Dardanos: Map 7.8.7, AX.
7.3.19a "Such as others . . . received": probably Herakleides is referring especially to Alcibiades, a key figure in Athenian politics in the second half of the Peloponnesian War, who acquired various forts in Thrace, including Bisanthe and New Fort (the former mentioned at 7.2.38, both at 7.5.8; see n. 7.5.8a). Alcibiades retired to a Thracian fort in 406–405 when in exile from Athens but had died in 404/3. Note too that Miltiades, the victor of the battle of Marathon in 490, owned a hereditary principality in the Chersonese.

greater the gifts you give to Seuthes, the more good things you will receive back from him." On hearing this, Xenophon was at a loss, for he had crossed over from Parium with nothing except a slave boy and enough money for the journey.

[21] The most powerful of the Thracians present, the generals and captains of the Greeks, and any embassy that was present from a Greek city all went inside for the evening meal. They found their seating for the meal arranged in a circle, and then three-legged tables were brought in for all of them; there were as many as twenty of these, laden with portions of meat and great loaves of leavened bread that had been skewered onto the meats.[a] [22] Moreover, the tables in front of the guests were continually set with more food, for such was the custom. Seuthes led the way in what one was supposed to do. He picked up the loaves of bread laid out near him, tore them into small pieces, and threw them around to chosen people as he saw fit, and similarly with the meat, leaving just a taste for himself. [23] Then the others by whom the tables were laid out set about acting in the same way.[a] One particular Arcadian, Arystas by name, a ferocious eater, would have nothing to do with throwing the food around, and, taking into his hands a loaf as large as three quarts[b] and adding meat to it, he proceeded to eat his meal on his lap. [24] They were carrying drinking horns of wine around, and everyone received one; but when the wine pourer arrived at Arystas' side carrying the drinking horn, Arystas said, looking at Xenophon, who was no longer eating, "Give it to him over there, for he is already past the serious business and I am not finished with it yet." [25] When Seuthes heard Arystas' voice, he asked the wine pourer what he was saying, and the wine pourer, who understood Greek, told him. At this, not surprisingly, there was laughter.

[26] When the drinking was already in full flow, a Thracian man came in with a white horse, and, taking a full drinking horn, he said, "I drink to you, Seuthes, and make you a present of this horse. Mounted on him, you will capture whomever you may want to when you pursue, and when you retreat, you will definitely have no fear of the enemy." [27] Another person brought in a slave boy and made a present of him in the same way, with a toast to Seuthes, and yet another brought clothes for Seuthes' wife. Then Timasion drank to Seuthes' health and made him a present of a silver bowl

7.3.21–25
December 400?
COASTAL THRACE
Seuthes presides
over a feast.

7.3.26–28
December 400?
COASTAL THRACE
Presents are given
to Seuthes.

---

7.3.21a  See Figure 7.3.21, a banquet scene from the fourth-century Thracian tomb of Kazanlak.

7.3.23a  Seuthes' personal distribution of food showed his audience who was highest in his favor and so had a political function. But in Appendix F: Thrace, §10, Zosia Archibald warns against inferring that the customs of the court of the Odrysian high king would have been as boisterous.

7.3.23b  Three quarts/3 liters: the Greek text refers to the loaf as a *trichoinikon* (a three-*choinix* loaf); on the *choinix*, see

Appendix O: Measurements, §20. It was normal for the ancients to use measures of capacity, like quarts and liters, in many cases where we would use measures of weight. One *choinix* of wheatmeal could be thought of as a daily ration. It would expand during the process of turning it into bread, but ancient bread-making processes did not involve the dough rising nearly as much as today. A three-*choinix* loaf of bread was a very large amount to eat at a sitting. Arcadia: Map 1.2.1, AX.

FIGURE 7.3.21. LATE
FOURTH-CENTURY WALL
PAINTING FROM THE
KAZANLAK TOMB IN
THRACE DEPICTING A MEAL
EATEN FROM A THREE-
LEGGED TABLE (TRIPOD).
THIS FEAST IS A MODEL OF
DECORUM, UNLIKE THE
ONE DESCRIBED BY
XENOPHON.

7.3.29–33
December 400?
COASTAL THRACE
Xenophon, slightly
drunk, announces that his
gift is the assistance of the
Greek army.

and a carpet worth ten minas.[a] [28] A certain Gnesippos, an Athenian, stood up and said it was an old and very honorable custom that the haves should make gifts to the king to honor him while the king gave to the have-nots. The effect of that would be, he said, that "I too might then be in a position to make presents to you and to honor you."[a]

[29] Xenophon was at a loss as to what to do, especially since, as a mark of honor, he happened to be seated in the chair closest to Seuthes. Herakleides was telling the wine pourer to hand Xenophon the drinking horn when Xenophon, already somewhat drunk, took the horn, stood up boldly, and said, [30] "My gift, Seuthes, is myself and these companions of mine here, to be faithful friends to you; and none of them are unwilling, but all want to be friends with you even more than I do. [31] And here they are now, not asking you for anything further but freely offering themselves to labor on your behalf and to go ahead in danger. With their assistance, if the gods so will it, you shall obtain a great deal of land, some of it your ancestral domain recovered once more and some of it new land now acquired by you; and you shall also acquire many horses, and many men and beautiful women, whom there will be no need for you to carry off as plunder but who will come forward of their own accord, bearing gifts to you." [32] Seuthes

7.3.27a  Ten minas: see Appendix O: Measurements, §§10–11. Thus, Timasion's carpet was said to be worth around forty Cyzicene staters, over three years' pay for an ordinary soldier and ten months' pay for a general. One wonders how Xenophon thought he knew this was the value.

7.3.28a  All gift-giving customs over time involve reciprocity somehow, though this may be in terms of intangible rewards for the donor, like prestige. In Thrace, apparently (7.3.18), gifts to the prince customarily preceded corresponding anticipated benefits from him, for example from the booty of a future campaign. Gnesippos is suggesting that in the case of poor men like him, the prince must give first. Perhaps he is hoping that the traditional Thracian order of things will be set aside, but more likely he is making a joke in the hope that he will get a little something for his wit.

stood up, drank with Xenophon out of the horn, and poured the dregs down over him.[a]

After all this people came in blowing on horns—such as they use for giving signals—and on wind instruments made of raw oxhide, trumpeting tunes with split octave notes.[b] [33] At this, Seuthes himself stood up, raised a loud war cry, and leapt from his place very nimbly, as if avoiding a missile. Then clowns came in.

[34] As the sun was on the verge of setting, the Greeks stood up and said that it was time to post night guards and give out the password. They told Seuthes to give instructions that none of the Thracians were to enter the Greek camps at night, "since," they said, "our enemies are just 'Thracians' to us, as are you, our friends."[a]

[35] As they were going out, Seuthes[a] stood up at the same time and did not seem drunk at all. He came out too, called the generals over, and said, "Men, our enemies do not yet know of our alliance. So let's attack them before they take precautions against being captured or make preparations to defend themselves. Then we should be extremely likely to seize both people and possessions." [36] The generals all approved of this idea and told him to act as their leader. He said, "Make your preparations and wait. At the right moment, I myself will come to you, and, having picked up my peltasts as well as you, I will take the lead with the horses."

[37] At this point Xenophon said, "Well, then, if we are to make our way by night, consider whether the Greek custom is not superior. During the day the section that leads the army in its journeys is whichever may seem appropriate on each occasion, depending on the terrain, whether it be the hoplites, the peltasts, or the cavalry. But at night it is a Greek custom for the slowest to lead, [38] for in this way armies are least strung out and the sections are least likely to fail to notice if they stray in different directions. Often troops that are strung out fall foul of each other and in their ignorance do each other harm."

[39] Seuthes in reply said, "What you say is right, and I will follow your custom. I will also give you as guides those from our oldest troops who have the most experience of this part of the country, while I myself follow behind with the horses. I will quickly make my appearance at the front if it is necessary." They gave out "Athena" as the password, in recognition of their kinship,[a] and after this conversation retired to rest.

7.3.34–39
December 400?
COASTAL THRACE
At sundown the banquet ends, and Seuthes and the Greek generals agree to make a surprise attack on the Thynoi.

FIGURE 7.3.37. THRACIAN FOURTH-CENTURY BRONZE HELMET FOUND NEAR SHIPKA, BULGARIA.

7.3.32a According to Byzantine dictionaries citing this passage, it was a Thracian custom to pour out the last dregs of the wine over the clothes of one's drinking companion. Xenophon's contemporary Plato also alludes to it (*Laws* 1 637e).

7.3.32b Wind instrument: probably a type of bagpipes, with different drones set to play an octave apart. This effect was called *magadin*, and there were other ancient instruments, called *magadeis*, that played notes an octave apart, one a twenty-stringed harp and another a kind of pipe.

7.3.34a Seuthes and his men came from one Thracian tribe, the Odrysae, while the enemy were from another, the Thynoi, so they could have made the distinction even at night. But the Greeks are saying that, to them, all Thracians are the same.

7.3.35a On Seuthes, see Appendix W: Brief Biographies, §30.

7.3.39a For this mythical relationship between Odrysae and Athenians, see n. 7.2.31a.

7.3.40–43
December 400?
INTERIOR THRACE
The two armies make a
successful night march to
the mountains.

[40] When it was about the middle of the night, Seuthes turned up with the cavalry, wearing breastplates, and the peltasts, fully armed. And after he had handed over the guides, the hoplites led the way, the peltasts followed, and the cavalry guarded the rear.[a] [41] When day came, Seuthes galloped up to the front and praised the Greek custom, for, he said, it had often happened to him when making his way by night, even with only a few troops, that he and the cavalry had been separated from the infantry. But on this occasion, day revealed them to be all together, as they should be. "Now you stay here and rest; I shall come back when I have looked around a bit." [42] With these words he rode on, taking a byway through hill country. When he reached a large expanse of snow, he looked around to see whether there were any tracks of people leading either onward or in the opposite direction. When he had seen that the route had not been used, he came swiftly back again and reported: [43] "Men, there will be a fine outcome, God willing, for when we attack, we shall catch the people unawares. But now I will take the lead with the horses so that if we should see anyone, he shall not make his escape and signal our presence to the enemy. You follow, and if you get left behind, follow the track of the horses. When we have crossed over the mountains, we shall come to many prosperous villages."[a]

7.3.44–45
December 400?
INTERIOR THRACE–
THYNIAN PLAIN
*Heights above plain (75)*
Seuthes reconnoiters the
Thynian plain from the
heights above it.

[44] When midday came, Seuthes was already on top of the heights,[a] and after looking down on the villages, he came riding back to the hoplites and reported: "I will immediately send down the cavalry to cover the plain at a gallop and the peltasts to run and attack the villages. As for you, follow as quickly as you possibly can, so that if anyone stands his ground, you can repay him in full for it."

[45] When Xenophon heard this, he dismounted from his horse. At this Seuthes asked him, "Why are you dismounting when we must hurry?" "I know," Xenophon said, "that you don't want just me alone. The hoplites will run more quickly, and willingly, if I too am on foot when I lead them."

7.3.46–48
December 400?
THYNIAN PLAIN VILLAGES
With Greek help, Seuthes
captures control of the
plain.

[46] After this exchange Seuthes set off, and Timasion set off alongside him with roughly forty Greek cavalry. Xenophon passed the word to the more mobile troops, those up to thirty years old, to go forward from their companies. He himself dashed along with these, while Kleanor[a] led the rest. [47] After they had reached the villages, Seuthes rode up with about thirty cavalrymen and said, "This has turned out, Xenophon, just as you were saying.[a] The people are under our control. But my cavalry have gone on unsupported, one pursuing here and another there, and I am afraid that

7.3.40a　See Figure 7.4.4 (left) for a Thracian peltast.
7.3.43a　They were going to cross a ridge west of the Thynian plain: Map 7.3.44 (though this location is disputed and it is not listed in the *Barrington Atlas*).
7.3.44a　Heights above plain, the probable location for Seuthes' reconnaissance over the plain: Map 7.3.44, *Halting place 75;* see Figure 7.3.44.
7.3.46a　On Kleanor, see Appendix W: Brief Biographies, §19.
7.3.47a　"Just as you were saying": Xenophon has not in fact reported himself as saying anything that exactly fits the situation, but perhaps this refers to his remarks at 7.3.37–38 about cavalry losing touch with the infantry at night if the cavalry takes the lead.

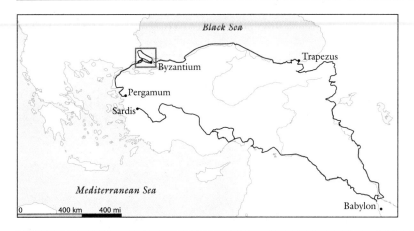

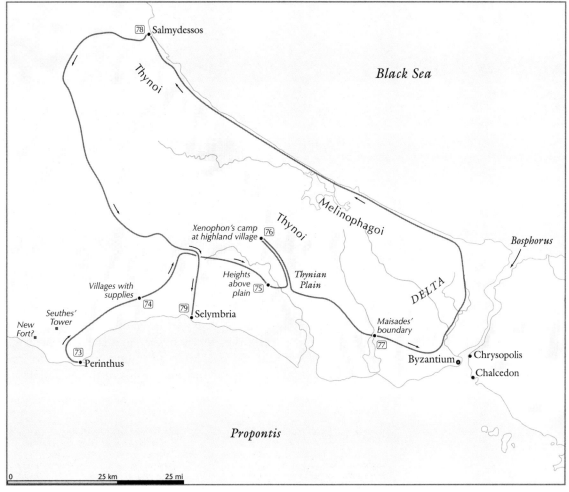

MAP 7.3.44. XENOPHON'S CAMPAIGNS IN THRACE: FROM PERINTHUS TO SELYMBRIA, *HALTING PLACES 73–79*.

FIGURE 7.3.44. THE THYNIAN PLAIN AS SEEN IN SUMMER FROM THE HILLS FROM WHICH SEUTHES AND THE GREEKS LOOKED DOWN ON IT WHEN COVERED IN SNOW.

the enemy will make a stand together somewhere and do us some harm. And some of us must also be left in the villages, as they are full of people."

[48] "Well, then," said Xenophon, "I will occupy the heights[a] with the troops I have here; you tell Kleanor to extend the phalanx[b] through the plain beyond the villages."

When they did so, about a thousand slaves were taken, two thousand cattle, and ten thousand sheep and goats. Then they bivouacked there for the time being.

[1] On the next day, Seuthes burned the villages down completely and left no house standing, in order to instill fear in the other tribesmen about what would happen to them if they did not obey him, and then he came away again. [2] He also sent Herakleides to Perinthus[a] to dispose of the booty so that there might be pay for the army, while in the meantime he

7.4.1–6
December 400?
THYNIAN PLAIN VILLAGES
Amid extreme cold, Seuthes occupies the plain and then attacks the Thynoi again.

7.3.48a  There were heights on three sides of this plain, and it is not clear which ones Xenophon means here. It would be odd for the Thynoi to flee to the heights to the southwest, from which the army has just descended, and Kleanor was closer to these heights than Xenophon was, so guarding them should have been assigned to him. The heights mentioned at 7.4.2, which were still accessible to the inhabitants, were probably to the northwest (see n. 7.4.11b). So the heights mentioned here are probably those across the plain to the north and east, which would explain why the advance party under Xenophon is likely to occupy them.
7.3.48b  Phalanx: a body of troops drawn up across a broad front in close formation; for more, see Appendix H: Infantry and Cavalry in *Anabasis*, §§13–15.
7.4.2a  Perinthus: Map 7.3.44.

FIGURE 7.4.4. TWO THRACIANS WEARING CHARACTERISTIC HIGH LEATHER BOOTS AND LONG PATTERNED CLOAKS CALLED *ZEIRAI*, AS DEPICTED ON FIFTH-CENTURY GREEK BOWLS. THE PELTAST (LEFT) CARRIES A LIGHT CRESCENT-SHAPED SHIELD OR *PELTĒ*. THE FIGURE ON THE RIGHT WEARS THE *ALŌPEKIS*, A POINTED FOXSKIN HAT.

and the Greeks set up camps throughout the Thynian plain. The inhabitants abandoned the plain, fleeing to the mountains. [3] There was deep snow, and it was cold, to such an extent that the water being carried in for the evening meal would freeze, as would the wine in its containers, and many of the Greeks found that their noses and ears were rotting off with frostbite. [4] Then it became clear why the Thracians wear foxskin caps on their heads and over their ears, and tunics not only around the chest but also around the thighs, and why when on horseback they have *zeirai*[a] down to the feet rather than short cloaks. [5] Seuthes sent some of the captives away to the mountains with the message that unless the people there came down to settle and obeyed him thereafter, he would burn down their villages too and their grain, and they would perish from hunger. As a result, women and children and older males did come down; the younger males continued to bivouac in the villages under the brow of the mountain. [6] When Seuthes observed this, he told Xenophon to take the youngest of the hoplites and follow him. They rose during the night and at daybreak arrived at these

7.4.4a    The *zeira* was a robe fastened around the loins and and extending below the knee, often (as with the ones mentioned here) as      far as the feet. Herodotus (7.69) gives the same name to an Arabian garment. See Figure 7.4.4.

villages. Most of the inhabitants made their escape, for the mountain was close by; those Seuthes captured, he speared mercilessly.

[7] In Xenophon's detachment was one Episthenes of Olynthos,[a] who had a passion for boys. He saw a handsome boy, just in the first flush of adolescence and carrying a *peltē*,[b] who was on the point of being killed, and he ran up and entreated Xenophon to go to the boy's aid. [8] Xenophon went to Seuthes and asked him not to kill the boy, explaining Episthenes' proclivities and that he had in the past recruited an entire company using as the sole criterion whether those in question were handsome; Xenophon added that with these troops he proved himself a good man.

[9] Seuthes asked him, "Episthenes, would you even be willing to die on behalf of this boy?"

Raising his chin, he stretched out his neck and said, "Strike, if the boy so bids you and he is going to feel gratitude toward me!"

[10] Seuthes then asked the boy whether he should strike Episthenes rather than him. The boy would not consent to that but begged and prayed him to put neither of them to death.

Thereupon Episthenes put his arms around the boy and said, "The hour has come, Seuthes, for you to fight it out with me to the end over this boy—for I will not give him up." [11] Seuthes laughed and let the matter go.[a]

Seuthes decided to stay there temporarily so that those on the mountain should not draw supplies from these villages. He himself went down a bit lower and set up quarters in the plain, while Xenophon with his picked troops did so in the highest village under the mountain, and the other Greeks settled down in quarters nearby among the Thracian highlanders, as they are called.[b]

[12] After this not many days had passed when the Thracians from the mountain came down to Seuthes to make arrangements for a truce and for hostages. Xenophon too came and spoke at length to Seuthes, his concern being that their quarters were in useless locations and the enemy were close by. He said it would be more agreeable to bivouac outside in secure places rather than stay with a roof over their heads at risk of their lives. Seuthes reassured him, telling him to have no fear; and he showed him the hostages they had taken from the enemy. [13] Some of those who were coming down from the mountain also asked Xenophon himself to help them obtain the truce. He agreed to do so, telling them to have no fear, for he gave his word that they would not suffer harm in any way if they obeyed

7.4.7a  Episthenes of Olynthos: although Amphipolis and Olynthos (Map 5.3.7, AX) were close together in northern Greece, this Episthenes is probably different from the Episthenes of Amphipolis who commanded the peltasts at the battle of Cunaxa (1.10.7), as he is introduced in a way that implies we have not met him before.

7.4.7b  *Peltē*: the light crescent-shaped shield typically carried by peltasts; see Appendix H: Infantry and Cavalry in *Anabasis*, §4. See also Figure 7.4.4 (left).

7.4.11a  This incident (7.4.7–11) is discussed in Appendix K: The Noncombatant Contingent of the Army, §16.

7.4.11b  On Map 7.3.44, *Halting place 76* represents our suggested location for Xenophon's camp. This is in an extensive highland area in the hills to the northwest of the Thynian plain, and it would be natural for the inhabitants of the plain to retreat there so as to link up with their fellow tribesmen farther north.

Seuthes. But in reality they were saying all this only as a cover for spying.

[14] That was what happened during the day, but that night the Thynoi emerged from the mountains and mounted an attack on them. The master of each house acted as a guide to it, for it was difficult to find the houses within the villages in any other way because of the darkness, and moreover they were fenced all around with great stakes in order to keep in the animals. [15] When they arrived at the doors of any given house, some of them proceeded to throw javelins into the house and others to strike out with cudgels, which people said they had in order to knock lance heads off spear shafts; yet others set the houses on fire, calling on Xenophon by name and telling him to come out and be killed or else, they said, he would be burned alive then and there. [16] Already the fire could be seen coming through the thatch, and Xenophon's companions inside the house had put on their body armor and equipped themselves with shields and sabers and helmets, when Silanos of Makistos,[a] who was about eighteen years old, blew a signal on the trumpet. At this they immediately rushed out with their swords drawn, and so did the other Greeks from their quarters. [17] The Thracians fled, as indeed is their way, shifting their small shields around to their backs. Some Thracians, whose shields became entangled with the stakes as they scrambled over the palisade, were captured as they dangled there. Others were killed because they entirely mistook the ways out. The Greeks continued to pursue them out of the village, [18] but some of the Thynoi turned back in the darkness and started to throw javelins at some Greeks running past a burning house, throwing out of the darkness and toward the light. They wounded Hieronymos of Epitalion and Theogenes of Locris,[a] both captains, but nobody was killed: however, the clothes and equipment of some people were destroyed by the fires. [19] Seuthes arrived, coming to the rescue, and he had seven horsemen with him as an advance party, together with his Thracian trumpeter. From the moment Seuthes learned the news and for the whole time he was coming up to help, he had the horn sounded; so this too helped to instill fear in the enemy. On arrival, he shook their hands and said he had thought he would find many of them dead.

[20] As a result, Xenophon asked Seuthes to hand the hostages over to him, and either to make a sortie jointly with him to the mountain or, if he did not wish to participate, to let Xenophon make the foray on his own. [21] So on the following day, Seuthes handed over the hostages, men who were already rather elderly—the most powerful of the highlanders, so they said—and he too came on the sortie with his forces. Seuthes now had forces that were three times their original size, since on hearing what he was achieving,

7.4.14–19
December 400?
THYNIAN PLAIN
*Xenophon's highland
camp (76)*
The Thynoi mount a
night attack on Xenophon
and his men, but Seuthes
comes to the rescue.

7.4.20–24
December 400?
THYNIAN PLAIN
Seeing the great
combined forces of
Seuthes and Xenophon,
the Thynoi come down
from the mountain and
sue for peace.

7.4.16a  Makistos: Map 1.2.1, AX.
7.4.18a  This Hieronymos is probably the same
         person as Hieronymos of Elis, referred to
         at 3.1.34, 6.4.10, and 7.1.32. Epitalion
         was a village Sparta made independent of
         Elis around this time, probably in 400.
         The change in ethnic could well reflect
         Hieronymos' own discovery that this had

happened, perhaps when he was in
Byzantium. (Note, however, that "Epitalion" has been restored to the text by a
nineteenth-century emendation: the
manuscripts name two different places,
neither of which is otherwise known.)
Epitalion, Elis: Map 1.2.1, AX. Locris:
Map 5.3.7, BX.

troops kept coming down from the Odrysae[a] in great numbers to campaign alongside him. [22] When the Thynoi saw from their mountain the many hoplites, many peltasts, and many horsemen who had gathered, they came down and sued for peace, agreeing to do everything he said and urging him to receive their pledges. [23] Seuthes called Xenophon over and explained to him what they were saying, and he said he would not make the peace treaty if Xenophon wanted to take revenge on them for the recent attack.

[24] Xenophon said, "Well, I personally think that I have sufficient recompense as things stand if from now on they become slaves instead of a free people." However, he added that his advice to Seuthes was that the hostages he took for the future should be the people who were most capable of doing some harm, leaving the old ones at home.

So all the people in that area submitted, and [1] Seuthes and the Greeks now crossed over a ridge to the region known as the Delta to attack the Thracians above Byzantium.[a] This was beyond what had been the domain of Maisades, though it had been ruled by Teres the Odrysian.[b] [2] Herakleides was there too, with the proceeds of the booty. From this Seuthes sorted out three pairs of mules (in fact, three was the total number of these) and also teams of oxen; then he called Xenophon over and told him to take his pick and to divide the rest among the generals and captains.

[3] Xenophon said, "Well, I for my part am content to receive something later on; instead, make your gifts to these generals who followed me and to the captains."

[4] So Timasion the Dardanian received one of the pairs of mules, as did Kleanor the Orchomenian and Phryniskos the Achaean, while the teams of oxen were divided up among the captains.[a] But as for the pay, they handed out only twenty days' worth, though already a whole month had elapsed, for Herakleides maintained that the profit had been no greater than that.

[5] At this Xenophon became annoyed and said, with an oath, "You seem to me, Herakleides, not to care for Seuthes as much as you should. For if you cared for him, you would have brought the full amount of the pay with you when you came. You should have borrowed the extra money if you really were unable to raise it any other way, and even parted with your own clothes."

[6] Herakleides was annoyed at this, and afraid of being expelled from Seuthes' circle of friends; and from that day onward, he would malign Xenophon to Seuthes as much as he could. [7] The soldiers now blamed Xenophon because they did not have their pay, while Seuthes was annoyed

7.4.21a  Odrysae/Odrysian territory: Book 7 map.
7.5.1a   The Delta, previously mentioned at 7.1.33, was presumably so called because its boundaries formed a triangle, like the Greek letter delta (Δ). Delta (probable though disputed location), Byzantium: Map 7.3.44 (the Delta is not listed in the *Barrington Atlas*).
7.5.1b   Teres the Odrysian was probably not the Teres of 7.2.22 but a later local princeling by that name, contemporary with Maisades. The probable point at which the army crossed from what had been Maisades'

territory into the Delta is labeled Maisades' boundary on Map 7.3.44, *Halting place 77*.
7.5.4a   The highest quality mules could be worth ten times as much as oxen, or even more. It is not clear what, if anything, the other generals, Philesios and Xanthikles, received, or whether they had left since their last mention at 7.2.1. From 7.6.19 it would appear that some of the captains did not receive anything. Dardanos: Map 7.8.7, AX. Orchomenos, Achaea: Map 1.2.1, AX.

with him too because he insistently demanded the pay for the soldiers. [8] Up until then Seuthes had constantly mentioned that when he left for the coast, he would hand Bisanthe and Ganos and New Fort[a] over to him, but from this point on, he no longer mentioned anything about them, as Herakleides had also in his malice spoken against this idea, saying that it was not safe to hand over forts to a man with an army.

[9] As a result, Xenophon started to ask himself what course of action should be taken about campaigning still farther into the interior, but Herakleides took the other generals to see Seuthes and was urging them to say that they themselves could lead the army just as well as Xenophon. He promised them that within a few days their full pay for two months would be forthcoming, and he was urging them to carry on campaigning with Seuthes [10] when Timasion said, "Now I, for my part, would not go on a campaign without Xenophon even if there were going to be pay for five months," and Phryniskos and Kleanor expressed their agreement with Timasion. [11] Seuthes thereupon took to abusing Herakleides for not inviting Xenophon as well, and the result was that they invited him to come by himself. But Xenophon, knowing Herakleides' evil cunning and that he wanted to have an opportunity to malign him to the other generals, arrived with all the generals and the captains.

[12] When they had all been persuaded, they proceeded with the joint campaign. Keeping the Black Sea on their right and passing through the land of the so-called Millet-Eating Thracians, they went as far as Salmydessos.[a] Many of the ships sailing into the Black Sea come aground there and are wrecked, as the shallows extend over a very great expanse of sea.[b] [13] The Thracians who live thereabouts plunder the wrecks cast up in their own districts, having put up stone slabs to mark their respective territories. (People said that in the past, before they set up the markers, many of those looting the wrecks would die at each other's hands.) [14] Many couches are found there, many little boxes, and many books, also the many other things that shipowners carry in wooden chests.[a] When they had subdued these lands, Seuthes' army and the Greeks came back again.[b]

7.5.9–11
December 400?/
January 399?
THE DELTA
Another campaign farther north in Thrace is agreed upon.

7.5.12–14
December 400?/
January 399?
BLACK SEA COAST–
SALMYDESSOS
*Salmydessos (78)*
The campaign is carried out successfully. Xenophon notes the Thracian practice of plundering shipwrecks.

---

7.5.8a    Bisanthe alone was named in this connection previously, at 7.2.38. Like Bisanthe and several other Thracian strongholds, New Fort had been in the hands of the Athenian Alcibiades (see n. 7.3.19a) some years prior to this. Bisanthe, Ganos, New Fort: Map 7.2.7 (New Fort is Neon Teichos in the *Barrington Atlas*).

7.5.12a    Melinophagoi (Millet-Eating Thracians) territory, Salmydessos (*Halting place 78*): Map 7.3.44 (the Melinophagoi are not listed in the *Barrington Atlas*).

7.5.12b    The same information is given by the first-century geographer Strabo (1.3.4, 1.3.7), who attributes the phenomenon to shoals of mud brought down by the rivers; but apparently it is no longer true, though the coast is still treacherous because of the many difficult capes, and there are still

some reefs in the vicinity.

7.5.14a    A "sail locker" was found in a wreck of this period, the *Kyrenia*, excavated in 1970. It contained rings for the sails, spare parts for the rigging, bundles of iron ingots, remains of many different types of small items of food such as nuts, and a portable altar.

7.5.14b    The campaign to Salmydessos sounds like a less important campaign than the earlier one, but it is the only Thracian campaign reported in Diodorus' account of the Cyreans (14.37.2–3; in Appendix S: Selections from Diodorus) and is indeed the point at which Diodorus first mentions Xenophon. For more on the relationship between the accounts of Diodorus and Xenophon, see Appendix M: Other Ancient Sources on the Ten Thousand.

[15] And now Seuthes had an army that was more numerous than the Greek troops, for far more of the Odrysae had come down and more and more tribesmen were submitting all the time, further increasing the combined force. They were bivouacked down in the plain above Selymbria, about three and a half miles[a] from the sea. [16] No pay had yet been seen, and the soldiers were extremely angry with Xenophon, while Seuthes no longer continued on friendly terms with him; on the contrary, whenever Xenophon wanted to come and meet him, many obstacles from alleged business would now be put up.

[1] During this period, when almost two months had elapsed,[a] Charminos the Laconian and Polynikos arrived from Thibron.[b] They said that the Lacedaemonians had decided to campaign against Tissaphernes, and Thibron had sailed out to wage the war;[c] he wanted this army too and said that there would be pay for each soldier of a daric per month,[d] with double for the captains and double again for the generals.

[2] When the Lacedaemonians[a] arrived, the moment that Herakleides learned that they had come for the Greek army he said to Seuthes that something really splendid had happened. "The Lacedaemonians want the army, and you don't want it anymore. If you give up the army, you will be making yourself agreeable to the Lacedaemonians, and the soldiers will no longer demand pay; instead, they will leave the country."

[3] When he heard this, Seuthes told him to bring in the envoys; and when they said that they had come to fetch the army, he said in the course of his reply that he would give it up to them, that he wanted to be their friend and ally, and that he was inviting them to a banquet as a formal mark of his friendship. He put on the banquet in magnificent style, but he did not invite Xenophon, nor any of the other generals.

7.5.15a About 3.5 miles/5.5 kilometers: the Greek text says 30 stades; see Appendix O: Measurements, §5. Selymbria: Map 7.3.44, *Halting place 79.*

7.6.1a These two months are probably the time the Greeks spent in Selymbria since their return from Salmydessos, rather than their entire service time with Seuthes, which more likely totaled three months, though they expected to be paid only for the first two, for which they had been specifically hired.

7.6.1b Polynikos was also a Laconian (translated at 7.6.7 as "Lacedaemonian delegate" for reasons explained in the Translator's Notes, §6). For the difference between "Laconia" and "Laconian," referring to a geographical area and its inhabitants, and "Lacedaemon" and "Lacedaemonian," referring to the state that originated there and its citizens, see Appendix B: Xenophon and Sparta, §§18–19, which also explains the relationship between Lacedaemon and Sparta. On Thibron, see Appendix W: Brief Biographies, §35. Laconia: Map 1.2.1, BY.

7.6.1c On the Spartans' about-face at this point, see Appendix B: Xenophon and Sparta, §8.

The campaign was initially against Tissaphernes, now again the Persian satrap (governor) in Sardis, because his new demands on the Greek cities of Asia led them to complain to Sparta (Xenophon, *Hellenika* 3.1.2). For Tissaphernes' career before and after the events of *Anabasis*, see Appendix W, §37. The Spartans sent Thibron to protect them, and he came to Asia to campaign in 399, probably arriving at the beginning of the normal campaigning season for 399, in March (in our terms). Sardis: Map 7.3.44, locator. Lacedaemon: Map 1.2.1, BX.

7.6.1d Seuthes had promised the men a Cyzicene stater per month (7.3.10); on darics and their close relationship with Cyzicenes, see Appendix O, §§13–15. Even if, as is possible, a daric was worth slightly less in this part of the Greek world than a Cyzicene, the men would still think themselves better off with the Spartans, as they were more likely actually to receive the pay they had been promised. See Figure 5.6.3 for a Cyzicene stater and Figure O.13 for a gold daric.

7.6.2a The Lacedaemonians here are just Charminos and Polynikos.

[4] When the Lacedaemonians asked what sort of man Xenophon was, Seuthes answered that he was not so bad in other respects, but he played the soldiers' friend, and because of this he was the cause of problems for himself.

They asked him, "You mean the man curries favor with the men, as if they were equals?"[a] to which Herakleides replied, "Oh, yes, very much so."

[5] "You do not think," they said, "that he will oppose us about the troops' departure, do you?"

"Well," said Herakleides, "if you assemble the troops and promise them their pay, they will run off with you, paying little attention to him."

[6] "So how," they said, "might they be assembled for us?"

"Early tomorrow," said Herakleides, "we will bring you to them. And I know," he said, "that when they see you, they will happily run to a meeting."

In this way that day came to an end, [7] and on the following day, Seuthes and Herakleides brought the Lacedaemonian delegates to the army, and the troops assembled. The two Lacedaemonian delegates said to them, "The Lacedaemonians have decided to wage war on Tissaphernes, who wronged you, so if you come with us, you shall have your revenge and each of you shall draw a daric per month,[a] a captain double, and a general double again."

[8] The soldiers were happy to hear this, and right away one of the Arcadians[a] stood up and denounced Xenophon. Seuthes was present too, as he wished to know what was going to be done, and he stood within earshot with an interpreter, though he himself understood Greek for the most part. [9] What the Arcadian said was this: "You know, Lacedaemonians, as far as we are concerned, we would have been in your service long ago if Xenophon had not used his persuasive powers to bring us away here, to this place with its dreadful winter, through all of which we have never ceased to campaign both by day and by night. He has the fruits of our labors: Seuthes has enriched him personally but deprives us of our pay. [10] So," he said, "if I could see him stoned to death, paying the penalty for the way he has dragged us around, it seems to me that I would then have my pay and not be at all weighed down by the toils we have endured." Following him, another soldier stood up in the same vein and then another.

In response, Xenophon spoke as follows: [11] "Well! Human beings must expect anything and everything, so it seems! Otherwise, how could I now be getting the blame from you in this business, where I think I can testify, at least to my own satisfaction, that I have shown the greatest zeal on your behalf. In the first place, I turned back when I had already set off for home, not under the impression—no, by Zeus, not at all—that you were doing well but, rather, because I was hearing that you were in difficulties and I wanted to help you in any way I could. [12] And then when I

7.6.4–6
March 399
SELYMBRIA
Herakleides takes the opportunity to disparage Xenophon to the Spartans.

7.6.7
March 399
SELYMBRIA
The Spartan proposals to the army.

7.6.8–10
March 399
SELYMBRIA
An Arcadian denounces Xenophon for having kept the army out of Spartan service.

7.6.11–15
March 399
SELYMBRIA
Xenophon's defense.

---

7.6.4a   Even for Xenophon, not shy of repetition of words, the close repetition of "man" and "men" here is striking; "as if they were equals" has been added in translation to represent the point behind it. (Translator's note)

7.6.7a   A daric per month: see n. 7.6.1d.

7.6.8a   Arcadia: Map 1.2.1, AX.

arrived, and Seuthes here was sending messenger after messenger to me[a] and making me many promises if I persuaded you to go to him, I did not try to do any such thing, as you yourselves know. Instead I led you to where I thought you would cross over to Asia the most quickly, since I believed that that was best for you and I knew that it was what you wanted. [13] But when Aristarchos came with his triremes and prevented us from sailing across, as a result I called you together—which was, of course, exactly the right thing to do—to discuss what action we should take. [14] Well, then, when you heard on the one hand that Aristarchos was commanding you to make your way to the Chersonese[a] and on the other that Seuthes was seeking to persuade you to campaign with him, you all spoke in favor of going with Seuthes, and you all voted for that. So in what way, then, did I do wrong in bringing you to where you had all decided to go? [15] After that Seuthes did indeed begin to tell lies about your pay. I do not praise him for that: if I were to do so, you would justly both blame me and hate me. But on the contrary, I was previously, above all others, his particular friend, and I am now, above all others, the one who is on the worst terms with him. How, then, when I have chosen you rather than Seuthes, could I still justly get the blame from you on the very point on which I am on bad terms with him?

7.6.16–22
March 399
SELYMBRIA
Xenophon denies having received any money or other gifts from Seuthes.

[16] "But you may say that it is possible that I am being crafty and have taken for myself from Seuthes what is really yours. On that basis this much is clear: if Seuthes was really paying me anything, of course his object in making the payment would not be to lose what he gave me and still have to settle up with you some other way. No, I suppose that if he had been making me any gifts, he would have given them with the aim of giving me a relatively small amount in order to avoid giving away a larger amount to you. [17] If, then, you think that this is the situation, you can in an instant make the whole business completely pointless for us both by exacting payment from him. For it's clear that if I have had something from him, Seuthes will demand it back from me, and surely his demand will be a just one if I previously took a bribe and now I fail to carry through for him the business for which it was paid.

[18] "But on the contrary, I think I am far from having what is yours, for I swear to you by every one of the gods and goddesses that the real truth is that I have nothing of what Seuthes promised me for my personal reward. He himself is present, and as he is listening, he can bear witness as to whether I am swearing false oaths. [19] To increase your astonishment still more, I further swear that I have not received what the other generals have received— not even as much as some of the captains. [20] And why, you may ask, did I act in this way? Because, men, I thought that the more I shared his previous poverty with him, the more of a friend he would be to me whenever

7.6.12a The narrative told of only two messages (7.1.5, 7.2.10; referred to again at 7.2.24–28). In his speech, Xenophon is

perhaps expressing the facts in a more rhetorically effective way.

7.6.14a Chersonese: Map 7.8.7, AX.

he became powerful enough. Only now, when I see him flourishing, do I recognize all too clearly how his mind works. [21] Someone might indeed ask, 'Aren't you ashamed to be so stupidly deceived?' Yes, by Zeus I certainly would have been ashamed if I had been deceived by an enemy. But in the case of a friend, as here, it seems to me to be more disgraceful to deceive than to be deceived, [22] since (if it really is right to talk in terms of being on guard against friends) I know that we took every precaution not to provide him with any just cause to avoid giving us what he promised. We did not wrong him in any way, we did not mismanage his affairs at all, and we certainly did not show cowardice in any enterprise to which he summoned us.

[23] " 'But,' you may say, 'you should have received the proper pledges so that he could not have deceived you in any way if he wanted to.' In reply to this argument, then, hear me say something that I would never have said in his presence if you had not seemed to be totally lacking in feeling, or at least in gratitude, toward me. [24] Remember in what sort of difficulties you found yourselves, from which I extracted you when I brought you to Seuthes. If you approached the city of Perinthus, wasn't Aristarchos the Lacedaemonian refusing to let you in, having shut the gates?[a] You were encamped outside in the open air, it was the middle of winter,[b] and you were dependent on the market, though you saw that there were few enough things to buy and you had little enough money to buy them. Remaining in Thrace[c] was unavoidable, [25] since a blockade of triremes was stopping you from sailing across to Asia; and yet for anyone who remained there, it was also inevitable that they would be in enemy country, in a place where there were many horsemen and many peltasts on the opposing side. [26] We did have a hoplite force with which, if we had kept together as we attacked the villages, we might perhaps have been able to seize some small amount of food. But it would not have been possible for us to pursue and capture either people to enslave or herds of animals, for I found you no longer had an organized force of cavalry or peltasts among you. [27] So if, in this great necessity of yours, I had adopted Seuthes as an ally for you—even without having demanded any pay at all from him in addition, since he had what you needed, both cavalry and peltasts—would I really have seemed to you to have planned things badly on your behalf?

[28] "For, of course, as a result of your joint action with these people, you found food in greater abundance in the villages, because the Thracians were all the more forced to flee in haste, and you have had a share in a greater number of animals and slaves. [29] Also, when the cavalry was added to our number, we no longer saw any of the enemy, though previously they had been boldly following us close behind, and by means of their cavalry and

7.6.23–27
March 399
SELYMBRIA
Xenophon reminds the soldiers of the difficulties they faced before joining Seuthes.

7.6.28–32
March 399
SELYMBRIA
Xenophon points out the benefits they have gained from their association with Seuthes.

7.6.24a   We have not been told before that Aristar-chos shut the gates. Perinthus: Map 7.3.44, *Halting place 73.*
7.6.24b   They were probably near Perinthus in November and early December, rather than strictly in midwinter, so in his speech

Xenophon seems to have heightened his language for rhetorical effect. For the chronology of Book 7, see Appendix Q: The Chronology of the March, §14.
7.6.24c   Thrace: Book 7 map.

peltasts, they had altogether prevented you from spreading out in small groups and so obtaining more abundant food supplies. [30] If, then, by his assistance he has provided you with this degree of safety but has not added very much pay for achieving it, is this indeed the terrible tragedy as a result of which you think that I should surely be put to death?

[31] "And now, as things stand, how are you placed as you leave? Haven't you passed the winter with an abundance of food supplies, and with anything you received from Seuthes coming over and above that, as it is the enemy's property that you have been using up? Furthermore, in the course of your exploits, you neither had to endure the sight of the dead bodies of any men from your own ranks nor did you lose any men through their being captured alive. [32] If you have achieved something honorable against the barbarians in Asia, haven't you not only preserved that achievement but also now added further glory to those deeds, since on top of what happened before, you have overcome the Thracians in Europe against whom you campaigned? I say that though you are angry with me on account of all this, by rights you should feel gratitude to the gods for these benefits.

7.6.33–38
March 399
SELYMBRIA
Xenophon finishes his
defense with reflections
on his own situation.

[33] "Such is the state of your affairs. But now, in the name of the gods, come and consider how mine stand. When I was going home on that earlier occasion, I started on the return journey much praised by you and, through you, with a glorious reputation in the eyes of the other Greeks. And I was trusted by the Lacedaemonians; otherwise they would not have sent me back to you. [34] But now I am going away maligned by you to the Lacedaemonians and an object of hatred to Seuthes on your account, when I had been hoping that as I had done well for him with your assistance, I would be securing a place that could serve as a noble refuge not only for myself but also for my children, if I were to have any.ᵃ [35] And you, for whose sake I have in so many ways annoyed people much more powerful than myself, and on whose behalf I have even now not yet ceased to labor to do whatever good I can—you have such an opinion of me as this!

[36] "Well, then, you have me in your power here. And that isn't because you took me in open flight or caught me trying to steal away. If you do what you say, be aware that you will have put to death a man who spent many, many nights awake for your sake; who toiled alongside you and put himself in danger both when it was his duty and also beyond it; who in addition, by the grace of the gods, set up with your assistance many, many trophiesᵃ over the barbarians; and who contended against you, in every way I could, to prevent your making yourselves enemies to any of the Greeks. [37]

---

7.6.34a  Xenophon had two sons, Diodoros and
          Gryllos (killed fighting heroically for
          Athens and Sparta against the Thebans at
          the battle of Mantineia in 362). They were
          nicknamed the Dioskouroi, referring to the
          mythical twins Kastor and Polydeukes, so
          probably they were twins. We do not know
          when they were born. It's possible they
          were conceived before he left Athens, but

it's just as likely that they were born after
his return to Greece in 394.

7.6.36a  A trophy was a memorial set up by the
          victors of a battle, usually consisting of a
          post on which armor from the vanquished
          was hung; for more, see the Glossary. For
          instances of battlefield trophies Xenophon
          records, see 4.6.27 and 6.5.32.

Indeed, as a result, it is now possible for you to make your way wherever you choose to go by land and by sea without blame from anyone. And now, when your situation appears entirely free from difficulties and you are sailing to the very place where you have long wished to be; when those with the greatest power stand in need of you, pay is in prospect, and leaders who are reputed to be the best have come here[a]—does now really seem to you to be the time to put me to such a death as soon as possible? [38] It was certainly not like this when, during our time of difficulties, you used to call me father—you people who have the most excellent memories!—and promised to remember me forever as a benefactor. But these people here who have now come to fetch you are not stupid, so I don't think you are improving their opinion of you when you behave like this toward me." And with this he stopped.

[39] Then Charminos the Lacedaemonian stood up and said, "Now, by the Twin Gods,[a] men, you don't seem to me to be angry with this man with any justice at all. I myself am in a position to testify on his behalf, since when Polynikos and I asked Seuthes what sort of man Xenophon was, he did not criticize him in any other respect but said that he was too much the soldiers' friend, and that because of this it was the worse for him in relations with us Lacedaemonians and with Seuthes himself."

[40] At this point Eurylochos of Lousoi stood up and said, "It also seems to me, men of Lacedaemon,[a] that your first act as our generals should be to extract our pay for us from Seuthes, whether he is willing or no, and not to lead us away until we have it."

[41] Polykrates of Athens, prompted by Xenophon, said, "Look over there, men. I see Herakleides present here too—Herakleides, who took into his own hands the rich booty for which we worked hard and, when he had disposed of it, failed to surrender the proceeds either to Seuthes or to us. Instead he stole them, and still keeps them himself. So if we are prudent, we shall hold on to him. It's not as if he is a Thracian," he said. "No—he's a Greek who treats Greeks unjustly."

[42] When Herakleides heard this, he was extremely panic-stricken. He went up to Seuthes and said, "If *we* are prudent, we will get away from here, out of the power of these people." And they mounted their horses and went galloping away, off to their own camp. [43] From there, Seuthes sent Abrozelmes, his interpreter, to Xenophon and urged him to remain in his service with a thousand hoplites, and he promised to give him the strongholds on the coast and the other things he had previously promised. He also made out that he had a great secret to tell, and then said that he had heard from Polynikos that if Xenophon came into the hands of the Lacedaemonians,

7.6.39
March 399
SELYMBRIA
Charminos supports Xenophon.

7.6.40–44
March 399
SELYMBRIA
The Greeks turn on Seuthes and Herakleides, who gallop off hastily.

7.6.37a   Xenophon is referring here to the Spartans.
7.6.39a   The Twin Gods Kastor and Polydeukes, twin sons of Zeus and the mythological Spartan queen Leda. They were also known as the Dioskouroi and were partic-

ularly important in Spartan cult. Leda was the mother of Helen, whose beauty caused the Trojan War.
7.6.40a   Lousoi, Lacedaemon: Map 1.2.1, AX, BX.

he would certainly be put to death by Thibron. [44] Many others also sent such messages to Xenophon, to the effect that he had been maligned and needed to be on his guard. Hearing all this, he took two sacrificial victims and set about offering sacrifice to Zeus the King to inquire whether it would be better and more fitting to remain at Seuthes' side on the basis that Seuthes was proposing, or to leave with the army. The god directed him to leave.[a]

[1] Thereafter Seuthes moved his camp farther away, and the Greeks took up new quarters in villages, with the intention of collecting plentiful rations from them before going back to the coast. These villages had been given by Seuthes to Medosades. [2] So when Medosades saw the Greeks using up what was in the villages, he was angry, and, taking with him about thirty cavalry and an Odrysian[a] man who was one of the most powerful of those who had come down from the interior, he came to the Greek camp and called Xenophon out from the army. Xenophon took some of the captains and other supporters of his and went to meet Medosades. [3] Medosades then said, "Xenophon, you people are behaving unjustly in pillaging our villages. So we give you advance warning, I on behalf of Seuthes and this man here, who has come from Medokos,[a] the king of the interior, to go away from our land. If you don't, we will not give in to you; instead, if you damage our land, we will defend ourselves as we would against enemies."

[4] When Xenophon heard this, he said, "Well, now, when you say such things, it is difficult to endure giving any answer to you. However, for the sake of this youth here,[a] I will speak out, in order that he may know what sort of people you are and what sort we are. [5] In our case," he said, "before we became your friends, we made our way through this land wherever we wished, pillaging if we wanted to, burning if we wanted to, [6] and whenever you yourself came to us on an embassy, you bivouacked among us without fear of any of the enemy. But you never used to come here into this country in numbers, or if you did ever come here, you bivouacked as one does in land belonging to stronger forces, with your horses ready bridled. [7] Then you became our friends and are in possession of this land because of us, together with the aid of the gods, yet now you are driving us out of this same land! We were holding it through our own strength when you received it from us, for, as you yourself know, certainly the enemy were insufficient to drive us out. [8] And yet so far are you from thinking it right to present any gifts to us before you send us away, or to provide us with benefits in return for the

---

**7.7.1–3**
March 399
VILLAGES NEAR SELYMBRIA
Medosades, accompanied by an Odrysian noble, gives Xenophon an ultimatum.

**7.7.4–10**
March 399
COASTAL THRACE
Xenophon makes a robust response.

7.6.44a Although skilled seers professed to be able to read complex messages from entrails, the procedure usually led to simple yes/no answers. Xenophon here takes two sacrificial victims because he had two questions to ask, as Michael Flower explains in Appendix G: Divinity and Divining, §12. We are not told which question he asked first or whether he needed to sacrifice both victims. See

Figures 2.1.9 and 6.5.2.
7.7.2a Odrysae/Odrysian territory: Book 7 map.
7.7.3a On Medokos, see Appendix W: Brief Biographies, §22.
7.7.4a "This youth here" must refer to the very powerful Odrysian from the interior (7.7.2), but it is odd that he was not said to be rather young when first mentioned.

benefits you have received, that even as we make our way out of the area, you try as best you can to stop us from bivouacking here at all under shelter for even a short time. [9] In speaking like this, you show no shame, either before the gods or before this man, who can see that you are rich now but that before you became friends with us, you made your living from brigandage, as you yourself used to say.

[10] "But in any case," he said, "why do you direct your remarks to me? It is no longer I who am in charge here but the Lacedaemonians, to whom you handed over the army to lead away. Nor did you invite me to be present, you most extraordinary people, so that, just as I incurred their hatred when I led the army to you, I might now get their thanks for giving it back."

[11] When the Odrysian heard this speech, he said, "When I hear these things, Medosades, I for my part sink down into the earth from shame. If I had known earlier, I would certainly not have accompanied you, and now I am going away. King Medokos would not praise me at all if I drove out our benefactors." [12] With these words he mounted his horse and rode away, and with him the other horsemen except for four or five.

Medosades continued to be upset by the fact that his land was being pillaged, and he told Xenophon to summon the two Lacedaemonians. [13] So Xenophon, taking the most useful people with him, went over to Charminos and Polynikos and said that Medosades was summoning them in order to state publicly what he had just said to Xenophon: that they were to leave his land. [14] "So I think," Xenophon said, "that you would receive the pay that is owed to the army if you were to declare that the army had asked you to assist in extracting it from Seuthes whether he was willing or unwilling, and that the soldiers say that if they succeeded in this, they would eagerly follow you. And you might add that they seem to you to be saying what is right, and that you promised to depart when, and only when, the soldiers have what they are rightly owed."

[15] When the Lacedaemonian delegates heard this, they replied that they would indeed say that and would add whatever else of great weight they could, and they immediately began to make their way over, together with all the important people. When they arrived, Charminos said, "If you have something to say to us, Medosades, or for that matter if you do not, we have something to say to you." [16] Medosades replied, very submissively indeed, "Well, what I say," he said, "and Seuthes says the same, is that we think that these villagers who have become our friends should not suffer harm at your hands. The harm you do to them, by the same token you do to us, for they belong to us."

[17] "Well, then, we would go away as you wish," the Lacedaemonian delegates said, "if and when those whose actions have achieved your present position for you[a] receive their pay. But if they don't receive it, we are even

7.7.11–12
March 399
COASTAL THRACE
The Odrysian nobleman rides off in shame.

7.7.13–14
March 399
COASTAL THRACE
Xenophon relays to the Spartans Medosades' demand to see them and advises them as to how to reply.

7.7.15–19
March 399
COASTAL THRACE
The Spartans speak robustly to Medosades, who responds submissively.

7.7.17a Xenophon makes the Spartans refer to the Greek mercenaries in a rather roundabout way, especially given the Spartan simplicity of speech; perhaps this is intended to sound more menacing.

now coming to help them, and to take revenge on men who wronged them, contrary to their oaths. And indeed if you too are people of that sort, we will begin here and now to exact what justice requires."

[18] Xenophon added, "Medosades, you might want to turn the decision over to these people in whose land we are—since you say that they are friends of yours—for them to vote whether it is appropriate for us to leave their land or for you to do so."[a] [19] Medosades declined this proposal. Instead he strongly pressed the two Lacedaemonian delegates to go themselves to Seuthes about the pay, and said he thought Seuthes would listen. But if they wouldn't go themselves, he told them to send Xenophon along with him, and promised his own cooperation. He asked them not to burn the villages.

[20] Consequently they sent Xenophon and, along with him, those who seemed likely to be the most useful. When Xenophon arrived, he said to Seuthes, "I am not here, Seuthes, in order to lay claim to anything. Instead I want to teach you, if I can, [21] that you were unjustly annoyed with me because I kept asking you, on behalf of the soldiers, for what you had previously been promising them so readily. I did so because I thought that it was quite as advantageous to you to give it to them as it was to them to receive it.

[22] "First, then, I know that, with the aid of the gods, these troops raised you to an eminent position, since they made you king of extensive lands and many people; and so it is impossible for you to escape notice, either when you do something noble or when you do something disgraceful. [23] It seems to me that for a man in your position, it is important to avoid being thought to have dismissed without thanks men who have been your benefactors. It is likewise important to be spoken well of by six thousand people.[a] And it is most important not to render yourself at all untrustworthy in what you say. [24] For I observe that the words of the untrustworthy are empty, powerless, and devoid of prestige, failing to achieve their goal; whereas in the case of those who evidently make a practice of truthfulness, their words—when they ask for something—are able to obtain just as much as others can by force. If they want to bring certain individuals to their senses, I know that threats from such people have just as sobering an effect as actual punishment at the hands of others. If men of this sort promise something to anyone, they accomplish just as much as others do by paying cash down.

[25] "Recall for yourself what you had paid us in advance when you took us as allies: nothing, as you know. But because you had won our trust in the truth of what you said, you induced all these people to go campaigning with you and to acquire for you a realm worth not just the thirty talents that they

---

**7.7.20–27**
**March 399**
COASTAL THRACE
Xenophon goes to Seuthes and points out the effects on his reputation of paying or not paying the Greeks as he promised.

7.7.18a Xenophon implies that, as far as the local inhabitants are concerned, Medosades and Seuthes are considered not friends but unwanted interlopers.

7.7.23a There were probably not that many Greek soldiers at this point. A figure of 5,300 is posited in Appendix I: The Size and Makeup of the Ten Thousand, §13.

think they should now be receiving[a] but many times that amount. [26] So, then, in the first place, hasn't this ability of yours to attract trust, by means of which you acquired your kingdom, been in effect sold by you for this sum of money? [27] Come, now, recall how you then thought it would be a great thing to gain the domain that you subjected and now have in your possession. I for my part know full well that you would have prayed to have the outcome that has been achieved for you rather than to come across many times the amount of money you are withholding.

[28] "To my way of thinking, it seems more damaging and more disgraceful to fail to hold on to this territory now than it would have been then to fail to acquire it, in just the same way as it is more irksome to become poor after being rich than not to become rich in the first place, and in the same way as it is more grievous to have to appear in public as a private individual after being a king than not to have become a king in the first place. [29] Well, then, you know for a start that those who have now become your subjects have been persuaded to accept your rule not through any friendship for you but through necessity, and that they would try to become free again if fear of some sort were not restraining them. [30] So suppose they were to see the soldiers so well-disposed toward you that they would continue to stay here if you told them to, or alternatively would come back quickly should there be a need for that, and suppose they also saw that, whenever you wanted them, more soldiers would quickly stand by you as a result of hearing many good things said about you by these troops. Don't you think that that would make your subjects more afraid and more prudent where you are concerned than if they suspected that, because of distrust resulting from what has now happened, no more troops would come to you, and that these soldiers would actually be better disposed toward them than toward you?

[31] "But in truth they submitted to you not because they fell short of us in numbers but because of their lack of leaders. Consequently there is now this additional danger: that they take as their leaders some of those who think they are being treated unjustly by you, or people still stronger than those—the Lacedaemonians. And that might indeed happen if the soldiers promise that they will campaign with the Lacedaemonians more enthusiastically should the Lacedaemonians now exact these dues from you, and the Lacedaemonians grant this to the soldiers through their need for the army. [32] It is quite clear that in reality the Thracians who are now subjected to you would much more enthusiastically make attacks on you than alongside you. For while you win, their lot is slavery; but if you are defeated, it will be freedom.

7.7.28–34
March 399
COASTAL THRACE
Xenophon mentions further disadvantages that will come to Seuthes from not paying the soldiers.

7.7.25a  Thirty talents was a very large sum of money; see Appendix O: Measurements, §§10–11. For further implications of this figure for the number of troops at this point, see Appendix I: The Size and Makeup of the Ten Thousand, §13.

[33] "Don't you think that you should already be planning ahead for the land, as being your own property? If so, then which do you suppose would leave it free from evils to a greater extent: if these soldiers received what they claim they are owed and so departed, leaving a state of peace here, or if the soldiers were to remain here as if in hostile territory and you were to try to assemble a force in opposition to them, larger than theirs and also in need of food supplies? [34] Would more money be lost if these troops were given what was owed to them than if the debt remained outstanding and it were necessary for you to pay other troops, stronger than these?

7.7.35–42
March 399
COASTAL THRACE
Xenophon contrasts Herakleides' penny-pinching advice to Seuthes with the candid friendship Xenophon himself had offered.

[35] "But be that as it may, to Herakleides—as he used to make clear to me—this money seemed a very large sum. In reality, it is a much smaller matter now for you to obtain this amount and pay it over than it was for you to obtain and pay over an amount one-tenth the size during the time before we joined you. [36] For it is not the absolute number that determines what is large and what is small but the resources of the person who is giving and receiving, and your annual revenue now will be greater than all the assets put together that you previously owned.

[37] "That, Seuthes, was how for my part I used to think ahead for you, as being my friend, so that you should seem worthy of the benefits the gods had given you and I might not lose standing with the army. [38] For be well aware that at present I should not be able to use this army to harm one of my enemies if I wished to, nor should I be in a position to come to your aid if I once again wanted to do so, such is the army's attitude toward me. [39] And yet I make you yourself my witness, along with the gods (who know the truth), that I do not have anything that came from you for the soldiers, that I never asked for what was really theirs to be diverted to me personally, and that though you made me promises, I did not demand their fulfillment. [40] I swear to you that if you had tried to give me something, I would not have taken it, unless the soldiers too were going to receive what was theirs at the same time. How disgraceful it would have been to set my own affairs straight while overlooking the fact that theirs were in a bad way, especially in view of the honor in which I was held by them!

[41] "And yet to Herakleides, by contrast, everything seems to be rubbish compared to obtaining money by every possible means. However, Seuthes, I think there is no finer and more resplendent thing for a man, and especially for a ruler, than to have personal merit and justice and nobility. [42] He who has these is rich, in that he has many friends, and also rich in there being others who want to become his friends. If he does well, he has people who will share his triumph; if he were to slip up in some respect, he would not lack people to come to his aid.

[43] "But be that as it may, if you did not learn from my deeds that I was a friend to you from the bottom of my heart, and you cannot gather it from my words, all the same you should surely consider the words of the soldiers, for you were present and heard what was said by those who wished to find fault with me. [44] They denounced me to the Lacedaemonians for setting a higher value on you than I did on the Lacedaemonians, and they charged me for their own part with taking more care to see your business prosper than theirs. And they said that I had presents from you. [45] And yet do you think that they would accuse me of having these alleged gifts from you if they had seen me display any animosity against you? On the contrary, they made their accusations because they had observed my enthusiasm toward you!

[46] "I suppose all human beings think it necessary to display goodwill to the person from whom they receive gifts. In your case, before any service was done for you, you gave me a pleasant welcome, in your looks, your tone of voice, and your tokens of friendship; and whatever it might be, you did not stint in promising it to me. And now, after you have achieved what you wanted and you have become as great a figure as I could make you, can you now endure to overlook the fact that I am dishonored among the soldiers? [47] But in truth I trust that time will teach you to decide to hand over the money, and indeed that you yourself will not bear to see those who freely did you good make accusations against you. So I ask you, when you do hand the money over, to exert yourself to restore me to the same standing that I held in the eyes of the soldiers as I did when you took me up."

[48] When Seuthes heard this speech, he cursed the individual who was the cause of his not having handed over the pay long before, and everyone suspected that he meant Herakleides. "For it was never my intention," he said, "to deprive you of it, and I will hand it over."

[49] At this Xenophon spoke again: "So since you intend to hand it over, I now ask you to hand it over through me, and not to overlook the fact that because of you my position with the army is now quite different from what it was when we came to you."

[50] Seuthes said, "No, you will not be less honored among the soldiers because of me, and if you remain at my side with just a thousand hoplites, I will hand over to you the strongholds and the other things that I promised."

[51] In reply Xenophon said, "That things could happen like that is impossible. Just send us away."

"And yet," said Seuthes, "I know that it would at any rate be safer for you to remain with me than to go away."

[52] "Well," Xenophon replied, "I applaud your concern, but it is not possible for me to remain. Still, please think that it would also be to your own benefit if I were held in greater honor."

7.7.43–47
March 399
COASTAL THRACE
Xenophon reminds Seuthes of the hostility the soldiers have shown him because of his friendship with Seuthes and asks him to take action to restore his position.

7.7.48–54
March 399
COASTAL THRACE
Seuthes undertakes to hand over what he can and offers Xenophon a safe refuge.

[53] At that Seuthes said, "I have only a small amount of money to hand, and that I give to you: one talent.[a] Also six hundred oxen, four thousand sheep and goats, and about 120 slaves. Take these; also add the hostages who came from those who wronged you,[b] and go on your way."

[54] Xenophon laughed and said, "So if these do not cover the pay, whose talent am I to say I have? Since it is a positive source of danger for me, on leaving you, would I not be well-advised to take precautions against being stoned? You heard the threats."

Just for the time being, he remained there. [55] But on the following day, Seuthes handed over to them what he had promised and, along with it, sent people to act as cattle drivers. Up until then the soldiers had been saying that Xenophon had gone off to live with Seuthes and receive what had been promised to him, but when they saw him coming, they were pleased and ran out to meet him.

[56] When Xenophon saw Charminos and Polynikos, he said, "These too[a] have been kept safe for the army because of you, and I hand them over to you. When you have disposed of them, distribute the proceeds to the army." So they took them over, appointed booty-sellers, and set about selling them, and much blame they had as a result.

[57] Xenophon did not have anything to do with the sale but openly made preparations to go home, for no motion regarding his exile had yet been put to the vote at Athens.[a] His closest supporters in the camp came to him and asked him repeatedly not to leave until he had brought the army away and handed it over to Thibron.[b]

[1] From there they sailed over to Lampsacus, and there Xenophon was met by Eukleides, a seer from Phleious, who was the son of that Kleagoras who painted the facade in the Lyceum.[a] He congratulated Xenophon on his safe return and asked him how much gold he had. [2] Xenophon solemnly swore to him that in truth he would not have even enough money for the journey home unless he sold his horse and what he had about his own

7.7.53a  On talents, see Appendix O: Measurements, §§10–11.
7.7.53b  Xenophon was previously reported (7.4.21) as already having these hostages in his possession, but perhaps he handed them back to Seuthes at the conclusion of the treaty recorded at 7.4.24. Alternatively, Seuthes means that these hostages, who were to be returned assuming good behavior by their sponsors, may now, if he wishes, be sold into slavery without further ado.
7.7.56a  By "these too," Xenophon means the animals that Seuthes gave him. It's possible that some words have been lost here, perhaps recording that Xenophon had first handed over Seuthes' talent to the two Spartans. For scribal omissions of this kind in Xenophon's manuscripts, see the Translator's Notes, §13.
7.7.57a  For discussion of Xenophon's exile, see the Introduction, §3; this passage is discussed

at §3.2–3.3, where Shane Brennan supports those who infer from it that Xenophon was exiled not long afterward.
7.7.57b  On Thibron, see Appendix W: Brief Biographies, §35.
7.8.1a  Kleagoras is otherwise unknown, and the text is uncertain. The reference to painting the facade in the Lyceum is a modern conjecture based on a corrupt word. The Lyceum was a public gymnasium in the precinct of Apollo Lykeios in the southeast quarter of Athens; later in the fourth century the philosopher Aristotle famously gave lectures there. In the fifth and fourth centuries, it was the muster point for Athenian hoplites and cavalry. There are almost no visible remains at the site today. There is no other evidence for such paintings in the Lyceum, though it is not unlikely. Lampsacus: Map 7.8.7, AX, *Halting place 80.* Phleious: Map 1.2.1, AX.

person. Eukleides did not believe him. [3] But when the Lampsacenes sent tokens of friendship to Xenophon and he was performing a sacrifice to Apollo, he had Eukleides stand next to him, and when Eukleides saw the sacrificial signs,[a] he said that now he did believe that Xenophon had no money. "But I know," he said, "that even if there was ever about to be money for you, some impediment would appear—if nothing else, you would stand in your own way." [4] Xenophon agreed with this. Eukleides then said, "Zeus Meilichios is impeding you," and he asked if he had already sacrificed to him "in the way," he said, "in which I was accustomed to offer sacrifice at home with you and your family, sacrificing an entire animal as a burnt offering."[a] Xenophon said that he had not offered sacrifice to this god in the whole time since he went abroad. So Eukleides advised him to offer a sacrifice in the accustomed way and said that things would turn out for the better.

[5] On the following day, Xenophon went to Ophryneion[a] and set about his sacrifice, a burnt offering of whole piglets according to his ancestral custom, and favorable omens were obtained. [6] And on that very day, Biton and Naukleidas[a] arrived to give money to the army, and they entered into guest-friendship with Xenophon. They had bought back the horse he had disposed of at Lampsacus for fifty darics,[b] for they suspected that he had sold it because of his straitened circumstances, since they had heard that he was fond of the horse; and they gave it back to him and would not allow him to reimburse the price.

[7] From there they set about making their way through the Troad, and when they had crossed over Mount Ida, they first came to Antandros, and then, making their way along the coast, to the Plain of Thebe.[a] [8] From there they traveled by way of Adramyttium and Kertonion past Atarneus, and on reaching the Caicus plain, they occupied Pergamum in

*7.8.5–6*
*March 399*
THE TROAD
*Ophryneion (81)*
Xenophon makes the suggested sacrifice, and his affairs immediately improve.

*7.8.7–11*
*March 399*
THE TROAD–AEOLIS–MYSIA
*Antandros (82)–*
*Pergamum (87)*
Hellas entertains Xenophon and suggests making the Persian nobleman Asidates the target of a kidnapping.

7.8.3a  For the signs visible to seers in the entrails of sacrificed animals, see Appendix G: Divinity and Divining, §§2–5, 8–13, 15; see also Figure 2.1.9. This is an unusual case, because the sacrifice was not "offered" for the sake of obtaining divinatory guidance (note that Eukleides is not said explicitly to be acting as a seer at the sacrifice, as is usual with Xenophontic seers) but "performed" for some other reason, perhaps as a thanksgiving sacrifice.

7.8.4a  Zeus Meilichios (Zeus the Gentle) was an avatar of Zeus who appeared in the form of a serpent and was regarded as the bestower of riches. At about this time of year, late March, the Athenians sacrificed to him at the Diasia, a festival to propitiate the dead; Eukleides' reference to the sacrifice he used to offer with Xenophon's family could well refer to this festival, when different Athenian localities made idiosyncratic offerings, according to Thucydides 1.126.6 as now understood (the Crawley/Landmark translation of this passage reflects an older understanding).

7.8.5a  Xenophon probably delayed making the

prescribed sacrifice until he reached Ophryneion because it was a sacrifice to Zeus Meilichios to propitiate the dead that the army had slain, and the tomb of the Trojan hero Hector was said to be there. Ophryneion: Map 7.8.7, AX, *Halting place 81*.

7.8.6a  From the fact that Xenophon gives no further details on introducing Biton and Naukleidas, not even the usual indication of their city or country of origin, these two representatives of Thibron would seem to be very well-known people of the period; for possible identifications, see Appendix W: Brief Biographies, §25.

7.8.6b  Presumably Xenophon sold the horse between meeting Eukleides and leaving Lampsacus for Ophryneion. Fifty darics (see Appendix O: Measurements, §§13–14) is an extremely good price for a horse, though not beyond the evidence for very high quality horses.

7.8.7a  The following locations appear on Map 7.8.7, BX: Troad, Mt. Ida, Antandros (*Halting place 82*), Plain of Thebe (*Halting place 83;* Thebes Pedion in the *Barrington Atlas*).

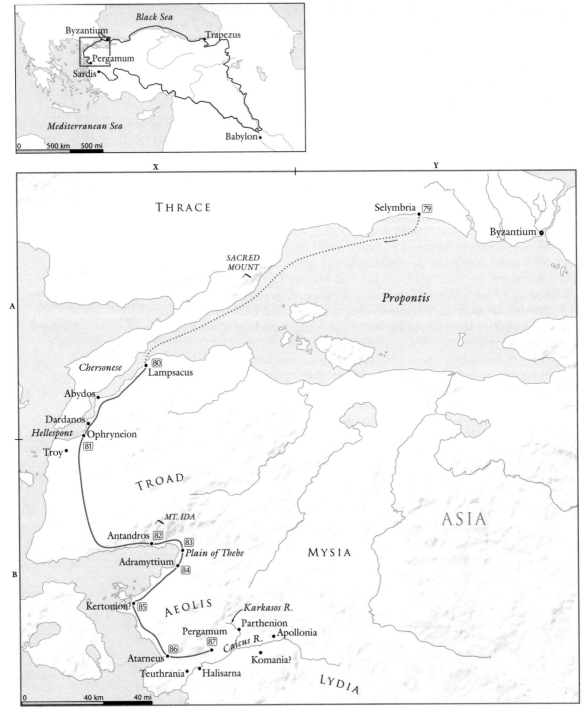

MAP 7.8.7. THRACE, THE TROAD, AND MYSIA: FROM SELYMBRIA TO PERGAMUM, *HALTING PLACES 79–87.*

Mysia.[a] There Xenophon was warmly received at the house of Hellas, the wife of Gongylos the Eretrian and mother of Gorgion and Gongylos;[b] [9] she pointed out to him that Asidates, a Persian man, lived in the plain, and she said that if Xenophon went by night with three hundred men, he would capture him, and not only him but his wife and children and store of wealth—and there was a lot of it. She sent her cousin and Daphnagoras, whom she was accustomed to rate very highly, to guide Xenophon there. [10] So with these two alongside him, Xenophon set about offering a sacrifice; and Basias the Eleian,[a] who was there acting as seer, said that the sacred signs were very favorable toward him and the man should be easy to capture. [11] After Xenophon had dined, he set out on his way, taking with him the captains who were his closest associates and those soldiers who had proved themselves reliable throughout, in order to do them a good turn. About six hundred other people forced themselves on him and tried to come along too, but the captains drove them off, thinking it was easy money and not wanting to have to divide their own share.

[12] They arrived about midnight. The slaves who lived in the region of the tower ran away from them, as for the most part did the livestock that Asidates owned, but they paid no attention to them in their effort to catch Asidates himself and his family. [13] When they proved unable to take the tower by direct assault (for it was high and large and was defended by battlements and many warlike men), they tried to tunnel through the ramparts. [14] The mud-brick wall was eight bricks thick, but they completed the tunnel just as the day broke. As soon as the sunlight shone through it, someone from inside struck a blow with an ox spit right through the thigh of the nearest Greek, and thereafter they fired arrows out through the hole, ensuring that it was no longer safe to approach that way. [15] What with their shouts and lighting of beacons, Itabelis[a] with his own personal force came out to help them, as did Assyrian hoplites and Hyrcanian cavalry from Komania, about eighty of them, these being in the King's pay, and in addition about eight hundred peltasts; and also some troops from Parthenion and others, including cavalry, from Apollonia and the nearby strongholds.[b]

7.8.12–19
March 399
NEAR PERGAMUM
Initially the kidnapping of Asidates fails because of the intervention of Itabelis.

7.8.8a   The following locations appear on Map 7.8.7: Adramyttium (*Halting place 84*), Kertonion (possible location, *Halting place 85*), Atarneus (*Halting place 86*), Caicus River, BX; Pergamum (*Halting place 87*), BX and locator; Mysia, BY (Kertonion is listed as Kytonion?/ Kertonos? in the *Barrington Atlas* and is placed farther inland on its maps than the route the army takes here would imply).

7.8.8b   For how this family (referred to as the Gongylids) came to be Persian landowners and for their continuing self-identification as Greeks, see Appendix W: Brief Biographies, §16. Eretria: Map 1.2.1, AY.

7.8.10a   Elis: Map 1.2.1, AX.

7.8.15a   Itabelis was evidently a non-Greek grandee living in the area; see Sekunda 1998. His name, suggesting a Babylonian origin, implies he had been posted here by the

central government. There is some evidence that, probably a little later than this, he was appointed satrap of Mysia.

7.8.15b   As Assyria and Hyrcania are far from western Anatolia, these troops presumably represent detachments on a long-term posting from their home areas, or possibly military colonists whose ancestors originally came from there. Komania would be the place in the Caicus valley where they are now based, but its precise location is not at all clear to us. For all these Persian forces, see Appendix C: The Persian Empire, §22; Appendix D: The Persian Army, §§6, 18–19. Assyria: Book 3 map. Hyrcania: Ref. Map 9, BY. Komania (possible location), Parthenion (probable location), Apollonia: Map 7.8.7, BX (Komania is not listed in the *Barrington Atlas*).

[16] Then of course it was time to consider how they were going to make their retreat. They seized as many cattle and sheep as were there and began to drive them off, and slaves as well, having first put them all inside a hollow rectangle.[a] They did this not because they still had their minds on the booty but in order to prevent the retreat turning into outright flight. That could have happened if they had left the booty there and made off, as this would have made the enemy bolder and disheartened the soldiers; but as it was, they were withdrawing as if they would make a fight of it for the sake of the booty. [17] When Gongylos saw how few were the Greeks and how many those attacking them, he came out himself, despite his mother's objections, with his personal force, wishing to share in the good work; and Prokles, the descendant of Damaratos, also brought help from Halisarna and Teuthrania.[a] [18] By now Xenophon's troops were very hard-pressed by the arrows and slingstones, and they were making their way forward in a circular formation, so that their shields might provide protection against the arrows; with difficulty they crossed the river Karkasos,[a] about half of them wounded. [19] There too Agasias the Stymphalian[a] captain was wounded, all the time continuing to fight against the enemy. But they came through safely, with about two hundred slaves, and sheep enough for sacrificial victims.

[20] On the following day, Xenophon offered sacrifice, and then, during the night, he marched out with all the army in order to go as far into Lydia[a] as possible; the idea was that people would then be off their guard, instead of being afraid because they knew the Greeks were close. [21] But Asidates had heard that Xenophon had again offered a sacrifice to inquire about attacking him and that he was coming with the whole army, and he moved out temporarily to some villages that lie below the township of Parthenion. [22] Xenophon's troops fell in with him there by pure chance and captured him and his wife and children, his horses, and all his possessions, and thus the earlier sacred signs were fulfilled. [23] Then they went back to Pergamum. There Xenophon saluted the god, since the Laconians and the captains and the other generals and the soldiers joined together in arranging for him to have his pick of the horses and teams of oxen and the rest of the booty, with the result that there was enough for him now to do someone else a good turn as well.

[24] After this Thibron made his appearance and took over the army; and having combined it with the rest of the Greek forces, he made war against Tissaphernes and Pharnabazos.[a]

**7.8.20–23**
**March 399**
PERGAMUM–VILLAGES
NEAR PARTHENION–
PERGAMUM
On a second attempt, Xenophon succeeds in kidnapping Asidates and thus makes his fortune.

**7.8.24**
**March 399**
PERGAMUM
Thibron takes over the army.

7.8.16a   On the hollow rectangle, see n. 3.2.36a.
7.8.17a   Prokles was referred to at 2.1.3 as the ruler of Teuthrania and a supporter of Cyrus. For the origin of his name and his ultimate allegiance to Greece, see Appendix W: Brief Biographies, §28, which also contains information about Damaratos. Halisarna, Teuthrania: Map 7.8.7, BX.
7.8.18a   Karkasos River: Map 7.8.7, BX.

7.8.19a   Stymphalos: Map 1.2.1, AX.
7.8.20a   Lydia: Map 7.8.7, BX (the *Barrington Atlas* labels Lydia well to the south of where our map places it, but the text here suggests that the border between Mysia and Lydia was the Caicus River).
7.8.24a   On Tissaphernes and Pharnabazos, see Appendix W, §§37, 27.

[25] [These were the names of the rulers of the King's land through which we traveled: Artimas of Lydia, Artakamas of Phrygia, Mithradates of Lycaonia and Cappadocia, Syennesis of Cilicia, Dernes of Phoenicia and Arabia, Belesys of Syria and Assyria, Rhoparas of Babylon, Arbakas of Media, Tiribazos of the Phasianoi and Hesperites.[a] The Kardouchoi and Chalybes and Chaldaioi and Makrones and Kolchoi and Mossynoeci and Koitoi and Tibareni are independent.[b] Korylas was the ruler of Paphlagonia, Pharnabazos of Bithynia, Seuthes of the Thracians in Europe.[c]][d]

[26] [The count of the whole journey, both up to the interior and back down to the sea, is 215 days' marches, 1,150 parasangs, 34,255 stades.[a] The full time taken in the journey to the interior and back again was a year and three months.][b]

7.8.25a On Tiribazos, see Appendix W: Brief Biographies, §36. The following locations appear on Ref. Map 7: Lycaonia, Cilicia, CX; Cappadocia, Western Armenia, BY; Lydia, BW; Phrygia (meaning Greater Phrygia), Assyria, CY; Babylon, DZ; Media, CZ. Phoenicia: Ref. Map 5, DY. Arabia (in this context): Ref. Map 9, CX. Phasianoi territory: Map 4.7.1, BY (Phasioi in the *Barrington Atlas*). The Hesperites are referred to by this name only here and are not listed in the *Barrington Atlas;* perhaps they are to be identified with the western Armenians of 4.5.9–11, 4.5.24–36, who are not given a specific name there, but the matter is debatable.

7.8.25b The [Eastern] Chalybes and the Chaldaioi are probably the same people. The Koitoi are mysterious, but perhaps they are to be identified with the Mossynoeci who became allies of the Greeks, since their penchant for public sex (5.4.33) would fit with a plausible interpretation of the name in Greek. Kardouchoi territory: Map 4.4.3. [E.] Chalybes (probable location), Makrones, Kolchoi territories: Map 4.7.1, BX. Mossynoeci, Tibareni territories: Map 5.4.1 (the *Barrington Atlas* locates the [Eastern] Chalybes differently; see n. 4.3.4b).

7.8.25c Pharnabazos was satrap (governor) of Hellespontine Phrygia rather than of Bithynia, which was semi-independent. On Seuthes, see Appendix W, §30. Paphlagonia: Book 6 map. Hellespontine Phrygia, Bithynia/Bithynians, Thrace: Book 7 map.

7.8.25d Almost all editors agree that this section and the two similar lists of Greek office-holders that appear in Xenophon's later work, *Hellenika*, were added in antiquity. But that does not mean that this list or the other two are necessarily inaccurate, although the section adds some rulers' names to the narrative. Conversely, Orontas of eastern Armenia has gone missing, perhaps in transmission. The Taochoi and Skythenoi, mentioned in the narrative, are not named here. The material presumably comes from another fourth-century historian. Armenia: Map 4.4.3. Taochoi, Skythenoi territories: Map 4.7.1, BY, BX.

7.8.26a The paragraph disagrees slightly with the two previous summaries at 2.2.6 and 5.5.4 and should probably be brought into line by altering the text to "1,155 parasangs, 34,650 stades." The corrected stades figure is equivalent to about 4,000 miles/ 6,430 kilometers. The figures seem somewhat at odds with the narrative: see n. 5.5.4c. On the parasang (a Persian unit for measuring travel) and the stade, see Appendix O: Measurements, §§7–8, 5, respectively.

7.8.26b Editors generally agree that this count, together with its predecessors at 2.2.6 and 5.5.4, is not by Xenophon but was added in antiquity. Despite its position here at the end of the work, it does not cover the complete journey but only as far as Kotyora (Book 5 map, *Halting place 66*). For the aftermath of the march, see the Epilogue.

# EPILOGUE

## Shane Brennan

§1. With Cyrus and his rebellious force out of the way, the King consolidated his power and subsequently went on to enjoy a long reign (405/4 to 359/8)—the longest of any Achaemenid ruler. In spite of persistent difficulties with Egypt, which rose against him after his accession, Artaxerxes came to be the dominant figure in the eastern Mediterranean in the first half of the fourth century.[a] The King's Peace of 387/6 gave him unfettered control of the cities in western Anatolia, and with the subjection of the island of Cyprus shortly afterward, a century of Greek naval ascendancy on the seas was reined in.[b] Artaxerxes had three sons by his wife, Stateira, to whom he was said to be greatly devoted, and by one report 115 illegitimate ones by concubines.[c] He lived into his nineties.

§2. The King's mother, Parysatis, an eager supporter of Cyrus' attempt on the throne, exacted vengeance on all believed to have had a hand in her favorite son's death. A Carian who claimed he was the one who had killed Cyrus was put on the rack for ten days, had his eyes gouged out and molten brass poured into his ears until he died; Masabates, a eunuch of the King who had cut off the head and right hand of Cyrus, was flayed alive.[a] Parysatis was influential too in the later decision taken by the King to eliminate Tissaphernes, who was assassinated while taking a bath in Colossae, his severed head delivered in a bag to the court.[b] With his death she had avenged herself on the one whom she must have regarded as being the major cause of Cyrus' failure to rise to the kingship. Showing a softer side Parysatis provided provisions for Klearchos while he was in prison in Babylon following his capture by

NOTE:  Locations mentioned in the Epilogue can be found in the Reference Maps section.

Epi.1a  Egypt had been a Persian satrapy since 525.

Epi.1b  A reckonable Greek presence in the Aegean and eastern Mediterranean had been established through the success of the Delian League, founded in 478 in the wake of the Persian Wars.

Epi.1c  Artaxerxes' sons: Justin, *Epitome* 10.1.1. On Justin (second or third century C.E.), see Ancient Sources Cited in the Edition. Plutarch says the king had 360 concubines: *Life of Artaxerxes* 27.2. On Stateira, see Parysatis, §26, in Appendix W: Brief Biographies of Selected Characters in *Anabasis*.

Epi.2a  For the executions of the Carian and Masabates, see Plutarch, *Life of Artaxerxes* 14 and 17 respectively.

Epi.2b  Execution of Tissaphernes: Plutarch, *Life of Artaxerxes* 23, Diodorus 14.80.6–8.

Tissaphernes, and after the Spartan's execution in 400, in a touch that recalled Cyrus' love of gardening, she had palm trees planted on the place of his burial.[c] In later years the Greek accounts report that she came to exert great influence on Artaxerxes.

§3. Around 5,300 of the original 13,000 or so mercenaries who marched up-country with Cyrus remained at the conclusion of Xenophon's narrative in Thrace.[a] As Xenophon's own situation at that point showed—he had to sell his horse to pay for his proposed return to Athens[b]—in terms of financial gain the expedition had been generally disappointing. In spite of all their efforts to secure wages and booty over the course of the journey, few seem to have had much to their name in the end.[c] The offer of employment from Sparta to fight in Asia reported near to the end of *Anabasis* would thus have been attractive; the pay of a daric per month[d] indeed was the same as they had originally accepted from Cyrus, and there was the added bonus that they would fight against Tissaphernes, their old enemy.[e] Led by Xenophon, the group crossed back from Europe to Asia and joined Thibron and his forces in spring 399 for the campaign. The showdown with Tissaphernes did not come until 395, by which time the army was led by King Agesilaos himself. Marshaling his forces on the plain of Sardis, where most of the Ten Thousand had joined Cyrus six years before, Agesilaos inflicted a striking defeat on the Persians.[f] The Cyreans later returned to Greece with the king and fought on the Spartan side at the battle of Coronea in 394. We do not hear of them again as a separate unit.

§4. As we know from his flash-forward in *Anabasis*, the Spartans settled Xenophon on an estate near Olympia in the Peloponnese.[a] It is probable he resided there from the late 390s to 371, when he was forced to leave following the collapse of Sparta's power in the region. Diogenes in his biography reports that he made his way to Corinth and lived there, but some modern scholars think he returned to Athens, where the decree of exile against him which he mentions in *Anabasis* had by that time been withdrawn.[b] Wherever he lived, it is apparent that he was writing until the mid-350s, which is thought by many to be when he died. His extraordinary literary output was to a notable degree shaped by his early life experiences, prominent among these his time with the Ten Thousand and his contact with the philosopher Socrates. Xenophon had two sons that we know of, one of whom, Gryllos, was killed at the battle of Mantineia in 362.

Epi.2c  Klearchos' seizure by Tissaphernes: *Anabasis* 2.5.31–32. Imprisonment and execution in Babylon: Ctesias in Photius, §69 (in Appendix U: Photius' Synopsis of Ctesias' *Persika*). Cyrus and gardening: Xenophon, *Oikonomikos* 4.20–22.

Epi.3a  Appendix I: The Size and Makeup of the Ten Thousand discusses the army's changing size over the course of the expedition and retreat.

Epi.3b  Xenophon's sale of his horse: 7.8.6.

Epi.3c  Exceptions include the soothsayer Silanos, recipient of 3,000 darics from Cyrus (1.7.18), who sailed away at Heraclea on the Black Sea (6.4.13); the general Timasion, who we learn acquired valuable oriental cups, bowls, and carpets (7.3.18, 7.3.27; see 4.4.21 for their possible origin); and in the end, Xenophon himself, who benefits from a raid on a wealthy Persian in western Anatolia (7.8.9–22).

Epi.3d  Spartan offer of employment: 7.6.7. Soldiers' pay: 1.3.21.

Epi.3e  Following his treacherous capture of their generals at the Zapatas River, Tissaphernes had funneled the Greeks into the hostile mountains of eastern Anatolia, doubtless believing they would succumb to the harsh weather and fierce tribes.

Epi.3f  This success was one factor in the King's decision to eliminate Tissaphernes, mentioned in §2. On Agesilaos, see Appendix W: Brief Biographies, §2.

Epi.4a  Xenophon in the Peloponnese: 5.3.7.

Epi.4b  Xenophon mentions decree of exile: 5.3.7, 7.7.57. Xenophon goes to Corinth: Diogenes Laertius 2.53 (in Appendix V: Diogenes Laertius' *Life of Xenophon*). On the repeal of the exile decree, see n. Intro. 3.5d.

§5. The march of the Ten Thousand earned a special place in the minds of Greeks of the fourth century. The army's feat of marching into the King's heartland and returning as a unit, if a much depleted one, won them widespread admiration and offered inspiration for later expeditions to the east. Prior to the battle at Issus against the Persians in 333, Alexander the Great is said to have rallied his troops by reminding them of the achievement of Xenophon's men, who he pointed out were less in number and less complete as a fighting force, not even having cavalry for the battle in Babylonia.[a] But even before *Anabasis* itself became available the Ten Thousand were being held up as a proof of Persian weakness and Greek power. According to Plutarch, the Spartans were spurred to their campaign in Asia by the Cyreans' success,[b] while Isocrates invokes them several times in his writings in support of a panhellenic campaign against Persia. "Let me sum up the whole matter," he writes in the *Panegyrikos*, "these men did not set out to get plunder or to capture a town, but took the field against the King himself, and yet they returned in greater security than ambassadors who go to him on a friendly mission."[c]

§6. That the memory of the event endured in public consciousness beyond the fourth century and the extraordinary successes of Alexander is a testament to its being on an important level a story of human triumph in the face of great adversity. Numerous references are made to the march through antiquity, perhaps most poignantly by the Roman general Mark Antony, whose huge army suffered great losses in a retreat through eastern Anatolia following a campaign against the Parthians in 36. Seeing the suffering all around him, Antony is said to have often recalled the fortitude of the Greeks. "Many perished thus, and the Parthians would not desist, and Antony, as we are told, would often cry: 'O the Ten Thousand!' thereby expressing his admiration of Xenophon's army, which made an even longer march to the sea from Babylon, and fought with many times as many enemies, and yet came off safe."[a]

Epi.5a  Arrian, *Anabasis Alexandrou* 2.7.8–9.

Epi.5b  Plutarch, *Life of Artaxerxes* 20.1–2 (in Appendix T: Selections from Plutarch).

Epi.5c  On Isocrates (c. 436–338), see Ancient Sources Cited in the Edition. *Panegyrikos* 4.149, published around 380 (Norlin/Loeb translation).

Epi.6a  Plutarch, *Life of Antony* 45.6 (Perrin/Loeb translation). For the reception of the Ten Thousand from antiquity through to modern times, see Appendix R: The Legacy of Xenophon's *Anabasis*. Tim Rood starts his appendix with this passage.

# APPENDIX A

## *Xenophon and Socrates*

§1. At the start of Book 3 of *Anabasis*, in a rare moment of overt autobiography, Xenophon introduces himself and tells us how he came to be in the army. A family friend, Proxenos of Thebes, had written to invite him to join an expedition and had sung the praises of Cyrus the Younger—brother of the Persian King Artaxerxes II—who would lead it.[a] Xenophon was attracted by the proposition, but first he asked Socrates' advice. Socrates was concerned that working for Cyrus might make Xenophon extremely unpopular in Athens, since Cyrus' support for the Spartans had helped them defeat Athens only a few years earlier.[b] He suggested, therefore, that Xenophon go to Delphi[c] to ask the famous oracle what he should do. And Xenophon did go to Delphi—but he did not ask the question Socrates had advised him to ask. Instead he asked, as he wrote in *Anabasis*, "to which of the gods he should perform sacrifices and offer prayers in order to make the journey that he had in mind in accordance with the best and most honorable course of action, and then, his mission honorably accomplished, to reach safety again."[d]

§2. A curious story, which raises two obvious questions: Why did Xenophon consult Socrates—and why did he disobey him in part?

### Who Was Socrates?

§3. Simply put, Socrates was the most famous wise man, or sophist, in Athens at the time. When Xenophon consulted him, in 401, Socrates had been famous for at least thirty years. Athenian comedy of the time commented in a satirical fashion on contemporary public figures, and Socrates was prominent enough by the end of the 430s to have begun attracting this kind of attention, as in a fragment by the comic poet

---

A.1a  On Proxenos, Cyrus the Younger, and Artaxerxes, see Appendix W: Brief Biographies of Selected Characters in *Anabasis*, §§29, 10, 6. Thebes: Ref. Map 2, BZ.

A.1b  Athens, Sparta: Ref. Map 2, CZ, DY.

A.1c  Delphi: Ref. Map 2, BY.

A.1d  Socrates' advice to Xenophon: 3.1.4–6 (the quotation is at 3.1.6).

Callias from around this period, in which a female character, asked why she is so stuck up, says that Socrates is the cause of it.[a]

§4. Unfortunately, while this kind of thing tells us that Socrates was well enough known for playwrights to expect that jokes about him would go down well with an audience of several thousand ordinary Athenians, it does not tell us exactly what he was famous for. Nor is the situation improved even by the fact that a few years later, in March 423, Socrates featured in two of the three comedies that competed at the Athenian festival called the City Dionysia. About the second-placed play, *Connus*, by Ameipsias, we know virtually nothing. The last-placed play, however, was *Clouds*, by Aristophanes, and thanks to his subsequent great fame, it has survived complete. Matters are slightly complicated by the fact that the text we have is not the first edition. Aristophanes was annoyed at having placed third; he redrafted the play, and the text we have is this revised edition. There is little chance of knowing in much detail how it differed from the original.

§5. At any rate, we have a complete play in which Socrates features prominently, written by a fellow Athenian during Socrates' lifetime. Despite this bright promise, it is a great disappointment as a source for Socrates' life and work. Aristophanes' purpose was not to write biography but to raise laughter, and that is what he uses the figure of Socrates for. His "Socrates" is obsessed by trivial intellectual problems (such as how many flea-feet a flea can jump) and sows dangerous ideas in the minds of his students—especially ideas that would undermine orthodox moral and religious practices. He is an all-purpose figure, made to bear as many as possible of the mockable aspects of the New Thought[a] that was popular among the young men of Athens at the time. There must be elements of the portrait that are true to life if the play is satire rather than farce, but they are most likely limited to physical and personal features, such as his ugliness and his professed poverty. As far as his thought is concerned, the character Socrates resembles Diogenes of Apollonia[b] (a natural scientist on whose supposedly atheistic work Aristophanes drew for the play) or Protagoras (whose rhetorical teaching was taken to undermine morality by making it possible to argue both sides of a case without regard for right or wrong) as much as he does the historical Socrates.

§6. Corroboration of the idea that Aristophanes was just being funny comes from other plays of his in which Socrates is mentioned. In *Birds* (produced in 414), for instance, Aristophanes portrays Socrates as a necromancer, but no one has shown an inclination to believe that picture.[a] Why, then, believe the other? It would be absurd to do so just because it is painted on a larger canvas—a full play rather than a few lines.

§7. Aristophanes is the only witness to Socrates' life and thought who wrote during Socrates' lifetime. After Socrates' death (he was executed by the Athenian democracy in 399 for reasons discussed below), writing about him became a minor

A.3a   Callias 1 fragment 15, as numbered in Storey 2011.
A.5a   New Thought: a blend of proto-scientific speculation, new argumentative methods, and radical ideas about human religious, cultural,

and political institutions.
A.5b   Apollonia Pontica: Ref. Map 3, BZ.
A.6a   Socrates the necromancer: Aristophanes, *Birds* 1553ff.

industry. Many who had known him put pen to paper to try to give an impression of the man at work, interacting with others in conversation and as a wise adviser. Much of this work survives in fragments at best, but we have the complete Socratic writings of two of his students, Plato and Xenophon. What do they tell us about Socrates?

§8. This is an area of enormous scholarly controversy. Optimists hold, with considerable reasonableness, that wherever Plato and Xenophon (and any of our other more remote witnesses, especially Aristotle) agree on some point of doctrine or personality, we are entitled to find a trace of the historical Socrates. Pessimists, on the other hand, hold that such similarities are not responses to the historical Socrates but are due to intertextuality—the habit ancient authors had of shaping their texts in response to those of others. In other words, if Xenophon's Socrates is in any respects similar to Plato's Socrates, that is because Xenophon was deliberately responding to what he read in Plato; he was not, or not only, checking his memories of the historical Socrates in deciding what to write.

§9. Moreover, there are very good grounds for thinking that none of the portraits the Socratics gave are accurate, or at least that we have no way of telling: this genre of writing was fictional,[a] and in any case the accounts contradict one another, so whom do we trust? It seems that each Socratic writer had his own mission: Plato's was to establish philosophy as the one valid form of higher education, and so his Socrates is a philosophically stimulating and ruthless arguer; Xenophon's was to ground traditional morality on Socratic practice, and so his Socrates is more conventional.[b] There is common ground between these portraits, but there are also great differences.

§10. Plato's portrait of Socrates contains further puzzles. On the one hand, there is a group of dialogues (which are plausibly considered, on stylistic grounds, to have been composed early in his writing career, perhaps in the 390s and 380s) in which Socrates is very prominent but almost entirely as a questioner. Typically he confronts an individual—a self-styled expert in some walk of life or moral quality, such as courage—and, by ruthless questioning and argument (occasionally concerned more with sheer refutation than with the rules of logic), exposes inconsistencies in the other's set of beliefs. The dialogue typically ends there, without establishing, except perhaps implicitly, how we are more constructively to think about the concept being investigated. On the other hand, many of Plato's later works are also dialogues run by Socrates, but in these Socrates is not a self-confessed ignoramus who perforce can only ask questions but, rather, a man who constantly develops bold ideas—precisely the ideas that we think of as constituting Platonic philosophy.

§11. There has been a very strong tendency among scholars in recent decades to think that the portrait of Socrates in Plato's early dialogues is true to life and that

---

A.9a   Socratic dialogues fictional: Aristotle, *Poetics* 1447b, in context: he is talking about various kinds of fiction.

A.9b   We have a few substantial fragments of one other Socratic writer, Aeschines of Sphettos (Ref. Map 2, CZ), but not enough for us to be able to characterize his mission.

the Socrates of the later dialogues, who departs from purely ethical concerns and develops metaphysical and other ideas, is simply a mouthpiece for Platonism, while Xenophon's Socrates voices Xenophon's own concerns.[a] If you were to read a modern book on Socrates, the chances are very high that the portrait on offer would be the Socrates of early Plato.[b]

§12. Unfortunately there are serious problems with this view. Above all, we really have no grounds for saying that Plato's earlier portrait is true to life while the later one is not. We simply have two different portraits that just happen to have come from the pen of the same man. The very fact that they are different is relevant, because, as far as we can tell, every portrait of Socrates from every Socratic writer was different. That seems to have been the nature of the game: to put "Socrates" in various conversational contexts and imagine what, on this particular version of "Socrates," the man might have said or done. Under such circumstances, none of these portraits can be precise biographical documents.

§13. And so Xenophon's depiction of Socrates is very different from Plato's—from *either* of Plato's. Xenophon's Socrates rarely descends to pungent argument and certainly never ascends to highbrow metaphysics. His words are still generally directed at individuals but in a sternly avuncular fashion: in Xenophon, Socrates confronts his interlocutors with plain, practical advice on how to get on in public life, or how to think of friends, or how to acquire self-discipline; his general theme is how to improve oneself and become useful to society. He often punctures conceits, as early Plato's Socrates does, but far more gently and constructively; Xenophon's Socrates tends to deliver homilies rather than expose contradictions.

§14. The problem—known in academic circles as the Socratic Problem—is now plain to see. The only strictly contemporary portrait of Socrates we have, that of Aristophanes, is not trustworthy, and neither are the versions from Plato and Xenophon. They were writing fiction or, at the very best, what Socrates might have said or done, and their portraits are quite different, with no way of telling which, if any of them, is to be preferred as a historical portrait. Xenophon's has no better claim than any other to be true, then, but he is at least consistent with himself. In *Memorabilia* (*Recollections of Socrates*) he portrays Socrates as a wise adviser, and that is exactly how he appears in *Anabasis* too: as a man to whom you could turn in a crisis for advice. Xenophon would not have turned to early Plato's Socrates for advice, because the kind of analysis undertaken by early Plato's Socrates would have left him, in practical terms, no better off.

§15. There is, however, more that can be said about the Socratic Problem if we turn from literary presentations to the historical context. The most solid, historical fact about Socrates is that he was put on trial by the Athenian democracy in the spring of 399. The charge was impiety or, more precisely, not recognizing or worshipping the gods of the city but introducing new gods and corrupting the youth of

A.11a  On this view Xenophon's and the later Plato's use of "Socrates" would be an acknowledgment that although they may be going beyond their teacher, even in places contradicting him, their ideas still owe a lot to those of Socrates.

A.11b  The most forceful and foundational statement of this view is contained in Vlastos 1991.

the city (with such irreligious notions). He was condemned to death and died after drinking the poison hemlock.[a]

§16. About the trial there is again a great deal of controversy. Was Socrates guilty as charged? Do the charges disguise any hidden political agenda? To answer these questions, one must understand the charges in their original context. The charge of impiety was a tool used frequently by the Athenian democracy to get rid of undesirables, especially intellectuals, whose work could easily be made out to run contrary to traditional religious and moral practices.[a] "Impiety" in this context means little more than "un-Athenian activity."

§17. Impiety was a serious charge in ancient Athens—a potentially capital charge, as Socrates found out. Why was it taken so seriously? For us in the liberal West today, religious beliefs and practices are personal, and the state has little or no right to interfere in them. This was not the case in Classical Athens. In general, the state was involved in many matters that nowadays would fall within the sacrosanct zone of one's private life. It was a matter of concern to the Athenian state, for instance, that citizens should produce citizen children and that these children should be brought up to contribute to the success of Athens. In particular, the prosperity of Athens (as of any community) was held to depend on the benevolence of the gods, and the citizen body earned that benevolence not just by participating properly in public festivals but by performing private prayers and acts of worship too. To accuse someone of impiety, then, was to accuse him of undermining Athenian society in general; to accuse him of corrupting the youth was to accuse him of trying to see that the next generation of politicians rejected the customs and practices that had stood Athens in good stead for so long. The charge of impiety was, in the context of ancient Athenian society, a directly political charge; there was no hidden agenda.

§18. Socrates died, then, on this view, because he was held by the Athenian democracy to be *politically* undesirable. And there is further evidence that he and his circle were regarded as politically suspect. A couple of lines from Aristophanes' *Birds* again give us a starting point: "Everyone was mad about Sparta in those days: they wore their hair long, starved themselves, never washed, aped Socrates."[a] Socrates' circle intersected to a considerable extent with an upper-class, pro-Spartan element in Athenian political life. Such men were antidemocratic and occasionally even worked for the downfall of the democracy. In 415, in the hysteria following a failed oligarchic coup, a number of people from Socrates' group found it wise to take themselves off into exile. In 411–410 an oligarchy did briefly rule Athens, and more members of Socrates' circle were involved in the coup, especially the notorious Alcibiades (who had been Socrates' lover at the end of the 430s). Then the brutal Thirty, as they soon came to be called, who took power for a few months in 404–403, also included several people who were close to Socrates. It is, in fact, extremely

A.15a  This form of execution was favored by the Athenians at the time; in being self-administered, it absolved the state of bloodguilt.

A.16a  There is some evidence for Athenian prosecution of intellectuals (Anaxagoras, Protagoras) for impiety toward the end of the fifth century, and better evidence that this was the charge brought against

both Aristotle and his successor Theophrastus toward the end of the fourth century, when the issue was actually their unpopular political stance in favor of Macedonia (Ref. Map 3, CX).

A.18a  "Everyone was mad": Aristophanes, *Birds* 1281–82 (author's translation).

unlikely that Socrates was sympathetic to oligarchy (see §20), but there were certainly grounds for thinking he was.

§19. If Socrates' trial—our solid, historical fact—was politically motivated, we can return on this basis to our sources for Socrates and try to determine the historical Socrates' political position. There is, in fact, a great deal of common ground between Xenophon and Plato in the political ideas they attribute to Socrates, and it is clear that, while these ideas fall far short of any kind of political program or elaborated political philosophy, they are critical of aspects of the Athenian democracy. Plato and Xenophon attribute to Socrates, above all, the thought that governing should be left to experts, who would be professional, long-term rulers, and they therefore from time to time have him condemn the Athenian way of relying on an annual lottery to choose many officials.[a]

§20. Given the fictional nature of the Socratics' writings, we cannot be certain that these ideas were Socrates' rather than Plato's and Xenophon's, but given the political nature of the trial, it is a reasonable guess that they were. The best way to reconstruct their fragmentary remarks and put them together with the overriding ethical concerns of Socrates as portrayed in our sources is to think that Socrates wanted to see the moral regeneration of Athens under a regime of wise, Socratically trained rulers.[a] Strictly speaking, then, Socrates was neither an oligarch nor a democrat. He was a different kind of elitist: he wanted to see the best men rule, whatever their wealth or social status. These are some of the ideas Xenophon would have heard from him.

## Xenophon, Socrates, and *Anabasis*

§21. So much for Socrates' views. But what was Xenophon's relationship to him? Xenophon consulted Socrates on the expedition with Cyrus in 401, and later in his life he wrote a number of works featuring Socrates: four books of recollections of Socrates (*Memorabilia*); a book on domestic economy (*Oikonomikos*), much of which is in the form of a Socratic dialogue, with Socrates ironically playing the role of the person being instructed rather than that of the teacher; *Symposion*, showing Socrates in conversation with other guests at an upper-class Athenian party; and the short *Apologia Sokratous*, purporting to reproduce some of what Socrates said in his defense at his trial and explain why he said it. Unfortunately we have no other good evidence that might help us uncover the extent or nature of Xenophon's association with Socrates. The third-century C.E. author Diogenes Laertius wrote a "conversion story"[a] describing how Socrates first turned Xenophon's mind to philosophical inquiry, but it strikes me as a fabrication (perhaps originally by another Socratic writer) that came to be accepted as historical truth. We also hear, from Cicero,[b] that Xenophon featured in one of the Socratic dialogues written by Aeschines

A.19a  Experts should rule: Xenophon, *Memorabilia* (*Recollections of Socrates*) 3.1.4, 3.6–7, 3.9.10; Plato, *Crito* 47a–d, *Apology* 25b, *Republic* 473c–541b. Criticism of the lottery: Xenophon, *Memorabilia* 1.2.9; Aristotle, *Rhetoric* 1393b.
A.20a  As in Plato's *Republic*, which is a development of

Socratic political ideas.
A.21a  Diogenes Laertius 2.48 (in Appendix V: Diogenes Laertius' *Life of Xenophon*).
A.21b  Cicero, *On the Composition of Arguments* (*De inventione*) 1.51.

of Sphettos. But, like the conversion story, this tells us no more than that Xenophon studied with Socrates; it does not tell us anything about the intensity of the relationship.

§22. All we can say, then, is that Xenophon knew Socrates well enough to be mightily impressed by him—impressed enough to have spent a great deal of his later life writing about him and protecting his memory from slander,[a] and to have turned to him for advice in 401, rather than to those who would be the normal givers of advice in his culture, his father or some other male relative. Evidently Xenophon was a member of the Socratic circle (whatever exactly that might mean) long enough for Socrates to make a deep and lifelong impression on him.

§23. But Socrates' influence on Xenophon appears in more subtle ways too. On the face of it, it is easy to characterize Xenophon's mind-set as conservative: He constantly stressed the importance of theological orthodoxy and correct religious practice. He devoted treatises to such upper-class pursuits as hunting and horse breeding. He promoted the canonical virtues of courage, self-discipline, freedom, and fair dealing. And his distinctly unrevolutionary ideal was that people should be useful to their friends and communities.

§24. A more charitable and less superficial approach to Xenophon's work, however, reveals surprising depths beneath the apparent conservatism. He did not want people just to ape the moral behavior of their forebears; he wanted them to develop an internal state of self-discipline that would enable them to be detached from materialistic and egoistic goals. Without this, he argued, people would never be properly free, or able to do good for their friends and community.[a] The freedom that he wanted for himself and others consisted not in the traditional social freedoms of the Athenian upper classes; rather, it was an internal state of nonattachment. The stated goal of all or most ancient Greek ethical theories was happiness (*eudaimonia*); Xenophon believed that the way to achieve happiness was to have less, not more. If you reduce your desires and needs, it is easier to be happy, because you are not suffering from a compulsion to pursue illusory goals.

§25. It may seem obvious that we would all be happier if we did not want more than we could have, but it is extremely difficult to put this into practice throughout one's life. Xenophon portrays Socrates as a man who had attained this kind of enlightenment: he is someone who can consistently live with reduced desires, free from temptation, and in full control of his wants and expectations. It is no wonder that it was Xenophon's Socrates, rather than Plato's, who became the ideal sage for the later school of Stoic philosophers. That consistency, that degree of enlightenment, is what Xenophon holds out to his readers as his ideal. It forms a true Socratic layer to his work.

§26. Can we detect a Socratic flavor to *Anabasis*? In *Anabasis* Xenophon portrays

A.22a  This is the express goal of *Memorabilia* (*Recollections of Socrates*), right from its first page.

A.24a  Need for self-discipline: see, for example, Xenophon, *Memorabilia* 1.5.1, 2.6.16–28; *Oikonomikos* (*On the Management of the Household*) 1.18–23.

himself as in possession of all the standard virtues, but there is really no trace in the text of the kind of Socratic reflection on these virtues, and on how to make them stable personal qualities, that was outlined in §25; this reflection occurs more in Xenophon's explicitly Socratic works. However, given the idea that Socrates was a political idealist who wanted to see Socratically trained leaders in charge of things, we are struck by the strong emphasis on leadership in *Anabasis*.[a] By both explicit comment (as in the obituaries of 2.6) and implicit portrayals of leaders in action, Xenophon lets the reader know what qualities a good leader should have—he should be knowledgeable but flexible, god-fearing, trusted by his men, farsighted and good at planning, and so on—and sets himself up as just such an exemplar. Now, it may be tempting to think that in *Anabasis* Xenophon shows himself on a personal journey toward some kind of enlightenment, or at least toward wise leadership, but in fact no real learning curve is involved: as soon as Xenophon appears fully on the scene, at the beginning of Book 3, he has what it takes to be a good commander, as is demonstrated by his confident speeches at 3.1 and 3.2 and by their success. He springs fully formed as a leader into the narrative, like the goddess Athena born in armor from the head of Zeus.

§27. But this scene from the beginning of Book 3 is part of the Socratic episode of the book. Xenophon introduces himself, tells the Socrates story, and then immediately begins to reflect on his qualifications for leadership. Considering the whole context, then, it is plausible to suggest that he is presenting himself as someone who, as a result of time spent with Socrates, already has what it takes to be a good leader. And so for the rest of the book we see Xenophon in action as a wise commander. It is not surprising that, as a student of Socrates, he wanted to form a colony on the Black Sea, with himself as founder; he was uniquely placed to fulfill Socrates' dream of the expert as ruler.[a] This was thwarted, as so much else was on the Black Sea, by the greed and malice of some of Xenophon's colleagues, but it is equally unsurprising to find Xenophon *turning down* two further occasions when he could have become a sole ruler.[b] In both cases he does so because accepting the offer would endanger the men, and a good leader eliminates risk as much as possible.

§28. Many other passages in *Anabasis* could demonstrate Xenophon's skills as a leader; I have chosen these two because the contrast between right and wrong leadership makes the point clearly. It is not far-fetched, then, to suggest that we are supposed to see Xenophon throughout *Anabasis* as a Socratic leader in action.[a] This was no theoretical conversation initiated by Socrates in comfortable circumstances in prosperous Athens; this was real life, with all its attendant dangers, where a leader had to prove himself moment by moment as a capable commander. And I should say, finally, that if it is right to think that one of Xenophon's purposes in *Anabasis* was to portray himself between the lines as a Socratic leader, this is typical of the way he works. He does not trumpet the points he wishes to make, but often lets the reader come at them

A.26a  Leadership as a theme of *Anabasis:* see the Introduction, §8.2–5.
A.27a  Black Sea colony: 5.6.15–18. Expert as ruler: see §19. Black Sea: Ref. Map 1, AX.
A.27b  At 6.1.25 and 7.1.21.
A.28a  This would form an aspect of the defensive function of *Anabasis* (see the Introduction,

§§8.6–14): not only did Xenophon want to defend his own memory by portraying himself as an exemplary leader; he also wanted to defend the memory of Socrates (Introduction, §8.12–14) by showing that the latter could turn out responsible and effective leaders such as Xenophon.

by more oblique or subtle routes, in this case by reading a narrative of action rather than a theoretical disquisition on leadership. Xenophon learned well from Socrates.

## Why Did Xenophon Disregard Socrates' Advice?

§29. The final question facing us is this: If Xenophon saw Socrates as a wise adviser, why did he not take his advice in 401? We have so little knowledge of Xenophon's life, let alone access to his inner thoughts, that any answer to this question is bound to be speculative and circumstantial.

§30. Since Socrates was wise, we might be supposed to think that he was right—that Xenophon should not have assumed from the start that he was going to go on the expedition. Consistent with the views Xenophon attributes to Socrates elsewhere,[a] the latter wanted to leave a decision about the unknowable future to the gods. That leaves open the possibility that Xenophon might have stayed in Athens. If so, we might speculate that, accepting the gods' decision, Socrates might have put Xenophon to work toward fulfilling Socrates' ideals for Athens itself, or perhaps finding some accommodation with the restored democracy.

§31. But that did not happen: Xenophon left Athens and did not return for thirty or forty years, if at all.[a] So another line of speculation, especially plausible for those who are attracted by a reading of *Anabasis* as Xenophon's personal odyssey toward wise leadership, might be that the story is meant to underscore his immaturity before the expedition by contrast with his maturation over the course of the book.

§32. But perhaps a more plausible answer arises simply from recalling a few significant facts from what little we know of Xenophon's younger life. We know that he belonged to a wealthy Athenian family; we know that he served in the Athenian cavalry; it is very likely that he was an enforcer for the Thirty.[a] This strongly suggests that when the democracy was restored in 403, Xenophon (along with others of his class) would find himself well out of sympathy with it.

§33. However, not only was Xenophon out of sympathy with the democracy, but the democracy was also out of sympathy with him: Athens was infected by prejudice against him and his kind and against the whole Socratic circle, which was suspected of being pro-Spartan and oligarchic.[a] There are signs of a purge of Xenophon's class in Athens not long after the fall of the Thirty: a considerable number of cavalrymen were sent abroad in 399, ostensibly to serve their allies but the democracy also wanted to be rid of them, and their unpopularity lingered for a long time afterward.[b] We also hear (though the story may be unreliable) that in 399, immediately after Socrates' trial and death, Plato and other Socratics found it sensible to spend some time away from the city.[c]

§34. Xenophon came to be officially exiled from Athens sometime in the 390s.[a]

A.30a  Decisions about the uncertain future to be referred to the gods: Xenophon, *Memorabilia* (*Recollections of Socrates*) 1.1.6–9.
A.31a  On Xenophon's exile from Athens, see the Introduction, §3.2–6.
A.32a  On Xenophon's younger life and activities under the Thirty, see the Introduction, §§2.6–8, 2.15–16.
A.33a  On Xenophon's attitude toward Sparta, see Appendix B: Xenophon and Sparta.
A.33b  On the unpopularity of the cavalry, see the Introduction, §§2.16, 3.1.
A.33c  Diogenes Laertius, *Lives of Eminent Philosophers* 3.6.
A.34a  The precise date is controversial. I incline toward 394, but see the Introduction, §3.2–3.4.

The Athenians had various good grounds for this: he was pro Spartan; he had been a friend of enemies of Athens, such as Cyrus; and he was a real or suspected opponent of Athenian democracy. So the answer to the question of why Xenophon chose not to take Socrates' advice could be that already in 401 he could read the writing on the wall. He had made up his mind to go, perhaps even before consulting Socrates but certainly before consulting the oracle at Delphi, even if that meant disobeying the man he took to be his mentor.

Robin Waterfield
Lakonia, Greece

# APPENDIX B

## *Xenophon and Sparta*

§1. Xenophon's *Anabasis* raises in an acute form questions of generic placement and authorial intention, and is very hard to pin down: Is it a disguised apologetic autobiography, an authentic firsthand adventure story, a political or ethical tract, a comparative ethnography-cum-geography, or even a work of history? Undoubtedly it is some—and the sum—of all these, but whether or not it is any one of them more than the rest, the writing and publishing of *Anabasis* must have been affected by the author's peculiar and peculiarly intense relationship with Sparta and certain Spartans.[a]

§2. In 401, seeking an excuse to leave an Athens where life in a restored democracy was not at all comfortable for a formerly active oligarch, Xenophon, then quite possibly in his late twenties, had in effect exiled himself by taking employment as a mercenary in the pay of the Persian pretender to the imperial throne, Cyrus the Younger, whose cause the Spartans favored (see §5).[a] Later Xenophon was condemned formally to a long political exile, possibly because in 394 he had fought—as an officer (and former commander) of the remnant of the "Ten Thousand" mercenaries who had campaigned with Cyrus—on the side of Sparta and against his native Athens.[b] It was certainly thanks to the Spartans and in particular to King Agesilaos II (r. c. 400–360/59) that he was able to enjoy a relatively comfortable exile for twenty years or more on a Spartan-gifted estate at Skillous, not far from Olympia in the northwestern Peloponnese[c]—as he himself describes in loving detail in *Anabasis* (5.3.7–13).

§3. This privileged, special relationship with the major player in the eastern Greek world of his day was a mixed blessing for a chronicler, let alone a historian,

---

NOTE: All references to *Hellenika* in this appendix refer to Xenophon's work.

B.1a  On Xenophon's relationship with one Spartan in particular, see Strassler 2009, Appendix G: Agesilaos, also by Paul Cartledge. Sparta: Ref. Map 2, DY.

B.2a  On Cyrus the Younger, see Appendix W: Brief Biographies of Selected Characters in *Anabasis*, §10. Athens: Ref. Map 2, CZ.

B.2b  The more likely reason for the decree of exile, hinted at perhaps in 3.1.5, is that he had enlisted in the service of Cyrus, whom, since 407, the Athenians had with good reason considered a mortal enemy. (For further discussion of the date of exile and the reasons for it, see the Introduction, §3.1–3.)

B.2c  On Agesilaos, see Appendix W, §2. Skillous, Olympia, Peloponnese: Ref. Map 2, CX.

and there has been much dispute among scholars as to whether or not Xenophon can be labeled as simply—or predominantly—pro-Spartan. He certainly considered himself one of "those who wanted what was best for the Peloponnese,"[a] as he imagined the Spartans generally to have too, at least when led by his hero Agesilaos; but such was his unbending and overriding piety that he could also berate the Spartans (though not Agesilaos, whom Xenophon rather amazingly lets off the hook) for committing an egregious act of sacrilege in 382 by invading and occupying Thebes in peacetime, thereby breaking a solemn oath.[b] In *Anabasis* he does not disguise his personal indebtedness to the Spartans, but neither does he suppress or even mitigate his criticism of individual Spartans' brutality and high-handedness.

### Sparta's History and Its Place in the World in 401–399

§4. Spartans then had great opportunities and temptations to walk none too softly and not just to carry but to wield vigorously a big imperial stick. For after 404—but no longer by the time Xenophon was composing *Anabasis*—Sparta was the leading power in Aegean Greece,[a] following its victory in what is typically today called the Peloponnesian War, though it would be more aptly named the War of the Athenians and the Peloponnesians or the Atheno-Peloponnesian War. Xenophon refers back to this generation-long conflict (fought on and off between 431 and 404) several times,[b] in the last two cases in speeches that he attributes to himself—writing as ever in the third person, so that it is always "Xenophon"[c] did or said such-and-such, not "I" did or said. In one of those speeches, at 7.1.27, he enumerates Athens' naval and other economic resources (three hundred triremes on the stocks, an annual revenue of one thousand silver talents),[d] thus somewhat, but not exactly, echoing Thucydides' Pericles. He does so, however, to opposite effect, in order to emphasize the gulf between the Athenians' situation at the height of their navy-based power and the depths to which they had sunk following their defeat by Sparta: not only did they then have to face the fact of Sparta's leadership of the Greek world, but the Spartans also forced them to acknowledge Spartan hegemony over Athens itself.[e]

§5. What Xenophon does not need to say in *Anabasis*—but did need to in *Hellenika*, his history of Greece between 411 and 362, written in part to complete the truncated masterpiece of his great predecessor Thucydides[a]—is that it was largely due to Persian money, channeled by that very same Cyrus the Younger, that Sparta had eventually triumphed over Athens in the Peloponnesian War, and triumphed,

B.3a  "Those who wanted": *Hellenika* 7.4.35 (Marincola/ Landmark translation). The sentiment is repeated at 7.5.1.

B.3b  Xenophon berates Sparta: *Hellenika* 5.4.1. The oath referred to is that sworn at *Hellenika* 5.1.35. Thebes: Ref. Map 2, BZ.

B.4a  Leading power in Aegean Greece: 6.1.26–28, 6.6.9, 6.6.12–14, 7.1.26–28, 7.1.30. But no longer so: 6.6.9. See also §11. Aegean Sea: Ref. Map 2, BZ.

B.4b  References to Peloponnesian War: 3.1.5, 5.6.24, 6.1.27–28, 7.1.27.

B.4c  Here and elsewhere in this appendix, "Xenophon" (in quote marks) indicates Xenophon the character in *Anabasis*, as distinct from Xenophon the author of the narrative.

B.4d  Thucydides' Pericles: Thucydides 2.13, in particular 2.13.3. Triremes: long warships with three banks of oars; for more, see the Glossary. On talents, see Appendix O: Ancient Greek and Persian Units of Measurement, §§10–11.

B.4e  Spartan hegemony over Athens: 6.1.27, 7.1.28.

B.5a  On Thucydides, see Ancient Sources Cited in this Edition.

paradoxically for a notoriously landlubbing people, on the alien element of the sea. What he does say in *Anabasis* (3.1.5) is that Cyrus had supported Sparta in the war, but very striking are the differences between *Anabasis*' rather shy account of the relations between Cyrus and Sparta and the account at *Hellenika* 3.1.1: the latter forthrightly reveals Sparta's overt collaboration with Cyrus in his war for the Persian imperial throne against his older full brother, who had reigned since 405/4 as Artaxerxes II (the Greek form of his name).[b] *Hellenika* also uses a different name for the Spartan naval commander (one or the other name looks like a nickname), more clearly identifies him as *nauarchos* (admiral of the fleet) at that time (401),[c] and makes a more robust statement about the effect of the fleet on Syennesis (the hereditary Cilician[d] ruler and a Persian subject) than does *Anabasis*.

§6. However that may be, the Spartans supported Cyrus' bid for the Persian throne in more than one way. Klearchos,[a] a renegade Spartan commander about whom Xenophon had mixed feelings, was one of Cyrus' principal recruiting officers for the Ten Thousand. Several high-ranking figures among the mercenaries came from Sparta's home territory, including the full Spartan Cheirisophos, whose relationship with Klearchos was no less complicated than that with Xenophon himself.[b] In 401 not only did Cheirisophos offer Cyrus his support, but so too did a Lacedaemonian (Spartan) fleet.[c] Which all prompts the question: What did Sparta think it was doing in 401? Why was it risking the antagonism of the Great King of Persia, and more immediately of the King's key man in the far west, the satrap (governor) Tissaphernes?[d] A similar problem is raised—but not explicated or explained—by 7.2.8: Does the behavior of ex–admiral of the fleet Anaxibios[e] toward Xenophon here indicate foreign-policy divergences among the Spartan elite or simply personal spite? What does it say about Spartan governmental control of overseas officials?

§7. No doubt, the conduct of foreign policy at this moment was a major problem, whatever the conflicting personalities or political outlooks involved. At the same time as Sparta was attempting to maintain its imperial interests in Thrace and—through garrisons at Byzantium and Chalcedon and possibly elsewhere—around the Hellespont, it is not impossible that the city was also having to fight, literally, to maintain imperial control much nearer to home, indeed in its own Peloponnesian backyard, specifically against Elis.[a] Elis, an important member of Sparta's Peloponnesian League, was also superintendent of the symbolically vital Olympia site and the Olympic Games festival—from which, in an act of revenge, Elis had gone so far as to exclude the Spartans in 420, besides imposing a huge fine on them.[b] The Spartans' war on Elis of 402–400 (the most plausible dating, according

B.5b  On Artaxerxes, see Appendix W: Brief Biographies, §6.

B.5c  *Anabasis* appears to be ambiguous as to whether he was the supreme *nauarchos* or an admiral of just that particular contingent; on the *nauarchia*, see further §14.

B.5d  Cilicia: Ref. Map 5, CY.

B.6a  On Klearchos, see Appendix W, §20.

B.6b  Cheirisophos' command, independent of Klearchos: 1.4.3. On Cheirisophos, see Appendix W, §7.

B.6c  Lacedaemonian fleet: 1.2.21, 1.4.2. On the relationship between Lacedaemon and Sparta, see §§18–19.

B.6d  On Tissaphernes, see Appendix W, §37.

B.6e  On Anaxibios, see Appendix W, §3.

B.7a  Sparta's imperial interests in Thrace: 2.6.2, 5.1.15, 7.1.13, 7.2.2. Garrisons at Byzantium and Chalcedon: 7.1.20. Thrace, Hellespont: Ref. Map 3, CY, DY. Byzantium, Chalcedon: Ref. Map 4.1, AY. Elis: Ref. Map 2, CX.

B.7b  Peloponnesian League: a name given by modern scholars to those city-states, most of them within the Peloponnese, that swore to have the same friends and enemies as Sparta and to follow the Spartans wherever they might lead.

to some scholars), described in some detail in *Hellenika,* was designed both to exact compensation for that past slight and to overthrow an existing, antipathetic regime and—in line with Sparta's normal policy toward subordinate allies—instead impose a conveniently friendly oligarchy;[c] this successful but possibly shortsighted war of containment may have an echo at *Anabasis* 7.4.18.[d]

§8. The Anabasis Project, if we may so call it, was a resounding failure. The Greek mercenaries won their part of the battle of Cunaxa (near Babylon),[a] but Cyrus himself was killed, thereby robbing the expedition of its entire point. Woe followed upon woe as the Greeks' leading commanders, including Klearchos, were tricked by Tissaphernes and murdered on his orders, leaving the Ten Thousand temporarily leaderless. What ensued constitutes the heart of Xenophon's version, as told in *Anabasis,* until we learn at 7.6.1 that, in one of those extraordinary about-faces of Spartan foreign policy, the Spartans have decided to make war on Great King Artaxerxes, ostensibly in the cause of the freedom of the Greeks of Asia from Persian suzerainty—although it was the Spartans themselves who had sold that very liberty to Persia back in 411 in exchange for gold and eventual victory over Athens. After the recall of the ineffectual Thibron, the key role on the ground in Asia between 399 and 396 was played by the crafty Spartan Derkylidas,[b] who spearheaded the Spartan war effort as area commander in chief of forces that included the remnant of the Ten Thousand, still at this point led by Xenophon. Derkylidas' activities are described in some detail in *Hellenika* (3.1.8–3.2.20); his earlier operations in the Peloponnesian War under the satrap Pharnabazos[c] (with whom he fell out) are referred back to at *Anabasis* 5.6.24.

§9. At 5.3.6, in the chapter where Xenophon is speaking autobiographically of what he did with his share of the Ten Thousand's mercenary spoils, he reports laconically that he returned from Asia to mainland Greece "with Agesilaos" to take part in the campaign against the Boeotians.[a] That was in 394. But behind those few sparing words lies a rich and original history. In, I believe, 400, Agesilaos had obtained the Eurypontid throne of Sparta[b] only with the support of the controversial Lysander (an old ally of the Persian prince Cyrus the Younger, and the principal architect of Sparta's victory over Athens in 404) and in the teeth of fierce opposition from a supposed son of Agesilaos' older half brother Agis II. Agesilaos had since distanced himself from Lysander, and though lame from birth and already about fifty years old, he managed in 396 to persuade the authorities in Sparta[c] to appoint him successor to Derkylidas as commander in chief of the Persian campaign. Agesilaos thus became the first Spartan king ever to take the field on the continent of Asia and, moreover, the first to be put in command simultaneously of both the army and the associated naval forces.[d]

B.7c  Sparta's normal policy: Thucydides 1.19.
B.7d  See n. 7.4.18a, where David Thomas suggests that a change in the ethnic designation of one of the officers reflects the Spartans' "liberation" of his village from Eleian control.
B.8a  Battlefield of Cunaxa, Babylon: Ref. Map 6, DZ.
B.8b  So cunning was Derkylidas that he earned the nickname Sisyphus, after a mythical king of Corinth who managed to trick even the god of death in Hades. On Thibron and Derkylidas, see Appendix W: Brief Biographies, §§35, 12.

Corinth: Ref. Map 2, CY.
B.8c  On Pharnabazos, see Appendix W, §27.
B.9a  Boeotia: Ref. Map 2, BY.
B.9b  Sparta had two royal families, the Eurypontids and the Agiads; see further §13.
B.9c  Authorities in Sparta: what Xenophon in *Anabasis* calls *ta en Spartēi telē* (2.6.4) and *ta oikoi telē* (7.1.34). Exactly who these authorities were is uncertain: possibly just the ephors, or perhaps the ephors and the Gerousia (see §16) combined.
B.9d  On the Spartan kingship, see further §13.

§10. Predictably, the campaign was not a success, either by land or, especially, by sea. In 394 Agesilaos was urgently recalled to Sparta to head up the Peloponnesian and other forces required to quell a major uprising that was jeopardizing Sparta's overall hegemony of mainland Greece. The uprising was engineered by a quadruple alliance of the Boeotians (Boeotia was a federal state dominated by Thebes), the Corinthians, the Athenians, and the Argives.[a] And it was funded, not surprisingly, by Persia: if Sparta could switch its allegiance, the Persians could likewise redirect their cash at will to Sparta's enemies. The participation of Athens and Argos, both democracies, was only to be expected, but the Boeotians and the Corinthians were former Peloponnesian League allies of Sparta, oligarchically run, and their defection was critical. If Xenophon at 5.3.6 chooses to refer only to the Boeotians, that is partly because it was against them in particular that he would fight under Agesilaos, at Coronea,[b] in Boeotia; but the choice of wording also reflected Agesilaos' personal animus against the Boeotians, besides enabling Xenophon to suppress a direct mention of his own treachery in fighting against his fellow Athenians (see §2). Nor was it only members of the Quadruple Alliance who resented Sparta's hegemony or, at any rate, the mode of its operation. Among Sparta's other Peloponnesian League allies, the next most important were those in Arcadia; at 6.1.30, where a named Arcadian from Stymphalos[c] is allowed a personal voice, we get a strong hint of Arcadian animosity toward Spartan pretensions.

§11. It was noted in §4 that after 404 Sparta was the leading power in Aegean Greece, but that was no longer so by the time Xenophon was composing *Anabasis*. Scholars differ considerably over when exactly that was. One strong possibility is that it was sometime soon after Sparta's disastrous defeat at the battle of Leuktra,[a] in 371. At any rate, the fact that Xenophon's contemporaries needed to be reminded of the Spartan hegemony's past existence would suggest that it seemed by then to belong to a different world.

**Spartan Political and Military Institutions**

§12. The ancient Greeks themselves found it notoriously difficult, once they became concerned about such things, to classify the Spartan *politeia* (polity, political system).[a] One obstacle was what Thucydides frustratedly called "the secrecy of the *politeia*,"[b] but the main causes of the difficulty were the nature of the system of governance itself and the process of its evolution. Was Sparta a funny kind of democracy? After all, it was the *damos* (Spartan dialect for what is generally referred to as the *dēmos*, the "people"; that is, the assembly of full Spartiate citizens) that had the

B.10a  Corinth, Argos: Ref. Map 2, CY.
B.10b  The battle is described at *Hellenika* 4.3. Coronea: Ref. Map 2, BY.
B.10c  Arcadia, Stymphalos: Ref. Map 2, CX, CY.
B.11a  Leuktra: Ref. Map 2, CY.
B.12a  See Strassler 2009, Appendix E: Spartan Government and Society, §§13–17, for more on the Spartan political system, and Appendix F: The Spartan Army (and the Battle of Leuctra) on the Spartan army and navy. Both are by Paul Cartledge.

B.12b  Thucydides 5.68.2.

*kratos* ("power") to make decisions of peace and war. Was Sparta a funny kind of oligarchy? The members of the Gerousia, an aristocratic council of thirty elders, had tenure for life; most executive officials, such as the ephors (see §16), were elected by the people, not selected by the characteristically democratic process of the lot, and they wielded extensive but ill-defined magisterial powers unrestrained either by written law or by an administrative council with teeth. Was Sparta a kingship? There were, after all, not just one but two legally constituted kings, who both could exercise great executive power and were hedged around with a powerful, divinely authorized charisma. Or was Sparta, finally (almost a counsel of despair), a "mixed constitution," combining some element or aspect of all of these—if, that is, a genuinely mixed or balanced constitution can ever, anywhere, be a practical reality?

§13. Sparta was unique in Greece in preserving an age-old dual kingship into the Classical era—and well beyond. A kingship divided meant that each of the two kings was relatively less powerful than he would have been had he reigned alone, and the division of rule was furthered by a permanent, hereditary animosity between the two aristocratic houses that by divine right enjoyed the regal estate and wielded the royal powers.[a] But the long reign of the Eurypontid Agesilaos showed, as had that of the Agiad Kleomenes I (r. c. 520–490) before him, just how effectively powerful a king could make himself. A king's formal powers were considerably greater in wartime than in peacetime, for only a king could command a Spartan or allied army. From the late sixth century on, some restrictions on that automatic power of command were successively imposed. After 506 a Spartan or allied army could be commanded by only one king, not by both together, and from 478 onward we hear that a commanding king would be accompanied and presumably supervised by two of the city's chief executive officials, the ephors. Yet still his powers while in the field remained almost unrestricted; it was only on his return to Sparta that he might be reprimanded, indeed on occasion fined or otherwise punished for misdemeanors, and in some extreme cases deposed from office. Agesilaos managed to avoid all such recriminations, despite a number of serious failures in the field; but even he felt it politic more than once to declare himself unavailable in advance for a particular command. In *Anabasis* Xenophon refers to Agesilaos by name just the once (at 5.3.6) but does not label him "king"; this relatively light touch was heavily overcompensated for by the posthumous laudation (*Agesilaos*) he published soon after the king's death in 360/59.

§14. Naval command was another matter. Sparta did very little militarily at sea at all before 525. When a Spartan force was sent to Athens' territory by sea in 512, it was under the command of a nonroyal Spartan citizen. The first Spartan king to exercise command of a fleet was Leotychidas, in 479; but that was of a Hellenic—not just a Spartan—fleet, the enemy was Persia, not another Greek power, and the really important component of the allied naval force was the Athenian ships com-

B.13a   Hereditary animosity: Herodotus 6.53.

manded by the Athenian "general" Xanthippos, the father of Pericles. It was not until the Peloponnesian War—and more specifically its last phase, beginning in 413—that Sparta was required to go down to the sea in earnest aggression. In Classical Greek *nauarchos* could mean generically "naval commander" or "admiral," but in Spartan Greek from about 412 onward it meant specifically the holder of the office of the *nauarchia*, or something like "admiral of the fleet." The *nauarchia* was an elective office, and its holder was the most senior naval officer, able, at least in theory, to direct any other Spartan naval commanders there might be. Unwilling for this top executive office to become a springboard or launchpad for excessive power, the Spartans strictly limited tenure to one year—in practice, one summer campaigning season—and made it nonrenewable. They therefore had to get around their own law in 405 when they wanted Lysander to serve a second term, following his first, in 407, at a year's interval. They did so by creating him de jure vice admiral, although de facto it was he who took the helm and finished off the Peloponnesian War; indeed, he was still in the post the following spring and by then was operating far more politically than militarily. Moreover, as Aristotle observed, the *nauarchia*—at least as exercised by Lysander—was "almost…another kingship,"[a] which no doubt partly explains why Agesilaos in 396 was so keen to make sure that it was under his control, whether directly or indirectly (he nepotistically appointed an incompetent brother-in-law to the post).[b]

§15. Another Spartan military-political innovation of the Peloponnesian War was the office of harmost (*harmostēs*, "fixer"), an office with a specifically imperial function. The harmost system in general is referred to in a speech by "Xenophon" himself at 6.6.13; the implication is that harmosts are the chief agents of Sparta's imperial power in the western Asiatic sphere and that they wield exceptional power and influence. Precise interpretation depends on whether the sphere of harmosts' authority was defined geographically or whether, alternatively, they each had authority at large, though being based in different places. It is not possible to decide that definitely. At 7.2.13 the harmost of the key city of Byzantium, one Aristarchos, is shown as willing to exercise his power some distance from his base.[a] Relations between *nauarchos* and harmosts are seemingly thrown into an odd light by 7.2.6, where Kleandros[b] disobeys the *nauarchos* Anaxibios without apparent reprisal, and 7.2.7, where the satrap Pharnabazos intrigues with the harmost on the spot, Aristarchos, rather than waiting for the *nauarchos* Polos.

§16. The chief executive officials of the Spartan state, apart from the kings, *nauarchoi*, and harmosts, were the five annually elected ephors (overseers or superintendents). Though elected individually (by an idiosyncratic form of popular acclamation that Aristotle found "laughable"[a]), they served collectively as a board from autumn to autumn and could not be reelected. Where a collective decision of the board was required, it might be reached by majority vote, but they voted as indi-

B.14a  Aristotle, *Politics* 2 1271a41–42 (Rackham/Loeb translation).
B.14b  The *nauarchia* is referred to at 5.1.4, 6.1.16, 6.6.13, 7.1.2, 7.2.5, 7.2.7; probably also at 1.4.2, though here the translation leaves open the alternative thought that the word is being used to mean the admiral of this particular fleet rather

than the holder of the defined office.
B.15a  Particular harmosts are also mentioned at 6.2.13 (again proposing to go a long way from his base of Byzantium), 7.1.8, 7.2.5, 7.2.16.
B.15b  On Kleandros, see Appendix W: Brief Biographies, §18.
B.16a  Found "laughable": Aristotle, *Politics* 2 1270b28.

viduals when the ephorate served as an adjunct body to the standing, permanent aristocratic council of the Gerousia (twenty-eight members elected for life from the over-sixties, also by popular acclamation, together with the two kings ex officio)—for example, when acting as a supreme court in trying a king. At home their powers were, as noted, both extensive and ill-defined. But the individuals wielding them might be relatively humble or poor persons, since every Spartan citizen in good standing was eligible for the office, and some of those might have been concerned not to offend any of the permanently empowered officeholders and dignitaries. As regards foreign affairs, it was the ephors who formally declared war—on Persia in 399, for example, thereby empowering Thibron with the state's military authority. At 2.6.2–3 there is a mention of the exceptionally bellicose Spartan Klearchos' dealings with different boards of ephors both during and after the Peloponnesian War; in the latter case, not unpredictably, he found himself seriously at odds with them.

§17. One final Spartan office that deserves brief mention is that of the *laphuropōlai* (booty sellers). Xenophon does not actually refer to Spartans holding that office as such in *Anabasis*, but at 7.7.56 he relates that "Xenophon" told two Spartan officials to appoint people of that title to sell booty raised in Thrace, and in the *Lakedaimonion Politeia* (*Constitution of the Lacedaemonians*), a work he devoted specifically to the politics, society, and culture of Sparta, he mentions that officers of that title were attached to the commanding king's staff on campaign.[a] For a state such as Sparta, which refused to levy much in the way of tax on its citizens in either peace or war, all war booty and any other external sources of income were especially valuable.

## Spartan Social Structure and Customs

§18. Confusingly, ancient Greek has several terms that can, according to context, be translated "Spartan."[a] Thus Charminos is a "Laconian" (*lakōn*) at 7.6.1 but at 7.6.39 a "Lacedaemonian" (*lakedaimonios*). The former, arguably, has more of an ethnic flavor—from it comes the adjective *lakonikos*, which could be applied to custom (for example, theft; see §20) and mode of speech (whence our "laconic")—whereas *lakedaimonios* is the adjective of *Lakedaimōn*, which could refer to the Spartan state either as a political entity (as we might say "Sparta" did this or that) or as a geographical entity, the territory controlled by the Spartan *polis* (city-state), including Messenia[b] as well as Laconia. However, although *lakedaimonios* could therefore be used to mean "citizen of Sparta," as in the case of Charminos, it could also be used to refer to adult males who, though Greek and free and living within the borders of the Spartan state, were not citizens of Sparta but belonged to the status group known collectively as *perioikoi*, or "outdwellers." There were more than fifty of these communities of *perioikoi*, which counted as *poleis* but were politically subordinate to Sparta. Two individual *perioikoi* are named as such in *Anabasis:* Neon from Messenian Asine[c] at 5.3.4 and Dexippos (local origin unspecified) at 5.1.15.

B.17a  Xenophon, *Lakedaimonion Politeia* (*Constitution of the Lacedaemonians*) 13.11; compare *Hellenika* 4.1.26.
B.18a  See further Strassler 2009, Appendix E: Spartan Government and Society, §§9–12.

B.18b  Messenia: Ref. Map 2, DX.
B.18c  Asine: Ref. Map 2, DY.

§19. In order to distinguish between these two kinds of "Lacedaemonians," Spartan citizens might also be referred to as *Spartiatai;* for instance, Drakontios is twice formally labeled *Spartiatēs* (4.8.25, 6.6.30), despite his inferiority within the command structure. Finally, just to complicate things even more, in order to distinguish full Spartan citizens within Sparta from various kinds and degrees of free and Greek sub-Spartiates, the former might be referred to as *homoioi*, as for instance at 4.6.14. Here in context "Xenophon" is engaging in a bit of ethnocentric banter with the Spartiate Cheirisophos, to which we shall return in the next paragraph. But it remains first to add that *homoios* means literally "same-ish," same in one or more but not in all respects. Though regularly translated into English as "equals," a better translation of *homoioi* would be "peers."

§20. The cross-cultural point "Xenophon" is making at 4.6.14–15 is that the Spartans are alleged to have officially tolerated, indeed encouraged, theft. This was a crime other Greek states sought to guard against or aimed to counteract by harsh legal means. Moreover, Xenophon wishes to emphasize that the Spartans practiced it from childhood onward (*ek paidōn*), which is a coded reference to the fact that Sparta, uniquely, had a state-imposed and state-regulated comprehensive educational curriculum for boys from the age of seven until political-social adulthood (at eighteen), a system of *paideia* (education) described elsewhere in some detail by Xenophon.[a] Here, to draw the comparative cultural contrast as strongly as possible, "Xenophon" twice refers to "law" at Sparta: once to the alleged fact that Sparta considered it actually honorable to steal anything not forbidden by law, the second time to the alleged fact that in Sparta legal sanction was imposed not for stealing but for incompetence in being caught doing so. The Sparta of "Xenophon" was an alien place indeed, as I believe we too should imagine it to have been.

Paul Cartledge
A. G. Leventis Senior Research Fellow
Clare College, Cambridge
A. G. Leventis Professor of Greek Culture Emeritus
Faculty of Classics
University of Cambridge
Cambridge, UK

B.20a  Xenophon, *Lakedaimonion Politeia* (*Constitution of the Lacedaemonians*) 2–4 (for theft specifically, by teenagers, 2.6–9).

# APPENDIX C

## *The Persian Empire*

§1. There are strands to *Anabasis* that have little or nothing to do with Persia or Persians, and it does not touch on everywhere even in their western empire.[a] Caria, Lycia, Phoenicia, and Palestine are a blank, and Egypt is merely an offstage locus of rebellion (2.1.14, 2.5.13) and an ethnic attribute of troops settled in Babylonia (1.8.9).[b] Nonetheless, the work offers eyewitness evidence, sometimes unique, about certain imperial regions, in particular Mesopotamia and eastern Anatolia,[c] and circumstantial information of a broadly institutional sort is embedded more or less incidentally in the narrative.

§2. Greek writers sometimes described the eastern power that attacked the Aegean and was defeated in 480–479 as Median.[a] In *Anabasis*, however, Media and the Medes appear only in a strict geographic sense, and the empire within whose territory much of *Anabasis* is played out is a Persian one. Its profile in *Anabasis* can be viewed in terms of the royal family and wider elite, satraps (see §9) and other local authority figures, geographic entities (cities and smaller settlements or focal points) and the long-distance routes connecting them, systems for extracting tributary or other profit, and the military structure that kept it all safe. Military matters are addressed in Appendix D: The Persian Army, but the other issues are reviewed below.

### The Royal Family and the Wider Elite

§3. The power of the Persian King, sometimes referred to as the Great King, ruler of a vast ancestral realm, makes even King Artaxerxes' brother Cyrus a slave,[a] at least in

NOTE: All references to *Hellenika* in this appendix refer to Xenophon's work.

C.1a Persian Empire: see Ref. Map 9, and for selected sites, Map C.1 and locator.

C.1b Caria: Ref. Map 4.2, DY. Lycia: Ref. Map 4.1, DY. Phoenicia, Palestine, Babylonia: Map C.1. Egypt: Map C.1, locator.

C.1c "Anatolia" is roughly synonymous with "Asia Minor," another term often used by modern writers; neither term was yet in use in Classical antiquity. Mesopotamia: Map C.1. Anatolia: Map C.1, locator.

C.2a Aegean Sea: Ref. Map 2, BZ. Media: Map C.1.

C.3a Great King: 1.2.8, 1.4.11, 1.7.2, 1.7.13. Vast realm: 1.5.9, 1.7.6. Brother as slave: 1.9.29, 2.5.38. On Artaxerxes and Cyrus the Younger, see Appendix W: Brief Biographies of Selected Characters in *Anabasis*, §§6, 10.

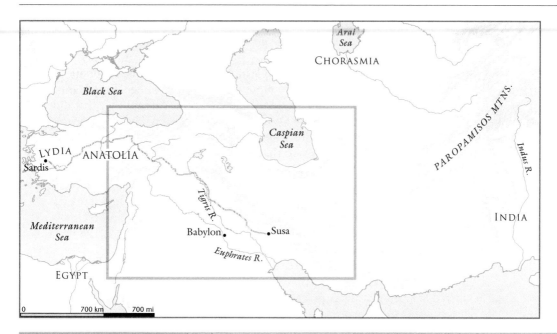

Map. C.1. Selected sites in the central Persian Empire in the early fourth century.

a Greek perception further reflected in the almost Hellenic desire for freedom attributed to Cyrus at 1.7.3.[b] Some cite the trial of Orontas[c] at 1.6.6–8 as evidence that hierarchical relationships within the elite should be construed in terms of medieval vassal rituals; while such a view does not work in detail, it is also inappropriate to conjure up images of chattel slavery. When, more than a century earlier, King Darius I used the word *bandaka* of a satrap or general in the Bisutun Inscription,[d] that did not implicitly restrict the man's capacity for autonomous action to the degree characteristic of the human property of Greek slave owners. Another Greek perception on show in *Anabasis* is that the *proskynēsis* that the King and others receive is proper only between man and god.[e] Its actual importance as a status marker is vividly, if fleetingly, captured in special circumstances at 1.6.10 and 1.8.21.

§4. The King's uniqueness is marked by his upright tiara,[a] but all high-ranking Persians are gorgeously appareled, something memorably evoked at 1.5.8. This is not least because the fine clothing, jewelry, and gold objects they wear (1.8.29) are among the customary gifts of honor from the King, as referred to at 1.2.27[b]—a passing allusion to a central feature of Achaemenid kingship:[c] the giving and receiving of gifts. A different example of the symbolic value of clothing is provided at 1.6.10, where Orontas' belt is grasped as a sign of his condemnation to death.

§5. The *Anabasis* story involves conflict at the heart of the royal family. We get a fleeting sense of the role of other family members in the figures of Parysatis (mother of Cyrus and Artaxerxes), Orontas, and the unnamed bastard brother, brother-in-law, and daughter of the King—but only a fleeting one, and it is the King's friends, not just his family, who provide the empire's satraps.[a] The passing appearance of the brothers of Ariaios and Tissaphernes[b] at 2.4.1 and 2.5.35, respectively, is a reminder that family relations might matter elsewhere in the wider Persian elite. One thing that the wider elite shared with the royals was education "at the King's Gates,"[c] where boys learn self-discipline, respect, an ability to rule and be ruled, riding, use of weapons, and the normative effects of royal praise and blame. Xenophon also touches, somewhat differently, on Persian education in *Kyroupaideia* (*The Education of Cyrus*; 1.2.3–16); and

C.3b   Compare Agesilaos' attempt to stir up this desire in the Persian nobleman Pharnabazos (on whom, see Appendix W: Brief Biographies, §27), as reported in *Hellenika* 4.1.36.

C.3c   This Orontas is a nobleman related to Artaxerxes by blood.

C.3d   The Bisutun Inscription may be found in translation in Kuhrt 2007, 141–58, where *bandaka* is translated as "subject." Bisutun: Map C.1.

C.3e   *Proskynēsis* proper only to a god: 3.2.13. *Proskynēsis* describes a gesture of obeisance, sometimes involving prostration, made when approaching a social superior (Herodotus 1.134). Since Cyrus would receive *proskynēsis* from those around him in any case, the phrasing of *Anabasis* 1.8.21 (where he now receives it "as King") confirms that the degree of physical abasement varied with the social gulf. See Figure 3.2.13 for a frieze depicting a Persian official performing *proskynēsis* to the Great King.

C.4a   Upright tiara: 2.5.23. The tiara (or *kurbasia*) was a type of soft felt headgear characteristically associated with riding costumes. It covered the neck and ears as well as the crown of the head and had flaps

that could be tied beneath the chin. The material of the body of the hat was usually doubled over, so that it did not project much, if at all, above the top of the head; but the King (and the crown prince, once designated as his successor) wore the tiara with the material undoubled, so that it was considerably taller. A story in Plutarch, *Life of Themistocles* 29.8, implies that an ordinary tiara could be converted into a royal one. See further Tuplin 2007.

C.4b   For gifts of honor from the King, see also Xenophon, *Kyroupaideia* (*The Education of Cyrus*) 8.2.8.

C.4c   Achaemenid kingship: the Persian Kings of this period claimed descent from a possibly mythical figure called Achaemenes. For more on the Achaemenids, see the Glossary.

C.5a   Parysatis: 1.1.4. Orontas: 1.6.1. King's brother: 2.4.25, 3.4.13; brother-in-law: 2.3.17; daughter: 2.4.8, 3.4.13. King's friends provide the satraps: 1.7.6. On Parysatis, see Appendix W, §26.

C.5b   On Ariaios and Tissaphernes, see Appendix W, §§4, 37.

C.5c   Education "at the King's Gates" (in this translation rendered "in the King's palace"): 1.9.2–5.

it was a topic in which other Greek writers took an (often moralizing) interest.

§6. "The King's Gates," taken literally, evokes the physical setting of kingship.[a] Also pertinent here are the palaces of Cyrus and Xerxes at Kelainai and those of various satraps.[b] *Anabasis* gives no architectural descriptions of such places or of the Cilician ruler's palace; ironically the ruined Assyrian royal cities of Nimrud and Nineveh fare better,[c] as does the tower of Asidates, with its battlements and eight-brick-thick walls.[d] But the environs of palaces are variously said to contain parks for hunting or ornamental trees (*paradeisoi*, from which comes our "paradise"), water sources, an acropolis, or villages.[e] The *paradeisoi* are a distinctively Persian feature, first recorded in surviving Greek texts by Xenophon.

§7. Taken less literally, the term "the King's Gates" (it recurs at 2.4.4)[a] evokes the royal court as human institution. Of that we see something in the friends of the King, in particular Tiribazos, the man whose unique right it was to assist the King to mount his horse,[b] and also in Cyrus' table companions and mace-bearers.[c] The mace-bearers are a category encountered in royal contexts in Xenophon's *Kyroupaideia*,[d] and they appear on the Apadana frieze at the King's palace at Persepolis, but we have no Persian term for them. In *Kyroupaideia* at least some mace-bearers are eunuchs,[e] but eunuchs are not explicitly part of the Persian world of *Anabasis*.

§8. There are also titular royal personages not in the King's immediate environs. At 1.2.20, at Dana, Cyrus executes Megaphernes, a royal scribe. The word used (*phoinikistēs*) reflects an informant from the eastern Aegean or Anatolian Greek world; a man in a comparable position is described by Herodotus as a royal secretary (*grammatistēs*), in this case to a *hyparchos*.[a] The "royal" sobriquet perhaps indicates that the man was appointed by the King and/or was meant to act as a protector of the King's interests, rather as Achaemenid and Neo-Babylonian kings had royal officials in temple administrations.

## Satraps, Subgovernors, and Others

§9. The most striking figure is Cyrus, satrap of Lydia, Greater Phrygia, and Cappadocia and general, or *karanos*, of those who assemble at the plain of Kastolos.[a] The Iranian term *karanos* appears only in *Hellenika*, and its significance should not

C.6a Monumental gates still stand today at the royal palaces of Persepolis and Pasargadae (Map C.1), the latter seemingly purely symbolic, as there are no walls adjoining the gates.

C.6b Palaces at Kelainai: 1.2.7–9. Palaces of satraps: 1.4.10, 3.4.24, 4.4.2, 4.4.7. On Xerxes, see Appendix W: Brief Biographies, §38. Kelainai: Ref. Map 4.1, CZ.

C.6c Nimrud (under Xenophon's name for it, Larisa) and Nineveh (under Xenophon's name for it, Mespila): 3.4.7–12. Cilicia: Map C.1. Assyria, Larisa (Nimrud), Mespila (Nineveh): Ref. Map 7, CZ.

C.6d Asidates' tower: 7.8.12–13.

C.6e Parks: 1.2.7, 1.4.10. Water sources: 1.2.8, 1.4.10. Acropolis: 1.2.8. Villages: 3.4.24, 4.4.1, 4.4.7.

C.7a At 2.4.4 this translation renders it "at [the King's] own doors."

C.7b Friends of the King: 1.7.6. Tiribazos' right to act as royal groom: 4.4.4. On Tiribazos, see Appendix W, §36.

C.7c Table companions: 1.8.25, 1.9.31; see further

Herodotus 3.132, 5.24, 7.119; Heraclides (No. 689 in F. Jacoby, *Die Fragmente der griechischen Historiker*) F2. Mace-bearers: 1.6.11, 1.8.28.

C.7d *Kyroupaideia* (*The Education of Cyrus*) 8.1.38, 8.3.15, 8.4.2.

C.7e Some mace-bearers are eunuchs: *Kyroupaideia* 7.3.15, 8.4.2.

C.8a Royal secretary (*grammatistēs*): Herodotus 3.128.3. *Hyparchos*: see the Glossary for a discussion of the various meanings of this word. Dana: Ref. Map 5, CY.

C.9a Cyrus' position: Xenophon, *Anabasis* 1.1.2, 1.9.7, *Hellenika* 1.4.3. Other similar characterizations: Diodorus 14.12.8, 14.19.2, 14.26.4 (in Appendix S: Selections from Diodorus); Plutarch, *Life of Artaxerxes* 2 (in Appendix T: Selections from Plutarch's *Life of Artaxerxes*); Justin 5.5.1. Lydia: Map C.1, locator. Cappadocia: Map C.1. On Greater Phrygia, see n. 1.2.6a. Greater Phrygia: Ref. Map 4.1, BZ. Plain of Kastolos: Ref. Map 4.2, BY.

be overstated; the distinctive thing is the reference to the plain of Kastolos.[b] Whether Cyrus replaced existing satraps of Lydia, Phrygia, and Cappadocia or was placed over them has been debated. "Satrap" (*xšaçapāvan-*, "protector of the realm") is an intrinsically fluid term, so coexisting satraps of unequal status in a region are quite possible. (We see this more mundanely at 3.4.31 and 3.5.16.) Either way Tissaphernes remains on hand to give Artaxerxes prior warning of Cyrus' rebellion at 1.2.4. Apart from Cyrus, the most interesting governors are probably Tiribazos, Orontas (a different person from the Orontas of 1.6.1 mentioned in §§3–5), and Belesys.[c] Tiribazos (*hyparchos*, here equivalent to lieutenant governor) and Orontas controlled Western Armenia and Armenia, respectively,[d] a hierarchic distinction that recurs in sources from the period of Alexander the Great (r. 336–323). Belesys, in charge of Syria,[e] is exceptional in the ranks of high-level satraps, being of Babylonian origin (the correct form of his name is Belšunu). Xenophon indicates that he was no longer in office—having presumably been replaced by Abrokomas—when Cyrus' army wrecked his palace and gardens on the Dardas River.[f] The change was recent (among numerous cuneiform documents excavated in Babylon that relate to Belesys' business affairs, the latest to designate him as governor is dated January 10, 401), but the reason for his displacement is unknown. Tamos the Egyptian is known elsewhere as a regional lieutenant, and perhaps had such a role under Cyrus, but is only a fleet commander in *Anabasis;* the two are not incompatible, especially in the context of armed rebellion.[g]

§10. Other kinds of local authorities, substantial and modest, appear in *Anabasis.* Korylas in Paphlagonia[a] and Syennesis in Cilicia—subjects of the King, though flexible or downright insubordinate in how they interpreted that subjection in practice—certainly belong in the first category. So too, probably, does the second man executed at 1.2.20, referred to in the Greek as a *hyparchos.*[b] On a much smaller scale, the army's encounter with the village chief responsible for a group of Armenian villages is a unique revelation of the very local implications of imperial rule.[c] Both he and the village women speak "Persian," but unfortunately one cannot tell whether this was the language of the imperial heartland or a local Iranian dialect with pre-Achaemenid roots. Among other small-scale figures, the most interesting are the Demaratids and Gongylids, descendants of Demaratos and Gongylos, two Greeks whose support of Xerxes was rewarded with territory in Aeolis and who could be described as ruling or holding small towns there.[d]

C.9b  *Karanos:* for more on this term, see the Glossary. For more on the scope of the muster, see Appendix D: The Persian Army, §10.

C.9c  Other high-ranking satraps mentioned are Tissaphernes and Pharnabazos (certainly), Abrokomas (presumably), Arbakes (probably): 1.7.12, 7.8.25; Plutarch, *Life of Artaxerxes* 14. Gobryas (*Anabasis* 1.7.12) may be the governor of Babylon already known in 420–417. For Xenophon's references to Abrokomas and further discussion of his position, see Appendix W: Brief Biographies, §1, where a more hesitant view is taken as to his precise office. Babylon: Map C.1 and locator.

C.9d  *Hyparchos:* see the Glossary. Tiribazos: 4.4.4. Orontas: 3.5.17. Armenia, Western Armenia: Map C.1.

C.9e  Syria: Map C.1.

C.9f  Cyrus wrecks Belesys' palace: 1.4.10. Dardas River, possible location: Ref. Map 5, CZ.

C.9g  Tamos: as regional commander, Thucydides 8.31, 8.87; perhaps also under Cyrus, Diodorus 14.19.6 (in Appendix S: Selections from Diodorus); as fleet commander, *Anabasis* 1.2.21, 1.4.2; Diodorus 14.19.5 (in Appendix S). On Tamos, see Appendix W, §16.

C.10a  Paphlagonia: Ref. Map 7, AX.

C.10b  The word *hyparchos* is translated "subordinate official" at 1.2.20 in this edition.

C.10c  Village chief in Armenia: 4.5.10–4.6.2.

C.10d  Ruling: *Anabasis* 2.1.3. Holding: *Hellenika* 3.1.6. On the Gongylids, see Appendix W, §16. Aeolis: Ref. Map 4.1, BX; Ref. Map 4.2, BY.

§11. *Anabasis* does not convey much detail about how the empire was governed by the practical interplay between the King and those in whom authority was vested at lower levels. But one broad principle of royal rule articulated in *Kyroupaideia* (*The Education of Cyrus*)—that members of the elite can serve as a check on one another—is exemplified, if in a rather aggravated case, when Tissaphernes reports Cyrus' suspiciously extensive mercenary recruitment.[a] The dynamic of competitive relationships within the elite is reflected in a different way by the fact that Ariaios knows he is not of high enough status ever to aspire to be King.[b]

## Landscape and Geographic Extent

§12. Within the landscape of *Anabasis*, we come across cities (*poleis*), villages, forts, and a set of fortified natural "gates," as well as open countryside and royal estate land; both examples of this last category belong to Queen Parysatis, one designated as a bridal gift.[a] Subtle terminological distinctions among regions, especially in eastern Anatolia, may or may not reflect a conscious judgment of diversity on Xenophon's part; but the issue is only marginally relevant, as the salient areas largely look to be divorced from direct Persian control. The word *polis* can embrace everything from the capital cities of Susa and Ecbatana, through Tarsus and Kelainai or Iconium, and not forgetting Keramon Agora (Potters' Market) and Issus,[b] down to the "many large cities" that lay west of the Tigris River,[c] most of which cannot have been at all large, or the metropolis (mother city) of the Mossynoeci.[d] The quasi-formulaic description of some cities as "populous" (*oikoumenai*) resists reliable decoding: here too it is doubtful whether Xenophon is deploying an intelligible or useful template. But he had heard reports that Ecbatana was where the King spent the summer[e]—the earliest surviving item in a dossier of Greek texts about systematic royal seasonal relocation.

§13. Focal places are joined by roads, of whose character *Anabasis* gives surprisingly little detail. Pontoon bridges are mentioned occasionally.[a] Looking across the Kentrites River into Armenia, the Greeks see a road that seems man-made,[b] but we never learn whether it actually was, and the issue barely recurs elsewhere. Xenophon's rhetorical flourish at 3.2.24 about the King building a road fit for four-horse chariots in Mysia presupposes the idea of royal roads, but he evinces no awareness of the Royal Road described by Herodotus,[c] although the Greeks crossed its line in northern Assyria,[d] or of other similar purpose-built long-distance routes. There were many of these, and the army must have marched along some of them. The surveillance and security measures indicated in Herodotus[e] may be compared with a chilling report in

C.11a  Tissaphernes reports on Cyrus' activities: 1.2.4.
C.11b  Ariaios' nonroyal status: 2.2.1.
C.12a  Natural "gates": 1.4.4. Royal estate land: 1.4.9, 2.4.27.
C.12b  Susa: Map C.1 and locator. Ecbatana: Map C.1. The following locations appear on Ref. Map 7: Potters' Market, probable location, BW (Keramon Agora in the *Barrington Atlas*); Tarsus, Iconium, CX; Issus, CY.
C.12c  "Many large cities": 2.4.21. Tigris River: Map C.1 and locator.
C.12d  Metropolis of the Mossynoeci: 5.4.15. Mossynoeci

territory: Ref. Map 5, AZ.
C.12e  King's summer in Ecbatana: 3.5.15.
C.13a  Pontoon bridges: 1.2.5, 2.4.13, 2.4.24.
C.13b  Man-made road: 4.3.5. Kentrites River: Ref. Map 7, BY.
C.13c  Herodotus 5.52–54. For the Royal Road's course, see Map C.1 and locator. Mysia: Ref. Map 4.1, BY; Ref. Map 4.2, BZ.
C.13d  The Royal Road is referred to, but not by name, in *Anabasis* at 3.5.15 (the route to Lydia and Ionia).
C.13e  Security measures: Herodotus 5.35, 5.52.

*Anabasis* (1.9.13) that Cyrus guaranteed safe travel by displaying maimed criminals along major routes. Outside that passage we see little of nonmilitary travelers,
perhaps only Queen Epyaxa of Cilicia in her covered carriage (but she *is* on a diplomatic mission, with a bodyguard) and the Euphrates valley inhabitants who sell millstones in Babylon.[f] Any other hint of the special status and administrative management
of particular roads depends on the rather speculative inference, from Xenophon's
systematic count of parasangs, that information about distances was displayed by
the roadside.[g]

§14. At 1.7.6 Cyrus is made to describe the empire as bounded by the limits of
human habitability,[a] a plain untruth that we need not assume any Persian ever actually
uttered, though it might match the onetime aspiration of Persian kingship. The true
outer limits in Xenophon's time are not in all cases clear: the state of things in Cyrenaica, south of the Nile's first cataract, beyond the Hindu Kush, or in the Chorasmian
environs of the Aral Sea is debatable—and well beyond Xenophon's scope.[b] What he
*does* offer is evidence of discontinuity of imperial control somewhat closer to hand.

§15. The Kardouchoi (their territory was between Mesopotamia and Armenia)
were not Persian subjects, despite intermittent periods of satrapal truce and recipro-
cal relations.[a] There were similar situations in upland Mysia and Pisidia (see §17)
and with the Kadousioi, who lived by the Caspian Sea and are referred to by Xenophon
in *Hellenika* (2.1.13).[b] Furthermore, it seems from other sources that the King regularly made "gifts" to the Ouxioi, Elymai, and Cossaeans, who lived between Persepolis and Ecbatana, and also to the Mardoi, in return for passing through their territory.[c]
But the Kardouchoi, unlike most of these other peoples, never appear in Persian service, even as mercenaries.

§16. There is no sign of Persian authority in northeastern Anatolia beyond Armenia. The Chaldaioi (perhaps the same people as are elsewhere referred to as the
Chalybes, for example at 4.7.15) and the Taochoi are certainly nonsubject,[a] though
not necessarily hostile to the Persians (some serve as mercenaries), and the people farther north seem even more detached, though Xenophon offers no systematic comment; that is left to the later scribe who inserted 7.8.25 into Xenophon's text, who
designates the Makrones, Kolchoi, Mossynoeci, Koitoi, and Tibareni as autonomous.[b]

C.13f  Epyaxa travels: 1.2.16. Millstone makers: 1.5.5.
On Queen Epyaxa, see Appendix W: Brief
Biographies, §14. Euphrates River: Map C.1 and
locator.

C.13g  On the parasang, a unit of measurement of travel,
see the Introduction, §7.3–5, and Appendix O:
Ancient Greek and Persian Units of Measurement, §§7–8. For more on Xenophon's route, see
Appendix P: The Route of the Ten Thousand.

C.14a  Xenophon as narrator says the same at *Kyroupaideia* (*The Education of Cyrus*) 8.6.21.

C.14b  Cyrenaica, Nile River: Ref. Map 1, CW, DX. The
Hindu Kush was called the Indian Caucasus or
Paropamisos in ancient times. Paropamisos,
Chorasmia, Aral Sea: Map C.1, locator (the last
two are beyond the scope of the *Barrington
Atlas*).

C.15a  Kardouchoi's status: 3.5.16. Kardouchoi territory: Map C.1.

C.15b  Pisidia: Ref. Map 4.1, CZ. Kadousioi territory:

Map C.1. Caspian Sea: Map C.1 and locator.

C.15c  From other sources: the principal source here is
the first-century geographer Strabo (11.13.6),
whose work also includes much historical information. Ouxioi, Elymai, Cossaeans, territories:
Map C.1. Mardoi territory, possible location: Ref.
Map 6, AY.

C.16a  Chaldaioi and Taochoi not the King's subjects:
5.5.17. The Chaldaioi are not shown as such on
any map in this edition. [E.] Chalybes, Taochoi
territories: Ref. Map 6 AY. (The *Barrington
Atlas* does not locate the [Eastern] Chalybes on
its maps and locates the Chaldaioi differently, at
Map 87 E4 [Chaldia].)

C.16b  Scribal insertion: on this, see n. 7.8.25d. Makrones, Kolchoi territories: Ref. Map 6, AX. Tibareni
territory: Ref. Map 5, AZ. The Koitoi are not
shown separately from the Mossynoeci (see n.
7.8.25b).

The reference to Byzantium at 7.1.29 as "the first Greek city we reach" should not be taken to imply that Xenophon counts Greek cities in northern Anatolia as "barbarian," that is, Persian imperial subjects, and there is no hint of this in the narrative. Independent information about the region is virtually nonexistent for the decades around 400. Relations between the army and northern Anatolian cities were awkward, and there is no reason why Xenophon should have concealed their Persian-subject status if it had been the case. That fits in with Xenophon's representation of neighboring Paphlagonia, where Korylas had rejected Persian authority.[c] It is difficult to say how precisely this fits with other signs of Paphlagonian rebelliousness farther west in the 390s and 380s, the presence of one thousand Paphlagonian horsemen in Cyrus' army in 401, or Diodorus' reference to a Paphlagonian "satrap" circa 404,[d] but north-central Anatolia was plainly not a stable part of the imperial system. Farther west, the Bithynians invoked Pharnabazos' help, but relations were often strained, and the clear implication of *Anabasis* is that the region northeast of the Propontis was not directly controlled imperial territory.[e]

§17. At 3.2.23 Xenophon says that Mysians and Pisidians "inhabit many great and prosperous cities in the land of the King against the King's will" and that the Lycaonians have seized "strong points in the plains" and exploit the Persians' land—which is why Cyrus let his army loot it, "on the ground that it was enemy territory."[a] The remarks about Mysia and Pisidia cohere with other evidence of their troublesome independence in *Anabasis* and elsewhere in Xenophon,[b] though "great and prosperous cities" is an exaggeration. The remark about Lycaonia (a region largely ignored in classical sources) is without parallel but articulates a distinctive state of affairs in the steppe east of Iconium and at the foot of Mount Boratinon.[c]

§18. The existence of persistently detached regions is one thing; the fact or apprehension of revolt within mainstream imperial territory is another. Xenophon alludes to the Egyptian defection—a new development at the time of the events of *Anabasis* but a long-standing one, despite a number of attempts at reconquest, by the time people were reading the book. More remarkably, at 3.2.24–25 he makes his younger self claim implausibly that the King feared the Greek army's capacity to be the focus for an insurgency in eastern Babylonia.

## Exploitation

§19. The Persian realm, even if discontinuous, was an empire of plenty.[a] Although Xenophon's stress is on Cyrus' relationship with his agents, not on improvement of landscape or "economy," Cyrus' insistence on profit maximization chimes with an understanding that fostering agricultural productivity was a fiscal and ideological good.[b]

C.16c  Korylas rejects Persian authority: 5.6.8.
C.16d  Rebelliousness: this involved a ruler variously named as Otys, Gyes, or Thuys. Horsemen: 1.8.5. Paphlagonian "satrap": Diodorus 14.11.3.
C.16e  Pharnabazos' troops come to aid Bithynians: *Anabasis* 6.4.24, 6.5.30. Relations strained: *Hellenika* 3.2.2. Bithynia, Propontis: Ref. Map 4.1, AZ, AY.
C.17a  Cyrus allows it to be looted: 1.2.19. Lycaonia:

Ref. Map 5, CX.
C.17b  Mysian and Pisidian independence: *Anabasis* 1.1.11, 1.2.1, 1.6.7, 1.9.14, 2.5.13; *Hellenika* 3.1.13; *Memorabilia* (*Recollections of Socrates*) 3.5.26.
C.17c  Mt. Boratinon: Ref. Map 5, CX.
C.19a  Empire of plenty: 3.2.25.
C.19b  Cyrus' profit orientation: 1.9.19.

§20. About tribute payment *Anabasis* offers rather little. From 1.1.8 we see that individual Greek cities are tributary units and infer that the duty to transmit tribute was personal to the relevant satrap. When Cyrus took de facto control of Tissaphernes' cities, he was not *obliged* to send their tribute to the King: it is as though tribute is not a city's bureaucratic obligation to the King that the satrap or some other official has to administer but a satrap's personal debt to the King relating to the extent of authority the King has granted him.

§21. In Armenia we encounter horses reared as *dasmos* ("tribute" or, more literally, "share") for the King;[a] other Greek authors offer direct analogies for this in Cappadocia, Media, Cilicia, and Aspendos,[b] while Persepolis Fortification documents[c] link *baziš* (Old Persian: *baji-*), which corresponds to *dasmos*, with animals of other sorts. But Strabo, one of those Greek authors, also tells us that Armenia annually dispatched twenty thousand animals for sacrifice at the Mithrakana, a Mithra festival with royal associations.[d] (At it the King got drunk and performed the so-called Persian dance.)[e] If we can legitimately combine Xenophon and Strabo (and the role of a horse "sacred to the sun" at 4.5.35 *might* favor this, as Mithra had strong connections with the sun), the result is a reminder that, though royal *dasmos* may be an expression of political subordination, nothing follows for sure from that about how the King's allocation is consumed. Any inclination to see horses as a military resource is unduly narrow-minded; and funding religious observance was, after all, simply another way of securing a political outcome—namely, the empire's continued well-being. Regrettably, *Anabasis* offers few other hints about the Persian religious environment, though it provides an intriguing oath-affirming ritual at 2.2.9 and a striking example at 1.6.7 of the willingness of Persians to acknowledge the power of non-Iranian gods. There is also the remarkable fact that the *neokoros* (temple warden) of Artemis' temple in Ephesus had a Persian title.[f]

§22. The Persepolis Fortification archive referred to in §21 discloses large numbers of dependent workers (many of them from distant parts of the empire) and a complex system of collection, storage, and distribution of food commodities; but there are no unequivocal signs of this in *Anabasis*. The people in Parysatis' Mesopotamian villages mentioned at 2.4.27 might have resembled Persepolitan laborers or the branded workers of Arshama's Egyptian estate,[a] but Tissaphernes' refusal to allow their seizure hardly proves it; and their description here as slaves (*andrapoda*) refers to their condition if seized, not necessarily their prior condition. Actual *andrapoda*

C.21a  Horses as King's tribute (*dasmos*): 4.5.24.
C.21b  Horses as tribute: in Cappadocia and Media, Strabo 11.13.8; in Cilicia, Herodotus 3.90; in Aspendos, Arrian, *Anabasis Alexandrou* 1.26.3. Aspendos: Ref. Map 4.1, DZ.
C.21c  The Persepolis Fortification documents form an archive of many thousands of inscribed clay tablets, predominantly dating from 509 to 494 (but with at least one text dating from as early as 518/17), that were discovered in the northwest fortifications of the Persepolis terrace. They are bureaucratic records dealing with the collection, storage, and disbursement of locally produced commodities (primarily foodstuffs) intended for consumption at all levels of society. Kuhrt 2007, 770–801, contains a representative selection of documents from this archive.
C.21d  Twenty thousand animals: Strabo 11.14.9 (on Strabo, see n. C.15c). In Persian religious belief, the god Mithra was associated with covenants (oaths were sworn by him) and light (especially sunlight).
C.21e  A much less exalted person performs this at a banquet in Paphlagonia at 6.1.10.
C.21f  Megabyzos the temple warden: 5.3.6–7. Ephesus: Ref. Map 4.1, CX; Ref. Map 4.2, DY.
C.22a  Workers in Egypt: Kuhrt 2007, 819. Arshama was satrap of Egypt for over twenty-five years in the late fifth century, and a dossier of documents relating to him has survived: see Tuplin and Ma 2020.

do appear around Asidates' tower in Aeolis: in a region of military colonization,[b] they might represent an artificially organized labor force, but one can really draw no firm conclusion about their status. As for storage and distribution, the army did encounter extra-urban places (generally, "villages") containing significant amounts of food. The villages at 3.4.31, which are associated with a palace (*basileion*) and where supplies of wine and cereal products have been collected for the satrap of the region, may have been places where someone with correct documentation could have drawn on official resources. Whether the sinews for cord making and the lead discovered at earlier villages[c] reflect an official arms depot is much less certain, and the status of the place's plentiful food supply is a matter of speculation, as it is in other salient cases.

## Conclusion

§23. Such gaps or uncertainties are natural in a text that is the product of contingent experience, not deliberate or systematic observation of the empire. We meet the same phenomenon in the modest information offered about Achaemenid Persian religion, or the invisibility of administrative interplay between different levels of officialdom, or the failure to evoke in any detail the physical environment (natural or man-made). The historian's reaction must be to celebrate the things that *are* to be found in *Anabasis* and the fact that, if it is poor at providing an analytical description of imperial institutions, it is good at offering vivid circumstantial examples of specific elements in the infrastructure of such institutions. It is also good at provoking important questions: for example, what does it say about Achaemenid kingship and relations within the Persian elite that Artaxerxes tolerated conflict between Cyrus and Tissaphernes or admitted Ariaios and other rebels back into favor?[a] The sources for Achaemenid history as a whole illuminate some localities and/or phenomena very brightly while leaving comparable ones in darkness; *Anabasis* does not buck the trend, and it would be astonishing if it did.

Christopher Tuplin
Gladstone Professor of Greek
Department of Archaeology, Classics, and Egyptology
University of Liverpool
Liverpool, UK

C.22b  Slaves (*andrapoda*): 7.8.12, 7.8.19. Military colonies in Aeolis: 7.8.14–15.
C.22c  Sinews and lead: 3.4.18.

C.23a  Conflict tolerated: 1.1.8. Rebels readmitted to King's favor: 2.4.1, 3.3.2–5, 3.3.7, 3.4.2–6; see also *Hellenika* 4.1.27.

# APPENDIX D

## *The Persian Army*

§1. "The Persian army" is a convenient, if slightly misleading, shorthand for the various forces that, irrespective of precise ethnic composition, were intended to protect the interests of the Persian King—though they might on occasion be used against him, as by Cyrus in Book 1 of *Anabasis*, or by one elite figure against another.[a] The army is represented in *Anabasis* by three types of forces: the multi-origin royal force that fought at the battle of Cunaxa,[b] an ad hoc force under Tissaphernes assembled after Cunaxa, and a series of satrapal or subsatrapal forces associated with Cyrus, Abrokomas, Orontas, Tiribazos, Pharnabazos, and Itabelis.[c] *Anabasis* provides valuable information about the mobilization, tactical character, and strategic deployment of the relevant groups of soldiers, analysis of which can tell us much about the Persian military establishment. Some of this information is unique: the military environment of Armenia under Artaxerxes and other Achaemenid Kings is otherwise unknown, and although that of western Anatolia is illuminated by various sources, there is nothing quite like the description of troops in the Caicus valley at 7.8.15.[d] What follows concentrates on summarizing the material in *Anabasis* rather than providing detailed comparisons with similar material elsewhere.

### Mobilization

§2. Artaxerxes' army at Cunaxa provides the occasion for the only surviving itemized account of a Persian royal army between the Persian expeditions to Greece of

D.1a One elite figure against another: 1.1.8, 1.3.20, 1.6.6–7. On Cyrus the Younger, see Appendix W: Brief Biographies of Selected Characters in *Anabasis*, §10. Persian Empire: Ref. Map 9.

D.1b See Appendix L: The Battle of Cunaxa, where more sophisticated tactics are tentatively attributed to the Persians than were understood by Xenophon or envisaged in this appendix. Battlefield of Cunaxa: Ref. Map 6, DZ.

D.1c Satrapal: that is, coming from the province of a particular satrap (governor); for more on satraps, see Appendix C: The Persian Empire, §9. On Tis-

saphernes, Abrokomas, Orontas, Tiribazos, and Pharnabazos, see Appendix W, §§37, 1, 25, 36, 27. For more on Itabelis, see §6 and n. 7.8.15a.

D.1d On Artaxerxes, see Appendix W, §6. Achaemenid: of the Persian Kings who claimed descent from a possibly mythical Achaemenes; for more, see the Glossary. "Anatolia" is roughly synonymous with "Asia Minor," another term often used by modern writers; neither term was yet in use in Classical antiquity. Armenia: Map C.1. Anatolia: Map C.1, locator. Caicus River: Ref. Map 4.2, BY.

480–479 and Alexander the Great (r. 336–323). At 1.7.11–12 the army consists of four equal sections, commanded by Tissaphernes, Gobryas, Arbakes, and Abrokomas. Since Abrokomas was, perhaps, satrap of Syria[a] and set out for Cunaxa with forces from his province (though he failed to arrive in time), one might infer that each of the sections is a regional levy. That interpretation is supported by the statement at 1.8.9 that "all these" troops were "arranged by ethnicity [*kata ethnē*]," although the troops referred to there might possibly be just the ones directly facing the Greeks. At 1.7.11–12 there is no difficulty in seeing Arbakes as commanding a regional levy,[b] but it is more of a problem to see how Gobryas and Tissaphernes fit into the pattern. At first sight Gobryas seems a good candidate for a Mesopotamian levy, as a man of this name was governor of Babylon early in Darius II's reign.[c] Similarly, although Tissaphernes can hardly be in charge of an Anatolian levy, since he arrived from there with just five hundred horsemen,[d] the most obvious solution would seem to be that he had been put in charge of troops from somewhere else, such as Persia. But there is a difficulty with this distribution of roles. At 1.8.9, where the battlefield formation is described, Tissaphernes is with horsemen in white cuirasses who are adjacent to *gerrhophoroi* (troops carrying wicker shields) and "Egyptian" hoplites, whose proximate origin is probably Babylonia,[e] since Egypt itself was in revolt against the Persians at this time. Perhaps, then, he belongs with a Mesopotamian army group and it was Gobryas (whose Babylonian connection did lie some way in the past) who led the putative regional levy from Persia. The force under the King's unnamed bastard brother that reached the Tigris River thirty-six days after Cunaxa can then represent a levy from eastern Iran or farther afield (Diodorus Siculus mentions India in this connection).[f] But these inferences are rather speculative. Perhaps it is wrong to try to make 1.7.11–12 and 1.8.9 perfectly consonant with each other or to think that either passage can be altogether trusted. (After all, the numbers supplied are absurd, and 1.8.9 details only those troops directly facing the Greeks, before tailing off into generalities.) However that may be, organization by ethnic group and the levying of regional units would at any rate correspond broadly with the world of royal armies in Herodotus and the Alexander historians; and the late arrival of Abrokomas and Artaxerxes' bastard brother shows that those who actually fought at Cunaxa came from at most Mesopotamia, western Iran, and Armenia.

§3. In addition to his generals' troops, the King himself was in the middle of his army (a customary Persian practice, ensuring security and ease of communication), screened by six thousand cavalry, and there were 150 scythed chariots in front of the whole array.[a] The six thousand cavalry presumably represent an elite unit (their reported rout by Cyrus' six hundred cavalry casts them as a rather poor elite but should be treated with caution—or perhaps the figure six thousand is a gross exaggera-

D.2a  Syria: Map C.1.
D.2b  Plutarch, in *Life of Artaxerxes* 14.2, calls Arbakes a Mede (Media: Map C.1).
D.2c  On Darius II, see Appendix W: Brief Biographies, §11. Mesopotamia: Map C.1. Babylon: Map C.1 and locator.
D.2d  Five hundred horsemen: 1.2.4.
D.2e  Egypt: Map C.1, locator. Babylonia: Map C.1.
D.2f  Thirty-six days after Cunaxa: 2.4.25. Mentions

India: Diodorus 14.22.1 (in Appendix S: Selections from Diodorus). Tigris River: Map C.1 and locator. Iran (a modern term): Ref. Map 8, BZ. India: Map C.1, locator.
D.3a  King in the middle of the army: 1.8.22. Six thousand cavalry: 1.7.11, 1.8.12–13, 1.8.21–26. Scythed chariots: 1.8.9. Scythed chariots have scythes attached to the axles and the undercarriage.

tion), but there is no hint of an infantry equivalent, such as the Immortals mentioned by Herodotus.[b] Perhaps this is another sign of the patchiness of Xenophon's picture.

§4. After Cunaxa, Tissaphernes formed a composite subroyal army. This included the bastard brother's eastern Iranian force and most of Cyrus' defeated army except the Greek mercenaries. He also received soldiers from the King.[a] If these came from the Cunaxa army (perhaps reinforced by Abrokomas' men once they had arrived), that would explain the presence of a unit belonging to the Armenian satrap and royal son-in-law Orontas.[b] Klearchos and Xenophon suggest that the accumulated army was especially rich in cavalry, but although cavalry appear in the narrative, it is impossible to assess overall proportions reliably.[c] (But note that once the Greeks form a small cavalry unit of their own, the Persian cavalry cease to be prominent in the action.) Meanwhile, the only infantry explicitly present are archers and slingers.[d]

§5. Satrapy-defined forces appear in several additional places, often in association with mercenaries (as was also true of Abrokomas' Syrian troops of 1.7.12, since 1.4.3 tells us he also had Greek mercenaries, some or all of whom deserted). There are two such groups in Armenia: one at 4.3.3–23, ascribed to Orontas (the satrap) and Artouchas (perhaps a *hyparchos*, or lieutenant), and the other at 4.4.4–21, ascribed to Tiribazos, *hyparchos* of Western Armenia.[a] The latter group consists of Tiribazos' "own force" plus Chalybian and Taochian mercenaries.[b] The mercenaries (of relatively local origin but not direct Persian subjects) are probably all foot soldiers, while Tiribazos' "own force" includes cavalry and archers; at least one of the archers is specifically a Persian, and that might be the case with the whole "own force." The Orontas/Artouchas group guarding the Kentrites River crossing is a cavalry and infantry force comprising Armenians, Mardoi, and Chaldaioi[c]—that is, entirely composed of locals. The Chaldaioi are mercenaries, again from outside imperial territory; the Armenians and Mardoi, a levy from provincial subjects. The two eastern Anatolian groups are thus similar in including mercenaries but may differ in the origin of their other component. (Orontas has his "own force" in Babylonia at 2.4.8, but there is no guarantee that either he or they were at the Kentrites crossing.) Neither group is quantified, but the course of events does not suggest that either is particularly large.

§6. Something a bit structurally similar turns up in the Caicus valley.[a] The attack on Asidates' estate brings out Itabelis and his "own force," plus other troops from various neighboring localities: what Xenophon here refers to as "Assyrian hoplites" and also Hyrcanian cavalry (who are said to be in the King's pay), alongside peltasts and other cavalry.[b] But this time the mercenaries are *not* local, and we have both an

D.3b Immortals: Herodotus 7.83.1.
D.4a Tissaphernes' army: 3.4.13; bastard brother's force, 2.4.25; nonmercenary elements of Cyrus' army, 2.2.7, 2.4.9, 2.4.24, 2.5.35; soldiers from the King, Diodorus 14.26.5 (in Appendix S: Selections from Diodorus).
D.4b Orontas: 2.4.8, 3.4.13.
D.4c Klearchos: 2.4.6. Xenophon: 3.2.18. Cavalry appear in the narrative: 2.5.32, 2.5.35, 3.3.1, 3.3.6–7, 3.4.2–5, 3.4.24, 3.4.34–35. On Klearchos, see Appendix W: Brief Biographies, §20.
D.4d Archers and slingers: 3.3.6–7, 3.4.2, 3.4.14, 3.4.25–26.
D.5a On the *hyparchos*, see the Glossary. Western Arme-

nia: Map C.1.
D.5b [Eastern] Chalybes, Taochoi territories: Ref. Map 6, AX, AY. The *Barrington Atlas* does not locate the Eastern Chalybes.
D.5c The Chaldaioi do not appear on the maps as such; the editors tentatively identify them with the Eastern Chalybes: see n. 4.3.4b. The *Barrington Atlas* locates the Chaldaioi differently, at Map 87 E4 (Chaldia). Kentrites River, Mardoi territory (possible location): Ref. Map 6, BY.
D.6a Caicus valley: 7.8.15–18.
D.6b Peltasts: light-armed infantrymen; see Appendix H: Infantry and Cavalry in *Anabasis*, §§4–5. Assyria: Ref. Map 6, CY. Hyrcania: Map C.1.

Iranian official's "own force" (as in Western Armenia) and troops provided by local subjects (as at the Kentrites crossing). It is hard to decide whether Itabelis is a high-level regional *hyparchos* (like Tiribazos) or belongs to a more restricted territory. Either way, the principles upon which local defense forces are formed seem broadly similar to those in eastern Anatolia.

§7. Another salient episode takes us to northern Anatolia, where the Greeks met resistance near Kalpe Harbor from Pharnabazos' cavalry and Bithynian peltasts and horsemen.[a] Pharnabazos himself is not present; instead Spithridates and Rhathines[b] have come with "the force"—that is, Pharnabazos' "own force,"[c] temporarily under his subordinates' command. This force is entirely composed of horsemen (like the groups of horsemen Alexander the Great faced at the Granicus River),[d] prompting speculation that all these "own forces" are built around a core of Persian or Persian-style cavalry. The Bithynians fighting beside them are neither mercenaries nor imperial subjects but an autonomous (sometimes troublesome) group who have solicited Pharnabazos' help. The episode thus provides a further variation on defense of imperial interests against local threats. The same goes for the Cilicians and Aspendians serving the Cilician ruler Syennesis and his wife.[e] At this date there is no satrap of Cilicia, merely a native dynast, whose forces seem to be entirely non-Persian. In Herodotus (3.90) Cilician tribute funded a regional cavalry garrison, but there is no sign of this in *Anabasis*.

§8. The most powerful recruiter of satrapal forces in *Anabasis* is Cyrus. His royal status, authority over multiple regions, and rebellious intentions make him unusual. But the formation of his army—whose alleged purpose was internal defense—rests on familiar principles, for it consists of mercenaries from outside imperial territory (Greeks and a few Thracians, almost all foot soldiers) and a cavalry and infantry force provided by the territories of which he was satrap (Lydia, Greater Phrygia, and Cappadocia) and presumably commanded by those about whose military competence Xenophon tells us he took such care.[a] There was also Paphlagonian cavalry, posted alongside the Greek mercenaries at Cunaxa,[b] but they are perhaps to be seen as external allies—dissident imperial subjects but not part of Cyrus' satrapal realm. Preoccupied with the mercenaries, Xenophon offers almost no information about the rest of the army (apart from an implausible claim that they numbered one hundred thousand), but Diodorus' reference to Persians and "other barbarians," in particular but presumably not exclusively Phrygians and Lydians, sounds reasonable.[c]

§9. One detail Xenophon *does* provide is that Cyrus was general of "all those whose

---

D.7a  Pharnabazos' cavalry and Bithynian peltasts: 6.4.24, 6.5.7–32. Kalpe Harbor, possible location, Bithynia: Ref. Map 4.1, AY, AZ.

D.7b  Spithridates and Rhathines: 6.5.7; for more on them, see Appendix W: Brief Biographies, §33.

D.7c  "the force" is a literal translation of the Greek text, and "Pharnabazos' 'own force'" is a paraphrase. The Landmark translation of 6.5.7 follows Christopher Tuplin's interpretation of the Greek expression in context but uses a different paraphrase, "with the standing army of the satrapy." (Translator's note)

D.7d  Cavalry at the battle of the Granicus River: Diodorus 17.19.4–5. Granicus River: Ref. Map 4.2, AX.

D.7e  Syennesis and his wife: 1.2.12, 1.2.25. Cilicia: Ref. Map 5, CY. Aspendos: Ref. Map 4.1, DZ.

D.8a  Cyrus' army: 1.2.16, 1.8.1–7, 1.8.21–27, 1.9.31; Diodorus 14.19.7–9 (in Appendix S: Selections from Diodorus). Cyrus' concern for military effectiveness: 1.1.5. On Greater Phrygia, see n. 1.2.6a. Thrace: Ref. Map 3, CY. Lydia: Ref. Map 4.1, CY; Ref. Map 4.2, CZ. Greater Phrygia: Ref. Map 4.1, BZ. Cappadocia: Ref. Map 5, BY.

D.8b  Paphlagonian cavalry: 1.8.5. Paphlagonia: Ref. Map 5, AX.

D.8c  One hundred thousand: 1.7.10. Diodorus' reference: Diodorus 14.22.5–6 (in Appendix S). The Phrygians here came from Greater Phrygia.

muster point was the plain of Kastolos,"ᵃ The plain of Kastolos is in eastern Lydia, between two routes from Sardisᵇ to Phrygia. That is rather peripheral as a muster point for purely Lydian resources, whether for inspectionᶜ or for more vigorous purposes. It is more central to a combination of Lydian and Phrygian territory, but this does not help, since Cyrus also controlled Cappadocia, and scholars usually see the title as traditional, not one peculiar to the special circumstances of Cyrus' appointment.

## Deployment and Strategy

§10. Xenophon's account of Cunaxa provides the first written reference to scythed chariots in an uncontentiously historical episode, though not one that redounds to their credit as tactical weapons.ᵃ But elsewhere in *Anabasis*, Persian land forces consist simply of cavalry and/or infantry units. Naval forces are scarcely visible.ᵇ

§11. In Klearchos' viewᵃ most of the enemy were (high-quality) cavalry, but Xenophon offers no sound evidence about the proportions of cavalry and infantry; numbers are provided only intermittently (and sometimes absurdly), and no single composite force is fully quantified. Some cavalrymen carry bows and perhaps slings.ᵇ Others (those with Cyrus at 1.8.3, 1.8.6–7) have helmets, breastplates, and thigh protectors; ride horses fitted with head and chest armor; and wield spears (*palta*) and Greek sabers.ᶜ But most are not described in any detail. The breastplates perhaps had a neck guard, as shown on the Çan Sarcophagus, found near Troy, in western Turkey; and for thigh protectors we may look, for example, to the Payava Sarcophagus in the British Museum.ᵈ

§12. The King's infantry at Cunaxa includes *gerrhophoroi* with wicker shields and "Egyptian" hoplites with "shields reaching to their feet."ᵃ With this pairing we may compare Xenophon's *Kyroupaideia* (*The Education of Cyrus*) 7.1.33–34, which confirms that the *gerrhophoroi* carry relatively small shields, not the large rectilinear *gerrha* used at the battles of Plataea and Mycale to form protective walls.ᵇ In *Kyroupaideia* (where the *gerrhophoroi* are the standard Persian line infantry), they wear breastplates and carry swords,ᶜ and this presumably applies in *Anabasis* as well. Elsewhere in *Anabasis* infantrymen fighting for the Persians are normally archers or slingers, but there are also mercenary Chaldaian and Chalybian spearmen in eastern Anatolia, allied Bithynian peltasts near Kalpe Harbor, and peltasts and Assyrian hoplites in the Caicus valley.ᵈ

D.9a "All those whose muster point": 1.1.2, also see 1.9.7; Xenophon, *Hellenika* 1.4.3. Plain of Kastolos: Ref. Map 4.2, CZ.
D.9b Sardis: Ref. Map 4.1, CY; Ref. Map 4.2, CZ.
D.9c On Persian troop inspection, see Xenophon, *Oikonomikos* (*On the Management of the Household*) 4.6–7; perhaps implied for the plain of Kastolos at *Kyroupaideia* (*The Education of Cyrus*) 6.2.11.
D.10a Scythed chariots: 1.7.11, 1.8.10; on their ineffectiveness, 1.8.20.
D.10b Naval forces: 1.1.7, 1.4.2.
D.11a Klearchos' view: 2.4.6.
D.11b Cavalrymen with bows and slings: 3.3.7, 3.3.10; perhaps also implicit in 4.3.6, 4.3.17–18.
D.11c Cyrus' *palta* (spears): 1.5.15, 1.8.3. Persians with breastplates: also 2.5.35.
D.11d Breastplates with neck guard: Sevinç et al. 2001;

note esp. figures 11 and 12. Thigh protectors: Demargne 1974, plates 40 and 41. Troy: Ref. Map 4.2, AX.
D.12a *Gerrhophoroi* (troops carrying wicker shields) and (other) shields reaching down to the feet: 1.8.9. On *gerrhophoroi* and "Egyptian" hoplites, see §2.
D.12b Shield walls: Herodotus 9.61, 9.99, 9.102; Plato, *Laches* 191C. Plataea: Ref. Map 2, CY. Mycale: Ref. Map 4.2, DY.
D.12c Breastplates and swords: *Kyroupaideia* (*The Education of Cyrus*) 1.2.13, 2.1.9, 2.1.16, 2.1.21, 2.2.9, 2.3.17–18. Breastplates (swords not mentioned): *Kyroupaideia* 5.3.36, 5.3.37, 5.3.52, 6.3.24, 7.1.10.
D.12d Chaldaian and Chalybian spearmen: 4.3.4, 4.4.18; details of their accoutrements, 4.3.4, 4.7.15–16. Bithynian peltasts: 6.5.19. Peltasts and hoplites in Caicus valley: 7.8.15.

The peltast armed with a javelin (*akontion*) is encountered quite often in *Kyrou-paideia*, in Persian and non-Persian forces, so it is interesting that the term "peltast" is rarely used in *Anabasis* of Persian-employed troops. Perhaps Xenophon wished to avoid confusion with the peltasts of the Greek mercenary force. Or perhaps Persian-employed peltasts really were rare: there is little sign of them even where the term is not present, the spear-throwing skirmishers at 3.4.25–26 being a rare possible exception. As for the more plentiful archers and slingers, we learn little except that they use bows and slings. The Persian bow is relatively large and outshoots the Cretan one,[c] and a Persian archer at 4.4.16 also carries an Amazon-style axe (*sagaris*). Persian slingers use hand-size sling stones and outshoot Greek javelin-men but are outperformed by Rhodians with lead sling bullets.[f] *Anabasis* provides the earliest evidence of slingers in a Persian military context (see also 7.8.18). What archers and slingers wear is not explicitly described, but they are "very nimble . . . and highly mobile" (3.3.6) and thus cannot have much protective equipment.

§13. Various incidental features of military practice deserve mention. In battle a cavalryman might wear a gold *akinakēs* (short sword or dagger),[a] an honorific object but one with which a throat can be cut. (Cyrus also received gifts "for war or . . . finery"[b]—or both at once?) There are fire signals at 7.8.15 and a royal standard at 1.10.12. Troops fight under the whip at 3.4.25; Herodotus said the same of Xerxes' troops at Thermopylae,[c] but *Anabasis* is describing archers in a situation of tactical and topographical advantage who do not have to be forced into dangerously close contact with the enemy, so deployment of the whip seems strange. Cavalry horses are tied up at night, a tactical disadvantage (the Greeks exploit it to win two days free of harassment)[d] but necessary to prevent nighttime stampedes—a special danger, perhaps, because of the comparatively large numbers of horses present. Xenophon certainly presents it as a distinctive Persian phenomenon. Nighttime activity by infantry is not, however, precluded.[e] On the logistical front, we meet baggage animals in Artaxerxes' army and wagons in Cyrus' army.[f] Food could be supplied commercially[g] or by seizure, but we do not hear explicitly of provisions coming from official store-houses. Persian armies (like others) may wreck the property of those whom they are theoretically protecting.[h] The commanders of satrapal forces in Armenia travel with opulent tents and other appurtenances; presumably this was true of Cyrus and the King, although Xenophon does not comment beyond mentioning Cyrus' concubines.[i] It says something about the expected diversity of the "Persian army" when, at 4.5.10, Armenian villagers initially accept that a force of Greek soldiers (surely an entirely novel sight) is on its way to the local satrap.

§14. The presence of eastern Anatolian mercenaries in Armenia is a reminder that

D.12e  Persian bow: 3.3.7, 3.4.17. Crete: Ref. Map 1, CX.

D.12f  Relative performance of slingers: 3.3.7, 3.3.16–17. Rhodes: Ref. Map 4.1, DY.

D.13a  *Akinakēs* (ceremonial dagger): 1.8.29. See Figure 1.8.29.

D.13b  "For war or . . . finery": 1.9.23.

D.13c  Troops at Thermopylae: Herodotus 7.223. Thermopylae: Ref. Map 2, BY.

D.13d  Tied up at night: 3.4.35. Free of harassment: 3.4.37.

D.13e  Nighttime activity by infantry: 3.4.37, 4.4.17, 4.5.18.

D.13f  Artaxerxes' baggage animals: 2.2.15; Diodorus 14.22.4 (in Appendix S: Selections from Diodorus). Cyrus' wagons: 1.5.7, 1.10.18.

D.13g  Food supplied commercially: 1.2.18, 1.3.14, 1.5.6, 2.3.26–27, 3.1.2; Diodorus 14.19.9 (in Appendix S).

D.13h  Property destroyed by Persian army: 2.2.16.

D.13i  Opulent tents: 4.3.25, 4.4.21. Cyrus' concubines: 1.10.2.

Persian mercenary use is not just a matter of Greeks employed in the west, though they are the most prominent category across our sources, and Cyrus' accumulation of so many of them was without Persian precedent. All satraps were presumably entitled to hire mercenaries if they could find and afford them; Cyrus' actions became suspicious only when the scale exceeded the putative purpose.ᵃ A remarkable Greek of mercenary character is Phalinos, a man in Tissaphernes' entourage who claimed expertise in tactics and weapons training.ᵇ Had he come from Anatolia when Tissaphernes fled with his five hundred horsemen? Or was he a Greek who was already in Mesopotamia or Persia and became attached to Tissaphernes during the preparations for Cunaxa? His military contribution is a matter for conjecture, but he was ineffective as a negotiator after the battle.ᶜ

§15. A few broader observations can be made about Persian military strategies and tactics. That Cunaxa was fought where it was entails two decisions on Artaxerxes' part. The first was that Mesopotamia was the farthest west Cyrus could be confronted, given the time available, and that anywhere farther east would cede too much to the aggressor (Plutarchᵃ claims that Tiribazos convinced the King of this). The second was that the relevant area along the Euphrates Riverᵇ was a suitable battlefield. Unfortunately it is impossible to judge how wide a choice of such locations there may have been. The suggestion at 1.7.14 that Artaxerxes' forces were once farther west than Cunaxa, if true, would imply that he changed his mind on the point. But it is improbable that the ditch at 1.7.14–16 was ever intended to be part of the King's strategic or tactical planning.

§16. As for the battle itself, Xenophon ascribes to Artaxerxes no complex plan (the encirclement Cyrus fears at 1.8.23–24 is a product of disparity of numbers), though he does claim that after an attack on Cyrus' camp, the King regrouped his troops for an unsuccessful second-phase attack on the Greek mercenaries.ᵃ Meanwhile, Cyrus' troops entered battle in some disarray, having been caught unawares, and his strategy eventually turned on a make-or-break personal attack on the King.ᵇ The only other more-or-less formal battle involving Persian forces, that near Kalpe Harbor at 6.5.7–32, is notable for the way Pharnabazos' cavalry (which happily attacked scattered foragers at 6.4.24) chooses not to get involved, leaving the fighting against the Greek army to the Bithynians.

§17. This strategy of nonengagement is echoed on a larger scale by Pharnabazos' subsequent failure to do anything about the Greek army except pressure his Spartan contacts to get them out of Anatolia.ᵃ On a still larger scale, Tissaphernes preferred to harass the Greeks in the Tigris valley rather than force a decisive battle.ᵇ Tiribazos adopted a similar approach in Western Armenia.ᶜ How far their decisions were purely military is perhaps debatable, though Tiribazos at least probably lacked suffi-

---

D.14a  Cyrus' out-of-scale hire of mercenaries: 1.2.4.
D.14b  Phalinos: 2.1.7.
D.14c  Tactical cunning is attributed to Tissaphernes in Appendix L: The Battle of Cunaxa, §18. Phalinos an ineffective negotiator: 2.1.7–23.
D.15a  *Life of Artaxerxes* 7.2 (in Appendix T: Selections from Plutarch's *Life of Artaxerxes*).
D.15b  Euphrates River: Ref. Map 6, DZ.
D.16a  Attack on Cyrus' camp: 1.10.2–3, 1.10.7, 1.10.18. King regroups troops: 1.10.9–10.

D.16b  Caught unawares: 1.7.19–1.8.1. Personal attack on the King: 1.8.12, 1.8.24; compare Diodorus 14.23.5–7 (in Appendix S: Selections from Diodorus); Plutarch, *Life of Artaxerxes* 10–11 (in Appendix T).
D.17a  Pressure to remove the Ten Thousand from Anatolia: 7.1.2, 7.2.4–7.
D.17b  Tissaphernes restricts himself to harassment: 3.3.6–3.5.6.
D.17c  Tiribazos harasses Greeks: 4.4.18, 4.5.12, 4.5.17.

cient forces for any real alternative. (One doubts that the projected ambush at 4.4.18 could have had a really devastating effect.) Xenophon gives us some information about the methods of harassment,[d] none of it especially surprising—though there is a reference at 3.3.10 to what was later known as the Parthian shot.[e] That the Greeks made any progress at all in the first stage northward from the Zapatas River[f] after losing almost all their generals suggests that, even in ideal circumstances, Persian skirmishers could not operate completely continuously. Elsewhere we hear of other indirect strategies, such as destruction of food resources, disinformation, and manipulation of watercourses for psychological impact[g]—though the last two occur during a period of supposed truce.

§18. One possible surprise of *Anabasis* is that, although the narrative embraces large amounts of imperial territory, we see so little by way of local military occupation. The Caicus valley episode at 7.8.8–23 is famous because, uniquely, it details the military presence in a particular locality.[a] Otherwise we hear of forces mobilized at or close to regional borders (Armenia and Western Armenia) or sent beyond regional borders (Pharnabazos' cavalry) but are left with an impression of the countryside and its roads as devoid of systematic armed surveillance or fixed guard posts or garrison posts. Even at the Cilician Gates, the defenders had been in tents.[b] We cannot assess the permanence of the Cilician force that annihilated two Greek companies farther to the west[c] or be sure what military infrastructure facilitated the brutal (but apparently unusual) displays of mutilated "wrongdoers" at 1.9.13.

§19. But the impression may be partly illusory. Xenophon's journey was largely through imperial territory that was either essentially friendly (Anatolia) or on a war footing (Syria, Mesopotamia, Armenia). In the former case, local defense forces are irrelevant, granted that Xenophon's business is narrating the army's experiences, not describing Achaemenid infrastructure for its own sake.[a] In the latter case, soldiers who were usually scattered across the landscape either had been mobilized into the larger defense forces we *do* see or were weak and thus not expected to take any action against a serious military incursion and so, once again, did not become a matter of narrative interest. This explains why there was no resistance at the Syrian-Cilician Gates.[b] The defenders had gone, either because Abrokomas was taking them to Babylonia or because they knew it was impossible to hold the position against a large army with naval support and so withdrew. (A consideration of the latter sort had prompted Syennesis' earlier abandonment of the northerly Cilician Gates.)[c] The Syrian-Cilician Gates are the only dedicated nonurban fortified military site in *Anabasis*. Any others

D.17d  Methods of harassment: 3.3.6–10, 3.4.1–5, 3.4.14–15, 3.4.18, 3.4.25–33, 3.4.37–49.
D.17e  A Parthian shot is one fired backward from a fast-moving horse or, more generally, while the archer is in real or feigned retreat.
D.17f  Zapatas (modern Greater Zab) River: Map C.1.
D.17g  Persians destroy food resources: 1.6.2, 3.5.2–3. Engage in disinformation: 2.4.22. Manipulate watercourses: 2.3.13.
D.18a  Military presence: 7.8.15.
D.18b  Defenders in tents: 1.2.22. The Cilician Gates are to be distinguished from the similar gates at the

other end of Cilicia, on the Syrian border, the Syrian-Cilician Gates. Both locations appear on Ref. Map 5, CY (both labeled Kilikiai Pylai in the *Barrington Atlas*: Cilician Gates, 66 F2, Syrian-Cilician Gates, 67 C3).
D.18c  Annihilation of two Greek companies: 1.2.25.
D.19a  That is why we *do* hear a bit about Cilicia: the region's slightly uncertain response to Cyrus had practical consequences.
D.19b  Syrian-Cilician Gates: see n. D.18b.
D.19c  Abandonment of the Cilician Gates: 1.2.21.

thc Greeks saw must have been unoccupied or, if occupied, capable of being ignored and bypassed.[d] We hear about the Syrian-Cilician Gates only because they could theoretically have posed a military threat and Cyrus' army actually had to physically pass through their fortifications. Most of the imperial landscape was not like that, and so we hear more of the provisions found in towns and villages than about the soldiers who were supposed to protect them. Similarly we hear about the Caicus valley because the salient enemy incursion was by a few hundred men, not the entire Greek army, and because no central mobilization of resources had yet occurred against either that army or Thibron's[e] expeditionary force.

§20. But although there may be an element of illusion, it remains implicit in the explanation just given that the landscape was not heavily militarized or intended to provide a series of immediate local checks to major military attack. This is part of what lies behind Xenophon's famous observation that one could penetrate deep into imperial territory provided that one moved quickly:[a] regional resistance takes time to mobilize from dispersed resources, and there is no other option. Nothing in Xenophon's generic model for provincial defense in *Oikonomikos* and *Kyroupaideia*[b] and nothing implicit in the mysterious people "whose muster point was the plain of Kastolos" can stand against this. The inclination to deal with the detachment of the Mysians, Pisidians, Lycaonians, and Kardouchoi[c] by a mixture of laissez-faire and occasional attack rather than conquest and permanent occupation presupposes an essential realism about what could be achieved without a large, transregional, institutionally uniform, and multifunctional army—precisely the thing of which our sources provide no real sign at this period.

§21. Greeks do not always get the better of non-Greeks in *Anabasis*.[a] But elements of the Persian army never get the upper hand for long: the first day north of the Zapatas went very badly, but the situation is completely reversed the next day against a much larger attack thanks to the recruitment of just two hundred slingers and fifty horsemen.[b] Later problems are dealt with by tactical deployment.[c] The Kardouchoi cause much greater suffering than Tissaphernes ever did, but the Greeks get through their territory, whereas an entire Persian army had once allegedly been annihilated there.[d] Artaxerxes' forces at Cunaxa may not have made the undisciplined noise Cyrus predicted, but they reportedly twice ran away from the Greeks before striking a single blow.[e] The King is subsequently portrayed as nervous about camping too close to the Greeks, and a year later Pharnabazos' cavalry avoided them

---

D.19d  The fortified Armenian village (4.5.9–10) and Asidates' "tower" (7.8.12–13) are not specifically military, and the status of the fortress where the population of Tarsus took refuge (1.2.24) and of the Armenian towered houses at 4.4.2 is debatable. The Tarsian refuge was no threat to the Greeks, while there was nobody in Armenia to keep the Greeks from getting the food supplies they wanted. Tarsus: Ref. Map 5, CY.

D.19e  On Thibron, see Appendix W: Brief Biographies, §35.

D.20a  Penetrability of imperial territory: 1.5.9.

D.20b  Provincial defense systems: Xenophon, *Oikonomikos* (*On the Management of the Household*) 4; *Kyroupaideia* (*The Education of Cyrus*)

8.6.1–3, 8.6.9, 8.6.16.

D.20c  Mysia, Pisidia: Ref. Map 4.1, BY, CZ. Lycaonia: Ref. Map 5, CX. Kardouchoi territory: Map C.1.

D.21a  Non-Greek successes: see, for example, Menon's unit in Cilicia, 1.2.25; Drilai, 5.2.3–27; Mossynoeci, 5.4.16–20; Caicus valley raid, 7.8.12–19. Drilai, Mossynoeci territories: Ref. Map 5, AZ.

D.21b  First day north of the Zapatas: 3.3.6–11. Recruitment of slingers and horsemen: 3.3.20, 3.4.1–6.

D.21c  Tactical deployment: 3.4.24–30, 3.4.37–49.

D.21d  Kardouchoi cause suffering: 4.3.2. Persian army annihilated: 3.5.16.

D.21e  Undisciplined noise: 1.7.4, 1.8.11. Persians run away: 1.8.19, 1.10.10.

on the battlefield.[f] *Anabasis* does not, in short, give a very supportive picture of the Persian army, nor is there anything to correspond to Herodotus' insistence that the Persians fought bravely at Plataea despite having the wrong equipment to face Greek hoplites.[g] On the contrary, Cyrus himself is made to criticize non-Greek fighters, and at Tyriaion we hear how the Greeks stage a spectacle to bring out non-Greek inferiority.[h]

§22. Xenophon's account of the Persian military environment is partial in every sense. But if it is easy to recognize the bias, it is not so easy to correct for it. The thought experiments with idealized models of Persian military practice in other of Xenophon's works (*Oikonomikos* 4, *Kyroupaideia*) do not involve Persians fighting Greeks, and there are few Persian successes against Greeks in *Hellenika*. Some readers may suspect that particular fights were closer-run than they are made to appear or may discern realistic avoidance of poor odds rather than cowardice or systematic weakness. Others may think systematic weakness was precisely the issue—and that Persians' use of more and more Greek mercenaries in the fourth century was an intelligent response to that weakness, not a sign of moral surrender. But the all-embracing history of the Persian army that might finally settle such an issue remains to be written.

Christopher Tuplin
Gladstone Professor of Greek
Department of Archaeology, Classics, and Egyptology
University of Liverpool
Liverpool, UK

D.21f  King nervous: 2.2.17–18, 2.3.1. Cavalry avoids Greeks: 6.5.30.
D.21g  Herodotus 9.62.

D.21h  Cyrus criticizes non-Greek fighters: 1.7.3–4. Spectacle: 1.2.15–18. Tyriaion: Ref. Map 5, CX.

# APPENDIX E

## *Panhellenism*

§1. The word "panhellenism" is a compound of the Greek words for "all Greek." It implies the notion of Greekness but more particularly is understood as the notion of the unification of Greece in a war of conquest against the East, which was governed by the Persians from the sixth to the fourth century. The Persians posed a constant threat to the freedom of the Greeks on the Aegean coast, and indeed twice invaded mainland Greece, in 490 and 480–479, as was recounted later in the fifth century by Herodotus.[a] The Greek conquest of the East was sometimes explicitly associated with winning wealth and remedying the relative poverty of the Greeks at home, through the acquisition of plunder or settlement in colonies in the conquered land. There was also the potential for imposition of Greek values on the East after conquest, through occupation and governance. The fourth-century orator Isocrates made the most explicit appeal for panhellenism, in works of rhetoric that sought to persuade the powers of his time—Athens in his Speech 4 (*Panegyricus*), Macedonia in his Speech 5 (*Philippus*)[b]—to settle differences between the states of Greece and lead them in unity on such an expedition. In *Panegyricus* he suggests that the idea was widespread when he refers to others "who teach us that we must put an end to our wars and turn against the barbarian, who list all the disadvantages of the wars between ourselves and the advantages that will come from the expedition against him."[c]

§2. But unity was not something that came naturally to Greeks. Herodotus (8.144) had the Athenians point to their common blood, common language, and common religious cults and practices in a speech designed to explain their resistance to the Persians, yet Greek history shows that it was much more normal for Greek city-states to be at war with one another than to live in harmony. The formation of empires and leagues, such as the Peloponnesian League[a] in the late sixth century and

E.1a  Persian Empire: Ref. Map 9. Aegean Sea: Ref. Map 2, BZ.
E.1b  Isocrates (436–338) was an influential Athenian rhetorician and a contemporary of Xenophon's. Athens: Ref. Map 2, CZ. Macedonia: Ref. Map 3, CX.
E.1c  Author's translation.
E.2a  Peloponnesian League: a name given by modern scholars to those city-states, most of them within the Peloponnese, that swore to have the same friends and enemies as Sparta and to follow the Spartans wherever they might lead.

the Athenian Empire in the mid-fifth century, did unify parts of the Greek world; but it was not until the mid-fourth century that the greater number of the city-states of mainland Greece were brought into line. This was the achievement of Philip of Macedonia, who defeated the most powerful of these and imposed unity on the mainland Greek states through his creation of the League of Corinth[b] (338/7). Then indeed it could be said that panhellenism bore real fruit: Philip's son Alexander went on to lead an expedition of Greeks and Macedonians against the Persians and succeeded in transferring their kingship to his own person. He hellenized the East (at least to an extent) by blending Macedonian and eastern royal protocols, establishing cities along Greek lines, and imposing Macedonian governors alongside Persian ones, as well as through intermarriage. But the successes of Philip and Alexander lay sixty years and more in the future when the Ten Thousand (a force of Greek mercenaries) fought their way through the Persian Empire, as recorded in Xenophon's *Anabasis.*

§3. Xenophon has been thought to have encouraged panhellenist ambitions against Persia, both as the author of *Anabasis* and in what he says as a character within it. Since it has been argued that panhellenism was a widespread ideology already in the fifth century, we have special reason to expect to find it in a fourth-century text in which a large number of Greek soldiers go on an expedition to the East. Xenophon himself says in *Hellenika* 3.4.2 that when, less than half a decade after this expedition, the Spartan Lysander proposed that King Agesilaos[a] should lead an expedition against Persia, he referred to the survival of the Ten Thousand as a reason for being confident of success. Yet examination of the text of *Anabasis* reveals little that might constitute a traditional panhellenic theme. Some, therefore, emphasizing the flexibility of the notion, have found that *Anabasis* as a whole demonstrates Xenophon's own interpretation of the theme, so that panhellenism is to be found in the working of the community of the Ten Thousand. The panhellenic need for unity among Greeks against the East is thus said to be reflected in Xenophon's emphasis on how unity within the army gave them success, while disunity meant failure. So, for example, Xenophon's plan to found a city, outlined at *Anabasis* 5.6.15, becomes a "panhellenic" reaction to remedy their increasing disunity.

§4. To begin at the beginning: Cyrus the Younger's original plan to use the Ten Thousand to depose his brother Artaxerxes II has some intimations of panhellenism.[a] Cyrus was a Persian, who might have liked to draw on a united Greece in the struggle against his brother but took the best men he could find from Greece's separate regions, in particular Thessaly, Arcadia, and Laconia.[b] Nevertheless he seems to champion the superiority of Greekness at 1.7.2–4, where he tells the Greeks that he prefers them to barbarian[c] troops because of the superiority they possess in their "freedom," which he says he would swap for everything he possesses. This championing

E.2b   Corinth: Ref. Map 2, CY.
E.3a   On Agesilaos, see Appendix W: Brief Biographies of Selected Characters in *Anabasis*, §2. Sparta: Ref. Map 2, DY.
E.4a   On Cyrus the Younger and Artaxerxes, see Appendix W, §§10, 6.

E.4b   The following locations appear on Ref. Map 2: Thessaly, AY; Arcadia, CX; Laconia, DY.
E.4c   Barbarian: for a discussion of the nuances of this word in Greek as compared to English, see the Introduction, §5.1.

of "hellenism" is a regular ingredient of panhellenism, but of course the evidence is compromised, because Cyrus is encouraging the Greeks to follow him, and the barbarians he is referring to do not include his own close Persian associates, who perform so heroically alongside him at the battle of Cunaxa.[d] Cyrus offers another aspect of panhellenic thought when, at 1.7.7, he appears to promise to give the Greek leaders provinces to rule over if he is successful against his brother. That might look like the hellenization of the East that was to come with Alexander, when governorships of provinces were given to Macedonians and even some Greeks. But Cyrus' promised rewards were a way of keeping his Greeks loyal rather than a deliberate hellenization of the East. Some believe that his freedom speech is undermined by the greed that the Greeks show for his promised rewards; while this may go too far, it is evident that in offering such rewards, Cyrus is tailoring his speech to suit his audience.

§5. Xenophon certainly does promote the virtues of the Ten Thousand in *Anabasis*, but he does not include a panhellenic crusade in his summary of their various motives for joining Cyrus.[a] According to this summary, they joined the expedition because of Cyrus' reputation for generosity and for material reward. That generosity is confirmed in the obituary for Cyrus at 1.9. The later obituaries for the Greek generals[b] confirm that some were in it to get rich and famous, by fair means (Proxenos) or foul (Menon).[c] Klearchos, exceptionally, loved fighting even above making money and spent what money he had on making war, as Xenophon puts it.[d] These motives encourage us to see any panhellenism within the Ten Thousand as an accidental by-product of other motives.

§6. Once Cyrus is killed, in the battle of Cunaxa, Klearchos as leader wants to use the army to put another candidate on the throne: in the first instance Ariaios, and then he is duped into thinking that Tissaphernes might be a candidate.[a] But Klearchos then abandons the idea of kingmaking and thinks, as a regular mercenary would, of serving the Persians in a campaign to subdue Mysia or Egypt;[b] that seems far from panhellenic. This notion too comes to nothing and soon gives way to a desire on the part of the army to return to Greece. At 2.4.3–4, however, the Greeks explicitly see their achievement against the King as encouragement for a panhellenic crusade: they convey to Klearchos their concern that the King will annihilate them because he will not want them to make him a laughingstock by letting them return home and report that so few are needed to defeat him. This looks promising for the panhellenic thesis, but Klearchos in his reply does not comment on it, and the theme goes undeveloped.

§7. Xenophon's concern when he comes into the action after the generals have been seized by Tissaphernes is a safe return home for himself and the army. He has no ambitions for the army to serve the Persians as mercenaries. In his first speech to the army, at 3.2.7–32, he does hint that they might remain and settle in the East,

E.4d　Heroism of Cyrus' Persian associates: 1.8.21–28. Battlefield of Cunaxa: Ref. Map 6, DZ.
E.5a　Motives for joining Cyrus: 6.4.8.
E.5b　Obituaries of Greek generals: 2.6.
E.5c　On Proxenos and Menon, see Appendix W: Brief Biographies, §§29, 23.
E.5d　Klearchos' love of war: 2.6.6–7. On Klearchos, see Appendix W, §20.

E.6a　Putting Ariaios on the throne: 2.1.4. Klearchos duped: 2.5.23; n. 2.5.23a discusses rival interpretations of the passage. On Ariaios and Tissaphernes, see Appendix W, §§4, 37.
E.6b　Possible campaigns against Mysia or Egypt: 2.5.13. Mysia: Ref. Map 4.1, BY; Ref. Map 4.2, BZ. Egypt: Ref. Map 1, DX.

but the context compromises the message. Settlement is first presented as something they should pretend to be considering, so as to encourage the King to facilitate their departure rather than harbor such enemies. But he says that if they did that, they might be tempted by the lovely big Persian women and forget all about returning home, like the lotus-eaters in Homer's *Odyssey*. So, finally he suggests that they should go back home, in order to persuade the Greeks there to remedy their poverty by going east and becoming wealthy. The transfer of populations and consequent remedying of poverty that Xenophon mentions here are panhellenic ideas, but it is hard to work out whether he actually supports them when his purpose is mainly to put some heart into the men. In any case he again leaves the ideas undeveloped: he breaks off and says that "all these good things" come to those who conquer,[a] and he gets down to the business of getting home safely by burning all the excess baggage, including what contributes to the easy life, such as wagons. The references to the substantial Persian women suggest a light touch to the idea of settling that would prevent anyone from taking this altogether seriously.

§8. Xenophon does point to weaknesses in the eastern power structures, and his narrative manner when he comments on these at 1.5.9 ("anyone who considered the matter carefully…") seems to encourage the audience to reflect on them. These are part of panhellenic thinking. He notes here, for instance, the distances that had to be covered for effective action against an invader, which is the problem of a highly centralized empire. He later points to the weakness of the Persian cavalry army at night, because the horses are tethered.[a] But these comments just explain matters in the text: why Cyrus was moving so fast, and why the Greeks were able to put distance between themselves and the Persians as they were striking camp. They are suggestions, no more than that, which might make the audience start to wonder about whether an invasion might possibly not be so difficult.

§9. After the death of Cyrus, there is no further offensive military activity against the Persians, which is, after all, the central ingredient of "normal" panhellenism. The Greeks confront other nations as they make their way home; but though these others are often disaffected from the Persians (for example, the Kardouchoi),[a] the Greeks make no attempt to gather these other peoples into a larger force to fight against Persia, which is a panhellenic idea, and what Agesilaos subsequently tried to do in Paphlagonia.[b] Nor is the spirit of panhellenism evident at all when the Ten Thousand arrive on the coast of the Black Sea[c] and have to deal with the Greek colonists there. It has been noted that Diodorus Siculus conceals tensions between troops and colonists in his own account of events,[d] but Xenophon is candid in his revelations. In the relations between the Ten Thousand and the Greeks at Heraclea, Sinope, and Byzantium,[e] he portrays "business as usual," which means hostility and

---

E.7a  "All these good things": 3.2.26 ("All these good things belong to those who are the stronger").

E.8a  Persian horses tethered at night: 3.4.35.

E.9a  Disaffection of the Kardouchoi: 3.5.16, 4.1.8. Kardouchoi territory: Ref. Map 6, BY.

E.9b  During his expedition against Persia of 396–394, Agesilaos sought to bring over local powers to his side: Xenophon, *Hellenika* 4.1; at 4.1.2 Xenophon writes that Agesilaos "had for a long time wanted

to induce some nation to revolt from the Persian King" (Marincola/Landmark translation). Paphlagonia: Ref. Map 5, AX.

E.9c  Black Sea: Ref. Map 1, AX.

E.9d  Diodorus 14.19–31 (in Appendix S: Selections from Diodorus).

E.9e  Heraclea, Byzantium: Ref. Map 4.1, AZ, AY. Sinope: Ref. Map 5, AY.

suspicion. The colonies did not welcome the entry into their territory of an army in need of shelter and provisions, and one now inclined to violence if those needs are not met. The people of Sinope do appeal to their common Greekness in a speech designed to protect their interests against the Ten Thousand, but they threaten to ally with a local Paphlagonian chief against their fellow Greeks if they do not get their way, and the Ten Thousand respond by asserting that if they are provoked, they will make an ally of the Paphlagonian ruler against them.[f]

§10. On the arrival of the Ten Thousand at Byzantium, panhellenism is again lacking. Xenophon describes at 7.1.25–31 how a section of the army wants to use violence against the city and how he appealed to the soldiers' affinity with other Greeks in order to make them desist. He indicates their folly in alienating the Spartan governor when they already have so many other enemies, and says how right the Greeks of the area would be to turn against them when, though the Ten Thousand never once tried to take a foreign city, they now want to plunder the first Greek city they come across (which is, of course, an exaggeration, suited to the emotional context of his speech). His advice is that they should get what they want by obeying the Spartans, not plundering the places the Spartans govern. There is no panhellenism in their relations with Sparta, either: in the very antithesis of panhellenism, the new Spartan governor sells four hundred of the Ten Thousand into slavery.[a] Perhaps the most we can say of these passages is that they serve as negative paradigms, as a warning to any future panhellenic force that they will have problems with other Greeks if they mean to traverse their territory.

§11. One of the passages many have linked to panhellenic sentiments on Xenophon's part is his proposal to found a city on the coast of the Black Sea, where those on the expedition could settle.[a] Xenophon's thoughts here encompass the extension of Greek territory, which is a panhellenic notion; but this "colony" is not in the heartland and not directed against the Persians, and, it could be argued, it looks like just another colony in the Pontic region, alongside Heraclea and the rest. There is also un-panhellenic opposition to the notion from within the army, from those who do not want to stay or those who suspect Xenophon's motives, and also from the cities already occupying the region, Sinope and Heraclea, whose immediate response is to offer money and ships to remove the Greeks from their territory.[b] Xenophon gives in because of this opposition, insisting on his perennial theme that the army must stay together at all costs or risk separate annihilation in diminished numbers.

§12. Should we see Xenophon's drive for unity in the army as a reflection of the need for unity among the cities of Greece in the panhellenic vision of Isocrates, in which putting an end to intra-Greek wars was a necessary precondition of success against the barbarian? When Xenophon describes the disunity within the army at Kotyora, he appeals to notions of togetherness, asking his troops how they can fight their enemies when they kill one another, and what cities, knowing of their internal lawlessness, will receive them.[a] The lesson certainly is that they fail when their unity

E.9f   Sinopean threat: 5.5.12. Response of the Ten
       Thousand: 5.5.23.
E.10a  Sold into slavery: 7.2.6.
E.11a  Possible foundation of Black Sea city: 5.6.15.

E.11b  Sinope and Heraclea offer inducements to depart:
       5.6.21.
E.12a  Appeals to solidarity: 5.7.32–33. Kotyora: Ref.
       Map 5, AZ.

fails. The most notable instance of this is at 6.2.9–12, when the Arcadians and Achaeans leave the coalition.[b] These two groups drew a natural unity from the close proximity of their homelands in the Peloponnese,[c] but when they split from the main force in the later stages of the expedition, they endangered themselves and the common cause. Xenophon worked hard to preserve unity in the interests of the common security of the whole army, and by 6.4.11 the previous dissidents have sworn not to split again, in the interests of security. Yet the dangers arising from Greek disunity were visible much earlier than Isocrates and Xenophon; they can be seen clearly in Herodotus' narrative of the Persian Wars of the early fifth century. If we do interpret the recognition of the dangers of disunity as a form of panhellenism in *Anabasis*, then it just repeats the lessons that should have been learned from the Persian Wars and is as much and as little of a panhellenic tale as Herodotus' account of that earlier experience.

§13. The humiliation of the Persian King's infantry by the Ten Thousand at Cunaxa showed that Greek hoplites[a] could, under the right leadership, make their way into the heart of Persia and defeat their eastern opposition. This may well have encouraged fourth-century panhellenists to think that, with a larger force and better leadership, they might achieve a more complete success against Persia. And the safe return of the Ten Thousand to the coast might have encouraged them to think that, even were they to fail and suffer severe hardships, they need not be annihilated. But at no point is this encouragement explicit in the work. In *Anabasis* Xenophon mentions elements in the ideology of panhellenism, such as the common identity of Greeks and the founding of colonies in the East, even the remedying of their poverty thereby, but he does not develop these ideas, and the lack of development suggests that he is not interested in actively pursuing panhellenic themes. It has even been suggested that his description of the expedition shows what a panhellenic expedition should do its best to avoid. This is, certainly, reflected in the army's relations with the Greeks of the Black Sea, which shows moreover that panhellenism can at least on occasion be an opportunistic front for self-interest or an argument directed against indiscipline. It is also reflected in the tendency toward disunity, which Xenophon emphasizes was true of the army after the initial journey down to the sea.

§14. By contrast, Xenophon's account of the expedition of Agesilaos in 396–394 in *Hellenika* represents an eastern panhellenic crusade more positively. Here Peloponnesians and Asiatic Greeks unite under a Spartan king and make inroads into the East by creating a strong cavalry, winning battles over the Persians, and forging alliances with disaffected rulers against the Persian King. But here too initial success is undermined by disunity when the Greeks on the mainland, financed by Persian gold, unite to make war against the Spartans rather than join their crusade against the Persians. This forces Agesilaos to return to defend Sparta and its allies against their Greek foes. Xenophon's recognition of panhellenic elements in Agesilaos' expedition makes it all the more significant that he does not develop them in *Anabasis*.

E.12b  Arcadia, Achaea: Ref. Map 2, CX.
E.12c  Peloponnese: Ref. Map 2, CY.
E.13a  Hoplites: heavily armed infantrymen; see Appen-
         dix H: Infantry and Cavalry in *Anabasis*, §§2–3.

He seems to have been more interested in other themes, such as the nature of leadership, so evident in his treatment of Cyrus and himself.

§15. There were other writers who employed the idea that the march of the Ten Thousand exposed the military weakness of the Persians, and made it the focus of a more central panhellenic theme. Isocrates did so in encouraging his own crusade in *Panegyricus,* and again in *Philippus,* an open letter he wrote much later to Philip of Macedonia.[a] Arrian, the historian of the Macedonian conquest of Persia, said that Alexander the Great referred to it in a speech to his men before the battle of Issus in 333, in which he declared that Xenophon and his Ten Thousand had routed the King with his whole power near Babylon.[b] The theme is taken up again in the second century by the historian Polybius, who argued that the failure to mount head-on opposition to Xenophon's return march from Mesopotamia was the ultimate cause of Alexander's invasion.[c] Yet any development of the idea in Xenophon's *Anabasis* needs to be explored irrespective of the later achievements of Philip and Alexander, which Xenophon could not have had in mind when he wrote, and without the assumption that one can read the views of Isocrates into the narrative of Xenophon.[d]

Vivienne J. Gray
Professor Emeritus
Department of Classics and Ancient History
University of Auckland
Auckland, New Zealand

E.15a  Isocrates refers to the Ten Thousand in support of his advocacy of crusade: in *Panegyricus,* 4.145–149; in *Philippus,* 5.90–98.
E.15b  Alexander's speech: Arrian, *Anabasis* 2.7.8–9. Issus: Ref. Map 5, CY. Babylon: Ref. Map 6, DZ.
E.15c  Polybius 3.6.10. Mesopotamia: Ref. Map 6, CX.
E.15d  For more on the subject of panhellenism in Xenophon's *Anabasis,* see Dillery 1995; Flower 2000, 2012; Mitchell 2007, esp. p. 23; Tim Rood, "Panhellenism and Self-Presentation: Xenophon's Speeches," in Lane Fox 2004, 305–29.

# APPENDIX F

## *Thrace*

§1. Xenophon's ability to sketch a scene with a few precise details has ensured that his memoir contains references and circumstantial evidence of a kind that has not survived from classical antiquity in any other way. At least, the informal character of his narrative has immortalized characters and details that most other writers evidently thought of little interest or value. Nevertheless the detail can be deceptive, especially if one makes the mistake of thinking that Xenophon's subject in Book 7 is the peoples and cultures of southeastern Europe and of the Asiatic shores of the Propontis[a] and the straits at each end of it. Rather, his intention was simply to tell the story of the mercenary army.

§2. Seuthes, the Thracian about whom we hear the most in *Anabasis*, provides a useful example of Xenophon's approach in this narrative.[a] In 400 this man was a minor ruler or princeling of the dominant Thracian tribe, the Odrysae.[b] He is also referred to in Xenophon's more wide-ranging history, *Hellenika*.[c] In *Anabasis* we do not really get to know much about Seuthes' political profile. He is presented in the context of a local campaign, conducted with the help of Xenophon's surviving mercenary army, in the hinterland of Byzantium.[d] We learn more about him in *Hellenika*, where Xenophon describes his collaboration with other leading contemporary figures operating in the north Aegean, including the Spartan general Derkylidas and the Athenian general Thrasyboulos.[e] But the Seuthes of *Hellenika* seems to be a rather different kind of leader from the man presented in *Anabasis*. In *Hellenika* he

NOTE: All references to *Hellenika* in this appendix refer to Xenophon's work.

F.1a   Propontis: Ref. Map 3, CZ.
F.2a   On Seuthes, see Appendix W: Brief Biographies of Selected Characters in *Anabasis*, §30. Thrace: Ref. Map 3.
F.2b   Odrysae territory: Ref. Map 3, CY.
F.2c   *Hellenika* 3.2.2, 3.2.9. Two inscriptions from Athens that have been dated to around 389 refer to individual Thracian leaders mentioned in *Anabasis*: Seuthes in *Inscriptiones Graecae* (*IG*), vol. 2, 2nd ed., no. 21 (the fragmentary text men-

tions an alliance between the Athenians and Seuthes; the Athenian general Chabrias is twice mentioned as a witness for the Athenians) and Medokos in *IG*, vol. 2, 2nd ed., no. 22 (also very fragmentary).
F.2d   Hinterland of Byzantium: Map 7.3.44.
F.2e   Derkylidas: *Hellenika* 3.2.2–5. Thrasyboulos: *Hellenika* 4.8.26; see also Diodorus 14.94.2. On Derkylidas, see Appendix W, §12. The following locations appear on Ref. Map 2: Aegean Sea, BZ; Sparta, DY; Athens, CZ.

is presented as a reasonably effective regional commander, dealing with senior representatives of major foreign powers in an apparently constructive spirit. In *Anabasis* Seuthes is a more ambiguous figure, whose motives are never explored, whose relations to other political actors are not investigated in any detail, and whose behavior is sometimes enigmatic. Princes, such as Seuthes and another local princeling named Teres, coexisted with the paramount king of the Odrysian Thracians, represented by the figure of Medokos[f] in Xenophon's story. Medokos is based far into the interior, twelve days' journey inland, and interstate embassies, such as the emissaries bearing gifts from the city of Parium,[g] are directed to him. But in neither work does Xenophon provide a physical description or political analysis of Thrace. He simply presents a series of incidents in succession.

§3. Partly for this reason, it is controversial where the balance of power lay between Seuthes and Medokos. An earlier high king, Sitalkes, had been very much the dominant figure over the whole of Thrace, and indeed the eastern Balkan area more widely, and had been able to raise huge armies, as the contemporary historian Thucydides tells us in connection with his expedition of 429.[a] His immediate successor, Seuthes I, who reigned in the generation before Xenophon's Seuthes, was able to raise even more taxation than Sitalkes had done from his Thracian subjects.[b] But Medokos seems a somewhat distant figure in *Anabasis*, and Xenophon's Seuthes refers to a time of troubles in which Seuthes' father, Maisades, lost control of his princedom over three non-Odrysian tribes.[c] Many scholars consider Medokos to have had less control over the princelings of the periphery, like Seuthes, than his predecessors had had, and indeed eventually Seuthes did rebel against him.[d] However, the evidence of material culture shows that central regulation was strong in the final third of the fifth century and the first half of the fourth. An inscription (c. 350) referring to an *emporion* (trading station) at Pistiros, in central Thrace, and at other locations in the interior reinforces this impression.[e] The time of troubles was in the past and could have been quite brief. Seuthes may well have had a degree of autonomy (as suggested at 7.3.16); but his sidekick Medosades' reference to Medokos as king of the interior at 7.7.3, and the active intervention of a senior Odrysian officer at this juncture on Medosades' behalf, show that the wider pattern of authority was operating in 400/399, irrespective of Seuthes' campaign. Indeed, the relationship between Seuthes and Medokos need not have been anything other than cordial at this point. Medokos had given Seuthes the resources to regain his father's former command, and Seuthes acknowledged Medokos as king.[f] There is no reason to think that Seuthes' frustrations in 400, voiced at 7.2.32–33, were directed at Medokos rather than at the rather shadowy, unnamed persons or groups who had deprived his father, Maisades, of his inheritance.

F.2f    Teres: *Anabasis* 7.5.1, n. 7.5.1b. Medokos is given an initial "A" in other works (*Hellenika* 4.8.26; Isocrates 5.6). Other references to him may be found at Diodorus 13.105.3, 14.94.2 (not in Appendix S: Selections from Diodorus). On Medokos, see Appendix W: Brief Biographies, §22.

F.2g    Emissaries from Parium: 7.3.13–16. Parium is mentioned a number of times in the story as one of the chief stopping-off points on the Asiatic coast of the straits (7.2.7, 7.3.20); archaeological evidence from inland Thrace confirms the close cooperation between it and the Odrysian kings. Parium: Ref. Map 4.2, AX.

F.3a    Thucydides 2.98.3–4.

F.3b    Seuthes' tax revenues: Thucydides 2.97.3.

F.3c    Maisades lost control over tribes: 7.2.32.

F.3d    Seuthes' rebellion: Aristotle, *Politics* 5, 1312a14.

F.3e    For the Pistiros inscription, see Chankowski and Domaradzka 1999. Pistiros: Ref. Map 3, CX. This location is disputed; others place it on the coast as Pistyros (*Barrington Atlas*, Map 51 D3).

F.3f    Seuthes acknowledges Medokos as king: 7.2.32.

§4. Though there is a mention of Seuthes in passing at 5.1.15 and there are preliminary references to him at 7.1.5 and 7.1.14, the narrative of *Anabasis* first turns
our attention more fully to him in 7.2. Here he is introduced as a local ruler, or
would-be ruler, who receives the principal officers of the mercenary army at night in
a fortified aerie. Some of the specific information given in connection with this fortified residence (dubbed a tower at 7.2.21) is the sort of graphic detail that only
Xenophon, among ancient historians, provides. He and a small group of fellow officers set off by night on horseback to meet up with Seuthes. Xenophon describes the
fires the men come across, which they soon realize were intended to enable easy
detection of intruders. The Greeks were expected to identify themselves to invisible
Thracian sentries over the course of about seven miles to Seuthes' nighttime location.[a] At some undisclosed distance from their destination, they were escorted by
two hundred peltasts, who had been notified by one of the sentries.[b] Evidently
Seuthes' troop dispositions were intended to keep a close watch on any developments that took place at any time of the day or night, and he was well aware of the
various movements of Greek and Persian soldiers on either side of the Propontis. We
know from *Anabasis* that he was assisted in this by bilingual speakers.[c] In view of the
amount of coming and going between the mercenaries and various military and
commercial personnel, it would seem that there were quite a few of these, particularly in coastal areas, quite apart from official ambassadors like Medosades.[d]

§5. Seuthes offered Xenophon and the remaining Cyreans (former mercenaries
of Cyrus[a]) a paid contract on the European side of the Propontis. He evidently
tempted the mercenaries with plentiful booty and various kinds of material induce-
ment: a Cyzicene stater[b] a month for each soldier, with captains getting twice the
pay and generals four times a soldier's pay, as well as land, herds of cattle, and a
coastal fort.[c] Xenophon himself was offered further personal distinctions: not only
three of Seuthes' forts but also Seuthes' own daughter in marriage, together with a
bride-price for a daughter of Xenophon's, should he have one,[d] but we hear nothing of any further negotiations about women. This exceeds what a mercenary captain or general might expect as a reward for a single campaign, and it implies that
Seuthes was not just interested in a temporary arrangement but had other, longer-
term plans only hinted at in Xenophon's account. The Cyreans eventually stayed in
Seuthes' employ, however, for only about two months.

§6. The normal role of Greek mercenaries was as trained infantrymen, who could
stand up to both cavalry and infantry in battle when deployed in the deep ranks of
the phalanx[a] formation. But Seuthes did not expect Xenophon's mercenaries to
function in that way. So much is apparent when at 7.3.43–44 Seuthes describes the
tactics he intends to use in taking "enemy" villages. The speed of the Thracian cav-

F.4a  Journey to Seuthes' location: 7.2.17–19. About 7
miles/11 kilometers: the Greek text says 60 stades;
see Appendix O: Ancient Greek and Persian Units
of Measurement, §5.
F.4b  Peltast escort: 7.2.20. Peltasts: light-armed
infantrymen; see Appendix H: Infantry and Cavalry in *Anabasis*, §§4–5.
F.4c  Use of interpreters: 7.2.19.
F.4d  Medosades: used by Seuthes as an envoy: 7.1.5,

7.2.10, 7.2.23; also appears at 7.7.1–19.
F.5a  On Cyrus the Younger, see Appendix W: Brief
Biographies, §10.
F.5b  For Cyzicene staters, see Appendix O, §§12, 15.
F.5c  Seuthes' offers to Cyreans: 7.2.36.
F.5d  Seuthes' offers to Xenophon: 7.2.38.
F.6a  Phalanx: a body of troops drawn up across a broad
front in close formation; for more, see Appendix
H, §§13–15.

alry was essential to surprise and overwhelm a lowland community; peltasts then followed up the cavalry. The Greek mercenaries were expected to provide a support force to hold the positions and property taken by the Thracian cavalry and peltasts. This tactic seems to have worked well on a number of occasions.[b]

§7. As the late historian Brian Bosworth remarked, "The . . . campaign in Thrace was notable for its lack of military action";[a] hence it is difficult for us to assess Thracian fighting tactics from Xenophon's narrative. The mercenary army was largely engaged in attacks on civilian populations, not in combat against Thracian troops. Even then Xenophon is less interested in precise topographical details or cultural distinctions than he is in the thrill of the action. So we hear about one occasion when javelins are hurled into houses and clubs are raised against any potential spears, before the houses are fired within their stake enclosures (neither houses nor enclosures are described in a way that can be visualized). The raiders then flee, throwing their light curved shields (*peltai*) over their backs.[b] Similarly, when Xenophon remarks at 7.4.4 on the appropriateness of winter gear in the mountains of southeastern Thrace—notably the traditional foxskin caps (*alōpekides*), which covered the head and ears, knee-length tunics, and ankle-length cloaks (*zeirai*) instead of the much shorter *chlamys* more familiar to a Greek audience—this brief reference is not a preliminary to any digression on Thracian dress, tactics, or weaponry. He does not even fill it out by mentioning the calfskin boots and the colorfulness of the stripe-patterned *zeirai* noted by Herodotus and depicted by Athenian vase painters.[c]

§8. Xenophon does, however, reveal something in passing about Thracian armor, for at 7.3.40 he points out that Seuthes' cavalrymen wore breastplates. Some exceptional examples of Thracian body armor have come to light in recent excavations, including a spectacular outfit, composed of iron scales on a leather backing, that would have covered the entire torso of a man, with flaps over the abdomen and thighs and a matching iron, leather-backed pectoral.[a] So the Greeks whom Xenophon records at 7.4.16 as putting on body armor might have acquired all or part of it locally. They might even have acquired the kinds of very striking armor that archaeology has unearthed. The narrative makes clear that large quantities of mobile wealth were in regular circulation and might get sold and resold at markets in towns like Perinthus and Byzantium.[b] This makes it likely that many soldiers, whether Thracian or Greek, had access to many different sorts of equipment and weapons. The kinds of weapons and armor excavated from hundreds of Thracian burials of the fifth and fourth centuries imply that this was true of Thracian cavalrymen in particular. Iron tools, spear and javelin heads, axes, bronze arrowheads, and some knives often follow local traditions, while swords commonly follow well-known Greek forms. They might, nevertheless, have been made by smiths in a wide range of settings and com-

F.6b   Success of combined operations: 7.3.47–48,
       7.4.4–21.
F.7a   Bosworth 1996, 26, n. 74.
F.7b   Thracian raiders: 7.4.15, 7.4.17.
F.7c   *Zeirai* (Thracian cloaks): colorful, Herodotus 7.75;
       stripes, see Figure 7.4.4.
F.8a   This suit of armor, from a particularly notable col-
       lection of weapons and body armor found in
       southeastern Bulgaria (Ref. Map 8, AX), is illus-
       trated and discussed (along with the rest of the

collection) in Agre 2011; for this armor, see that
work's pp. 72–84.
F.8b   Markets for booty: 7.3.48, 7.4.2, 7.5.2. Perinthus:
       Ref. Map 3, CZ.

missions, from unique pieces made for particular leaders to standard designs for ordinary Greek or Thracian soldiers.[c]

§9. Xenophon also provides us with some plausible detail about Thracian social interactions. At the initial meeting between Xenophon and Seuthes, which was the prelude to official negotiations between Seuthes and the mercenaries, horns of wine were exchanged.[a] The drinking horn was a common prestige vessel, though by no means the only type of cup used at Thracian banquets. The following day, after most of the mercenaries had agreed to Seuthes' terms of employment and had set up camp in order to have a decent meal, Seuthes invited the captains and generals to dinner in one of the nearby villages. The meal evidently took place indoors, though Xenophon tells us nothing specific about the location. It was a relatively formal occasion, insofar as the company included local men of rank, who are not described or otherwise referred to again, and some visiting ambassadors, also largely unidentified.[b] While the guests waited to be admitted, they were approached by one Herakleides of Maroneia, a man who is given a rather unflattering portrait elsewhere in Xenophon's story, especially where he sells booty and where he returns with the proceeds of the sale.[c] What happened next has a slightly unsavory feel. Herakleides' first move was to approach some visiting ambassadors from Parium,[d] whom he tried to persuade to stop off to stay with Seuthes rather than go inland to see his overlord, Medokos, as had been their intention. This distasteful behavior taints his subsequent approaches to the Greek officers, when he prompted them to offer presents to Seuthes. Later, at the dinner, we witness various Thracians bringing other gifts to Seuthes: a white horse; a young boy; garments for Seuthes' wife.[e] In each case the donor drinks to the recipient's health while offering his gift. This description does not have the unpleasant feeling of Herakleides' earlier touting for presents and chimes more closely with other data about gift giving among the Odrysian Thracians. The tantalizingly throwaway remark about Timasion the Dardanian's drinking cups and "barbarian" (Persian) carpets, evidently regarded as suitable gifts, has the ring of truth about it.[f]

§10. The description of the meal offers some interesting insights. First, there is the circular organization of the seating plan. About twenty three-legged tables were arranged in a circle to enable the visitors to reach the food easily—generous servings of meat, skewered onto loaves of bread and washed down with wine.[a] While these tables, being three-legged, would seem to have been round, representations of tables from tombs in Thrace and Macedonia are generally rectangular, though there are round stone examples from both regions.[b] The custom of pouring the last drops over fellow guests[c] seems authentic enough. The description of Seuthes throwing pieces of bread and meat to his fellow diners is rather more difficult to

F.8c  See Archibald 1998, 197–209, for a detailed bibliography of armor and weapons up to 1995. Finds of similar items have continued to accumulate since then. See n. F.8a.

F.9a  Horns of wine exchanged: 7.2.23.
F.9b  Other guests at the banquet: 7.3.21.
F.9c  Herakleides: 7.3.16; sent to sell booty, 7.4.2; returns with the proceeds, 7.5.2, 7.5.6; also appears in a poor light at 7.5.9, 7.5.11, 7.6.2, 7.6.41–42. Maroneia: Ref. Map 3, CY.

F.9d  Ambassadors from Parium: 7.3.16.
F.9e  Thracian gifts for Seuthes: 7.3.26–27.
F.9f  Timasion's gifts: 7.3.18, 7.3.27. Dardanos: Ref. Map 4.2, AX.
F.10a  Seating arrangements: 7.3.21.
F.10b  Andrianou 2009, 50–63. Macedonia: Ref. Map 3, CX. For a depiction of a three-legged table in a Thracian tomb, see Figure 7.3.21.
F.10c  Last drops of wine: 7.3.32.

comprehend, at least in the way that Xenophon presents the custom.[d] The broader context implies that the gesture was intended to symbolize the traditional generosity of a prince, and this seems to be what the Athenian Gnesippos has in mind, in his comments following Seuthes' actions, when he stands up to applaud the tradition of gift giving.[e] But it would be dangerous to extrapolate from this depiction of a rustic banquet to the courtly protocol of the high king of the Odrysae.

§11. The description of the sales of booty provides better insight into pan-Thracian conditions, just as it exposes the emptiness of Xenophon's rhetoric of freedom in the speech he makes to put pressure on Seuthes to guarantee the mercenaries' pay by threatening to liberate the villagers—villagers who in fact had been taken away as captives, evidently to be sold as slaves.[a] Xenophon put the figure at around a thousand, alongside twice as many cattle and perhaps tens of thousands of other small animals, mainly sheep and goats. These people ended up being sold by Herakleides in the market at Perinthus,[b] on the coast west of Byzantium. Context is provided for us by a law from Abdera, dating from around 350, that regulates the sale of people and pack animals, stipulating that a seller needed to provide a surety (presumably in case the sale fell through).[c] These sales of booty provide the best indication of a vibrant, at times intense, exchange between the inhabitants of the continental interior and those of the coastal fringes.

Zosia H. Archibald
Department of Archaeology, Classics, and Egyptology
University of Liverpool
Liverpool, UK

F.10d  Custom of throwing food to guests: 7.3.22.
F.10e  Gnesippos' comments: 7.3.28.
F.11a  Xenophon's rhetoric of freedom: 7.7.29–32.
       Captive villagers gathered together: 7.3.48.

F.11b  Perinthus as market for slaves: 7.4.2, 7.5.2.
F.11c  Abdera law: *Supplementum Epigraphicum Graecum* 47, 1026; Loukopoulou et al. 2005, E3, 186–190 and plate 1. Abdera: Ref. Map 3, CY.

# APPENDIX G

## *Divinity and Divining*

§1. It may come as a surprise to many readers of *Anabasis* that despite its emphasis on the importance of honoring the gods, on keeping one's oaths, and on the centrality of divination to decision-making, there is no word in ancient Greek for "religion." Nor was there an authoritative "sacred text" (the equivalent of the Bible or Qur'an) that could be used to prescribe belief and practice. This does not mean that the Greeks were not as "religious" as *Anabasis* seems to indicate. On the contrary, religious practices, beliefs, and rituals were so deeply embedded in all aspects of life that there was no conceptual category of "religion" as something set apart from warfare, politics, or everyday activities. This "embeddedness" makes *Anabasis* an essential source for Greek "religion" as it was practiced during Xenophon's lifetime.

§2. The most conspicuous manifestation of religion in *Anabasis* concerns divination. Divination comprises the various means by which mortals try to obtain a sign from the gods that indicates their wishes or advice. In ancient Greece divination provided answers to perplexing and difficult questions and facilitated decisive action in cases in which an individual or group might otherwise have been at a loss how to act. When individuals were faced with alternative courses of action, divination allowed them to bypass indecision and proceed confidently with a specific plan. Many different methods of divination appear in *Anabasis:* consultation of the oracle of Apollo at Delphi;[a] interpretation of the movements, behavior, and cries of birds (augury); interpretation of dreams and portents; and, most frequently, examination of the entrails of a sacrificed animal. In warfare two types of sacrificial divination were of immense importance: the campground sacrifice (*hiera*) and the battle-line sacrifice (*sphagia*). Performing *hiera* involved examining the entrails, especially the liver, of the victim (usually a sheep). In a sacrificial context, *hiera* can usually be translated as "sacred signs" (as has been done in this translation of *Anabasis*) or "omens" (mean-

G.2a   Delphi: Ref. Map 2, BY.

ing the signs or omens discovered by inspecting the entrails). Performing *sphagia* consisted of slitting the throat of the victim (usually a goat or ram) while observing its movements and the flow of blood. Accordingly, *sphagia* can be translated as "blood sacrifice."[b] On one occasion, when the army was about to force its way across the Kentrites River, the seers let the blood of the victims flow directly into it.[c]

§3. Systems of divination are usually flexible enough to allow space for reinterpretation or repetition (for instance, a Greek seer could sacrifice up to three times on the same day in order to get a better result). It is controversial whether divination ever kept someone from a course of action he or she was firmly determined upon, but there appear to be examples in *Anabasis* of this happening. The inability to obtain favorable omens from sacrifice allegedly kept the Greeks from attacking the Tibareni or from leaving their camp at Kalpe Harbor.[a] The reader, of course, can never be sure of the extent to which Xenophon the historical actor, as opposed to Xenophon the character in *Anabasis*, really let divination guide his actions.

§4. The rites of divination were usually performed by a professional seer (*mantis* in Greek), and several seers appear by name (Silanos, Arexion, Eukleides, and Basias). Seers were itinerant ritual specialists who provided their services for a fee to anyone willing to hire them. No Greek army ever went into the field without one or more seers in attendance, and it was usually up to individual generals to choose their own (long-term relationships between seers and generals seem to have been fairly common). The seers on the expedition could perform other rituals too. With Xenophon's approval they recommend a purification of the army after a period of internal dissension.[a] And when a harsh north wind was blasting the soldiers' faces as they were marching through Armenia, one of the seers told them to make a blood sacrifice to the wind.[b] It may seem surprising that Cyrus, being a Persian,[c] employed a Greek seer, but this was by no means unprecedented. The Persian commander Mardonios had a famous Greek seer in his service at the battle of Plataea, in 479.[d]

§5. Although Xenophon was not himself a seer, he claims that he sacrificed frequently and knew a great deal about how to interpret the results.[a] We also see him deciding by himself on the meaning of dreams (at 3.1.11–12 and 4.3.8) and of signs (the sneeze at 3.2.9). Diogenes Laertius, author of a biography of Xenophon, describes him as pious, fond of sacrificing, and competent to interpret the omens from sacrifice.[b] Even if this is merely an inference from Xenophon's writings, it sums up very well the image that the author Xenophon has constructed of Xenophon the character. The opinion of a professional seer, however, was always more authoritative than Xenophon's own interpretation of sacred signs. For that reason he frequently employed the services of the seers present on the expedition concerning both military operations and personal matters. When Xenophon was deciding issues

G.2b  For a divination scene of the examination of a liver (*hiera*), see Figure 2.1.9; and for a depiction of a prebattle blood sacrifice (*sphagia*), see Figure 6.5.8.
G.2c  At the crossing of the Kentrites: 4.3.17. Kentrites River: Ref. Map 6, BY.
G.3a  For more on the incident at Kalpe Harbor, see §§13–14. Tibareni territory: Ref. Map 5, AZ. Kalpe Harbor, possible location: Ref. Map 4.1, AZ.
G.4a  Seers recommend purification: 5.7.35.
G.4b  Blood sacrifice to the wind: 4.5.3–4. Armenia:

Ref. Map 6, AY.
G.4c  On Cyrus the Younger, see Appendix W: Brief Biographies of Selected Characters in *Anabasis*, §10. Persian Empire: Ref. Map 9.
G.4d  Greek seer at Plataea: Herodotus 9.37. Plataea: Ref. Map 2, CY.
G.5a  Xenophon's claims to knowledge about divination: 5.6.29.
G.5b  Diogenes Laertius 2.6.56 (in Appendix V: Diogenes Laertius' *Life of Xenophon*).

that affected him personally (whether to discuss the founding of a colony, whether to accept sole command of the army, whether to return home to Athens, whether to lead the army to the Thracian princeling Seuthes,[c] and whether to remain with Seuthes or stick with the troops), he made these difficult and perplexing decisions by sacrificing a victim to the gods and examining its entrails. Even though divination is a means whereby the gods give advice, not orders, the constant referral of these important decisions to divine arbitration does tend to mitigate Xenophon's personal responsibility for the consequences of his choices.

§6. The most authoritative method of divination in the ancient world, however, was the consultation of an oracle at the sanctuary of a god, the most famous being the oracle of Apollo at Delphi. There a priestess, called the Pythia, became possessed by Apollo and acted as his mouthpiece. On Socrates' recommendation Xenophon consulted Delphi before setting out to join Cyrus on his expedition, but he famously asked the wrong question of the god:[a] instead of inquiring whether it was better for him to go or to stay at home, he asked to which of the gods he should sacrifice and pray in order to have a successful trip and return safely. Although this was not an unusual form of question for oracular consultations, Xenophon nevertheless formulated his query in such a way as to almost guarantee the response he wanted by restricting the range of possible answers that the god could give. He obviously did not want to give Apollo the opportunity to tell him that he should stay in Athens.

§7. The Greeks also believed that the gods, apart from providing advice and guidance, could take a more active hand in human affairs, especially by punishing the wicked and assisting the pious. Xenophon repeatedly asserts in his speeches in Book 3 that the gods will be hostile to the Persians as oath breakers but be allies of the Greeks, since they kept their oaths.[a] In some incidents we can glimpse divine agency at work, such as in the dream that roused Xenophon to action after the arrest of the generals by Tissaphernes and in the spontaneous house fire that saved the Greeks when they were trying to escape from the Drilai, a tribe dwelling near the Black Sea.[b] The most explicit acknowledgment of divine intervention occurs when Xenophon rallies his men to save the Arcadians when surrounded by Bithynian Thracians and on the verge of annihilation.[c] He tells them: "Perhaps it is the god who is bringing this about, in his wish to humble those who boasted of their superior wisdom, and to give us the position of greater honor, since we make the gods our starting point."[d] People who begin with the gods are those who trust in divination rather than in their own mere human wisdom.

§8. *Anabasis* contains a particularly vivid portrait of the type of itinerant seer who accompanies armies on campaign. Silanos from Ambracia, who acts as Cyrus' personal seer, first appears when Cyrus is marching with his entire army in battle order

G.5c    On Seuthes, see Appendix W: Brief Biographies, §30. Athens: Ref. Map 2, CZ.

G.6a    For this incident, see 3.1.5–7. For further discussion of Socrates' exchanges with Xenophon on this occasion, see the Introduction, §2.10, and Appendix A: Xenophon and Socrates, §§21, 27, 29–34.

G.7a    Gods will support Greeks against Persians: 3.1.21–22, 3.2.10.

G.7b    Xenophon's dream: 3.1.11–13. Fire among the

Drilai: 5.2.24. On Tissaphernes, see Appendix W, §37. Drilai territory, Black Sea: Ref. Map 5, AZ.

G.7c    Arcadia: Ref. Map 2, CX. Bithynia/Bithynians: Ref. Map 4, AY.

G.7d    "Perhaps it is the god": 6.3.18.

toward the Persian King.[a] When the King does not appear, Cyrus summons Silanos and gives him three thousand gold darics, because when sacrificing eleven days previously, the seer predicted that the King would not fight within ten days and Cyrus promised to give him ten talents if the prediction proved true.[b] Silanos' prediction that ten days would pass without a battle is not the kind of information that was normally obtained by inspecting the liver and entrails of a sacrificial victim. Usually the signs were either favorable or unfavorable for a particular course of action or, more rarely, revealed impending danger. Xenophon has displaced this scene in order to create dramatic suspense before the battle of Cunaxa,[c] but we can easily infer that the context was the campground sacrifice. If so, then Silanos need have said no more than that the sacrifice was propitious for marching out or, more boldly, that the King would not fight on that particular day. Obviously he took a gamble of sorts and made a much more elaborate prediction than was expected of someone with his expertise. And this gamble paid off handsomely: ten talents was a huge fortune, making Silanos the equivalent of a millionaire in today's world.

§9. A good example of the way in which sacrificial divination usually worked is when Cyrus asks Xenophon at Cunaxa to "say to everyone that the sacred signs [*hiera*] from the main sacrifice were favorable and the omens from the blood sacrifice [*sphagia*] were favorable too."[a] Yet the fact that Cyrus was killed does not seem to have caused any doubts about the validity of divination. When a seer proclaimed that the sacred signs or omens were favorable, this did not mean that success or victory was guaranteed, since the whole point of a divinatory sacrifice was to ascertain whether the movement toward an engagement with the enemy should proceed. The gods were indicating their will but were not promising victory if their will was followed.

§10. When Xenophon was thinking of founding a colony on the coast of the Black Sea, he decided to make a preliminary divinatory sacrifice before bringing up the subject with the army.[a] Silanos assisted him with this sacrifice; but since Silanos wanted to get back to Greece as soon as possible with the money that Cyrus had given him, he reported Xenophon's scheme to the army. The modern reader will reasonably wonder why Silanos did not simply tell Xenophon that the omens were unfavorable for discussing a colony. When Xenophon is forced to defend his actions before the assembled troops, we discover the reason why Silanos had been unable to lie: because he knew that Xenophon had a lot of experience with sacrifices.[b] Since no two livers look exactly alike, there was a subjective element in a seer's evaluation of a particular liver's size, shape, texture, and color. Yet there were some fixed rules of interpretation (for example, if a liver was missing a lobe, that was always an extremely bad sign), and Xenophon apparently knew enough to be able to read livers and entrails on his own.

§11. In one episode several different modes of divination intersect and reinforce

G.8a  Silanos' first appearance: 1.7.18. Ambracia: Ref. Map 2, BX.
G.8b  The gold daric, equivalent to 25 Attic drachmas, was the standard large coin of the Persian empire. For more on darics and on talents, see Appendix O: Ancient Greek and Persian Units of Measurement, §§13–14, 10–11. In n. O.14c Thomas Martin points out that other evidence suggests that 3,000 gold darics would equate to 10 Persian talents, meaning that Cyrus paid exactly what he had promised.
G.8c  Battlefield of Cunaxa: Ref. Map 6, DZ.
G.9a  "The sacred signs": 1.8.15.
G.10a  Preliminary divinatory sacrifice: 5.6.16.
G.10b  Silanos' knowledge of Xenophon's expertise: 5.6.29.

one another. When Xenophon is trying to decide whether to accept the sole command of the Ten Thousand,[a] he places two victims next to himself and sacrifices them to Zeus the King, the very god, we are now told, to whom the oracle at Delphi recommended that he sacrifice. He thinks that Zeus the King was also the god who sent the dream to him after the arrest of the generals, and he also recalls a portent—an eagle (Zeus' bird) sitting by the side of the road—that occurred on his journey to join Cyrus (an ambiguous omen, because eagles are attacked by other birds when not in flight). When Xenophon sacrifices, Zeus indicates to him very clearly neither to ask for the command nor, if they should elect him, to accept it. In this scene Xenophon combines four different divinatory experiences that took place at different times in order to justify his decision not to take the command that was being offered to him.

§12. When the troops would not accede to Xenophon's arguments as to why he was not the best choice, he addressed them again, telling them about the results of his sacrifice.[a] This new argument put an end to the debate, and the army chose the Spartan Cheirisophos.[b] Xenophon depicts the evidence of the sacrifices as decisively settling the issue of the command in the eyes of the troops. For the average Greek hoplite, the evidence of divination was far more authoritative than so-called rational arguments, insofar as Xenophon had already explained at length why it was not a good idea for the command to be given to an Athenian in preference to a Lacedaemonian.[c] Why does Xenophon here (as again at 7.6.43–44, when he is trying to decide whether to stay behind with Seuthes in Thrace) sacrifice two victims? It is not because one of them is merely held in reserve in case the answer is not clear during the first sacrifice, for the wording at 6.1.22 indicates that Xenophon has sacrificed both victims. We need to infer that Xenophon asked different questions of each victim as a type of checking: while sacrificing one victim, he must have asked, "Is it better for the army to entrust the command to me?" and while sacrificing the other, "Is it better for me to turn down the command?" Only the sequence "yes-no" or "no-yes" would count as a reliable answer.

§13. The most seemingly problematic incident in which divination played a key role surrounds the events that took place at Kalpe Harbor, on the Black Sea coast. The Ten Thousand are depicted as being restricted to their camp at Kalpe for three days without provisions and in great hardship because the sacred signs were not favorable for marching out.[a] This leads to a rather tense situation in which Xenophon is the target of the soldiers' frustrations. They even accuse him of bribing the seer Arexion to say that the sacrifices were unfavorable for departure.[b]

§14. Despite the fact that the gods continued to warn the army against leaving camp, the general Neon led out two thousand men on his own initiative. Five hun-

G.11a  Xenophon considers accepting sole command: 6.1.22–24.
G.12a  Xenophon reveals results of sacrifice: 6.1.31.
G.12b  On Cheirisophos, see Appendix W: Brief Biographies, §7.
G.12c  Hoplite: a heavily armed infantryman; see Appendix H: Infantry and Cavalry in *Anabasis*, §§2–3. Xenophon had already explained: 6.1.26–29.

Lacedaemon: Ref. Map 2, DY. The terms Lacedaemon and Sparta are nearly synonymous. Lacedaemon is a state and territorial designation. Sparta was the most important city within it; see Appendix B: Xenophon and Sparta, §§18–19.
G.13a  Greek hardship: 6.4.12–6.5.21.
G.13b  Accusations of bribery: 6.4.14.

dred of them were cut down by a cavalry force that, unbeknownst to the Greeks, had been sent by the Persian satrap Pharnabazos to prevent any attempt by the army to cross into Phrygia.[a] Xenophon performed the *sphagia* (the blood sacrifice made immediately before battle) and went to the rescue. The following day, the fourth day of this incident, the Greeks fortified a base camp on the Kalpe peninsula and a boat arrived bringing food and sacrificial victims. Now that the Greeks had received provisions and occupied a secure position to which to retreat in case of a defeat, the sacred signs (*hiera*) about leaving camp to face Pharnabazos' forces proved favorable with the first victim, and the seer Arexion saw an auspicious eagle (a sign sent by Zeus).[b] When the enemy appeared, the blood sacrifice was also favorable with the first victim. A little later Xenophon encouraged his men to join battle with the enemy by pointing out that all three types of omens were favorable: the sacred signs, the bird omens (*oinōnoi*), and the blood sacrifice.[c] The Greeks then went on to win a decisive victory.

§15. The role of divination is particularly emphatic at the end of *Anabasis*, where it again serves to validate the narrator's construction of Xenophon's character and actions. At Lampsacus, on the southern shore of the Propontis, Xenophon encounters the seer Eukleides of Phleious,[a] who apparently had been employed by his family back in Athens. Eukleides informs Xenophon that his current poverty is due to his failure to sacrifice to Zeus Meilichios (Zeus in his capacity as the gracious and gentle recipient of propitiatory sacrifices). The next day Xenophon does so (burning whole pigs according to his ancestral custom), and almost immediately his fortunes begin to change.[b] The final narrative sequence, in which Xenophon at long last enriches himself, is also framed by divination.[c] While at Pergamum,[d] he was informed that if he attacked by night, he could capture a wealthy Persian named Asidates with his family and possessions. Xenophon sacrificed, "and Basias the Eleian, who was there acting as seer, said that the sacred signs were very favorable toward him and the man should be easy to capture."[e] The expedition did not go as smoothly as Xenophon had anticipated, but in the end Asidates was indeed captured, and the narrator concludes, "And thus the earlier sacred signs were fulfilled,"[f] referring to the initial sacrifice made by Basias. *Anabasis* itself, moreover, neatly ends with a statement that brings the narrative full circle to Xenophon's initial encounter with the seer Eukleides. After the army had returned to Pergamum, "Xenophon saluted the god" (Zeus Meilichios) and was awarded his pick of the plunder.[g]

§16. The religious aspects of warfare were by no means restricted to prebattle sacrifices. After the omens proved favorable for battle, the Greeks sang the paean to Apollo

---

G.14a  Defeat by Persian cavalry: 6.4.24. On satraps, see the Glossary. On Pharnabazos, see Appendix W: Brief Biographies, §27. By Phrygia, here Hellespontine Phrygia is meant (see n. 1.2.6a): Ref. Map 4.1, BX; Ref. Map 4.2, AY.
G.14b  Auspicious eagle: 6.5.2.
G.14c  Three types of omen favorable: 6.5.21.
G.15a  Xenophon meets Eukleides: 7.8.4–5. Lampsacus: Ref. Map 4.2, AY. Propontis: Ref. Map 4.1, AY; Ref. Map 2, AY. Phleious: Ref. Map 2, CY.
G.15b  Sacrifice to Zeus Meilichios initiates change of

fortune: 7.8.5–6.
G.15c  Final narrative sequence: 7.8.8–23.
G.15d  Pergamum: Ref. Map 4.1, BX; Ref. Map 4.2, BY.
G.15e  "Basias the Eleian": 7.8.10. Elis: Ref. Map 2, CX.
G.15f  "And thus the earlier sacred signs": 7.8.22.
G.15g  "Xenophon saluted the god" and received the pick of the plunder: 7.8.23.

and then charged as they raised the battle cry to Enyalios, a name for Ares.[a] Religion was equally important outside the context of battle. When the Greeks were at Kerasous, on the Black Sea, they sold their prisoners, and a tenth of the profits was distributed to the generals, who were to use the money to make dedications to Apollo, and to Artemis of Ephesus.[b] In a substantial flash-forward, we learn that Xenophon eventually placed a dedication in the treasury of the Athenians at Delphi and established a temple, estate, and festival for Artemis at Skillous, in the Peloponnese.[c]

§17. In the Greek world, the most important communal means of honoring the gods was through public sacrifices followed by competitions. Under the conditions of the march, it was not easy for the Ten Thousand to perform elaborate religious rituals, but they did so on a few occasions. The general Xenias, an Arcadian, held the Lykaian festival (in honor of Lykaian Zeus, who was worshipped in Arcadia) while the army was at Peltai.[a] After their arrival at the Greek city of Trapezus, on the Black Sea, they held an athletic contest and offered the sacrifice to the gods (including Zeus the Savior and Herakles) that Xenophon himself, in response to an ominous sneeze, had earlier proposed that they make whenever they first arrived at a friendly land.[b] During their forty-five days at Kotyora, the Ten Thousand made sacrifices to the gods, and each of the various ethnic groups apparently held their own processions and athletic games.[c] Because the army was made up of Greeks from many different cities and regions as well as of different ethnicities (Arcadians constituted the single-largest ethnic group), they sometimes held joint religious celebrations (as at Trapezus) and at other times each group performed its own local rituals (as at Peltai). Even so, it was highly unusual that the annual Lykaia should be celebrated outside Arcadia.

§18. Another important communal ritual was burial of the dead. Although views varied greatly among the Greeks as to precisely what happened to the soul (*psychē*) of the deceased, all agreed that it was imperative for corpses to receive proper burial. Otherwise the ghosts of the unburied would be unable to enter the Underworld and would remain restless and potentially dangerous. Whenever possible, the army and its commanders made every effort to retrieve the bodies of the dead and to bury them, even if this meant making a truce with the enemy in order to get the bodies back or burying the corpses from a previous conflict while marching in battle formation.[a] There was an implicit understanding among the Ten Thousand that none of their number be left unburied and that customary funeral rites be performed as fully as possible, although sometimes these duties were impossible to discharge.[b] They once requested others (the Kerasountians) to perform the burial; and on another occasion, near Kalpe Harbor, they erected a cenotaph for those corpses that could not be found.[c]

G.16a  Paean sung: 1.10.10. Battle cry to Enyalios raised: 1.8.18, 1.10.10, 5.2.14.
G.16b  Tenth for Apollo and Artemis: 5.3.4. Kerasous: Ref. Map 5, AZ. Ephesus: Ref. Map 4.1, CX; Ref. Map 4.2, DY.
G.16c  Skillous, Peloponnese: Ref. Map 2, CX.
G.17a  Lykaian festival: 1.2.10. "Lykaian" derives from Mt. Lykaion (Ref. Map 2, CX), an important site for pan-Arcadian rituals associated with Zeus. Peltai, approximate location: Ref. Map 4.1, CY (not listed in the *Barrington Atlas*).

G.17b  Athletic contest: 4.8.25–28. Vow of sacrifice: 3.2.9. Trapezus: Ref. Map 5, AZ.
G.17c  Sacrifices and games at Kotyora: 5.5.5. Kotyora: Ref. Map 5, AZ.
G.18a  Truce to recover bodies: 4.2.23. Burying old corpses: 6.5.5–6.
G.18b  Implicit understanding: 4.2.23, 6.4.9. Burial of comrades thwarted: 4.1.18–19.
G.18c  Kerasountians to bury soldiers: 5.7.30. Cenotaph: 6.4.9.

§19. If the Ten Thousand were in some sense a Greek *polis* (city-state) on the move, they replicated, as far as they could, the normative ritual practices of life and death. But they were not a typical *polis*, coming as they did from many different locales and representing a variety of ethnicities, each of which practiced its own variations of the phenomena that we conveniently, for want of a better term, call ancient Greek religion.

Michael A. Flower
Department of Classics
Princeton University
Princeton, New Jersey

# APPENDIX H

## *Infantry and Cavalry in* Anabasis

§1. In his *Anabasis* Xenophon gives us an unparalleled look at a Greek army as it marches from Sardis to Cunaxa to the Black Sea and finally to Europe, covering more than four thousand miles[a] in fifteen months, fighting enemies, burying the dead, choosing new leaders, making friends, sacrificing to the gods, looting property, capturing people to use as scouts and slaves, making love, dancing after dinner, competing in athletic events. It's a remarkably rich description of Greek hoplites, peltasts, archers, slingers, and horsemen, both in and out of action (Xenophon himself distinguishes these five parts of the army at 5.6.15).

§2. A Greek hoplite (*hoplitēs*) took his name not from his shield, which he called an *aspis*, but from his equipment in general. The root *hopl-* originally meant a tool or, in the plural, a set of tools, not necessarily military. By the Classical period, *hopla* most often meant a set of military gear. For a military review that Cyrus held at Tyriaion, the Greek hoplites lined up four-deep, each wearing a bronze helmet, a red tunic, and greaves (bronze shin guards), and carrying his shield and spear.[a] Tunics were normally worn underneath bronze breastplates or linen corselets, so unless the soldiers were wearing the tunics on top that day, they had dispensed with their body armor during the review. Shields were made of wood, sometimes faced with a thin layer of bronze, more for show than for added protection. Hoplites carried thrusting spears, about eight feet[b] long with an iron spearhead and a bronze spike on the butt, and usually a short iron sword as a secondary weapon. For a long time, scholars estimated the total weight of this panoply at seventy or more pounds,[c] but recent work, based partly on the results achieved by reenactors, has shown that this estimate is

---

H.1a  Army covers more than 4,000 miles/6,435 kilometers: 7.8.26, with n. 7.8.26a; the Greek text says 34,255 stades. On stades, see Appendix O: Ancient Greek and Persian Units of Measurement, §5. The following locations appear on Ref. Map 7: Sardis, BW; battlefield of Cunaxa, DZ; Black Sea, AX.

H.2a  Review at Tyriaion: 1.2.16; see nn. 1.2.16a, b for

a brief discussion of the red tunic and greaves. On Cyrus the Younger, see Appendix W: Brief Biographies of Selected Characters in *Anabasis*, §10. Tyriaion: Ref. Map 5, CX.

H.2b  Eight feet/2.5 meters.

H.2c  For an illustration of a panoply, see Figure 1.2.16. Seventy pounds/32 kilograms.

too high. A panoply weighed no more than fifty pounds and perhaps as little as thirty[d] if one opted for a corselet instead of a breastplate, as had become normal by Xenophon's day. A man who chose a *pilos* (a conical metal, leather, or felt cap) rather than a helmet and went without a breastplate and greaves could decrease his load to twenty pounds.[e]

§3. The most distinctive piece of this equipment was the shield, so much so that eventually (the first explicit case occurs in Xenophon's *Hellenika* 2.4.25) the singular *hoplon* sometimes came to be used for an *aspis*. Round or oval, concave with an offset rim, made not of hardwood but of lighter and more flexible poplar or willow, with a central armband through which the hoplite put his left arm up to the elbow so he could grab a leather strap close to the right edge, this shield protected him effectively; but like any shield carried on the left arm, it protected him better against an enemy coming from his left than one coming from his right. At about three feet in diameter, the shield was large enough that it could cover two men in a pinch, as Xenophon appreciated personally when another hoplite gave him cover after his shield-bearer deserted, taking his shield (two men behind one *aspis* would resemble two people under one umbrella, neither completely protected).[a] The shield's shape allowed a hoplite to rest it on his shoulder. Back home hoplites often had slaves carry their shields until the moment they really needed them. On this campaign, however, most mercenaries were carrying their own stuff. After they reached the Black Sea, one Antileon of Thurii pronounced himself so tired of packing and marching and carrying his gear that he wanted to sail home lying on his back.[b]

§4. A peltast took his name from his *peltē*, a crescent-shaped shield smaller than an *aspis*. Peltasts could wear helmets, and their shields could be faced with bronze: gleaming bronze *peltai* once gave away the position of ten Cretans pretending to set an ambush.[a] Peltasts wore less body armor than hoplites, and those called *gymnētes* ("naked," translated "light-armed" in this edition) wore no armor at all. Peltasts were quicker than hoplites. When Xenophon describes assaults on Thracian villages, he can explain the fact that many villagers got away simply by noting that they were peltasts against hoplites.[b] When the Greeks were desperate to capture a mountain held by the Kolchoi, it was no surprise that the peltasts outran the hoplites and reached the top first.[c]

§5. A peltast's distinctive weapon was the javelin. When Xenophon deployed peltasts and wanted them ready for action at any moment, he ordered them to advance "with fingers through the throwing loop,"[a] that is, the leather strap Greeks used to increase spear-throwing range. The range of an ancient javelin is uncertain: perhaps one hundred yards, and certainly less than that of a Greek bow, though Xenophon can mention both archers and javelin throwers in the same breath as fail-

H.2d  Fifty or 30 pounds/23 or 14 kilograms.
H.2e  Twenty pounds/9 kilograms.
H.3a  Three feet/1 meter. Two men behind one shield (*aspis*): 4.2.20–21.
H.3b  Journey by sea better than by land: 5.1.2. Thurii: Ref. Map 1, BW.
H.4a  Gleams give away ambush detachment: 5.2.29.

H.4b  Thracian peltasts speedier than hoplites: 6.3.4. Thrace: Ref. Map 3.
H.4c  Peltasts outrun hoplites uphill: 4.8.18. Kolchoi territory: Ref. Map 6, AX.
H.5a  "With fingers through the throwing loop": 4.3.28, 5.2.12. See Figure 4.3.28.

ing to reach the enemy archers and slingers,[b] At one point he notes that the Greeks picked up Kardouchian arrows, which were about three feet long, fitted them with throwing loops, and used them as javelins.[c] Like hoplites, peltasts carried a short sword.

§6. The Greeks brought few archers, only two hundred Cretans,[a] probably because Cyrus had so many archers himself. Cretan archers could not shoot as far as Persian archers, as Xenophon observes,[b] because the Greeks used wooden bows, which were less powerful than the Persian composite bows, made of wood, bone, and sinews glued together. When Greek archers were under fire, they needed to be protected by hoplites, because they did not wear armor.[c] Persian bows could not shoot three or four stades (600–800 yards); they could reach three or four *plethra* (100–133 yards) but not much more, as is shown at the crossing of the Kentrites River.[d] In this last incident, it is unclear precisely where the enemy archers were stationed. A common estimate puts the effective range of a composite bow at 175–190 yards.[e]

§7. Xenophon credits himself with suggesting that the Greeks respond to the enemy superiority in archers by creating a corps of slingers.[a] The sling was a simple, inexpensive weapon: a small piece of leather with strings on either side. After loading a stone or a lead bullet from his supply,[b] the slinger whirled the sling around his head, released the string on one side, and sent the missile flying toward his target. Xenophon claims that Rhodians in the army knew how to use a sling and had twice the range with their lead bullets as the enemy slingers with their hand-sized stones.[c] When his expectation that the Rhodians would have their slings with them proved to be correct, two hundred slingers were assembled overnight.[d] They stopped the damage from Persian archers and slingers, because they could sling farther than most Persian archers could shoot, as is shown by 3.4.16. However, some Persian arrows must have reached them, though weakly, or the Greeks could not have reused Persian arrows as they did at 3.4.17. But when the Persians held a hill above the Greeks, they were able to pin the Greek archers and the slingers inside the ranks of hoplites, since slingers, like archers, lacked protective gear.[e]

§8. The Greeks also managed to assemble a small cavalry force. Originally Klearchos brought more than forty horsemen, mostly Thracian, but forty deserted after the battle of Cunaxa.[a] Xenophon quotes himself as telling the troops not to worry that they have no horsemen, because "nobody ever dies in battle from being bitten or

H.5b    One hundred yards/91 meters. Range of javelin less than that of Greek bow: Thucydides 3.98.1. Greek archers and javelin throwers fail to reach enemy: *Anabasis* 3.3.15.

H.5c    Kardouchian arrows used as javelins: 4.2.28. Three feet/1 meter. Kardouchoi territory: Ref. Map 6, BY.

H.6a    Cretan archers: 1.2.9. Crete: Ref. Map 1, CX.

H.6b    Cretan archers' range less than Persians': 3.3.7, 3.3.15. Persian Empire: see Ref. Map 9.

H.6c    Hoplites protect archers: 3.3.7.

H.6d    Six hundred yards/550 meters beyond range of Persian bows: 1.8.17–19. Persian arrows reach 100 yards/91 meters or so: 4.3.1, 4.3.3, 4.3.6. Persian arrows fall short at Kentrites crossing:

4.3.17–18. On stades and *plethra*, see Appendix O: Measurements, §§5, 2–3. Kentrites River: Ref. Map 6, BY.

H.6e    One hundred seventy-five to 190 yards/160–175 meters.

H.7a    Slinger corps suggested: 3.3.16.

H.7b    Loading a sling: 5.2.12.

H.7c    Rhodians' use of slings: 3.3.16–17. Rhodes: Ref. Map 4.1, DY.

H.7d    Recruitment of Rhodian slingers: 3.3.20.

H.7e    Archers and slingers pinned inside hoplite ranks: 3.4.25–26.

H.8a    Klearchos' Thracian horsemen: 1.5.13. Forty horsemen desert: 2.2.7. On Klearchos, see Appendix W: Brief Biographies, §20.

kicked by a horse."[b] If the men were convinced by his brave face, they learned differently the very next day, when the Greeks progressed barely more than three miles due to harassment from Mithradates' horsemen, archers, and slingers.[c] From the horses the Thracians left behind, others brought along by officers such as Xenophon, and still others they captured, the Greeks reconstituted a cavalry contingent of fifty horsemen.

§9. The Greeks supplied their volunteer horsemen with soft leather jerkins and corselets[a]—vitally important, because horsemen did not use shields. At 3.4.48 Xenophon says that he had a difficult time keeping up with the hoplites after he dismounted and took a shield, noting that he was wearing a cavalry corselet,[b] which suggests that his cavalry corselet was heavier than what the hoplites were wearing. Perhaps it had metal scales attached. Horsemen probably wore open helmets, as recommended by Xenophon in his work *Peri Hippikes* (*On Horsemanship*) 12.3. Xenophon there recommends various other pieces of armor for horse and rider. He favors a slashing saber rather than a thrusting sword, along with two javelins of cornel wood, one to throw and one to thrust.[c] His experiences in Asia probably prompted these recommendations.

§10. The Cyreans' new cavalry contingent proved its worth the very day after it was constituted, when it led a charge that routed Mithradates' one thousand horsemen and four thousand archers and slingers, if Xenophon's numbers are to be believed.[a] The Greeks killed many enemies as they fled, and captured eighteen horsemen alive.[b] This success deterred the Persians from getting too close again. Xenophon notes two later occasions on which the Greeks acquired horses—twenty from the camp of Tiribazos and subsequently seventeen colts being reared in a village as tribute for the Persian King[c]—though he does not say whether the size of the small cavalry contingent increased as a result.

§11. At the outset Cyrus' recruiters commanded the men they brought. These contingents, which varied in size, remained in place until most of the generals were tricked, captured, and killed after the battle of Cunaxa.[a] After choosing new generals, the Greeks also seem to have equalized the size of the forces each commanded. From the start the hoplites were organized into *lochoi* (companies), each led by a *lochagos* (captain). Captains may have recruited their own troops, either (as Cyrus asked them to do) as garrison commanders in Ionia,[b] or when generals such as Klearchos recruited large forces by delegating the job to individuals charged with

---

H.8b   "Nobody ever dies in battle": 3.2.18.

H.8c   Three miles/5 kilometers. Greeks harassed by Mithradates: 3.3.6–11. Mithradates had been a supporter of Cyrus but had at this point returned to his allegiance to the Great King and was acting as a subordinate of Tissaphernes, on whom see Appendix W: Brief Biographies, §37.

H.9a   Volunteer cavalry supplied with protective clothing: 3.3.19–20.

H.9b   While the Greek *thōraka...hippikon* at 3.4.48 is translated here as "cavalry corselet," I have retained the traditional translation "cavalry breastplate," but this relates only to what I regard as Xenophon's own likely dress choices and is with-

out prejudice to whether cavalrymen generally would wear breastplates or, as suggested here, corselets with metal scales. (Translator's note)

H.9c   Xenophon's recommendations: *Peri Hippikes* (*On Horsemanship*) 12.11–12.

H.10a   Size of Mithradates' forces: 3.4.2.

H.10b   Persian horsemen captured: 3.4.5.

H.10c   Horses acquired from Tiribazos: 4.4.21. Capture of colts: 4.5.24, 4.5.35. On Tiribazos, see Appendix W, §36.

H.11a   Arrest and execution of the generals: 2.5.30–2.6.1.

H.11b   Cyrus asks garrison commanders to recruit troops: 1.1.6. Ionia: Ref. Map 4.1, CX; Ref. Map 4.2, CY.

finding one *lochos* each. Xenophon relates an incident involving Episthenes, who had once recruited a *lochos* on the basis of good looks (though the passage reads as if Episthenes had assembled this *lochos* for some other campaign).[c] The two companies lost in the Taurus Mountains numbered about 50 each,[d] but since the whole army originally had about 120 captains and light-infantry officers (about 100 captains and light-infantry officers remained after 20 captains were killed by Tissaphernes[e]), the army began with roughly 100 companies of hoplites averaging about 100 men each.[f] By the time the Greeks came within sight of the Black Sea, the hoplites were reduced to about 80 companies of about 100 men each,[g] presumably after some redistributing.

§12. Xenophon pays less attention to the peltasts and their organization. Originally he records numbers and sometimes origins of the contingents brought by individuals.[a] He names Episthenes of Amphipolis as the commander of the peltasts at Cunaxa.[b] They must have been organized into smaller units, but the only ones Xenophon mentions specifically are the three divisions, each of six hundred peltasts and archers, employed in the land of the Kolchoi; he names Aischines of Acarnania as the commander of one of these divisions.[c] Still smaller units might have combined to form these divisions, but such smaller units are never mentioned. Xenophon names Stratokles as the leader of the Cretan archers[d] but does not mention who commanded the Rhodian slingers. The cavalry receive more attention: Miltokythes led Klearchos' original forty horsemen; Lykios the Athenian, and subsequently Timasion the Dardanian, commanded the cavalry that was formed after the generals had been seized.[e]

§13. Although the words "hoplite" and "phalanx" are much older, *Anabasis* contains the earliest-attested use of the phrase "hoplite phalanx" (literally, "the phalanx of the hoplites").[a] Xenophon describes this phalanx both during a military review arranged to impress the queen of Cilicia[b] and several times as it deployed for battle. For the review Cyrus ordered the Greeks to deploy as they normally did for battle. They lined up four-deep, with Menon[c] and his men on the right, Klearchos and his men on the left, and the other generals in the center. At the trumpet's signal, the men pointed their spears forward and advanced, going faster and faster until they broke into a run and frightened the queen. Xenophon does not mention the peltasts, archers, or cavalry here, though the peltasts made up more than one-fifth of the mercenary force.

H.11c Episthenes' recruitment criterion: 7.4.7–11.
H.11d Two companies total 100 men: 1.2.25. Taurus Mountains: Ref. Map 5, CY.
H.11e Captains killed by Tissaphernes: 2.5.30. Number remaining: 3.1.33.
H.11f For discussion of the total size of the hoplite contingent, see Appendix I: The Size and Makeup of the Ten Thousand, §§3–4 and Table I.4.
H.11g Eighty companies of 100 men each: 4.8.15.
H.12a Numbers in peltast contingents: 1.2.3, 1.2.6, 1.2.9.
H.12b Episthenes of Amphipolis: 1.10.7. Amphipolis: Ref. Map 3, CX.
H.12c Three divisions of peltasts: 4.8.15. Aischines of Acarnania: 4.8.18. Acarnania: Ref. Map 2, BX.
H.12d Stratokles: 4.2.28.
H.12e Miltokythes: 2.2.7. Lykios the Athenian: 3.3.20, 4.3.22, 4.7.24. Timasion the Dardanian (as cavalry leader): 6.3.14, 6.3.22. Athens: Ref. Map 2, CZ. Dardanos: Ref. Map 4.2, AX.
H.13a "Hoplite phalanx": 6.5.27.
H.13b Military review for queen of Cilicia: 1.2.14–18. Cilicia: Ref. Map 5, CY.
H.13c On Menon, see Appendix W: Brief Biographies, §23.

§14. Four-deep, however, was a thinner line than usual. When Xenophon wanted to quiet the men in the agora of Byzantium, he ordered them to get in formation, and the hoplites quickly arranged themselves eight-deep, with the peltasts on the sides.[a] (At Cunaxa the divisions of peltasts were all on the right side.)[b] As to the width of the phalanx, Xenophon provides little help. He stresses, again and again, the importance of remaining in formation,[c] but he does not say how tight the formation was. It was loose enough at Cunaxa that the Greeks could open gaps to allow the Persian scythed chariots to go through.[d]

§15. Greek hoplites and phalanxes are not inextricably bound together. Xenophon sometimes describes non-Greeks in *Anabasis* as forming a "phalanx," and indeed he sometimes refers to non-Greeks as "hoplites."[a] Likewise, Greeks can fight in other formations. When facing the Kolchoi on a mountain, Xenophon gives himself a speech on the disadvantages of the phalanx formation:[b] on difficult terrain the line will be broken; if the formation is many ranks deep, it will be outflanked; if it is only a few ranks deep, it might well be cut through. The Greeks accepted Xenophon's recommendation that they should instead form deep columns with spaces between them, deploying the peltasts and archers on both flanks and in the center. "It will not be easy for the enemy to get into the gaps," Xenophon says, ". . . with our companies on both sides of them."[c] This plan worked. In order to match the width of the Greek line, the Kolchoi moved to the right and the left, opening a gap in the middle. When the peltasts ran into that gap, all the Kolchoi fled.[d]

§16. Against Pharnabazos[a] the Greeks adopted another of Xenophon's recommendations. This time he advised establishing a reserve force a hundred feet behind the phalanx, with the peltasts on the sides.[b] Pharnabazos' men routed the peltasts, who charged first, but when the Greek hoplites came on, the enemy fled.[c] The results were similar when the mercenaries assaulted the main stronghold of the Mossynoeci.[d] They were routed the first day, when they approached without orders from their generals and in no sort of order, provoking an admonishing lecture from Xenophon on the importance of good order.[e] However, the second day, when they advanced in column behind the peltasts, with archers in the spaces between the columns, the Mossynoeci fought the peltasts but fled when the hoplites got close.[f]

§17. Despite the impression given by Xenophon's frequent emphasis on "order," hoplites were not limited to fighting in formation. They served as garrison troops;

H.14a  Quiet the men in the agora: 7.1.19 (this edition translates the Greek *agora* as "the marketplace" in this passage). Army arranges itself in formation: 7.1.23. Byzantium: Ref. Map 4.1, AY.
H.14b  Divisions of peltasts at Cunaxa: 1.8.5.
H.14c  Importance of remaining in formation: see, for example, 1.8.19, 5.4.20.
H.14d  Gaps for chariots to pass through: 1.8.20. The scythed chariots themselves are described at 1.8.10.
H.15a  Non-Greek phalanxes: 4.8.9, 6.5.7 (in both places this edition renders the Greek word *phalanx* as "line of battle"). Non-Greek hoplites: Egyptians, 1.8.9; Assyrians, 7.8.15. Egypt: Ref.

Map 1, DX. Assyria: Ref. Map 6, CY.
H.15b  Disadvantages of phalanx formation: 4.8.10–13.
H.15c  "It will not be easy": 4.8.13.
H.15d  Column formation succeeds: 4.8.19.
H.16a  On Pharnabazos, see Appendix W: Brief Biographies, §27.
H.16b  Reserve force: 6.5.9–11. Peltasts on sides of phalanx: 6.5.25. One hundred feet/30 meters.
H.16c  Success of hoplites rectifies peltast failure: 6.5.27–28.
H.16d  Mossynoeci territory: Ref. Map 5, AZ.
H.16e  Rout of disorderly mercenaries: 5.4.16–18. Lecture by Xenophon: 5.4.19–21.
H.16f  Success of orderly hoplites: 5.4.22–26.

they besieged cities, such as Miletus; they set an ambush.[a] They charged up a hill, each making his way as best he could.[b] They forded a river as fast as they could, each man keeping his own position so the hoplites did not get in one another's way—but then Xenophon says the best man was the one who got across first, which gives quite a different impression of how orderly the crossing was.[c] *Anabasis* shows hoplites adapting to all sorts of conditions. Of all the peoples the mercenaries met, only the Chalybes were willing to stand and fight charging Greek hoplites.[d] Everyone else preferred flight to hand-to-hand combat, whether the Greeks were charging in a phalanx, scrambling up a hill, sloshing across a river, or running out of a burning house with swords drawn, fully armed with corselets, shields, swords, and helmets.[e]

§18. Versatile though they were, the hoplites would not have survived without the supporting troops. The critical crossing of the Kentrites River, for example, would not have been possible had the cavalry and peltasts not chased away the enemy cavalry on the far side.[a] Good commanders know how to use different kinds of troops. Xenophon makes the point most clearly in his narrative of what happened to the Arcadians and Achaeans, all hoplites, after the army split into three divisions.[b] Thracian peltasts annihilated one Arcadian company, killed all but eight men in another, and penned the rest up on a hill. Xenophon notes that since the Arcadians had no archers or javelin throwers or horsemen, the Thracians could approach, throw their javelins, and escape without suffering any losses. Heroic efforts by Xenophon and his men saved the day. He sent the cavalry ahead to see what they could, and he sent the peltasts to the flanks and the heights, where they could signal if they saw anything. Horsemen, peltasts, and hoplites set fires as they advanced, to give the impression of a large army. The Thracians withdrew as they approached.

§19. These events in Bithynian Thrace fulfilled Xenophon's earlier prediction that if the Greeks split up into small detachments, they would not be able to get food and escape intact, while together they would receive respect and obtain provisions.[a] The story of the Thracian king Seuthes[b] in the last book of *Anabasis* confirms the point. Defending his alliance with Seuthes, Xenophon says that when he returned to the troops after his abortive attempt to sail home, he found the army without any organized contingents of horsemen or peltasts left. By allying with Seuthes, they acquired those very troops as allies and were able to get not only provisions but also more cattle and captives.[c] In their first joint action, Seuthes and the Greeks seized a thousand captives, two thousand oxen, and ten thousand other animals.[d]

H.17a   Hoplites: as garrison troops, 1.1.6, 1.4.15; besiege Miletus, 1.1.7; set ambush, 4.7.22. Miletus: Ref. Map 4.1, DX.
H.17b   Hoplites climb hill out of formation: 4.2.12.
H.17c   Hoplites ford river: 4.3.29–34.
H.17d   Chalybes face charging Greek hoplites: 4.7.15–16. These Chalybes are the more warlike of two so-named tribes. [E.] Chalybes territory: Ref. Map 6, AX (not listed in the *Barrington Atlas*).
H.17e   Hoplites charge out of burning house: 7.4.16–17.
H.18a   Cavalry and peltasts chase away enemy cavalry: 4.3.22.
H.18b   Arcadian and Achaean misadventures: 6.3.

Arcadia, Achaea: Ref. Map 2, CX.
H.19a   On Bithynian Thrace, see n. 6.2.17a. Need to remain united: 5.6.32. Bithynia: Ref. Map 4.1, AZ.
H.19b   On Seuthes, see Appendix W: Brief Biographies, §30.
H.19c   Success in alliance with Seuthes: 7.6.24–29.
H.19d   Initial fruits of cooperation: 7.3.48.

§20. So divided they fell; united they stood. Xenophon writes with a hint of regret about his ill-fated idea of founding a city on the Black Sea. The idea occurred to him, he says, when he saw the large number of Greek hoplites, peltasts, archers, slingers, and horsemen, all of them proficient because of their experience.[a] It would become a great city, he thought—but the men disagreed among themselves, the project didn't come off, and the great adventure ended with a whimper rather than a bang.

Peter Krentz
W. R. Grey Professor of Classics
Davidson College
Davidson, North Carolina

H.20a    Army gives Xenophon idea of founding colony:
       5.6.15.

# APPENDIX I

*The Size and Makeup of the Ten Thousand*

§1. The Greeks in Cyrus'[a] army have been referred to as the Ten Thousand (*myrioi* in Greek) since antiquity. But the name is something of a misnomer. It is not used by any of the contemporary sources, including Xenophon, who refers to the mercenaries in *Hellenika* (3.2.7) as "the Cyreans."[b] The readiest explanation may be simply that later writers chose 10,000 as a suitably round number. At any rate, it does not correspond to the actual number of Greeks in any of the enumerations that were taken on the march.

§2. In Book 1 of *Anabasis*, Cyrus' army in fact contains about 13,000 Greeks; 8,600 of these are reported at 5.3.3 as having survived the march from Mesopotamia to Kerasous, on the Black Sea, and about 5,000 were still serving with the army in Thrace in Book 7, as explained in §§12–13.[a] Although these broad figures are clear, the numbers of Greek soldiers given at various points in the manuscripts of Xenophon's text present many difficulties, as they do not square with one another.

## The Size of Cyrus' Greek Army When First Assembled

§3. Greek troops join the army at 1.2.3, 1.2.6, 1.2.9, and 1.4.3. At 1.7.10, in a review of the Greek troops just before the battle of Cunaxa, Xenophon says there were 10,400 hoplites and 2,500 peltasts, a total of 12,900 soldiers.[a] Previously only one significant loss has been reported (at 1.2.25): 100 men did not complete the passage through the mountains of Cilicia.[b] On the basis of this, 13,000 Greeks

---

I.1a  On Cyrus the Younger, see Appendix W: Brief Biographies of Selected Characters in *Anabasis*, §10.

I.1b  "the Cyreans" (*Kyreioi* in Greek): the Marincola/Landmark translation of *Hellenika* paraphrases this as "the men who had fought with Cyrus."

I.2a  The following locations appear on Ref. Map 7:

Mesopotamia, CY; Kerasous, AY; Black Sea, AX; Thrace, AW.

I.3a  Hoplites: heavy-armed infantrymen; see Appendix H: Infantry and Cavalry in *Anabasis*, §§2–3. Peltasts: light-armed infantrymen; see Appendix H, §§4–5. Battlefield of Cunaxa: Ref. Map 6, DZ.

I.3b  Cilicia: Ref. Map 5, CY.

FIGURE I.3. RELIEF OF
A PHALANX OF HOPLITES,
C. 370–50, TOMB OF
PERIKLES OF LYCIA, FROM
LIMYRA, ANATOLIA.

joined the army during the march from Sardis[c] to Cunaxa. Superficially this number might seem confirmed by the fact that, according to the manuscript text, 13,000 is also the total of the soldiers reported at 1.2.9 as present at the review at Kelainai; very nearly the total of the individual contingents mentioned at 1.2.3, 1.2.6, and 1.2.9; and the number of Greek mercenaries given by Diodorus 14.19.6–7.[d] But between Kelainai and Cunaxa, two further Greek contingents joined the army, together adding 1,100 more hoplites, as we are told at 1.4.3. So the numbers do not in fact agree.

§4. Furthermore, there is something wrong with the details of the individual contingents given in the manuscripts, as they report Sophainetos of Stymphalos[a] as arriving with his 1,000 hoplites both at 1.2.3 and at 1.2.9. This edition follows the nineteenth-century scholar Ludwig August Dindorf in deleting the reference to Sophainetos at 1.2.3. The individual contingents now do square with the total at the pre-Cunaxa review at 1.7.10, although, to make the match complete, we have to assume that 200 hoplites have been reclassified as peltasts, perhaps as a consequence of losing some part of their equipment. Now, though, they no longer square with the total at Kelainai given at 1.2.9. It is possible that the manuscripts here are wrong, but because the manuscripts of the narratives of these events in both Xenophon and Diodorus give the same wrong figure, the most likely explanation is that Xenophon himself got confused between the two reviews. In this edition, therefore, we have let the manuscript figures at 1.2.9 stand. The table of Greek contingents details the makeup of the 13,000 troops, of whom 100 perished in Cilicia and 12,900 fought at the battle of Cunaxa.

I.3c   Sardis: Ref. Map 4.1, CY; Ref. Map 4.2, CZ.
I.3d   In Appendix S: Selections from Diodorus. Kelainai:
       Ref. Map 4.1, CZ.
I.4a   On Sophainetos, see Appendix W: Brief Biogra-
       phies, §33. Stymphalos: Ref. Map 2, CY.

## Table I.4. The Greek Contingents of Cyrus' Army

| Bk./Chap. | Commander | Joined at | Contingent |
|---|---|---|---|
| 1.1.9 | KLEARCHOS OF LACEDAEMON<br>Raised and maintained a force for Cyrus in the Thracian Chersonese. | Kelainai, 1.2.9 | 1,000 hoplites<br>800 peltasts<br>200 archers |
| 1.1.10,<br>1.2.1,<br>2.6.28 | MENON OF THESSALY<br>Cyrus had originally given Aristippos, a guest-friend,[b] pay for 4,000 troops for a campaign in Thessaly. Cyrus ordered him to bring these to Sardis, but he did not come himself. Menon is subsequently attested as the general of Aristippos' mercenaries and evidently brought only some of the 4,000 troops that Cyrus had paid for. | Colossae, 1.2.6 | 1,000 hoplites<br>500 peltasts |
| 1.1.11 | PROXENOS OF BOEOTIA<br>Guest-friend of Cyrus; asked by him to raise a force for a campaign against the Pisidians. | Sardis, 1.2.3 | 1,500 hoplites<br>500 *gymnētes*[c] |
| 1.1.11 | SOCRATES OF ACHAEA<br>Guest-friend of Cyrus; asked by him to raise a force for a war on the Persian satrap[d] Tissaphernes. | Sardis, 1.2.3 | 500 hoplites |
| 1.1.11 | SOPHAINETOS OF STYMPHALOS<br>Guest-friend of Cyrus; asked by him to raise a force for a war on Tissaphernes. | Kelainai, 1.2.9 | 1,000 hoplites |
| 1.2.1 | XENIAS OF ARCADIA<br>Head of Cyrus' garrison troops in western Anatolia. | Sardis, 1.2.3 | 4,000 hoplites |
| 1.2.3 | PASION OF MEGARA<br>Commander in the campaign against Tissaphernes at Miletus. | Sardis, 1.2.3 | 300 hoplites<br>300 peltasts |
| 1.2.9 | SOSIS OF SYRACUSE | Kelainai, 1.2.9 | 300 hoplites |
| 1.4.3 | CHEIRISOPHOS OF LACEDAEMON<br>Cyrus sent for him, Xenophon says; see also Diodorus 14.19.4–5 (in Appendix S). | Landed by Spartan ships, Issus, 1.4.3 | 700 hoplites |
| 1.4.3 | COMMANDER NOT NAMED<br>Mercenaries of the Persian satrap Abrokomas deserted him and joined Cyrus. | Issus, 1.4.3 | 400 hoplites |
| | | | 10,700 hoplites<br>1,600 peltasts<br>500 *gymnētes*<br>200 archers |
| | | Total | 13,000 troops |

NOTE: All locations mentioned in the table can be found in the Reference Maps. Further information on Abrokomas, Aristippos, Cyrus the Younger, Klearchos, Menon, Proxenos, Tissaphernes, and Sophainetos can be found in Appendix W: Brief Biographies.

I.4b  Guest-friend: someone with whom there is a bond of ritualized friendship of a type that was common between prominent men of different cities; for a full discussion, see the Glossary.

I.4c  *Gymnētes:* infantry without protective clothing.

I.4d  Persian satrap: a provincial governor.

337

## The Biggest Single Disaster
## for the Ten Thousand

§5. Following the defection of 300 Thracian peltasts shortly after the battle of Cunaxa,[a] 12,600 Greek troops set off on the journey home. At 5.3.3 Xenophon says 8,600 troops were counted at Kerasous,[b] on the Black Sea coast. So 4,000 of the 12,600 had perished on the way to the Black Sea or in their first few weeks after reaching it. Many of those will have fallen at the hands of the Persians or because of the snow in Armenia,[c] but a surprisingly large number can be shown to have died not so long before they reached Kerasous. At 4.8.15 we are told that almost 8,000 hoplites and about 1,800 peltasts attacked the Kolchoi in the last engagement before they reached Trapezus,[d] so between Trapezus and Kerasous, at least 1,200 soldiers died—30 percent of the casualty total over the whole march out of Mesopotamia.

§6. Some of these 1,200 men will have died from sickness, as mentioned at 5.3.3, but Xenophon there emphasizes that such deaths were few. Others will have died in incidental skirmishes, in particular the failed raid of Kleainetos (5.1.17), which might have led to casualties of 100 or so, as there were two companies involved, totaling about 200 men, and heavy losses among them. A few more may have deserted alongside Dexippos[a] in the fifty-oared ships mentioned at 5.15. But there is really only one occasion that can account for the great bulk of the 1,200—namely, the attack under Xenophon's personal leadership on the Drilai,[b] recounted at 5.2. Xenophon took half the army on this expedition,[c] so if he lost, say, 1,000 men, that amounted to about a fifth of the troops he was leading. He is therefore being tendentious when he says at 5.2.32, "In this way they all arrived safe back in the camp," diverting attention from the army as a whole to the small contingent that assisted the Mysian[d] whose adventures are singled out here.

§7. Indeed, according to the text of most manuscripts at 5.2.4, accepted by many modern editors, the total number of casualties at this late stage may have been even larger than this. In these manuscripts (though not in our text; see §8), we are told there that more than 2,000 peltasts and spearmen foolishly ran ahead of the hoplites across a ravine in the country of the Drilai. On this basis it would seem that something like 1,500 men died between Trapezus and Kerasous rather than 1,200. True, at 4.8.15 there appear to be only 1,800 peltasts and archers, but this is not a strong objection to there being more than 2,000 peltasts and spearmen at 5.2.4: the balance could be spearmen, presumably held back behind the main formation at 4.8.15 and so not included in the number given there. Such spearmen would presumably be the remnant of the *gymnētes* (very light-armed men) mentioned at 1.2.3, originally 500 in number. Usually these people appear to be counted toward totals of peltasts, but they are sometimes referred to separately, for example at 5.2.16.

I.5a  Defection of 300 peltasts: 2.7.2.
I.5b  Kerasous: Ref. Map 5, AZ.
I.5c  Armenia: Ref. Map 6, AY.
I.5d  Kolchoi territory, Trapezus: Ref. Map 6, AX.

I.6a  On Dexippos, see Appendix W: Brief Biographies, §13.
I.6b  Drilai territory: Ref. Map 5, AZ.
I.6c  Half the army involved in attack: 5.2.1.
I.6d  Mysia: Ref. Map 4.1, BY; Ref. Map 4.2, BY.

§8. All the same, there is a strong argument against the figure of 2,000 at 5.2.4: it implies implausible differential attrition rates between hoplites and peltasts. As there were fewer than 8,000 hoplites at 4.8.15, more than 2,400 had perished on the way to Trapezus, out of a total of 10,400 hoplites reviewed shortly before Cunaxa—a casualty rate of more than 23 percent. But if more than 2,000 peltasts and spearmen remained at 5.2.4, when there had been only 2,500 with the army at Cunaxa, 300 of whom deserted almost immediately, then no more than 200 non-hoplite soldiers had perished on the march to Trapezus—a casualty rate of only 9 percent. Such a discrepancy in favor of the peltasts is surely impossible. So there seems to be something wrong with the figure of 2,000 peltasts and spearmen at 5.2.4. And indeed, one of the three earliest manuscripts reads here "more than 1,000" rather than "more than 2,000," which would solve the problem. So this edition, in common with some others, uses the figure 1,000 at 5.2.4, and we need think of "only" 1,200 casualties between Trapezus and Kerasous.

## The Size of the Army When It Divided into Three Parts on the Black Sea Coast

§9. The army split into three parts while it was at Heraclea, as recounted at 6.2.16 (it reunited at Kalpe Harbor not long after).[a] The details of this split cause problems. The two smaller sections, both about the same size, were those of Xenophon and Cheirisophos.[b] Xenophon had 1,700 hoplites, 300 peltasts, and 40 cavalry, for a total of 2,040. Cheirisophos had 1,400 hoplites; the number of his peltasts varies between manuscripts (see further §11). But the main problem lies with the largest division, that of the Arcadians and Achaeans,[c] all hoplites, who, we are told at 6.2.10, "totaled more than half of the army." At Kerasous 8,600 soldiers had been counted, so at that point there were more than 4,300 Arcadians and Achaeans, probably quite a lot more, since if the number had been close to 4,300, Xenophon could have been expected to say "about half" rather than "more than half." The difficulty comes when we ask how many Arcadians and Achaeans there were by the time they reached Heraclea.

§10. At 6.2.16 some manuscripts say there were "more than 4,500" Arcadians and Achaeans at Heraclea and others say there were "more than 4,000." Modern editors are fairly evenly split between these two figures. But in order for "more than 4,000" to have been an appropriate way of referring to the Arcadians in this context, where Xenophon seems to be counting in hundreds rather than thousands or even five hundreds, there would have to have been 300 to 400 casualties between Kerasous and Heraclea, which is more than seems likely. There was fighting against the primitive Mossynoeci, and we are also told of raids by Paphlagonians,[a] but the way Xenophon refers to casualties in these cases does not suggest losses of anything like

I.9a   Heraclea, Kalpe Harbor (possible location): Ref. Map 4.1, AY, AZ.
I.9b   On Cheirisophos, see Appendix W: Brief Biographies, §7.
I.9c   Arcadia, Achaea: Ref. Map 2, CX.
I.10a   Mossynoeci territory, Paphlagonia: Ref. Map 5, AZ, AX.

this magnitude. Furthermore, while the failed raid of Kleuretos mentioned at 5.7.16 would have had a bigger impact, to be successfully kept secret from the senior officers it could not have involved many hundreds of men, and there were seemingly a reasonable number of survivors. Probably there were also some deaths among the sick who are mentioned at 5.3.1 and 5.5.20. But there is no great argument for reckoning them to be as many as the several hundred required to fill the numerical gap. That would imply a much higher mortality rate from illness for this stretch of the journey than for the rest of it.

§11. On the other hand, putting "more than 4,500" Arcadians together with the usual readings for the numbers of non-Arcadian soldiers produces the opposite problem, as it implies casualties between Kerasous and Heraclea of an absolute maximum of 25, a scale that seems too small to cover Kleuretos' failed raid. However, while most manuscripts and all editors give the number of Cheirisophos' peltasts at Heraclea as 700, two manuscripts instead make the number 600, and this would allow all the figures to be fitted together, assuming rounding here and there. On this basis there could have been perhaps 40 to 60 casualties from Kleuretos' raid. So this edition has adopted "more than 4,500" as the number of Arcadians and Achaeans at Heraclea and 600 as the number of Cheirisophos' peltasts, giving a total size for the army at Heraclea of more than 8,500.[a]

## The Number of Greeks Who Eventually Joined Thibron

§12. This figure of more than 8,500 was further depleted over the winter in Thrace.[a] At 7.7.23 Xenophon reproves Seuthes[b] in words that imply that there were 6,000 Greek soldiers witnessing his behavior. But the fallout since Heraclea had been greater than this. Between 6.2.16 and 7.7.23, Xenophon records the loss of almost 2,500 men, through either dying in battle, being sold into slavery by the Spartans, or departing with Neon.[c] On top of this, many men had left the army in Byzantium,[d] and perhaps some had died of illness, though Xenophon doesn't say so. Thus we should get down well below 6,000. Indeed, Diodorus 14.37.1[e] says that about 5,000 Greeks under Xenophon joined Seuthes.

§13. The truth may well lie between these two figures. At 7.7.25 we are told that the Greeks think they should be receiving 30 talents from Seuthes for their services. The troops were promised pay for two months (7.5.9) but received only twenty days' pay (7.5.4), so they are owed pay for about one month and 10 days at 1 Cyzicene stater/about 25 drachmas per month (7.2.36), thus about 33 drachmas per

I.11a  A subsidiary problem here concerns the fact that these 600 peltasts are said to have been "Klearchos' Thracians." Although it is not literally impossible that this was true of all of them, it would, since they had originally numbered 800 (1.2.9), imply a much lower rate of attrition among "Klearchos' Thracians" than among the other peltasts. So it is more likely that Klearchos' remaining Thracians formed merely the core of the group that Cheirisophos now commanded.

I.12a  Thrace: Ref. Map 3.
I.12b  On Seuthes, see Appendix W: Brief Biographies, §30.
I.12c  Dying in battle: 6.3.5 (bearing in mind that the Arcadians seem to be operating with ten unusually large "companies"), 6.4.24. Sold by Spartans: 7.2.6–7. Departing with Neon: 7.2.11. Sparta: Ref. Map 2, DY.
I.12d  Troops leave Byzantium: 7.2.3–4. Byzantium: Ref. Map 4.1, AY.
I.12e  In Appendix S: Selections from Diodorus.

man. Thirty talents equals 180,000 drachmas, so there are about 5,400 soldiers, or, rather, about 5,300 once one has allowed for the higher pay of the officers. This should give the correct order of magnitude, but precision is inappropriate: 30 talents could be a round number, and the exchange rate between Cyzicene staters, made of electrum, and drachmas, made of silver, was not constant.[a]

§14. To sum up, 13,000 Greeks originally joined up with Cyrus, but only about 5,300 remained to join Thibron's[a] army a year and a half later.

David Thomas
Buckinghamshire, UK

I.13a   For all these units of currency and how to com-
        pare them with modern units, see Appendix O:
        Ancient Greek and Persian Units of Measurement,
        §§9–19.
I.14a   On Thibron, see Appendix W: Brief Biographies,
        §35.

# APPENDIX J

## *A Soldier's View of the March*

§1. Xenophon's *Anabasis* provides a vivid portrait of the mercenaries of Cyrus—the Cyreans, as they were known in antiquity.[a] While it above all emphasizes leadership and tactics, it also offers numerous incidental descriptions of life on the march. Taken together, these brief snapshots of such activities as camping, foraging, cooking, and eating enable us to discern the military and social structures that shaped the daily lives of ordinary Cyrean soldiers and to understand their experience of the campaign.

§2. The Cyreans were highly diverse. Their ranks included exiles, ex-slaves, aristocratic adventurers, such as Xenophon himself, and even a former professional boxer.[a] The troops ranged in age from about eighteen to fifty.[b] A noticeable proportion were forty or older,[c] so that, overall, more than half the army may have been over thirty. Given their ages, most of the mercenaries were probably veterans rather than raw recruits. Most had joined Cyrus in search of profit, but not all were poor.[d] The men hailed from more than two dozen Greek cities, regions, or tribes. More than half came from Arcadia and Achaea on the Peloponnese, regions renowned for their mercenaries.[e] There were also many non-Greeks in the army, among them eight hundred Thracians as well as others from various parts of Anatolia.[f] Regional animosities or perceived ethnic differences sometimes caused serious friction, but otherwise the army tolerated and even celebrated its diversity.[g] At critical moments soldiers worked together despite differences in age, social status, and ethnicity.

§3. The mercenaries began their service with Cyrus as members of seven individually recruited and organized forces, each led by its own general; indeed Xenophon

---

NOTE: All references to *Hellenika* in this appendix refer to Xenophon's work.

J.1a Cyreans: *Hellenika* 3.2.7, 3.4.20. The Greek word is *Kureioi* (Κύρειοι) in both places, but translators often use longer explanatory phrases. On Cyrus the Younger, see Appendix W: Brief Biographies of Selected Characters in *Anabasis*, §10.
J.2a Exile: *Anabasis* 4.8.25. Ex-slave: 4.8.4. Boxer: 5.8.23.
J.2b Eighteen: 7.4.16. Fifty: 2.6.15.
J.2c Over forty: 5.3.1, 6.5.4.
J.2d Not all poor: 6.4.8.

J.2e More than half from Arcadia and Achaea: 6.2.10. How many soldiers this amounted to is discussed in Appendix I: The Size and Makeup of the Army, §§9–11. For the fame of Arcadian mercenaries, see *Hellenika* 7.1.23. Arcadia, Achaea, Peloponnese: Ref. Map 2, CX.
J.2f Thracians: 1.2.9. Various Anatolians: 4.8.4, 5.2.29, 6.1.9–12. Thrace: Ref. Map 3. Anatolia: Ref. Map 1, BX.
J.2g Interethnic friction: 3.1.31, 6.1.30, 6.2.9–12. Celebration of ethnic diversity: 6.1.5–13.

even refers to them as independent armies.[a] Before the battle of Cunaxa,[b] these forces marched and camped separately, although all looked to Cyrus to provide them with markets or rations. Nor did the men of each army necessarily recognize the authority of generals other than their own. At one point on the way down the Euphrates River, Klearchos' and Menon's armies nearly came to blows after Klearchos disciplined one of Menon's men.[c] After Cunaxa, changes in leadership, the selection of volunteers for special units or missions,[d] and the overall exigency of the retreat helped erode the boundaries between the original armies, so that they began to function more as divisions subordinate to the command of all the generals than as independent entities. Yet generals continued to encamp separately with their divisions, and some men's loyalties to specific divisions and generals never entirely disappeared.[e] By the end of the campaign, although multiple generals remained as a vestige of the troops' original organization in separate contingents, the Cyreans had become an integrated single army.[f]

§4. While the army's overall command structure changed over time, soldiers tended to remain with the same company (*lochos*) throughout the campaign. Mustering about a hundred men, a company was the basic fighting and marching unit of the Cyrean hoplites.[a] A *lochagos*, or captain, led each company; many captains probably had personally recruited their troops.[b] Some captains had a lieutenant (*hypolochagos*) or perhaps a trumpeter (*salpinktes*)[c] to convey orders, but there was otherwise little or no formal structure within a company. Only the six picked companies created in Mesopotamia during the initial stages of the retreat had designated subofficers and formal subunits.[d] Companies could form four ranks deep in an unbroken phalanx battle order or maneuver independently on rough ground.[e] Light infantry (slingers, archers, peltasts) and cavalry were organized in units (*taxeis*) of up to several hundred men apiece, each under a group commander (*taxiarchos*).[f]

§5. For long marches the Cyreans traveled in company columns, normally four men abreast.[a] They could spread out into several parallel columns for speed or form a hollow rectangle to protect against flank attacks.[b] The mercenaries also became adept at night marches.[c] At pinch points or in the mountains, it could take hours for the whole army to pass a spot.[d] Pack animals, porters, and other noncombatants

J.3a   Seven separate forces: 1.1.9–1.2.3. "Army" as one of them: 1.1.9, 1.1.10, 1.2.1. For a listing of the contingents, see Appendix I: The Size and Makeup of the Army, Table I.4.
J.3b   Battlefield of Cunaxa: Ref. Map 6, DZ.
J.3c   Conflict between Klearchos' and Menon's armies: 1.5.11–17. On Klearchos and Menon, see Appendix W: Brief Biographies, §§20, 23. Euphrates River: Ref. Map 6, CX.
J.3d   Leadership changes: 3.1.47. Volunteers for special units: 3.3.18. Volunteers for missions: 4.1.27.
J.3e   Separate encampments: 4.5.23. Continuing loyalties: for example, 7.2.11, 7.3.2.
J.3f   Multiple generals within integrated army: 7.2.35.
J.4a   Company (*lochos*) of about 100 men the basic unit: 3.1.32–33, 4.8.15. Hoplites: heavily armed infantrymen; see Appendix H: Infantry and Cavalry in *Anabasis*, esp. §§2–3. See Figure 1.2.16 for an illustration of a hoplite.
J.4b   Captains personally recruit their companies (*lochoi*):

7.4.8; *Hellenika* 4.2.5.
J.4c   Lieutenant: 5.2.13. Trumpeter: 4.3.29, 4.4.22. See Figure 4.2.1 for an illustration of a *salpinx* (trumpet).
J.4d   Subunits of picked companies: 3.4.19–23; similarly, 4.3.26. Mesopotamia: Ref. Map 6, CY.
J.4e   Line of battle: 1.2.14–18 (in a review), 1.8.14. Companies maneuver independently: 4.2.4–13, 4.8.9–13. On the phalanx, see the Glossary.
J.4f   Peltasts organized into units: 4.3.22. Groups of slingers and cavalry: 3.3.20. *Taxiarchos* (translated "group commander" in this edition): 3.1.37, 4.1.28. For more on light infantry, including peltasts, and cavalry, see Appendix H, esp. §§4–10.
J.5a   Marching in column: 4.6.5–6; similar movement from column to line, 1.8.14. Four men abreast: inferred from 2.4.26 (unusually, two abreast for a special reason).
J.5b   Parallel columns: 3.4.30. Hollow rectangle: 3.2.36.
J.5c   Night marches: 2.2.7–8, 3.4.36–37, 7.3.40–41.
J.5d   Restricted passages: 1.7.14–16, 4.1.10.

marched alongside the company to which they belonged.[c] Xenophon's narrative often records the army's marches in parasangs, a measure that the troops themselves probably used.[f] Clearly, whatever the precise meaning of "parasang," the troops' progress depended on terrain, weather, and the amount of available daylight. The average day's march from Sardis to Thapsakos was six parasangs, but on some stretches the army made up to ten a day.[g] On the winter retreat through northern Mesopotamia and eastern Anatolia, Xenophon records less progress than that: often only five parasangs a day for stretches of thirty days or more[h] and indeed sometimes less still.[i] At day's end each company encamped as a unit, along with the other companies under a single general's command.[j]

§6. Though companies were reduced in number by deaths, injuries, and desertions, troops were not arbitrarily shuffled about just to keep companies at full strength. Kallimachos' company, for example, fought well against the Taochoi even though it mustered only seventy of its original one hundred men.[a] Some soldiers did transfer to new units, and the remnants of severely mauled companies may have been combined into a new company or used to replenish understrength companies.[b] As a result the army had about a hundred hoplite companies just after Cunaxa, but several months later only eighty remained.[c]

§7. Cyreans who lived together in the same company day and night for the duration of the campaign could develop strong bonds with one another and with their captain. The captain Agasias, for example, rescued one of his men from arrest solely on the ground that the man was part of his company.[a] Some captains competed with one another in displays of valor, inspiring the men of their companies to follow.[b] Others set a poor example by deserting.[c]

§8. Within each company soldiers organized themselves into small, informal mess groups (*suskēniai*; literally, "tent-sharings"). The members of each group called one another messmates (*suskēnoi*)[a] and shared in the daily routines of camping, foraging, cooking, and eating. Informal soldiers' communities of this sort were common in Classical Greek armies, which lacked centralized logistical services; the Spartans[b] were exceptional in having formal messes and supply officers. As the size of Cyrean mess groups was not formally regulated, their numbers may have varied widely, from two or three messmates up to perhaps fifteen, and group compositions may have changed over the course of the campaign.

§9. Because they could not count on the army to provide rations, medical care,

J.5e Proximity of baggage train to soldiers on march: 2.2.4. On noncombatants among the army's baggage train, see Appendix K: The Noncombatant Contingent of the Army.

J.5f On parasangs, see the Introduction, §7.3–5; Appendix O: Ancient Greek and Persian Units of Measurement, §§7–8.

J.5g Ten parasangs a day: 1.2.11. Sardis: Ref. Map 4.1, CY; Ref. Map 4.2, BY. Thapsakos, possible location: Ref. Map 6, CX (not listed in the *Barrington Atlas*).

J.5h Five parasangs a day: 4.4.1, 4.4.3, 4.4.7, 4.5.2, 4.6.4, 4.6.5, 4.7.19; six parasangs a day, 4.7.1.

J.5i Fewer than five parasangs a day: for example, 3.3.11 (25 stades, about 1 parasang or perhaps a bit less), 3.4.13, 4.8.1, 4.8.22; also, according to many editors (including this Landmark edition), 4.5.3 and,

by conjecture in this edition, 4.7.15.

J.5j Companies encamp with others with the same general: 4.4.8.

J.6a Kallimachos' company numbers seventy: 4.7.8–9. Taochoi territory: Ref. Map 6, AY.

J.6b Transfers to new units: 3.3.16–20, 3.4.19–23. Severely mauled company: 4.2.17. For combinations of soldiers from different units, compare *Hellenika* 1.2.15–17.

J.6c One hundred companies: 3.1.33. Eighty companies: 4.8.15.

J.7a Agasias rescues one of his soldiers: 6.6.7, 6.6.17.

J.7b Competitions in valor: 4.7.8–12, 5.2.11.

J.7c Captain Kleairetos deserts: 5.7.15–16.

J.8a Messmates: 5.7.15, 5.8.5.

J.8b Sparta: Ref. Map 2, DY.

equipment, or other support, messmates had to rely on one another. The social bonds that developed among them could foster unit cohesion and morale, making the company to which they belonged more effective in combat. Yet Cyrean mess groups should not be idealized as "bands of brothers." Disputes about property, arguments over women or boy-favorites, and drunkenness could lead messmates to blows; such fights certainly occurred in the army.[a] Tensions between mess groups also arose, as some hoarded food and even prevented outsiders from sharing the warmth of their fires.[b] An extreme case of mess group loyalty appears in Xenophon's story of the mule-driving soldier who, forced to carry a dying stranger at the cost of protecting his messmates' gear, chose to abandon the stranger.[c] Devotion to comrades could also hinder the entire army: on at least one occasion, some soldiers abandoned their posts in battle to look after the needs of their mess group, while other groups deserted altogether.[d]

§10. Some Cyreans had personal slaves or servants, but the army overall had very few such noncombatants before Cunaxa.[a] The lack of slaves and servants forced soldiers to do their own chores in cooperation with their messmates.[b] During the retreat to the sea, the mercenaries acquired both male and female captives; the generals forced the men to release many of them before entering the territory of the Kardouchoi, but some soldiers smuggled desirable boys and women past the generals.[c] As these boys and women shared the rigors of the retreat, they were assimilated into the army's mess groups, becoming soldiers' companions rather than captives.[d] Some of these relationships endured even after the campaign ended.[e] Along the Black Sea coast, the troops enslaved and sold numerous prisoners.[f]

§11. Regardless of company or mess group, every soldier had to cope with the physical realities of life on the march. Weapons and armor were probably lighter than scholars previously thought, but men also needed clothing, cooking gear, food, water, and other personal effects. The average hoplite, therefore, may have carried about sixty-eight pounds, while light infantrymen carried up to forty-four pounds.[a] The troops began the expedition with tents but burned them before commencing their retreat.[b] Since the army had no central equipment reserve, some men made use of captured weapons.[c] The lack of any central stock of replacement clothing made soldiers keen to steal clothes, and losing clothing was a misfortune deserving specific mention.[d] Many men wore out their sandals and had to improvise rough animal-hide moccasins.[e]

§12. To ease their burdens, some Cyreans used donkeys or asses and mules as pack animals.[a] Messmates could choose one of their number to safeguard their pack

J.9a   Fights between soldiers: 1.5.11, 5.8.4, 6.6.6–7.
J.9b   Tension between mess groups: 4.5.5.
J.9c   Messmates' gear chosen over stranger's life: 5.8.4–11.
J.9d   Posts temporarily abandoned: 4.3.30. Permanent desertion: 5.7.15–16.
J.10a  See Appendix K: The Noncombatant Contingent of the Army, §3, for a similar argument.
J.10b  Soldiers do own chores: 4.3.11, 5.1.2.
J.10c  Acquisition of captives: 3.5.14, 4.1.12–13, 4.6.1–3, 7.4.7. Captives smuggled past generals: 4.1.14–15. Kardouchoi territory: Ref. Map 6, BY.
J.10d  Captives become companions: 4.3.19, 4.8.27, 5.4.33, 6.1.11–13.
J.10e  Enduring relationship: 4.6.3.
J.10f  Captives taken, enslaved, and sold: 6.3.3, 6.6.38,

7.3.48, 7.8.19. Black Sea: Ref. Map 1, AX.
J.11a  Sixty-eight pounds/31 kilograms, 44 pounds/20 kilograms. In Appendix H: Infantry and Cavalry in *Anabasis*, §2, Peter Krentz estimates the weight of the armor within these overall figures as 30 pounds/13.6 kilograms for many hoplites and 20 pounds/9 kilograms for light infantrymen.
J.11b  Burning of tents: 3.3.1.
J.11c  Reuse of captured weapons: 3.4.17, 4.2.28.
J.11d  Theft of clothes (from outsiders): 4.3.12, 5.8.23. Loss of clothes: 7.4.18.
J.11e  Improvised footwear: 4.5.14.
J.12a  Pack animals: unspecified, 1.7.20; donkeys, 2.1.6. Donkey loose among the baggage: 2.2.20.

animal and the gear it carried.[b] The army began the march with an uncertain number of pack animals and ox-drawn carts;[c] these seem to have been provided by the soldiers themselves rather than officially issued. The carts were burned following the seizure of the generals near the Zapatas River, but the soldiers obtained others after reaching the Black Sea coast.[d] During the march the soldiers acquired livestock, horses, oxen, and mules as booty or gifts and used some of them to carry baggage.[e]

§13. Caring for animals required time and attention each day. Soldiers could let their animals out to graze around camp or bring them fodder.[a] Some men also had to shepherd captured livestock.[b] Every morning pack animals had to be loaded before the march could begin. There were designated signals for packing and loading animals.[c] Although the Greeks knew of wood-frame packsaddles, most animals probably carried their loads in simple panniers or baskets, secured with leather straps.[d] Animals suffered terribly from hunger and weather during the march[e] and were sometimes eaten when supplies gave out. One striking aspect of *Anabasis* is the attention that Xenophon, an experienced animal handler, gives to the experiences of the army's animals. He even has them take part in the joyous scene when the army first catches sight of the sea.[f]

§14. The search for food and cooking fuel was another constant of campaign life. On the way toward Babylon, troops could buy provisions from traveling merchants who accompanied the army; Cyrus also let the mercenaries acquire supplies from settlements en route.[a] During the tense truce following Cunaxa, the Persians provided the Cyreans with access to local markets or allowed the mercenaries to requisition from settlements.[b] During the retreat across eastern Anatolia, the troops were reduced to plundering and foraging. When supplies ran short, men bartered with one another for food and firewood.[c] On the Black Sea coast, some cities again provided markets, but the troops continued to plunder where they could and also extracted "gifts" from the locals.[d]

§15. When the army stopped to rest, messmates likely slept as a group, at first in their tents but, during the retreat, sometimes huddled together in the snow.[a] A covering of fresh, dry snow could act as insulation. As Xenophon remarks, soldiers were reluctant to get up from under such a snow blanket.[b] Deep snow and high winds, on the other hand, were a recipe for frostbite, blindness, and death, especially when soldiers were wet from crossing rivers.[c] Villages offered warmth and security, especially in the Anatolian winter.[d] During spring and summer on the Black Sea coast, troops

J.12b  Some soldiers guard pack animal and gear: 1.10.3, 5.8.5.
J.12c  Carts: 1.7.20.
J.12d  Carts burned: 3.2.27. Army has carts again: 6.4.22. Zapatas (modern Greater Zab) River: Ref. Map 6, CY.
J.12e  Animals acquired as booty or gifts: 3.5.2, 3.5.9–12, 4.4.21, 4.5.24, 4.5.35, 4.7.14, 7.5.4.
J.13a  Fodder: 1.5.7, 1.9.27.
J.13b  Captured livestock: 3.5.2, 4.7.14, 6.6.37.
J.13c  Designated signals: 2.2.4.
J.13d  Straps ("ropes" in this Landmark translation) used with pack animals: 3.5.10.
J.13e  Animals' suffering: 1.5.5, 4.5.4, 4.5.12.
J.13f  Animals participate in rush to see the sea: 4.7.24.

J.14a  Traveling merchants: 1.3.14, 1.5.6. Cyrus permits supplies to be acquired from settlements: 1.4.19. Babylon: Ref. Map 6, DZ.
J.14b  Access to local markets: 2.3.24, 2.4.9. Requisitioning from settlements: 2.3.14, 2.4.27.
J.14c  Barter for food and firewood: 4.5.5–6.
J.14d  Gifts from Black Sea cities: 6.1.15, 6.2.3.
J.15a  Sleep in tents: 3.3.1. Huddled together in the snow: 4.5.19–20.
J.15b  Soldiers in snow reluctant to get up: 4.4.11.
J.15c  Death from exposure: 4.5.3–4. Frostbite and snow blindness: 4.5.12–13.
J.15d  Villages in the winter: 4.1.11, 4.4.8, 4.4.14, 4.5.23, 4.5.30–33.

often preferred to sleep outside even when villages were available.[e] Sentry duty became a regular feature of soldiers' camp life after Cunaxa.[f]

§16. Typically the Cyreans ate their morning meal (*ariston*) around midmorning, often after marching or some other activity.[a] The second main meal (*deipnon*, translated "evening meal" in this edition) came in the late afternoon or early evening before sunset.[b] Soldiers probably often ate leftovers of previously cooked meals in the morning but kindled fires to cook their second meal. Making a fire required not only fuel but also a way to start it—not always easy to do in a world without matches or lighters.[c] During the Anatolian winter, being caught outside overnight without fire could mean freezing to death.[d]

§17. The soldiers' staple food was grain, typically barley or wheat, purchased from markets or taken from settlements en route.[a] Unmilled grain could be boiled as porridge or parched over a fire; flour or meal could be baked into bread.[b] Bread could also be purchased[c] or plundered. When grain was unobtainable, the men ate whatever they could get their hands on, from their own baggage animals to native foods, such as salted dolphin and bread made of boiled hazelnut meal.[d] Most Classical Greeks ate little meat, but the Cyreans happily ate it whenever they could; eating nothing except meat, though, was a hardship.[e] The troops relished drink even more than food. During the march they sampled everything from date-palm or grape wine to barley beer.[f] Some even ate honey that proved psychoactive,[g] perhaps precisely for the high it offered; such honey was probably produced by bees feeding on rhododendron pollen. Xenophon himself boasted of his drinking prowess and described the depths of the retreat as being without even "a sniff of wine."[h]

§18. Injured or ill Cyreans could expect rudimentary medical care at best. Early in the retreat, the army appointed eight "doctors" (*iatroi*),[a] but what if any training or supplies these men possessed is unclear. Skilled doctors could have coped with arrow wounds and broken bones but not with massive internal injuries or infections.[b] During the retreat up the Tigris River,[c] the Cyreans at first tried carrying their wounded along with them. Doing so, however, slowed the army's pace too much.[d] Thereafter Xenophon never mentions carrying the wounded; the vehemence with which he attacks the soldier who abandoned a sick stranger[e] belies the uncomfortable truth that incapacitated men without help from their messmates must often have been left behind to die. Only after the Cyreans obtained ships on the Black Sea could they easily transport their sick and injured.[f]

§19. Weather and lack of supplies could inflict more harm than enemy action. In

J.15e  Troops prefer to sleep on beach: 6.4.7.
J.15f  Sentry duty: 2.3.2, 2.6.10, 3.1.40, 7.3.34.
J.16a  Morning meal: 1.10.19 (shortly before noon, 1.8.1), 3.3.1, 4.1.14, 6.5.1, 7.3.9–10.
J.16b  Evening meal: 1.10.15–19, 3.1.3, 3.5.18, 4.6.22, 6.3.21, 6.4.26.
J.16c  *Hellenika* 4.5.3–4 reveals one method of carrying fire over short distances.
J.16d  Freezing to death: *Anabasis* 4.5.11.
J.17a  Grain: bought in markets, 1.5.6; taken from settlements, 4.4.9, 4.5.26, 6.6.1.
J.17b  Wheat and barley baked into bread: 4.5.31.
J.17c  Purchases of bread: 1.5.10.
J.17d  Baggage animals: 2.1.6. Dolphin, nut bread: 5.4.28–29.

J.17e  Meat consumption: 4.5.30–31. Pure meat diet a hardship: 1.5.6, 4.7.17.
J.17f  Palm wine: 1.5.10, 2.3.14. Grape wine: 2.4.28, 3.4.31, 4.2.22, 4.4.9. Barley beer: 4.5.26–27, n. 4.5.26a.
J.17g  Psychoactive honey: 4.8.20–21.
J.17h  Drinking prowess: 5.8.19. "Sniff of wine": 5.8.3.
J.18a  "Doctors": 3.4.30, n. 3.4.30a.
J.18b  Arrow wounds: 3.3.7. Broken bones: 4.2.20, 4.7.4–5. Massive internal injuries: 2.5.33.
J.18c  Tigris River: Ref. Map 6, CZ.
J.18d  Army slowed by carrying wounded: 3.4.31–32.
J.18e  Abandonment of a sick stranger: 5.8.8–10.
J.18f  Transportation of sick and injured by sea: 5.3.1, 5.5.20, 7.2.6.

Mesopotamia the army often marched at night or early in the morning, probably to avoid the blazing summer sun.[a] In the Anatolian winter, soldiers suffered from exposure, hypothermia, frostbite, and snow blindness.[b] Some fell ill from lack of food, while others succumbed to disease.[c] Some sick Cyreans who sought refuge in Byzantium were sold into slavery.[d] Ultimately only about five thousand of the more than twelve thousand who set out in 401 were still together under arms in the spring of 399.[e]

§20. The mercenaries honored their dead as best they could. Even during the retreat, they buried fallen comrades whenever possible, sometimes negotiating with hostile locals so they could retrieve their dead.[a] On the Black Sea coast, the army made special missions to gather and bury fallen soldiers.[b] At Kalpe Harbor the men also erected a cenotaph and laid wreaths to honor dead comrades whose bodies could not be found.[c]

§21. Assemblies, speeches, and other scenes of communal decision-making are prominent features of *Anabasis*, especially at key turning points in Xenophon's narrative. Following the capture and execution of many of their officers in Mesopotamia, after reaching the sea at Trapezus,[a] and repeatedly along the Black Sea coast, the Cyreans gathered to deliberate over their next steps. As a result, modern studies of *Anabasis* have often emphasized the political aspects of the army, portraying it as a sort of moving city-state, an outpost of Greek democracy in barbarian lands.

§22. Yet a closer look reveals a more complicated reality. Early on, some Cyreans addressed their concerns about unpaid wages directly to Cyrus, not through an assembly.[a] When the troops went on strike in Tarsus because they suspected the true goal of the expedition, their first action was to throw stones at Klearchos rather than to engage in rational discussion.[b] Only in response, and in collusion with Cyrus, did Klearchos call an assembly intended to persuade the mercenaries to advance. Soon men from other divisions were joining Klearchos and selecting emissaries to attend meetings with Cyrus.[c] The ploy worked, and the march resumed. When Cyrus revealed his plans at Thapsakos, the generals assembled the entire army and overcame the soldiers' misgivings with promises of more than a year's bonus pay.[d] Menon went further, convincing his men that being the first across the Euphrates would win them special favor from Cyrus.[e] After Cunaxa, in contrast, Klearchos took the lead among the generals without seeking any mandate from the other officers, much less from the ordinary soldiers.[f]

J.19a  Mesopotamian night-marches: 1.7.1, 2.2.4–8. Editors' note: here John Lee follows an "early" chronology for the march, in contrast to the "late" chronology adopted by the editors of this Landmark edition (see Appendix Q: The Chronology of the March).
J.19b  Effects of winter weather: 4.5.4, 4.5.11–12, 4.5.15–17.
J.19c  Fainting from starvation: 4.5.7–9. Death by disease: 5.3.3.
J.19d  Sick soldiers sold into slavery: 7.2.6. Byzantium: Ref. Map 4.1, AY.
J.19e  Five thousand Cyreans in 399: Diodorus 14.37.1 (in Appendix S: Selections from Diodorus). See further Appendix I: The Size and Makeup of the Ten Thousand, §§12–13.

J.20a  Burial of dead soldiers on retreat: 4.1.18–19, 5.8.9. Retrieval of corpses by negotiation: 4.2.23.
J.20b  Special missions to gather and bury dead: 6.4.9–11, 6.5.3–6.
J.20c  Cenotaph: 6.4.9. Kalpe Harbor, possible location: Ref. Map 4.1, AY.
J.21a  Trapezus: Ref. Map 5, AZ.
J.22a  Direct complaints about pay to Cyrus: 1.2.11.
J.22b  Troops begin to stone Klearchos: 1.3.1–2. On Klearchos, see Appendix W: Brief Biographies, §20. Tarsus: Ref. Map 5, CY.
J.22c  Collective representations to Cyrus: 1.3.1–21.
J.22d  Promises of bonus pay: 1.4.12–13.
J.22e  Menon's successful argument: 1.4.13–17. On Menon, see Appendix W, §23.
J.22f  Klearchos takes charge: 2.2.5.

§23. The capture and execution of Klearchos and four of his colleagues[a] opened the way for new leaders, among them Xenophon. Still, these new commanders were selected by the surviving generals and captains rather than by the army as a whole.[b] When the entire army assembled to discuss preparations for the retreat, Xenophon reports that the soldiers unanimously agreed with the generals' proposals, but his narrative needs to be balanced against the story of the captain Apollonides, who was driven from the army for expressing an unpopular opinion.[c] Other Cyreans who might have wanted to speak out may have kept quiet for fear of similar treatment. During the march across Anatolia to the Black Sea, the generals and captains made all decisions without putting them to a vote.[d] The ordinary soldiers responded not by insisting on an assembly but by simply disobeying decrees they did not like.[e]

§24. After reaching Trapezus, most if not all of the soldiers just wanted to go home, preferably with some profit to show for their sufferings.[a] As the army made its way westward toward Byzantium, various commanders used assemblies in attempts to keep the army together or to increase their own power and influence.[b] Meanwhile, those who had the resources or opportunity simply deserted.[c] For men without the means or desire to leave, the army now began to represent strength in numbers.[d] The troops exercised communal power to put generals on trial and to fine them.[e] They also developed rules to distinguish between private plunder and common army property.[f] Later the men assembled to discuss whether to take service with the Thracian dynast Seuthes, and later still whether to join the Spartans.[g] Even so, they never quite got over the habit of throwing stones at those with whom they disagreed.[h]

§25. In the end, while the army assembly did sometimes come to the fore, most of the time the ordinary soldier's view of the march was defined by his overlapping and sometimes conflicting loyalties to company and messmates and by the daily routines of life in the field. The extraordinary experiences the men shared marked them apart, both physically and mentally. Indeed, upon returning to western Anatolia, many of the survivors took up service there with the Spartans, returned with the Spartan army to mainland Greece, and were still a cohesive unit more than five years afterward.[a] In later years aging survivors probably traded memories of their experiences. Others besides Xenophon may also have set down their reminiscences in writing, as the general Sophainetos of Stymphalos is said to have done.[b]

§26. Examining soldiers' lives in *Anabasis* helps us understand much about the Classical Greek military experience. Yet we must remember that *Anabasis* is a selec-

J.23a  Execution of the generals: 2.5.31–32.
J.23b  Selection of new commanders: 3.1.15, 3.1.32–34, 3.1.46–47, 3.2.1.
J.23c  Alleged unanimous support for generals' proposals: 3.2.9, 3.2.33. Apollonides driven out: 3.1.26–32.
J.23d  Decision by generals and captains alone: 3.5.7–12.
J.23e  Actual or anticipated disobedience by ordinary soldiers: 4.2.12–14.
J.24a  Soldiers' desire to go home: 5.1.2–3. Preferably with profit: 6.1.17–18, 6.2.4.
J.24b  Various commanders use assemblies to try: to keep army together, 5.1.5–13; to increase individuals' power, 5.6.21–33, 6.2.9–10.
J.24c  Actual and attempted desertions: 5.7.14–16, 6.4.13, 7.2.3–4.

J.24d  Strength in numbers: 5.6.32–33.
J.24e  Trials of generals: 5.7.34, 5.8.1.
J.24f  Rules about ownership of plunder: 5.1.12, 6.6.27–28.
J.24g  Service with Seuthes: 7.3.13–14; with the Spartans: 7.6.7–8. On Seuthes, see Appendix W: Brief Biographies, §30.
J.24h  Stoning or the threat thereof: 5.7.21, 7.6.10, 7.7.54.
J.25a  Later history of the Cyreans: 7.8.24; *Hellenika* 4.3.15, 4.3.17.
J.25b  On Sophainetos' reported memoirs, see Appendix M: Other Ancient Sources on the Ten Thousand, §§12–15. On Sophainetos, see Appendix W, §32. Stymphalos: Ref. Map 2, CY.

tive record, shaped by Xenophon's own memories and purposes. Sometimes his narrative can best be understood by placing it in conjunction with evidence from other ancient texts, archaeological material, and historical comparisons with other armies.[a] Moreover, the particular circumstances of the Cyreans—on the move in hostile territory over many months and thousands of miles—were unique, so it is important not to generalize too broadly from their experience. Nonetheless Xenophon's *Anabasis*, with its indelible images of men struggling for daily survival in the face of enemies, weather, and terrain, remains essential reading for anyone seeking to understand warfare in the Classical world.

John W. I. Lee
Associate Professor
Department of History
University of California, Santa Barbara

---

J.26a   For more on the topics examined in this appendix,
        see Lee 2007.

# APPENDIX K

*The Noncombatant Contingent of the Army*

§1. Noncombatants were a standard feature of ancient armies. Camp followers encompassed an astonishingly diverse collectivity that followed the army in various statuses and capacities: free and slave, young and old, male and female. They came in various ethnicities, in various degrees of connection to the army, and with various and shifting motivations. Such noncombatants might fulfill crucial logistical functions: selling food and supplies to soldiers, attending to and carrying luggage, driving the pack animals, foraging for food. They might supply a range of personal and sexual services. In providing entertainment and companionship, they might also play a valuable role in boosting morale and mitigating the tedium of the march and extended periods away from home. Some followers (male shield-carriers, females serving as nurses or courtesans) were well placed to supply psychological support and develop genuine friendships with individual soldiers, and as such might become quite integrated within the army. In addition to these noncombatants in the strict sense, the term may perhaps be extended to cover others whose primary function was to contribute in some specialized capacity, though they might also fight on occasion, or perhaps even routinely; these would be individuals working closely with the highest command (advisers), playing critical roles on the fringe of battle (seers, trumpeters), or enabling communication and reconnaissance (interpreters, scouts).

§2. Ancient historians, for the most part, refrained from specifying the numbers of camp followers, so the topic attracts much conjecture today. In some cases such "shadow armies" may have approached the size of the combat force itself: on the Greek mainland in the Classical period, an Athenian hoplite typically enjoyed the service of a slave-attendant to carry his shield and in other ways assist, sometimes even to fight alongside him, while a Spartan hoplite relied on the services of one (or more) state-owned slaves (helots).[a] During his campaigns the Achaemenid Persian

---

K.2a    Hoplite: a heavily armed infantryman; see Appendix H: Infantry and Cavalry in *Anabasis*, §§2–3.
       Athens, Sparta: Ref. Map 2, CZ, DY.

King carted along his entire family and household, countless attendants—cooks, bakers, cupbearers, grooms, and so forth—and luxurious household furniture and other paraphernalia to create a suitably royal setting on the march.[b] Other Persian generals did likewise, though less extravagantly.[c] Despite Alexander the Great's best efforts to minimize the number of noncombatants behind his Macedonian[d] army, it was trailed by an enormous mass of followers: seers, Greek philosophers and historians, geographers, as well as slaves, merchants, and dealers and attendants of various sorts, not to mention the siege and supply trains. An average ratio of one noncombatant to three combatants is perhaps a reasonable conjecture for his army when it first set off (with the ratio of noncombatants naturally climbing higher thereafter as locals, attracted by economic opportunities, joined the expedition). The Romans' even more highly professionalized military force reduced the ratio to perhaps one noncombatant for every four soldiers.

§3. The Ten Thousand of the *Anabasis*—Greek mercenaries serving in the Persian prince Cyrus'[a] army—have traditionally been assumed to have been shadowed by a noncombatant contingent of (approximately) another ten thousand: a vast horde of personal slaves and servants, seers, salesmen, dealers, grooms and other menials, prostitutes, doctors, and countless captives. But there is little evidence in Xenophon's text for the existence of such a horde: Xenophon mentions a "great crowd"[b] (*polus ochlos*) at 3.2.36, but this refers not only to camp followers but also to the incapacitated (sick and wounded soldiers). We hear of no professional doctors on the campaign: soldiers (or possibly slaves) are appointed to supply medical services when the need arises.[c] Presumably other skilled craftsmen and professionals (such as barbers and shoemakers) could likewise be found within the ranks of the Ten Thousand and called upon as necessary. Most tellingly, the Cyreans (as Cyrus' mercenaries are sometimes called) are described as often undertaking the chores, such as carrying weapons and baggage, for which personal slaves or attendants might have been expected to take responsibility if they were present in great numbers.[d] In this respect they surely provided a model for the slimmed-down war machines that were the Macedonian armies of Philip and Alexander. And so many thousands of followers doubtless would have posed a logistical nightmare: double the mouths to feed (and double the resulting waste needing disposal); constant anxiety at the potential desertion of baggage- and weapons-carriers (with consequent loss of supplies and arms); hoplites drawn away from the fight to serve as supervisors; the inevitable slowing of the pace of the march. More persuasive, then, is the idea of a smaller noncombatant contingent that waxed and waned and in other ways shifted

---

K.2b  On the Achaemenid dynasty, see the Glossary. Admittedly, the portrayal of Persian Kings and nobles with large, unwieldy trains depends on Greek sources. Achaemenid documents suggest that at least some ordinary troops had to carry and manage their own gear; Plutarch's account of Cyrus' death attests that some men followed the royal army to perform menial services (Plutarch, *Life of Artaxerxes* 11.5–6; in Appendix T: Selections from Plutarch's *Life of Artaxerxes*).

K.2c  Persian generals bringing household on campaign: for example, Tiribazos at 4.4.21.

K.2d  Macedonia: Ref. Map 3, CX.

K.3a  On Cyrus the Younger, see Appendix W: Brief Biographies of Selected Characters in *Anabasis*, §10.

K.3b  "Great crowd" is a literal translation. In this edition, *polus ochlos* has been translated more freely as "throng of noncombatants."

K.3c  Ad hoc "doctors" appointed: 3.4.30.

K.3d  See, for example, 5.1.2; also see Appendix J: A Soldier's View of the March, §10, on soldiers carrying out their own chores, indicating a lack of servants brought from home.

character in response to the different circumstances and terrain over the course of the Cyreans' march.

§4. While Cyrus led the army and was in charge of its provisioning, the camp following to some extent will have mirrored Persian royal practice. It included at least two Greek concubines from Cyrus' harem; his seers, priests, and attendants; and a substantial baggage train (including four hundred carts laden with flour and wine).[a] Also present were numerous individuals come to exploit the economic opportunities that any large army represents: merchants attached to the market found within the non-Greek contingent of the army,[b] as well as craftsmen and other specialists. Much of this noncombatant force connected to and organized by Cyrus must have dissolved at his death, or soon thereafter have deserted to the Persian King Artaxerxes (along with Cyrus' satrapal forces and some of the Greek mercenaries),[c] especially in view of his far greater numbers and power.

§5. To cope with the dearth of intelligence that followed Cyrus' death and the exposure of the treachery of Tissaphernes (who, in the period after the battle of Cunaxa, had provided the Greeks with guides), the army regularly seized individuals for brief periods—days or weeks—to supply local knowledge of topography; occasionally a local ruler supplied a guide.[a] In the period after Tissaphernes seized the generals, the Cyreans also extensively plundered the villages of northern Mesopotamia.[b] Here considerable numbers of local inhabitants (free and slave, male and female, no doubt greatly varied in age) were captured and enslaved, to serve as human booty alongside the inanimate sort. Though presumably exploited in the interim for labor and sex, these individuals were destined for the most part not to be retained but to be sold as soon as the opportunity presented itself. Indeed, after the demise of Cyrus, the Cyreans' paymaster, the sale of such booty was their only reliable source of income. Prior to pressing on through the mountains of the Kardouchoi, the generals enforced baggage restrictions on the soldiers in the form of a mass jettisoning of human captives and plunder for the sake of the army's efficiency.[c] Other captives perished along the way.[d] Some individuals of slave status did, however, remain connected to the army for far longer periods—most notably, the attendants brought from home by generals and officers, Xenophon included,[e] and perhaps by some of the hoplites. Individual captives who had been smuggled through the baggage restrictions and who survived the grueling march that followed may even have developed enduring relationships with their erstwhile captors (see further in §§11–16) and have remained with them for the remainder of the expedition and beyond.

§6. While on the move, the noncombatant contingent proceeded as a group,

K.4a  Cyrus' concubines: 1.10.2–3. Four hundred carts: 1.10.18.
K.4b  Merchants: 1.2.18, 1.3.14, 1.5.6.
K.4c  Satrapal forces join the King: 2.4.9, 3.2.17. Thracians desert: 2.2.7. Greeks desert: 3.3.5. On Artaxerxes, see Appendix W: Brief Biographies, §6. On satraps, see the Glossary.
K.5a  Prisoners taken for topographical knowledge: 4.1.22, 4.4.16–19, 4.5.28, 4.6.17. Local ruler supplies guide: 4.7.19. On Tissaphernes, see Appendix W, §37. Battlefield of Cunaxa: Ref. Map 6, DZ.
K.5b  Tissaphernes seizes the generals: 2.5.31–2.6.1.

Plundering Mesopotamian villages: for example, 3.4.18. Mesopotamia: Ref. Map 6, CY.
K.5c  Captives and baggage jettisoned: 4.1.13; for jettisoning baggage, see also 3.2.28, 3.3.1. Kardouchoi territory: Ref. Map 6, BY.
K.5d  Captives perish: for example, 4.5.4.
K.5e  Xenophon's personal attendants: 4.2.20, 7.3.20.

together with the temporary noncombatants (sick and wounded soldiers), secure within a hollow rectangle of troops marching on all four sides of them, or protected by hoplites in front and behind, as during the crossing of the Kentrites River.[a] Most of this number, including "youngsters and women" (presumably both girls and boys, mainly but not exclusively captives), were put aboard the available ships at Trapezus along with older soldiers and others less fit for combat and marching, under the supervision of the older generals, to cruise along the final stretch of the journey back toward Greece.[b] This suggests some concern on the soldiers' part for the safety of their noncombatant followers.

§7. Noncombatants are not the focus of Xenophon's account, but at various points they slip from the shadows into the light, so that we glimpse their importance to the Cyreans and find them playing significant roles in his story. Undoubtedly the most important are the seers, free individuals who stood on the cusp of combat, exercising extraordinary authority over whether and when combat or withdrawal could take place[a] and whether certain actions were permissible or essential, such as the purification of the army at 5.7.35. Indeed, beyond serving in their specialist capacity, they seem very often to have engaged in actual combat as well—in which case they were not strictly noncombatants. A handful of such seers likely served the Cyreans.[b] As communicators with and appeasers of the divine, they (like military chaplains of more recent times) also exercised considerable influence on the crucial matter of the soldiers' morale.[c] Silanos of Ambracia, a Greek seer who had served as Cyrus' diviner and remained with the army, comes to the fore in the narrative as Xenophon first turns to him in moments of desperation when the gods' help is required.[d] A free agent motivated by a desire to reach home as soon as possible with his huge fortune (given by Cyrus for a correct prediction),[e] he shares with the men Xenophon's nascent reflections on the possibility of founding a colony, thus scuppering any such plan. When the Cyreans reach the Black Sea, he slips away as soon as possible, in contravention of the army's decree against such desertion.[f] Silanos' selfish motives and greed serve as a narrative foil to Xenophon's promotion of the common good.

§8. Heralds, likewise, appear in crucial roles: the pronouncement of Tolmides of Elis, "the best herald of his day," calms troops seized by panic in the night.[a] With Xenophon's interest in cross-cultural communication and its logistics, he underscores also the key role of interpreters, who might be free or slaves, on the march. We find them relaying essential commands, supplying the Cyreans with crucial information gleaned from locals, and opening up important lines of communication.[b]

§9. Xenophon's narrative also vividly conveys the impression made on the Greek

---

K.6a   Hollow rectangle: 3.2.36. Noncombatants at the crossing of the Kentrites: 4.3.15. Kentrites River: Ref. Map 7, BY.

K.6b   "Youngsters and women" and others put on ship: 5.3.1. Trapezus: Ref. Map 5, AZ.

K.7a   Seers' authority over choice to attack: 5.2.9, 5.5.3.

K.7b   For more on seers, see Appendix G: Divinity and Divining, esp. §§4–5, 8.

K.7c   Positive effect on morale: 4.5.4.

K.7d   Silanos of Ambracia turned to by Xenophon:

5.6.16. Ambracia: Ref. Map 2, BX.

K.7e   Cyrus rewards Silanos: 1.7.18, 5.6.18.

K.7f   Silanos' desertion: 6.4.13. Black Sea: Ref. Map 1, AX.

K.8a   "Best herald of his day": 2.2.20–21. Elis: Ref. Map 2, CX.

K.8b   Relaying essential commands: 1.2.17, 1.8.12. Supplying local information: 2.5.35, 4.5.10, 4.5.34–36. Opening lines of communication: 4.2.18, 5.4.5, 7.2.19.

soldiers and others by another category of noncombatants: women. Their individual and collective presence is felt at key moments of the narrative and doubtless served to remind the Greek mercenaries (as it reminds Xenophon's readers) of the settled life that the Cyreans had left behind.

§10. Cyrus' Phocaean concubine, "said to be wise and beautiful," is captured by Artaxerxes' troops in the aftermath of Cunaxa, as is her younger Milesian counterpart, whose initiative and verve are clear in the report of her escaping undressed over to the Greek side.[a] Other women too were perhaps present on the first stage of the march, from Sardis to Babylon:[b] Xenophon mentions the wives and children of two generals left behind in Tralles in Caria, but other soldiers' wives may have accompanied the army, and there was more than one opportuny for plunder on the way to Cunaxa.[c] The march through Mesopotamia that followed presented plenty of further opportunities for accumulating plunder, and Xenophon observes the particular allure of "the big and beautiful Median and Persian women and girls."[d] When the army reached the mountainous terrain of the Kardouchoi, excess baggage and bodies, including the recently acquired females, came to present a severe liability, and so the generals made the decision to discard them.[e] But the ranks of the noncombatant contingent swelled again during the march along the southern shore of the Black Sea, which presented further chances for seizing human plunder. During the final stretch—the expedition in Thrace, before the Greeks' arrival back on the coast of western Anatolia—most villagers ran away, were executed by the Greeks' Thracian ally Seuthes, or killed themselves, and so eluded captivity.[f]

§11. The scrutiny of baggage in the foothills below the mountains of the Kardouchoi appears to have marked a moment of some transformation in the relationships between soldiers and their captives. Here, we are told, the troops complied with the generals' order to abandon captives and superfluous baggage, "except where someone had concealed something, like a boy he especially fancied or a good-looking woman."[a] A soldier's decision thus to preserve the life of a captive (saving him or her from death or enslavement at the hands of the barbarous Kardouchoi or from a perilous journey back home) was a decision to support (and keep warm, and feed) an individual for himself through the arduous next stage of the march, retaining him or her as a valued companion rather than as expendable booty. The next stage of the march indeed proved the toughest of the entire expedition so far,[b] and in the shared struggle to survive, men and women doubtless came closer.

§12. After the punishing march through the land of the Kardouchoi, when the army had to contrive a fiercely contested crossing over the Kentrites River, we thus find the women of the army working in harmony with and in support of the men:

---

K.10a "Wise and beautiful": 1.10.2. Milesian concubine escapes: 1.10.3. Phocaea, Miletus: Ref. Map 4.2, DY.

K.10b Sardis: Ref. Map 4.1, CY; Ref. Map 4.2, CZ. Babylon: Ref. Map 6, DZ.

K.10c Generals' wives left in Tralles in Caria: 1.4.8. Opportunities for plunder: in Lycaonia, 1.2.19; in Cilicia, 1.2.26, 1.3.14. Tralles, Caria: Ref. Map 4.2, DY. Lycaonia, Cilicia: Ref. Map 5, CX, CY.

K.10d "Big and beautiful . . . women and girls": 3.2.25.

Media: Ref. Map 6, CZ. See Figure 3.2.25 for a depiction of a Persian woman on an engraved gemstone.

K.10e Made the decision to discard them: 4.1.12–14.

K.10f Thrace: Ref. Map 3. Western Anatolia: Ref. Map 4.1. On Seuthes, see Appendix W: Brief Biographies, §30.

K.11a "Except where someone had concealed something": 4.1.14.

K.11b Toughest so far: 4.3.2.

when the sacrifices turn favorable, every one of them joins her voice to the battle cry of the soldiers.[a] Xenophon emphasizes the impact of the women's presence with his arresting comment that "there were a lot of *hetairai* with the army."[b] The ambiguous term *hetairai* ("kept women" or "courtesans" but alternatively "female companions") was perhaps deliberately chosen to imply that the women are now indeed true companions. Later, in the games put on at Trapezus to celebrate the arrival at the Black Sea, the courtesans again cheer on the soldiers, this time in sport: their presence and gaze raise the ante, generating rivalry on the part of the male contestants.[c]

§13. That the women as a collective make such an impression on outsiders as well is suggested by the Mossynoeci's professed desire to have sex with them in public.[a] Sexual mores are a category of culture and a reflection of character that also fascinated Xenophon's predecessor Herodotus, and here as elsewhere Xenophon dons his ethnographer's hat. The sensational detail confirms and underscores the soldiers' judgment that the Mossynoeci are the most uncivilized of peoples, with customs most unlike those of the Greeks, to have been encountered on the entire march.[b]

§14. One accomplished individual female Xenophon brings to our attention is the dancing slave girl who performs at the after-dinner symposium the Greeks put on for a foreign embassy.[a] Noting the Paphlagonians' amazement at how the Greeks dance in armor, one of the Cyreans urges his Arcadian comrade to bring in his dancing girl (a category of female generally of lower status than a courtesan).[b] Clad in the finest raiment (just as the soldier dancers had been), light shield in hand, she performs the Greek Pyrrhic (war) dance elegantly and to rapturous applause. At this startling spectacle of strength combined with beauty, and male-female complementarity, the foreign representatives ask whether the Greeks' women also fight by their side. With a joke on the stereotype of the effeminate barbarian, the Greeks reply that "these were the women who had chased the Great King out of the camp"![c] (The joke stands in the tradition also of Greek appreciation of the concept of manly women fighting womanly men.) The girl's performance is the climax and conclusion of the evening, and Xenophon notes that a treaty with the Paphlagonians followed the next day.[d] Not only has the girl clearly been providing the mercenaries with high-quality entertainment (whether from the beginning of the expedition or since being acquired in one of the Greek cities on the Black Sea), but on this occasion she has helped them to convey an impression of martial strength. The soldiers' identification of these women accompanying them in Paphlagonia with the women in the camp at Cunaxa leaves the impression again of females on the march as a group that is visible as a collective, and perhaps even indicates that some of them were present as companions of the distinguished members of the Greek army who participated in

K.12a  Women join battle cry: 4.3.19.
K.12b  "A lot of *hetairai*" (*hetairai* is translated as "kept women" in this edition): 4.3.19.
K.12c  Spectators spur on contestants: 4.8.27. Emily Baragwanath here reads "female companions" (ἑταιρῶν; *hetairōn*), as conjectured by the early modern scholar Brodaeus. The manuscript tradition has the same word with a different accent (ἑταίρων), which makes it masculine: hence this edition translates the word as "companions"

here without specification of gender. (Translator's note)
K.13a  Mossynoeci desire sex: 5.4.33. Mossynoeci territory: Ref. Map 5, AZ.
K.13b  Soldiers' judgment on Mossynoeci: 5.4.34.
K.14a  Dancing slave girl at banquet: 6.1.12–13.
K.14b  Paphlagonia: Ref. Map 5, AX. Arcadia: Ref. Map 2, CX.
K.14c  "These were the women": 6.1.13.
K.14d  Treaty with Paphlagonians: 6.1.14.

this dinner.ᶜ Interestingly, by the end of Xenophon's narration of the episode, the divisions between different statuses of female—strict divisions indeed in the world of mainland Greece—appear to have broken down, with the women labeled just "women" (*gunaikes*, a word that can also mean "wives"). Perhaps the great variety of identities (ethnicities and backgrounds) among the mercenaries did indeed have the effect of breaking down the rigid status differentiations among other groups, not least those of the female noncombatants.

§15. Another significant presence among noncombatants is the boy slaves, who—as Xenophon reveals in the context of the boys' stadium race at the Trapezus Games—constituted another distinct collectivity among captives.ᵃ Following capture, they might be used in various capacities or sold. Just as beautiful women represented desirable booty,ᵇ so did lovely boys, but the focus of Xenophon's narrative is again on relationships rather than sex. (By contrast with women and children, adult men were more often killed than taken captive, since they presented more of a risk.) The boys' role comes to the fore in two episodes. The first concerns a village chief's son, who is taken hostage in a bid to ensure that his father will be a reliable guide. When the father runs away, the Greek soldier Pleisthenes "fell in love with the boy, and when he got back home with him, found him very faithful,"ᶜ a brief sentence evoking a relationship that lasted beyond the end of the long march.

§16. Another of the Cyreans, Episthenes, saves a captive boy from death in an episode whose charm and humanity are accentuated by its savage backdrop (the Thracian prince Seuthes' indiscriminate killing of all human prisoners). Spotting the beautiful boy, Episthenes pleads with Xenophon that he might be spared. Xenophon in turn petitions Seuthes, describing the soldier's partiality for beautiful boys and recounting how the soldier once assembled a battalion according to looks alone and displayed great valor while fighting with it. (The story aims to undermine possible assumptions on the Thracian's part of incompatibility between heroism and appreciation for beauty.) Asked by Seuthes whether he would die for the boy, Episthenes affirms that he would; the boy, asked by Seuthes whether he should strike Episthenes in his stead, pleads that both he and Episthenes be spared; finally Episthenes embraces the boy and expresses his intention to fight for him and not give him up.ᵃ The relationship was in reality profoundly asymmetrical—the boy had no choice, if he wanted to save his life—but Xenophon presents it in terms of supreme mutuality: man and boy each preserve the other's life.

§17. Xenophon's *Anabasis* thus offers us a precious glimpse of the noncombatant contingent of the Cyreans' army. We see individuals and groups serving in a variety of capacities and representing an important part of the community on the march. Xenophon's narrative is shaped by a desire to write a gripping account of the march

K.14e  Soldiers at banquet individually invited as "the most appropriate": 6.1.3.
K.15a  Boys' stadium race: 4.8.27.
K.15b  Women as booty: 4.1.14, 4.3.30.
K.15c  Pleisthenes "fell in love with the boy": 4.6.3.
K.16a  Episthenes saves a Thracian boy: 7.4.7–11.

and of his own and others' leadership, and by his own practical and philosophical interests. It is also shaped by his literary concerns and is therefore selective; like the other ancient historians, he at times prefers paradigmatic presentation to tedious repetition, which means that a single description of a phenomenon (such as the behavior or character of an individual or group) may stand for multiple instances. Xenophon's account of the great march, like his other literary works, reveals his keen appreciation of the contribution that can be made by a diverse stripe of humanity, and his desire to embrace that rich diversity within his thinking on human character and relations.

Emily Baragwanath
Associate Professor of Classics
The University of North Carolina at Chapel Hill

# APPENDIX L

## The Battle of Cunaxa

§1. Xenophon's narrative of the battle of Cunaxa in *Anabasis* is probably the most detailed eyewitness account we possess of any pitched battle fought by Greeks in the Classical period.[a] What is more, accounts by six other ancient authors either have come down to us or are specifically attested by name. Incorporated in Plutarch's *Life of Artaxerxes* and in the epitome of the Byzantine cleric Photius are substantial fragments from the account of another eyewitness, the Persian King Artaxerxes' physician, Ctesias; Plutarch also tells us briefly about the version of the fourth-century historian Dinon; and we have an account from the first-century historian Diodorus Siculus that gives a detail ascribed to his fourth-century predecessor Ephorus.[b] This Landmark edition presents this material in translation in Appendices S (Diodorus), T (Plutarch), and U (Photius). It would be a reasonable hope that comparing Xenophon's version with the others would throw light on his purposes and general credibility. But it is far from easy to make out what actually happened and why.

### Xenophon's Account

§2. Xenophon's account is shown schematically in the diagrams in Book 1, representing the earlier and later stages of the battle.[a] According to Xenophon, Cyrus' army—composed of about thirteen thousand Greeks and (he says) one hundred thousand Persians and others—was marching somewhat carelessly toward Babylon when it was surprised to see the much larger army of Cyrus' brother Artaxerxes, said to consist of nine hundred thousand men.[b] When the battle started, Artaxerxes' army was advancing in orderly formation, whereas Cyrus' army was in disorder;

---

NOTE: All citations of Diodorus are included in Appendix S: Selections from Diodorus.

L.1a   Battlefield of Cunaxa: Map 1.5.1 and inset.
L.1b   For more on all these authors, see Appendix M: Other Ancient Sources on the Ten Thousand. On Artaxerxes, see Appendix W: Brief Biographies of Selected Characters in *Anabasis*, §6.

L.2a   The battle of Cunaxa is described at 1.8–10. See Diagram 1.8 for the phases of the battle.
L.2b   For the composition of Cyrus' Greek forces, see Appendix I: The Size and Makeup of the Ten Thousand. On Cyrus the Younger, see Appendix W, §10. Babylon: Ref. Map 6, DZ.

indeed, his left wing may still have been coming up into line. On his right wing, Cyrus placed his Greek hoplites, with the Paphlagonian horsemen yet farther to the right and the Greek and Thracian peltasts[c] beyond them, next to the Euphrates River; he himself took the center, and his principal lieutenant, Ariaios, commanded the left wing.[d] Artaxerxes also took his position in the center of his army, but because his army was so much larger, his position was not directly opposite Cyrus but some way to his left.[e] Cyrus ordered the principal Greek general, Klearchos,[f] to attack Artaxerxes personally, but instead the Greek hoplites charged straight ahead and ran their opponents off the battlefield. Nor did Ariaios' troops, which were the ones directly facing Artaxerxes, engage him; indeed, Artaxerxes was able to direct his right wing to bend around so as to threaten to take Ariaios on the flank. Consequently Cyrus personally charged at his brother, which he did in a brave if rash manner, and succeeded in wounding him. But Cyrus was himself then wounded by one of Artaxerxes' entourage, and in a confused melee he was killed, together with the leading nobles around him. In the meantime Cyrus' old enemy Tissaphernes,[g] on the King's extreme left, had ridden with his cavalry unit down the edge of the battlefield, where he met with no resistance from the Paphlagonian horsemen and the Greek peltasts—they, while maintaining good order, had prudently stepped out of his way.

§3. Cyrus' death marks the beginning of the second stage of the battle. When Ariaios heard of it, he fled with the entirety of Cyrus' left wing. The Greeks—ignorant of what had happened, since they had charged off the battlefield and had not kept in touch with Cyrus' center—continued to maintain their formation but did not engage the enemy again. According to Xenophon, the King, recovered from his wound, met Tissaphernes in Cyrus' camp, and the King's army as a whole (except for the part of his left wing that the Greeks had chased off the field) then turned and advanced in the direction from which it had come. The Greeks initially thought that the King's men were advancing directly toward them, and subsequently that Artaxerxes intended to take them in the flank; hence the Greeks planned to turn through ninety degrees so as to face the flank attack, but in fact the King maneuvered past the Greeks. Then, Xenophon says, the King got into much the same position as he had been in at the beginning of the battle and threatened to advance on the Greek line; but when the Greeks showed they were not cowed but were still prepared to engage the Persians, the Persian army withdrew, leaving the Greeks in possession of the battlefield. Of course, though the Greeks had thus achieved a tactical triumph, they were in a hopeless strategic situation, as the enemy now possessed an even greater numerical advantage, the Greek supply lines had been cut, and they had no Persian candidate to be a credible challenger against the King. A mixture of obtuseness and bravado may have obscured this to some extent from the Greeks at the time, but Xenophon's narrative reveals it clearly enough, even if his speeches show he was good at putting on a brave face when in difficulties.

L.2c   Hoplites: heavily armed infantrymen; peltasts: light-armed infantry; see Appendix H: Infantry and Cavalry in *Anabasis*, §§2–3, 4–5. Paphlagonia: Ref. Map 5, AX. Thrace: Ref. Map 3. Euphrates River: Ref. Map 6, CY.

L.2d   On Ariaios, see Appendix W: Brief Biographies, §4.

L.2e   This is the configuration of forces depicted in Diagram 1.8, Phase 1.

L.2f   On Klearchos, see Appendix W, §20.

L.2g   On Tissaphernes, see Appendix W, §37.

## Internal Problems with
## Xenophon's Account

§4. The main outline of Xenophon's account, considered by itself, may appear fairly straightforward. However, it does present some internal problems. The main ones are these:

§5. Xenophon has doubtless given the correct numbers for the Greek contingents, but the logistic realities show that he has exaggerated the number of Persians involved—grossly so (perhaps by as much as a factor of ten) in the case of Artaxerxes' forces, and to a considerable extent as regards the Persians on Cyrus' side. But correcting for this does not touch the rest of his account.[a]

§6. Many modern scholars say that Xenophon places Artaxerxes beyond the left of Cyrus' army at the outset of the battle. On this basis, when Cyrus ordered Klearchos to charge against Artaxerxes personally, he was telling him to charge from almost the extreme right to beyond the extreme left of Cyrus' army, meanwhile necessarily presenting his flank to the advancing enemy. Cyrus may have been reckless, but that would have been an insane order to give. Artaxerxes, being at the center of his army, was obviously to the left of the Greeks, and he was also no doubt placed to the left of Cyrus personally; but he cannot have been beyond the left wing of Cyrus' whole army. However, Xenophon should not be accused of making a mistake here. The manuscripts at 1.8.13, the key passage that has led to this accusation, give the required sense that Artaxerxes was beyond the *Greek* left wing; but most editors have wrongly followed the nineteenth-century scholar F. K. Hertlein in deleting the word for "Greek."[a]

§7. According to Xenophon's account, while Tissaphernes certainly proved his loyalty to Artaxerxes,[a] his contribution to the King's victory was not distinguished. The left wing, where he was stationed, did not perform well. The cavalry, of which he is represented as being in personal command, succeeded in reaching the enemy camp, but it had not engaged the enemy on the way and did not impact on their possession of the field. The camp subsequently had to be relinquished to the Greeks; its occupation may have given them a hungry evening, but it did not affect their military viability. Tissaphernes also surely had responsibility for the infantry on the left wing, since he was one of four generals in the King's army, a status that could not be applied to the mere commander of a cavalry unit; but these infantrymen fled from the Greek charge. If Xenophon was right, Tissaphernes had comparatively little to do with the fact that the King was now secure on his throne. Yet it emerges from Xenophon's subsequent narrative, and from the course of history over the next few years, that Tissaphernes had reached a pinnacle of royal confidence and favor. Has Xenophon perhaps misunderstood Tissaphernes' true role?

L.5a  On the logistic realities, see briefly the Introduction, §5.3. A similar problem arises with Herodotus' numbers for Xerxes' expeditionary force in 480; see Michael Flower's detailed discussion in Strassler 2007, Appendix R: The Size of Xerxes' Expeditionary Force.

L.6a  If any change in the manuscript tradition is to be made, it should be the deletion of the word for "wing" at 1.8.23, which would make it clearer that Xenophon refers to the left of Cyrus personally. This is the course I have adopted in this edition.

L.7a  Unlike two of his three fellow commanders: Abrokomas, who turned up late (perhaps he had tried his best, but Artaxerxes might reasonably have suspected him of hedging his bets); and Arbakes, who, it seems from Plutarch, *Life of Artaxerxes* 14.2, actually deserted during the battle (presumably, to judge from the King's moderate reaction, Arbakes did so only on hearing of Artaxerxes' wound and believing that he had been killed). On Abrokomas, see Appendix W: Brief Biographies, §1.

## Accounts by Other Authors

§8. The other accounts complicate the situation further. In bare outline the story as told in Plutarch and Diodorus agrees fairly well with Xenophon: Artaxerxes' army is much larger than Cyrus', the Greeks form Cyrus' right wing and drive the enemy opposite them off the field, Cyrus charges Artaxerxes and wounds him but is himself killed, Tissaphernes plays a large part in the battle, and the Greeks remain unchallenged but in a hopeless situation. But at the next level of detail, there are considerable variations, making us wonder whether we should believe Xenophon or Ctesias or (perhaps) others, such as the sources behind Dinon. Xenophon may indeed be deliberately correcting Ctesias, since he refers to his account at 1.8.26 and thereby rules out that the differences arise from ignorance on Xenophon's part. But that does not necessarily mean Xenophon was right.

§9. In one respect Ctesias certainly has the advantage. According to Plutarch, *Life of Artaxerxes* 13.3,[a] Ctesias gave a figure of four hundred thousand for Artaxerxes' army, which is still higher than is logistically feasible but is less absurd than Xenophon's figure of nine hundred thousand. According to Diodorus 14.22.2, Ephorus also gave this four hundred thousand figure.

§10. Plutarch includes a lot of detail about the hand-to-hand confrontation between the two brothers and the death of Cyrus, and to some extent it differs from Xenophon's fairly brief remarks. One version Plutarch gives, on the authority of Dinon, is that while Cyrus had indeed wounded Artaxerxes, Artaxerxes then remounted and killed Cyrus. This is evidently the official Persian story, a convenient lie. By contrast, the detail given by Ctesias here is not obviously fabricated. Ctesias and Xenophon disagree about where Cyrus was first wounded (under the eye, according to Xenophon; on the temple, according to Ctesias) and when (at the very time Cyrus threw his spear at Artaxerxes, according to Xenophon; later, according to Ctesias). However, it must have been difficult to discover the precise truth about what happened in the middle of the battle. It is dangerous to draw inferences from this about the general credibility of either source.

§11. However, Ctesias is surely romanticizing when he says that Cyrus' lieutenant Ariaios was at Cyrus' side when the latter charged at the King, Ariaios himself casting the first spear at Artaxerxes. Such a direct assault by Ariaios on Artaxerxes seems unlikely, since the King subsequently not only showed mercy to Ariaios but actually restored him to favor. Xenophon, implicitly contradicting Ctesias, says at 1.9.31 that Ariaios commanded Cyrus' left wing, evidently at some distance; and Diodorus 14.24.1 more explicitly places him some way away, though he gives his name as Aridaios. Cyrus' left wing was opposed to the forces directly in front of Artaxerxes, but this does not imply that Ariaios attacked these forces, much less Artaxerxes himself, for Xenophon remarks at 1.8.23 that the forces directly in front of Artaxerxes were not under attack until Cyrus turned to his left and charged them. Perhaps (contrary to Ctesias' account) Ariaios—and indeed the Persians generally, other than Cyrus himself—were reluctant to confront the person of the King.

L.9a   In Appendix T: Selections from Plutarch's *Life of Artaxerxes*.

§12. It is important to note that Diodorus here is not simply repeating Xenophon's account, for he adds that Aridaios fought stoutly against the King's encircling troops until he heard of Cyrus' death—a detail not in Xenophon and at variance with his tone. While Diodorus' account of the Ten Thousand generally is quite close to Xenophon's and for some stretches very close indeed, perhaps here we have a sign of an ultimate eyewitness source who was neither Xenophon nor Ctesias. If so, it would provide independent support to Xenophon in his disagreement with Ctesias here—though admittedly the difference between Diodorus and Xenophon might not be due to Diodorus' source, as he is capable of introducing casual variations of his own into his material.

§13. Ctesias also claims that Artaxerxes' wound meant he had to be taken out of the battle to recover, though he subsequently returned and even cavorted around brandishing Cyrus' head. As Ctesias was present as the King's personal physician, he was certainly in a position to know, but unfortunately this does not guarantee that he told the truth, for the worse the wound, the more it would redound to Ctesias' credit as a physician if he healed it promptly.

§14. This matters, because Diodorus 14.23.6 says that when Artaxerxes retired from the battle, Tissaphernes succeeded to the command. If this is true, Xenophon must be wrong to say that Tissaphernes rode with his cavalry along the Euphrates to Cyrus' camp and only there joined up again with the King: to take over command; Tissaphernes would have to have been closer to the center than the main body of his cavalry was and to have never lost communication with Artaxerxes. But all sources agree that the Greeks chased away the infantry stationed on the right of Tissaphernes' cavalry. Therefore, if Diodorus is correct here, Tissaphernes must have been on the other side of these infantry detachments, able to step away from them to rejoin Artaxerxes.

§15. At first sight Diodorus' implicit placement of Tissaphernes at or near the center makes it even odder that Tissaphernes was especially honored by the King after the battle, something Diodorus (14.26.4) emphasizes yet more strongly than Xenophon. In Xenophon's account, at least Tissaphernes demonstrated his personal worthiness by leading his cavalry into Cyrus' camp; whereas if Diodorus is right, not only did he not do any such thing, but he also abdicated responsibility for trying to stem the rout of the infantry under his command. As we shall see, there is a possible explanation, although it is one that, if accepted, would show that Xenophon completely misunderstood what was going on.

### The Truth about Cunaxa?

§16. Cyrus' rebellion was a desperate gamble, but it was not completely hopeless, despite Artaxerxes' greater legitimacy and ability to call on far more resources. Cyrus had the potential support of the Queen Mother Parysatis,[a] which he could expect would complicate Artaxerxes' situation in the event of a military standoff and might mitigate his own punishment if he lost on the battlefield. He also had two things on

---

L.16a   On Parysatis, see Appendix W: Brief Biographies,
       §26.

his side militarily. His first advantage, as Xenophon points out at 1.5.9, was his comparative speed and flexibility, the upside of his smaller army. His opponents evidently expected him to go by the usual route, through northern Mesopotamia and so down the Tigris River[b] or on to Persia itself. But by marching down the northern bank of the Euphrates despite the inferior road and severe problems in obtaining supplies, he had a chance of reaching Babylon before his brother mobilized effectively; if he could enter Babylon and entrench himself there, he could hope to play on Babylonian resentments and the divisions at the Persian court to bring about his brother's downfall. Cyrus' second advantage was his Greeks, because when properly supported by cavalry and light infantry, the hoplite phalanx[c] was extremely effective on unbroken ground. So great was the fear they inspired that he could plan on having them fight at half their normal depth—at any rate, that is what is implied when in the review at Tyriaion they paraded four-deep rather than the normal eight-deep.[d] Thus he could hope to compensate for his smaller numbers by lengthening his line of battle, making it more difficult for the King's army, if it did catch him before he reached Babylon, to outflank him. If he formed up as he planned, the Greeks would have to veer only slightly to the left to attack Artaxerxes personally; and whatever might be true of Cyrus' Persian supporters, the Greeks would be free of any legitimist inhibitions about doing so.

§17. Two things went wrong for Cyrus, nullifying these advantages. First, the King did indeed succeed in mobilizing enough of his resources sufficiently quickly to catch Cyrus still on the open plain of Mesopotamia, though it was a close-run thing—not only Abrokomas but also the King's unnamed bastard brother were late for the battle.[a] To make things worse for Cyrus, after exemplary efforts to push the army on and improve its discipline, at the end he slackened his grip, so he had to form up for battle in a rush. Probably his left wing was not in good order, and possibly he had to plant his center where he happened to be, bunching the Greeks between it and the river, rather than setting himself opposite Artaxerxes and extending the Greek line to fill the available space. Thus Artaxerxes was out of range of the Greek phalanx unless either it charged diagonally—a dangerous feat, which it is not surprising Klearchos declined to perform—or it first defeated the opponents directly in front of it and then turned through ninety degrees to attack the enemy center. Well-trained hoplites could execute such a maneuver: seven years later the Spartans did so at the battle of Nemea.[b] But the second thing that went wrong for Cyrus was that the Greeks, apparently quite oblivious both then and later to the fact that they were doing anything untoward, carried on with their pursuit of their fleeing opponents and thus were of no use in delivering force where it really mattered.

§18. Some scholars have suggested that this was a matter not just of Greek tactical folly but also of Persian tactical cunning.[a] They argue that the flight of the infantry on the Persian left was a stratagem by Tissaphernes, deliberately designed to draw the

---

L.16b  Mesopotamia, Tigris River: Ref. Map 6, CY, CZ.
L.16c  Phalanx: a body of troops drawn up across a broad front in close formation; see Appendix H: Infantry and Cavalry, §§13–15.
L.16d  Review at Tyriaion: 1.2.15. Tyriaion: Ref. Map 5, CX.

L.17a  Late for battle: Abrokomas, 1.7.12; the King's bastard brother, 2.4.15.
L.17b  Spartan maneuver at the battle of Nemea: Xenophon, *Hellenika* 4.2.20–22. Sparta, Nemea: Ref. Map 2, DY, CY.
L.18a  Wylie 1992, 129–30; Ehrhardt 1994.

Greek phalanx away from Cyrus and the Persian center. Tissaphernes had had a decade or more to observe and ponder Greek battle habits, and a winning stratagem on his part could be the reason Artaxerxes especially honored him subsequently. This theory and Diodorus' account can be used to bolster each other: if Tissaphernes intended two-thirds of his division to withdraw swiftly, then he should have been where Diodorus implies he was—at the junction of the withdrawing division and the center—to ensure that the withdrawal was, despite appearances, orderly and that the apparent rout did not upset the other troops, who had to stay put and be ready in case the Greeks were not taken in by the feint but turned to the center after all.

§19. If Diodorus is right here, the truth about Tissaphernes' position—though not necessarily about the plans of the Persian high command—was surely in Ctesias. So, as we saw in §8, it would have been known to Xenophon, who refers to Ctesias' account at 1.8.26 and therefore had evidently read it. Xenophon, then, either would be lying or erroneously thought he knew better. In the light of his general performance as a source,[a] the latter is more likely. When the baggage handlers in the Greek camp saw among them the King, Tissaphernes, and Tissaphernes' cavalry, they could have been confused about whether Tissaphernes arrived on the scene with the King or with his cavalry. Xenophon might then have been unduly influenced by what his own contacts had told him at the time, as against what he read in Ctesias. It is characteristic of Xenophon to overvalue his own limited pool of witnesses.

§20. Proof as to what really happened at Cunaxa is lacking. Ctesias is not trustworthy when blowing his own trumpet about his prowess as a doctor; Diodorus is capable of blunders; Tissaphernes certainly proved his loyalty, whether or not he also demonstrated his undoubted cunning. But the theory that Tissaphernes set a trap for the Greeks is very attractive: the Persians were not nearly as stupid and militarily ineffective as the Greeks, including Xenophon, liked to believe.

David Thomas<br/>Buckinghamshire, UK

---

L.19a  Xenophon as a source: Thomas 2009, §§14–15,
       esp. §§14.1, 15.1.

# APPENDIX M

## *Other Ancient Sources on the Ten Thousand*

§1. Xenophon was not the only ancient author to narrate the story of the Ten Thousand though he almost certainly told their tale at much greater length than any other writer.[a] Some of these writers' works have largely been lost, but this Landmark edition contains three appendices with translations of parts of surviving works by writers that covered some or all of the story:

*Appendix S:* Diodorus Siculus, a first-century compiler; passages from Book 14 of his forty-book universal history.

*Appendix T:* Plutarch, philosopher and antiquary (second century C.E.); extracts from his *Life of Artaxerxes*—which incorporates material from both the *Persika* of Ctesias of Cnidus, a Greek physician to Artaxerxes who was present at the battle of Cunaxa, and from Dinon of Colophon, a later fourth-century writer about matters Persian.[b]

*Appendix U:* Photius, ninth century C.E. Byzantine scholar;[c] part of his epitome (brief abridgment) of Ctesias' *Persika*.

The extracts from Plutarch and Photius concern only the first part of Xenophon's narrative, principally the battle of Cunaxa, which is the subject of Appendix L: The Battle of Cunaxa, and therefore they will hardly be touched on here.[d] Diodorus, however, also covered the march back from Mesopotamia to the Black Sea and on to Thrace,[e] and he and his possible sources are the focus of this appendix.

§2. Diodorus is not a satisfactory historian; but valiant efforts have been made to defend him in recent years, and it is clear that he should not be dismissed as a mere mechanical compiler. Nevertheless, while he planned his work on a very grand scale, claimed to have spent many years composing it, and tried to structure much of it

M.1a  On Cyrus the Younger and Artaxerxes, see Appendix W: Brief Biographies of Selected Characters in *Anabasis*, §§10, 6.

M.1b  For more on Ctesias, see Appendix W, §8. Cnidus: Ref. Map 4.1, DX. Colophon: Ref. Map 4.2, DY. Battlefield of Cunaxa: Ref. Map 6, DX.

M.1c  Photius produced 279 summaries of books he had read. These are valuable today because about half

of these books are now lost. Byzantium: Ref. Map 4.1, AY.

M.1d  See, however, the entry for Menon in Appendix W, §23, for discussion of a discrepancy between Photius and Xenophon about the betrayal of the Greek generals to Tissaphernes.

M.1e  Mesopotamia: Ref. Map 6, CY. Black Sea: Ref. Map 3, BZ. Thrace: Ref. Map 3.

around what should have been a useful chronological scaffold, he was a hasty, care-less, and uncritical writer, prone to blunders and to confusion about chronology, at least in the section of his work on the fifth and fourth centuries. However, there are considerable stretches of Greek and Sicilian history of which his is the main surviving account, and he very often used good sources, so if they can be disentangled from his own misapprehensions, he can give us valuable information.[a]

## Non-Xenophontic Material in Diodorus' Account of the Ten Thousand

§3. Diodorus' account parallels Xenophon very closely except for what he says about Klearchos' earlier tyrannical behavior in Byzantium.[a] Not only is his outline of the events of the march the same; he also gives us similar details about the weapons of the Kardouchoi, the march through the Armenian snow, the soldiers' reaction to seeing the sea, the effects of "mad honey," and the customs of the Mossynoeci.[b] Most of such small differences as there are could reasonably be explained away, either as rhetorical variations or as unimportant slips.[c] However, there are exceptions. A very striking one is that Diodorus does not mention Xenophon during the journey from Mesopotamia via Trapezus to Byzantium but introduces him later, when he makes war on the Thracians of Salmydessos.[d] This is very different from Xenophon's emphasis on his own importance from Mesopo-tamia onward; Xenophon's account does not even suggest that the campaign directed at Salmydessos was his most important campaign in Thrace. There is a similar difference between the two writers' treatment of the Spartan general Cheirisophos.[e] According to Diodorus,[f] after Tissaphernes seized the Greek gener-als, the Greeks appointed Cheirisophos the supreme commander, whereas in Xenophon he is only first among equals, except for a very brief period on the Black Sea coast. Since eyewitnesses could not have told Diodorus this, living as he did centuries later, many have thought that he drew this material from another written account, which deliberately downplayed Xenophon's role, perhaps with some degree of justice.

§4. Diodorus also gives us several other possible pointers to having used a non-Xenophontic source. If we compare the first book of *Anabasis* to Diodorus' account, the latter contains three important pieces of information about the march to Mesopotamia that are not found in Xenophon. First, in several passages he convinc-ingly stresses the involvement of the Lacedaemonian state in Cyrus' venture and the

M.2a   Diodorus is also discussed in Thomas 2009, §7. Sicily: Ref. Map 1, BW.

M.3a   Klearchos in Byzantium and nearby Selymbria: Diodorus 14.12.2–7 (unless otherwise noted, all Diodorus passages cited in this appendix are trans-lated in Appendix S: Selections from Diodorus). On Klearchos, see Appendix W: Brief Biographies, §20.

M.3b   Kardouchoi territory, Armenia: Ref. Map 6, BY, AY. Mossynoeci territory: Ref. Map 5, AZ.

M.3c   Rhetorical variations might include hail as well as wind and snow in Armenia, or the detail that the Mossynoecian towers were seven stories high.

Unimportant slips could be small variations in the forms of names, and perhaps also Diodorus' attri-bution to Proxenos of remarks Xenophon assigns to Theopompos (a different person from the his-torian Theopompus discussed elsewhere in this appendix): Diodorus 14.25.4, Xenophon, *Anaba-sis* 2.1.12. On Proxenos, see Appendix W, §29.

M.3d   First mention of Xenophon: Diodorus 14.37.1. Trapezus: Ref. Map 7, AY. Salmydessos: Ref. Map 3, CZ.

M.3e   On Cheirisophos, see Appendix W, §7.

M.3f   Appointment of Cheirisophos: Diodorus 14.27.1.

duplicity it showed.ᵃ Second, Diodorus explicitly and plausibly makes the army pass through the Cilician Gates (but that might not show independent information, as it was an easy enough guess).ᵇ And third, he gives credible details not in Xenophon of how Syennesis of Cilicia tried to hedge his bets between Cyrus and Artaxerxes.ᶜ Diodorus then goes on to present two major variations from Xenophon's narrative of the battle of Cunaxa:ᵈ first, he writes that Tissaphernes took over the supreme command of the Persians when Artaxerxes was wounded; but in Xenophon's account of the matter, Tissaphernes was at this point on another part of the battle-field, riding through the Greek peltasts;ᵉ second, he also says that Aridaios (his name for Xenophon's Ariaios) fought stoutly at Cunaxa until he heard of Cyrus' death,ᶠ something that cannot be gathered from Xenophon.

§5. Some of Diodorus' detailed information about the subsequent journey through the Anatolian highlandsᵃ differs from Xenophon's, and in two instances his version does have some plausibility. One of these plausible variations is that Diodorus says that the army delayed for four days by the Phasis River and that, after defeating the Chaoi and the Phasianoi, they spent fifteen days in the farms they had seized from the natives; Xenophon does not report either of these delays,ᵇ but it seems nat-ural enough for the army to take a break in both locations. Again, Diodorus tells us that it took fifteen days to march from Gymnasia to the place where they saw the sea from Mount Chenium; Xenophon says, with some emphasis, that it took five days from Gymnias before the soldiers saw the sea from Mount Theches.ᶜ Presumably Gymnasia is to be equated with Gymnias and Chenium with Theches, but more seri-ous is the discrepancy between the fifteen days and the five. The general opinion is that fifteen days is just a slip, but in my view Diodorus is quite likely right. For one thing, according to Xenophon, their guide from Gymnias said as soon as he first met them that they could kill him if they failed to see the sea within five days. It was odd for him to have taken such a big risk on the very first day that he met the Greeks, for even if he honestly expected that they would see the sea that soon, rival natives or weather might easily have caused a delay, making his undertaking a personal cata-strophe for him. His promise would have been much more natural if in reality he had been leading the Greeks for some time and they were getting fed up with detours against the enemies of Gymnias. More generally, Xenophon's indications of the time spent on the march amount to somewhat less than the full period between a November date for the battle of Cunaxaᵈ and a mid-to-late May arrival in the

M.4a Lacedaemonian state involvement: Diodorus 14.19.4, 14.21.1–2, 14.22.5. Lacedaemon: Ref. Map 2, DY; also see the Glossary.
M.4b Cilician Gates named and described: Diodorus 14.20.1; compare Xenophon, *Anabasis* 1.2.21–22. Cilician Gates, Cilicia: Ref. Map 5, CY. See Figure 1.2.22 for a photograph of the Cilician Gates.
M.4c Details about Syennesis: Diodorus 14.20.3.
M.4d The first of these variations is discussed at greater length in Appendix L: The Battle of Cunaxa, §§11–12, 15.
M.4e Tissaphernes' position: compare Diodorus 14.23.6 with Xenophon, *Anabasis* 1.10.7. Peltasts: light-armed infantrymen; see Appendix H: Infantry and Cavalry in *Anabasis*, §§4–5.
M.4f Bravery of Aridaios: Diodorus 14.24.1. On Ari-aios, see Appendix W: Brief Biographies, §4.
M.5a Anatolia: Ref. Map 1, BX.
M.5b Reports of delays: Diodorus 14.29.1. Xenophon does not report them: the relevant places could be at 4.6.4–5 and 4.6.27 (or perhaps immediately after 4.7.14). Phasis River, Phasianoi territory: Ref. Map 6, AY (Phasioi in the *Barrington Atlas*). Diodorus' Chaoi are presumably equivalent to the Taochoi: Ref. Map 6, AY.
M.5c Fifteen days' march: Diodorus 14.29.3. Five days: *Anabasis* 4.7.20. Possible locations of Gymnias, Mt. Theches: Ref. Map 6, AX.
M.5d The November date for the battle of Cunaxa is argued for in Appendix Q: The Chronology of the March.

vicinity of Trapezus.[c] A few more days at Diodorus 14.29.1 and ten extra days at 14.29.3 would help fill that gap.[f]

§6. At this point in the argument, we need to distinguish between Diodorus' immediate sources and his ultimate sources. It is incredible that he would not have mentioned Xenophon in the main part of his narrative if he had been summarizing Xenophon's own account, for he was not a critical historian and he was prone to seeing history in terms of "great men." So almost all scholars agree that he was relying on another source who stood between Xenophon and himself. The issue is whether that intermediary used Xenophon and only Xenophon as a source. If the intermediary had read Xenophon with critical acumen, he might well have become suspicious of the all-important role Xenophon assigned to himself even if he had no other contemporary source to call on. So the most striking of all the differences between Diodorus' narrative and *Anabasis* turns out not to help much in determining whether there was a second ultimate source (and the similar variance in their treatments of Cheirisophos could be an oversimplification by Diodorus himself).

§7. It is possible to find explanations for each of the other specific instances of variations between the texts of Xenophon and Diodorus. Some of them, such as the three pieces of extra information about the march to Mesopotamia mentioned in §4, might conceivably be due to imaginative development of Xenophon's narrative by someone else, perhaps an intermediary between Xenophon and Diodorus. Others, especially where Xenophon and Diodorus give different numbers of days for this or that stretch of the journey, could be simple errors, perhaps by Diodorus himself. The discrepancies involving the battle of Cunaxa are a special case, since Ctesias' account of it in his *Persika* was available to all the possible intermediary sources to copy or to blend in; so the Cunaxa discrepancies may not help us determine how the sources interacted elsewhere. But when one considers the large number of possible and plausible instances in the round, it does look probable that genuine non-Xenophontic material about the Ten Thousand did reach Diodorus, not only from Ctesias but also from others.

## Other Fourth-Century Sources:
## More General Historians

§8. When trying to work out who Diodorus' non-Xenophontic sources might have been, some degree of speculation is unavoidable. There were at least three fourth-century historians who could have covered the battle of Cunaxa and given at least an outline of the Ten Thousand's return to the Greek world—namely, Ephorus of Cyme, Theopompus of Chios, and Cratippus of Athens.[a] The works of all three survive only in fragments,[b] none of which give an extended narrative of the relevant

M.5e  The mid-to-late May date for the arrival would be when the "mad honey" found by the soldiers at 4.8.20–21 would have been newly laid down by the bees and at its strongest. See Appendix Q: The Chronology of the March, §§8–10.

M.5f  But other ways of finding the days to fill this gap are possible, and indeed in the side notes of this Landmark edition, they have been distributed in a

different but plausible way.

M.8a  Cyme, Chios, Ref. Map 4.2, CY, CX. Athens: Ref. Map 2, CZ.

M.8b  The fragments are collected in the great work of Felix Jacoby, *Die Fragmente der griechischen Historiker* (Jacoby 1923–58). Ephorus is historian number 70, Theopompus 115, Cratippus 64.

events; but in the case of two of them, the fragments do contain evidence of overlap with *Anabasis*. As we shall see, it is not possible to choose one of them with confidence as the one that Diodorus used.

§9. Ephorus is the usual candidate for Diodorus' immediate source on the Ten Thousand. In the middle to late years of the fourth century, he wrote a massive history, thirty books long, which began with the legend of the return of the descendants of Herakles to the Peloponnese and ended with the siege of Perinthus undertaken by Philip of Macedonia in 340.[a] As well as the history of the Greek mainland, it covered Sicily[b] and matters Persian, and the reference to Ephorus at Diodorus 14.22.2 shows that it included an account of the battle of Cunaxa. Indeed, most scholars believe that Ephorus' history was Diodorus' chief—perhaps virtually sole—narrative source for the whole period from around 500 or even earlier to the mid-350s.[c] The main argument for this belief is that Diodorus has special problems with the chronology of this period, which are most easily explained if his main source did not divide up its narrative into successive years as Diodorus himself does, probably taking his system over from a chronological handbook. Since it is known that Ephorus did not use this kind of annalistic framework, it is a natural explanation for the confusions in Diodorus' chronology that he had a problem adapting Ephorus' continuous narrative into his own year-by-year system. Ephorus was a serious historian, and it is likely that he used Ctesias and Xenophon and any other written source that was available, exercising his intelligence in reworking the material. Elsewhere he tried to avoid following the obvious source too closely, and this would give him a motive for trying to downplay or even eliminate Xenophon from much of the story of the Ten Thousand. He also no doubt gathered oral evidence for events within his adult lifetime, but by the time he came to research the battle of Cunaxa, the remnants of the Ten Thousand will have been elderly and few.[d] So it is much more likely that Ephorus did not interview them, but relied on another written source (or sources) to supplement Xenophon; and if, as most scholars suppose, Diodorus was using Ephorus here, we would have in turn to consider where this further written material might have come from.

§10. Theopompus is less often considered as a possible source for Diodorus, but his claims should not be overlooked. He wrote his most famous work, the fifty-eight-book *Philippika*, centered on the reign of Philip II of Macedonia (360–336), at much the same time as Ephorus was composing his universal history.[a] But previous to *Philippika*, Theopompus had produced his twelve-book *Hellenika*, continuing the narrative of Thucydides' history of the Peloponnesian War[b] from where it left off, in 411, to the battle of Cnidus, in 394. He may well have been working on it as early as the 370s. Theopompus' *Hellenika* formed an important source for these

M.9a  Macedonia: Ref. Map 3, CX. Perinthus: Ref. Map 4.1, AX.
M.9b  Sicily: Ref. Map 1, BW.
M.9c  There is less agreement about Diodorus' sources for the history of Sicily.
M. 9d  Ephorus was still writing his history in the 320s. It is controversial when he started it; some scholars have thought it was as early as the 350s. But even so he would not have reached the march of the Ten Thousand until around 345 at

the earliest, so any surviving soldiers would have been in their seventies and eighties.
M.10a  Scholars differ on when Theopompus was born. The two ancient sources that give dates for his birth disagree: I support the earlier of the two dates, the period 408–405. (The rival date is 378/7.)
M.10b  Thucydides (late 450s–390s): Athenian historian. For more on him see Ancient Sources Cited in this Edition.

years for both Plutarch and another author who wrote in the second century C.E., Pausanias.[c] Although there is no direct evidence that Theopompus' *Hellenika* featured the Ten Thousand, the fragments include references to Kalpe and the Thynoi, familiar from Xenophon's *Anabasis*, and to Kytonion, which many scholars have argued is the true name of a place that the manuscripts of *Anabasis* call Kertonion; Kalpe and Kytonion are said to occur in Theopompus' eighth book, which would be the appropriate chronological place.[d] Theopompus is not usually regarded as a likely source for Diodorus, and his *Philippika* was diffuse, digressive, and confusingly arranged and so would have been difficult for Diodorus to use; but *Hellenika* was probably much more straightforward, to judge from a comparison of the surviving fragments of the two works. We might add that Diodorus certainly used another source in addition to Ephorus for his account of the murder of the Athenian politician Alcibiades in 403,[e] just before the events of *Anabasis*. Theopompus was of a sour disposition and did not care for Athenians, so Diodorus' omission of Xenophon from the most heroic part of the story of the Ten Thousand might well be the indirect result of Theopompus' bias. Unlike the case of Ephorus, if we accept Theopompus as Diodorus' source, that does not necessarily mean that we then have to look for another written source behind him. For although Theopompus will naturally have made use of any literary sources that were available, and he was indeed accused in late antiquity of widespread plagiarism of Xenophon's *Hellenika*, he was also known as an indefatigable researcher; and if he started research even in the 360s, he should still have been able, unlike Ephorus, to interview witnesses of the events of 400.

§11. Cratippus is the third fourth-century historian to consider. He was another continuator of Thucydides, earlier than Theopompus, but little is known for sure about him beyond this, except that his work definitely continued beyond the end of the Peloponnesian War (431–404), to at least 394. However, most modern scholars agree that he is the likeliest candidate to be the author of *Hellenica Oxyrhynchia*, a modern name for a history of the 400s and 390s that survives in extensive papyrus fragments.[a] It was written within fifty years of the latest events we know it recounted, but we cannot be certain about the identity of the author. Its narrative was divided up into separate years and gave considerable detail on the topics that it covers; it seems to be the product of a good deal of research among eyewitnesses. Whoever the author was, all scholars agree that it is the ultimate source of Diodorus' account of the Spartan king Agesilaos'[b] campaign in Asia in 395. But there is a big obstacle to seeing *Hellenica Oxyrhynchia* as Diodorus' immediate source for these years, for Diodorus' chronology for the period 404–393 is very confused, and it should not

M.10c  Pausanias (c. 110–after 180 C.E.): Greek travel writer. For more on him see Ancient Sources Cited in this Edition.

M.10d  Kalpe: Theopompus F15; Xenophon, *Anabasis* 6.4.1. The Thynoi: Theopompus F16; *Anabasis* 7.2.32, 7.4.2, 7.4.14. Kytonion: Theopompus F17; compare Kertonion at *Anabasis* 7.8.8. Kalpe/Kalpe Harbor, possible location: Ref. Map 4.1, AY. Thynoi territory: Ref. Map 3, CZ. Kertonion: Ref. Map 4.2, BX. (Kertonion is not listed in the *Barrington Atlas*. It locates Kytonion tentatively on Map 56 E3, but in a different location from the one this edition adopts

for Kertonion.)

M.10e  Murder of Alcibiades: Diodorus 14.11.1 (not in Appendix S: Selections from Diodorus).

M.11a  The modern name for this work derives from the ancient Upper Egyptian city Oxyrhynchus (Ref. Map 1, DX), on the outskirts of which the fragments were discovered in a rubbish pile. The main alternative theory is that the fragments of *Hellenica Oxyrhynchia* are really from Theopompus' *Hellenika*, a view that still commands impressive, if minority, scholarly support.

M.11b  On Agesilaos, see Appendix W: Brief Biographies, §2.

have been if his narrative was directly based on an explicitly annalistic source like *Hellenica Oxyrhynchia*. As I said above (§9), the usual explanation is that Diodorus was using Ephorus, who had recast *Hellenica Oxyrhynchia* into nonannalistic form, perhaps with variations. Accordingly, the twentieth-century scholar H. D. Westlake argued that *Hellenica Oxyrhynchia* is the ultimate source, via Ephorus, of Diodorus' account of the Ten Thousand as a whole,[c] and though that is unlikely because of the great degree of overlap between Diodorus and Xenophon on the topic, the work could be the source of some or all of Diodorus' non-Xenophontic material about the Ten Thousand. If that is so, Diodorus' account would be worthy of considerable respect, as the general credit of this work stands high.[d] *Hellenica Oxyrhynchia* very likely came out prior to *Anabasis*—at least if Cratippus was the author—which makes it possible that Xenophon wrote *Anabasis* as a conscious reaction to it.[e]

### Other Fourth-Century Sources:
### A Dedicated Monograph?

§12. Although it is thus possible that behind Diodorus' non-Xenophontic material there is genuine eyewitness testimony given orally to either Theopompus or Cratippus, many modern scholars have believed that Diodorus' work might in part derive from a written account by one of the other generals on the march, namely Sophainetos of Stymphalos. This is the so-called Sophainetos Hypothesis.[a] Over a thousand years later, the sixth-century C.E. lexicographer Stephanus of Byzantium cites a work called the *Anabasis of Cyrus* by Sophainetos four times for the names of places or peoples. Two of them are apparently at variance with Xenophon's text and one adds to the information he gives. Some of Diodorus' additional material supports this theory—specifically, the details of the journey through the Anatolian highlands, since these would, if genuine, naturally be thought to derive ultimately from one of the Ten Thousand. It is plausible to characterize this suggested eyewitness source as hostile to Xenophon. At many points in Xenophon's narrative, he writes defensively, as if answering criticisms of which he expects his audience to be aware. This is readily explained if a colleague had already put such criticisms into circulation, and Sophainetos is a plausible candidate to be this hostile colleague. He was the oldest of the generals and might well have downplayed Xenophon's part, serving as a model for Diodorus' minimizing presentation. Perhaps it is in retribution for this that Xenophon persistently denigrates Sophainetos. According to Xenophon, Sophainetos was left behind in camp in Armenia, given a cushy job when the army reached the Black Sea, subsequently fined for dereliction of duty, and made to look a fool on a later sortie.[b] These arguments come nowhere near showing that Diodorus' account represents Sophainetos to the exclusion of Xenophon; but one might be drawn to think

M.11c　Westlake 1987.

M.11d　For more on *Hellenica Oxyrhynchia*, see Thomas 2009, §7, but I am not as confident now as I was then that Cratippus was the author.

M.11e　Thomas 2009, §10.6–7, argues that much of the first half of Xenophon's *Hellenika* was a conscious reaction to *Hellenica Oxyrhynchia*.

M.12a　More detailed argument for and against the Sophainetos Hypothesis may be found in the respective chapters by Cawkwell and Stylianou in Lane Fox 2004. On Sophainetos, see Appendix W: Brief Biographies, §32. Stymphalos: Ref. Map 2, CY.

M.12b　Left behind: 4.4.19. Cushy job: 5.3.1. Fined: 5.8.1. Made to look a fool: 6.5.13. Armenia: Ref. Map 6, AY. Black Sea: Ref. Map 1, AX.

that Diodorus' intermediate source, whether Ephorus or Theopompus, blended Sophainetos and Xenophon together. Nevertheless, probably the majority of scholars at the present time reject the Sophainetos Hypothesis.

§13. The above arguments for the theory are certainly not conclusive. Perhaps Diodorus' extra details about the journey are errors, or information gleaned by Theopompus or Cratippus from other eyewitnesses. When Xenophon reacts defensively, the critics to whom he reacts might have spread their hostile comments by word of mouth rather than in writing, and indeed those criticisms that concern details of the Thracian campaign in Book 7 of *Anabasis* are not likely to have been spread by any memoirs composed by Sophainetos: his name is absent from the list of generals at 7.2.1, so he was probably no longer with the army at this point. Diodorus' silence about Xenophon can be explained without reference to Sophainetos: as we saw, if the source was Theopompus, he hated Athenians; if it was Ephorus, he perhaps reacted against the extent to which Xenophon had singled himself out compared to the other generals. Finally, Xenophon does denigrate Sophainetos, but that is not in itself a proof that the latter attacked him in a written account; the pair might just have fallen out during the march, if indeed we are right to see personal animosity at all.

§14. Stephanus' four citations from Sophainetos' alleged monograph also fall short of proof that it was written by someone whose information was personal to the writer and also good. Stephanus actually notes that Sophainetos and Xenophon use the same name for the Kardouchoi, so that is no evidence that the two works were independent. Xenophon's Taochoi become Taoi in Stephanus' report of Sophainetos and Chaoi in Diodorus, but this might be the result of corruption in the manuscripts.[a] Sophainetos is said to have given Physkos as the name for the city on the Physkos River that Xenophon calls Opis: that might be accounted for by a misunderstanding of what Sophainetos said.[b] Finally, it is true that when the monograph that Stephanus attributes to Sophainetos mentions that Charmande was opposite the Babylonian Gates,[c] it is certainly going beyond what Xenophon says about the place—but this is hardly proof that the monograph really was written by an eyewitness like Sophainetos, for the statement is arguably false, and even if it were true, it may have been quite widely known. Either way, it would not be good evidence for a genuine monograph by Sophainetos.

§15. The skeptics about Sophainetos' monograph usually say that it must have been a late literary exercise, akin to the many forged or at least fictional letters in antiquity. They claim that it is improbable that a genuine fourth-century monograph by Sophainetos should survive for over a thousand years without anyone referring to it prior to Stephanus of Byzantium. However, there are in fact about half a dozen other historians—all too obscure for it to be worth anyone's while to foist forged works upon them—who seem to have lived five hundred years or more before

M.14a  Taochoi: Xenophon, *Anabasis* 4.6.5, 4.7.1. Chaoi: Diodorus 14.29.1 according to the manuscripts (in Appendix S: Diodorus, Peter Green emends to "Taochoi"). Kardouchoi, Taochoi territories: Ref. Map 6, BY, AY.

M.14b  Xenophon's Opis: 2.4.25. Opis was really elsewhere; the view taken in this edition is that Xenophon confused Opis with Sittake: Ref. Map 6, CZ. (Sittake is not listed in the *Barring-ton Atlas*. The Physkos is probably to be identified with the *Atlas'* Radani River.)

M.14c  Charmande: 1.5.10. The location for Charmande is disputed, but our chosen site is not opposite the Babylonian Gates, taken to mean the town of Pylai, whose name is Greek for "gates." It is, however, possible that Charmande really was near Pylai. Charmande (not listed in the *Barrington Atlas*), Pylai: Ref. Map 6, DY, DZ.

Stephanus but whose first extant citation is in his lexicon; it is true, though, that Sophainetos would be the most extreme case. It also seems to me unlikely that if one were going to write, as a literary exercise, an account of the Ten Thousand from the standpoint of a general other than Xenophon, one would choose Sophainetos; Kleanor,[a] Timasion, or Neon were more prominent figures and offer more opportunities to show events in a different perspective. So my personal view is that some of Diodorus' information does ultimately come from a monograph by Sophainetos, which Diodorus' immediate source—Ephorus or (maybe) Theopompus—has blended with Xenophon and perhaps with other material, whether oral or written.

## Does It Matter?

§16. With all this uncertainty, nonspecialists may be tempted to wonder whether they should care about the sources of Diodorus' rival account. There are three reasons why this is important. The first may be more applicable to people interested in Greek history generally than to readers specifically of *Anabasis*. Diodorus is one of our two main narrative historians for the fifty years from 411 to 362 and almost our only narrative historian for several other periods in the fourth century. So his own sources, their credibility, and what he did with them are very high up on the issues that have to be confronted in trying to make out what happened in that period, the age of Athenian democracy, its times of trial, and its ultimate suppression. The second reason is likewise about assessing what actually happened, this time specifically about what happened on the march. Only by estimating the nature and worth of Diodorus' sources can the student of the Ten Thousand decide on the credibility of Xenophon as a narrator and witness. Conclusions about the probable course of the battle of Cunaxa and the exact number of days spent here and there in eastern Anatolia have implications for what we are to make of Xenophon's testimony more generally when we do not have another source to measure it against.

§17. The third reason—probably the most important one for many modern readers of *Anabasis*—is that there are consequences for our appreciation of Xenophon's purposes and degree of success as a writer. If Xenophon had in front of him an earlier account of the march, whether Sophainetos or *Hellenica Oxyrhynchia* or both, so did many of the initial audience for whom he wrote. To grasp Xenophon's intentions, we would need to be constantly alert to catch the ghostly voice of his interlocutor, the criticisms Xenophon might be meeting, the occasions when his candor may not be as great as it appears.

David Thomas
Buckinghamshire, UK

M.15a  On Kleanor, see Appendix W: Brief Biographies,
　　　§19.

# APPENDIX N

*Xenophon and the Development of
Classical Historiography*

§1. Assessing Xenophon's place in the development of Classical Greek historiography is at once easy and difficult—easy because for years he was regarded as inferior to his great predecessor Thucydides, as if this were a sufficient description of his historical work; difficult because his historiography, as with his philosophical and occasional (or minor) writings, is extremely varied and multitextured, indeed genre-breaking in many regards. As it will surely be of more interest to the reader to hear about what Xenophon's historical writing is rather than what it is not (that is, not Thucydides), I have elected to go with the more difficult assessment here. Although it is inevitable that Xenophon's *Hellenika*—continuation of and in some sense rival to Thucydides—will be a main focus of attention, account needs also to be taken of other Xenophontic works with a historical perspective, in particular *Anabasis*.

§2. *Hellenika*, a history of "Greek Affairs," starts in 411, where Thucydides' history of the Peloponnesian War left off, and extends down to 362 and the battle of Second Mantineia, which confirmed Sparta's inability to re-create its once-unquestioned supremacy, even in the Peloponnese.[a] Since *Hellenika* starts where Thucydides stops, it has long been thought to have been meant formally to complete the earlier account and hence also to imitate its methods to some degree. Xenophon was not the only one to do this. *The Life of Thucydides* that has been transmitted to us under the name of Marcellinus mentions the fourth-century historian Theopompus (whose work survives only in fragments) as another continuator of Thucydides, in addition to Xenophon.[b] Also, the *Hellenica Oxyrhynchia* (preserved incomplete on papyri only) is self-evidently a continuation of Thucydides; its author is unknown, but it cannot be by Theopompus.[c] Those who see in Xenophon not just a continuator of Thucydides but an imitator of him in *Hellenika* note that, especially in the early por-

NOTE: All references to *Hellenika* in this appendix refer to Xenophon's work.

N.2a The following locations appear on Ref. Map 2: Mantineia, Peloponnese, CY; Sparta, DY.

N.2b Marcellinus, *Life of Thucydides* 45.

N.2c This is the general but not universal consensus. For more on the *Hellenica Oxyrhynchia* and on Theopompus, see Appendix M: Other Ancient Sources on the Ten Thousand, esp. §§10–11.

tions of the history, through 2.3.10, Xenophon seems to mark the passage of time in the war in a way similar to Thucydides and also is careful to report in precise numbers, particularly in connection with the sizes of fleets of warships. Less often noted but no less important is that, remarkably for an ancient historical work, *Hellenika* lacks a preface, a detail that also suggests that the work was meant in some sense to continue Thucydides.

§3. But if Xenophon envisioned *Hellenika* as the completion of Thucydides' history of the Peloponnesian War, he clearly changed his mind at some point, because the work goes well beyond the end of the war in 404. One of Xenophon's major contributions to the genre of contemporary or near-contemporary history was to see that it did not have to be built around the narrative of a single conflict or other theme. When we move beyond the part of *Hellenika* that completes the account of the war, we see Xenophon correspondingly move away from what have been deemed more Thucydidean concerns. A passage that reveals this reorientation can be found at the start of Book 5, where Xenophon recounts in almost cinematic terms the departure of a Spartan commander named Teleutias from his troops. Pausing to defend his decision to highlight the moment, Xenophon observes: "Now I well know that in narrating these events, I do not record anything about funds expended, dangers confronted, or stratagems employed. And yet, by Zeus, I think it worthwhile for a man to consider what it was that Teleutias had done that so disposed the men he commanded to behave like that. For this is truly an achievement for a man, more worthy of being recorded than spending a great deal of money or encountering many dangers."[a] "Funds expended," "dangers confronted," and "stratagems employed" are signature historiographic concerns of Thucydides, but while by no means absent in the second, longer portion of *Hellenika* after the "completion,"[b] they have to make room for Xenophon's own interest in paradigms of leadership and model communities (good and bad), among other themes.

§4. While some will want to question such surgical precision, it does seem fair to say that with Xenophon Greek historical writing underwent something of a shift in focus and purpose from what Thucydides was aiming at. If individuals are important and play a significant role in shaping Thucydides' narrative, it could be said that in Xenophon they dominate. The treatment of the actions and thinking of King Agesilaos[a] of Sparta, to take the most obvious case, virtually replaces the narration of the activities of Sparta for good stretches of text. Furthermore, Xenophon not infrequently judges individuals' actions in a way that seems to have a strong didactic function,[b] in this being unlike Thucydides—though the latter no doubt had his eye on posterity and the future utility of his history to it.[c] In both regards—making the actions of individuals the focus of historical narrative, and the didactic purpose of his treatment—Xenophon can be seen to anticipate important developments later.

---

N.3a  "Now I well know": *Hellenika* 5.1.4 (Marincola/ Landmark translation).

N.3b  Second, longer portion: *Hellenika* 2.3.11–7.5.27.

N.4a  On Agesilaos, see Appendix W: Brief Biographies of Selected Characters in *Anabasis*, §2.

N.4b  Xenophon's didactic judgments: for example, *Hellenika* 5.3.7, 6.2.32, 6.2.39.

N.4c  Thucydides' eye on posterity: see esp. Thucydides 1.22.4.

§5. Insofar as he seems to have followed closely in the footsteps of Thucydides, scholars have tended to view Xenophon as chiefly in dialogue with him. And yet, to paint with a big brush, one could say that *Hellenika* also has distinct aspects in common with Thucydides' predecessor Herodotus, historian of the early-fifth-century wars between Greeks and Persians. At the micro level, there are some close verbal similarities that turn up in both authors: so, for instance, Phillidas of Thebes in *Hellenika* happens to be "on some business or other,"[a] which puts him in the right place at the right time to advance a major plot of revenge, and the same is true of Hermotimos of Pedasa in Herodotus[b]—the strong implication in both cases being that it was not chance at all that put them in such an ideal spot to launch their plans. At the macro level, too, there are what look like deliberate attempts by Xenophon to write in a Herodotean register. Phillidas' scheme to eliminate the pro-Spartan oligarchs of Thebes looks very much like a similar episode in Herodotus, where the Macedonian prince Alexander engineers the murder of Persians: in both cases youths dressed as highborn women kill enemies of their state, who think they are to be entertained by these "women" after an evening of heavy drinking.[c] On very rare occasions, Xenophon, like Herodotus, can claim that the divine was responsible for the outcome of an event.[d]

§6. This accent on the divine as a historical agent links up with religious views found in Xenophon's philosophical works, especially in connection with Socrates: what look like expressions of traditional piety in *Memorabilia* 1.4 and 4.3 can at the same time be seen as evidence for an unconventional belief in an all-powerful, all-knowing divine being whose influence in history is not hard to imagine. Of particular importance to Xenophon was adherence to one's oaths: Agesilaos expresses this view in *Hellenika* when he thanks the satrap Tissaphernes for breaking his oath, thereby making the gods, who oversee oaths, the enemies of Persia and allies of the Greek army operating in Asia.[a] Curiously, Xenophon himself expresses the same sentiment in *Anabasis* in a speech to his fellow mercenaries.[b] In Xenophon humans, too, are aware of the historical consequences of unethical behavior, policed as it is by the gods.

§7. It is important, finally, to note, in connection with Xenophon's *Hellenika*, that it has a very problematic ending. Herodotus has a very carefully crafted end that takes us in a flashback to the reign of Cyrus the Great but in a way that is clearly meant to make us think about the ambitions of the Persians and how they dictated, for good and ill, their actions in subsequent years, right down to the failure of Xerxes' invasion of Greece and very likely even beyond that.[a] Notoriously Thucydides' history is incomplete (indeed, remember that Xenophon and others in some sense "completed"

N.5a   "On some business or other": *Hellenika* 5.4.2 (Marincola/Landmark translation). Pedasa: Ref. Map 4.1, DX. Thebes: Ref. Map 2, BZ.

N.5b   Herodotus 8.106.1.

N.5c   Murder of Persians: Herodotus 5.20. Murder of pro-Spartan oligarchs: *Hellenika* 5.4.4–7. Macedonia: Ref. Map 3, CX.

N.5d   Divine responsibility asserted: most famously at *Hellenika* 5.4.1 but note also *Hellenika* 4.4.12. Compare Herodotus 1.34.1, 7.12–19.

N.6a   Agesilaos thanks Tissaphernes for oath-breaking: *Hellenika* 3.4.11. On satraps (provincial governors), see the Glossary. On Tissaphernes, see Appendix W: Brief Biographies, §37.

N.6b   Xenophon regards Persian oath-breaking as advantageous: 3.2.10.

N.7a   Flashback to Cyrus: Herodotus 9.122. On Cyrus the Great/Cyrus the Elder and Xerxes, see Appendix W, §§9, 38.

it). But had he finished it, I cannot help thinking that there would have been a significant point of closure, and I am not alone in thinking so. Xenophon quite deliberately ends his *Hellenika*, but he specifically refuses to find closure. Discussing the outcome of the battle of Second Mantineia, when Thebes soundly defeated Sparta but at a very heavy price, Xenophon observes that while nearly everyone in Greece expected the battle to be literally decisive in determining the ordering of power in the Greek world, no such clarity of settlement was forthcoming: "In Greece as a whole there was more uncertainty and disturbance after the battle than there had been before."[b]

§8. For a man devoted to the principle of order, to find that the epochal battle of his time brought no ordering to his world must have distressed and disoriented him. Meaning in history, to extend the thesis advanced by the German philosopher Karl Löwith as regards Christian and post-Christian historians,[a] depends on our ability to find closure—an end point that explains what has gone before. Virtually all the subsequent historians of Greco-Roman antiquity can be said to have been animated by the desire to find such closure. Some, like Xenophon, were clearly challenged in their belief that the explanation was what they thought it was. The great second-century Greek historian Polybius, for instance, thought that the history of his age was explained by the establishment of Roman power from one end of the Mediterranean to the other; it was the defining event of his time—even allowing for the workings of *to paradoxon* (the unexpected) to upset things.[b] But after the final destruction of Carthage, in 146, Polybius recognized that people's understanding of the nature of Roman rule was not a settled matter but still contingent: whether Rome's dominion was worthy of praise or blame was still unclear.[c] Hence the vantage point he had when he started his history fundamentally changed; uncertainty now had to be accounted for. Panhellenic accents can be found throughout *Hellenika*, and yet its final message seems to have to do with the impossibility of the Greeks' uniting under the leadership of a single *polis* (city-state).[d]

§9. We should now briefly look at Xenophon's encomium of King Agesilaos. As with *Anabasis* (see §§12–15), nothing like Xenophon's *Agesilaos* had been written before, and little like it was afterward. It is routine to point out that it vies for the honor of being the first biography in the Greek literary tradition with only one other work: Isocrates' *Evagoras*, an epideictic oration (display speech) written for Nicocles, the son of King Evagoras of Cyprus[a] (ruled c. 411–374). It is certainly true that both works have as their principal aim the praise of a recently deceased ruler.[b] But unlike Isocrates' display speech, *Agesilaos* is divided into two distinct parts: a historical narrative, which runs through Agesilaos' "deeds" (in Greek, his *erga*), and a section devoted to his "virtue" (in Greek, his *aretē*, under several different heads: Piety, Justice, and so on), which concludes with a summary that reca-

N.7b   "In Greece as a whole": *Hellenika* 7.5.27 (Marincola/Landmark translation).

N.8a   Löwith 1949, esp. p. 5.

N.8b   Defining event, but unexpected: Polybius 1.1.3–5.

N.8c   Judgment on Rome still unclear: Polybius 3.4–5. Carthage: Ref. Map 1, CW.

N.8d   Panhellenic accents in *Hellenika*: see Appendix E:

Panhellenism, §§3, 14.

N.9a   Epideictic oration: one written purely as a display of a writer's rhetorical prowess. Cyprus: Ref. Map 1, CX.

N.9b   At *Agesilaos* 10.3, Xenophon refers to his work by the Greek equivalent of "encomium," *enkōmion*; Isocrates 9 (*Evagoras*) 8 uses the corresponding verb to describe what he is doing.

pitulates his outstanding qualities.[c] The historical narrative covers Agesilaos' life from his accession to the throne, in 400, when he was about forty-four years old, to his last year, when, at the age of eighty-four, he was serving as a mercenary leader in Egypt and Libya during an Egyptian revolt from Persian rule.[d] Many passages from this section are virtually identical to sections in *Hellenika* that deal with the king. What is noteworthy is that Xenophon omits Agesilaos' first years and much of his earlier adulthood from this narrative, as well as his death, presumably because they did not do his subject credit: Agesilaos was born with a birth defect, was not in line to succeed to the throne, and was involved in an unseemly succession dispute; and he died in Libya while leading a mercenary army, an episode that involved his abandoning his first employer. (But the king's death is mentioned in the final recapitulatory section of the work.)

§10. Two points seem to be especially important in connection with *Agesilaos*. First, if it is correct to characterize later biographical writing in antiquity as splitting into two distinct types—the so-called Plutarch type, which features essentially only a diachronic narrative of the hero's deeds, and the Suetonius type, which has both a historical narrative and a summation of the hero's virtues and vices[a]—Xenophon can be seen to have pioneered both, for insofar as he produced a life of Agesilaos that obviously conforms to the latter type, he also devoted the first part of *Agesilaos* to a historical review of the king. Second, with *Hellenika* and *Agesilaos* set side by side, we are in a unique position to be able to compare two historical narratives by the same author covering the same material. While disagreement persists, it is fair to say that the biography of the king is clearly encomiastic, whereas the history, though containing many of the same details and scenes, casts a much more complex light on Agesilaos, one that should make modern readers skeptical that Xenophon was quite the blind Spartan apologist he is sometimes made out to be.

§11. It is natural to compare *Agesilaos* with Xenophon's *Apologia Sokratous* (*Defense of Socrates*) and *Apomnemoneumata* (*Recollections of Socrates;* in Latin, *Memorabilia*), insofar as all three works are in some sense biographical. In these two works, as in his *Symposion* (*The Drinking Party*), Xenophon sought to preserve the memory of Socrates, his character and ways of thought, as did other followers of Socrates.[a] Indeed, Greek biography may well have received an important early stimulus, if not actual inspiration, from this process.

§12. It is high time I moved on to an evaluation of *Anabasis* as a historical work and its relation to previous and subsequent historiography. It is vital to observe first that *Anabasis* is not, strictly speaking, a history—if by that we mean something like what Herodotus or Thucydides wrote, or even Xenophon himself in *Hellenika*. A "card catalog" description of *Anabasis* would run something like the following: "a narrative of the activities of the Greek mercenary army of Cyrus the Younger from

N.9c  Agesilaos' deeds: *Agesilaos* 1.6–3.1, marked by use of the word *erga* at the opening and close. Agesilaos' virtue: *Agesilaos* 3.1–11.16. (The summary referred to forms chapter 11.)

N.9d  Egypt, Libya: Ref. Map 1, DX, CX.

N.10a For more on Plutarch and Suetonius, see Ancient Sources Cited in this Edition.

N.11a Plato is the most familiar example, but there were other writers of Socratic dialogues whose work is lost, for example Antisthenes. For more on Socrates and a somewhat different approach to Xenophon's aims in his Socratic writings, see Appendix A: Xenophon and Socrates.

401 to 399 in western Anatolia and Thrace,[a] told from a third-person perspective by one of its members." Nothing on this scale had been written before in Greek literature (though Thucydides does include his own actions, told in the third person, in his narrative), and few authors wrote anything like it later, except that the lost history of Alexander the Great by his subordinate general Ptolemy must have been somewhat similar, as (even more so) were Julius Caesar's *Commentaries, De Bello Gallico* (*Gallic War*) and *De Bello Civili* (*Civil War*)—crucially, all three works told in the third person. Admittedly, memoir literature had been composed before (for example, in the fifth century by Ion of Chios and Stesimbrotus of Thasos); and later powerful men, often military leaders, would write up accounts of their activities, as Aratus of Sicyon did in his lost *Hypomnemata* (*Memoirs*) and Augustus Caesar did in his *Res Gestae* (*Achievements*);[b] but these were all written in the first person rather than in the third.

§13. It is hard to overstate the importance of this feature of *Anabasis*: perspective, in the form of the voice of the narrator, is everything. If, for instance, the crucial beginning of Book 3 of *Anabasis* had been told from a first-person perspective instead of in the third person, Xenophon's rallying first of himself, then of his fellow commanders, and finally of the army would look very different. As a narrative about a decisive chain of events in the collective life of the Ten Thousand—the army coming together when faced with extinction and reconstituting itself as a fighting force determined to ensure its survival and return home—*Anabasis* presents Xenophon as the architect of this new resolve, himself spurred to action by an admonitory dream.[a] This looks so very Homeric, very like the problematic attempt by Agamemnon to stir the Achaeans to action after the departure of Achilles in Book 2 of the Iliad:[b] a dream, followed by a call to action, and even the timely punishment of a dubious scapegoat figure that follows in both Xenophon and Homer.[c]

§14. It is natural to assume that one of Xenophon's reasons for telling this story in the third person—indeed, the main one—was to avoid the odium of praising himself, a fear all Greeks had, and a motive that is cited by Plutarch when explaining Xenophon's decision to go with a third-person narrator in *Anabasis*.[a] This explanation gains further plausibility if in *Anabasis* Xenophon had apologetic aims: he wanted to defend himself and his actions. You don't have to be a lawyer to know the difference between third-person testimony and first-person assertion.

§15. But these explanations get us only so far. They are not sufficient, to my mind, to account for the scale of what Xenophon attempted in *Anabasis*. No other expressly apologetic work from antiquity is anywhere near the size of *Anabasis*. Rather, it is quite literally a personal history of the Ten Thousand. It would not have taken much for even a fairly dim reader to make the connection between Xenophon

N.12a  On Cyrus the Younger, see Appendix W: Brief Biographies, §10. Western Anatolia: Ref. Map 4.1, BY. Thrace: Ref. Map 3.

N.12b  For more on Aratus and Augustus, see Ancient Sources Cited in this Edition. Chios: Ref. Map 4.2, CX. Thasos: Ref. Map 3, DX. Sicyon: Ref. Map 2, CY.

N.13a  Xenophon's dream: 3.1.11–14.

N.13b  Agamemnon stirs the Achaeans to action: Homer, *Iliad* 2.16ff.

N.13c  In *Anabasis* (3.1.32) Apollonides is driven away from the army; in the *Iliad* (2.265ff.) Thersites is punished by Odysseus.

N.14a  Odium of self-praise: for example, Demosthenes, *On the Crown* 3. Reason for third-person narration: Plutarch, *Moralia* 345e.

the author of *Anabasis*, Xenophon its narrator, and Xenophon its main historical agent. To be sure, Xenophon himself created something of a smokescreen in *Hellenika* when, at 3.1.2, he attributed an account of the Ten Thousand to one "Themistogenes of Syracuse"; but this deception, if a deception it was, would have deceived no one—it certainly didn't fool Plutarch (as shown in the passage cited in §14). Insofar as *Anabasis* is a historical narrative told, at least from Book 3 onward, primarily through the thinking and action of one man of almost heroic stature—Xenophon—we can see it as an important precursor to histories produced only a few years later that were centered on the careers of great kings of Macedon: the lost *Philippika* of Theopompus and the numerous lost histories of Alexander the Great (by Callisthenes, Ptolemy, Aristobulus, and Cleitarchus, for instance). One (much later) historian of Alexander, Arrian of Nicomedia, writing in the second century C.E., even titled his history *Anabasis Alexandrou*, the "*Anabasis of Alexander*"—the account of another hero's expedition "up country" and back in Persian territory, on a much larger scale and with much greater consequences, to be sure, but nonetheless similar in some ways also to Xenophon's story, as the title announces.[a]

§16. In connection with famous and idealized leaders, it is important to see that, as in *Hellenika*, in *Anabasis* there is a distinct focus on what constitutes good and bad leadership. In the first book, we have the paradigm of Cyrus; in the first and second books, the several Greek unit commanders receive summarizing capsule biographies at the notice of their deaths.[a] Throughout the bulk of the remaining books, we see Xenophon, naturally, providing noteworthy leadership at several points, as well as moments when individuals signally fail (notably Kleairetos and Neon).[b] We are even treated to moments when junior officers achieve great things for the benefit of the whole army and places where heroic accomplishment and a "beautiful" death are recorded, almost in Homeric fashion, with a brief death notice.[c]

§17. It is important also to see that there is a strong political component in the story Xenophon's *Anabasis* tells—namely, of the growth and decay of an idealized community: the Ten Thousand themselves, a "*polis* on the move." Now, it would be folly to allege that Herodotus and Thucydides did not have a strong political focus in their historiography: one has only to look at Herodotus' famous Constitutional Debate (3.80–82) and numerous passages from Thucydides (for example, the Mytilenian Debate at 3.36–49, the Melian Dialogue at 5.84–111, or the extensive analysis of the Oligarchy of the Four Hundred within the narrative of its rise and fall at 8.45–98) to see how their works could be read as politico-philosophical treatises as well as histories. But even so, these authors do not permit political analysis and speculation to shape their texts in quite the same way Xenophon has done in *Anabasis*. The narrative of the successes and failures of the Ten Thousand, under the leadership of Xenophon and others, can be read as a profoundly political story—a study, really, of self-governance, leadership, and collective action. As such, it can

N.15a   Arrian's *Anabasis Alexandrou* survives and has been translated in Romm 2010; that volume's Appendix A: Arrian's Sources and Reliability deals with Arrian's predecessors. Nicomedia: Ref. Map 4.1, AY.

N.16a   Cyrus: 1.9. Capsule biographies: 2.6.
N.16b   Kleairetos: 5.7.14–16. Neon: 6.4.23–26.
N.16c   Achievements of junior officers: for example, 4.7.10–12. Death notices: 4.1.18, 4.7.13–14.

be connected not just to similar elements in the writing of such historians as Theopompus and Polybius but even to such philosophical authors as Plato and Aristotle. Indeed, Xenophon's own *Kyroupaideia* (*The Education of Cyrus*), *Hieron*, *Hipparchikos* (*Cavalry Commander*), and *Poroi* (*Ways and Means*) can all be said to have some overlap with his political thinking in *Anabasis*. It is good to remember in this context that to many in antiquity, Xenophon was first a philosopher and only secondarily a historian.[a]

John Dillery
Professor of Classics
University of Virginia
Charlottesville

---

N.17a See, for instance, Quintilian, *Institutio Oratoria* (*Training in Oratory*) 10.1.75.

# APPENDIX O

### *Ancient Greek and Persian Units of Measurement*

§1. In Xenophon's time, different-sized units of measurement were used by Greeks, Persians, and the other peoples living in different regions of the Mediterranean and southwestern Asian world (the geographical setting for *Anabasis*). This had been true for as far back as our archaeological and historical records extend.[a] A variety of ancient sources provide information concerning these ancient units, but the different standards in use in different locations and the disconcerting fact that at least some of these standards were changed over time can make it difficult to reach secure conclusions about the units mentioned in a particular text. Despite scholars' ongoing efforts, the state of our knowledge remains largely as uncertain as an eminent archaeologist described it as long ago as 1952 in her study of balance weights excavated at ancient Corinth: "Although literary and archaeological evidence is abundant [for ancient weights and measures], the results are generally confusing and often baffling."[b] Therefore, it is important to be aware that different modern reference works can provide different absolute values for the same ancient units; the table at the end of this appendix must be read with this limitation in mind.

## Distance

§2. Greek and other Mediterranean and Southwest Asian units for measuring distance were originally based on assumed lengths of parts of the human body, as the Roman architect and engineer Vitruvius noted: "The calculations of the units of measure, which are seen to be necessary in all [building] projects, are drawn from the parts of the human body, as the finger, the palm, the foot, the cubit."[a] The first surviving specification of Greek units of distance comes in the fifth-century historian Herodotus' description of the two pyramids standing in the middle of Lake Moeris

---

O.1a The Greeks mostly derived their standards of weight, for example, from those of the older civilizations of the eastern Mediterranean. Mediterranean Sea, Mesopotamia: Ref. Map 1, CX, BY.

O.1b Davidson 1952, 203. Corinth: Ref. Map 2, CY.
O.2a Units of measure derived from human body: Vitruvius *De Architectura* (*On Architecture*) 3.1.5 (author's translation).

383

FIGURE O.4. THIS METROLOGICAL TRIANGULAR STONE SLAB CARVED IN RELIEF SHOWS STANDARD DIMENSIONS FOR A MEASUREMENT OF THE FOOT, THE PALM, THE FINGER (INCH), A FATHOM (OUTSTRETCHED ARMS), AND A CUBIT (ELBOW TO FINGERTIP). SCHOLARS AGREE THAT IT WAS PROBABLY CARVED SOMETIME BETWEEN 460 AND 430. ITS PROVENANCE IS UNKNOWN.

in Egypt: "One hundred fathoms equal just a stade or 6 *plethra;* the length of a fathom is equal to 6 feet or 4 cubits; 4 palms equal 1 foot, and 6 palms equal 1 cubit."[b] Xenophon in his *Anabasis* refers to five of these Greek units of distance, namely the **stade** (*stadion:* first at 1.4.1), the **plethron** (plural *plethra;* a measure of 100 feet: first at 1.2.5), the **fathom** (*orguia,* from the tips of the fingers of one outstretched arm to those of the other: first at 1.7.14), the **cubit** (*pēchus,* from the elbow to the tips of the fingers: first at 4.2.28), and the **foot** (*pous:* first at 1.2.8).[c]

§3. The relationships between these Greek units of distance were as follows:[a]

$$
\begin{aligned}
1 \text{ foot} &= 16 \text{ fingers or 4 palms} \\
1 \text{ cubit} &= 24 \text{ fingers or 1.5 feet} \\
1 \text{ fathom} &= 6 \text{ feet or 4 cubits} \\
1 \ plethron &= 100 \text{ feet or 16.67 fathoms} \\
1 \text{ stade} &= 600 \text{ feet or 6 } plethra
\end{aligned}
$$

§4. Scholars have calculated absolute values for Greek units of distance from the lengths of the distance between the start and finish lines in running tracks in ancient Greek athletic stadiums; the dimensions and construction marks of surviving buildings, especially on the Acropolis in Athens;[a] the depiction of length standards related to the male body carved on surviving metrological relief sculptures (see Figure O.4); and ancient builders' measuring tools.

O.2b  Herodotus 2.149 (Purvis/Landmark translation). Lake Moeris, Egypt: Ref. Map 1, DX.
O.2c  All distances in the *Anabasis* text have been converted to their US equivalents. US and metric equivalents of all the units discussed in this appendix can be found in the table in §23.
O.3a  Herodotus also provides information on the ratios between various units of distance at 2.6, 2.9, 4.41, 4.86, 5.53, 6.42.
O.4a  Acropolis: the citadel or high point of a city. For more, see the Glossary. Athens: Ref. Map 2, CZ.

§5. To indicate distances Xenophon frequently cites the **stade**, which Herodotus explicitly equates with 600 feet/about 183 meters.[a] This unit was apparently the distance established for a traditional footrace in Greek athletic contests, but the absolute length of the stade is as unclear as ever. It has been shown that ancient writers were often as uncertain as modern ones about the absolute length of the stade, and indeed excavations on the Peloponnese have shown that at Halieis it equaled 546 feet/166 meters, while at Olympia it measured 631 feet/192 meters.[b] Xenophon does not specify the standard for the foot that he is using; however, since he was an Athenian, it seems plausible that he is referring to the length of the foot often assumed to have been a standard at ancient Athens,[c] the so-called **Attic foot**. The absolute length of this foot remains a subject of disagreement among scholars. Many think that it was 11.7 inches/296 millimeters, the same as the length deduced from archaeological evidence for the Roman foot, while others calculate that the Attic foot equaled approximately 12.1 inches/308 millimeters.

§6. Xenophon also refers to longer measures of distance.[a] The *stathmos* (plural *stathmoi;* literally "station") was a Greek term that meant (among other things) a stopping place or lodging for animals and people. When Xenophon uses the term in *Anabasis,*[b] it refers to a single day's march and it is translated accordingly in this edition.[c] Earlier, Herodotus used the term to refer to royal stations with guesthouses maintained for messengers and other official travelers as they made the long trip along the so-called Royal Road of the Persian Empire that connected western Anatolia with the imperial headquarters in what is today central Iran.[d] Presumably, these stations were intended to provide overnight accommodation and were therefore established a day's journey from each other; the actual distance between them must have varied depending on the terrain and where the best location was, within the right range, to build appropriate accommodation. That the absolute distance between stations varied is implied by the figures that Herodotus gives at 5.52–53 in describing the distances between locations along the Royal Road, which he indicates both by the number of stations separating them and by the number of parasangs (on which see §§7–8). The ratios of parasang to station that he lists vary from 3.7 to 5.2. This suggests that the distance between stations could vary by up to 40 percent (assuming that the parasang was a fixed unit of distance—but see §§7–8 for doubts about this).

§7. The **parasang** was a Persian measure (*parasaggēs*) that is, however, so far attested

O.5a  Equivalence between stade and 600 feet: Herodotus 2.149.
O.5b  The source for these figures is Romano 1993, 17. The following locations appear on Ref. Map 2: Halieis, Peloponnese, CY; Olympia, CX.
O.5c  Athens: Ref. Map 2, CZ.
O.6a  For the disputed issue of how Xenophon came up with the figures that he gives, see the Introduction, §7.
O.6b  The first instance is at 1.2.5.
O.6c  Editors' note: Xenophon habitually groups together several *stathmoi* or days' marches and gives the location of the opening and closing stopping places, several days' march apart, without necessarily saying anything about points in between. Often but not always the stopping places Xenophon singles out are where the army paused for some time or where it reached some territorial marker such as a major river or tribal border. Xenophon himself does not use any generic term for these inflection points on the journey, but in this edition they are referred to in the editorial material as "Halting places" and marked with numbers on the route maps.
O.6d  Herodotus 5.52. Royal Road: Ref. Map 9. Iran: Ref. Map 8, BZ. Anatolia: Ref. Map 1, BX.

for the Achaemenid period only in Greek sources.[a] Xenophon uses it at 1.2.5 (and in many other places) to refer to the length of man-made constructions, the distance between armies, and, above all, the length of journeys and marches. Scholars continue to dispute whether the parasang signifies the distance traversed in a unit of time or a distance representing an extent of measured space. Herodotus states that 1 parasang was equal in distance to 30 stades.[b] He therefore evidently regarded the parasang as a spatially measured distance.[c] Some later Greek writers agree with Herodotus' reckoning, but seriously conflicting reports on the absolute distance of the parasang also exist. The geographer Strabo says that different sources variously equated the parasang with lengths of 30, 40, and 60 stades,[d] while the Roman writer Pliny reports that the Persians had different lengths for the parasang.[e] Some modern scholars argue that the parasang was a measure of time—namely the distance that infantrymen could march in an hour.[f] Also of note is that the name of the modern Persian unit of distance, the *farsang* or *farsakh*, recalls that of the parasang, and that this unit is generally reckoned at about 3.7 miles/6 kilometers. The view of the parasang taken in this volume is that it was a partly time-based measure, which is to say that its value was dependent on the nature of the landscape being traversed. So in harsh terrain such as desert wadis or mountains we expect to see high parasang figures relative to the actual distance.[g]

§8. Xenophon uses the parasang to indicate distances some fifty or more times in the first four books of *Anabasis*.[a] One difficulty with assuming that the parasang was a unit of a fixed amount in Xenophon is that this assumption, it has been argued, yields calculations of distance in his account that seem not to reflect accurately the actual distances involved. For example, at 1.2.19–20 Xenophon reports that Cyrus' army marched 30 parasangs from Iconium, the last city in Phrygia, through Lycaonia and then 25 parasangs through Cappadocia to Dana.[b] Some scholars[c] maintain that the former distance is actually some 28 miles/45 kilometers shorter than the latter. But others are less sure that we know enough of the precise routes to use them to undermine the notion of the parasang as a fixed unit.[d] And indeed three passages in *Anabasis* (2.2.6, 5.5.4, 7.8.26) speak for a more-or-less exact equivalence

O.7a   On the Achaemenid dynasty of Persian kings, see the Glossary.
O.7b   Herodotus 2.6, 5.53, 6.42.
O.7c   Tim Rood (Rood 2010b, 53) has suggested that Herodotus' phrasing at 5.53 indicates that he knew of alternate absolute distances ascribed to the parasang.
O.7d   Strabo 11.11.5.
O.7e   Pliny, *Natural History* 6.124.
O.7f   As Christopher Tuplin points out (Tuplin 1997, 404), one issue making it difficult to understand how the parasang could have been linked to the hour as a unit of time is that the length of the hour as calculated in antiquity varied according to the amount of daylight throughout the year. He also notes (on p. 415) that there is no ancient evidence for the interpretation of the parasang as a measurement of an hour's journey.
O.7g   Also see the Introduction, §7.4.
O.8a   The first instance occurs at 1.2.5.
O.8b   For this part of the route, see Map 1.2.13: Ico-

nium–Dana, *Halting places 10–12;* the unnamed point 30 parasangs from Iconium and 25 from Dana is labeled "Army divides," *Halting place 11.* Lycaonia, CX; Cappadocia, BY; Phrygia (Greater Phrygia), AX. On Cyrus the Younger, see Appendix W: Brief Biographies of Selected Characters in *Anabasis*, §10.
O.8c   Williams 1996, 285.
O.8d   Tricia King (King 1988) believes that this particular topography is not sufficiently well identified to make precise calculations and that Xenophon's measurements of distance, where they can be reliably checked on the ground, fall within an acceptable margin of error for calculations based on the parasang as a fixed unit. Note also that in the maps in this edition, the somewhat controversial view is taken that the army took the long way south of Mount Boratinon (Map 1.2.13, AX) rather than a more direct route; according to this view, the problem here would not arise.

between the parasang and 30 stades, but these passages are generally regarded by editors as interpolated by later scribes.[e] Thus the nature of the parasang in *Anabasis* remains uncertain, but the terrain-based theory offers perhaps the most plausible basis for reconciling the evidence.

**Currency**

§9. Greek currency consisted of coins (there were no bills) minted in gold, silver, or bronze. Greeks identified their coinages by images (called "types" in numismatics) and inscriptions ("legends") on the coins, but these pictorial and written messages often lacked any indication of a particular coin's value as currency; users were expected to know, or find out for themselves, how much each piece of currency was worth. Scholars estimate that approximately 95 percent of the transactional value of ancient gold and silver coins minted by a public authority came from the intrinsic, bullion value of the precious metal in each coin. The remaining 5 percent of the value came from the implicit guarantee that the authority issuing the coins would enforce their acceptance as legal tender in its home region; that is, possessors of coins could be confident that they could use this currency in financial transactions and that sellers had to accept this money and could not legally demand an alternate (and more costly to the buyer) medium of payment. The issuing authority of official coinage was identified by the types and (sometimes) the legends stamped onto coins. Bronze coins, which had much less intrinsic value, were used as small change, circulating almost exclusively in the region where they were minted and being exchanged at rates established by the government. Bronze coinage was therefore essentially a form of fiduciary local currency.

§10. For calculating large sums of money, Greeks used units of accounting called the **mina** (first mentioned in *Anabasis* at 1.4.13) and the **talent** (first mentioned at 2.3.20). The terms "mina" and "talent" could designate both monetary values and weight. The modern equivalences of ancient Greek weight standards can be established, at least in part, from the study of surviving standardized units, such as molded and (sometimes) inscribed and sculpted pieces of metal. A mina was a unit of 100 drachmas (see §11), which on the Attic standard would amount to about 430 grams/15 ounces[a] or perhaps a bit more. On the heavier Aeginetan standard (named after the Greek city-state on the island of Aegina[b]), a mina weighed approximately 615 grams/22 ounces. A Greek talent was a unit of 6,000 drachmas (equal to 60 minas), which on the Attic standard would weigh about 25.8 to 25.9 kilograms/56.9 to 57.1 pounds; this weight for the talent was the same on the Euboic standard (named after the island of Euboea).[c] Therefore this standard is sometimes referred to as the Euboic-Attic standard.

§11. The monetary values of the talent and the mina are most easily quantified by reference to the numbers of **drachmas** to which they were equivalent. The term

---

O.8e    This edition follows the opinion of most editors that the passages are interpolated. See nn. 2.2.6d, 5.5.4c, 7.8.26b for further discussion.

O.10a    Modern numismatists use metric weights, so those, rather than US weights, are given first here.

O.10b    Aegina: Ref. Map 2, CZ.

O.10c    Euboea: Ref. Map 2, BZ.

FIGURE O.13. ACHAEMENID GOLD
DARIC DEPICTING GREAT KING WITH
SPEAR, FOURTH CENTURY.

"drachma" (meaning "handful") designated a commonly minted silver coin (and also a unit of weight). The drachma (not mentioned in *Anabasis*) was the equivalent of 6 silver **obols**. Xenophon in *Anabasis* mentions the obol, but only once, along with the half obol (1.5.6). Since a drachma on the Attic standard weighed on average 4.3 grams/0.15 ounce, an obol was a tiny coin, weighing less than a gram.

§12. Xenophon refers (at 5.6.23 and elsewhere) to a Greek denomination in electrum (an alloy of silver and gold) known as a **Cyzicene statēr**. (The Greek word *statēr*, meaning literally "weight," indicates a currency system's largest denomination.) Weighing an average of about 16.1 grams/0.57 ounce each, "Cyzicenes" were named after Cyzicus, a city-state on the shore of the southern part of the Propontis.[a] They became an important trade currency in Greece and western Anatolia.[b] The best estimate is that 1 Cyzicene had a value that ranged (depending on local exchange rates) from approximately 21 drachmas and 4 obols to 28 drachmas on the Attic standard.

§13. At 1.5.6 Xenophon makes his only reference (and indeed the only extant undisputed reference in Classical Greek literature) to a Persian denomination in silver known to Greeks as a *siglos* (plural *sigloi*), which weighed about 5.6 grams/0.2 ounce. Xenophon more frequently (1.1.9 and elsewhere) mentions another, much more valuable Persian denomination, the **daric**; the term "daric" usually indicates a gold coin.[a] The Greeks thought the name derived from that of the Persian king Darius I (r. 522–486), though it seems more likely that it comes from a Persian word meaning "golden." In Xenophon's time this gold coin weighed about 8.4 grams/0.3 ounce.

§14. Gold coins were naturally the most valuable pieces of currency. Their high value made it easier to use them to pay large lump sums, as, for example, the cumulative pay for several months' service by mercenaries if paid all at once on a single

---

O.12a  Cyzicus, Propontis: Ref. Map 4.2, AY. Propontis: Ref. Map 4.1, AY. See Figure 5.6.23 for an example of a Cyzicene stater.

O.12b  Western Anatolia: Ref. Map 4.1.

O.13a  Silver as well as gold darics are mentioned in Plutarch, *Life of Cimon* 10.

occasion or to make an expensive purchase, such as a fine horse—one is said to have fetched 50 darics![a] Herodotus calculates the ratio of value between gold and silver in his time as 13 to 1.[b] On the weight system of Persian coinage in use at that point, 1 gold daric was equal in value to 20 silver *sigloi*. So as Xenophon says at 1.5.6 that a *siglos* was equal in value to 7.5 Attic obols, that is, 1.25 drachmas, that would make a daric worth 150 obols or 25 drachmas.[c]

§15. In *Anabasis* the usual monthly rate of pay for rank-and-file mercenaries is either a gold daric or a Cyzicene, while officers received double or quadruple that amount, depending on rank.[a] The implication, therefore, is that these two denominations were roughly equivalent in value. Since, however, the exchange ratio between gold and electrum varied regionally, soldiers would have preferred to have been paid in whichever currency had a higher value in the region where they intended to spend their wages. When the mercenaries who survived the grueling march up-country finally reached the Black Sea region, Xenophon reports that certain locals offered them pay of a Cyzicene stater a month to sail away (and leave their territory unharmed).[b] Pay in this currency represented an attractive choice for an international contingent of mercenaries who found themselves in what amounted to a monetary zone in the Black Sea region where Cyzicenes were particularly valuable, since electrum tended to trade at a higher value with respect to gold in western Anatolia.

§16. The only meaningful way to measure the value of ancient money in its own time is to compare wages and prices. Since wages and prices in antiquity were as variable over time and space as they are today, generalizations about them cannot be authoritative. The best-documented evidence for prices and wages in everyday circumstances in ancient Greece comes from Athens in the fifth and fourth centuries. During the earlier fifth century, a worker in Athens could expect to earn perhaps 2 obols per day; by the end of the century, in the conditions of the Peloponnesian War, some could receive a drachma (6 obols) as a daily wage. Enough barley (a dietary staple for most people that was somewhat cheaper than wheat) to feed a family of five for a day's meals cost 1/48 of a drachma, while a gallon of olive oil went for 3 drachmas. Consumers paid 5 to 20 drachmas for a cloak and 6 to 8 drachmas for a pair of shoes.[a]

§17. The context of Xenophon's *Anabasis* is, however, not everyday circumstances but, rather, the extraordinary situation of a mercenary army on the march and at war in hostile territory. Thucydides' description of the siege of Poteidaia in 428 contains the earliest extant reference to a precise rate of pay for hoplites, some of

O.14a  On a single occasion: 1.2.11. Horse fetches 50 darics: 7.8.6.

O.14b  Gold/silver ratio: Herodotus 3.95.

O.14c  *Anabasis* 1.7.18, where Cyrus richly rewards the seer Silanos for a successful prophecy, arguably provides a problem for this conclusion, since it seems to equate 10 talents with 3,000 darics, which at 6,000 drachmas to the Attic talent would suggest that a daric was worth 20 drachmas rather than 25. But as the giver is Cyrus, the talent here may not be the Attic talent but the denomination that played an equivalent part in the Persian system. The Persian name for this is not known, but there is other evidence that it was heavier than the Attic talent.

O.15a  Soldiers paid a gold daric per month: 1.3.21, 7.6.1. Soldiers paid a Cyzicene per month: 5.6.23; see also 7.2.36, 7.3.10 (period not explicit). Officers paid multiples: 7.2.36, 7.6.1.

O.15b  Offer of a Cyzicene stater a month: 5.6.23. Black Sea: Ref. Map 1, AX.

O.16a  Loomis 1998, 259–320, conveniently tabulates the specific evidence from Classical Athens.

whom, it has been argued, were mercenaries:[a] these soldiers each received 1 drachma per day for themselves and 1 for their attendant (*hypēretēs*). This rate was apparently high; in 413 the Athenians sent home as too costly the Thracian mercenaries whom they had agreed to remunerate with 1 drachma per day.[b] In a treaty among several city-states made in 420, Thucydides reports that a lower rate of pay was set for hoplites and other infantrymen:[c] 3 Aeginetan obols (equals 4.5 Attic obols or 0.75 drachma) per day.

§18. As previously mentioned, Xenophon records that the nonofficer mercenaries in Cyrus' army were originally hired at a rate of 1 daric per month. The prince, however, had to promise to raise their wages by 50 percent once the soldiers realized that he intended to lead them all the way to the Euphrates River.[a] If a daric was the equivalent of 25 Attic drachmas (see §14) and a month was reckoned at thirty days, then the daily rate of pay was 5 obols per day.[b] How far the pay of Cyrus' mercenaries went toward providing them with a decent subsistence is hard to say. Scholars' opinions on the value of this rate of pay range from "low" to "not bad." The mercenaries' best hopes for financial gain from their service apparently lay in obtaining booty and bonuses.

§19. The troops most likely had to provide the majority of their own food; the commander's responsibility was apparently only to make sure that markets were available at which the men could purchase supplies. It has been estimated that, on average, a soldier needed to spend about 2 obols or a bit more per day on food to maintain his normal level of activity. The prices charged by the merchants selling to the soldiers could be exorbitant: in the one such instance that Xenophon documents (1.5.6), the asking price for wheat and barley meal—based on the information on currency and units of capacity that he records in this passage—works out to the equivalent of 120 Attic drachmas per *medimnos* (a unit of capacity; see §20).[a] The usual price for this amount of grain in Athens in the early fourth century seems to have been in the range of 5 to 6 drachmas. As Xenophon reports, the soldiers, when faced with this famine-level price for their preferred staple, had to subsist on meat, which was evidently (and unusually) cheaper in their current circumstances, perhaps because they relied on hunting or on slaughtering some pack animals. As for the mercenaries' equipment, it is not clear what they had to supply on their own and what Cyrus provided for them; it may well be that the troops had to provide most or even all of their weapons and armor from their own resources.

## Capacity

§20. Xenophon in *Anabasis* mentions units of capacity on Greek and Persian standards. As with other ancient units of measurement, we cannot be sure of the precise absolute values of these units. In describing amounts of barley at 6.1.15 and

O.17a  Precise pay for hoplites: Thucydides 3.17.4.
Hoplites: heavily armed infantrymen; see Appendix H: Infantry and Cavalry in *Anabasis*, §§2–3. Poteidaia: Ref. Map 2, AY.
O.17b  Thracians too costly: Thucydides 7.27.2. Thrace: Ref. Map 3.
O.17c  Lower rate: Thucydides 5.47.6.
O.18a  Euphrates River: Ref. Map 5, CZ.

O.18b  Polybius reports (6.39.12) that, two hundred years later, a Roman infantry soldier was paid 2 obols per day, a centurion 4 obols, and a cavalryman 1 drachma or 6 obols.
O.19a  Using Persian units equated with Greek units, Xenophon says that 2 *choinikes* (see §20) of grain cost 30 Attic obols, which amounts to 120 drachmas per *medimnos*.

6.2.3, he refers to the large Greek dry measure called a ***medimnos*** (plural *medimnoi*), which was approximately 51.5 liters; an American bushel, by comparison, is about 35 liters. Polybius reports that a Roman soldier received as his food ration "about two thirds of an Attic *medimnos* of wheat" a month, while a cavalryman got 7 *medimnoi* of wheat and 2 of barley.[a] Xenophon also mentions the smaller dry measure called a ***choinix*** (plural *choinikes*), at 1.5.6 and 7.3.23; the latter passage refers to a "triple *choinix.*" One *choinix* equaled ¹⁄₄₈ of a *medimnos* and therefore a little more than 1.8 pints/1 liter in volume. Some idea of what this quantity of grain represented in terms of nutrition can be gleaned from Herodotus' statement that a *choinix* of wheat represented a daily ration for one person.[b] Finally, at 1.5.6 Xenophon refers to a Persian measure (*kapīč*), which the Greeks called a ***kapithē***; he explicitly equates it with 2 (Attic) *choinikes*, while the calculations of the second-century C.E. military writer Polyaenus make it the equivalent of 1 *choinix.*[c] The evidence from Persian sources is not sufficiently clear to resolve this discrepancy with certainty.

§21. The Greek liquid measure that Xenophon mentions at 6.1.15 and 6.2.3, referring to amounts of wine, is a ***keramion*** (plural *keramia*). However, he does not specify a quantity for the term, which literally means "container made from clay" and is translated in this edition as "jar of wine." Scholars assume that whatever its exact quantity, it was less than that of a ***metrētēs*** (plural *metrētai;* equals 12 *choes*). Neither of these measures is mentioned in *Anabasis*, but their size is clearer to us than that of the *keramion:* the *metrētēs* was a measure amounting to perhaps some 10.3 gallons/39 liters. If a *keramion* was equivalent to 8 ***choes*** (singular *chous*) as has been suggested in a discussion of a fourth-century text,[a] then it would be approximately 7 gallons/26 liters.

§22. Although the word does not appear in *Anabasis*, mention should also be made of the ***kotulē*** (plural *kotulai*), a unit that is referred to by Plutarch in a passage from his *Life of Artaxerxes*.[a] There were 144 *kotulai* in a *metrētēs*, so at 10.4 gallons/39.39 liters to a *metrētēs*, a *kotulē* would amount to about 270 milliliters, or rather more than half a US pint.

Thomas R. Martin
Department of Classics
College of the Holy Cross
Worcester, Massachusetts

O.20a   Roman soldier's food ration: Polybius 6.39.13.
O.20b   *Choinix* of wheat one day's food ration: Herodotus 7.187.2. Triple *choinix:* translated in this edition as 3 quarts; see n. 7.3.23b.
O.20c   *Kapithē* equals 1 *choinix:* Polyaenus *Strategemata* 4.3.32 (using a variant spelling *kapizē*).
O.21a   Hypothesis that 1 *keramion* equals 8 *choes:* Pritchett and Pippin 1956, 201, discussing

[Demosthenes] *Oration* 35, §§10, 18.
O.22a   *Kotulē:* Plutarch, *Life of Artaxerxes* 12.3 (in Appendix T: Selections from Plutarch's *Life of Artaxerxes*).

## §23. Units of Measurement in *Anabasis* and Their Modern Equivalents

### Distance

| | |
|---|---|
| foot (*pous*) | = 11.6 or 12.1 inches = 296 or 308 millimeters |
| cubit (*pēchus*) | = 17.5 or 18.2 inches = 444 or 462 millimeters |
| fathom (*orguia*) | = 5.8 or 6.1 feet = 1.78 or 1.85 meters |
| *plethron* | = 97.1 or 101 feet = 29.6 or 30.8 meters |
| stade (*stadion*) | = 600 feet |
| | = 6 plethra |
| | = 584 or 607 feet = 178 or 185 meters |
| parasang (Persian, *parasaggēs*) | = 30 stades[a] |

### Currency and Weight

| | |
|---|---|
| 6 obols | = 1 drachma = 0.7 grams = 0.25 ounce |
| drachma | = 4.3 grams = 0.15 ounce |
| *siglos* | = 5.6 grams = 0.2 ounce |
| daric | = 8.4 grams = 0.3 ounce |
| Cyzicene stater | = 16.1 grams = 0.57 ounce |
| mina | = 100 drachmas |
| | = 430 grams = 15.68 ounces = 0.94 pound |
| talent | = 6,000 drachmas = 60 minas |
| | = 25.8 to 25.9 kilograms = 56.88 to 57.10 pounds |

### Capacity (Dry)

| | |
|---|---|
| *choinix* | = $\frac{1}{48}$ *medimnos* |
| | = 0.98 quart = 1.08 liters |
| *kapithē* | = 1.96 quarts = 2.16 liters (?) |
| *medimnos* | = 11.46 US bushels = 51.5 liters |

### Capacity (Liquid)

| | |
|---|---|
| *kotulē* | = 0.57 pint = 270 milliliters |
| *keramion* | = 5.7 gallons (?) = 26 liters (?) |

NOTE: As explained in §1, all these equivalences must be regarded as approximate. Allowing for the difference in scholarly opinion discussed in §5, the first metric equivalence listed in each row of this table is calculated at 1 Attic foot = 296 millimeters/0.296 meter, the second at 1 Attic foot = 308 millimeters/0.308 meter. The question marks indicate where the evidence leaves even greater room for uncertainty than in the other cases, where the order of magnitude may be regarded as certain even if the precise equivalents are not.

O.23a According to Herodotus (see §7); for the parasang as instead being terrain-based and therefore of no fixed distance, see the Introduction, §7.3–5.

# APPENDIX P

## *The Route of the Ten Thousand*

§1. Arrian begins his *Periplus*, a report of a journey along the Black Sea coast written for the emperor Hadrian in the 130s C.E., with his arrival at Trapezus and a reference to Xenophon's sighting of the sea with the Ten Thousand.[a] We learn that earlier Hadrian, too, had stood and looked out at the sea "from the same spot" as Xenophon had, and that a statue of the emperor pointing toward the sea had been set up.[b] Although Arrian and Hadrian may have been among the first to seek out locations from the march, they were not the first who in the course of their journeys called the Ten Thousand to mind: Alexander the Great and Mark Antony had done likewise, a testimony to the power that the story held in antiquity.[c] A later, notable phase of interest in the expedition came in the eighteenth and nineteenth centuries, when antiquarians and travelers began to search for evidence of the Classical past. As regards Xenophon and his men, an objective for many was to stand on the very spot from where the army saw the sea, named by Xenophon as Mount Theches. Yet while locating Theches has arguably been the outstanding quest for investigators of the route, there are a number of other uncertainties and problems surrounding it, and in this appendix I look at some of the most important of these. I begin with an overview of the process behind uncovering the army's tracks, turning then to examine specific route issues, including the identity of Mount Theches.

§2. The general course of the route taken by the Ten Thousand on their long march is well known.[a] Beginning at Sardis, in western Anatolia, they cross the south-

P.1a  Arrian of Nicomedia, an ethnic Greek, was an outstanding politician, military man, and writer of his day. His most famous work is his history of Alexander, *Anabasis Alexandrou*. Nicomedia: Ref. Map 4.1, AY. Black Sea, Trapezus: Map P.3.

P.1b  Hadrian and Xenophon: Arrian, *Periplus* 1.1–3. Arrian is ambiguous, perhaps deliberately, in his opening, where he talks about sighting the sea and the location of the statue of Hadrian. It would perhaps be odd for the said statue to have been set up in the mountains, and some scholars imagine it at a vantage point above the city. For discussion about the true identity of Mt. Theches, see §§11–14.

Map P.3 shows a selection of sites identified by scholars over the years as the mountain.

P.1c  The Ten Thousand remembered: Arrian, *Anabasis Alexandrou* 2.7.8–9; Plutarch, *Life of Antony* 45.6. See further Appendix R: The Legacy of Xenophon's *Anabasis*.

P.2a  Ref. Map 7 shows all the places and rivers named in this paragraph. The journey is often described in terms of an *anabasis*, or march inland (Sardis to Cunaxa, Book 1); *katabasis*, march down-country (Cunaxa to Trapezus, Books 2–4); and *parabasis*, march along the coast (Trapezus to Byzantium, Books 5–6).

ern part of the landmass into Syria and travel down along the Euphrates River to Babylonia; turning northward after the battle with the Persian King, initially along the Tigris River and then via the rugged highlands of historical Armenia, they eventually descend to the Black Sea shore at Trapezus. From there they continue on foot and by ship west along the seacoast to Byzantium, with a winter in European Thrace before the remnants of the army return to Ionia. In his account of the march, Xenophon provides us with a record of their progress and so a means to inscribe a more precise line across the territory traversed. From the outset he supplies information about starting and ending points, distances, and rest days.[b] While not every stage of the route is described in all these terms, the record furnishes enough information to enable most of the way to be approximately retraced. The process of recovering the route involves identifying waymarks named in the text— cities, natural features, territorial boundaries—and joining these up by means of the detail and descriptions given by Xenophon. This task is aided by the fact that, up until the twentieth century and the onset of modern roadbuilding, routes were historically stable, following what we might term an optimal path. We can think of this as having evolved over time from the different possibilities available; changes in political boundaries and physical geography could and would have shifted certain routes, but aside from this, networks were relatively fixed.[c] It bears mention that a weakness of reading route maps is that it may give an impression of certainty, that the army traveled from A to B to C as if part of a planned route, whereas in reality, for much of the time the way ahead was unknown, determined in the end by a combination of factors. Often we are told what these are by Xenophon, but sometimes not.

§3. Although much of the army's route is recoverable, some real uncertainties remain about the location of places named and about how the army got from one named point to the next. One complication is the frequency with which place-names changed: often there is a trail in the historiography or archaeological evidence, but sometimes not. Another factor is that natural features and especially river courses can change markedly over time. The middle course of the Tigris River, for example, is known to have shifted its channel eastward in later antiquity, meaning that a route marked alongside it today would not in fact be the same as that followed by the army on its retreat. A further complication worth emphasizing is that Xenophon, of course, is not immune to errors, so for instance, as is almost certainly the case with Opis and Sittake in central Mesopotamia,[a] locations in the record can be mixed up, making reconstruction harder. But continuing to build knowledge of the route is important as, on the one hand, it serves to help test the veracity of the record, and on the other it brings us nearer to the experience of the march.

§4. Although commentators disagree about several points in the march across Anatolia, arguably the first major challenge in retracing the route comes on the

P.2b   Distances are given in days of march, parasangs, and, occasionally, stades. On these, and in particular for the problem of assigning a value to the parasang, see Appendix O: Ancient Greek and Persian Units of Measurement, §§7–8, and the Introduction, §7.3–5.

P.2c   There is evidence that road networks existed in

Anatolia from at least the Neolithic period; by the third millennium, these are known to have extended beyond the region and were key to commercial and cultural development in the Near East.

P.3a   The following locations appear on Ref. Map 6: Opis, DZ; Sittake, CZ; Mesopotamia, CX.

fringe of Mesopotamia. Leaving the Mediterranean at Myriandos,[a] Cyrus led his army inland toward the Euphrates River, intending to cross into Mesopotamia and then to travel down along the riverbank to Babylonia.[b] The route taken to the river was a frequently used one, if in parts arduous, but thereafter much of it is nonstandard, with a particularly long stretch crossing barren and difficult terrain.[c] However, this was about the quickest way to Cyrus's destination, and as we learn from Xenophon, speed was a vital element in his plan.[d] The problem for modern commentators is the location where Cyrus crossed the Euphrates.

§5. Xenophon names the Euphrates crossing place as Thapsakos, describing it as "a great and prosperous city."[a] Alexander crossed here coming from Phoenicia on his way to hunt down Darius in 331,[b] and the third-century geographer Eratosthenes used Thapsakos as a zero-point for measuring distances to locations throughout Asia.[c] Yet for all its evident significance in Achaemenid[d] and Hellenistic times, it is practically unheard of in later antiquity, and archaeologists have not been able to locate it. Thapsakos, it's worth noting, is not unique in this regard. A number of cities appearing in the historical record of the region remain unidentified, a situation partly explained by a dearth of in situ epigraphic testimony and one compounded in the modern era by the construction of dams on the Euphrates. Our approach has been to try to follow Xenophon's travel figures as closely as possible, taking into account the desert terrain, the nature of the parasang, and settlement history in the area. On this basis it seems to us that the crossing place is more likely to have been on the lower section of the Middle Euphrates, where it turns from a southerly to an easterly course in the Syrian desert. This would have been a more natural transit site for travelers, such as Cyrus and Alexander, coming from the Mediterranean coast.[e] Those coming from central Anatolia, and on the opposite side from northern Mesopotamia, would have naturally centered on the more northerly stretch from Zeugma to Carchemish,[f] which was also a transit zone in ancient times and indeed is favored by some scholars as the likely location of Thapsakos. As to the mystery of its seeming disappearance, it may in fact be right there before our eyes but under a different name. In this regard we can note that Zeugma was founded as Seleucia-on-the-Euphrates but soon after became known as Zeugma ("bridge" in Greek);

P.4a  Mediterranean Sea: Map P.1, locator. Myriandos: Ref. Map 5, CY.
P.4b  Euphrates River, Babylonia: Ref. Map 6, BX, DZ.
P.4c  Difficult terrain: Xenophon, *Anabasis* 1.5.5–8. Arrian fills in for us detail absent in Xenophon about the normal route onward from the river crossing. "When he [Alexander] set out from the Euphrates, he did not take the road that led directly to Babylon, since everything was more practicable for the army on the other road: it was easier to obtain green fodder for the horses and provisions for the men, and the heat was not so intense" (Arrian, *Anabasis Alexandrou* 3.7.3).
P.4d  Speed vital to Cyrus: 1.5.9.
P.5a  See 1.4.11. Thapsakos, possible locations: Map P.1.
P.5b  Arrian, *Anabasis Alexandrou* 3.7.3. After his defeat by Alexander at Issus in 333, Darius fled here with a number of his courtiers (2.13.1). Phoenicia: Map P.1. Issus: Ref. Map 5, CY.

P.5c  The work of Eratosthenes only survives in fragments and is reported here by the geographer Strabo (2.1.24) writing in the early first century C.E.
P.5d  On the Achaemenid (Persian) dynasty, see the Glossary.
P.5e  In *Anabasis* (1.4.9–11) Xenophon marks the distance from Myriandos to Thapsakos at twelve days, while the Roman historian Curtius (*Histories of Alexander* 4.9.12) says Alexander marched eleven days to the Euphrates crossing (from Phoenicia). Arrian (*Anabasis Alexandrou* 3.7.1) tells us that Alexander crossed the Euphrates at Thapsakos, so he was a day quicker than Cyrus. This information favors a lower location for Thapsakos, given that Alexander's departure point from the Mediterranean was well to the south of Xenophon's.
P.5f  Zeugma, Carchemish: Map P.1. Carchemish is not listed in the *Barrington Atlas*.

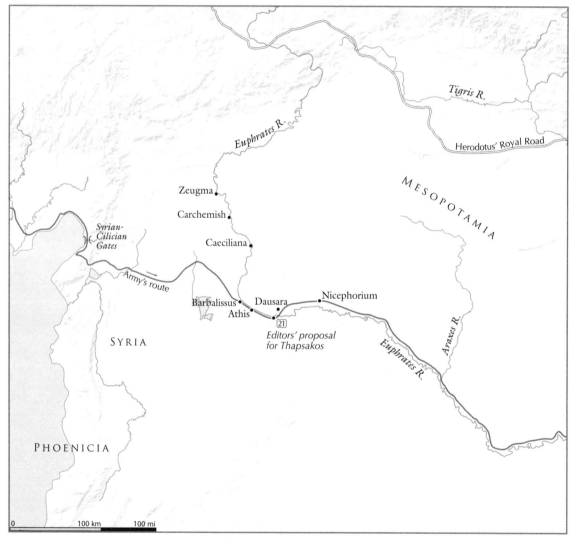

MAP P.1. SOME OF THE POSSIBLE LOCATIONS FOR THAPSAKOS, SITE OF THE EUPHRATES RIVER CROSSING. DIFFERENT LOCATIONS IMPLY DIFFERENT ROUTES FOR CYRUS' ARMY.

Thapsakos (from the Aramaic *tipsha*, "crossing place") might similarly have become Roman Dausara, the site assigned to Thapsakos on our maps.

§6. Rivers, as we'll see, feature prominently as route determiners in the army's retreat to the sea from Babylonia following the battle of Cunaxa.[a] Having realized they could not go back the way they had come, since supplies along the desert stretch of the Euphrates had been exhausted, the Greeks proceeded along the Tigris, coming after several weeks to a road junction, probably in the vicinity of modern Cizre, in southeast Turkey.[b] We are told in *Anabasis* that there were routes going east and west from here, and also one going north into the mountains. West was the way the army would certainly have wanted to go, but as we learn from Xenophon, the depth of the river and the presence of the enemy on the far bank made this crossing impossible.[c] For this reason they pressed on north through the mountains, which, while potentially hostile territory, was not under the control of the King. They believed that once they had crossed them and reached Armenia, they would be able to choose a way westward.[d]

§7. It is striking that when they were actually in Armenia and a westward route presented itself, they did not take it; equally striking is that Xenophon does not explain the reason why they did not follow the seemingly natural course of action, as he did at the Tigris junction. We can identify the area in question as the modern Muş Plain, a vast valley floor cut through by the Euphrates. From the heart of the plain, the army should have sought either to go southwest to the Mediterranean, where ships would be available, or to cross the river and proceed directly into central Anatolia.[a] Instead we can estimate from the distances in the text that they most likely came close to the river, but then changed direction and crossed it some way upstream to the northeast, eventually becoming lost. Xenophon's failure to fully explain the situation on the plain, which was the base of the satrap of Western Armenia, with whom the Greeks had apparently come to an agreement, is an instance of his silence on matters we would very much like to know more about.[b] It could be that some of these omissions are unintentional, an eventuality that speaks against the modern theory that he maintained a diary during the march,[c] while in other cases the author might reasonably expect that his readers would read between the lines and infer from the circumstances what was not spelled out: here, plausibly, that agreements with

P.6a   Battlefield of Cunaxa: Ref. Map 6, DZ.

P.6b   Supplies exhausted: 2.2.11; and see n. P.4c. Tigris road junction (Map 3.5.15)/modern Cizre (Map P.2). This would probably be the junction that Alexander arrived at following his crossing at Thapsakos, so one prospective route for the army would see them go in the opposite direction to him, then retrace their path to Myriandos and the sea.

P.6c   Going west impossible: 3.5.7–12. When Alexander crossed the Tigris in pursuit of Darius in 331, the current made his passage notably difficult (Arrian, *Anabasis Alexandrou* 3.7.5). If this was not at the same place where the retreating Greeks contemplated crossing, it would have been in the same general area.

P.6d   Reasons for northward route: 3.5.17. Armenia: Ref. Map 6, AY.

P.7a   In either case the Greeks would soon have connected with an established routeway; it's even possible that a branch of the Royal Road passed through this area. Its course in this region is disputed. We locate the Royal Road a fair distance farther to the west than the location of the army at this point (see Ref. Map 9 for its course), but an alternative view would have it go from Siirt via the Bitlis Valley and the Muş Plain to modern Bingöl. More generally, we can recall the report of the captives at the crossroads, which emphasized that once in Armenia "it was easy to travel to wherever anyone wanted to make his way" (3.5.17). Bingöl: Ref. Map 8, BY. Muş Plain, Siirt, Bitlis Valley: Map P.2.

P.7b   Agreement reached with satrap: 4.4.5–6. Historical Western Armenia: Map P.2. On satraps (provincial governors), see the Glossary.

P.7c   On whether Xenophon kept a diary, see the Introduction, §7.6–12.

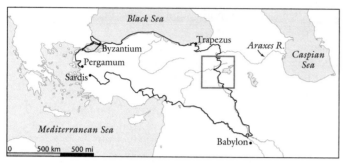

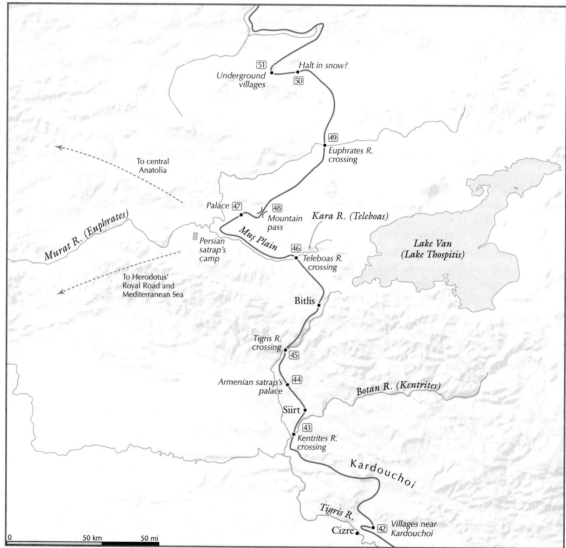

MAP P.2. HISTORICAL WESTERN ARMENIA SHOWING MODERN AND ANCIENT PLACE-NAMES.

the satrap at 4.4.6 compelled them to go the way they did.[d] Others, however, point out that selective silence is part of Xenophon's literary armory, typically deployed when he prefers not to confront a situation or a particular set of circumstances. Here it could be that the Greeks opted not to challenge the Persians to win the best route home, a decision that, in light of the extreme hardships they subsequently endured, and the far greater length of their journey, could have reflected poorly on the leadership, especially if the Persian force had not been a formidable one.

§8. Even though we are not fully informed about what went on in the Muş Plain, we are able to make educated guesses. As emphasized earlier, it's important to keep in mind that the onward direction of the retreat was very often decided by the situation on the ground rather than a planned itinerary. Notably, up until this point, there is no evidence in the text that any real thought had been given to the alternative of traveling northward to the Black Sea. It may be that even as they turned in that direction, the idea was not under consideration, but rather it was assumed that another opportunity to go west would present itself.

§9. A major difficulty with tracing the army's route north beyond the Muş Plain is the lack of geographical detail in the narrative. From its crossing of the Euphrates high up on its course to the arrival at Trapezus on the Black Sea, only one settlement (Gymnias), one mountain (Theches), and two rivers (Phasis, Harpasos) are named.[a] This, together with a lack of general agreement on the identification of these features except for Trapezus, has led to a range of route suggestions for this long stretch: no other part of the journey has so divided scholarly opinion. The lack of regional knowledge on the part of the Greeks that is implied by Xenophon's text would explain why the army needed guides and why they seem to have got lost in the highlands after their Armenian one had run away.[b] The author tells us that they followed the Phasis River for seven days[c] and that they then undertook a two-day march to a mountain pass. This pass would have been on the northern side of the Phasis and probably lay on the watershed of the Black and Caspian Sea basins.[d] What we could infer from this northward turn is that the Greeks had realized that the river they were following flowed into the Caspian Sea, not in the direction in which they now wanted to go. A prominent theory is that, having

P.7d   The objective of the Persians after the battle of Cunaxa must have been to prevent or seriously hamper the return of the Greeks to Ionia (Ref. Map 4.1, CX; Ref. Map 4.2, BX) so that their plight would serve as a warning to future aggressors. Pursuant to this Tiribazos, the satrap, might have indicated that an attempt to go directly southwest, or to cross the river in the vicinity, would be resisted by his forces and those of the neighboring satrap, whereas if the Ten Thousand marched north, they could obtain supplies from tribal areas and would not be at risk of attack from royal forces. The men's desire for booty from these lands should not be underestimated.

P.9a   Euphrates crossing (4.5.2): Map P.2. Phasis River (4.6.4): Ref. Map 6, AY. Harpasos River (4.7.18), Gymnias, possible location (4.7.19), Mount Theches (4.7.21), Trapezus (4.8.22): Map P.3. For these stages of the journey, see also Map 4.7.1, *Halting places 49–61*.

P.9b   Guide: 4.6.1–3. But this region was not as empty as the impression Xenophon gives in his narrative. Infrastructure and settlement in much of the region were well developed since the second millennium. One explanation for Xenophon's approach could be literary, that he sought to reflect a sense of disorientation in the army, another that he wished to omit detail from the account in order to gloss over certain events on the ground, for example, an error on the geography of the river they followed after the guide fled. See further the Introduction, §7.17.

P.9c   Followed Phasis River: 4.6.4.

P.9d   See Map 4.7.1. The relevant pass is labeled "Pass to plain," *Halting place 54*, on the more westerly of the two possible routes shown on the map. It is known today as the Çakirbaba Pass (Ref. Map 8, AZ). The choice between the westerly and easterly routes is discussed in §10. Caspian Sea: Ref. Map 1, AZ.

come to a Phasis River, the army's command took it to be the same as the one in Colchis, which empties into the eastern Black Sea.[e] In fact, the river was most probably the Araxes, though it is conceivable that the branch the Greeks initially picked up was known as the Phasis River:[f] the Phasianoi lived in this region, mostly along the Araxes valley, and it may be that the relevant section of the river carried their name or that the Greeks inferred the name from the presence of the tribe.[g] It was only when they subsequently crossed the watershed, which was held by three of the regional tribes, including the Phasianoi, that they knew they were on track to reach the Black Sea.[h]

§10. Taking account of the difficulties posed by text and landscape in this stretch, in Map 4.7.1 we also show an alternative for the Phasis march, running between route numbers 52 and 55. While the main route illustrated has been selected because the section of it running north from the valley of the Phasis/Araxes is the most natural way for a traveler seeking to reach the Black Sea from the Araxes valley to choose, it leaves the problem that the following march—from the mountain pass to the Taochian fort, as we have identified it[a]—covers much less ground than what Xenophon recorded for the stage at 4.7.1: just 40 miles/64 kilometers when more commonly a stretch of thirty parasangs would work out to around 100 miles. Seeking to fill out the distance given in the text, a number of commentators have taken the Ten Thousand more directly to the Araxes River valley than we have, and then considerably farther to the east along the valley before turning first north and then back west. Although this would mean that the army went very far out of its way and would imply a surprising inability to obtain proper local knowledge from captives, it would be a much better fit for the parasang indications that Xenophon gives for the march from the pass to the Taochian fort. Accordingly we have identified a particular pass on the modern Turkish-Armenian border near Ani as another possibility for the place where the Greeks outflanked the three native tribes.[b] There are no doubt other more or less viable places, but all contenders for the right route come with disadvantages.

§11. The high point of the journey came at Mount Theches, the much-celebrated height from which the Greeks looked out on the Black Sea. The occasion is immortalized by Xenophon at 4.7.21–26 through his descriptions of the approach to the vantage point and of the joy felt by the men as they realize that they are close to being only a sea voyage away from home. As noted at the start of this appendix, the mountainous area south of Trapezus was already in antiquity a draw for those familiar with the story, and in the modern era a steady mix of scholars and travelers have sought to stand on the same spot and relive the moment. Quite apart from its significance in the story, it is an important landmark on the route, marking the effective conclusion of this leg of the journey and enabling some conjecture about the course of preceding stages to be made. There is not, however, any consensus as to which of

P.9e   Phasis River in Colchis: Map 4.7.1, AY.
P.9f   For this part of the Phasis (?) River, see the river system near the northern border of Map P.2. Phasis/Araxes River: Map 4.7.1, BY.
P.9g   The name of the modern Turkish town of Pasinler (Ref. Map 8, AZ) and the surrounding eponymous plain are said to reflect the presence of the

ancient people.
P.9h   Pass held by Phasianoi and others: 4.6.5.
P.10a  Taochian fort, possible location: Map 4.7.1, BY.
P.10b  Three tribes outflanked: 4.6.5. Ani is a place-name attested here only in late antiquity. The names of the settlements here in 400 are unknown. Pass near Ani: Map 4.7.1, BY.

400

the many heights extending east from the Zigana Pass, south of the Turkish city of Trabzon (ancient Trapezus), was the one from which the army saw the sea.[a]

§12. The first thing to say about Mount Theches is that it must have been a well-known vantage point, or else their guide would not have pledged to give his life should he fail to get them to a place from which they would see the sea within five days.[a] We can probably assume that the height was situated close to a recognized trade route winding its way over the mountains and down to the sea; given its size the army must always have preferred established routes unless these were blocked by an enemy.[b] Further, the mountain should offer regular views of the sea at that time of year, an inference arising from the guide's confidence that the Greeks would see the sea and from the fact that they did see it. This is important, as several of the putative sites for the mountain offer only periodic glimpses of the sea even at times of the year favorable for visibility. Fog is a factor especially in spring and summer.[c] It's worth emphasizing that the mountain's prominence need not have derived from its height or shape but may be due to the fact that it constituted a key waymark on the trail.

§13. The location identified as Mount Theches in this edition, the northwesterly spur of Polut Dağı, fulfills the criteria outlined above. Although lower (7,595 feet/2,315 meters) than most candidates for Theches, and not especially striking as one approaches from the south, it sits closer to the shoreline than most of the others (about eighteen miles, or twenty-nine kilometers, direct distance) and its expansive summit commands an exceptional view down the valley and on to the sea. Accessible to men and horses alike, it is a site that, as the large cairn near the north edge indicates, has attracted both locals and travelers, the latter able to take in the panorama as part of their journey to the coast.[a] While it would not be safe to identify the current cairn with an ancient one, the abundance of stones on the summit makes it easy to imagine how a monument as described by Xenophon at 4.7.25 could have been raised on this spot; similarly, the impression from the same passage that many men gathered on the height fits with the physical extent of the place.

§14. Any location for Mount Theches should, in addition, fit with the author's report that on the first day down from the mountain, the Greeks arrived at a river confluence (at 4.8.1), one river forming a boundary between the Skythenoi and the Makrones.[a] Such a feature is not distinctive on the seaward side of the mountains, where numerous streams flow into one another as they descend through the valleys. In this case, we take the river that forms in the "Theches valley" to be the tribal boundary, the larger and fast-flowing river which it meets at its opening being the modern Karadere.[b]

§15. On arriving at the port of Trapezus, the army expected that it would soon be on its way home by ship. As one of the soldiers put it, "What I long for now is to have

P.11a  Zigana Pass and a selection of candidates for Mt. Theches: Map P.3.

P.12a  Guide's "five days" pledge: 4.7.20.

P.12b  See 4.1.20–24 and 4.6.5–12 for instances where the army was blocked by enemies.

P.12c  See further Appendix Q: The Chronology of the March, §5.

P.13a  For the editors' proposed location, see Map P.3. The *Barrington Atlas* locates it at modern Deveboynu Tepe (Map P.3). For a photograph taken

from the editors' proposed site for Mt. Theches, see Figure 4.7.25.

P.14a  Confluence of the Hyssos and tribal boundary rivers, Skythenoi, Makrones territories: Map P.3, Map 4.7.25.

P.14b  Karadere (ancient Hyssos) River: Map P.3. The problem is actually quite complicated as, for instance, it could be argued that the larger river is the boundary one, a reading that would reconfigure the tribal territories.

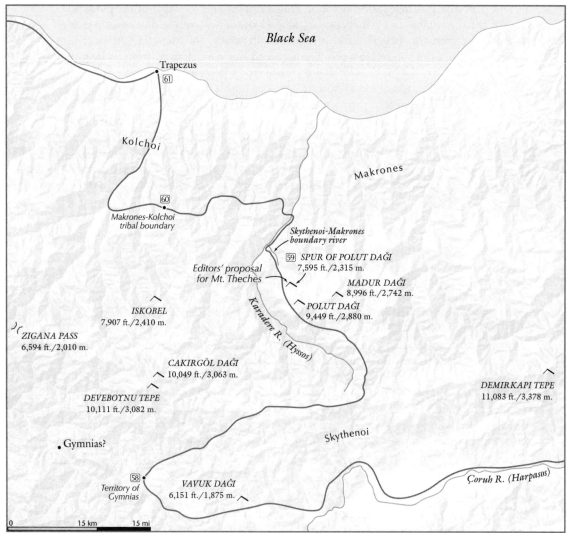

MAP P.3. SOME OF THE POSSIBLE LOCATIONS FOR MOUNT THECHES. DIFFERENT LOCATIONS IMPLY DIFFERENT ROUTES
FOR THE ARMY.

no more of these troubles, since we have reached the sea, and instead to sail the rest of the way and arrive in Greece stretched out at my ease, like Odysseus."[a] Up until the second half of the twentieth century, ships were indeed the standard means of travel in this area, as the coastal topography made land journeys very difficult. Xenophon says as much when the army is deliberating on its plans for the rest of the journey: "In case our efforts do not after all succeed in providing enough merchant ships, it would be a good idea for us to instruct the cities along the coast to mend the roads, which we hear are in poor condition for travelers."[b] As it turned out, they were unable to acquire a sufficient number of vessels, and most of the force was obliged to continue on foot.

§16. While Xenophon may have persuaded settlements along the coast to repair their roads,[a] the land journey was still evidently arduous. It took almost three days to reach Kerasous, a distance of less than thirty miles/forty-eight kilometers,[b] while the eight days' march through Mossynoeci territory, we guess from the description, would have been along steep inland paths.[c] It is likely that this route would not have been as difficult or slow as the one following the contours of the coast, which would have sometimes entailed upstream diversions to ford rivers. For the rest of their time traveling through the southern Black Sea littoral, the army kept within range of the coastline, whether by land or ship (Kotyora to Sinope, Sinope to Heraclea), thus making their journey largely traceable.[d]

§17. A particular problem is the site of Kalpe Harbor. Although Xenophon describes this in some detail at 6.4.1–6, the homogenous topography of the coastline means that there are several sites that could feasibly fit with the narrative. There are further complicating factors, one being that the area sits in a seismically active zone, another that Xenophon's writings are to a notable degree shaped by paradigm; that is, he often represents people and places in an idealized rather than a realistic way, usually with the aim of bringing out a moral point or a point of instruction on leadership.[a] At Kalpe Harbor the men suspect that certain people wished to found a city there,[b] and Xenophon, if he was not one of these people, certainly paints a picture of an ideal settlement. Thus the physical setting, which might still be identifiable through a considered description, is transformed almost beyond recognition. Against this background we have chosen a site, modern Kerpe, which seems to fit best with the detail of the march record, notably being roughly at the halfway point between Heraclea and Byzantium, as Xenophon reports.[c]

P.15a   Soldier wants to travel by sea: 5.1.2.
P.15b   Roads need repairing: 5.1.13.
P.16a   Roads repaired: 5.1.14.
P.16b   Three days from Trapezus to Kerasous: 5.3.2. The experience of a nineteenth-century traveler, J. M. Kinneir, illustrates the arduous nature of overland journeys in this vicinity. He writes that while at (modern) Ordu (Xenophon's Kotyora), the aga of the place stated, "as it was madness to think of travelling by land, he had ordered a felucca [boat] to carry us to Keresoun" (Kinneir 1818, 324). (Kinneir was traveling along the Turkish Black Sea coast in the reverse direction to the army, in Classical terms from Kotyora toward Trapezus.) Kinneir's Keresoun is today called Giresun. Incidentally, although the name is similar to Xenophon's Kerasous, and there are

scholars who identify the two, on our reading of the march record we place Xenophon's Kerasous at modern Kirazlik, much closer to Trapezus than is Giresun. Trapezus, Kotyora, Kerasous: Ref. Map 7, AY. Modern Ordu, Giresun, Kirazlik: Ref. Map 8, AY.
P.16c   Eight days' journey through Mossynoeci territory: 5.5.1; see Map 5.4.1.
P.16d   Kotyora to Sinope to Heraclea: Ref. Map 7, AY–AX.
P.17a   On paradigm in Xenophon's writings, see the Introduction, §6.10, and for leadership, §8.2–5.
P.17b   Kalpe Harbor, possible location: Ref. Map 7, AW, Map 6.4.1, corresponding to modern Kerpe (Ref. Map 8, AW).
P.17c   Halfway point: 6.4.3. For the segment between Heraclea and Byzantium, see Ref. Map 4.1, AY–AZ.

§18. Some writers consider that the army's journey ended with its crossing out of Asia to Byzantium, which Xenophon refers to as the first Greek city they reached.[a] As one nineteenth-century commentator, William Ainsworth, wrote, "The retreat of the Ten Thousand may in reality be said to end at this point, for the kind of business which they became engaged in after crossing the Bosphorus, has nothing to do with that on which they were originally taken from their homes by the ambition of Cyrus."[b] Nonetheless, Xenophon's narrative breaks off not at this point but several months later, at Pergamum, the intervening period in Thrace being charted in Book 7.[c] The route the army took while in Thrace is uncertain in many details, more so than in most of the preceding marches, and the chronology too is problematic. While previous stages were markedly affected by geographic and military exigencies, the journey here was strongly influenced by political factors—both Persia and Sparta, wary of the army, sought at different times to disband and control it—and by the desire of the men to acquire booty before returning home. Just as the need for a livelihood had drawn the mercenaries to Sardis from across the Greek world in 401, so too it brought them out of Thrace and back again to Ionia in 399 for service with a new overlord and a renewed cycle of confrontation with Persians.[d]

Shane Brennan
Associate Professor of History
American University in Dubai
United Arab Emirates

P.18a First Greek city: 7.1.29. Byzantium, Bosphorus: Ref. Map 4.1, AY.
P.18b Ainsworth 1854, 337.
P.18c Pergamum: Ref. Map 4.1, BY; Ref. Map 4.2, BX. Thrace: Ref. Map 3.
P.18d For more on the route of the Ten Thousand, see Hamilton 1842, Layard 1853, Ainsworth 1854, Manfredi 1986, Lendle 1995, Mitford 2000, Waterfield 2006, Brennan 2008.

# APPENDIX Q

## *The Chronology of the March*

§1. Xenophon's *Anabasis* does not specify the time frame within which the events it describes took place. In the text there are no references to archon years, panhellenic festivals, or local calendars, any of which could have helped establish fixed (absolute) dates. The opening of the book does, however, provide historical information on the background to Cyrus' rebellion and some detail can be dated from other sources. Diodorus Siculus, the first-century writer who compiled a universal history down to his own day, gives the year of Cyrus' recall to Persia to see his father as 405; moreover, in his summary of the march, he gives the year in which the expedition started as 401.[a] Diodorus is not infallible when it comes to chronology, but for these events there is corroborating material, including, by way of editorial interpolations, Xenophon's *Hellenika*.[b]

§2. We know, then, that Cyrus' expedition began in Sardis in 401 and, from the march detail provided in *Anabasis*, that it finished back in western Anatolia just under two years later, when the remnants of the Ten Thousand were absorbed into a Spartan expeditionary force.[a] What is not certain is the precise chronology of the march since no calendrical date is given in *Anabasis* or elsewhere to which the march can be anchored. A traditional view puts the start on March 6, 401, with the travel detail proceeding from this date: in this scheme the battle of Cunaxa is fought in September of that year, with the army reaching the Black Sea in February 400, Byzantium in August, then crossing back to western Anatolia from Thrace after winter 400/399.[b] However, while this approximate end date is secure—the incidence of major snowfalls

---

Q.1a Diodorus: year of Cyrus' recall to Persia, 13.104.1–4; start date of the expedition, 14.19.1–2 (in Appendix S: Selections from Diodorus). Xenophon refers to Cyrus' recall at 1.1.1–2. Diodorus' *Universal History*, in particular those parts of it that touch on the expedition, is looked at by David Thomas in Appendix M: Other Ancient Sources on the Ten Thousand. On Cyrus the Younger, see Appendix W: Brief Biographies of Selected Characters in *Anabasis*,

§10. Persian Empire: Ref. Map 9.

Q.1b Dates by reference to Athenian archons (see the Glossary) were inserted into the *Hellenika* narrative by later editors. For more on this subject, see Thomas 2009, Appendix C: Chronological Problems in the Continuation (1.1.1–2.3.10) of Xenophon's *Hellenika*, §§5–9.

Q.2a Sardis, western Anatolia: Ref. Map 4.1, CY, BY. Sparta: Ref. Map 2, DY.

Q.2b Cousin 1905.

405

in Xenophon's narrative shows that two winters elapse between start and finish[c]—there is no compelling reason to settle on the March 401 start date, even if some support for it does come from the fact that ancient expeditions tended to begin in early spring, when weather conditions became favorable. In more recent times, two further views on the chronology have been put forward, one arguing that the expedition started in early February, the other that it started in late May.[d] The reasoning behind these opposing arguments is looked at in §§4–10. The view we take on the march chronology is important as it affects how we understand the experience of the march. For instance, in the "early" scheme, the battle of Cunaxa is fought in debilitating summer heat, prompting commentators subscribing to this time frame to assert that the army would have suffered from heatstroke casualties and exhaustion. In contrast, the "late" chronology has the battle take place under a softer autumnal sun, which would not have exacted the same toll on combatants and consequently could not have been a factor in the outcome of the battle, as the summer heat could have been in the early scenario.

## Chronological Pointers

§3. One way of trying to establish the chronology is to look for time-of-year clues in Xenophon's account. On his journey he often remarks on the world around him, and on occasion his reports provide grounds for conjectures about time. For instance, when at 4.5.3 he writes of deep snow in Armenia, we know it is winter, probably late winter, when snow levels are highest; and when at 1.4.17 he describes how the army crosses the Euphrates at Thapsakos on foot, we can be confident that this must have been at a time in the river's cycle when it was at or close to its ebb in autumn.[a] By combining the details of distance and days' march Xenophon gives us with these seasonal clues, a picture of the army in time as well as space emerges; by identifying further environmental and physical pointers, we can refine the chronology and at the same time impose a check on the record.[b] If Xenophon's descriptions are accurate and his record is complete, then the various pointers should all line up, reflecting the progress of the army in the account and leaving us with a reasonably precise chronology for the march.[c]

## The Early Chronology

§4. Reports on the physical and natural worlds are not the only potential clues to time embedded in *Anabasis*. Early on in the story, Xenophon tells us that at Peltai,

Q.2c  Elapse of two winters: at 4.4.8, 4.4.11, February 400; at 7.3.42, 7.4.3, winter 400/399. The following locations appear on Ref. Map 7: Battlefield of Cunaxa, DZ; Black Sea (Pontus Euxinus in the *Barrington Atlas*), AX; Byzantium, Thrace, AW.
Q.2d  For the early chronology see, for example, Glombiowski 1994, for the late, Brennan 2008. For a comparison of the different chronologies, see the table, §16.
Q.3a  Armenia: Ref. Map 6, AY. Thapsakos, possible location: Ref. Map 6, CX; Map 1.4.1, *Halting place 21*.
Q.3b  Chronological pointers in *Anabasis*: the crossing of the Euphrates, 1.4.17–18; mud in the desert, 1.5.7–8; suspicions about flooded irrigation chan-

nels, 2.3.13; date harvest in northern Babylonia (Ref. Map 6, DZ), 2.3.14–16; the state of the Tigris River near modern Cizre (Ref. Map 8, CZ), 3.5.7; snow in historical Western Armenia (Ref. Map 6, AX, Map P.2), Book 4 throughout; visibility of the sea from Mt. Theches, Appendix Q, §11 and n. Q.11c, and the erection of a cairn at or near its summit, 4.7.20–25 (Mount Theches, possible locations: Map P.3); honeycombs, 4.8.20–21; grain stores on the Black Sea, 5.4.27. The relevant text footnotes in most of these cases briefly outline the chronological content of the episodes.
Q.3c  On the veracity of Xenophon's record, see the Introduction, §§7.13–18.

in western Anatolia, the army celebrated the Lykaia, an Arcadian festival that honored Zeus.[a] Sacrifices were made, and Cyrus himself attended the festival's athletic games.[b] It has been argued that this festival was held annually on the vernal equinox, March 21–24, and accordingly that the Arcadian contingent of Cyrus' force celebrated the occasion at this time. Working back through the march record to the beginning at Sardis, we have the army setting out at the beginning of February; on this basis it then crosses the middle Euphrates in late June, enters Babylonia at the beginning of August, and makes its way through northeastern Anatolia[c] in December before the full onset of winter.

§5. There are some difficulties with this view. It is not certain that the festival was celebrated on a fixed date, and even if it was, the date may not have been on the vernal equinox. At this time Mount Lykaion, in Arcadia, where the Lykaia was held,[a] would usually still be covered in snow, a fact that leads some to believe that the festival was celebrated in summer. The early scheme, moreover, does not fit well with several of the putative chronological pointers in the text, notably the crossing of the Euphrates at Thapsakos in Book 1 (but see §11) and the descriptions of heavy snow in Armenia in Book 4: the first snowfalls arrive in Armenia in November, and it would be unusual to have heavy snow before that, as the early chronology requires. A difficulty also arises with the sailing season in the Aegean, which usually ran from May to September with the wider window from March to early November dependent on conditions and the willingness of sailors. But in the favor of both the early and traditional chronology is that fog in the period September through January would be less of a potential obstacle to the sighting of the sea from Mount Theches than it would be in May when in the late chronology the army would have arrived there.

## The Late Chronology

§6. The late scheme is based on a range of chronological pointers in the text. As mentioned, a number have been identified,[a] and most of these have been evaluated by commentators. Lined up, they leave a picture of the army setting off from Sardis in late May, crossing the Euphrates in October, fighting at Cunaxa in late November, and crossing the mountains of northeast Anatolia in May.[b] Two pointers used to support the late chronology are weather conditions in northeast Anatolia and the curious episode of "mad honey" (see §8) just before the army reaches the Black Sea.

§7. At their eastern end, the mountains of northern Anatolia rise sharply and press in toward the sea, so that within a short distance of the coast they reach heights in excess of 10,000 feet/3,060 meters. Crossing these entailed significant effort, and in winter the passes were blocked. On the heights the first snows arrive as early as October, and they remain on the highland pastures until May or June. Under these conditions it seems unlikely that a large army would have been able to cross the range without undue risk either until winter had begun to fade or before it had set in.

Q.4a  Army celebrates Lykaia: 1.2.10. Peltai: Ref. Map 4.1, CY (not listed in the *Barrington Atlas*). Arcadia: Ref. Map 2, CX.
Q.4b  Festival's athletic games: 1.2.10.
Q.4c  Anatolia: Ref. Map 7, BX.

Q.5a  The hippodrome where the games were held stands at nearly 4,000 feet/1,200 meters above sea level. Mt. Lykaion: Ref. Map 2, CY.
Q.6a  For these pointers, see n. Q.3b.
Q.6b  Route of the Ten Thousand: Ref. Map 7.

Notwithstanding the comparatively more favorable condition for visibility, this consideration undermines the traditional chronology, which would have the army cross these mountains in late January and arrive at the Black Sea in early February.

§8. A subsequent encounter with toxic honey may further weaken the traditional chronology and undermine the early one. After the army had crossed over the range and was on its way down to the sea, it happened upon some villages. Xenophon recalls:

> And though there was nothing else that at all surprised them, there were many swarms of bees thereabouts, and all of the soldiers who ate the honeycombs began to behave crazily, started to vomit, and were subject to diarrhea, and none of them could stand up straight.[a]

The men had eaten what is known locally today as *deli bal*, "mad honey." Modern science has identified the poisonous agent as acetylandromedol, a toxin that inhibits breathing and agitates the nervous system, setting in train a series of effects, such as hypotension, cardiac rhythm disorders, nausea, dizziness, and impaired consciousness. The chemical is found in this region in yellow rhododendrons (*Rhododendron luteum*), which grow on hillsides among the purple variety of the flower (*Rhododendron ponticum*).

§9. It has been argued that the toxin is active only in fresh honey, in which case, to produce the described effects, the honey must have been eaten during the period when bees produce their food. In the eastern Black Sea region, this occurs from late April to late June, when the rhododendrons are in flower.[a] So if the men had come to these villages in January or February 400, as in the early and traditional chronologies respectively, they could not have eaten fresh honey but, rather, would have eaten the store made by the bees for winter from the previous season. That said, anecdotal evidence and some medical studies indicate that the toxin in fact remains active for a prolonged period, even if its potency might lessen over time. This would make it possible for the army to have eaten the honey in winter—or indeed for the Kolchoi, with whom the Greeks had just fought, to have deliberately left out bowls of it to poison their enemy, as later in antiquity their neighbors the Mossynoeci would do.[b]

§10. Xenophon's report nevertheless seems to imply that the bees were noticeable, or intrusive, as they would be in the flowering season, so when this further argument is added to the mix, the mad honey episode reinforces the late chronology.[a] A still stronger reinforcement for it arises on the Black Sea. As the Greeks progress through the land of the Mossynoeci, they plunder the stores of one of the hostile factions and find newly harvested grain,[b] which implies we have reached July at the earliest.

§11. A general weakness of the late scheme is that not all of the pointers are solid. Some may, as with the honey episode, be valid for extended periods. In other

Q.8a   "Swarms of bees": 4.8.20.
Q.9a   Beekeepers today normally harvest the honey in early July; but its production by the bees is gradual, so from early in the flowering season, it is possible to remove and ingest it. Only a spoonful is needed to cause hallucinations.
Q.9b   Mossynoeci leave honey out intentionally: Strabo 12.3.18. Kolchoi territory: Ref. Map 6, AX. Mos-

synoeci territory: Ref. Map 5, AZ.
Q.10a  The Greek word used at 4.8.20, *smēnē*, can mean either "swarms" or "hives." "Swarms" was chosen for the translation because the soldiers, in the area for only a short time, were more likely to notice highly active bees than stable colonies, and thus be led to their honey.
Q.10b  Newly harvested grain: 5.4.27.

cases Xenophon's narrative might be argued to be slippery. For example, the extraordinary crossing of the Euphrates at Thapsakos[a] in Book 1, rather than serving as part of a reliable record of the journey, could be paradigmatic, intended to give the impression of Cyrus as divinely favored. Xenophon was conscious that his participation in a rebellion spearheaded by mercenaries did not sit well with his standing as a follower of Socrates, and he took pains throughout the work to justify his involvement with Cyrus;[b] painting the prince in the best possible light was one way of achieving this end. Another criticism of the late chronology is that, as mentioned with regards to Mount Theches, fog would probably be more of a hindrance to visibility in May than it would in December and January.[c] It bears recalling as well that ancient expeditions tended to begin in early spring (§2), at the first opportunity following winter. Cyrus' case, though, was unusual: surprise was a cornerstone of his plan, and he sought to outwit the King however he could.

### The "Snow Lacuna" Theory

§12. The systematic character of Xenophon's record leaves the impression that it is complete—that all stages of the journey have been accounted for. Scrutiny supports this impression, as the number of days Xenophon records the army as marching throughout is largely consistent with the distances in question if we measure these independently. For instance, the number of march days given for the journey from the army's entry into the territory of the Kardouchoi[a] to its arrival at the Black Sea (about sixty-seven—Xenophon's narrative is not wholly clear in places) is reasonable in light of the known distance. Nonetheless it could well be that there are days missing from the record of the twenty-two-month-long march from Sardis to Pergamum.[b] One apparent omission is the crossing of the Lesser Zab River in Upper Mesopotamia; the failure to mention this implies that a period has been left out, although the control of fixed points suggests that this would amount to no more than a couple of days.[c] Of more concern is the subsequent crossing of eastern Anatolia. It could be that in the wilderness (as Xenophon portrays the region) and the harsh conditions of this march, the army became lost and wandered for days, even weeks, before regaining its path. In this scenario time spent going around in circles, so to speak, would not add anything to the actual progress of the journey, though it would extend its

Q.11a  Crossing of the Euphrates at Thapsakos: 1.4.17–18. Thapsakos, possible location: Ref. Map 6, CX, Map P.1.

Q.11b  Xenophon's justification for his service with Cyrus: see the Introduction, §8.10–11. On Socrates, see Appendix W: Brief Biographies, §31.

Q.11c  Our candidate for this mountain is closer to the sea than other ones, so reducing the risk of a view being blocked by fog. See Appendix P: The Route of the Ten Thousand, §13.

Q.12a  Kardouchoi territory: Ref. Map 6, BY.

Q.12b  The army's march: Ref. Map 7. Sardis, Pergamum: Ref. Map 7, BW.

Q.12c  Omission of Lesser Zab River crossing: the distance between Opis (Xenophon's Sittake) and the junction of the Zapatas and Tigris rivers is approximately 230 miles/370 kilometers (see Book 2 map), which in terms of progress broadly fits with the fourteen days of travel—roughly 5 parasangs per day—reported by Xenophon. However, moving upstream along the Zapatas to the ford where we believe the army crossed (modern Kellek, Ref. Map 8, CZ) extends the distance by about 25 miles/40 kilometers and suggests that one or possibly two days are missing; the lacuna may or may not be related to the omission of the Lesser Zab. On parasangs, see Appendix O: Ancient Greek and Persian Units of Measurement, §§7–8, and the Introduction, §7.3–5. The following locations appear on Ref. Map 6: Lesser Zab River (Zabas Mikros in the *Barrington Atlas*), CZ; Mesopotamia, CY; Opis (Xenophon's Sittake), DZ; Zapatas (modern Greater Zab) River, Tigris River, CZ.

length. Arguing for this, the Italian scholar Valerio Manfredi suggests that there are up to three months missing from the record, and that Xenophon chose to pass over the episode because, as one of the army's leaders at this point, he incurred blame for its having lost its way. According to this theory, which draws on the climatic and environmental evidence, the army sets out in early March but does not cross the North Anatolia mountains until May; the gap in the record is explained by Xenophon's having deliberately omitted a period of time in the crossing of Armenia, which he narrates in 4.5–6.[d]

§13. Manfredi's idea, subsequently refined as the "snow lacuna" theory by Robin Lane Fox, has its attractions; as Lane Fox puts it, it fits neatly with a picture of Xenophon as "evasive, apologetic, and a master of leaving unwelcome things out."[a] More concretely, since we know that the region in question had been administered by successive civilizations—Assyrian, Median, and Achaemenid[b]—it cannot have been as empty as Xenophon's threadbare reporting indicates. Against the theory of the gap in the record, since self-defense is generally considered to be a prominent element in the text, it might be expected that Xenophon would have taken some opportunity to defend himself against such a substantial charge of neglect or incompetence. At 5.8.1–12, he goes to great lengths to justify his harsh treatment of a baggage carrier during the segment of the retreat narrated in 4.5–6. It's hard to explain as well how ripples from such a setback didn't surface in later accounts of the march. Of no less weight is the fact that the late chronology makes the theory unnecessary. Fitting with the internal evidence of the text, it does not require postulating any substantial gap. Some gap does not raise issues of credibility, since, recalling the example of the Lesser Zab River, we should expect the cumulative effect of minor errors to result in some difference to the actual time frame as revealed by the chronological pointers.

### The Campaign in Thrace

§14. Although some consider the march to have concluded at Byzantium, which Xenophon describes as the first Greek city they came to on the retreat, his narrative continues beyond this point.[a] Book 7 describes how, after leaving the city of Byzantium, the army campaigned in Thrace for several months, probably crossing back to western Anatolia in March 399. We have based our reconstruction of the chronology for Book 7 on three more or less fixed points derived from normal climatic conditions for the Aegean Sea[b] and for Thrace. We assume that Anaxibios would not

---

Q.12d  See the comparative table at the end of this appendix for dates. If one were to subscribe to the view that Diodorus, who included a summary of the march in his universal history (14.19–31, 14.19.37; in Appendix S: Diodorus), had a source independent of Xenophon, then it might seem that the theory had some textual support as well, as Diodorus (14.29.3; in Appendix S) gives fifteen as the number of travel days between Gymnias and Mt. Theches, whereas Xenophon has just five (4.7.19–21). However, in the wider frame of this stretch of the retreat—from the Armenian villages to Trapezus (4.6.1–4.8.22)—the number of days taken up by the journey given in the respective accounts is quite close. Thus even if Diodorus is

independent, he more or less bears out Xenophon's account. For more on Diodorus' account of the march, see Appendix M: Other Ancient Sources on the Ten Thousand, §§3–7. Gymnias (possible location) to Mt. Theches: Map 4.7.1, BX, *Halting places 58–59*. Armenian villages (Guide runs off) to Trapezus: Map 4.7.1, BY–BX, *Halting places 52–61*.

Q.13a  Lane Fox 2004, 45.

Q.13b  Assyria, Media: Ref. Map 6, CY, CZ. For the Achaemenid dynasty of Persian Kings, see the Glossary.

Q.14a  First Greek city: 7.1.29. Byzantium: Ref. Map 4.1, AY.

Q.14b  Aegean Sea: Ref. Map 2, BZ.

have attempted the sea voyage that he begins at 7.2.5 more than a few days after the beginning of November, that the snow recorded at 7.3.42 and 7.4.3 fell after the beginning of December, and that Thibron's army, which is reported to be on its way by sea at 7.6.1, would not have set sail before the beginning of March at the earliest, since fleets would not move across the Aegean during the winter except in dire necessity. The events recounted by Xenophon from Kalpe Harbor[c] to the end of Book 7 have then been distributed around these three fixed points on the basis of what seems most likely. The estimates of time on the move are reasonably reliable, but while the total time spent inactive will be more or less correct, there is a degree of guesswork involved in how long they waited at each of the various locations where we are told about delays; we suggest a further short delay at one location, Salmydessos,[d] where Xenophon does not explicitly mention a pause, but which most probably required the army to overawe the inhabitants for several days to subdue them sufficiently. The main uncertainty is how long they stayed near Perinthus[e] at 7.2.11–15: Xenophon's narrative suggests it was only a few days, but it must have been a good deal longer in view of the above fixed points.

## Conclusions

§15. The traditional view that Cyrus' army started out from Sardis in March 401 and arrived at the Black Sea in February of the following year has now been put aside by most commentators, rendered untenable by weather conditions in northeastern Anatolia in winter. The early chronology, in which the army begins its march in February, avoids this problem by having the men cross before the onset of full winter. However, this view is based principally on an argument that the festival the army celebrated not long after the expedition began is tied to one that was held in Arcadia at the spring equinox. This argument is not watertight, and the view tends to overlook or unduly stretch various chronological pointers. A further issue for both the traditional and the early chronology is the reference at 5.4.27 to new grain in the Black Sea area, pointing to July or later for this episode. The "snow lacuna" theory allows for the army to begin in March but not arrive at the sea until May the following year. The late arrival at the Black Sea is explained, in this theory, by an omission in the record, some three months during which the army wandered about in eastern Anatolia. But the late chronology, produced from Xenophon's descriptions of the world around him on his journey, indicates that there is no such gap in the record. The army begins their march at Sardis in late May 401, crosses the North Anatolia mountains in May 400, and arrives at the Black Sea later the same month. These accordingly are the dates used in the chronological indications given in this Landmark edition.

Shane Brennan
Associate Professor of History
American University in Dubai
United Arab Emirates

Q.14c  Kalpe Harbor, possible location: Ref. Map 4.1, AY.

Q.14d  Salmydessos: Ref. Map 3, CZ.

Q.14e  Perinthus: Ref. Map 4.1, AY.

## §16. Overview of March Chronologies

| Year Bk/Chap. | Event | Traditional | Early | "Snow Lacuna" | Late/Landmark |
|---|---|---|---|---|---|
| **401** | | | | | |
| 1.2.1 | Start of expedition | March 6 | February 6 | March | Late May |
| 1.4.17 | Euphrates crossing at Thapsakos | July 27 | June 27 | | October |
| 1.8 | Battle of Cunaxa | September 3 | August 3 | Early September | Late November |
| 4.4.8 | Heavy snow in Armenia | November 28 | October 28 | November/ December | February 400 |
| **400** | | | | | |
| 4.8.20 | Encounter with bees in Kolchian villages | January | December | May | May |
| 4.8.22 | Arrival at Trapezus | February 5 | January 5 | Late May | May |
| 5.4.27 | Discovery of new grain harvested by Mossynoeci | April 1 | March 1 | July | Early July |
| 7.1.7 | Arrival at Byzantium | August 7 | July 7 | Autumn | Late October |
| **399** | | | | | |
| 7.8.24 | Thibron's expedition: the remnants of the army join Sparta's campaign in western Anatolia. | Spring | Spring | Spring | Spring |

SOURCES FOR CHRONOLOGIES OF THE MARCH:

>    Traditional:   Cousin 1905. Cousin's early March date came to be
>                   adopted by many as the conventional starting date for
>                   the expedition.
>          Early:   Glombiowski 1994, Lee 2007.
> "Snow lacuna":    Manfredi 1986, Lane Fox 2004.
>           Late:   Gassner 1953, Brennan 2008.
>                   The Landmark editors follow a late chronology.

# APPENDIX R

## *The Legacy of Xenophon's* Anabasis

§1. The classic status of Xenophon's *Anabasis* as an account of military endeavor and perseverance in exotic lands was established in antiquity. Particularly poignant is a story told in Plutarch's *Life of Antony* about Mark Antony's own difficult retreat across much of the same winter landscape as was traversed by the Ten Thousand, the Greek mercenaries fighting in Cyrus' Persian army: at one point, Plutarch relates, Antony gasped, "O, the Ten Thousand!" in admiration of Xenophon's Greeks.[a] Given Xenophon's theme, however, it is no surprise that the Ten Thousand's exploits in Asia were evoked most often in connection with Greek relations with Persia. Even before Alexander of Macedonia conquered the Persian Empire in the 330s, the Athenian orator Isocrates claimed, in a work addressed to Alexander's father, Philip II, that the Greek soldiers' performance at the battle of Cunaxa had demonstrated the weakness of the Persian King.[b] The same message had earlier appeared in Isocrates' *Panegyricus*, composed around 380, where he lowered the Greeks' numbers to six thousand and claimed they were all of low social status in order to castigate more strongly the Persians' failure to prevent the Greeks' escape.[c] Xenophon himself provides further evidence in his *Hellenika* (finished in the 350s) that the Greeks' successful escape from the heart of the Persian Empire was used to promote the cause of a panhellenic attack on Persia.[d]

§2. Allusions by fourth-century writers to the events described by Xenophon's *Anabasis* do not necessarily show that they had read *Anabasis* itself: the allusions could be based on general oral reports about those events or on other written accounts (if any existed). Indeed, Isocrates' *Panegyricus* was almost certainly composed before *Anabasis*, and it has often been thought that it was Xenophon responding to Isocrates rather than Isocrates commenting on Xenophon. But while there is good contem-

R.1a "O, the Ten Thousand!": Plutarch, *Life of Antony* 45.12. On Cyrus the Younger, see Appendix W: Brief Biographies of Selected Characters in *Anabasis*, §10.
R.1b Weakness of the Persian King: Isocrates 5 (*Philippus*) 90. Macedonia: Ref. Map 3, CX. Battlefield of

Cunaxa: Ref. Map 6, DZ.
R.1c Castigation of Persian failure: Isocrates 4 (*Panegyricus*) 145–49.
R.1d Promotion of panhellenic attack: Xenophon, *Hellenika* 3.4.2, 6.1.12.

porary evidence for Xenophon's fame in his lifetime (in particular, the honors paid to his son Gryllos after his death in battle), firm evidence for the influence of *Anabasis* itself can first be found later in antiquity. In the second century B.C.E., the historian Polybius made an explicit causal link between "the retreat of the Greeks under Xenophon from the upper satrapies" and Alexander's conquest of the Persian Empire.[a] Here the (admittedly inexact) reference to Xenophon as leader suggests a reading of *Anabasis* itself. Later, in the second century C.E., Arrian entitled his account of Alexander's expedition *Anabasis Alexandrou,* the *Anabasis of Alexander,* and made Alexander appeal in a speech to the memory of the Ten Thousand.[b] Writing at a time when Xenophon's style was widely admired and imitated, Arrian went further than his contemporaries by modeling his literary career on Xenophon's.

§3. The fortunes of Xenophon's *Anabasis* have had their ups and downs since antiquity. His account was still read in the Greek East during the Byzantine era, but it was much less known in the Latin West. During the Renaissance, when Xenophon became more widely known in Western Europe, his most admired works were *Oikonomikos,* a dialogue on household management; *Hieron,* a dialogue on tyranny; and above all *Kyroupaideia* (*The Education of Cyrus*), a didactic work on leadership. Machiavelli, for instance, refers to both *Hieron* and *Kyroupaideia,* but there is no evidence that he knew *Anabasis.* But *Anabasis* did become more familiar with time as more printed editions were published. Francis Bacon, for instance, cited Xenophon in *The Advancement of Learning* (1605) as an example of a man who was expert in both warfare and philosophy—a theme also promoted by a long essay in Latin by the sixteenth-century French scholar Henri Estienne (usually referred to as Stephanus) that was printed in some editions of Xenophon's work. Shakespeare may also have known *Anabasis:* it has been suggested that Fluellen's speech in *Henry V* comparing Macedon to Monmouth ("There is a river in Macedon; and there is also moreover a river at Monmouth . . . and there is salmons in both")[a] was inspired by Xenophon's comparison at *Anabasis* 5.3.8 between the estate he bought for the goddess Artemis at Skillous and her sanctuary at Ephesus, both of which had rivers running through them stocked with fish.[b]

§4. By the eighteenth century, *Anabasis* was more widely read and praised, but it was still not Xenophon's most highly regarded work. That position was now held by his *Memorabilia* (*Recollections of Socrates*), which was admired for its depiction of Socrates—generally held then to be the equal of or superior to Plato's—and for the parable (taken from the sophist Prodicus) of Herakles at the crossroads choosing between the easy route to Pleasure and the tough road up to Virtue. On the basis of Xenophon's account of his life at Skillous and his known fondness for hunting, he was also regarded at this time as an ancient prototype of the English country squire.

§5. It was in the nineteenth century that *Anabasis* came to be regarded as Xenophon's masterpiece. This change in the work's fortunes came at a time when the areas Xenophon had traveled through were becoming more accessible to Euro-

R.2a  Link between Xenophon's retreat and Alexander's conquest: Polybius 3.6.9–12 (Paton/Loeb translation).
R.2b  Alexander refers to the Ten Thousand: Arrian, *Anabasis Alexandrou* 2.7.8–9. Paul Cartledge

makes the same point somewhat more expansively in his Introduction to Romm 2010, §1.1–3.
R.3a  Act 4, scene 7.
R.3b  Skillous: Ref Map 2, CX; Ephesus: Ref. Map 4.1, CX; Ref. Map 4.2, DY.

pean explorers and of some strategic importance. It was also a time when Xenophon's account of his encounters with tough opponents like the Kardouchoi[a] had great resonance for European and North American soldiers engaged in conflicts with contemporary "savages."

§6. The fame of *Anabasis* was spread above all by its adoption as a school text. Its widespread use in US schools began in the 1840s—in the same decade that the United States' victory over Mexico led to the extension of its rule across the continent. One American scholar who played an important role in promoting Xenophon's claims at this time was Cornelius Felton, a professor of Greek at Harvard. In his popular *Greek Reader for the Use of Schools* (1840), he introduced a selection from Xenophon's writings by praising the "illustrious writer" for his military exploits: surmounting "innumerable" difficulties "from the hostility of the natives, the want of provisions, and the occasional severity of the weather," Xenophon had led a retreat that "has justly been considered one of the most memorable recorded in the annals of war" and then had written *Anabasis*, "one of the finest specimens of military history." The actual experience of schoolchildren reading *Anabasis* was often, however, a sorry one: for them, the early stages of Xenophon's account of the march upcountry were designed as a grueling test of Greek grammar, not as an exciting adventure or an insight into the cultural conflict between Greece and Persia.

§7. One sign of the new fame of *Anabasis* was the increasing use of the Ten Thousand in military comparisons. Aligning a modern march with the exploits of Xenophon's heroic Greeks was a common mode of panegyric. In the American War of Independence, marches by George Washington and Benedict Arnold were compared with Xenophon's. The same honor was given a century later to the long retreat of the Nez Perce under Chief Joseph, the "Indian Xenophon." It was in the Mexican War (1846–48), however, that Xenophon attained his greatest prominence. An expedition across the prairies to Mexico by a group of volunteers from Missouri led by Alexander Doniphan was frequently compared with the march of the Ten Thousand in newspaper articles and public speeches. The appeal of Xenophon at that time came from a range of deep and complementary impulses. The expanse of the American West was read in terms of the Asiatic deserts crossed by Xenophon. Soft Mexicans and hard Indians were viewed in terms similar to the Persians and the mountain tribes of antiquity. American manhood was defined in terms of Greek ideals of freedom and democracy. Much was made too of the similar sound of the names "Xenophon" and "Doniphan." The Americans also saw themselves as surpassing the achievements of the Greeks: Doniphan had marched farther than Xeno-phon, and his expedition had been an advance, not a retreat.

§8. The trend of comparing *Anabasis* with modern expeditions continues in the twenty-first century. One of the first accounts published after the Anglo-American invasion of Iraq in 2003 was entitled *The March Up* and inspired by *Anabasis*. This account (written by two Vietnam veterans, Ray Smith and Bing West) presents the

R.5a   Kardouchoi territory: Ref. Map 6, BY.

modern US Marines as the Ten Thousand reincarnated: they are "today's hoplites," "the inheritors of Xenophon's code of bravery and camaraderie." At the same time, such scholars as Victor Davis Hanson have achieved a huge following with works that openly exploit ancient history for political arguments about the present; Hanson, as the title of his 2001 best seller puts it, has even claimed that the qualities displayed by the Ten Thousand can help explain "Why the West Has Won."

§9. The fame of Xenophon's account in the past two centuries has been marked above all by the recurrence of three key motifs: the concept of *anabasis*, which has been taken to mean both an advance, in line with the proper Greek meaning of the word, and a retreat, because the march to the sea is the most famous part of Xenophon's expedition; the joyous shout of "*Thalatta! Thalatta!*"—"The sea! The sea!"—raised by the Ten Thousand on Mount Theches when they first caught sight of the Black Sea;[a] and parasangs, the Persian unit of measurement used by Xenophon to track the army's progress into and retreat from Mesopotamia.[b]

§10. The idea of *anabasis* was often used in the nineteenth century to glorify the expansion of the United States across the continent. In 1856, for instance, Cornelius Felton supported the campaign of John Charles Frémont, the presidential candidate for the Republican Party, with a speech in which he claimed that Frémont had written "an Anabasis—California!" Since the early 1840s, Frémont had cultivated a heroic persona as leader of several expeditions mapping and exploring routes into the American West; he was hailed as the conqueror of California thanks to his role in the war against Mexico. So Felton's allusion to *Anabasis* was implying that in the Republican candidate's famed trips seeking routes across the Rocky Mountains, he had conquered difficulties similar to those Xenophon faced.

§11. The term *anabasis* has been used in many other nationalistic contexts. A memoir by a German soldier, F. von Notz, describing a retreat inland through the Balkans at the end of the First World War, was entitled *Deutsche Anabasis 1918*. After drawing several parallels with the retreat of the Ten Thousand, von Notz ended his memoir with this thought: "The German people will have another great Anabasis: Escape, Ascent, Resurrection!" The allure of *Anabasis* manifested itself at the same time in celebrations of the feats of the Czech Legion in Siberia. This army had been stranded behind Russian lines after the Russians made peace with the Austro-Hungarian Empire in 1917. Like the Ten Thousand after the battle of Cunaxa, it refused orders to disarm; instead, it set off toward Vladivostok in the hope of joining the newly formed Czech national army fighting on the Western Front. This widely admired Czech "*anabasis*" was in turn used to advance the Czech claim for a nation-state. Xenophon was also cited at the climax of the British evacuation from Dunkirk on June 4, 1940, when the London *Times* ran a lead editorial headed ANABASIS, aligning the retreat to Dunkirk with the retreat of the Ten Thousand.

§12. The examples above illustrate the ambiguity (advance or retreat?) central to the modern reception of the *anabasis* motif. This ambiguity was exploited to the

R.9a  Joyous shout: Xenophon, *Anabasis* 4.7.21–24. Mt. Theches, possible location (located differently in the *Barrington Atlas*), Black Sea: Ref. Map 6, AX.
R.9b  For the meaning of "parasang," see the Introduction, §7.3–5; Appendix O: Ancient Greek and Persian Units of Measurement, §§7–8; Rood 2010b discusses parasangs' literary function. Mesopotamia: Ref. Map 6, CY.

full in one of the most controversial modern military expeditions: Sherman's march through Georgia in the US Civil War. Sherman's march was often compared with Xenophon's in contemporary reports. But while supporters of the North saw it as an advance through enemy territory, Confederate supporters tried to present it as a desperate retreat. This split view of Sherman's position was accompanied by a split view of the Ten Thousand: their retreat was presented either as a demonstration of Greek strength or as a desperate flight. In later years, after the end of the Civil War, Sherman's march came to influence the way Xenophon's expedition was conceived: instead of being generally described as the "Retreat of the Ten Thousand," it was now described, like Sherman's, as a "March to the Sea." This way of conceiving of the Greeks' march promoted triumphalist readings of *Anabasis;* far less attention was paid to Xenophon's more negative portrayal of the Ten Thousand during the march along the Black Sea coast. In antiquity, by contrast, later sections of the *Anabasis* had attracted as much interest as the earlier books: in Athenaeus' *Deipnosophists* (*Learned Banqueters*) of around 200 C.E., he includes references to the symposia scenes from Books 6 and 7 of *Anabasis;* while the pseudonymous *Letters of Chion* include a fictional eyewitness account of Xenophon calming the mutinous troops in Byzantium—a display that encourages the narrator to believe that the same man can be both a philosopher and a man of action.

§13. While the *anabasis* motif has also played an important role in the artistic and literary reception of Xenophon through the centuries, the main influence of *Anabasis* on creative artists has come through the shout "Thalatta! Thalatta!" This shout first became popular in the Romantic period. Heinrich Heine began his *North Sea* poems (1827) with:

> Thalatta! Thalatta!
> Greetings to you, o eternal sea!
> Greetings to you ten-thousandfold.[a]

With the spread of the railways, the cry was often invoked in accounts of increasingly popular visits to the seaside, and sometimes even shouted. Its widespread appeal was playfully exploited by James Joyce in his modernist masterpiece *Ulysses* (1922). In the opening scene, Joyce mocks the shout's romantic aura as he presents the pompous Buck Mulligan exclaiming, "*Thalatta! Thalatta!* She is our great sweet mother," as he looks out on Dublin Bay. This shout is then picked up in a much less assertive register in Molly Bloom's concluding monologue: "O that awful deep-down torrent O and the sea the sea crimson sometimes like fire and the glorious sunsets."

§14. The shout of "The Sea! The Sea!" was used in military contexts too as an emblem of triumph after long toil. War memoirs by British prisoners of war held in Turkey in the First World War portrayed it as having been in their thoughts as they

---

R.13a  The translation is by Hal Draper, slightly modi-
     fied.

managed to escape, like Xenophon to the Black Sea; they had earlier followed Xenophon's route in reverse after their capture at Kut,[a] in Mesopotamia. The shout was also evoked in the London *Times* editorial on the British army's retreat to Dunkirk in 1940, where it was associated with a distinctively English feeling for the sea. But while it has often been linked with the English spirit of adventure, represented by such men as T. E. Lawrence (Lawrence of Arabia) and the traveler and writer Peter Fleming, it was also cited in von Notz's account of his German *anabasis* (to bring out his joy on seeing a railway line) and in portrayals of the emotions of Sherman's troops as they approached Savannah.

§15. While "The Sea! The Sea!" has had a particular appeal since the Romantic age, the third of the key *Anabasis* motifs, parasangs, was already picked up in antiquity. The second-century C.E. satirist Lucian started one of his dialogues, the *Icaromenippus*, by placing a pastiche of travel writing in the mouth of a character who computes the length of his recent journey among the stars: "It was three hundred stades [sixty thousand yards], then, from the earth to the moon, my first *stathmos* [day's travel]; and from there up to the sun perhaps five hundred parasangs."[a] This draws an exasperated response from a friend: "For a long time now I have been following you about and listening to your outlandish talk about . . . those outworn topics, *stathmoi* and parasangs." It is a sign of the obsession with Xenophon in this period that *stathmoi* and parasangs, even when displaced to outer space, could be "outworn topics."

§16. Xenophon's parasangs have been most powerfully exploited by the Northern Irish poet Louis MacNeice. In *Autumn Journal*, a poem written in 1938, he implicitly uses Xenophon to comment on the world position in his own day. But whereas the parasang formula in *Anabasis* re-creates the Greeks' steady progress toward the sea, MacNeice writes:

> And all of Xenophon's parasangs
> Would take us only an inch from danger.

(He went on to compose his BBC radio play *The March of the Ten Thousand* soon after the Dunkirk evacuation.) In a more purely personal poem, "Round the Corner," which includes memories of childhood visits to the sea, MacNeice presented the moving image of "Xenophon crusted with parasangs," knowing that he was home. And he turned again to Xenophon and his parasangs in an emotional passage in his autobiography, *The Strings Are False*, where he describes a different sort of homecoming, his shout at the first sight of the sea off the west coast of Ireland, the area where his father grew up: "Thalassa! Thalassa! . . . the endless parasangs have ended."

§17. The popularity of Xenophon's parasangs also speaks to a sense that the Ten Thousand are to be admired more as emblems of endurance than for the transient triumph of their return. This idea is best expressed in a short essay on *Anabasis* by Italo

R.14a Kut: Ref. Map 8, DZ.
R.15a "It was three hundred stades": Lucian, *Icaromenippus* 1 (Harmon/Loeb translation). On

stades, *stathmoi*, and parasangs, see Appendix O: Measurements, §§5–8.

Calvino in his volume *Why Read the Classics?:* "The Greek army, creeping through the mountain heights and fjords amidst constant ambushes and attacks, no longer able to distinguish just to what extent it is a victim or an oppressor,...inspires in the reader an almost symbolic anguish which perhaps only we today can understand."[a] The Ten Thousand have become existential heroes.

§18. This short account of the extraordinary afterlife of Xenophon's *Anabasis* has focused on three key motifs. But it is fitting to close with what is now the single most popular example of Xenophon's influence: Walter Hill's 1979 film *The Warriors*, based on Sol Yurick's gritty 1965 novel of the same name. The story of *Anabasis* is here transferred to New York: after an inspiring figure named Cyrus, who wants to unify all the gangs of New York, is shot dead in the Bronx, a Coney Island gang called the Warriors is wrongly accused of killing him and pursued by other gangs on its way home. Innocents on the run, the Warriors finally make it back to Coney Island. The film ends with them standing on a beach, looking out at the sea: "When we see the ocean, we figure we're home, we're safe." The Ten Thousand as Xenophon portrays them were not so innocent, and not so safe either, when they reached the sea. But their recasting as modern gang members is a compelling transformation that keeps the story alive for many thousands of viewers whose knowledge of Xenophon's *Anabasis* itself is at most confined to coming across its title in one of the numerous online discussions of Hill's cult film.[a]

> Tim Rood
> Professor of Greek Literature
> St. Hugh's College
> Oxford, UK

---

R.17a   Calvino 1999, 23.
R.18a   Further information about all the modern writers
            discussed in this appendix can be found in Rood

2004 or (for US writers) Rood 2010.

# APPENDIX S

*Selections from* The Library of History
*of Diodorus Siculus* * *Relevant to* Anabasis

Translated by Peter Green

## Klearchos' Rule in Byzantium
## Prior to Cyrus' Expedition: 14.12

**14.12.** [1] When this year's events were concluded, the archon in Athens[a] was Eukleides [403/2]. . . . [2] . . . The Byzantines, being both split by factional strife and also at war with their Thracian[a] neighbors, found themselves in serious trouble. Since they were unable to resolve their internal rivalries, they asked the Lacedaemonians for a general. To restore order in their city, the Spartans[b] sent them Klearchos. [3] Entrusted by the Byzantines with authority in all matters, he proceeded to enroll large numbers of mercenaries, so that he was their protector no longer but, rather, their *tyrannos*.[a] First he invited their leading officials to some festival or other and put them all to death. This left the city without a governing body. In its absence, he rounded up thirty of the most prominent Byzantines, put cords around their necks,

*NOTE: Diodorus Siculus (fl. first century B.C.E.), an essential source for Greek and Sicilian history in the fourth century, wrote about Cyrus' expedition and the march of the Ten Thousand. For further biographical information, see Ancient Sources Cited in this Edition. Diodorus' own sources are discussed in Appendix M: Other Ancient Sources on the Ten Thousand.

These selections are drawn from Peter Green's *Diodorus Siculus, The Persian Wars to the Fall of Athens: Books 11–14.34 (480–401 B.C.E.)*. The translation of Diodorus 14.35–37, also by Green, has not been previously published. His translation is based chiefly on the Budé edition, as well as on the Teubner and Loeb editions. See the Bibliography for details on all these works. With Peter Green's kind permission, some changes have been made to conform with the style of this Landmark edition. These include proper-noun spellings, except where they represent differences between Diodorus' and Xenophon's texts. Green's editorial notes have been relocated from the body of the text to footnotes and designated by his name in parentheses. The Landmark editors have made a very few additional changes in the translation, added footnotes referring the reader to the maps in this edition, and made a small number of editorial comments.

S.14.12.1a  The archonship at Athens was a magistracy that changed every year in midsummer. For more on archons, see the Glossary. Athens: Ref. Map 2, CZ.

S.14.12.2a  Byzantium: Ref. Map 4.1, AY. Thrace: Ref. Map 3.

S.14.12.2b  Sparta was the principal city of Lacedaemon. Sparta, Lacedaemon: Ref. Map 2, DY.

S.14.12.3a  A *tyrannos* was an absolute, usually unconstitutional or extraconstitutional, ruler, whose exercise of power was unrestrained. In Greek of the fifth and fourth century, the term did not necessarily designate a tyrant in the modern English sense, but that meaning came to predominate, as it does here.

and strangled them, after which he appropriated all their property for himself. He then made a list of the wealthiest citizens and brought various false charges against them. Some he executed; others he exiled. In this way he got possession of a great deal of money, which he used to hire numerous mercenaries and thus safeguard his authority.

[4] When his savagery and tyrannical power became matters of public knowledge, the Lacedaemonians first of all sent representatives to him to persuade him to give up his dictatorial rule; but since he took no notice of their request, they then sent an expeditionary force against him, with Panthoedas as its commander. [5] On learning of his approach, Klearchos removed his own troops to Selymbria,[a] another city under his control, figuring that, with his record of offenses against the Byzantines, he would have not only the Lacedaemonians but every man in the city as his enemy. [6] So, having decided that Selymbria would make a safer base from which to conduct the war, he transferred both his funds and his armed forces there. On being informed that the Lacedaemonians were near at hand, he went out to meet them and fought an engagement with the force led by Panthoedas near what is known as "The Ford" (*poros*). [7] The battle went on for a long time, but the Lacedaemonians fought brilliantly, and the forces of the *tyrannos* were destroyed. Klearchos himself, with a few comrades, at first took refuge in Selymbria and was besieged there; but after a while he became scared, slipped out by night, and sailed away to Ionia,[a] where he became a close friend of Cyrus, the Great King's brother, and got to command his troops. [8] Cyrus, who had been designated as commander in chief of the maritime satrapies,[a] was full of ambition, and indeed had plans to lead an expedition against his brother Artaxerxes. [9] So, seeing that Klearchos was a man of bold and natural audacity, Cyrus provided him with cash and gave him the job of enlisting as many mercenaries as he could, convinced that in him he would have an apt partner for his daring enterprise.

## Cyrus' Expedition, the Battle of Cunaxa, and the March Back to the Greek World: 14.19–31

**14.19.** [1] When this year came to an end, Xenainetos[a] was archon in Athens [401/0]. . . . [2] About this time Cyrus, the commander in chief of the maritime satrapies, was implementing a long-meditated scheme to take the field against his brother Artaxerxes.[a] A highly ambitious young man, he had a by no means ineffectual appetite for the contests of war. [3] When an adequate corps of mercenaries had been assembled and all preparations for the campaign were in place, he still did not tell his troops the truth but said he was taking this force to Cilicia[a] to deal with the *tyrannoi* who had revolted against the King. [4] He also sent ambassadors to the Lacedaemonians, to remind them of the service that he had rendered them during their war

S.14.12.5a  Selymbria: Ref. Map 3, CZ.
S.14.12.7a  Ionia: Ref. Map 4.1, CX; Ref. Map 4.2, CY.
S.14.12.8a  Satrapy: the province of a satrap (governor) within the Persian Empire. Cyrus was responsible for more than one of the traditional provinces. For more on satraps, see the Glossary.
S.14.19.1a  Diodorus' manuscripts give a slightly different name for Xenainetos, which has been

corrected on the basis of fourth-century sources.
S.14.19.2a  From here to chapter 31, Diodorus' narrative should be read in conjunction with the detailed (and largely eyewitness) account of these events provided by Xenophon in his *Anabasis* (Peter Green).
S.14.19.3a  Cilicia: Ref. Map 5, CY.

against the Athenians[a] and to solicit their alliance. The Lacedaemonians, reckoning that this war would be to their advantage, decided to support Cyrus and at once sent envoys to Samos,[b] their admiral, instructing him to do whatever Cyrus might ask of him. [5] Samos had twenty-five triremes, with which he sailed to Ephesus,[a] to Cyrus' admiral, prepared for any kind of joint action with him. They also dispatched a force of eight hundred infantry under the command of Cheirisophos. The commander of the barbarian fleet, Tamos, had fifty magnificently equipped triremes; when the Lacedaemonians arrived, they all put to sea together, setting course for Cilicia.

[6] Cyrus, meanwhile, assembled in Sardis both the contingents from Asia and thirteen thousand mercenaries.[a] As governors of Lydia and Phrygia, he appointed Persian kinsmen of his, but for Ionia, the Aeolid, and surrounding regions, he chose Tamos, his trusted friend and a native of Memphis.[b] He himself and his army set out as though making for Cilicia and Pisidia,[c] spreading the word that certain inhabitants of those regions were in revolt. [7] From Asia he had a total of seventy thousand troops, including three thousand cavalry; from the Peloponnese[a] and the rest of the Greek mainland, the thirteen thousand mercenaries. [8] The troops from the Peloponnese, except for the Achaeans, were commanded by Klearchos the Lacedaemonian; those from Boeotia, by Proxenos of Thebes; the Achaeans, by an Achaean, Socrates; and the Thessalian contingent, by Menon of Larissa.[a] [9] The junior officers of the *barbaroi*[a] were Persians, while Cyrus himself was commander in chief of the entire force. By now he had revealed to his senior commanders that this expedition was in fact directed against his brother, but he still kept the troops at large in the dark,[b] fearing that the vast scale of the campaign might drive them to abandon his undertaking. Consequently, with an eye to future events, he went out of his way on the march to keep the rank and file happy, treating them courteously and ensuring that they were well provisioned.

**14.20.** [1] After traversing Lydia and Phrygia and the regions bordering on Cilicia, he reached the frontier of Cilicia itself, the defile at the Cilician Gates.[a] This defile is both narrow and precipitous, some two and a quarter miles[b] long, closely

S.14.19.4a  Diodorus has previously covered this at 13.70.3 under the year 407/6 (Peter Green).
S.14.19.4b  Called Samios in Xenophon, *Hellenika* 3.1.1, and Pythagoras (*sic*) at *Anabasis* 1.4.2, where Xenophon also differs on the number of Lacedaemonian triremes (thirty-five) and troops (seven hundred), besides giving Tamos a smaller fleet (twenty-five triremes) (Peter Green). Triremes: long warships with three sets of oars; see the Glossary.
S.14.19.5a  Ephesus: Ref. Map 4.1, CX; Ref. Map 4.2, DY.
S.14.19.6a  This number, which agrees with Xenophon's figure at 1.2.9 at a slightly later point in time, is discussed in Appendix I: The Size and Makeup of the Ten Thousand, §§3–4. Sardis: Ref. Map 4.1, CY; Ref. Map 4.2, CZ.
S.14.19.6b  Lydia: Ref. Map 4.1, CY; Ref. Map 4.2, CZ. Phrygia (Greater Phrygia): Ref. Map 4.1, BZ. The Aeolid/Aeolis: Ref. Map 4.1, BX; Ref. Map 4.2, BY. Memphis: Ref. Map 1, DX.
S.14.19.6c  Pisidia: Ref. Map 4.1, CZ.
S.14.19.7a  Peloponnese: Ref. Map 2, CX.
S.14.19.8a  Diogenes Laertius 2.6.50 (in Appendix V: Diogenes Laertius' *Life of Xenophon*) says

that Menon came from Pharsalus, another Thessalian city, rather than Larissa. On Menon, see n. S.14.27.2a. On the composition of the Greek contingent in Cyrus' army, see Appendix I, Table I.4, which sets out the evidence in Xenophon's text. Xenophon does not link the origins of the various contingents with the origins of their commanders as strongly as Diodorus does here. The following locations appear on Ref. Map 2: Achaea, CX; Boeotia, Pharsalus, BY; Thebes, BZ; Thessaly, Larissa, AY.
S.14.19.9a  *Barbaroi:* translated as "barbarians" in this edition.
S.14.19.9b  Including the Greek mercenaries. Klearchos (*Anabasis* 1.2.1–21) seems to have been the only one among them privy to Cyrus' plans (Peter Green).
S.14.20.1a  Cilician Gates: Ref. Map 5, CY.
S.14.20.1b  Two and a quarter miles: the Greek text says 20 stades/about 3.6 kilometers). On stades, see Appendix O: Ancient Greek and Persian Units of Measurement, §§2–5.

flanked on both sides by exceptionally high and impenetrable mountains. Walls, again on both sides, run down from the mountains to the road, on which gates have also been constructed.[c] [2] Cyrus led his army through the defile and debouched on what is, without exception, the most beautiful plain in Asia. Across this plain he advanced to Tarsus,[a] the largest city in Cilicia, which he quickly occupied. When Syennesis, the ruler of Cilicia, heard reports of the size of the enemy forces, he was in something of a quandary, being no match for them if it came to a fight. [3] So when Cyrus sent for him with pledges of safe conduct, he went. On learning the truth about the war, he undertook to ally himself with Cyrus against Artaxerxes and sent one of his sons, together with a sizable contingent of Cilicians, to join the expedition. Being a crafty rogue by nature, he insured himself against the uncertainties of Fortune by secretly dispatching his other son to the King, to report on the forces massed against him and to explain that he, Syennesis, was allied with Cyrus only out of necessity; that he was actually a loyal subject still; and that when an opportunity arose, he would desert Cyrus and join the King's forces.[a]

[4] Cyrus rested his troops in Tarsus for twenty days. But when he then struck camp, the rank and file suspected that the expedition was really aimed at Artaxerxes. As each man calculated the distances to be covered and the number of hostile tribes through whose territory they would have to make their way, he became acutely worried, for the word had got around that it was a four-month march for an army to Bactria[a] and that more than four hundred thousand troops had been mustered to serve the King. [5] They were thoroughly scared, and this made them resentful. Indeed, they became so furious with the way they had been treacherously deceived that they were all set to murder the leaders responsible. However, when Cyrus made an urgent appeal to them all and assured them that he was leading the army not against Artaxerxes but to deal with a satrap in Syria,[a] the troops were convinced and—after receiving a pay raise—resumed their original goodwill toward him.

**14.21.** [1] After traversing Cilicia, Cyrus reached Issus,[a] which is by the sea and the last city in Cilicia. About the same time, the Lacedaemonian fleet also put in there. They went ashore, met with Cyrus, and informed him of the Spartans' favorable reaction to his plans. They also disembarked the eight hundred foot soldiers who had come with Cheirisophos and turned them over to him. [2] They pretended that it was Cyrus' friends who had sent these mercenaries, but in actual fact everything had been done with the approval of the ephors.[a] The Lacedaemonians were not yet openly committed to this war, but they still kept their intentions secret, waiting on the turn of events.

Cyrus struck camp and set out with his army, making for Syria and ordering his

14.20.1c  Diodorus' report of fortifications constructed across the pass is almost certainly false, at least for 401, and is probably just a misunderstanding of the name of the pass.
S.14.20.2a  Tarsus: Ref. Map 5, CY.
S.14.20.3a  Xenophon (*Anabasis* 1.2.12, 1.2.26–27) gives further details of Syennesis' double-dealing, reporting inter alia that he sent his wife Epyaxa to Cyrus before Cyrus reached the Cilician Gates, with back pay for his troops and herself (it was widely believed)

for his bed (Peter Green).
S.14.20.4a  Bactria: Ref. Map 9, AZ.
S.14.20.5a  The satrap referred to was Abrokomas: *Anabasis* 1.3.20 (Peter Green). Syria: Ref. Map 5, DZ.
S.14.21.1a  Issus: Ref. Map 5, CY.
S.14.21.2a  Ephors: annually elected magistrates at Sparta who determined Spartan foreign policy and broad strategy; see further Appendix B: Xenophon and Sparta, §16.

naval commanders to accompany him by sea, with the entire fleet. [3] When he reached what are known as "The Gates" and found the place unguarded, he was overjoyed, having had serious concerns that troops might have already occupied it. The site is a narrow and precipitous pass, easily guarded by a few men. [4] The mountains on either side of it lie close to each other, the one being rugged, with beetling crags, while the other—the largest in the region, called Amanus and running the whole length of Phoenicia—comes right down to the road.[a] The open space between the mountains is about one-third of a mile[b] in length, walled throughout, and with gates so designed as to leave only a narrow opening.[c] [5] After passing through the Gates unopposed, Cyrus sent back to Ephesus the part of the fleet that had accompanied him; since he was about to strike inland, he would no longer have any use for it. A twenty days' march brought him to Thapsakos, a city on the Euphrates River.[a] [6] Here he stopped for five days, and after ingratiating himself with the troops by a generous distribution of provisions and booty from foraging, he summoned them to an assembly and disclosed the true purpose of the expedition. When the soldiers reacted to his speech with hostility, he begged them all not to desert him and promised (among other munificent rewards) that when he got to Babylon,[a] he would give every man there five silver minas.[b] Elated by this prospect, the rank and file were persuaded to follow him.[c] [7] When Cyrus had crossed the Euphrates with his army, he force-marched nonstop until he had reached the frontier of Babylonia,[a] and there he rested his troops.

**14.22.** [1] King Artaxerxes had been informed earlier by Pharnabazos that Cyrus was covertly assembling an army with which to attack him; and now, on hearing he had set out for the interior, the King summoned contingents from every quarter of the empire to Ecbatana in Media.[a] [2] When those from the Indians[a] and certain other peoples were slow in arriving because of the distance they had to travel, he set out to confront Cyrus with such troops as were already mustered. He had in all, according to Ephorus,[b] not less than four hundred thousand men, cavalry included. [3] On reaching the Babylonian plain, he pitched camp along one bank of the Euphrates, with the intention of leaving his baggage there: he had heard that the enemy forces were not far off, and [reports of] their dangerous recklessness made him nervous. [4] He therefore had a protective ditch dug, sixty feet wide and ten deep, and encircled [his camp] with the covered wagons that accompanied him, like

S.14.21.4a I accept Vogel's emendation *megiston* ("largest") for the (in context) meaningless reading of Diodorus' manuscripts, and Wesseling's topographically acute "*Amanos*" for the manuscript reading "*Libanos*" (Peter Green). "On either side of it" has been added to the translation to clarify the meaning. Amanus (Mtns.), Phoenicia: Ref. Map 5, CY, DY.
S.14.21.4b One-third of a mile: the Greek text says 3 stades (0.33 miles/about 0.53 kilometers).
S.14.21.4c This is the modern Bahçe pass, known in antiquity as the Amanic Gates. Darius III came down this pass behind Alexander's troops and cut off his line of retreat before the battle of Issus (fall 333); see Diodorus 17.32.1–4 (Peter Green). Peter Green thus takes it that Diodorus and Xenophon disagree about the

route of the army, as Xenophon does not take it through the Amanic Gates (Ref. Map 5, CY; Amanikai Pylai in the *Barrington Atlas*); modern Bahçe Pass: Ref. Map 8, CY.
S.14.21.5a Thapsakos, possible location, Euphrates River: Ref. Map 5, CZ. (Thapsakos is not listed in the *Barrington Atlas*.)
S.14.21.6a Babylon: Ref. Map 6, DZ.
S.14.21.6b On minas, see Appendix O: Measurements, §§10–11.
S.14.21.6c See *Anabasis* 1.4.11–18.
S.14.21.7a Babylonia: Ref. Map 6, DZ.
S.14.22.1a Ecbatana, Media: Ref. Map 9, CX.
S.14.22.2a India: Ref. Map 9, CZ.
S.14.22.2b For this fourth-century historian, see Appendix M: Other Ancient Sources on the Ten Thousand, §9.

a rampart. Then, leaving behind in camp both the baggage and a crowd of noncombatants, together with an adequate detachment to guard them, he set out at the head of his army, marching light, to meet an enemy that was now close at hand.[a]

[5] When Cyrus saw the King's forces approaching, he at once drew up his own troops in battle order. His right wing, flanking the Euphrates, was held by the Lacedaemonian infantry and some of the mercenaries, under the general command of Klearchos the Lacedaemonian, and supported by the cavalry contingent from Paphlagonia,[a] a thousand and more strong. The other wing consisted of troops from Phrygia and Lydia, together with about a thousand cavalry under the command of Aridaios.[b] [6] Cyrus stationed himself in the center of the phalanx,[a] with the finest troops of the Persians and other *barbaroi*, some ten thousand in number. Deployed in front of him was a crack cavalry regiment, a thousand strong, splendidly equipped with Greek cuirasses and dirks. [7] Artaxerxes stationed large numbers of scythed chariots[a] along the entire front of his phalanx, at the midpoint of which he took up his own position, having at his command not less than fifty thousand picked troops. He also appointed Persians as commanders of the wings.

**14.23.** [1] When the armies were about three *stadioi*[a] apart, the Greeks launched into their paean,[b] and to begin with advanced at an easy pace; but as they came within bowshot range, they broke into a fast run. They had been ordered to do this by Klearchos the Lacedaemonian, his idea being that not running for too great a distance would keep the combatants physically fresh for battle, while moving at the double when at close quarters would cause arrows and other missiles to fly over them. [2] And indeed, as Cyrus' troops drew near the King's army, they became the target for such a volley of missiles as one might well expect from a horde four hundred thousand strong. Nevertheless, they spent comparatively little time fighting with javelins, after which they battled it out hand to hand. [3] From the very first moment of engagement, the Lacedaemonians and the other mercenaries astounded the *barbaroi* arrayed against them, both by the excellence of their equipment and by their evident expertise, [4] since the *barbaroi* themselves were protected only by small bucklers, and most of their divisions were light-armed troops. Furthermore, they were not battle hardened; whereas the Greeks, because of the length of the Peloponnesian War,[a] had been engaged in nonstop fighting and thus were experienced veterans by comparison. As a result, they routed the *barbaroi* straight off and killed large numbers of them during the subsequent pursuit. [5] It also so happened[a]

S.14.22.4a  For a full eyewitness account of the battle of Cunaxa (the name of the site has been preserved by Plutarch, *Life of Artaxerxes* 8.2 [in Appendix T: Selections from Plutarch's *Life of Artaxerxes*]), see *Anabasis* 1.7.14–1.8.29, 1.10.1–16, on which Diodorus' narrative largely relies, with additional details from Ephorus and Ctesias (Peter Green). Here Peter Green implies that Diodorus used Xenophon directly. See Appendix M: Other Sources on the Ten Thousand, §6, for a different view. On Ctesias, see Appendix W: Brief Biographies of Selected Characters in *Anabasis*, §8.

S.14.22.5a  Paphlagonia: Ref. Map 5, AX.
S.14.22.5b  This is the same man whom Xenophon calls Ariaios.

S.14.22.6a  Phalanx: a body of troops drawn up across a broad front in close formation; see Appendix H: Infantry and Cavalry in *Anabasis*, §§13–15.
S.14.22.7a  Scythed chariots: see *Anabasis* 1.8.10.
S.14.23.1a  Three *stadioi* equals about 580 yards/530 meters.
S.14.23.1b  Paean: a solemn chant, especially (as in this case) a battle hymn.
S.14.23.4a  The Peloponnesian War, between Athens and Sparta and their respective allies, began in 431, and fighting continued, with a couple of short breaks, until 404.
S.14.23.5a  In fact, this was a well-established Persian tradition; see *Anabasis* 1.8.22 (Peter Green).

that both men competing for the kingdom had taken up a position in mid-phalanx, so that when they realized this fact, they made for each other in an ardent desire to decide the outcome of the battle by themselves. Fortune, it would seem, was bringing the brothers' rivalry for supreme power to the test of single combat, as though in imitation of that braggart encounter long ago—the theme of so many tragedies[b]— between Eteocles and Polyneices. [6] Cyrus made the first move. He hurled his javelin from a distance, hit the King, and laid him low; but Artaxerxes' attendants quickly picked him up and carried him away, out of the battle. The Persian warrior Tissaphernes at once took over the King's command, rallied the rank and file, and himself fought heroically, making good the setback caused by the King's elimination, showing up everywhere with his elite troops and killing large numbers of the enemy, so that his presence was noted even at a distance. [7] Cyrus, elated by the success of his troops, charged impetuously into the thick of the enemy, and at first, thanks to his boundless daring, slew many of them. But then, exposing himself too recklessly, he was struck by a common Persian soldier and fell, mortally wounded. With his death, the King's men regained confidence for the fight. In the end, through a mixture of resolute courage and superior numbers, they overwhelmed their opponents.

**14.24.** [1] On the other wing Aridaios—Cyrus' satrap who had been appointed to that command—to begin with, vigorously withstood the attacks of the *barbaroi;* but later, hemmed in by their extended battle line and learning of Cyrus' death, he withdrew with his own troops to one of his earlier way stations, which provided a passable refuge for them. [2] Klearchos, observing that not only the allies' center but the rest of their line had been routed, stopped the pursuit, recalled his troops, and deployed them in battle order, fearing that the entire enemy force might now descend on the Greeks, encircle them, and wipe them out to the last man. [3] The King's troops, after routing their opponents, first pillaged Cyrus' baggage and then, night already having fallen, launched a general assault on the Greeks; but when the latter stoutly fought off the attack, the *barbaroi* resisted for a short while only, and very soon turned and fled, overcome by the Greeks' daring and expertise. [4] Klearchos' troops slaughtered a good many of the *barbaroi*, and then, it now being dark, retired and set up a trophy.[a] At some time around the second watch,[b] they made it safely back to their camp.

[5] Such was the outcome of this battle. The losses of the King's army totaled more than fifteen thousand, most of them killed by the Lacedaemonians and mercenaries with Klearchos. [6] On the other side of Cyrus' troops, there fell about three thousand, while not a single Greek (we are told) was killed and only a few were wounded. When the night ended, Aridaios (he who had withdrawn to the way station) sent word to Klearchos, inviting him to bring his troops over, so that together they could get safely through to the coast. Now that Cyrus was dead and the King's forces

---

S.14.23.5b   Best known today from Aeschylus' *Seven*
             *Against Thebes.* Eteocles and Polyneices were
             two sons of Oedipus who engaged in a fratri-
             cidal civil war over the succession, killing one
             another in the battle for Thebes (Peter Green).
S.14.24.4a   Trophy: a memorial set up by the victors of a
             battle, usually consisting of a post on which

armor from the vanquished was hung; for
more, see the Glossary.
S.14.24.4b   The Greeks divided the night, from dusk to
             dawn, into five watches (*phylakai*). These
             varied in length according to the time of year
             (Peter Green).

were everywhere in the ascendancy, acute anxiety afflicted all those who had had the temerity to join an expedition for the object of overthrowing Artaxerxes' royal power.

**14.25.** [1] Klearchos now called a meeting of generals and other commanders to discuss the current situation. While they were about this business, there arrived an embassy from the King, in which the chief ambassador was a Greek named Phalynos,[a] a Zacynthian[b] by birth. Introduced into the meeting, they reported King Artaxerxes' words as follows: "Since I have defeated and killed Cyrus, surrender your arms, make your way to my doors, and find out how you may win my favor and thus get some benefit." [2] To this pronouncement each of the generals gave a reply much like that of Leonidas, made when he was guarding the pass of Thermopylae[a] and Xerxes sent messengers ordering him to lay down his arms. [3] At that time Leonidas told them to take this message back to the King: "We are of the opinion that, even should we become friends to Xerxes, we shall be better allies with our arms in our possession; and if we are forced to fight him, we shall, likewise, fight better if armed."[a] [4] After Klearchos had made a very similar response, Proxenos the Theban said: "We have now lost virtually everything else, save only our valor and our arms. So we believe that if we hang on to the latter, our valor, too, will be of some use to us, whereas if we surrender them, valor alone will avail us nothing." He therefore told them to take this message back to the King: "If he is planning some kind of trouble for us, we will use our arms to contend with him for our common good." [5] One of the commanders, Sophilos, is also on record as having said he was surprised at the King's words, "for if he thinks himself more than a match for the Greeks, let him come here with his army and take our arms from us; but if he prefers persuasion, let him state what favor he will grant us that is a fair return for them." [6] Next after these, Socrates the Achaean said that he found the King's behavior in their regard quite extraordinary, "since what he wants of us he demands on the spot, whereas what will be given us in return he orders us to enquire of him later. In brief, then: if it's in ignorance of who actually won that he's telling us to obey his orders as though we were the losers, let him bring his vast host here and find out whose the victory was; but if he's lying to us in full awareness that we were the victors, then how can we trust any future promises he may make?"[a] [7] On getting these responses, the messengers departed, and Klearchos marched his men to

S.14.25.1a  *Anabasis* 2.1.7 (Peter Green).
            Xenophon spells the name Phalinos.
S.14.25.1b  Zacynthus: Ref. Map 2, CX.
S.14.25.2a  The battle in question was fought in 480
            between a very large army under the Persian
            King Xerxes and a much smaller force under
            Leonidas, king of Sparta, trying to resist
            Xerxes' entry into central and southern
            Greece. The Spartans fought on to the last
            man, and Greeks subsequently greatly admired
            their heroism. Thermopylae: Ref. Map 2, BY.
S.14.25.3a  See Diodorus 11.5.5 (Peter Green).
S.14.25.6a  Diodorus' account of this exchange differs in
            several respects from Xenophon's. The speech
            that the latter attributes to Theopompos
            [*Anabasis* 2.1.12], Diodorus gives to Proxenos;
            that of Proxenos in the *Anabasis* Diodorus puts
            in the mouth of Sophilos; and he adds an inter-
            vention by Socrates the Achaean. Neither of

these last two figures in Xenophon's account.
M. Bonnet points out on p. xxvi of the Budé
edition of Diodorus Book 14, of which she is
co-editor (Bonnet and Bennett 1997), that
Diodorus' version (unlike Xenophon's) claims
knowledge of events on the Persian side
(14.22.1–4, 14.24.5–6, 14.26.4–5). Though
Diodorus clearly drew on Xenophon (for a
striking instance, see 14.30.1–2 and compare
*Anabasis* 4.8.20–21), he also, equally clearly,
had access to a version (perhaps that of his fellow commander Sophainetos, now lost) that
remembered the meeting differently and could
draw on Persian-controlled sources (Peter
Green). On Sophainetos, see Appendix M:
Other Ancient Sources on the Ten Thousand,
§§12–15, which is more tentative about
whether Sophainetos really did write his own
account than Peter Green is here.

the way station where those troops that escaped the battle in safety had found refuge. When the entire force was assembled there, they deliberated together about how they were to manage their retreat to the sea and what route they should take. [8] They decided that they should not return the same way as they had come, since much of it was barren countryside where they could not expect to find provisions, especially with a hostile army in pursuit of them. They therefore determined to make for Paphlagonia, and the whole force accordingly set out in that direction, traveling at an easy pace, to let them procure provisions en route.

**14.26.** [1] The King was by now somewhat recovered from his wound, and when he learned of the enemy's retreat, he got the impression that they were in flight and hastened to pursue them with his own forces. [2] Since they were making slow progress, he soon caught up with them. But by then night had fallen, so he encamped nearby. When day broke and the Greeks began to array their forces for battle, he sent messengers to them and arranged a temporary three-day truce. [3] During this period they reached an agreement. He would arrange a peaceful passage through his territory to the sea for them and furnish them with guides to that end, while the mercenaries under Klearchos and all the troops commanded by Aridaios would commit no offenses in the course of their march.[a] [4] After this the Greeks took to the road, and the King led his army back to Babylon. There he fittingly honored each individual who had distinguished himself in the battle and judged Tissaphernes to have been the most courageous of them all. So he gave him rich rewards in recompense, as well as his own daughter in marriage, and from then on continued to treat him as his most faithful friend. He also gave him the command that Cyrus had held over the maritime satrapies.[a]

[5] Tissaphernes, observing the King's fury at the Greeks, offered to destroy them all for him, provided he gave him the men to do it and made a deal with Aridaios, being convinced that this was a man who would betray the Greeks during the course of their march.[a] The King received his proposal with pleasure and let Tissaphernes select, from the whole of his army, as many of the top warriors as he might need for his project. [6] <Tissaphernes then proposed to Klearchos and>[a] the other leaders that they should come and discuss matters with him in person. So almost all the generals, together with Klearchos and a score or so of captains, went to meet Tissaphernes, and there followed them some two hundred soldiers who wanted to visit the market. [7] Tissaphernes invited the generals into his tent while the captains waited outside. After a little while, a red flag was hoisted from Tissaphernes' tent; he had the generals inside arrested, while a specially assigned group descended on the captains

S.14.26.3a Diodorus has run two stages of the negotiations into one. The three-day truce was to let the Greeks seek provisions in the villages (*Anabasis* 2.3.1–16); there followed a longer discussion, with Tissaphernes as broker, to set up guidelines for the march south (*Anabasis* 2.3.17–29) (Peter Green).

S.14.26.4a Though he became Cyrus' virtual successor in Asia Minor (Xenophon, *Hellenika* 3.1–3), Tissaphernes did not marry Artaxerxes' daughter (Diodorus here confuses him with his colleague Orontas, the satrap of eastern Armenia; *Anabasis* 2.4.8), and after his

defeat by Agesilaos at Sardis in 395, he was summarily executed (Diodorus 14.80.6–8) (Peter Green). Asia Minor is called western Anatolia elsewhere in this volume.

S.14.26.5a He was right; see *Anabasis* 2.5.35–40 (Peter Green).

S.14.26.6a There is a lacuna in the manuscripts here, though the sense (as inserted) remains clear enough. Diodorus' account of the episode that follows is narrated at great length by Xenophon in *Anabasis* 2.5.2–27 (Peter Green).

and killed them, and others finished off those soldiers who had come for the market, all except for one man, who got away back to camp with news of the disaster.

**14.27.** [1] On learning what had happened, the troops were momentarily panic-stricken. They all hastened to arm themselves, but in great disorder, since they had no commanders. When no one came to trouble them, however, they chose a number of generals and gave the supreme command to Cheirisophos the Lacedaemonian. [2] These men organized the army as seemed best to them for the march and pushed on toward Paphlagonia.

Tissaphernes handcuffed the generals and sent them off to Artaxerxes, who had them all executed, with the single exception of Menon, since he alone, because of his disagreements with his allies, was thought to have been ready to betray the Greeks.[a] [3] Tissaphernes and his forces followed close on the heels of the Greeks, yet he dared not engage them face-to-face in battle from fear of the crazy recklessness of desperate men. Though ready to harass them when the terrain was advantageous, he could not do them any serious harm but simply kept in pursuit, inflicting minimal damage, as far as the country of a people called the Kardouchoi,[a] at which point, [4] unable to do anything further, he and his army took off for Ionia.

It took the Greeks seven days to cross the mountain passes of the Kardouchoi, during which they suffered a great deal from the attentions of the local inhabitants, who were both aggressive and familiar with the terrain. [5] They were an independent tribe, hostile to the Great King, and well practiced in military matters; in particular, they trained themselves to use exceptionally large stones as missiles for their slings, as well as large arrows. Employing these, they kept up a lethal fusillade against the Greeks from high ground, killing large numbers of them and seriously injuring not a few others. [6] For their arrows, more than three feet[a] long, penetrated both shields and cuirasses, and no defensive armor could withstand their force. The arrows they used, it is said, were so large that the Greeks wound thongs around spent ones and threw them back, treating them like javelins.[b] [7] Having thus, with much difficulty, made their way through the aforesaid country, they reached the Kentrites River and by crossing it entered Armenia.[a] The satrap there was Tiribazos: they made a treaty with him and passed through his territory as friends.

**14.28.** [1] As they were negotiating the mountain passes of Armenia, they were caught in a heavy snowstorm and barely escaped perishing to the last man. When the air was disturbed, to begin with, the snow fell so lightly from the sky that the progress of the march was in no way hampered; but then a wind arose and the snowfall became heavier and heavier, blanketing the ground until not only the road but every landmark was completely invisible. [2] Discouragement and fear now spread among the rank and file. No one wanted to turn back, which meant certain destruction; yet because of the massive snowfall, further progress was impossible. As the storm gathered intensity, there came fierce gusts of wind and heavy hail, blow-

---

S.14.27.2a  A view shared by Xenophon; see *Anabasis* 2.5.8, 2.6.29. This is the same person as the Meno who figures as the protagonist in Plato's dialogue of that name, where his guest-friendship with the Great King is mentioned (78D) (Peter Green). See further n. 14.19.8a.

S.14.27.3a  Kardouchoi territory: Ref. Map 6, BY.

S.14.27.6a  Three feet: the Greek text says two *pēcheis*. On *pēcheis* (cubits), see Appendix O: Measurements, §§2–3, 23.

S.14.27.6b  See *Anabasis* 4.2.27–28 (Peter Green).

S.14.27.7a  Peter Green notes that it was specifically western Armenia the Greeks were entering. Kentrites River, Armenia: Ref. Map 7, BY.

ing directly into their faces and bringing the entire column to a halt. Each individual, unable to endure the hardships of this march any further, was stopped dead in his tracks, wherever he happened to be. [3] Though all lacked even the barest necessities, they endured the rest of that day and the following night in the open, suffering intensely. The unending snowfall covered up their weapons, and their bodies were chilled through by the freezing air. The hardships they endured were such that they got no sleep all night. Some managed to light fires and found a measure of relief from that; but others were so chilled throughout their bodies, with almost all their extremities frostbitten, that they gave up any hope of rescue. [4] Thus, when the night was over, it turned out that most of the beasts of burden had perished, while of the men many were dead; a considerable number, though still conscious, could not move their frozen bodies; and some were blinded because of the cold and the reflected glare off the snow. [5] Undoubtedly they would all have perished had they not gone on a little farther and found villages with supplies in abundance. These villages had special underground entry tunnels for the beasts of burden, and others, with ladders, for the inhabitants.... <In the>ᵃ houses the cattle were provided with fodder, while their owners had a plentiful store of all the necessities of life.

**14.29.** [1] After spending eight days in these villages, they pressed on to the Phasis River,ᵃ where they stopped for another four days. They then passed through the territory of the Taochoi and Phasianoi.ᵇ When the local inhabitants attacked them, they defeated them in battle, killing a good many. They then occupied their properties, which had good things in plenty, and spent fifteen days there. [2] Marching on from there, they passed through the territory known as that of the Chaldaioi in seven days and reached the Harpagos River,ᵃ which is about four hundred feetᵇ wide. Their route then took them through the territory of the Skytinoi,ᶜ across a plain where they rested for three days, enjoying every necessity in abundance. After this they marched on and by the fourth day reached a large town called †Gymnasia†.ᵈ [3] At this point the local ruler made an agreement with them and provided them with guides as far as the sea.

After fifteen days they reached Mount Chenion, and when those at the head of the column glimpsed the sea, in their delight they raised such a hullabaloo that the rearguard assumed there had been an enemy attack and rushed to arms.ᵃ [4] But

---

S.14.28.5a Another textual lacuna: the sense is clear from the parallel description by Xenophon at *Anabasis* 4.5.25 (Peter Green).

S.14.29.1a Phasis River: Ref. Map 6, AY.

S.14.29.1b Taochoi, Phasianoi territories: Ref. Map 6, AY (Phasioi in the *Barrington Atlas*). Taochoi is Peter Green's correction of the Chaoi in Diodorus'manuscripts, retained by many scholars.

S.14.29.2a Chaldaioi, perhaps the same as the Eastern Chalybes. Eastern Chalybes; Harpagos/ Harpasos River: Ref. Map 6, AX. The *Barrington Atlas* does not locate the Eastern Chalybes on its maps and locates the Chaldaioi differently, at Map 87 E4 (Chaldia).

S.14.29.2b Four hundred feet: the Greek text says 4 *plethra* (Peter Green). On *plethra*, see Appendix O: Measurements, §§2, 3, 23.

S.14.29.2c Skytinoi/Skythenoi: Ref. Map 6, AX.

S.14.29.2d Gymnasia, which Peter Green places in dag-

gers to indicate that he is not confident it is what Diodorus wrote here, is presumably to be identified with Xenophon's Gymnias at *Anabasis* 4.7.19. For the Landmark editors' proposed location, see Gymnias, possible location: Ref. Map 6, AX. Peter Green tentatively suggests identifying it with Gizenenica: Map 4.7.25.

S.14.29.3a The occasion is famous from *Anabasis* 4.7.21–26 ("Thalassa! Thalassa!"), yet its details remain obscure; for example, the identity and precise location of the mountain ("Theches" in Xenophon) are still uncertain (Peter Green). For the Landmark editors' view, see Appendix P: The Route of the Ten Thousand, §§12–14, and Map P.3. For the famous cry "Thalassa! Thalassa!" ("The sea! The sea!"), see Appendix R: The Legacy of Xenophon's *Anabasis*, §§9, 13–14.

when they had all got up to the point from which the sea was visible, they raised their arms to the gods in gratitude, convinced that they now had reached safety. They gathered a great mass of stones and built them into two huge cairns, on which they dedicated spoils taken from the *barbaroi*, being determined to leave behind an undying memorial of their expedition.

Their guide they presented with a silver bowl and a Persian robe; and he, after showing them the road to the Makrones,[a] took his leave. [5] The Greeks then entered the territory of the Makrones, with whom they concluded an agreement. As a pledge of good faith, they received from them a native spear and gave them a Greek one in exchange. The *barbaroi* assured them that this tradition, handed down to them from their forefathers, was the strongest known guarantee of good faith. On leaving the frontiers of this people, they found themselves in the country of the Kolchoi.[a] [6] When the local inhabitants banded together against them, they defeated them in battle, killed large numbers of them, and seized a hilltop stronghold from which they plundered the surrounding territory. The booty thus acquired they brought back to the stronghold, and rested themselves in the midst of plenty.

**14.30.** [1] In this region there were to be found vast numbers of beehives,[a] which yielded a rare and costly kind of honey. But all those who sampled it experienced the strangest affliction: after eating some, they lost consciousness, fell down, and lay on the ground like so many corpses.[b] [2] Since its special sweetness had led many to try it, the number of the fallen soon came to resemble the victims of a military rout. For the rest of that day, the troops were much disheartened, taken aback both by the strangeness of the incident and by the multitude of those affected. But the next day, at about the same time, they all came round, gradually regained their faculties, and got to their feet; their physical state resembled that of someone recovering from a dose of poison.[a]

[3] After three days' recuperation, they marched on to the Greek city of Trapezus, a colony of the Sinopians within Kolchian territory.[a] There they stayed for thirty days, entertained splendidly by the local inhabitants. They offered sacrifice to Herakles and Zeus the Deliverer and held a gymnastic contest at the place where, it is said, *Argo* put in with Jason and his crew.[b] [4] From here they sent off their leader, Cheirisophos, to Byzantium to obtain transport vessels and triremes, since he reckoned himself a friend of Anaxibios, the Byzantine naval commander.[a] Him they dispatched in a light craft, and then, taking over a couple of oared skiffs from the men of

S.14.29.4a  Makrones territory: Ref. Map 6, AX.
S.14.29.5a  Kolchoi territory: Ref. Map 6, AX.
S.14.30.1a  *Anabasis* 4.8.20–21 (Peter Green). The word that both Diodorus and Xenophon use in referring to the bees here, *smēnē*, is ambiguous between "hives" (used here) and "swarms" (used in the translation of Xenophon's account in this edition).
S.14.30.1b  The local bees harvested the blossoms of the yellow-flowered *Rhododendron luteum*; the resultant honey, when still fresh in the comb, would produce just the toxic effect described by Diodorus and Xenophon (Peter Green). See further *Anabasis* n. 4.8.20b and Appendix Q: The Chronology of the March, §§8–10.
S.14.30.2a  Dose of poison: the same word, *pharmako-*

*posia*, is used by Xenophon and at 4.8.21 is translated in this edition as "enchanted potion." The word can mean alternatively, and indeed simultaneously, "a dose of medicine."
5.14.30.3a  Marched on in May/June 400 (Peter Green). Trapezus, Sinope: Ref. Map 5, AZ, AY.
S.14.30.3b  Diodorus here confuses the Colchis at the eastern extremity of the Black Sea (which was where Jason reputedly landed) with the territory of the Kolchoi immediately to the south of Trapezus (Peter Green). On Jason and the Argonauts, see *Anabasis* n. 6.2.1a.
S.14.30.4a  This is a mistake: Anaxibios was a Spartan and commanding the Spartan fleet, though he was based at Byzantium at this point. Byzantium: Ref. Map 4.1, AY.

Trapezus, they proceeded to despoil the neighboring *barbaroi* by both land and sea.

[5] So for thirty days they awaited Cheirisophos' return, but when he still delayed and provisions for the men were running short, they left Trapezus and two days later reached the Greek city of Kerasous,[a] a colony of the Sinopians. After stopping there for a few days, they moved on into the territory of the Mossynician tribe.[b] [6] When these *barbaroi* gathered to attack them, they defeated them in battle with great slaughter. The Mossynoeci then retreated to a stronghold where they resided and had a number of wooden towers seven stories high. The Greeks launched a series of assaults on it and took it by storm. This stronghold was the capital of all their other defensive positions, and in it, at its very summit, their king had his dwelling. [7] They have a traditional custom that the king must stay in it for his entire life and issue his edicts to the masses from there. The troops declared that this was the most barbarous tribe they had ever encountered, reporting that the men had congress with their women in public; that even the wealthiest people's offspring were fed on boiled nuts; and that they were all, as children, tattooed with various designs on both back and breast.

The Greeks got through this region in eight days, and the next, called Tibarene,[a] in three.

**14.31.** [1] From there they came to a Greek city called Kotyora,[a] a colony of the Sinopians. They spent fifty days there, raiding the Paphlagonians and other *barbaroi* in the area. The inhabitants of Heraclea[b] and Sinope sent them transport vessels, in which they and their baggage animals were ferried over to Sinope.[c] [2] Sinope, a colony of the Milesians situated in Paphlagonia, had the greatest renown of any city in the area and was where, in our own times, the Mithradates who fought the Romans had his largest palace.[a] [3] Another arrival there was Cheirisophos, whose mission to secure triremes had come to nothing. The Sinopians nevertheless entertained them all generously and sent them on by sea to Heraclea, a colony of the Megarians.[a] The entire convoy anchored off the peninsula of Acheron,[b] where (the story goes) Herakles brought Cerberus up from Hades. [4] From here they made their way overland through Bithynia,[a] at some risk to themselves, since the local inhabitants kept harassing them for the whole course of their march. So it was with difficulty that these survivors of the Ten Thousand, now some 8,300 in number, made it through to the Chalcedonian city of Chrysopolis.[b] [5] From there on, further travel was easy, and some got safely home to their own countries; but the remainder assembled in the Chersonese and plundered the adjacent territory of the Thracians.[a] This, then, was the conclusion of Cyrus' campaign against Artaxerxes.[b]

S.14.30.5a  Kerasous: Ref. Map 5, AZ.
S.14.30.5b  The Mossynician tribe: see *Anabasis* 5.4.1–26 (Peter Green). Mossynoeci territory: Ref. Map 5, AZ.
S.14.30.7a  Tibarene, evidently the territory of the Tibareni: Ref. Map 5, AZ.
S.14.31.1a  Kotyora: Ref. Map 5, AZ.
S.14.31.1b  Heraclea: Ref. Map 4.1, AZ.
S.14.31.1c  "To Sinope" has been added in the translation for clarity.
S.14.31.2a  Mithradates VI (r. 120–63) of Pontus, of which Sinope was the capital, fought two major wars against Rome: in 89–85, defeated

by Sulla, and in 73–66, defeated by Lucullus and Pompey (Peter Green). Miletus: Ref. Map 4.1, DY.
S.14.31.3a  Megara: Ref. Map 2, CY.
S.14.31.3b  Peninsula of Acheron/Acherousian Chersonese: Ref. Map 4.1, AZ.
S.14.31.4a  Bithynia/Bithynians: Ref. Map 4.1, AZ.
S.14.31.4b  Chalcedon, Chrysopolis: Ref. Map 4.1, AY.
S.14.31.5a  Chersonese, Thrace: Ref. Map 3, DY, CY.
S.14.31.5b  This chapter is a perfunctory note covering events that take up the whole of Books 6 and 7 in *Anabasis* (Peter Green).

## Tissaphernes, Thibron, and the Greeks
## Who Had Been in Cyrus' Army: 14.35–37

**14.35.** [1] When this year was over, the archon in Athens was Laches [400/399]. . . . The 95th Olympiad took place, in which Minos of Athens won the *stadion*.[a] . . . [2] At this time Artaxerxes, the king of Asia, now that he had defeated Cyrus, sent out Tissaphernes[a] to take over the command of all the maritime satrapies. Because of this the satraps and cities that had allied themselves with Cyrus were in a state of considerable anxiety, fearing reprisals for their offenses against the King. [3] So all the other satraps sent ambassadors to Tissaphernes, paid court to him, and to the best of their ability arranged their affairs to please him; the single exception was Tamos, the most powerful of them all and the governor of Ionia,[a] who shipped aboard his triremes all his possessions and all his sons, except for one, called Glos, who later became commander in chief of the King's armies. [4] Tamos, therefore, in fear of Tissaphernes, took his fleet to Egypt and sought asylum with the Egyptian king, Psammetichos, a descendant of the famous Psammetichos.[a] Since he had earlier rendered this king good service, he figured he would now find in him a safe haven against the reprisals of Artaxerxes. [5] Psammetichos, however, taking no account either of the service done him or of the sacred obligations due to a suppliant, had this man—both suppliant and friend—slaughtered, together with his children, in order to get possession of his goods and his fleet.

[6] The Greek communities of Asia, on learning of Tissaphernes' imminent arrival and being deeply concerned for their own safety, sent ambassadors to the Lacedaemonians, begging them not to stand by and let their cities be laid waste by the barbarians. The Lacedaemonians promised them support and sent ambassadors to Tissaphernes with a request that he not take any hostile military action against the Greek cities.

[7] But Tissaphernes and his army, on arrival at the nearest city, that of Cyme,[a] laid waste all the surrounding countryside and took large numbers of prisoners. He then corralled the Cymaians in their city and laid siege to it. However, since, by the time winter was approaching, he had still not managed to reduce it, he ransomed his prisoners at a stiff price and raised the siege.

**14.36.** [1] The Lacedaemonians appointed Thibron commander of the war against the King, gave him a thousand men from their own citizen body, and instructed him to recruit such troops from their allies as he should consider expedient. [2] Thibron marched to Corinth[a] and there issued his requests for allied troops. He then sailed

---

S.14.35.1a  *Stadion:* a footrace run over the distance of one stade (two hundred yards/about 183 meters).

S.14.35.2a  The manuscripts read "Pharnabazos": the correction [to Tissaphernes] is Wesseling's. From 14.26.4 and what follows the present passage, it is clear that Diodorus here confuses the two satraps (Peter Green).

S.14.35.3a  Ionia: Ref. Map 4.1, CX; Ref. Map 4.2, CY.

S.14.35.4a  Psammetichos (Psamtek) I (r. 664–611) was the famous Saite founder of the Twenty-Sixth Dynasty [Sais: Ref. Map 9, DW]. He used Greek mercenaries and developed com-

mercial links with the Greek world through a licensed trading enclave at Naucratis [Ref. Map 9, DW]. In 400 the pharaoh was Amyrtaios, the sole ruler of the Twenty-Seventh Dynasty. There is no homonymous descendant of Psamtek's on record in the feuding and chaotic Twenty-Eighth Dynasty, but it is not impossible that he existed. There is, however, a Psammuthis, with one regnal year c. 390, and Diodorus or his source may have confused the two names (Peter Green).

S.14.35.7a  Cyme: Ref. Map 4.2, BX.

S.14.36.2a  Corinth: Ref. Map 2, CY.

to Ephesus[b] with a total force of not more than five thousand. On arrival he enlisted some two thousand men, both from the cities that adhered to him and from other cities, so that when he set out, his total forces numbered more than seven thousand. A march of about fifteen miles brought him to Magnesia,[c] which was governed by Tissaphernes. He took this city at the first assault and then made straight for Tralles,[d] in Ionia, where he set about besieging the citadel; but when he failed to make any headway because of its strong defenses, he returned to Magnesia. [3] Now this city was unwalled, and Thibron feared that once he was gone, Tissaphernes would, as a result, regain control of it. He therefore relocated it to a nearby hill, known as Thorax. He then made a sortie into enemy territory, thus procuring for his troops a glut of every sort of booty. However, when Tissaphernes appeared with a strong cavalry force, Thibron felt it prudent to return to Ephesus.

**14.37.** [1] About the same time, of those men who had campaigned with Cyrus and managed to get back safely to Greece, some now returned to their own countries, but the majority, about five thousand[a] in all, who had grown accustomed to a soldier's life, chose Xenophon as their general.[b] [2] He took this force and promptly set off to make war on the Thracians dwelling in the region around Salmydessos.[a] This city's territory extends for a considerable distance up the left [that is, west] coast of the Black Sea and is the cause of numerous shipwrecks.[b] [3] Consequently the Thracians from those parts were in the habit of lying in wait for the merchants who were cast ashore and taking them prisoner. Xenophon and the troops he had mustered now moved into their territory, defeated them in battle, and burned most of their villages. [4] After this Thibron offered to hire them,[a] so they marched off to join him and helped the Lacedaemonians carry on their war against the Persians.

S.14.36.2b Ephesus: Ref. Map 4.1, CX; Ref. Map 4.2, DY.
S.14.36.2c Fifteen miles: the Greek text says 120 stades/ about 24 kilometers. Magnesia: Ref. Map 4.2, DY.
S.14.36.2d Tralles: Ref. Map 4.2, DY.
S.14.37.1a The figure of 5,000 troops with Xenophon in Thrace is discussed in Appendix I: The Size and Makeup of the Ten Thousand, §§12–13.
S.14.37.1b See, by way of comparison, *Anabasis* 7.2.8–10. For whatever reason, Diodorus never mentions Xenophon during the retreat of the Ten Thousand. Drawing on an alternative source (perhaps Sophainetos) has been

suggested, but that alone would not explain the omission, since Diodorus knew Xenophon's work well: 1.37.4, 13.42.5, 15.76.4. The events Diodorus records in this paragraph are covered in detail in *Anabasis* Book 7 (Peter Green). For a different view of the relationship between Xenophon's account and Diodorus', see Appendix M: Other Ancient Sources on the Ten Thousand.
S.14.37.2a Salmydessos: Ref. Map 3, CZ.
S.14.37.2b See *Anabasis* 7.5.12 (Peter Green).
S.14.37.4a Compare *Anabasis* 7.6.1 (Peter Green).

# APPENDIX T

*Selections from Plutarch's* Life of Artaxerxes[*]
*Relevant to* Anabasis

Translated by Pamela Mensch

## Artaxerxes' Succession to the Throne and His Relations with His Brother Cyrus: 1–4

**1.** [1] The first Artaxerxes,[a] who surpassed all Persian Kings in gentleness and magnanimity, was surnamed the Long-Armed, because his right arm was longer than his left, and was the son of Xerxes. The second Artaxerxes, who is the subject of the present account, was surnamed Mnemon and was the maternal grandson of the first.[b] For Darius and Parysatis had four sons, the eldest being Artaxerxes, followed by Cyrus and two younger sons, Ostanes and Oxathres. [2] Cyrus was named after Cyrus the Elder, who they say was named for the sun (for the Persian word for "sun" is *cyrus*). Artaxerxes, however, was originally called Arsikas. Though Dinon says he was called Oarses, it is unlikely that Ctesias—even if in other respects he has filled his books with a hodgepodge of wild and incredible tales—did not know the name of the King in whose household he served as physician, attending the King, his wife, his mother, and his children.[a]

**2.** [1] Now Cyrus, from his earliest youth, was eager and impetuous, whereas his elder brother seemed gentler in every way and naturally weaker in his impulses. He (Arsikas) married, at his parents' behest, a beautiful and noble woman, and shielded her in opposition to their wishes; for the King, after slaying her brother, wished to do away with her as well; [2] but Arsikas, beseeching his mother and shedding many

*NOTE: Plutarch of Chaeronea, in Boeotia (late first–early second century C.E.), wrote many philosophical and biographical works. For more on him, see Ancient Sources Cited in this Edition. The work translated here consists of extracts from his life of Artaxerxes II (r. 405/4–359/8). Chaeronea, Boeotia: Ref. Map 2, BY.

T.1.1a  The dates of reign of the Persian Kings mentioned by Plutarch: Cyrus the Great/Cyrus the Elder, c. 557–530, king of Anshan in Persia and founder of the Persian Empire; Xerxes, 486–465; Artaxerxes I, 465–424/3; Darius II, 424/3–

405/4; Artaxerxes II, 405/4–359/8. For more on Cyrus, Xerxes, Darius II, and Artaxerxes II, see Appendix W: Brief Biographies of Selected Characters in *Anabasis*, §§9, 38, 11, 6, respectively.

T.1.1b  Artaxerxes II was not only Artaxerxes I's maternal grandson but also his paternal grandson, since his parents Darius II and Parysatis were half-siblings, Artaxerxes I being father of both but with different mothers. For Parysatis, see Appendix W, §26.

T.1.2a  On Dinon and Ctesias, see Ancient Authors Cited in this Edition.

tears, finally persuaded her that they should neither kill her nor separate her from him.[a] His mother, however, who was devoted to Cyrus, loved *him* more and wished him to be King. And that was why, when his father fell ill and Cyrus was summoned from the coast, he traveled home in the expectation that through her efforts he would be named heir to the throne. [3] For Parysatis made use of the specious argument (the one Xerxes the Elder had used, on Demaratos' advice)[a] that she had borne Arsikas to Darius when he was a private citizen but Cyrus when he was King. She failed to convince him, however, and the elder son was proclaimed King, having taken the name Artaxerxes, while Cyrus remained satrap of Lydia[b] and commander of the coastal forces.

**3.** [1] Shortly after Darius died, the King rode out to Pasargadae[a] to receive the royal initiation from the Persian priests. The ceremony is performed at the shrine of a warlike goddess whom one might liken to Athena. [2] The candidate must enter the sanctuary, remove his robe, and don the one that Cyrus the Elder wore before he became King; he must then eat a cake of figs, munch some pistachio nuts, and drink a cup of sour milk. Whatever else they do is unknown to outsiders. [3] When Artaxerxes was about to perform the rite, Tissaphernes arrived with one of the priests: the man who had served as Cyrus' supervisor in the traditional training of boys and had instructed him in Magian lore,[a] and was thought to be more disappointed than anyone that his pupil had not been proclaimed King. This was why his accusation was credited; [4] for he accused Cyrus of planning to lie in wait in the shrine until the King had removed his robe and then to attack and kill him. Some say that his charge led to Cyrus' arrest, others that Cyrus had actually entered the shrine and concealed himself and was betrayed by the priest. [5] But when Cyrus was about to be put to death, his mother clasped him in her arms, enveloping him with her tresses and pressing his neck against hers; and by her piteous lamentations and cries, she moved the King to spare him, and sent him back to the coast. But he was not content with that office, nor did he even recall his release but only his arrest; and his anger only deepened his desire for the kingdom.

**4.** [1] Some say that it was because his stipend did not suffice for his daily bread that Cyrus revolted from the King—a foolish notion, surely, if for no other reason than that his mother was on his side and pressed him to draw upon her own resources to any extent he wished. And it is a proof of his wealth that he maintained mercenary forces in many places through his guest-friends and intimates, as Xenophon has reported.[a] For

T.2.2a   Arsikas married Stateira, who came from one of the most senior of the Persian noble families. Her brother was called Teritouchmes, and for unclear reasons he dishonored his wife, Darius' daughter Amestris, and revolted from the King. When the revolt was put down, it seems that not only Teritouchmes but also almost all of his close relatives were killed, although, as Plutarch relates here, not his sister Stateira. The story is found in Photius' synopsis of Ctesias' *Persika*, chapter 55 (not in Appendix U: Selections from Photius' Synopsis of Ctesias' *Persika* Relevant to *Anabasis*).

T.2.3a   The story is told in Herodotus 7.3. Xerxes I was not the oldest son of his father, Darius, but he was the first born after his father became King, and he used this argument to obtain appointment as crown prince. He then reigned as King from 486 to 465. He is called Xerxes the Elder here because another Xerxes was King very briefly in the winter of 424/3. The story of Damaratos can be found in Appendix W: Brief Biographies, §28, under his descendant Prokles.

T.2.3b   Lydia: Ref. Map 4.1, CY, Ref. Map 4.2, CZ.

T.3.1a   Pasargadae: Ref. Map 9, CY.

T.3.3a   Magian lore: the Magi were Persian (Herodotus says specifically Median) ritual experts, especially as regards sacrifices, although their functions were wider; for example, they seem to have educated the nobility. Media: Ref. Map 9, CX.

T.4.1a   Xenophon has reported: *Anabasis* 1.1.6–11. Guest-friends: those who share a bond of ritualized friendship; for more, see the Glossary.

he did not bring the mercenaries together while his preparations were still being kept secret but retained, in various places and on many pretexts, recruiters of foreign troops. [2] Meanwhile the King's mother, who was present at court, allayed suspicions, and Cyrus himself always wrote to the King courteously, sometimes making requests, sometimes rebutting Tissaphernes' accusations and claiming that it was the latter who was the target of his rivalry and struggle.

[3] Furthermore, the King had a natural tendency to procrastinate, which most saw as a sign of his clemency. In the beginning he seems to have been intent on rivaling the gentleness of Artaxerxes his namesake, making himself agreeable to the people he met, bestowing favors and honors beyond their deserts, divesting all punishments of insult or vindictive pleasure, and, when he received and bestowed favors, appearing no less gracious and kindly to the givers than to the recipients. [4] For no present, however small, failed to elicit his ardent acceptance; he even said to a certain Omisus, who had brought him a single pomegranate of surpassing size, "By Mithra,[a] this man would soon make a minor city important were he entrusted with it."

### Cyrus' Revolt and the Battle of Cunaxa: 6–13

**6.** [1] But men who were innovative and restless felt that state affairs needed Cyrus—a man who had great spirit, exceptional skill as a warrior, and love for his companions—and that the greatness of empire required a King who possessed judgment and ambition. [2] Accordingly, Cyrus, in launching the war, trusted those at the center of the Persian realm no less than the men of his immediate circle. He also wrote to the Lacedaemonians,[a] inviting them to aid him and supply him with men, to whom he said he would give horses if they were infantrymen, chariots if they were horsemen, villages if they had farms, and cities if they had villages; and promised that the soldiers' pay would not be counted but measured out.[b] [3] Among his many boasts, he said he had a sturdier heart than his brother, had a better understanding of philosophy and Magian lore, and could drink more wine and hold it better, whereas Artaxerxes was so cowardly and soft that he could sit neither his horse in hunts nor his throne in times of danger. The Lacedaemonians accordingly sent a *skytalē*[a] to Klearchos ordering him to give Cyrus every assistance. [4] Thus Cyrus marched against the King with a large barbarian force and nearly thirteen thousand Greek mercenaries,[a] offering a variety of pretexts for his expedition. But its actual

T.4.4a   Mithra was one of the three principal Persian gods at the time of Artaxerxes, who may have increased emphasis on him. He was not only a warrior god to whom horse sacrifice was appropriate, but also the protector of the crops and fields, which explains the King's invocation of him in connection with the enormous pomegranate.

T.6.2a   Lacedaemonian foreign policy at this point is discussed in Appendix B: Xenophon and Sparta, §§6–7 (Sparta was the principal city within Lacedaemon). Lacedaemon, Sparta: Ref. Map 2, DY.

T.6.2b   Not counted but measured out: that is, the number of coins to be paid to each soldier would be so great that, rather than being counted out individually, they would be weighed.

T.6.3a   A *skytalē* (literally, "staff") was an official dispatch

of the Spartan authorities, so named because it was encoded by being written on a strip of leather wrapped around a baton, so that when separated from the baton, it was unintelligible; the recipient then decoded it by wrapping it around a similar baton that the Spartan authorities had previously given to him.

T.6.4a   The figure of just under 13,000 Greek mercenaries is given twice by Xenophon (or at least by his manuscripts), at 1.2.9 (the review at Kelainai) and 1.7.10 (the review just before the battle of Cunaxa). As is explained in Appendix I: The Size and Makeup of the Army, §§3–4, the figure at 1.2.9 must be wrong. Probably Plutarch did not notice that the two figures, superficially agreeing with one another, were in fact inconsistent.

object did not escape notice for long; for Tissaphernes soon went to the King to inform him of it in person. A great uproar overwhelmed the court, Parysatis bearing most of the blame for the war, and her friends being suspected and accused. [5] But Parysatis was particularly vexed by Stateira,[a] who in her distress at the war would cry, "Where now are those pledges of yours? Where are the entreaties with which you rescued the man who has plotted against his brother, only to plunge us into war and trouble?" From then on Parysatis hated Stateira; and since she was naturally sullen, and barbaric in her anger and vindictiveness, she plotted against the queen's life. [6] Now Dinon says that the plot was carried out during the war, whereas Ctesias says it occurred later; and seeing that the latter was not likely to be ignorant of the time, since he was present during the action, and he had no reason to purposelessly change the time of the deed in his narration (despite the fact that his account often suffers when it veers away from the truth toward the mythological and dramatic), it will have, in this account, the place he gave it.

**7.** [1] As Cyrus advanced, rumors and reports reached him that the King had decided not to fight at once and that he was not eager to come to blows with him but would wait in Persia until his forces had congregated there from all sides. For he had cut a trench through the plain about sixty feet in width and the same in depth,[a] extending about forty-five miles;[b] yet he had permitted Cyrus to cross it and to advance to within a short distance from Babylon.[c] [2] And they say that it was Tiribazos who dared before anyone else to tell the King that he should not shun battle, nor, upon withdrawing from Media or Babylon or even Susa,[a] hide himself in Persia, given that he possessed a force many times more numerous than that of the enemy and countless satraps and generals better able than Cyrus to deliberate and conduct a war. And thus he incited the King to fight as soon as possible.

[3] At first, appearing suddenly with nine hundred thousand men[a] splendidly arrayed, he so astounded and distressed the enemy, who were marching along in disorder and unarmed (owing to their confidence and contempt for the King), that Cyrus could hardly manage, amid a great uproar and shouting, to bring them into formation; and then, by leading them onward slowly and in silence, he amazed the Greeks with their good order, since the Greeks were anticipating, in so large a throng, disorderly shouting and leaping, great confusion, and gaps in their lines. [4] Furthermore, Artaxerxes wisely posted the strongest of his scythed chariots in front of his own phalanx[a] and opposite the Greeks, so that before the two sides engaged at close quarters, these might break through the enemy ranks by the force of their charge.

**8.** [1] Though many have described that battle, with Xenophon all but bringing

---

T.6.5a  Stateira is Artaxerxes' wife.
T.7.1a  Sixty feet/18 meters: the Greek text says 10 *orguiai;* see Appendix O: Ancient Greek and Persian Units of Measurement, §§2, 23. Compare the much more plausible figures given by Xenophon, *Anabasis* 1.7.14. The origin of Plutarch's error is not known.
T.7.1b  About forty-five miles/72 kilometers: the Greek text says 400 stades; see Appendix O, §§2, 23.
T.7.1c  Babylon: Ref. Map 9, CX.

T.7.2a  Tiribazos was a Persian nobleman whom Xenophon later encountered in Western Armenia. For his career, see Appendix W: Brief Biographies, §36. Media, Susa: Ref. Map 9, CX, CY.
T.7.3a  On the large figures given by the sources for the Persian army, see *Anabasis* n. 1.7.13a.
T.7.4a  Scythed chariots: see *Anabasis* 1.8.10. Phalanx: a body of troops drawn up across a broad front in close formation; see Appendix H: Infantry and Cavalry in *Anabasis*, §§13–15.

it before our very eyes and by the vividness of his account always enabling his reader to share its emotions and dangers, as if the action belonged not to the past but to the present, it would not be the part of a sensible man to narrate its events, except when Xenophon has omitted anything noteworthy. [2] The site, then, where the pitched battle was fought is called Cunaxa, a place about fifty-five miles from Babylon.ᵃ It is said that before the battle, when Klearchos urged Cyrus to remain behind the combatants and not risk his life, Cyrus said, "What do you mean, Klearchos? I am aiming for the kingdom—do you order me to act in a manner that is unworthy of being a king?" [3] But if Cyrus committed a serious error by plunging rashly into the fray and not guarding against its danger, Klearchos was at least as mistaken, if not even more so, in refusing to station the Greeks opposite the King, choosing instead to post his right wing by the river, lest it be surrounded. For if he were seeking perfect security and thought it of the utmost importance not to suffer anything, he would have done best to stay at home. [4] But he had journeyed well over a thousand milesᵃ from the sea under arms, though nothing compelled him to do so, in order to seat Cyrus on the royal throne; and then, by scouting around for a battleground and position where he would be able, not to save his leader and paymaster, but to fight safely and at his ease, he resembled a person who, panicked by fear of immediate danger, has thrown aside the plans formed to serve his overall strategy and abandoned the premise of his expedition. [5] For none of the men arrayed around the King would have stood their ground had the Greeks charged at them; instead, when the King's men had been driven off and the King had either fled or fallen, it would have been possible for Cyrus, on prevailing, to procure his own safety and the kingdom, as is evident from how the action unfolded. Klearchos' timidity is therefore more to blame than Cyrus' rashness for the failure of their cause and the loss of Cyrus himself. [6] For had the King tried to find a place to post the Greeks where he would render their attack least injurious to him, he would have found none other than the spot farthest from himself and his suite, since he remained unaware that he had been defeated, and Cyrus was cut down before he could take advantage of Klearchos' victory. [7] Cyrus himself knew what should be done and ordered Klearchos to post his men in the center. But Klearchos, though he said he would take care to do what was best, ruined everything.

**9.** [1] For the Greeks were overpowering the barbarians to their hearts' content and pursuing them a long distance. But Cyrus, mounted on a headstrong and restive thoroughbred whose name, according to Ctesias, was Pasaces, was approached at a

T.8.2a  About fifty-five miles/89 kilometers: the Greek text says 500 stades; see Appendix O: Measurements, §§2, 23. This Plutarch passage is the first extant reference to Cunaxa as the location of the battle. At *Anabasis* 2.2.6, the distance from the battlefield to Babylon is given as 360 stades (about 40 miles/64 kilometers); see n. 2.2.6c. Although this passage is a later scribal insertion and not by Xenophon himself, it accords better with the other indications in Xenophon's text,

and this edition has located the battlefield in line with it (on Ref. Map 6, DZ) rather than with what Plutarch says.

T.8.4a  Over a thousand miles: the Greek text says 10,000 stades, which equals 1,136 miles/1,828 kilometers at 200 yards/about 183 meters to the stade. On the conversion rate, see Appendix O, §§2, 23.

gallop by Artagerses, the leader of the Kadousioi,[a] who shouted, [2] "Oh, most unjust and senseless of men, who disgraces the name of Cyrus, the noblest in Persia, you have come with wicked Greeks on a wicked journey to plunder the goods of Persia, and hope to slay your master and brother, who has ten thousand times ten thousand slaves who are better than you. You'll find the proof of this right now, for you'll lose your own head here before you set eyes on the face of the King." [3] So saying, he hurled his spear at Cyrus. But Cyrus' breastplate resisted it firmly, and he was not wounded, though he reeled under the force of the blow. And when Artagerses had turned his horse away, Cyrus hurled his own weapon, hit Artagerses, and drove the head of his spear through the man's neck near the collarbone.

[4] Almost everyone agrees that Artagerses was killed by Cyrus. As for Cyrus' own death, since Xenophon speaks of it simply and briefly[a] (as he himself was not present), it may not be amiss for me to report what Dinon and, in turn, what Ctesias says about it.

**10.** [1] Dinon says that when Artagerses fell, Cyrus charged out boldly against the men stationed in front of the King and wounded the King's horse, and that the King slipped to the ground; and when Tiribazos soon mounted the King on another horse and said, "Sire, remember this day, for it deserves not to be forgot," Cyrus attacked with his horse and threw Artaxerxes down. [2] Then the King, infuriated by the third charge and telling his attendants that it was better not to live, charged blindly and rashly at Cyrus, who was rushing toward the weapons of the enemy. The King himself then hit him with his spear, while the King's attendants hurled their weapons at him. [3] Thus Cyrus fell, as some say, by the King's hand; but others maintain that a Carian[a] struck the blow, a deed the King rewarded with the privilege of carrying a golden cock upon his spear in front of the first ranks in all his campaigns; for in fact, the Persians refer to the Carians as cocks on account of the crests with which they adorn their helmets.

**11.** [1] Ctesias' account, which we give in a condensed form, is as follows: On killing Artagerses, Cyrus rode to the King and the King to him, both in silence. Ariaios, a friend of Cyrus', hurled his spear before Cyrus did but failed to wound him. The King, hurling his spear, missed Cyrus but hit and killed Satiphernes, a nobleman and Cyrus' trusted friend. [2] Cyrus, throwing his spear at the King, pierced his breastplate and wounded his chest, the dart penetrating nearly two finger-breadths, whereupon the King fell from his horse. When the men who attended him fled in confusion, he himself stood up and, with a few men (of whom Ctesias was one), took possession of a nearby hill and stayed there quietly. Though Cyrus was in the thick of the enemy, his spirited horse carried him forward a long way; and now that it was dark, his enemies failed to recognize him and his friends could not find him. [3] Elated by his victory and full of eagerness and courage, he charged through the enemy ranks, shouting, "Stand aside, wretches!" He shouted this many times in Per-

T.9.1a  Kadousioi: Artaxerxes' predecessor Darius II
        had recently warred with this fierce tribe, who
        lived on the edge of the Persian Empire, to the
        southeast of the Caspian Sea, and Artaxerxes
        himself subsequently led troops against them.
        But it would seem that at this point they were
        loyalists. Kadousioi territory, Caspian Sea: Ref.
        Map 9, BX. Artagerses and his troops are men-

        tioned at 1.7.11 and 1.8.24.
T.9.4a  *Anabasis* 1.8.26–27.
T.10.3a Caria: Ref. Map 4.2, DY.

sian; some stood aside and made obeisance, though Cyrus' tiara[a] fell from his head. And running past him, a young Persian named Mithradates struck him with his spear on the temple near his eye, unaware of who he was. [4] Blood gushed from the wound, and Cyrus, dizzy and dazed, fell from his horse. The horse, escaping, was wandering about, but an attendant of the man who had hit Cyrus took up his felt saddlecloth, which had slipped to the ground, drenched with blood. As Cyrus had difficulty recovering from the blow, some eunuchs who were present tried to seat him on another horse and save him. [5] But as he was unable to ride and wished to walk by himself, they held him up and carried him along. Though he staggered and slipped, he thought he was victorious, because he heard the fugitives addressing him as their King and begging him to spare them. Meanwhile some poor, penniless Caunians[a] who accompanied the King's army as menials found themselves among the men accompanying Cyrus and assumed they were friends. [6] But eventually, noticing their purple tunics (whereas all the King's men wore white ones), they realized that these men were enemies. Then one of the Caunians, not knowing who Cyrus was, dared to hit him from behind with a spear. The vein behind his thigh being severed, Cyrus fell; and when his wounded temple hit a rock, he died. Such is Ctesias' account, in which, as if he had sought to kill the man with a blunt sword, it is only eventually that he succeeds in killing him.[a]

   **12.** [1] When Cyrus had died, Artasyras, the King's Eye,[a] happened to ride past on horseback. Coming upon the eunuchs lamenting, he asked the most trusted of them, "Who is this, Pariskas, whom you sit here mourning?" He replied, "Do you not see Cyrus dead, Artasyras?" Astonished, Artasyras urged the eunuch to take heart and to guard the corpse. [2] Then, hastening to Artaxerxes, who by now had despaired of his cause and was suffering from thirst and his wound, he joyously reported that he had himself seen Cyrus' corpse. The King at once rose up, commanding Artasyras to lead him to the place; but as there was much talk about the Greeks and fear that they were pursuing and conquering and prevailing everywhere, he decided to send a larger party to see. Thirty men were sent, carrying torches. [3] Meanwhile, since the King was almost dead from thirst, the eunuch Satibarzanes ran about to find him something to drink; for the place had no water and was far from the camp. He finally met one of the poorer Caunians, who had a cheap wineskin containing about four pints[a] of foul and polluted water; taking the skin, he brought it to the King. And while Artaxerxes was gulping it down, Satibarzanes asked whether he did not find it utterly disgusting. [4] The King then swore by the gods that he had never yet found any wine or even the lightest and purest water so pleasant to drink. "So if I am unable," he said, "to find the man who gave this to you and to repay him, I pray that the gods may make him happy and prosperous."

T.11.3a  For the significance of the tiara, see Appendix C: The Persian Empire, §4, and n. C.4a. See also Figure 2.5.33.

T.11.5a  Caunus: Ref. Map 4.1, DY.

T.11.6a  Plutarch, seemingly placing literary considerations above accurate reporting, is criticizing Ctesias' account for being long-winded.

T.12.1a  King's Eye: an official, equivalent to the head of the intelligence service, referred to by several fifth-century Greek sources. Xenophon, however, in his *Kyroupaideia* (*The Education of Cyrus*) 8.2.10–12, denies that there is one particular person so called, so the matter is controversial.

T.12.3a  About four pints: the Greek text says almost 8 *kotulai;* see Appendix O: Measurements, §22.

**13.** [1] Meanwhile the thirty messengers rode up to Artaxerxes, beaming and joyous, to report his unexpected good fortune. Heartened by the vast numbers of soldiers who ran back together and stood around him, he descended from the hill in the bright light of many torches. [2] When he halted beside the corpse, and its head and right hand were cut off in accordance with some Persian custom, he ordered that the head be brought to him; and grasping it by the hair, which was long and shaggy, he displayed it to those who were still in doubt and meditating flight.[a] These men were astonished and made obeisance; and consequently Artaxerxes was soon surrounded by seventy thousand men, who returned with him to the camp. [3] He had marched out originally, according to Ctesias, with four hundred thousand men, though Dinon and Xenophon say that many more bore arms in the battle.[a] Ctesias says that the corpses brought to Artaxerxes numbered nine thousand, though the King himself thought there were no fewer than twenty thousand. The matter, accordingly, is controversial; but by now it is clear that Ctesias spoke falsely when he said that he himself was sent to the Greeks along with Phalinos the Zacynthian[b] and some others. [4] For Xenophon knew that Ctesias lived at court, since he mentions him and is clearly familiar with his books. So if Ctesias had gone as an interpreter to such important talks, Xenophon would not have left him nameless, whereas he mentions only Phalinos. But apparently Ctesias, being extraordinarily eager for glory and no less fond of the Lacedaemonians and Klearchos, always makes room in his narrative for himself, and there he will recall many fine things about Klearchos and Lacedaemon.

### The Arrest and Death of Klearchos and Other Greek Generals: 18

**18.** [1] When Tissaphernes deceived Klearchos and the other generals, and in violation of his oaths arrested and sent them bound in shackles to the King, Ctesias says that Klearchos asked him for a comb and, on receiving one and tending to his head, was so pleased with Ctesias' service that he gave him his seal ring as a token of friendship that he could show to his kinsmen and friends in Lacedaemon. (The device carved on the ring depicted a group of Caryatids[a] dancing.) [2] The rations sent to Klearchos were appropriated and consumed by his fellow prisoners, who gave only a small quantity to Klearchos. Ctesias says that he himself remedied this, seeing to it that more was sent to Klearchos and that the soldiers were given separate provisions. He says that he supplied and provided these things at the benevolent suggestion of Parysatis.[a] [3] He mentions that ham was sent to Klearchos daily to

---

T.13.2a  Plutarch agrees with Xenophon here (*Anabasis* 1.10.1), though Xenophon does not speak of Artaxerxes' personally brandishing Cyrus' head. According to Photius' summary of Ctesias (Appendix U: Photius, §64), the King himself cut off Cyrus' head and right hand, but at §66 it seems it was actually done by an underling, as Plutarch states.

T.13.3a  See *Anabasis* 1.7.11–12.

T.13.3b  Zacynthus: Ref. Map 2, CX.

T.18.1a  Caryatids: the priestesses of Artemis at Karyai, a village in Laconia. The word has come to be

used more generally of statuesque draped female figures, especially in the form of architectural columns. For more on Tissaphernes, see Appendix W: Brief Biographies, §37. Karya, Laconia: Ref. Map 2, DY.

T.18.2a  The Persians told the Greek army a different story, according to Xenophon 2.5.38, namely that Klearchos was killed immediately, but Xenophon himself does not vouch for this. Photius' summary of Ctesias also includes this detail (Appendix U: Photius, §69).

supplement his rations and that Klearchos advised and instructed him to conceal a small dagger in the flesh and send it to him and not allow his fate to depend on the cruelty of the King. But Ctesias was afraid and would not agree. When Parysatis entreated the King not to put Klearchos to death, Ctesias says that Artaxerxes consented and promised under oath that he would not do so; but then, persuaded by Stateira, he had all the generals except Menon put to death.[a] [4] It was for this reason, according to Ctesias, that Parysatis plotted against Stateira and prepared to poison her. But the story is implausible and imputes an absurd motive to Parysatis, implying that it was for the sake of Klearchos that she dared to perform so terrible and dangerous a deed as to kill the King's lawful wife and the mother of children being reared for the throne. [5] But it is obvious that Ctesias was exaggerating in this instance out of regard for the memory of Klearchos. For he even reports that when the generals were put to death, the corpses of the others were torn apart by dogs and birds, but in the case of Klearchos, a gale of wind carrying a great quantity of earth heaped a mound over his body and concealed it; and that when some dates had fallen there, a marvelous palm grove[a] grew up and overshadowed the place, with the result that the King deeply regretted having slain Klearchos, a man beloved by the gods.

## Consequences of the Escape of Cyrus' Greek Soldiers: 20

**20.** [1] Though the King was no less eager to capture the Greeks who had come up with Cyrus than he had been to overcome Cyrus himself and retain possession of his own kingdom, he did not succeed; for though they had lost Cyrus, their leader, along with their generals, they nevertheless got away safe from the palace itself, as it were, and provided conclusive evidence that the empire of the Persians and their King, though abounding in gold, luxuriousness, and women, was in all other respects vain and pretentious. [2] Thereupon all of Greece took heart and scorned the barbarians, with the result that the Lacedaemonians thought it would be strange if now, at any rate, they did not free the Greeks who dwelled in Asia and end their abuse at the hands of the Persians. After entrusting the conduct of the war first to Thimbron and then to Derkyllidas (neither of whom accomplished anything noteworthy), they appointed their king Agesilaos as general.[a] [3] And he, after crossing with ships to Asia, went to work at once and won great renown; and when he had been victorious in a pitched battle with Tissaphernes, he roused the cities to revolt.

T.18.3a Xenophon, like Ctesias, says that Menon was not executed along with the other generals, but according to him, he was tortured to death later (2.6.29).
T.18.5a According to Photius' summary of Ctesias (Appendix U: Photius, §71), the palm trees had been planted by Parysatis' eunuchs at her command, so it seems that Plutarch is being unfair to Ctesias here in suggesting he made it out to be a miracle.
T.20.2a Thimbron: a variant spelling for Thibron (Thimbron is the form given by many *Anabasis*

manuscripts too). Derkyllidas: a variant spelling for Derkylidas. For more on Thibron, see Appendix W: Brief Biographies, §35; Derkylidas, §12; Agesilaos, §2.

At that point Artaxerxes, who had given thought to how he should conduct the war, sent Timokrates of Rhodes[a] to Greece with a great deal of gold, ordering him to bribe the cities' most powerful men and rouse the Greeks to go to war with the Lacedaemonians. [4] When Timokrates had done so and the largest cities had formed a league and the Peloponnese[a] was in turmoil, the archons ordered Agesilaos home from Asia. That is when he is said to have remarked to his friends as he departed that the King was driving him from Asia with thirty thousand archers; for the coins of Persia are stamped with the image of an archer.

T.20.3a  Rhodes: Ref. Map 4.1, DY.
T.20.4a  Peloponnese: Ref. Map 2, CY.

# APPENDIX U

*Selections from Photius' Synopsis of Ctesias'* Persika*
*Relevant to* Anabasis

Translated by Pamela Mensch

57. In his nineteenth book, [Ctesias] recounts how Ochus, otherwise known as Darius,[a] died of an illness in Babylon after reigning for thirty-five years.[b] Ochus was succeeded by Arsaces, who changed his name to Artaxerxes....

59. Cyrus is denounced by Tissaphernes to his brother Artaxerxes; he flees to his mother, Parysatis, and is acquitted of the charge. Dishonored by his brother, Cyrus departs to his own satrapy[a] and foments a rebellion....

63. A revolt of Cyrus from his brother and a mustering of a Greek and barbarian army, Klearchos commanding the Greeks. How Syennesis, the king of the Cilicians, is simultaneously allied with Cyrus and Artaxerxes.[a] How Cyrus exhorts his army, and Artaxerxes his own. Klearchos the Lacedaemonian, the Greeks' commander, and Menon the Thessalian,[b] who were accompanying Cyrus, were constantly quarreling, because Cyrus consulted Klearchos about all matters but took no account of Menon.

Many deserted the ranks of Artaxerxes to join Cyrus, but no one left Cyrus to join Artaxerxes. That is why Arbarios, who sought to join Cyrus and was denounced, was plunged into a room filled with ashes.[c]

*NOTE: This appendix contains extracts from the *Persika* of Ctesias of Cnidus, Artaxerxes II's personal physician, as sketchily summarized by the ninth-century C.E. scholar Photius along with synopses of many other books he had read. The parts translated here are selected from Photius' summaries of Books 19–23 and cover the parts most relevant to Cyrus' rebellion. For more on both Ctesias and Photius, see Ancient Authors Cited in this Edition. Cnidus: Ref. Map 4.1, DY.

U.57a  Ochus was his birth name; Darius (II) was his throne name.

U.57b  Thirty-five years: this is an error. Ochus reigned for nineteen years (Diodorus 13.108.1, borne out by other evidence). Darius II's death is mentioned by Xenophon in *Anabasis* 1.1.1, 1.1.3. Babylon: Ref. Map 6, DZ.

U.59a  See *Anabasis* 1.1.3–6. Satrapy: the province of a satrap (governor) within the Persian Empire. For

more on satraps, see the Glossary.

U.63a  Xenophon's more detailed account at 1.2.12 and 1.2.21–27 has a different slant. Cilicia: Ref. Map 5, CY.

U.63b  Lacedaemon, Thessaly: Ref. Map 2, DY, AY.

U.63c  Room filled with ashes: this was a recognized punishment among the Persians and had been administered to Sekundianos (regarded as a usurper), the immediate predecessor of Cyrus and Artaxerxes' father, Darius II. The room filled with hot ashes had no roof; the victim was pushed into the ashes from the top of a wall or sat on the wall until he was overcome by sleep and toppled in. Of this Arbarios, nothing more is known for sure, but it is possible that he should be identified with a man of the same name who assisted Darius II Ochus (the father of Artaxerxes and Cyrus) in seizing power in 424, and who is also known to have had estates in Babylonia (Ref. Map 6, DZ).

64. Cyrus' attack on the King's army and Cyrus' victory, but also the death of Cyrus as a result of his having disobeyed Klearchos, and the mutilation of the body of Cyrus by his brother Artaxerxes. The King himself cut off the head and the hand he had used to strike against him, and he triumphed.[a]

65. A retreat by night of Klearchos the Lacedaemonian with the Greeks who accompanied him, and an occupation of one of the cities of Parysatis.[a] Then a treaty between the King and the Greeks.

66. How Parysatis arrived in Babylon, mourning for Cyrus, and how with difficulty she obtained his head and hand, gave them funeral honors, and sent them to Susa.[a]

The story of Bagapates,[b] who, by order of the King, had cut the head from Cyrus' corpse. How Cyrus' mother, after playing at dice with her son[c] and winning, received Bagapates, who was the stake; and in what manner, after he had been flayed, he was impaled by Parysatis. It was then, at Artaxerxes' urgent entreaty, that Parysatis ceased mourning for Cyrus.

67. How Artaxerxes offered gifts to the man who had brought him Cyrus' saddlecloth; and how Artaxerxes honored the Carian[a] who was thought to have struck Cyrus; and how Parysatis had the honored Carian tortured and put to death.

How Artaxerxes, at Parysatis' request, gave her Mitradates, who had boasted at table that he had killed Cyrus; and she, upon receiving him, put him cruelly to death.[b]

So much for books nineteen and twenty.

68. As for books twenty-one, twenty-two, and twenty-three (the last concludes the work), they cover the following events: how Tissaphernes plotted against the Greeks; how he associated himself with Menon the Thessalian, through whom, by guile and oaths, he overpowered Klearchos and the other generals. Klearchos had at the same time foreseen the plot and sought to foil it. But the multitude, deceived through Menon, compelled him against his will to appear before Tissaphernes; and Proxenos the Boeotian,[a] himself already misled by the deceit, seconded their advice.

69. How Tissaphernes sent Klearchos and the others, in shackles, to Artaxerxes in Babylon, and how everyone streamed together to set eyes on Klearchos. How Ctesias himself, being Parysatis' physician, did much, thanks to her, to please and look after Klearchos when he was in prison.[a] And Parysatis would have freed him from his bonds and released him had Stateira not persuaded her husband, Arta-

U.64a  Plutarch (13.2; in Appendix T: Selections from Plutarch's *Life of Artaxerxes*) and Photius himself, in §66, say that the King got one of his underlings to carry out the mutilation for him. Xenophon puts it more vaguely at *Anabasis* 1.10.1.

U.65a  Cities of Parysatis: presumably to be identified with the "villages of Parysatis" mentioned by Xenophon at *Anabasis* 2.5.27.

U.66a  Parysatis presumably wanted to have Cyrus' head close to her, implying that she normally lived at this point in Susa, site of royal palaces and the location most often mentioned in our sources in connection with the King's diplomatic business. Susa: Ref. Map 9, CY.

U.66b  Bagapates is called Masabates by Plutarch, *Life of Artaxerxes* 17.

U.66c  "Her son," that is, Artaxerxes.

U.67a  A fuller version of Ctesias' story of the Carian and his miserable fate is given by Plutarch in *Life of Artaxerxes* 10.3, 14.3–5 (the former passage is in Appendix T). Caria: Ref. Map 4.2, DY.

U.67b  Mitradates (variant spelling of Mithradates): his boast and punishment are recounted in *Life of Artaxerxes* 11.3 (in Appendix T), 14.3–4, 15.1–5, 16.1–4.

U.68a  Boeotia: Ref. Map 2, BY.

U.69a  Fuller details of Ctesias' dealings with Klearchos in prison are given by Plutarch, *Life of Artaxerxes* 18 (in Appendix T). The Persians told the Greek army a different story, according to Xenophon 2.5.38, namely that Klearchos was killed immediately, but Xenophon himself does not vouch for this.

xerxes, to execute him. Klearchos was executed, and something marvelous occurred over his corpse. All by itself, a violent wind heaped a great burial mound over him. The Greeks who had been sent with him were also executed, except for Menon.[b] . . .

71. The tomb of Klearchos, after eight years, appeared covered with palms, which Parysatis, at the time of his death, had had secretly planted by her eunuchs.

U.69b   Xenophon, like Ctesias, says that Menon was not
        executed along with the other generals, but
        according to him, he was tortured to death later
        (2.6.29).

# APPENDIX V

## *Diogenes Laertius'* Life of Xenophon

### Translated by R. D. Hicks

### 2.48–59

[48] Xenophon, the son of Gryllos, was a citizen of Athens and belonged to the deme Erchia;[a] he was a man of rare modesty and extremely handsome. The story goes that Socrates met him in a narrow passage, and that he stretched out his stick to bar the way, while he inquired where every kind of food was sold. Upon receiving a reply, he put another question, "And where do men become good and honorable?" Xenophon was fairly puzzled; "Then follow me," said Socrates, "and learn." From that time onward he was a pupil of Socrates. He was the first to take notes of, and to give to the world, the conversation of Socrates, under the title of *Memorabilia*. Moreover, he was the first to write a history of philosophers.

Aristippus,[b] in the fourth book of his work *On the Luxury of the Ancients*, declares that he was enamored of Kleinias, [49] and said in reference to him, "It is sweeter for me to gaze on Kleinias than on all the fair sights in the world. I would be content to be blind to everything else if I could but gaze on him alone. I am vexed with the night and with sleep because I cannot see Kleinias, and most grateful to the day and the sun for showing him to me."[a]

He gained the friendship of Cyrus in the following way.[b] He had an intimate friend named Proxenos, a Boeotian, a pupil of Gorgias of Leontini[c] and a friend of

NOTE: This translation is taken from *Lives of Eminent Philosophers*. Diogenes Laertius, vol. 1 (Books 1–5). R. D. Hicks. Cambridge, Harvard University Press, 1972 (first published 1925), Loeb Classical Library. It is here reprinted under Creative Commons License BY–SA 3.0 US. We have added footnotes and conformed the titles of Xenophon's works and some spellings of proper names to our usage. The original footnotes are identified by the translator's name (Hicks). For more on Diogenes, see Ancient Sources Cited in this Edition.

V.2.48a The territory of Athens was divided into demes ("districts" or "parishes"). Erchia was close to Boeotia. For more on demes, see the Glossary. The following locations appear on Ref. Map 2: Erchia, Athens, CZ; Boeotia, BY.

V.2.48b Aristippus was a Socratic philosopher who appears in Xenophon's *Memorabilia* (*Recollections of Socrates*); see Ancient Sources Cited in this Edition.

V.2.49a Kleinias was the son of the famous Athenian politician Alcibiades. In Xenophon's *Memorabilia* (1.3.8–13), he depicts another man, Critoboulos, as smitten with Kleinias' beauty; but he also represents himself as happy enough to kiss Kleinias if he got the chance.

V.2.49b See *Anabasis* 3.1.4–9.

V.2.49c On Gorgias, a famous sophist and rhetorician, see Appendix W: Brief Biographies of Selected Characters in *Anabasis*, §17. Xenophon refers to Proxenos' being his pupil at 2.6.16. Leontini: Ref. Map 1, BW.

Cyrus. Proxenos, while living in Sardis[d] at the court of Cyrus, wrote a letter to Xenophon at Athens, inviting him to come and seek the friendship of Cyrus. [50] Xenophon showed this letter to Socrates and asked his advice, which was that he should go to Delphi and consult the oracle.[a] Xenophon complied and came into the presence of the god. He inquired, not *whether* he should go and seek service with Cyrus, but *in what way* he should do so. This offended Socrates, yet at the same time he advised him to go. On his arrival at the court of Cyrus he became as warmly attached to him as Proxenos himself. We have his own sufficient narrative of all that happened on the expedition and on the return home. He was, however, at enmity with Menon of Pharsalus,[b] the mercenary general, throughout the expedition, and, by way of abuse, charges him with having a favorite older than himself. Again, he reproaches one Apollonides with having had his ears pierced.[c]

[51] After the expedition and the misfortunes which overtook it in Pontus and the treacheries of Seuthes, the king of the Odrysians,[a] he returned to Asia,[b] having enlisted the troops of Cyrus as mercenaries in the service of Agesilaos, the Spartan king,[c] to whom he was devoted beyond measure. About this time he was banished by the Athenians for siding with Sparta. When he was in Ephesus and had a sum of money, he entrusted one half of it to Megabyzos, the priest of Artemis, to keep until his return, or if he should never return, to apply to the erection of a statue in honour of the goddess.[d] But the other half he sent in votive offerings to Delphi. Next he came to Greece with Agesilaos, who had been recalled to carry on the war against Thebes.[e] And the Lacedaemonians[f] conferred on him a privileged position.

[52] He then left Agesilaos and made his way to Skillous, a place in the territory of Elis not far from the city.[a] According to Demetrius of Magnesia[b] he was accompanied by his wife Philesia, and, in a speech written for the freedman whom Xenophon prosecuted for neglect of duty,[c] Dinarchus mentions that his two sons Gryllos and Diodoros,

V.2.49d Sardis: Ref. Map 4.1, CY, Ref. Map 4.2, CZ.
V.2.50a The oracle of Apollo at Delphi was the most famous oracle in the Greek world. Delphi: Ref. Map 2, BY.
V.2.50b This information about Menon's place of origin is not in *Anabasis* but is very likely true. On Menon, see Appendix W: Brief Biographies, §23. Pharsalus: Ref. Map 2, BY.
V.2.50c *Anabasis* 3.1.26–31 (Hicks).
V.2.51a The misfortunes in "Pontus" and the treacheries of Seuthes are recounted at *Anabasis* 5.7.7. Pontus was the name subsequently given first to an independent kingdom and then to a Roman province on the southern coast of the Black Sea, but it was not in use with this meaning in Xenophon's time, when the area was divided between many different tribes, so is not labeled on our maps. Odrysians/ Odrysae territory: Ref. Map 3, CY.
V.2.51b Xenophon's return to Asia is described at 7.8 and shown on Map 7.8.7.
V.2.51c Diogenes here runs together Xenophon's joining the Spartans under Thibron in 399 with his continuing to serve in Asia under Agesilaos in 396–4. For more on Agesilaos, see Appendix W, §2. For more on Sparta, see Appendix B: Xenophon and Sparta. Sparta: Ref. Map 2, DY.
V.2.51d *Anabasis* 5.3.6. Ephesus: Ref. Map 4.1, CX,

Ref. Map 4.2, DY.
V.2.51e This war, otherwise known as the Corinthian War, was fought from 395 to 386. Thebes was just one city in a wider coalition opposed to Sparta. Thebes: Ref. Map 2, BZ.
V.2.51f Lacedaemon was the official name of the state of which Sparta was the principal city: Ref. Map 2, DY.
V.2.52a *Anabasis* 5.3.7. Skillous, Elis: Ref. Map 2, CX.
V.2.52b Demetrius lived in the mid-first century and wrote a work entitled *On Homonyms*, which survives only in fragments (most of them within the text of Diogenes Laertius). It is not known from which of the several places called Magnesia Demetrius came.
V.2.52c Suits for neglect of duty were brought by slave owners against slaves they had freed, alleging that the latter had failed to observe the duties a freedman owed to his former master. However, it is not certain that this is what Diogenes is referring to. Some scholars say the speech was written "against Xenophon for desertion" (Hicks). The Loeb translator has gone beyond Diogenes' text by taking into account the speech's title as reported by the first-century scholar Dionysius of Halicarnassus, namely "Defense of Aischylos against Xenophon in the neglect of duty case." Halicarnassus: Ref. Map 4.1, DX

the Dioscuri as they were called, also went with him.[d] Megabyzos having arrived to attend the festival, Xenophon received from him the deposit of money and bought and dedicated to the goddess an estate with a river running through, which bears the same name Selinous[e] as the river at Ephesus. And from that time onward he hunted, entertained his friends, and worked at his histories without interruption. Dinarchus, however, asserts that it was the Lacedaemonians who gave him a house and land.

[53] At the same time we are told that Phylopidas the Spartan sent to him at Skillous a present of captive slaves from Dardanos, and that he disposed of them as he thought fit, and that the Elians marched against Skillous, and owing to the slowness of the Spartans captured the place, whereupon his sons retired to Lepreon with a few of the servants, while Xenophon himself, who had previously gone to Elis, went next to Lepreon to join his sons, and then made his escape with them from Lepreon to Corinth[a] and took up his abode there. Meanwhile the Athenians passed a decree to assist Sparta, and Xenophon sent his sons to Athens to serve in the army in defense of Sparta. [54] According to Diocles[a] in his *Lives of the Philosophers*, they had been trained in Sparta itself. Diodorus came safe out of the battle without performing any distinguished service, and he had a son of the same name (Gryllos) as his brother. Gryllos was posted with the cavalry and, in the battle which took place about Mantineia,[b] fought stoutly and fell, as Ephorus relates in his twenty-fifth book,[c] Cephisodoros being in command of the cavalry and Hegesilaus commander in chief. In this battle Epaminondas[d] also fell. On this occasion Xenophon is said to have been sacrificing, with a chaplet on his head, which he removed when his son's death was announced. But afterward, upon learning that he had fallen gloriously, he replaced the chaplet on his head. [55] Some say that he did not even shed tears, but exclaimed, "I knew my son was mortal."[a] Aristotle mentions that there were innumerable authors of epitaphs and eulogies upon Gryllos, who wrote, in part at least, to gratify his father. Hermippus too, in his *Life of Theophrastus*, affirms that even Isocrates wrote an encomium on Gryllos.[b] Timon, however, jeers at Xenophon in the lines:

V.2.52d  Dinarchus was a late-fourth-century speechwriter, but his career did not overlap at all with Xenophon's life. The explanation may be that the Xenophon against whom Dinarchus spoke was not our Xenophon but his grandson, and Dinarchus was trying to undermine any appeal the latter might make to the glorious memory of his grandfather. The original Dioscuri/ Dioskouroi were the mythological twins Kastor and Polydeukes, brothers of Helen of Troy, who were important cult figures at Sparta.

V.2.52e  The Selinous River near Skillous is not shown on the maps owing to scale. The Selinous River near Ephesus: Ref. Map 4.2, DY. .

V.2.53a  This passage might be more literally translated "and Xenophon himself went first to Elis and then came to Lepreon to join his sons, and from there made his escape with them to Corinth . . ." Thus Xenophon went to Elis only after Skillous had been captured. Dardanos: Ref. Map 4.2, AX. Lepreon, Corinth: Ref. Map 2, CX, CY.

V.2.54a  Diocles is often said to have lived in the mid-late first century, but the evidence for this is very poor indeed. All our information about his work comes from Diogenes Laertius, who cites him about twenty times. See further Ancient Sources Cited in this Edition.

V.2.54b  The battle of Mantineia occurred in 362 between the Thebans and their allies and the Spartans, Athenians, and their allies. The Thebans won but lost their general: the result was in effect a draw. The campaign is described in Xenophon, *Hellenika* 7.5. Mantineia: Ref. Map 2, CY.

V.2.54c  Ephorus was an important fourth-century historian whose *Universal History*, in thirty books, survives only in fragments, though most modern scholars also believe it underlies much of the narrative of Diodorus Siculus. For further discussion of this, see Appendix M: Other Ancient Sources on the Ten Thousand, §9.

V.2.54d  Epaminondas was the general of the Theban army opposed to Sparta and Athens in this battle.

V.2.55a  Or, "I fathered him, so I knew he was mortal." Had he been the son of a god, he might have been immortal.

V.2.55b  Hermippus was a mid- to late-third-century author whose work survives only in fragments. Isocrates was a fourth-century orator, pamphleteer, and teacher of rhetoric; fifteen of his speeches/pamphlets survive, but not this one.

A feeble pair or triad of works, or even a greater number, such as would come from Xenophon or the might of Aeschines, that not unpersuasive writer.[c]

Such was his life. He flourished in the fourth year of the 94th Olympiad,[d] and he took part in the expedition of Cyrus in the archonship of Xenainetos in the year before the death of Socrates.

[56] He died, according to Ctesiclides[a] of Athens in his list of archons and Olympic victors, in the first year of the 105th Olympiad, in the archonship of Callidemides,[b] the year in which Philip,[c] the son of Amyntas, came to the throne of Macedonia. He died at Corinth, as is stated by Demetrius of Magnesia, obviously at an advanced age. He was a worthy man in general, particularly fond of horses and hunting, an able tactician as is clear from his writings, pious, fond of sacrificing, and an expert in augury from the victims; and he made Socrates his exact model.

He wrote some forty books in all, though the division into books is not always the same,[d] namely:

[57] The *Anabasis* (*The March Upcountry*),[a] with a preface to each
    separate book but not one to the whole work.[b]

    *Kyroupaideia* (*The Education of Cyrus*).

    *Hellenika* (*History of Greece*).

    *Memorabilia* (*Recollections of Socrates*).

    *Symposion* (*The Drinking Party*).

    *Oikonomikos* (*On the Management of the Household*).

    *On Horsemanship* (*Peri Hippikes*).

    *On Hunting* (*Kynegetikos*).

    *On the Duty of a Cavalry General* (*Hipparchikos; Cavalry Commander*).

    *A Defense of Socrates* (*Apologia Sokratous*).

V.2.55c Timon of Phleious was an early-third-century skeptical philosopher. Timon fragment 26, standard edition, H. Diels, *Poetarum Philosophorum Graecorum Fragmenta*. It is not known who was the immediate target of Timon's remarks. He is criticizing Xenophon and Aeschines indirectly, as he says that feeble works would come from the pens of both of them. The references to Aeschines' might and persuasiveness are presumably sarcastic. On this Aeschines, see Ancient Sources Cited in this Edition. Phleious: Ref. Map 2, CY.

V.2.55d In 401–400 B.C.E. (Hicks). This is also the date of the archonship of Xenainetos; on archons, see the Glossary.

V.2.56a Ctesiclides [the manuscripts call him Stesikleides] is known to us from Athenaeus, who cites his *Chronology*, vi. 272 C, x. 445 D. It may seem rash to intrude him here; but compare iv. 5, where a similar error is certain (Hicks).

V.2.56b In 360–359 B.C.E. (Hicks). This is too early: Xenophon was certainly still alive in 356 and probably still in 355. Furthermore, the Athenian archon's name for 360/59 was really Kallimedes: this second slip, however, is that of a scribe rather than of Diogenes himself.

V.2.56c Philip of Macedonia, the father of Alexander the Great. Macedonia: Ref. Map 3, CX.

V.2.56d Diogenes names fourteen works but says there are forty books. Where a work is divided into several books, as is the case with *Anabasis*, he must be reckoning it book by book. However, even so his total of forty does not agree with the medieval manuscripts used in our modern editions, where the number of books totals thirty-seven. There is some evidence for a different division of books in antiquity in the case of *Hellenika*.

V.2.57a Titles shown in parentheses are the translations and Greek spellings used in this edition adapted to conform to Diogenes' text where that differs from the manuscripts of Xenophon's. For more on these titles, see the List of Xenophon's Writings.

V.2.57b Almost all modern scholars regard these prefaces as scribal insertions. Diogenes' comment shows that they had already been added by the time he wrote around 200 C.E. In our manuscripts, Book 6 lacks a preface, though 6.2.1 is somewhat similar: probably Books 5 and 6 circulated as a single book at the time the prefaces were composed and Diogenes wrote about them.

> *On Revenues (Poroi; Ways and Means).*
>
> *Hieron* or *Of Tyranny.*
>
> *Agesilaos.*
>
> *The Constitutions of Athens and Sparta (Athenaion Politeia, Lacedaimonion Politeia).*

Demetrius of Magnesia denies that the last of these works is by Xenophon.[b] There is a tradition that he made Thucydides famous by publishing his history, which was unknown, and which he might have appropriated to his own use. By the sweetness of his narrative he earned the name of the Attic Muse. Hence he and Plato were jealous of each other, as will be stated in the chapter on Plato.

[58] There is an epigram of mine on him also:[a]

> Up the steep path to fame toiled Xenophon
> In that long march of glorious memories;
> In deeds of Greece, how bright his lesson shone!
> How fair was wisdom seen in Socrates![b]

There is another on the circumstances of his death:

> Albeit the countrymen of Cranaus and Cecrops condemned thee, Xenophon, to exile on account of thy friendship for Cyrus, yet hospitable Corinth welcomed thee, so well content with the delights of that city wast thou, and there didst resolve to take up thy rest.[c]

[59] In other authorities I find the statement that he flourished, along with the other Socratics, in the 89th Olympiad,[a] and Ister affirms that he was banished by a decree of Eubulus and recalled by a decree of the same man.[b] [...][c]

V.2.57b The medieval manuscripts of Xenophon's works contain both a *Constitution of the Athenians* (*Athenaion Politeia*) and a *Constitution of the Lacedaemonians* (*Lakedaimonion Politeia*). Modern scholars almost all agree that the former is not by Xenophon, though it probably dates from the late fifth century and perhaps there was a copy of it in Xenophon's papers. It is possible that Demetrius of Magnesia was really talking about just this work, or it may be, while rightly suspicious of it, he wrongly extended his suspicions to the parallel work on the Lacedaemonians.

V.2.58a *Anthologia Palatina* vii. 97 (Hicks). The *Palatine Anthology* is a collection of epigrams of the period 100 B.C.E.–c. 560 C.E. made around 940 C.E.

V.2.58b Or in plain prose: "Not only for Cyrus' sake did Xenophon go up to Persia, but because he sought the path which leads to the abode of Zeus. For, having shown that the great deeds of Greece are the outcome of his training, he recalled what a beautiful thing was the wisdom of Socrates" (Hicks).

V.2.58c *Anthologia Palatina* vii. 98 (Hicks). The countrymen of Cranaus and Cecrops, mythical kings of Athens, were Athenians.

V.2.59a This would be 424–420 B.C.E., a date obviously absurd as the *floruit* for either Xenophon or Plato (Hicks). On the subject of Xenophon's age, see n. Intro.2.6a.

V.2.59b Ister was a late-third-century antiquarian, writing chiefly about Athens, whose work survives only in fragments. There was a famous Athenian politician named Eubulus in the mid-fourth century, but too late to have moved the decree for Xenophon's banishment. It has been attractively suggested that the name here should be Euboulides, the Athenian archon of 394/3.

V.2.59c The last paragraph of the biography, which lists six other people called Xenophon, is omitted here.

# APPENDIX W

*Brief Biographies of Selected Characters*
*in* Anabasis

David Thomas

## Abrokomas

§1. Abrokomas, Persian general and a personal enemy of *Cyrus the Younger, brother of King *Artaxerxes. Artaxerxes had placed Abrokomas in command of a large army, located at least temporarily in Syria in 401, but he arrived late for the battle of Cunaxa. Presumably this was because, after crossing the Euphrates River, he had marched along the more northerly route to Mesopotamia—considerably longer than the southern route that Cyrus himself took but an easier march and much better for supplies—though it is conceivable that he dawdled to hedge his bets between Cyrus and Artaxerxes. The precise post Abrokomas held is not clear. It has been suggested that he was satrap[a] of Phoenicia, from where he is said to be marching at 1.4.5, but the unknown scribe who added a note at 7.8.25 says that Dernes was the satrap of Phoenicia and Arabia. The satrapy of Syria is another possibility,[b] though this would imply that its boundaries took in Phoenicia as a sub-satrapy. A quite attractive alternate theory is that the reason Abrokomas had a large army under his control in 401 was that he was supposed to be organizing the reconquest of Egypt, which was in rebellion from 404 under Amyrtaios, a local dynast (it was not reconquered by the Persians until 343–342); if that was the case, perhaps he was not in charge of any other specific satrapy. Whether or not he was focused on Egypt in 401, he was subsequently one of three Persian generals put in charge of an unsuccessful expedition there, perhaps in 390–388, about which we are badly informed, so it seems he was forgiven for being too late for Cunaxa.

---

NOTE: An asterisk (*) next to a name indicates that a separate entry for that person will be found in this appendix. With the exception of some villages near Pergamum in §§16.4, 16.5, all locations and peoples mentioned can be found the Reference Maps section. All mentions of *Hellenika* in footnotes in this appendix refer to Xenophon's work.

W.1a Satrap: governor of a province of the Persian Empire; for more, see the Glossary.

W.1b Abrokomas satrap of Syria: as tentatively proposed by Christopher Tuplin in Appendix C: The Persian Empire, §9.

## Agesilaos

§2. Agesilaos II (444?–360/59), king of Sparta from (probably) 400 to 360/59. From 396 to 394, he led the Spartan expedition against Persia, from which he was recalled to campaign in mainland Greece against the recalcitrant Thebans and others, including the Athenians. He pursued aggressively anti-Theban policies for the rest of his life; these led to a decisive defeat for Sparta at the battle of Leuktra in 371, which gave the Thebans the opportunity to end Spartan hegemony even in the Peloponnese. Xenophon became Agesilaos' protégé in the 390s and wrote a eulogy of him after his death; he also extensively featured him in *Hellenika*, his partial history of the period 411–362.[a]

## Anaxibios

§3.1. Anaxibios (died c. 389), Spartan *nauarchos* (admiral)[a] for 401/400. In summer 400 he had stationed himself in Byzantium. When the Greek expeditionary force was at Kotyora, *Cheirisophos, at the time its leading figure, claimed to be a friend of Anaxibios and tried unsuccessfully to use this connection to arrange onward sea transport for the troops. Anaxibios saw this large body of ill-disciplined soldiers as a potential menace and planned to manipulate them by false promises of pay to come to Byzantium, thus avoiding any disruption to the (at this point) friendly relations between Sparta and the local Persian satrap *Pharnabazos. He then planned to hurry them away from this strategically vital but politically fragile city as fast as possible. His repeated deceit precipitated the soldiers' violent takeover of Byzantium that was no doubt his nightmare, and he ignominiously fled to the citadel, but Xenophon managed to coax the troops to withdraw. It was now the end of Anaxibios' year of office as *nauarchos*, and his successor was near at hand, so he set off for home by ship, having been with some difficulty persuaded to let Xenophon accompany him.

§3.2. Xenophon insinuates that Pharnabazos had offered Anaxibios a bribe to get the Greek army out of Asia but, once Anaxibios was no longer in charge, refused to pay up. At any rate, Pharnabazos unexpectedly snubbed him, with momentous consequences. Anaxibios performed a quick about-face: he ordered Xenophon to go back to the Greek army and keep it together, which he did immediately, and to invade Asia, which he did eventually. Even more important, Anaxibios' return to Sparta full of animosity against Pharnabazos coincided with a debate there about a request from the Ionian Greeks for help against the Persians. This led to a major change in Spartan foreign policy and war between Sparta and Persia from 399 to 386. Anaxibios was again a commander in the Hellespontine area, as harmost at Abydos, around 389, when he was careless on the march and consequently was ambushed and killed by the Athenian general Iphikrates.[b] Xenophon stresses Anaxibios' bravery in the face of death, which suggests that his apparently poor performance when Byzantium was stormed was not the result of cowardice.

W.2a   For more on Agesilaos, see Appendix B: Xenophon and Sparta, §§2, 9, 13. For a more detailed account, see Strassler 2009, Appendix G: Agesilaos.

W.3a   *Nauarchos:* chief admiral of the Spartan fleet for the year; for more, see Appendix B, §14.

W.3b   Harmost: a technical term (literally, "fixer") for a

Spartan official resident abroad; for more, see Appendix B, §15. Anaxibios: harmost at Abydos: *Hellenika* 4.8.32; careless on march and killed, 4.8.35–39.

## Ariaios

§4.1. Ariaios (also called Aridaios by Diodorus Siculus), the most prominent Persian supporter of *Cyrus the Younger and commander of the left wing of Cyrus' forces at the battle of Cunaxa. According to Diodorus,[a] to begin with, he fought bravely. (We must reject the report of *Ctesias, passed on by Plutarch, that Ariaios stood next to Cyrus and cast the first spear at King *Artaxerxes.)[b] However, after hearing of Cyrus' death, Ariaios fled the battlefield, intending to return to Ionia. The Greek general *Klearchos offered to place him on the royal throne—a completely unrealistic aspiration given the military situation—but he wisely rejected the offer on the ground that there were many Persian noblemen senior to him. Nevertheless, initially he cooperated with the Greeks, offering to lead them back to the Aegean coast, swearing an oath of mutual loyalty, and camping close by them. But under pressure from his family and assured of the forgiveness of the King, he gradually disassociated himself from the Greeks, camped instead with the King's leading supporters, *Tissaphernes and *Orontas, and was suspected of intriguing against Klearchos. The final break came after the arrest of Klearchos and four other Greek generals, when Ariaios' accusations against Klearchos and demand that the Greeks hand over their weapons were met with repeated vitriolic denunciations. A stray reference to him thereafter (3.5.1) shows that he stayed with Tissaphernes to harry the Greeks on their progress up the Tigris River. Eventually he returned to the Aegean seaboard, perhaps with Tissaphernes in 400.

§4.2. It seems that, following the arrest of the Greek generals, Ariaios was initially able to protect one of them—*Menon, his guest-friend,[c] with whom (Xenophon insinuates at 2.6.28) he had a homosexual relationship, such being his general proclivity. But although the matter is not free from doubt, as the biased Xenophon is the only source to touch on Menon's subsequent grisly fate, it seems that Ariaios could not protect him indefinitely. Nevertheless, Ariaios was able to sustain his own position—the King did not go back on his promise of clemency, which, Diodorus tells us,[d] Tissaphernes had persuaded the King to offer in return for Ariaios' key service in the betrayal of the Greeks. As it turned out, the King's favor toward the repentant rebel Ariaios outlasted even his gratitude to the key loyalist Tissaphernes: when the order for the latter's removal came down from the King in 395, it was Ariaios, still a satrap, who assisted in carrying it out by seizing Tissaphernes in his bath,[e] and who, after Tissaphernes' execution, was appointed a general in command of the coast; not much later he received the surrender of another rebel, *Spithridates, who hoped that Ariaios' own rebellion would make him sympathetic.[f] His history after that is unknown.

## Aristippos

§5.1. Aristippos, dynast of Larissa in Thessaly and a guest-friend of *Cyrus the Younger's. He requested help from Cyrus against his political opponents and was

W.4a  Diodorus 14.24.1 (in Appendix S: Selections from Diodorus).
W.4b  Plutarch, *Life of Artaxerxes* 11.1 (in Appendix T: Selections from Plutarch's *Life of Artaxerxes*); for more, see Appendix L: The Battle of Cunaxa, §8.
W.4c  Guest-friend: someone with whom there is a bond of ritualized friendship of a type that was common

between prominent men of different cities; for more, see the Glossary.
W.4d  Diodorus 14.26.5 (in Appendix S).
W.4e  Seizing Tissaphernes in his bath: Diodorus 14.80.8 (in Strassler 2009, Appendix O: Diodorus).
W.4f  Make him sympathetic: *Hellenika* 4.1.27.

sent six months' pay for four thousand mercenaries, twice the numbers he had asked for. But when Cyrus asked for the mercenaries to be sent to him, Aristippos sent only one thousand hoplites and five hundred locally sourced peltasts[a] (under his fellow Thessalian *Menon), presumably because he was under even more pressure from his opponents than when he first asked for help. In Xenophon's hostile obituary of Menon, he insinuates that Aristippos gave the command of these troops to Menon because of a sexual relationship between them (2.6.28). More likely, the move was politically motivated.

§5.2. As Aristippos' actions show, Thessaly was in a highly disordered state of affairs in the late fifth century. The Aleuads, the leading family in and around Larissa, to which Aristippos belonged, had been dominant in Thessaly in the late sixth century and had set up some pan-Thessalian institutions, the precise nature and nomenclature of which are disputed. During the course of the fifth century, it seems that the largest cities of Thessaly had grown in importance relative to the nobles of the countryside, that among the cities Pharsalus and Pherai had grown in power relative to Larissa, that the pan-Thessalian assembly and head of state had become much weaker (we do not know even the name of the Thessalian head of state between about 410 and 375 or so), and that the grip of the Aleuads over Larissa itself had probably also slackened. External powers, in particular Sparta and King Archelaus of Macedon (r. 413–399), periodically exercised a strong influence over Thessaly or even intervened directly. It has been suggested that the opponents against whom Aristippos required help all came from Larissa itself, possibly more moderate oligarchs whose views are reflected in a much-disputed pamphlet, "On the Constitution," transmitted to us as a work of the second-century C.E. rhetorician Herodes Atticus. However, the numbers of mercenaries that Aristippos needed on a continuing basis make it more likely that external enemies were also involved, in particular Lykophron of Pherai, a rival Thessalian dynast who had won a great battle over the Larissaeans and others on or around September 4, 404.[b] War was still going on in 395 between Lykophron, supported by the Spartans, and Aristippos' successor as the leading dynast in Larissa, Medios.[c] Presumably Aristippos died at some point between 401 and 395.

## Artaxerxes

§6.1. Artaxerxes II, Great King of Persia from 405/4 to 359/8. The eldest son of *Darius II and Darius' half sister *Parysatis, he was born well before Darius became Great King in 424/3, perhaps around 445. His birth name, according to *Ctesias, was Arsaces or Arsikas,[a] but when he became King on Darius' death, he took the throne name Artaxerxes, becoming the second King of that name. The succession had been disputed by his brother *Cyrus the Younger, who had been born "in the purple" after Darius' accession and, perhaps for that reason, was preferred by the Queen Mother, Parysatis. But Artaxerxes seems to have succeeded easily enough,

---

W.5a   On hoplites (heavy-armed infantry) and peltasts (light-armed infantry), see Appendix H: Infantry and Cavalry in *Anabasis*, §§2–3, 4–5.
W.5b   Lykophron's victory: *Hellenika* 2.3.4.
W.5c   War between Lykophron and Medios: Diodorus

14.82.5 (not in Appendix S: Diodorus).
W.6a   Arsaces: Photius §57 (in Appendix U: Selections from Photius' Synopsis of Ctesias' *Persika*).
Arsikas: Plutarch, *Life of Artaxerxes* 1.2 (in Appendix T: Plutarch).

though there were allegations that Cyrus plotted to assassinate him during the coronation ceremonies; these accusations had to be smoothed over by Parysatis.[b] Xenophon narrates in detail Cyrus' subsequent rebellion against Artaxerxes and their respective fortunes at Cunaxa, where Artaxerxes offered battle and commanded the royal forces in person from the center of his line. Cyrus charged and wounded him but was himself killed in the resultant melee. Further, and in some respects divergent, detail is given by Plutarch and Ctesias.[c] According to Ctesias, Cyrus' head and right hand were cut off either by Artaxerxes himself or on his orders, and Plutarch says Artaxerxes took Cyrus' head by the hair and swung it about, though Xenophon is not explicit about this. Artaxerxes seems to have found it fairly easy to forgive Cyrus' open supporters, such as *Ariaios; he was readier to see punishment meted out to those who slighted his dignity by contradicting his version of the clash with Cyrus or who, like *Tissaphernes in 395, were suspected of secret treachery.

§6.2. Artaxerxes subsequently had the longest reign of any of the Persian Kings, which was very successful for at least the first thirty-five years. The high point was when, in 387/6, under the terms of the King's Peace (renewed 375/4, 372/1, and 366/5), the mainland Greek states accepted that he ruled the Greek cities in western Anatolia and that, while he did not rule mainland Greece itself, he chose the Spartans to exercise hegemony there and it was thus formally within his sphere of influence. Xenophon's *Hellenika* gives many particulars from a Greek perspective and does not disguise the position in 387/6, although he does tend to downplay Persian involvement in subsequent King's Peaces. However, Artaxerxes' forces failed several times in expeditions to reconquer Egypt, which had rebelled in 404/3, and the last decade of his life was plagued by episodes of serious disaffection in western Anatolia, known as the Satraps' Revolt, which greatly diminished his standing in Greece; by a plot against him by his eldest son, Darius, and his close counselor *Tiribazos (mentioned as his friend at *Anabasis* 4.4.4); and by the bloodstained intrigues of the son who eventually succeeded him, Artaxerxes III Ochus. Xenophon's comments in Book 8 of *Kyroupaideia* (*The Education of Cyrus*) and in *Agesilaos* show that by the end of the 360s, he had come to despise Artaxerxes, but his attitude in *Anabasis*, though negative, does not seem so extreme, whether from the difference in genre between these works or because the determining factor in his views was Artaxerxes' switch away from supporting Spartan hegemony in mainland Greece, which became definitive only with the Peace of 366/5.

### Biton, see Naukleidas and Biton

### Cheirisophos

§7.1. Cheirisophos the Lacedaemonian,[a] Spartan general and the leading figure in the Greek expeditionary force from the time of the Persian arrest of *Klearchos and

W.6b  Cyrus' alleged assassination plot: Plutarch, *Life of Artaxerxes* 3.3–6 (in Appendix T: Plutarch); compare *Anabasis* 1.1.3–4.
W.6c  See Appendix L: The Battle of Cunaxa.
W.7a  The terms Lacedaemon and Sparta are nearly syn-

onymous. Lacedaemon is a state and territorial designation. Sparta was the most important city within it; see Appendix B: Xenophon and Sparta, §§18–19.

four other generals at the Zapatas River to his death, from sickness, at Kalpe Harbor in Bithynia about seven months later (in September 400). He had originally joined *Cyrus the Younger at Issus with seven hundred hoplites. Xenophon does not explain how this came about, but according to Diodorus,[b] the Spartan authorities appointed him to this command, thus coming down on Cyrus' side. These hoplites will not have been Spartan citizens, however, though a couple of the senior ones were *perioikoi*.[c] Doubtless Cheirisophos fought at Cunaxa, though this is not stated explicitly, and after the battle he was among the deputation sent to *Ariaios to offer to make him King of Persia. He was not one of the generals whom the Persians arrested at the Zapatas River, being then engaged in extracting supplies from a Babylonian village, and was still absent when a Persian deputation came to the Greeks after the arrest. Although *Anabasis* represents Xenophon as initiating, and then doing most of the talking at, the midnight meeting of the officers that followed, Cheirisophos assumed the role of chairman of the meeting in his brief praise of Xenophon's speech and his dismissal of the officers, instructing them to choose new leaders of sections of the army that had lost their previous generals. It was he who the next day spoke first to the assembled Greek soldiers, advising them to prepare for war, and who actually put Xenophon's main body of proposals to the vote. On (it is said) Xenophon's motion, he was subsequently assigned to lead the vanguard. Here and hereafter, Xenophon represents Cheirisophos as first among equals, and down to 6.1.33 no more than that, but Diodorus claims that he was given the supreme command at this point, immediately after the arrest of the other generals.[d] It can be calculated from *Anabasis* 3.3.37[e] that he was the third-youngest of the seven generals, so presumably he was around thirty-five.

§7.2. Books 3 and 4 of *Anabasis* give a full account of Cheirisophos' performance as head of the vanguard and of his interactions with Xenophon, the joint head of the rearguard. They are depicted as having had a good enough relationship to incorporate give-and-take in criticism and mutual joshing. But the general impression Xenophon gives us, whether fairly or not, is that Cheirisophos, though not actually incompetent and certainly not deficient in personal bravery, lacked tactical imagination and skill in managing men. On reaching Trapezus, Cheirisophos planned to arrange sea transport back to Greece, and sailed away to Byzantium to obtain help in so doing from the *nauarchos* (admiral) *Anaxibios, who he claimed was an old friend of his, but he brought only one trireme[f] with him when he finally rejoined the Greeks at Sinope. He was chosen as commander in chief of the Greek army following Xenophon's refusal to stand for the post, but this role lasted only a few days because, having disagreed with the soldiers' attempts to extort money from the Heracleans, he was deserted by the Arcadians and Achaeans and consequently lost his command. Sick at heart, he was persuaded by his deputy Neon to refuse to continue in company with Xenophon, and instead traveled, with the troops personally loyal

W.7b   Diodorus 14.19.5 (in Appendix S: Diodorus).
W.7c   *Perioikoi*: free inhabitants of Laconia, inferior to the citizens of Sparta; see Appendix B: Xenophon and Sparta, §18.
W.7d   Diodorus 14.27.1 (in Appendix S: Diodorus). On this claim and what some have inferred from it

about Diodorus' sources, see Appendix M: Other Ancient Sources on the Ten Thousand, §§3, 6, 9.
W.7e   In the version of the text followed in this edition.
W.7f   Trireme: long warship with three banks of oars; for more, see the Glossary.

to him, from Heraclea to Kalpe Harbor. Already ill, he died shortly after his arrival. According to Xenophon, Cheirisophos' death was due to the effects of a medicine he took for a fever, but his general failure with both the Spartan authorities and the army may have been a factor too. Strikingly, Xenophon does not give him an obituary, as he has earlier done for senior leaders. This may be a sign that Xenophon thought him insignificant or unworthy; but note that the recipients of obituaries in *Anabasis* all died as the result of enemy action of one kind or another, and it was the Spartan custom that only those who die in battle are entitled to be named on inscriptions to commemorate them.

## Ctesias

§8.1. Ctesias of Cnidus, the Great King *Artaxerxes' personal physician. Ctesias' father, Ctesiochos, was also a physician, and it is likely that medicine had been the family profession for generations. We are told by later sources that Ctesias came to the Persian court as a prisoner of war and remained for seventeen years, in which case he arrived during the previous reign, that of *Darius II, but some modern scholars doubt both these statements. He was present at the battle of Cunaxa, where he treated Artaxerxes successfully for the wound that he received at the hands of Cyrus. Ctesias also claimed that he had been part of the King's deputation to the Greek army that was led by Phalinos, but Xenophon states that Phalinos was the only Greek on it. Subsequent to Cunaxa, Ctesias had dealings with the Greek general *Klearchos during the latter's imprisonment; Ctesias' account, retailed by Photius, of how Klearchos fatally came to put himself into the hands of the Persian commander *Tissaphernes may well reflect Klearchos' own story. Ctesias acted as a go-between when, in response to the Spartan invasions of western Anatolia from 399, Artaxerxes entered into arrangements with the Cypriot king Evagoras and his protégé the Athenian Konon, who became the commander of the Persian fleet in Caria and the Aegean. Then, in 398/7, at a time when, it seems, ambassadors whom the Spartans had sent to Artaxerxes were held incommunicado, the King sent Ctesias on a diplomatic mission to Sparta; most probably he never returned to Persia. Although details of the evidence are confused, the Spartans seem to have arrested him and brought him to trial—possibly on the ground that he had helped conceal from them the seriousness of Persian contacts with Konon—but he was acquitted; very likely it helped that he could produce the ring Klearchos had given him in return for his services to him in captivity.

§8.2. Ctesias wrote *Persika*, a history of Assyria, Media, and Persia from legendary times to 398/7, in twenty-three books; and *Indika*, an account of India, in one book. His narrative in *Persika* was particularly rich on the court intrigues of his own day. Ctesias had a poor reputation for truthfulness in ancient times; Plutarch's accusation that he lied when he said he was part of the deputation to the Greek army after the battle of Cunaxa is only one instance among many of his reputed untruths. The early books of *Persika* were more romance than serious history, he can undoubtedly be convicted of exaggeration or error in other respects, and many modern scholars suspect his lurid representation of Persian court politics of being unbalanced sensationalism; but more recently his stock has risen somewhat.

### Cyrus the Elder/Cyrus the Great

§9. Cyrus the Elder, king of Anshan in Persia (r. 559–530) and founder of the Persian Empire. Having succeeded his father, Cambyses, as king of Anshan, he successively conquered Media, Lydia, Ionia, and Babylonia (which brought with it Syria and Palestine) in the course of just over a decade (550–539). The fifth-century historian Herodotus in Book 1 of his *Histories* relates a legend regarding Cyrus' early life but is fairly trustworthy about his period of conquest and his death at the hands of the Massagetai, a Scythian tribe. The speed of his rise and the extent, power, and durability of his empire made a great impression on the Greeks, and he was considered the quintessential prince by the late fifth- to early fourth-century philosopher Antisthenes, whose lost work *Cyrus* was doubtless important in the formation of Xenophon's own long historico-philosophical romantic novel *Kyroupaideia* (*The Education of Cyrus*). Xenophon refers to Cyrus the Elder in *Anabasis* at 1.9.1 as the most kingly of Persian monarchs.

### Cyrus the Younger

§10.1. Cyrus the Younger (424/3–401), Persian prince and would-be Great King, the central figure in Book 1 of *Anabasis*. He was the second son of King *Darius II and his wife and half sister, *Parysatis; unlike his elder brother, *Artaxerxes, he was born after Darius had become the Great King, at the earliest in December 424. He was put in overall command of Persian forces in the west and made satrap of Lydia, Greater Phrygia, and Cappadocia at some point between spring 408 and spring 407, most probably at the latter date, when he had just turned sixteen.[a] He retained these appointments until his father's death, in the winter of 405/4. Xenophon recounts in some detail in *Hellenika* how—unlike *Tissaphernes, who had previously been the principal Persian strategist in the west—Cyrus unambiguously backed the Spartans against the Athenians in the last phase of the Peloponnesian War, which had been running on and off since 431. While no doubt this was in origin his father's policy, which he had been sent to the west to implement, he seems to have gone beyond his instructions in the resources he was prepared to invest in Sparta, partly because of a warm personal rapport with Lysander, Sparta's naval commander in 407/6 and (de facto) 405/4. These resources enabled the Spartans to outspend Athens in maintaining their fleet, making it likely that they would eventually win the war, although in fact their crucial victory at Aigospotamoi was due not to this but to Lysander's superior generalship. Cyrus may well have already been preparing the ground for a bid to supplant his elder brother as his father's successor: an interpolator at *Hellenika*

W.10a   That he was already sixteen at this point is suggested by *Anabasis* 1.9.6–7, which seems to tell of      his hunting prior to his departure for the west. On Greater Phrygia, see n. 1.2.6a.

2.1.8–9 says that he put to death two of his first cousins for failing to give him a ceremonial gesture that was by rights given only to the King. Darius summoned Cyrus back to court in mid-405, either for this reason or simply because he was dying, as Xenophon says at *Anabasis* 1.1–2; it is at this point that the action of *Anabasis* begins. Tissaphernes accused Cyrus of plotting against the new King, Artaxerxes II; Xenophon means us to understand from his report (*Anabasis* 1.1.3) that Cyrus was guiltless, but others thought differently.[b] In any event, the sources agree that, following his arrest, it was only through the influence of the Queen Mother that he was reprieved and sent back to the west, where he started to plan armed rebellion, although taking care to remit tribute to Artaxerxes regularly. According to Xenophon, he was assisted by the continuing support of Parysatis.

§10.2. The whole of *Anabasis* Book 1 is a continuous narrative of the progress of Cyrus' rebellion. This begins with his arrangements to have friends loyal to him, notably the Spartan exile *Klearchos, muster troops in various locations. He concealed the real reasons for assembling his army, partly through pointing to a quarrel he was having with Tissaphernes about control of the Ionian cities and partly through claiming that his intention was to campaign against the Pisidians. Xenophon supplies a detailed account of Cyrus' march from Sardis to Babylonia, during which Cyrus tried to take Artaxerxes by surprise by marching southeast along the banks of the mid-Euphrates—a direct but difficult route through desert country—rather than along the normal road, which ran across to the Tigris River and then south along the Tigris valley. In Babylonia he fought a pitched battle against the royal forces, conventionally known as the battle of Cunaxa.

§10.3. After the battle had begun, Cyrus impetuously charged Artaxerxes and wounded him but was killed in the subsequent melee. A version of this confrontation and its end, much longer than Xenophon's, was given by *Ctesias, and a somewhat different one, representing the official Persian version, by Dinon.[c] In this final conflict, Cyrus' entourage showed conspicuous loyalty to him, even to death; but the victors cut off his head and right hand, and his surviving Persian supporters were subsequently reconciled to Artaxerxes' regime.

§10.4. Xenophon provides a long, formal obituary for Cyrus, stressing his virtues from boyhood onward, above all his generosity, and not admitting any deficiencies. However, we are not bound to accept this as an accurate estimation of the man, and indeed it is not fully borne out by Xenophon's own narrative. While his account gives chapter and verse for some of Cyrus' good qualities—when recounting his magnanimity toward the deserters Xenias and Pasion, the discipline he exerted on the nobles in his entourage, and the way in which he separated warring Greek generals—it also reveals defects. Cyrus was slack in the immediate approach to the battle with his brother; his sense of what the hoplite phalanx[d] could reasonably be expected to do was poor, as shown in the order he gave Klearchos to march across the battlefield to attack Artaxerxes personally; and in the battle itself, his reckless impetuosity

W.10b Others thought differently: see Plutarch, *Life of Artaxerxes* 3 (in Appendix T: Plutarch).

W.10c Both versions are found in Plutarch, *Life of Artaxerxes* (Ctesias' at 9.1–3, 11; Dinon's at 9.4, 10; in Appendix T).

W.10d Phalanx: a body of troops drawn up across a broad front in close formation. For more, see Appendix H: Infantry and Cavalry in *Anabasis*, §§13–15.

brought about his death. Recent scholars have also pointed out that Xenophon is unusually reticent about Cyrus' piety when one compares what he says about other favorite leaders, such as *Cyrus the Elder and King *Agesilaos of Sparta (and himself). Nor is Cyrus' treason against his brother very attractive, especially given the latter's clemency.

§10.5. Cyrus may have alienated only a fairly small number of his direct subordinates. Xenophon dwells in particular on Orontas, put to death for plotting to desert with a troop of cavalry despite—like Cyrus himself—having been forgiven for earlier disloyalty; the only other disaffected Persian named is Megaphernes, whom Cyrus executed at Dana. But it is noteworthy that Cyrus gained no outright adherents from other members of the Persian nobility, such as *Pharnabazos, the satrap of Hellespontine Phrygia. The most he got before the battle of Cunaxa was people hedging their bets, as was done by Syennesis,ᵉ the ruler of Cilicia, and perhaps by the Persian general *Abrokomas. In the battle itself, another of Artaxerxes' generals, Arbakes, may have switched sides,ᶠ but probably only because he mistakenly thought that it was all over for Artaxerxes. Other Persian nobles were and remained resolutely opposed to him, chief among them Tissaphernes.

**Darius II**

§11. Darius II, Great King of Persia from 424/3 to 405/4. He was the son of King Artaxerxes I (r. 465–424/3) and a Babylonian concubine, Kosmartidene. His birth name was Ochus; Darius (II) was the throne name he took on succeeding his father after a power struggle in which Artaxerxes' only legitimate son, Xerxes II, was assassinated and Xerxes' half brother Sogdianos, who was responsible for this, was overcome by Ochus. Before his accession, Ochus had married his half sister *Parysatis. Xenophon records two sons of theirs: Arsaces, Darius II's successor as *Artaxerxes (II), was born before Ochus became Great King, *Cyrus the Younger afterward. Plutarch tells us of two other surviving sons, and Xenophon refers at *Anabasis* 2.4.25 to an unnamed bastard son, loyal to Artaxerxes, as being in command of troops. We are not well informed on the events of Darius II's reign until, as a consequence of Athens' foolish support for the rebel Amorges, in 413/12 the Persians began to back the Spartans in the second half of the Peloponnesian War; this, however, was done wholeheartedly only with Darius' appointment of Cyrus as *karanos* (commander) in western Anatolia in (probably) spring 407.ᵃ A further possible reference to Darius in *Anabasis* occurs at 1.1.6, where it is said that the King had "of old" given the Ionian cities to *Tissaphernes; this is usually taken to be a grant by Artaxerxes II in 404, but in the opinion of this writer, it is more likely to be a grant by Darius II sometime during the period 413–408.

**Derkylidas**

§12. Derkylidas, Spartan general. He campaigned in Aeolis, the Troad, and Hellespontine Phrygia in the final years of the Peloponnesian War, inducing Abydos and

---

W.10e  On Syennesis, see *Anabasis* n. 1.2.22a.
W.10f  On Arbakes, see n. 1.7.12b.
W.11a  *Anabasis* 1.1.2, 1.9.7, but more informatively in

*Hellenika* 1.4.3. On the term *karanos*, see the Glossary and Appendix C: The Persian Empire, §9.

Lampsacus to revolt in 411[a] and serving as harmost at Abydos in 407. At this time he acted as a subordinate of Sparta's great general Lysander and was humiliatingly disciplined by Sparta's then ally *Pharnabazos, the Persian satrap of Hellespontine Phrygia, whom, as a consequence, Derkylidas hated. Subsequently, after the events in *Anabasis,* Derkylidas succeeded *Thibron as commander of Sparta's troops in Anatolia, a post he held from late 399 to early 396, when he was replaced by King *Agesilaos. Xenophon gives a fairly full account of Derkylidas' campaigns in *Hellenika* (3.1.8–3.2.20). Xenophon himself participated in these campaigns, since Derkylidas took over from Thibron the remnants of the Greek mercenaries who had fought for *Cyrus the Younger; these mercenaries are even referred to as "Derkylidas' mercenaries" in the *Hellenica Oxyrhynchia*.[b] Derkylidas returned to Sparta in 396; but when Agesilaos himself returned from Anatolia in 394, he asked Derkylidas to go back, and he once again became harmost at Abydos, where he is said to have done a good job until superseded by *Anaxibios in 389.[c] Derkylidas was famous for his serpentine cunning.

### Dexippos

§13.1. Dexippos, a Laconian *perioikos*[a] among the Ten Thousand. Xenophon regarded him with great hostility (seen most clearly at *Anabasis* 5.1.15), but perhaps there are two sides to the story, as the facts of his earlier life put him in a more favorable light. A few years before the expedition of *Cyrus the Younger, Dexippos was living in Gela, in Sicily, perhaps having come there from the Aegean in the train of the Syracusan exile Hermokrates, who died attempting a coup d'état in Syracuse in 408. In 406 Dexippos led a force of mercenaries from Gela to assist another Sicilian city, Acragas, against the Carthaginians; this campaign led to four of the five Acragantine generals' being stoned to death for not pressing their advantage against the enemy and, partly on the advice of Dexippos, to the Acragantines' having to evacuate their city. Dexippos does not seem to have taken the blame for the fiasco, since he was then entrusted by Syracuse (the dominant Greek city in Sicily) with garrisoning Gela, which was expected to be the Carthaginians' next target. He refused to cooperate with Dionysius of Syracuse in his aim of establishing a tyranny in Syracuse, and on the latter's success, Dexippos was sent back to Greece.

§13.2. It is not known whether Dexippos came to the army as part of the official Spartan contingent led by *Cheirisophos or independently, either by himself or perhaps with the renegade Spartan general *Klearchos. To judge from *Anabasis* 6.1.32, it seems that he resented the fact that he was not a general when Xenophon and Timasion were. He first surfaces in Xenophon's narrative at 5.1.15, where we are told that on being put in command of a small warship, he deserted and sailed out of the Black Sea. Evidently he went to the Spartan authorities in Byzantium: Cheirisophos, the most senior Spartan among the Ten Thousand, subsequently told the army that

W.12a  Derkylidas induces Abydos and Lampsakos to revolt: Thucydides 8.61.1, 8.62.1.
W.12b  *Hellenica Oxyrhynchia* fragment 24.2 in Chambers' edition, translated in Strassler 2009, Appendix P: Selected Fragments of the *Hellenica Oxyrhynchia* Relevant to Xenophon's *Hellenika* (fragment 21.2 in Bartoletti's edition).
W.12c  Derkylidas: asked to go back to Anatolia, *Hellenika* 4.3.1–3; harmost at Abydos, 4.8.3–6; superseded by Anaxibios, 4.8.32.
W.13a  *Perioikos:* a free inhabitant of Laconia, inferior to the citizens of Sparta; see Appendix B: Xenophon and Sparta, §18.

Dexippos had been trying to prejudice the Spartan *nauarchos* (admiral), *Anaxibios, against Xenophon. Dexippos returned to the army in the company of the Spartan harmost *Kleandros and, according to Xenophon, tried to interfere with the prescribed arrangements about booty. This caused a riot, for which he sought to put the blame indirectly onto Xenophon by denouncing Xenophon's close ally Agasias. Ultimately, however, Kleandros preferred to deal with Xenophon rather than foist Dexippos on the army, and it is noteworthy that even the hostile Anaxibios and Aristarchos (the harmost of Byzantium) made no attempt to make the remnant of the Ten Thousand accept him. Subsequently, though it is not clear how much later, Dexippos tried to carry on an intrigue at the court of the Thracian princeling *Seuthes and was killed by another Lacedaemonian, Nikandros; the full circumstances are not known.

## Epyaxa

§14. Epyaxa, wife of Syennesis of Cilicia. She joined *Cyrus the Younger at Kaystroupedion as he approached Cilicia from the north and allegedly became his lover; shortly thereafter he held a review of his troops at Tyriaion for her benefit, in the course of which the charge of the Greek phalanx alarmed her. Cyrus then sent her on to Cilicia with a detachment led by *Menon, and she reached Tarsus ahead of the main army. Once there, she seems to have championed Cyrus' cause with her husband, persuading him to meet Cyrus. Although there is no direct evidence for her outside *Anabasis*, it has been argued on the basis of her name that she was probably a descendant of a mid-sixth-century monarch of the Cilician mountain area, Appuašu of Pirindu, and, as such, perhaps had a power base independent of Syennesis. Possibly, then, she was pursuing a pro-Cyrus policy in contrast to the reservations of her husband, but equally likely is that this was a show and they were collaborating in trying to hedge Syennesis' bets between Cyrus and *Artaxerxes.

## Eteonikos

§15. Eteonikos, senior Spartan officer of considerable experience but limited luck. He is first heard of in connection with an unsuccessful Spartan campaign against Lesbos in 412.[a] Subsequently (the year is disputed), he was harmost in Thasos (or possibly in Iasos), from which he was thrown out, together with the pro-Spartan faction.[b] In 406 he commanded a reserve force left besieging Mytilene on Lesbos when the main Spartan fleet sailed out to meet the Athenians; Xenophon tells us of his resourcefulness in extricating himself when the Spartans lost the battle of Arginousai and in taking his ships to comparative safety, as well as in dealing with indiscipline among his starving troops on Chios shortly afterward.[c] The following year he was one of the commanding officers at the battle of Aigospotamoi, where the Spartan general Lysander decisively destroyed the Athenian fleet; he was later sent by Lysander to mop up resistance on the coast of Thrace.[d] *Anabasis* finds him

W.15a  Campaign against Lesbos: Thucydides 8.23.4.
W.15b  Eteonikos thrown out as harmost: *Hellenika*
       1.1.32.
W.15c  Eteonikos: besieging Mytilene, *Hellenika*
       1.6.26; at Arginousai, 1.6.35–38; on Chios,
       2.1.1–5.
W.15d  Eteonikos: at Aigospotamoi, Diodorus 13.106.4

(in Strassler 2009, Appendix O: Diodorus); on
the Thracian coast, *Hellenika* 2.2.5.

with the *nauarchos* (admiral), *Anaxibios, in Byzantium, where rioting soldiers forced him to flee ignominiously to the citadel. Thereafter he served on the island of Aegina, to which he returned in (probably) 389 in the course of the Corinthian War, though the following year he again had trouble with mutinous troops there.[c]

**Glous,** see **Tamos and Glous**

**Gongylids, the**

§16. A family of Greeks living in and near Pergamum for most of the fifth century:

§16.1. **Gongylos I** of Eretria, placed in charge of Byzantium by the Spartan regent Pausanias in the aftermath of the Persian King *Xerxes' great expedition against Greece in 480. Subsequently he acted as a go-between in treasonable contacts between Pausanias and the Persians. He was banished from his native Eretria for supporting the Persians and was given a fiefdom by Xerxes—so before the latter's death in 465.[a]

§16.2. **Gongylos II**, his son, who also identified himself as Gongylos of Eretria, although he had perhaps never been to Eretria himself. He was dead by 399.

§16.3. **Hellas of Pergamum**, Gongylos II's wife. She entertained Xenophon at her home in spring 399 and advised him to kidnap the rich Persian landowner Asidates. From her name, which means "Greece," it seems she came from another family of Greek exiles, possibly the Spartan family to which her neighbor *Prokles belonged.

§16.4. **Gongylos III**, a son of Gongylos II and Hellas of Pergamum. Xenophon describes him as lord of Myrina and Gryneion[b] (a little south of Pergamum). He came to aid in the Greek assault on Asidates and subsequently joined the Spartan general *Thibron in open opposition to Persian rule.

§16.5. **Gorgion**, Gongylos III's brother, whom Xenophon describes as lord of Gambreion (a little east of Pergamum) and Palaigambreion (location unknown, but presumably close by).[c] Coins minted by him have survived. He joined Thibron with his brother; it is not known what happened to them when the Spartans eventually withdrew from the area.

**Gorgias**

§17. Gorgias of Leontini (in Sicily), rhetorician and sophist (c. 485–c. 380).[a] Xenophon reports at *Anabasis* 2.6.16 that his friend the general *Proxenos studied under him; the passage shows that Xenophon thought the experience had made Proxenos altogether too complacent about his own competence and cleverness. Nevertheless, Xenophon himself had evidently been influenced in his youth by Gorgias, at least as regards his views on style, since he imitates him at length in the ornate and rather precious introductory passage of *Kynegetikos* (*On Hunting*), probably Xenophon's earliest work.

W.15e  Eteonikos: on Aegina, *Hellenika* 5.1.1; trouble with mutinous troops, 5.1.13.

W.16a  Gongylos I given a fiefdom: *Hellenika* 3.1.6.

W.16b  Gongylos III lord of Myrina and Gryneion: *Hellenika* 3.1.6.

W.16c  Gorgion lord of Gambreion and Palaigambreion: *Hellenika* 3.1.6.

W.17a  The extant fragments of Gorgias' work may be found, as DK 82, in the standard edition of the works of the pre-Socratics, H. Diels and W. Kranz, eds., *Die Fragmente der Vorsokratiker*, 6th ed. (Berlin: Weidmann, 1951–52). Two complete short showpieces have survived.

Indeed, the influence may have continued, since it has been plausibly suggested that at *Memorabilia* (*Recollections of Socrates*) 4.1.4 Xenophon is closely paraphrasing a passage by Gorgias. The philosopher Plato introduces Gorgias as a character in the Socratic dialogue that bears his name, where he is portrayed relatively sympathetically.

## Kleandros

§18.1. Kleandros, Lacedaemonian harmost (governor) of Byzantium. He came to check out the Greek army at Kalpe Harbor after its presence on the Black Sea coast had been reported by its leading general, *Cheirisophos, to the authorities in Byzantium, of whom Kleandros would have been the second most senior, after the *nauarchos* (admiral) *Anaxibios. The men had thought he would bring enough ships to carry them home, but he brought only two triremes. He also brought the former army officer *Dexippos, regarded by Xenophon (perhaps unfairly) as a deserter, who immediately intervened in a dispute within the army over plunder and thus provoked a riot in which Xenophon's friend Agasias played a prominent part. Though there are some small signs in Xenophon's text that Kleandros himself had had reservations about Dexippos from the start, the riot threw him completely off balance; he fled to the seashore and then threatened to have the soldiers shut out of all Greek cities. However, he changed his tune when, on Xenophon's advice, Agasias delivered himself up and the Greek generals collectively humbled themselves. At this Kleandros agreed to release those accused of rioting and offered to take charge of the army for its march to Byzantium, though he changed his mind after receiving unfavorable omens. He was now well-disposed toward the Greek army: he and Xenophon became guest-friends, and he exchanged gifts with the army before he departed for Byzantium. Once they were all in Byzantium, he helped Xenophon plan his return to mainland Greece and treated with compassion those soldiers who remained in the city following Anaxibios' expulsion of the army as a whole.

§18.2. According to Plutarch,[a] Kleandros had previously been an adviser to Kallikratidas, the Spartan *nauarchos* for 406, and Kallikratidas made him his deputy in the event of his own death, which did in fact occur during the sea battle of Arginousai.[b] Kallikratidas had strongly resented the fact that the Spartans had to take Persian gold in order to overcome Athens, and he is represented by Xenophon in *Hellenika* as a panhellenist.[c] It would be reasonable to assume that Kleandros, being the officer Kallikratidas appointed as his deputy, held similar views, which will have made it easier for Kleandros to regard Xenophon positively.

## Kleanor

§19. Kleanor of Orchomenos (in Arcadia), Greek officer. Though not one of the original Greek generals on the expedition, he was evidently a very senior officer from the beginning, presumably as a result of his age and long experience. He is said to

W.18a   Plutarch, *Sayings of the Lacedaemonians* 222f (Kallikratidas, §6).
W.18b   Diodorus 13.98.1 (in Strassler 2009, Appendix O: Diodorus) assigns Klearchos this deputizing role, but Plutarch is a better authority, especially as regards names, which Diodorus has a track record of confusing.

W.18c   On panhellenism, see Appendix E: Panhellenism.

have been the oldest person present—at least after the temporary departure of the leading Greek general, *Klearchos—when Phalinos came to the Greek camp after the battle of Cunaxa as an envoy from the Persians; and he took the lead, despite the presence of several generals, in vehemently rejecting the Persian demand that the Greeks surrender their weapons. After the arrest of Klearchos and the other generals, Kleanor acted as a general, alongside *Sophainetos (the sole actual general in the Greek camp at this point), in receiving a Persian deputation, on which occasion he made another passionate outburst, this time to accuse Cyrus' former lieutenant *Ariaios of oath-breaking. The following day he was formally elected general in place of Agias. He is referred to many times on the subsequent journey. Characteristically, he spoke to the soldiers of Persian bad faith, and with similar forthrightness he advocated an immediate attack on the Chalybes, the Taochoi, and the Phasianoi, a step Xenophon showed was poor tactics. It is no surprise that, much later, Kleanor was one of the three generals who bluntly put a stop to the attempt of the itinerant military expert *Koiratadas to take over the army; or that he was among those who wished to maintain the army's independence and advocated a course of action likely to involve prolonged active campaigning—namely, signing up with the Thracian princeling *Seuthes. But despite his age, he did not confine himself to blunt words: he is recorded as having led the hoplites[a] against the Kolchoi up a mountain, and as leading the troops over age thirty in the battle in support of Seuthes for the Thynian plain. Kleanor's role in the breakaway of the Arcadians and Achaeans in Heraclea is not specified, but it is perhaps because he was an Arcadian, and therefore trusted by the army's very large Arcadian contingent, that he was specially chosen to perform a vital sacrifice at Kalpe Harbor, which proved unsuccessful. Despite a number of run-ins with Xenophon over time and generous gifts from Seuthes, when the two fell out, Kleanor refused to campaign with Seuthes unless Xenophon participated. Xenophon builds up an attractive picture of this brave, loyal, outspoken, but perhaps not very clever old soldier.

## Klearchos

§20.1. Klearchos the Lacedaemonian (c. 450–400), ultimately the leading Greek general within the army of *Cyrus the Younger. He came from a senior family in Sparta: his father, Ramphias, with two others, delivered Sparta's ultimatum to Athens in early 431, just before the outbreak of the Peloponnesian War.[a] In summer 412 Klearchos was sent to the Hellespont to assist Sparta's then ally *Pharnabazos, satrap of Hellespontine Phrygia, against the Athenians.[b] This was a natural place to deploy him, as he was Byzantium's *proxenos*[c] at Sparta. Byzantium duly defected from Athens,[d] and subsequently he brought nearby Cyzicus over as well. Then, in early 410, he was one of the key officers of the Spartan *nauarchos* (admiral) Mindaros at a major naval battle off Cyzicus, which Sparta lost disastrously. According to Xenophon,[e] later that year the Spartan king Agis sent Klearchos back from Sparta to

---

W.19a  Hoplites: heavy-armed infantry; for more, see Appendix H: Infantry and Cavalry in *Anabasis*, §§2–3.

W.20a  Sparta's ultimatum: Thucydides 1.139.3.

W.20b  Klearchos sent to Hellespont: Thucydides 8.8.2.

W.20c  *Proxenos:* a man who, while still residing in the city-state of which he was a citizen (and to which

he was expected to have his primary loyalty), was appointed to act in support of the citizens of a particular foreign state in their dealings with the *proxenos*' city; for more, see the Glossary.

W.20d  Caused Byzantium to revolt: Thucydides 8.80.1–3.

W.20e  *Hellenika* 1.1.35–36.

Byzantium to throttle Athens' main grain supply, which passed through the Hellespont. He was a stern authoritarian as Spartan harmost (governor) of Byzantium, for example depriving the citizens of food in order to feed the garrison when the city was under siege; consequently, in (probably) 408, influential Byzantines betrayed the city to the Athenians, and a Spartan court subsequently decided that their behavior had been understandable.[f] Klearchos may have been under something of a cloud after this, as he is not recorded as one of the senior officers of the Spartan *nauarchos* Lysander, who in 405 won the decisive battle of Aigospotamoi.

§20.2. After the war, probably in 403, the Byzantines asked the Spartans to send them a general not only to help in a war against the Thracians but also to compose their internal divisions.[g] Despite earlier events, Klearchos persuaded the ephors[h] to send him; and though they thought better of it before he had even left the Peloponnese, he ignored their order to turn back, gathered a mercenary army, and demanded admission to Byzantium. The Byzantines refused, and the ephors followed up their recall order by formally condemning him for disobedience. However, the Byzantines were then besieged by the Thracians and, desperate for help, approached Klearchos, who was still in the area. He persuaded the Byzantine army to board ship (ostensibly to outflank the Thracians), invited the two key Byzantine generals to join him in a tavern, secretly murdered them, and then occupied the city with his mercenaries. After putting thirty leading citizens to death and committing other outrages, he ruled as an arbitrary dictator. The Spartans actually had to send an army to dislodge him, first from Byzantium and then from nearby Selymbria, near which he lost a pitched battle against them. Shortly afterward, a disgraced exile, he fled to Cyrus in Ionia. We know about his Byzantine atrocities not from Xenophon but partly from Diodorus[i] and partly from a later author, Polyaenus. Cyrus commissioned Klearchos to raise an army for him in the Thracian Chersonese, which he used to wage war on the Thracians. Polyaenus tells further anecdotes about this war, in particular that Klearchos terrified the Thracians into submission by making them believe that he literally ate the enemy for dinner.

§20.3. When Cyrus summoned him, Klearchos brought his army to join him at Kelainai. He knew from the outset that Cyrus' real objective was to march to Babylonia to attack King *Artaxerxes; according to Xenophon, Klearchos was the only general who knew so early, but this seems unlikely. That he was on the left wing at the army review in Tyriaion shows that, to start with, Cyrus did not regard him as his leading general, since the normal place of command in Greek armies was on the right wing; but he overtook his rival, *Menon, when by cunning manipulation he overcame the soldiers' initial opposition to going on from Tarsus. Later in the march, the harsh discipline Klearchos applied to one of Menon's soldiers led to a violent confrontation with Menon's troops, which Cyrus personally had to put a stop to. But by now Klearchos was clearly Cyrus' preferred general, the one Greek Cyrus chose to take part in the trial of the traitor Orontas, and was therefore posted

W.20f   Betrayal of Byzantium: *Hellenika* 1.3.14–22.
W.20g   Asked the Spartans to send them a general: Diodorus 14.12.2 (in Appendix S: Diodorus).
W.20h   Ephors: the chief elected magistrates of Sparta and heads of the government, exercising military

discipline over individual Spartan citizens; for more, see Appendix B: Xenophon and Sparta, §16.
W.20i   Activities in Byzantium and Selymbria: Diodorus 14.12.2–7 (in Appendix S: Diodorus).

on the right wing at the battle of Cunaxa. As the battle started, Klearchos ignored Cyrus' order to charge Artaxerxes himself, which would have meant marching at a slant, and instead directed the Greeks straight ahead; he then allowed them to advance far beyond the rest of Cyrus' line. The course of the battle, and Klearchos' performance, is discussed in Appendix L: The Battle of Cunaxa.

§20.4. After the battle, left in control of his own sector of the battlefield, Klearchos claimed victory over Artaxerxes' army and, on hearing of the death of Cyrus, offered (absurdly) to make Cyrus' ally *Ariaios King. More reasonably, when Phalinos, the intermediary sent by the Persians, demanded that the Greeks hand over their weapons, Klearchos made Greek success in the battle a ground for refusal, handling Phalinos with great skill and apparent nonchalance. After a day's delay, he linked up with Ariaios' men. By now he was the undisputed leader of the whole Greek army. On the subsequent march through Babylonia, he further demonstrated his cunning by a fake announcement to quiet a nighttime panic in the Greek camp. After putting up a show of reluctance, he accepted a truce from the Persians and the assistance of the Persian general *Tissaphernes for the return journey. Xenophon gives examples of his severe but hands-on leadership style on the onward march at *Anabasis* 2.3.11–12.

§20.5. Relations between Greeks and Persians were seen to deteriorate continually as they journeyed northward along the Tigris River. Klearchos tried to convince Tissaphernes of his good faith, but at the same time he explained to suspicious Greeks that his cooperation with the Persian general was based only on current necessities. Although Xenophon recounts subterfuges on both sides during the march, he represents Klearchos as sincere when, after they had reached the Zapatas River, he approached Tissaphernes to improve their relations, offering him Greek help in the west. He voiced his suspicions that a slanderer was trying to poison their relationship, and then agreed to a further meeting at which the troublemakers would be named. According to Xenophon, Klearchos was naïve in trusting Tissaphernes' reassurances and was key in persuading the Greeks to send most of their officers to this meeting, hoping that Menon would be revealed as the troublemaker and Klearchos would thus be free of this rival. By contrast, Ctesias says[j] that Klearchos did not want to go to the second meeting but was talked into it by his fellow generals *Proxenos and Menon; the latter had indeed been conspiring with Tissaphernes and had gulled Proxenos. Ctesias was very likely told this by Klearchos himself, whom he met later,[k] but Klearchos was probably trying to disguise his own folly. Tissaphernes may well have always planned a coup once the Greeks were safely at a distance from Babylon. Whatever the truth, at the meeting Tissaphernes arrested Klearchos and the four other Greek generals who attended. Klearchos was kept in prison for a time, cold-shouldered by his fellow Greek captives. He was eventually executed, as were the other arrested generals, following a power struggle between Artaxerxes' mother, *Parysatis, who tried to save him, and Artaxerxes' wife, Stateira, who prevailed.

W.20j   In Photius §68 (in Appendix U: Photius).
W.20k   Met later: Photius §69 (in Appendix U).

§20.6. Xenophon's obituary of Klearchos[l] emphasizes Klearchos' keenness for warfare, his grimness, and his severity but also his reassuring professionalism. But by suppressing Klearchos' appalling behavior in Byzantium, by raising probably unjustified suspicions against Menon, and by failing to reckon with the possibility that Klearchos was outgeneraled at Cunaxa, Xenophon's account, though by no means wholly positive, gives far too kind an impression of him.

### Koiratadas

§21. Koiratadas of Thebes, alleged military expert who traveled around hiring himself out as a general. He persuaded the remnant of the Ten Thousand in Byzantium to hire him, but it almost immediately became evident that he did not have enough supplies to feed them all, and his tenure came to a swift end. Previously, probably in 408, Koiratadas had been a subordinate of the Spartan *Klearchos when the latter was harmost[a] at Byzantium during the later stages of the Peloponnesian War against Athens; and while entrusted with responsibility for the city in Klearchos' absence, he succeeded in losing it to the Athenians because the Byzantines opened the gates to them at night. His name is restored by a plausible emendation in *Hellenica Oxyrhynchia*[b] as a leading supporter of the pro-Spartan party at Thebes in 395, at which time this group was outwitted by its pro-Athenian opponents, who led Thebes into war alongside Athens against Sparta. These two incidents help explain Xenophon's evident contempt for him; they also show him to have been a Spartan loyalist, which strongly suggests that he was not simply pursuing his career in his approach to the army but had been put up to it by the Spartan *nauarchos* (admiral) *Anaxibios, currently resident in Byzantium, in order to lure the army out of the city.

### Medokos

§22. Medokos, king of the Odrysae, the dominant Thracian tribe. Known in other sources as Amadokos or Amadokes, he succeeded Seuthes I during a period of difficulties for the Odrysae and reigned for twenty years or so around the turn of the fifth to the fourth century. His orphaned cousin *Seuthes was brought up at his court, which was far in the interior of Thrace (but perhaps not quite as far as the twelve days' journey alleged by Seuthes' sidekick Herakleides); subsequently Medokos gave him some troops to reestablish himself in the principality in eastern Thrace from which Seuthes' father, Maisades, had been expelled. Already in *Anabasis* there are signs of strain in the relationship between Medokos and Seuthes, since Herakleides tries to dissuade gift-bearing envoys from Parium from their proposed journey to see Medokos; still, Medosades, another of Seuthes' henchmen, refers to Medokos respectfully, and an Odrysian nobleman who declares his allegiance to Medokos is cooperating with Seuthes. However, from other sources we learn that in the end

W.20l   Obituary of Klearchos: *Anabasis* 2.6.1–15.
W.21a   Harmost: a technical term (literally, "fixer") for a Spartan official resident abroad; for more, see Appendix B: Xenophon and Sparta, §15.
W.21b   *Hellenica Oxyrhynchia* fragment 20.1 in Chambers' edition, translated in Strassler 2009, Appendix P: Selected Fragments of the *Hellenica*

*Oxyrhynchia* Relevant to Xenophon's *Hellenika* (fragment 17.1 in Bartoletti's edition).

Seuthes overtly rebelled against Medokos and claimed kingship over the coastal areas of Thrace in his own right, and they were still in conflict when in (probably) 390 the Athenian general Thrasyboulos intervened to reconcile them and confirm or establish them both as Athenian allies.[a] It seems likely that Medokos died shortly afterward, as an inscription dating from 386/5 shows a different man, Hebryzelmis, as king of the Odrysae and an Athenian ally, but it is possible that political authority among the Odrysae had fractured still further in the early 380s. However, Medokos' branch of the family retained some power, as it is presumably his son who is attested, under the name Amadokos, as taking an independent line as a Thracian princeling in 359.

## Menon

§23.1. Menon the Thessalian (d. 400), leader of a contingent of 1,500 troops in *Cyrus the Younger's army, which he joined at Colossae. Despite his youth, Menon had been given this appointment by *Aristippos, the dynast of Larissa; Xenophon claims[a] that this was because of a homosexual relationship between them. However, Menon was not himself from Larissa but from another Thessalian city, Pharsalus.[b] Menon was a very suitable person for Aristippos to send, as he was a guest-friend[c] of *Ariaios, the commander of Cyrus' non-Greek troops, a relationship Xenophon also interpreted sexually; and, according to the philosopher Plato (one of whose Socratic dialogues is named after Menon), also a hereditary guest-friend of the Persian King himself. It seems that, to start with, Menon was the Greek commander Cyrus honored most, since he assigned him the right wing at a review at Tyriaion, but he subsequently lost ground to *Klearchos the Spartan. Perhaps this was partly because when Menon was sent with a detachment to escort the Cilician queen *Epyaxa to Tarsus by a special route, he lost two companies on the way and his men ran amok in Tarsus on arrival there; but presumably it was mostly the result of Klearchos' obvious military competence and persuasiveness with the troops. Menon was first to cross the Euphrates at Thapsakos, perhaps trying to regain lost ground; but though he obtained praise and gifts from Cyrus, his influence does not seem to have increased, and he had a violent quarrel with Klearchos on the march through Mesopotamia. Relations with Klearchos cannot have been helped by Menon's Thessalian background, for it is likely that, like Larissa, Pharsalus was at this point hostile to Lykophron (of Pherai, the third Thessalian city), who was supported by the Spartans; eventually the Spartans garrisoned Pharsalus to prevent it from obstructing Lykophron.[d] Menon led the Greek left wing at the review before Cunaxa and in the battle itself, thus being formally downgraded behind Klearchos to the post of second honor. After the battle the Greeks tried to utilize Menon's special relationship with Ariaios, making him part of a delegation to the latter, with whom he remained for some time. But the relationship started to become a source of suspicion, at least to

---

W.22a  Thrasyboulos intervenes: *Hellenika* 4.8.26.
W.23a  *Anabasis* 2.6.28.
W.23b  Menon from Pharsalus: according to Diogenes Laertius 2.50 (in Appendix V: Diogenes Laertius' *Life of Xenophon*). Thus the statement at Diodorus 14.19.8 (in Appendix S: Diodorus) that Menon was from Larissa must be a slip.

W.23c  Guest-friend: someone with whom there is a bond of ritualized friendship of a type that was common between prominent men of different cities; for more, see the Glossary.
W.23d  Spartans garrisoned Pharsalus: Diodorus 14.82.5–6 (in Strassler 2009, Appendix O: Diodorus).

Xenophon; more importantly, Klearchos became convinced that Menon was maligning him to the Persians.

§23.2. According to *Ctesias,[c] Menon was indeed plotting with the Persian commander *Tissaphernes, and when Klearchos was invited to what turned out to be a fateful meeting with the latter, he did not want to go but succumbed to pressure from Menon. However, Xenophon's account is different, and it has been suggested that, since Ctesias had dealings with Klearchos in his subsequent captivity, Ctesias' story represents Klearchos' own self-exculpatory recharacterization of events. Menon was one of the other generals who went to the meeting with Tissaphernes and was arrested there. The Persians claimed that he had given them information about Klearchos' plotting and was being well treated, and that he was spared at this point is confirmed by Diodorus (with a slightly different explanation) and by Ctesias.[f] According to Xenophon, Menon nevertheless came to an especially bad end, as unlike the other Greek generals, who were given the swift death of beheading, he was tortured to death over the course of a year; but the other sources do not confirm this. Xenophon gave Menon an outstandingly negative obituary, branding him a liar, slanderer, scoffer, money-grubber, and sexually aberrant individual, and it would be natural to think that Xenophon thought Menon had betrayed the Greeks, although he does not make that accusation directly. However, it has been well argued that there is no good evidence that Menon did any such thing. The more favorable treatment he received from his Persian captors at least initially might be due to his relationship with Ariaios, whom the King seems to have forgiven completely; and Xenophon's attitude might be driven chiefly by Menon's personal rudeness to him, which seems implied by some of the complaints in the obituary. Plato, in his *Meno*, says that Menon had been a pupil of the rhetorician *Gorgias and bears out Xenophon's complaints to some extent by making him spoiled and imperious and by having Socrates hint that he is greedy for money; but he is made to speak both spiritedly and sensibly, and there is no hint that he was to become a traitor.

### Naukleidas and Biton

§24.1. Naukleidas was a Spartan and one of the five ephors[a] in 403. Along with the Spartan king Pausanias, he pursued a policy of détente toward the Athenian democrats[b] and was subsequently prosecuted by Lysander, the general who had been key to Sparta's success against Athens in the Peloponnesian War. This Landmark edition proposes that it was Naukleidas who was sent as an envoy to Xenophon from the Spartan commander *Thibron in 399 and who became Xenophon's guest-friend (7.8.6); the manuscripts of *Anabasis* confuse this person with Eukleides, mentioned a little earlier in the text, and previous editors have printed "Nausiklides" from a marginal comment in two late manuscripts. Nausiklides would be otherwise unknown, except that the second-century C.E. anthologist Athenaeus cites a disparaging remark about the Helle-

W.23e    In Photius §68 (in Appendix U: Photius).
W.23f    Diodorus 14.27.2 (in Appendix S: Diodorus).
        Ctesias in Photius §69 (in Appendix U).
W.24a    On ephors, see n. W.20h.
W.24b    Policy of détente: *Hellenika* 2.4.35–36.

spontine area by a man named Nausiklides, perhaps also a scribal error for Naukleidas. The man ought to have been quite well-known at the time Xenophon wrote, since the latter gives no ethnic or other identifying information, as he usually does. If this proposal is correct, it is an important indication that it was the supporters of King Pausanias rather than of his colleague, King *Agesilaos, who initially backed Sparta's turn against Persia in late 400. Since Naukleidas had shown that he was friendly to Athens in 403, he will have been chosen by Thibron to reassure Xenophon about his intentions.

§24.2. Similarly, his fellow envoy **Biton**, who by the same argument ought to be well-known to contemporaries, might reasonably be identified with the Biton of Syracuse who in 397–396 commanded a garrison of Sicels (native Sicilians) on behalf of the tyrant Dionysius of Syracuse.[c] If in 399 this man was a commander of mercenaries in Sparta's service, he too could have been a very suitable person to reassure Xenophon. (However, one family of Xenophontic manuscripts calls him Bion rather than Biton.)

## Orontas

§25.1. Orontas, son-in-law of King *Artaxerxes and son of Artasyras (named by Plutarch as "the King's Eye" at the battle of Cunaxa);[a] said to have been of Bactrian stock. Others imply that he was a descendant of Hydarnes, one of the seven Persian conspirators who put Darius I on the throne in 522. He evidently fought at Cunaxa and around this time married Artaxerxes' daughter Rhodogyne.[b] Either then or earlier, he was appointed satrap[c] of Armenia. Most of Xenophon's references to him occur in the context of his journey with Rhodogyne to his satrapy, during which he helped *Tissaphernes first to escort and then to harry the Greeks as they traveled northward. Troops of his unsuccessfully tried to prevent the Greeks from crossing the Kentrites River into Armenia. Thereafter it seems that he left the Greeks to his lieutenant governor (*hyparchos*),[d] *Tiribazos.

§25.2. Orontas' later career was something of a roller coaster, many aspects of which are controversial. In the late 380s, he commanded the Persian forces fighting against the rebel Evagoras, king of Salamis on Cyprus, probably in a joint command with Tiribazos at first but subsequently subordinated to him. Their consequent quarrel and Orontas' accusations against Tiribazos initially led to temporary disgrace for the latter, but in the end Tiribazos triumphed and Orontas was expelled from the list of King's Friends and demoted from the satrapy of Armenia. Instead, it seems he was made *hyparchos* of Mysia, headquartered at Pergamum, which was probably his position at the time Xenophon completed *Anabasis;* this means he would have been a familiar figure to Xenophon's initial readers. During the 360s a series of satraps in central and western Anatolia rebelled against the King, attempting to force concessions from him about their various positions. Fairly late in this movement, Orontas joined the rebels and is said to have become their leader. Artaxerxes was now very old, and Orontas probably feared Tiribazos' very strong influence over the crown

W.24c  Biton of Syracuse: Diodorus 14.53.5 (not in Appendix S: Diodorus).

W.25a  King's Eye: Plutarch, *Life of Artaxerxes* 12.1 (in Appendix T: Plutarch). The evidence is unclear whether the King's Eye was a single official, the head of intelligence, or whether it was a title applied to all Persian intelligence officers.

W.25b  Artaxerxes' daughter Rhodogyne: Plutarch, *Life of Artaxerxes* 27.7 (not in Appendix T: Plutarch).

W.25c  Satrap: governor of a province of the Persian Empire; for more, see the Glossary.

W.25d  *Hyparchos:* for discussion of the various meanings of this word, see the Glossary.

prince, Darius. But Darius and Tiribazos tried to hasten Artaxerxes' demise, and both were put to death themselves. Orontas accepted generous terms offered by Artaxerxes and surrendered his soldiers and cities to the King, thereupon receiving a wider command in the west. He seems to have died not long after.

### Parysatis

§26. Parysatis, Persian queen, then Queen Mother. She was the daughter of Artaxerxes I, Great King of Persia (r. 465–424), and the half sister and wife of his son and eventual successor, *Darius II. *Artaxerxes II and *Cyrus the Younger were their sons, Artaxerxes born before Darius unexpectedly succeeded to the throne, Cyrus shortly afterward. (According to Ctesias,ᵃ Parysatis and Darius II had ten more children after Cyrus, but only two of these survived infancy.) Parysatis supported Cyrus' claims to succeed Darius on the ground that being born a King's son was more important than being the firstborn. When Artaxerxes obtained the throne despite this, she successfully pleaded with him to ignore accusations against Cyrus made by *Tissaphernes, his subordinate in the western provinces, and to reinstate Cyrus there. She also backed Cyrus' claim to be officially given the Ionian cities that had revolted from Tissaphernes to him. Xenophon seems to assert that Parysatis even continued to support Cyrus in his efforts to displace Artaxerxes. On their march the Greeks twice passed through villages owned by Parysatis: the first villages were in Syria, said to have been given to her to pay for her girdles; the second were in the mid-Tigris valley, and these Tissaphernes (spitefully, according to Xenophon) gave the Greeks permission to plunder. Cuneiform tablets survive with administrative records of other estates of hers in Babylonia. Parysatis was a tough, ruthless, and cunning woman, and nowhere is this clearer than in her horrible revenge on those who had been directly concerned in the death of Cyrus. Ctesias also says she poisoned Artaxerxes' queen, Stateira, allegedly because Stateira bested her over the execution of Cyrus' general *Klearchos, whom Parysatis had tried to save; but their enmity went back two decades before that. For this crime against his wife, Artaxerxes merely banished his mother from court, and that only temporarily. She remained a key influence on him: he sent her the head of Tissaphernes when the latter fell from favor and was put to death in 395, and Parysatis is said to have been instrumental in persuading Artaxerxes to marry his own daughter, Atossa. The idea of increasing the concentration of royal blood fits with Parysatis' own sibling relation to Darius II and with her support for Cyrus because he was born the King's son; it also perhaps partly indicates insecurity because of Darius' comparatively weak claim on the throne.

### Pharnabazos

§27.1. Pharnabazos, satrap of Hellespontine Phrygia.ᵃ Pharnabazos succeeded his father, Pharnakes, as satrap in 413. Hellespontine Phrygia was almost a hereditary satrapy, already in the hands of a relation of Pharnabazos' in 478; the family were

W.26a  Ctesias, Photius §51 (not in Appendix U: Photius).
W.27a  Not Bithynia, despite the scribal insertion at *Anabasis* 7.8.25: see *Hellenika* 3.2.2.

distant cousins of the royal house. On his appointment Pharnabazos and his rival and colleague *Tissaphernes (satrap of Lydia and Caria) were instructed to recover tribute from the Greek cities of Asia; as Thucydides recounts in detail,[b] they opened rival negotiations with Sparta, then waging the Peloponnesian War against Athens. Pharnabazos was a much stauncher ally of Sparta than Tissaphernes, but the battles of Abydos, Cyzicus, and Chalcedon, in which he fought alongside the Spartans,[c] were all won by the Athenians. In subsequent campaigns in Hellespontine Phrygia, Pharnabazos again cooperated with the Spartans, under Lysander, but his complaints against *Derkylidas, a senior Spartan officer, permanently alienated the latter. In winter 404/3, after Lysander had brought the Peloponnesian War to a triumphant end, Pharnabazos denounced him too and caused his recall by the Spartan government. Around the same time, Diodorus tells us,[d] Pharnabazos warned the new Persian King, *Artaxerxes, that *Cyrus the Younger was plotting against him, but it would seem that Artaxerxes discounted this, since Xenophon reports Tissaphernes' warning to Artaxerxes in 401 as if it were the first, and it was Tissaphernes to whom the King was grateful subsequently, subordinating Pharnabazos to him and removing Aeolis from Pharnabazos' satrapy to give to Tissaphernes.[e]

§27.2. Pharnabazos was hostile to the remnants of Cyrus' troops when they appeared near his province in late 400. He sent cavalry to assist the Bithynians in attempting to keep them out, and his troops later directly attacked the Greeks, though unsuccessfully. He asked the Spartan *nauarchos* (admiral), *Anaxibios, to make the Greek army cross out of Asia, which Anaxibios duly arranged. But despite this and what should have been the gratifying subsequent disintegration of the army, Pharnabazos snubbed Anaxibios on his way back to Sparta, switching his attention to the newly arrived Spartan harmost of Byzantium, Aristarchos. While Aristarchos fell in with Pharnabazos' wishes, Anaxibios was enraged and sent Xenophon back to the army to lead it back to Asia, though Aristarchos managed to block this for the time being. Pharnabazos had alienated too many people in Sparta now, and antipathy toward him will have been a factor in the Spartans' positive response at this point to an appeal from the Greeks of Asia: although the Asian Greeks were complaining particularly of Tissaphernes, the Spartan commander *Thibron campaigned against both satraps in 399.

§27.3. Xenophon's *Hellenika* recounts how Thibron was followed as Spartan commander in Asia by Pharnabazos' enemy Derkylidas,[f] who—with some encouragement from Tissaphernes—particularly targeted Pharnabazos. In 395 Derkylidas' successor, *Agesilaos, was likewise encouraged by Tissaphernes' successor, Tithraustes, to switch from his initial attack on Lydia to harassing Pharnabazos instead. By then Pharnabazos had organized a fleet, entrusted in 397 to the Athenian admiral Konon, which subsequently ended Spartan naval power in the Aegean at the battle of Cnidus (394). This bolstered Athens, which rebuilt the fortifications of its port, Peiraieus, and the Long Walls connecting the port with the main city partly with

W.27b  Persian satraps' rival negotiations: Thucydides Book 8 generally, but see especially 8.5.4–8.6.2, 8.39.1–2, 8.43.2–4, 8.80.1–2, 8.99.

W.27c  Pharnabazos supports Spartans: at Abydos, *Hellenika* 1.1.6; at Cyzicus, 1.1.14; at Chalcedon, 1.3.5.

W.27d  Diodorus 14.11.3 (in Strassler 2009, Appendix O: Diodorus).

W.27e  Aeolis given to Tissaphernes: *Hellenika* 3.2.13.

W.27f  Derkylidas succeeds Thibron as commander: *Hellenika* 3.1.8–10.

Pharnabazos' money; but the victory also secured Persian domination along the eastern Aegean seacoast and cemented Pharnabazos' position with Artaxerxes. By 387 he had left Hellespontine Phrygia to go to the Great King's court to marry Artaxerxes' daughter Apame. He was appointed to command two expeditions to recover Egypt for the Persians, from whom it had revolted shortly before 400. The first time, when he shared command with two others, was perhaps in 390–388; the second appointment was in 380 or 379, but the invasion itself did not occur until 373. Both expeditions achieved little or nothing, and Pharnabazos is thought to have died shortly after the second one.

### Prokles

§28. Prokles, ruler of Teuthrania, a small principality near Pergamum. Prokles was ethnically, and perhaps also culturally, a Greek, descended from Damaratos, king of Sparta at the turn of the sixth to the fifth century, whose story would have been familiar to Xenophon's first readers from Herodotus. The Spartans had a dual kingship, with two royal houses, the Agiads and the Eurypontids;[a] Damaratos, a Eurypontid king, was deposed as a result of an intrigue by his co-king, the Agiad Kleomenes. Sometime later, in 480, Damaratos accompanied the expedition against Greece mounted by the Great King *Xerxes. It seems that Damaratos received a small principality in Asia near the Aegean seaboard, and that his descendants continued to stress their royal Spartan origins: Prokles was given the name of the father of Eurypon, the legendary founder of the Eurypontids. Prokles was a supporter of *Cyrus the Younger but brigaded with his Persian troops rather than with the Greek army. After Cyrus' death he acted as an intermediary between Cyrus' erstwhile lieutenant *Ariaios and the Greek army and evidently followed Ariaios in returning to his allegiance to Artaxerxes. Nevertheless, when, almost eighteen months later, Xenophon arrived in Pergamum, Prokles burned his boats with the Persians by helping Xenophon escape from his first, unsuccessful, attempt to kidnap the rich Persian Asidates. The regional satrap *Tissaphernes had taken a tougher line with the Asian Greeks on his return to the west in 400; perhaps this disaffected Prokles. Prokles then joined the Spartan commander *Thibron in the war against the Persians.[b] His subsequent history is unknown.

### Proxenos

§29.1. Proxenos (d. 400), guest-friend of *Cyrus the Younger's and leader of one of the largest contingents of troops within the Ten Thousand. Though in general Xenophon refers to him as a Boeotian, at one point he mentions him as coming specifically from Thebes, the largest city in Boeotia and the dominant force within the Boeotian confederation. Proxenos was one of the friends Cyrus commissioned to assemble troops for him, which Proxenos duly brought to Sardis and led on the expedition. He also recruited Xenophon, who was another of his guest-friends; Xenophon is at pains to emphasize that at this stage Proxenos did not know Cyrus'

---

W.28a   Spartan kingship and royal houses: for more, see     W.28b   Prokles joins Thibron: *Hellenika* 3.1.6.
        Appendix B: Xenophon and Sparta, §13.

true intentions, but this may be naïveté on Xenophon's part, unconsciously left unquestioned out of a desire not to spoil the memory of their friendship. During the march to Babylonia, Proxenos tried to intercede in a violent dispute between his fellow generals *Klearchos and *Menon, but the would-be combatants were parted only by Cyrus' personal intervention. To judge from his position on Klearchos' immediate left at Cunaxa, Proxenos ranked third among Cyrus' Greek generals. After the battle Xenophon records him as querying the Persian requirement that the Greeks should surrender their weapons. Ctesias alleges[a] that Proxenos joined with Menon in putting pressure on Klearchos to go to the fatal interview at which the Persian commander *Tissaphernes arrested all the Greek generals who attended; the Persians subsequently put them to death. Ctesias acquits Proxenos (but not Menon) of actually being a party to a conspiracy against Klearchos and says he was himself deceived by a trick. Xenophon does not record this pressure at all—indeed, according to him, Klearchos went completely voluntarily—but perhaps *Anabasis* 2.6.20 suggests that he agreed that Proxenos had been gulled by Menon. More generally, the obituary that Xenophon gives him emphasizes his sense of honor and decency but also the weakness of his style of leadership.

§29.2. Information about Proxenos outside *Anabasis* chimes with Xenophon's emphasis on his pride in his education by the sophist *Gorgias. Diodorus[b] assigns to Proxenos the "philosophic" speech that Xenophon puts into the mouth of Theopompos of Athens at 2.1.12. A source from the early third century C.E., Philostratus, mentions that Xenophon was for a time a prisoner in Boeotia but was given parole, and that this enabled him to attend the lectures of the sophist Prodicus of Keos: it has been attractively suggested that Xenophon met Proxenos at this time, and that it was through Proxenos, also interested in philosophy, that Xenophon obtained the necessary parole.

**Rhathines,** see **Spithridates and Rhathines**

**Seuthes**

§30.1. Seuthes (d. 384/3?), Thracian princeling and subsequently king of the Odrysae (as King Seuthes II). Seuthes was a descendant of the Teres who founded the dynasty that ruled the Odrysae, the most powerful tribe in Thrace, from the first half of the fifth century. Seuthes' father, Maisades, had a principality and ruled over the Melanditai, the Tranipsai, and the Thynoi but was expelled, probably in the 410s, leaving his child to be brought up at the court of his cousin the Odrysian king *Medokos. Seuthes was unhappy about his subservient position, and Medokos provided the resources for him to try to reinstate himself in his father's principality. He must already have had some success in this by 405, because Diodorus reports[a] that in that year the Athenian ex-general Alcibiades referred to him, as well as to Medokos, as Thracian kings whose support would be useful to the Athenians. But when Xenophon and his troops arrived in the area, his position seems to have been much more

---

W.29a   Photius §68 (in Appendix U: Photius).
W.29b   Diodorus 14.25.4 (in Appendix S: Diodorus).

W.30a   Diodorus 13.105.3 (in Strassler 2009, Appendix O: Diodorus).

precarious, despite his having retrieved certain Thracian strongholds on Alcibiades' death (in 403).

§30.2. Book 7 of *Anabasis* is largely concerned with the Greek army's relations with Seuthes. These initially led to a transformation of his position when the Greeks helped him conquer the Thynoi, both in the Thynian plain and at Salmydessos, but were subsequently soured by his unwillingness or inability to give them the full pay that he had promised. He is shown as delighted when the army is taken off his hands by emissaries sent from the Spartan commander *Thibron. However, while the narrative and especially Xenophon's own speeches within it emphasize Seuthes' duplicity and faithlessness, and no doubt he was a slippery character, he had genuine difficulties in turning into sufficient cash the resources in land and population that the Greeks had helped him take over. Xenophon's narrative depicts Seuthes as allowing his aide Herakleides to undermine Medokos' position with foreigners, and it shows that after Seuthes' victory he attracted followers who had previously been in Medokos' directly controlled territory. However, as we see from the behavior at 7.7.11 of one of the most powerful of these men (not given a name by Xenophon), this was still compatible with loyalty to Medokos, leaving Seuthes' own position ambiguous for the moment. *Anabasis* gives the strong impression that it was the initial conquest of the Thynian plain that was key to his rise, but Diodorus[b] ignores it and instead emphasizes Xenophon's part in taking Salmydessos.

§30.3. Seuthes is recorded as having helped the Spartan general *Derkylidas against the Thracians of Bithynia in 399 and as having entertained him in 398 when the latter was en route to fighting the Thracians of the Chersonese, which it would thus seem Seuthes did not control at this time.[c] At some point in the 390s, Seuthes openly rebelled against the less militarily experienced Medokos. The two were still actively hostile to each other when (probably in 390) the Athenian general Thrasyboulos reconciled them and made them both, or confirmed them as, allies of Athens against Sparta.[d] Subsequently the Athenian general Iphikrates married one of Seuthes' daughters and took up residence at his court around the time of the King's Peace of 387/6, which temporarily put an end to military ventures by the Athenians. Iphikrates entered Seuthes' service, with very positive results for both Seuthes and his son and successor, Kotys. The relationship with Athens was, however, more complex than might be suggested by Iphikrates' good relations with Seuthes in the mid-380s and Seuthes' professions of goodwill to Athenians recorded by Xenophon. The sources here are fragmentary and disputed by scholars, but the Roman author Seneca the Elder, presumably referring to this Seuthes, says that Iphikrates twice defeated a Thracian king, afterward making a treaty with him and marrying his daughter; and other sources seem to indicate that Seuthes had at some point wiped out an Athenian force in the Chersonese and that he had put military pressure on Athens to fall in with the King's Peace. Seuthes probably died in 384/3, most likely outliving Medokos, since an Athenian inscription of 386/5 mentions one Hebryzelmis as king of the Odrysae. It is not clear whether Seuthes ever became undisputed king of the Odrysae,

W.30b  Diodorus 14.37.2 (in Appendix S: Diodorus).

W.30c  Seuthes helps Derkylidas: *Hellenika* 3.2.2; entertains him, 3.2.9–10.

W.30d  Allies of Athens: *Hellenika* 4.8.26.

but his son Kotys certainly did. The Odrysian kings' attitude toward Athens was a very topical subject in the Athens of the 360s, when *Anabasis* was probably written.

## Socrates

§31. Socrates the Athenian (469–399), philosopher. Socrates is the best-known of all the characters in *Anabasis* because of the tremendous influence he had on the development of ancient Greek (and subsequent) philosophy, though he himself left no writings behind him. At 3.1.4–7, Xenophon reports asking for his advice on joining Cyrus and then circumventing it. See Appendix A: Xenophon and Socrates for a discussion of the differences in the three contemporary sources (namely, Aristophanes, Plato, and Xenophon) for Socrates, his thought, and his method of approach and also of the meaning of the charges on which he was condemned to death by drinking hemlock. For his relationship with Xenophon, see also the Introduction, §§2.9–12, 8.12–14.

## Sophainetos

§32.1. Sophainetos the Stymphalian,[a] a guest-friend of *Cyrus the Younger's and one of the original Greek generals in the army, who brought his troops to join Cyrus at Kelainai. At 6.5.13, he is said to be the oldest of the (then) generals; at 5.3.1, one of the two oldest generals. If we are to take this literally, it should mean Sophainetos was not present at the interview with the King's envoy Phalinos after the battle of Cunaxa, which is recounted at 2.1.10, since *Kleanor, who was a general during the events of Book 6, is said to have been the oldest Greek in the group of officers who received Phalinos. However, in Diodorus' account of this interview,[b] he assigns to "Sophilos" (probably a mistake for Sophainetos) the sentiments that in Xenophon are expressed by Xenophon's friend *Proxenos. It is not clear whether this reflects rival eyewitness testimony (not necessarily accurate, of course) or is a later confection, perhaps by someone who wanted to show his independence from Xenophon.

§32.2. Since Sophainetos did not attend the fateful interview with the Persian commander *Tissaphernes, he was not arrested with *Klearchos and most of the other generals but instead is recorded as having received a Persian deputation shortly afterward. Thus he survived to be a general on the journey back to the Black Sea and along its coast. Xenophon seems to mention Sophainetos largely in contexts that are somewhat derogatory: left behind to guard the camp at 4.4.19, detailed to travel by sea from Trapezus rather than through potentially hostile territory at 5.3.1, fined for dereliction of duty at 5.8.1, being pusillanimous about attacking over rough ground in Bithynia at 6.5.13. As our text stands, he is not mentioned in Book 7, so possibly he died or (more likely) left the army at Byzantium, though it is conceivable that he remained a general and his name has dropped out at 7.2.1, where there is something amiss with the text. The sixth-century C.E. lexicographer Stephanus of Byzantium gives four citations from what he alleges is Sophainetos' *Anabasis of*

W.32a  Stymphalos was a small city in Arcadia.
W.32b  Diodorus 14.25.5 (in Appendix S: Diodorus).

*Cyrus;*[c] if Sophainetos was indeed its author, it would prove that he survived, though not that he stayed with the army past Byzantium.

### Spithridates and Rhathines

§33.1. Spithridates was a senior officer in the army of *Pharnabazos, satrap of Hellespontine Phrygia; he unsuccessfully attacked the Greek army as it passed through Bithynia. A man of this name was one of the three generals who suppressed the rebel satrap Pissuthnes, perhaps in 422/1. Subsequent to the events of *Anabasis*, Spithridates fell out with Pharnabazos, and in 395, together with his handsome son Megabates, he was persuaded to join the Spartan king *Agesilaos in his campaign against Pharnabazos. Spithridates suggested to Agesilaos that he should try to enlist the king of the Paphlagonians to his cause; Agesilaos then arranged for the king to marry Spithridates' daughter (though Spithridates may have been less eager for this than Agesilaos and the Paphlagonian king). But this backfired against Agesilaos when Spithridates and the Paphlagonians, thinking themselves poorly treated in the distribution of booty, returned to their Persian allegiance, with Spithridates using *Cyrus the Younger's old supporter *Ariaios as an intermediary to obtain mercy.[a]

§33.2. By contrast, Spithridates' fellow officer Rhathines remained loyal to Pharnabazos. Xenophon records at *Hellenika* 3.4.13–14 that he defeated Agesilaos' cavalry in a skirmish in Phrygia in 396. He is presumably the same man as the Persian Rhathanes in *Hellenica Oxyrhynchia*,[b] who put up a spirited defense of the city of Gordion a year later when it was attacked by Agesilaos. This meant Rhathines was directly opposing his former colleague Spithridates, since this was within the period when the latter was assisting Agesilaos.

### Tamos and Glous

§34.1. Tamos (pronounced Tamōs; d. 400), who came from Egypt, was lieutenant governor (*hyparchos*) to *Tissaphernes in Ionia in winter 412/11; and when the latter absented himself for a time, he gave Tamos the thankless responsibility of providing (nonexistent) finance for the Spartan fleet.[a] Perhaps it was not surprising that, set up in this way as a scapegoat, Tamos, together with his son Glous (d. 380 or 379),[b] subsequently sided with *Cyrus the Younger against Tissaphernes. Diodorus[c] states that Cyrus made Tamos satrap of Ionia and Aeolis, though it is not clear how this fits in with Xenophon's report of his command of Cyrus' fleet as it made its way from Ephesus to Issus. Glous was evidently a senior member of Cyrus' entourage, twice mentioned during the march to Babylonia as executing his orders. When, after the battle of Cunaxa, Tissaphernes returned in triumph to Sardis, Tamos fled with all his children except Glous to Egypt, where he expected to be given asylum by a

W.32c   For a discussion of this work, see Appendix M: Other Ancient Sources on the Ten Thousand, §§12–15.

W.33a   The most detailed account of all this is given by Xenophon in *Hellenika* 3.4.10, 4.1.1–28. The matter is touched on in *Hellenica Oxyrhynchia*, fragments 24.4, 25.1 in Chambers' edition (fragments 21.4, 22.1 in Bartoletti's edition), translated in Strassler 2009, Appendix P: Selected Fragments of the *Hellenica Oxyrhynchia* Relevant to Xenophon's *Hellenika*.

W.33b   *Hellenica Oxyrhynchia* fragment 24.6 in Chambers' edition (fragment 21.6 in Bartoletti's edition), translated in Strassler 2009, Appendix P.

W.34a   Tamos lieutenant governor in Ionia: Thucydides 8.31.2; Tamos' failure to provide adequate finance, 8.87.1–3, 8.99.1.

W.34b   Glous is spelled Glōs by Diodorus, and this is a common spelling among scholars today.

W.34c   Diodorus 14.19.6 (in Appendix S: Diodorus).

rebel prince Diodorus calls Psammetichos; instead, the latter killed him and his children for their money.

§34.2. Meanwhile Glous quickly made his peace with King *Artaxerxes, along with Cyrus' leading supporter, *Ariaios, and is recorded as keeping watch, on Artaxerxes' behalf, over the Greeks as they crossed the Tigris River; he remained in the Great King's service after his father's flight. In the 380s Artaxerxes appointed Glous to command the fleet against another rebel—Evagoras, king of Salamis, on Cyprus—in an expedition under the overall command of Glous' father-in-law, *Tiribazos. Glous won a major though not completely conclusive sea battle; but when, probably in 380, Tiribazos fell temporarily into disgrace for allegedly negotiating too leniently with Evagoras, Glous was afraid for his own position and revolted from the King. He fomented trouble among the Greeks of Asia, allied himself with Psammetichos' successor in Egypt, Acoris, and sought help from the Spartans, but he was assassinated before the Spartans made any overt move.

## Thibron

§35. Thibron (d. 391), Lacedaemonian general. He was sent out in spring 399 as the first commander of the Spartan expedition requested by the Greek cities of Ionia to protect them from *Tissaphernes, then the most important Persian in western Anatolia. He sent his subordinates Charminos and Polynikos ahead of him to *Seuthes, the Thracian princeling who had hired the remnant of the Greek expeditionary force, to request that he allow Thibron to hire the troops instead. It seems he had been initially prejudiced against Xenophon, who was warned that he would be executed by him; but when Xenophon did bring the army across to Asia, he received money and reassurance from *Naukleidas and Biton, presumably sent by Thibron, and was allowed to retain command of his troops when he finally handed them over. Nevertheless, in *Hellenika* Xenophon gives a sour account of Thibron's period of command; the parallel narrative of Diodorus shows that he did have some success at the outset, but the authors agree that he was recalled by the Spartans for incompetence.[a] Xenophon suggests that a prime factor in his recall was indiscipline among the troops, perhaps especially the Ten Thousand, leading to complaints to the home government from plundered allies. In 391 Thibron once more led an army to western Anatolia against the Persians but was surprised by the Persian satrap Struthas and killed in the battle. Again, comparison of Xenophon's brief narrative with that of Diodorus shows that Xenophon has left out Thibron's successes, played up his ineptitude, and added scandalous suggestions about his being a passive homosexual.[b] Xenophon evidently hated Thibron, who had not given him his confidence and, though he had kept Xenophon in his post, presumably tried to undermine his authority with

W.35a  *Hellenika* 3.1.4–8, 3.2.1. Diodorus 14.36 (in Appendix S: Diodorus). Diodorus 14.38.2 in Strassler 2009, Appendix O: Diodorus.
W.35b  *Hellenika* 4.8.17–19. Diodorus 14.99.1–3 in Strassler 2009, Appendix O.

the Ten Thousand. The fourth-century philosopher and polymath Aristotle mentions a Thibron who (like Xenophon) wrote a *Constitution of the Lacedaemonians*, which praised the Spartan lawgiver for designing a successful military state. If this is the same man (as is most often accepted), Thibron was an unusually intellectual Spartan, which makes it even more striking that he and Xenophon did not get on.

### Tiribazos

§36.1. Tiribazos (d. 362/1?), lieutenant governor (*hyparchos*) of Western Armenia at the time of the events of *Anabasis;* a scribal insertion claims that his province included the Phasianoi. According to Plutarch, Tiribazos encouraged King *Artaxerxes to offer battle to *Cyrus the Younger at Cunaxa, and according to what seems to be the official account of the battle, after the King was thrown by his horse, Tiribazos provided him with a fresh mount.[a] When the Greeks entered his territory, he approached them to arrange a truce while they crossed through it; nevertheless, he dogged their footsteps as they proceeded, planning to ambush them in the Armenian mountains—perhaps not unreasonably, as they had broken the terms of the truce by burning down an Armenian village. The ambush plan was foiled by a surprise attack by the Greeks that captured Tiribazos' luxuriously appointed camp, but Tiribazos continued to keep very close to them for some time thereafter.

§36.2. Tiribazos' position as *hyparchos* in 400 was a fairly junior one: though Herodotus uses the term *hyparchos* to cover people who must have been satraps, elsewhere it indicates a lower status, and so here Tiribazos will have been subordinate to the overall satrap of Armenia, *Orontas. But subsequently Tiribazos' career prospered: as Xenophon mentions (4.4.4), he was a friend of Artaxerxes' and was given the special privilege of helping him mount his horse, which sounds as though it is connected with Plutarch's story of his providing a new mount for the King at Cunaxa. (We are told by Diodorus[b] that Tiribazos also once saved the King's life during a lion hunt.) He is next found in command in Ionia in 392, when he turned against the Athenians, whom the King had been supporting against the Spartans for the previous few years but who were now showing signs of trying to revive their fifth-century control of the Aegean islands and the coast of western Anatolia. Upon the refusal of the Athenians and their Greek allies to break off war with the Spartans, Tiribazos secretly funded the Spartans; arrested the Athenian admiral Konon, who had won the battle of Cnidus for the Persians; and tried to persuade Artaxerxes to commit to the Spartan side.[c] Artaxerxes was not yet ready to jettison his previous policy, and Tiribazos may have been under a cloud for a time; but he was again in Ionia in 388 when the Spartans once more tried to obtain Persian support, this time successfully, and it was Tiribazos who read out the terms of the pro-Spartan King's Peace of 387/6 to the Greek delegates at Sardis.[d]

§36.3. Tiribazos is found shortly afterward in a senior position in the Persian

W.36a  Tiribazos: encourages the King to do battle, Plutarch, *Life of Artaxerxes* 7.2; provides a fresh mount, 10.1 (in Appendix T: Plutarch).

W.36b  Diodorus 15.10.3 (not in Appendix S: Diodorus).

W.36c  Tiribazos' activities in Ionia in 392: *Hellenika*

4.8.12–17.

W.36d  Tiribazos in Ionia in 388: *Hellenika* 5.1.6, 5.1.28; reads the terms, 5.1.30–31.

expedition against the rebellious King Evagoras of Salamis (on Cyprus). Probably but not certainly, this was initially a co-command with his former boss, Orontas, but Tiribazos persuaded Artaxerxes that it would be more efficient to subordinate Orontas to himself: when the campaign stalled, Orontas took his revenge and successfully denounced Tiribazos for (in effect) trying to make himself independent of central control through intriguing with Evagoras, the Spartans, and his own senior officers. Artaxerxes recalled and disgraced Tiribazos and gave the command to Orontas instead. However, Tiribazos' disgrace did not last. Orontas was no more successful militarily than Tiribazos had been and was ultimately forced to accept Evagoras' surrender on terms that Tiribazos had rejected. Tiribazos was also able to point to a brilliant diplomatic coup that he had pulled off when participating in a campaign personally undertaken by Artaxerxes against the Kadousioi, a tribe that lived near the Caspian Sea, thus bringing to a successful close a venture that had previously gone badly wrong. Hence Tiribazos was rehabilitated in a show trial and promised the hand of one of the King's daughters in marriage. Unfortunately, Artaxerxes twice let Tiribazos down here, instead adding first one promised daughter and then another to his own harem.[c] Tiribazos became embittered and, probably in 362/1, plotted with the crown prince, Darius, to assassinate Artaxerxes. The plot was disclosed; Tiribazos was killed in a skirmish within the palace, and Darius was executed subsequently.

## Tissaphernes

§37.1. Tissaphernes (d. 395), son of Hydarnes; satrap in Lydia and probably Caria for most of the period 421 to 395. He was very likely a descendant of the Hydarnes who was one of the seven noblemen who conspired to put Darius I on the throne in 522, probably through yet another Hydarnes, who was general over the peoples of the Asian seaboard of the Aegean in 480.[a] The father of Stateira, the wife of the Great King *Artaxerxes, was also called Hydarnes, and although this was not the same man as Tissaphernes' father,[b] quite possibly Tissaphernes and Stateira were cousins in some degree.

§37.2. Prior to his service as satrap, Tissaphernes was instrumental in putting down a revolt by the previous satrap in Sardis, Pissouthnes (perhaps in 422/1). From then on, for almost thirty years, Tissaphernes was the most important Persian in the west, except for the brief period (407–405) during which *Cyrus the Younger held the position of *karanos*[c] for the area. In 413, as the Athenian Empire seemed to be crumbling, the Great King *Darius II demanded of Tissaphernes and *Pharnabazos, his colleague to the north, the tribute of the Greek cities of the seaboard. It was probably at this point that the King awarded the Ionian cities to Tissaphernes,[d] although most scholars place it later, in 405–404. In Book 8 of Thucydides' history, he details the partly competitive efforts of Tissaphernes and Pharnabazos over the

W.36e  Endogamy was a common practice within the Persian royal family, but these are particularly extreme examples, apparently unparalleled.

W.37a  Hydarnes: one of the seven noblemen, Herodotus 3.70.2; the general: 7.135.1.

W.37b  *Anabasis* 2.4.28 mentions one of Stateira's brothers alongside Tissaphernes without indicating that the latter was also her sibling.

W.37c  *Karanos:* see the Glossary and Appendix C: The Persian Empire, §9.

W.37d  King awards Ionian cities: *Anabasis* 1.1.6.

following few years (413–411), and Xenophon continues the story more sketchily in Book 1 of *Hellenika*. Tissaphernes initially gave straightforward support to the Spartans in their war against Athens, negotiating a treaty with them in which they conceded Persian claims in Asia in return for Persian military assistance and subsidies; but he soon began to temporize. According to Thucydides, this was in order to avoid the Spartans' simply replacing the Athenians as the dominant power in the Aegean. In (probably) 407 Darius rejected half measures in favor of a return to fully backing the Spartans, and sent his son Cyrus to the west to implement it. Tissaphernes was not, however, disgraced, although subordinated to Cyrus and, it seems, retaining the fullness of his satrapal position only in Caria. Indeed, Tissaphernes was in Cyrus' entourage when the latter went back to his father's deathbed, and Cyrus was evidently surprised when Tissaphernes accused him of plotting to kill his brother, the new Great King, Artaxerxes.

§37.3. Although Artaxerxes forgave Cyrus through the intervention of their mother, *Parysatis, and sent him back to the Aegean seaboard, he no longer placed Cyrus over Tissaphernes. A private war broke out between the two, in particular over control of the Ionian Greek cities, which, with the exception of Miletus, Cyrus took over from Tissaphernes in accordance with the cities' wishes. However, Cyrus had to besiege Miletus, because Tissaphernes had preemptively purged Cyrus' partisans there. Cyrus used this war as his initial pretext to gather troops, with the ultimate aim of rebelling against Artaxerxes himself; but eventually the scale of the preparations was such that Tissaphernes was able to convince Artaxerxes of the true state of affairs and induce him to begin countermeasures. Tissaphernes was given the command of one-quarter of Artaxerxes' army, taking personal charge of a cavalry unit on the left wing at the battle of Cunaxa. When the Greeks routed the infantry in front of them, Tissaphernes (according to Xenophon) was at the head of these cavalrymen when they rode past the Greek flank and into the lightly guarded enemy camp, where he joined up with Artaxerxes. But Appendix L: The Battle of Cunaxa, especially §§7, 14–15, 18–19, argues that although the cavalry charge was real enough, Tissaphernes actually stayed with the main body of the Persian army, since Diodorus[e] says that he took over temporary command of the whole army when Artaxerxes was wounded and had to leave the battlefield; the appendix further supports the theory that Tissaphernes staged the disorderly retirement of the Persian infantry when charged by the Greeks, in order to remove the latter from the main action.

§37.4. After the battle Artaxerxes put Tissaphernes in charge of dealing with the unbeaten Greeks in Cyrus' army. He was for a long time conciliatory toward them, claiming that Artaxerxes had given him permission to help them because of his part in the battle, swearing a more detailed truce with them, and promising to lead them out of Babylonia and provide them with supplies. He did indeed lead them out of Babylonia but remained an object of suspicion and mysterious rumors as they all marched along the Tigris River. Suspicions reached their height at the Zapatas

W.37e   Diodorus 14.23.6 (in Appendix S: Diodorus).

River; the leading Greek general, *Klearchos, tried to improve their relations with offers of Greek assistance in the west, but he was unscrupulously manipulated by Tissaphernes, who played on his hostility to his fellow general *Menon to trick him into persuading the Greeks to send most of their officers to a meeting in Tissaphernes' tent. At this meeting Tissaphernes showed his true colors by arresting the Greek generals and killing their entourage. Most likely this coup had been planned from the beginning, to happen once the Greeks were far enough away from Babylon for safety.

§37.5. Despite initially conciliatory noises from the Persians, it was now clear to the Greeks that Tissaphernes was an open enemy, and Persian attacks started very soon after the Greek army had crossed the Zapatas River in their continuing march north. Tissaphernes often directed these in person. His harassment of the Greeks continued intermittently for over a fortnight and included following a scorched-earth policy in the northern Tigris plain. He did not, however, pursue the Greeks farther once they turned into the territory of the Kardouchoi, and perhaps his intention had always been to push them out of Mesopotamia rather than to take the risk of a decisive confrontation in order to destroy them. That would fit with his failure to resist their initial Zapatas crossing.

§37.6. Diodorus[f] reports that Artaxerxes honored Tissaphernes more than anyone else after the battle. Tissaphernes returned to the west in early 400 with his authority enhanced to cover Cyrus' domains; perhaps already at this point he was also made senior to Pharnabazos and awarded Aeolis, previously part of Pharnabazos' satrapy, as was certainly true in 397.[g] Tissaphernes thereupon demanded that the Ionian cities acknowledge his overlordship, but instead, in mid-400, they requested help from Sparta. The Spartans responded during the winter of 400/399, when they reversed their attitude toward the Persians and decided to send out *Thibron to campaign against Tissaphernes; he arrived in (probably) March 399 and, adding Xenophon's troops to his own, began to make war. Later in 399 Thibron was superseded by *Derkylidas, and in 396 the Spartan king *Agesilaos himself came out.

§37.7. From 399 to 396, Tissaphernes was fairly successful at limiting the Spartans' incursions into his territories, but largely through deflecting them into the softer target of Pharnabazos' satrapy. In 398 Pharnabazos began a more activist policy of building a fleet so as to interfere with Spartan naval supremacy in the Aegean,[h] and Artaxerxes must have begun to think that he had preferred the wrong man. Tissaphernes was no doubt already in deep trouble with the King when his forces were defeated by Agesilaos just outside Sardis in 395, soon after which—too soon for the defeat to be the key factor Xenophon assumes it was—Artaxerxes sent one of his courtiers, Tithraustes, down to the west. With the assistance of *Ariaios, Cyrus' former lieutenant, Tithraustes arrested Tissaphernes and cut off his head, which he dispatched to the King. Artaxerxes sent it on to the Queen Mother, Parysatis, who had pressed him to execute Tissaphernes, since she blamed him for the fate of Cyrus, her

W.37f   Diodorus 14.26.4 (in Appendix S: Diodorus).
W.37g   Tissaphernes: authority enhanced, *Hellenika*
         3.1.3; senior to Pharnabazos, 3.2.13.

W.37h   Building a fleet: Diodorus 14.39.1–3 (in Strassler
         2009, Appendix O: Diodorus).

favorite son.[i] If he was also a member of the extended family of Artaxerxes' queen, Stateira, whom Parysatis is said to have poisoned (probably in the early 390s), that will only have added to Parysatis' hatred for him, and (after Stateira's death) perhaps also to Artaxerxes' suspicions that Tissaphernes was pulling his punches where the Spartans were concerned.

§37.8. Tissaphernes is depicted by both Thucydides and Xenophon as a wily dissimulator. His policy in 411–407 of trying to wear down both Athens and Sparta was surely the correct one for Persia; his strategy for dealing with the Greeks in Cyrus' army was effective and, depending on one's views about the course of the battle of Cunaxa, may have been truly masterly. But from 399 onward, his reputation for slipperiness reduced his effectiveness with both Greeks and Persians and made him vulnerable to almost certainly untrue accusations of disloyalty to Artaxerxes.

### Xerxes

§38. Xerxes, Great King of the Persians from 486 to 465. In Greek accounts, of which the most extensive surviving is that of Herodotus, the most important event of Xerxes' reign was his attack on mainland Greece in 480, when he succeeded in defeating the Spartans at the battle of Thermopylae and in occupying Athens and burning down the sanctuaries on the Acropolis.[a] But despite his personal oversight, his fleet was defeated by the combined Greek fleet at the battle of Salamis (also in 480);[b] the following year his close relation and lieutenant Mardonios was defeated on land at Plataea, allegedly on the same day the Persians lost a second naval battle, at Mycale, on the southwestern coast of Anatolia; and despite periodic pushbacks, further Persian defeats followed, in particular around 466 at the Eurymedon River, on the southern coast of western Anatolia. Xerxes was murdered in a palace coup, about which our evidence is confused. It should be borne in mind that in trying to establish Xerxes' own priorities and in assessing his reign as a whole, we are hampered by the Graecocentric nature of the literary sources. For the Greeks whose cities had resisted Xerxes, especially the Spartans and the Athenians (such as Xenophon), their stand against him was fundamental to their perception of themselves.

W.37i  Tissaphernes' execution: *Hellenika* 3.4.25. Diodorus 14.80.7–8 (in Strassler 2009, Appendix O).
W.38a  Acropolis: the citadel or high point of a city; for

more, see the Glossary.
W.38b  The Persian defeat at Salamis is referred to twice in *Anabasis*, at 1.2.9 and 3.2.13.

# TRANSLATOR'S NOTES

David Thomas

## Xenophon's Style and the Issues It Poses

§1. It has been an unexpected bonus from undertaking this Landmark translation that having to think about every word, clause, and sentence in *Anabasis* has greatly increased my respect for Xenophon not only as an effective narrator but also—despite the surface appearance of effortless plainness that the work may give—as a conscious and quite subtle stylist.

§2. There is in fact some direct evidence that Xenophon paid close attention to his style. He wrote up his patron King Agesilaos' part in the warfare of the 390s in two different works, namely *Hellenika* (a narrative history) and *Agesilaos* (a eulogy of the dead king). The two accounts run in parallel for pages at a time, but they are not identical. The rhetorical surface of the encomium has been polished more than that in the history, a fact that would be especially striking if—as the evidence on balance suggests—the history came second, meaning Xenophon has set about toning it down. Part of the difference is that the account in *Agesilaos* is more elevated in vocabulary but that in *Hellenika* is more strictly correct in terms of Attic, the dialect of Greek prevalent in the city of Athens and the surrounding countryside (Attica). Another difference is that in his parallel narratives of the same events, Xenophon has taken trouble to modify several of the verbs from one form of the past tense to another (if *Agesilaos* came first, the so-called aorist tense to the imperfect) and has reformulated his sentences in other fairly subtle ways. So if much of his work gives an impression of transparent lucidity that has, so to speak, written itself, this was in fact the product of careful toil. In the introductory section of what may have been his first work, *Kynegetikos* (*On Hunting*), Xenophon proved that he could write in the consciously high style of the contemporary master, Gorgias; in the rest of the piece, he proved he could fit his style to the function he wished it to perform. We can also see that he could exercise control over the details of his style: most of his work includes many particles (words that perform similar functions in Greek to English expressions such as "at any rate" or "so then," or to italics used for emphasis), but for whatever reason they are much less evident in the opening section of *Hellenika* (1.1–2.10), often referred to now as the "Continuation" (of Thucydides). So I should not have been surprised to find that *Anabasis* rewarded close scrutiny—even if it is not always possible to convey Xenophon's effects in translation.

§3. The forms of the words that Xenophon uses in *Anabasis* overwhelmingly reflect the Attic dialect, which he was brought up to speak and which was establishing itself in the fourth century as the single most important Greek dialect for literary purposes. However, his choice of words is more eclectic. Xenophon uses many words that are unknown or rare in Attic prose; quite a lot of them seem to be poetic words or otherwise heightened expressions, but some, by contrast, may have been neologisms, and there are a good number that come from other dialects without, apparently, carrying any poetic implications in themselves, though it may be relevant that tragic and lyric poetry readily admitted words and forms from other dialects.

§4. The basic study of Xenophon's nonstandard vocabulary was carried out a century ago by Léopold Gautier.[a] Gautier looked at the contexts in which Xenophon used a non-Attic expression, but only very rarely could he see any specific reasons why it might have been appropriate to diverge from Athenian usage. He therefore concluded that there were no literary implications in the choice; it was just that Xenophon had lived for a long time outside Attica, so his natural vocabulary was wider than pure Attic. But it is more likely that Xenophon regarded adherence to strict Attic as parochial, a denial of history's origins in authors who wrote in the Ionic dialect (such as Herodotus), perhaps even a slap in the face for panhellenic sentiments, and wanted the literary language to be open to words from a variety of social contexts. He is particularly prone to preserving usages that had died out of Attic in the fourth century but still occurred elsewhere. His neologisms and technical terms show that this was not just a matter of preferring to be old-fashioned; rather, it is as if he is refusing to cooperate with what he sees as the narrowing of Athenian horizons and the rejection of the common past of the Greeks as a whole. So there can be literary implications even when there is no specific point in the use of a rare expression in the particular place where it occurs. Similarly, the sprinkling of poetic and sometimes specifically Homeric expressions is intended to give a heroic patina to the narrative. Some of Xenophon's unusual vocabulary certainly has a particular point in its context: for example, words and expressions typical of the Doric dialect are especially prone to appear in the mouths of Spartans.[b] This may seem natural enough, but it was not the usual practice outside comedy. More generally, one should regard with suspicion claims that words or forms characteristic of different dialects are used in different places solely out of a desire to avoid repetition: so, for example, when at 6.6.28 an unnamed (but non-Spartan) soldier uses the word *rhētra*, the proper term for Spartan laws, to refer to what might more normally be called *dogma* ("decree" or "judgment"), this is surely not because Xenophon

TransNotes.4a   Gautier 1911. Huitink and Rood 2019 includes a fine supplementary study of Xenophon's diction, which independently takes the same line as I do here but with much more detail.

TransNotes.4b   In the mouths of Spartans: see 3.2.3, 6.6.36, 7.1.8, 7.6.39.

wishes to vary his vocabulary for the sake of it but because the soldier is speaking to a Spartan, who responds by calling him a *toros*, seemingly also a Spartan expression,[c] in this case for a sharp fellow or smart guy.

§5. Variation for its own sake was in truth a most unlikely fault to attribute to Xenophon, who is not in the least shy about repetition. There are well over thirty instances in which, sometimes with evident rhetorical point and sometimes with none that is obvious, a noun, adjective, or verb is repeated three or more times within a few sentences. Striking examples of this are the repetition of Cyrus' name at 1.4.2–3, perhaps marking the fact that he is, after an interruption, once again firmly in the driver's seat; the repetition of different verbs with the common core of *agō* (lead) at 1.6.10–11, as Orontas is taken from his place of trial to his place of execution; the repetition of *aphthonos* (abundant) at 7.6.28–31. And then there is the constant refrain in Books 1–4 that the army traveled for X *stathmoi* (here translated "days' march") over Y parasangs.[a] The very constancy of this particular repetition means that we notice when these terms are absent and so look for an explanation when *stathmoi* and parasangs are not mentioned as the army journeys through the land of the Kardouchoi and after it has emerged from the mountains of Anatolia. The verb within the formula changes from *exelaunei* when Cyrus is in charge (here translated "he pushed on") to *eporeuonto* (singular *eporeuto*) after Cyrus has died (here translated "they made their way"); again the constancy of each repetition shows that the change must signify something, and therefore the translation should also mark the change somehow.[b] Both words are conventionally translated "march," but neither carries the implication of rhythmic walking in formation that "march" does, so these translations may convey too strong an impression of a coherent, disciplined body (the word is even used at 1.7.20, where the slack conduct of the men is emphasized), especially during the arduous journey from Mesopotamia to the Black Sea. *Eporeuonto* is also frequently used in *Anabasis* in circumstances in which it cannot be translated "march." What it actually conveys is the idea that the army is traveling purposefully and making progress; this is the undertone that its repetition promotes, both within the standard formula and beyond it. When a small detachment is to be broken off to scale a mountain (3.4.41–42) or the soldiers scramble up rough terrain so steep they have to pull each other up (4.2.8), when a delegation is sent to Kleandros to offer to surrender Agasias for trial (6.6.19), they are not marching, but they are still making their way forward. The word is also linked with *aporia*, a state in which one does not know the way forward (both literally and metaphorically), but I have not found it possible to demonstrate this linkage in the translation.

§6. Although I have tried to avoid breaking up the patterns created across the work by word repetitions and distinctions, English idiom is often at odds with this. The translator has to make judgments about which of these features were meant to convey a point or to bring out an emphasis, in which case English idiom and authorial

---

TransNotes.4c  See Xenophon, *Lakedaimonion Politeia* (*Constitution of the Lacedaemonians*) 2.11.

TransNotes.5a  The parasang is a Persian unit for measuring travel, but it is controversial whether it measures hours spent traveling, distance traveled, or a combination of the two; see the Introduction, §7.3–5, and Appendix

O: Ancient Greek and Persian Units of Measurement, §§7–8.

TransNotes.5b  The basic insight in this sentence and the previous one is that argued for by Rood 2010b, 56 (*eporeueto*), 57 (*exelaunei*). However, he translates both verbs differently.

intention may have to be weighed up against one another. There are also a number of words or groups of associated words where Xenophon's choices may not be deliberately making a point but where I have tried to reflect them in English so that the Greekless student has a better chance of seeing how the Greek concepts work. To this end, in this edition, "good" always translates *agathos* and cognates and never translates any quasi-synonym; in particular it never translates *kalos* ("fine, noble, beautiful") (I wish it were also possible to translate *kalos* univocally, but it isn't). Similarly, "man" and "men" standing by themselves virtually always translate *anēr*, "a male person," and never *anthrōpos*, "a human being" or some less definite expression.[a] In addition, I have chosen and stuck with different words in English to correspond to the different words and expressions that Xenophon uses for offering sacrifice and obtaining good or bad sacrificial omens.[b] In 7.6 and 7.7 there are references to Charminos and Polynikos sometimes as Laconians and sometimes as Lacedaemonians. Strictly speaking, the former indicates the inhabitants of the relevant territory and the latter indicates the citizens of the relevant state. Although Xenophon may perhaps be using the two words interchangeably, I have thought it right to preserve a distinction in the translation; but as literal translation seemed potentially confusing to the nonspecialist reader, I have translated "Laconian" in this section as "Lacedaemonian delegate" (except at its first occurrence at 7.6.1).

§7. There are some aspects of Xenophon's usage that it is impossible to convey in English because of basic differences in grammar between the two languages. Greek verbs have five tenses that can represent the past (the pluperfect, perfect, aorist, imperfect, and historic present), and while the distinctions between the first four can be conveyed in English with more or less success, the historic present is problematic in literary English. One ancient commentator on style said Xenophon used it to create immediacy; a recent theory is that it is used to bring out the structure of the narrative; but whatever the correct interpretation, the translator is unable to reflect it. Similarly, Xenophon sometimes prefixes proper names with a definite article and sometimes not; although one can't be quite sure, because the manuscripts are especially liable to disagree with one another about the presence of the article, this looks like a device that slightly increases the audience's focus on the person named with the article—a bit like the difference between filming a scene in long shot and filming it as a series of close-ups on one or more actors. But English has no comparable device. However, Xenophon has a related device that English *can* imitate: sometimes he prefixes adjectives indicating place of origin with a definite article ("Xenophon the Athenian") and sometimes not (literally, "Xenophon Athenian"; more freely, "Xenophon of Athens"), and I have taken care to follow suit.

§8. There are other similar, though less extreme, problems for the translator. Xenophon's style is rich in particles, which connect expressions and shade their meaning. Often, undue expansion or emphasis is produced by trying to convey the

TransNotes.6a  However, 3.2.2. and 3.2.11 defeated me. Also, at 4.1.24 and 4.5.24, *anēr* is used in the narrower sense of "husband." I have also permitted myself sometimes to translate *anthrōpos* as "mankind."

TransNotes.6b  There are exceptions at 6.4.20 and 6.5.2.

Except in these places, I translate *hiera*, literally "sacred things," as "sacred signs." But in these two places I translate the word as "sacred rites," since here it is the process of sacrifice rather than its outcome that is being referred to.

precise shade in English, so Xenophon appears to be either wordier or less nuanced than he really was. Also, as we saw above, he frequently uses words from other dialects and words with a poetic flavor. One might hope that as English too is rich in variants from different parts of the world and from its long literary history, it would be possible to convey this, and I have tried to take some steps in this direction; but the result can risk sounding quaint or pretentious, partly because for us poetry no longer plays the central cultural role that it did for fifth- and fourth-century Greeks and partly because in any case English poetry has increasingly turned its back on poetic diction over the last two hundred years. Sometimes, however, Xenophon himself must have sounded a bit odd to an Athenian reader, which is why I have occasionally taken the risk, especially where it is possible there was a point being made. So, for example, at 4.1.16, "many a time" translates *thamina*, a word with Homeric overtones used here in the narrative of deeds of heroism (similarly "draw nigh" is used to translate *pelasai* at 4.2.3); at 4.3.13 the dative case rather than the accusative is used with *keleuō*, also a Homeric usage in a particularly solemn context, and so I translate the word as "bade"; at 7.1.33 "attained their destination" is used for *molōsin*, a pompous phrase that fits the speaker, Koiratadas, "all mouth and no trousers." A related issue is whether one should try to make speech sound as it would in a novel written today, where it is likely to consist of shorter sentences and be simpler in syntax than the surrounding narrative; the reverse was true in much Classical Greek prose, where oratory was an art form in itself. Here I have not concealed the overtly rhetorical finish of Xenophon's Greek in the longer speeches; a higher style is also evident in his obituaries (one near the end of Book 1, three at the end of Book 2).

§9. Finally, I should mention that, despite the relative simplicity and usual clarity of Xenophon's style, there are still quite a few places where commentators and translators differ about exactly what he means, and occasionally I have ventured to differ from the consensus or even to make a new suggestion in a problematic passage.[a] However, where there are differences between this translation and others, they are more usually due to my adopting a different Greek text in the first place, and I now turn to outlining the factors that create textual diversity.

### The History and Reconstruction of the Text

§10. Translations of classical works may seem to offer a bland surface of certainty to the reader, but behind them lie not only the difficulties intrinsic to all translation in rendering what the author wrote into a different language, but also a complex process of estimating what the author wrote in the first place. The manuscripts on which modern editions of *Anabasis* are based differ in several thousand places from each other, and partly as a result, there are many hundreds of differences between the two modern editions that readers are most likely to come across, those of E. C. Marchant for the Oxford Classical Text series (1904) and of John Dillery for the Loeb Classical Library (1998), the latter being based on the now out-of-print text edited by Karl Hude for the Teubner series (1931, reprinted with notes by J. Peters in 1972).

§11. The very earliest evidence we have is a few scraps of papyri covering the odd

TransNotes.9a   Instances are at 4.1.26, 4.5.27, 5.2.12, 6.6.16.

chapter and sentence here and there, and these date to the second century C.E., about six hundred years after Xenophon wrote his book. Around eight hundred years after the papyri, in the tenth century C.E., comes the first extant manuscript covering the whole work (often referred to as F).[a] We next have two manuscripts from around four hundred years after that. One of them, originally dating from 1320 but subsequently much altered, is often referred to as C (the original version as $C_1$, the altered version as $C_2$). The other, probably slightly later and often referred to as M, largely agrees with F, the combination being conventionally referred to as FM; but FM differ from $C_1$ in about four thousand places. Although $C_1$ dates from 1320, it contains an introductory poem that shows that it descends from a manuscript presented to the Byzantine emperor Leo VI (886–912), who prided himself on his learning and culture; this presentation manuscript could be the prize copy of a new, consciously created edition earlier than F and M, and this has boosted $C_1$'s status in the eyes of many scholars.

§12. Different modern editors therefore also disagree with each other, both about how to reconstruct the most recent common ancestor of our existing manuscripts (the technical term for which is the "archetype") and about how far the text had deteriorated between Xenophon's time and the time of the archetype, which may perhaps have been copied as much as a millennium later. There are thus about a thousand differences between Marchant's text and Hude's, though many of these make little or no difference to the meaning. Marchant was committed on principle to manuscript $C_1$ and departs from it only where he considers it more or less impossible; Hude was committed on principle to weighing up the two main groups of manuscripts word by word and phrase by phrase (in fact, he still ends up preferring $C_1$ more of the time than FM, but it's a fairly close thing). Hude in 1931 worked with eleven manuscripts, but a year later Luigi Castiglioni published a report on four further manuscripts, two of which (his b and g) he argued were important. Peters mostly accepted his claim, and Dillery's edition reflects Peters' position on this. Partly for this reason, although Dillery's text is much closer to Hude's than to Marchant's, it differs from Hude's text in over two hundred places. Dillery also strikes the balance between C and FM rather more in C's favor than Hude had done.

§13. Much is mysterious about the process by which the text that Xenophon wrote turned over time into the fifteen different manuscripts about which one can learn in the pages of Marchant, Hude, and Castiglioni. Quite a lot of scribal error seems to have entered the tradition in its first millennium: in all extant manuscripts there are phrases and sentences that have been added and other phrases and sentences that have been omitted, and it is generally agreed that the archetype already had such interpolations and lacunas. In particular, Diogenes Laertius in the second or third century C.E. reports that the separate books had prefaces; almost all scholars regard these as interpolations, and the need to write prefaces to individual books to my mind suggests that for some time previously the books had been circulating sep-

TransNotes.11a  The usual modern designations for the majority of the manuscripts derive from the editions of the nineteenth-century scholar Ludwig Dindorf; the locations and up-to-date catalog numbers may most conveniently be found in Huitink and Rood 2019, 39. Dindorf ranked the manuscripts according to his view of how valuable they were and assigned capital letters accordingly. As stated in §12, in 1932 Luigi Castiglioni added several more manuscripts, assigning lowercase letters (a, b, g) to three of them.

arately as well as all together. Shortly after this, whole texts became much more convenient to produce as copyists gave up papyrus rolls and substituted stitched and bound volumes (codices), but separate circulation of individual books may perhaps have continued in subsequent centuries alongside whole texts, perhaps for school use, as has been the case in more modern times. In the early ninth century, there was a major change in the way high-quality Greek manuscripts were written: prior to then, they were written in capital letters, afterward in lowercase letters (minuscule). Some kinds of mistakes scribes make are characteristic of copying capital letters, and some are characteristic of copying minuscule script. Comparing the mistakes that different manuscripts have made, it looks to me as though there may have been some books of *Anabasis* where the archetype for that book was written in capital letters, but other books where it was written in minuscule. If this is right, at least some of our manuscripts are derived from a tradition that took material from books that were circulating separately from each other. But this is admittedly a speculative suggestion.

§14. As mentioned above, the big divide in our manuscripts is between the traditions represented by FM (and most other extant manuscripts) on the one hand and $C_1$ (and four other extant manuscripts) on the other. There is a smaller divide within the FM tradition, where there is a group of four late manuscripts that stand together and arguably represent a subtradition of equal weight to F and M, preserving correct readings that they had lost; the best of them seems to be Castiglioni's manuscript b. Readings from both main traditions are intermingled in the papyri and in the indirect evidence provided by quotations and excerpts elsewhere. The divergence seems to have occurred around the time of the aforementioned change from capital letters to minuscule in the early ninth century, for some books a little before and for others at precisely this point or very shortly afterward. The idea that $C_1$ may reflect a ninth-century edition would be boosted if, as suggested above, at least one of the two traditions was taking material from books that were circulating separately, for that would imply that the scribe was trying to assemble the best text he could from different sources available to him. Of course, $C_1$ is not itself the manuscript that was presented to Leo VI: it dates from over four hundred years later, giving many opportunities for things to be miscopied on the way. But we may have some help in reconstructing the presentation manuscript. In my view, the main scribe who added corrections to $C_1$ and also the scribe who stands behind Castiglioni's manuscript g were consulting, in addition to $C_1$, another manuscript, now lost, which also descended from the ninth-century edition, but by an independent route.[a]

§15. It is important to realize that reconstructing the ninth-century edition does not in itself allow us to read Xenophon's original text. The ninth-century editor was not infallible in his choices, which still have to be weighed up against the tradition represented by FM to work out what was in the archetype. And the archetype itself certainly had errors in it, and all editors make changes going beyond the variant

TransNotes.14a  This was not Castiglioni's own view. He thought the amendments to $C_1$ and the non-C material in g all come from a lost manuscript of the same family as FM. But while there may have been some contamination between the two main traditions, in my opinion there has not been much. However, detailed argument would be out of place here.

manuscript readings or what may be put forward to explain the variations. There are around four hundred such changes to be made, the precise number depending on the views of the individual editor. About a quarter of these just correct spellings, for example by using evidence from inscriptions contemporary with the author, and some others delete scribal glosses that have intruded into the text from the margins (which, if the scribe got his gloss right, do not change the meaning). But some are conjectural emendations, designed to remove or replace something that has puzzled the editor about the transmitted text. And sometimes we can only recognize that there is a difficulty, without being sure how to cure it; this is especially true in the case of possible omissions in the archetype, one of which is generally recognized at 5.8.1 and others may be discerned at the ends of 4.2 and 6.3.14 and in 7.7.56. Naturally, conjectural emendations are particularly contentious, both as regards whether emendation is necessary at all and as regards the particular emendation adopted.

§16. The reader may wonder how much all of this really matters to our comprehension of the work. Quite a few manuscript variations, where not self-evidently scribal slips, make virtually no difference at all to the meaning or tone, and for good reasons it is rare for Xenophontic scholars to suggest conjectures that move on from clarifying what "must be" the sense to offering hitherto unsuspected information of substance or beauties of expression. But it is worth spending time trying to get the text right. Despite his "plain man's" style, Xenophon, as remarked earlier, is actually a conscious and subtle stylist who is precise in his choices. So the right editorial calls should enhance the reader's appreciation even on small points on which manuscripts differ, such as employing one tense of a verb rather than another, using sometimes "you" and sometimes "we" when addressing colleagues or fellow soldiers, or (for readers of the Greek text only) the presence or absence of the definite article with proper names. On a larger scale, scribes, and sometimes editors, have a tendency to smooth away the unexpected—to remove touches of character in speeches and to soften oddities of custom. Conversely, eye slips by scribes or physical accidents to manuscripts can make the author seem more illogical or careless than was really true: in particular, such factors seem already by the time of the archetype to have made havoc of the internal logic of several speeches. And we shall think worse of Xenophon as a narrator if we accept as his the premature disclosure of information offered by all but one scribe ($C_1$) in what ought to be a carefully considered highlight at 4.7.21, or the premature disclosure of misinformation offered by the entire tradition at 5.7.2.

§17. More specifically, textual confusion has clouded the precise route or duration of the march at 3.4.24, 4.3.2, and 4.5.3, and manuscript variation or error has affected several passages about the size of the army and the leadership of its contingents (1.2.3, 1.2.9, 5.2.4, 6.2.16; possibly 1.7.10). It has also made it more difficult to be sure of the identity or movements of some of the second-rank players: Is the lover of boys at 4.6.1 and 4.6.3 Episthenes, like the lover of boys at 7.4.7, or a different man, Pleisthenes? Is there a general or generals missing from the list at 7.2.1? Where did the Hieronymos mentioned at 7.4.18 come from?[a] What were the names of the envoys from the Spartan army sent to Xenophon at 7.8.6, a matter of some historical significance if I am right to suggest one of them was Naukleidas, an important figure in Sparta about whom we know from other sources? At 2.1.12 there is a thematically central exchange between an Athenian soldier of a philosophic turn of phrase and Phalinos, a renegade Greek who has come as the Persians' emissary. Manuscript C here names the Athenian as Theopompos, but the rival tradition headed by FM makes the man Xenophon himself: which we choose has evident implications for Xenophon's self-representation in the work. Editors have also worried away at whether scribal error at 1.8.13 has added to the difficulties of making sense in detail of the battle of Cunaxa. The single most important manuscript variation is at 5.3.7, referring to Xenophon's exile from Athens, where the tense of the key verb differs between C and FM, thus adding further murk to the already murky subject of the date of the decision by the Athenians.[b]

§18. This Landmark edition does not exactly follow any existing edition in the text that it translates. Lying behind my translation is an "implied text" that I have constructed from a reconsideration of the readings reported in the apparatuses to the editions of Marchant, Hude, and Peters, and also the older edition by Breitenbach. This has been supplemented by Castiglioni's reports, my own inspection of one manuscript (manuscript D) and of digitized copies of two others (Castiglioni's manuscripts b and g), a limited amount of consideration of other scholars' published conjectures and readings, and a few conjectures that appear here for the first time.[a] The published text that is closest to my "implied text" is John Dillery's, but there are about four hundred differences. Although I have sometimes preferred the reading of C and its close allies where Dillery adopts the reading of FM, on balance (and by quite a long way) I have shifted my "implied text" in the direction of FM. Not unconnected with this is that more than a third of the changes I have made are reversions to the Hude text, which was Dillery's own starting point. I have also been somewhat more negative about the state of the archetype than Dillery and therefore readier to admit editorial conjectures into the text.

§19. Almost 250 of my variants from Dillery are listed in the table below. These constitute all the variants that have had a discernible effect on the translation, though often only a small one. (The 150 or so other variants are mostly matters of spelling or the like.) The table shows whether my reading is a modern conjecture or is to be found in one or more of the manuscripts. Almost 150 of the listed variants are reversions to the text as printed by Hude, Marchant, or both. About a fifth of the remainder are my own contribution, and the others are backed by a variety of other scholars.

TransNotes.17a  Hieronymos' place of origin as stated at 7.4.18 was the subject of a brilliant emendation by the nineteenth-century scholar Schenkl. See further n. 7.4.18a.

TransNotes.17b  This edition follows the text and interpretation argued for by Tuplin 1987, though not the particular date for the exile that he advocates. The subject is discussed further in the Introduction, §6.1.

TransNotes.18a  I am grateful to Leofranc Holford-Strevens for his conjecture at 7.3.3. The other new conjectures are my own.

| Passage | Loeb text | Landmark implied text | Authority | Supporting scholars |
|---------|-----------|-----------------------|-----------|---------------------|
| 1.1.5 | ἀπεπέμπετο | ἀνεπέμπετο | FM | vulgate, Liddell and Scott |
| 1.1.7 | ἀποστῆναι πρὸς Κῦρον | Deleted | Wolf | Hude |
| 1.2.3 | Σοφαίνετος δὲ ὁ Στυμφάλιος ὁπλίτας ἔχων χιλίους | Deleted | Dindorf | Gemoll |
| 1.2.9 | Σοφαίνετος ὁ Ἀρκὰς | Σοφαίνετος Ἀρκάδας | cgbD | Marchant |
| 1.2.17 | τῶν βαρβάρων φόβος πολύς τε καὶ ἄλλοις, καὶ ἡ Κίλισσα (Persson) | τῶν δὲ βαρβάρων φόβος πολὺς καὶ ἡ τε Κίλισσα | cgbD | Hude, Marchant |
| 1.2.21 | τό τε Μένωνος στράτευμα | τὸ Μένωνος στράτευμα | cgbD | Marchant |
| 1.2.21 | ὅτι τριήρεις | τριήρεις | Hertlein | |
| 1.2.21 | Τάμων ἔχοντα | Deleted | Weiske | |
| 1.2.22 | ἐπίρρυτον καὶ | καὶ ἐπίρρυτον [καὶ] | fg | Castiglioni, Bevilacqua |
| 1.2.22 | περιεῖχεν | περιέχει | FMC$_2$g | Hude |
| 1.3.12 | ἄξιος | ἄξιος φίλος | All except C$_1$A | Hude |
| 1.3.14 | οὗτος μὲν | οὗτος μὲν δὴ | FM | Hude |
| 1.3.16 | τὸν στόλον | στόλον | FMEg, compare C$_1$ | vulgate |
| 1.3.17 | αὐταῖς ταῖς τριήρεσι | ταῖς τριήρεσι | C$_1$Db | Marchant |
| 1.4.6 | ἔμεινεν | ἔμειναν | All except C$_1$ | Hude |
| 1.4.7 | ἐπεὶ δ' | ἐπεὶ δ'οὖν | FMb | Breitenbach |
| 1.5.10 | σκεπάσματα | στεγάσματα | All mss | Marchant |
| 1.5.11 | τῶν τέ του Μένωνος (Madvig) | τού τε τῶν Μένωνος | Thomas | |
| 1.5.11 | τῶν τοῦ Κλεάρχου | του τῶν Κλεάρχου | Rehdantz | Masqueray |

NOTE: The relevant works of the scholars are cited either directly in the Bibliography under "Editions and Commentaries" or "Specialized Books, Journals, and Articles," or may be found in the bibliographies of Breitenbach 1867, Hude/Peters 1972, or Bevilacqua 2002. "Thomas" indicates my own conjectures.

"Vulgate" means the universal or near-universal reading of editors from the sixteenth to the early nineteenth century (and sometimes later), but I have generally not recorded this where there is the name of a late nineteenth-century or twentieth-century editor to include instead.

TABLE HEADS

**Landmark implied text:** Thomas, translator's reading, see §18 for explanation.

**Authority:** scholar(s) who first proposed the relevant emendation. Manuscripts designated by capital letters are per Hude 1931 or Marchant 1904; by the lowercase letters a, b, and g, Peters' revision of Hude 1931; by lowercase c, all of CABE; by lowercase f, all of FMDb and possibly others; see §§11–12.

KEY TO SYMBOLS

[ ]   Words that appear in the manuscripts but that modern editors believe are later additions, not by Xenophon.

< >   Material taken from supplements by modern scholars.

***   Lacuna in text

| Passage | Loeb text | Landmark implied text | Authority | Supporting scholars |
|---------|-----------|----------------------|-----------|---------------------|
| 1.6.1 | ἴχνη ἵππων | ἴχνια ἵππων | cab | Marchant |
| 1.7.3 | ἀνθρώπων ἀπόρων βαρβάρων συμμάχους ὑμᾶς | ἀνθρώπων ἀπόρων συμμάχους ὑμᾶς | Bisschop | Hude |
| 1.7.15 | ἔνθα | ἔνθα δὴ εἰσὶν | All except $C_1$ | vulgate |
| 1.7.15–16 | ἦν δὲ παρὰ τὸν Εὐφράτην ... τὸ εὖρος• ταύτην δὲ τὴν τάφρον ... προσελαύνοντα | ταύτην δὲ τὴν τάφρον ... προσελαύνοντα. ἦν δὲ παρὰ τὸν Εὐφράτην ... τὸ εὖρος. | Thomas | |
| 1.8.10 | ἐλθόντων | ἐλώντων | f | Hude |
| 1.8.13 | τοῦ εὐωνύμου (Hertlein) | τοῦ Ἑλληνικοῦ εὐωνύμου | All mss | Marchant |
| 1.8.23 | κέρατος | Deleted | Thomas | |
| 1.9.16 | πλουσιωτέρως (misprint) | πλουσιωτέρους | All mss except perhaps $C_1$ | Hude |
| 1.10.1 | τοῦ αὐτῶν στρατοπέδου | τοῦ αὐτῶν στρατοπέδου | gD (and others?) | Marchant |
| 1.10.6 | προσιόντος | προσιόντα | gb | Castiglioni |
| 1.10.12 | ἐπὶ πέλτῃ | ἐπὶ πέλτης | f | Hude |
| 2.1.3 | περιμείνειεν ἂν αὐτούς | περιμένοιεν αὐτούς | $C_1$ | Marchant |
| 2.1.12 | Ξενοφῶν | Θεόπομπος | cg, in marg. DV | Marchant |
| 2.1.15 | Κλέαρχος | καὶ Κλέαρχος | f | Hude |
| 2.1.17 | λεγόμενον (Cobet) | ἀναλεγόμενον | All mss | Breitenbach |
| 2.1.19 | συμβουλεύω σώζεσθαι ὑμῖν | συμβουλεύω σώζεσθαι | fg | Hude |
| 2.2.12 | μὴ δυνήσεται βασιλεὺς (Cobet) | μὴ δύνηται βασιλεὺς | All mss | Marchant |
| 2.3.8 | ἐδόκει τὰς σπονδὰς (misprint) | ἐδόκει ταχὺ τὰς σπονδὰς | f | Hude, Marchant |
| 2.3.12 | Κλέαρχον | καὶ Κλέαρχον | f | Hude |
| 2.3.18 | τῆς πάσης Ἑλλάδος | τῆς ἄλλης Ἑλλάδος | g, compare Suidas | Castiglioni, Bevilacqua |
| 2.3.19 | ἐδίωξα | ἐδίωξε | $C_1$ | Marchant |
| 2.3.25 | καίπερ πολλῶν (Gemoll) | καίπερ πάνυ πολλῶν | All mss ($C_1$ omitted but then restored) | Hude, Marchant |
| 2.4.3 | Τί μένομεν ἤ | Τί μένομεν; ἤ | Editors generally | |

| Passage | Loeb text | Landmark implied text | Authority | Supporting scholars |
|---------|-----------|----------------------|-----------|---------------------|
| 2.4.6 | ἀποκτείναιμεν (misprint) | ἀποκτείναιμεν; | Editors generally | |
| 2.4.6 | ἡττωμένων δὲ | ἡττωμένων γε μὴν | b | Kruger |
| 2.4.8 | Ὀρόντας τὴν ἑαυτοῦ δύναμιν• ἦγε | Ὀρόντας τὴν ἑαυτοῦ• ἦγε | g | Castiglioni |
| 2.4.14 | οὐ μέντοι | οὐ μέντοι γε | FMb | Hude |
| 2.4.26 | ἦν ἀνάγκη | ἀνάγκη | f, Suda | Hude |
| 2.5.3 | Ἐπειδὴ δὲ ξυνῆλθον | Ἐπειδὴ δὲ συνηλθέτην | Thomas, compare συνελθέτην Db | |
| 2.5.11 | τὴν σαυτοῦ ἀρχὴν | τὴν σαυτοῦ | g, Rehdantz | Hude, Marchant |
| 2.5.13 | ὑμᾶς γιγνώσκω | ὑμᾶς νῦν γιγνώσκω | All except C₁ | Hude |
| 2.5.18 | βουλοίμεθα | βουλώμεθα | cg | Marchant |
| 2.6.9 | ἐκολαζέ τε ἰσχυρῶς | ἐκολαζέ τε αἰεὶ ἰσχυρῶς | fC₂g | vulgate, Masqueray |
| 2.6.19 | καλῶν κἀγαθῶν | καλῶν μὲν κἀγαθῶν | All mss have μὲν | Hude, Marchant |
| 3.1.20 | ἤδη (Schneider) | ἤδη | All mss | Marchant |
| 3.1.24 | ταῦτ' | ταὐτὰ | Hug | Marchant |
| 3.1.38 | ὀνῆσαι | ὠφελῆσαι | cg | Marchant |
| 3.2.4 | Κλεάρχῳ καὶ | Κλεάρχῳ γε καὶ | Bornemann | Hude |
| 3.2.11 | αὐτοὶ Ἀθηναῖοι | αὐτοῖς Ἀθηναῖοι | All mss except C₁ | Hude |
| 3.2.12 | καὶ ἔτι νῦν | καὶ ἔτι καὶ νῦν | f | Hude |
| 3.2.17 | ὅτι οἱ Ἀριαίου (Hug) | εἰ οἱ Πέρσαι οἱ | Erbse 1960 | |
| 3.2.20 | ἁμαρτήσονται (Schenkl) | ἁμαρτάνουσι | All mss but C₁ | Hude |
| 3.2.22 | πάντες γὰρ | πάντες μὲν γὰρ | All mss but C₁A | vulgate |
| 3.2.22 | οἱ ποταμοί | ποταμοί | C₁Ag | Marchant |
| 3.2.22 | προσιοῦσι | προιοῦσι | g (and B?) | Hude |
| 3.2.23 | ἐν βασιλέως χώρᾳ | ἐν τῇ βασιλέως χώρᾳ | All mss but C₁ | Hude |
| 3.2.23 | βασιλέως χώρᾳ πολλὰς κτλ | βασιλέως χώρᾳ ἄκοντος βασιλέως πολλὰς κτλ | g, compare f | Castiglioni |
| 3.2.23 | τὴν τούτων χώραν | τὴν τούτου χώραν | f | Hude |

| Passage | Loeb text | Landmark implied text | Authority | Supporting scholars |
|---------|-----------|----------------------|-----------|---------------------|
| 3.2.31 | ψηφίσασθαι | ἤδη ψηφίσασθαι | Thomas, compare ἦν CBgTZ | |
| 3.2.33 | πάντες | ἅπαντες | f | Hude |
| 3.2.37 | δύο τὼ πρεσβυτάτω στρατηγώ (Cobet) | δύο τῶν πρεσβυτάτων Omitted [στρατηγοὶ] | Thomas, compare mss readings | Compare Masqueray; Huitink and Rood |
| 3.3.7 | οἱ δὲ ἀκοντισταὶ | οἵ τε ἀκοντισταὶ | f | Hude |
| 3.3.15 | οἱ πολέμιοι | οἱ μὲν πολέμιοι | All except C₁ | Hude |
| 3.3.16 | σφενδονητῶν | σφενδονητῶν τε | FMD | Hude |
| 3.3.18 | καὶ τούτων τῷ μὲν | καὶ τούτοις μὲν | Cobet | Huitink and Rood |
| 3.3.18 | ἐντεταλμένῳ | ἐν τῷ τεταγμένῳ | CABg | Marchant |
| 3.3.19 | ὁρῶ δὲ | ὁρῶ δὲ καὶ | f | Hude |
| 3.4.1 | αὐτοὺς διαβῆναι | διαβῆναι | DVab | Hude |
| 3.4.8 | ἥλιον δὲ νεφέλη προκαλύψασα (Brodaeus) | Ἥλιος δὲ νεφέλην προκαλύψας | All mss | Huitink and Rood |
| 3.4.11 | τοῦ δὲ τείχους ἡ περίοδος | τοῦ δὲ κύκλου ἡ περίοδος | f | Hude |
| 3.4.13 | ἱππέας ἦλθεν | ἱππέας ἤγαγεν | Gemoll | |
| 3.4.15 | οἱ Σκύθαι τοξόται | οἱ τοξόται | Krüger | Hude, Marchant |
| 3.4.16 | τῶν τοξοτῶν | τῶν πλείστων τοξοτῶν | All except C₁ | vulgate, Lendle |
| 3.4.17–18 | | Last sentence of 3.4.17 transposed to follow ἦν γὰρ πολὺς σῖτος ἐν ταῖς κώμαις | Huitink and Rood (in commentary) | |
| 3.4.19 | Ἔνθα δὲ | Ἔνθα δὴ | fEg | Hude |
| 3.4.19 | ἢν συγκύπτῃ | ἢν μὲν συγκύπτῃ | All except C₁ | vulgate, Lendle |
| 3.4.24 | ὑφ' ᾧ | ἐφ' ᾧ | MZbg | Schenkl; Huitink and Rood |
| 3.4.24 | ἦσαν (Schenkl) | ἦν | All mss | Hude |
| 3.4.24 | αἱ κῶμαι (Schenkl) | Deleted | Thomas | Huitink and Rood |
| 3.4.35 | χαλινῶσαι δεῖ | χαλινῶσαι, δεῖ | Marchant | |
| 3.4.36 | οὐ γὰρ ἐδόκει | οὐδὲ γὰρ ἐδόκει | V | Hude |
| 3.5.1 | ἐστρατοπεδεύοντο | ἐστρατοποδεύσαντο | f | Hude |

| Passage | Loeb text | Landmark implied text | Authority | Supporting scholars |
|---|---|---|---|---|
| 3.5.4 | βοηθείας (both times) | βοηλασίας | Gemoll | |
| 3.5.4 | ἀπήντησαν οἱ Ἕλληνες | ἀπήντησαν | Bornemann | Hude |
| 3.5.7 | ἀπῆλθον | ἦλθον | cg | Marchant |
| 3.5.13 | εἰς τοὔμπαλιν (Reiske) | εἰς τοὔμπαλιν ὡς πρὸς Βαβυλῶνα | b for ὡς; πρὸς Βαβυλῶνα in all mss with different words before it | Castiglioni |
| 3.5.13 | τὰ ἐπιτήδεια ἦσαν (Rehdantz) | τὰ ἐπιτήδεια ἦσαν | All mss | Hude |
| 3.5.18 | παραγγέλλῃ | παραγγείλῃ | f | Hude |
| 4.1.10 | ὀλίγοι ὄντες | ὀλίγοι τινὲς ὄντες | f | Hude |
| 4.1.14 | τὰ δέ τι ἀναπαυόμενοι | τὰ δὲ καὶ ἀναπαυόμενοι | f | Hude, Marchant |
| 4.2.3 | πταίοντες (Schneider) | παίοντες | All mss in varying positions | Marchant |
| 4.2.27 | αὐτοῖς τοῖς ἀναβᾶσι | αὐτοῖς ἀναβᾶσι | Pantazides | Hude |
| 4.3.1 | ἀνέπνευσαν (Hug) | ἀνεπαύσαντο | All mss except perhaps C$_1$ | Hude |
| 4.3.8 | περιρρυῆναι | περιρραγῆναι | fg | vulgate |
| 4.3.32 | στρέψαντες ἔσπευδον (Castiglioni) | στρέψαντες ἔφευγον | All mss | Hude, Marchant |
| 4.4.16 | καὶ Ἀμαζόνες | καὶ αἱ Ἀμαζόνες | g, Schneider | Marchant |
| 4.5.15 | αὐτόθεν | αὐτόθι | cg | Marchant |
| 4.5.16 | οὐ γὰρ ἂν δύνασθαι | οὐδὲ γὰρ ἂν δύνασθαι | f | Hude |
| 4.5.27 | πόμα | πῶμα | Dindorf | Marchant |
| 4.5.29 | πάντες οἱ στρατιῶται | οἱ στρατιῶται | f | Hude |
| 4.6.1 | Ἐπισθένει | Πλεισθένει | cg | Marchant |
| 4.6.3 | Ἐπισθένης | Πλεισθένης | cg | Marchant |
| 4.6.20 | Ἀριστέας Χῖος | Ἀριστέας ὁ Χῖος | cg | Marchant |
| 4.7.11 | οὐδὲ Εὐρύλοχον | οὔτε Εὐρύλοχον | Schneider | Hude |
| 4.7.13 | Αἰνέας ὁ Στυμφάλιος | Αἰνέας Στυμφάλιος | cg | Marchant |
| 4.7.15 | πεντήκοντα | πεντεκαίδεκα | Thomas | |

| Passage | Loeb text | Landmark implied text | Authority | Supporting scholars |
|---------|-----------|----------------------|-----------|---------------------|
| 4.7.16 | ἀποτέμνοντες | ἀποτέμοντες | Matthiae | Hude, Marchant |
| 4.7.18 | ἐκ τούτου | ἐκ τούτων | C₁Ag | Marchant |
| 4.7.21 | καὶ κατεῖδον τὴν θάλατταν | Omitted | C₁ | Gemoll, Masqueray, Bevilacqua |
| 4.8.11 | ὑπ' ἀθρόων καὶ βελῶν | ὑπ' ἀθρόων πη καὶ βελῶν | All mss except Ag | Breitenbach |
| 4.8.11 | καὶ ἀνθρώπων πολλῶν | καὶ ἀνθρώπων | f | Hude |
| 4.8.12 | οἱ ἔσχατοι λόχοι | Deleted | Cobet | Marchant |
| 4.8.28 | ἐκυλινδοῦντο | ἐκαλινδοῦντο | Cobet, for different reasons | Hude, Marchant |
| 5.1.1 | πορεία | ἀποπορεία | Fᶜ | |
| 5.1.2 | Λέων | Ἀντιλέων | f | Hude |
| 5.1.9 | Ἐννοεῖτε δὲ | Ἐννοεῖτε δὴ | All mss except Ab | Hude, Marchant |
| 5.2.4 | δισχίλιοι ἄνθρωποι | εἰς χιλίους ἀνθρώπους | M | Hude |
| 5.2.29 | λαβὼν | λαβὼν τέτταρας ἢ πέντε καὶ | f (except for καὶ) | Bornemann |
| 5.2.31 | καλινδούμενοι | κυλινδόμενοι | M | vulgate: κυ- form |
| 5.4.22 | μεταξὺ τῶν λόχων ὀρθίων | μεταξὺ τῶν λόχων | Lion | Marchant |
| 5.4.26 | φυλάττοντα | φυλάττουσιν | Brunck | Marchant |
| 5.4.29 | τούτων καὶ πλείστω | τούτῳ καὶ πλείστω | f | Hude |
| 5.5.4 | ἄποικον, ὄντας δ' (compare Hude) | ἀποίκους οἰκοῦντας | f | Breitenbach |
| 5.5.13 | ἦν δυνατὸν | ἦν ἡμῖν δυνατὸν | ab | Lion |
| 5.5.14 | καὶ εἴ τις | καὶ μὴν εἴ τις | Mb Aldine | Hude |
| 5.5.20 | τὰ αὑτῶν δαπανῶντες | τὰ αὑτῶν δαπανῶντες | BE | Marchant |
| 5.6.1 | μόνοι γὰρ ἂν ἐδόκουν | μόνοι γὰρ ἐδόκουν | f | Hude |
| 5.6.5 | ἕξομεν | ἕξομεν ἡμεῖς | b | Castiglioni |
| 5.6.12 | πορείαν | τὴν πορείαν | Bisschop | Cobet, Masqueray |
| 5.6.15 | χώραν καὶ δύναμιν | καὶ χώραν καὶ δύναμιν | f | Hude |
| 5.6.19 | βούλεται | βουλεύεται | fC₂g | vulgate |

| Passage | Loeb text | Landmark implied text | Authority | Supporting scholars |
|---------|-----------|----------------------|-----------|---------------------|
| 5.6.25 | ὥστε τῷ βουλομένῳ ἐνοικεῖν | ὥστε εἶναι τῷ βουλομένῳ ἐνοικεῖν | Marchant in textual apparatus only | Compare Rehdantz, Masqueray, Bevilacqua: ὥστε τῷ βουλομένῳ εἶναι ἐνοικεῖν |
| 5.6.35 | τῆς μισθοφορᾶς | Deleted | Krüger | Marchant |
| 5.7.2 | ὅσοι γὰρ μὴ εἰς θάλατταν κατέφυγον κατελεύσθησαν | Deleted | Rehdantz (cg omit γὰρ) | Marchant |
| 5.7.5 | ἀδικοῦντες | ἀδικεῖν | cg | Marchant |
| 5.7.9 | ἐξηπατηκὼς εἰς ὑμᾶς, | ἐξηπατηκὼς εἰς, | cg | Marchant |
| 5.7.10 | καὶ ἠλιθίων | ἠλιθίων | f | Hude |
| 5.7.12 | φανῶμεν | ἀποφαινώμεθα | cg | Marchant |
| 5.7.13 | ἐπώλουν ὑμῖν | ἐπώλουν ἡμῖν | MDbEg | Hude, Marchant |
| 5.7.18 | κελεύειν [αὐτοὺς] θάπτειν | κελεύειν αὐτοὺς θάπτειν | c | Marchant |
| 5.7.35 | ἔδοξε καθῆραι | ἔδοξε καὶ καθῆραι | f | Hude |
| 5.8.1 | αἱρεφεὶς κατημέλει | αἱρεθεὶς *** κατημέλει | Leonclavius | Hude, Marchant |
| 5.8.12 | ἀνέκραγον | ἀνέκραγον πάντες | f | Hude |
| 5.8.25 | ἐπεκούφισα (Reiske) | ἐπεκούρησα | All mss | Marchant |
| 5.8.26 | καλόν γε καὶ δίκαιον | καλόν τε καὶ δίκαιον | cgM | Marchant |
| 6.1.5 | ἔπεσε | ἔπαισε | fEg | vulgate, Castiglioni |
| 6.1.21 | καὶ κίνδυνος | κίνδυνος | f | Hude |
| 6.1.26 | οὔτε ὑμῖν μοι δοκεῖ | οὔτε ὑμῖν οὔτε ἐμοὶ δοκεῖ | f | vulgate |
| 6.2.1 | παραπλέοντες ... τοῦτον δὲ | Deleted | Krüger | Breitenbach, Lendle |
| 6.2.16 | οὕτω | καὶ οὕτω | b | Castiglioni |
| 6.2.16 | ἑπτακοσίους (the first time) | ἑξακοσίους | ab | Castiglioni |
| 6.3.3 | περιεβάλοντο | περιεβάλλοντο | All mss except Cᶜ (and VZ?) | Marchant |
| 6.3.3 | διαφυγόντες (I. Vossius) | διαπεφευγότες | Castiglioni | Peters |
| 6.3.3 | διέφυγον | διέφευγον | cgD | Marchant |
| 6.3.5 | τοὺς ἄλλους πάντας | τοὺς ἄλλους ἅπαντας | ab | Castiglioni |

| Passage | Loeb text | Landmark implied text | Authority | Supporting scholars |
|---------|-----------|----------------------|-----------|---------------------|
| 6.3.6 | οἱ ἄλλοι δὲ λοχαγοὶ | οἱ ἄλλοι δὲ λόχοι | Pantazides | Marchant |
| 6.3.14 | Transposed after 6.3.18 (Rehdantz) | Retained original ms order | All mss | vulgate |
| 6.3.16 | ἡμεῖς γὰρ ἀποδραίημεν ἂν οὐδαμοῖ ἐνθένδε | *** ἡμεῖς γὰρ ἀποδραίημεν ἂν οὐδαμοῖ ἐνθένδε | Thomas | |
| 6.3.22 | οὔτε φίλιον στρατεύμα οὔτε πολέμιον | οὔτε τὸ φίλιον στρατεύμα οὔτε τὸ πολέμιον | First τὸ fg, second τὸ all mss except A | Hude |
| 6.3.22 | (καὶ ταῦτα ... στράτευμα) | Transposed to end of sentence after καταλελειμμένους | Bothe | Cobet |
| 6.3.23 | ἔπειτα δὲ καὶ | ἔπειτα δὲ | f | Hude |
| 6.3.23 | ἔωθεν καὶ τοὺς Ἕλληνας δὲ | ἔωθεν δὲ καὶ τοὺς Ἕλληνας | f | Hude |
| 6.4.6 | ἐλαῶν (Dindorf) | ἐλαιῶν | All mss | Breitenbach |
| 6.4.9 | τὰ ἱερὰ καλὰ | τὰ ἱερὰ | FMD, compare b | Hude |
| 6.4.12 | δῆλον ὅτι | Omitted | g, Krüger | Marchant |
| 6.5.2 | γίγνεται τὰ ἱερὰ | γίγνεται καλὰ τὰ ἱερὰ | f | vulgate |
| 6.5.13 | οὐκ ἄξιον εἴη διαβαίνειν τοιοῦτον ὂν τὸ νάπος | βουλῆς οὐκ ἄξιον εἴη εἰ διαβατέον ἐστι τοιοῦτον νάπος | cg | Marchant |
| 6.5.18–19 | Θαυμάζω ... χωρίων stands after σωτηρία as the first sentence of §19 | Transposed to follow ἐφέπεσθαι as the first sentence of §18 | Thomas | compare Hartman |
| 6.5.29 | δεξίον | δεξίον αὖ | f | Hude |
| 6.6.5 | ἄλλοι ἄλλῃ (Schneider) | ἄλλοι | All mss | Marchant |
| 6.6.22 | Δέξιππον (the second time) | Deleted | Cobet | Gemoll, Masqueray, Bevilacqua |
| 6.6.23 | ἀπολώλαμεν | ἀπολώλαμεν πάντες | f | Hude |
| 6.6.25 | ἀξιοῦτε, | Deleted comma | Thomas | |
| 6.6.26 | νῦν μὲν οὖν | νῦν οὖν | cg | Marchant |
| 6.6.31 | ἐλθὼν | ἐλθόντων | Krüger | Matthiäs |
| 6.6.32 | κόσμιοί εἰσι | κόσμιοί εἰσιν ἅπαντες | b | |
| 6.6.35 | συνεβάλοντο (Stephanus) | συνεβάλοντο | All mss as regards imperfect | Marchant as regards imperfect |
| 7.1.1 | πορείᾳ | ἀποπορείᾳ | F (only) | |

| Passage | Loeb text | Landmark implied text | Authority | Supporting scholars |
|---------|-----------|----------------------|-----------|---------------------|
| 7.1.12 | Καὶ ἄρδην παντες | Καὶ ἤδη τε πάντες | f | vulgate, compare Cobet |
| 7.1.12 | γένοιντο πάντες | γένοιντο ἄρδην πάντες | Ast | Hirschig |
| 7.1.15 | ἐν ᾧ δὲ | ἐν ᾧ δὲ οὗτοι | f | Hude |
| 7.1.15 | οἱ στρατιῶται | οἱ γε στρατιῶται | Hutchinson | |
| 7.1.17 | οἳ ἐτύγχανον | οἳ ἔτι ἐτύγχανον | Gemoll | |
| 7.1.34 | ἐπαγγελλόμενα | ἀπαγγελλόμενα | All mss except b | Hude, Marchant |
| 7.2.1 | καὶ Φρυνίσκος ὁ Ἀχαιὸς | καὶ Φρυνίσκος ὁ Ἀχαιὸς <καὶ Κλεάνωρ ὁ Ὀρχομένιος> | Poppo | Lendle |
| 7.2.3 | ταὐτὰ ἐβούλοντο (Zeune) | ταῦτα ἐβούλοντο | All mss | vulgate, Stronk |
| 7.2.3 | ἀποδιδόμενοι | ἀποδόμενοι | Cobet | |
| 7.2.3 | οἱ δὲ καὶ (Muretus) | οἱ δὲ καὶ διαδόντες | Bornemann, based on mss οἱ δὲ καὶ διδόντες | Kühner |
| 7.2.3 | Mss have τὰ ὅπλα κατὰ τοὺς χώρους εἰς τὰς πόλεις omitted by Loeb (Muretus, partly following DV) | τὰ ὅπλα εἰς τὰς πόλεις (omitting just κατὰ τοὺς χώρους) | Breitenbach (in footnote) | |
| 7.2.8 | ἐκ τούτου ὁ Ἀναξίβιος | ἐκ τούτου δὴ ὁ Ἀναξίβιος | Bornemann, compare FMD | |
| 7.2.12 | ὁ ἐκ Βυζαντίου (Schaefer) | ἐκ Βυζαντίου | All mss | vulgate, Masqueray |
| 7.2.12 | ἁρμοστής | Deleted | Thomas | |
| 7.2.25 | εἰ ἀληθῆ ταῦτ' εἶπεν | εἰ ἀληθῆ ταῦτα εἴη | cg | Marchant |
| 7.2.33 | ἀποβλέπων | ἀποβλέπων ὥσπερ κύων | f | Hude |
| 7.3.2 | καὶ λοχαγούς | Omitted | cg | Marchant |
| 7.3.3 | …πωλήσειν ἔτι ὑμᾶς… | …πωλήσειν ἔτι ἡμᾶς… | C₁gA | |
| 7.3.3 | ἔτι ὑμᾶς, ἀλλὰ λήψεσθαι | ἔτι, ἀλλὰ λήψεσθαι ὑμᾶς | Holford-Strevens (personal communication) | |
| 7.3.3 | μισθόν, | μισθὸν μᾶλλον, | f | Hude |
| 7.3.6 | ὅτῳ, ἔφη | ὅτῳ ὑμῶν, ἔφη | b | Muretus |
| 7.3.10 | τοῖς στρατιώταις | Omitted | f | Hude |

| Passage | Loeb text | Landmark implied text | Authority | Supporting scholars |
|---------|-----------|----------------------|-----------|---------------------|
| 7.3.21 | οἱ λοχαγοὶ | λοχαγοὶ | f | Hude |
| 7.3.32 | συγκατεσκεδάστο μετ' | κατεσκεδάστο κατ' | Pantazides | |
| 7.3.32 | μαγάδι | μάγαδιν | Athenaeus | Barker 1982 |
| 7.4.6 | κατέλαβον | ἔλαβε | cg | Marchant |
| 7.4.9 | ἐπανατείνας | ὑπερανατείνας | cg | Marchant |
| 7.4.17 | τρόπος ἦν αὐτοῖς | τρόπος αὐτοῖς | f | Hude |
| 7.4.18 | Εὐοδέα | Ἐπιταλιέα | Schenkl | |
| 7.5.3 | ἐμοὶ τοίνυν | ἐμοὶ μὲν τοίνυν | f | Hude |
| 7.5.14 | ηὑρίσκοντο (Dindorf) | εὑρίσκονται | f | vulgate |
| 7.6.3 | λέγει | ἔλεγεν | c | Marchant |
| 7.6.7 | ἔληξεν | ἔληξε | All mss except CAZ | Hude |
| 7.6.10 | ἐγὼ μὲν | ἐγὼ μὲν, ἔφη | f | vulgate |
| 7.6.12 | οὐκ ἐπεχείρησα | οὐδ' ἐπεχείρησα | MZ | Hude |
| 7.6.18 | πάσας | πάσας ἦ μὴν | b | Castiglioni |
| 7.6.21 | ἐξαπατᾶσθαι. ἐπεὶ | ἐξαπατᾶσθαι, ἐπεὶ | Thomas | |
| 7.6.29 | ἡμᾶς | ὑμᾶς | CABg | |
| 7.6.36 | καὶ γὰρ νῦν (Gemoll) | καὶ γὰρ οὖν νῦν | f | Hude, Marchant |
| 7.6.37 | Λακεδαιμόνιοι | Deleted | Cobet | Hude |
| 7.7.8 | ἐναυλισθῆναι | ἐγκαταυλισθῆναι | Dindorf | |
| 7.7.19 | πεῖσαι | ἀκοῦσαι | f | vulgate |
| 7.7.20 | πάρειμι σε | πάρειμι | cg | Marchant |
| 7.7.26 | πιπράσκεται. | πιπράσκεται; | Zeune | Hude |
| 7.7.34 | κρείττονας | κρείττονας τούτων | f | Hude |
| 7.7.36 | τοῦ λαμβάνοντος | λαμβάνοντος | All mss except M and possibly B | Marchant, Bevilacqua |
| 7.7.37 | δοκοίης | δοκῆς | cg | Kühner |
| 7.7.42 | καὶ ἄλλων | ἄλλων | All mss except BZ | Hude, Marchant |

| Passage | Loeb text | Landmark implied text | Authority | Supporting scholars |
|---|---|---|---|---|
| 7.7.46 | ἀποκεῖσθαι | ἀποδείκνυσθαι | All mss except M | Marchant, Bevilacqua |
| 7.8.1 | ἐντοίχια (Bornemann) | ἐνώπια | Toup | Zeune |
| 7.8.6 | Ναυσικλείδης | Ναυκλείδας | Thomas | |
| 7.8.7 | πορευόμενοι τῆς Μυσίας (Poppo) | πορευόμενοι | Rehdantz | Marchant |
| 7.8.8 | Ἑλλάδι | παρ' Ἑλλάδι | f | Hude |
| 7.8.10 | ἁλώσιμος εἴη | ἂν ἁλώσιμος εἴη | MDb | Hude |
| 7.8.11 | ἄλλους πιστοὺς (Hug) | τοὺς στρατιώτας τοὺς πιστοὺς | Thomas after Hug's alternative | |
| 7.8.15 | Ἰταμένης (Dindorf) | Ἰταβέλις | FMZa, compare D | Sekunda 1998 |
| 7.8.22 | συντυγχάνουσιν | συμπεριτυγχάνουσιν | FDVab | vulgate |

# ANCIENT SOURCES

## Cited in this Edition

**Aeschines of Sphettus/Aeschines Socraticus** (early fourth century B.C.E.): author of philosophical dialogues, most of which involved Socrates as a character. Seven of these dialogues are known by name, but extensive fragments survive from only two of them (*Aspasia* and *Alcibiades*). Sphettus is a deme of Athens. Aeschines of Sphettus is to be distinguished from another, better-known Aeschines, who was a politician and orator later in the fourth century.

**Aeschylus** (525/4?–456/5 B.C.E.): Athenian dramatist. In antiquity seventy to ninety plays were attributed to Aeschylus, but only seven have been transmitted complete to us under his name. Six powerful tragedies, dating from 472 to 458, are certainly by him; many scholars deny that he wrote the seventh, *Prometheus Bound*, although it likewise dates from the fifth century and is also a masterpiece. In addition, many fragments of his other plays, including substantial parts of two of them preserved on papyrus, have survived.

**Ameipsias** (late fifth century B.C.E.): comic dramatist of Athens, during the period of the so-called Old Comedy. Names of seven of his plays are known, but only thirty-nine brief fragments survive. *Aristophanes refers to him with scorn.

**Antisthenes** (450s?–360s? B.C.E.): Athenian philosopher, associate of Socrates. Sixty-two titles of works by him are known, but apart from *Aias* and *Odysseus*, two display speeches (ones written as literary exercises), only brief and puzzling fragments remain. He appears as a character in Xenophon's *Symposion* (*The Drinking Party*), and two of Xenophon's works have titles, *Oikonomikos* (*On the Management of the Household*) and *Kyroupaideia* (*The Education of Cyrus*), that echo those of works by Antisthenes.

**Aratus** of Sicyon (271–213 B.C.E.): statesman. His memoirs—over thirty books long, covering his life to 220—served as a defense of his policy and actions as the leading figure in the Achaean League of independent Greek states. Only fragments survive, but a fair amount is known about the work, as it formed the basis for the narrative of the period given by *Polybius and also for *Plutarch's *Life of Aratus*.

**Aristippus** of Cyrene (late fifth/early fourth century B.C.E.): philosopher, associate of Socrates. The most important sources for him are a long passage in Xenophon's *Memorabilia* and a life of him by *Diogenes Laertius. This life names around thirty dialogues, essays, and treatises, and

NOTE: An asterisk (*) next to a name within an entry indicates that an entry for that person will be found elsewhere in Ancient Sources Cited in this Edition.

507

one standard collection of citations is more than 165 pages long; but it is not clear how much of this should really be assigned to him. He had a luxurious, even licentious, lifestyle, and some sources say (and others deny) that he identified pleasure (seemingly, immediate pleasure) as the aim of life. Scholars dispute whether he was a serious philosopher, as we understand the concept, but several recent studies have strengthened the case for this.

**Aristobulus** (early third century B.C.E.): historian of Alexander the Great. He had served in Alexander's army and is attested as beginning to write his history at the age of eighty-four, finishing it sometime after 301 (he is also attested as having lived to beyond ninety). Sixty-two fragments of his work survive; he was also one of the two chief sources for *Arrian's *Anabasis Alexandrou*.

**Aristophanes** (c. 455–c. 386 B.C.E.): the most famous playwright of the so-called Old Comedy at Athens. Eleven of his plays survive, plus nearly a thousand fragments and citations.

**Aristotle** (384–322 B.C.E.): philosopher, polymath, and tutor of the young Alexander the Great. He was born in the city of Stageira in Northern Greece. Aristotle's many extant writings cover a vast range of subjects, including poetics, politics, ethics, zoology, cosmology, metaphysics, and logic. A few of the works attributed to him in antiquity have been generally recognized by modern scholars as being composed by others and passed off as Aristotle's.

**Arrian** of Nicomedia, in Bithynia (85?–c. 163 C.E.): prolific Greek writer on philosophy and history. He attained high office in the service of the philhellene emperor Hadrian, becoming consul in 129? C.E. and legate of Cappadocia c. 131–137. His philosophic work the *Discourses of Epictetus* survives. Of his historical works, his major composition, the seventeen-book *Parthica*, on Trajan's Parthian War, is lost, but several others survive, most important among them seven books of *Anabasis Alexandrou*, about Alexander the Great. As the title *Anabasis* implies, Arrian saw himself as a second Xenophon; for example, he, like Xenophon, wrote a *Kynegetikos* (*On Hunting*), which has also come down to us in full.

**Athenaeus** (c. 200 C.E.): Greek writer from Naukratis in Egypt, the author of *Deipnosophistai* (*Learned Banqueters*), a miscellany in fifteen books, twelve and a half of which survive in full, the first two and a half only in extracts and summaries. The work recounts a very long banquet at which the participants exchange snippets from a huge number of authors about banqueting and food generally. In many cases Athenaeus' extracts are one of the main sources of evidence we have for the authors in question.

**Augustus Caesar** (63 B.C.E.–14 C.E.): Roman emperor. A great-nephew of *Julius Caesar, he was adopted by him in his will as his heir. In a series of ruthless campaigns between 44 and 30, he defeated all rivals to become the master of the Roman world, a position consolidated by his constitutional settlement of 27 and assumption of the name Augustus. He remained Roman emperor until his death over forty years later. His *Res Gestae* (*Achievements*) was composed to be read to the Roman Senate after his death and then inscribed on stone monuments around the empire; one of these inscriptions survives in full in the Turkish capital, Ankara.

**Aulus Gellius** (120s–after 178 C.E.): Roman author. He wrote *Noctes Atticae* (*Attic* [Athenian] *Nights*), a miscellany of notes and excerpts from a wide variety of Roman (especially early Roman) and Greek authors, set in the framework of learned conversations between partly fictitious characters and partly real contemporaries. The work, twenty books long, survives almost complete.

**Callias** (attested as writing between 446–430 B.C.E.): comic dramatist at Athens during the period of Old Comedy. Names of eight of his plays are known, but only forty brief fragments survive.

**Callisthenes** (died 327 B.C.E.): historian. A kinsman and student of Aristotle, he was the first to write about the conquests of Alexander the Great, whom he accompanied in his war against Persia as the official recorder of the event. His *Deeds of Alexander* (of which only a few brief fragments remain) was a eulogistic and flattering work, but eventually Alexander put Callisthenes to death for opposing his increasing wish to be treated with the ceremony appropriate to the Persian King. We also know of three other historical works by Callisthenes, written before he went on the expedition.

**Cassius Dio** (c. 164–after 229 C.E.), often referred to as "Dio": a Greek from Bithynia who had a distinguished career in the Roman Senate, including serving twice as consul, and who wrote, in Greek, a *Roman History* in eighty books. Books 36–54, covering 68–10 B.C.E., survive complete; very substantial fragments of books 55–60 (9 B.C.E.–46 C.E.) and books 78–79 (217–c. 220 C.E.) also survive. The rest of the work is represented by two fairly full summaries by Byzantine scholars, plus other excerpts, one of which concerns the topography of Byzantium. Modern editors have reconstructed the distribution of the fragments of the later books in two different ways, which can give rise to problems in citing or following up references.

**Chion:** one of the assassins of the tyrant Klearchos of Heraclea, the Black Sea city, in 353/2 B.C.E. The *Letters of Chion* are a work of fiction narrating events leading up to the murder. Xenophon's actions in Byzantium as described in *Anabasis* are anachronistically brought into the epistolary narrative of events forty-five or so years later. The letters were actually written centuries after their dramatic date as a literary exercise during the time of the Roman Empire, though scholars differ as to whether the late first or the fourth century C.E. is the likelier period for their composition.

**Cicero/Marcus Tullius Cicero** (106–43 B.C.E.): leading Roman politician of the late Republican period and an outstanding orator. Many of his speeches survive, together with hundreds of letters, almost all of them not written for publication and therefore uniquely valuable as a source. He also wrote extensively on philosophy, as well as on rhetoric.

**Cleitarchus** (late fourth century B.C.E.?): author of a history of Alexander the Great, which most scholars believe was written between 310 and 300. There is some evidence that he later became keeper of the records of Alexandria in Egypt. His history represents a tradition substantially different from that of *Arrian, both less eulogistic and more sensational. While only thirty-seven brief fragments of this work survive, it is known to have contained at least twelve books and is generally agreed to have been the foundation of the accounts of *Diodorus Siculus, *Curtius, and certain other later historians.

**Cratippus** of Athens (active early fourth century B.C.E.): historian who wrote a continuation of *Thucydides' narrative of the Peloponnesian War, starting in 411 and continuing until at least the late 390s. Very few citations or fragments of this work survive, unless, as many scholars believe, the remains of *Hellenica Oxyrhynchia* come from Cratippus' history. A little more information about *Hellenica Oxyrhynchia* and Cratippus is given in Appendix M: Other Ancient Sources on the Ten Thousand.

**Ctesias of Cnidus** (late fifth/early fourth century B.C.E.): physician to the Persian King Artaxerxes II; on his return to Greece in the 390s, he wrote *Persika*, in twenty-three books, covering both Assyrian and Persian history. His narrative continued to his own day and included a detailed account of the battle of Cunaxa, mentioned by Xenophon in the course of his own narrative of the battle (*Anabasis* 1.8.26). Substantial fragments of this work and of Ctesias' *Indika* (*Indian Affairs*) survive in *Diodorus, *Plutarch, and other later authors; both works were summarized book by book by *Photius. Extracts relating to Ctesias' narrative of Artaxerxes' reign are included in translation in Appendix T: Selections from Plutarch's *Life of Artaxerxes* and Appendix U: Selections from Photius' Synopsis of Ctesias' *Persika*. He has often been criticized in both ancient and modern times for sensationalism, superficiality, and inaccuracy amounting to falsification, though some scholars more recently have been less unsympathetic.

**Ctesiclides/Ctesicles** (third century B.C.E.?): author of a work entitled *The List of Archons and Olympic Victors*, which, it seems, was not simply a list but, rather, an Olympiad chronicle, a chronological record of events throughout the Greek world organized by reference to successive Olympic Games. It was in three books or possibly more and continued at least to 241; scholars guess it was written not very long after this date. Three fragments are all that have come down to us, two in *Athenaeus and one in *Diogenes Laertius' *Life of Xenophon*, though Athenaeus gives the work a different title and the manuscripts of Diogenes transmit the name as "Stesiclides." The recognition that the three fragments refer to the same author and work is due to the late nineteenth-century German scholar Wilamowitz.

**Curtius/Quintus Curtius Rufus** (first century C.E.?): Latin historian, probably to be identified with a rhetorician of the same name as well as with the Roman consul of 43 C.E. He wrote a highly rhetorical history of Alexander the Great in ten books (the first two are lost, together with some sections of the remainder). It is generally believed by scholars that his main source was *Cleitarchus.

**Demetrius** of Magnesia (active c. 50 B.C.E.): author of a work entitled *On Homonyms*, distinguishing between people and places of the same name. This survives only in a few fragments, chiefly in *Diogenes Laertius.

**Demosthenes** (384–322 B.C.E.): Athenian politician and the greatest of the Athenian orators. Demosthenes was one of the principal speakers in the Assembly at Athens from the 340s to the 320s and was its dominant figure in the period 343–338, when he bitterly opposed the ultimately successful attempts of Philip of Macedonia to dominate Greece. He was also a prolific orator in the law courts. Sixty-one surviving speeches are ascribed to him in our manuscripts. About one-third are regarded by some or all editors as composed by other people.

**Dinarchus** (361/60–c. 290 B.C.E.): speechwriter from Corinth who lived most of his life in Athens as a resident alien. All but one of the sixty speeches ancient scholars recognized as his were written to be delivered by other people, generally (perhaps always) in civil or criminal trials. One speech from 323 has survived in full, and we have extensive parts of two other speeches made the same year, together with brief fragments of or references to several more made at other times.

**Dinon** of Colophon (late fourth-century B.C.E.): author of a rather sensational history of Persia in at least eight books (probably many more), which went down at least to the reconquest of Egypt in 343/2. He seems to have had sources close to the Persian court but was prone to accept propaganda and to embroider his material. His work survives only in fragments: directly attested fragments are mostly preserved within the writings of *Plutarch, including but not limited to the *Life of Artaxerxes*, but wider influence, both on Plutarch and on other authors, is plausibly suspected.

**Dio of Prusa/Dio Chrysostom** (Golden Mouth) (early 40s–120? C.E.): Greek orator from Bithynia. Seventy-eight speeches and essays of his survive, covering political and moral topics as well as exhibitions of showy cleverness, such as an argument that Troy was not captured by the Greeks. Many of his speeches were simply display pieces, but some deal with the real situation in the Anatolia of his day.

**Diocles** of Magnesia (date uncertain): historian of philosophy. Our knowledge of him comes from *Diogenes Laertius, for whom he was a major source and who cites him almost twenty times. It is often said that there is a reference to him when young in the poet Meleager, which shows that his work dates from the mid- to late first century B.C.E.; but the evidence for this identification, and therefore for Diocles' dates, is not very strong.

**Diodorus,** often referred to as Diodorus Siculus (the Sicilian) (first-century B.C.E.): Greek author of *Bibliotheke Historike* (*Library of History*), a universal history in forty books starting with the mythological period and continuing into Diodorus' lifetime (stopping in 60), it covered Egypt, the Middle East, and India but concentrated chiefly on Greece, Sicily, and Rome. Though we have substantial fragments from throughout the work, only fifteen books (1–5, 11–20) survive in full. Books 1–5 survey lands outside the Greek world and mythical times in Greece. Books 11–20 narrate Greek and Sicilian history from 480 to 302; while often confused and prone to error, they are an essential source for much of this period, especially for the fourth century, as a result of the loss of the primary historians on whom Diodorus relied. Translations of passages of Diodorus relevant to *Anabasis* appear in Appendix S: Selections from Diodorus. He covered Cyrus' expedition and the march of the Ten Thousand in sections of his Book 14, to which Appendix S adds an earlier section of that book covering some of the earlier career of Klearchos, Cyrus' principal Greek general. More about his reliability and possible sources can be found in Appendix M: Other Ancient Sources on the Ten Thousand. Further passages relevant to the period of Xenophon's adult life appear in *The Landmark Xenophon's* Hellenika, Appendix O: Selections from the *Histories* of Diodorus Siculus Relevant to Xenophon's *Hellenika*.

**Diogenes Laertius** (early third century C.E.?): writer on the lives and doctrines of the philosophers of the Classical and Hellenistic periods; all ten books have survived. His life of Xenophon appears as part of Book 2. A translation can be found in Appendix V: Diogenes Laertius' *Life of Xenophon*. It is generally believed that, apart from the Hellenistic philosopher Epicurus, whom he treats last and at greatest length, Diogenes had himself read very few of the philosophers he discussed. Instead, he took his material from preceding compilers and commentators, but fortunately he used a wide variety of these and often names his direct and indirect sources. The ancient biographic tradition for literary figures is often accused of being based largely on inferences, often false, from the works of the subjects of the biographies. However, this is demonstrably untrue of Diogenes' life of Xenophon, where his immediate authorities derived material from at least six other fourth-century sources and from a collection of Athenian decrees. The result of the process certainly contains error and misconception, but it does also include truth not attested elsewhere.

**Dionysius of Halicarnassus** (late first century B.C.E.): Greek historian, rhetorician, and literary critic. His *Roman Antiquities* recounted early Roman history (to the early third century) in twenty books; the first eleven survive in full, along with excerpts from others. Also extant is his series of valuable essays on the style and historical context of various Greek writers of the Classical period.

**Dioscorides** (late first century C.E.): pharmacologist from Cilicia who wrote *Materia Medica*, a treatise in Greek in five books on the preparation, properties, and testing of medicinal drugs. The product of considerable original research into plants, combined with clinical observations and a sophisticated typological arrangement, the work survives in full and covers over one thousand natural drugs, including Xenophon's "mad honey."

**Ephorus** of Cyme (mid-fourth century B.C.E.): author of a massive history, thirty books long, covering events throughout the Archaic and Classical periods in Greece, Sicily, and Persia. The work itself is lost, but fairly numerous fragments remain, and he is believed to have been a key source for *Diodorus and certain other later historians.

**Gellius:** see **Aulus Gellius.**

**Hecataeus** of Miletus (late sixth/early fifth centuries B.C.E.): mythographer, genealogist, and geographer. His *Historiai*, or *Genealogiai*, attempts to systematize the body of Greek myths in a rational way; only about thirty fragments of the work survive. He was also the author of a geography (*Periodos gēs*), a description of the earth in two parts, Europe and Asia; over three hundred fragments survive, but most are just citations of place-names. In addition, he is said to have produced a map of the world, but we have no knowledge of the form it took.

**Hellenica Oxyrhynchia; Oxyrhynchus Historian/"P":** *Hellenica Oxyrynchia* is a detailed history of the period from 411 to at least 395 B.C.E., substantial fragments of which were discovered in the twentieth century in papyri of the Roman imperial period found at Oxyrhynchus, in Egypt. Hence, its author is known to modern scholars as the Oxyrhynchus Historian or simply "P" for papyrus. Who this was is disputed, the most popular candidate being *Cratippus. The main alternative theory is that the fragments are really from *Theopompus' *Hellenika*. It looks as though the author sees himself as continuing the history of the Peloponnesian War by *Thucydides, which broke off in 411. *Hellenica Oxyrhynchia* passages are translated in *The Landmark Xenophon's* Hellenika, Appendix P: Selected Fragments of the *Hellenica Oxyrhynchia* Relevant to Xenophon's *Hellenika*.

**Heraclides of Cyme** (mid-fourth century B.C.E.): author of a history of Persia in five books, and *Paraskeuastika* (*Preparations* or *Resources*) in at least two books. (Many scholars think that the latter work was part of the former.) Only a few fragments of Heraclides' writings survive, the longest and most important of which are preserved by *Athenaeus. He is generally regarded as one of the most reliable writers on Persian affairs.

**Hermippus** of Smyrna (mid- to late third century B.C.E.): author of *Lives of Those Distinguished for Culture*, a series of biographies of philosophers, writers, and lawgivers. Although he was a highly diligent scholar, meticulous in citing sources, the results are unreliable, since he was more interested in sensationalism than truth; indeed, some outright invention on his part is also possible. His work survives only in fragments, of which there are about eighty-five.

**Herodotus** of Halicarnassus (mid-fifth century B.C.E.): historian of the Graeco-Persian wars of the early fifth century. His work, *Histories*, in nine books (which have survived in full), also contains a long digression on Egypt and much material on the earlier history of various Greek states and of Persia. The Roman writer *Cicero described him as "the father of history," a sobriquet that has stuck.

**Homer:** The ancient Greeks believed that their two oldest literary works, the long epic poems *Iliad* and *Odyssey*, were both written by the same man, a blind poet called Homer. Both poems consist of twenty-four books, though the *Iliad* has almost one-third more lines. It recounts incidents from the ninth year of the legendary ten-year Trojan War, while the *Odyssey* tells of the adventures of Odysseus in his journey back from the war and his eventual homecoming. The date most commonly assigned to them is the late eighth century B.C.E., but modern scholars have disagreed among themselves not only about this but also about whether the poems were composed orally or in writing, whether each epic was composed by one author or put together out of the compositions of several people, and whether the same person was the principal composer of both works.

**Ion of Chios** (c. 485–c. 422 B.C.E.): dramatist, poet, and prose author. His most notable work was *Epidemiai*, or *Visits*, which recorded his meetings and conversations with leading politicians, dramatists, and other public figures of his day. Only fragments survive of this and of his other writings.

**Isocrates** (436–338 B.C.E.): Athenian orator, pamphleteer, and teacher of rhetoric. Six law court speeches written for others between 403 and 393 survive, together with fifteen display speeches or pamphlets and nine letters written subsequently. He continued writing into his extreme old age. Twenty-five of these thirty speeches and letters have been preserved in full. A recurrent theme was the need for all Greeks to unite in a war of revenge and conquest against the Persians.

**Istrus/Ister** (late third century B.C.E.): scholar of Athenian antiquities, of whose work seventy-seven fragments remain. He was chiefly concerned with the cult and institutions of Athens in the mythical period, but (as his reference to Xenophon's banishment and recall shows) not exclusively so.

**Julius Caesar** (100–44 B.C.E.): the famous Roman politician and general. He conquered Gaul (modern France) between 58 and 51 and then won the Civil Wars of 49–45 but was assassinated on the Ides of March 44. His narratives of the Gallic Wars (*De Bello Gallico*) in seven books (with an eighth by his subordinate Aulus Hirtius) and of the Civil War (*De Bello Civile*) from 49 to 48 in three books (subsequently continued by others) survive in full.

**Justin/Marcus Junianius Justinus** (second or third century C.E.): Roman historian known mainly through his extant summary (*epitome*) of *Philippic History* (on the foundation and history of the Macedonian empire), composed under Augustus by Pompeius Trogus.

**Lucian** (second century C.E.): satirical writer and wit who came from Samosata on the Euphrates River (as with many others in eastern Turkey, the site has now disappeared under dam waters). He wrote with great accomplishment in the imitation of Classical Greek that was characteristic of his period (the so-called Second Sophistic). Around eighty dialogues and essays attributed to him have survived, generally with a strong comic element in them, and most though not all of these are believed by modern scholars to be genuine.

**Lysias** (459/8?–c. 380 B.C.E.): prolific speechwriter for the Athenian courts in the time of the restored democracy (after 403). He himself was not an Athenian citizen, so virtually all his compositions were written for others to deliver. We are told that ancient critics regarded 233 speeches as correctly attributed to him; of these, twenty-nine have survived in full, twenty-eight written for courtroom delivery and one display oration. We also have substantial extracts from five more, plus over three hundred quotations from over one hundred further speeches. He was remarkable for the lucidity of his style and for his skill in narrative.

**Marcellinus** (sixth century C.E.): scholar who gave the final form to a life of *Thucydides assembled from several earlier elements.

**Oxyrhynchus Historian/"P":** see *Hellenica Oxyrhynchia*

***Palatine Anthology*** (*Anthologia Palatina*): collection of epigrams of the period 100 B.C.E.–c. 560 C.E., made around 940 C.E. by expansion of an earlier collection. It contains around 3,700 short poems.

**Pausanias** (c. 110–after 180 C.E.): Greek author from Lydia who wrote a *Periegesis* (*Description* or *Tour*) of Greece in ten books, probably between 165 and 180 C.E. This gave exhaustive coverage of Greek cities and villages in Attica, the Peloponnese, and other areas south of Thermopylae, with their surviving monuments (especially those from the Archaic and Classical periods), and was the product of Pausanias' extensive travels in the area. His recording of inscriptions and description of sites and monuments have been largely verified by modern archaeology: where he adds historical material from literary sources, its accuracy can be more dubious, but it is often still valuable.

**Philostratus** (c. 170–c. 247 C.E.): Athenian author of biographies and various other works. His longest composition was a partly fictional life in eight books of a first-century sage and miracle worker (or charlatan) called Apollonius of Tyana; he also wrote *Lives of the Sophists* in two books, covering fifty-nine philosophers and litterateurs. The great majority of these come from the first and second century C.E. and form what is known to modern scholars as the Second Sophistic, after a phrase used by Philostratus. But the work also includes some lives of early sophists; in that of *Prodicus, there is a reference to Xenophon attending his lectures.

**Photius** (c. 810–c. 893 C.E.): eminent scholar in the time of the Byzantine Empire and twice patriarch of Constantinople (858–867 C.E., 878–886 C.E.). He played an active and unscrupulous part in court politics and ecclesiastical affairs. At the same time, he was the most learned man of his day, a time that saw a major revival of learning. His principal extant work, the *Bibliotheke* or *Library*, consists of a summary, with sometimes acute critical comments, of 279 books that he had read, about half of which have since been lost. In many cases Photius' account is therefore the best or sole source for these works. One of them is the *Persika* of *Ctesias. Extracts covering Cyrus' rebellion are translated in Appendix U: Selections from Photius' Synopsis of Ctesias' *Persika*.

**Plato** (427–347 B.C.E.): Athenian philosopher, a pupil of Socrates. Plato's dialogues, along with Xenophon's *Memorabilia* (*Recollections of Socrates*) are our chief source for Socrates' ideas and methods, since he wrote nothing himself. However, it is highly controversial to what extent they reflect his true views rather than Plato's own theories building on Socratic foundations. All Plato's published compositions have survived, the principal ones being thirty-four dialogues (a few of which some scholars doubt are genuine). The dialogues vary in length from a few pages to the ten books of *Republic* and the twelve books of *Laws*, his last and longest work. Socrates is the principal character in most of these; Plato himself never appears.

**Pliny the Elder** (23/4–79 C.E.): Latin author of the encylopedic *Natural History* in thirty-seven books, which survives in full. He died during the eruption of Mount Vesuvius that destroyed Pompeii, as a consequence of approaching too closely in order to observe the phenomenon better.

**Plutarch** of Chaeronea (c. 45–shortly after 120 C.E.): biographer and author of many works on popular philosophy and other topics. Some 128 survive—and this represents only about half his total output. Seventy-eight of them, on various topics, are often referred to collectively as *Moralia* (about two-thirds of the *Moralia* have perished). But his crowning achievement was his forty-eight "parallel lives" of eminent Greek and Roman generals and statesmen, of which forty-six survive. Four other "lives" have also been transmitted to us, one of which is his *Life of Artaxerxes*. Extracts related to *Anabasis* are translated in Appendix T: Selections from Plutarch's *Life of Artaxerxes*. Plutarch was writing biography, designed to bring out character, rather than a comprehensive history of the times he covered. Nevertheless, he read very widely, sought to avoid error, and applied intelligence to his sources, which he frequently identifies for us, as he does in the *Life of Artaxerxes*.

**Polyaenus** (late second century C.E.): Macedonian author of eight books of *Stratagems*—a collection of military maxims and ingenious tactical devices, employed mostly by historical Greek commanders—which survive in full.

**Polybius** (c. 200–c. 118 B.C.E.): Greek statesman and author of a forty-book history describing and seeking to explain Rome's swift rise to dominance of virtually the whole world as Polybius knew it. The work was centered on the period from 220 to 167, but the first two books deal with events prior to 220 and books 30–39 continue the narrative to 145, just as Rome completed its conquest of Greece. Only the first five books survive in full, but at least some fragments, often very extensive ones, remain from thirty-three of the other thirty-five books.

514

**Prodicus** of Keos (late fifth century B.C.E.): philosopher. No complete works of his survive, and virtually no direct quotations, but Xenophon's *Memorabilia* provides a long paraphrase of Prodicus' story about Herakles' choice between Virtue and Vice, and a fair amount can be reconstructed about him from *Plato's dialogues and other sources. The most recent edition of what is extant of Prodicus' works includes and discusses ninety citations or fragments.

**Ptolemy** (367/6–283/2 B.C.E.): Macedonian general, ruler of Egypt from 323 (styled king from 306/305 and crowned as successor to the pharaohs in 304). He was the founder of the Ptolemaic dynasty, which ruled Egypt down to Cleopatra in 30. He also wrote a detailed account of Alexander's campaigns, which, while it does not itself survive, was one of the two main sources for *Arrian's *Anabasis Alexandrou.*

**Quintilian/Marcus Fabius Quintilianus** (late first-century C.E.): advocate in the Roman courts and teacher of rhetoric in Rome. His surviving work, written under the emperor Domitian (81–96 C.E.), is *Institutio Oratoria* (*Training in Oratory*) in twelve books, which survives complete. It ranges from the education of infants and adolescents through technical rhetorical precepts to discussion of past exemplars to study.

**Seneca the Elder/Lucius Annaeus Seneca** (c. 50 B.C.E.–c. 40 C.E.): writer in Latin on declamation, a method of training public speakers through the composition and delivery of rhetorical exercises. Five of the ten books of his *Controversiae* (speeches in fictitious lawsuits) survive, along with one book of his *Suasoriae* (deliberative speeches). There is also an abridgment covering much of what otherwise has been lost. His work consists partly of extracts from various speakers and partly of commentary on them, with incidental anecdotes. In the course of this, genuine historical information is sometimes included—for example, to set the scene for the fictitious speech.

**Sophainetos** of Stymphalos: a general in Cyrus the Younger's army. *Stephanus of Byzantium cites four very short fragments from what he claims is Sophainetos' account of the expedition of the Ten Thousand. Many modern scholars regard this as a later fabrication, probably as a literary exercise. For discussion of his authorship, see Appendix M: Other Ancient Sources on the Ten Thousand; for more on the man, see Appendix W: Brief Biographies of Selected Characters in *Anabasis.*

**Stephanus of Byzantium** (sixth century C.E.): lexicographer. His work *Ethnika*, on the names of places and peoples, comprised as many as sixty books. It survives only in summaries, which, while providing extensive lists of names and citations, omit most of Stephanus' comments.

**Stesimbrotus** of Thasos (late fifth century B.C.E.): biographer of the Athenian politicians Themistocles, Pericles, and his rival Thucydides son of Melesias (not to be confused with the historian *Thucydides). His work survives only in a few brief fragments.

**Strabo** (64? B.C.E.–24 C.E.): Greek geographer from Amaseia, in Pontus. He was the author of *Geographia* in seventeen books, which has survived almost in full. After an initial section giving theoretical perspectives on geography, it consists of a virtual tour through more or less all the world as the Greeks and Romans knew it, with descriptions of many locations (often derived from earlier authors and representing previous conditions). Considerable amounts of valuable historical information are included on the way.

**Suetonius/Gaius Suetonius Tranquillus** (c. 70–early 130s? C.E.): Roman biographer, man of letters, and senior imperial administrator. His *De Vita Caesarum* (*Lives of the Caesars*), almost all of which survives, consists of twelve fairly short biographies covering *Julius Caesar and the eleven emperors from *Augustus Caesar to Domitian. Though each life has at least some chronological elements, for most, the material is mainly arranged by topic rather than date, like the second half of Xenophon's *Agesilaos*. A substantial number of lives from Suetonius' *De Viris Illustribus* (*On Famous Men*) also survive—in particular those of teachers of grammar and rhetoric and good extracts from those of poets—but these are much briefer. Titles are known of many other biographic, antiquarian, and miscellaneous works. His lives are anecdotal and often scurrilous, but recent work has emphasized his scholarship.

**Theopompus** of Chios (fourth-century B.C.E.): historian. He was extremely prolific: his principal works were the twelve-book *Hellenika* (a history of Greece from 411 to 394) and the fifty-eight-book *Philippika*. The core of the latter was an account of Philip of Macedon's rise to power over Greece in the mid-fourth century, but it contained very extensive material on other aspects of fourth-century history as well. These works, and some more minor ones, are generally agreed to have been lost except for about four hundred short fragments, though some scholars believe that part of *Hellenika* survives in the form of the *Hellenica Oxyrhnchia*. For discussion of what he may have said about Cyrus' expedition and its aftermath, see Appendix M: Other Ancient Sources on the Ten Thousand.

**Thucydides** (late 450s–390s B.C.E.): Athenian general and historian. The eight books of his history of the Peloponnesian War between Athens and Sparta survive in full, though he did not live to complete the work.

**Timon** of Phleious (c. 320–230 B.C.E.): philosopher. His most important work was the *Silloi*, three books of lampoons written in hexameter verse ridiculing all philosophers (including Xenophon) except for the skeptic Pyrrhos. Only fragments survive.

**Vitruvius** (first century B.C.E.): Roman architect and military engineer, author of *On Architecture* in ten books, all of which survive. This goes well beyond building construction methods and aesthetics to encompass, for example, measuring things more generally, geometry, and astronomy.

# GLOSSARY

## David Thomas

**Achaemenids:** the dynasty of Persian kings that ruled Iran, Mesopotamia, Syria, almost all of Anatolia, and sometimes Egypt from Darius I (r. 522–486) to Darius III in the 330s, named after a possibly fictitious royal ancestor of Darius I's, Achaemenes. This was also the name of the clan from which all Persian kings came, including Cyrus the Great (559–530) and his predecessors, so the term is often applied to the whole period of the Persian Empire, starting with Cyrus.

**acropolis:** the citadel or high point of a city. Often it was the site of the original settlement; in historical times it was well stocked with temples and other sacred sites and often enclosed by its own set of defensive walls within the walls of the city.

**apologia:** a defense of one's actions or conduct.

**archon** (literally, "ruler"): a title for one of the most important offices in ancient Greek city-states. In Classical Athens there were ten archons, serving for a year at a time; after 487/6 the final choice was made by lottery, and by Xenophon's time the archons' functions were confined to religious and judicial matters. Each civil year was named after the person chosen to be the so-called eponymous archon.

**blood sacrifice** (*sphagia*): a sacrifice in which omens were derived not (as usual) from examining the victim's entrails but from observing the flow of blood from the knife wound to the throat by which the victim was killed. As this was a much quicker business than the full campground sacrifice (*hiera*) and did not involve setting up an altar, it was used for the standard sacrifice just before battle was joined; but it could also be used on other occasions when an emergency procedure was justified. See Figure 6.5.2 and Appendix G: Divinity and Divining, §§2, 9.

**deme:** a village, township, or urban or rural district, especially in Attica (the home territory of Athens). Attica was divided into 139 demes of widely varying sizes; they played a vital role in the operation of the Athenian constitution in the fifth and fourth centuries, since representation within the Athenian Council of Five Hundred was based on the demes as units, with the number of representatives varying according to the size of each deme.

**emmer** (Greek *zeia*): a hulled wheat, so called because the kernel is enclosed in the hull, unlike almost all modern wheats where it pushes out of the hull, making their separation easier. It is still grown to some extent in mountainous areas of Europe and as a specialty produce in the US.

NOTE:  For units of measurements of distance, currency, weight, and capacity, see Appendix O: Ancient Greek and Persian Units of Measurement.

**ephor** ("overseer" or "superintendent"): member of a board of annually elected Spartan officials with high executive authority. They were superior for their year of office even to the two Spartan kings (except that they could not give direct orders on the conduct of a campaign to the king at the head of the army when abroad). One of the ephors gave his name to the year in which he was in office, and the assembly of Spartan citizens was presided over by an ephor. See Appendix B: Xenophon and Sparta, §16.

**guest-friend** (*xenos*): a man with whom a Greek from a different *polis* or country had gone through a ritual involving a formal declaration, sealed by a handshake, that created long-term obligations of mutual hospitality and expectations of assistance between them. It was possible to be a foreigner's friend (*philos*) without necessarily being his guest-friend, the latter being a stronger relationship (at least in principle).

Two guest-friends did not necessarily have a personal emotional bond with one another, if only because the relationship was often carried forward between families for generations. It seems unlikely that all four of the generals whom Xenophon says were Cyrus' guest-friends (1.1.10, 1.1.11) were more than acquaintances on good terms with him; the relationship was doubtless primarily based on mutual self-interest. Similarly, Biton and Naukleidas, the two emissaries sent by the Spartan commander Thibron to see Xenophon after he had brought the army from Thrace to Asia, became Xenophon's guest-friends on the day they met him (7.8.6), primarily for political reasons, though the effect was to add their personal assurances of his safety to those they must have brought from Thibron. On the other hand, in at least two cases people seem to have become Xenophon's guest-friends in order to institutionalize and make permanent the personal friendship they and Xenophon had formed, namely Proxenos (3.1.4, 5.3.5), the general who invited Xenophon to join him in Cyrus' army, and Kleandros (6.6.35), the Spartan harmost whom Xenophon met on the Black Sea coast.

Related to *xenos* is *xenia* (tokens of hospitality), diplomatic gifts that were intended to show the friendship of the city or tribe making them and acceptance of which implied that the recipients would likewise treat the donors as friends. Another related word is *proxenos*.

Guest-friendships with foreigners played an important part in the culture of the groups with the highest status in Archaic and Classical Greece and are an important feature of *Anabasis*. Xenophon also explores several similar, though weaker, relationships of trust and fidelity, such as the one that should have been formed between Klearchos and Tissaphernes by eating at the same table, which the senior Greek officer Kleanor says (3.2.4) it was an offense against Zeus Xenios for Tissaphernes to break, and also the *philia* ("simple" friendship) with Xenophon that the Thracian princeling Seuthes abused (7.6.20–22). Related to this theme is the faithfulness that the Armenian village headman's son showed to Pleisthenes of Amphipolis (4.6.3).

**harmost** (*harmostēs*, literally "fixer"): a Spartan official who was posted abroad with the responsibility of sorting out problems in his vicinity. *Harmostēs* is sometimes translated "governor," and generally harmosts were resident in a particular city with command of its garrison; but their role seems not to have been as strictly confined geographically as that may suggest. See Appendix B: Xenophon and Sparta, §15.

**hoplite:** heavy-armed infantryman, often bearing a characteristic round shield, who fought in close formation. See Appendix H: Infantry and Cavalry in *Anabasis*, §§2–3, also Figures 1.2.16 and 5.4.12.

*hybris:* the English word "hubris," derived from the Greek, denotes an attitude of overweening pride and arrogance and is applied particularly to the overconfidence of the tragic hero before disaster strikes him. This is a genuine Greek usage. But at 5.8.1–3 Xenophon uses words from the same stem, also in accordance with normal Greek usage, to refer to willful actions, often involving violence, that are intended to convey contempt for the victim; in Athens *hybris* was a specific category of crime with its own legal form of indictment, and it was a very serious charge because of the need within the democracy to prevent poor free men from being treated like slaves. This Landmark edition translates the word in this passage as "arrogant willfulness." In the same passage, donkeys are stated to be especially prone to *hybris;* this is presumably because they are stubborn and willful animals that can be prone to kick and that, when they show their teeth and bray, could be imagined to be laughing at those around them.

*hyparchos:* as the term is used by most classical authors, including Xenophon, a subordinate administrator within the Persian Empire, either a lieutenant governor of a territory (as with Tiribazos at 4.4.4) or a senior member of staff (as at 1.2.20). However, in Herodotus it refers to officials who are clearly subordinate only to the Great King himself, people whom other authors such as Xenophon would call satraps.

*kaloi kagathoi* ("good and honorable people"): a phrase with both moral and class overtones in Classical Greek, like "gentleman" in Victorian English; it depends on the context which sound louder. At 2.6.19 Proxenos' relationship with his officers is compared with his relationship with his ordinary soldiers, and here the class overtones predominate; but at 2.6.20 his true friends (such as Xenophon) are compared with those who manipulated him, among whom Xenophon is obviously thinking especially of Proxenos' fellow general Menon, and here the moral overtones come to the fore. *Kaloi kagathoi*'s moral overtones can refer in suitable contexts especially to military virtues, and then the class overtones can be virtually absent, as at 4.1.19.

*karanos:* this word occurs in Xenophon's description of Cyrus the Younger's status in western Anatolia around 407 at *Hellenika* 1.4.3, where he is said to be *karanos* of all those who muster at Kastolos. The expression, evidently Persian in origin, is there glossed with a Greek word that means "master of" or "having authority over," while the parallel passages in *Anabasis* (1.1.2, 1.9.7) refer to Cyrus as the "general" of this muster. Very recently a word apparently reflecting the same underlying Persian term has been found in an Aramaic archive from the northeastern province of Bactria (in modern terms, northwest Afghanistan). Scholars disagree about whether the word simply means "general" or, alternatively, signifies someone who had authority over several satrapies (see **satrap**), as Cyrus did. There is also controversy over the degree of permanence of the role of "*karanos* of all those who muster at Kastolos." Amid the uncertainty it is at any rate clear, both from the Xenophon passages and the etymology, that it indicates senior military authority.

**Lacedaemon/Lacedaemonian(s):** the state in occupation of the territory of Laconia, whose chief city was Sparta. The terms Lacedaemon and Sparta are nearly synonymous for most purposes, but strictly speaking, Lacedaemon is a state and territorial designation, and Sparta was the most important city within it. The Spartans monopolized political power within the Lacedaemonian state. See Appendix B: Xenophon and Sparta, §§18–19; also see *perioikoi*.

**millet:** a word used for two types of cereal grass. Foxtail millet (in Greek, *melinē;* in Latin, *panicum*), sometimes called Italian millet, has a seed head that forms a long, compact cluster; in antiquity the seeds were sometimes made into a kind of bread. Proso millet (in Greek, *kegchros;* in Latin, *milium*), a similar cereal grass but thought by the ancients to be more nutritious, has a floppy seed head; the seeds were often made into bread or porridge. They are rarely used for human consumption nowadays.

*nauarchos:* "admiral" in Classical Greek generally, but in Sparta, at any rate from a point in the late fifth century, it specifically referred to the person who was appointed annually as the most senior officer of the fleet. In theory this man could not serve twice, though the Spartans found a way around the law when they wanted to. During the Spartan *nauarchos*' period of office, his role was the naval equivalent of the king's over the land army. See Appendix B: Xenophon and Sparta, §14.

**parasang:** a Persian unit for measuring travel, but it is controversial whether it measures hours spent traveling, distance traveled, or a combination of the two. See the Introduction, §7.3–5, and Appendix O: Ancient Greek and Persian Units of Measurement, §§7–8; for the modern reception of the word, see Appendix R: The Legacy of Xenophon's *Anabasis*, §§15–17.

**peltast:** light-armed infantryman, typically carrying a light, crescent-shaped shield called a *peltē*, though Xenophon sometimes uses the term more generally to cover yet lighter infantry. See Appendix H: Infantry and Cavalry in *Anabasis*, §§4–5, and Figure 7.4.4 (left).

*perioikoi* (literally, "outdwellers"): those Lacedaemonions who were not inhabitants of Sparta, the dominant city in Lacedaemon, but free citizens of the roughly fifty other towns and villages in Laconia and the neighboring territory of Messenia (for distinctions among Lacedaemon, Sparta, and Laconia, see **Lacedaemon/Lacedaemonian[s]**). Each of these towns managed its own municipal affairs but was subordinate to Sparta regarding military matters and external relations. It was nevertheless possible for individual *perioikoi* to be appointed to the command of ships and troops within the Lacedaemonian forces, and not only in the rather special circumstances of the command that was held by the *perioikos* Neon, the lieutenant and successor to the Spartan general Cheirisophos, and aspired to by the *perioikos* Dexippos, whose long-running rivalry with Xenophon is illustrated in *Anabasis*. See Appendix B: Xenophon and Sparta, §18.

**phalanx:** a body of troops (usually but not necessarily hoplites) drawn up in a close formation much broader than it is deep. See Appendix H, Infantry and Cavalry in *Anabasis*, §§13–15.

*polis* (plural, *poleis*): a city-state, the predominant but not exclusive form of state organization in Classical Greece (the Greeks also used the word for non-Greek city-states). The central concept was of a self-governing urban settlement with a rural hinterland of limited extent—a day's journey from the center to any of the borders has been proposed as the practical upper limit for the homeland of a *polis*, though some *poleis* were far smaller than this. The principle of self-government could be weakened in practice through aggrandizement by powerful neighbors, including other city-states, or by more or less voluntary associations with other city-states, but it remained key to the self-image of a *polis* and its citizens. At least a thousand Greek city-states have been identified, over half of them in mainland Greece south of Thessaly, on the Aegean islands, or on the coast of western Anatolia.

*proxenos* (plural, *proxenoi*): a man who, while still residing in the city-state of which he was a citizen (and to which he was expected to have his primary loyalty), was appointed to act in support of the citizens of a particular foreign state in their dealings with the *proxenos*' city. In particular, he looked after them when they visited the city, whether as official envoys or in a purely private capacity. He would entertain prominent visitors from the foreign state, introduce their ambassadors to the authorities of his city, and facilitate the foreign citizens' access to his city's courts. The appointment was almost always made by the foreign state, which granted the status partly as an honorific recognition of individuals for providing support in the past and as an encouragement to them to continue to identify with the interests of that state. Several thousand examples of people appointed to this status by Greek city-states between the late sixth and the first century B.C.E. are known through literary references and especially through inscriptions, and almost certainly the role went even further back into the past.

The two examples of *proxenoi* in *Anabasis* are unusual in that the foreign state is not Greek. In the case of the Trapezountian Timesitheos (5.4.2), it is a non-Greek tribe, the Mossynoeci; in the case of the Sinopean Hekatonymos (5.6.11), it is a non-Greek dynast, Korylas, the ruler of the Paphlagonians. There are a fair number of examples in other sources of non-Greek city-states' appointing a Greek *proxenos* in a Greek city-state, and half a dozen inscriptions record such appointments by non-Greek dynasts. Appointment by a non-Greek tribe seems to be otherwise unknown, and the tone of Xenophon's narrative about the Mossynoeci suggests, though perhaps misleadingly, that they would have lacked the necessary sophistication. However, Herodotus says (6.57.2) that in Sparta the kings chose *proxenoi* from among Spartan citizens, evidently to act for particular foreign cities assigned to them. It therefore cannot be excluded that it was the people of Trapezus, from where the army had just come, who had appointed Timesitheos, in effect as a liaison officer.

A modern office with similarities to the *proxenos* is that of the consul, a resident of a foreign country whom states appoint to assist their people on holiday or on business while in that country. Consuls are normally paid, which the *proxenos* was not; but honorary consuls are often also appointed, though these are sometimes citizens of the appointing country who are resident abroad, which was never true of the *proxenos*. The *proxenos* did not merely give the consular type of assistance, however: as the Greeks did not maintain permanent embassies in foreign states, he was also expected to operate at a political level in support of his sponsoring state and would therefore typically be a prominent politician.

The role of *proxenos* is related to, and doubtless originated from, the status of *xenos* (see **guest-friend**), though being a *xenos* was personal in nature rather than institutional.

**satrap:** in the Persian Empire during this period, the governor of a territory—usually a province or a group of provinces—assigned to him by the Great King of Persia, whose chief representative in the territory he thus became. However, on occasion the title is used for senior administrators who may be reporting to the Great King via a more senior satrap; and at least in works by late Greek authors, it can appear to indicate high status generally rather than territorial responsibilities. The original meaning of the word in Old Persian (*xšaçapāvan-*) was "protector of the realm." See Appendix C: The Persian Empire, §9.

**Sparta/Spartans:** the chief city within the state of Lacedaemon. The Spartans monopolized political power within Lacedaemon, and modern works usually use Sparta and Spartans rather than Lacedaemon and Lacedaemonians to refer to the history and actions of the state. There were several different classes of Spartan, the Spartiates being the group with full political privileges and powers. See Appendix B: Xenophon and Sparta, §§18–19.

**trireme:** a long warship with three banks of oars, the standard vessel of the period for use in battle. The main sea battle technique was to ram the opponent's ship with a bronze ram that was fixed on the prow. In addition to a small crew of officers and sailing experts (sixteen on Athenian triremes), the ship required a large number of rowers—typically 170 on an Athenian vessel. Though the Athenians also customarily supplied a trireme with ten hoplites and four archers, the ship was less suitable for carrying heavy-armed or specialist troops in large numbers; merchant ships, with a rounder shape and deeper draft, were used for this purpose. See Figure 5.8.20; also see Strassler 2009, Appendix K: Trireme Warfare in Xenophon's *Hellenika*.

**trophy** (*tropaion*): a memorial placed by victorious Greeks on the battlefield (or, in the case of naval victories, on a nearby coast) to establish the fact of their control over the area, to commemorate it thereafter, and to thank the gods for granting them the victory. The trophy would consist of a helmet, a shield, and other captured pieces of armor nailed to a tree or post. Because it was regarded as sacred, the defeated enemy, if they were Greeks, would not remove it even if they regained control of the place where it was located.

# SELECTED BIBLIOGRAPHY

FOR THE GENERAL READER OF *ANABASIS*

Akurgal, Ekrem. 1983. *Ancient Civilizations and Ruins of Turkey: From Prehistoric Times until the End of the Roman Empire.* Translated by John Whybrow and Mollie Emre. 5th ed. Istanbul: Haşet Kitabevi. Reprint, London: Routledge Kegan Paul, 2002.

Anderson, J. K. 1974. *Xenophon.* London: Duckworth.

Brennan, Shane. 2005. *In the Tracks of the Ten Thousand: A Journey on Foot through Turkey, Syria and Iraq.* London: Robert Hale.

Briant, Pierre. 2002. *From Cyrus to Alexander: A History of the Persian Empire.* Translated by Peter Daniels. Winona Lake, IN: Eisenbrauns.

Calvino, Italo. 1999. "Xenophon's *Anabasis.*" In *Why Read the Classics?*, translated by Martin L. McLaughlin, 19–23. New York: Pantheon Books.

Cartledge, Paul. 1987. *Agesilaos and the Crisis of Sparta.* London: Duckworth.

Casson, Lionel. 1974. *Travel in the Ancient World.* London: Allen and Unwin. 2nd ed.: Johns Hopkins University Press (Baltimore and London, 1994).

Cawkwell, George. 1972. Introduction to *Xenophon: The Persian Expedition*, translated by Rex Warner, 2nd ed., 9–48. Harmondsworth, UK: Penguin Books.

Dillery, John. 1995. *Xenophon and the History of His Times.* London and New York: Routledge.

Flower, Michael A. 2008. *The Seer in Ancient Greece.* Berkeley and Los Angeles: University of California Press.

———. 2012. *Xenophon's* Anabasis, *or* The Expedition of Cyrus. New York: Oxford University Press.

———, ed. 2017. *The Cambridge Companion to Xenophon.* Cambridge: Cambridge University Press.

Hall, Jonathan M. 2002. *Hellenicity: Between Ethnicity and Culture.* Chicago: University of Chicago Press.

Higgins, W. E. 1977. *Xenophon the Athenian: The Problem of the Individual and the Society of the Polis.* Albany, NY: SUNY Press.

Kuhrt, Amélie. 2007. *The Persian Empire: A Corpus of Sources from the Achaemenid Period.* London and New York: Routledge.

Lane Fox, Robin, ed. 2004. *The Long March: Xenophon and the Ten Thousand.* New Haven, CT, and London: Yale University Press.

Lee, John W. I. 2007. *A Greek Army on the March: Soldiers and Survival in Xenophon's* Anabasis. Cambridge: Cambridge University Press.

Morrison, Donald R., ed. 2011. *The Cambridge Companion to Socrates*. Cambridge: Cambridge University Press.

Rood, Tim. 2004. *The Sea! The Sea! The Shout of the Ten Thousand in the Modern Imagination*. London and New York: Duckworth Overlook.

Strassler, Robert B., ed. 1996. *The Landmark Thucydides: A Comprehensive Guide to the Peloponnesian War*. Translated by Richard Crawley. New York: Free Press.

———— 2007. *The Landmark Herodotus: The* Histories. Translated by Andrea L. Purvis. New York: Pantheon Books.

———— 2009. *The Landmark Xenophon's* Hellenika. Translated by John Marincola. New York: Pantheon Books.

Strauss, Barry S. 1986. *Athens after the Peloponnesian War: Class, Faction and Policy 403–386 BC*. London and Sydney: Croom Helm.

Talbert, Richard J. A., ed. 2000. *Barrington Atlas of the Greek and Roman World*. Princeton, NJ, and Oxford, UK: Princeton University Press.

Thomas, David. 2009. Introduction to Strassler 2009.

Trundle, Matthew. 2004. *Greek Mercenaries: From the Late Archaic Period to Alexander*. London and New York: Routledge.

Van Wees, Hans. 2004. *Greek Warfare: Myths and Realities*. London: Duckworth.

Waterfield, Robin. 2006. *Xenophon's Retreat: Greece, Persia, and the End of the Golden Age*. London: Faber and Faber.

————. 2009. *Why Socrates Died: Dispelling the Myths*. London: Faber and Faber.

Wiesehöfer, Josef. 2001. *Ancient Persia: from 550 BC to 650 AD*. Translated by Azizeh Azodi. 2nd ed. London: I.B. Tauris.


## SPECIALIZED BOOKS, JOURNALS, AND ARTICLES

Ainsworth, W. F. 1854. "A Geographical Commentary on the *Anabasis* of Xenophon." In *Xenophon: The* Anabasis, *or* Expedition of Cyrus, *and the* Memorabilia *of Socrates*, translated by Rev. J. S. Watson, 263–338. London: H. G. Bohn.

Andrae, Walter. 1938. *Das wiedererstandene Assur*. Leipzig: J. C. Hinrichs. Reprint, Munich: C. H. Beck, 1977.

Andrianou, Dimitra. 2009. *The Furniture and Furnishings of Ancient Greek Houses and Tombs*. Cambridge: Cambridge University Press.

Archibald, Zalina H. 1998. *The Odrysian Kingdom of Thrace: Orpheus Unmasked*. Oxford: Clarendon Press.

Badian, E. 2004. "Xenophon the Athenian." In *Xenophon and His World: Papers from a Conference Held in Liverpool in July 1999*, edited by Christopher Tuplin, 33–53. Stuttgart: Franz Steiner Verlag (Historia Einzelschriften 172).

Barker, Andrew. "The Innovations of Lysander the Kitharist." *The Classical Quarterly* 32, no. 2 (1982): 266–69.

Bigwood, J. M. "The Ancient Accounts of the Battle of Cunaxa." *The American Journal of Philology* 104, no. 4 (1983): 340–57.

Bivar, A. D. H. 1985. "Achaemenid Coins, Weights and Measures." In *The Cambridge History of Iran*, vol. 2, *The Median and Achaemenian Periods*, edited by Ilya Gershevitch, 610–39. Cambridge: Cambridge University Press.

Bosworth, A. B. 1996. *Alexander and the East: The Tragedy of Triumph*. Oxford: Clarendon Press.

Bradley, P. J. 2001. "Irony and the Narrator in Xenophon's *Anabasis*." In *Essays in Honour of Gor-*

*don Williams*, edited by E. I. Tylawksy and C. G. Weiss, 59–84. New Haven, CT: Henry R. Schwab. Reprinted in Gray 2010, 520–552.

———. 2011. "Xenophon's *Anabasis:* Reading the End with Zeus the Merciful." *Arethusa* 44, no. 3 (Fall): 279–310.

Breitenbach, H. R. 1967. "Xenophon (6): Xenophon von Athen." In *Paulys Real-Encyclopädie der klassischen Altertumswissenschaft*. Vol. 9 A2, edited by Georg Wissowa, Wilhelm Kroll, Karl Mittelhaus, 1567–1928, 1981/2–2051, 2502. Stuttgart: Alfred Druckenmüller Verlag.

Brennan, Shane. 2008. "Chronological Pointers in Xenophon's *Anabasis*." *Bulletin of the Institute of Classical Studies* 51, no. 1 (December): 51–61.

———. 2016. "Did the Mossynoikoi Whistle? A Consideration of the Distance between *Poleis* in the Black Sea Mountains Given at *Anabasis* 5.4.31." *Greece & Rome* 63, no. 1 (April): 91–105.

———. 2022, *forthcoming. Xenophon's* Anabasis*: A Socratic History*. Edinburgh: Edinburgh University Press.

Briant, Pierre, ed. 1995. *Dans les pas des Dix-Mille: Peuples et pays de Proche-Orient vus par un Grec*. Toulouse: Presses Universitaires du Mirail (Pallas 43). Reviewed in Tuplin 1999.

Brown, Truesdell S. 1986. "Menon of Thessaly." *Historia* 35, no. 4: 387–404.

Bunbury, E. H. 1879. *A History of Ancient Geography among the Greeks and Romans from the Earliest Ages till the Fall of the Roman Empire*. 2 vols. London: John Murray.

Buzzetti, Eric. 2008. Introduction to *Xenophon: The Anabasis of Cyrus*, translated and annotated by Wayne Ambler, 1–35. Ithaca, NY: Cornell University Press.

Castiglioni, Luigi. 1932. "Studi intorno alla storia del testo dell' *Anabasi* di Senofonte." *Memorie del Reale Istituto lombardo di scienze e lettere: Classe di lettere, scienze morali e storiche* 24 (15 of Series 3), Fasciculo 3: 109–54.

———. 1933. Untitled review of two editions of *Anabasis:* Masqueray 1930/31 and Hude 1931. *Gnomon* 9, no. 12 (December): 638–648.

Comfort, Anthony, and Rifat Ergeç. 2001. "Following the Euphrates in Antiquity: North–South Routes around Zeugma." *Anatolian Studies* 51: 19–49.

Cousin, Georges. 1905. *Kyros le jeune en Asie Mineure (Printemps 408–Juillet 401 avant Jésus-Christ)*. Paris and Nancy: Imprimerie Berger-Levrault & Compagnie.

Curzon, Robert. 1854. *Armenia: A Year at Erzeroom and on the Frontiers of Russia, Turkey, and Persia*. London: John Murray.

Dalley, Stephanie. 2013. *The Mystery of the Hanging Gardens of Babylon: An Elusive World Wonder Traced*. Oxford: Oxford University Press.

Danzig, Gabriel. 2007. "Xenophon's Wicked Persian, or What's Wrong with Tissaphernes? Xenophon's Views on Lying and Breaking Oaths." In *Persian Responses: Political and Cultural Interaction with(in) the Achaemenid Empire*, edited by Christopher Tuplin, 27–50. Swansea: Classical Press of Wales.

Ehrhardt, C. T. H. R. 1994. "Two Notes on Xenophon's *Anabasis*." *Ancient History Bulletin* 8, no. 1 (January–March): 1–4.

Erbse, Hartmut. 1960. "Textkritische Bemerkungen zu Xenophon." *Rheinisches Museum für Philologie* 103, no. 2: 144–68.

———. 1966. "Xenophons *Anabasis*." *Gymnasium* 73: 485–505. Translated into English as "Xenophon's *Anabasis*" in Gray 2010, 476–501.

Flower, Michael A. 2000. "From Simonides to Isocrates: The Fifth-Century Origins of Fourth-Century Panhellenism." *Classical Antiquity* 19, no. 1 (April): 65–101.

Gassner, Gustav. 1953. "Der Zug der Zehntausend nach Trapezunt." *Abhandlungen der Braunschweigischen Wissentschaftlischen Gesellschaft* 5: 1–35.

Gautier, Léopold. 1911. *La langue de Xénophon*. Geneva: Georg & Co.

Gawlikowski, Michal. 1996. "Thapsacus and Zeugma: The Crossing of the Euphrates in Antiquity." *Iraq* 58: 123–33.

Głombiowksi, Krzysztof. 1994. "The Campaign of Cyrus the Younger and the Retreat of the Ten Thousand: The Chronology." *Pomoerium* 1: 37–44.

Graf, David F. 1994. "The Persian Royal Road System." In *Achaemenid History 8: Continuity and Change: Proceedings of the Last Achaemenid History Workshop April 6–8, 1990—Ann Arbor, Michigan*, edited by Heleen Sancisi-Weerdenburg, Amélie Kuhrt, and Margaret Cool Root, 167–89. Leiden: Nederlands Instituut voor het Nabije Oosten.

Gray, Vivienne J., ed. 2010. *Oxford Readings in Classical Studies: Xenophon*. Oxford and New York: Oxford University Press.

———. 2011. *Xenophon's Mirror of Princes: Reading the Reflections*. Oxford: Oxford University Press.

Green, P. M. 1994. "Text and Context in the Matter of Xenophon's Exile." In *Ventures into Greek History*, edited by Ian Worthington, 215–27. Oxford: Clarendon Press. Reprinted in Peter Green, *From Ikaria to the Stars: Classical Mythification, Ancient and Modern* (Austin: University of Texas Press, 2004), 133–43.

Hamilton, William J. 1842. *Researches in Asia Minor, Pontus and Armenia: With Some Account of Their Antiquities and Geology*. 2 vols. London: John Murray. Reprint, Cambridge: Cambridge University Press, 2012.

Harman, Rosie. 2016. "Colonisation, Nostos and the Foreign Environment in Xenophon's *Anabasis*." In *The Routledge Handbook of Identity and the Environment in the Classical and Medieval Worlds*, edited by Rebecca Futo Kennedy and Molly Jones-Lewis, 133–50. London: Routledge.

Herman, Gabriel. 1987. *Ritualized Friendship and the Greek City*. Cambridge: Cambridge University Press.

Hirsch, Steven W. 1985. *The Friendship of the Barbarians: Xenophon and the Persian Empire*. Hanover, NH, and London: University Press of New England.

Hobden, Fiona, and Christopher Tuplin, eds. 2012. *Xenophon: Ethical Principles and Historical Enquiry*. Leiden: Brill (Mnemosyne Supplementary Volume 348).

Hornblower, Simon. 2000. "Sticks, Stones, and Spartans: The Sociology of Spartan Violence." In *War and Violence in Ancient Greece*, edited by Hans van Wees, 57–82. London: Duckworth and the Classical Press of Wales.

Humble, Noreen M. 1997. *Xenophon's View of Sparta: A Study of the* Anabasis, Hellenica *and* Respublica Lacedaemoniorum. Dissertation, McMaster.

Hyland, John. 2010. "The Desertion of Nicarchus the Arcadian in Xenophon's *Anabasis*." *Phoenix* 64, no. 3/4 (Fall/Winter): 238–53.

Keaveney, Arthur. 2012. "The Trial of Orontas: Xenophon, *Anabasis* I, 6." *L'Antiquité Classique* 81: 31–41.

King, Tricia. 1988. "How Many Parasangs to Babylon?" *Journal of the Ancient Chronology Forum* 2: 69–78.

Kinneir, John Macdonald. 1818. *Journey through Asia Minor, Armenia and Koordistan in the Years 1813 and 1814: With Remarks on the Marches of Alexander and Retreat of the Ten Thousand*. London: John Murray. Reprint, London: British Library, 2011.

Krasilnikoff, Jens A. 1993. "The Regular Payment of Aegean Mercenaries in the Classical Period." *Classica et Mediaevalia* 44: 77–95.

Layard, Austen H. 1853. *Discoveries among the Ruins of Nineveh and Babylon; With Travels in Armenia, Kurdistan and the Desert: Being the Result of a Second Expedition Undertaken for the Trustees of the British Museum*. New York: G. P. Putnam & Co.

Lewis, D. M., John Boardman, Simon Hornblower, and M. Ostwald, eds. 1994. *The Cambridge Ancient History*, vol. 6, *The Fourth Century B.C.* 2nd ed. Cambridge: Cambridge University Press.

Loomis, William T. 1998. *Wages, Welfare Costs and Inflation in Classical Athens*. Ann Arbor: University of Michigan Press.

Löwith, Karl. 1949. *Meaning in History: The Theological Implications of the Philosophy of History.* Chicago: University of Chicago Press.

MacLaren, Malcolm, Jr. 1934. "Xenophon and Themistogenes." *Transactions and Proceedings of the American Philological Association* 65: 240–47.

Mack, William. 2015. *Proxeny and Polis: Institutional Networks in the Ancient Greek World.* Oxford: Oxford University Press.

Manfredi, Valerio. 1986. *La strada dei diecimila: Topografia e geografia dell' Oriente di Senofonte.* Milan: Jaca Book.

Mayor, Adrienne. 1995. "Mad Honey!" *Archaeology* 48, no. 6: 32–40.

McCloskey, B. 2017. "Xenophon the Philosopher: *E Pluribus Plura.*" *American Journal of Philology* 138, no. 4 (January): 605–40.

Millender, Ellen. 2012. "Spartan 'Friendship' and Xenophon's Crafting of the *Anabasis.*" In *Xenophon: Ethical Principles and Historical Enquiry*, edited by Fiona Hobden and Christopher Tuplin, 377–426. Leiden: Brill (Mnemosyne Supplementary Volume 348).

Mitchell, Lynette. 2007. *Panhellenism and the Barbarian in Archaic and Classical Greece.* Swansea: Classical Press of Wales.

Mitford, Tim. 2000. "Thalatta, Thalatta: Xenophon's View of the Black Sea." *Anatolian Studies* 50: 127–31.

O'Connor, Stephen. 2016. "The *agoranomoi* at Cotyora (Xen. *An.* 5.7.21–9): Cerasuntians or Cyreans?" *The Classical Quarterly* 66, no. 1 (May): 84–99.

Pernot, Laurent. 2014. "La réception antique de Xénophon: Quel modèle pour quels orateurs?" In *Xénophon et la Rhétorique*, edited by Pierre Pontier, 281–94. Paris: Presses de l'Université Paris-Sorbonne.

Powell, Anton, and Nicolas Richer, eds. 2020. *Xenophon and Sparta.* Swansea: Classical Press of Wales.

Pritchett, W. Kendrick, and Anne Pippin. 1956. "The Attic Stelai: Part II." *Hesperia* 25, no. 3 (July–September): 178–328.

Purves, Alex C. 2010. *Space and Time in Ancient Greek Narrative.* Cambridge and New York: Cambridge University Press.

Reade, Julian Edgeworth. 2015. "Xenophon's Journey through Babylonia and Assyria." *Iraq* 77: 173–202.

Romano, David Gilman. 1993. *Athletics and Mathematics in Archaic Corinth: The Origins of the Greek Stadion.* Philadelphia: American Philosophical Society.

Romm, James, ed. 2010. *The Landmark Arrian: The Campaigns of Alexander.* Translated by Pamela Mensch. New York: Pantheon Books.

Rood, Tim. 2010a. *American Anabasis: Xenophon and the Idea of America from the Mexican War to Iraq.* London and New York: Duckworth Overlook.

———. 2010b. "Xenophon's Parasangs." *Journal of Hellenic Studies* 130: 51–66.

———. 2014. "Space and Landscape in Xenophon's *Anabasis.*" In *Space, Place and Landscape in Ancient Greek Literature and Culture*, edited by Kate Gilhuly and Nancy Worman, 63–93. Cambridge: Cambridge University Press.

Ross Murray, Steven, William A. Sands, and Douglas A. O'Roark. 2011. "Throwing the Ancient Greek Dory: How Effective is the Attached *Ankyle* at Increasing the Distance of the Throw?" *Palamedes. A Journal of Ancient History* 6: 137–151.

Roy, J. 1967. "The Mercenaries of Cyrus." *Historia* 16, no. 3 (July): 287–323.

———. 1968. "Xenophon's Evidence for the *Anabasis.*" *Athenaeum* 46: 37–46.

Sekunda, N. V. 1998. "Itabelis and the Satrapy of Mysia." *American Journal of Ancient History* 14, no. 1: 73–102.

Stolper, Matthew W. 1987. "Belšunu the Satrap." In *Language, Literature and History: Philological and Historical Studies Presented to Erica Reiner*, edited by Francesca Rochberg-Halton, 389–402. New Haven, CT: American Oriental Society.

Tamiolaki, Melina. 2012. "Virtue and Leadership in Xenophon: Ideal Leaders or Ideal Losers?" In

*Xenophon: Ethical Principles and Historical Enquiry*, edited by Fiona Hobden and Christopher Tuplin, 563–89. Leiden: Brill (Mnemosyne Supplementary Volume 348).

Tuplin, Christopher. 1987. "Xenophon's Exile Again." In *Homo Viator: Classical Essays for John Bramble*, edited by Michael Whitby, Philip Hardie, and Mary Whitby, 251–81. Bristol, UK: Bristol Classical Press.

———. 1997. "Achaemenid Arithmetic: Numerical Problems in Persian History." *Topoi* Supplément 1: 365–421.

———. 1998. "The Seasonal Migration of Achaemenid Kings: A Report on Old and New Evidence." In *Studies in Persian History: Essays in Memory of David M. Lewis* (*Achaemenid History* XI), edited by Maria Brosius and Amélie Kuhrt, 63–114. Leiden: Nederlands Instituut voor het Nabije Oosten.

———. 1999. "On the Track of the Ten Thousand." Review of Briant 1995. *Revue des Études Anciennes* 101, nos. 3–4: 331–66.

———. 2003. "Xenophon in Media." In *Continuity of Empire (?): Assyria, Media, Persia*, edited by Giovanni B. Lanfranchi, Michael Roaf, and Robert Rollinger, 351–89. Padua, Italy: S.a.r.g.o.n. Editrice e Libreria.

———, ed. 2004. *Xenophon and His World: Papers from a Conference Held in Liverpool in July 1999*. Stuttgart: Franz Steiner Verlag (Historia Einzelschriften 172).

———. 2007. "Treacherous Hearts and Upright Tiaras: The Achaemenid King's Head-dress." In *Persian Responses: Political and Cultural Interaction with(in) the Achaemenid Empire*, edited by Christopher Tuplin, 67–97. Swansea: Classical Press of Wales.

———. 2010a. "All the King's Horse: In Search of Achaemenid Persian Cavalry." In *New Perspectives on Ancient Warfare*, edited by Garrett G. Fagan and Matthew Trundle, 101–82. Leiden: Brill.

———. 2010b. "All the King's Men." In *The World of Achaemenid Persia: History, Art and Society in Iran and the Ancient Near East*, edited by John Curtis and St. John Simpson, 51–61. London and New York: I.B. Tauris.

Tuplin, C. J., and J. Ma, eds. 2020. *Aršāma and His World: The Bodleian Letters in Context*. Oxford: Oxford University Press.

Valeva, Julia, Emil Nankov, and Denver Graninger, eds. 2015. *A Companion to Ancient Thrace*. Malden, MA, and Chichester, UK: Wiley-Blackwell.

Vlastos, Gregory. 1991. *Socrates, Ironist and Moral Philosopher*. Cambridge: Cambridge University Press.

Wheeler, Everett L. 2007. "Herodotus and the Black Sea Region" (Appendix E), "Rivers and Peoples of Scythia" (Appendix F), and "The Continuity of Steppe Culture" (Appendix G). In Strassler 2009.

Williams, Frank. 1996. "Xenophon's Dana and the Passage of Cyrus' Army over the Taurus Mountains." *Historia* 45: 284–314.

Wylie, Graham. 1992. "Cunaxa and Xenophon." *L'Antiquité Classique* 61: 119–34.

## Selected Editions and Commentaries of *Anabasis*

Bevilacqua, Fiorenza, ed. 2002. *Anabasi di Senofonte*. Turin: Unione Tipografico-Editrice Torinese.

Breitenbach, Ludovicus, ed. 1867. *Xenophontis* Anabasis. Halle, Germany: Libraria Orphanotrophei.

Brownson, Carleton L., ed. and trans. 1922. *Xenophon* Anabasis. Cambridge, MA, and London: Harvard University Press (Loeb Classical Library). Rev. Loeb ed. (corrected reprint of 1998 revision), with Introduction, by John Dillery, 2001.

Hude, Carolus, ed. 1931. *Xenophontis Expeditio Cyri*. Leipzig: Teubner. Rev. ed. by J. Peters, Leipzig: Teubner, 1972.

Huitink, Luuk, and Tim Rood, eds., comm. 2019. *Commentary on Xenophon* Anabasis *Book III*. Cambridge: Cambridge University Press.

Lendle, Otto. 1995. *Kommentar zu Xenophons* Anabasis. Darmstadt, Germany: Wissenschaftliche Buchgesellschaft.

Marchant, E. C., ed. 1904. *Xenophontis Opera Omnia*, vol. 3, *Expeditio Cyri*. Oxford: Clarendon Press (Oxford Classical Texts).

Masqueray, Paul, ed. and trans. (into French). 1930/31. *Xénophon,* Anabase. Paris: Les Belles Lettres (Budé ed.).

Stronk, Jan P., ed., trans., comm. 1995. *The Ten Thousand in Thrace, An Archaeological and Historical Commentary on Xenophon's* Anabasis, *Books VI.iii–vi–VII*. Amsterdam: J. C. Gieben.


FURTHER MATERIAL ON AUTHORS TRANSLATED
IN APPENDICES S, T, U, AND V

*Ctesias and Photius*

Lenfant, Dominique, ed. and trans. (into French), with Introduction. 2004. *Ctésias de Cnide:* La Perse, L'Inde, *autres fragments*. Paris: Les Belles Lettres (Budé ed.).

Llewellyn-Jones, Lloyd, and James Robson, trans., with Introduction. 2010. *Ctesias' History of Persia: Tales of the Orient*. London and New York: Routledge.

Stronk, Jan P., ed., trans., comm. 1995, with Introduction. 2010. *Ctesias' Persian History*, part 1. Düsseldorf: Wellem.

Wilson, N. G., trans. 1994. *Photius: The* Bibliotheca: *A Selection*. London: Duckworth.


*Diodorus Siculus*

Bonnet, Martine, and Eric R. Bennett, eds. and trans. (into French). 1997. *Diodore de Sicile* Bibliothèque Historique *Livre XIV*. Paris: Les Belles Lettres (Budé ed.).

Green, Peter, trans. 2006. *Diodorus Siculus Books 11–12.37.1: Greek History 480–431 B.C. The Alternative Version*. Austin: University of Texas Press.

———. 2010. *Diodorus Siculus: The Persian Wars to the Fall of Athens: Books 11–14.34 (480–401 BCE)*. Austin: University of Texas Press.

Oldfather, C. H., ed. and trans. 1954. *Diodorus of Sicily* Library of History *Volume VI (Books XIV–XV.19)*. Cambridge and London: Harvard University Press (Loeb Classical Library).

Stylianou, P. J., comm. 1998. *A Historical Commentary on Diodorus Siculus Book 15*. Oxford: Clarendon Press.

Vogel, Fredericus, ed. 1893. *Diodori Bibliotheca Historica*. Vol. 3. Leipzig: B. G. Teubner.

Westlake, H. D. 1987. "Diodorus and the Expedition of Cyrus." *Phoenix* 41, no. 3 (Autumn): 241–54.


*Diogenes Laertius*

Dorandi, Tiziano, ed., with Introduction. 2013. *Diogenes Laertius: Lives of Eminent Philosophers*. Cambridge: Cambridge University Press.

Hicks, R. D., ed. and trans. 1972. *Diogenes Laertius: Lives of Eminent Philosophers.* Vol. 1, *Books 1–5*. Rev. ed., with Introduction by Herbert S. Long. Cambridge, MA, and London: Harvard University Press (Loeb Classical Library). Originally published 1925.

Mejer, Jørgen. 1978. *Diogenes Laertius and His Hellenistic Background*. Wiesbaden, Germany: F. Steiner (Hermes Einzelschriften 40).


*Plutarch*

Beck, Mark, ed. 2014. *A Companion to Plutarch*. Malden, MA, and Chichester, UK: Wiley-Blackwell.

Perrin, Bernadotte, ed. and trans. 1926. *Plutarch* Lives *Volume XI (Aratus, Artaxerxes, Galba, Otho)*. Cambridge, MA, and London: Harvard University Press (Loeb Classical Library).

Scott-Kilvert, Ian, and Timothy E. Duff, trans. 2011. *The Age of Alexander: Ten Greek Lives by Plutarch.* Harmondsworth, UK: Penguin Books.


ARCHAEOLOGICAL REPORTS AND
EDITIONS OF INSCRIPTIONS AND FRAGMENTS

Agre, Daniela. 2011. *The Tumulus of Golyamata Mogila near the Villages of Malomirovo and Zlatinitsa.* Sofia, Bulgaria: Avalon.

Chankowski, Véronique, and Lidia Domaradzka. 1999. "Réédition de l'inscription de Pistiros et problèmes d'interprétation." *Bulletin de Correspondance Hellénique* 123, no. 1: 246–58.

Davidson, Gladys R. 1952. *Corinth XII: The Minor Objects.* Princeton, NJ: American School of Classical Studies at Athens.

Demargne, Pierre, ed. 1974. *Fouilles de Xanthos Tome 5, Tombes-maisons, tombes rupestres et sarcophages.* Paris: Klincksieck.

*Inscriptiones Graecae* (*IG*). Berlin: G. Reimer, then De Gruyter, 1873–.

Jacoby, Felix, ed. 1923–58. *Die Fragmente der griechischen Historiker* (*FGrH*); parts 1–3 in 15 vols. Berlin (Weidmann) and Leiden (Brill). Jacoby Online includes rev. and enl. parts 1–3, edited by Ian Worthington, as well as new parts 4 and 5.

Loukopoulou, Louiza D., and others, eds. 2005. Epigraphes tēs Thrakēs tou Aigaiou metaxy tōn potamōn Nestou kai Evrou (nomoi Xanthēs, Rhodopēs kai Evrou). Inscriptiones antiquae partis Thraciae quae ad ora maris Aegaei sita est: praefecturae Xanthes, Rhodopes et Hebri. Athens: Kentron Hellēnikēs kai Rōmaikēs Archaiotētos (*IThrAeg*).

Sevinç, Nurten, Reyhan Körpe, Musa Tombul, Charles Brian Rose, Donna Strahan, Henrike Kiesewetter, and John Wallrodt. 2001. "A New Painted Graeco-Persian Sarcophagus from Çan." *Studia Troica* 11: 383–420.

*Supplementum Epigraphicum Graecum* (*SEG*). Leiden: Sijthoff, 1923–71. Amsterdam: J. C. Gieben, 1979–2005. Leiden: Brill, 2006–.

Storey, Ian C., ed. and trans. 2011. *Fragments of Old Comedy.* 3 vols. Cambridge, MA: Harvard University Press (Loeb Classical Library).

# FIGURE CREDITS

Frontispiece   Ali Hassan Mohammed.
Intro.2.9   Azoor Photo/Alamy Stock Photo.
Intro.4.2   Alberto Paredes/Alamy Stock Photo.
Intro.5.1   Museum für Kunst und Gewerbe Hamburg, CC0 1.0 Universal.
1.1.6   © The Trustees of the British Museum.
1.2.4   Shane Brennan.
1.2.16   Livius.org, Jona Lendering, CC0 1.0 Universal.
1.2.19   Shane Brennan.
1.2.22   New York State Archives Digital Collection.
1.5.5   Shane Brennan.
1.5.10   Shane Brennan.
1.8.9   © bpk/Antikensammlung, SMB/Johannes Laurentius.
1.8.29, left   A. Davey, Flickr, 2010, CC BY-2.0.
1.8.29, right   Livius.org, Marco Prins, CC0 1.0 Universal.
2.1.9   akg images/Erich Lessing.
2.3.15, top   Zev Radovan/www.BibleLandPictures.com/Alamy Stock Photo.
2.3.15, bottom   Jim Gordan, US Army Corps of Engineers, US National Archives, public domain.
2.3.28   © De Agostini Editore/G Dagli Orti.
2.4.13   *L'Illustration*, No. 4034, June 26, 1920, 387, public domain.
2.4.28   © The Trustees of the British Museum.
2.5.23   Lucas, Flickr/Wikimedia.org, CC BY-SA 2.0.
3.2.13   Livius.org, Marco Prins, CC0 1.0 Universal.
3.2.25   © The Trustees of the British Museum.
3.4.7, top   Gertrude Bell Archive, Newcastle University, L_192.
3.4.7, bottom   Courtesy The British Institute for the Study of Iraq.
3.5.15   Shane Brennan.
4.2.1   © The Trustees of the British Museum.
4.3.1, top   Shane Brennan.
4.3.1, bottom   Gts-tg, CC BY-SA 4.0, Wikipedia.org, Ashmolean Museum.
4.3.28   © The Trustees of the British Museum.
4.3.28, bottom   Photo by Dr. Steven Ross Murray, adapted.
4.4.21, left   The Metropolitan Museum, Fletcher Fund, 1954.
4.4.21, right   The Metropolitan Museum, Rogers Fund, 1947.
4.5.14   Carole Raddato, Flicker, CC BY-SA 2.0.
4.5.25   © Nevit Dilmen, Wikimedia.org, CC BY-SA 3.0.

# INDEX

**Abrokomas,** a Persian general, claimed by Cyrus to be located at the Euphrates and to be the target of his march, 1.3.20; his forces in Syria include Greek troops who desert to Cyrus, 1.4.3; his men have been posted at the "gates" on the coastline between Cilicia and Syria, 1.4.5; withdraws his army from north Syria rather than confront Cyrus, 1.4.5, 1.4.18; though intended to be one of Artaxerxes' four principal commanders at the battle of Cunaxa, arrived late for the battle, 1.7.12; *see also* Appendix W, §1

**Abrozelmes,** interpreter to Seuthes the Thracian warlord, relays a message from Seuthes to Xenophon, 7.6.43

**Abydos,** Chersonese located opposite, 1.1.9

**Acarnania,** *see* **Aeschines**

**Achaeans,** break away from Greek army along with Arcadians, 6.2.9–12, 6.2.16; reunited with Xenophon's troops in Bithynia, 6.3.24; *see also individual Achaeans* **Lykon; Philesios; Phryniskos; Samolas; Socrates the Achaean; Xanthikles**

**Acherousian Chersonese,** *see* **Chersonese, Acherousian**

**Adramyttium,** Xenophon travels through, 7.8.8

**Aeolis,** Timasion promises to guide Greek soldiers around, 5.6.24

**Agasias** of Stymphalos (in Arcadia), a captain of the rearguard, urges his fellow soldiers in Proxenos' contingent to drive the defeatist Apollonides away, 3.1.31; volunteers for service on an advance party in the mountains, 4.1.27; moves forward against a stronghold of the Taochoi and competes with other captains to capture it, 4.7.9, 4.7.11–12; climbs up stockade around settlement of Drilai, 5.2.15; urges Xenophon to become commander in chief, 6.1.30; contrary to Xenophon's own policy, serves as an ambassador from the soldiers to make threats against the Heracleans, 6.2.7; plays leading role in ending Arcadian secession and thus reuniting the Greek army at Kalpe Harbor, 6.4.10; becomes involved in a dispute at Kalpe Harbor between different groups of soldiers over plunder, which culminates in a riot witnessed by the Spartan har-

most Kleandros, who demands the surrender of the troublemakers, 6.6.7–11; accepts Xenophon's advice to turn himself over and is accompanied by the generals to an interview with Kleandros, 6.6.15–28; initially retained by Kleandros in custody, 6.6.26; released after further representations, 6.6.34–35; wounded in a raid on the tower of the rich Persian Asidates, 7.8.19; his mutual friendship with Xenophon emphasized, 6.6.11

**Agesilaos,** King of Sparta, accompanied by Xenophon when recalled from Asia to campaign in mainland Greece against the Thebans, 5.3.6; *see also* Appendix W, §2

**Agias** of Arcadia, Greek general, arrested by Tissaphernes and subsequently put to death, 2.5.31–2, 2.6.1; briefly obituarized, 2.6.30; succeeded as a general by Kleanor, 3.1.47

**Aietes,** Phasianoi (of Colchis) ruled by grandson of, 5.6.37

**Aineias** of Stymphalos (in Arcadia), a captain, dragged to his death by a Taochian, 4.7.13–14

**Ainians,** join Cyrus' army at Colossae, 1.2.6; dance at banquet for Paphlagonians, 6.1.7–8

**Aischines** of Acarnania, leader of a unit of peltasts, pursues Persian cavalry into the highlands on the far side of the Kentrites River, 4.3.22; leads his detachment to the top of a ridge occupied by the Kolchoi, 4.8.18

**ally/allies**
  *of Greek army:*
    Ariaios, backed by oaths, 2.2.8; no longer, 3.2.2
    Cyrus, his reasons for being, 1.7.3
    the gods, 3.2.10
    Mossynoecian faction, 5.4.3–11, 5.4.16, 5.4.18, 5.4.30
    Paphlagonians, potentially, as threatened by Xenophon to Sinopeans, 5.5.22–23
    Seuthes, circumstances in which chosen as, 7.6.27, 7.7.25
    Tissaphernes, potentially, 2.5.13
  *of Klearchos:* says he regards his troops as his friends and allies, 1.3.6
  *of Lacedaemonians:* army will be declared to be at war with, as well as with Lacedaemonians themselves, 7.1.26; role of

---

NOTE: All dates are B.C.E (Before the Common Era). Additional information on selected characters can be found in Appendix W: Brief Biographies of Selected Characters in *Anabasis.*

**ally/allies** *(cont'd)*
in war against Athens, 7.1.27; present state of alliance, now including Athens and her allies, 7.1.28; Seuthes wishes to be, 7.6.3
*of Paphlagonians:* Sinope, potentially, as threatened by Hekatonymos, 5.5.12, 5.5.22; Greek army, as counter-threatened by Xenophon, 5.5.22–23
*of Tissaphernes:* the Great King's power is, 2.5.11; Greek army could be, for use against rebel Egyptians, 2.5.13

**Amazons,** battle axe typical of, found on captive taken in Armenia, 4.4.16

**ambassador(s):** threatened by undiscipline of Greeks, 5.7.27; from the Great King: come to Greeks after Cunaxa, 3.1.28; to Heraclea: to make extortionate demands, 6.2.5–8; from Kolchoi in mountains: visit Kerasous following Greek attack, are killed by Greek soldiers, 5.7.17–19, 5.7.30; from Paphlagonia: sent to Greeks, 6.1.2–4; entertained to dinner and dance show, 6.1.3–13; come to agreement with Greeks, 6.1.14; from Seuthes, Medosades used as, 7.2.23; from Sinope: visit army in Kotyora, 5.5.7–12; eventually establish good relations with army, 5.5.24–25; asked for advice about journey on from Kotyora, 5.6.2; to Sinope, sent by army to make transport arrangements, 5.6.13–14

**Ambracia,** *see* **Silanos of Ambracia**

**ambush,** natives captured in, near Theches, 4.7.22; fake, set to deceive Drilai as Greeks retreat, 5.3.30

**Amphikrates** son of Amphidemos of Athens, a captain of the rearguard, killed in action by the Kardouchoi while defending a ridge to which Xenophon had posted him, 4.2.13, 4.2.17

**Amphipolis,** *see* **Pleisthenes**

**Anaxibios,** Spartan *nauarchos,* Cheirisophos claims to be friend of, sails to Byzantium to get to help with sea transport, 5.1.4; though unable to supply ships, willing to pay troops, according to Cheirisophos, 6.1.16; under the influence of Dexippos and therefore prejudiced against Xenophon, prompted by Pharnabazos, asks Greek army to cross out of Asia and promises pay, 7.1.2–4; orders army to leave Byzantium, withholds its pay and tries to close gates against it, 7.1.7, 7.1.10–13; flees from incoming army to the acropolis via a short passage by sea, 7.1.20; negotiations with, opened under Xenophon's influence, 7.1.31–2; agrees to report favorably to the Spartan authorities about army's conduct, 7.1.34; again closes Byzantium city gates against them once outside, 7.1.36; pleased on hearing of disintegration of army, 7.2.4; orders any soldiers from the army found in Byzantium to be sold into slavery, 7.2.6; on expiry of term of office as *nauarchos,* allows Xenophon to accompany him away from Byzantium, 7.1.39; snubbed by Pharnabazos at Parium, 7.2.5–7; orders Xenophon to go back to the Greek army and keep it together to attack Pharnabazos, 7.2.8; his orders countermanded by Aristarchos, 7.2.13; *see also* Appendix W, §3

**anger, evinced by,** ships' officers with crew during stormy weather, 5.8.20; those who are poor having once been rich, 7.7.28
*Cheirisophos:* with Armenian village headman for not taking army via villages, 4.6.2
*Cyrus:* at difficulties with wagons in mudslides (feigned), 1.5.8

*Greek troops:*
in Menon's army, having lost two companies in Cilician mountains, 1.2.26; believing generals knew Cyrus' true aims all along, 1.4.12; in Menon's army, at Klearchos for beating one of their number, 1.5.11; believing Xenophon is trying to take them back to Phasis, 5.7.2; when sacrifices do not produce omens favorable for departure from Kalpe Harbor, 6.4.16; at being deceived by Anaxibios in Byzantium, 7.1.25, 7.4.14; at Xenophon for not obtaining their pay from Seuthes, 7.5.16; at Xenophon, unjustifiably, for what has happened to them in Thrace, 7.6.32, 7.6.39;
Klearchos, as a result of being heavily stoned by troops, 1.5.14; often when inflicting punishment, 2.6.9;
Lacedaemonians, if non-Lacedaemonian master of ceremonies is chosen (sarcastic suggestion by Agasias), 6.1.30;
Medosades, at Greeks for removing supplies from his villages, 7.7.2;
Tissaphernes, with Egyptian rebels, 2.5.13;
Xenophon, with sick soldiers who refuse to move despite enemy pursuit, 4.5.16; with Medosades for his ridiculous accusations, 7.7.4

**animal(s)**
draft: attacked by mutinous Greek soldiers, 1.3.1; die on Cyrus' march through Arabia, 1.5.5; Cyrus' soldiers load many of their weapons onto, 1.7.20; in shortage after Cunaxa, slaughtered by Greeks for food, 2.1.6; loaded up by Greeks for march to Ariaios, 2.2.4; seen grazing near Artaxerxes' camp, 2.2.15, but subsequently no longer visible, 2.2.18; Xenophon advises Greeks not to be hindered by, 3.2.27; move forward in center of hollow-square formation, 3.3.6; to replace horses in Greek baggage train, 3.3.19; many left behind by Greeks for journey through mountains, 4.1.12–13; path suitable for, 4.1.24; travel with Greek rearguard through Kardouchoi territory, 4.2.9, 4.2.10, 4.2.13; cross Kentrites River between two halves of Greek army, 4.3.15, 4.3.26; stragglers among, captured by Greeks from Persians fleeing Kentrites River heights, 4.3.25; distract many Greek troops from combat duties, 4.3.30; suffer during snowfall in Armenia, 4.4.11, 4.5.4; Xenophon searches among to requisition food, 4.5.8; stolen from Greeks by Armenians during march through snow, 4.5.12; brought into Armenian houses through dug-out entrances, 4.5.25; Armenian headman gives Greeks advice on traveling through snow with, 4.5.36; able to pass through mountain territory of [Eastern] Chalybes, Taochoi, and Phasians, 4.6.17; urged on to summit of mountain above Black Sea, 4.7.24; also cared for during Xenophon's festival for Artemis in Skillous, 5.3.11; taken by Greeks to carry plunder from Bithynian countryside, 6.6.1; *see also* **donkeys; mules; oxen**
other livestock: Persians' abundance of, 3.1.19; proposal to cross Tigris River involves using skins of and ropes used with, 3.5.9–10; of various kinds, kept in underground Armenian houses, 4.5.25; kept in strongholds by Taochoi, 4.7.2; captured by Greeks with Taochian stronghold, providing food for march through [Eastern] Chalybes' territory, 4.7.14, 4.7.17; spotted by peltasts at main Drilai stronghold, 5.2.4; captured in Thynian plain, 7.3.48; fenced in by Thynoi in their homesteads, 7.4.14; Greeks outside

Perinthus without means to capture, but needed Seuthes' help, 7.6.26–28; given to Xenophon by Seuthes for Greek soldiers, 7.7.53; run away as Greeks attempt to kidnap Asidates, 7.8.12; seized by Greeks from Asidates, 7.8.16, 7.8.19; *see also* **cattle; goats; goose; pigs; poultry; sheep;**

for sacrifice: obtained by Greeks in Armenian villages, 4.4.9; at pasture in Skillous, used in festival, 5.3.8; sold to Greeks, by mountain people near Kerasous, 5.7.13; army runs short of at Kalpe Harbor, 6.4.25; sent to army at Kalpe Harbor by Heracleans, 6.5.1; supplied by Koiratadas but taken away by him without being used, 7.1.40–41; *see also* **cattle; goats; oxen; pigs; sheep;**

wild: Cyrus' skill at hunting, 1.2.7; in palace park at Kelainai, 1.2.7; wild asses, bustards, gazelles, ostriches in Syrian desert, 1.5.2–3; Cyrus' courage in hunting, attacked by, kills bear, 1.9.6; boar, deer, plentiful for hunting near Selinous River in Greece, 5.3.8–10;

various: boar, bull, ram, wolf killed for swearing of oaths between Ariaios and Greeks, 2.2.9; taken by Greeks from abandoned Drilai strongholds, 5.2.3; *see also* **bees; dolphins; doves; eagle; fish; hares; horses; mussels**

**Antandros,** Xenophon arrives at, 7.8.7

**Antileon** of Thurii, trooper, advocates travel by sea for the journey onward from Trapezus, 5.1.2

**Apollo** (god), said to have flayed Marsyas at source of Marsyas River, 1.2.8; tells Xenophon the names of the gods to whom he should sacrifice, 3.1.6, 8; Greek generals divide up tithe reserved for, 5.3.4; Xenophon has votive offering made from his share of tithe for, 5.3.5; sacrifice to, performed by Xenophon in Lampsacus, 7.8.3

**Apollonia,** Asidates receives military support from, 7.8.15

**Apollonides,** captain, gives defeatist speech after arrest of the Greek generals, 3.1.26; found to have pierced ears, is driven away as being a Lydian, 3.1.31

**Arabia,** Cyrus' army marches through, 1.5.1–3; ruled by Dernes, 7.8.25

**Araxes River** (Syria), Cyrus' army replenishes supplies at, 1.4.19; *see also* **Phasis River (in Armenia)**

**Arbakes/Arbakas,** one of the four commanders of Artaxerxes' army, 1.7.12; named as satrap of Media (with variant spelling Arbakas), 7.8.25 (scribal insertion)

**Arcadians**

numbers of, in army: together with Achaeans, form majority of army, 6.2.10; more than 4,500, all hoplites, join together, 6.2.16; Sophainetos brings one thousand to join Cyrus' army at Kelainai, 1.2.9;

history of breakaway: institute split-up of Greek army at Heraclea, 6.2.9–12, 6.2.16; journey from Heraclea to Bithynian Thrace, 6.2.17; face difficulties in Bithynian Thrace, 6.3.2–9; Xenophon's contingent travels into Bithynia to aid, 6.3.10–22; leave hill in Bithynia where they had been under siege, 6.3.22–23; survivors reunited with Xenophon's troops in Bithynia, 6.3.23–26; dead, buried by special expedition, 6.4.9–10; oldest amongst, lead full reunion of Greek army at Kalpe Harbor, 6.4.10–11;

other incidents involving: reach top of Kolchian mountain, 4.8.18; at banquet for Paphlagonians, dance themselves and also provide dancing-girl, 6.1.11–12; accuse Xenophon of keeping soldiers out of service of Lacedaemonians, 7.6.8–10;

*see also* **Lykaian sacrifices;** *and see individual Arcadians*

Agasias; Agias; Arexion; Aristonymos; Arystas; Basias; Eurylochos; Hegesander; Kallimachos; Kleanor; Nikarchos; Pyrrhias; Smikres; Xenias; *see further* Aineas; Sophainetos (both also from an Arcadian city, but not explicitly stated by Xenophon to be Arcadians)

**Archagoras** of Argos, a captain of the rearguard, left by Xenophon to guard a ridge against the Kardouchoi, 4.2.13; reports dislodgement of troops with severe casualties, 4.2.17

**archer(s),** generally have shorter range than Rhodian stone slingers, 3.4.16; Arcadian contingent of Greek army lacks, 6.3.7;

Cretan: join Cyrus' army at Kelainai, 1.2.9; have shorter range than Persians, 3.3.7, 3.3.15; hold off Tissaphernes' troops, 3.4.15; collect and practice with enemy arrows, 3.4.17; when mingled with noncombatants, unable to retaliate against Persians, 3.4.26; utilized during Kentrites River crossing, 4.3.27–28; put into formation for fighting Kolchoi, 4.8.15; given orders to fire at Drilai stronghold on signal, 5.2.12; placed in position for Greek attack on Mossynoeci stronghold, 5.4.22–23; Xenophon contemplates great experience of, 5.6.15;

Kardouchoi, great skill of, 4.2.28;

Persian: move forward in Artaxerxes' army, 1.8.9; Cyrus, eager as a boy to learn how to be an, 1.9.5; in Mithradates' attack on Greeks, 3.3.6–7; have longer range than Greek archers, 3.3.7, 3.3.15; in Mithradates' second attack on Greeks, 3.4.2, 3.4.4; ordered by Tissaphernes to harass Greeks, 3.4.14; have shorter range than Rhodian slingers, lose arrows to Cretans, 3.4.16–17; attack Greeks in high hills, 3.4.25–26;

*see also* **arrows**

**Arexion** of Parrasia (in Arcadia): acts as seer at Kalpe Harbor, 6.4.13, 6.5.2; and before a battle in Bithynia against Pharnabazos' troops, 6.5.8

*Argo,* on voyage from Sinope to Heraclea, Greeks pass reported anchorage of, according to scribal insertion, 6.2.1

**Argos,** *see* **Archagoras**

**Ariaios** (also called Aridaios by Diodorus), the most prominent Persian supporter of Cyrus, commands left wing of Cyrus' forces at the battle of Cunaxa, 1.8.5; on hearing of Cyrus' death, flees the battlefield, 1.9.31, 1.10.1, 2.1.3; informs Greeks of his intention to return to Ionia, 2.1.3; offered royal throne by Klearchos, 2.1.4–6; rejects offer as being inferior to many other Persian noblemen, 2.2.1–2; offers to lead Greeks back to the Aegean coast, 2.2.1–2; swears oath of mutual loyalty with Greeks, 2.2.8–9; advises Greeks to retreat as fast as possible, 2.2.10–15; initially camps close to Greeks; put under pressure by his family and assured of Artaxerxes' forgiveness, 2.4.1–2; makes clear to Greeks that he will not support them if they break post-battle truce, 2.4.5; camps with Tissaphernes and Orontas, 2.4.9; sends suspect message to Proxenos and Klearchos warning of prospective barbarian attack, 2.4.15–16; suspected by Klearchos of assisting Menon in misrepresenting Greek intentions to Tissaphernes, 2.5.28; following arrest of Greek generals, approaches remaining Greeks to accuse Klearchos of perjury and conspiracy, and demands Greeks' weapons in the name of the King, 2.5.38, 2.5.40; denounced to his face by Kleanor for treachery, 2.5.38–39; denounced to Greek

**Ariaios** *(cont'd)*

  army by Cheirisophos and Kleanor, 3.2.2, 3.2.5, 3.2.17; campaigns with Tissaphernes against Greeks, 3.5.1

  relationship with Menon: Menon his guest-friend, 2.1.5, 2.4.15; Menon insinuated to be his paramour, 2.6.28; *see also* Appendix W, §4

**Aristarchos,** Spartan harmost of Byzantium in succession to Kleandros: having been instructed by Anaxibios to sell as slaves any Cyrean soldiers he finds in Byzantium, carries out instructions vigorously, 7.2.5–6, 7.3.3; enters into agreement with Pharnabazos about Greek army, cutting out Anaxibios, 7.2.7; forbids Xenophon from leading army back into Asia, 7.2.12–13; plots to arrest Xenophon, 7.2.14, 7.2.16; repeatedly orders Xenophon to take the army to the Chersonese, 7.2.15, 7.3.2–3, 7.3.7–8, 7.6.12–14, 7.6.25; refuses army access to Perinthus, 7.6.24

**Aristeas** of Chios, commander of light-armed troops: his military value, 4.1.28; volunteers for advance party in the Kardouchian mountains, 4.1.28; leads light-armed troops against [Eastern] Chalybes, Taochoi, and Phasianoi, 4.6.20

**Aristippos,** dynast of Larissa in Thessaly, a guest-friend of Cyrus, asks for help against political opponents and is sent double the help requested, 1.1.10; requested by Cyrus for mercenaries, 1.2.1; sends, under Menon's command, much less help than Cyrus had funded, 1.2.6; places Menon in command, 1.2.6; his motive in choosing Menon insinuated to be their sexual relationship, 2.6.28; *see also* Appendix W, §5

**Ariston** of Athens, sent as ambassador to Sinope, 5.6.14

**Aristonymos** of Methydrion (in Arcadia), a captain of the rearguard: volunteers for advance party in Kardouchian mountains, 4.1.27; leads hoplites against [Eastern] Chalybes, Taochoi, and Phasianoi, 4.6.20; competes successfully against three other captains to be the first to reach Taochian stronghold, 4.7.9–12

**Armenia/Armenians**

  geography of: headwaters of Tigris in, 4.1.3; separated from land of Kardouchoi by Kentrites River, 4.3.1; road across Kentrites leads into, 4.3.20; as confirmed by headman, underground villages are part of, 4.5.34; bordered by land of [Eastern] Chalybes, 4.5.34;

  rulers of: Orontas, governor of, 3.5.17; Tiribazos lieutenant-governor of Western, 4.4.4–6; *see also* **Orontas; Tiribazos**

  and Greek army: Greek generals decide to travel through Kardouchoi territory in order to reach, 3.5.17; Orontas' troops, including Armenians, attempt to stop Greeks crossing into, 4.3.3; journey through, notable especially for snow, 4.4.1–4.6.3; Greeks use boys of, to wait on them in native costume, 4.5.33

**armor,** weighs Xenophon down as he leads troops to summit, 3.4.48; pierced by Kardouchoi arrows, 4.2.28; put aside by Greek soldiers to climb Drilai stockade, 5.2.15

  worn or put on by: Cyrus' army, to fight battle of Cunaxa, 1.8.3, 1.8.6; horses in Cyrus' army, 1.8.7; Persians accompanying Ariaios to conference with Greeks, 2.5.35; Xenophon when addressing Greek soldiers, 3.2.7; newly appointed Greek cavalry, as a result of special issue, 3.3.20; Orontas' cavalry, 4.3.3; [Eastern] Chalybes, 4.7.15–16; dancers at banquet for Paphlagonians, 6.1.11; Greeks during attack by Thynoi, 7.4.16

**arrows**

  used against Greeks: causing sole Greek casualty at the battle of Cunaxa, 1.8.20; by Persians after Zapatas crossing, 3.3.7, especially cavalry, 3.3.10; at longer range by Persians than Greek archers can manage, 3.3.15; penetration of Greek ranks by, signal for Greek rearguard charge, 3.4.4; in high hills north of Tigris plain, by barbarians, 3.4.25; by Kardouchoi, 4.1.10, 4.1.16, 4.2.12, 4.2.27, 4.3.30, 4.3.33; kill two Greeks, 4.1.18; length of, as used by Kardouchoi, 4.2.28; by Persians as Greeks cross Kentrites River, 4.3.6, 4.3.18; from Asidates' tower, 7.8.14, 7.8.18

  used by Greeks: gathered from battlefield by Greeks for firewood, 2.1.6; against Tissaphernes' troops, successfully, 3.4.15; collected from Persians by Cretan archers, 3.4.17; of Kardouchoi, reused as javelins, 4.2.28; in feint at Kentrites crossing, held as if ready to shoot, 4.3.28; fired at Drilai stronghold, 5.2.12, 5.2.14; interchange of fire of, between Drilai and Cretans during Greek retreat, 5.2.32; *see also* **archers**

**Artagerses,** commander of Artaxerxes' cavalry bodyguard at the battle of Cunaxa, 1.7.11; said to have been slain by Cyrus personally, 1.8.24

**Artakamas,** satrap of Phrygia, 7.8.25

**Artaozos,** a Persian supporter of Cyrus, subsequently reconciled to Artaxerxes alongside Ariaios, is twice involved in diplomatic communications with the Greek army, 2.4.16, 2.5.35

**Artapatas,** leader of Cyrus' mace-bearers: tent of, used for execution of the traitor Orontas, 1.6.11; kills himself on top of Cyrus' corpse with the *akinakes* that Cyrus had awarded to him, 1.8.28–29

**Artaxerxes (II),** Great King of Persia

  *family:* elder brother of Cyrus, both being sons of Parysatis, succeeds his father Darius as King, 1.1.1–3; Orontas, satrap of Armenia, is married to daughter of, 2.4.8; Greeks encounter bastard brother of, 2.4.25, 3.4.13; his brother-in-law joins Tissaphernes in swearing pledge to Greeks, 2.4.28

  *background information:* enormous resources of, 3.1.19; spends summer and spring each year in Susa and Ecbatana, 3.5.15; Kardouchoi hostile to, 3.5.16, 4.1.8; Armenians rearing horses as tribute for, 4.5.24, 4.5.34; Paphlagonian cavalry said to have refused to attend on, 5.6.8; his paid mercenaries garrisoned near Pergamum, 7.8.15; rulers in land of, listed, 7.8.25

  *feud and war with Cyrus:* arrests Cyrus but releases him at request of Parysatis, 1.1.3–4; Cyrus, with Parysatis' support, begins plotting against, 1.1.4–6, 1.1.8; asked by Cyrus for rule over Ionian cities, 1.1.8; warned by Tissaphernes of Cyrus' plans, makes counter-preparations, 1.2.4–5, 2.3.19; prior to Cyrus' arrival in area, holds Syrian side of walls along Cilician border, 1.4.4; Cyrus announces his campaign against, 1.4.11; Cyrus moves to mount a swift attack on, 1.5.9; Cyrus prepares for battle with, 1.7.1, 1.7.9, 1.7.14; battle position of, 1.7.11, 1.8.12, 1.8.21–23; makes trench to defend against Cyrus' army, 1.7.14–16; will not fight within ten days, Silanos correctly prophesies, 1.7.18; charged and wounded by Cyrus, 1.8.21–27; said by some to have ordered Artapatas' slaying on top of Cyrus' body, 1.8.29; breaks into Cyrus'

other captains to capture a Taochian stronghold, 4.7.11–12; sent to Anaxibios on behalf of the soldiers, 7.1.32; asks Lacedaemonians to get pay due to the Greeks from Seuthes, 7.6.40

**Eurymachos** of Dardanos, delegate of his fellow Dardanian Timasion to Heracleans and Sinopeans, 5.6.21

**faithfulness,** *see* **trust/trustworthiness, faithfulness**

**fear:** hubbub and din commonly caused by extreme, 2.2.19; can cause irreparable damage between collaborators even if unjustified, Klearchos says, 2.5.5; in Ariaios, of the gods, absent since he breaks pledges, Kleanor says, 3.2.5; *actually or potentially inspired by Greek army:*

in Persian enemies: extreme, in Artaxerxes as Greek army approaches, 2.2.18, 2.3.1; lest Greeks fail to agree to truce, played on by Klearchos, 2.3.9; intended by Greek soldiers mutilating enemy corpses, 3.4.5; lest Greek detachment cut them off, 3.4.29; of night attacks, leading them to camp at distance from Greeks, 3.4.34; in cavalry at Kentrites River, lest intercepted, 4.3.21; causes enemy to throw themselves down Armenian snowy slope, 4.5.18; in Pharnabazos, 7.1.2; in Asidates, Xenophon seeks to damp down by march in opposite direction, 7.8.20;

in other non-Greeks: great, in barbarian supporters of Cyrus at Tyriaion review, 1.2.17–18; attempts to induce in Kardouchian captive fail, 4.1.23; wrongly attributed to Kardouchoi as motive for leaving their position, 4.2.15; in Drilai, by fake ambush, 5.2.30; in Kerasountians witnessing madness of rioting troops, 5.7.22, 5.7.26; in Bithynians besieging Arcadians, at signs Xenophon's detachment is approaching, 6.3.25; to extreme extent, by Bithynian cavalry, 6.5.29–30;

in Greeks, including army's own officers: in Proxenos by his troops, rather than vice versa, 2.6.19; in Greek cities along Black Sea coast, causing them to repair roads, 5.1.13; extreme, in Timasion and Thorax, at likely reaction to nonfulfillment of promises of pay, 5.6.36; in some generals, at riot in Kotyora, 5.7.22; in Xenophon, at prospect of looting of Byzantium, 7.1.18; extreme, by Herakleides at army's reaction to speech by Polykrates denouncing him, 7.6.42;

*inspired by Greek generals:* extreme, in Menon and Menon's troops when attacked by Klearchos with Thracians, 1.5.13; in Klearchos' troops, by Klearchos more than by the enemy, as Klearchos wishes, 2.6.10; in Klearchos' troops by fear of punishment, producing good effects, 2.6.14;

*not inspired by Greek general when it might have been expected:* not by Proxenos in his troops, rather than vice versa, 2.6.19;

*inspired by Persian King or army:* in Klearchos, because of possible encirclement, 1.8.13; in Cyrus, lest Artaxerxes cut off Greek units from the rest of his army, 1.8.24; in Greeks at battle of Cunaxa, at prospect of possible maneuver, 1.10.9; in rank-and-file Greeks, lest Persians fail to agree to truce, admitted by Klearchos, 2.3.9; in Greece generally, if Greek army destroyed by Artaxerxes, 2.4.3; in Klearchos, lest army be cut off by Persians breaking down bridge over Tigris, 2.4.18; in Greek army, dissipated, Klearchos says, by Tissaphernes' being with them, 2.5.10; in potential enemies, by torturing Greek prisoners, or so

Artaxerxes wishes, so Xenophon says, 3.1.18; needlessly, according to Xenophon, giving reasons, 3.2.16; in Mithradates, he claims, since he is consorting with Greeks, 3.3.2; in Greeks, lest they be attacked while crossing gully, 3.4.1; in Greek peltasts, of Persian cavalry, 6.5.29;

*not inspired by Persian King or army when it might have been expected:* Xenophon says army will show Klearchos how it lacks, 6.6.32;

*inspired in or by Seuthes:*

inspired in Seuthes: of Thynoi, prompts special precautions with horses, 7.2.21; of being left unsupported against Thynian counterattack, 7.4.47;

not inspired by Seuthes, given certain circumstances: of enemy pursuit, not relevant if riding swift horse, its donor says, 7.3.26; *compare* Medosades, not afraid of enemy while bivouacking with Greeks, 7.7.6;

inspired by Seuthes: burns down Thynian villages to instill, 7.4.1; needless regarding further retaliation, Xenophon tells Thynoi, 7.4.13; horn sounded by, to instill in attacking Thynoi, 7.4.19; in Herakleides, of being expelled from friendship, 7.5.6; necessary to restrain his subjects from revolt, 7.7.29; more likely in Seuthes' subjects if Seuthes and Greek army on good terms, 7.7.30;

*inspired by Cyrus:* in Klearchos, claiming to fear retribution, 1.3.10; in soldier fearing to follow guide provided by Cyrus, if army leaves him to go home, 1.3.17; in Milesians, because of Cyrus' loyalty to their exiles, 1.9.9;

*inspired by other non-Greeks:* in Greek generals, lest Kardouchoi forestall army by occupying pass into their land, 3.5.18; by Kardouchoi, Taochoi, and Chaldaioi, but not so as to prevent Greeks campaigning against, 5.5.17;

*inspired by other causes:*

in Xenophon: by dream, 3.1.12; by continuation of truce with Persians, he says, 3.1.20; by thought that Greek soldiers will prefer to stay with Persian women rather than go home, 3.2.25; by possible death of horse sacred to sun god, 4.5.35; regarding location of his quarters, needlessly, according to Seuthes, 7.4.12;

in other individuals: in Agasias, of being beaten in race for Taochian stronghold, 4.7.11; in Cyrus, of being short of rewards for supporters if victorious, absent, 1.7.7; in Menon, of perjurers and wrongdoers as proof against attack, 2.6.25; in Silanos, of plan to found Black Sea colony, 5.6.17; in Zelarchos, of being lynched, 5.7.29;

in Greek soldiers: groundlessly while camping at night in Babylonia, dissipated by Klearchos' announcement about a loose donkey, 2.2.19–21; of journey with Cyrus on from Cilicia toward Babylon, 3.1.10; of speaking out in assembly, should be overcome, 3.2.32; in besieged Arcadians, of being left unsupported by Xenophon, 6.3.26; of Lacedaemonian reaction to army's cooperation with Seuthes, 7.2.37;

in others: in cavalry, of falling off their horses, or so Xenophon says, 3.2.19; in plowman in bandit country, mimicked as part of Thessalian dance, 6.1.8;

*not shown:*

by travelers in Cyrus' domain concerning robbers, 1.9.13; by Ariaios, of the gods, given that he breaks pledges, Kleanor says, 3.2.5

*see also* **cowardice**

**figs,** grown near Kalpe Harbor, 6.4.6; carried off by Greeks, 6.6.1

**finger rings,** given by Greeks to guide who led them to Black Sea, 4.7.27

**fire(s),** in Xenophon's dream, 3.1.11–12; lit by Greeks to burn surplus equipment, 3.3.1; sticks to kindle gathered by two young Greeks, 4.3.11; lit by Greeks on snowy morning, 4.4.12; arranged as signal for Greeks taking heights from Chalybes, Taochoi, and Phasianoi, 4.6.20;

set for destructive purposes: by Cyrus to palace of Belesys, 1.4.10; by Artaxerxes' cavalry to land in front of Greeks, 1.6.1; as threatened by Tissaphernes, to destroy Greeks' food supply, 2.5.19; by Persians to drive Greeks from land, 3.5.3–6; by Greeks to Kardouchoi villages, negotiated to abstain from, 4.2.19; by some Greeks to houses in Armenian villages, recklessly, 4.4.14; by Drilai to own settlements in scorched-earth tactics, 5.2.3; sweeps through Drilai settlement, allowing Greeks to escape, 5.2.24–27; by Xenophon's troops in Bithynia, 6.3.15, 6.3.19; by Thynoi attacking Greeks by night in mountain villages, 7.4.15–16, 7.4.18;

set at nighttime: by Greeks after battle of Cunaxa, kindled with debris from battle, 2.1.6; neglected by Greeks in despair after arrest of generals, 3.1.3; by Kardouchoi in hilltops, 4.1.11; by Kardouchoi guarding side route, 4.2.5, 4.2.14; many reported to be ablaze during night in Armenia, 4.4.9, but are not substantiated when followed up, 4.4.15–16; kept burning by Greeks to survive snowy conditions, 4.5.5–6; some Greeks in exposed conditions unable to light overnight, 4.5.9, 4.5.21; by Chalybes, Taochoi, and Phasianoi in defense against Greeks, 4.6.22; by Bithynian enemy, seen by Xenophon's men, 6.3.20; by Xenophon's troops in Bithynia, first lit, then extinguished, 6.3.20–21, 6.3.25; by Seuthes' army in front of their pickets, 7.2.18

**firebrands,** thrown by Greeks at Drilai stronghold, 5.2.14

**fish,** in Chalos River considered sacred by Syrians, 1.4.9; in the two Selinous rivers, of Ephesus and of Skillous, 5.3.8

**food,** not eaten by many Greeks on evening after arrest of generals, 3.1.3; soldiers occupy themselves with obtaining and cooking while officers hold strategy meetings, 3.5.7, 3.5.14; Greeks promise to replenish Armenian headman's house with, 4.5.28; kept in strongholds by Taochoi, 4.7.1;

*acquisition of:*

by Greeks/Cyrus' army: Klearchos foresees difficulties in, if Greeks separate from Cyrus, 1.3.11; claimed possible only in market in Cyrus' camp, 1.3.14; from Araxes River villages, 1.4.19; stocking up on, reason for Cyrus to pause in his swift march along mid-Euphrates, 1.5.9; from Charmande, through crossing Euphrates River on rafts, 1.5.10; Cyrus' concern and good planning for, 1.9.27, 1.10.18;

made condition of Greek truce with Artaxerxes, 2.3.5–9, 3.1.28; from Persian villages, 2.3.14–16, 3.4.18, 3.4.31; Tissaphernes gives Greeks instructions about, 2.3.26–27; need for cooperation between Greeks and Tissaphernes over, 2.4.5, 2.5.9; possible in area between Tigris River and canal, 2.4.22; from Parysatis' villages, 2.4.27; involving crossing Tigris at Kainai in rafts, 2.4.28; Klearchos' special expertise in, 2.6.8;

Xenophon does not wish to rely on Persian-organized markets for, 3.2.20–21; Xenophon suggests villages suitable for, 3.2.34; in Tigris plain, 3.4.18; from villages near satrap's palace 3.4.31;

from Kardouchoi villages, 4.1.8–9, 4.2.22; in Kentrites plain, 4.3.2; from Armenian villages between Kentrites and Euphrates Rivers, 4.4.2, 4.4.7, 4.4.9, 4.4.14; promised by Tiribazos, 4.4.6; in Skythenoi territory, 4.7.18; in Kolchian villages, 4.8.19; gifted by Trapezountians, 4.8.23, 5.5.14;

while awaiting transport home from Trapezus, Xenophon makes proposals for, 5.1.6–8; intraday expeditions from Trapezus for, 5.2.1; from Drilai stronghold, sought 5.2.4, and achieved, 5.2.28; in Paphlagonian and Kotyorite territory, through forage rather than by purchase, 5.5.6; need for makes army treat certain peoples as enemies, 5.5.16–17; requires Greeks to travel as one large group, 5.6.13, 5.6.32; needed for voyage out of Black Sea, 5.6.19, 5.6.20;

through military action in Bithynia, 6.4.23–24, 6.5.7, types listed, 6.6.1;

directed by Anaxibios to go to Thracian villages for, 7.1.13; promised by Koiratadas, 7.1.33, 7.1.35; promised by Aristarchos, 7.3.3; Xenophon advises soldiers to choose between Aristarchos and Seuthes only after, 7.3.4–5, 7.3.8; promised by Seuthes, 7.3.8–9, 7.3.10, 7.3.13; Xenophon reminds Greeks of Seuthes' assistance in, 7.6.28, 7.6.29, 7.6.31;

by others: sought by Persian coming from Tiribazos' camp, 4.4.17; by eagle only in flight, 6.1.23;

*availability:*

in abundance: Cyrus' gifts of to friends, 1.9.26; for Persians generally, 3.1.19; in underground Armenian houses, types specified, 4.5.25–26, 4.5.30–31; provided by Artemis for Xenophon's festival in Skillous, types specified, 5.3.9; plentifully stored by Mossynoeci, types specified, 5.4.27–29; as crops grown in Bithynian countryside near Kalpe Harbor, types specified, 6.4.6; at Seuthes' banquet, 7.3.21–23;

shortage of: for Cyrus' army in mid-Euphrates deserts, 1.5.4–6; alleviated by Cyrus, 1.9.27; for Greeks following battle of Cunaxa, 1.10.18–19, 2.1.6, 2.2.3, 2.2.16; for Ariaios' men, 2.2.11–12; generally on march to Zapatas, even prior to the generals' arrest, 3.1.20; Persian scorched-earth tactics could result in, 3.5.3, 3.5.5; cause need for Greeks to press on through Kardouchoi territory, 4.1.15; in Armenia, afflicts Greek troops starving during march through snow, 4.5.7, 4.5.11, 4.5.21, 5.8.3; but partly alleviated by sharing food, 4.5.5; and by special distributions organized by Xenophon, 4.5.7–9; in Taochian territory, 4.7.1, 4.7.3; in Chalybes' territory, 4.7.17; causes army to leave Trapezus, 5.3.1; at Heraclea to some extent, 6.2.3–4; at Kalpe Harbor, 6.4.9, 6.4.12, 6.4.16, 6.4.17, 6.4.19, 6.4.23, 6.5.20; needs to be overcome before army can depart Byzantium, 7.1.9; not met adequately by Koiratadas, 7.1.40–41; soldiers traveling to Chersonese will face, 7.2.15; at or near Perinthus, 7.3.3–5, 7.3.13, 7.6.26, 7.6.29;

*importance of:* emphasized by Klearchos, 1.3.11; Xenophon

says should be a priority in choice of baggage to transport, 3.2.27–28; animals, captives, and noncombatants require large amounts of, 4.1.13;

*see also* **animals,** other livestock; **animals, wild; bread; cattle,** consumed; **crops; market**

**ford:** generally available near sources of rivers, 3.2.22;
of Euphrates River: at Thapsakos, 1.4.17–18; in Armenia, 4.5.2; of Halys River, not available, 5.6.9;
of Kentrites River: difficulties at the regular, 4.3.6; passibility of alternative, 4.3.10–23;
of Parthenios River, not available, 5.6.9;
of Tigris River, not available in plain, 3.5.7, 4.1.2

**formation, military**
column, use of: for uphill charge against Kardouchoi, 4.2.11; for crossing Kentrites River, 4.3.17; on march, line of battle substituted when close to enemy tribesmen, 4.6.7; after discussion, rather than line of battle in uphill attack on Kolchoi, successfully, 4.8.10–19; in attack on Mossynoeci, 5.4.22; in expedition to bury corpses near Kalpe Harbor, details of mode of operation, 6.5.5–6;
hollow rectangle: adopted at Xenophon's instigation for onward march from Zapatas River, 3.2.36–38; disadvantages of, 3.4.19–20; modified by addition of flexible response units, 3.4.21–23; used in retreat from assault on Asidates' tower, 7.8.16;
on night march: infantry to lead, 7.3.36;
reserves: used by Xenophon in Bithynia when attacking Pharnabazos' men, 6.5.9–11;

*see also* **phalanx; platoon**

**friend(s)/friendship(s),** having many friends, the fruit of personal merit, justice, and nobility, 7.7.42;
*of Artaxerxes:* Orontas, in past and, he hopes, to come, 1.6.3; Tiribazos, 4.4.8; the Greek army, potentially—in Proxenos' sarcastic speculations, 2.1.10; in the hopes of some soldiers, 2.1.14; in Klearchos' riposte to Phalinos, 2.1.20;
*of Cyrus:* Tissaphernes, so Cyrus initially believes, 1.1.2; visitors from Artaxerxes' court, 1.1.5; Klearchos, 1.3.5; Orontas' judges, 1.6.6; not Orontas ever again, by his own admission, 1.6.8; not Orontas, contrasted with the willing by Klearchos, 1.6.9; Ariaios, 2.2.3; Xenophon, as promised by Proxenos, 3.1.4; the Greek army generally, as Kleanor says, 3.2.5; *see also* under **guest-friend(s);**
benefits of his friendship: stressed by Klearchos, 1.3.12; by a Greek soldier, 1.3.19; by Menon, 1.4.14–15; Cyrus promises to substitute his own friends for Artaxerxes', as satraps, 1.7.6–7; Cyrus' loyalty in particular to Milesian exiles, 1.9.10; Cyrus' generosity in, 1.9.20–28; loyalty shown to Cyrus by his friends, 1.9.28–30; dubious in Xenophon's case, according to Socrates, 3.1.5;
*of Klearchos:* Cyrus, 1.3.5; Tissaphernes, or so Klearchos maintains, 2.5.8, giving reasons why suitable, 2.5.11–14, 2.5.24, and as he indeed believes, 2.5.27; his own soldiers, more important to him (he says) than Cyrus, 1.3.6; but, according to the narrator, not in fact, 2.6.13;
benefits of his friendship: none, he says, if no longer the leader of his troops, 1.3.6; his friends given information on trial of Orontas, 1.6.5;
*of Menon:* Tissaphernes, Menon intends, or so Klearchos

says, 2.5.28; both Greeks and Persians, so Persians say, 2.5.41; the powerful, or so he wishes for bad reasons, 2.6.21; his evil methods for obtaining, 2.6.26; his two-faced attitude toward, 2.6.23–24; his mockery of, 2.6.26;
*of Proxenos:* with both Greeks and Persians, Persians are implying 2.5.41; with leading men already, he believes, 2.6.17; *see also* **guest-friend(s);**
*of Seuthes:*
Greek army: might become, Greeks speculate, 7.1.2; pledged to him as, by Xenophon, 7.3.30; his situation before and after army became, 7.7.5–7, 7.7.9;
Athenians generally, Seuthes suggests, 7.2.31;
Lacedaemonians, Seuthes requests, inviting to banquet, 7.6.3;
Thynoi, not the motive for their submission, 7.7.29; *note also* discussion as to whether Thracian villagers are truly friends of Medosades, sidekick of Seuthes, 7.7.16, 7.7.18;
Xenophon: so Seuthes promises, 7.2.25; was treated as, prior to arguments about troops' pay, 7.6.15, 7.7.46; subsequently treated inappropriately for, 7.6.20–22; had noble intentions as, he reminds Seuthes, 7.7.37, 7.7.43;
*of Greek army, non-Greek:* none, if Greeks leave unilaterally, Klearchos says, 2.4.5; duplicitous Ariaios a false, Kleanor says, 2.5.39; inadvisable for Greeks, according to Xenophon, 3.2.8; Mithradates a false, 3.3.2, 3.3.7; Kardouchoi not prepared to be, 4.1.8–9; Kolchoi, give cattle as tokens of friendship, 4.8.24; western Mossynoeci faction, 5.4.21, 5.4.32, 5.5.1; Tibareni, offer tokens of friendship, 5.5.2–3; various barbarian tribes, 5.5.14–15, 5.5.18; the Paphlagonian ruler, so Xenophon threatens, 5.5.22, 23; certain mountain barbarians, so they supposed, 5.7.14; none between Byzantium and Heraclea, 6.4.2; potentially, Bithynians with army, 6.6.4;
*of Greek army with Greek cities:*
Heraclea: offer Greeks tokens of, criticized by Lykon as insufficient, but ground for Cheirisophos and Xenophon to resist making threats, 6.2.3–6;
Kotyora: not initially, to Xenophon's regret, 5.5.19; subsequently, 5.5.24–25; Sinope: becomes, after initial problems, 5.5.24–25; always intended to be, Hekatonymos claims, 5.6.3; sends tokens of friendship, 6.1.15;
Trapezus:
gives army cattle, barley meal, and wine as tokens of, 4.8.23, 5.5.14;
warnings about reactions of: Xenophon fears army's mayhem and rioting has dishonored in eyes of, 5.7.12; Xenophon doubts any city will be, none taking in misbehaving army, 5.7.33; Xenophon warns army that its activities in Byzantium are provoking war against itself from its own, 7.1.29;
*of Xenophon, beyond passages cited above:* Xenophon weighs up positive reaction of his, to his becoming commander, 6.1.20; Agasias with Xenophon, 6.6.11; Xenophon with soldiers, inappropriately, Herakleides says to Lacedaemonians, 7.6.4, 7.6.39; Lampsacenes offer Xenophon tokens of, 7.8.3; Xenophon chooses captains for kidnapping expedition who are his special, 7.8.11;

**gods** *(cont'd)*

escape from Drilai through setting houses on fire, 5.2.24–25; to Greek army in its battles, 6.5.23, 7.6.36; to Seuthes and Medosades, 7.7.7; to Seuthes, 7.7.37;

hoped for or anticipated: by Kleanor, 3.2.6; by Klearchos, 2.3.23; Xenophon sees as source of success, 3.2.7; by Xenophon, 3.2.8–14, who believes gods are on the side of the Greeks, 3.1.21–23, 3.2.8–11, 3.2.14, 3.3.14;

need for, referred to: by Seuthes in passing, 7.2.34; by Xenophon in passing, 3.2.7, 7.3.31, 7.3.43, 7.7.22; by Xenophon and Kleandros, 6.6.32, 6.6.34;

*attitudes toward:*

respect: Klearchos gives consequent shame before, as reason Greeks did not desert Cyrus, 2.3.22; Tissaphernes stresses he would not perjure himself to, 2.5.20–21; by Xenophon's men, perhaps the explanation of contrast with plight of Arcadian detachment, Xenophon says, 6.3.18;

disrespect: Kleanor surprised that Ariaios is not ashamed before, 2.5.39; Kleanor stigmatizes Tissaphernes as having no belief in or regard for, 2.5.39; reverence for, normally regarded as reason for self-congratulation, but not by Menon, 2.6.26; Kleanor denounces Ariaios' disregard for, 3.2.5; Xenophon accuses Medosades of lacking shame before, when slandering army, 7.7.9;

likely consequences of disrespect: Klearchos refuses to believe Tissaphernes would needlessly swear false oaths by, 2.4.7; Klearchos reminds Tissaphernes that neither of them could escape from wrath of, 2.5.7, 2.5.8; Xenophon warns army of its danger of seeming dishonorable to, 5.7.12; inability of impious to sacrifice gladly, 5.7.32;

*consulted and/or offered sacrifice:* various, nominated by Apollo of Delphi, offered sacrifices by Xenophon prior to journey, 3.1.6, 3.1.8; thanksgiving sacrifices to all, vowed, 3.2.9, and duly offered, 4.8.25; when consulted in sacrifice, veto attacks on Tibareni strongholds, 5.5.3; sacrificed to, at Kotyora, 5.5.5; consulted by Xenophon about his becoming commander in chief, 6.1.22, 6.1.31; and about their support if he goes to Seuthes, 7.2.15;

*see also* **sacrifice(s)**; *and see specific gods:* **Apollo; Artemis; Athena; doves** (Syrian); **Enyalios; fish** (Syrian); **Helios; Herakles; Twin Gods; Zeus**

**gold,** coronets offered by Cyrus as prizes made from, 1.2.10; gifts given by Cyrus to Syennesis made from, 1.2.27; promised to Greeks by Cyrus, 1.7.7; given to Silanos by Cyrus, 1.7.18; Artapates' dagger made from, 1.8.29; used on Persian royal standard, 1.10.12; Persians' abundance of, 3.1.19; Artemis' effigy at Ephesus made from, 5.3.12; Xenophon's lack of, 7.8.1–2; *see also* **darics**

**Gongylos of Eretria/Gongylos (II),** dead husband of Hellas [of Pergamum], 7.8.8; *see also* Appendix W, §16

**Gongylos the Younger/Gongylos (III),** son of Gongylos of Eretria and Hellas of Pergamum, 7.8.8; comes to aid Greek assault on Asidates, 7.8.17; *see also* Appendix W, §16

**goose,** Cyrus passes to friends remainder of delicious, 1.9.26

**Gorgias** of Leontini (in Sicily), rhetorician and sophist, Proxenos a pupil of, 2.6.16; *see also* Appendix W, §17

**Gorgion,** son of Gongylos of Eretria and Hellas of Pergamum, 7.8.8; *see also* Appendix W, §16

**Great King,** Kelainai palace of, 1.2.8, 1.2.9; *see also individual Great Kings* **Artaxerxes (II); Darius (II); Xerxes**

**greaves** (bronze shinguards), worn by, Cyrus' army during Tyriaion review, 1.2.16; Chalybes, 4.7.16; Drilai, 5.2.22

**Greece/Greeks,** lies beyond Black Sea to the south, 5.7.7;

Greek language: Pategyas shouts message in, as well as in Persian, 1.8.1; Seuthes' wine-pourer understands, 7.3.25; Seuthes understands to a fair extent, 7.6.8;

customs, flora, and other characteristics: Cyrus' cavalry have sabers typical of, 1.8.7; date palms in, inferior to those of Babylonia, 2.3.15; methods of irrigating millet in, 2.4.13; pierced ears uncharacteristic of, 3.1.31; land of free cities, 3.2.13; lance of type usual in, 4.8.7; use of olive oil by, contrasted with Mossynoeci's use of dolphin fat, 5.4.28; Mossynoeci the people regarded by Greek soldiers as most removed from customs of, 5.4.34; plenty of spare land, Thorax claims, 5.6.25; Greek custom when hoplites, peltasts, and cavalry march together at night, 7.3.37–38, 7.3.41;

history of: Xerxes' defeat by, 1.2.9, 3.2.13; repeated Persian defeats when fighting against, 3.2.11–13;

people or cities identified as: Phalinos, by narrator, 2.1.7, by Klearchos, 2.1.16; Trapezus, 4.8.22, 5.1.1, 5.5.14; Kerasous, 5.3.2; Kotyora, 5.5.3; Heraclea, 6.2.1; none between Heraclea and Byzantium, 6.4.2; Byzantium, the first such that army has reached according to Xenophon, 7.1.29; ambassadors present at Seuthes' banquet, 7.3.21;

referred to as a single people: able to travel without fear in Cyrus' domains, 1.9.13; Apollonides viewed as disgrace to, 3.1.30; poverty of, according to Xenophon could be alleviated by emigration into lands currently Persian, 3.2.26; Xenophon contemplates founding of Black Sea city for, 5.6.15–18; Bithynians maltreat captured, 6.4.2; traders come to army in Bithynia from cities of the, 6.6.3; Lacedaemonians are rulers over, 6.6.9, 6.6.12–14, 7.1.30; Kleandros threatens to exclude soldiers from, 6.6.9–10, 6.6.12–14, 6.6.16; Koiratadas hawking his alleged skills around, 7.1.33;

referred to as a unitary audience: Cyrus' popularity among Greeks, 1.9.28; Klearchos reminds Phalinos that his advice will be reported in, 2.1.17; Tissaphernes, being a neighbor to, claims to want gratitude of, 2.3.18, *see also* 3.2.4; Greek soldiers argue that their destruction would put an end to campaigns against the Great King by, 2.4.3; Artaxerxes will not allow soldiers to return to, in order to report their triumph, 2.4.4; Klearchos supposes Tissaphernes cares about his reputation for trustworthiness in, 2.4.7; Tissaphernes claims an intense desire to seem trustworthy to, 2.5.22; Xenophon says sacking Byzantium will result in harsh consequences from, 7.1.29–30; Xenophon's general reputation previously high in, 7.6.33; Xenophon reminds soldiers of his help in securing their reputation in, 7.6.36;

fellow Greeks, solidarity among: Klearchos uses his army in Hellespont region to aid, 1.1.9, 1.3.3, 2.6.2; Klearchos speciously professes his loyalty to, 1.3.5; Hekatonymos applauds the soldiers as, 5.5.8, and urges consequent claims of mutual respect, 5.5.9; Xenophon speaks of treatment of soldiers by, 5.5.14; soldiers remind Sinopeans that they are, 5.6.2; Xenophon and Cheirisophos do not believe army should make monetary demands of, if friendly, 6.2.6; Xenophon urges nobility of saving, 6.3.17; Polykrates accuses Herakleides of injustice toward, 7.6.41;

as source of army: Cyrus gathers troops from, 1.1.6–8, 1.1.9–11;

army's return to: soldier pretends to be anxious for quick, 1.3.14; Xenias' and Pasion's troops want, 1.4.7; Tissaphernes promises army safe, under his leadership, 2.3.26, 2.3.28; Artaxerxes will block, 2.4.4; Greek soldiers long for, though distant, 3.1.2, 3.1.3; Xenophon on balance advocates, 3.2.26; race against enemy to command mountaintop should be seen as race toward, Xenophon says, 3.4.46; the goal of army, rather than the territory of the Makrones, 4.8.6; Antileon wishes to achieve by sea at leisure, 5.1.2; generals explain to Mossynoeci as their goal, 5.4.5; Silanos wants for himself, 5.6.18; should be soldiers' keenest wish, Timasion says, 5.6.22; supported by Xenophon, 5.6.33; Phasis expedition could not be confused with, Xenophon argues, 5.7.6–9; soldiers, now close to achieving, consider how to enhance their prospects once secured, 6.1.17; soldiers long for, 6.4.8; in Bithynia, Xenophon reminds soldiers how close, 6.5.23, 6.6.12; Agasias accuses Dexippos of knowing difficulties of, if by land, 6.6.22; Kleandros offers to lead personally, 6.6.34;

*see also* **captains, Greek; cavalry,** Greek; **generals, Greek; hoplites,** Greek; **Ionia; mercenaries,** Greek; **Peloponnese/Peloponnesians; peltasts,** in Cyrus'/Greek army

**guest-friend(s),** Aristippos and Cyrus, 1.1.10; Proxenos and Cyrus, 1.1.11; Sophainetos, Socrates, and Cyrus, 1.1.11; Cyrus becomes Klearchos', 1.3.3; Ariaios and Menon, 2.1.5, 2.4.15; Proxenos and Xenophon, 3.1.4, 5.3.5; Zeus' protection of, 3.2.4; Kleandros and Xenophon become, 6.6.35, 7.1.8; Xenophon says if Seuthes provides supplies, he will be behaving like, 7.3.8; Biton and Naukleidas become Xenophon's, 7.8.6

**Gymnias,** reached by Greeks, 4.7.19

**Halisarna,** Greeks assaulting Asidates receive help from, 7.8.17

**Halys River,** Hekatonymos describes difficulty of crossing, 5.6.9; on voyage from Sinope to Heraclea, Greeks (allegedly) pass mouth of, 6.2.1

**hand(s),** Cyrus has those of wrongdoers cut off, 1.9.13; victorious Persians cut off the dead Cyrus' right, 1.10.1, 3.1.18; tokens representing, sent by Artaxerxes to Ariaios, 2.4.1; said by Klearchos to have been preferred by Artaxerxes, 2.4.7; raised in voting by Greek soldiers, 3.2.9, 3.2.33, 3.2.28, 5.6.33, 7.3.6; brigand's, tied behind his back by victorious plowman in Thracian dance, 6.1.8; *see also* **handshakes**

**handshakes,** exchanged between: Cyrus and Orontas, 1.6.6; Greek officers and Tissaphernes and Artaxerxes' brother-in-law, 2.3.28, 3.2.4; Greek delegates and Seuthes at end of meeting, 7.3.9; Greeks and Seuthes when latter comes to rescue, 7.4.19

**hand-to-hand fighting,** Kardouchian equipment unsuited for, 4.4.31; Greeks victorious against tribesmen in,

4.6.24; [Eastern] Chalybes prepared to engage in, 4.7.15; initially attempted by Mossynoeci, 5.4.25

**hares,** Armenian headman's son-in-law absent hunting, 4.5.24

**Harmene,** Greeks arrive in Sinope at port of, 6.1.15, 6.1.17

**harmost(s),** Spartan official(s) based abroad: will act together to exclude Greek army reported to be hostile to Sparta, 6.6.13; Kleandros, resident in Byzantium, identified as, 6.2.13, 6.4.17, 7.1.8; Aristarchos, replacement for Kleandros, identified as, 7.2.5, 7.2.7, 7.2.13; responsible for Spartan interests in the Chersonese, will demand obedience from soldiers sent there, 7.2.15

**Harpasos River,** reached by Greeks, 4.7.18

**hats,** of foxskin, worn by Thracians, 7.4.4

**headcount review,** of Greek army: at Kelainai, 1.2.9; taken at midnight in Babylonia, 1.7.1, 10; at Kerasous, 5.3.3; allegedly to be taken outside Byzantium, 7.1.11; *compare also* numbers given for Greeks assaulting Kolchoi position, 4.8.15; numbers and proportions given for army as it split up at Heraclea, 6.2.10, 6.2.16

**headman:** captured by Polykrates in Armenian village, 4.5.24; promises to help Greeks, 4.5.28–29; accompanies Xenophon through Armenian villages, 4.5.30, 4.5.32; provides Greeks with useful information, 4.5.34–36; given to Cheirisophos as a guide, is mistreated and runs away, 4.6.1–3

**Hegesandros,** general in the breakaway Arcadian contingent, one of only eight survivors of Bithynian attack on his unit, 6.3.5

**Hekatonymos,** a Sinopean: reputed to be a clever speaker, 5.4.7; acts as spokesman of a Sinopean deputation criticizing the army for its occupation of Kotyora, 5.4.7–12; crushingly rebutted by Xenophon, 5.5.13–23; urges army to travel by sea rather than across Paphlagonia, 5.6.3–10; suspected by some of being motivated by friendship for Korylas, the Paphlagonian ruler, 5.6.11

**Helios,** sun god, assists Cyrus the Elder to take Larisa, 3.4.8; sacrifice of horses to, 4.5.35

**Hellas** [of Pergamum], wife of Gongylos of Eretria, entertains Xenophon in Pergamum and advises him to kidnap Asidates, 7.8.8; *see also* Appendix W, §16

**Hellespont,** Klearchos' army receives financial support from cities around, 1.1.9; against Spartan orders, Klearchos voyages to, 2.6.3; Polos approaches, 7.2.5

**helmets,** worn by: Cyrus' Greek army during Tyriaion review, 1.2.16; all of Cyrus' Persian cavalry troop (except Cyrus himself), during battle, 1.8.6; Chalybes, 4.7.16; Drilai, Paphlagonian-type, 5.2.22; Greeks during Thynoi attack, 7.4.16; Mossynoeci, similar to Paphlagonian, 5.4.13

**Heraclea/Heracleans**
location: Sinope situated on coastal route from Kotyora to, 5.6.10; Xenophon's contingent, not far from Kalpe Harbor, long way from, 6.3.16; Asian (Bithynian) Thrace extends from Black Sea mouth to, 6.4.1; voyage from Byzantium to, 6.4.2, 6.4.3;

and Greek army: Timasion and Thorax attempt to extort money from, 5.6.19; offer Timasion money to get army to leave Black Sea region, 5.6.21, 5.6.26; Xenophon believes army should take offer of ships from, 5.6.31; provide army with merchant ships, but refuse to give money,

**leader(s),** Herakles the Leader, object of sacrifices and chosen as watchword, 6.3.15, 6.5.24–25; infantry to be placed leading cavalry at night, 7.3.37–39;

*Cyrus:* his magnanimity toward the deserters Xenias and Pasion, 1.4.8–9; his vigorous direction of Persian nobles when wagons stuck in mud, 1.5.8–9; his action to separate warring Greek generals, 1.5.15–17; summary of his leadership qualities, 1.9.1–31;

*Klearchos:* after Cunaxa, undisputed as, 2.2.5; his style of leadership exhibited in march through trench-crossed Babylonia, 2.3.11–13; characterized generally, 2.6.8–15;

*Xenophon as:* offers himself to Proxenos' officers as, 3.1.25; claims not to obstruct election of other, 5.7.10; considers but rejects idea of becoming sole, 6.1.19–24; is urged by rioting soldiers to lead takeover of Byzantium, but cools the men down and declines, 7.1.21–31; leads army to Seuthes, 7.3.6–7; in effect defends his record as, in army's dealings with Seuthes, 7.6.7–38;

his style of leadership: Books 3–7 throughout, esp. sharing the men's toils, 3.4.46–49, 7.3.45–46; accessibility, 4.3.10; compassionate but firm behavior in march through snow, 4.5.7–9. 4.5.15–21, 5.8.1–26; his opinions about: indispensable, 1.1.38; elected, will have no authority on current trends, 5.7.28; Lacedaemonian position as leaders of Greece must be respected, 6.1.27–28, 7.1.30, 7.6.37;

*other Greeks:* new generals chosen to be, 3.1.47, 3.2.1; Stratokles the, of the Cretan archers, 4.2.28; of Greek army, Tiribazos asks to speak to, 4.4.5; Aischines the, of peltasts supporting Arcadians, 4.4.18; Kleanor, of Arcadian hoplites, 4.8.19; collectively army consensus reached on need for single, 6.1.18, 6.1.25; debates on identity of single, 6.1.19–33; Cheirisophos elected, rejected, 6.1.32, 6.2.12, 6.3.1; Kallimachos and Lykon ringleaders of Arcadian breakaway, 6.2.9; of reserve units, named, 6.5.11; army will be obedient to Kleandros as their, Xenophon tells him, 6.6.32; Kleandros wishes to be army's, but the sacrificial omens block it, 6.6.35–36; Koiratadas' failed attempt to become army's, 7.1.33–37, 7.1.40–41;

*others among or of non-Greeks:* of Mossynoecian faction, come to conference with Greeks, 5.4.3–11; Greek generals agree Seuthes should act as, in assault on Thynoi, 7.3.36; lack of, crucial weakness of Thynoi, 7.7.31; Seuthes in danger of Thynoi choosing strong Greek leaders, 7.7.31

**Leontini,** *see* **Gorgias**

**libation(s),** offered in thanks for news of how to cross Kentrites River, 4.3.13–14; offered at banquet for Paphlagonians, 6.1.5

**light-armed troops** (Greek *gymnētes*), in Proxenos' army joining Cyrus, 1.2.3; comprising slingers and archers, shut up in hollow square, 3.4.26; on ascent to land of Kardouchoi, Cheirisophos has all in van, Xenophon none in rearguard, 4.1.6; group commanders of, asked for volunteers for special mission, Aristeas responds, 4.1.28; ambush and capture potential guides on march north of Phasis River, 4.6.17; Aristeas again responds, with Nikomachos, to call for volunteers for special mission with their, 4.6.20; as slingers in attack on Drilai, 5.2.12; more mobile from, deployed by Xenophon in Bithynia for reconnaissance, 6.3.15; *see also* **lighter-armed troops; peltasts**

**lighter-armed troops** (Greek *psiloi*), of Cretan archers, 3.3.7; of troops rushing into Drilai stronghold besides peltasts, 5.2.16

**Locris,** *see* **Theogenes**

**logs,** thrown at Greeks by Drilai, 5.2.23; used by Greeks to spread fire in Drilai settlement, 5.2.26; hollowed out for use by Mossynoeci in canoes, 5.4.11

**Lousoi,** *see* **Eurylochos**

**Lycaonia/Lycaonians:** plundered by Greeks as Cyrus' army marches through, 1.2.19; inhabit land in Persian Empire against Artaxerxes' will, 3.2.23; (allegedly) ruled by Mithradates, 7.8.25

**Lydia/Lydians:** Cyrus' army marches through, 1.2.5; sell grain to Cyrus' army, 1.5.6; Cyrus' appointment as satrap of, 1.9.7; Apollonides' appearance suggests he comes from, 3.1.31; as west of Tigris plain, 3.5.15; Asidates not fooled by Greek ruse of marching into, 7.8.20–21; ruled by Artimas, 7.8.25

**Lykaian sacrifices,** offered by Xenias the Arcadian at Peltai, 1.2.10

**Lykios son of Polystratos** of Athens: appointed commander of newly formed cavalry unit, 3.3.20; pursues Persian cavalry into highlands near Kentrites River, 4.3.22; captures Persian animals and supplies, 4.3.25; accompanies Xenophon to viewpoint on Mount Theches, 4.7.24

**Lykios the Syracusan,** horseman, sent by Klearchos to reconnoiter after battle of Cunaxa, 1.10.14

**Lykon** of Achaea, a troublemaker: speaks against Xenophon's Black Sea city plan, 5.6.27; criticizes generals for not obtaining payment for army, 6.2.4; sent as ambassador from soldiers to extort money from Heracleans, 6.2.7; one of the leaders of the breakaway Arcadian/Achaean group, 6.2.9

**Lykos River,** flows through Heraclean plain, 6.2.3

**mace-bearers,** Artapatas is most faithful of Cyrus', 1.6.11

**Maeander River:** Cyrus' army crosses, 1.2.5; flows through palace park in Kelainai, 1.2.7; Marsyas River empties into, 1.2.8

**Magnetes,** dance at banquet for Paphlagonians, 6.1.7–8

**Maisades,** father of Seuthes the Thracian: held principality over Thynoi, Melanditai, and Tranipsai, but not extending as far as the Delta of Thrace, 7.2.32, 7.5.1; having lost principality during generally difficult period for Odrysae, dies, leaving the child Seuthes to be brought up at the court of his kinsman, king Medokos, 7.2.32

**Makistos,** *see* **Silanos of Makistos**

**Makrones,** Greeks reach land of, 4.7.27; prepare to fight Greeks, 4.8.1–3; soldier in Greek army by origin one of the, 4.8.4; reach agreement with Greeks and provide market to them, 4.8.4–8, 5.5.18; as independent tribe, 7.8.25

**maligning,** *see* **defamation**

**Mantineians,** dance at banquet for Paphlagonians, 6.1.11

**Mardoi,** act as mercenaries for Orontas, 4.3.4

**Mariandynoi,** Heraclea is situated in land of, 6.2.1

**market(s):** time of day measured by reference to attendance in, 1.8.1; following arrest of generals, Greek soldiers concerned about access to, 3.1.2; army willing to be friendly with those who will provide, 5.5.17–18; will not be provided to undisciplined soldiers, Xenophon foresees, 5.7.33;

**sick, the,** afflicted with cold, snowblindness, and frostbite in the Armenian highlands, 4.5.12, 4.5.17–18, 4.5.21, 22; put on board ship at Kerasous, 5.3.1; people of Kotyora refuse to take in, but are compelled to do so, 5.5.6, 5.5.20; incident of the sick man rescued by Xenophon from being buried alive, 5.8.6–11; Kleandros compulsorily quarters on Byzantines, 7.2.6

**Sicyon/Sicyonians,** grumbling Soteridas comes from, 3.4.47; *see also* **Soteridas**

**Silanos of Ambracia,** seer: richly rewarded by Cyrus for success of prophecy that Artaxerxes would not confront Cyrus' army during the following ten days, 1.7.18, 5.6.18; acts as Xenophon's seer in reading sacrificial omens about founding Greek city on Black Sea, 5.6.16, 5.6.29; reveals Black Sea city plan to soldiers in misleading form, 5.6.17–19, 5.6.29; opposes Xenophon's proposal that all soldiers must travel back to Greece as one group, 5.6.34; deserts Greek army at Heraclea, 6.4.13.

**Silanos of Makistos** (in Elis), a young trumpeter, 7.6.16

**silver**
  used for money: promised to Greek soldiers participating in Cyrus' campaign, 1.4.13; promised to those giving information about a disturbance in camp, 2.2.20;
  objects made from: feet of couches in Tiribazos' tent, 4.4.21; drinking horn given to guide from Gymnias, 4.7.27; bowl presented by Timasion to Seuthes, 7.3.27

**Sinope/Sinopeans:** lies on coastal route between Kotyora and Heraclea, 6.1.10;
  colonies from: Trapezus, 4.8.22; Kerasous, 5.3.2; Kotyora, 5.5.3; army's presence in Kotyora alarms, 5.5.7–12; army's behavior in Kotyora defended to, 5.5.15–23;
  and Paphlagonians: threaten to form alliance with Paphlagonians, 5.5.12, 5.6.3; instead, establish good relations with army, 5.5.24–25; advise army not to travel by land through Paphlagonia, but to go by sea, 5.6.1–11; Hekatonymos is Korylas' *proxenos* at, 5.6.11;
  dealings with army subsequent to Hekatonymos' speeches about Paphlagonia: army arranges to receive merchant ships from, 5.6.12–14; Timasion and Thorax attempt to extort money from, 5.6.19; offer Timasion money to get army to leave Black Sea region, 5.6.21, 5.6.26; Xenophon believes army should take offer of ships from, 5.6.31; army arrives at, 6.1.15; army sails to Heraclea from, 6.2.1

**Sitalkas,** past king of the Odrysae, commemorated in song, 6.1.6

**Sittake,** Greeks camp near, 2.4.13–14; *see also* **Opis**

**Skillous,** Xenophon creates precinct for Artemis in, 5.3.7–13

**Skythenoi,** Greeks pass through land of, 4.7.18; separated from Makrones' territory by river, 4.8.1

**slave(s)**
  in Persian Empire: Cyrus gives Cilicians right to recover those taken as booty, 1.2.27; Cyrus' generosity to brave volunteers showed he thought bad men fit to be their, 1.9.15; Cyrus the King's, 1.9.29, 2.5.38; many in Tissaphernes' entourage, 2.3.13; in the villages of Parysatis in Media, Greeks prohibited from taking, 2.4.27; Greek army's aim had been to make Artaxerxes a, 3.1.17; run away as Greeks attempt to kidnap Asidates, 7.8.12; seized by Greeks from Asidates, 7.8.16, 7.8.19;
  among or of Greeks: at Zapatas River, killed by Persian cav-

alry alongside Greek freemen, 2.5.32; perish during snowfall in Armenia, 4.5.4; former, claims to have originally been a Macronian and acts as go-between with them, 4.8.4–5; if army is ever outnumbered, it will be in position of, Xenophon says to Sinopeans, 5.6.13; dancing-girl is, of an Arcadian, 6.1.12; remain at Kalpe Harbor while soldiers go out on expedition, 6.5.3; taken by Greeks to plunder Bithynian countryside, 6.6.1; one only brought by Xenophon from Parium to Perinthus, 7.3.20;
  among or of Thracians: among gifts made to Seuthes at banquet, 7.3.27; Xenophon satisfied if Seuthes makes Thynoi, 7.4.24; fate of Thynoi if Seuthes is victorious, 7.7.32;
  acts of enslavement: seized by Arcadians from Bithynian villages, 6.3.3; captured by Greeks in Bithynian countryside, 6.6.38; Anaxibios orders Greek soldiers remaining in Byzantium to be made, 7.1.36, 7.2.6; Aristarchos sells Greek soldiers as, 7.2.6; Aristarchos promises no longer to sell Greek soldiers as, 7.3.3; captured in Thynian plain, 7.3.48; Greeks outside Perinthus did not have means to capture, 7.6.26; Xenophon reminds soldiers of Seuthes' help in acquiring, 7.6.28; given to Xenophon by Seuthes for Greek soldiers, 7.7.53

**slingers, Greek:** Xenophon suggests creating units of, using lead shot as well as stones, 3.3.16–18; appointed following Xenophon's suggestions, 3.3.20; hold off Tissaphernes' troops, 3.4.15, 3.4.16; unable to retaliate against Persians in high hills, 3.4.26; sent by Cheirisophos to Xenophon to assist in fighting Kardouchoi, 4.3.27; given orders to fire at Drilai stronghold on signal, 5.2.12; and do so, 5.2.14; Xenophon notes competence of, 5.6.15; *see also* **stone slingers**

**Smikres,** an Arcadian, general in breakaway Arcadian contingent, killed by Bithynians, 6.3.4–5

**sneeze,** thought by Greeks to be sign from gods, 3.2.9

**snow**
  *in Armenia:*
    creates difficult conditions for Greeks: apathy, animals unable to move, 4.4.8–13; causes windburn, numbness, starving faints in Greeks, 4.5.1, 4.5.3–9; snow blindness, frostbite, apathy, 4.5.11–21;
    Armenian headman: gives Greeks advice on traveling with animals through, 4.5.36; leads Greeks through, 4.6.2;
    main cause, besides enemy action, of Greek deaths on the march, 5.3.3;
    Xenophon denies that he was unnecessarily harsh when Greeks were beset by, 5.8.3, 5.8.14–15;
  *in Thrace:* Seuthes looks for enemies' tracks in, 7.3.42; makes conditions unpleasant for Greeks in Thynian plain, 7.4.3

**Socrates the Achaean,** Greek general: one of the generals in charge of the cities in Ionia which Cyrus garrisoned against Tissaphernes, 1.1.11; joins Cyrus' army mustering at Sardis, 1.2.3; one of five generals arrested by Tissaphernes and subsequently put to death, 2.5.31; obituarized, 2.6.30; replaced as general by Xanthikles, 3.1.47

**Socrates the Athenian,** the famous philosopher: asked for advice about joining Cyrus by Xenophon, 3.1.5; his advice circumvented, 3.1.7; *see also* Appendix W, §31; Appendix A

# REFERENCE MAPS

## Directory

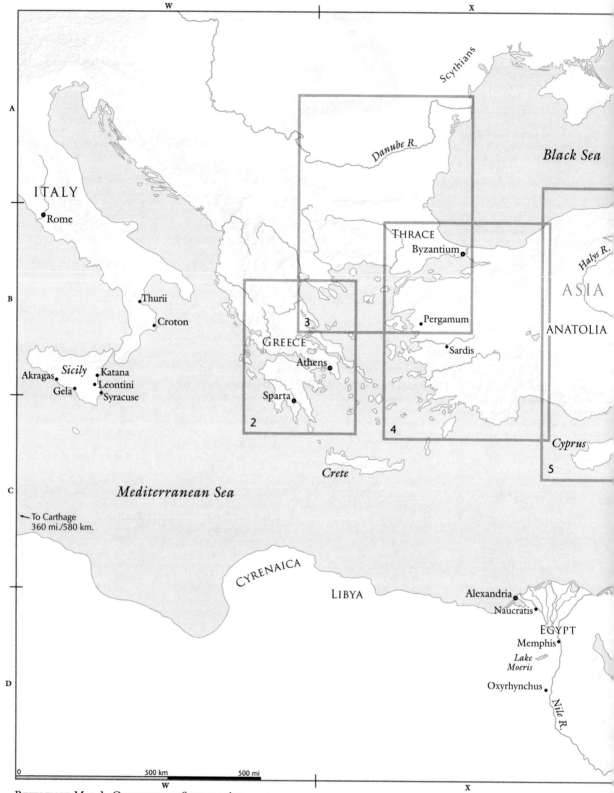

W               X

Scythians

Danube R.

*Black Sea*

A

ITALY

Rome

THRACE

Byzantium

*Halys R.*

ASIA

B

Thurii

Croton

3

Pergamum

ANATOLIA

GREECE

Sardis

Athens

*Sicily*

Akragas •   • Katana

Gela •   • Leontini

     • Syracuse

Sparta

2

4

*Cyprus*

5

*Crete*

C

*Mediterranean Sea*

← To Carthage
360 mi./580 km.

CYRENAICA

LIBYA

Alexandria

Naucratis

EGYPT

Memphis

*Lake Moeris*

Oxyrhynchus

*Nile R.*

D

0        500 km       500 mi

W              X

REFERENCE MAP 1: OVERVIEW OF SITES IN *ANABASIS*

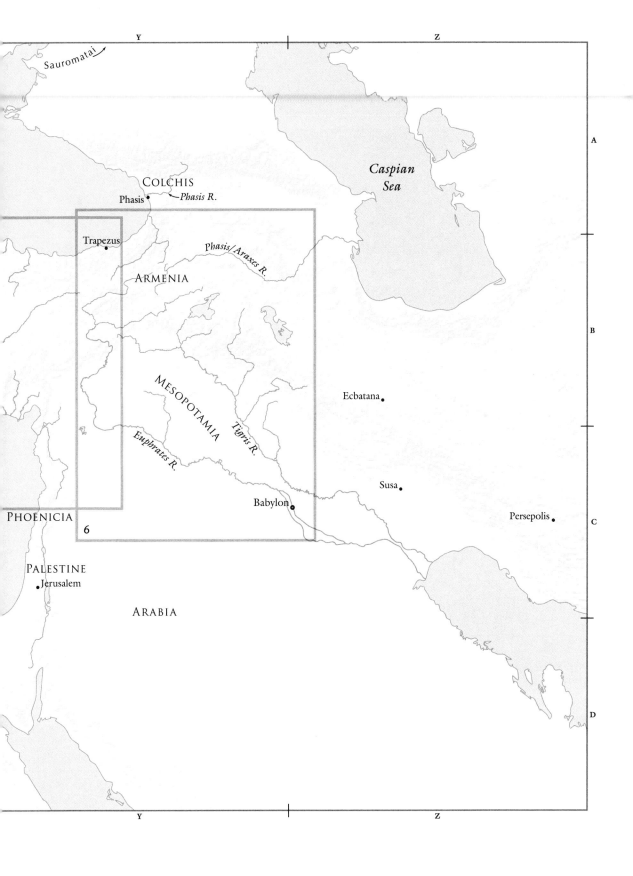

Y
Z

Sauromatai

A

Caspian
Sea

COLCHIS
Phasis • *Phasis R.*

Trapezus •

*Phasis/Araxes R.*

ARMENIA

B

Ecbatana •

MESOPOTAMIA

*Tigris R.*

*Euphrates R.*

Susa •

PHOENICIA

Persepolis •

C

6

Babylon •

PALESTINE
• Jerusalem

ARABIA

D

Y
Z

X          Y          Z

CHALCIDICE
• Olynthos
Poteidaia •

A

Aegean
Sea

Larissa •

MAGNESIA

THESSALY          • Pherai

Pharsalus •

AMBRACIA

DOLOPIA

AINIS
AETOLIA          MT. OETA          • Oreos

B          Thermopylae ✕          LOCRIS
ACARNANIA

BOEOTIA

Euboea

Delphi ⋔          Chaeronea          • Eretria
Coronea ✕          • Thebes
Ithaca          Leuktra ✕          • Plataea

ACHAEA          Marathon ✕

Zacynthus          Pellene •          Isthmus of Corinth          Megara •          Athens
Lousoi •          Sicyon •                              Erchia •
ELIS          Stymphalos •          Corinth •          Salamis ✕          • Sphettos
Phleious •
ARCADIA          Nemea ✕          Aegina
C          MT. PHOLOE          • Orchomenos
Epitalion •          Olympia ⋔          Methydrion •          Argos •
Skillous •          • Makistos          Mantineia •          Keos
MT. LYKAION          • Megalopolis          Halieis •
Lepreon •
PARRASIA          Karyai •
PELOPONNESE

MESSENIA          • Sparta
LACEDAEMON
Sphakteria          LACONIA

• Asine

D

0     50 km     50 mi

Cape Tainaron

REFERENCE MAP 2: GREECE

X   Y   Z

A

Danube R.

Triballi

B                                                    Black Sea

Court of
Medokos?                            Apollonia
                                           Pontica
⌃                              Tranipsai?
MT. SKOMBROS
           Pistiros?                         Melanditai?
                        Odrysae
                                           Salmydessos
S
t
r
y
m
o
n
 
R
.                    THRACE              Thynoi   Melinophagoi

C                                              Selymbria   Thynian
                                                          Plain
MACEDONIA                          New Fort?        Byzantium
                                      Bisanthe   Perinthus
           Abdera   Maroneia    SACRED
Amphipolis                        MOUNT ⌃ Ganos   Propontis

Stageira
                 Thasos
                        Chersonese
                    Aigospotamoi

                    Hellespont          TROAD

D

Aegean Sea

0   75 km   75 mi

REFERENCE MAP 3: THRACE

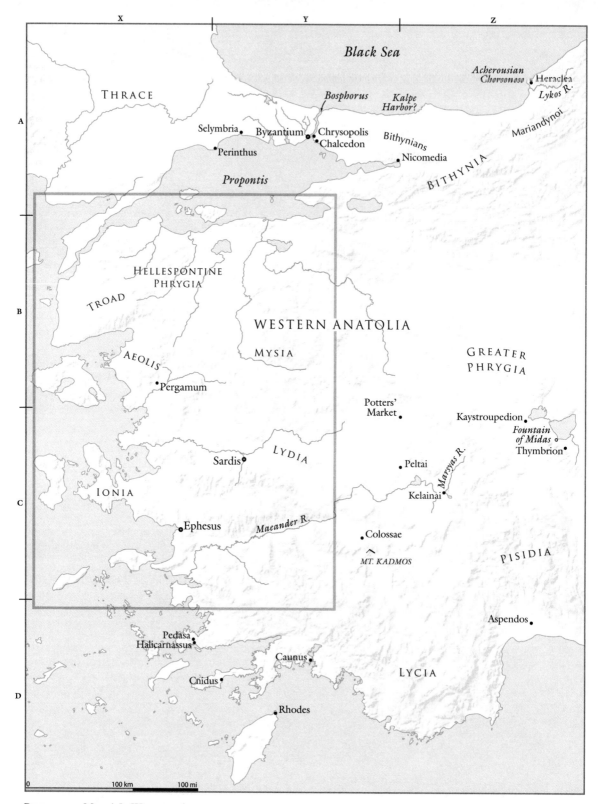

REFERENCE MAP 4.1: WESTERN ANATOLIA

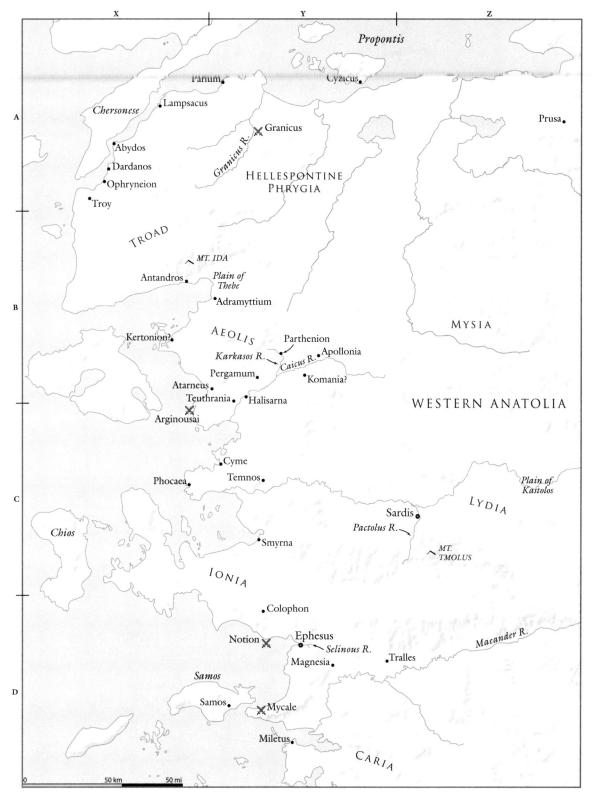

| X | Y | Z |

**Propontis**

*Chersonese*

Parium •

Cyzicus •

Prusa •

Lampsacus •

Granicus ✕ • Granicus

*Granicus R.*

Abydos •
Dardanos •
Ophryneion •

**HELLESPONTINE PHRYGIA**

Troy •

**T R O A D**

⌄ *MT. IDA*

*Plain of Thebe*

Antandros •

Adramyttium •

**M Y S I A**

Kertonion? •

**A E O L I S**

Parthenion

*Karkasos R.*

Apollonia •

*Caicus R.*

Pergamum •

Komania? •

Atarneus •
Teuthrania •
• Halisarna

**WESTERN ANATOLIA**

✕ Arginousai

Cyme •

Temnos •

Phocaea •

*Plain of Kastolos*

**L Y D I A**

Sardis •

*Pactolus R.*

*Chios*

⌄ *MT. TMOLUS*

Smyrna •

**I O N I A**

Colophon •

*Maeander R.*

Notion ✕

Ephesus ◉
← *Selinous R.*

Magnesia •

Tralles •

*Samos*

Samos •

✕ Mycale

Miletus •

**C A R I A**

0   50 km   50 mi

REFERENCE MAP 4.2: INSET OF WESTERN ANATOLIA, IONIAN COAST

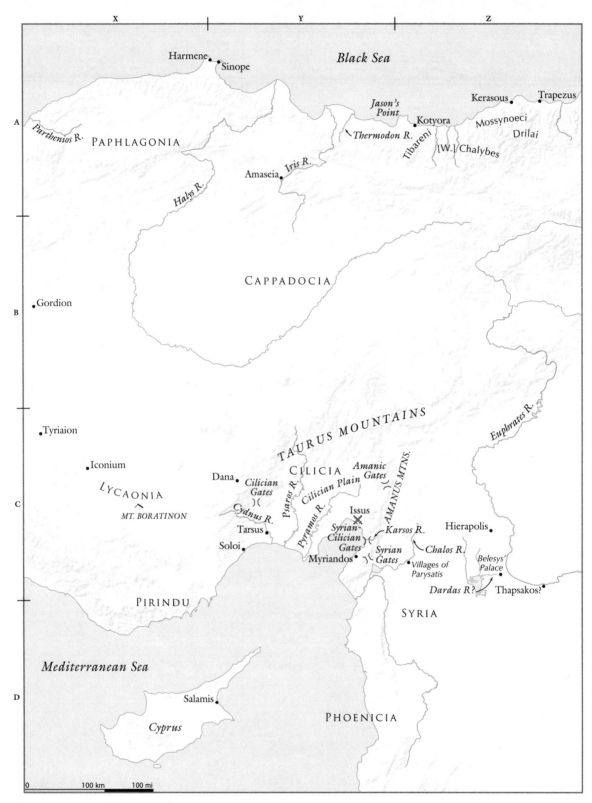

X        Y        Z

*Black Sea*

Harmene
Sinope

*Jason's Point*
Kerasous    Trapezus

A

*Parthenios R.*

PAPHLAGONIA

*Thermodon R.*
Kotyora
Mossynoeci
Tibareni
[W.] Chalybes
Drilai

*Halys R.*

Amaseia   *Iris R.*

CAPPADOCIA

*Euphrates R.*

Gordion

B

Tyriaion

TAURUS MOUNTAINS

Iconium

Dana
CILICIA
*Cilician Gates*
*Psaros R.*
*Amanic Gates*

LYCAONIA

*MT. BORATINON*

*Cilician Plain*

*Cydnus R.*

AMANUS MTNS.

Tarsus

Issus

C

Soloi

*Syrian Cilician Gates*
*Karsos R.*
Hierapolis

*Pyramos R.*

Myriandos
*Syrian Gates*
*Chalos R.*

*Belesys' Palace*

*Villages of Parysatis*

PIRINDU

*Dardas R.?*
Thapsakos?

SYRIA

*Mediterranean Sea*

D

Salamis

PHOENICIA

*Cyprus*

0   100 km   100 mi

REFERENCE MAP 5: EASTERN ANATOLIA

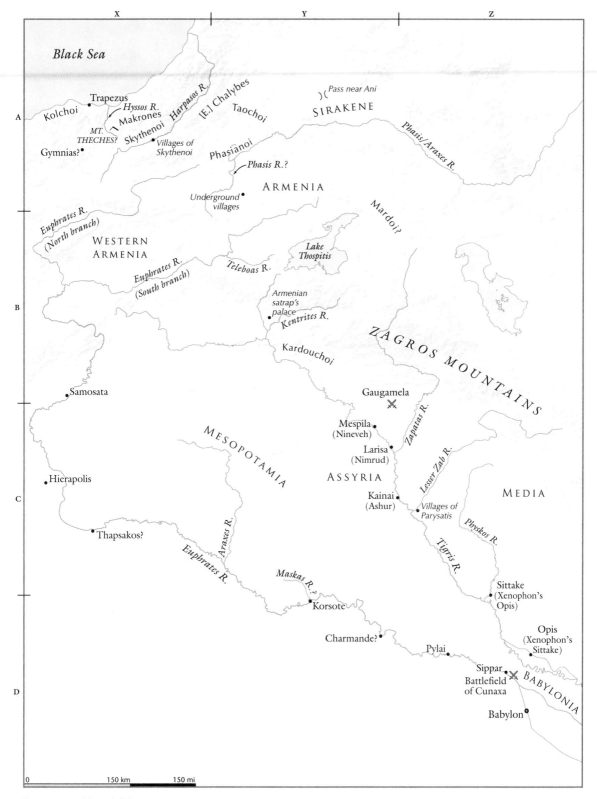

Black Sea

X  Y  Z

A

Kolchoi
Trapezus
*Hyssos R.*
Makrones
*MT.
THECHES?*
Skythenoi  *Harpasos R.*
*[E.] Chalybes*  Taochoi
*Villages of
Skythenoi*
Gymnias?
Phasianoi

*Pass near Ani*
SIRAKENE

*Phasis/Araxes R.*

*Phasis R.?*

ARMENIA

*Underground
villages*

*Mardoi?*

*Euphrates R.
(North branch)*

WESTERN
ARMENIA

*Lake
Thospitis*

B

*Euphrates R.
(South branch)*  *Teleboas R.*

*Armenian
satrap's
palace*
*Kentrites R.*

Kardouchoi

ZAGROS MOUNTAINS

Samosata

Gaugamela

Mespila
(Nineveh)
Larisa
(Nimrud)

*Zapatas R.*

MESOPOTAMIA

ASSYRIA

*Lesser Zab R.*

MEDIA

Hierapolis

Kainai
(Ashur)

*Villages of
Parysatis*

*Physkos R.*

C

Thapsakos?

*Araxes R.*

*Euphrates R.*

*Maskas R.?*

*Tigris R.*

Korsote

Sittake
(Xenophon's
Opis)

Charmande?

Pylai

Opis
(Xenophon's
Sittake)

Sippar
Battlefield
of Cunaxa

BABYLONIA

D

Babylon

0    150 km    150 mi

REFERENCE MAP 6: MESOPOTAMIA

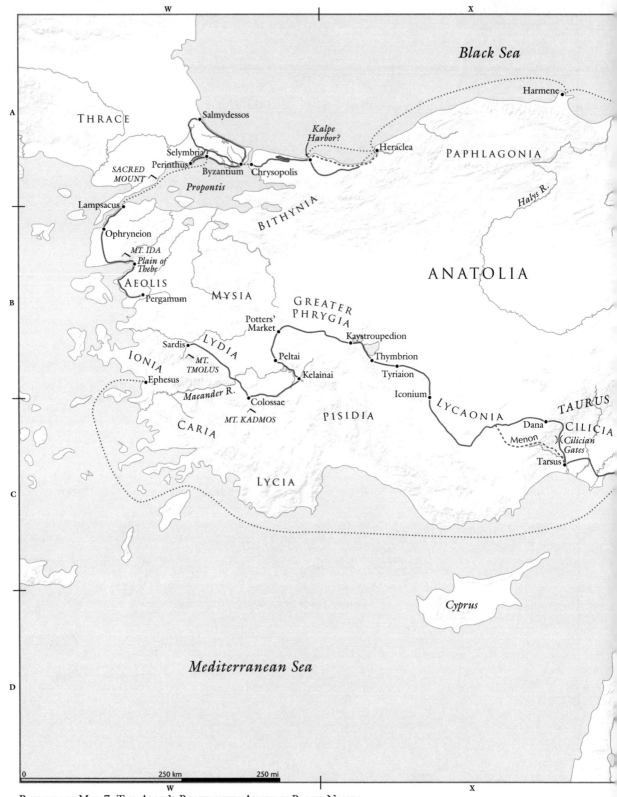

*Black Sea*

Harmene

A

THRACE

Salmydessos

*Kalpe Harbor?*

PAPHLAGONIA

Selymbria

Perinthus

*SACRED MOUNT*

Byzantium

Chrysopolis

Heraclea

*Propontis*

Halys R.

BITHYNIA

Lampsacus

Ophryneion

*MT. IDA*
*Plain of Thebe*

ANATOLIA

AEOLIS

Pergamum

MYSIA

GREATER PHRYGIA

B

Potters' Market

Kaystroupedion

Sardis

LYDIA

Thymbrion

IONIA

*MT. TMOLUS*

Peltai

Tyriaion

Ephesus

Kelainai

Iconium

LYCAONIA

*Maeander R.*

TAURUS

Colossae

Dana

CILICIA

*MT. KADMOS*

PISIDIA

Menon

*Cilician Gates*

CARIA

Tarsus

LYCIA

C

Cyprus

*Mediterranean Sea*

D

REFERENCE MAP 7: THE ARMY'S ROUTE WITH ANCIENT PLACE-NAMES

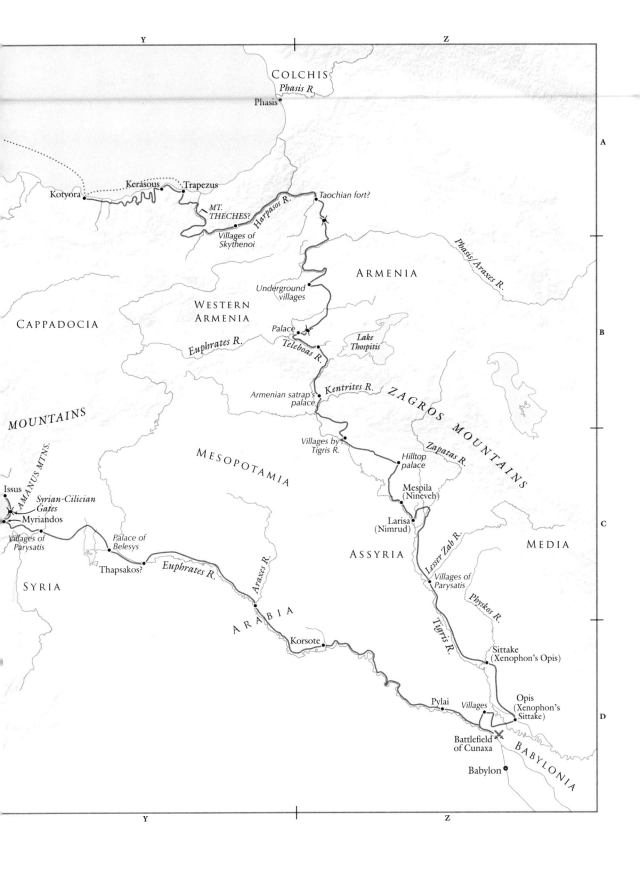

COLCHIS

*Phasis R.*

Phasis

Y                                Z

Kotyora   Kerásous   Trapezus                                          A

*MT.*
*THECHES?*                    *Harpasos R.*   Taochian fort?

*Villages of*
*Skythenoi*

ARMENIA

*Underground*
*villages*                                    *Phasis/Araxes R.*

CAPPADOCIA

WESTERN
ARMENIA

*Euphrates R.*        Palace

*Teleboas R.*      *Lake*                                           B
*Thospitis*

*Kentrites R.*        Z A G R O S

Armenian satrap's
*palace*                                  M O U N T A I N S

*Villages by*
*Tigris R.*                  *Hilltop*      *Zapatas R.*
*palace*

MOUNTAINS

*AMANUS MTNS.*         MESOPOTAMIA           Mespila
(Nineveh)

Issus

*Syrian-Cilician*
*Gates*
Myriandos                                Larisa                      C
(Nimrud)
*Villages of*
*Parysatis*          Palace of                    MEDIA
*Belesys*                  ASSYRIA
SYRIA                                         *Lesser Zab R.*

Thapsakos?   *Euphrates R.*                   *Villages of*
*Parysatis*

*Araxes R.*                                   *Physkos R.*

A R A B I A

*Tigris R.*

Korsote                                     Sittake
(Xenophon's Opis)

Pylai   *Villages*                          Opis
(Xenophon's
Sittake)                   D

Battlefield
of Cunaxa                 B A B Y L O N I A

Babylon

Y                                Z

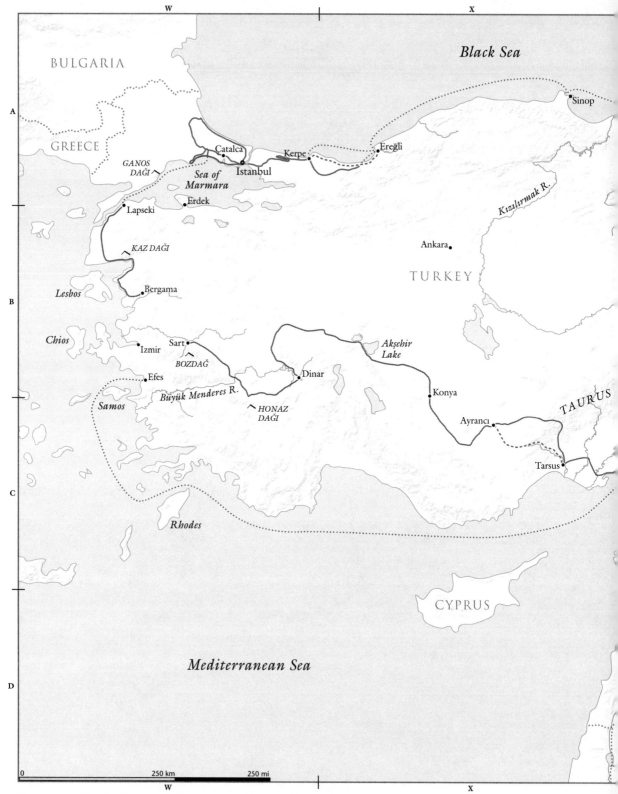

REFERENCE MAP 8: THE ARMY'S ROUTE WITH MODERN PLACE-NAMES

Y                                    Z

*Rioni R.*

GEORGIA

A

AZERBAIJAN

ARMENIA

Ordu •
Kirazlik •        • Trabzon          *Penek R.*
Giresun •                            • Kars
         Kuşköy •   *POLUT*      *Oltu R.*
~ *Yeşilırmak R.*  *DAĞI*
         *Zigana Pass* (          *Çakırbaba*   *Aras R.*
Gümüşhane •                        *Pass*
         Bayburt •   *Çoruh R.*
              Pasinler •
         Erzurum •

SÜPHAN
DAĞI                                 B
Bingöl •        *Euphrates (Murat) R.*   *Lake*
         Muş •                      *Van*
         Bitlis •                         IRAN

MOUNTAINS              *Botan R.*
         *Tigris (Dicle) R.*        ZAGROS MOUNTAINS

*Bahçe*                   Mardin •     Cizre •
*Pass*                                            *Greater Zab R.*
         *NUR DAĞLARI*      MESOPOTAMIA
• Dörtyol
• İskenderun                         Mosul •     • Kellek        C
*Belen*
*Pass*   • Aleppo   *Lake*
              *Assad*   Raqqa •      *Lesser Zab R.*
              *Khabur R.*
         *Euphrates (Furat) R.*      Baiji •     *Adhaim R.*

SYRIA                                IRAQ

LEBANON                    Jubbah •
                                     Samarra •
         • Damascus        Hit •
                      Falluja •   Baghdad •        D
                                 *Tigris (Dicle) R.*   Kut •

Y                                    Z

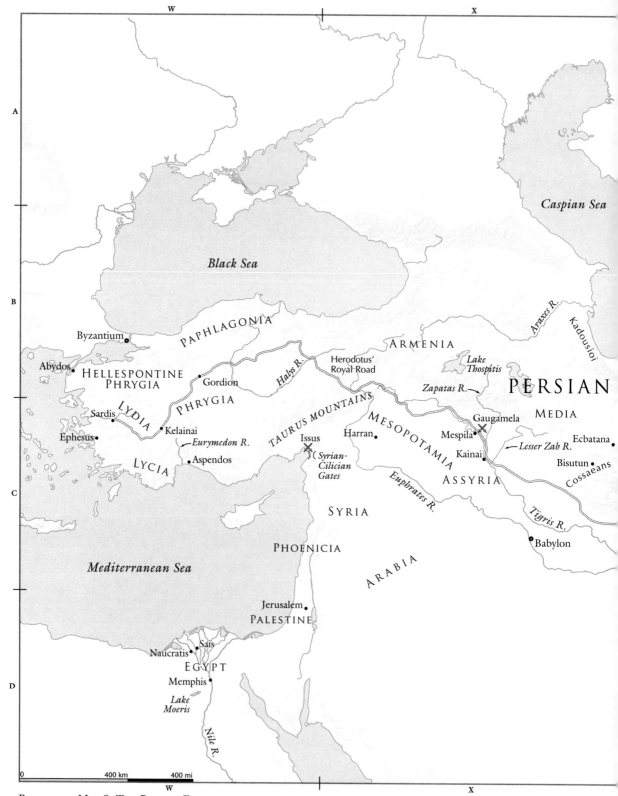

W                                    X

A

Caspian Sea

Black Sea

B

Byzantium

PAPHLAGONIA                    ARMENIA                    Avaxes R.            Kadousioi

Abydos                                                      Lake
HELLESPONTINE                Herodotus'          Thospitis          PERSIAN
PHRYGIA           Gordion       Royal Road
                                        Halys R.        Zapatas R.              MEDIA
Sardis        LYDIA    PHRYGIA                      TAURUS MOUNTAINS        Gaugamela
                    Kelainai                                      MESOPOTAMIA    Mespila          Ecbatana
Ephesus                  Eurymedon R.        Issus    Harran                    Lesser Zab R.
                                              Syrian-                  Kainai        Bisutun
LYCIA        Aspendos              Cilician                    ASSYRIA          Cossaeans
C                                        Gates        Euphrates R.
                                    SYRIA                                        Tigris R.

PHOENICIA                                      Babylon

Mediterranean Sea                    ARABIA

Jerusalem
PALESTINE

Sais
Naucratis
EGYPT

Memphis

D                          Lake
                        Moeris

                              Nile R.

0        400 km      400 mi
          W                                    X

REFERENCE MAP 9: THE PERSIAN EMPIRE

Aral
Sea

CHORASMIA

Oxus R.

Massagetai

BACTRIA

PAROPAMISOS MOUNTAINS

PARTHIA

HYRCANIA

Indus R.

ARACHOSIA

EMPIRE

DRANGIANE

INDIA

ZAGROS MOUNTAINS

Elymai
Ouxioi
•Susa

PERSIS

•Pasargadae
Anshan •  •Persepolis

Persian Gulf

Y          Z          A

B

C

D

Y          Z

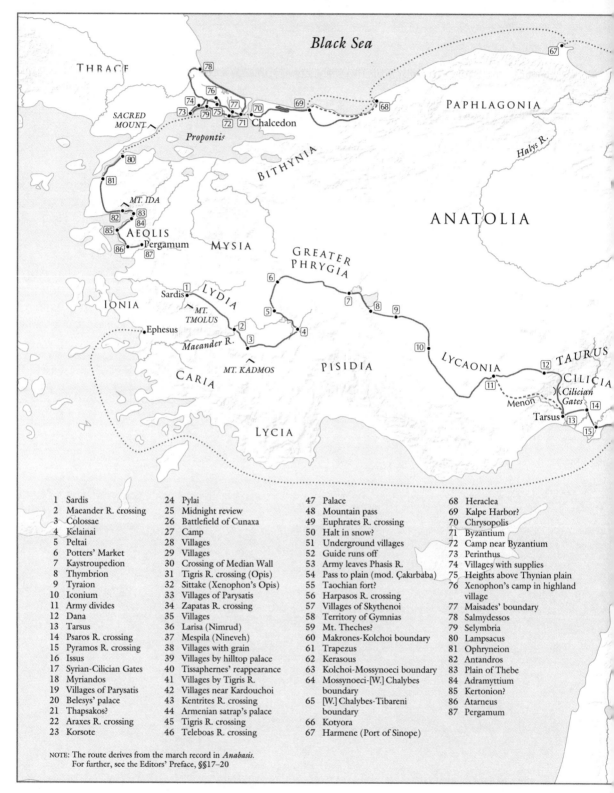

| | | | |
|---|---|---|---|
| 1 | Sardis | 24 Pylai | 47 Palace | 68 Heraclea |
| 2 | Maeander R. crossing | 25 Midnight review | 48 Mountain pass | 69 Kalpe Harbor? |
| 3 | Colossae | 26 Battlefield of Cunaxa | 49 Euphrates R. crossing | 70 Chrysopolis |
| 4 | Kelainai | 27 Camp | 50 Halt in snow? | 71 Byzantium |
| 5 | Peltai | 28 Villages | 51 Underground villages | 72 Camp near Byzantium |
| 6 | Potters' Market | 29 Villages | 52 Guide runs off | 73 Perinthus |
| 7 | Kaystroupedion | 30 Crossing of Median Wall | 53 Army leaves Phasis R. | 74 Villages with supplies |
| 8 | Thymbrion | 31 Tigris R. crossing (Opis) | 54 Pass to plain (mod. Çakırbaba) | 75 Heights above Thynian plain |
| 9 | Tyraion | 32 Sittake (Xenophon's Opis) | 55 Taochian fort? | 76 Xenophon's camp in highland |
| 10 | Iconium | 33 Villages of Parysatis | 56 Harpasos R. crossing | village |
| 11 | Army divides | 34 Zapatas R. crossing | 57 Villages of Skythenoi | 77 Maisades' boundary |
| 12 | Dana | 35 Villages | 58 Territory of Gymnias | 78 Salmydessos |
| 13 | Tarsus | 36 Larisa (Nimrud) | 59 Mt. Theches? | 79 Selymbria |
| 14 | Psaros R. crossing | 37 Mespila (Nineveh) | 60 Makrones-Kolchoi boundary | 80 Lampsacus |
| 15 | Pyramos R. crossing | 38 Villages with grain | 61 Trapezus | 81 Ophryneion |
| 16 | Issus | 39 Villages by hilltop palace | 62 Kerasous | 82 Antandros |
| 17 | Syrian-Cilician Gates | 40 Tissaphernes' reappearance | 63 Kolchoi-Mossynoeci boundary | 83 Plain of Thebe |
| 18 | Myriandos | 41 Villages by Tigris R. | 64 Mossynoeci-[W.] Chalybes | 84 Adramyttium |
| 19 | Villages of Parysatis | 42 Villages near Kardouchoi | boundary | 85 Kertonion? |
| 20 | Belesys' palace | 43 Kentrites R. crossing | 65 [W.] Chalybes-Tibareni | 86 Atarneus |
| 21 | Thapsakos? | 44 Armenian satrap's palace | boundary | 87 Pergamum |
| 22 | Araxes R. crossing | 45 Tigris R. crossing | 66 Kotyora | |
| 23 | Korsote | 46 Teleboas R. crossing | 67 Harmene (Port of Sinope) | |

NOTE: The route derives from the march record in *Anabasis*.
For further, see the Editors' Preface, §§17–20

REFERENCE MAP 10: THE ROUTE OF THE TEN THOUSAND GREEKS WITH HALTING PLACES OF THE MARCH

Black Sea

Trapezus

MT.
THECHES?

Harpasos R.

Phasis/Araxes R.

ARMENIA

CAPPADOCIA

WESTERN
ARMENIA

Euphrates R.

Teleboas R.

Lake
Thospitis

Kentrites R.

ZAGROS

MOUNTAINS

AMANUS MTNS.

Zapatas R.

MESOPOTAMIA

MOUNTAINS

ASSYRIA

MEDIA

SYRIA

Euphrates R.

Araxes R.

Lesser Zab R.

Physkos R.

ARABIA

Tigris R.

BABYLONIA

Babylon

0          250 km          250 mi

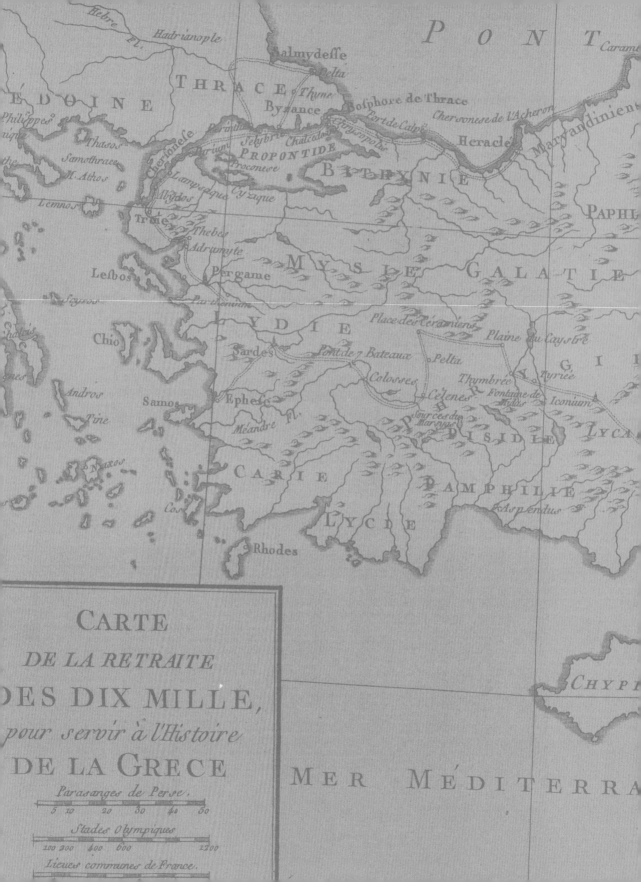

P O N T

Caram...

Hebre Fl.

Hadrianople

THRACE

Salmydesse

Delta

Thyne

Byzance

Bosphore de Thrace

Chersonese de l'Acheron

EDOINE

Philippes

...que

...the

Thasos

Samothrace

M. Athos

Perinthe

Chersonese

Byzium

Selybrie

Chalcedon

Port de Calpé

Chrysopolis

Heraclé

Maryandiniens

PROPONTIDE

Proconese

Lampsaque

Cyzique

Abydos

Troie

Thebes

Adramyte

Lemnos

B I T H Y N I E

M Y S I E

G A L A T I E

PAPHL

Lesbos

Pergame

Parthenium

Sestos

L Y D I E

Chio

Sardes

Pont de 7 Bateaux

Place des Céramiens

Pelta

Plaine du Caystre

G I

Tyriée

Colosses

Thymbrée

Andros

Tine

Samos

Ephese

Celenes

Sources du

Fontaine de

Midas

Iconium

LYCA

Méandre Fl.

P I S I D I E

...es

...ales

Naxos

C A R I E

P A M P H I L I E

Cos

Aspendus

L Y C I E

Rhodes

CHYPI

CARTE

DE LA RETRAITE

DES DIX MILLE,

pour servir à l'Histoire

DE LA GRECE

Parasanges de Perse.

5  10    20    30    40   50

Stades Olympiques

100 200  400  600          1200

Lieues communes de France.

MER MÉDITERRA